THE TRANSFORMATION
OF IRELAND

DIARMAID FERRITER

THE OVERLOOK PRESS
WOODSTOCK & NEW YORK

For Sheila Maher: my love, my life

First published in the United States in 2005 by
The Overlook Press, Peter Mayer Publishers, Inc.
Woodstock & New York

WOODSTOCK:
One Overlook Drive
Woodstock, NY 12498

NEW YORK:
141 Wooster Street
New York, NY 10012

Manufactured in the United States of America
ISBN 1-58567-681-0

CONTENTS

ACKNOWLEDGEMENTS

Many people contributed to the gestation and completion of this book, not least my colleagues in the History Department at St Patrick's College: Dáire Keogh, Carla King, Marion Lyons, Matthew Stout and especially James Kelly, who provided friendship, professional support and sound advice. Yet again, I have to thank my family from the bottom of my heart, for years of warmth, love, understanding, humour and loyalty. They are as important as friends and confidants, as parents and siblings. I can't express in words my gratitude to them – Nollaig and Vera, Cian, Muireann and Tríona. As the family has grown, so has the love and companionship, and I am indebted to Deirdre Mulligan, Lar Joyce, Lucy and Catherine Maher, Rose Cottam, Luan, Síofra, Liberty and Rachel. Tom and Anne Maher have been dream in-laws; I am constantly humbled by their generosity and kindness. Kevin Maher, the jewel in the crown of Ireland's Diaspora, has been there from the beginning – a better and closer friend one couldn't hope for; his friendship is accompanied by a creative mind that is unique and powerful, and a humour that is absorbing and addictive. Ronan, Carmel, Karen and Rachel Furlong have a special place in the Ferriter hearts; their sustained friendship over many years has been inestimable.

Catriona Crowe has advised, encouraged and enthralled in equal measure; her suggestions have always been humane, insightful, clever and fun, as is her friendship. Colm Tóibín and Deirdre McMahon read the earlier drafts and made invaluable suggestions; they put a lot of effort into the manuscript; their contribution, friendship and generosity have been immense and are much appreciated. Greg Prendergast has been there through thick and thin; providing laughter, insight and companionship, as have Mark Duncan, Stephen Cullinane, Paul Rouse, Paul Murphy, Aisling Caden, Adrienne Egan, Martin Walsh, Anne Marie Kearney, Lisa Finnegan, Mark Hyland, Katie and Seàn Condon, Leo Casey, Michelle Thomas, Pat Leahy, Gráinne Gavigan, Gráinne Seoige, David Whelan, Antoinette Prout, Feargal de Fréine, Heather and Euan Randall, John Rouse, Seán Kearns, William Murphy, Maeve Coogan, Dave and Annalise Heron, Georg Grote, Lindsey-Earner Byrne, David Maguire, Tom, Anna, Carla and Melanie Briggs, and Peter and Olivia Casey.

Mary Daly and Margaret MacCurtain have encouraged and advised me for many years, as have Tim O'Neill and Maeve Bradley; once again I want to record my gratitude. Michael Laffan, Eoin O'Sullivan, Tom Garvin, Ger Garland, Victor Laing, the late Peter Young, Michael Kennedy, Susannah Riordan, Philip Harvey, Fearghal McGarry, Brian Hanley and Pauric Travers have always been generous with their time and thoughts.

The friendship, advice and assistance of many others have helped me in many ways over the years. I am grateful to Tom Bartlett, Ronan Fanning, William Mulligan, Eunan O'Halpin, Séamus Helferty, David Craig, Aideen Ireland, Peter Mooney, Teri Garvey, Declan Roe, Tony and Catherine Sweeney, Donal and Carmel Ó Loinsigh, Brendan O'Donoghue, David Doyle, Tadgh Ó hAnnracháin, Susan Conlon, the late Albert Lovett, Art Cosgrove, Monica Cullinane, Brendan Barrington, Brendán MacSuibhne, Seymour Philips, Bernadette Whelan, John McCafferty, James McGuire, James Quinn, Pauric Dempsey, Jude McCarthy, Catherine Brosnan, Catherine Cox, Seán Gallagher, Ronan Gallagher, Gavin Aherne, Eimear Kilrane, Mary Byrne, Therese Manley, Paul Brett, Tom, Dermot and Roísín Mulligan, Ronán O'Brien, Madelene Humphreys, Brian Somers, Eamon O'Flaherty, Seán Duffy, Howard Clarke, Damien Brady, Enda Delaney, Fergus Campbell, Joost Augusteijn, Marnie Hay, Ivar McGrath, Patsy and Dolores Rouse, Niav Gallagher, Barry Gaffney, Kay Sheehy, Linda Longmore, Maurice Bric, Sheila O'Donnellan, Karen Carleton, Bernard McGuckian, Micheál MacGréil, Nuala O'Neill, Bernadette Comerford, Alex White, Jane Ohlmeyer, Sineád McCoole, Ciaran Brady, Paddy Sarsfield, Lorcan Farrell, Fiona Poole, Cormac Kinsella, Justin Kavanagh, Pat Wall, Orna Hanley, Fergus D'arcy, Fr Stephen Redmond, Rob Somerville Woodward, Seán McGreal, Mary Clarke, Marie Clarke,

Brian Donnelly, Mary Shine Thompson, Therese Dooley, Colm Hefferon, Joseph Dunn, Ray Topley, Tom Halpin, Alan Titley, Fionnuala Waldron, Diane Ryan, Eileen McDevitt, Theresa O'Farrell, Gerry O'Reilly, Maurice O'Reilly, Mary Pluck, Maura Sheehan, Noemi Rigney, Ciarán Sugrue, Alan English, Philomena Donnelly, Annette Jordan, Liam Mac Mathuna, Ciarán Mac Murchaidh, Yvonne Marshall, the staff of the UCD Archives Department, the staff of the Public Records Office of Northern Ireland, the staff of the National Library of Ireland, the staff of the Derry City Council Museum, the staff of the National Archives of Ireland, the staff of the library at UCD and the staff of the library at St Patrick's College.

Peter Carson, who suggested I write this book, along with his colleagues at Profile Books, especially Penny Daniel, Helen Williams and Andrew Franklin, have been patient, encouraging, professional and a pleasure to work with from start to finish. Particular thanks are due to Mark Handsley and Ruth Killick for their help, expertise and professionalism.

This book is dedicated to Sheila Maher, Queen of the Dolphins, soul mate, lover and best friend, who represents all that was best about Ireland from 1970 onwards. It would take another book to do justice to her many qualities. They include her passion, wit and wisdom; her anger; her probing mind; her devilish sense of humour and savage tongue; her capacity for love, tolerance and companionship; her courage in the midst of adversity; and her unrivalled assessments of contemporary radio, literature, film, politics and hypocrisy. This book could not have been written without you, and is as much yours as mine.

GLOSSARY

Selected Terms

Pronunciation and translation of Irish terms appear in parentheses.

Acronyms

CnB / Cumman na mBan (*cuman na mawn*—'*Association of Women*'): The female division of the Irish Volunteers, launched in Dublin in April 1914. Its central branch was based in Parnell Street, Dublin. By 1916 it had 43 branches and supported the 1916 Rising, in which many members participated. Its membership included several of the leading Republican women of the period, and it was active in the War of Independence. A majority of its membership rejected the Anglo-Irish Treaty.

CnG / Cumann na nGaedheal (*cuman na nwaol*—'*Association of Irish People*'): The main political party that supported the Anglo-Irish Treaty of 1921. Previous members of Sinn Fein established it in April 1923. Led by William Cosgrave, it formed the first government of the Irish Free State until 1932. In 1933 it merged with other groups to become Fine Gael, which then became the main opposition party.

GAA / Gaelic Athletic Association: An amateur sporting organisation established in 1884 in Thurles, County Tipperary, to promote Irish football, hurling, handball and camogie. It became the most successful sporting organisation in twentieth century Ireland.

GPO / General Post Office: Located in the middle of Dublin City's main thoroughfare, O'Connell Street, the GPO provided the main base for the Easter rebels in

1916 and the location for the reading of the Proclamation of the Irish Republic at the beginning of the Rising.

ICA / Irish Citizen's Army: Founded as a workers defence corps by James Connolly and James Larkin during the 1913 lock-out to protect workers from attack by police. Its aim was the establishment of a workers republic, and it participated in the 1916 Rising.

IPP / Irish Parliamentary Party: Developed from the Home Rule League, the IPP was established in 1873, and later led by Charles Stewart Parnell. The party was divided after his death, but reunited in 1900 and then dominated Irish representation at Westminster until 1918, when it was decimated by the success of the Sinn Fein party.

IRA / Irish Republican Army: Became the army of the Irish Republic during the War of Independence, and had its origins in the Irish Volunteers. The IRA split over the Anglo-Irish Treaty, and was declared illegal in 1936, but a minority of Republicans continued to recognise its legitimacy.

IRB / Irish Republican Brotherhood: Founded in Dublin in 1858, at the same time the Fenians were established in New York, this was a secret society that aimed to overthrow British rule in Ireland. The IRB staged an unsuccessful rebellion in 1867. Younger men revived it in the early years of the twentieth century. It infiltrated the Irish Volunteers, and its military council planned the 1916 Rising.

RIC / Royal Irish Constabulary: An armed police force, formed in 1836. Members were recruited from among the tenant-farmer class. During the early stages of the War of Independence, it was the primary target of the IRA. It was disbanded in March 1922.

RUC / Royal Ulster Constabulary: A police force established in Northern Ireland in June 1922. It lacked support from the nationalist community. After 1968, over 300 of its members were killed during the Troubles.

SDLP / Social Democratic and Labour Party: Founded in August 1970 by nationalist, labour and civil rights groups, and led the opposition in the Northern Ireland parliament. The SLDP played a leading role in bringing about a settlement of the Northern Ireland Troubles, and advocated a system of joint sovereignty over Northern Ireland by the British and Irish governments, with a locally elected assembly and executive.

UDA / Ulster Defence Association: A loyalist paramilitary organisation founded in Belfast in September 1971 in order to combat the IRA.

UDR / Ulster Defence Regiment: A British army regiment established in January 1970. It was divided into full- and part-time sections and assisted the RUC and British Army.

UVF / Ulster Volunteer Force: Established in January 1913 to resist the implementation of Home Rule, due to come into force in September 1914. The UVF was funded by businessmen and wealthy landowners and became armed in April 1914. They disbanded after the Government of Ireland Act (1920). The name was revived in 1966 for use by a loyalist paramilitary force.

Terms

Ancient Order of Hibernians: Emerged in 1838 as a Catholic reaction to the Orange Order. Supported the struggle for Home Rule in the late nineteenth and early twentieth century, and during the 1920s attempted to guard Catholic rights in Northern Ireland.

Bloody Friday (1972): On 21 July 1972, 20 IRA bomb explosions killed 11 and injured 130 in just one hour in the centre of Belfast city.

Bloody Sunday (1920): On 21 November 1920, the IRA shot dead 14 British officers. It provoked a reprisal by Black and Tans at Croke Park Dublin, where a football match was being played. The soldiers opened fire on the spectators, killing 12 and wounding 60.

Bloody Sunday (1972): On 30 January 1972, 13 unarmed people were shot dead and 17 injured by British soldiers of the Parachute Regiment in the Bogside area of Derry during an anti-internment rally organised by the Derry Civil Rights Association.

Clann na Poblachta (*clan na publackta- 'Family of the Republic'*): Political party established in Dublin in July 1946. It included many who had been active in the IRA and presented itself as a modern party demanding social change. It won 10 seats in the 1948 general election and participated in the first coalition government, 1948-51. Dissolved in 1965.

Clann na Talmhan (*clan na talon—'Family of the Land'*): Political party established in July 1939, in Galway, to advocate the interests of western farmers. It won 11 seats in the general election of 1944 and participated in the Coalition government (1948-51). Its parliamentary representation ended in 1965.

Cumann na Saoirse (*cumin na searsha—'Association of Freedom'*): A short-lived breakaway group of women from Cumann na mBan, formed in Dublin in March 1922. Its members supported the Anglo-Irish Treaty.

Dail Eireann (Dail) (*dawl airin—'Assembly of Ireland'*): The Irish parliament, first established in Dublin in January 1919 in defiance of British rule in Ireland. Initially, it claimed an all-Ireland jurisdiction. After 1922 it was the parliament of the 26-county Irish Free State (known as the Republic of Ireland since 1949).

Easter Rising: Planned by the military council of the IRB, it began on 24 April 1916, and was confined almost exclusively to Dublin. Its leaders occupied the GPO and declared an Irish Republic. The fighting lasted for a week, after which the insurgents surrendered to the British army. Official casualty figures were 450 killed. Fifteen of its leaders were executed and over 3,400 people arrested in its aftermath.

Famine (Great) (1845-49): Caused by the failure of the potato crop as a result of blight. The worst catastrophe of modern Irish history, as for one-third of the population the potato was their sole food. It caused the death of approximately one million people and forced another million to emigrate.

Fenian Movement: The Fenians were an oath-bound Republican secret society established in New York on 17 March 1858, at the same time as the establishment of the IRB. They were named after na Fianna, the warrior bands of Irish mythology.

Fine Gael *(feena gale—'Clan of Irish People')*: Founded in September 1933, from a merger of Cumann na nGaedheal and other, smaller parties opposed to Fianna Fail. Traditional supporters included substantial farmers and the business community. They were the main party in coalition governments in 1948-51, 1954-57, 1973-77, 1982-87 and 1994-97. They are the main opposition party in the current Dail.

Fianna Fail *(feena fall—'Warriors of Destiny')*: Political party established by Eamon De Valera in May 1926, when he broke with Sinn Fein. Its aims were the reunification of Ireland, economic self-sufficiency and promotion of the Irish language. One of the most successful political parties in western Europe, it was initially in power from 1932-48. It also formed governments from 1951-54, 1957-73, 1977-81, and was the lead coalition party from 1987-94, and 1997 to the present.

Gaelic League: Established in 1893 by Irish language scholars to promote the speaking and writing of Irish. An important organisation in the cultural revival of the late nineteenth- and early twentieth centuries.

Gaeltacht *(galetockth—'Irishness' or 'Irish-speaking People')*: A term used in English to mean an Irish-speaking district.

Garda Siochana *(garda shecawna—'Guardians of Peace')*: The national police force, established in 1922, originally under the title Civic Guard. Women were admitted after 1958.

Home Rule: A term first used in the 1860s to describe the Irish demand for an autonomous Irish parliament. Some of its promoters wanted to retain a connection with the British parliament, which would have responsibility for imperial affairs.

Independent Orange Order: A breakaway group from the Orange Order, founded by T.H. Sloan in June 1903. It had a predominantly working-class membership, which was critical of the ruling elite within the Ulster Unionist Party.

Irish Volunteers: Founded in November 1913 in response to the formation of the UVF and within a year had 80,000 members. The Irish Volunteers were a defence force that wanted to ensure the implementation of home rule. The organisation split when a minority of members rejected support for Britain in the First World War.

This minority group was infiltrated by the IRB, who used it as a front organisation when planning the 1916 Rising. In August 1920 the Volunteers took an oath to the Republic and became the IRA.

Magdalen homes/ laundries: The Irish version of the eighteenth-century female penitentiary movement led to the establishment of Magdalen homes, originally established to rehabilitate prostitutes. Beginning in the nineteenth century they were run by the Good Shepherd Sisters to accommodate so-called fallen women—often unmarried mothers or abused women who were usually held against their will. Inmates laboured in the laundries attached to the convents and many were detained illegally for life.

Republican: In Ireland, used to describe those supporting a republican form of government and a united Ireland.

Sinn Fein (*shin fane*—'We Ourselves'): A political movement that emerged in 1905, under the leadership of Arthur Griffith, with the stated intention of making England 'take one hand from Ireland's throat and the other out of Ireland's pocket'. Did not become a mass movement until 1917-18, when it succeeded in replacing the IPP as the main vehicle of Irish nationalist and Republican opinion. The party split over the Anglo-Irish Treaty in 1921; Fine Gael and Fianna Fail can trace their origins to this split. The party survived as a small Republican grouping, became more left wing in the 1960s, and split again in 1970 in response to the outbreak of the Troubles, with the minority group becoming the political wing of the IRA. In 1986 Sinn Fein ended their traditional abstentionist policy with regard to the Dail and was active in working-class politics north and south. They gradually came to support the peace process and a move towards the political mainstream. Following the IRA ceasefire in 1994, their electoral support increased, north and south.

Taoiseach (*teeshock*): Irish prime minister.

TD (Teachta Dala) (*teeockta dawla*): Member of the Irish parliament.

Troubles: Term used to describe the war in Northern Ireland (1969-94) following attacks on nationalist areas and the resumption of the IRA's military campaign in 1969 to force British withdrawal from Northern Ireland.

Ulster Unionist Council: The governing body of the Ulster Unionist Party, formed in 1905 to defend the interests of unionists and to draw together disparate groups within the wider unionist movement.

INTRODUCTION

I

This book was written during a period of great upheaval in Irish society at the very beginning of the twenty-first century, when contemporary debate provoked much thought on the extent of change and continuity in the course of modern Irish history. The research of many historians in the 1980s and 1990s had moved away from a narrow focus on the high drama of Irish politics in the direction of social and cultural history. Their labours revealed the extent to which many of the 'pillars' of Irish society – including the Church, the controllers of state power and the family – had not been scrutinised sufficiently. They also exposed the degree to which, despite the attention given to cultural studies, modernity and national identity, the analysis of class and economic issues had been neglected. It also seemed that many of the labels associated with particular years of Irish history – 'Plato's cave' (the period of the Second World War), 'The decade of the vanishing Irish' (the 1950s) and the 'Best of decades' (the 1960s)[1] – were not satisfactory in the light of ongoing research and newly available sources, while there was still a tendency to begin general histories of Ireland in the twentieth century between the years of 1912 and 1922 rather than in 1900.

Numerous specialised studies published in the 1980s and 1990s now need to be incorporated into a new interpretation of the twentieth century, as does an assessment of newly released files such as those from the Bureau of Military History – nearly 2,000 statements taken from participants in the events of 1913–21, released only in 2003, as well as state papers covering numerous events from the 1930s to the 1960s, but available to researchers only in the 1990s. The 1986 National Archives Act stipulated that state papers could be released after a period of thirty years had lapsed, but the last two decades have witnessed a large amount of information being brought into the public domain as a result of investigative journalism, and of a demand for transparency that culminated in the Freedom of Information Act of 1997. There is thus ample material available to justify a history of twentieth-century Ireland that goes beyond the 1970s.

In the past decade, questions concerning what constitutes legitimate research material have frequently been raised, particularly in the context of what it felt like to grow up in twentieth-century Ireland and the need to inject a greater degree of humanity into the study of Irish history. The renowned historian of Ulster A. T. Q. Stewart suggested in 1993: 'If you look at history, it is about humanity and it is about emotions and some historians write as if it were not. Their view has become terribly narrow.'[2] This observation was particularly apt in light of the many difficult, challenging and sometimes horrendous aspects of Irish life in previous decades that were unearthed and exposed in the 1990s. Their exposure highlights the need to re-examine critically the framework of interpretation scholars have employed to date. In August 2000 one of Ireland's most popular journalists, Con Houlihan, wondered: 'Is the Republic a nation today? The question is rhetorical. In the concluding years of the twentieth century it seemed that some hidden forces administered a powerful emetic to our state. Part of the dirty underbelly was exposed.'[3]

There was nothing uniquely Irish or entirely new in what was exposed – child abuse, cover-ups, a web of powerful and venal people engaged in massive tax evasion, contempt shown for the gravely ill. Many were issues that had been alluded to, or indeed explicitly articulated by, investigative journalists, novelists and crusaders of reform of various hues over the course of the century. But the sheer volume of the revelations and a willingness finally to debate and confront them also meant the idea that the silent spirit of the people was the source of all great things was comprehensively and ruthlessly shattered.

The challenge in terms of the writing of Irish history is how to contextualise these discoveries, a task made more difficult because the past seemed to impinge so directly on contemporary life as the century drew to a close. The Irish journalist Fintan O'Toole pointed out in the *Irish Times Book of the Century* that in the 1990s 'the gap between history and current affairs seemed at times almost to narrow to nothing. Only now was it becoming possible to understand the nature of the state that had emerged from the nationalist struggle.'[4] This in turns leads to the question: what was the nature of that state and its governors, and were the harsh judgements of Joe Lee, for example, at the end of the 1980s in his seminal *Ireland 1912–85*, justified?[5] A year before Lee's book was published, T. J. Barrington of the Institute of Public Administration had suggested: 'for a long time now this has been a very badly governed country, partly because of sustained political failure, but also because Irish government has failed to take seriously the task of developing our state institutions and the welfare state struggles to evolve into the welfare society.'[6]

In the same year Roy Foster's *Modern Ireland 1600–1972* was refreshing in its determination to move away from the grand narrative of Irish history; the story of Ireland, as new specialised studies were making clear, could no longer be told as 'a morality tale'. Foster's book was a narrative with a strong 'interpretative level' that stressed themes as much as events, a welcome approach given the amount of areas then under re-evaluation. Foster began an important process which involved not the drawing of definite conclusions, but the highlighting of ideas and areas that needed more probing. While his survey was biting and controversial in relation to certain themes, particularly in the context of the legitimacy of Irish republicanism, in the words of one reviewer it went far in attempting to 'see the mental bones beneath the physical skin' and in 'explaining the relativeness of historical understanding by reference to perception ... and in seeking to retain a sense of chaotic authenticity within a framework where both reason and generalisation still have significant roles to play'.[7]

Ten years later, Seán Ó Mordha, an acclaimed Irish documentary-maker, revealed that what struck him most about Ireland, in his research for *Seven Ages*, a documentary series on twentieth-century Ireland, was its poverty, and the daunting task facing those who wished to build a nation. He concluded that by the end of the century Ireland had approached maturity, if not quite wisdom.[8] In response to such an observation it could be argued that too much attention has been devoted to the 'daunting task' school of interpretation of Irish history and not enough to assessing the huge opportunities squandered. This book seeks to address some of these questions and ultimately to offer more questions – it does not purport to be a definitive history of twentieth-century Ireland based on decades of archival research but something of a stock-taking exercise and will suggest new departures and revisions.

Historians of course are heavily influenced by the contemporary environment in which they write, and this is all the more significant when that environment has been transformed in a remarkably short space of time. In May 1988 the *Economist* magazine, in a special edition on Ireland, under the photograph of a beggar on Dublin's O'Connell Street, referred in its headline to the 'poorest of the rich nations'. Only eight years later the same publication replaced the headline with 'Ireland: Europe's shining light'.[9] It also posed the question of whether traditional Irish values had changed – had a people who had often been presented as representing the antithesis of materialistic values become greedy and profit-obsessed? Those who suggested that traditional allegiances were replaced by a negative individualism were in turn faced with a simple question: did they want a return to the sad old days of dole and emigration queues?

While historians can take a much broader view of this issue, there are also traps into which they can fall. In the mid-1990s Joe Lee, in a challenging piece of historical revisionism, urged a re-examination of the sentiments expressed in Eamon de Valera's 1943 'Ireland that we dreamed of' speech. One of the most famous broadcasts of the century, it was an articulation of traditional, non-material, rural values. In light of contemporary Irish society and priorities, Lee suggested: 'De Valera's model emphasised the essential links between the generations as he identified his ideal for the dependent ages in society – childhood, youth and old age. Giving was as important as receiving, service as important as wealth. It was a society in which rights were balanced by responsibilities, in which adults of materially productive years acknowledged non-material obligations both to those who came before and to those whom were coming after, the generations woven together into a seamless social fabric.'[10] Lee's observation was a reminder of the danger of automatically dismissing the social vision articulated by an earlier generation. But there is also the danger here of acute nostalgia; of shelter from modern-day concerns by taking mid-century political rhetoric and promises at face value, and applauding a revolutionary generation for the dignity of their aspiration rather than their concrete achievements. But Lee's was also a timely reminder of the danger of reading history backwards and of imparting present-day values to past situations, and, in turn, bringing to an assessment of twentieth-century Ireland a corrosive cynicism that does scant justice to its complexities.

Nowhere is this complexity more evident than in relation to the family. Scholars seem to concur that twentieth-century Ireland nurtured a caring community bound together by a high degree of social consensus, underpinned by an underdeveloped but viable economy, a stable multi-party political system and a distinctive foreign policy. But if the family is placed at the top of this achievement, why hasn't it been subjected to more sustained examination? A central component of historiographical enterprise has to be to assess the changing dynamic of the Irish family, a work ably commenced by economist Finola Kennedy in her book *Cottage to Crèche*. Her research confirmed that most of the change in family life was driven by economic desire and necessity, or as she put it: 'central to this study is the idea that changes in family patterns have been driven by economic factors which, when they gained sufficient strength, tended to outweigh those of tradition'. Equally significant, she maintained that 'institutional changes were frequently introduced to accommodate choices already made by the people'.[11]

Irish readers over the course of the century remained enthralled by the family. The novelist John McGahern, interviewed after the publication of *Amongst Women* in 1990, commented: 'you don't have a proper society. The whole country is made up of families. Each family is a kind of halfway house between the individual and the society. The clichés we use about the family have the force of law: "you know how he is" or "you'll never change her". They condone everything but they mean nothing.'[12] But officially, perhaps the family was not a private institution but a political entity, or as the Irish Constitution of 1937 put it, 'the natural and fundamental unit' or 'a national institution possessing inalienable and imprescriptible rights'. Fintan O'Toole pointed out that during the divorce referendum of 1986 'the evidence, of course, is that we were always prepared to allow this ideal constitutional notion of the family to remain above and beyond economic realities. Real state support for the family has always been minimal in comparison with that of our supposedly less family-oriented neighbours.'[13] The idea of the family and its components as central to the Irish soul, and the idea of social and moral consensus around it, was not something which was questioned only in the 1980s. For all the celebrated modernity and material progress of the 1960s, for example, there was much more that was not tackled. During this decade Michael Viney, one of the most outstanding journalists of his generation, became almost a one-man department of sociology as he explored Ireland's dark corners. He concluded in 1967 in his publication *Growing Old in Ireland*: 'The fact is that we are becoming more selfish as our standards improve. We are becoming more censorious too. If there is a social or moral stigma attached to a family or an individual, the neighbours are almost certain to keep far away.'[14]

This would suggest growing liberalism and affluence did not lead to more openness or to a greater willingness to tackle the fundamental inequities and institutional disgraces that existed. That Minister for Education Brian Lenihan's comment on a visit to Artane Industrial School in 1968 (home to hundreds of Irish boys, some of whom were suffering harsh abuse) was 'Get me out of this fucking place'[15] said much about what a government and society wanted and did not want to see, acknowledge and act on. Of course, politically soothing rhetoric was necessary by the end of the century in response to what went on in Ireland in the past. In her inauguration speech as President of Ireland in 1997, Mary McAleese acknowledged: 'our own history has been hard on lives young and old'.[16]

What needs to be investigated by historians is how this came to be, particularly when, after the creation of the Free State in 1922, blaming outside forces was no longer credible. Memoirs are crucial in this regard; an important and legitimate source material if treated with the same care and sometimes scepticism that we should treat all documentary evidence. But it also seems to be the case that in placing them alongside 'official' documentation we can have a history that is ultimately more complete and human.[17] By 2001 *Angela's Ashes* by Frank McCourt, detailing harrowing poverty in Limerick in the 1930s and 1940s, was available in 32 languages, having sold millions of copies. But it had plenty of detractors also. Was it just that many people felt he was exaggerating poverty or was there also a discomfort in being forced to confront and engage with a difficult past?

The way in which it raised these questions was hugely important. The condescension that was a feature of the backlash to its success seems unduly trite, failing to acknowledge that for many experiencing destitution the desperate measures resorted to, such as a move to America at the first available opportunity, were a necessity rather than a choice. This is a reminder of how poor Ireland was, and historians have a duty not to forget

this. Nor should they close their eyes to the fact that it is difficult for historical research alone to succeed in getting a society to come to terms with
its own identity without the help of other disciplines.

II

This raises the issue of class, another neglected aspect of Irish history
writing. In a seminal article in the intellectual journal *Studies* in 1964, a
Labour Party activist, David Thornley, noted that 'we have no large-scale
study of class structure in Ireland'.[18] A year earlier, a district court judge in
Limerick had contended that class distinctions were almost entirely absent
in Ireland, in refusing to accept counsel's argument that there was a class
difference between farmers and farm labourers.[19] This capacity for self-
delusion in the 1960s was widespread, compounded perhaps by the fact
that so many of the working class were forced to emigrate in the previous
decade. Dublin's Abbey Theatre rejected the Irish playwright Tom
Murphy's play *Whistle in the Dark* on the grounds that the dispossessed
class, the characters he wrote about, did not exist. Unfortunately there is a
tendency for such issues to be lumped under the general heading 'literary
censorship' instead of focusing on the denial of class, and historians need
to re-place these questions centre stage. As the Irish novelist Colm Tóibín
pointed out in writing about the work of Murphy:

> As Ireland gained its freedom, there was no inclination to dwell on the
> fact that a whole class of people had been dispossessed in the previous
> seventy years (by the new farmer's class) and they were left unfree in
> a free Ireland, full of resentment, bewilderment and pain, not sharing
> any of the beliefs in nationalism, religion or social progress with the
> rest of the country, nor themselves attaining any class solidarity.[20]

Class differences were in fact blatantly enunciated well after
independence. The social historian Tony Farmar quotes the Irish feminist
Monica Barnes reflecting on small-town provincial life: 'The small town
snob system was remarkably complex, very subtle. It rarely came out
in the open but everyone knew their place ... it was most visible at the
reading out in church of the annual collection and if you paid beyond your
amount, people talked about you getting beyond your station.'[21] Long
after the era when Frank McCourt's begging mother was humiliated by
public officials, there were degrading manifestations of Irish snobbery.

Even in the mid-1960s, Liam Ryan, a Cork sociologist, in examining a suburb of one of the larger cities (a caustic indictment of the disastrous planning of the 1950s housing estates) wrote about the operation of public assistance. He recorded the experiences of those applying, in this case a deserted wife and her family:

> So he's gone away from you, you couldn't keep him, couldn't you? And he abuses everyone in public, and as well, we are made to stand in a queue in public and let the whole street see that we are beggars. That's no way to treat people and that's where a lot of the trouble comes from, from that element – tuppence halfpenny worth looking down on tuppence.[22]

Double standards in relation to class were reflected in other ways. Both the Irish Housewives Association and the Irish Countrywomen's Association, for example, remarked to the Commission on Emigration, which sat between 1948 and 1954, that the domestic worker in Great Britain got more recognition as a human being than she did at home. Central to this was denial – in this case, by the middle class in Ireland which was not comfortable with Catholic women cleaning for Protestant families in England. What was ignored was the fact that the women were often breaking their backs in their own backyard in Ireland. In rejecting proposals for increased access to healthcare in the late 1940s J. J. McElligott, Secretary to the Department of Finance, noted:

> There was at one time in this country the belief – perhaps it still persists – that to take 'a red ticket' involved a certain loss of caste and that the doctor should be paid if the money could be found at all. That very proper pride will surely be steadily diminished if the farmers' sons and daughters can get this medical benefit without any transfer of cash. I am not activated by financial considerations when I say that it is a pity it should be helped to disappear.[23]

III

The 1980s must loom large in any analysis of the twentieth century because in many respects it was the decade when the delusion and the denials were exposed, if not always confronted successfully. There are many examples that could be given to highlight the pretence that Ireland was exceptionally morally intact. None was more poignant than the death of 15-year-old Ann Lovett, after giving birth to a child under a grotto in Granard, County Longford, in February 1984. Some days later on the radio show of Ireland's most popular and accomplished broadcaster, Gay Byrne of RTÉ, there were 50 minutes of extraordinary ground-breaking radio. The broadcaster read out letters he had received from women with deep and dark secrets. One listener depicted it as 'a controlled but relentless onslaught of terrible intimacies … a sort of secret history of modern Ireland emerged that day with stories from everyday since the 1940s, stories that had been told to no-one; stories that had been bottled up and swallowed down'.[24] The phrase 'a secret history of modern Ireland' was well chosen, but some of the secrets had now entered the public realm and were not going to go away. The influence of the media in this regard was significant. Although sometimes depicted as the single most important agent of modernisation in Irish society, Gay Byrne made the key point in his autobiography that 'we would never impose a discussion on a society that is not ready for it, because it would be fruitless to do so'.[25]

But there was still much room in the 1980s for a denial of many of the problems that had not been confronted since independence, including emigration, child abuse, poverty, marriage breakdown and sexuality. Following the 1983 abortion amendment campaign, which succeeded in inserting a 'pro-life' clause in the Irish Constitution, and the 1986 divorce referendum, when the proposal to legalise divorce was defeated, the political scientist Tom Garvin suggested that 'denial was a mechanism which protected people against the necessity to confront change and permitted a politics of cultural defence which could ignore change'.[26] But the 'politics of cultural defence' had been building for many years, partly because contemporaries, and indeed some historians, preferred to lay stress on the question of denying access to outside influences rather than focus on the issues under their own noses. In March 1929 the *Irish Times* suggested that, especially in the south and west:

> there is irony in the fact that, at this very time, when the Free State government has declared war on English newspapers, the Irish newspapers are forced almost daily to touch matters which are both wicked and disgusting. The standards of sexual morality are lamentably low. The abominable crime of rape figures often in the police reports. Infanticide is common – one judge has described it as a national industry.

The editorial went on to suggest that 'it is a sad misfortune that the public mind has been put upon a false track by the Free State government's absurd censorship Bill. The decay is home-grown.'[27] The extent to which abuse continued to be home-grown, and indeed family-based, was revealed in *Sophia's Story* by Susan McKay, published in 1998 after a Sligo woman's father was convicted in 1995 of raping and abusing his children over a 20-year period which ended only in 1993.[28]

Perhaps historians have fallen into the trap of becoming consumed with what Irish people were supposedly not permitted to do as opposed to what they actually did; and what they actually read as opposed to what was banned. In this context it was an Anglo-American culture that dominated. The interest in the British royal family was just one manifestation of this. In the 1990s Irish cleric Mark Hederman wrote entertainingly about the Wallis Simpson abdication crisis in 1936. His mother was well informed about this, despite a news blackout in Ireland:

> when my mother began to tell people at parties in Dublin, they thought she was off her head. Being a conscientious Catholic she asked a Jesuit priest whether it was libel, detraction or scandal to be spreading news that was common knowledge in America but completely unknown over here. 'I'm not quite sure which it is,' he said, 'but it's very interesting, tell me more.'[29]

Two bestsellers in Ireland in the 1930s were a handbook on the King's coronation and the *Irish Independent*'s handbook on emigration to England. Indeed, it has been suggested that publishers in Ireland in the 1930s could have performed better if they had tapped into the potential appetite for the lowbrow.[30]

When contemporary Irish cultural policies were clearly failing, a common reaction was to look to the past rather than acknowledge what Irish people were doing at the time. In March 1937, when a Fine Gael politician, James Dillon, attacked a Fianna Fáil minister, Frank Aiken, for his use of the Irish language in the Dáil chamber, reading a civil servant's script he did not understand himself, Aiken retorted that Dillon 'was quite a young man when this country required soldiers. Where was he then?'[31] Dónal Mac Amhlaigh, an Irish labourer in Britain in the 1940s and 1950s, wrote about a fellow emigrant trying to sell the *Irish Democrat* newspaper: 'he stretched it out to one man who snarled, "clear off with your 'oul paper,

the church doesn't approve of it." The *News of the World* was sticking out
of the man's pocket at the time. The man with the *Democrat* merely said,
"just how mixed up can Irishmen get?"[32] Similarly, John Horgan, in the
most recent history of the Irish media, noted that 'the Irish mass audience
for TV has never found it difficult to combine a deeply rooted and at times
even visceral republicanism with a deep fascination with the activities of
the House of Windsor'.[33]

IV

Another point made by David Thornley in 1964 was that 'incomprehen-
sibly we have not as yet any professional study of the Catholic Church in
Ireland as a social and political influence'. Significant advances were made
in the following decades with the work of John Whyte, Tom Inglis and
Patrick Murray among others. Much of this work was concerned with
Church–state relations, though the more recent work of Mary Kenny
focused on the social and cultural impact of the Church also.[34] But there
is still a great deal to be done to place the revelations of the 1990s, which
have resulted in much justifiable anger being directed at the Church, into
a legitimate historical framework.

Assessing the mid-century Church in the light of the reaction to a
sordid underbelly of Irish Catholicism exposed in the 1990s is laced with
difficulties. The fact that the journalist John Cooney's biography of John
Charles McQuaid, Archbishop of Dublin from 1940 to 1972, was marketed
on the basis that it exposed him as a paedophile in the absence of reliable
evidence to back up the single incident alleged is a case in point.[35] The
truth is that there are many aspects of the Church and its figures we know
precious little about. Victims of clerical abuse who published in the 1990s
were also capable of seeing a wider picture. Patrick Touher, a resident
at Artane Industrial School in Dublin, wrote of his experiences that 'the
majority of the brothers were truly dedicated to our care; of course a few
bad eggs emerged as in any institution, but I know that on the whole the
Brothers were doing their best within limited circumstances in hard times
and with frightening numbers'.[36] He also pointed out that much was done
to ensure the boys learned a trade and that hard work made sure institutions could be self-sufficient while paid a limited subsidy by the state, and
were thus saving the state money at a time of economic depression.

But it has also been shown that the managers of some schools operated
a deliberate policy of secrecy and obstruction with regard to information

concerning how they ran their institutions and how they treated what are quite accurately referred to as their 'inmates'. This was the case with the penitential Magdalen laundries for young female 'offenders'. And what of the snobberies and hypocrisies of the society that co-operated with these institutions by sending children to them and subsequently deliberately turned a blind eye to their plight? This was not a process the Church could oversee in isolation; and the historian should not attempt to analyse it in isolation.

The interest in McQuaid is understandable given his dominance (and enormous personal archive), but why have individuals like bishops Cornelius Lucey of Cork, Michael Browne of Galway and Peter Birch of Kilkenny eluded researchers? All were members of the Catholic Hierarchy who outside the arena of sexual morality could be radical and even social-ist. How did their own education influence this generation of powerful prelates? Whatever about his own bias, at least Cooney acknowledges that how they were educated plays an important role:

> It is clear from private conversations which McQuaid had with Mrs Simms [the wife of the Church of Ireland Archbishop of Dublin] that he made an attempt to understand the changing attitudes of a younger generation towards organised religion, but that he was incapable of transcending the theological approach which he had been taught as a student.[37]

The same was true of subsequent archbishops of Dublin.

More exploration of the intellectual formation of this generation of Irish Catholics is necessary, as is research into the influence of the mod-ernist movement on early twentieth-century Catholicism, and the impact of papal encyclicals. Garret FitzGerald, Irish Taoiseach (prime minister) from 1982 to 1987, insisted in recent years that 'the institutional Church lost virtually all credibility with the great majority of people ... by its insistence on elevating the issue of the possible impact of contraception on sexual mores to the level of an absolute that must take precedence over all other considerations'.[38] There is some truth in this, but there is a danger too of the historian becoming too preoccupied with the Church's seeming obsession with sexual morality at the expense of looking at the wider context, a point well made and illustrated by Mary Kenny in *Goodbye to Catholic Ireland*. It is also important to look at the clerical response to social issues in the pre-independence era because they were among the few people who were writing about such problems. A clerical commentator on the social problems of Cork, in *Studies* in 1915, suggested, in remarking on the resilience of the Irish poor: 'how these poor people live, or rather, how they manage to die so slowly' was worthy of inquiry and 'could social workers find some means of publication their accounts could be even more shocking'.[39]

Alcohol abuse was endemic in Irish society by the end of the nineteenth century, but it was the Church rather than the state that was most vocal and active in attempting to combat it in the early years of the new century. But did this momentum with regard to welfare remain after independence? How committed were Catholic Church leaders to bringing pressure to bear on the state to solve the problem of slum housing in Dublin, where, to quote the historian Janet Nolan: 'overcrowding among the poorest third of the city's population was so severe that although officials set the minimum amount of human living space at 400 cubic feet per adult, the laws regulating dairies mandated 800 cubic feet of space for each Irish cow'.[40] Or was it the case that the Church impeded progress owing to its own desire to control and its over-emphasis on the sanctification of deprivation?

And what of the noble influence of Irish Catholic teaching? Did it make Irish politicians more honest in the early decades of the century? The overwhelming majority of public representatives throughout the century did not become wealthy from careers in politics. The memoirs of an Irish senator, Joseph Connolly, 'describes his bank manager in 1916 advising him to give creditors 10 shillings in the pound though he could pay more. Connolly said this was contrary to Catholic and Sinn Féin principles; he would sooner lose everything than cheat them.'[41] As the historian James Donnelly has pointed out, we need to look not just at liberal and secular international ideas that the Catholic Church in Ireland rejected, but also the conservative political and religious ideas that they enthusiastically welcomed, such as Marian devotion. We also need to give attention to the determined and successful attempts (and again Cooney's work on McQuaid is instructive in this regard, as is research on the Pioneer temperance association given its failure to influence legislation) to keep the Church out of politics, rather than accepting at face value the 'Church–state clash' labels. Who is to say that the opinion of Liam O'Bríain, an academic and Fine Gael supporter, was not more widespread, when he wrote to the Fine Gael

TD (member of parliament) Michael Hayes in June 1951: 'Do you know, I think an element in this recent election was a feeling that of all politicians, de Valera is the one most ready to say "No!" to the Bishops if driven to it.'[42] And finally, to what extent did the imposition of the Church's moral authority come at the expense of a durable intellectual contribution? In 1960 the *Observer* newspaper suggested that 'a nation, proud of its Roman Catholicism, has been curiously complacent that its contribution to Catholic thought has been perhaps the smallest of all the nations of Europe'.[43]

V

Also significant in this regard was the failure of Catholic social theory to take root in a country that supposedly had impeccable credentials for it. The reasons for the failure are manifold, but at the heart lay a determination to keep Ireland a strongly centralised state and this theme, and its relation, the distribution of power in twentieth-century Ireland, needs much consideration. Through looking at the history of local government in twentieth-century Ireland, one not only gets an insight into the failure to make Ireland more equitable and socially a better place in which to live, but also the manner in which all political parties stripped away local-government powers. By the end of the century the concept of local autonomy had lost much of its meaning. Those who came to control the politics of independent Ireland did not suddenly become exponents of centralisation; it was a feature of political culture prior to independence. Eunan O'Halpin noted that what the leading constitutional nationalist leaders of the first decades of the century, such as John Redmond, John Dillon and others, wanted 'was a government machine absolutely under the control of a small group of ministers. A Home Rule Ireland would be run on centralised lines, with a strong finance department the dominant force in government.'[44] Sinn Féin shared this view, as did both Cumann na nGaedheal (later Fine Gael) and Fianna Fáil, making a mockery of the insistence of Constance Markievicz, Irish republican and the first woman to be elected to the House of Commons, that 'we have thought and done differently from other nations. We never produced a tyrant. There was something that prevented any man or woman ever desiring to conquer all Ireland – a sort of feeling for decentralisation.'[45] In 1969 Charles McCarthy, in a book published by the Irish Public Administration, *The Distasteful Challenge*, insisted quite the opposite: 'An Irish man sees authority as something conferred on him from above. There is no tradition which says that a man must first govern himself – dynamism from below has never been a feature of Irish society.'[46]

This is a measure of the success of the main political parties in a small country of fostering clientelism and the belief that a strong centre was the best option. Irish voters came to know nothing else and seemed to embrace it wholeheartedly. In 1966 a small survey found that 71 per cent of Dubliners agreed that 'a few strong leaders would do more for the country than all the laws and talk'.[47] Privately, individuals like the Fianna Fáil minister Seán Lemass, in the 1930s and 1940s, believed it was necessary to counteract what he called the Irish people's 'fissiparous tendencies' with strong central government.[48] The rhetorical ideal of political and cultural self-sufficiency did not in practice extend to the people exercising much power themselves. Those who sought a restructure were either ignored, dismissed or, as in the case of the Vocational Commission, established in 1939 to investigate the possibility of alternative power structures in Ireland, sent off to compile lengthy reports that government ministers insisted would lead to anarchy if implemented. And of course, as the research of Susannah Riordan has illustrated, contempt breeds contempt; as in other European countries in the 1930s: 'the tendency of the vocational movement – whether or not it was ultimately undemocratic – to foster a climate of contempt for the existing parliamentary forms – should not be underestimated'.[49]

It would be churlish not to applaud Irish democrats for resisting Irish versions of the more extreme far-right European movements, but one could also give numerous examples of the victims of state centralisation and lack of autonomous power; again they belong to another history of hidden Ireland. One of the most symbolic was that of the island communities, who, as supposedly the guardians of the ultimate Gaelic Ireland, were left stranded. Just who was responsible for such a precious heritage, that declined from 211 inhabited islands in 1841 to 61 in 1991; from a population of 38,138 to 9,700 people?[50] Officially it seemed no one. In the *Irish Times* of August 1931 a resident of the Loughrea Islands noted that when looking for assistance 'we were referred from Herod to Pilate until we didn't know where to go. The local-government department referred the matter to the Minister for Fisheries and that department in turn said it was not a matter for them and referred it to the department for industry and commerce. This department also stated it was not their province.'[51]

This did not mean that, as the century progressed, powerful and often unaccountable interest groups did not emerge. David Thornley has also commented that 'we have not a single study of the informal decision-making bodies like pressure groups and virtually none of our community elites – a vital subject in the analysis of power'. Particularly interesting has been the huge growth in the power of the legal profession and its enormous influence over politics and the ensuing creation of vast personal wealth, along with more historically established interest groups like the Vintners. Much more about these groups needs to be explored.

VI

And what of the political parties themselves? Again, it is notable how little has been written in this regard but this has as much to do with the late opening of party political archives as with lack of interest on the part of researchers. Over the course of the century Irish voters remained remarkably loyal to the party political system as it emerged out of the Civil War and one of the main themes of independence was its political stability. Although the extent to which the initial security of the state was under threat in the early years of the state has been disputed, Irish voters were comfortable with a democratic system of proportional representation dominated by the three bigger political parties – Fianna Fáil, Labour and Fine Gael. Michael O'Riordan remained the longest-serving leader of a communist party anywhere in Europe precisely because Irish Communist Party membership numbers did not necessitate regular change.

But in comparison to other countries, perhaps the narrow range of political focus brought benefits also. There is much food for thought for historians in the journalist Mary Holland's reflection in 2002. In the midst of another requiem about the end of Civil War politics, she felt it should be acknowledged that there was little appetite for the politics of the far right:

> I've written plenty of columns complaining about the lack of any real left–right divide in Irish politics and the consequent deadening effect of virtual consensus on most social and economic issues. But, at this period of transition, it is perhaps time to acknowledge that Civil War politics served this state well. The fact that the political debate was rooted in whose grandfather shot who in the early years of

the last century was a major factor in enabling us to escape the worst extremes of some of our more sophisticated neighbours. At a time when Margaret Thatcher was intent on destroying the trade union movement in Britain and proudly proclaimed that 'there is no such thing as society' the political leadership of this state opted for partnership between government, employees and unions. At the same time, many community organisations – some of the most important attached to the Catholic Church – ensured that the principle of 'greed is good' could not be elevated into a core principle of any political party, not even the allegedly Thatcherite Progressive Democrats.[52]

This raises the question of ideology and the extent to which, historically, there were any real differences between the Irish political parties. James Dillon asked the Dáil in 1951: 'what ideological differences, if words retain their meaning, divide any two deputies on any side of this house?'[53] In this regard it is clearly time for histories to be written of all the political parties and great advances were made in the 1990s in terms of political parties taking their archives seriously. Ireland's oldest political party, the Labour Party, has been acknowledged as the most difficult of the Irish political parties to understand; and indeed, for much of the twentieth century it seemed to have difficulty understanding itself. This raises questions about the political maturation or otherwise of the republic, as the left seemed to be trapped by the legacy of the division over the Treaty in Irish politics. But other parties too need more sustained exploration, particularly given that at the end of the century members of the Fine Gael party interviewed by the political scientist Michael Marsh suggested the main difference between themselves and Fianna Fáil was that Fine Gael 'were more honourable'.[54]

Politicians across the spectrum were exceptionally cautious about being tainted as radicals. Dan Spring's election posters, for example, did not even acknowledge his membership of the Labour Party when he stood for election in North Kerry in the 1950s and 1960s. Garret FitzGerald recorded that in 1967/8, in the midst of talk about a possible merger between Fine Gael and Labour, the Labour Party leader, Brendan Corish, suggested he would be glad to see prominent Fine Gael members in the Labour Party.[55] This raises interesting questions about the way the political parties saw themselves – left, right or centre – and the extent to which these divisions were relevant to political debate in Ireland. In a series of debates in the early 1960s, TDs of each party claimed that their party was to the left of their opponents.[56]

The two main parties both retained elements of the traits that they had exhibited in the 1920s up to more recent times. In 1923 William Cosgrave, leader of Cumann na nGaedheal and first President of the Executive Council (prime minister) of the Free State, insisted in an election address in Kilkenny: 'the motto for this election is safety first'.[57] There is much truth in the historian John Regan's assertion that the pro-Treaty party was 'defined by external factors rather than internal ideological agenda', and inevitably that emphasis on an external threat and safety meant that grassroots activism and constituency work was not always a priority. Cosgrave admitted in a letter to Michael Hayes after his retirement: 'But we must be candid. In the sphere that we considered the least important but which was the most important, we failed; viz.: to retain popular support.'[58]

Fianna Fáil's approach to the electorate on the other hand was utterly pragmatic and often deliberately ambiguous. During the election campaign of 1932, in which Fianna Fáil triumphed and began a period of sixteen years in office, their leader Eamon de Valera's skill was evident in this regard. On 6 February he insisted: 'the state has the right to interfere when private property is being abused and worked against the interests of the community'. Six days later according to the *Irish Independent* he made a solemn pledge 'that the person and property of every citizen will be safeguarded as well as by a Fianna Fáil government as by a government of Cumann na nGaedheal'.[59]

Private property developers never had to worry in any case – there is huge irony in the fact that the Irish social revolution of the late nineteenth century, in which the political and social power of the landed elite was broken by the tenantry, was succeeded a hundred years later by a class of landowners and speculators who were to exercise their domination of land in an even more invidious way than some of the most wretched nineteenth-century landlords. Many of them were closely tied to the political parties.[60] The language used by political parties, suggested Fintan O'Toole, evolved from nineteenth-century romanticism, and was 'sustained by the need to evade social realities'. This rhetoric was an attempt to make real divisions in Irish society invisible and resulted in, amongst other things, contradictory statements about wealth redistribution and the causes of poverty.[61]

But at a broader level, many of the assessments we have of the period dominated by Fianna Fáil are still too generalised and imply there was a vigorous commitment to ideological thinking in the ranks of Fianna Fáil. Take, for example, the certainty implied in novelist John Banville's sweeping assertion that de Valera's Ireland was 'a demilitarised totalitarian state in which the lives of its citizens were to be controlled not by a system of coercive force and secret policing but by a kind of applied spiritual paralysis maintained by an unofficial federation between the Catholic clergy, the judiciary, the civil service and politicians'.[62] Timidity, conservatism, pragmatism and paternalism do not necessarily imply totalitarianism. In Banville's assessment one can see the dangers of reaching exaggerated conclusions by focusing primarily on the example of literary censorship. But the 'unofficial federations' Banville writes of were important. We clearly need more information on the civil service given that only two authors have tackled the history of government departments.[63] We need more political memoirs also, Irish politicians being slow to take up this task. As the veteran political analyst Brian Farrell pointed out: 'In retirement almost all have maintained a virtual Trappist-like custody of the tongue.'[64] Another gap in the historiography is the lack of any sustained historical analysis of the legal system and the judiciary. All in all though, it is a measure of the innate conservatism of Irish politics that the only proposals for changes to a political institution that people responded to – and voted for Mary Robinson, a candidate with a radical new vision of its role, in 1990 – concerned the Irish presidency, an office with little real power.

VII

Both main parties emerged from the same republican movement of the 1916–21 period, and a growing number of regional studies of the revolution have forced the reassessment of many assumptions.[65] A. T. Q. Stewart suggested that Irish history will continue to be a discipline which is easily politicised, 'which adds a great edge to historical debate … that is part of the mindset of the country and is also a product of the continuing conflict within the island which uses and relates to history in such an obvious and potent way'.[66] That is why the writing of the history of 1916–23 will remain controversial. There has been a tendency to place work on the early twentieth-century revolution in the context of the North's troubles. Peter Hart points out, for example, that 'one striking conclusion is that Cork experienced one "political death" for every 530 people between 1917 and 1923 as compared with a figure for Northern Ireland between 1969 and 1975 of one for every 1,200 people'.[67] But whatever about the merit of such comparisons (they were after all very different conflicts), Peter Hart's seminal work, *The IRA and Its Enemies*, illustrates the level of painstaking research and detective work involved in reconstructing the War of Independence and Civil War in even a single county. It is no wonder a definitive answer still cannot be given to the question of how many died nationally during the revolution. Hart's work nonetheless has revealed the multitude of layers within the republican movement as social and cultural divisions interacted with and shaped political attitudes.

This sense of a much more complex society with strong sectarian divisions is significant, particularly in terms of what republicans failed to do. One of the Catholic Church's senior prelates, Cardinal Cahal Daly, officiated at the state funerals in October 2001 of ten War of Independence IRA volunteers who had remained buried in Mountjoy after their execution. In his homily Daly suggested that celebrating the historical contribution of those seen as noble, pious and brave young men was one thing, but there was also an obligation to acknowledge that the promises about social equality in the 1916 Proclamation and the first Dáil's Democratic Programme, were promises not kept, and that there was no excuse now for blaming outsiders. It was a timely reminder of the need to acknowledge some of the failures of the Irish revolution.[68]

Historians still have to tease out the culture of republicanism during this period. David Fitzpatrick observed in 1998 that 'the ideology of Irish republicanism has never been much contested or even debated by its proponents',[69] or as Seán O'Faoláin's wife put it more acidly: 'You are all abstract fanatics.'[70] Ernie O'Malley, a War of Independence and Civil War IRA veteran, who later wrote powerfully about the period, remembered: 'I saw a certain hardness in our idealism. It made us aloof from ordinary living, as if we were above it.'[71] Many republicans of this era who had been born in Victorian Ireland shared many and varying cultural inheritances. As articulated by Richard English, Ernie O'Malley's influences moved between 'marginalised Anglophobia and Anglocentric Anglophobia, between the rural and the urban, between the popular and the elitist between the modern and the anti-modern ... between the parochially distinctive and the internationally distinguished'.[72] This was a somewhat inevitable result of Ireland's colonial legacy. Another part of that legacy was confusion as to the measure of independence that was conferred at the end of the War of Independence. Deirdre McMahon, an expert on Anglo-Irish affairs during this period, noted that:

> Ireland, unlike Canada, was a dominion by revolution, not evolution. Furthermore, the dominion settlement suffered from fatal flaws; as a concept dominion status was still in the process of evolution; the Irish had never asked for it; it came too late, it was imposed, and it was accompanied by partition and civil war. The surprise is that it lasted as long as it did.[73]

These aspects of the colonial legacy underline the need to know more about the Ireland in which Ernie O'Malley and his contemporaries grew to adulthood. The first twenty years of the century have been relatively neglected, given the tendency of some histories of twentieth-century Ireland to begin around 1920. As the work of Senia Paseta suggested: 'the attention lavished on one particular mind – republican – has obscured numerous other political and social developments which shaped the evolution of Ireland in the new century'.[74] Patrick Maume's dissection of Irish political culture in *The Long Gestation* identifies the deep internal divisions in the aggressive contemporary journalism and tensions in the co-operative movement, the Irish Parliamentary Party and the labour movement, and the difficulty of finding a consistent nationalist or republican philosophy.[75]

There is still a tendency to overestimate the importance of individuals like Michael Collins and Eamon de Valera at the expense of movements, as Colm Tóibín noted:

> those central moments in French history are communal and urban, but the critical moments in Irish history seem more like a nineteenth-century novel in which the individual, tragic hero is burdened by the society he lives in. We have no communards, no rabble in the streets. Instead we have personal sacrifice as a metaphor for general sacrifice.[76]

In terms of what the 'rabble' were doing, there is a need for more reflection on sport and leisure that is not just seen through the lens of political upheaval; the historian John A. Murphy pointed out in relation to the Gaelic Athletic Association that 'on per capita basis the attendances at major Gaelic games would rival those at Melbourne Football, the largest in the world at the time'.[77]

Understanding the complexity of Ulster unionism as a movement which was not nearly as monolithic or singularly strident and focused as its detractors would maintain is central to any historical analysis of the North in the early years of the century. Similarly, only in the last decade has a thorough examination of the fate of Ulster nationalists in the period up to the 1920s been attempted.[78] Stereotypes abounded in relation to how Ulster was depicted. Understandably, given the sheer intractability of the Northern Ireland problem for much of the century, and the bloody birth of its state, the Troubles after 1969 spawned thousands of books and articles. But a preoccupation with the republican–unionist rivalries of these periods has resulted in neglect of the period from the 1930s to the 1960s and indeed the social history of Ulster, a study of which reveals how the working classes of both communities shared many of the same burdens. In this sense, perhaps the focus of scholars has been too narrow also in their lack of attention to ordinary life and ordinary people.

The conflict in the North from 1969 onwards led to debate amongst historians about the role of violence in Irish history and the consequences of the Anglo-Irish connection, a debate that became pointedly political from the end of the 1970s and into the 1980s. In 1977 T. W. Moody of Trinity College Dublin, reflecting on the subject of 'Irish history and Irish mythology', argued that popular historical understanding was not generally derived from the labours of academic historians but from popular traditions and institutions – the myth – as distinct from what he referred to as 'scientific history'. He suggested that myths could be both benign and malignant, with his particular concern the myths of Orange loyalism and predestinate nationalism. This was particularly significant, he suggested, in the context of the identification of the modern nation with Gaelic civilisation and seven hundred years of struggle with Britain, which neglected constitutional nationalism and equated armed republicanism with the will of the people, a myth revived by the IRA from 1969 to depict the war as being waged on Britain as opposed to Northern Protestants.[79]

Critics of such revising saw the tendency to question the historical legitimacy of violent opposition to British rule as a convenient marriage of government opposition to the IRA's renewed campaign and hostile academics who were, according to Desmond Fennell, 'dabbling amateurishly in contemporary politics',[80] in a bid to undermine the moral legitimacy of a previous generation of Irish republicans. Ronan Fanning was to maintain that those running scared of the debate on 'revisionism' were fearful that the faith of nationalism would be undermined. Such debates were necessary and legitimate – they had been neglected far too long, and Roy Foster, in maintaining that 'we are all revisionists now' in the sense that history should be about constant questioning of assumptions and revisiting, was wise to eventually broaden the parameters of this debate.[81]

But the sniping at times became fractious, heated and narrowly focused and seemed almost a re-run of the debate about the Anglo-Irish Treaty of December 1921. There was a danger too of revisionists making the same mistakes they were criticising – establishing a framework of historical interpretation based on history as a morality tale of wrong and right. Unwittingly perhaps, those involved may in fact have pushed younger scholars, weary of the continued obsession of the Anglo-Irish axis, in the direction of neglected social and cultural history. The novelist Séamus Deane, in his *Reading in the Dark*, wrote powerfully about a classmate in school in 1948 who composed an essay about mealtime; a mother and children waiting for their father, a jug of milk and a dish of potatoes. 'Now that,' said the Master, 'that's writing. That's just telling the truth.' 'I'd never thought such stuff was worth writing about,' wrote Deane. 'It was ordinary life – no rebellions, or love affairs or dangerous flights across the fields at night.' It is a lesson historians of modern Ireland could learn much from.[82]

VIII

The two decades with supposedly the most contrast – the 1950s and 1960s – remain under-researched. There are many who will disagree with the thesis of Brian Fallon in his book *An Age of Innocence*, in which he disputes the idea that Ireland was a cultural wasteland in the 1940s and 1950s, or as he put it, Ireland was 'not a chauvinistic statelet shutting its doors and windows on international currents'. Even more may disagree with his contention that 'what is overlooked is that this national oddity, ingrownness and tendency towards self-contemplation may have had their positive sides – that they may even be linked umbilically and organically to the achievements of Irish writers and artists'.[83] But Fallon's thesis is significant in encouraging a more open mind in approaching a decade traditionally presented as relentlessly dull. There is plenty to suggest that a questioning culture emerged in the 1950s and that debate about change does not belong solely to the 1960s. Issues that had not been mentioned or challenged were at least being questioned, even if it was with cautionary qualification. In 1955, Cecil Barrett, Director of the Catholic Social Welfare Bureau, writing about the 10,000 dependent children in Irish society without homes, questioned the merits of placing healthy children in institutions, while adding: 'I do wish to be critical of those who manage children's institutions.'[84] There was a recognition, too, that it was time to acknowledge that much of the Irish revolution's rhetoric had been utterly aspirational – that there was no one grand inclusive programme for Irish development. Declan Kiberd suggested this was reflected in the work of Samuel Beckett, who saw Irish society as a mere pastiche with 'no overall purpose' and his response was to put despair and futility on stage for people to laugh at. The poet Patrick Kavanagh contrasted this attitude with that of 'academic writers ready to offer a huge illuminating symbol as if society were a solid, unified Victorian life'.[85]

And what of the 1960s? The decade of the rising tide that promised to lift all boats? The 'best of decades'?[86] Undoubtedly there were new opportunities and they should not be underestimated, but the assumption of positive modernisation needs to be qualified. The National Archive state papers relating to the 1960s that were released in the 1990s illustrate that the break with the past was not as clear-cut as some would maintain. More significantly, fundamental priorities did not alter in terms of Ireland remaining an unequal society with scant regard for its most vulnerable citizens. Much attention, for example, has rightly been given to the Fianna Fáil minister Donogh O'Malley's decision to introduce free secondary education in 1967; but little attention has been given to the case of David Moore in the summer of the following year, written about in the *Daily Telegraph*. The newspaper reported that David, nine years old, partially deaf and blind, was brutally beaten in a school in Inchicore in Dublin by a Christian Brother who subsequently became the first member of a religious order to be prosecuted for assaulting a pupil. The parents were punished, it seemed, for taking the case, by being awarded one shilling in damages but not costs and were forced subsequently to emigrate to Canada.[87] Also in the area of child welfare the Tuairim ('opinion') research group, composed of younger academics and researchers looking for solutions to Irish social, economic and political problems, pointed out in 1966 that 'it may come as a shock to some people to learn that we are still caring for deprived people under legislation passed nearly sixty years ago, which has long been discarded in the country of its origin'.[88]

Sharing the new economic wealth created by programmes for economic expansion was kept off the agenda, establishing a precedent for an approach to wealth distribution that lasted for the rest of the century. In January 1965, a Fianna Fáil minister, Kevin Boland, wrote to the Minister for Finance: 'I assure you that my suggestion that after eight years spent in promoting economic expansion something reasonably substantial should now be done for social welfare is not an effort to wreck the second programme for economic expansion.' He also wrote of 'a general feeling that we have not paid sufficient attention to the weaker sections of the community and that there has not been an equitable distribution of the increased prosperity to which we point as an achievement.'[89] Taxpayers' money was still being used as a massive subsidy to middle and upper-middle classes in Irish education. The Taoiseach, Jack Lynch, in 1969 insisted: 'we in this country are secure in the tenure of our land and homes so long as no alien philosophies creep in on us',[90] which was similar to the sentiments expressed in Justice Department files of the 1920s documenting the government's belief that it was not wise to introduce 'reckless reforms' to cater for the worst aspects of the urban landlord system on the basis that 'hard cases make bad law'.[91] Presumably, then, even at the end of the 'best of decades' the concepts of redistribution and equality were 'alien philosophies'.

IX

Finally, it is worth looking at the assessments of those in the 1980s and 1990s who insisted that twentieth-century Ireland had no shortage of achievements to its credit, in contrast to Joe Lee's view that there had been a preponderance of the 'possessor principle', a 'feeble sense of public morality' and the lack of 'a viable civic culture'.[92] Lee has been criticised for his failure to be clear on how such things can be defined or to relate his claims to what it felt like to be a part of Irish society during the years of his study (1912–85). But he deserves praise for forcing historians to develop a more critical framework of interpretation and for his brilliant political analysis. Lee also warned, in responding to specific criticisms of areas of Irish life not dealt with in the book, that there is a danger in 'chasing the latest politically correct fashion which would be to prostitute history to propaganda'.[93] But this defence could be taken too far, particularly regarding the failure to write about women solely because they were not numerous in parliament. Whether or not Ireland was a gendered state after the 1920s is worthy of scrutiny. The Irish writer Nuala O'Faoláin reflected the views of many feminists when criticising the seminal *Field Day Anthology of Irish Writing* in 1991, as being 'immensely wounding' in its exclusion of women. She suggested: 'while this book was demolishing the patriarchy of Britain on a grand front, its own native patriarchy was sitting there smug as ever'. But the response – a separate voluminous women's edition eventually published in 2002 – revealed the vibrancy of women's studies in Ireland and the extent of the role they had played in Irish history. It provided, in the words of the literary critic Catriona Crowe, 'an almost overwhelming set of contexts for understanding how women lived in Ireland', and demonstrated the degree to which feminist activists were responsible for winning many victories, along with the sheer range of primary source material that documented those struggles.[94]

Martin Mansergh, adviser to a succession of Fianna Fáil taoisigh in the 1980s and 1990s, writing at the very end of the century, suggested an altogether more positive framework of interpretation than that offered by Lee, praising the excitement and intellectual fervour of the early twentieth century, the Irish creation of a model of anti-imperialist struggle, progressive aspects of Catholic social theory and the ability to make social partnership work:

> Ireland is ending the twentieth century on a high note. Of course, national self-understanding is constantly evolving, nurturing and developing, but broadly, the national project has been successful. There have been difficulties and serious failures along the way, leading to major course connections, but there has also been a lot of positive progress at many points. We have gradually carved out a path of our own that does not fall too easily into conventional political, economic or sociological categories. There is no sense of helplessness vis-à-vis the serious problems we still have to overcome.[95]

This assessment is overly optimistic and selective. Mansergh was writing about a country in which the last general election of the century was fought on the grounds that taxation of the middle classes was a form of unacceptable persecution, while public services and health care remained in a lamentable state despite a decade of extraordinary wealth. The same country where the writer Michael O'Loughlin, returning to Ireland after twenty years away, found 'on the one hand a burgeoning underclass racked by drugs, gangsterism and poverty and on the other, spectacular wealth, vulgarity and indifference'.[96] The gulf between these two assessments needs to be explored, and it needs to be explored using a variety of sources, in an effort to assess whether Ireland by the end of the twentieth century was still aspiring to rather than delivering on the confident nationalist predictions of a hundred years previously.

- ONE -

1900–1912

Ireland would be like 'soft wax' for years to come

Politically and socially, the island of Ireland was, on the surface at least, relatively calm in 1900. The previous half-century had witnessed considerable turmoil and trauma, most notably in the form of the Great Famine (1845–9), which resulted in widespread death and emigration. The population of the small island, which covers an area of 32,595 miles, and is divided into the provinces of Ulster in the north, and Leinster, Munster and Connaught in the east, south and west, plummeted from 8,175,124 in 1841 to just 4,456,546 in 1901.

A land war which commenced in the late 1870s began the process of the demise of the landlord class, and moves towards land ownership for the masses, in what was an overwhelmingly agricultural country. Socially and economically, a new middle class of farmers was cementing its gains and political authority, though the campaign in the 1880s to achieve Home Rule, a limited form of independence from the United Kingdom, had been unsuccessful. In the north of the country, the unionists of Ulster had demonstrated outright opposition to Home Rule, and in the process had emphasised their political bonds with the British Conservative Party, which had been in power since 1895.

The unionists' distinct identity was also cultural and religious. The three southern provinces were homogeneously Catholic, with 89.6 per cent of their population Catholic by 1911, and more confident since the granting of Catholic emancipation in 1829, under the leadership of the 'Liberator', Daniel O'Connell. In contrast, by 1911, Protestants in Ulster accounted for 56.33 per cent of the population. Many were descended from the original planters of the seventeenth century, one of Britain's colonising projects, which had resulted in the 'planting' of a large number of English and Scottish Protestants in Ulster, taking land previously held by Catholic 'old English' and Irish natives. Ulster was also distinct in its degree of industrialisation and urbanisation; in contrast, the industrial revolution had made little impact elsewhere. Though united against Home Rule, the unionist movement was often divided on class and religious lines, reflecting its complicated heritage and the level of inequality that existed in Ulster society.

Despite the evolution of organised political nationalism in the south in the late nineteenth century, at the dawn of the twentieth century there was considerable support in both Ireland and England for the maintenance of the Act of Union of 1800. This Act had been the response to an Irish insurrection in 1798, and had created the United Kingdom of Great Britain and Ireland, with 100 Irish MPs representing Ireland in the House of Commons. It resulted in the abolition of the Irish parliament, which had existed in various forms, though not without interruption, since the thirteenth century, following England's conquest of Ireland in the twelfth century. Throughout the eighteenth century, the Irish parliament had represented the interests of the Protestant propertied classes.

Gerald Balfour, who as Chief Secretary in 1900 was effectively head of the Irish administration in Ireland, which had its headquarters in Dublin Castle, was answerable to the British parliament for some 29 government departments in Ireland. Though he denied it, he was said to have coined the phrase 'killing Home Rule with kindness' to describe the Conservative government's reforms in the areas of land ownership, local government, infrastructure and agricultural development, working on the age-old assumption that economic improvement would dilute the potential for radical nationalism in Ireland.

Despite the failure of Charles Stewart Parnell and his nationalist Irish Parliamentary Party to achieve Home Rule in conjunction with the British Liberal Party in the 1880s, a sense of Irish nationalism and a distinct Irish identity was apparent in many ways in the south of Ireland in 1900. At the turn of the century, the renowned Irish poet W. B. Yeats predicted that Ireland would be like 'soft wax' for years to come, as it was entering 'a new period of political activity'. A new sense of cultural vibrancy, in the form of a distinctive language, literature and history, was very much in evidence; the Irish Literary Theatre had been established, and James Joyce was submitting his earliest work for publication. The country was endowed with writers of excellence, and the level of cultural debate was intense and intellectually challenging, reflected in the endeavours of the Gaelic League, founded to promote the Irish language, and its numerous publications. Ideas of an 'Irish-Ireland' abounded.

The republican Fenian movement of the nineteenth century, dedicated to overthrowing British rule in Ireland when circumstances would permit, was undergoing a process of rejuvenation, and the Irish Parliamentary Party reunited in 1900, after experiencing division and faction in the 1890s. The outbreak of the Boer War in 1899 provided advanced Irish nationalists with an opportunity to galvanise anti-British and pro-Boer sentiment, and to suggest there were lessons to be learned regarding how to take on the might of the British Empire. But it was also the case that thousands of Irish men were loyal servants of the army of that empire, whether out of conviction or economic necessity. The aged Queen Victoria visited Ireland in 1900, for the first time in thirty-seven years, and although advanced nationalists protested loudly, she was well received by most. Majority nationalist opinion, it seemed, was content to aspire to a Home Rule settlement that would see Ireland stay within the empire.

Many Irish nationalists in 1900 thus had something of a dual attitude to British rule in Ireland; while they would not mourn its passing and while many would work towards its destruction, most were also culturally and politically comfortable with the trappings of empire. The middle classes had also inherited distinctly 'Victorian' attitudes when it came to social issues and the alleviation of poverty and inequality, and all classes had absorbed English popular culture and literature.

Class tension still abounded in many rural areas, which a new agrarian body, William O'Brien's United Irish League, was keen to exploit. Many of the agricultural labourers were landless, there were still people living in mud cabins, and the average life expectancy was little beyond fifty. Most Irish farmsteads were minuscule, and 32,000 people had emigrated in 1899 alone, reflecting a higher emigration rate than existed elsewhere in Europe.

Nearly 25 per cent of children born in the capital city, Dublin, would not live to the age of one, and diseases such as TB were rife. The failure or partial failure of the potato crop was still capable of generating near-famine conditions, and in the absence of social welfare measures the last refuge for many was still the despised workhouse, imposed on Ireland by the Irish Poor Law Act of 1838, which had divided the country into 130 unions, each with a workhouse. Many inhabitants of the cities, north and south, were living in appalling slum conditions, and labour and trade union leaders were keen to engender a sense of working-class hegemony. Irish women, both unionist and nationalist, were also becoming more involved in public life and organised for specific political and cultural purposes, a minority becoming the first generation of Irish women to benefit from access to third-level education. But despite political agitation, a degree of social discontent and class tension, and the observations and predictions of Yeats and others, few could have predicted the scale of the transformation of Ireland in the first twenty years of the twentieth century.

'inventing, criticising, attempting and doing'

In the late nineteenth and early twentieth centuries, some nationalist political activists made optimistic predictions about Ireland's prospects in the new century. This was despite the passing of the era of Charles Stewart Parnell. Though he had united national sentiment in the south of Ireland at the height of his career in the 1880s, Parnell had failed to deliver Home Rule. But the idea that a wholesale transference of energy from the life of politics to the life of culture occurred as a result does scant justice to the many forces at work in Irish society at this time. The most recent research suggests that the Irish 'cultural revival' of this period was a relatively coherent mass movement, despite differences in religion, class, gender and political conviction. But far from political pessimism, there was also, among the educated Catholic elite, a dynamism and confident outlook, with a vision of a Home Rule Ireland taking a central place in the British Empire.[1] Alongside this, a nationalist tradition stretching back two centuries was being communicated to a newly literate mass audience, and sometimes reinterpreted. One aspect of that tradition was a belief in the use of violence to achieve Irish independence from Britain. Adherents of the various philosophies of Irish nationalism were exceptionally active in the opening decade of the twentieth century, and often borrowed freely from each other's discourse.[2]

A year after the death of Parnell, in 1892, a small pamphlet was published in Dublin entitled *Ireland in the Twentieth Century*, in which the writer T. J. Clancy contended that the coming century, being the 'heir of all ages', would witness Ireland taking its place among the nations of the world. He made a number of predictions for the future of the country, suggesting Ireland's nineteenth-century bond with America had illustrated that the country's central and most favourable geographical position would be the source of great advantage in the coming century, having already brought Ireland from the confines of civilisation to its very centre.

Clancy was less concerned with lamenting the years of persecution, suffering and loss than with emphasising Ireland's potential for development, particularly if the issues of peasant proprietorship of land and Home Rule were solved satisfactorily. In his view, there was no natural or physical reason why Ireland should be a poor country; nor was there any evidence of poverty in the intellectual and moral characteristics of the people. Rather, natural resources and a favourable trading location, close to the great consuming centres of Europe, meant that Ireland could become a rich nation. Indeed, he suggested the country could develop an industrial base to make it capable of supporting a population of between eight and ten million, ensuring, with adequate, paternal state policies, rather than relying on the political economy, that the country could produce and manufacture enough not just for its own population but for export. He predicted that standards of living would increase, as would life expectancy, and placed emphasis on the brilliant scholastic tradition of the Irish, while acknowledging that they had much ground to make up in technical and scientific education.[3]

This optimism needed to be complemented by a crusade, according to the first edition of the *Leader* newspaper in 1900, to prove Ireland was capable of the task of self-government and intellectual political and cultural self-reliance, harnessing all the resources of the country, and 'inventing, criticising, attempting and doing'.[4] This was perhaps an Irish version of the coming unbridled Edwardian optimism, in the sense that the Edwardians, seeing themselves as a liberal society, believed in progress by compromise with decisions arrived at by constitutional methods, rather than political battle being waged on the streets.

Allowing for exaggeration, there were many reasons for optimism in late nineteenth- and early twentieth-century Ireland. The social transformation of the nineteenth century had been characterised by the increasing organisation of larger agricultural holdings, complemented by a growth in banking and the development of railways. A development of pasturage, at the expense of tillage, had revealed the possibility for an increase in the exportation of cattle to Britain. (There were over 800,000 cattle exported annually early in the century.[5]) The net result, according to F. S. L. Lyons, one of the first Irish historians of the modern era to write a history of post-Famine Ireland, 'was to substitute a rural bourgeoisie for a rural proletariat'.[6]

By the dawn of the twentieth century there was little doubt that the material conditions of life had improved in rural Ireland, with more security of tenure and the threat of endemic starvation no longer an annual fear. But it came at a significant cost, not only in the context of political struggle, but also in the demography and structure of rural society. This was reflected in late and arranged marriages and the continued emigration of a substantial part of the young population.

'Don't let us have an argument on our way home from your father's burial'
The historian Patrick Maume has convincingly revised the accepted wisdom about the nature of Irish politics during the post-Parnell period. Maume's assessment of the continued evolution of the nationalist tradition is built around a detailed examination of the interaction of various nationalist elements, their champions and foes and their discourse. He demonstrates the intricacies of politics at local level and the importance of the development of communications to spread various ideas – some old, some borrowed, some new – to a newly literate mass audience. He highlights the multitude of layers that underpinned the reunification of the Irish Parliamentary Party, the various machinations of William O'Brien's agrarian protest body the United Irish League, and the rise of a small Sinn Féin ('ourselves alone') movement as a competitor to the Parnellite tradition in Irish politics. Along the way he gives many valuable and original insights into the personalities, major and minor, that fuelled much of the debate of the period.[7]

Maume's research underlines the importance of the communications revolution and in particular the increase in the number of nationalist provincial newspapers. These were partly a consequence of the late nineteenth-century campaign to displace or co-opt the professional and commercial elite that dominated contemporary Catholic society. Much infighting and personal antagonism characterised the politics of the period and there was growing awareness of the development of the local in Irish politics. In this sense the assumption of F. S. L. Lyons of an 'extraordinary transference of

energy from the life of politics into the life of culture'[8] needs to be qualified. Similarly, the contention in 1911 of the writer Lady Gregory, one
of the leaders of the cultural revival (in a view shared by her mentor, the
poet W. B. Yeats), that 'Young men were no longer tied up in leagues
and politics, their imagination called out for something more',[9] was only
partly true.

The Irish Parliamentary Party was indeed facing difficulties and at
times indifference. The discipline its members had historically imposed on
themselves and the obedience they marshalled in their followers was under
severe threat, and political victory seemed unlikely, as the party's problems
were compounded by quarrelling among its leaders. Issues like local-government reform were crucial in strengthening intermediate organisation
at the expense of centralised leadership, and the United Irish League disrupted the traditional balance of power between the British government
and Catholic and lay clerical elites. There was also a lower-middle class
they were out of touch with; this was manifest in the development of a new
nationalist self-image by those outside the existing patronage networks,
reflected in the pages of Arthur Griffith's *United Ireland* and D. P. Moran's
the *Leader*. These journalists had differences in approach, given Griffith's
reliance on eighteenth- and nineteenth-century Irish patriotic reasoning,
and Moran's tendency to be aggressively contemporary, but both aimed at
similar audiences.

Another spirited publication, though short-lived, was the *Irish
Peasant*, which commenced publication in 1903, and the activities of
various organisations such as the Ancient Order of Hibernians and the All
for Ireland League also contributed to the dynamism of local agitation.
Most were later to find a common home in the Irish Volunteer movement,
established in 1913 in response to the Ulster Volunteer Force formed
by Ulster unionists to prevent the implementation of Home Rule. The
British government was to remain tolerant of the many manifestations of
discontent, which was to prove costly during the period of the First World
War.

The reality of politics in post-Parnell Ireland was that his death
exposed the degree to which he and his handlers had successfully managed
potential divisions and schisms by creating an icon that shrewdly masked
the internal tensions. 'We created Parnell,' insisted Tim Healy, one of his
parliamentary contemporaries, 'and Parnell created us. We seized very
early in the movement the idea of this man with his superb silences, his

historic name, his determination, his self-control, his aloofness – we seized that as the canvas of a great national hero.'[10] Expectations were not only too high; it was also the case that his tragic, romantic and speedy passing ensured that a subsequent generation of nationalists would grow to political maturation with a memory of the squabbles his ousting gave rise to.

One of Ireland's most celebrated playwrights, Seán O'Casey, detailed in his memoirs the capacity of the fractious Parnell debates to dominate the discourse of even the most delicate family situations:

'I wonder will the home rulers ever be able to turn the Royal Bank of Ireland into an Irish House of Parliament,' murmured the mother, as she glanced out the window. – 'God forbid they'd ever be able to turn such a beautiful building into a rendezvous of rowdyism,' said Ella fervently. 'Parnell's the only gentleman in the whole gang,' said Tom. 'They were watching their chance for fifty years and Kitty O'Shea [the married woman with whom he had an affair, prompting his downfall] is only an excuse for downing him. If they throw him over, clowns and pantaloons in a pantomime parliament are all they can hope to be.' 'Oh,' said the mother pleadingly. 'Don't let us have an argument on our way home from your father's burial.'[11]

Maud Griffith, wife of the future Sinn Féin leader Arthur, in a statement to the Bureau of Military History in the 1950s (see Chapter 3), revealed the extent to which such squabbles could turn a person off politics altogether, even though she was married to the most prolific political propagandist of the era: 'he never talked to me about politics as I did not want to, having been brought up in a family in which my father was an ardent Parnellite and my mother a follower of William O'Brien, with consequent frequent disputes on political matters.'[12]

'for the first time I saw the whole of Ireland'

It was not surprising a new generation tired of such debates, a point worth bearing in mind when examining the resurgence of the Irish Republican Brotherhood, a secret oath-bound society that had ignited a failed rebellion in 1867, but which was now reorganising through the labours of a new generation. It seemed that 'younger separatists who had not experienced the triumphs of the 1880s and who judged politics only by the faction-fighting of the Irish Parliamentary Party split were impatient with

Griffith's attempts to reinvent Parnellism and they found in the IRB a
nucleus for supporters of pure and simple republicanism'.[13] At the level
of popular politics, some of the social and literary clubs and recreational
societies which the nineteenth-century Fenians had cultivated could, if
revitalised, continue to act as political bases for the artisans who sought to
keep some semblance of the physical-force tradition alive.

But not all young men who joined the IRB were conscious of any
grand political plan and, whether out of boredom, or the wish to be
included in local socialising, needed little persuading or political tutelage.
Some of the statements to the Bureau of Military History imply a great
degree of casualness in the manner in which men joined inactive branches
and the extent to which dominant families in a particular parish could
heavily influence the nationalist sentiment of their neighbourhood. John
Flanagan from West Clare, for example, remembered being persuaded to
join by a member of the most dominant family in his parish: 'I agreed to
join that evening during which he swore me in as we were standing beside
Owen Doyle's pump in Henry Street, Kilrush ... The business, as I now
remember it, consisted mostly of discussion on the recruitment of new
members and the circulation of the paper *Irish Freedom*.'[14]

The Gaelic Athletic Association and in particular the Gaelic League
were also important in drawing young people into the national movement,
and political advancement and cultural enrichment seemed to necessitate
membership of both organisations. A member of the Supreme Council of
the IRB, Patrick Sarsfield, referred to his experience of the League at the
Munster Féis in 1902: 'Something in the songs ... something in the music
... something in the atmosphere gripped me and I seemed to be put in
touch with something far back in the race ... for the first time I saw the
whole of Ireland.'[15] Patrick Higgins, Gaelic League member and future
Irish Volunteer, suggested 'the whole Volunteer movement in Cork and
the position it created grew out of the activities of a relatively small group
of men and women who had been working in different ways to promote
one or other various aspects of the Irish-Ireland movement'.[16]

Coinciding with this, the emergence of a substantial Catholic middle
class and Catholic urbanised merchants was a direct product of advanced
employment and economic opportunities. Their support of moderate
nationalism was reflected in the pages of the *Freeman's Journal*. The late
nineteenth-century alliance between the British Liberal Party and the Irish
Parliamentary Party ensured that Irish politics of the period remained

multi-layered. But Irish Parliamentary Party representatives came to be more frequently lambasted for perceived selfishness, corruption and laziness. Those looking for a new direction in Irish politics dismissed the idea that there was any great difference between the British Liberal or Conservative parties, accusing the Irish party of being intent on merely replacing one ascendancy with its own.

This was Irish politics at national level, but it was on the local arena that the polemicists often focused their attention. One notable question being posed at the beginning of the decade was the extent to which the nation belonged to the MPs or the people, a consideration given added weight by the campaigns of William O'Brien. Rival policies were certainly gestating. Patrick Maume has noted:

> D. P. Moran combined cultural revivalism, criticism of the party's anti-intellectualism and authoritarianism and the politics of Catholic grievance to provide a rationale for a populist version of the traditional Catholic 'Whiggery' that placed Catholic middle-class interests above political nationalism. Arthur Griffith drew on the ideology of Young Ireland and on artisan traditions of self-help and anti-deferentialism to combine a reinvented separatism with the Parnellite legacy and the 'Hungarian policy' as the course to be taken by a new Parnell when the party finally reverted to corruption and chaos. The agrarian agitation was, however, making it harder for the British government to manage Ireland.[17]

At national level, the administration of Ireland under the Union involved the workings of a multitude of departments, boards and officers, presided over by a titular head, the Lord Lieutenant or Viceroy. But in practice, administrative power lay in the hands of the Chief Secretary, who was answerable for the activities of a number of departments which were operating in many instances autonomously. Other important posts included the Lord Chancellor, the Attorney General, and the Under Secretary, who was in effect the permanent head of the Chief Secretary's office in Dublin. Overseeing the administration of British rule in Ireland was a frustrating experience that few ambitious politicians cherished. The relationship of government departments to each other was ill defined and chief secretaries often found themselves powerless in dealing with government agencies. The Treasury's patent disdain of Irish government departments exacerbated the difficulties as did a lack of appetite for the implementation of structural and operational reform. This was a reluctance that seemed to be shared by Irish politicians who focused on the idea of controlling rather than improving the administration of government in Ireland.[18]

In the 1890s, administrative bodies deliberately placed outside the control of Dublin Castle included the Congested Districts Board and the Department of Agriculture and Technical Instruction. Though they were often in conflict with other government departments and unsure of their administrative function, they did instil some appreciation of what would later come to be known as 'regional development'. Transfer of land also became an essential administrative responsibility following the passing of Land Acts in 1881 (which established the Land Commission) and 1885, and the most significant, the Wyndham Act of 1903. The legislation of the late nineteenth century initially advanced to tenants the sum necessary to purchase their holdings, repayable over a period of years, and established an independent commission to determine equitable rents, while the Wyndham Act finished off landlord control over tenants and made it easier for tenants to purchase land. A defect in the act was that ratepayers had to meet the financial shortcomings arising from land purchase. The act was eventually revised by the Liberal government in 1909, not only altering the finances of the land purchase scheme but also providing 'for compulsory purchase orders against reluctant landlords in the congested western districts, and gave coercive power to the Land Commission for the first time'.[19]

By the end of the 1890s, British management of Ireland also included the introduction of representative local government, seen as one manifestation of the Conservative government's attempt to 'kill Home Rule with kindness'. Irish politicians treated the implementation of the Local Government (Ireland) Act of 1898 with relative caution. William O'Brien was apt to speak of it as a stepping stone, seeing it as a further argument to complete the fabric of constitutional liberty, and a measure which would in no sense divert Irish nationalist leaders from their ultimate aim of Home Rule. Prior to 1898, local-government authority in Ireland had been confined to a Protestant elite. In a system characterised by elitism and stagnation, power had rested with grand juries, Poor Law boards, boards of works and county sheriffs. The new local-government system had both a financial and a political importance. Under the terms of the act, local government was now to be distributed between county councils, urban and rural district councils and boards of guardians. The act made the parliamentary electorate the local-government electorate, which meant that male householders and those occupying part of a house now had the vote. Significantly, the new poor rate was to be charged to the occupier rather than the landlord, which undoubtedly made it easier for them to swallow the pill of losing their administrative grip. With the first elections held in April 1899 there had been an opportunity for more nationalist control and the practice of democracy on a scale never experienced before. Nationalists won 300 seats, with the unionists taking 83, the significance of which can be gauged by the fact that prior to 1899 nationalists had filled only 47 out of 704 grand jury positions. Four women were returned as district councillors and 26 as rural district councillors (women were not permitted to run as county councillors until 1911).

'Redmond and his whole party would be kicked into space'

Nationwide, pre-election speeches had focused on Home Rule sentiments and the over-taxation of Ireland. During their first meetings most councils insisted on passing motions on these themes, while the rehousing of evicted tenants and demands for a Catholic university also featured prominently. Many, however, were astute enough to appoint unionist members to the financial committees, recognising their greater practical experience in such matters. In Tullamore, County Offaly, one councillor was chided for the absurdity of his motion proposing the abolition of landlords.

As this suggests, the councils of Ireland were to be by no means hotbeds of belligerent radicalism. It is quite accurate to view the introduction of modern democratic councils as an important starting point in the development of the local in Irish politics; particularly in the context of extending patronage and strengthening local organisation at the expense of House of Commons-based leadership. There were negative aspects also, and for all the talk of the abolition of the old boards of guardians and the disappearance of the landlord class from the administration of local affairs, there is validity in the argument that one oligarchy was merely replaced by another, that of the substantial farmer and his attendant mindset, which was slow to change and reluctant to spend money. The first parliamentary leader of the Ulster Unionists, Edward Saunderson, had perceptively noted that 'when an Irishman is confined within the lines of common sense and shown that if he chooses to indulge in eccentricity he will find it an expensive enjoyment, that Irishman is seen to be as sensible as any other man'.[20]

The proof of Saunderson's prediction was evident in the fact that councillors who were extravagant and inefficient in expenditure were liable to be voted out of office in 1902 and 1905. Ironically, given nationalists' castigation of previous local government, councillors were also in the long run to gain a reputation for jobbery and petty corruption which was not seriously challenged until after independence in 1922. George Wyndham (Chief Secretary 1900–1905) attempted further rationalisation of the administration, particularly in the context of land reform. Although Wyndham privately made noises about being theoretically predisposed to the idea of Home Rule, he also believed it was not 'as yet within the range of practical politics',[21] and his belief in taming nationalist sentiment through fairer administration was to be his undoing. His political career in Ireland was destroyed by opposition to his proposed measures of devolution.

Three quarters of the Irish constituencies were returning Home Rulers of one kind or another early in the century, and the victory of the Liberals in 1907 seemed to hold hopes of progress being made in the direction of self-government. Nonetheless, an Irish Council Bill, proposed in 1906, providing for a Council of 106 to administer eight of the most important Dublin departments came to nothing. The demise of this initiative had much to do with the failure to consult adequately with Irish politicians, illustrating for John Redmond (as leader of the Irish Parliamentary Party) that it was dangerous to co-operate with the Liberals on reform measures that fell short of Home Rule. Augustine Birrell, writing in 1907, recognised in relation to Redmond that:

> He can't rest on his oars for a single moment … the impression is general in Ireland that the parliamentary party have allowed Home Rule to be shoved under and that it can't emerge for at least a decade. Were the impression to become a belief, Redmond and his whole party would be kicked into space … if he can't gain our support then he must fight nail and tooth and at least half his supporters would be just as well pleased if he decided to fight us.[22]

This episode raised interesting questions about the Liberal Party's approach to Irish affairs. Alan O'Day has questioned why such a resourceful generation in many respects proved so resourceless when it came to managing Ireland. The Liberal historian George Dangerfield saw the failure to deal with Ireland satisfactorily as playing a central role in the demise of Victorian Liberal England. Presumably it was seen as important to solve the Irish issue as it would have a significant impact on the whole of the United Kingdom. One of their dilemmas was whether to approach Ireland on the basis that there were two races on the island or only to admit to 'differences of degree'.[23] The reality was that most Liberals could not create a viable alternative to the nineteenth-century policy of Gladstonian Home Rule; though equally, they could blame Redmond for his insistence on Home Rule and any resultant unpopular legislation. But crises always had the potential to derail Anglo-Irish relations and the Home Rule question did highlight the political and constitutional 'ailments' of the age. According to O'Day the Edwardians had 'a reasonably coherent view of what was meant of themselves as a liberal society' that lay 'in discussion, compromise, rationality and the acceptance of decisions arrived at by legally constituted authority. Dissent was openly condoned but any political battle was to be waged in newspaper columns, on platforms and in parliament – not on the streets.'[24] But it was also true that by the outbreak of the First World War it was in fact the streets that mattered most in Irish politics, raising serious questions about Liberal Party mismanagement and the difference in Irish conditions.

The return of a Liberal government to power opened up new political possibilities and had the capacity to reveal the practical political limitations of voluntary action or cultural revival. There was always the possibility of Irish MPs profiting from parliamentary arithmetic, and a constitutional crisis in Britain after Lloyd George's Budget of 1909 resulted in the removal of the House of Lords veto and its replacement with a delaying power of only two years.

But despite this development, which made the passing of a Home Rule bill possible, and though the Irish Parliamentary Party was capable of the occasional use of extremist rhetoric, there was a body of opinion that was becoming increasingly sceptical of the narrow political ambitions of the Home Rule supporters. A contemporary well-educated Catholic, John Moynihan, remarked in a letter to his brother in 1912 that:

> The whole scheme of the present Bill is calculated to push the power into the hands of the most dangerous and inefficient class in the country. All the indicators are that the Irish parliament will be similar in character to the present Dublin Corporation, which is shunned by

all decent men and instead of being an object of pride is an object of contempt to the citizens.[25]

'badgers in the glen'

William O'Brien had become a pivotal player in Irish politics by the turn of the century, channelling the new political energy evident at local level. His United Irish League, formed in Westport, County Mayo, in January 1898, which aimed at securing the redistribution of land to small western farmers, had, by the summer of 1900, spread its network countrywide and was instrumental in reuniting the IPP. O'Brien was anxious to involve Parnellites and present his league as a constitutional movement acting within the law, although he was determined to keep it quite separate from the Parliamentary Party. However, after 1900 it became the main constituency and fundraising organisation for the IPP.

It was also his intention that it should be the anchor of a new phase in the Irish land war, and denunciations of landlordism, land legislation and land-grabbers (as the grazers and ranchers were often referred to) soon followed. Crucially, local issues tended to dominate the speeches and resolutions associated with the League though O'Brien, in the absence of the old Land League organisers, was very much on his own in organisational terms. It was difficult to secure the co-operation and support of people like John Dillon, who wanted the movement to be subordinate to the Party (unlike O'Brien, who insisted the party 'can only be saved or united from outside'), and veteran land campaigner Michael Davitt, always more comfortable with the notion of an extra-parliamentary movement. Given the pressures on O'Brien it was unsurprising that he had to delegate a lot of authority to local organisers. Like the Land League before, O'Brien had to contend with lack of support from affluent nationalists. But he succeeded in overcoming Church hostility and recruited the support of Parnellites in many local areas, and in particular used the local-government elections of April 1899 to secure a power base, reminding the new electorate that they were no longer 'badgers in the glen'.[26]

'a way which caught the multitude'

A convention at Claremorris in January 1899 was endorsed by both Church and different factions of the IPP and produced a constitution for the League which, while prioritising the cause of national self-government for Ireland, was still dominated by agrarian concerns. Most of O'Brien's

subsequent speeches echoed this by calling for the abolition of landlordism. The message of the League reached an even wider audience with the
production of the *Irish People* newspaper in September 1899, the work on
which, combined with everything else, was taking its toll on O'Brien's
health. It may have been tempting for O'Brien, with a view to courting
Irish-American support, to have engendered more militant, if not illegal,
League activities. But throughout 1900 this line of action was broadly
avoided, perhaps because political developments in 1900 heralded the
reunification of the Irish Party under the leadership of John Redmond and
a general election in the autumn of that year. A memorandum from the
Chief Secretary's office suggested that O'Brien could be viewed as having
achieved much, because he was the only man who had a programme, while
'the other Irish leaders in parliament occupied themselves watching, and
quarrelling with each other. They dealt in generalities, but they never
proposed anything that would appeal to the people. Mr O'Brien turned to
the old question of the land, and presented it in a way which caught the
multitude.'[27]

O'Brien was exceptional in his ability to act as a catalyst for political action, seemingly loyal to the dictum that rhetorical extremism was
a means of securing a hearing for moderation. Many of his ventures –
newspaper editor, MP, land war leader who became an advocate of conciliation towards landlords – were the product of his fertile imagination,
which helped to ensure the balance on which the survival of constitutional
nationalism depended. Having opposed the reunion of the parliamentary
factions in 1900 he advocated a more conciliatory approach after the Land
Act of 1903, being pragmatic about the impact it would have, and in this
context what was politically feasible. This was a political recognition that,
socially, things were improving for many.

Given the bitterness of the Parnell split during the 1890s, the reunification of the Irish Parliamentary Party in 1900 under John Redmond
was an important turning point. He was to lead the party for the next
17 years, an extraordinary feat given the continuing factionalism within
the party and the growing dissent outside. The election of 1900 saw 72
MPs elected who were pledged to supporting the League. They included
O'Brien, who now saw the function of the party as 'making the wrongs of
the remotest country village' heard in London, another indication that the
era of the local had arrived, which was underpinned by the Parliamentary
Party's espousal of compulsory land purchase.

However, the party preoccupied itself with other matters, the Church remained tepid in its endorsement of League activities, and the government seemed intent on conciliating rather than provoking. Although League activity was stepped up in 1902, particularly in the context of a vigorous withholding rents campaign, the Conservatives had begun to make moves in the direction of a new land purchase bill. The relationship between O'Brien and the party was coming under increasing strain owing to the disturbed state of much of the country. For some dissident unionists also, a creed likely to 'fray at the edges' when Home Rule was not a serious threat, the demise of landlordism was to be heartily striven for. As the Ulster land agitator T. W. Russell put it in *The Irish Land Question* (1902): 'The union is best maintained and preserved by doing away with those grievances which imperil its existence. Chief of these is the Irish land system. And he is a true unionist who seeks, as I do, to destroy it.'[28]

'unable to marry until the exuberance of life has gone out of them'

The emigration initiated by the Famine continued into the twentieth century and proved to be one of the great formative factors in modern Irish history. It is a reminder that twentieth-century Irish history cannot be understood merely in terms of Ireland alone and those who were left behind. By 1911 one third of all people born in Ireland were living elsewhere. The figures were truly remarkable – by the last decade of the nineteenth century only three fifths of those born in Ireland were still at home, and three million were overseas, and return migration was rare. In County Mayo, for example, the population dropped from 388,887 in 1841 to 192,177 in 1911. More women than men were leaving towards the end of the nineteenth century, and in the period 1901–11, the number of females emigrating per 1,000 males was 1223.[29]

As the new century dawned, Irish men married at an average age of 30 and women at 26 but, by 1911, 27 per cent of men and 25 per cent of women in the age range 45–54 had never been wed. In the early years of the century 90 per cent of those emigrating were single, and unskilled. The writer Robert Lynd, in his *Home Life in Ireland*, published in 1909, depressingly concluded that 'Ireland is largely a country of late marriages and of few marriages. Emigration has drained the country to an unnatural degree of the young men and women of marrying age, and those who remain are ... frequently unable to marry until the exuberance of life has gone out of them.'[30] The unparalleled migration of the nineteenth century established a pattern of reaction from economists, politicians, priests and nationalists which was ultimately ambivalent, a characteristic which continued for much of the twentieth century. This was despite the fact that in the dying years of the nineteenth century and the early years of the twentieth some Irish were assisted in emigrating through a mixture of state, local and philanthropic aid, because the alternative at home was destitution, which placed its own burden on local resources.

What attention was given to the problem tended to focus on the consequences for the future of rural life rather than on the causes. The Catholic Hierarchy in 1902 issued a resolution on the matter which was more concerned with the supposed female delusion that there was 'some bright vision beyond the Atlantic' and the recklessness of males in entering a depressed American employment market.[31] Much of the rhetoric employed by Cardinal Manning in the late nineteenth century was based on the idea of the horrors of industrialisation, set against the tranquillity of the emigrants' former environment. Speaking of destitute Irish girls in London, he said: 'What were they a little while ago? Daughters of our noble peasantry in the country, born in green villages and hamlets, growing up in innocence, coming to England in the hope of industry and employment.'[32] The Catholic Church, however, did not favour restricting the free movement of people; the *Irish Catholic*, a paper that had decried population loss, was still happy to accept advertisements in 1911 which aggressively recruited intending emigrants. A measure of what members of the Hierarchy thought the 'noble' peasants should tolerate was reflected in the views of Dr Denis Kelly, the Catholic bishop of Ross, who had been a member of the Poor Law commission of 1909. He declared himself in favour of the quarter acre clause, a measure introduced during the Famine in 1847 stipulating that any family holding more than a quarter of an acre could not be granted relief, either in or out of the workhouse, until they gave up their land. Kelly believed that the existence of the clause was 'an incentive to self-reliance' and that it kept large numbers of the population 'on the right side of the border line which separates poverty from actual pauperism'.[33]

Although the phrase 'peasant extermination' occasionally appeared in nationalist rhetoric in relation to emigration, silence was a more notable feature of nationalist reaction, or, alternatively, proposals to make rural life less dull through educational classes and entertainment. These suggestions did little to promote a realistic approach to the social and economic issues which gave rise to emigration, and instead were absorbed into the broader 'Gaelic revival' movement. The *Irish Peasant* took a more aggressive line, with some arguing that emigration agents should be boycotted, though interestingly, those suggesting such a course of action were rebuked in 1906 by a contributor to the paper who suggested that a boycott would be counterproductive and misfocused. It was asserted that 'emigration is a fact, and society must order itself to meet facts'.[34] This was to be the more prevalent, though often unstated, position in relation to Irish emigration.

Demographically, Ireland was also unique. Farm labourers born around the turn of the century had the lowest marriage rate of any social class, with about half still unmarried by 1950, while life expectancy for men and women in 1900 was just under 50 years. Infant mortality rates stood at 99 per 1,000 live births. In the first decade of the century 6,500 children under the age of one year died on average each year.

As unskilled labourers and domestic servants, Irish emigrants naturally clustered in slum areas. As David Fitzpatrick noted: 'Throughout the post-Famine century, emigration represented an expected stage in the cycle of life – the Irish equivalent of moving out of the parental household into lodgings in the modern city. Children were reared as potential emigrants, and when they reached adulthood, many knew that they "must travel"', partly as a result of the 'stem-family' succession system, which saw the eldest son inherit the farm.[35] These 'push' factors were further strengthened by the growing dependence of those at home on emigrant remittances. In 1908, Louis Paul-Dubois in his book *Contemporary Ireland* referred to emigration as the 'fundamental characteristic of contemporary Ireland'. He examined the region of Clifden, in County Galway, where it was estimated that £10,000 per annum was received in emigrants' remittances, which was over half the amount owed for rents from the 3,300 families in the district: '... throughout the West of Ireland, the landlord's rents are often merely a tax levied on the filial piety of child emigrants from the peasant families'.[36] Jeremiah Murphy, in his memoir of a childhood in Kerry in the opening years of the century, recalled:

> The century was new and economic conditions were improving in many parts of the world. People who had emigrated from Ireland to the United States, England or Australia frequently sent money home to their aged parents and it was interesting to hear the old people

boast about the gifts. Naturally, the ones with the largest families in America had the most reason to boast ... many of them saved some money and returned for a trip or desired to settle down on a farm in their native land. The girls especially were prime targets of the young farmers contemplating matrimony and they provided almost unfair competition for the other girls who left home. They were smart looking, well dressed and their manners and speech were a distinct asset. However, when asked if they were going to marry a farmer, some retorted, 'I guess I'm too wise for that.'[37]

One historian of Irish female emigration, Janet Nolan, noted that many Irish women emigrated independently of husbands or fathers; well before the 1880s the pattern of unmarried women travelling alone to foreign cities had been established. Almost 82,000 more females than males left Ireland between 1885 and 1920, with almost 700,000 women leaving. Nolan acknowledged there was much suffering, but also suggested: 'the reappearance of pre-Famine roles within the Irish-American family enabled emigrant women and their daughters to emerge as active forces in their new communities. Their emigration signified their active choice to regain lost social and economic power, while domestic service speeded the process of assimilation.'[38]

'something less valuable than a plough'

For those who did not emigrate, owing to their tender years, there was another way in which they could be utilised to add to the family income. Patrick MacGill's *Children of the Dead End*, published in London in 1914, gave an unsentimental insight into the loss of childhood by those who were taken out of elementary schooling in depressed parts of rural Ireland. They were brought to hiring fairs and rented out to farmers, who, as he noted, treated them 'rather less kindly than their animals'. The money that they earned was sent home and given to the landlord and the priest. MacGill was frank about the fact that many children of his generation and background were born and bred merely to support their parents, and that parents took great care to drive that fact into their minds from infancy. As for his 'Master', the farmer who hired him out, and worked him to the bone, he noted that 'to him I was not a human being, a boy with an appetite and a soul. I was merely a ware purchased in the market place, something less valuable than a plough, and of no more account than a barrow.'[39] Such treatment was by no means unique to Irish children, but it ironically coincided with a time when some of Ireland's cultural and literary nationalists sought to make childhood a sort of 'expendable cultural object': in plays and literature, childhood, like Ireland itself, had to be re-created as a place of innocence.[40]

The Victorian interest in the plight of the vulnerable child had a knock-on effect in Ireland, but it was also countered by delusion, as evidenced by the fact that some Dubliners had objected to the establishment of a Dublin Society for the Prevention of Cruelty to Children in 1889. Journals such as the *Social and Statistical Inquiry Society of Ireland*, along with newspapers, pamphlets and books, drew attention to issues relating to child welfare. Members of Dublin Corporation, in conjunction with organisations such as the Women's National Health Association and the police-aided Clothing Society, initiated a number of welfare schemes for mothers, infants and children, and Irish philanthropic efforts improved the lot of many. But reformers were also resented by some as upper- and middle-class interfering philanthropists. Indeed, one of the arguments which had been used in attempting to prevent the establishment of the DSPCC was a repudiation of any claim that Dublin children were maltreated, it being suggested that to admit to the existence of cruelty would destroy the image of Ireland as 'the maternal isle'. Just over 300 people were charged with neglect of children in 1900 (by 1918 the number had dropped to 150).[41]

'devoted to lucrative laundry work'
Many of the Magdalen laundries, charged with the reform of Ireland's 'fallen and immoral' girls, had evolved in the nineteenth century in response to the problem of prostitution, an initiative spearheaded by nuns with a missionary passion. In the Magdalen asylum at New Ross, there were 45 selected 'fallen women' in 1901, while in the same year there were 196 'vagrant' girls at the Good Shepherd institution in Cork, whose nuns were in receipt of £3,157 from the state. A contemporary critic of their *modus operandi*, Michael McCarthy, in *Priests and People in Ireland* (1902) suggested: 'the nuns' Magdalen asylums do not decrease female immorality. They are devoted to lucrative laundry work, which must enhance the wealth of the religious.'[42] Some of these women ended up incarcerated for life, often deliberately not educated, obliged to wear clothes designed to be as asexual as possible, and suffering daily humiliation.

Children remained the main victims of slum conditions, and indeed a century that some believed would herald the 'age of the child' proved to be anything but for those Irish children who were born into poverty, neglect or dysfunctional families. Given the emphasis on the family in Irish life, it might have been thought that Irish society in the twentieth century would be particularly conscious in this regard. The writer G. K. Chesterton famously remarked that 'wherever there is Ireland there is the family and it counts for a great deal'.[43] At the beginning of the century, children were beginning to be noticed as individuals susceptible to neglect and ill-treatment, and in Edwardian England social investigators like Charles Booth and Seebohm Rowntree were attempting to quantify poverty, analysing its causes and consequences. The Royal Commission on the Poor Law and relief of distress noted in 1904 that more than 50 per cent of the 1,250 families it investigated had less than the necessary minimum income of £1 per week to support a family of two adults and two children.[44] While the Children Act of 1908 was regarded as a fundamental step in extending child protection, incorporating in one statute a host of amending laws and piecemeal legislation which emphasised the social rights of children, it was in practice more parent-centred (in the sense of bringing them to account for neglect) than child-centred. The Act also dictated that 'the courts should be agencies for the rescue as well as the punishment of children'. It was this Act which Ireland was to rely on in dealing with the problems of child welfare for almost the entire twentieth century. Rather than a serious culture of child welfare developing, as elsewhere, the institutional option was relied on in Ireland, where there was eagerness to develop the Victorian structures that had been pioneered for children in Britain, with the Church playing a crucial part in their management.

The first reformatory school had opened in Ireland in 1858, with industrial schools following in 1869. Right from the beginning their welfare record was dismal – between 1869 and 1913, 48,664 children were admitted to industrial schools in Ireland, and 2,623 died while in custody. An inspector of the schools had noted in 1900 that conditions in many of these schools were 'better imagined than described'. Middle-class children were more liable to be sent to orphanages, maintaining a class divide.[45]

The treatment of mental illness was also affected by class considerations. Elizabeth Malcolm has suggested that:

In Ireland committal had little to do with industrialisation or urbanisation. What it more reflected was the growing power and prosperity
of the small-farming class. Committal was a method by which families
of this class could control and neutralise their strident members; those
who had not emigrated, but who still sought to resist the demands
of the family backed by the Church. And as [Seán] O'Casey also suggested, committal worked: its victims were reduced to 'shadows'; a
living dead, no longer a threat to familial authority. Labelled as suffering from incurable, hereditary disorders, such people were shunted in
and out of asylums by their families until large numbers of them were
eventually left there to die.[46]

Between 1906 and 1909 there were three separate commissions on services
to the insane in Ireland, but conditions were slow to improve.

'Some celebrated the event by having a few drinks and were injured'

For the elderly, however, life was considerably improved by the introduction
of old-age pensions in 1909. Jeremiah Murphy wrote wryly that 'all
the old timers, male and female, who were able to walk, collected the
first payment. For many it was the last. Some celebrated the event by
having a few drinks and were injured, while others contracted colds or
pneumonia.'[47] Contemporary newspapers reported that in Roscommon
neighbours carried 'cartloads of aged female pensioners' to the post office,
while in Ennis, County Clare, the police were called to keep order. The
sum of five shillings was considerable, given that an unskilled labourer
in Ireland might earn no more than double that in a week. While the
original act excluded those on outdoor relief, this was changed in 1911,
and economic historian Cormac Ó Gráda has suggested that it was
'arguably the most radical and far-reaching piece of welfare enacted in
Ireland in the twentieth century'. By February 1909, 177,000 pensions
were granted in Ireland (4.1 per cent of the population) compared with
370,000 in England (1.1 per cent), and since compulsory registration of
births began only in 1864, determination of age was open to debate.[48]
While there were more older people and poverty in Ireland, there were
undoubtedly many bogus claims – by 1911 there were 243,000 recipients
in the 32 counties. Indeed, the underestimation of how many people in
Ireland would claim was one of the reasons for Lloyd George's 'People's
Budget' in 1910 that led to a constitutional crisis over the House of

Lords' veto, and with its loss one of the impediments to Home Rule was gone. It was thus ironic, given its impact in Ireland, that it did not feature strongly in pre-1908 political debates, and had not been sought by Irish nationalists. In 1911, following the 'purging of thousands of bogus claims', Ireland's share was still 22.2 per cent of those claiming (in 1910, 38,495 pensions were revoked in Ireland, against 29,217 in the rest of the UK). The *Irish Times* commented sarcastically on 1 January 1909 that 'with fewer inhabitants than Scotland by a quarter of a million, Ireland has established claims to nearly 74,000 more pensions. This surely is a major tribute to the longevity of our race and to the healthy character of our much-abused climate.'[49]

'the hidden Ireland'

Towards the end of the nineteenth century bleak assessments of urban squalor were still commonplace. In 1896 the travel writer C. W. Gedney described the poverty of Limerick:

> Nothing more squalid than the cabins which flank this thoroughfare could be found in Ireland. Wretched hovels with heaps of manure and slush at their doors, ducks, goats and pigs grubbing in search of offal, liquid manure running across the paths into the road, mud-begrimed half-naked children, women in rags and tatters.[50]

But there had been progress made in the area of rural housing and by 1914 nearly 50,000 cottages had been built for agricultural labourers, mostly with a subsidy from the Imperial Exchequer, which had been substantially increased after new legislation saw the state meeting 36 per cent of loan repayments. In the years 1910–11 an unprecedented 6,223 dwellings were completed. By 1900 over 80 per cent of the total debt incurred by rural authorities was for Labourers Acts loans, Michael Davitt suggesting they were 'a rational principle of state socialism'.[51] After an Irish Housing Act of 1908 the question of urban housing problems received more attention. Before the First World War, Ireland had in the region of 1.3 million urban inhabitants, the largest centres being Dublin with 305,000, Cork with 76,000 and Limerick with just under 40,000. In Dublin 20 per cent were classed as general labourers. Between 1891 and 1911 the population of the city grew by over 20,000 yet only 2,600 new dwellings were built.

In 1911, 66 per cent of the city's working-class population of 128,000 were deemed to be living in substandard housing, while 118,000 Dublin poor were packed into just over 5,000 tenement houses. Fifteen hundred of these were deemed totally unfit for human habitation. The subsidy under the 1908 act encouraged urban municipalities to become involved in housebuilding, but slum collapses as late as September 1923 seemed to confirm the observation of Seán O'Casey that they were vaults hiding the dead instead of homes sheltering the living. They were, he maintained, 'the hidden Ireland'.[52]

Particularly in Dublin city, the rate of mortality was alarmingly high, in both domestic and comparative terms. In 1899 it reached the figure of 33.6 per 1,000, compared to figures of 19.7 for London, 19.6 for Edinburgh and 21.6 for Glasgow. Of the 9,000 people who died in Dublin city in 1901, 1,600 died in the workhouses.[53] These institutions were a product of the 1838 Poor Law, which had divided the country into 130 unions, each with a workhouse at its centre. (The workhouse infrastructure had been designed to cater for 80,000 people, but the Famine years witnessed them become overcrowded centres of disease and destitution – in March 1851, 250,611 people were paupers receiving poor relief in the workhouses,[54] ensuring that they would become, in the eyes of Irish nationalists, a detested symbol of British mismanagement in Ireland.) According to the census of 1901, 159 Poor Law unions catered for 43,043 paupers and another 58,365 were dependent on outdoor relief.

Outbreaks of diphtheria, measles and smallpox were an intrinsic part of the Dublin slum experience, prompting a series of health and housing reports during the first two decades of the century. The Dublin slums were unique in not being a product of the industrial revolution, and progress in dealing with the problem was slow. Unlike in Belfast, which was characterised by two-up, two-down Victorian housing, speculators (or 'house jobbers') purchased many of the larger and dilapidated buildings in Dublin city. Such edifices, particularly on the Northside, had once been highly fashionable and at the hub of commercial activity, which had now moved to the other side of the city; and having purchased them, landlords tended to let individual rooms to families. Paul-Dubois estimated that the percentage of families living in one-room tenements in 1901 was 36, compared to 15 in London, and as little as one in Cork and Belfast.[55] Those intent on reform through slum clearance and new construction often found their plans were overshadowed by the desire to contain contagious disease within the slums and the continued ghettoisation of the poor, who were often depicted as being morally as well as materially in dire straits, by both state and charity organisations.

On the eve of the new century, the *Daily Nation* had warned of the need to face up to the slum evil 'or else punishment neither light nor pleasant will follow as a consequence of their apathy and neglect'.[56] There was no shortage of outrage expressed at such conditions in the opening years of the twentieth century and, indeed, there was much analysis, particularly in response to particular episodes and tragedies. In 1900 Sir Charles Cameron, the city's Medical Officer, drew attention to the malnourishment of mothers and to the fact that infant mortality among the labouring classes was five times higher than those of the upper classes, and he recommended the clearing of certain slum areas. While Dublin Corporation had acquired powers in the late nineteenth century to regulate private housing in the context of sanitation, they had only tinkered at the margins of the housing crisis, as had the small Dublin Artisans Dwelling Company and the Iveagh Trust. In 1911, 22.9 per cent of Dublin's population lived in one-room tenements with the only large centres of population getting near that figure being Finsbury in London (14.8) and Glasgow (13.2).[57] In contrast, it has been suggested Ireland's rural labourers were:

> among the best housed of their class in Western Europe ... as late as 1921 it was reported that 48,000 cottages had been provided in rural Ireland since 1883, with a total expenditure of £8.5 million, whereas under the urban housing acts only £5 million had been spent and just 10,000 houses built.[58]

In 1903 the Mansion House Conference on housing had suggested the provision of new housing on the outskirts of the city, and Dublin Corporation was faced with the problem of a small rateable base because of the subsequent drift to the suburbs. Reform of Dublin's urban problems was hampered by the complexity of the relationship between the ownership of land and property and municipal politics, and the low rateable value of much of the property in the city.[59] Undoubtedly, some members of the Corporation did well out of the housing crisis, though it has been argued that the role of the slum owners within nationalist politics has been exaggerated, given the links between the Irish Parliamentary Party and the Town Tenants League.[60] The early years of the century saw the beginning of many debates about moving the population out to the suburbs and there were policy debates about the nature and location of housing. The historical geographer Ruth McManus has suggested that as well as borrowing ideas from Europe there was much blurring of the distinction between public and private housing, and that 'both speculative builders and Dublin Corporation needed each other'. But it was during this era that the decisions were made which gave the modern city its low-rise and low-density shape, meaning that by the end of the century Dublin was to be very much a twentieth- as opposed to an eighteenth-century city, with less than 15 per cent of the housing stock at the end of the century predating 1919.[61] The existence of independent townships hindered the orderly development of the city, and given the site value of the tenements, landlords had little incentive to rebuild their property. Nonetheless, the impetus towards state subsidy was more advanced in Ireland than elsewhere, with a national policy of state housing based on centrally subsidised municipal dwellings and recommended design, and British legislation dealing with the Irish housing question created concern about the potential for British municipalities to demand the same.[62]

The work of oral historian Kevin Kearns has drawn on the rich sense of dialogue, community spirit and resourcefulness of those who lived in the tenements, and there is truth in the observation that life in the tenements was 'philosophically accepted' by many. But there is also a danger of succumbing to romanticisation in this regard; alongside triumphs of human spirit and the communal system of mutual dependency, there was also much alcoholism, prostitution and violence against women. One woman pointed out in Kevin Kearns's history of the Dublin tenements: 'Anyone who says they were good old days is a headcase. It'd make you sick to think of them.'[63]

'a pestilent jungle inhabited only by consumptive patients'

Tuberculosis remained a huge killer, but it was only in the last decade of the nineteenth century that it became a major concern of public-health officials, no doubt encouraged by the fact that it was in decline as a cause of mortality in England and Wales. By contrast, it was on the increase in Ireland, peaking in 1904, when it accounted for nearly 13,000 deaths, or 16 per cent of all deaths in Ireland, and despite the insistence of local-government welfare bodies on the segregation of tubercular from non-tubercular patients, this practice remained only nominal.

The Women's National Health Association, formed in 1907, did much to highlight the problem, but the Tuberculosis Act of 1908 was adopted by only a small minority of local authorities. In the first decade of the century it could not be said that Ireland had anything approaching a comprehensive TB service, with most of the beds for victims of TB located in the workhouses, which meant that the main challenge facing those intent on changing attitudes and practices in the field of welfare and health care in Ireland would be to break the link between poor assistance and medical care.

More significantly in the long term, the growing publicity given to TB was instrumental in the construction of social taboos about what constituted 'clean' behaviour in the matter of public health. Simultaneous with the first moves being made to provide purpose-built hospitals for consumptives and increased local-authority involvement in this whole area was the feeling that public-health campaigns impinged aggressively and unnecessarily on private lives. Some medical professionals, backed by politicians, were reluctant to make the notification and registration of TB sufferers compulsory, resenting the impression being given that Ireland was 'a pestilent jungle inhabited only by consumptive patients'.[64] Greta Jones has noted, in relation to the period up to 1914, that:

> Given the scale of the problem in Ireland and the resources available in 1899–1914, it was impossible that all TB sufferers could be notified, treated at a dispensary or segregated if necessary, in purpose-built sanatoria. Although campaigners held out this as their eventual goal, they fell back upon spreading the hygienic gospel to the public at large and transforming the treatment of the tubercular within the family as well as the community. Ironically, as the annual toll of TB deaths fell in Ireland and the TB services expanded, a greater proportion of sufferers were brought within their compass and notification; the dispensary and the sanatorium became a routine part of the experience of the disease in inter-war Ireland. Even then, there remained a large minority who either deliberately or inadvertently avoided all contact with the TB services and suffered – and often died – quietly and privately beyond the gaze of officialdom.[65]

It can be legitimately argued that creating a public-health discourse narrowly centred around TB was also a convenient way of shirking the broader social questions of poverty and social reform. Unfortunately, perhaps owing to a combination of all the above factors, private sufferance and endurance remained the lot of many. The *Irish Times* fairly pointed out in 1911 that without meaningful changes in local policy 'the slums of Dublin will still be there whether we get Home Rule or not'.[66]

The attitude of the Irish Parliamentary Party towards the issue of medical benefit was cautious, with a belief that comprehensive medical insurance schemes were extravagant and unsuited to Ireland, as a rural country. In 1913, 15.9 per cent of the population was insured. Politicians complained about 'penal taxation' and pointed to the small number of Friendly Societies in Ireland. The Church, too, added its voice of concern. The historian of health reform Ruth Barrington noted that the bishops 'did not seem to be aware of the 800,000 industrial workers and domestic servants in the labour force who stood to benefit from the [proposed medical insurance] Bill'.[67] The fact that insurance-based medical benefit was not introduced to Ireland meant that doctors avoided a system of payment by capitation fee, and loss of private practice. But this rejection of a major foundation of the welfare state had negative long-term implications given the lack of central financing for general practice and hospital services.

Despite the bleak conditions endured by many, there were improvements made in the city of Dublin, notably in terms of street paving, draining and the introduction of a successful water system. Municipal structures were certainly more advantageous to the city than the early nineteenth-century patchwork of parish and vestry organisations.

'one of the heresies of our time'

Drunkenness continued to be a problem that attracted the attention of both natives and newcomers. Historically, Ireland had not been short of observers, both domestic and foreign, on the curious and pervasive Irish relationship with alcohol. The country had experienced a short-lived but massively popular temperance crusade in the 1830s led by a Capuchin friar, Fr Theobald Matthew, and in the later nineteenth century the attribution of excessive drinking to an external agent (the British) and the identification of Ireland's political liberation with the moderation of this drinking had become a propaganda weapon in the hands of some nationalist politicians. At the turn of the century, however, it was as serious a problem as at any time previously, and one which prompted the establishment of the Pioneer Total Abstinence Association, which went on to become the largest Catholic lay movement in twentieth-century Ireland, and indeed, as a percentage of the population, one of the largest movements of its kind in the world. There was over £13 million being spent annually on drink in the last decade of the nineteenth century, and in 1891–2 an astounding 100,528 arrests for drunkenness.

Although temperance groups tended to see their work as more important in the context of saving souls and making religious sacrifice (members of the Pioneers offered their pledge to the benefit of the Sacred Heart), it was also the case that temperance entered the wider lexicon of Irish cultural progress in the opening years of the century, a revival of the nineteenth-century idea that 'Ireland sober' would be 'Ireland free'. The Gaelic Athletic Association, for example, referred to an ideal Gael as one who would be 'a matchless athlete, sober, pure in speech and deed, self-possessed and self-reliant'; an ironic aspiration in many ways given the squabbles, injury and drunkenness that accompanied some fixtures.

Despite the efforts of reformers, alcohol continued to be central to communities in sickness and health, poverty and wealth. Paul-Dubois drew attention to the town of Tralee in County Kerry, where there were 117 pubs for 9,367 inhabitants, and noted the enormous social power of the publican. Interestingly, he also suggested that the physical constitution of the Irish, weakened by poverty and hunger, was less likely to cope with alcoholic stimulants than that of the Anglo-Saxon. It was also the case that drunkards were indulged. In any case, at a political level, nationalists, particularly those in the Irish Parliamentary Party, were not prone to much analysis of the social ills induced by excessive drinking because of the importance of the alcohol trade in the commercial life of Ireland. The proposal to increase taxes on spirits in Lloyd George's 1909 budget united nationalist politicians, and indeed some unionist distillers, in opposition, and they were ensured a sympathetic audience in the Catholic Hierarchy. By 1908 it was estimated that there were nearly 23,000 licensed retail outlets in the country, of which 17,223 were public houses, highlighting the extraordinarily liberal approach to the granting of licences.[68]

Those intent on promoting total abstinence were also sometimes in danger of appearing fanatical, given that temperance had traditionally been more associated with the Protestant rather than the Catholic religion.

The Father Matthew Union, an organisation for abstaining priests, was reminded by the Bishop of Elphin, John Clancy, that while the Church imposed celibacy, it did not impose abstinence from drink and 'teetotallers must not lay the flattering unction to their souls that, because they are teetotallers they are, therefore, superior to all others. That is one of the heresies of our time, and the sooner it is consigned to the limbo of uncelestial repose, the better.'[69] Those who were determined to continue the waking of the Irish dead seemed to thoroughly agree.

'no isolation of the quarrel'?

The lot of urban workers in Dublin remained difficult, particularly for the unskilled. The Irish Congress of Trade Unions had been formed in 1894, and an aggressive socialism was expounded by labour organiser James Connolly in the *Workers' Republic* (1898–1903). It has been traditionally thought that the organised workers in the capital city were moderate and lacking in aggression in the opening years of the century in contrast to the violent agitation of the Dublin Tradesmen's Union in the early decades of the previous century. Certainly, by the later years of the nineteenth century Dublin tradesmen's unions had adopted a more moderate stance that had achieved a certain degree of success by the 1890s. Tradesmen's unions were more likely to maintain a higher level of organisation and defend their established conditions of work, but the more serious unemployment that afflicted the unskilled labourers limited the militancy of their unions. Extensive dock disputes marked the opening year of the century, but the enforcement of established rules of work seemed to be more important at this stage than militant action. Though there were exceptions, like the bricklayers' lockout of 1904, Dublin employers did little to interfere with established conditions of work for skilled labourers. For the unskilled, the closing years of the nineteenth century had been demoralising, and despite being well organised railway workers were defeated in industrial disputes in 1894 and 1897, as were the coal and dock labourers in 1900.

William Martin Murphy, the most successful Irish service sector entrepreneur of the late-Victorian and early-Edwardian period, and later to be a detested employer of Dublin's working class in the eyes of socialists, had been prepared to act as an arbitrator in trade clashes for the Dublin Trades Council in the early 1890s, but was completely opposed to new or general unionism for the unskilled. Owner of both the Dublin Tram Company and

the Great Southern and Western Railway, and soon to take over the ailing
Irish Independent, he would not tolerate any attempt to organise unskilled
workers and had trenchantly resisted railwaymen's demands in the 1890s
for a nine-hour day (they were working up to 14 hours a day). Given
that there was little to indicate that a revitalisation of unionism amongst
the labourers was imminent, and given that unionism amongst labourers
seemed incapable of overcoming the obstacles created by general unemployment, the reaction of Dublin trade unionists to the struggles of the
Belfast workers was hugely important. The subsequent inauguration of
James Larkin's Irish Transport and General Workers' Union in January
1909 heralded a new chapter in Irish industrial relations.

One of the most legendary of modern Irish history's personalities,
Larkin emerged as a trade union leader after what was in effect the second
wave of the 'new unionism' to emerge in Ireland after the failed attempts
of the opening years of the century. Recessions of the early 1890s and
again from 1900 to 1904 revealed that the emergence of a new unionism
was very much bound up with trade cycles. Another challenge facing
those attempting to organise trade unions was the question of how to deal
with the British connection. Could a coherent and successful indigenous
movement be created in this regard? Or if a new wave of organisation was
to transpire, would it engage tactically with the nationalist movement or
develop an exclusively trade union politics? Answers to such questions
were never going to evolve overnight, but what was clear up to 1909 was
that the Irish Congress of Trade Unions was dominated by small, semi-
skilled societies, and their proceedings seemed to be more concerned with
rhetorical gestures, pomp and ceremony than effective representation.

What proved instrumental in the appeal of Larkin was the dissemination of a syndicalist idea, based on a denunciation of party politics as
the machine of self-serving elites who betrayed their base. The aim was to
revolutionise trade union practice by evolving the notion of sympathetic
solidarity or all-out action, accompanied by the rhetoric of moral resurrection which was very much Larkin's forte.

Irish trade unionists were undoubtedly influenced by developments
abroad. James Connolly had left Ireland in 1903 after the relative failure
of his Irish Republican Socialist Party; 'more syllables than members'
was the unkind comment of some cynics.[70] He returned from America in
1907, where he had been deeply influenced by American syndicalism. Significantly, the idea of sympathetic action meant that the whole base of the

Irish trade union movement had to broaden from the actions of transport workers in particular to include general workers. Transport dominated Larkin's earlier battles in Belfast in 1907 and Dublin and Cork in 1908 and 1909, and it was not yet the case that there was an integrated national trade union movement. Larkin became associated with a pattern in union disputes that involved militant workers, an excessive reaction by employers and an attendant violence. Vilified as Larkin was by press, clergy and employers, the challenge for him was to develop a new departure in terms of a general union approach. Arnold Wright had commented that 'It is the essence of Larkinism, as of the syndicalism of which it is the child, that there shall be no isolation of the quarrel.'[71] Making the quarrel communal set the tone for the most famous dispute in Irish labour history: the Dublin Lockout of 1913 (see Chapter 2).

Aside from unionisation in the labour force, another significant trend of the opening years of the century was a 'buy-Irish' campaign, a reaction to the increased reliance on imported manufacturing materials. This was strongly supported by the *Irish Daily Independent*, who saw it as a very practical form of patriotism, while the Irish Congress of Trade Unions regarded technical education as the most effective way of countering the effects of foreign competition. Meanwhile, the Irish Socialist Republican Party condemned the impact of mechanisation on workers. In addition to the trade unions, the Dublin-based Irish Industrial League, an organisation established to promote industrial development, also agitated against importation. Interestingly, some manufacturers complained of importation to facilitate church-building. In 1905 one manufacturer suggested: 'the truth is the people will not lay the lesson to heart till all the clergy, all over Ireland, preach from their altars and pulpits the vital necessity of supporting home manufacturers'.[72]

Nationalists were aware by the early years of the century that they needed to take on the concerns of the labour sector. In 1899 labour representatives were elected to Dublin Corporation, but were lambasted by the Dublin Trades Council as being inefficient and corrupt, and while a Labour Electoral Alliance of 1901 predicted a bright future for the labour movement, this seemed misplaced optimism. Connolly was scathing about the members of the first labour grouping in Dublin Corporation because of their inactivity on labour issues and involvement in political factions. The failure to establish an independent Labour Party seemed to be caused by a lack of distinct political aims, and it was notable, for example, that Dublin trade unionists seemed to have little interest in attacking the operation of the Poor Law system.

In terms of the wider economy, substantial improvements were made in the living conditions of many, which were manifested in improved levels of literacy, higher-quality housing and greater tobacco, tea and sugar consumption. Trends in small savings rose significantly from the 1880s to the 1910s. Bank deposits, which had amounted to £8 million in 1850, rose to £43 million by 1900. But post-Famine prosperity in the economy was by no means even or uninterrupted. Linen and shipbuilding continued to be important, as did brewing and distilling, though the drinks industry (Irish whiskey accounted for one quarter of UK output) was not to provide major employment. Only a small increase in industrial output had been recorded by the 1910s, and while it could be argued that Irish industry held its own, industrial progress was disappointing relative to Britain, whose output quadrupled during this period.

Surprisingly, because its raw material was imported, at the time of the 1907 Census of Production tobacco manufacturing was one of Ireland's largest industries, one of a small number of industries which were net exporters, including linen, textiles, shipbuilding, food processing and alcoholic drinks.[73]

Many reasons have been put forward for Ireland's lack of industrial progress in this regard, including lack of entrepreneurship, an anti-business Catholic ethos and lack of venture capital. Cormac Ó Gráda has convincingly argued that many of these traditional arguments remain unproven, particularly when the sophistication of the Irish banking system is taken into account and the impressive figures for savings. More important factors may have been lack of resources, particularly coal and iron, and Ireland's closeness to the highly industrialised British economy. But Tom Inglis, in his sociological examination of Irish Catholicism, *Moral Monopoly*, maintained that if modernisation is defined by industrialisation and the development of a modern economy, the Catholic Church delayed modernisation because of its opposition to 'materialism, consumerism and individualism'.[74]

'in dread that some neighbour should hear of it and cast an envious eye on it'
Many improvements were evident in the conditions of rural Ireland by the late nineteenth and early twentieth centuries. The Famine had resulted in the consolidation of farm holdings, with one in four farms disappearing as

a result of the catastrophe, and the decline was concentrated on holdings of less than 15 acres. The percentage of farms containing 15 acres and less dropped from 49 to 40 between 1851 and 1911. Farm productivity increased, aided by mechanical innovations and creameries. Livestock increased in number and value, and tillage was slowly declining.

Landlords in the post-Famine period still had a collective income that was more than the public revenue of Ireland, and during the late nineteenth and early twentieth centuries were very much wedded to the conservative alliance that dominated British politics, a class favourably immortalised in the fiction of Edith Somerville and Martin Ross. There were approximately 20,000 landlords in late nineteenth-century Ireland, but half the land was in the hands of 1,000 major landlords. Lord Lansdowne, for example, owned 120,000 acres in six different counties, while the Duke of Devonshire held 60,000 acres in Cork, Waterford and Tipperary. There were in the region of 500,000 tenants, one third occupying 'congested' or uneconomic holdings, with about two and a half million acres of untenanted land.

The early twentieth century, however, was to herald the end of landlordism in Ireland, owing to legislation which facilitated the transfer of about 9 million acres. By 1914, 75 per cent of occupiers were buying out their landlords, mostly under the Land Acts of 1903 and 1909. The Wyndham Act of 1903 stipulated that landlords were to be paid in cash, rather than in land stock as had previously been the case, and they were given a bonus of 12 per cent to encourage sale. The Act also introduced the principle of selling whole estates with tenants agreeing common terms rather than piecemeal sales; the Land Commission also made provision for the purchase of estates and the resale of untenanted lands to uneconomic holders or evicted tenants. Because of the collapse of government credit the implementation of the Act encountered financial problems – the Treasury limited annual advances to £5 million; but, by 1909, £50 million worth of sales had been agreed and were awaiting payment. By 1908, 7 million acres had been sold under the Wyndham Act. The old man in Daniel Corkery's *A Munster Twilight* (1916) reminds his son after the Wyndham Act: 'You won't have to face what I had to face; the struggling with landlords and the law – the law that would leave a rich man poor and a poor man broken.'[75] The 1909 Birrell Act sought to rectify the financial defects; losses on land stock for pending agreements were to be paid by the Treasury, and payment in stock was reintroduced. Under the pre-1921 British Land Acts, primarily the 1903 and 1909 Acts, over 316,000 tenants purchased holdings amounting to 11.5 million acres out of a total of 20 million acres in the country.[76] Figures for the changes in owner-occupied land give an indication of what amounted to a social revolution in rural Ireland – in 1870, 3 per cent of rural dwellers were owners; this had risen to 29.2 per cent in 1906 and 63.9 per cent by 1916. Martin Waters described the importance and long-term impact of such measures in practical material terms, in contrast to the idealised notion of the timeless and anti-materialistic Irish peasant:

> In effect, the nineteenth century witnessed a massive social transformation characterised by larger holdings increasingly organised in response to market demands, the operation of which was facilitated by the growth of banking and the development of the railroads. The change was reflected in emigration statistics and in the decline of tillage and the growth of pasturage, a prerequisite for an enormous increase in the exportation of cattle to Britain. Aside from linking the Irish economy more closely to Britain's … few aspects of Irish life – whether religious, political, literary or marital – were unaffected. The notion then of an 'Irish peasantry' with a peculiar ethos somehow remaining outside the dynamics of Irish history, except in the sense of it vanishing through emigration or of its being fundamentally modified through the adoption of a market orientation, is untenable.[77]

Robert Lynd had gathered as much in 1909 when he noted that:

> suddenly finding themselves in possession of their own land, or at least with a good prospect of possessing their own land, after a struggle of many generations, they are like men who have come upon a fortune and are in dread that some neighbour should hear of it and cast an envious eye on it.[78]

But there were losers also. Michael Davitt had been quite perceptive in predicting that the ultimate outcome of the land war would be the trading of one inequality for another and the rise of new social tensions. The number of landless labourers declined dramatically – from over 700,000 in 1851 to just under 260,000 in 1901. Although by the early years of the century their living conditions had improved, their working conditions lagged far behind most of those in rural society, and indeed far behind their own aspirations. Rural unemployment and the numerical weakness of labourers, lack of finance and limited organisational skill also inhibited their capacity to organise. A rural proletariat, but also farmers without land, the articulation of their grievances was often ambiguous, as they seemed unsure whether to concentrate their energy on agitation for an improvement in working conditions and wages, or to demand land also, but their enfranchisement in 1884 had seemed to make relatively little impact on their political muscle.

Labourers in Munster, particularly in Cork, tended to take the organisational lead on behalf of labourers generally, as evidenced by the emergence of the Irish Land and Labour Association in 1894. The number of branches increased from 98 in 1901 to 144 in 1904 and they were largely confined to Cork, Limerick and Tipperary. To many involved it seemed, particularly after the Wyndham Act which had catered for the tenant farmers, that legislation to cater for their needs would be the next logical step. But they were to discover that being caught in the crossfire caused by the wider battle for political allegiance in rural Ireland between William O'Brien and John Redmond militated against their own unity and generated splits and factions. Notwithstanding, Labourers Acts in 1906 and 1911 greatly assisted cottage-building for labourers.

Increased prosperity was also reflected in housing conditions for tenant farmers. Only 17 per cent had lived in houses with five or more rooms in 1841; by 1901 the percentage was 56. In 1861 one rural family in ten still lived in what were classed by the census as 'fourth class' accommodation, essentially meaning one room per family; by 1911 only 1 per cent of families did. In short, the long-term effect of the Famine was a rural Ireland that was more sparsely populated but better off. This had enormous long-term consequences for Irish society, not just in terms of class and social relations, but also regarding how the Famine was remembered, denied, distorted or ignored. At the end of the twentieth century Colm Tóibín argued:

> there began a great silence about class division in Catholic Ireland …
> An entire class of Irish Catholics survived the Famine; many indeed
> improved their prospects as a result of it and this legacy may be more
> difficult for us to deal with in Ireland now than the legacy of those who
> died or emigrated.[79]

'there is practically no criminal class in Ireland'

Lawlessness was certainly not the problem it had been in rural Ireland, reflected in particular in the relative tranquillity of the professional lives of many members of the Royal Irish Constabulary. During the late nineteenth and early twentieth centuries resident magistrates of the British administration in Ireland not only became better trained in the law but also more representative of the Irish population as a whole. The entire Irish prison population in 1899 had amounted to only 322, 19 of them women. A report on policing in 1902 suggested that 'while political agitation kept the Irish police on their toes, there is practically no criminal class in Ireland'.[80] Samuel Waters, who retired from the RIC in 1906, having achieved the rank of assistant inspector general, served in 11 stations in nine counties, and was one of the few members of the force to leave memoirs behind. He recalled generally friendly relations between police and people. Most recruits were the sons of tenant farmers or rural labourers, attracted to the force by the security of regular employment and a pension, though the creation of an officer class ensured a significant class barrier existed between officers and ordinary policemen, sergeants joined priests, teachers and 'gombeenmen' (money-lenders) as the main players in a typical Irish village hierarchy. The impression given by Waters was that during periods of social peace the policing of rural Ireland could be performed by a normal civil police force that could be flexible and pragmatic in the administration of its affairs, being relatively well integrated into local communities. Though the onslaught of a more militant nationalism was ultimately to be the undoing of the RIC, prior to that, policing was perhaps not too arduous a task – 'more akin to house-keeping than peace-keeping' was the summation of one historian[81] – and its composition was an accurate reflection of the socio-structure of Irish society. Samuel Waters concluded his comparison with English and Irish policing by noting that 'The Irish policeman is a more philosophic man. He considers before he attempts to enforce a law, where the balance of convenience lies.'[82] One of the century's most influential writers, Seán O'Faoláin, recalled of his father, a long-established member of the force: 'My father said he used to pass the night producing hard words to spell, or, if it were a clear night, reading the stars.'[83]

Many ex-RIC men gave statements to the Bureau of Military History in the 1940s and 1950s, and some were adamant that there was nothing incompatible between their membership and a nationalist identity. The lure of respectability as well as parental approval was reason enough for joining – J. J. McConnell, who joined in 1907, and later became a sergeant, was defensive, insisting he had 'realised my childhood ambition. Indeed it was the dream of all my boyhood pals to join the force that was greatly admired and respected throughout the country.' He noted that even his Fenian father approved of him joining. Regarding his duties in the early days, he remembered a quiet time, occasionally punctuated by drink-induced disorder: 'whiskey was popular, cheap and deadly ... a man with a shilling in his pocket could quickly get fighting drunk ... so the police had their hands full at every public gathering.'[84]

There were 27,000 soldiers stationed in Ireland in 1900 in addition to 12,000 armed RIC men, making Ireland the most densely militarised area of the British Empire in peacetime. The mobilisation caused by the Boer War undoubtedly hardened moderate opinion against the Empire, and helped the radicals in Irish politics to reach a wider audience, but it also obliged many Irish soldiers to fight against the Boers. David Fitzpatrick makes the point that in the early twentieth century 'the common rhetoric of militarism transcended political divisions in Ireland throughout the turmoil of the period between the Anglo-Boer war of 1899–1902 and the Anglo-Irish settlement of 1921–2. For unionists, nationalists and republicans alike, soldiery was an ideal to be extolled rather than a menace to be confronted.' In the 1901 wartime British army, there were 50,000 Irishmen; natives of Ireland accounted for 12 per cent of the overall population of the United Kingdom but 13.5 per cent of soldiers and non-commissioned officers.[85] If the Boer War was a formative influence on many Irish nationalists, it also invigorated the imperial aspect of Ulster Unionism. The historian of Ireland's involvement in the Boer War, Donal McCracken, suggested it also inflamed Irish-American opinion, marking its arrival as a major force in Irish politics.[86] Major John McBride's pro-Boer Irish Brigade may have been praised by the anti-recruiting campaign in Ireland, but the bravery of the soldiers in the Irish regiments serving in South Africa was also acclaimed.

'because weeds spring spontaneously from the ground'

For those who avoided urban or military life, land ownership could also breed complacency, and much remained depressing about the rural hinterland. A caustic observer in the late nineteenth century had suggested that the Irish working the land did not see the connection between the theory and practice of agriculture, 'and expect that because weeds spring spontaneously from the ground ... that their knowledge of farming is to be acquired without any culture or labour of their brains'.[87] Many of the themes which dominated 'ruralism', a subject which was reflected on by all those with an interest in Ireland, including the organisation of rural communities, the challenge posed by the flight from the land and the constant demand for redistribution, were in evidence at the very beginning of the century. Filson Young, a provocative commentator on Irish agricultural affairs, suggested that the interest of many in the land was morbid and hypochondriacal, while the remedies proposed were generally insignificant and useless.

Some of this was fair criticism. The question of bringing a modern system of state-aided education to Irish agriculture had been considered by the Recess Committee established to make recommendations on the Agriculture and Industries (Ireland) Bill of 1897. Having examined modern agricultural states in countries like Denmark, Belgium and as far afield as Canada and Australia, they had recommended that an agricultural board needed to consist of men 'directly acquainted with the circumstances of the country, outside the influence of red tape and routine'. The response was the creation of the Department of Agricultural and Technical Instruction. A writer in the *New Ireland Review*, however, in 1905, lamented the fact that in Ireland the idea of special education for agriculture was treated as a 'palpable absurdity', with many potential pupils refusing to attend DATI courses. It was an important admission, highlighting the extent to which ultimately it was the rural population themselves rather than their political masters who would decide the pace of progress on agricultural reform.[88]

Despite poverty, there was a need for a positive belief that a balance could be struck between the ideal of a nation of small farmers and social and economic reality, a balance at the heart of the acerbic debate between Horace Plunkett, the Protestant agricultural reformer, and the Catholic writer Monsignor O'Riordan. O'Riordan replied to Plunkett's *Ireland in the New Century* with his *Catholicity and Progress in Ireland*, which, among other things, refuted Plunkett's contention that the application and industriousness of Irish peasants was questionable, and accused Plunkett of fishing for the reasons for emigration 'in the realm of poetry'.[89] Plunkett was to find that his attempt to apply an Irish version of what was a wider European anti-urban and rural revitalisation movement became subsumed in more narrowly focused debates centred around Irish nationalism. O'Riordan's dismissive conclusion was that 'we must not identify human or social progress with these material or industrial progresses'.[90]

The majority of the Irish rural population were doubtless unmoved by either of their theories, but the early years of the century witnessed many pleas for the rural community to adopt an approach of self-help, rather than relying on external aid. Plunkett's task was frustrating. He was a pioneer of the concept of systematic rural development, who, in spite of his role in Irish affairs being often overlooked, influenced many international reformers, and can be credited as one of the few who had a long-term vision for the development of rural Ireland.[91] He was apt to remind audiences that even if full peasant proprietorship was achieved and Home Rule implemented, rural underdevelopment would still have to be faced. Class conflict intervened to frustrate much of what he sought to do. If it was true that one of the aims of the co-operative movement was to smooth class differences between tenants and landlords, it also emphasised the class differences between farmers and shopkeepers.

Plunkett estimated that there were 800 co-operative societies in the country in 1903, but given the movement's lack of appeal to those involved in the cattle industry, there were always going to be limits to its success. The statistics of co-operative endeavour, though indicating progress, were not inspiring. In 1890 there was only one agricultural co-operative in the whole country. In 1903 there were 370 dairy societies, 201 co-operative banks and 146 agricultural societies under the auspices of the Irish Agricultural Organisation Society, and by 1914 there were over 1,000 societies and nearly 90,000 members.

The experience of Plunkett and the co-operative movement generally also raised a fundamental issue which was to be the thorn in the side of many of those who sought organisational and ideological change in rural communities, or indeed those who demanded an alteration in the distribution of power in Ireland, or a greater measure of decentralisation. How was one to satisfactorily define a suitable balance between the encroachment of state and voluntary initiative? To what extent would bureaucracy impinge? The difficulty of negotiating a suitable balance was one of the reasons for disputes between the Irish Agricultural Organisation Society and the Department of Agricultural and Technical Instruction, with the IAOS paying the price of government support by losing subscriptions from farmers. This, in turn, made the co-operative movement more dependent on government support, with a resultant loss of autonomy.[92]

In 1899 Plunkett had become secretary of the DATI and initiated a state subsidy for the IAOS and the establishment of co-operative credit unions, of which there were 477 in 1899. Plunkett fell foul of both the Catholic Church and the petty snobberies and resentments of middle rural Ireland, and in 1906 the halting of the grant to the IAOS by the new Liberal government effectively killed off co-operatism. The co-operative credit banks also suffered, though this was also due to bad business practice – the interest rates under which they were operating were simply not viable.

Alliances between large farmers and smallholders had been a notable feature of the Irish land war, but in many ways it was an uneasy, vulnerable alliance that had dissipated by the beginning of the new century. This was reflected in the United Irish League's bitter denunciations of the ranchers, particularly in Connacht, ultimately leading to a 'ranch war' in the opening years of the century. This conflict had its origins in the fundamental redistributive aims of the UIL and led to no-rent campaigns being conducted on many estates, particularly in areas like Roscommon from 1900 to 1903, with ranchers in particular who rented untenanted land being seen as the greatest obstacle to division of these lands. Though the lines of conflict seemed obvious, there was much blurring at their edges. One of the reasons why the UIL was unable to maintain a consistent commitment to the unrest conducted against the rancher community was that the ranchers were heavily integrated into the community because of the important role they played in the lives of the smallholders who were dependent on them to buy the cattle which paid their rent. As well as assuming positions of leadership, they were culturally and financially important to the Church. It was also the case that individual trade and property jealousies could be acted on under the cover of UIL agitation, highlighting the factionalism which was a consequence of the individual economic, social and political ambition that heralded the dawn of a measure of modernisation in rural Ireland. At the peak of the 'ranch war' in 1907–8, there were over 1,000 cattle drives and a significant amount of organised, collective non-payment of rent. This would suggest the war was not solely to displace grazers or ranchers, but also about tenants deliberately targeting landlords in order to sell their land, at a time when only 26 per cent of tenants' land had been purchased. This pressure contributed

to the Birrell Act of 1909, which would ultimately transform social relationships in rural areas but also contribute to the demise of the United
Irish League.[93]

Rural revitalisation was also one of the reasons behind the publication of the short-lived *Irish Peasant*, which first appeared in 1903, the
editor W. P. Ryan insisting it was the only newspaper that advocated the
redress of peasant farmers' grievances. But it also called on rural communities to create their own prosperity, agriculturally and industrially. In
the words of Ryan, the paper was not 'against Home Rule but for preparing for it'.[94] He was quick to denounce self-labelled patriotic movements
which did little to alleviate the immediate social and economic difficulties
of Irish peasants and was not averse to criticising the Church for the same
reasons (forcing the paper's eventual closure). He provocatively queried
the Church's role in fostering rural development and challenged their lack
of identification with the tillage farmer. Ideals, in Ryan's view, were not
enough if there was not a concerted push for the creation of the social and
economic conditions in which they could be realised.

Failure to bring prosperity to the west of Ireland remained a barrier
to rural progress. Paul-Dubois drew attention to County Mayo, where, at
the beginning of the twentieth century, the 36,000 families involved in
agriculture were settled on 94,000 acres out of a total county acreage of 1.3
million.[95] Admittedly, the emergence of the Congested District Board in
1890 had demonstrated a commitment to state intervention in the west,
encouraging amalgamation of land holdings, resettlement and industrialisation. Between its foundation and 1915, nearly 30,000 holdings were
improved. Yet as it attempted to improve rural conditions, an intense
distrust of bureaucracy was being sown, as co-operative movements began
to bemoan the red tape which they felt stymied the pace of progress and
brought them into conflict with an excessively centralised policy of relief.
Paul-Dubois also noted that the board did not have the energy or the
freedom to apply relief on a large scale. The Royal Commission on conges-
tion, which sat between 1906 and 1908, had to reiterate that the interests
of small farmers should prevail when it came to framing a policy for the
west.

'half gombeenmen, half political priests'

Class was crucial in this regard, as were changes in the rural–urban divide
within Irish society, though trying to discern the extent to which the

lower and middle strata of Irish society (rural and town labourers, tenant farmers, traders and small businessmen) consolidated their position is difficult. The middle-peasantry seemed to consolidate its status – as the number of holdings of this nature from the Famine in 1845 to 1910 rose from 276,000 to 303,500, along with a strengthening in the position of capitalist farmers. But equally significantly, as pointed out by Liam Kennedy, was the rise of traders and an increased reliance on the market which forged new links between town and countryside. A mere 15 per cent of the population lived in towns of at least 1,500 inhabitants in 1841, but this figure had risen to 32 per cent by 1901.[96] Tom Garvin saw this as 'the classic Irish Victorian pattern of upward and outward mobility', in a move away from the farm and into retail trade which served the farming community.[97]

The *Irish Homestead*, the journal of the Irish Co-operative movement, under the editorship of poet and painter George Russell, elaborated on many similar themes challenging rural communities. Frequently giving attention to developments in European agriculture, it was effusive in its praise, for example, of Denmark's established system of education through popular high school, peasant ownership and wholesale farmer co-operation. It also frequently chided the rural community for its conservatism in refusing to use banks. The journal was generally optimistic about the potential for rural Ireland to develop, but only if the populace would organise in the manner of its European neighbours.

The co-operative movement produced its own heroes and inevitable tensions. Patrick Gallagher was a native of the Rosses district of County Donegal, having worked as a labourer in Scotland in the late nineteenth century like many of his contemporaries. He returned to Donegal at the turn of the century, determined to use the example of co-operatives in Scotland, and attempted, through establishing the Templecrone Co-operative Society, to defeat the financial stranglehold exercised by local gombeenmen.[98] Though he prompted the wrath of local traders, Gallagher's endeavours were particularly successful and indeed high profile, because he complemented his co-operative endeavours by immersing himself in local politics. In 1914, when giving evidence to a departmental committee on agricultural credit, he reflected on the activities of gombeenmen, who, in a district where 75 per cent of the population was illiterate, were acting as shopkeepers, producers, buyers and loan-sharks, with up to 150 per cent interest being charged in some areas to vulnerable small farmers whose land was then acquisitioned and auctioned when they failed to meet repayments. He insisted that the gombeenman, who 'can ruin any man who crosses him for he is all powerful in his own district',[99] was more harmful than any bad landlord. In 1910 the historian of the Irish Parliamentary Party, F. H. O'Donnell, complained not only that conventions of the United Irish League consisted of 'half gombeenmen and half political priests', but also that gombeenmen, regarded as the most respectable members of a community, were crucial in terms of the support base of Irish parliamentarians.[100] While he may have exaggerated their influence in this regard, it is noteworthy that similar complaints came from figures like George Russell and Horace Plunkett, who lamented the dominance in rural communities of shopkeepers, publicans and traders.

It is difficult to quantify the mental malaise which some authors observed as being a disturbing and pervasive part of Irish rural existence. Filson Young, writing in 1903, suggested that the spirit of rural Ireland was susceptible to being crushed by adherence to a strict Catholicism. He noted caustically that 'there may be no bastards in Ireland, but a hundred bastards would be a more gracious and healthy sign than one lunatic'.[101] But it has been fairly pointed out that it is unlikely that Catholic teaching would have had such widespread acceptance if it was fundamentally at variance with the economic and social needs of the rural peasantry, and that their acquiescence, at least superficially, may have been because it suited their material ambition.

'the modern virago instead of the gentle maid of Nazareth'

The *Irish Homestead* also frequently drew attention to the status of women in rural Ireland, reminding readers that the 'clinging dependence' of women on their farmer husbands was a thing of the past 'as it needed a background of wealth'.[102] This recognition was one of the reasons for the formation of the United Irishwomen in 1910, an organisation that encouraged women to approach their rural work in a business-like manner. As well as trying to improve conditions for themselves and their families in the development of the domestic economy and local markets, they also imparted information about welfare and became involved in promoting education.[103] Out of 8,000 national schools in Ireland at the beginning of the century, one quarter were single-sexed, for girls only, and national school teaching became an attractive career option for women; by 1900 they formed 45 per cent of the teaching force.[104] At third level, the case for co-education was boosted by the recommendations of the Robertson Commission (1903), and the decision of Trinity College in 1904 to admit women to the main male campus. After 1908, the universities were all open to women.

Although women were formally deprived of political power it is trite to assume that complete powerlessness was the hallmark of a woman's life in Ireland early in the new century. Religious orders of nuns had established hospitals, schools and orphanages on an unprecedented scale, managing their own institutions and finances with considerable skill and independence. In the changed economic circumstances of post-Famine Ireland, women had to display the same traits in the home place. Changes in female labour, and a decrease in the demand for women working outside the home, was certainly a feature of the post-Famine economy, and except at times of peak agricultural demand, women toiling in the fields was not a major element of the paid employment market. There was, however, more capital in circulation, much of which found its way into the domestic household. There is therefore much merit in the arguments of Joanna Bourke that women were able to assume a greater control over domestic finances and expenditure, as housework became more specialised and skilled, aided by the increasing number of courses being offered to women by such groups as the Board of National Education. The autonomy experienced by women in this regard, and the attendant exclusion of men from this sphere, was perhaps a subtle, though important change, and while in no sense a complete assault on patriarchy, did provide some women with an alternative to emigration and marriage abroad.[105]

According to the 1901 census, 193,300 women were engaged in domestic service throughout the country, accounting for one in every three women in employment (and outnumbering men in this work by 13 to one). Though the numbers were falling from their peak in the 1880s, they still accounted for 9 per cent of the country's total working population. It was very much the domain of the unmarried woman, and could be exceptionally isolating, in terms of the individual female's identity being subsumed into the employer's family. As employees, they were vulnerable to abuse, but in 1911 a bill that sought to regulate the wages and working conditions of the domestic servants was defeated in parliament.

The beginning of the twentieth century also witnessed an attempt by a minority of educated women to challenge their formal exclusion from male political culture. An Irish suffrage society had been established in

Dublin in 1876 and a Dublin Women's Suffrage Association in 1896. These were relatively genteel groups, and, it was not until the formation of the Irish Women's Franchise League in 1908 that the opportunity was created for a more militant and vigorous campaign for the vote. Throughout the last decade of the nineteenth century certain middle-class women were earning degrees for the first time, beneficiaries of the Intermediate Education Act of 1878, while at local-government level women were beginning to be involved in welfare associations. With the passing of the 1898 Local Government Act they won the right to sit and vote at district council level, although it was not until 1911 that they were allowed to serve as county councillors.

By 1900, 417 women had obtained arts degrees, with another 25 taking medical degrees. To a certain extent, the views of women on education – put forward by an Irish Association of Women Graduates, formed in 1902 – were subsumed into the wider debate about university education for Catholics. In the same way, the growing concern about the prospects of educated male professionals made it difficult for professional women to be heard, and they faced resentment from many quarters.[106] In 1913, Lambert McKenna, a prominent Jesuit priest who wrote on various social matters, asserted that women's intrusion into the public sphere contributed to the decline of the 'modern world', by propagating the notion of the 'modern woman'. It was clearly a term of derision for those who were taking advantage of new educational opportunities. He continued: 'In pressing women into the rough and tumble fight for existence, in putting before her, as her ideal, the modern virago instead of the gentle maid of Nazareth, in setting her up, not as a help but as a rival of man, the modern world is working its ruin.'[107] But as Senia Paseta has observed, the same educational developments which created this 'modern woman' – rising literacy, employment opportunities and urbanisation – were crucial in fuelling the wider cultural revival.[108]

Women were very much central to this revival, whether active in education, theatre, Irish language activism, politics or welfare issues. Maud Gonne, the daughter of a British army captain, found it difficult to be a prominent female nationalist working in a male tradition, but was wealthy enough to shake off the restrictions placed on women at this time. Her autobiography, A Servant of the Queen (1938), while often vain and tedious, does give a good insight into her anti-imperialist activities and her political life, which are often overlooked by biographers because of their obsession with her relationship with the poet W. B. Yeats.[109] In 1900 she established Inghinidhe Na hÉireann (Daughters of Erin), which aimed at Irish independence in all spheres of Irish life: political, economic and cultural. Twenty-nine women attended the first meeting and elected five vice-presidents, including Jenny Wyse Power, a former member of the Ladies' Land League in the 1880s, illustrating that a nineteenth-century precedent existed for female political activism. Lest their earnestness was doubted, 'one of the decisions taken at their first meeting was that members would stop wearing their hair puffed over their ears as this was deemed an English fashion'.[110] Members held classes on Irish history and the Irish language; warned women not to associate with English soldiers; and highlighted the dangers of venereal disease. The also formed a drama company that influenced W. B. Yeats. Sinéad McCoole has made the point that many who joined 'were young working women who discovered unprecedented freedom as they attended lectures, céilís [Irish dances] and monthly debates'.[111]

Many women accepted that their primary responsibility was to the home, but this did not have to exclude them from the Irish revival. Mary E. L. Butler, in *Irishwomen and the Home Language* (1900), published by the Gaelic League, argued that women had an important part to play in the language revival:

> Why? Because this language movement is not an academic one. It is a living one. What is wanted is to make the language living in the land; to do this it is necessary to make it the home language; and to make it the home language it is necessary to enlist the co-operation of woman – the home maker.[112]

Working-class women employed outside the home were also afforded opportunities to stake their claim to a place in the trade union movement during these years. In September 1911, a female trade unionist, Delia Larkin, reported with pride on the formation of the Irish Women's Workers' Union, through the 'women workers' column of the *Irish Worker*, the paper of the Irish Transport and General Workers' Union:

> It was, in reality, a surprise to all present. It has also been a source of conversation and comment to the general public, because an idea has always been uppermost in the people's minds that it was utterly

impossible to get a number of women to come together for any demonstration. In fact, I myself, have always felt that women were apathetic in their attitude towards their own betterment, but Tuesday's meeting has once and for all dispelled that feeling.[113]

'the fellow who spoke through his nose'

But formally, politics was dominated by nationalist males – the generation that grew to adulthood in Edwardian Ireland, some of whom later propelled the cause of Irish independence to unprecedented heights. Tom Garvin suggested that the cultural atmosphere in which these people were educated, and re-created, was suffused with a nationalist and anti-modernist romanticism. They rebelled against their elders but, according to Garvin, were sceptical about the possibility or desirability of mass democracy. He also suggested that their social thought was derived from ethics rather than politics, with intellectual guidance from the Church ensuring a middle-agrarian, small-town society outlook.[114] The Christian Brothers were to the fore in this regard, and the republican activist C. S. Andrews, born in Dublin in 1901, memorably recalled that 'This was the first generation of the men of no property among whom secondary education was sufficiently diffused to provide an effective leadership for a revolution.'[115] But such an education was no guarantee that its beneficiaries would be fawning in their attitude to the Catholic Church. Some of the Irish civil servants living in London between 1902 and 1913, such as P. S. O'Hegarty, Michael Collins and Bulmer Hobson, became active in the Irish Republican Brotherhood, and wanted no marriage of religion and politics. In 1904, P. S. O'Hegarty, later a prominent nationalist and historian, wrote to a contemporary:

> I don't hold that the priests are our natural enemies, but I do think strongly that they have acquired the habit and that nothing but strong determined attitudes will break them of it. They ruined every movement – directly or indirectly – since the passing of the Maynooth Grant in 1795 and we have to put them in their places if we are going to do anything ... most of the fellows here are anti-cleric to a greater or lesser degree ... it is only when a man leaves Ireland that he begins to see straight on some things, this among them.[116]

Andrews's memoir gives a particularly interesting insight into the class divisions operating in his native city at the turn of the century.

With a wry eye, he wrote of upper-class or 'Castle' Catholics, meaning the medical specialists, barristers and wholesale merchants, who had dinner in the evening and dressed for it: 'their accents were indistinguishable from those of the Dublin Protestants who held the flattering belief that they spoke the best English in the world'. The 'middle' middle classes 'had their dinner in the middle of the day and entertained themselves at musical evenings' and as medical doctors and grocers fervently wished for their own offspring to become Castle Catholics. Lower-middle-class Catholics were also described – the shopkeepers and publicans who lived over their business premises, and 'ate mid-day dinner, wore night-shirts rather than pyjamas and slept in feather beds. They took no holidays and seldom entertained.' Further down were the labourers and domestic servants, who sent their children to national schools for as short a time as possible, amused themselves in the pubs and took no interest in politics because 'their main concern was to provide food and lodging for their children; they frequently failed to do either'. They accepted misery as the will of God – their fortitude would be rewarded, they believed, in the next life.[117]

Regarding the cultural endeavours of individuals like the poet W. B. Yeats and Irish language activist Douglas Hyde, in relation to language and identity, Conor Cruise O'Brien in *States of Ireland*, suggested that 'most were too poor to concern themselves consciously with such things'. Many who were better off 'left all that behind them. You could be "for" English while being "against" England.' Cruise O'Brien noted Yeats's comment to his well-heeled friends – 'you must be baptized in the gutter' as being illustrative of a 'cultivated upper-middle class among raw lower-middle class'.[118] And what of the university elites who were being groomed to take over the job of running a Home Rule Ireland? The 'elite', according to Cruise O'Brien, who were being trained by the Jesuits? One of the issues that had repeatedly emerged in the post-Famine era was the demand for a Catholic university, and the need to shape any new institution along 'national' lines. It had become clear early in the century that university legislation based on an all-Ireland framework was unfeasible and the Irish Universities Act of 1908 was based on a partitionist and indeed sectarian rationale. It left Trinity College Dublin to its own devices, made Queen's University Belfast a university in its own right, and created the national university of Ireland, with constituent colleges in Dublin, Cork, Galway and Maynooth.

In writing the history of University College Cork, John A. Murphy discovered that one of the phrases which was often bandied about before the legislation of 1908 was the idea that what had been Queen's College Cork would now become 'the poor man's University'. This was a reference to the fact that the Act had envisioned the provision of scholarships to be provided by local authorities. This issue became dogged by disputes, as land and labour representatives on local authorities were cynical about making provision in striking the rates to enable children of ratepayers to secure college scholarships. They felt that rhetoric based on a flourishing classless university in Cork was clearly a case of putting the cart before the horse, given that the great majority of children had no access to secondary education, and it was clear that access to university would be confined to an already well-off minority. (By 1911 only 6 per cent of the school-going population were enrolled at secondary schools and the majority dropped out before finishing their final year.)

This was a view shared by national (primary school) teachers, but college authorities continued to delude themselves; the President of UCC in the first two decades of the twentieth century, Bertram Windle, made ridiculous and extravagant claims, insisting the college was not 'in any way closed to the children of the poorest worker'. A contemporary critic of Windle was perhaps more accurate in suggesting there was more likely to be a welcome 'for the fellow who spoke through his nose'.[119]

Those who were ultimately to benefit from the university legislation grew to political maturation between the fall of Parnell and the rise of a new republicanism, and it is fair to say that their fortunes have been generally overlooked, probably because it was the issue of education rather than political independence to which they devoted much of their energies. The university question not only became a forum for the articulation of grievances but also opened up debates about the right of women to enjoy the same status in universities as men.

While the university students expressed nationalist sentiments, they generally supported the IPP: indeed, Senia Paseta has argued that they may have been more 'nationally minded' than later republican propaganda allowed. But they also aped much that was prevalent in English public schools, and behaved at college debates like future parliamentarians at Westminster. Often, they were unashamedly elitist, conservative and moralistic, highlighting once again the class distinctions of Irish society. The economist George O'Brien, for example, ecstatically recalled the atmosphere at the King's Inns, training ground for future barristers:

The buildings dated back to the eighteenth century and had that air of aristocratic dignity which appealed to me so strongly. The ceremonial procedure at dinner, the elaborate uniforms of the servants, the procession of the benchers, the gallery of portraits of judges in the dining hall – all these things satisfied some sense of order and security.[120]

It was entirely appropriate that O'Brien had referred to the buildings of the eighteenth century, as this was the century when beautiful and elaborate edifices hid the extraordinary poverty and filth that permeated Dublin, and ensured its development as a city of extremes; a critic in the eighteenth century had labelled such buildings the 'Gorgeous mask of Ireland's distress'.[121]

Many of these people wanted to take a central part in an Ireland they could control, but one which had the trimmings and benefits of empire. This was a truth which latter republicans may have been slow to acknowledge or were quick to dismiss as irrelevant, and one which historians may have overlooked in their desire to understand the origins of modern Irish republicanism. But it was optimistic and proud, and crucial in shaping the outlook of many of those who were benefiting from the key changes of the early twentieth century. These were most noticeable in rising literacy, employment opportunities, urbanisation and social congregation, not to mention the links between Ireland and the United Kingdom: shared language, bureaucratic and professional institutions and the expansion of a middle class.

In Maynooth College, which housed the national seminary for Catholic priests, the beginning of spring was marked in the early years of the century by the preparing of tennis and croquet courts. The authorities looked more favourably on such pursuits than the Gaelic field games with their potential for roughness and manifestations of provincial rivalries, while staff recreation was centred around horse breeding. This is not to suggest that attention was not given to the dissemination of all things Irish; in 1906 the administrative council of the college was worried about the radical nationalist tone of many of the student debates, and there were fierce and prolonged rows about the issue of compulsory Irish.[122] Rather, it was another indication of the dual identity experienced by many involved at third-level education in Ireland.

'fat and comfortable in a mansion in Rathmines'

Middle-class Catholics were making other important and obvious advances, particularly in the professions, where they began to outnumber Protestants in the fields of law and medicine and in the civil service. The various boards, institutions and councils which the British government administered offered further avenues of advancement. Amongst the educated Catholic elite, class distinction was based on Victorian English norms, prompting the fear of journalist D. P. Moran that Catholic professionals would ultimately sit 'fat and comfortable in a mansion in Rathmines' (a suburb on the south of the city). Perhaps there is much truth in the assertion of Paseta that it was less a new world these people wanted than to dominate the old, and it is also the case that despite the vigour of the Gaelic movement Irish audiences showed little inclination to shun English popular culture. D. P. Moran worked hard to convince them otherwise with vigorous writing and robust criticism – in his view, Protestants could be Irish as long as they accepted that Ireland was a Catholic country. Often bigoted and utterly uninterested in the exchange of ideas, Moran nonetheless did not sink to the level of vituperation indulged in by J. J. O'Kelly in the *Catholic Bulletin*.[123]

'little sympathy for the clichéd shamrocks, wolfhounds and round towers'

In ridiculing the culture of cheap English newspapers and music hall entertainment Moran was in one sense a spokesman for the rising entrepreneurial class and small businesses. They were represented in a number of industrial development authorities established in some small Irish towns after 1903. His journalistic crusades also appealed to those Catholic graduates and ambitious white-collar workers who were denied access to official patronage. He launched campaigns bemoaning Protestant dominance in the higher civil service and the banks for example, and he championed a Catholic Association established in Dublin in 1902 to promote Catholic advancement above that of nationalism. He also distanced himself from the Irish Parliamentary Party, which he saw as utterly ineffective and hypocritical. Unlike Arthur Griffith, who he was to fall out with, 'he thought snobbery was inevitable and that nationalists should exploit it'.[124]

Griffith, on the other hand, unlike the present-centred Moran, believed that the eighteenth and nineteenth centuries provided unchanging terms of reference for nationalists. Moran, for example, attacked local authorities that gave contracts to non-Irish firms 'but criticised Griffith's protectionism and argued that customers should buy only Irish products that were "as good and as cheap" as competitors'. Griffith called this no protection at all and those who proposed it traitors.[125] Griffith, like so many polemical journalists in the early twentieth century, had an astonishing workrate – and could be narrow-minded but also imaginative. The historian of Sinn Féin, Michael Laffan, has pointed out that 'he was a gifted writer and a cantankerous politician, an obsessive compiler and manipulator of statistics, a theorist who revelled in past and present models for a future Irish state. Unlike most other radical Irish nationalists he was hard-headed and down-to-earth in his concern with economic questions, and he showed little sympathy for the clichéd shamrocks, wolfhounds and round towers which were cherished by so many of his contemporaries.'[126] His seminal *Resurrection of Hungary* was an argument promoting the merits of establishing Anglo-Irish relations along the lines of the Austro-Hungarian model of dual monarchy, recommending that Irish MPs should abstain from Westminster, in the same manner that Hungarian deputies had withdrawn from the imperial parliament in Vienna.

His National Council, formed in 1903 to mount a protest against the visit of Edward VII to Dublin, had the initial aim of the 'stamping out of toadyism and flunkeyism in this land' but was to develop into something more permanent. Meanwhile, young Ulster nationalists in 1905 launched the Dungannon Clubs, which were more extreme than Griffith's group. Interestingly, by 1906 it was being suggested that these various groups (including Cumann na nGaedheal – a loose federation of several lobbying groups that soon became an IRB front after its establishment in 1900) should combine to include both those who believed in the Constitution of 1782 'as a final settlement' (when the pre-Act of Union Irish Parliament had been granted legislative independence, though the executive continued to be headed by British politicians), and those who believed in full independence.[127] The Dungannon Clubs and Cumann na nGaedheal then established the 'Sinn Féin league', a title Griffith had begun using for his own newspaper in 1906. Soon afterwards his own National Council joined forces. A product of a Dublin artisan culture, Griffith sought to present his new movement as representing the antithesis of careerist corruption. He was also responsible for occasional anti-Semitism in deeming Jewish commercialism to be corrupting (though the Jewish community also had their staunch defenders such as Michael Davitt).

'if we today lack the guts to say Boo to any Protestant in the land'
By the beginning of the century, the Catholic share of the Irish population stood at 74.2 per cent. Of the 1.1 million Protestants in Ireland, 327,000 were in the 26 southern counties, being particularly heavily represented in the suburbs of Dublin. The European religious revival of the mid nineteenth century ensured that an Irish version would attempt to tackle the notorious indiscipline and general laziness within the administration of the Church. This tardiness was reflected in priests neglecting their duties, financial corruption and a reluctance to accept the authority of the Church Hierarchy. This led to many and varied internal disputes and an excessive localism within the Church, coupled with the tendency of priests to establish virtual independent fiefdoms within certain parishes or dioceses. The historical circumstances of eighteenth-century Irish Catholicism, which was subjected to 'Penal Laws' and the resultant operation of an underground church, were undoubtedly contributory factors to this general sorry state of affairs.

The repeal of the Penal Laws prompted a staggering increase in the number of nuns and brothers in Ireland in the nineteenth century, mirroring the explosion of vocations in England and France. In 1800 there had been only 120 nuns in six orders, but this figure had risen to 8,000 nuns in 35 orders and congregations by 1900.[128] Likewise, the Christian Brothers in 1831 had only 45 brothers, but nearly 1,000 in 1900 (and their number was to quadruple by the 1960s). Another significant indication of the robust state of the Catholic Church was that the first decade of the twentieth century marked the effective beginning of the missionary movement abroad, when a surplus of Irish priests became available to send away, with missionary magazines becoming a fixture in many Catholic homes.

Reforming bishops were the most obvious manifestation of change from the mid nineteenth century with a new emphasis on regular supervision, an increased devotion to religious instruction, financial scrutiny and new codes of behaviour for clerics. Particularly important was the promotion by Cardinal Paul Cullen (Archbishop of Dublin from 1852 to 1878) of ultramontanism, which, though by no means unchallenged, was characterised by political conservatism, an emphasis on papal authority and the acceptance of a combative and dogmatic theology. Political moderation did not mean that the late-nineteenth-century Irish Church was incapable of criticising political structures in Ireland, or indeed English mismanagement of Irish affairs, but it did mean an intolerance shown to secretive or armed republicanism. But it should not be assumed that the typical Irish Catholic would be dragged politically in a direction they did not want to go.

In material terms, the Church exploited the new-found prosperity of many of its adherents – particularly the middling farmers and shopkeepers – and indulged in a veritable orgy of church-building as well as setting up schools, orphanages and libraries.

It is undoubtedly significant that those who grew to adulthood in the early twentieth century were brought up in an era when the Church was thriving, directing, often controlling and nearly always educating. This created a culture dominated by a Catholic world view that was profoundly pessimistic on some levels, and whose chief intellectual mentors were the Catholic priests of Ireland who placed a strong emphasis on the values of the farm society. This gave rise to a distrust and revulsion at the prospect of city life, evidenced in literature such as Fr Peter O'Leary's *Mo Scéal Féin* ('my own story'). There was a certain snobbery in all this, depicted in James Joyce's *Dubliners* through the character of Miss Ivors, who was based on a woman Joyce had met through the Gaelic League. She was a character who admonished a contemporary for reading the *Daily Express*, wore conservative clothes and a Gaelic League brooch, and extolled the virtues of Irish lessons. But her commitment had to be seen to go further than that: 'Will you come for an excursion to the Aran Isles [Irish-speaking western islands] this month? We're going to stay for a whole month. It will be splendid out on the Atlantic.'[129]

Canon Sheehan's novels decried a decay in culture and manners, depicting city materialism as a retreat towards paganism, which priests, but also women, were central in combating. Fictional clerical characters were often depicted championing the development of cottage industry in their districts, as if to immunise the Church from any charge that their anti-urban bias was hindering economic development. Sheehan, for example, was adamant that it was the priests who had to take responsibility for the control of intellectual leadership in Ireland, particularly, as he warned in 1903, when the threat of the arrival of an educated layman who would discard the instructions of clerics was potentially around every corner.[130] As well as fiction, specifically Catholic newspapers and magazines such as the *Irish Messenger of the Sacred Heart*, the *Irish Catholic* and the *Irish Rosary* were part of the staple diet of the literate Irish Catholic by the turn of the century. It should not be assumed, however, that many of the popular, unofficial and sometimes pagan traditions which many Irish Catholics enjoyed could be ousted with ease.

The pontificate of Pope Leo XIII, in looking back to a pre-Industrial Revolution era, was pivotal in attempting to develop the concept of a social Catholicism which involved sympathetic rhetoric concerning the plight of the poor, tempered with a greater concern for the maintenance of public order. A Catholic intellectual from County Kerry, John Moynihan, in a letter to his brother Michael in 1909, suggested: 'You know well that the clergy would prefer the people to confine themselves in the matter of literature to the penny inanities of the Catholic Truth Society or the penny horribles of England rather than read a paper which might elevate their moral character.'[131] But what they had in mind for middle-class Catholics was different, as revealed by the Catholic Defence Society and the Catholic Association, which railed against Protestant discrimination in professional and business sectors – in 1902 the handbook of the Catholic Association insisted:

> There is no earthly use in people talking about what our forefathers suffered for the faith if we today lack the guts to say Boo to any Protestant in the land … we must fight with all our might until we have laid our hands on as much of the power, place and position of this country as our numbers, our ability and our unabated historical claims entitle us to demand.[132]

'an institution rather than a man'

The leadership of the Irish Catholic Church of the nineteenth and early twentieth centuries was dominated by exceptionally demonstrative archbishops of Dublin: Thomas Troy, Daniel Murray, Paul Cullen and, from 1885 until his death in 1921, William Walsh. At the end of his life a contemporary friend, Myles Ronan, observed that Walsh 'was wedded to so many movements and undertakings for such an extensive span of years that he seemed an institution rather than a man'.[133] By no means an effective orator, Walsh preferred the press over the pulpit, and there were few areas he did not see fit to tackle in his relentless quest to promote Catholicism, including politics, land, morality, temperance, labour issues and, perhaps most importantly, education

Well qualified to stake his claim as a moulder of public opinion and an authoritative critic on many affairs, his training in canon law and theology was put to good use and he seemed determined to be at all times polemical. Walsh's career was crucial in the continuance of the post-Famine trend of Church consolidation and spanned the Parnell era, the rise and fall of the Irish Parliamentary Party and the beginnings of the Irish pursuit of independence (all of which he expressed strong views on). That throughout his career political leaders, political parties and bishops were able to survive such changing fortunes was not only indicative of the key role the Church played in the consolidation of the modern Irish political system (and its contribution to, or control over, what was deemed acceptable or unacceptable); it also showed its determination to be a permanent feature of Irish secular as well as political life. This continued to be the trend after independence.

Paradoxically, Walsh was also an aloof loner, again indicative of a trend that was to persist – the extent to which the Irish Hierarchy was capable of staying culturally quite distant from its flock, while empathising with them politically. Walsh's real strength was his skill at assessing the popular mood and ensuring that any future independent Irish state would have to negotiate a social, cultural and educational infrastructure that was built and designed by the Church. As Thomas Morrissey, his most recent biographer, makes clear, this ensured that after independence the Church would see its role as that of mediator between different Catholic constituencies.[134]

Aside from his devotion to political issues, Walsh was also capable of showing great concern for the less well off in Irish society, but, crucially, was also aware of the Church's limitations in this regard. And they were many. Given the remarkable and fundamental reversals in the fortunes of the Catholic Church it is perhaps surprising that they failed to develop a social ideology that would have more belligerently attacked social neglect and decay. Were priests suitably equipped to adopt leadership roles in the pursuit of social Catholicism in early twentieth-century Ireland? The *Irish Peasant* in 1906 had rightly insisted that spiritually and socially the Irish Catholic Church had everything to gain by standing wholeheartedly for home development. But the problem for much of this period was that the definition of home development seemed rarely to extend to the formulation of a philosophy to combat poverty and public health, but rather employed the conveniently nebulous phrase, 'Irish-Ireland'.

It did sometimes seem that the role of the Catholic Church was to listen, guide and supervise without actually proposing solutions, or, as one critic put it: 'A Catholic who wants to be a critic may be one only on the condition that he reaches the conclusions which are prescribed by the Catholic Church.'[135] Quite simply, the Church was not specialising in social issues. The 'modernist movement' in the Church, inaugurated in 1891, seemed to have withered away after being condemned in the encyclical *Pascendi* (1907). A contributor to the *Irish Ecclesiastical Record* suggested *Pascendi* 'came as a disagreeable surprise' to those in the Irish Catholic Church, because, despite 'vague disquieting rumours' that all was not well in certain theological centres on the Continent, it was not recognised in Ireland that modernism as a movement was strong enough to merit a papal refutation. The author went on to reaffirm Irish Catholic abhorrence of modernism, rejecting the idea that God lived outside the mere phenomenal world and that man could not through intellectual powers acquire any valid knowledge about God's existence. This was regarded as an 'entirely false notion of philosophy'.[136]

But there were other obstacles facing those intent on reforming the Irish Church. Calling for social reform was relatively uncomplicated; the real difficulty was the form this change should take. The journalist W. P. Ryan, former editor of the *Irish Peasant* and thus no stranger to the wrath of an intolerant Church, had written in his book *The Pope's Green Isle* that 'On the place and rights of priests in the Irish social economy there were conflicting notions amongst the priests themselves and a still greater conflict of view as to the place and rights of the laics in the Church and elsewhere.'[137]

Bishops also found themselves divided on the issue of the agricultural co-operative movement, being at times supportive, at times in opposition, but mostly tepidly selective, for the simple reason that the machinations of the co-operative movement exposed contradictions in the social structure of rural Ireland. The difficulties in finding rural movements that could command unequivocal Church support were in evidence long before elements of the Catholic middle class of independent Ireland sought more robust Church sanction for their campaign for vocationalism, decentralisation and rural self-help. It was also the case that although the Church in early-twentieth-century Ireland was attempting to foster a parish consciousness, the poverty of much of the western seaboard was inimical to its development.

'the delicate-mindedness, or over-protectiveness, or mealy-mouthedness'

It was a problem that remained. Fr Joseph Flood, writing in 1915 on the role of the priest in social reform, noted enviously the *curies* in France turning presbyteries into co-operative societies and sewing guilds, and Dominican monks in Belgium going down mines in a spirit of Catholic unity. But he ruefully reflected that although Ireland was a land of peasant proprietors closely bonded to their clergy, and with a charitable disposition, they were forty years behind in Catholic social action 'due to mistrust'.[138] He might also have added class distinction and snobbery and an overriding concern with controlling public and sexual morality. Seán O'Faoláin, born in 1900, echoed in his autobiography a common complaint from those who grew to resent the excessive paternalism of Irish Catholicism:

> There is one thing I do blame, must blame, because it caused me so much suffering as a young boy – the delicate-mindedness, or over-protectiveness, or mealy-mouthedness, whichever it was, of the Irish church and the sentimental picture of Irish life, especially in relation to sex, that it presented to us through its teaching orders and from the pulpit, except when some tough Redemptorist [one of the most active preaching orders who organised regular retreats] took over to give us a bit of straightforward, realistic hell.[139]

The renowned poet Austin Clarke, born in 1896, remembered vividly the all-pervasive presence of religion when being reared in Dublin city: the book of sermons, the smell of frankincense and the richness of the ecclesiastical costume, and most significantly, the preoccupation with the next world:

> Certainly, as a child, I knew a great deal more about the next world than this one ... chief among those physical contacts with the next world was one which may have been unorthodox but was strangely moving. A tiny ringing in the ear meant that a poor soul in Purgatory was crying to us for aid ... all these self-attentions in the lifelong quest of eternal pleasure, that fearful last-minute rush of the Irish consciousness into the waiting mould of repentance and then that sad ultimate namelessness.[140]

If it is true that the Church continued to play an important role in debates about the land question and Ireland's constitutional relationship with Britain, it also played a pivotal role in the debate over the direction and control of education in Ireland. By the beginning of the twentieth century the need for reform regarding the needs and condition of Irish education was widely recognised. Indeed it was a debate, particularly the issue of denominational control of education, that had been ongoing for 50 years. The National Education system, established in 1831, had quickly become a denominational system and was a demonstration of the Church's ability to place itself to the forefront as official publicist of Catholic grievances, reflected in the concerns of such publications as *Irish Ecclesiastical Record* and *Irish Monthly*.

By the beginning of the twentieth century, for the majority of educated children, parochial organisation, denominational segregation and clerical management was the norm. There was a concomitant emergence of teacher and managerial organisations, while attendance figures for the national schools hovered at about 65 per cent, with a 'payment by results' system operating. By 1900 the Catholic Church was in control of nearly 9,000 national schools, which made significant advances in reducing the illiteracy of the population to just 12 per cent, though the same attention to physical maintenance was not affordable; in 1904, of the 167 national schools in Dublin, 104 had no toilet facilities.[141]

Few were educated to secondary level, in schools that were owned and managed by Church bodies, private individuals or teaching orders. Much depended on local circumstances, and, indeed, the degree of regional opulence. In 1901 there were 38,000 students in secondary schools, though only 8,000 were presented for examination at any level of the system. Of the 264 secondary schools operating in 1904, only 16 were located in Connaught. Although changes were introduced in the educational curricula at the turn of the century, there were no similar innovations in terms of state funding. As well as debate over the need for a central co-ordinating authority in conjunction with local government, another issue that dominated the early twentieth century was the status and employment of secondary teachers; in 1905 only 11.5 per cent of male and 8 per cent of female teachers in secondary schools possessed a degree.[142]

Dissatisfaction with the level of funding for education in Ireland was commented on in strong terms by Derry Corporation in 1907, when they insisted that Irish children were being treated unfairly:

we consider it a monstrous injustice to Ireland that the parliamentary grant for Irish primary education for the current year should be £578,909 less than the Scottish grant while the number of pupils to be educated in primary schools in these two countries is practically the same … we urgently ask an all round increase in the salaries of Irish teachers, as we believe the present starvation salaries are calculated to prevent the entrance of suitable candidates to the teaching profession as well as to drive away those who are already in, and that we see no reason whatever for denying to Irish teachers those civil rights which are freely conceded to the teachers of Great Britain.[143]

Four years later, Augustine Birrell was to admit in the House of Commons that 'the life of an ordinary assistant master in Ireland is detestable, the remuneration is miserably inadequate and he has no tenure of office at all'.[144] (Even in 1919, 30 per cent of lay teachers received salaries of less than £100 per annum.) At third level the debate about the need for a Catholic university had subsided after 1908. Alongside relatively well-endowed teacher-training colleges, provision for third level was confined at the beginning of the century to the old Dublin University (established in 1854) and the Queen's Colleges of Cork, Belfast and Galway, along with Trinity College Dublin. Between them they accounted for only about 1,000 students in 1908.[145] Two royal commissions, the Robertson of 1900 and the Fry of 1906, had sought to devise schemes but had failed to deliver proposals acceptable to all concerned, and it was a considerable achievement by Augustine Birrell, Chief Secretary in 1908, to create two new universities, meeting the desires of the Catholic Hierarchy while ensuring the continuing independent status of Trinity College. Given that the new colleges of the National University of Ireland were legally non-denominational, there were predictable accusations by Catholic extremists that they would turn out to be 'Godless Colleges', but the endorsement of the Catholic Hierarchy mitigated such sentiments. Perhaps Tim Healy was accurate in suggesting that 'the Bill is nobody's ideal'; it was not everything the Church wanted, but rather a clever compromise on the part of the Liberal government, and the NUI was to exhibit characteristics which were Catholic, but also democratic and utilitarian.[146]

Many educated Irish Catholics also immersed themselves in the novels of Canon Sheehan; the most famous of his books, *My New Curate*, was translated into a dozen languages. His books seem with the passing of time to be excessively sentimental and overly concerned with the disaster awaiting women who strayed from the path of righteous purity. But significantly it is now recognised that he also identified the discouragement of debate within the Church of his time, and *Luke Delmege* for example, published in 1901, was heavily criticised in clerical circles, suggesting that he could be seen by some of his peers as a critic advocating reform.[147] Likewise another priest-novelist, Gerald O'Donavan, in *Fr Ralph* (1913), dealt with the crisis of a young priest who felt he could not accept the terms of a papal encyclical and left the priesthood. The same author, in *Waiting,* examined the difficulties of a couple in a mixed marriage and implied a revulsion against the ways of the clergy in local politics and economics. Thus it is fair to see in the priestly fictions conflicting versions of what Ireland ought to be and that there was a market for careful and subtle criticism of the clergy.[148]

In 1912 a Limerick priest published the *Literary Crusade*, blaming literature for instances of insanity, suicide and crime, and was 'perplexed to be told by a newsagent that sales of "foreign magazines" newspapers and fictions were highest after Sunday mass'. Meanwhile the *Irish Messenger of the Sacred Heart*, expounding cultural and religious nationalism, had a circulation of 73,000 by the turn of the century. There had been a rise in literacy levels from 33 per cent in 1851 to 84 per cent in 1911, and 97.4 per cent of Irish emigrants to the United States between 1899 and 1910 (more than half of whom were women from the west and south-west) could read and write in English.[149]

'sucking the blood of other nations'

Incidents of anti-Semitism were a feature of communities where Jews had settled from the late nineteenth century, with most arriving from Lithuania. They became familiar fixtures – particularly the peddlers – in the South Circular Road district of Dublin and there were tensions between them and the more established Jews of the north side of the city. A degree of comfort is suggested by the fact that nearly all the Jewish homes listed in the 1901 census had a Roman Catholic servant.[150] Dublin possessed the largest Jewish community in Ireland, but there were about 25 families of Lithuanian Jews in Limerick in 1900.

Most of the County Inspector's reports dealing with their activities emphasised that while they loaned small amounts of money, they were not intent on acquiring land. But in 1904 the fact that Jews in Limerick were using the word 'pogrom' to describe their persecution was an indi-

cation of the hostility that could be engendered, when, as in this case, a
local Catholic priest insisted on dogmatic, revivalist and inflammatory
preaching. He suggested Jews were 'sucking the blood of other nations
and must not be allowed to do the same in Ireland', and they became easy
targets for those traders who were hostile to peddlers. The priest talked of
keeping the poor 'independent of the Jewish usurers', ensuring resentment
in working-class areas towards the Jewish peddlers, tradesmen and shopkeepers. His contentions were taken as a call for a commercial boycott,
which was reacted to incredulously by the local rabbi. He maintained that
they had lived in 'perfect peace and harmony with their Christian neighbours of all classes' while, now, Jewish children were being ostracised in
schools. It was a prejudice, according to James Joyce, which demonstrated
'the contempt people always show for the unknown'. The 1906 Aliens Act
restricted the number of Jews coming into the country.[151]

'a romantic notion of integrity?'

Perhaps it was appropriate that, at a time when the Irish people were
being urged to embrace the idea that they represented a historic community whose self-image predated the era of modern nationalism, there
was an intense debate on the status of history in the curriculum of Irish
schools. The literary critic Declan Kiberd has interpreted the debate about
national identity and anglicisation, generally accepted as having been
begun by Douglas Hyde and the Gaelic League in 1893, as posing the
choice between nationality or cosmopolitanism: 'Were the Irish a hybrid
people, as the artists generally claimed, exponents of multiple selfhood
and modern authenticity? Or were they a pure, unitary race, dedicated to
defending a romantic notion of integrity?'

The attempt to find an answer to such a fundamental question led
to the emergence of an extraordinary range of writing talent, as creative
artists sought to fill a certain vacuum or to make their mark in a country
that was, in the words of Yeats, 'like soft wax'.[152] The brilliance which
was the hallmark of many of the literary works was accompanied by much
bile. It was no coincidence, for example, that there was a dearth of images
of domestic harmony. If regeneration was the philosophy at work at this
stage, this too could be divisive, perhaps because the perpetration of the
idea that, in order to proclaim an ancient 'organic' Gaelic society, serious
criticisms of the shortcomings of contemporary society were necessary.

Thus Daniel Corkery rounded on the 'Ascendancy' perspective of professional historians who were, he felt, utterly removed from the 'hidden' (and thus real) Ireland. Likewise, D. P. Moran could be both creative as a pioneer of 'new journalism' in developing a framework for Ireland's new Gaelic obsessions and obnoxious in his ridicule of those who did not do enough to match the demise of the Ascendancy class with a significantly robust assertion of a culture based on Catholic and Gaelic lives.

The revival was a mass of contradictions, as indeed were those who sponsored and promoted it. Moran was shrewd and clever but narrow minded and hypocritical – he who lambasted city folk as lacking any serious identity rarely himself visited the Gaeltacht and did not learn to speak Irish.[153] What himself and Corkery perhaps failed to appreciate was that it was in the city where battles would be won – but cities were, according to Patrick Maume, beyond him: he looked to remote rural havens as James Joyce looked to Europe. Yet Corkery should not be dismissed, because in his idealism and his faults he represented an important generation. Nonetheless, looking to the poorest part of the country in order to imagine a purer and more creative Irish-language world was hopeless idealism.[154] Likewise Moran was perfectly legitimate in challenging what he called 'the accepted view that politics was the begin-all and end-all of Irish nationality', wryly noting that Irish men 'threw over Irish civilisation whilst they professed – and professed in perfect good faith – to fight for Irish nationality'. 'Our peasants have not gone into print – I know nothing of them,' he remarked.[155]

Alf Mac Lochlainn's summary of the 'Gaelic revival' was perhaps as good as any, when he wrote that it was a combination of 'romantic nationalism, second-hand radicalism, European radicalism, middle-class frustration and cultural awareness'.[156] It was inevitable it would be multi-layered given the impossibility of agreeing on one ready-made and fixed Irish identity. James Joyce, in 1903, when reviewing Lady Gregory's *Poets and Dreams*, suggested the storyteller from whom she took the stories had a 'feeble and sleepy mind' and that none of the stories had any satisfying imaginative wholeness, and he referred to the 'fullness of the senility' of the 'folk' ways.[157]

'himself his own father'
Declan Kiberd pointed out how ironic it was that the attempts to restore the Irish language coincided with the emergence of the literary greatness of Irish men writing in English, like Yeats, Joyce, J. M. Synge and George

Moore. For all the obsession with things rural it was also the case that it was in fact socialism that was the driving force behind so much of Irish writing. It was also a revival riddled with class differences. George Russell (Æ), one of the neglected Irish intellectuals of the early twentieth century, wrote widely on economic and cultural development, militarism and the role of labour. He took a communal view of the social order (which he shared with Connolly, Davitt and Plunkett) and articulated the notion that private property was an English imposition on a Gaelic society where the chieftains had held land in trust for the entire people. In holding that view he realised the extent and impact of class antagonisms, but also saw Irish intellectuals as part of a broader, international order – for him the acid test of success or failure for Ireland was if they could succeed in making democracy prevail in economic life. In other words, it was for the intellectuals to lead.[158]

But if a new generation were intent on being free to conceive of themselves, as distinct from accepting traditional definitions of national identity, this involved generational rejection; a revolt by young men against their fathers; men like Simon Dedalus, who in Joyce's words in *Portrait of the Artist* were defeatist and uncreative forward-looking 'praisers of their own past'. His son Stephen wanted instead to become 'himself his own father'. The historian Patrick O'Farrell suggested this was the real contribution made by writers in the initial decades of the century: not a smug version of national identity, 'but the assumption of a European perspective after a century of dreary provincialism. This revival was less an assertion of traditions long-denied than an insistence that Irish people have the freedom to conceive of themselves.'[159]

As George Moore saw it, Ireland may have been distinguished by a body of literature in which it appeared as a land of enchantment, but it was also 'as small as a pig's back'. Thus the dilemma he presented in his *Hail and Farewell Trilogy* (1911–14) was where Irish writers should locate themselves: at home or abroad; and furthermore, did Ireland have a unique culture then or in the past? Must Ireland settle for its provincial fate? As Colm Tóibín has pointed out, Joyce needed to find a language, form and style that was new and inventive so that his work would not be answerable to any earlier tradition. Thus sacred cows were ridiculed while the ordinary was to be championed: 'he set his masterpiece against any narrow idea of a nation. His nation of 1904 was made up of different people in the same place.'[160] Joyce, though, as G. J. Watson noted, was also coming to terms with a traditional culture as well as being dismissive. He was attempting to understand deprivation and inferiority in the Irish psyche, and to force people to face this honestly.[161]

Throughout the 1900s, W. B. Yeats was constantly excited by the potential that existed in Ireland for cultural revival. It was by no means an exclusively Irish preoccupation; as Roy Foster has demonstrated, Yeats's cultural enterprises in the early years of the century were centred in both Dublin and London. The ideas he had for a national theatre, realised in the form of the Abbey Theatre in December 1904, needed much input from others, including Lady Gregory, and the Fay brothers, highly conspicuous in fringe theatrical activity in Dublin at this time. The Fay brothers had 'more to offer than Gregory or Yeats allowed in later years'.[162] Some of the lectures that Yeats gave on a tour of America in 1903 reveal the sense of reawakening and cultural excitement of these years, and perhaps explain why politics played an important part in the choice of plays. The titles to the lectures included 'The intellectual revival of Ireland', 'Heroic literature of Ireland' and 'The theatre and what it might be'. Yeats wanted a national theatre to become a 'chief expression of Irish imagination', but he was also keen to control that expression, which led to much tension, as he saw himself, in the words of Foster, 'as a dictator in the cause of art, ready to dominate, divide and rule', and had a powerful sense of his own history.[163]

The literary revival was also about breaking with the tradition of nineteenth-century writers, who presented the rural population in accordance with their own natural understanding. Perhaps this was why J. M. Synge, in breaking with this, became a playwright of such perception but controversial brilliance. In urban environments, most notably at the Abbey Theatre, twice as many peasant as poetic plays were staged in the early years, stemming from the theatrical experiments of the Fay brothers. They proved enormously popular with audiences. The Abbey playwrights were suggesting, it seemed, that the exuberant language of the peasants, combined with a primitive grace and wilderness, prompted by their wild geographical environment, gave their lives a vividness and colour which was unique. The plays focused on the cottage, the outsider, matchmaking and rural marriage, emigration, family and land. But the extent to which the plays were truly depicting reality was controversial, as was reflected in the storm which greeted J. M. Synge's *Playboy of the Western World* in 1907, which the *Freeman's*

Journal decried as 'an unmitigated, protracted libel upon Irish peasant men, and worse still upon Irish girlhood'.[164]

What Synge had discovered, of course, in his attempt to portray rural life in all its manifold, and sometimes brutal, forms was that the demand that existed was not for truth, but idealised versions of the peasant. Someone of the genius of Synge, in being able to combine the poetic, the mythic and the real in his drama, and in creating the masterpieces of the genre, had perhaps exposed what was to be an enduring approach to the issues of rural Ireland throughout the century – the blatant gulf between the ideal and the practice. How the Irish coped with the violence themselves, as Kiberd pointed out, was Synge's real interest. The reaction to the play revealed huge ironies – the protestors physically assaulting the actors to prove, as some of them shouted, 'We are not a violent people'. They were of course merely proving the points made evident by Synge's characters – that those who are most insistent in opposing violence rhetorically are the most vicious in practice.[165] The propensity for violence, and the sexual frankness of the women, was particularly noticeable, suggesting that the Victorian gentility of the more opulent of Ireland's urban centres had yet to reach the wilds of the West. In any case, Declan Kiberd warned against being too hard on the kind of nationalist males who rioted at the Abbey, noting that 'few men anywhere in the Europe of 1907 could have coped with Synge's subversive gender-benders, least of all a group committed to the social construction of precisely the kind of Cuchulanoid heroism which the playwright was so mischievously debunking'.[166]

'bright and eloquent and witty'

The reaction to Synge was also virulent because the capacity for delusion about the 'Irish peasant' was undiminished in the opening years of the twentieth century. A contributor to the *New Ireland Review* of August 1901 suggested:

> It is universally acknowledged that the Irish peasantry are endowed with an inherent quickness of perception and possesses a peculiarly brilliant intelligence ... above the average of the other nations of western Europe. Whether these characteristics are the natural attributes of racial superiority, or have been acquired through those historic developments which are without parallel in the annals of any other people, it is not my task to examine. My purpose is to direct attention

to the fact that not merely are our countrymen bright and eloquent and witty, but that they also possess the more steadfast qualities which are necessary to profitable study and mature thought.[167]

This assertion was also defensive; L. P. Curtis, in his book *Anglo-Saxons and Celts* (1968), suggested that 'of the many pejorative adjectives applied by educated Englishmen to the Irish perhaps the most damaging, certainly the most persistent, were those which had to do with their alleged unreliability, emotional instability and mental disequilibrium'.[168]

On the face of it, there was ample evidence for this in Synge's work, but there is also much evidence of the power of the imagination in transcending the difficulties of life and the raw power of love. This was far removed from, in Roy Foster's words, 'respectable, provincial Victorian Ireland', those who were reared on Charles Kickham's *Knocknagow* and A. M. Sullivan's *Story of Ireland* 'all written in florid English, all nationalist, but certainly not new'.[169] Certainly new was the depiction of articulate and violent women, like Pegeen Mike ('and to think it's me speaking sweetly, Christy Mahon, and I the fright of seven townlands for my biting tongue. Well the heart's a wonder'[170]).

Another important component of the cultural regeneration became the quest to maintain the autonomy of art, as championed by Yeats, who in his own art was nonetheless capable of disingenuity. His was a multi-faceted life and it was he who was apt to impose artificial patterns on his life in retrospect, particularly in the context of his childhood.[171]

Yeats, like his close confidante Lady Gregory, was apt to revert to Ascendancy type when frustrated by the rabble. Following the riots over the *Playboy of the Western World*, Gregory suggested: 'It is the old battle between those who use a toothbrush and those who don't.' She, too, often held mutually contradictory positions; another example of the dilemma of those who prized Irish cultural independence and critical truth whilst disliking the excesses of the uneducated masses. This cultural confusion was widespread and in a sense applied to all classes. Colm Tóibín asserted in looking at Gregory at this time that 'It would be easy to suggest that Lady Gregory's attitudes in these years are tinged with a sort of hypocrisy or blindness to the strangeness of her own position. But such shiftings and turnings and dichotomies and inconsistencies are part of the history of Ireland in these years.'[172] Similarly, Fintan O'Toole pointed out in his survey of the century: 'by the end of the decade [1900–1910], neither the imperial claim to have pacified Ireland, nor the nationalist insistence that there was a clear, unified Irish culture was well founded. Many visions of what Ireland should be had begun to compete with each other.'[173] If there was ambiguity to the position of Yeats and Gregory, there was also a clear stand taken against censorship and in favour of artistic freedom, as witnessed by their insistence on staging the plays of Synge, George Bernard Shaw and Seán O'Casey, stagings that involved battling grassroots activists, the Church and the politicians. Yeats and Gregory had the class confidence and the belief in their case to do so.[174]

'Ireland is now plastic and will be for a few years to come'

Yeats in any case showed exceptional foresight in many of his ventures as he sought to resolve his own crisis of cultural identity, assessing an Ireland of both aristocrat and peasant, along with identifying Parnell and Synge and art collector Hugh Lane as three defining elements in his struggle with Ireland. The experience of the Abbey included struggles to define the Irish nation and to reconcile nationalism with a need for patronage and artistic creativity. Those promoting it, according to Roy Foster, often found themselves fighting the enemies within – insular constricting nationalist piety unable to absorb formal experiment or external influence – rather than the enemy without – British imperialism.[175] As far as Yeats was concerned, the enemies within were to the fore in frustrating attempts (ultimately unsuccessful) to provide a permanent home in Ireland for Hugh Lane's paintings, and Yeats's caustic observations on the failure to provide a gallery are a good indication of some of the disillusionment evident in his poetry in the second decade of the century. As Foster has pointed out, he identified the gallery campaign with Ireland's artistic and political maturity. In addressing a London audience in the summer of 1913, he chided the Irish aristocracy for abandoning the intellectuals and artists, suggesting Ireland's artistic independence was now threatened. The phrases and images he used on this occasion were repeated in his poetry and other writings for years:

> There is a moment in the history of every nation when it is plastic, when it is like wax, when it is ready to hold for generations the shape that is given to it. Ireland is now plastic and will be for a few years to come ... if Hugh Lane is defeated hundreds of young men and women all over the country will be discouraged – will choose a poorer idea of

what might be ... if the intellectual movement is defeated in Ireland, Ireland will for many years become a little huckstering nation, groping for halfpence in a greasy till. It is that, or the fulfilment of her better dreams. The choice is yours and ours.[176]

'she has begun to sing'

In November 1905 Douglas Hyde, originator of the Gaelic League in 1893, was presented to an audience in New York's Carnegie Hall as a successful 'missionary from Ireland'. He informed his audience that Ireland was no longer an old and poor woman but a beautiful woman who had begun 'to move and to play, she has begun to sing'. There was nothing quaint or amateurish about Hyde's plan for cultural independence; indeed Joe Lee went as far as to suggest that Hyde was 'one of the most remarkable [individuals] in Irish history whose stature as a cultural entrepreneur in European or indeed global terms has still to receive full recognition'.[177] Hyde could be justifiably proud of the League, established to vigorously promote the use of the Irish language. By February 1901 it had upwards of 200 branches, while four years later there may have been up to 500 branches, and the League played an important role in encouraging the publication of Irish-language books.

Hyde's fundraising tour of the United States was organised by the Irish-American philanthropist John Quinn and was an indication of the centrality of the United States in Irish affairs in the early years of the century. Similarly, Michael O'Flanagan, a prominent priest and social critic, also visited America regularly in an attempt to promote Irish industry and its funding (and was later during the Irish revolution to draw up a ten-point plan for land redistribution).[178] The travel writer Louis Paul-Dubois observed perceptively that the Gaelic League 'is occupied with propaganda, the application of its doctrine of a national renaissance on the basis of the national language. It intends to confer anew upon the country a psychological education.'

It would be easy to exaggerate the effect of an organisation that activated a relatively small minority of the population, but Paul-Dubois was perhaps accurate in seeing its true strength as being psychological, and it was in the area of education that its influence was most strongly felt. The Professor of Ancient History at Trinity College Dublin, John Mahaffy, had in 1899 launched a campaign to have the number of marks awarded for Irish in the intermediate certificate examinations reduced. He had been told, he maintained, by a 'higher authority' that 'it is almost impossible to get hold of a text in Irish which is not religious or which is not silly or indecent'.[179] That Irish was of no practical value was a common belief. This would help explain why, according to the 1891 census, only 66,000 people spoke Irish alone, a fact that undoubtedly galvanised the League, which was also important in promoting an appreciation (as opposed to the study) of Irish history, neglected in Irish schools until 1900.

Of the history literature that did exist, the *Leader* noted in 1900 that the majority of books avoided being connected closely to the present 'or being used for the purpose which they frequently lend themselves of throwing a searching criticism on our times'. Social historians of ancient Ireland preferred P. W. Joyce's *Concise History of Ireland* (1901), and histories that emphasised a consistency in Catholic reaction to the role of England. Study of history became compulsory in schools but did not yet perhaps arouse enough passion, which prompted an awareness of the decline of the oral tradition. Lady Gregory's researches among the Galway peasantry revealed a tradition not only of ghosts and fairies but of ancient Irish heroes and a love of the country 'stemming far beyond the days of the green flag'. She sought to refute the contention of Robert Atkinson of Trinity College that Irish literature represented 'the untrained popular feeling ... as there is very little idealism, there is very little imagination'.[180]

Dr William Delaney, president of University College Dublin, Stephen's Green, was later to ask why the language of the uneducated peasant should be a test for university education. The Gaelic League made the most of the controversy by depicting his stance as being akin to that of Mahaffy of Trinity College, and in opposition to the interests of Irish people; it would, they contended, encourage more people to take Irish in their final exams.[181] By 1908 Irish was an established subject in the national schools, while Michael O'Hickey, who held the chair of Celtic Language and Literature at Maynooth, became an able if equally controversial adversary of Delaney. In 1903 the trustees of Maynooth forced O'Hickey's resignation from the Gaelic League as a result of his pamphleteering in support of Irish in the curricula of the schools. In 1909 he was dismissed from his position at Maynooth after the heated campaign (ultimately successful) to have Irish made compulsory for matriculation in the newly established National University of Ireland. Maynooth had, he maintained, 'undoubtedly sent forth men who have achieved eminence in the field of

Irish historical and antiquarian research, but to purely Gaelic scholarship, however, it has given very few names and scarcely one, it must I fear be admitted, of the first rank'. There was a wider context to the O'Hickey controversy; not only was his language quite violent ('to be opposed by a section of our own, no matter how worthless and degenerate, is not to be endured'); but the administration of the college was worried about its impact on the student debating society to which he had contributed.[182] Nonetheless, the university campaign became another rallying point for the League and the occasion for mass demonstrations in Dublin, while many of the literary crew – Synge, Yeats, Edward Martyn and George Moore included – continued to champion the west of Ireland as the true repository of an ancient, unique and valuable Irish heritage.

The League also promoted the idea of economic nationalism and posed as a defender of Irish industry but quite skilfully maintained its political neutrality before 1915. They did perhaps give the answer to the reputed query of John Redmond in 1909: 'Why are the people taking such an interest in education?' Perhaps that was the significance of the League – its ability to become central to educational and cultural questions in the first decade of the century, rather than saving the language. It did manage to place pride in the cultural legacy of Irish, ensuring those not proficient could at least speak a little and perhaps read. But it was also significant in providing for many an antidote to the depression associated with much of the rural hinterland, particularly because of its cross-gender appeal – W. P. Ryan had noted in 1912 that the Gaelic League 'brought women into pride of place'.[183]

What constituted Irish dancing was another of its preoccupations in the early 1900s, and the debate as to what dances were and were not acceptable prompted much dispute and a letter war that raged in the columns of the League's newspaper, *An Claidheamh Soluis* ('the sword of light'). The fact that much of the League's involvement with dance emanated from London, with four- and eight-hand reels or 'figure dances', was attacked by the purists, the League going so far as to establish a commission of inquiry into the matter. Having heard evidence from all four provinces, the commission condemned the figure dances as not being Irish, though having spotted a couple in Mayo dancing the illicit moves, a contemporary wrote to a newspaper wondering if 'it were possible that in Gaelic Mayo there are some who still hanker after the fleshpots of Egypt?'[184]

'the vitality that lies inert in the common people'
Another important social outlet was the Gaelic Athletic Association,
which after initial bursts of popular and organisational enthusiasm in
the late nineteenth century (it was established in 1884) had gone into a
decline, with only 30 delegates attending the annual congress in 1900.
This prompted a thorough reorganisation in the first decade of the new
century. There has been a tendency to identify the GAA as merely a
political organisation, partly because of its ban on members partaking
in 'foreign' games. In truth the evolution of the GAA was not a narrow
pursuit in sporting Anglophobia but Irish sport embracing the British
model of sport codification and mirroring the European, African and Asian
trend of ball games becoming an important part of the social fabric. The
ban existed to ensure codification as well as self-preservation. In the words
of the sports historian Paul Rouse, the ban was 'an administrative necessity' rather than a mere statement of political ideology; or put another
way, while obviously nationalist, the debate around the GAA and political
nationalism was more fluid than generally recognised.[185]

While nationalism may have been central to its cultural role it could
not prosper unless it matured administratively, which was why the ban
returned with renewed vigour after 1902. This was one of the reasons
why it became so tightly controlled and ultimately the great success story
of twentieth-century Irish sport, with Kerry footballers and Kilkenny
hurlers becoming the first stars of the twentieth-century GAA. From
1900 on its regional and national administration was overhauled and the
entire infrastructure radically altered, while football and hurling were
transformed into fast, open team games, with ever-increasing attendance
and renewed clerical support. In 1906, a lapsed rule banning police participation that dated from the 1890s was reintroduced. The 1901 convention had called on 'the young men of Ireland not to identify themselves
with rugby or association football or any form of imported sport which is
likely to injuriously affect the national pastimes which the GAA provides
for self-respected Irishmen who have no desire to ape foreign manners or
customs'. In 1911, it extended such logic to the social lives of its members
by making ineligible for membership 'all who participate in dances or
similar entertainments got up by or under the patronage of soldiers or
policemen'.[186]

Ironically, as W. F. Mandle has shown, the GAA were keen to mould
their assessment of what made an ideal Irish athlete on the English cult

of Victorian manliness. But it was also as likely that Irish working-class boys would be playing soccer and the middle class following the fortunes of the Surrey and Kent cricket teams. The GAA structure, beginning in the smallest of parish clubs, also induced a satisfying tribal loyalty. As far back as 1956 Conor Cruise O'Brien estimated that the GAA was one of the most successful and original mass movements and that 'its importance has not even yet been fully recognised',[187] an analysis that was still to apply 50 years later. Daniel Corkery, too, suggested: 'The GAA might have easily turned into a sports association and nothing else. The extraordinary growth of this one humble enough association is really a measure of the vitality that lies inert in the common people. In spirit as in its achievement the GAA is not only unique but astonishing.'[188]

By 1910 there were over 400 soccer clubs in the country, and the national team defeated Wales in 1903 and Scotland in 1904, though it was to be some time before Ireland would repeat the success it had achieved on the rugby pitch in the 1890s, including a triple crown victory in 1899. Ireland alone of the four nations failed to win a triple crown in the period 1900–1914, but the establishment of the Lansdowne Road stadium in 1908 was something of a landmark.[189] The local handball court for many was a regular meeting place, while crossroad dances were common on Sunday afternoons. The special send-off given to the dead, despite Church condemnation, remained social as well as solemn occasions, Jeremiah Murphy commenting that 'whatever the respect the Irish people had for the living, it was not nearly as evident as the respect they seemed to have for the dead'.[190]

In 1903, in an initiative that had the backing of both nationalist and unionists, the Gordon Bennett Cup motor car race was held in Ireland because Britain did not have the necessary long stretches of road. It was the first international motor race to be held in Britain or Ireland, bequeathing a rich motor sport heritage which would later lead to the Irish Grand Prix series of the 1920s and 1930s. Commenting on contemporary cross-political support for the race, the *Northern Whig* contended that 'we see a wonderful blending of the orange and green. There is about this matter a unanimity of which some people considered Irishmen to be incapable.' Ironically, Eliot Zborowski, the Polish driver who helped to organise the race, suggested the British team use the colour green for the Irish race as a gesture to the host country, and it was to remain the official British racing colour.[191] Irishmen living in the United States made a big impact at the Olympics of 1904 and 1908. At the London Olympic games of 1908 native-born Irishmen won medals in 15 disciplines, including eight gold, and in revealing a penchant for weights and the hammer experienced success never to be repeated on such a scale by Irish Olympic participants.[192]

The appearance of a cinema in the round room of the Rotunda in 1909 promised the perfection of 'new living pictures'. The first Irish films, as seen in the production by Kalem Films of *The Lad from Old Ireland*, presented a sympathetic portrayal of Irish nationalism. They depicted the United States as an escape route from poverty and oppression, though Kalem were criticised by a priest in 1910 for being 'tramp photographers' and portraying the Irish as 'gypsies and ne'er do wells'. By 1916 there were 149 cinemas and halls listed as showing motion pictures.[193]

The newly established rural libraries of the early years of the century had fallen rapidly into decline as they were often in very poorly populated districts that were too small to support an independent service out of the rates, which had been limited to one penny in the pound. Lack of public funds was of course central to this neglect and, between 1900 and 1913, the philanthropist Andrew Carnegie helped to improve the situation by contributing approximately £150,000 for the development of libraries in Ireland, of which £108,000 was spent on buildings. Along with Carnegie grants, the passing of the Public Libraries (Ireland) Act of 1902 resulted in the establishment of public libraries in a number of cities and towns, but their size and content left a lot to be desired. Abbey playwright Lennox Robinson, the Carnegie Trust's organising librarian in Ireland, was later to comment in *The Bell* magazine that 'numerous villages managed to secure a small building which they boldly named a library and the librarian was only a badly-paid caretaker and there were four or five books'.[194] The first Library Association of Ireland was established in 1904.

Traditional music was also receiving serious scholarly attention with the publication in 1903 of Francis O'Neill's *The Music of Ireland* and in 1907 of *Dance Music in Ireland*. Significantly, the former, containing 1,850 tunes, was produced in Chicago and contributed to by many Irish immigrants in America, giving an indication of 'the wealth of music that was largely lost' during the nineteenth century, much of which had died with the musicians.[195] In 1905, in his *History of Irish Music*, Henry Grattan-Flood suggested that in the previous thirty years 'the investigations of erudite writers have cleared away the almost impenetrable haze which had so long obscured the state of civilisation as regards literature, art and music in pre-Norman and medieval days'.[196] But the challenge facing Irish composers, according to a teacher at the Royal Irish Academy of Music in 1906, was 'to master their art as musicians to the fullest extent, then go back to the wonderful store of folk melodies and build them into their music' – something easier said than done given the poverty of the Irish music education system and the danger of 'Irish music collapsing inwards under the pressure of its own cultural prestige'.[197]

'the English garrison in Ireland'?

By 1891 Belfast had overtaken Dublin to become the most populous city in Ireland. By 1911 there were 890,880 Protestants in Ulster out of a total population of 1.582 million. The first decade of the century in the North, owing to its industrial status and religious composition, differed from that of the rest of the island, though they were touched by many of the same issues and concerns. The difficulty of securing unionist and Protestant unity was very evident in political, economic and cultural disputes, and the allegiances of the Protestant population should not be assumed to have been narrow and monolithic. As Robert Lindsey Crawford, editor of the *Irish Protestant,* an evangelical newspaper in Dublin, put it in 1903: 'Irish Protestants should not wish always to be regarded as the English garrison in Ireland.'[198] This was a view given credence by something of a cultural renaissance in Ulster during this decade, as Crawford and others sought to bring Ulster Protestants beyond the idea of resistance to Catholic nationalism and towards some conception of their own duties and responsibilities as patriotic citizens.

It is evident that even very early in the new century, nationalists displayed an arrogance and naivety about what they perceived in Ulster Protestants as a complete lack of interest in or knowledge of their own past or their contemporary identity. Elizabeth Bloxham, who became an organiser of Cumman na mBan (the female wing of the Irish Volunteers) during the War of Independence, recalled a contemporary of hers in the 1900s expressing certainty about Ulster Protestants: 'at heart, they must be national. He was sure there was fine stuff in them and if only they were not kept in the dark about the history of their native country they would feel as we did.' Bloxham herself maintained that

the poorest and least educated Catholics had their symbols of national-

ity. At that time you rarely entered a house that had not a picture of
Wolfe Tone and Robert Emmet. 'Speeches from the Dock' in its green
paper cover, was well thumbed by some members of the family. There
was talk of the Land War and of 'old unhappy far off things and battles
long ago'. The Protestant mind had no such hinterland.[199]

'the child is old before it knows what it is to be young'

Industrialisation created as many problems as it created wealth, and
the work of scholars such as Jonathan Bardon and J. C. Beckett reveals
the extent to which, by the turn of the century, Belfast began to fall
behind the rest of the United Kingdom in the area of welfare provision. The operation of the Poor Law provided the lowest level of relief
in the kingdom; education was not yet compulsory; and there was a
reluctance to develop housing by-laws.[200] James Connolly was scathing
in the *Reconquest of Ireland* (1915) about the plight of the mill workers,
writing that 'In this part of Ireland the child is old before it knows
what it is to be young … in their wisdom our Lords and masters often
leave full grown men unemployed but they can always find use for the
bodies and limbs of our children.'[201]

Many Ulster women continued to toil at home, and were an essential
part of the cotton and linen industries until the early 1900s. The labour
of both mother and children was often necessary to sustain families, and a
1911 committee of inquiry into the linen and cotton making-up trades in
Northern Ireland concluded homework was an indispensable part of the
machinery of production, not only doubling the mother's responsibility
but also raising the question of the use of child labour.[202]

Though skilled wages were above the national average, there was
much welfare neglect. The Belfast Board of Guardian Minute Books for
1901 reveal that cardiac and respiratory diseases accounted for the highest
number of illnesses, with 20 inmates dying in the first week of that year,
and staff complaining of the need for more staff because of 'the enormous
growth which has taken place in the population of the city since the staff
of relieving officers was increased some 30 years ago'. They pointed to the
savings that could be made by making inmates perform work rather than
contractors, despite the Local Government Board insistence that this was
a 'gross irregularity'. Another common occurrence was the persecution of
husbands of inmates for leaving their wives and children chargeable to the
rates.[203] In the early twentieth century Belfast's death rate in the 15–20

age group was twice that of Manchester, 'itself a centre of the unhealthy cotton industry'.[204]

Ulster did not shy away from debates on what to do with the feeble-minded. A Belfast Eugenics Society emerged in 1911, the president of which, Charles Frederick D'Arcy, the Anglican bishop of Down and Connor, stressed the importance of preventing 'the marriage and multiplication of the unfit and almost anything would be worth doing to attain that end'. He approved of the vigour of forced sterilisation in the United States.[205]

Given the growing tensions between employed and employer it was perhaps understandable that trade unionists looked to Belfast to ignite popular strike action in the 1900s. The emergence of James Larkin in 1907 set in train events which by July of that year witnessed 100,000 trade unionists and their supporters marching on the streets, though ultimately sectarian unity proved elusive. There were many elements within Ulster society that frustrated efforts to build an independent labour movement. These included the Ancient Order of Hibernians representing Catholic interests and the Independent Orange Order representing the Protestant working class. The labour historian Austen Morgan suggested that James Connolly contributed to working-class polarisation in Belfast by arguing that socialists had a duty to support Home Rule.[206] While the events of 1907 were to reveal that the Protestant working class was not immune to class struggle, unionism and loyalists inflicted severe wounds on labour in Belfast (the trade unions received only £70 pounds from Dublin as against £48,000 from Britain). But the reality was that, in the years that followed, the British labour movement was utterly unwilling to challenge the sectarian assault on workers,[207] while historians may also have neglected the class consciousness and identity which existed among women textile workers – an activism with deep roots in the informal networks among working-class women which was sometimes as successful as the men's traditional trade union approach.[208]

From the end of the nineteenth century, unionist women had mobilised opposition to the threat of Home Rule and in 1909 unionist women in Derry city established the Women's Registration Society. Two years later the Ulster Women's Unionist Council was established, and though it had a huge membership (see Chapter 2), its leaders were 'largely content with their ancillary status within the unionist movement'.[209] Advocates of the enfranchisement of women were the exceptions to this rule. Edith Vane-Tempest, the 7th Marchioness of Londonderry, supported non-militant suffragists, and as a conservative from the upper classes was 'a rarity' amongst suffragists. One of her pamphlets on this issue, published in 1909, was entitled *Women's indirect influence, and its affect on character; her position improved by the franchise morally and materially*. It was a powerfully argued tract; what was needed, she surmised, was formal recognition to be given to the female contribution that already existed:

> It is all very well for those women who have comfortable homes to live in, and owing to these circumstances lead sheltered and protected lives, to pronounce in deprecating tones that 'women were not meant to compete with men'. But women, in these days are compelled to go out and work in their thousands, many have to support the home ... It is conceded how much influence women possess in these days, and they are encouraged in their political efforts by the men, their help is sought in elections, in canvassing, and in forming various leagues and societies ... Now, if women are allowed to exercise any influence at all, why in ordinary justice, should they always be subject to indirect methods? Surely it is a woman's right, as much as a man's, to exercise her influence whether in her political opinions or in ordinary life, in a direct and straightforward manner?[210]

The only female nationalist association of any significance was the Ladies' Auxiliary of the Ancient Order of Hibernians, established in 1910. It did nothing to encourage women to stand as parliamentary candidates, but instead immersed itself in electioneering, distribution of propaganda, charity and religious work.

The emergence of the Independent Orange Order under the guidance of the trade unionist T. H. Sloan was an indication of the potential for schism in the Orange ranks due to class tensions within unionism. In 1895 a secretary to one of the Loyal Orange Lodges had described the Orange Order as one 'which the Protestants of Ulster banded themselves together for the natural protection of their lives and property against the Celtic inhabitants of the country who looked upon them as confiscators'. But Robert Wallace, historian of the Orange Order in the late nineteenth century, had emphasised that Orangemen were generally from humble backgrounds and in welcoming all shades of Protestants had 'great psychological importance' in uniting Protestants. In 1899 he had written of a 'deep-rooted prejudice in the minds of Roman Catholics, high and low, against the Orange society – a prejudice which the Orangemen have not been able to eradicate, no matter what they say or do'.[211]

The Orange Order's fears were based on the idea of the threat of Roman Catholicism, confiscation of land and the destruction of prosperous industries, but it was significant that it was an internal rather than external threat which caused the most unrest in the opening years of the century. The Independent Orange Order had 68 lodges by 1906 under the leadership of T. H. Sloan, who ran for election and directed criticism at the leadership of the Ulster Unionists for neglecting working-class concerns.

Also important was the growing resentment at the landlord class as enunciated by T. W. Russell, who castigated their control of land as 'systemised and legalised robbery'.[212] In his history of Ulster, T. W. Moody pointed out that the Land Acts of 1903 and 1909 made it possible for 63,000 tenants in the province to become owners of their own land, three times the number provided by legislation of the late nineteenth century.[213] As in the South, local authorities often found tenants an ungrateful lot regarding the provision of labourers' cottages owing to the 'innumerable petty complaints constantly being received'. In County Londonderry, rural district councillors insisted 'a water supply 400 yards away could not be regarded as inaccessible and it was not expected that a pump should be provided at every plot'.[214] Disgruntlement within the ranks of unionism, and the desire of the Ulster Unionist Party to achieve local control and quell working-class and tenant grievances, was one of the main reasons for the creation of the Ulster Unionist council in 1905.

'smoke in secret, drink in secret and think in secret'

But there were other dissenting voices in Ulster as many sought to shake off smothering puritanical restrictions. The artist Paul Henry complained that 'I had to smoke in secret, drink in secret and think in secret. These were the three unpardonable sins. There was a fourth more deadly still, though it was never mentioned.'[215] It was significant that many Protestants with strong nationalist sympathies emerged from the North, such as Roger Casement, Robert Lynd and Bulmer Hobson. The latter was one of the leading lights behind the emergence of an Ulster Literary Theatre in 1902 – his response to the uninterested Yeats was: 'Damn Yeats we'll write our own plays.'[216]

Hobson insisted on an anti-sectarian editorial policy for his paper

The Republic, launched in 1906, while another journalist, James Good, criticised a unionist colonial mindset on the part of a people who supposedly cherished their independence. But there would be little sign of a sea change in unionist politics. The historian Flann Campbell suggested that:

> During the years 1905–8 there was a variety of powerful forces, not merely in the unionist party and among the city's employees and newspaper owners, pulling in several different directions. The 'Progressives' lacked any kind of ideological cohesion and held widely differing views as to the direction in which they should go. Liberals, Labour, tenant farmers, Irish nationalists and republicans and dissenters and would-be reformers of all types might broadly agree that they disliked the ruling class that dominated them, but in other respects they had not much in common … they were not likely to form a party that could effectively challenge the relatively monolithic unionist party.[217]

- TWO -

1912–1918

'*events crowd upon events*'

During the years 1912 to 1918, it seemed like a giant vacuum existed in Ireland, into which a variety of organisations and movements were being sucked, often with conflicting aims, personalities and visions of the future. By 1913, two extra-parliamentary forces existed in the country: in Ulster, the Ulster Volunteers, formed to prevent the implementation of Home Rule; and in the three other provinces, the Irish Volunteers, established to ensure Home Rule was implemented. Between them, they represented the views of over a quarter of a million people. The British government seemed unsure, even sleepy in its response. A variety of well-heeled and respected individuals, whose backgrounds would suggest little sympathy for Irish separatism, were caught up in the intense political awakening and excitement of this era. One of them, Constance Markievicz, a member of an Anglo-Irish aristocratic family, the Gore Booths of Lissadell in County Sligo, became the first woman to be elected to the British parliament, as a Sinn Féin candidate in 1918. In 1913, she had identified three great movements in Ireland: the nationalist, women's and labour movements.[1] But there were others, including the intense Ulster unionist resistance movement to Home Rule, a secret revolutionary Irish Republican Brotherhood, and the proponents of new ideas about the need for a distinct culture, history, language and education system.

Many, including Markievicz, moved freely between various minority movements, but competing, sometimes contradictory allegiances inevitably gave rise to tensions and class conflict. In his book *Irish Books and Irish People* (1919), Stephen Gwynn, a Protestant constitutional nationalist, lamented that the intellectual movement which had swept over Ireland 'has been both embittering and embittered' due to its inability to avoid politics. He concluded that the relationship between social change and culture was 'obscure, indefinite and intangible'; and this, after 25 years that had been 'the most formative in the country's history of any since Ireland became the composite nation that she is, or perhaps, has yet to become'.[2] Gwynn maintained the events of the previous few years, combined with continued British occupation of Ireland, proved that 'forces that, under normal and unhealthy conditions, would be purely beneficent, may easily grow explosive and disruptive'.

Five years later, Gwynn returned to an assessment of recent history, in his book *Ireland* (1924), and reflected on a period when 'events crowd upon events'. The Great War, the formation of the Ulster Volunteers and Irish Volunteers in 1913, the Dublin Lockout of 1913, the 1916 Rising, and a prodigious output of political speaking and newspaper articles had been a part of 'Ireland's melting pot'. Teachers, poets, soldiers, politicians and priests had played their part, and their grievances were not necessarily born of economic deprivation, nor were they rooted in traditional resentments about land ownership. 'Socially and economically', Gwynn wrote, 'the war brought floods of money into Ireland. There was no vast afflux of wealth to individuals, except in the North, because no great manufacturing centres existed. But agriculture had a golden time, and all the profits of agriculture went to the occupiers of land.'[3] Thousands of Irish soldiers, many of them nationalists, fought with the British army, suggesting a high degree of contentment with Ireland's place within the empire. At home, the minority of republicans who staged a rising in Dublin in April 1916 seemed strangely unrepresentative of national sentiment.

'like the death rattle of a nation'

A combination of all these factors contributed to the fermentation of ideas in Ireland during the war, and pose difficulties for historians in attempting to assess public opinion, and the extent to which there was a silent majority indifferent to, or resentful towards, advanced nationalists or republicans. Perhaps most significantly, 'all these separate activities were in touch with each other, by attraction or compulsion'.[4] Ireland, it seemed, could not remain immune from the growing cult of militarism throughout Europe. The Irish Volunteers, which claimed about 150,000 members, can be seen, according to Michael Laffan, 'as an Irish manifestation of Europe's "generation of 1914", young men who were dissatisfied with what they saw as a dull or decadent world, idealists who (in at least some cases) revelled in the excitement of militarism and the prospect of heroic conflict'.[5] One such young man, Liam Brady, a member of the Irish Volunteers, recalled in his contribution to the Bureau of Military History that 'the desire for drilling and marching got into my blood and without knowing the reason why, I kept looking for somewhere where I could drill, drill, drill'.[6]

But the appeal of militarism should not be seen as the only stimulus in the quest for Irish independence. This was also the era when characters of the intellectual calibre of the labour leader James Connolly emerged, with a version of Irish history to justify an attempt at achieving a workers' republic. His version was based on the idea that Ireland was by no means unique:

> history, in general, treats the working class as the manipulator of politics treats the working man – that is to say, with contempt when he remains passive and with derision, hatred and misrepresentation whenever he dares evince a desire to throw off the yoke of political or social servitude. Ireland is no exception to this rule. Irish history has ever been written by the master class – in the interests of the master class.[7]

Nor was the simple appeal of militarism enough to entice into Irish affairs the likes of Roger Casement, a knight of the British Empire, who was acclaimed for his work in exposing human-rights violations; or Erskine Childers, the famed novelist. And yet, in September 1913, Childers found himself having an intense conversation about Irish nationalism with Casement in Belfast, while 'climbing a lovely mountain just behind the town'.[8] Both were later executed for their devotion to the cause of Irish independence.

Though impossible to quantify exactly, the cultural renaissance of the previous decade – the abundance of books, plays, newspapers, poems and propaganda, and Irish language activism – undoubtedly influenced many nationalists. The result of the cross-fertilisation of all these ideas was, as recognised by P. J. Matthews, quasi-revolutionary.[9] J. M. Synge recognised that, when it came to speaking the Irish language, there was a gap between enthusiasm and competency, but he also accurately captured the collective emotional and political impact of the cultural crusade on its devotees. He wrote a striking account of his attendance at a Douglas Hyde play:

> at the beginning of the first night it was hard to keep a straight face at the sight of the beautiful Irish ladies of the Gaelic League all around the theatre talking non-stop in the most woeful Irish with their young clerks and workingmen who were quite pale with enthusiasm. But, it happened that during an interval in *Diarmaid and Gráinne*, according to local custom, the people in the Galleries started to sing. They sang old, well-known songs. Until that moment those melodies had never been heard sung in unison by so many voices with the ancient Irish words. A shiver went through the auditorium. In the lingering notes there was an incomparable melancholy, like the death rattle of a nation. One after another, faces could be seen leaning into their programmes. We wept.[10]

W. B. Yeats had also played his part. His 1902 play *Cathleen Ní Houlihán*, in which Maud Gonne starred, was a traditional allegorical personification of Ireland in the form of an old woman. She insists on the need of a young man at the time of the 1798 rebellion to sacrifice all for Ireland; and that dying in the process will ensure a patriot will be remembered for ever. At the end of the play she is transformed into 'a young girl and she had the walk of a queen'. The impact and legacy of this play troubled Yeats, particularly after the 1916 Rising. It also troubled Stephen Gwynn; so much so that: 'I went home asking myself if such plays should be produced unless one was prepared to go out and shoot and be shot. Miss Gonne's impersonation had stirred the audience as I have never seen another audience stirred.'[11]

'a little too self-conscious'?

Stephen Gwynn recognised, as did many other contemporaries and future historians, that it was the North of Ireland that had given the lead in an attempt to politicise and militarise the masses. Robert Lynd also insisted that the Ulster Volunteer Force 'burst open the gates, through which a flood of arms began to pour into the country'.[12] This development was central to one of the great ironies of political life in Ireland in the years preceding the outbreak of the First World War. While parliamentary politics seemed poised to deliver Home Rule, it was politics outside parliament that became more instrumental in shaping Ireland's future. This was initially at its most obvious in Ulster, though, given the history of dissent within unionism, the great unity shown in Ulster resistance to Home Rule was in many ways a response to a fear that dissent, if not contained, had the potential to destroy the coherence of opposition. Though the 890,880 Protestants of Ulster formed only 57 per cent of the province's population (1,581,696 in 1911), they were concentrated heavily in Antrim, Down, Derry and Armagh, forming compact communities, covering all social classes and groups. And yet, the image of Ulster opposition in 1912–14 was often brilliantly deceptive, papering over the cracks within the province.

Unionist tenacity was needed more than ever, it was believed, with the imminent threat of the British parliament passing Home Rule legislation. In 1909, the House of Lords had rejected the 'People's Budget', provoking a constitutional crisis; two general elections gave the Irish Parliamentary Party the balance of power in the House of Commons. A 1911 Act removing the veto of the House of Lords was eventually followed by the introduction of the third Home Rule bill, which offered an elected assembly subordinate to the United Kingdom in matters of finance and foreign affairs. The bill was eventually signed into law in 1914, but its implementation was delayed until the end of the war.

By 1914, Ulster unionists had done much to militarise the whole island, but as well as the threat to oppose Home Rule militarily, it seemed to many contemporaries they also had resource to a fundamental truth about democracy. In 1912, Harry Lawson MP posed the question: 'How are you in these days, these democratic days, in this democratic age, in this democratic country, to force a million men into a system which they refuse to join? How are you going to expel the Irish minority from citizenship of the UK?'[13] But unionists too were capable of actions and words that undermined any pretence to democracy. In a contribution to *Fortnight* magazine in 1991, Martin Mansergh wrote that 'even for the most revisionist historian, resistance to home rule is difficult to transform into a stand for liberal democratic ideas and enlightened values'.[14] The united front of 1912–14 went to the heart of the need to downplay divisions, socially and culturally, within unionism. Indeed, A. T. Q. Stewart maintained that it was a successful last-ditch effort by the Protestant Ascendancy in the North to salvage an alliance with the capitalists of Belfast, and to exploit the all-class structures of the Orange Lodge.[15]

Belfast certainly had its fair share of capitalists. It had been the fastest-growing urban centre in the United Kingdom in the nineteenth century; in 1851 it had a population of just 87,062, but the 1891 census confirmed that Belfast had a larger population than Dublin. By 1901 it had a population of just under 350,000. Observers noted, in the lead-up to the war, that 'in these crowded rushing thoroughfares we find the pulsing heart of a mighty commercial organisation whose vitality is ever augmenting and whose influence is already world-wide'. This was a fitting description of a city with the world's largest shipyard, and the largest ropeworks, tobacco factory and linen-spinning mill. Such industriousness prompted Louis Paul-Dubois in 1907 to suggest it resembled Liverpool or Glasgow rather than an Irish city.

It was certainly not without its tensions; A. T. Q. Stewart's observations are a reminder of the poisoned relations between labour and capitalism, which had erupted in the early years of the century. Jonathan Bardon suggested that the opulence of the City Hall, completed in 1906, 'seemed a little too self-conscious'.[16] Perhaps the same could be said of the *Titanic*, launched amid great fanfare in May 1911, in a display of shipbuilding prowess that astonished contemporaries. When it arrived in County Cork the local *Cork Examiner* noted:

> On the *Titanic* in brief, there is the atmosphere of community with all the delights of town. All of the advantages of the finest hotel, the desired comfort of home, the privacy of study in a fascinating marine setting ... safety is a first consideration with all voyagers and no excellence in other ways can compensate for lack of it. The *Titanic* is the last word in this respect; double bottom and water-tight compartments, steel decks, massive steel plates all in their way making for security, safety and strength ... all classes of passengers share equally in the benefits derivable and the security of one could not be achieved to the detriment of another.[17]

A contemporary merchant banker, having reflected on the pride of Ulstermen in witnessing its construction, suggested that with its sinking:

'It's the end of an era, an era of privilege. There were no lifeboats for the steerage passengers and the names of the dead on the *Titanic* memorial in Belfast appear in order of importance, unlike those on the war memorial beside it, which are in alphabetical order.'[18] The historian of Irish science John Wilson Foster suggested that the launching of the *Titanic* was 'a graphic culmination of the engineering genius of Belfast from the mid-Victorian to Edwardian times' and that its engineering staff from the Harland and Woolf shipyard were 'the largely unsung heroes of the tragedy'. Size, speed and power had, he suggested, become highly conscious cultural values at a time when Harland and Woolf employed 16,000 people. A visitor to the plant, the Irish gothic novelist Bram Stoker, saw 'genius, forethought ... experience and skill ... organisation complete and triumphant', and he took the dispensing of wages to 12,000 workers in ten minutes on Friday afternoon as proof of 'the perfection of the establishment's organisation'.[19]

'we should refrain from any expression of opinion on other policies'
Seven years earlier the founders of the Ulster Unionist Council had sought to perfect the organisation of Ulster unionism, and its inauguration was an institutional manifestation of the need to prevent unionism imploding through class tensions. In particular, it was an attempt by a leadership that was becoming aged, autocratic, contrary and out of touch to reassert its hegemony. It represented a recognition that incoherence or divided loyalties within the unionist family would dilute the effectiveness of their propaganda. It also seemed to indicate the declining significance of southern unionism (there were 256,699 southern Protestants), or the pretence of maintaining an all-Ireland unionism, as well as being a response to the growing vulnerability of a divided British Conservative Party.[20]

But it also presaged the declining status of parliament and the extent to which Ulster unionism in the parliamentary sense would be, in a manner similar to what had happened in the south, overshadowed by constituency concerns, and a loyalism that showed impatience with parliamentary methods and championed the move towards militarism.

Originally, the Home Rule crises of the 1880s and 1890s had elevated the issue of Ulster within political debate in the United Kingdom, and opposition to Home Rule had been accompanied by a growth of cultural and recreational organisations. This reflected a distinctive regional culture which, in particular, was being absorbed by many young men and women. Given the indications that unionism could be easily divided, the remarkable unity of 1912–14 was all the more significant. But in displaying such unity, it should not be assumed that unionists were fawning in their enunciation of Britishness. Edward Saunderson, the leader of parliamentary unionism, who died in 1906, in many ways represented a colonial elite who had a distrust and often distaste for the British. While desiring a gentry-dominated Unionist Party, he was a Whig who desired a degree of independence from the British political parties. Pressures from radical unionists, however, caused him to revert to 'a more narrowly class-based form of politics'.[21]

But whatever about difficulties with the British political establishment, the more immediate task was to maintain the cross-class alliance of unionism. 'Official unionism' survived, partly because sectional and sectarian and personal interests were able to reassert themselves. T. W. Russell and T. H. Sloan, in championing the agricultural and labour unionist interest respectively, may have exposed the class antagonisms within unionism, but there were perhaps far greater antagonisms that could unite. Russell may have highlighted an out-of-touch leadership, but that did not mean they could not descend from the heights of Westminster to the local Orange hall when pressed.

In any case, the squires were soon to be replaced by a younger generation, with different political methods and professional interests. Edward Carson, who took over the leadership of the Unionist parliamentary party in 1910, was the most obvious and important example. As Alvin Jackson has demonstrated, Ulster unionism was capable of both institutional and structural change, as well as being open to take-over by larger than life personalities.[22] Robert Lynd was being commendably optimistic, but overly naive, in maintaining in his book *Home Life in Ireland* (1909) that the youth of Ulster were coming to see more clearly that the fears of their fathers, 'intelligible in origin', were absurd. The people would unite, he suggested, but for the press, which was 'in the hands not of idealists, but of heated politicians and the same thing holds through to a great extent of the pulpit'.[23]

Ulster opposition to Asquith's third Home Rule bill in 1912 was more militant, politicised and middle class than previously. What was witnessed from 1912 to 1914 was a mass movement that, while triumphing on the streets and revelling in militarism, also had a constitutional and English focus, and included plans by the Ulster Unionist Council to delegate authority to a provisional Ulster government.

The Ulster Volunteer Force was formed in January 1913, with the aim of recruiting 100,000 members. Later that year, in September, an Ulster Provisional Government was constituted. Skilled political leadership was crucial during this dual period of political and military activity, exemplified by the sharpness of Edward Carson, but also by the likes of Walter Long, a prominent British Conservative MP who was the spokesman for southern unionism, and who assiduously used his network of British contacts. In the province itself, there was a notable revival of the Unionist Club Movement, which had fallen into decline after 1893, while the endorsement of Andrew Bonar Law, who had replaced Arthur Balfour in 1911 as leader of the Conservative Party, seemed to suggest an improvement in relations between the Tories and unionists.

The three southern provinces were pointedly absent from the unionist family picture at this juncture (in 1913, the Irish Unionist Alliance had fewer than 700 members), highlighting the fact that the increasing distinctiveness of Ulster unionism came inevitably at the expense of southern unionists. How could the minority in the south have possibly paralleled the overwhelming popular unionism of the north? Few would doubt the scale, determination and outward success of Ulster's mobilisation during 1912–14. But as with most carefully co-ordinated protest movements, it was also a many-headed monster that had the potential to be as damaging as it was successful.

Women were particularly active, having formed the Ulster Women's Unionist Council in January 1911. They viewed themselves as a steady and conservative movement, highlighting the potential threat of Home Rule to the sanctity of domestic life in Ulster, political action being seen as an extension of their maternal and protective responsibilities. The upper- and middle-class leaders were careful to avoid any wider debate about women's role in public life. Lady Dufferin wrote to Lady Londonderry, insisting: 'it is important that we should refrain from any expression of opinion on other policies'. In September 1912, while 218,206 men signed the Ulster Solemn League and Covenant, pledging resistance to Home Rule, 234,046 women did so.[24] But liberal or not, in terms of popular unionist politics – and this was the acid test of Ulster success in 1912–14 – the Ulster Women's Unionist Council, with a membership of between 40,000 and 50,000, was a formidable, if not overtly feminist, body. Rather than employing the semantics of political enfranchisement, they provided a supportive bulwark to male opposition. Significantly, during the First

World War, the Ulster Women's Unionist Council became increasingly frustrated with the general unionist suspension of political work, despite their conservativeness. In June 1918, six members met Edward Carson to formally register their discontent. Edith Wheeler, a former honorary secretary of the Council, outlined their grievances, including the fact that 'during the last four years of war, our opinion on any one political matter has never been asked. We ourselves have been mute, under what we consider has been a very insidious and slow disintegration of our power as Women Unionists.' The meeting resulted in the UWUC being granted twelve representatives on the Ulster Unionist Council.[25]

'Ulster's Stand for Union'

Growing militarism, reflecting a European glorification of arms-bearing, was championed in Ulster by veterans like James Craig and Fred Crawford, who had fought in the Boer War of 1899–1902. The Larne gun-running of 24–5 April 1914, when militant unionists led by Crawford success-fully landed 25,000 rifles and 3 million rounds of ammunition at Larne in County Antrim, was chronicled by the unionist Ronald McNeill in the energetic *Ulster's Stand for Union* (1922). But as Alvin Jackson has pointed out, it was more complex than its presentation as an outright military and political success would suggest. Patrick Buckland, writing in the 1970s, was perhaps correct in suggesting that there was a huge gulf in the aspira-tions of the UVF and the Ulster Unionist Party, in the sense that most of the political leaders of unionism hoped and thought that the UVF would not have to fight.[26]

Larne was a triumph only if it could be controlled, and extremists like Crawford did not in any sense receive blanket financial and politi-cal endorsement from the Ulster Unionist Council. It was, in a way, the failure of private negotiations between Carson and the British prime minister, Asquith, that gave the green light for the Larne exercise. As well as demonstrating the political and military muscle of the Ulster mili-tants, underpinned by Carson's apocalyptic rhetoric, the Larne incident was important in that it made a negotiated settlement more urgent, given the diverse quality of weaponry and, in overall terms, its relatively small quantity in relation to the size of the UVF. Charles Townshend noted that it would have been a military and logistical nightmare if pitched battle with British soldiers had taken place, not to mention the moral quandary of using German weapons to fight a British army while so many

Ulstermen were enlisting to fight Germans in the Great War.[27] Such a development would also have destroyed the effectiveness of the unionists' brilliant publicity campaign to gain sympathy for their cause, particularly in Britain.

'if you are not top dog, she will be'

The potential threats to unionist identity of Home Rule were of course widely and rudely circulated. However exaggerated, at their heart were understandable fears of religious discrimination, in particular the insensitivity of the *Ne Temere* papal decree, which stipulated that children of mixed marriage must be brought up as Catholics. This was a factor which made Home Rule seem even more obnoxious in unionist eyes than it had been previously. It is also fair to assert that the Gaelic League's triumph over more moderate nationalists in implementing its policy of compulsory Irish did little to negate a partitionist mindset. But the unionists, too, had their own aggressive dimension, James Craig suggesting: 'there can be no such thing as equality, for if you are not top dog, she will be'.[28]

Unionists also had understandable and legitimate fears about the consequences of Home Rule for northern industry, fears which historians (as pointed out by Paul Bew) can too easily gloss over.[29] James Logan, in *Ulster in the X-rays* (1922), suggested that the north-east enjoyed economic prosperity because of a particular type of Ulster grit and determination, with Belfast shipworkers 'staunch and determined, loyal and enthusiastic, hardworking and industrious', characteristics notably absent, it was presumed, elsewhere.[30]

The manner in which opposition to Home Rule evolved had much to do with the relationship between the media and mass politics. In particular, it was necessary to employ the services of the newly created advertising industry, which by the opening years of the twentieth century involved dozens of agencies in London. The general European media revolution was mirrored in Ulster, a testament to which were the unionist *Belfast News Letter*, under R. M. Sibbett, and the *Northern Whig* and *Belfast Evening Telegraph*, under Thomas Moles. James Craig's knowledge of marketing, gained from his family's connection with Dunville's Whiskey, was also important, as was his seemingly unlimited cash fund.

At this level, 1912–14 was essentially about a relentless two-year advertising campaign that left no stone unturned, no pole unadorned and no tree unclimbed. There were numerous target audiences, as the Ulster unionists did much to counteract the images of themselves as bigots. There were extreme examples of black propaganda, including the allegation that Belfast Catholics were conducting raffles for Protestant homes and jobs to be claimed by the winners on the day Home Rule became law.[31] Their campaigning also impacted on the British Liberal government. Augustine Birrell, following a tour of Ulster, recognised that some compromise was essential. The success of the campaign was not just due to a genuine belief that their culture was in peril, but also to its inclusivity; the simple message being that what they had in common was far more significant than their differences, and the incorporation of so many women into Ulster resistance was indicative in this regard.

'they had overcome through their own tenacity'
There were certain voices in the wilderness outside Ulster that accepted the legitimacy of the unionist arguments. Arthur Clery, later to be a defence lawyer for some of the 1916 insurgents, was one of the few nationalists of the era to advocate partition, simply because he regarded Ulster Protestants as a separate people entitled to self-determination. He even suggested that Protestants often had a more intense love of Ireland than he had observed among Catholics. While disliking Protestants intensely – denouncing them as 'bigoted aliens' – he had advocated partition as early as 1905, and in 1906 insisted:

> they have adopted precisely the same methods of propagating their opinions that we have ours. The press, the platform and the ballot box have all borne witness to their national faith and it seems to me that if these persons demand their national independence, and if they are, in truth, distinct in nationality, it requires a strong reason not to prevent them getting it. If we can prove that Irish freedom causes bondage to no man we shall have done much to help our cause.[32]

Clery was confronting what most nationalists of the era evaded. He seemed to accept that unionism was a serious political movement, as Patrick Maume notes: 'responding rationally to a distinctive set of loyalties and beliefs'. But in their passion to be excluded from Home Rule, unionists did not distinguish between the areas where they were in a majority and the areas where they were not. They were also open to the accusation that they were undermining the potential for moderation in

Irish politics (unionist and nationalist) by militarising Irish public life, and, in turn, doing much to militarise Irish republican thinking. Perhaps, as Michael Laffan noted, they had more in common with republican revolutionaries than with Home Rulers.[33] But Clery was correct in identifying a separate culture. It was more emotional and complex than some of the one-dimensional images associated with the era, that presented Ulster and its people as a homogeneous unit.

Much of the propaganda lay in an appeal to the past. Aside from the significance of their contribution to the Great War (examined below), writing a history that suited unionists' present pretensions was also important, particularly a history centred around the years of the 1641 massacre, or the Battle of the Boyne in 1690 to establish the Ulsterman as a particular type. This was seen in the work of Ernest William Hamilton, including the *Soul of Ulster* (1917), which depicted a strong race, brave and true with a clear conscience. The emphasis in this book, and in the work of W. A. Phillips, Professor of Modern History at Trinity College Dublin, and Ronald McNeill, was on unity, glossing over differences and articulating a common Protestant history. As Gillian McIntosh pointed out, these (along later with their 1916 war sacrifices) 'were the beacon buoys for unionists, marking the rocks on which Ulster Protestants had almost floundered in the past but which they had overcome through their own tenacity'.[34]

'the open secret of Ireland is that Ireland is a nation'

The need to assert such a strong regional identity was mirrored in the south, as was the growing militarism, reflected in particular in the establishment of the Irish Volunteers in November 1913, to match developments in Ulster. The new group had its origins in an article written by Eoin MacNeill, Professor of Early Irish History at University College Dublin. He had immersed himself in the promotion of the Irish language for the previous 25 years, and the basis of his nationalism was a 'vivid concept of the cultural nation of early Irish history'. An unlikely revolutionary, his 'heart was always telling him that his talents lay in scholarship and that his life should be spent among his books'.[35] Following persuasion by a member of the Gaelic League, his article 'The North Began' was published in *An Claidheamh Soluis*, the newspaper of the Gaelic League, on 1 November 1913. It threw down the gauntlet to nationalists to follow the lead given by Ulster unionists in their formation of the UVF. A public meeting followed, attended by 7,000 people, and the Irish Volunteers was established, shortly to be infiltrated by members of the IRB, though they had not been its main instigators.[36]

There was a huge response to the demand for recruits. One of the promoters of such recruitment, Patrick Pearse, later executed after the 1916 Rising, explained in 1915 the reasons for the establishment of the new force: 'What if conscription be forced upon Ireland? What if a Unionist or a Coalition British Ministry repudiates the Home Rule Act? What if it be determined to dismember Ireland? The future is big with these and other possibilities.'[37] But if, by 1915, these were the obvious contexts for any putative nationalist defence of Ireland, the issues had not been as clear-cut three years earlier. True, Thomas Kettle, poet and moderate nationalist politician, had asserted that 'the open secret of Ireland is that Ireland is a nation', a view given popular credence by the work of Alice Stopford Green in *Irish Nationality* (1911), which depicted the unbroken continuity of a national tradition in Irish history.[38]

But there were confusing signals from both Irish nationalists and the British sponsors of Home Rule legislation about the issue of nationhood. Speaking in the House of Commons in April 1912 on the provisions of the Home Rule bill, Balfour had talked of 'privileges which I think, if Ireland be a nation, are not nearly enough and which, if Ireland be not a nation, are far greater than you ought ever to have given'. Three months later, speaking in Dublin, Asquith maintained that 'in every relevant sense of the term, Ireland is a nation'. In contrast, Lord Hugh Cecil in the House of Commons suggested that Irish nationality, as the Irish Parliamentary Party would have it: 'can never be anything but shameful to themselves and dangerous to the empire. Let them feel the real pride of citizenship in the great nation to which they and we belong.'[39]

Earlier that year, in March, a mammoth Home Rule rally in Dublin included speakers on different platforms. While all spoke in favour of Home Rule, their emphasis differed. Patrick Pearse and Eoin MacNeill warned of the potential opposition if Home Rule was not granted, but MacNeill used much more restrained language than Pearse, indicating that something of a 'cross roads between constitutionalism and force' had been reached. Lurking in the background was the revitalised IRB, which a senior Dublin Castle official had suggested in 1903 was nothing 'but the shadow of a once terrifying name', but which had been actively recruiting, and was hostile to the small Sinn Féin party, whose founder, Arthur Griffith, supported the Irish Volunteers.

'it shook so much that it pointed everywhere at once'
Thomas Kettle's own life exemplified many of the dilemmas of those
loath to define nationalism too narrowly. Equally, there were difficulties
for those who tried to embrace too broad a definition. The leader of the
Irish Parliamentary Party, John Redmond, according to the memoirs of
playwright Seán O'Casey, though he 'kept his hand up to show the people
where to go, it shook so much that it pointed everywhere at once'.[40] Kettle
was a lawyer, constitutional nationalist and academic economist. In his
philosophy of politics, he had maintained the moral right of Ireland to
rebel, 'if it were possible', but he fought for Britain in the war, believing
Ireland in many ways was attempting to build an 'impossible future on
an imaginary past, which led English parties [in the past] to wipe her off
the slate of practical politics'. Yet as his friend Arthur Clery pointed out
after Kettle's death in combat: 'the idea of final self-sacrifice was as much a
haunting desire with him as it was with Patrick Pearse'.[41] In this tribute,
Clery sought to locate Kettle on Ireland's political map, making some
general observations on the direction of Irish politics between the 1890s
and the First World War:

> First there was the orthodoxy of the Irish party tracing its apostolic
> succession from Davitt to Parnell. It was powerful and popular. But
> its followers too often came to look on faith – faith in the party – as
> an all-sufficient substitute for personal good works. Over against them
> were the 'good workers' of various descriptions – language revivalists,
> industrial revivalists, men who devoted themselves to Irish poetry, Irish
> music, Irish pastimes, Irish drama or Irish art, many of them heretics
> or at least schismatic in matters political. But there was also a third
> movement which never advanced very far, but which influenced many
> thinking minds. A casual observer would describe it incorrectly by
> some such loose adjective as 'socialistic'. It was the effort to apply cos-
> mopolitan ideas of regeneration (often without any clear idea of what
> they were) to the social conditions of Ireland, more especially to the
> social conditions of its cities – in fact, an aspiration towards modern
> 'progress' of the less brutal kind. Kettle's effort was to combine the
> first school with the third – party or orthodoxy with social advance.
> He was as Mr [Robert] Lynd put it, European in his sympathies. With
> the second movement, on the other hand; with everything that could
> be described as 'Irish Ireland', though he sometimes gave it a nominal

support in words, he had a very minimum of agreement. He looked upon it as insular and unEuropean.[42]

These were sharp observations, recognising there was a school of political thought other than Redmondism that was squeezed out of the mainstream during the period of the Great War. Clery probably saw himself as belonging to this school. Historians writing in the 1970s and 1980s, in the shadow of the contemporary conflict in the North of Ireland, looked back to this period to question whether it would have been possible to rally behind a nationalism that stood for reconciliation as opposed to conflict; or as Paul Bew put it, whether Irish nationalism was capable of being more than simply the expression of the grievances of the Irish peasantry.[43] Finding a middle ground between reconciliation and conflict went to the heart of John Redmond's dilemma. British politicians – as seen from their differing definitions of Irish nationalism – were often similarly confused. What should not be overlooked was Clery's recognition that 'faith in the party' was not enough. The Irish Parliamentary Party was an old party during the war, with 50 of its 85 MPs in political life as a result of its exploitation of land issues, when land as an issue was no longer enough to sustain political dynamism.[44]

Redmond's faith in the Empire was also, it seems, born of a refusal to recognise its capacity for brutality; indeed he himself admitted the political focus of his party on land and self-government was far too narrow, with very little evidence of the concept of 'social advance'. But perhaps the social advance which Kettle wanted was not the Irish language issue, whose activists found Redmondism lacking, or indeed a new generation intent on affirming they were more ardent and sincere Catholics, who also found Redmondism wanting. The difficulty of Redmondites was that they wanted to be a part of the management structures they were attacking, and this went to the heart of the paradox of Irish nationalism.

'wherever the firing line extends'?

Redmond's decision to champion the war effort, and an attendant naivety about the real fears of unionists, meant he refused to face the reality that the best the Home Rule party could hope for after the war was not unity, but improved nationalist-unionist relations. During the war he mixed his rhetoric, speaking occasionally of reconciliation by uniting unionists and nationalists in the war effort, but undermining this with triumphalist assertions about the passing of a Home Rule bill. If Redmond was seen by many to be visionary because of his idea of inclusivity, of reconciling imperialism with nationalism, he also has to be seen as someone who had precious little vision or was indeed indifferent, when it came to the future of his own party, or indeed whether they had any future after the achievement of Home Rule. Leading a party that wanted to win Home Rule but would be too old to implement it was a measure of the limitations of the movement. Maturity had bred complacency, highlighting the stark generational differences that were shortly to come to the fore in Irish nationalism.

And where did John Redmond see northern nationalists if an all-Ireland Home Rule was not possible? The war was also a watershed for them. In the six counties that were to become Northern Ireland, a conference of nationalists in Belfast in June 1916 witnessed conflict between the old Home Rule party and Sinn Féin. Addressed by Redmond and organised by Joe Devlin, who represented West Belfast in parliament, it voted to accept Lloyd George's proposal for temporary exclusion of the six north-eastern counties, as the cost of the early implementation of Home Rule. But the delegates were divided by geography, with delegates from Fermanagh, Tyrone and Derry city voting solidly against it, and it was this east–west divide that was to be an important feature of northern politics for the foreseeable future.[45]

One of the ironies of Redmond's Woodenbridge speech in September 1914, when he urged Irish men to embrace the war effort and enlist in the British army, was that he referred to the 'spirit of Young Ireland', and said he was 'glad to see such magnificent material for soldiers around me', who should go 'wherever the firing line extends'.[46] Redmond was genuine in his belief that the war was one of good versus evil, but he was preaching to the converted. Others had their own ideas as to how to be soldiers; it was no coincidence that the text of 'The Soldier's Song', by Peadar Kearney and Patrick Heeney, later to become Ireland's national anthem, was first published by the young Bulmer Hobson in September 1912 and became increasingly popular as a marching and rallying song among the anti-recruitment Volunteers, confirming to themselves that they were soldiers rather than rebels.[47]

'The Lady at the helm'

By June 1914, Redmond was still in control of the Irish Volunteers, but they split as a consequence of his support for the war. He had moved to

place 25 of his nominees on the ruling committee, and was allowed to do
so in order to prevent divisions in the movement, but the eventual split, in
September 1914, could not be avoided, given his insistence that the Volunteers should volunteer for British army service. A majority, in the region
of 150,000, now called the National Volunteers, sided with Redmond,
with just under 8,000 siding with his opponent, Eoin MacNeill. (Alternative figures of 158,000 and 12,000 have also been cited.[48]) Before the split,
other developments had heightened military tension. In March, 58 British
cavalry officers at the Curragh camp, near Kildare, resigned their commissions rather than obey commands which they believed would involve
coercing Ulster into accepting Home Rule, or prevent the possibility of
armed unionist action. Although they were unofficially assured that this
would not happen, the incident 'was interpreted by nationalists as broader
evidence of the British army's partisanship; it was seen by unionists, on
the other hand, as the culmination of a plot to suppress their campaign
against Home Rule.'[49]

Shortly afterwards, the Howth gun-running, in May 1914, the auda-
cious nationalist version of the Larne episode, involved the importation
of 1,500 rifles and 45,000 rounds of ammunition. Bulmer Hobson, in his
history of the Volunteers, pointed to provocative Ulster rhetoric as one of
the reasons why the Irish Volunteers became determined to arm, quoting
Colonel Hackman, the Unionist MP for Wolverhampton, speaking about
the UVF: 'You may be quite certain that these men are not going to fight
with dummy muskets. They are going to use modern rifles and ammunition and they are being taught to shoot ... if the men will only hold them
straight, there won't be many nationalists to stand up against them.'[50]

The move to arm the Volunteers through the Howth gun-running
had been preceded by long marches into the country each Sunday morning
so the authorities would not regard the march to Howth as out of the
ordinary. There was no IRB involvement in the planning of this mission;
rather it involved the likes of Roger Casement, Erskine Childers and the
writer Darrell Figgis. Lady Gregory recorded in her diaries an account of
the gun-running mission, as told to her by Mrs Childers, wife of Erskine:

> ... they got a yacht and Darrell Figgis went over and bought the guns
> in Liege and they waited for them off Dover. 'We went up on the Welsh
> coast and lay outside Milford Haven, afraid of customs officers. Then
> for Holyhead and across to Ireland and sailed about the bay and outside

Howth till the boat came, when Erskine said "I am going to do it." It was just the hour when the tide was highest. We saw someone run up to a height and wave to us a signal. It was a young officer whose name I cannot tell. Then we saw the Volunteers coming down and when they saw us they broke into a run. The guns that had taken six hours to get on board were unloaded in a few minutes. As we left, there were cheers for "the Lady at the helm – it had been put into my hand".'[51]

A measure of the boldness of the move, and of the difficulties of curtailing militarism, was reflected in the attempt of the Assistant Commissioner of the Dublin police to disarm them on their way back. It was a somewhat farcical episode, according to Bulmer Hobson, but it well illustrated the difficulties the British government was facing in an increasingly armed island:

I told him that with great difficulty I had prevented our ammunition from being distributed though the men were clamouring for it, and that if he made any further move against us it would be distributed at once. I pointed out that this would mean that many men would be killed and wounded on both sides and that the responsibility would be entirely his. This finished what was left of Mr Harrel's resolution.[52]

Three civilians, however, were killed later that day, when British soldiers fired on an unarmed crowd at Bachelor's Walk in Dublin.

The political temperature was increased by Carson's proposal for the exclusion of the nine Ulster counties from the proposed Home Rule legislation, and the failure of negotiations at the Buckingham Conference in July 1914 meant that the enactment of the Home Rule bill came with a suspension in September 1914 for the duration of the war. The response of the British government to increased tension, and the militancy of both Ulster and Irish Volunteers, had been to stand idly by. If they were not going to resist Ulster defiance, they could scarcely be heavy-handed in dealing with nationalist Ireland. This inaction is partly explained by their preoccupation with international affairs, along with the belief that constitutional nationalists had sufficient control in the south of Ireland, and that it would be dangerous to create martyrs. When the coalition government was formed in 1915 in response to the First World War, they brought Carson to the heart of that government, where he served briefly as Attorney General, while John Redmond remained outside. The new consensus between Liberals and Tories thus completely undermined the value of the Irish Parliamentary Party

Redmond rejected an invitation to join the government, and was then humiliated by the refusal of the War Office to allow use of the National Volunteers for home defence or to sanction the formation of an Irish division within the British army. At the same time, there were estimated to be 1,700 IRB members in the country. Prior to the First World War, it had been revived by Tom Clarke, a veteran Fenian campaigner, who with his young disciples was planning to take advantage of the war to further the Brotherhood's aims. As witnessed by their statements to the Bureau of Military History, the young Turks had certain conflicting memories of these years. Denis McCullough, one such new recruit, had little time for a nostalgic and inactive Fenianism; he reminisced that 'I cleared out most of the older men (including my father), most of whom I considered of no further use to us'.[53] The IRB actively recruited in the North, but Séamus Dobbyn, involved in the Brotherhood in Derry, maintained that 'this attitude on the part of the younger men in the IRB was not due to any feeling that the older men were past their usefulness, but was the natural inclination of youth to take control'.[54] In the North they defined themselves in opposition to the dominant Ancient Order of Hibernians, who vigorously backed Joe Devlin of the Irish Parliamentary Party. Ernest Blythe recalled that during the early years of the century 'it was not possible to do much against the influence of Joe Devlin … the only thing we could do for a period was to meet weekly in Denis McCullough's workshop, sitting on benches and dismantled pianos and paying a shilling each towards liquidating the debt'.[55] The war years were to find them much more active.

'national unity and imperial unity and strength'?

Corrupt and deluded; honourable but naive? All such assessments have been made of John Redmond at some stage, and he sometimes accepted the criticisms of his political failures. What he should not be blamed for, as Patrick Maume notes, was the persistence of a sense of Irish separateness strong enough to limit willingness to make the necessary sacrifices if compromise with Britain was to be reached. What he could not be blamed for was that he inherited a divided party which was not going to allow itself to be placed under the autocratic rule which Parnell had enjoyed. Even at the height of his political prestige he had to tolerate the existence of small groups of nationalists repudiating his authority.[56] In short, the reunification of the Irish Parliamentary Party under John Redmond had been about survival rather than rejuvenation and regeneration. The same could be said about Redmond himself; the Liberal connection may have meant Home Rule (survival) but the form it would take was beyond the control of John Redmond (regeneration). Also, as Tom Garvin has pointed out, much of the politics of the era was artificial; the Irish Party was in the paradoxical situation of enjoying repeated electoral triumph and of never holding governmental office, a condition it shared with its Unionist counterparts, particularly after 1906.[57]

It is true that Redmond's travels to Australia and North America gave him an insight into the idea of a partnership with Britain in the Empire, but his belief that he could combine this with an all-embracing nationalism led to an unrealistic, if in the eyes of some noble, political vision for Ireland. This was summed up in his contention that Ireland could have 'national unity and imperial unity and strength'.[58] He was unlucky too in his relationship with the British government, given that by 1913–14, the most sympathetic minister, Augustine Birrell, was adrift from British policy-making and Redmond was receiving continually mixed signals from different ministers. Redmond was also unfortunate in being surrounded by egotistical colleagues, who, as Bew points out, tended to enter and exit stage when it suited them.[59] This gave more room to Joe Devlin and the Ancient Order of Hibernians (originally a nineteenth-century Irish-American benevolent society, now a Catholic political machine for the nationalist party under the presidency of Devlin, which attracted members because of its Freemason-style activities, its sectarianism and its rivalry with the Orange Order) to fill a political vacuum; the party's belief that the AOH would secure their political rear led them to drift further out of touch with popular opinion.

'to give them back their national liberties'?
The reality, and this was where Ulster unionists were more perceptive, was that Redmond was a parliamentarian at a time when parliament was becoming increasingly irrelevant to what was happening on the ground. This was a consequence of his immersion in a stagnant political culture; and his failure to recognise the significance of the strands in Irish political and cultural life, and the class divisions in Irish life. The shopkeepers and large farmers who formed much of the backbone of

the party's support were increasingly open to accusations that they were part of the establishment they decried.[60] Being delighted to stand where Parnell had stood (in the sense of having the parliamentary numbers to demand Home Rule) was a measure of Redmond's ignorance of the changes in the structure of Irish society since Parnell. In one of his last letters, Redmond, outlining the failure of his own project, foresaw only 'universal anarchy ... when every blackguard who wants to commit an outrage will simply call himself a Sinn Féiner and thereby get the sympathy of the unthinking crowd'.[61]

Justifiably seen by many as exemplifying tolerance, negotiation and commitment to the democratic process, these were also the words of one who was bound by an arrogance, and a generational inheritance that was a poisoned chalice. Fittingly, perhaps, his frustration culminated in the rejection of his party in 1918 by an Irish electorate who certainly could not be classed as unthinking. It was they, after all, who had begun to see through much that was hollow in Redmond's rhetoric, particularly in relation to the partition issue. It is also the case that, despite the fact that the structure of British government in Ireland was absurd, many of the problems continued to pulsate through Irish political life because there was precious little British political will to solve them, particularly among a generation of politicians who allowed English considerations to govern their stance on Ireland. But despite this, it is difficult to see how Redmond could have adopted any other course when it came to support for the war effort. In any case, Ireland's foreign policy would be determined by Britain, even in a Home Rule Ireland.

Joe Lee posed the question: 'What choice did Redmond have? Beggars can't be choosers, and the bottom line was that Irish nationalism, of all varieties, had only words to wave in the face of British and unionist guns.'[62] Like all others, Redmond believed it would be a short war and he concentrated on the idea that after the war there would be an Irish army, and that dying side by side with members of the UVF would lead to greater trust between unionists and nationalists. His manifesto for the war was based on the idea of a domestic Irish army and the achievement of liberty; as he put it: 'the democracy of Great Britain has finally and irrevocably decided to trust them, and to give them back their national liberties'.[63] But this reasoning was flawed, as Redmond greatly exaggerated the measure of independence an Ireland loyal to the Empire would be allowed to exercise.

'a glorious memory for the example of future generations'?
It was being recognised by the end of the twentieth century, particularly in the context of the Peace Process of the 1990s, that historical neglect of Southern Ireland's participation in the First World War was shameful. A 'collective amnesia' referred to by F. X. Martin as far back as 1967 came to be seen not only as immature, but as a denial of the true complexity of Irish political, social and cultural allegiances, during a period of shifting, and contradictory, loyalties. Underlining the work of the pioneers who broke this silence, in particular Keith Jeffery, was a belief that the war was the single most central experience in twentieth-century Ireland and that the events of the war years, whether in the General Post Office in Dublin at Easter 1916, or at the battle front in Europe, constituted a 'seamless robe' of Irish experience, a cautionary warning to those who view Irish history during this period as a history of 'differences'.[64] In the eight volumes of Ireland's memorial records produced in 1923, 49,435 Irish were listed as having died in the war, though the exact definition of 'Irish' remained uncertain. The Irish journalist Kevin Myers suggested a figure of 35,000 deaths, and he wrote with great passion about the scale of the official neglect of such huge loss of life and what it revealed about the selective culture of Irish nationalism.[65]

David Fitzpatrick has calculated that Ireland's aggregate male contribution to the wartime forces was 210,000. Enlistment figures revealed that 50,000 joined up in the first six months of the war and 90,000 in the succeeding 45 months, with a particularly remarkable response to the 1918 recruiting campaign, when between August and November 1918 alone 9,845 were recruited.[66] F. X. Martin made much of the fact that, according to the figures he used, in 1916 there were 150,183 Irishmen serving with the British forces, of which 99,837 were recruits who joined up after mobilisation in August 1914. There were also 1,121 members of the Dublin Metropolitan police and 9,501 members of the RIC and in addition 105,000 volunteers loyal to John Redmond – a total of 265,000 serving with, or in alliance with, the British forces, against about 12,000 Irish volunteers opposed.[67]

The reasons they joined in such numbers were manifold. Army officials were probably correct in believing social and economic factors were more important than political conviction. Tom Kettle, mentioned earlier, in a sonnet to his daughter, days before he was killed in the Somme in 1916, suggested that 'we fools' did not die for flag, nor King, nor emperor, 'but for a dream born in a herdsman's shed and for the secret scripture of the poor'. For many it was about a transition from boyhood to manhood; a shared excitement, despite the literature of disillusionment which followed the conflict, reflected in Michael MacDonagh's *The Irish on the Somme* (1917), which contended that 'this was a dastardly massacre and not manly warfare'. It was also another step in the growing militarisation of Ireland and indeed Europe, and the similar sufferings of both Irish and British soldiers would undermine the myth that the Irish were an exceptionally combative or martial race. Practical considerations were understandable in the decision to join; steady employment and (hopefully) a pension at the end. A typical volunteer was James English, a 38-year-old labourer from County Waterford, married with five children. By enlisting, he instantly increased his family's earnings by 154 per cent, and if anything was to happen to him, his wife was guaranteed a pension.[68]

Peer pressure in male environments undoubtedly played a part also, though Jeffery has suggested that 'the large numbers of Irish women engaged in undoubtedly less exciting, though still serious, wartime activities as yet constitute a kind of historically hidden Ireland'. There were, for example, 2,000 people employed at Kynoch's high-explosives plant in Arklow.[69] The divisions most obviously Irish were the 10th and 16th Irish Divisions and the 36th Ulster Division. Bryan Cooper in his history of the 10th Irish Division wrote of glorious death, 'yet there springs from their graves a glorious memory for the example of future generations'. For the fighting men from Ulster this was reflected hideously in just two days of the Battle of the Somme, when 5,500 of all ranks were killed, wounded or missing.

For unionists, the appeal of involvement in war was undoubtedly more politically focused: a public pledge reaffirming their imperial values, which in any case had formed such an important part of the battle against Home Rule to date. It was also something they expected a political return from. Gillian McIntosh wrote that 'the province's Protestant combatants were mythologised, transformed into historic figures from the past as the war became a version of the Battle of the Boyne transferred to a time (and a past) which bore no resemblance to the reality of the First World War'. McIntosh noted with regard to the unionists that:

> in their public presentation of events, Home Rule and German aggression came to embody parallel threats to the Empire which they had

been vociferously claiming to defend since 1886. Edward Carson's rhetoric about, and attitude towards, the empire (which epitomised that of unionists generally), like Redmond's, was complex, being both sincere and manipulative. Both political camps expected the gratitude of the British administration for their willingness to sacrifice themselves and the rank and file of their parties. Neither foresaw that in the First World War all special interests would be expendable.[70]

'A fearful scarlet ate up the hard spring darkness'

One of the key differences in the southern and northern Irish experiences was on their return home, it being particularly difficult for returning southern Irish soldiers, given the changed political circumstances. Many who subsequently allied themselves with Sinn Féin had seen active service in the British army. Tom Barry, for example, later one of the IRA's leading commanders in Munster in the War of Independence, had joined the British army in 1915 and served in the catastrophic Mesopotamian campaign in 1916. Erskine Childers and his cousin Robert Barry, both from Anglo-Irish backgrounds, served in the British army, but later became prominent republicans. IRA veteran Ernie O'Malley, author of two classic books about the 1916–23 period, *On Another Man's Wound* and the *Singing Flame*, had a brother in the British army and was planning to join up before the 1916 Rising shifted his allegiances. As pointed out by Deirdre MacMahon: 'these complex ties and allegiances, covering the First World War, the War of Independence and the Civil War, were repeated in hundreds of families'.[71]

It was the changed political circumstances when they returned home which ensured a degree of subsequent silence; the lost generation, so relevant to post-war Britain, was more associated in Ireland with the 'Big House'. The fate of these Anglo-Irish residences, when they became republican targets of hatred, was memorably encapsulated in Elizabeth Bowen's *The Last September*, when she wrote that 'the death, execution rather, of the three houses occurred in the same night. A fearful scarlet ate up the hard spring darkness. It seemed, looking from east to west at the sky tall with scarlet, that the country itself was burning.'[72] During the war, some Irish residents in Britain chose to return rather than be subject to conscription. They included the artist Seán Keating, who in his famous painting *Men of the West* (1916) sought to concentrate on images of ragged bandit Irish warriors; while it was years before the Irish theatre could deal with Seán

O'Casey's *The Silver Tassie*. Staging a play that expressed the horror of war and its aftermath was politically difficult in an Ireland that did not want to acknowledge participation in the Great War.

As Roy Foster has demonstrated, W. B. Yeats also found himself grappling with this issue, after the death in the war of Major Robert Gregory, son of his confidante, Lady Gregory. He actually wrote four poems about Robert Gregory, as much to figure out his own stage of artistic and personal development as to commemorate the dead pilot. In *An Irish Airman Foresees His Death*, it was significant that Gregory's commitment to fighting is somewhat existential, Yeats even suggesting he was alienated from the Empire, and he identifies Gregory with Galway and Ireland. But in another important poem, *In Memory of Major Robert Gregory*, a short life, joyously lived, is celebrated, the war hero given the accolade of achieving unity of being:

> Some burn damp faggots, others may consume
> All the combustible world in one small room
> As though dried straw, and if we turn about
> The bare chimney is gone back out
> Because the work had finished in that flare.
> Soldier, scholar, horseman, he,
> As 'twere all life's epitome,
> What made us dream he could comb grey hair?[73]

'The women were kept well plied with drink'

Southern Ireland in fact produced a considerable body of war literature, including Patrick MacGill's *The Red Horizon*, celebrating the positive interaction of Irish and British soldiers, while his 1921 novel *Fear* dealt with the grimness of the war. The poet Francis Ledwidge was also representative in both celebrating and deploring the war: 'a soldier's heart is greater than a poet's art and greater than a poet's frame, a little grave that has no name'.[74] The contemporary *Irish Catholic* newspaper revealed the existence of a certain contempt for pacifism in the South. One of their heroes was Fr Bernard Vaughan, the London preacher who denounced those 'shirking' from the war.[75]

Some of the young Irish men who joined the British army had undoubtedly been influenced by the wider concerns of the 'generation of 1914', believing they had been born into a crisis-ridden world, with a weakened older generation; war being viewed as a form of regeneration and catharsis.[76] Michael Moynihan, a native of Tralee, County Kerry, who had strong Fenian sympathies, joined the British army despite the opposition of his family, and kept up a regular correspondence with them. In a draft letter, he defended his decision by insisting the only way 'of serving Ireland is to fight for it' despite the 'empty words and irresolute deeds' of nationalist Ireland, in contrast to the 'strength of purpose and energy of resource' of its enemies. But Deirdre MacMahon, who has edited his letters, also suggests there was an element of spiritual crisis in his decision, reflected in the following lines:

> my idea of patriotism ... has nothing in common with later ideas of ordered progress and industrial development ... considerations such as these combined ... with a perhaps excessive distaste for peace and for modernity, have brought me to my present position which is far too bound up with my present philosophy to be shaken by petty criticism.[77]

Thousands of Irish women whose husbands were fighting with the British army were also enjoying a standard of living they could not have afforded but for their husbands' service, and they were often loud in their denunciation of Irish nationalists who decried their spouses' decision. Trade union organiser William O'Brien, when being brought to Richmond Barracks after the Easter Rising, remembered 'a considerable crowd assembled made up mainly of separation allowance women who booed and hissed us vigorously'. John Flanagan, active in canvassing for Sinn Féin at the East Clare by-election in 1917, recounted strong anti-Sinn Féin sentiment in Ennis:

> The women were kept well plied with drink by a number of the publicans who were supporters of the Irish party and in their drunken condition they were a frenzied and ferocious crowd to deal with. On a couple of occasions the volunteers were obliged to use the ash plant in order to protect Sinn Féin supporters from being mauled by these infuriated females.

Ernest Blythe, later a Free State government minister, recalled in his statement to the Bureau of Military History that after a Volunteer parade in Limerick:

the rabble of the city, particularly the 'separation women', got into the mood to make trouble and a large crowd of them gathered near the station to attack the Volunteers as they moved to the train. There was a certain amount of stone throwing and blows were struck at Volunteers as they passed by.[78]

'incapable of ruining women'

Nonetheless, there was also considerable opposition to the war in Ireland. It was a major theme in advanced nationalist propaganda and anti-war feelings were important in building limited support for republicans in the lead-up to the 1916 Rising. Even though it was but a small fraction of the total propaganda circulating in Ireland during the war, there were 12 nationalist newspapers with a national circulation, including *Sinn Féin, Éire Ireland, Irish Volunteer, Irish Freedom, Workers' Republic* and *Nationality*. But their reaction to the war also revealed contradictions and inconsistencies, given that many of the journalists were capable of demonstrating pride and sympathy with the Irish volunteers in the British army. The tendency to base some propaganda on the supposed sexual immorality of England and outsiders led one journalist to suggest that Irish men, in contrast, were 'incapable of ruining women', while Germany was elevated to the status of a 'morally and religiously pure' country like Ireland.[79]

In the battle for allegiance between pro- and anti-war sides, both saw the countryside as the true repository of the Irish spirit. The Department of Recruiting in Ireland went to great lengths to enlist farmers, informing them: 'every one of your farms is carefully mapped and recorded in Berlin'. In 1915, Arthur Griffith, when bemoaning Britain's control of the Irish food market, insisted: 'an Ireland ringed around with a wall of steel could not be starved. A besieged Ireland at the present time could feed a population of 7 million indefinitely.'[80] The brutalisation of discourse was becoming increasingly important in Ireland at this time, as was the lead Ulster had given in the call to arms of the Ulster Volunteers. But equally true was the fact that many of those who wrote in an extreme style were often practical moderates (very few actually participated in the Rising, for example).

'a very small minority, without influence; impotent'

Advanced nationalists like Desmond FitzGerald worried that a sense of Irish independence was being obliterated by a world war that was not being waged in the Irish people's interests.[81] The machinations of the Irish Republican Brotherhood in infiltrating the Volunteers, and secretly planning for a military rising, contingent on German help during the war, complicated the picture. No one would maintain that the insurgents who proclaimed a republic in Dublin during Easter 1916 had a popular mandate; but it has also been pointed out that there was an absence of democratic politics in Ireland during this period. Electoral politics was about sending (after often uncontested elections) representatives to Westminster, and Tom Garvin maintained that the constitutional relationship between Britain and Ireland prohibited normal democratic politics; that British policy in Ireland was not democratic in the sense that Ireland was ruled according to British contingencies.[82] There is a strong case to be made for the argument that 1916 forced the increasing democratisation of Irish life which British governments had prevented.

The Rising also occurred at a time when the British coalition government no longer sustained the Liberal/Nationalist axis. But as Garret FitzGerald pointed out in his *Reflections on the Irish State*, one of the paradoxes of the Rising becoming such an important event, and a reason why its legacy has been difficult to deal with in terms of 'democracy', was the fact that 'it was the mood of despair within nationalism' that provided the impetus for it, rather than a confident, popular republicanism. As FitzGerald's father, Desmond, realised, 'the Irish people had recognised themselves as part of England' and during the First World War, with Home Rule likely to be defeated again, 'There was no evidence to lead one to expect that the people could do more than shrug their shoulders and say they expected as much ... those of us who thought of Home Rule as something utterly inadequate were a very small minority, without influence; impotent.'[83]

Much of the strength of the Volunteer movement had been destroyed by the war. The split not only robbed it of much talent; it also left fewer moderates to be tediously argued with. Alvin Jackson suggested it was 'a legion of the excluded' that declared war on the British Empire at Easter 1916, with the rising led by those beyond the appeal of the Irish Parliamentary Party – Fenians, socialists, Gaelic Leaguers, politicised women and the young.[84] The IRB had fewer than 2,000 members, but harboured a youthful wing that was pleased to imitate Ulster militarisation in infiltrating the provisional committee of the Irish Volunteers. Certain 'respectable' members of the IRB may have been uneasy, but James

Connolly's Irish Citizens' Army, a small group established to protect the interests of Dublin's working class after the Lockout of 1913 (see below), needed a new agenda, James Connolly seeing the establishment of a socialist republic as facilitating the rise of the working-class underdog. Connolly took a more assertive leadership role in 1914, reorganising the ICA, adopting a constitution and appointing an army council. One of the main concerns of the IRB was that Connolly would attempt to instigate his own ICA rising, but he was eventually persuaded to work in conjunction with the IRB.

Cabals and further cabals abounded during this period, involving much deception, but also a divergence of views on what justified a rebellion, or, indeed, how 'respectable' that rebellion would be. This was particularly important given that a general revolutionary situation did not remotely exist in Ireland in the years immediately preceding 1916. It was also the case that relative government tolerance meant that those who wished to indulge in martial fervour could do so relatively unfettered. In the absence of conscription there was a noticeable lack of a framework of oppression that could be manipulated. In class-conscious Dublin city, which had provided 18,698 war recruits for the British army, some undoubtedly found the drilling of Volunteers embarrassing and irrelevant, just as Seán O'Faoláin had in Cork city. He recalled somebody:

> Drilling a shamble of 40 or 50 men in the open place between our windows in Half Moon Street – rudely accoutred fellows, with no uniform other than a belt around their ordinary working clothes, only a few bearing rifles. As I watched them fumble and stumble my blood had curled against them, they were so shabby, so absurd, so awkward, so unheroic looking. They were, as my father said, as the man would have said, disgracing our country; and this while real war was flashing and booming in Flanders and France.[85]

'In one room men and girls were methodically filling the last of the bombs'
But far removed from such sloppiness were the tactics of Seán Mac Diarmada and Tom Clarke, representing two generations of Irish republicanism within the Fenian movement. Plans for a rising through theirs and other clandestine cliques could conveniently operate under the cloak of planning a future response to a conscription threat or government efforts to disarm the Volunteers. But the failure of German aid to materialise meant a change

of plan and the duping of Eoin MacNeill, the Chief of Staff of the Irish Volunteers, by using the Volunteers as an army which would declare open war, unconcerned with the cost to themselves and others. Opinion on the merits of a rising was not unanimous. Clarke and Mac Diarmada formed a majority on the three-man executive of the IRB (the other member was Denis McCullough in Belfast), and bypassed the Supreme Council, forming a military council outside its control. This body eventually comprised seven, including Patrick Pearse. Not only were they thus a minority of a minority: 'only in early 1916 did the Supreme Council commit itself to a rebellion, but it did so in a vague manner and without deciding a date'.[86] Roger Casement had undertaken a clandestine mission to secure German assistance for the rising and attempted to recruit Irish prisoners of war who would form an Irish brigade, a mission that ended in failure. Although it is tempting to depict Eoin MacNeill as having his head too deeply buried in books, making him easy to deceive, he did illustrate an awareness of the mentality of the IRB radicals, as pointed out by Michael Laffan. His own position regarding the justification of rebellion was clear: it could be only a defensive reaction to a British attempt to disarm the Volunteers; and only if the rebels had a reasonable chance of success. By success, he meant 'success in the operation itself. Not merely some future moral or political advantage which may be hoped for as the result of non-success.'[87]

When he got wind of the plans he was immediately opposed to them but was informed that Casement was travelling back to Ireland with German arms (this was untrue – he was travelling to attempt to halt the rising because of the failure of his German mission), and was shown a document from Dublin Castle (a forgery), which suggested the British government was going to attempt to disarm the Volunteers. When he discovered the deception, he countermanded the order for Volunteers to assemble nationally on Easter Sunday, leading to the collapse of the plans for a nationwide rising. But in Dublin the IRB defied him, and pressed ahead with their plans to assemble Volunteers on Easter Monday. According to Laffan, the British government, which was keeping abreast of developments through, amongst other things, naval intelligence, believed that with all the mishaps there was no prospect of a rising, and no need to move against the ringleaders until after the Easter holiday.

In providing the rhetoric of justification, Pearse was not alone. Joseph Plunkett and Thomas MacDonagh, two other 1916 martyrs, were also exponents of the literature of blood sacrifice, ensuring the continuation of the separatist tradition. This was political but also a spiritual frame of reference, as seen in Pearse's overt Catholicism and language of devotional asceticism, once again epitomising a generation that saw its mission to be more ardent and better Catholics. Patrick Maume suggested that this was not the only way the Easter Rising grew out of a long-standing separatist culture:

> the rhetoric of Pearse drew on a separatist idiom, forged by Mitchell [John, a mid nineteenth-century patriot and polemicist] and Griffith and given credibility by the petty repressions, snobberies, hypocrisies and corruption of early twentieth-century Ireland. It appealed to the contrast between the ideals of the Irish party invoked against Unionists, Whigs and Castle Catholics and its own compromises with forces it claimed to oppose.[88]

One of these compromises had been the necessity of working with people like Eoin MacNeill, who did not believe that blood sacrifice was essential to the preservation of Irish nationality.

One of the main differences between the 1916 rebellion and previous ones was the ease of movement which the putative insurgents enjoyed through government inactivity. This allowed about 1,000 men and 200 women, members of the Volunteers, the ICA and the IRB, to answer the call of an Irish Republic, with Patrick Pearse as Commander-in-Chief of the Volunteers, and, in theory at least, president of the Provisional Government. The Republic was proclaimed and defended for nearly a week before surrender. Many of the women involved in 1916 considered themselves combatants and not auxiliaries, with Cumann na mBan, the female wing of the Irish Volunteers, formed in 1914, maintaining their own command structures. Winifred Carney, a Belfast woman, suffragist and trade unionist, was in Liberty Hall in Dublin city the night before Easter Sunday, and recalled:

> For those working-class families, dependent on their breadwinners and on their weekly wage, this matter of mobilisation for revolt was a wrenching part of their hold on life ... women of the citizen army ambulance unit came in. In one room men and girls were methodically filling the last of the bombs, working up to the last minute to increase the supply of munitions ... But there was no repining.

They kissed and shook hands, the women handing parcels and boxes of cigarettes.[89]

Other women were forced to accept the traditional gendered 'division of republican labour'. Kathleen Clarke, wife of IRB husband Tom, although she had 'begged' to march out with the insurgents, was forbidden by her husband, who insisted her role was 'to ensure the well-being of the dependants of those involved in the rising'.[90] Later in the century, women were completely written out of the narrative of the Rising. Brian Moore's poem 'Invisible Women' was a reminder of the women's historical neglect:

> For he sings of the bold Fenian men and
> the boys of the old brigade
> what about the women who stood there too?
> When history was made?
> Ireland, Mother Ireland with your freedom-loving sons,
> did your daughters run and hide at the sound of guns?
> Or did they have some part in the fight
> and why does everybody try to keep them out of sight?[91]

Bulmer Hobson acknowledged that a 'feeling against the presence of women in the organisation continued in varying degrees of intensity for many years and probably never completely disappeared'. As Mrs Tom Barry put it, when being told to go home and make sandwiches for the male Volunteers in 1916: 'you know the Volunteers, the kind of men they were; they thought that we should be away from all that danger'.[92]

'so good a European'?

The definitive history of the Rising has yet to be written, and many questions have been left unanswered. Much confusion abounded during Easter Week, on the part both of the rebels and of the British government. It is too simplistic to dismiss it as a hopeless blood sacrifice. True, James Connolly, when asked of the rebels' chances, replied: 'none whatever'.[93] But there was much more to Connolly, and indeed Pearse, than mystic notions about spilling blood for the benefit of future generations. As Michael Laffan points out, 'few of the conspirators actually sought martyrdom and they hoped and planned for a successful revolt'.[94] This would seem to contradict

Connolly's admission of hopelessness, but just serves to underline the degree of confusion, occasional optimism and pessimism that were a product of these years. Given the war, and the impending tumultuous events in places like Russia, and the contemporary cultural environment, there was reason for Connolly and others to believe they could transform political attitudes. Why, after all, did Connolly claim that Ireland was like a powder magazine waiting for someone to apply a match? Why did he feel it was necessary to align the labour and republican movements? Trying to analyse the rising from the perspective of the late twentieth century involves a deliberate down-playing of contemporary fixations.

Shortly after the execution of Connolly, Robert Lynd wrote a brilliantly perceptive introduction to Connolly's *Labour in Irish History* and *The Reconquest of Ireland*, in which, significantly, he praised him not as an Irish patriot, but as 'so good a European', because his principles were not applicable just to the Anglo-Irish struggle. Lynd also sought to get to the bottom of the question: why did someone of his intelligence get involved in a doomed rising? Part of the answer lay in Connolly's own writings, which focused on the history of the militancy of the Irish poor: 'he saw insurrection following insurrection apparently in vain, like wave following wave, but he still had faith in the hour when the tide would be full'.[95] Though he advocated class warfare, Lynd contended Connolly was interested in other things, including the recovery of the old Gaelic Ireland, which underlines the importance of the resort to history during these years. On the specific question of the rising, Lynd wrote:

> This question of Connolly's mood and purpose in the insurrection is one to which one returns in perplexity again and again. Did he expect to win? Did he expect the Germans to send assistance over the wreck of a defeated British navy? Did he imagine that Ireland would raise and defeat the most gigantic British army that is known to history? Did he really believe that a rifle was of any avail against modern artillery? I have discussed these questions with many people and everybody has his own answer.[96]

That there were so many answers being put forward by contemporaries is important; they were displaying none of the certainty that many future historians would express regarding how the Rising was viewed at the time.

'undersized products of the British slums'

The archives of the Bureau of Military History contain numerous accounts of first-hand experiences of the Rising. Given that it was mostly confined to Dublin, it is revealing to get the regional perspective on the Rising: countless statements record the frustration felt at the absence of reliable information from Dublin and the exaggerated accounts of what was going on. Across the country, Volunteers were called out, told to prepare, and then sent home again. The account of James Cullen, an Irish Volunteer captain in Enniscorthy, is typical:

> On Tuesday and Wednesday rumours of all kinds were circulating. Some said the Volunteers were sweeping the country, others that it was only the Citizen Army that had risen and that the Rising had been suppressed ... in the absence of any definite or authentic information it was very difficult to decide what to do ... Commandant Gilligan, who had gone to Dublin on Good Friday, arrived back in Enniscorthy late on Wednesday night. He had cycled all the way from Dublin.

Gilligan persuaded them to stage their own rising, which was short-lived and resulted in him and others 'being put on a cattle boat in the North Wall and taken to Holyhead'.[97]

Captain E. Gerard, a member of the British army in Ireland in 1916, was somewhat in awe of the Irish rebels and struck by their 'magnificent physique', remembering them as 'huge men', in contrast to the British troops stationed in Beggars Bush who were 'untrained, undersized products of the British slums'. He was later informed by the medical officer who attended the execution of the insurgents: 'they all died like Lions. The rifles of the firing party were waving like a field of corn. All the men were cut to ribbons at a range of about ten yards.'[98]

'I think Connolly was Commander-in-Chief'

The trade unionist William O'Brien maintained that afterwards, when the insurgents were rounded up in Richmond Barracks, Eamon de Valera, who commanded a battalion of troops in Dublin, 'said he was glad that he had no responsibility for deciding anything and that he simply obeyed orders given to him'. O'Brien's statement also refers to the hostility that existed between the Irish Volunteers and the Irish Citizens' Army. O'Brien estimated the Citizens' Army had only 339 members on its register by

Easter Week, and 'some of these only joined a short time before'. He referred to Constance Markievicz, one of the more high-profile republican women of the era, as being 'very irritable' and recalled that Tom Clarke expressed concern that 'she is too talkative. She cannot keep a secret.' Another female republican, Maud Gonne, was more sympathetic: 'I always think she does not get the credit she should.' Markievicz, according to Christopher Brady, a printer on the staff of the *Workers' Republic* who printed the '2,500 copies' of the 1916 Proclamation, arrived into the machine room with Eoin MacNeill's countermanding telegram, announcing: 'I will shoot Eoin MacNeill', to which he recalled James Connolly replying: 'You are not going to hurt a hair on MacNeill's head. If anything happens to MacNeill I will hold you responsible.' Regarding the authorship of the 1916 Proclamation, Brady insisted: 'It certainly was not Connolly's as I was familiar with his scrawl.'[99]

William O'Brien disputed the idea that Connolly was kidnapped by the IRB before the Rising in order to prevent the Citizens' Army from instigating its own rebellion, believing Connolly's forceful personality would have made this unlikely. 'I think Connolly was Commander-in-Chief … I think Pearse was only nominally Commander-in-Chief. I am positive about Connolly's position. Pearse had no capacity for that kind of work. He never decided anything in the post-office. Connolly was in charge of everything.' He also noted that 'Mrs Clarke is positive that Tom Clarke was president', adding that, regarding these leadership positions, 'something happened in the last few hours [before the Rising] that no one seems to know'.[100]

Pearse, in theory the Commander-in-Chief of the Irish Republic proclaimed at the outset of the Rising, was full of contradictions to the end. It was a measure of the success and assiduousness of Pearse in writing so much in the final years of his life that his name became most closely associated with the Rising, and thus revered in Irish republicanism.

Interestingly, at the beginning of the twenty-first century it was suggested that Pearse 'will find a place' in Irish history and commemoration, a measure of the extent to which veneration of the poet, school headmaster and Irish language activist had gone out of fashion. The truth was that, by the end of the century, both republicans and their critics could find the Pearse they wanted: warped genius, key figure of continuity republicanism, outstanding Irish historical martyr of the twentieth century, or anti-democrat and 'proto-fascist'. There were also warnings made of the danger of deliberate amnesia because of the fact the IRA had adopted Pearse and his rhetoric during the course of the Troubles. This was an element that so annoyed some academics and cultural commentators at the seventy-fifth anniversary of the Rising in 1991 that they were moved to collectively assert:

> Anniversaries are often problematic and few in recent times have been as loaded with ambiguities and contradictions as the 75th anniversary of 1916. The interpretation of this key event in modern Irish history has prompted fractures and disputes among historians, politicians and citizens; but outside the realm of embattled historiography open and general discussion has been curiously muted, not to say inhibited. There are those of us who feel that, as a reaction, amnesia, private or communal, is both unhealthy and dangerous.[101]

'to die will be an awfully big adventure'

Pearse in fact represented in person many of the contradictions of early-twentieth-century Irish republicanism. Born into a lower-middle-class family (who, like most, wanted to make it into the middle classes), from an early age he was transfixed with the idea of self-sacrifice and cultivated an exceptionally morbid imagination. But he was also caught between the desire for a truly Gaelic way of life and an Edwardian desire for respectability (which prompted him to qualify as a lawyer and build a holiday home in Connemara where he could act as an Irish-speaking gentleman amongst peasants). He always tried to act on his visions – of which he had an abundance – which led him in 1908 to establish a school, St Enda's in Rathfarnham in County Dublin, on the basis of his own personality. Here, myth and legend were an essential part of the curriculum, and Cú-Chulainn, an ancient mythical Irish warrior, in the words of a former pupil was 'almost a silent member of staff'. As well as idolising Peter Pan ('to die will be an awfully big adventure'), at one prize day at his school the winner of a poetry competition was rewarded not with a poetry book but with a rifle.[102]

It was the crippling debt of his school which prompted a lecture tour of the United States, where he fed off the exiles' republicanism and returned, many believe, a revolutionary. Wanting to make an impact on the IRB he was asked by Tom Clarke, via Clarke's wife Kathleen, to make the funeral speech for O'Donovan Rossa, a veteran exiled Fenian returned to Ireland for burial, 'as hot as hell', perhaps ironically for a patriot who believed he would go to heaven as a venerated Irish and Catholic warrior. Pearse was bound up with words; semantics to justify a revolution. Writing to a confidant, he noted that 'The O'Donovan Rossa funeral was wonderful',[103] and it encouraged him to write even more vociferously, much of his output revealing a reckless naivety.

One of his most quoted writings was in 1913 on *The Coming Revolution*, when he suggested: 'we may at first shoot the wrong people.' It is unlikely Pearse was capable of even shooting a rabbit in the wilds of Connemara, but over 500 people were killed and 2,500 wounded during the Rising, and its detractors understandably drew attention to the fact that in the units of the 16th Division in the same week 570 were killed on the battlefields of the Great War. The planned rising – and there are, most disappointingly, no documentary records of it – was more ambitious than that which occurred. This was a factor which actually sustained the iconography of Pearse, and ensured it was he who was key to the image of it, helped by him doing such a thorough job in preserving his own memory. This was done at the expense of the veteran Fenian Tom Clarke, who ideologically and generationally was perhaps the real president of the Irish republic in April 1916.[104]

'you inevitably find yourself back at the education question'

Pearse was a confused as well as a committed young man, and few have doubted his mystical earnestness, but it is also significant that he did not seem to know where his republicanism came from. In an unfinished biography, he crossed out words to the effect that his parents had made him a republican. He seemed asexual, but preservers of his memory constructed a tale of a lost fiancée.[105] His obvious devotion to young boys – seen in his poetry referring to 'fragrances in the kisses of their soft red mouths' – for some point to homosexuality, for others a typical Edwardian fascination with the cult of youthful masculinity. The suggestions of homosexuality were seen by his champions as just another attempt to smear a purist. Others were insistent that commemorating the 1916 Rising was no function of a late-twentieth-century democracy. Those who complained about the muteness of the seventy-fifth-anniversary celebrations in 1991, so far removed from the seemingly unbridled triumphalism of the fiftieth-anniversary state-sponsored events of 1966, refused to accept that just because the late-twentieth-century Republicans in waging war in the

North of Ireland borrowed his fundamentalism and rhetoric and made him their spiritual father, he should be erased altogether from the historical record. They too felt, it seemed, that to be ignored is nearly worse than to be attacked.

A man who continually wrote of the value of truth, Pearse revelled in deceiving MacNeill. He was a man who at times lauded, at times derided Germany. He also celebrated the sanctifying properties of bloodshed but was probably incapable of firing a revolver. Joe Lee has fairly pointed out that the reason for much of the confusion is too literal a reading of his many writings: '… there is a tendency to approach Pearse as a professional political philosopher. Yet he wrote not only as a conscious propagandist, but almost as a war propagandist.'[106]

There was an attractive side to Pearse as well. Seán O'Casey's subsequent drama, including *The Plough and the Stars*, was an acerbically realistic representation of the events of this period, but he was also able to write that 'Patrick Pearse, while filled with the vision of a romantic Ireland, was also fairly full of an Ireland, sensitive, knowledgeable, and graceful'.[107] Such thoughts are worth reflecting on in the context of his progressive views on education, which he believed was being botched by bureaucracy and usurped by the state at the expense of the individual. His writings on blood sacrifice have been given undue prominence, to the detriment of his worth as an educationalist, and as yet another nationalist who was utterly engaged with a sense of mission about not just political, but cultural awakening and who, like Connolly, looked to both past and future.

His writings on education for *An Claidheamh Soluis,* in editorials alone, amounted to a quarter of a million words. His career involved a quest for intellectual as well as political independence; as he put it in 1903: 'take up the Irish problem at what point you may, you inevitably find yourself back at the education question'. His *Murder Machine* (1916) was a compact and coherent work and was a reflection of new European thinking on education systems. It decried the snobbery of the Irish education system, which chose the select few who would go on to become civil servants, instead of 'fostering of the right growth of a personality'.[108]

But, ultimately, it was his invocation of the purifying power of violence with which he became most associated; it is also here that he seems at his most confused and contradictory. This was the same man who castigated Synge's *Playboy* for its 'brutal' glorification of violence; the same man who denounced Redmond for sacrificing to England 'as a peace holocaust the blood of 50,000 Irish men'.[109] Reality and rhetoric still sit uncomfortably alongside the name Patrick Pearse, and this largely explains why he represented many of the contradictions of violent twentieth-century Irish republicanism.

'necessary and inevitable'?

The rhetoric of the Rising was subsequently used selectively. It also went to the heart of the question of who knew the will of the people better than the people themselves, which was why, in the context of the North, the Rising became much derided in the 1970s and 1980s. As F. X. Martin noted long ago, it would be deceptive to insist that the Rising was 'necessary and inevitable' as far as contemporaries were concerned, as this imposes a pattern of events in the years preceding 1916 which was not visible even to extreme republicans. An *Irish Independent* poll in 1991 suggested that 65 per cent of Irish people looked back with pride to the Rising, but only 27 per cent felt it had made 'the Irish political situation any better'.[110]

'women with wispy, greasy hair ... walked around in evening dress'

Immediate reaction to the Rising has always been difficult to gauge, with anecdotal evidence abounding at the expense of hard fact. It is certainly worth noting the effect it had on future fighters for Irish freedom. Much depended on class. The disgust of the respectable O'Faoláins, who raged at the sense of betrayal, was matched by an indifference on the part of the middle class. Ernie O'Malley, newly arrived in Dublin, although very quickly converted, 'had no feeling about it. I might have been a foreign news correspondent who had just landed, knowing nothing about the country, the people or the cause of the present Rising.' Todd Andrews, on the other hand, wrote that 'my first act was to dash into the nearest church and say three "our fathers", three "hail Mary's" and three "glory be to the fathers" for the success of the rebellion', and more significantly, that he read Irish history no longer as a school subject but as something to know and understand. Later famed as a short-story writer, Frank O'Connor as a 13-year-old in Cork, recalled that:

> the daily papers showed Dublin as they showed Belgian cities destroyed
> by the Germans, as smoking ruins inhabited by men with rifles and

machine guns. At first my only reaction was horror that Irishmen could commit such a crime against England. I was sure that phase had ended with the Boer War in which father had fought, because one of his favourite songs said so – 'You used to call us traitors because of agitators but you can't call us traitors now.'[111]

How could a boy with a cultural diet of English public school comic books be expected to identify with the scenes at the GPO?

For some of Dublin's poor, on the other hand, the Rising provided an opportunity to loot, and they clamoured into destroyed buildings to secure whatever they could. Ernie O'Malley recorded that:

> Little girls hugged teddy bears and dolls as if they could hardly believe their good fortune. Kiddies carried golf bags and acted as caddies to young gentlemen in bright football jerseys and tall hats, who hit golf balls with their clubs, or indeed anything that came in their way. This was a holiday. Some of the women with wispy, greasy hair and blousy figures walked around in evening dress.[112]

The Belfast artist Muriel Brandt's *The Breadline* celebrated the gallantry of those unwittingly caught up in the fall-out from the Rising. There was a shortage of food, with what there was quickly bought up by the middle class, and her painting illustrated Irish Sisters of Charity handing out free government food.

'here, he knew a man who was respectable'
Ironically, James Connolly's bodyguard discovered him reading a detective story after his injury: 'a book like this, plenty of rest and an insurrection – all at the same time. This certainly is revolution de luxe.'[113] Connolly, shortly to be executed, may not have been too anxious about the afterlife; as far back as 1908 he had written to a friend that he had 'not the slightest tincture of faith left'.[114] But whatever about Connolly, seven of the 14 men executed as leaders of the 1916 Rising were products of a Christian Brothers education (as were three of the five executive members of the IRA in 1917 and five of the seven-man cabinet in 1921). The attitude of the Church nonetheless varied. The Archbishop of Dublin, William Walsh, was ill for most of the period, but he considered a rising without outside help to be fruitless, though not treacherous. He was not prepared

to condemn it publicly, conscious that if he did so he would be seen as siding with the government and was wary 'of being used by it'.[115]

The Rising presented the Catholic Church with its own problems, including a fear that it would undermine the bourgeois consensus between constitutional nationalism and the Church's representatives. Mrs Tom Barry's statement to the Bureau of Military History recorded that at the time of the Rising in 1916, Fr Michael O'Flanagan, later vice-president of Sinn Féin, had remarked to her of the fighters in the General Post Office: 'let these people burn to death, they are murderers', but he later relented and agreed to travel across town to assist with the injured. Barry was disgusted that when she and O'Flanagan were on their way to the GPO and they passed a drunken tramp who had been shot, 'the priest did not stop for him', but did give absolution to another wounded man. 'You see the difference,' she wrote, 'here, he knew a man who was respectable ... I said to Fr O'Flanagan, "Isn't it extraordinary you did not kneel beside the other man?"'[116]

But Church disapproval was by no means unanimous. Like their lay contemporaries, the clerics were often caught between conflicting loyalties. Class and respectability were not the only factors in determining the Church's attitude to the Rising. The Bureau of Military History statement of Fr Thomas Duggan, secretary to Bishop Daniel Cohalan of Cork, is illuminating in this regard. Many in the Church, and indeed in the republican movement, saw no contradiction in supporting Irish republicans and simultaneously administering to wounded Irish soldiers in the British army:

> My generation in Maynooth embraced the ideals of Easter Week 1916 with a hundred percent fervour. That did not prevent us from becoming Chaplains in the British Army. In the First World War there were well over 100,000 Irish Catholics in the fighting ranks ... everyone admitted that these boys were spiritually intractable to anyone save to an Irish priest. Hence, when in 1917 Cardinal Logue issued a special appeal for Irish Chaplains, I volunteered. And I went off to France with the blessing and encouragement of every friend I had in advanced Sinn Féin circles in Dublin.[117]

The preoccupation with respectability was not confined to the Church. It was as if there was an acceptance of the need to have respected middle-class men 'officially' at the helm, or in leadership positions, as seen in the case of Pearse (lawyer, headmaster) and Eoin MacNeill (university professor), while the socialists or Christian Brothers-educated boys actually called the shots. Stephen Gwynn observed that 'a curious complication in Irish social life is that the country as a whole outside of Belfast is strangely penetrated with aristocratic ideas'. Owing to Eoin MacNeill's academic standing, Gwynn asserted in 1924 that 'University College Dublin was the real focus of the movement which brought Ireland into armed insurrection'.[118] But this was only one layer of activism, and was Gwynn's attempt to rehabilitate the moderates. The poets, teachers, Fenians and labour activists were intent on more radical activity, while happy to have 'respected' figureheads who provided a cover for them. Such were the dynamics of this unusual coalition, and, as MacNeill was to discover, this necessitated much deception.

In his book *States of Ireland*, Conor Cruise O'Brien gives a good overview of the concern of his grandparents with class, and the extent to which, during these years of upheaval, social lines were being crossed. People were getting involved in pacifism, socialism and women's suffragism, 'English sort of things, really, grandmother thought'. The idea that these new alliances could actually result in marriage to the wrong 'type' troubled his grandmother, and the family was divided over O'Brien's parents' marriage. As he accurately summarised it: 'a simple exercise in parental authority could not stand against the spirit of the age ... [it was] an emotional division which tended to reflect wider divisions in the society'.[119]

Even amongst those who disagreed with the rising, there was horror expressed at the idea that it would be depicted as a grubby working-class episode which exposed the under-belly of the slums. The well-known pacifist and journalist Frank Skeffington was horrified at the looting in Dublin:

> It had to be stopped ... Seán O'Kelly, an officer of the Neutrality League who was assisting Connolly, had then been assigned a dozen men, armed with rifles and police sticks, to drive the looters out of Clerys. This they did but, just as soon as they went on to the next store, the looters swarmed back. O'Kelly reported to Connolly that he had never seen such industrious Irishmen in his life.

Skeffington wanted to organise a Citizens' Defence Force to police the area, but James Connolly reportedly said 'that will be one more problem for the British'.[120]

But whatever crumbs of comfort were to be handed out to Dublin's poor were not on offer to the captured insurgents. The Irish playwright in London George Bernard Shaw had suggested to the English media that the men after their surrender were prisoners of war; that it was entirely incorrect to slaughter them; and that an Irish man resorting to arms to achieve independence of his country was only doing what Englishmen would do if it was their misfortune to be invaded and conquered by the Germans during the war. The British government's reaction illustrated how prophetic were the words of Augustine Birrell, that 'it is not an Irish rebellion; it would be a pity if *ex post facto* it became one'. Military historian Charles Townshend makes the significant point that the Rising broke out in the twenty-first month of the war, when, in the context of conscription in England, the war became for Britain a total one, with Somme and Verdun grim reminders of what total war meant in practice.[121] Capital sentences were imposed on 16 of the Easter rebels by British military courts; Willie Pearse was executed simply because he was Patrick's brother. The executions were carried out in a protracted, semi-secret manner.[122]

The scale of the British reaction was certainly not presaged by their treatment of threats of violence prior to 1916, which they had left largely alone. This was perhaps in itself an encouragement to many to conclude that the legality of holding arms and drilling publicly was open to debate. When did subversion become rebellion? Was martial law an appropriate response in dealing with civil unrest? How could political and military aims be reconciled? It was of course the government's tendency to defer to the military (a product of the war), which made them believe that the executions were a matter of course; a fundamental concomitant of martial law. But the absence of political discussion of this matter is noteworthy; rather than a reassertion of political authority, the executions were for a British audience, again highlighting the manner in which Ireland could be governed according to British public opinion.[123]

'No more books by women please'
John Dillon quite rightly branded as lunacy the decision to round up everyone who might be a rebel sympathiser (where would one draw the line?). Heavily armed mobile columns scoured the country arresting 3,340 men and 79 women following the collapse of the Rising. Within a week

1,424 of the men and 73 of the women were released, while 1,836 men and five women were interned without trial, ensuring a scale of resentment against British rule in Ireland which was unprecedented. In an article written in 2000, Joe Lee suggested that what was striking about the reaction to the 1916 Rising was how few were executed given the extent of demonisation of Germans by British propaganda, and given that a war was being conducted in which the British army executed many of its own young soldiers. Sir John Maxwell was thus depicted as relatively mild, and he did after all commute most of the death sentences.[124] Michael Laffan also noted that 'The British response in May 1916 was relatively mild when compared with the repressive measures taken after the crushing of revolts in other major European cities' such as Paris in 1871 or Budapest in 1956.[125] In direct contrast, Charles Townshend insisted that:

> The suppression of the Irish rebellion must be judged to have been, by British standards, abnormally severe. It was an aberration generated by the pressure of the war. Only a much more rapid reassertion of political authority could have mitigated its impact, but it is clear that those who might have imposed such limits did not see the need to do so. They were after all British and no doubt represented in this the general opinion of the British public.[126]

The transcripts of the trials of the insurrection leaders reveal a mixture of fear, bravery and defiance. Those imprisoned after the Rising were often unsure what the future held for them. The humanity of the statement of Kathleen Lynn – medical doctor, first-aid lecturer to the Irish Citizens' Army and a member of Cumann na mBan in 1916 – is palpable, and reveals a mix of pride, innocence and sisterhood. In Mountjoy Prison after the Rising, she recalled:

> we were handled rather with joy by the wardresses because we were interesting prisoners, we were not like ordinary criminals. I got quite fond of the wardress who looked after me. She was quite kindly. We discovered that, when the suffragettes were there they had made little holes in the plaster under the pipes so that, if one lay down on the floor, one could talk to the person in the next cell. Countess Plunkett was in the next cell to mine. Of course, she was in a terrible state about her son having been executed and she used get awfully lonely and upset at

night. We would lie down on the floor and talk and that would make
her better. After a while, we were allowed visitors and parcels and then
we were inundated with all sorts of presents of luxuries. The only thing
we longed for was clean bread and butter … We had all sorts of cakes
and fruits etc., but we wanted something plain.[127]

In Brixton prison after 1916 Ernest Blythe was tormented by female
fiction:

The librarian warder, always changing my book when I was out at
exercise, gave me books by Mrs Henry Woods and Mrs Humphrey
Ward, which after a time I found it nearly impossible to read. I left a
note on my slate one day saying "No more books by women please",
after which I got boys' adventure stories and detective tales, which
were much better.[128]

Other statements to the Bureau from those imprisoned give a good
indication, not just of the suffering they experienced, but also their elation
at the impact their actions had made. Their resourcefulness in prison
was also notable. Arthur Griffith started a weekly manuscript journal
in Brixton prison and behaved, according to Blythe, 'Like a man having
a carefree holiday aboard a ship'. In the same prison Seán T. O'Kelly, a
future President of Ireland, started a choir. All grew beards, Blythe
maintained, except Terence McSwiney, who shaved because his girlfriend
visited regularly. Inmates in other prisons and internment camps were
enduring much more difficult conditions, but the incarceration provided
an opportunity for like-minded republicans to collectively plan for the
future. That it was being referred to by the British as a 'Sinn Féin rebellion'
(it was no such thing), and the public revulsion at the executions, meant
moderates like Arthur Griffith would have an opportunity to exploit the
new-found and misplaced fame of their small organisation, though where
exactly the more radical republicans would fit into the changed political
environment outside was far from clear.

In Dublin, contemporary chroniclers of the Rising exaggerated the
extent of German involvement, amongst other things. Hamilton Norway,
from a family of British imperial soldiers and civil servants, and in the city
for the duration of the Rising, believed that 'all the roads leading out of
Dublin are in the hands of the rebels'.[129] Norway also observed at the time

that 'people are appalled at the utter unpreparedness of the government. In the face of a huge body of trained and armed men, openly revolutionary, they had taken no precautions whatever for the defence of the city in the event of an outbreak.'

The failure of the German mission led to the capture of the celebrated human-rights campaigner Roger Casement, unaware that the *Aud*, carrying a consignment of 20,000 rifles from Germany for use in the Rising, had been intercepted by the Royal Navy. When he was hanged for high treason in August in Pentonville prison, the *Irish Times* lamented that 'Roger Casement's death is a miserable end to a life which for the greater part of its course was honourable and distinguished'.[130] Casement's late allegiance to the Catholic faith is the subject of one of the Bureau of Military History statements. Fr J. M. Cronin recalled Casement's last days in Pentonville prison, though he qualified his statement by saying that much of it was based on 'hearsay' and the facts needed 'to be well sifted'. The Westminster Curia had apparently demanded a written apology 'for any scandal Casement had given' before he could be received into the Church; but having written one under protest Casement then tore it up, maintaining 'he could not leave such a document behind him'. Priests reconciled him eventually, and Cronin heard of the 'voluntary penance that Casement imposed upon himself of taking off his shoes and socks and walking across his cell and kneeling and kissing the priest's [confessor's] feet'. A. M. Sullivan, Casement's defence lawyer, sent the Bureau a statement in which he maintained that Casement brought up the subject of his 'Black Diaries', detailing homosexual encounters which were being used at the time to discredit him: 'he was very nervous about it, and in spite of my efforts to avoid the subject, he intruded the observation that the matters recorded in the diary were inseparable from the manifestation of distinguished genius'.[131]

According to the Soviet leader, Lenin: 'the misfortune of the Irish was that they rose too soon, before the revolt of the European proletariat had matured'. Declan Kiberd pointed out that Conor Cruise O'Brien agreed when writing in 1966, suggesting that had they waited until 1918 they would have found a country united against the threat of conscription. The problem with all these assumptions is that they presuppose a popular desire for socialist revolt that was innovative and aggressively contemporary, whereas, as Kiberd himself admits, Irish innovations were dominated by the rhetoric of the past, because of the conservatism of the contemporary audience. James Connolly, for example, soothed fears of socialism with his claim in the *Reconquest of Ireland* that an Irish republic would simply mean a return to the Gaelic system of landholding, except that now the government rather than the chieftain would hold land in the name of the entire community.[132]

'unsung hero'

In the same year as the Rising, Tom Crean, one of the most inspirational and admirable individuals of twentieth-century Ireland, was completing a heroic journey: an epic 800-mile voyage in a 22½-foot boat in the world's most dangerous seas en route to South Georgia. Even more astonishing endurance was to be required in a march over the interior of South Georgia, attempting to rescue an Antarctic expedition gone wrong, in the company of the more famous Ernest Shackleton. There was much truth in the assertion of Shackleton that 'my name has been known to the general public for a long time and it has mostly been as leader, but how much depends upon the men'. None more so than Tom Crean, and his biographer noted that 'the four-mile long Crean Glacier on South Georgia and Mount Crean, which rises 8,360 feet above … Victoria Land on the Antarctic mainland, will forever perpetuate the memory of polar exploration's unsung hero'.[133]

Unsung, not least because of his own modesty but also because of the changed political environment in Ireland when he returned home as a member of the British Navy, having risen from the obscurity of a small farming community in Kerry to become one of the outstanding figures in the history of polar exploration. An added difficulty was the shooting of his brother, a member of the Royal Irish Constabulary. Crean served on three of the four momentous expeditions to the Antarctic, crossing many class boundaries in the process. From December 1914 he spent a total of 497 days on *Endurance* or adrift on the ice, before taking part in a successful mission to rescue the 22 men left behind on Elephant Island.

'Never a flower on their table'

Part of the text of the 1916 Proclamation of the Irish Republic read:

> The Irish Republic is entitled to, and hereby claims, the allegiance of
> every Irishman and Irishwoman. The Republic guarantees religious
> and civil liberty, equal rights and equal opportunities to all its citizens,

and declares its resolve to pursue the happiness and prosperity of the whole nation and of all its parts, cherishing all the children of the nation equally, and oblivious of all the differences carefully fostered by an alien government, which have divided a minority from the majority in the past.

The passage became one of the most quoted of twentieth-century Irish history, largely because of the failure of the promises to materialise, and because it was a useful one for socialists to quote in order to lambaste empty revolutionary sentiments.

Declan Kiberd pointed to the significance of the language of the Proclamation in addressing Irish women as well as men, given that most European women were still excluded from the franchise. He also suggested that 'by promising to cherish all the children of the nation equally, the rebels prefigured a welfare state, decades before the implementation of such a thing in Scandinavian countries or in post-war Britain'.[134] Written in the midst of the First World War, the Proclamation was also a reminder that the prosperity of the war years was by no means spread evenly.

During the years of the war there were signs that there was greater concern with issues of health, welfare and redistribution of wealth, while the Lockout of 1913 (discussed below) may have heightened awareness of the vulnerability of many labouring families in urban areas. This was matched by a growing number of surveys into poverty. Was the Church to take a lead in this regard and respond to the anger expressed by Seán O'Casey?

the poor he was told, were beloved by God. He didn't see any sign of his love here. Here he was a ripe young man and had never yet seen the poor satisfied with bread. Never a flower on their table ... never more than a faded newspaper to make the bare table look a richer thing; never a safer place to lie when sickness tossed us down, never a place to bathe away the dust and sweat mottling our uneasy bodies when the day's work was done; by the living God! those changing lies of life would have to go! He tightened his teeth and clenched his hands till the knuckles shone white.[135]

The commencement of the Jesuit periodical *Studies*, in 1912, provided some academics with a forum for highlighting the lack of attention to social work. The Professor of Education at University College Dublin, Timothy Corcoran SJ, reminded readers of what Catholic activists were doing in France and Germany, for example, and of the need to acquire further knowledge of what was being done in the field abroad. The message of various articles in this publication was that inequality was not being tackled. Corcoran listed a catalogue of failure: no diminution in the problem of purely precarious employment, or in the abuse of strong drink; and he suggested the school attendance of Ireland in city and country 'is a national scandal ... here and in many other ways, there is room enough for trained social workers; a thousand could find ample scope for well-directed energy in Dublin alone'.[136] The lack of appetite for confronting the housing crisis in the city was also noted, highlighting the divide between the rural and urban housing experiences. Labourers Acts had ensured that rural labourers made progress in the housing league during these years – indeed, it is not an exaggeration to term it a social revolution, in the sense that it was the first large-scale public-housing scheme in the country, with up to a quarter of a million housed under the Labourers Acts up to 1921. It was a development neglected by historians because the houses, rural-based and more scattered, were not as evident as the urban tenements that officialdom would not even look into, never mind raze to the ground.

The vast bulk of the labourers' cottages were erected by 1916 and TB, typhoid and scarlet fever were all declining as a result. In 1921, D. D. Sheehan, a past president of the Land and Labour Association (who had joined the British army during the war and lost two sons in the conflict), maintained that the labourers, as a result of these housing acts (particularly the landmark 1906 bill), 'were no longer a people to be kicked and cuffed and ordered about by the shoneens and squireens of the district; they became a very worthy class indeed, to be courted and flattered at election times and wheedled with all sorts of fair promises of what could be done for them'.[137]

'little evidence of conforming with modern ideas'

Following the outbreak of war in August 1914 and in the aftermath of the 1913 Lockout, a local government board inquiry heightened interest in the city's slums and their inhabitants, but ignored the fundamental connection between low wages and tenement housing. Recognising this correlation was a prerequisite to reform, alongside enforcing the existing bylaws (so many of which were disregarded) and educating tenement dwellers in matters of hygiene. The Housing Inquiry Report commented on the lack of social conscience on the part of certain members of Dublin Corporation, suggesting: 'want of a firm administration has created a number of owners with but little sense of their responsibilities as landlords ... it has helped much in the demoralisation of a number of the working classes and increased the number of inefficient workers in the city'. The report found that 60,000 people urgently required housing. A memorandum to the Housing Inquiry, at a time when it was felt that a move to housing people in the suburbs would be a better solution, suggested that 'The past schemes of the Corporation show little evidence of conforming with modern ideas. They have looked to a part and not to the whole of the city. The maximum number of houses has been put on each site and the resulting density of population perpetuates slum conditions.' But by focusing on suburbanisation, and a better class of housing, the Corporation was also in danger of neglecting those most in need. The response to the housing crisis, as revealed in this report, was a mixture of citizenship and goodwill but also deliberate segregation and manipulation. Charles Cameron, the Corporation's medical officer, in his reminiscences of 1913, assessed the status of a tailor in Dublin and the pathetic diet of dry bread and tea that his family lived on. He observed: 'it may appear strange that a tradesman could earn only 10 shillings per week; but such is often the case owing to irregular employment and the poor payment for making the cheaper kind of clothes'.[138] Ireland continued its dependence on Britain architecturally, the *Irish Builder* commenting in 1909 that Ireland was but a 'colourless imitation' of Britain in this regard and 'the probability is that she will continue to follow England as heretofore, at a respectful distance – the habit of imitativeness is too ingrained to be readily cast off'.[139]

In 1917, writing in *Studies*, a medical doctor suggested the two main challenges to improving living conditions were sanitation and the isolation and segregation of TB sufferers. It was revealing that he believed many would see as 'revolutionary' the suggestion that no person should be allowed to derive a profit from a house unless the house was in good sanitary condition and in good habitable repair.[140] What was the Church doing during this period to highlight such issues? The publication in 1914 of the English Jesuit Charles Plater's *The Priest and Social Action* certainly seemed to make some take notice, by highlighting the gulf between charity and social action. During this period Jesuits and the educated Catholic middle class did respond to an extent, producing articles and researching pamphlets, with, in particular, Lambert McKenna and Alfred O'Rahilly to the fore in invoking the writings of Frederick Ozanam, founder of the Saint Vincent de Paul Society.

Many were also politically inspired – to prevent socialism and communism – but ultimately it was not something the middle class as a whole responded to, while the working class remained obsessed with distinguishing between poor and poorer, or in Frank O'Connor's words the way in which going to a pawn shop in Cork for his mother 'meant an immediate descent in the social scale from the "hatties" to the "shawlies"; the poorest of the poor'. For O'Connor himself, nothing could persuade him that he belonged to a class to which boots and education came naturally.[141] Nor was poverty confined to Catholics; there were 92,328 Protestants living in Dublin city during this era, and they comprised 16 per cent of the white collar and manual workforce.[142] The historical geographer Jacinta Prunty suggested that the role of charitable and Church institutions in dealing with the Dublin poor was also marked by an at times virulent denominational struggle between Catholic and Protestant charities in the battle for the souls and bodies of the poorest slum dwellers.[143]

'a remarkable lack of concern for the living conditions of the patients'

There was a desire to make local authorities statutorily obliged to be more pro-active in caring for people suffering from mental illness, but there was no action taken in Ireland to correspond to the British Mental Deficiency Act of 1913. Little practical distinction was made between mentally ill and mentally handicapped. Treatment of lunacy was inadequate, divorced from medicine and from links with the care of the physically ill. At the beginning of the century there were over 20,000 insane in either asylums or workhouses, with thousands more housebound or 'vagrant idiots'. The problem was generally confined behind high walls, demonstrating the stigma of mental illness, with the priority to hide rather than to treat it. The number of patients admitted owing to 'insanity' between 1900 and 1914 increased from 21,169 to 25,180, a demand that local taxation was unable to meet. British Liberal governments paradoxically, in introducing social provisions which presaged (or started) the welfare state, appropriated funds available to support local authorities in Ireland and determined that any increased expenditure was to be met fully by local rates.

The idea of the native Irish being any more charitable in their treatment of this issue was undermined by the financial stringency shown in so many other regards at local level. Writing about asylum management committees at this level, Joseph Robins noted:

> Now that the native Irish were in charge of their own insane [after the introduction of local government], they were no more generous than the ascendancy governors who had for so long based their parsimonious management of the asylums on the just rights of property and on the belief that, in any event, institutions for pauper patients should reflect the grimness and discomforts of poverty. Reports of early twentieth century meetings of the new committees reveal a preoccupation with financial matters, opposition to wage increases, questioning of expenditure and a remarkable lack of concern for the living conditions of the patients themselves.[144]

The issue of workhouse and asylum separation, and the potential abolition of the structure of the Irish Poor Law machinery, was one thing in administrative terms; but it also encountered severe obstacles in the moral and ethical attitudes (not to mention class prejudices) of those who were called upon to consider such issues.

In 1915, a Cork cleric made a fascinating study of poverty in Cork city. He divided the 495 families earning under 21 shillings into two categories: those earning under 19 and those between 19 and 21. He found that 3 shillings was the difference between being acceptably and unacceptably poor. Those just over the 19 shilling threshold were noted for their determination to live respectably, sacrificing food for a better address, evident from the large shares of their income they spent on rent.[145] The continuing plight of the vulnerable child received limited attention during this period also. In an address to the Social and Statistical Inquiry Society, a contributor spoke of child life as a national asset, the pretext for which was the prominence given to the subject as a result of so many young men dying on the battlefields of Europe. The contributor shuddered at street-trading children and the loss to the nation of prospective wealth producers, pointing out that one baby in 11 born in Ireland in 1914 died within a year of birth. This was not the time for new legislation, it was suggested, but to implement what was already in existence.[146] (In July 1917 the *Weekly Irish Times* pointed out that the death of Irish babies exceeded the casualties of Irish soldiers during the war.) Though the strengthening of birth notification legislation in 1915 was a mark of progress, giving powers to Irish sanitary authorities to provide for the needs of mothers and children, experience was to show that giving powers to local authorities was one thing; getting them to use them quite another.

During the war, the national mortality rate was 90 per 1,000. In Dublin County borough, the infant mortality rate was 155.6 per 1,000, far higher than the 104 recorded for London and the 110 for Edinburgh; while both Dublin and Belfast had higher infant mortality rates in 1914 than in 1905. There was an increase in the number of voluntary organisations during the war attempting to address these difficulties, though a survey of welfare in the Dublin County borough in 1917 suggested much greater co-ordination was needed between the state and midwives, dispensary doctors and the insurance societies that administered maternity benefits. The Carnegie Trust suggested more ambitious legislation was needed in the area of welfare. The neglect of the Infectious Diseases (Notification) Act was also noted. In 1914, 4,784 children died between the ages of one and five from such diseases.[147]

'the children perish absolutely from want of food'

School attendance on paper seemed relatively satisfactory; according to the official annual report of the school attendance committee in 1914 there were 47,135 Dublin school children on the rolls, with an average attendance of 36,933 (or 78.2 per cent). But there were thousands more who were not on the school rolls and the nomadic tendencies of the poor in the city may have made it impossible to keep an accurate count.[148] A book called *The Blind Alley* (1915), by F. Ryan, suggested there were 8,000 children in Dublin city who were not on the rolls and that each year over 6,000 boys ended their school lives without having advanced beyond the second-lowest class of a national school.[149] School attendance laws were deemed insufficient without penal sanctions as severe as those in England, while greater facilities were needed for supplementary education that would help to save children from the fate that threatened the unskilled worker. By 1914 most large towns in Ireland had a technical school, but the Technical School Act of 1899 which legislated for them had made no specific provisions for accommodation, with the result that all classes of buildings were used, including disused jails, hospitals and chapels, and the situation was worse still in rural areas.

One of the reasons for there being a focus on poverty in Cork city was the activities of Alfred O'Rahilly, an academic from University College

Cork and champion of Catholic social activism. He had suggested that how the poor managed to die so slowly baffled both the economist and physiologist, and claimed attempts to ascertain poverty in Cork city tallied with the research of Booth in East London and Rowntree in York.[150] A particular concern during the war was the huge increases in the retail price of food, and T. A. Finlay had asserted categorically in the *Freeman's Journal* in May 1917 that:

> it is well demonstrated fact now that very large numbers of the children perish absolutely from want of food. That assertion has been called into question by some of the authorities. I have gone into the matter more fully and have got the actual facts, names and addresses. I maintain the assertion that children of the people are undoubtedly dying here merely for the want of nourishment.[151]

War had accentuated this process, an important reminder of the reality that lay behind the 'boom' in many districts. Drawing attention to a case where the local-authority medical officer in 1914 found a mother, father and seven adult siblings in one small room of 432 cubic feet, O'Rahilly asserted that in Cork there were 2,841 houses and tenements unfit for human habitation. O'Rahilly also gave a clue as to the issues frustrating social work, maintaining that 'could social workers find some means of publication their accounts would be even more shocking'. He made the important assertion, not shared by many of the middle class, that most of the poor were not in such conditions through any fault of their own. Announcing plans to establish a Catholic Social League, he took a swipe at middle-class snobbery, suggesting that the domestic ignorance of slum women was a social problem which could be solved by the 'leisured and educated women of Ireland – if they had the mind'.

'thousands all around us are perishing in the ocean of drink'

Most commentators on social conditions (and they were a small group) also drew attention to excessive drinking as a significant factor in contributing to the squalor of working-class communities. The founder of the Pioneer Association, Fr James Cullen, insisted in 1916 that 'the only thing wrong about Ireland is the excessive amount of drinking going on'. The war years had seen a rise in temperance activity, with protests by the National Total Abstinence Congress, and Cullen proudly announced that one fourteenth of the entire Catholic population had joined the Pioneer Association. But alongside this there was notable comment about increases in the number of females drinking (largely as a result of money being sent back from Irish soldiers in Europe). The column in the *Irish Catholic* newspaper devoted to the Pioneer Association remarked that 'In her case it is unspeakably worse. Somehow or other her degradation is more rapid and her demoralisation more complete.'[152] A whole raft of temperance literature was centred around the construction of a contradictory piety for women who were still seen as temperance's most ardent champions, but if they drank, as its most deplorable victims.

Proposals to initiate changes in the licensing laws generated debate about the merits of prohibition, compensation and local options. James Cullen continued, in the pages of the *Irish Catholic*, to make drink abuse a particular religious and spiritual concern. When the much-lauded *Titanic* sank, he wrote:

> They sank at night into their icy watery grave, and while we breathe a silent prayer of pity for their eternal repose, the awful thought is borne on us that not hundreds, but thousands all around us are perishing in the ocean of drink, and cry in vain for those who can, but will not, help them.[153]

Charity workers in the north of Ireland shared many of these concerns. The Women's Working Association, meeting in a Presbyterian church in Belfast in 1916, stressed the need for constant visitation after a woman had promised to abstain from alcohol. It was believed necessary for the women to stay sober 'so as to have her husband's meals ready when he comes home otherwise there is a row and the woman drinks more than ever'. It was also noted that 'the money that the soldiers' wives are getting is often largely spent on drink' but that 'better class women were harder to get at than the working-class people'.[154]

'defiance of any power strutting out to stand in the way of their march'

Temperance was also something which the legendary trade unionist James Larkin saw as one means towards improving the lot of the Irish labouring classes during this period. But sobriety on its own paled into insignificance when the magnitude of the overall labour question crystallised, culminating in the Dublin Lockout of 1913. The immediate issue in dispute was a requirement that workers should sign a document renouncing membership of the Irish Transport and General Workers' Union. The dispute was the culmination of a new generation of union leaders encouraging a more militant stance, replacing the more conservative craft officials on the Dublin Trades Council, following the craters strike of 1908. The trade unionists were pitted against the 404 employers of the Dublin Federation of Employers, with William Martin Murphy determined, it seemed, to seek conflict rather than encourage the development of a joint conciliation board. Ireland during this era was giving birth to various armies with banners and it seemed an appropriate time for trade unionists to make their pitch and declare their wars.

For his champions, Larkin brought orange and green together as never before; for his detractors he was a dangerous megalomaniac, oblivious to the cost of his actions. In his memoirs, Seán O'Casey recalled watching Larkin the orator:

> Aha, here now was the unfolding of the final word from the evolving words of the ages, the word of the modern, the word en masse and a mighty cheer gave it welcome. From a window in the building, leaning well forth, he talked to the workers, spoke as only Jim Larkin could speak, not for an assignation with peace, dark obedience or placid resignation, but trumpet-tongued of resistance to wrong, discontent with leering poverty and defiance of any power strutting out to stand in the way of their march onward.[155]

Historians have been relatively kind in their assessment of Larkin. Padraig Yeates, author of the definitive history of the Lockout, suggested: 'it was because his dedication to the workers' cause was so total, his love of Dublin's downtrodden class so obvious, his ability to convey ideas so magical that he was received with such rapt attention'.[156] But the role of the Dublin Trades Council in conducting the strike has been overshadowed by the attention given to Larkin. In January 1911 the Council passed a motion calling for the establishment of a labour representative committee, with an independent labour policy. This reflected a desire to forward the interests of the workers, an initiative that led to the formation of the Dublin Labour Party that put forward candidates for municipal elections for the next few years, with the support of the *Irish Worker* newspaper. They were not particularly successful – only five Labour councillors were elected in 1912 – and in the 1914 municipal elections, during the fifth month of the Lockout, 13 seats were contested, but only two won (though it should be noted that in 1911, in the UK as a whole, only approximately 60 per cent of the adult male population could vote at parliamentary elections, and in Dublin parliamentary divisions the figure was even smaller because of problems with the voter-registration process).[157]

In many ways Larkin has remained divisive, and there have been many labels attached to him: trade union organiser, flamboyant agitator, internationalist, man of action who also found himself meeting German intelligence agents in the US during the First World War (he refused to take their money) and was left sleeping rough in Mexico; a man intent, it seemed, on establishing risky contacts.[158] Many have emphasised his action, seeing it as more important than his ideology; others have maintained that while he may have been uninterested in deep Marxist debate, he was always fundamentally socialist.

Another consistent portrayal is that of a man who never counted costs, a heroic character with an indomitable spirit that no movement could crush, but whose strong ego, so effective when mobilised for the labour movement, could be destructive when used to attack his colleagues (and there were many such attacks). What has also been revealed was his instinctive commitment to the working class, over and above syndicalism, and his distrust of governmental and legislative experiments. Larkin's purpose during this period was to oversee the transition from craft-based trade unions to a new and general trade unionism. For some, this was not a case of him being a doctrinaire syndicalist in the classic European sense, but of being part of the English school of socialism where he had first put his beliefs into practice. But as Yeates points out, his syndicalist vision of enlisting secondary support for unions in Britain lacked the infrastructure of organisation.[159]

James Connolly was another towering labour figure from this era, the man who died an Irish republican in 1916 but had lived most of his life as an internationalist socialist. As already seen, he left behind a mass of writing (his ability to write about Irish history was quite exceptional), though teasing out a theory of permanent revolution from his writings has proved difficult. His martyrdom in 1916 may have obscured the significance of much of his political life (and made it convenient for future republicans to place a false unity on his life).[160] The impact he made on the socialist movement in Ireland, Britain and the United States was profound, though there is evidence, even in his earlier writings, of his attempt to deal with the tension between socialism and the constitutional or national question.

Ireland for Connolly was urban Ireland, and he had a clear faith in the value of industrialisation and the potential leading political role of the industrial working class. His essentially economistic understanding of socialism may have left many cold, but his assertion that you could not teach starving men Gaelic was also a reaction to the prevailing middle-class intellectualism that sometimes glossed over the living conditions of the masses of the population.[161]

Significantly, James Larkin's apprenticeship had been in Liverpool with the National Union of Dock Labourers, in the company of noted English trade unionists such as Tom Mann, Ben Tillet, James Sexton and Harry Gosling. Differences of approach, the bane of Larkin's industrial life, were evident from the beginning, particularly divisions between Larkin and James Sexton, who stood more for moral persuasion, and as a pioneer of the British labour movement sought evolutionary change and respect for the law rather than the revolution articulated by Larkin.[162] The Belfast Dockers and Traders strike of 1907, Larkin's next project, took place in the aftermath of the weakening of the labour movement there by the undermining of the unionist labour activist T. H. Sloan by the Ulster Unionist Council. Given the acute sectarian divisions within the Belfast shipyards (where huge production meant there were 25,000 employees in 1914), the challenge for Larkin's vision of the Irish labour movement was perhaps to blur divisions between Catholic employees and the specific identity of Protestant working-class unionists.

In view of the importance of production in the city, it was doubtful Belfast labour would abandon completely capitalism or the relationship with the local unionist political leadership. The dispute did, however, highlight the labour conditions of the unorganised workers and the differences within the working classes which were, it seemed, ignored by the existing leadership. Once again, Larkin was joined by a more moderate figurehead, this time Robert Morley of the Workers' Union. The violent nature of the Belfast dispute, which culminated in riots and deaths, undoubtedly weakened Larkin in his attempt to resist the pressure from Sexton's ITGWU for a settlement.[163]

If Larkin has been stereotyped into a caricature, much the same could be said about William Martin Murphy, the labour hate figure in Dublin in 1913. An image of him as a devouring capitalist hawk was relentlessly portrayed in Larkin's *Irish Worker* throughout 1913–14. This does have a touch of irony given that the self-made entrepreneur was seen by some employees as relatively liberal; though it is doubtful that he was unduly concerned at the caricature, given his unflappability and his ownership of the *Irish Independent*, which gave him a personal propaganda weapon.[164]

'blind Samsons pulling down the pillars of the social order'?

Even if a certain ambivalence in Murphy's outlook is allowed for, it cannot be denied that he could also be ruthless and antagonistic in his attitude towards trade unions, and for propaganda reasons labour activists could make the most of this, deriding the 'Irish Tsar of capitalism'. But the assertion of Markievicz after the infamous baton charge in O'Connell Street on 31 August 1913, when police attacked workers listening to Larkin speaking – that such scenes had only been rivalled in history by the Russian Bloody Sunday of 1905 – was delightful exaggeration. In any case Murphy was triumphalist about the defeat of the workers in 1913. The labour movement was not without its middle-class defenders, some of whose support went from tepid to hot, depending on the length and intensity of the dispute, and who were at pains to emphasise that this was labour as distinct from political agitation. Initially it seemed George Russell, for example, attempted to straddle a middle ground, suggesting that the tendency of the labour movement to 'substitute a rage for a policy' was facilitated by the authorities in Dublin, who allowed police brutality to go unchecked. But by September and October of 1913 Russell, in his journal the *Irish Homestead*, was asserting that labour discontent was 'nothing else than a passionate discontent with present conditions of wages, housing and unemployment ... labour is as guiltless of being socialist or syndicalist as Mr Murphy himself'.[165] In a letter to the *Irish Times*, he accused capitalists in Dublin of being arrogantly ignorant of the rights conceded to workers in the modern world:

> The men whose manhood you have broken will loathe you and will always be brooding and scheming to strike a fresh blow. The children will be taught to curse you. The infant being moulded in the womb will have breathed into its starved body the vitality of hate. It is not they – it is you – who are blind Samsons pulling down the pillars of the social order.[166]

Ultimately, however, it was Larkin's relationship with the British labour movement that held the key to the success or failure of the strike, and in December 1913, at a TUC Special Congress, this support was withdrawn, again not helped by the personality clashes between Larkin and some of the English trade union leaders. They had become increasingly unanimous in their condemnation of Larkin's style, and indeed his appeals to the rank and file over their heads. As trade unionists they were more amenable to constitutional challenges, a result of the English parliamentary tradition. Over £150,000 had been raised from various relief funds and it was badly needed. The lockout lasted over six months, involved 20,000 trade unionists and 1.7 million working days were lost.

A proposal by the English suffragist and social worker Dora Montefiore to get English families to provide holidays for the children of the strikers also caused uproar in sectarian-conscious Dublin. Larkin sharply asserted that it was a poor religion that could not stand a fortnight's holiday, seemingly indicating a 'casualness towards the intensity of religious feeling with respect to proselytism'. The Archbishop of Dublin, William Walsh, according to his biographer 'could no longer stand aside'. In a letter printed in all the main newspapers, he reminded Dublin's Catholic mothers that, as Catholics, they could be:

> no longer held worthy of the name of Catholic mothers if they so far forget that duty as to send away their children to be cared for in a strange land, without security of any kind that those to whom the poor children are to be handed over are Catholics, or, indeed, are persons of any faith at all.[167]

'I didn't take my eye away from people at any stage'

The Jesuit writer Lambert McKenna published a pamphlet dealing with the relationship between the Catholic Church and labour in 1913, and along with others insisted that the Church had its own idea that was neither liberalism nor socialism. It was suggested in the *Irish Monthly* in 1914 that the urgency of the social problem had not been brought home because all energy had been thrown into political and agrarian struggles, drowning the distant roar of the battle between capital and labour in evidence in the United States and England and on the Continent. The riddle McKenna could not seem to answer was that while the highest tribute could be paid to the 'magnificent' charity of Ireland, 'nowhere in Europe is social charity as distinguished from alms-giving charity less known or practised than in Ireland'.[168]

The most recent historian of the Lockout, Padraig Yeates, has suggested that:

> The myth has survived in large part because it has suited everyone. It gave the moral victory to the workers, while their material defeat underlined the comforting contention of the employers and other defenders of conservative ideologies that Larkinism, and by extension socialism, made for good rhetoric but was impractical. For the most part the Lockout was a far shabbier, bloodier and more mundane affair than the myth allows. Above all, it was an unnecessary dispute and probably would not have occurred but for the peculiarly perverse personalities of Larkin and the employers' leader William Martin Murphy. Few of the principals emerge well from this awful episode in Dublin's history. It was left to what Tom Kettle referred to as the 'second class people on both sides' to pick up the pieces. Of course, individual Dubliners of all classes and creeds, acting on the impulses of common humanity, did what they could to mitigate the worst aspects of the tragedy. So did thousands of workers in Britain who contributed almost £10,000 (the equivalent of £10 million today) to help their locked-out brethren. Nevertheless the Lockout raised passions that were by turn sectarian and nationalist. The help from Britain was often resented and, perversely, helped strengthen separatist tendencies within the Irish trade union movement.

Police attacks, most memorably in O'Connell Street, but also on Dublin Corporation buildings, were also conducive to the establishment of Connolly's Citizens' Army for the protection of Dublin's workers.[169]

But the humanity and personal suffering behind the dispute were something that lingered in the collective memory of working-class Dublin. The articulation of their woes, and indeed their dignity, was powerfully aired for the rest of the century, most notably in James Plunkett's novel *Strumpet City*, published in 1969 and later transferred to screen. A modest socialist born in 1920 in Irishtown, near the south inner city, Plunkett was reared in a location that symbolised a Dublin of extremes, Irishtown being a poor working-class area that bordered the opulent village of Sandymount and the extreme poverty of Ringsend. Like many socialists of his era

Plunkett revered Larkin, but it was his depiction of ordinary Dubliners of the period before the war that was the book's strongest feature. Unlike Joyce's Dublin of 'paralysis', Plunkett's characters had a vibrancy that moved them energetically around the dilapidated capital city. Despite the rags and the poverty, it was the dignity of the burdened that Plunkett excelled in portraying, combining artistic endeavour with a strong social conscience. But it was not a sentimental portrayal. Although Plunkett may have been lamenting the loss of an era of dignity, as a committed socialist he was also rejecting what he regarded as the contemporary tendency to accept poverty as divinely predestined. When asked to explain the success of the book, he suggested it was because 'I didn't take my eye away from people at any stage'.[170]

'increasing the labourer's sense of security'?

Did the tumultuous events of Dublin in 1913 have a knock-on effect outside the capital city? Trade unionism among farm labourers remained insignificant for the first two years of the First World War, an event that transformed the economic framework underpinning the mechanics of the labour market. Chronic pre-war unemployment was replaced by a demand for labour, which brought more security to the labourer (as had the building of houses) and a growing demand for food stuffs. Military recruitment had also disrupted the progress of unions catering for the unskilled: in the summer of 1915, 2,700 former Irish Transport and General Workers' Union members enrolled in the British army, at a time when contemporary membership was fewer than 5,000.[171]

On the eve of war, Irish labour was in a sorry state (it was suggested that the ITGWU was saved from bankruptcy in 1914 only by the members gambling at bingo); the syndicalist campaign had caused little disturbance outside the main cities, and the Irish Congress of Trade Unions met only occasionally and seemed to have little sense of coherence or purpose. Heavy unemployment in the towns affected between 6 and 9 per cent of the workforce in areas like shipbuilding, engineering and building, rates that were double those of the UK.[172]

The annual loss of workdays between 1914 and 1918 was less than one third of the annual losses of 1910–13, though some have maintained that the potency of class rhetoric did spread beyond towns, especially to the tillage and dairy farms of southern and eastern Ireland. But it was not until towards the end of the war that this would become more bellicose and organised in the wake of rampant inflation. In Connaught, for example, this involved relatively well-established trades councils in Sligo and Galway combining labourers, artisans, shop workers and public servants. Meanwhile in Kerry, the urban labour movement seemed capable of expansion in 1915 and 1916 because of its strong alliances with local Volunteers, an indication of a certain variation in the regional experiences of labour.[173]

The historian of rural labour Dan Bradley suggested that:

Trade unionism became successful among farm labourers in the years after 1917 because the Great War transformed the economic parameters governing the operation of the labour market. Shortage of manpower replaced chronic pre-war unemployment; thereby increasing the labourer's sense of security, while the growing demand for foodstuffs enhanced his position when demanding an improvement in conditions. Trade union growth remained insignificant for the first two years of the war for numerous reasons. Initial awe at the momentous events occurring in Europe, along with pleas for unity, had some effect. Separation allowances and regular wages were a novelty for a time for many working-class families. Then, too, it took time for the labourers to become conscious of how circumstances had altered in their favour and that agriculture was becoming increasingly prosperous.[174]

While Irish incomes averaged only 40 per cent of the British level in 1840, this proportion had risen to 60 per cent by 1913, surpassing the incomes of Finland, Italy and Portugal, and for a country commonly thought of as poor and undeveloped, its relative standing was surprisingly high. By 1918 the value of agricultural produce was nearly double what it had been in 1913, though this must be placed in the context of price and wage inflation. This had the potential to foster a fair degree of urban discontent, given that Ireland could not expect the industrial war expansion in employment that was a feature of Belfast and British cities. Some Dublin companies received contracts for clothing and engineering goods, and food exporters also received some valuable contracts. Between 1916 and 1918 there was a rise in the acreage under tillage of 1.7 million acres owing to an increase in the price for tillage products.[175]

'The cause of humanity'

The labour disputes impacted on a number of different levels, and given that 20,000 families were directly affected in Dublin in 1913, it was unsurprising that some middle-class campaigners reacted to contemporary events. Some notable women had begun to do this, whether as suffragists, pacifists, trade unionists or all three. For someone like Louie Bennett, for example, of the Irish Women's Workers' Union, the Lockout of 1913 was not only an event that dramatically sharpened the political consciousness, but also suggested that Home Rule, if achieved, would have little impact on the impoverished economic conditions of women workers. The women's movement, Bennett asserted, was not anti-nationalist but was greater than the cause of a nation because it was 'the cause of humanity'.[176]

Bennett's declaration is a reminder that many of the middle-class women who became politicised during this era had much broader frameworks of social and political interpretation than their male counterparts. Historians began to give them due recognition in the 1980s and 1990s following a long period of neglect. In 1978, in a pioneering collection of essays, the principal instigator of the Irish women's history movement, Margaret MacCurtain, suggested women were finding it difficult to learn about their historical identity or their historical role in the country through a lack of information or the skills of evaluation at their disposal.[177] This was to change dramatically in the next twenty years, but it still remained a specialist study, divorced from the narratives of the established texts. Joe Lee defended the absence of women in his account of *Ireland 1912–85* on the grounds that to suggest women had undue influence would be to impose a modern politically correct contention on a past situation where it did not exist. The abundant documentary evidence does not support his contention. In a provocative pamphlet, *The Missing Sex*, published in 1991, Margaret Ward posed the following question:

> Why has the Irish suffrage movement suffered such neglect by historians? Hanna Sheehy Skeffington calculated that in proportional terms it was as large as its British counterpart. It was certainly not concentrated in Dublin ... Neither is there any difficulty with source material, as the *Irish Citizen* ran between 1912 and 1920, and the Irish movement was often in the pages of British suffrage journals. It was also composed of educated women who wrote copiously.[178]

Almost 700,000 Irish women emigrated from Ireland between 1885 and 1920, 82,000 more than males; while between 1906 and 1914 only one tenth of those leaving were married.[179] For those not in the home, secure employment was scarce. Larkin had noted that poverty had made prostitution a fixture of city life, particularly on one side of O'Connell Street, owing to the fact that 'girl wage slaves' were driven to it; indeed, venereal disease became such an issue in the city that a special hospital for its treatment was built.[180]

For those intent on increasing the economic, political and social rights of women there was an abundance of obstacles, but it would be inaccurate to view politicised women as a homogeneous mass, as their politics frequently differed according to class. A Dublin Women's Suffrage Association formed in 1896 had fallen into genteel decline (only 43 members in 1908), and it was not until the formation of the Irish Women's Franchise League in 1908 by Hanna Sheehy Skeffington and Margaret Cousins that a more vigorous approach was contemplated. Some members were no doubt emboldened by their being the first generation to achieve third-level education. In 1912 Louie Bennett inaugurated the Irish Women's Suffrage Federation, the same year that saw the launch of the suffrage newspaper the *Irish Citizen* under the editorship of Francis Skeffington and James Cousins.

The Irish Women's Franchise League attracted those from the left and right of the political spectrum, across sectarian boundaries, which was to be both a help and a hindrance in the long term as they became dwarfed by the giants of unionism and nationalism. The organisation in no sense saw itself as the mere branch of an English movement, having its own constitution, newspaper and vision. Initially placing the suffrage claim above nationalism did little to endear them to the institutions of Irish nationalism. Some Irish politicians, like their English counterparts, saw suffrage as the beginnings of the end of civilisation as they understood it. It was the insistence on Home Rule that caused Irish suffragists difficulties, because for many it was imperative that female suffrage be included in a Home Rule bill. How to achieve this sparked differences of opinion, not just over militant tactics, but party affiliations and even eligibility for suffrage. Conflicting opinions were perhaps a measure of the success of mobilising such a strong, diverse body of women, who faced determined Church opposition for their rejection of the prevailing ethos of womanhood. The irony of the Irish party demanding Home Rule but not wishing to enfranchise women incensed many.

Hanna Sheehy Skeffington has enthused, sometimes dazzled, her biographers, and it is difficult to deny her iconic status in the history of Irish feminist political involvement. Her background was representative of many of those who came to dominate the Irish Suffrage Movement: solidly Catholic, nationalist, upper-middle class. Daughter of a Home Rule MP, she attended a French finishing school and was one of the first female graduates of University College Dublin. Her later conversion to republicanism never watered down her feminism, while her insistence that male politicians could no more be trusted with women's rights than the leprechaun with the crock of gold (the minute you take your eye off him he will slip away with it) was strikingly accurate. She and her radical husband Francis Skeffington (murdered as an innocent, pacifist bystander during the 1916 Rising by a British army captain) seemed, in pre-independent Ireland, to be sixty years ahead of their time: declaring agnosticism, refusing to baptise their child, taking each other's surnames and insisting on the wife's economic and political autonomy within marriage.[181]

'educated, articulate rowdyism'

But Sheehy Skeffington was also important as a symbol of the class-based nature of politics in early twentieth-century Ireland. Higher education was certainly opening the door to feminism and suffragism, but it also intellectually and socially underlined the barriers that existed between educated middle-class women and the majority of their fellow countrywomen. Their speech was overly class-conscious, despite the harsh experiences undergone by a minority in prison. Whether they liked it or not, they were considered ladies. And most of them did like it. Hanna's reflections on her time in prison reflected the aspirations and nobility of the suffrage movement as well as its fears, prejudices and inconsistencies.

As a stream of upper-class notables came to visit her, she remembered that 'educated, articulate rowdyism (as they would call it) from the comfortable classes, from respectfully dressed women, stupefied them'.[182] As with the Home Rule party, there was a tendency for Sheehy Skeffington to rally around a single issue with little examination of long-term aims. The suffragettes received little assistance from those who championed liberation in wider fields (James Larkin, unlike James Connolly, was notably mute), a reflection of a general hostility within the trade union movement, though some paid lip service. Louie Bennett suggested that the labour class had realised, as no other class had, the need for the economic and political freedom of women. This was the gradual realisation, as Sheehy Skeffington remarked, that it was 'votes for women and not just ladies' that they were pursuing. During the 1913 Lockout in which the suffragists were actively involved, the middle-class Louie Bennett recalled that she 'crept like a culprit into Liberty Hall to see Madame Markievicz in a big overall with sleeves rolled up, presiding over a cauldron of stew, surrounded by a crowd of gaunt women and children carrying bowls and cans'.[183] And yet it was also the trade unions that shabbily treated Delia Larkin, sister of James, because of her militancy, her independence, but above all her class.[184] Skeffington was more at ease with the comfortable class of ladies, and she had previously highlighted her prejudices by noting that consorting with servants was demoralising to one's social mood.[185] Despite public assertions that the cause broke down all social barriers, working-class participation remained minimal; working-class women had neither the education nor the leisure time.

But these women succeeded in keeping the issue in the public domain with an influence out of proportion to their numbers, as well as throwing down the gauntlet to the establishment in its attitude to female prisoners. Significantly, it was women who invented what became an essential moral and propaganda tool in the hands of future Irish republicans: the hunger strike. Skeffington noted that:

> at first Sinn Féin and its allies regarded the hunger-strike as a womanish thing … some held that political prisoners should take their medicine without whining and all that. Others regarded it as suicide. But the public at least was not apathetic and a feeling began to be voiced that there was something unreasonable in refusing women the vote.[186]

Hunger strike episodes and the question of political status meant a battle of wits, not just with prison governors and doctors but also with the authorities in Dublin Castle. Hanna in many ways also personified the difficulties imposed on many women by the conflicting claims of feminism and nationalism, exacerbated by the formation of Cumann na mBan, the female wing of the Irish Volunteers, in 1914. Groups like the Ancient Order of Hibernians, who were viciously anti-suffragist, were predictable in their reaction, accusing feminists of being pro-British and undermining independence.

The language used in the 1916 Proclamation suggested there were those who were amenable to the idea of female equality, but as nationalism became more practically politically important, the IWFL was to experience strained relations with male and female nationalists. For those like Hanna after the death of her husband, and Mary MacSwiney, following the death by hunger strike of her brother, British militarism became as much a barrier to feminist liberation as any domestic opposition. As early as 1914, MacSwiney had come to the conclusion that self-government was more important than suffragism: 'The fact that many Irish suffragists play the political ostrich and refuse to recognise the essential difference between this and English party questions, does not minimize that difference, it simply blinds their political intelligence and injures the cause they wish to promote.'[187]

Embracing Sinn Féin perhaps represented a move to mainstream politics, but it should not overshadow the precocious success of the IWFL in raising awareness about the issue of suffragism and in ensuring the rhetoric used in fighting for an Irish republic was the rhetoric of political equality.

The United Irishwomen, formed in 1910 to promote an improved standard of living for rural women, continued to meet during these years, and had 21 branches by the summer of 1912. Rather than focus on issues of political equality, as their minute books illustrate they were active in improving the health of the rural population, creating and advancing women's agricultural pursuits, initiating lectures and demonstrations in connection with women's work, and developing women's societies to work on co-operative lines. In 1913, their preoccupation with the welfare of young women was revealed in a resolution that emphasised the urgency of preventing the exploitation of 'imbecile' girls by unscrupulous men 'who were increasing the population of Ireland with children predestined to be idiots, lunatics or criminals, or girls who at best could not be useful citizens'.[188] The tone of many of their earlier meetings was professional and business-like, and sometimes strident; in 1914 they were prepared to take legal action against a member who refused to produce a receipt for a £30 lodgement she had made for the society. But they refused to get involved in the suffrage issue, turning down an invitation to speak on a suffrage platform in 1913 on the grounds that 'we must keep clear of anything controversial'; this was in keeping with their official status as a 'non-sectarian, non-political' organisation.[189]

'all tending towards a common objective'?
Patrick Pearse had predicted in November 1913 in *An Claidheamh Soluis* (the newspaper of the Gaelic League) that:

> there will be in the Ireland of the next few years a multitudinous activity of freedom clubs, young republican parties, labour organisations, socialist groups and what not. Good men and bad men, many of them seemingly contradictory, some mutually destructive, yet all tending towards a common objective ... the Irish revolution.[190]

The years 1917 and 1918 were dominated by efforts to ensure that the capacity for mutual destruction by all these groups would be contained, and to build a single movement around which a majority could rally. Despite all the activity from 1914 to 1916, there was, as yet, no unified 'Sinn Féin' movement, regardless of the repeated use of the phrase by those hostile to Irish republicans. Many of those labelled 'Sinn Féin' were dual monarchists and socialists and unsure of how to formulate their opposition to the existing state of affairs.

Throughout 1917, it was up to those sympathetic to the 'Sinn Féin' sentiment to rally the disparate members in order to defeat the Irish Parliamentary Party. Of huge help to Sinn Féin had been the release of the remaining 1916 prisoners in June, as part of Lloyd George's efforts to placate American opinion, coinciding with an Irish Convention which was doomed to failure from the beginning, since this attempt to find a solution to the Home Rule question was boycotted by republicans. It was a tremendously exciting time for many young political activists, even though many of them could not yet vote. In January 1917, Laurence Ginnell, shortly to join Sinn Féin, reassured Count Plunkett, the successful candidate in the North Roscommon by-election of that year, and father of Joseph Plunkett, who was executed after the 1916 Rising, that 'we have all the young, male and female'. It was significant that the Irish Volunteers were now applying their military discipline to canvassing, and roundly abusing the Irish Parliamentary Party while attempting to maximise sympathy for the 1916 rebels. Women were particularly important in this regard, spreading the new doctrine while many of their male colleagues were interned.

Kathleen Clarke had been left £3,000 by the Military Council of the IRB for relief aid in the aftermath of the Rising, and women were central to the collection and distribution of relief funds. They were also active in attempting to destroy hostile newspapers.[191]

It was by no means plain sailing, given the disagreements over the policy of abstention from the Westminster parliament and the contrary and egotistical behaviour of Count Plunkett. Michael Laffan has pointed out that:

> all parties shared the ideal of creating a united and widely based party which would coincide with the unorganised 'Sinn Féin' or separatist movement, and all were anxious to end the multiplicity of factions which had characterised separatism before the Easter Rising. Yet the next few months were marked by a series of bitter quarrels which at times made the achievement of such unity seem quite impossible.[192]

'the fad or the craze of 1917'

Ultimately, what was more important than their divisions was their shared aim of supplanting the Irish Parliamentary Party. Nonetheless, an attempt to reach agreement at a conference in April 1917 caused some acrimony amidst the competing voices. A compromise suggested was that each faction would preserve its distinct identity but co-operate with an organising committee. Feuding between radicals and moderates continued, but they now had new impetus, and by May it was fair to assert, in the words of Laffan, that 'Sinn Féin was the fad or the craze of 1917'. In subsequent by-elections both moderates and radicals co-operated, in the midst of much violence and intimidation by both Sinn Féin and the Irish Parliamentary Party. A victory in South Longford in May 1917 followed, and there were further successes in East Clare and Kilkenny, for two future Irish prime ministers, Eamon de Valera and William Cosgrave.[193]

In June 1917, a police inspector in West Cork had suggested that 'This Sinn Féinism is of a very undefined sort. It is anti-British, anti-Recruiting and above all anti-Redmondite. It is a voting, a shouting, a marching Sinn Féinism, but it is not a fighting one.'[194] This was a misjudgement. Marie Coleman has noted that in East Clare in 1917, following de Valera's victory, a banner declared: 'Irish party wounded in North Roscommon, killed in South Longford and buried in East Clare. RIP.' Indeed, the emergence of Longford as an IRA stronghold had much to do with seeds sowed during and directly after the 1917 by-election in Longford.[195] The mix of views within Sinn Féin did not seem overly problematic at this juncture. As Laffan points out, on de Valera's way to winning the East Clare by-election of 1918:

> the difference was one of degree rather than one of kind, and the lines between the groups were not clear cut. De Valera and Griffith provided the two poles, the one frequently stressing his republicanism and the other never going into details about systems of government, while the rest of the Sinn Féin leaders came somewhere between them.[196]

These elections were crucial in allowing a broad consensus to emerge. Wisely, suggests Laffan, their policies at the Sinn Féin October convention were left deliberately vague in order to avoid contentious issues until their hold over public opinion had been confirmed. At the convention, de Valera was elected President and promised the Irish people could decide after independence which form of government they wanted. It heralded a new unity, and by the end of 1917 the Volunteers and Sinn Féin seemed unassailable.

In the event, however, there were setbacks. Three by-election defeats followed in 1918, in South Armagh, Waterford and East Tyrone, suggesting in particular that Sinn Féin would have no clean sweep of the North. These developments also prompted them to train election workers. Given these reverses, the conscription crisis could not have come at a better time for Sinn Féin: the British government introduced the Military Service Bill in April 1918, extending conscription, which had existed in Britain since January 1916, to Ireland as well.

'a piece of rank raving madness'?

The conscription crisis was also significant, according to Joost Augusteijn, in that 'it changed the challenge to the authorities from open defiance of large groups of volunteers led by men who often invited arrest, to secret preparation for military conflict by a small group of dedicated volunteers'.[197] In June 1918, a number of women's organisations, including Cumann na mBan and the IWFL, pledged that their members would not take up posts vacated by conscripted males. They later declared that coercion had 'rendered the carrying out of suffrage activities impossible'. In the view of G. K. Chesterton, the decision to impose conscription in Ireland was 'a piece of rank raving madness', manufacturing German sympathisers 'steadily and systematically as if from a factory'. It was also a decision he believed would alter the mood of America.[198]

The arrival of the Catholic Church to the platform of opposition to conscription was particularly significant given their relative muteness prior to this, and the differences of opinion that existed within the Hierarchy concerning political involvement and the expression of political views. Efforts by the British Foreign Office to have the Pope restrain the Irish bishops failed. Interestingly, there was no significant debate about what the bishops' statement of opposition, which included the contention that opposition to conscription could take any form that was 'consonant with the laws of God', actually meant. They saw their influence as cementing opposition and preventing chaos. MacRory, the Bishop of Down and Connor, remarked that the opposition of the Hierarchy was based on the principle that a nation had to have a right to say when and why it would shed blood, 'and also on the ground that no power has any moral right to coerce young Irishmen to fight in the alleged interests of freedom until they have been allowed to enjoy freedom for themselves'.[199] Countless statements taken by the Bureau of Military History reflect the anger that the conscription threat generated, with many getting involved with the Volunteers precisely because of it. Eugene Bratton, a member of the Royal Irish Constabulary, claimed that members of the force 'resented [the proposed conscription] to a man'.[200] There was nothing exaggerated about these fears; they were clearly deeply felt, and contemporaries were struck by the level of intensity of what W. B. Yeats called 'the old historical passion'. Yeats was adamant about the damage conscription would do. He was persuaded to write a long, powerful letter to a senior Liberal politician, Lord Haldane:

> I have no part in politics and no liking for politics, but there are moments when one cannot keep out of them. I have met nobody in close contact with the people who believes that conscription can be imposed without the killing of men, and perhaps of women. Lady Gregory, who knows the country as few know it … is convinced that the women and children will stand in front of their men and receive the bullets. I do not say that this will happen, but I do say that there is in this country an extravagance of emotion which few Englishmen, accustomed to more objective habits of thought, can understand … I

find in people here in Dublin a sense of strain and expectancy which makes even strangers speak something of their mind. I was ordering some coal yesterday, and I said: 'I shall be in such and such a house for the next four months.' The man at the counter, a stranger to me, muttered: 'Who, in Ireland, can say where he will be in four months?' ... it seems to me a strangely wanton thing that England, for the sake of fifty thousand Irish soldiers, is prepared to hollow another trench between the countries and fill it with blood. If that is done England will only suffer in reputation, but Ireland will suffer in her character, and all the work of my life-time and that of my fellow-workers, all our effort to clarify and sweeten the popular mind, will be destroyed and Ireland, for another hundred years, will live in the sterility of her bitterness.[201]

In May 1918 the government, having decided to postpone the implementation of conscription in Ireland, decided instead to focus on Sinn Féin and arrested 73 prominent members, on the pretext that a German agent had been arrested off the coast of County Clare, and that there was a necessity to stamp out 'Pro-German intrigues' in Ireland. This also got rid of many of the moderates for some time (though Griffith in prison was elected in an East Cavan by-election), strengthening the hands of people like Harry Boland and Michael Collins, who had evaded arrest.[202] While, officially, conscription was postponed, in reality it had been abandoned.

'our unbroken tradition of nationhood'

The general election of 24–8 December 1918 witnessed Sinn Féin winning 73 of Ireland's 105 seats (25 of the Sinn Féin victories were in uncontested constituencies). Sinn Féin's manifesto for the election had stressed the unbroken history of Irish resistance to British rule, a very consistent and important message of this period (as it had been during the conscription crisis): 'It is based on our unbroken tradition of nationhood, on a unity in a national name which has never been challenged, on our possession of a distinctive national culture and social order, on the moral courage and dignity of our people in the face of alien aggression.'[203]

The election was important not just in terms of providing a political mandate for the Sinn Féin party, but also because about 75 per cent of Irish adults now had the vote, compared with 25 per cent previously. The Representation of the People Act extended the vote to men of 21 and women over 30 (those that had the requisite property qualifications). There was thus a three-fold increase in those able to vote in Ireland, from 698,000 to 1,931,000.[204] Sinn Féin received 47.5 per cent of the votes cast and unionists later used this figure to discredit the claim that on the basis of the 1918 result the creation of the Northern Ireland state was 'undemocratic' given that, nationally, Sinn Féin had not polled more than 50 per cent of the vote.[205] In any case, the mandate Sinn Féin received in 1918, undoubtedly influenced by their fight against conscription, was not a mandate for war, but for peace, many supporters having little interest in a republic or the constitutional status of Ireland. Sinn Féin also decided to run two female candidates, and thereby showed itself to be 'more radical than any other party in Britain or Ireland'. Their manifesto had also committed the party to using 'any and every means available to render impotent the power of England to hold Ireland in subjection by military force or otherwise'.[206]

A measure of the Parliamentary Party's weakness and complete divorce from the new culture of political activism was reflected in the view of their South Donegal MP, who had represented the constituency since 1887: 'I have too long been a member for this constituency to be able consistently with sincerity or self-respect to solicit as a favour votes to secure my election to parliament.'[207]

A radical Labour Party manifesto, promising to adopt the principles of the Russian Revolution, became redundant as a result of divisions in their own ranks about whether to contest the election. They eventually decided against, removing one more difficulty for Sinn Féin. Following intervention from the Catholic Church in Ulster, an equal division of seats to be contested by both the IPP and Sinn Féin was accepted, with four constituencies given to each, though there was still a reluctance to abandon seats candidates believed they could win. In the election 'perhaps the most revealing proof of the Parliamentary Party's demoralisation was its abandonment of 25 safe nationalist seats which it had held or challenged at the last election'. The Unionists also increased their representation by eight, now holding 23 of Ulster's seats.

Those elected members of Sinn Féin who were free to do so established Dáil Éireann (Irish parliament) on 21 January 1919 and declared independence, with de Valera elected president in April. By September, the British government declared the assembly a 'dangerous association'.

'death came with dramatic suddenness, often within 24 hours'

In the midst of all this political upheaval, devastation was caused by the outbreak of the influenza epidemic that ravaged the world between the spring of 1918 and early 1919. Distracted by the enormity of the political change, and the impending intensification of revolution, Irish historians have done little to assess its impact, and an analysis of it is long overdue. The contemporary Registrar-General, William Thompson, suggested that, since the Famine, no disease in Ireland had wreaked 'so much havoc'. Unlike in the rest of the UK, where comprehensive information on the dimension of the crisis was submitted to parliament, no report was submitted concerning Ireland, perhaps because of the political situation. It is probable that over 20,000 people in Ireland died as a result of the epidemic. It had a greater impact in some areas than others. In the fever hospitals of North Galway, deaths were averaging about ten a week, and:

> whole families were often affected, and the Galway papers carried many sad reports of both parents dying, leaving large families orphaned and destitute. Dr T. B. Costello, of Tuam, reported that doctors in North Galway often had to coffin the dead themselves, as no one in the area was fit enough to do so. The nuns in Tuam received high praise for their selfless nursing of the patients in their own homes.[208]

As elsewhere, the epidemic baffled the medical community. In delivering his presidential address to the Royal Academy of Medicine in Ireland in November 1918, Dr George Peacocke, of the Adelaide Hospital, noted that 'many believed that some yet undiscovered virus may be responsible'. In some cases he had used an influenza vaccine he had obtained from Trinity College Dublin, 'but no particular effect had been noticed'. During October in his hospital, there had been 497 admissions for influenza and 32 deaths, and 'in the most acute forms, death came with dramatic suddenness, often within 24 hours of the onset'.[209]

THREE

1918–1923

'*it would be a decided gain if they all took it into their heads to emigrate*'
In May 1921, William Cosgrave, Minister for Local Government in the
underground Dáil Éireann that had convened at the beginning of 1919,
sent a memorandum to Austin Stack, Minister for Home Affairs. Cosgrave
was later to become leader of the Irish Free State and a papal knight. Stack,
meanwhile, came to epitomise republican opposition to the Anglo-Irish
Treaty signed in December 1921. Cosgrave's concern was the feasibility
of organising the emigration of unwanted Irish orphans. He went on
to reflect on the plight of the young destitute in Ireland's workhouses,
institutions that the native illegal government, in attempting to supplant
British administration in Ireland, was committed to abolishing, in order
to get rid of what was regarded as a degrading and oppressive imposition
on Irish people. He wrote:

> As you are aware, people reared in workhouses are no great acquisition
> to human society. As a rule, their highest aim is to live at the expense of
> the ratepayers. As a consequence, it would be a decided gain if they all
> took it into their heads to emigrate. When abroad, they are thrown onto
> their own responsibilities and have to work whether they like it or not.[1]

It would be invidious to single out Cosgrave as having been particularly uncharitable or harsh in his social thinking. But this memorandum

highlighted the class bias of a revolutionary generation that had much more in common with the administration they were attempting to overthrow than they cared to admit. It seemed to suggest that Ireland's vulnerable children were an inconvenience to the conduct of the campaign for independence. This underlines the need to look behind the rhetoric of Sinn Féin during these years – a rhetoric often based on piety and righteousness, but also equality and justice. This particular memorandum also seemed to suggest that administrators and politicians were prepared to export the problems they found too difficult or inconvenient to deal with in a domestic context.

Historians have recently questioned the labelling of this period as the 'Irish revolution'. In 1990, David Fitzpatrick suggested it was a revolution in the sense that Ireland's 'major social and political institutions were turned upside down'. He also maintained that 'the alterations in Irish political organisation were sufficiently lasting and profound to merit the term revolution'. According to Charles Townshend, in its middle-class orientation and hostility to social revolution, it was perhaps more of a nineteenth- than a twentieth-century revolution.[2] Given the absence of Labour representation, the first Dáil was dominated by the lower-middle-class establishment, with virtually no working-class input.

But perhaps more important was that those who fought during these years felt they were living through a revolution, and as a result had 'a complicated relationship with democracy';[3] but their experience also infused their mission with a profoundly moral tone. In November 1919 a *Daily Herald* report declared that 'This invisible republic with its hidden courts and its prohibited volunteer troops exists in the hearts of the men and women of Ireland and wields a moral authority which all the tanks and machine guns of King George cannot command.' An Irish state was up and running in the face of massive opposition from a great power, and 'with massive popular support, the underground government of Dáil Éireann combined all methods, including violence, to emerge as the governing instrument of the Irish nation'.[4]

It could not, however, be achieved without ambiguity on many fronts. Neither could it be achieved, as pointed out by Michael Hopkinson, without 'the virtual collapse of British government in Ireland by 1920'. The weakness of British policy in Ireland was summed up by General Macready, commander of the British forces in Ireland, in a letter to the British prime minister Lloyd George's secretary and mistress in

June 1921, at the end of the conflict: 'There are, of course, one or two wild people about who still hold the absurd idea that if you go on killing long enough peace will ensue. I do not believe it for one moment, but I do believe that the more people are killed, the more difficult will be the final solution.'[5] This was a reminder of the difficulties of finding a uniform approach to the Irish problem.

Despite the extraordinary unity that Sinn Féin was able to achieve organisationally, and despite the general consensus that the commitment in the Proclamation of 1916 to equality should be reiterated at regular intervals, the real priority for republicans during the revolution was to ensure competing allegiances did not surface. This seemed to involve identifying external enemies and difficulties rather than a commitment to dealing with internal contradictions, something that historians began to grapple with in the 1980s and 1990s. The removal of halos from the participants has inevitably been a controversial part of this process, involving down-playing what were, on the face of it, extraordinary achievements. These included the destruction, politically and morally, of the Irish Parliamentary Party in the December 1918 general election; the waging of a military war of independence against the might of the British Empire which succeeded in forcing them to the negotiating table; and the partial success of supplanting the British administration in Ireland with a generation of talented, resourceful and boldly (sometimes bloodily) determined individuals. These achievements – and they do collectively merit the term 'revolutionary' – were underpinned by a rhetoric that to modern eyes seems quasi-spiritual.

'Seán and Séamus from Ballythis and Ballythat'

In March 2003, the files of the Bureau of Military History were finally opened to researchers, having remained under lock and key for fifty years. The Bureau had resulted from a government initiative in the 1940s to collect statements from those involved in the revolutionary era from 1913 up to the time of the Truce in July 1921 (the politically sensitive period of the Civil War was thus excluded from its remit). The Bureau, staffed mostly by serving army officers, and advised by leading Irish historians, was in existence until the end of the 1950s and amassed a collection of 1,773 statements. Although some were reluctant to co-operate with it, and historians were unhappy about the release embargo, it was a valuable exercise, and sheds much light on the reasons people got involved, along with their various triumphs and failures. Michael McDunphy, as Director of the Bureau, was the target of some criticisms but was determined to ensure not only that the material remained absolutely confidential, but also that the voice of the ordinary rank-and-file volunteer would be represented. He disagreed that only certain people should be earmarked for interview, seeing this as 'a form of snobbery', contending that 'an ordinary volunteer who served in the ranks and then returned to private life may often have a clearer and perhaps much more important story to tell than one who served with a titular rank, or whose subsequent career brought him into prominence or close contact with later developments'.[6] A measure of the perceived sensitivity of the statements was that one of the advisers to the Bureau believed they should not be made available to the general public, on the grounds that 'If every Séan and Séamus from Ballythis Ballythat who took major or minor or no part at all in the national movement from 1916 to 1921 has free access to the material it may result in local civil warfare in every second town and village in the country.'[7]

Some of the longer statements (and they run to over 200 pages in some cases) contain implausibly detailed recollections of precise incidents and conversations. Overall, however, the tone of the statements is measured, and while a number of witnesses were determined to settle old scores and indulge in hyperbole, many others seem to have approached the work of the Bureau in a highly scrupulous manner. Those directing the Bureau's affairs had an understandable preoccupation with getting information from well-known figures, but it may be that the true value of the witness statements lies in the testimony of the ordinary volunteers: what motivated them, what they did (and did not do), the extent to which they believed they were part of a national revolution, and the degree to which they triumphed and suffered. Given the volume of the material – 36,000 pages of evidence and 150,000 pieces in the confidential documents – it will be some time before it can be absorbed fully, but an initial examination suggests it has the potential to enhance or change our understanding of the period in a number of respects.

Historians have not before had access to such a nation-wide span of accounts of life in flying columns and the day-to-day activities and operations of the IRA. This is valuable in two ways. Given the new emphasis in historical research on regional histories of this period, those seeking to reconstruct the events of a particular county have an opportunity to consult a concentrated and detailed number of statements from that region and contrast them with information already in the public domain. Secondly, it will allow historians to broadly reconsider an issue that has not been explained fully to date: the degree of centralised control and co-ordination over IRA activities. The role of women in the conflict can also be reassessed, as can the impact of the First World War, and the influence of cultural organisations in the opening years of the century (which historians have only recently begun to research in depth) because many of the contributors place their statements in the wider context of the social, economic and cultural upheaval of these years. In recent years there has also been a new focus on policing in Ireland before 1922, and the numerous statements from those who served with the Royal Irish Constabulary provide an opportunity to analyse their relationship with nationalism, and interesting perspectives on the strength of policing in different counties. On a reading of these statements the relationship between the RIC and the communities they policed was more complex and multi-faceted than the history texts suggest.

The attitude of the Catholic Church to the crisis also deserves reassessment on the basis of these statements, given that some senior Church figures, often reluctant to comment publicly on the events of this period, were candid in their statements about divisions within their own ranks. Many of the statements are defensive in tone – inevitably, given the extent of the divisions that followed the negotiation of the Treaty – and it is often frustrating at the end of a particularly absorbing statement to find no information on the role the contributor played in the Civil War. The statements also contain evidence of widespread naivety concerning the position of Northern unionists; interesting material on Irish emigrants who assisted the IRA; and insights into the class and social divisions and snobberies of the period. Some of the statements would whet the appetite of a screenwriter, such was the excitement and drama of the period. Events such as the response to the conscription crisis are well documented, and the frequency with which this issue appears is testament to a depth of feeling that historians have perhaps neglected. History books tend to attribute the rise of Sinn Féin to the fallout from the 1916 Rising; but had there been no conscription threat, Sinn Féin might not have performed so well in the December 1918 election.

The statements suggest that the resourcefulness and commitment of this generation were exceptional. Theirs was overwhelmingly a revolution of the young; they were physically fit (they thought nothing of cycling from county to county) and, in the main, politically disciplined. Those looking for evidence of sophisticated ideological debate may be disappointed, but there is a huge amount of material of interest to the social historian. There was another overriding reason for many people's involvement: simple fun, socialising and recreation. For Elizabeth Bloxham, flirting and laughter were part and parcel of organising Cumann na mBan during the summer holidays: 'I have sometimes wondered if an invisible onlooker could have realised underneath our gaiety we were all in such deadly earnest.'[8]

'her long night of sorrow'

Many of the revolutionary generation grew to adulthood on a diet of propaganda and writing which had strongly emphasised Ireland's exclusivity in the annals of heroism and suffering; a tortured history that was merely a prelude to a new chapter of independence. Irish historical fiction in the late nineteenth and early twentieth centuries strongly invoked the Irish landscape, character, ancient Celtic genealogy and racial traits, and the continuity between past and present: a Gaelic and Catholic nation that was distinct and which could at best tolerate Norman and Anglo-Irish as exotic minority settlers. Also emphasised was an Irish political tradition which was communitarian rather than individualistic, and a civic tradition that was centred on order and justice. Order was synonymous with ownership of the land, the first stage of the Irish revolution which had, on the surface, been achieved by the beginning of this period; while justice was central in regulating social relationships between individuals. If fiction was anything to go by it was perhaps the latter that was to prove the most difficult.

For those intimidated, boycotted, ridiculed or forced out, there seemed little room for generosity in the strict definition of what constituted the 'Irish nation'. This was brought home sharply during the Irish revolution, though the bitter Civil War was to prove that the Irish were no more blessed or noble than their counterparts in many of the other divided parts of Europe. (It is worth noting that in 1919 up to 25 million Europeans found themselves in a minority situation in states that had been carved up as a result of the First World War, Czechoslovakia and Yugoslavia being but two obvious examples.) In 1913, the Irish novelist James Murphy had wondered where else Irish novelists could look for the lights and shadows necessary to a novel but in the strife between aggressive occupiers/exterminators and those resolved to holding on to their homes. Ireland's most popular novelist, Canon Sheehan, in his last novel, *The Graves at Kilmorna: A Story of '67* (1915), included a young prospective lawyer and revolutionary as a character involved in the 1867 Fenian rising. The landscape was central not only to imbuing him with an appreciation of Ireland's history, but also, it seemed, to opening the door to his (and Ireland's) future destiny. Ironically perhaps, given the extent to which women had to struggle to make their voices heard on the male nationalist platform during these years, Ireland and its landscape was invariably personified as a woman:

> As I thought of that Motherland, this Ireland of ours, with all her magic beauty – beauty of mountain and lake, of brown bog and sandy seashore, of her seas and her rivers – of all these things that grew into our lives and became a part of our being and then I thought of her long night of sorrow; how she has been trampled and shamed and degraded and then held up by her iron masters as an object of derision to the world – her masters who laughed at the hunger and ignorance they caused, her masters who held up her rags and fluttered them in the face of nations, who never knew or cared that it was these very masters who cut every weal into her body and took the bread from her mouth and snipped her garments into fragments, until I grew mad with the thought that perhaps the one chance of my life would escape me – to wreak vengeance on her foes, or save that motherland from further humiliation.[9]

Powerfully emotive, such passages gave scant recognition to the realities of rural life or communities that, in the midst of such pastoral beauty, were riddled with class tensions and difficulties. These were to be either suppressed or ignored, or solutions postponed until an independent Ireland would have the time and resources to devote to them. Initially, the newly organised Sinn Féin of late 1917 was also, it seemed, in the business of postponement in order to unify the disparate elements of nationalism and republicanism. On being elected President of Sinn Féin on 25 October 1917, Eamon de Valera had insisted he stood for an Irish republic as a monument to the dead, and that an Irish republic was the pious wish of every Irish heart. But the key aim was the international recognition of an Irish republic – de Valera insisted that, having achieved that, the Irish people should be allowed to decide on whatever form of government they wished. If they got a republic, he insisted, they could agree to differ afterwards. It is doubtful during these optimistic days that anyone could foresee just how savage these disagreements would be. But de Valera's discourse drew attention to two things that were to be again controversial: the need to secure international recognition, particularly in the context of the changed post-war world, and the question of the commitment to democracy.

'the last unliberated white community on the face of the globe'?

The extent to which the revolution was democratic, at both a political and a military level, has proved divisive, in the context of trying to define the character and representativeness of the Irish revolution. Here, too, the inevitable dethroning of heroes has occurred, raising the question of the extent to which this revolutionary generation were much more comfortable with defining enemies than with defining the polity for which they struggled. The extent to which there existed in the minds of the revolutionaries a classic conflict between the nostalgia as enunciated by Sheehan and the modern world is also worth exploring, as is the tension between an urban ideal and a rural reality, between parochial concerns and international contexts. Revisionists would add the conflict between democracy and anti-democracy, a tension not helped by the tradition of minority, secret, underground revolutionary activity which implied a certain distrust of popular consultation.

But depicting the revolution as a battle between democrats and autocrats, between pragmatism and idealism, is too simplistic. Antipathy was to be displayed by both sides after disagreement over the terms of agreement with Britain. The idea of one side having a virtuous regard for, or monopoly on, or indeed passion for democracy was certainly dispelled by the fact that after independence all shared a distrust of giving people too much autonomy, which was why the Irish state became so relentlessly centralised. Clues pointing to this distrust were in evidence before independence. In *What Sinn Féin Stands For* (1921), one of their chief propagandists, Aodh de Blacam, insisted that an Ireland in transition needed paternalistic and centralised control: an 'iron Bismarckian phase'.[10] This belief remained well after the transition period, as did the enduring influence of former gunmen. In any case, the danger of looking for a convenient split concerning democracy on the Irish side can conveniently ignore Britain's imposition of 'democracy' under threat of renewed war with the Empire. When voting in the general election of June 1922, the Irish electorate were in effect asked to endorse a treaty that British negotiators had insisted was their final offer in settling the War of Independence; the alternative, the prime minister Lloyd George maintained, was a renewed war.

In the event, neither Britain nor Ireland achieved their wishes. But the emphasis in the initial quest for independence on international recognition was hugely important, and whatever the various factors playing on the Irish patriot mind, it was not a conflict that could remain parochial, and resources were deployed cleverly in this regard. What did Ireland's case for independence mean in an international context? It is worth quoting in full a letter sent by writer and Irish republican Erskine Childers to the London *Times* on 5 May 1919 for the light it shed on these themes. Childers was later to be executed during the Civil War because of his anti-Treaty activities.

> I think it is true to say that in no country has the innermost aspiration of a national movement been so divorced from materialistic motives or so pure an outcome of a people's passionate will to be master of its own soil and destiny. Force, simple force is the reply; a military terror ... Ireland is an almost crimeless country in the ordinary sense. Judge after judge has been receiving white gloves for a white assize, while courts-martial fill the gaols with state created criminals guilty, or suspected of being guilty of offences, many grotesquely trivial and all directly attributable to the absence of the first condition of an orderly society, a government chosen by the people. A very few, a marvellously few, serious crimes occur; for the whole system is an invitation, an incitement to crime ... Ireland is now the only white nationality in the world (let us leave coloured possessions out of the discussion) where the principle of self-determination is not, at least in theory, conceded. It is the last of the 'problems', which were left in 1914, and it is incomparably the simplest. It is simplicity itself compared with those resulting from the collapse of Russia, Austria and Germany, where the intermixture of races, speaking different languages and the absence of clearly defined or maritime boundaries do cause difficulties of real complexity. Nevertheless, Great Britain is guaranteeing the boundaries of these new states, of which so little is known that the PM can joke in parliament about his ignorance till yesterday of the position on the map of one of the numerous 'Ulsters'. Is she, in the same breath, to decline to deal

with Ireland, whose uninterrupted historical identity and boundaries
nobody can mistake? Ireland, the last unliberated white community on
the face of the globe?

'It is your right to compel your tailor'

In this letter, Childers was attempting to encapsulate not only the significance of the international context, in terms of the First World War being
fought by the Allies in defence of the rights of small nations, but almost
all the arguments that were used to justify this revolutionary period: the
righteousness and exclusivity of an oppressed and historically distinct
people. To ignore Ulster unionist opposition was of course essential, as
it sullied such a simplistic canvas. But what was also interesting was the
insistence on non-materialistic values. In propaganda terms, Sinn Féin was
to give much thought to this during these years. The idea, as already
enunciated in the election manifesto (and later to be reiterated by Fianna
Fáil), was that Sinn Féin stood less for a political party than for the nation,
representing a tradition of nationhood handed on from dead generations;
that national self-interest should be heard above every class interest. Aodh
de Blacam was to add that every Irish social thinker envisaged Gaelic
Ireland as rural Ireland, and that the great crowded cities of Britain and
America were regarded in Ireland as perversions of the natural order; that
the 'average Irish man' was not attracted to the town, a sentiment deep-
rooted in the Irish mind.

This was a continuation of the line of thought in the *Ethics of Sinn
Féin*, published in 1917, which described the moral obligations of Sinn
Féin, which were, it seemed, many and restrictive:

> His conduct must be above reproach, his personality stainless. He
> must learn the Irish language, write on Irish paper, and abstain from
> alcohol and tobacco … give good example. Make examples of your
> life, your virtues, your courage, your temperance, your manliness. It is
> your right to compel your tailor, if he is unwilling, to make your coat
> of Irish cloth, to compel your grocer to sell you Irish eggs, to compel
> your public servants to acquire some knowledge of the Irish language
> and help Irish industries.[11]

This could be seen as highly contradictory when placed alongside the
insistence on non-materialism and ruralism. The hinterland, after all, was

full of a rural peasantry in no position financially or socially to be entertaining such notions. This was an indication that the directives seemed to be aimed at the educated class; the same class from which sprang those who would rather see the problem of Ireland's poverty exported than solved from within.

The first Dáil's Democratic Programme, presented at the first meeting of the Dáil in January 1919 in Dublin's Mansion House, was an indication that only a certain type of nebulous, ambiguous rhetoric concerning equality and redistribution would be tolerated by Sinn Féin. Tom Johnson, leader of the regularly sidelined Labour Party during these years, had included in his draft an insistence that 'all right to private property must be subordinated to the public right and welfare' and that capitalist assets not being used in the interests of workers be seized. This was omitted in favour of a general commitment to the development of Ireland's resources for the benefit of the Irish people; obligations which, in any case, were later to be postponed on the grounds that they were not capable of being delivered on while Ireland was in a state of transition.

The final version of the Democratic Programme also dropped the sentence: 'It shall be the purpose of the government to encourage the organisation of people into trade unions and co-operative societies with a view to the control and administration of the industries by the workers engaged in the industries.'[12] But the reality was that, as was pointed out by the few social activists who published during these years, Irish people were accustomed to seeing tenement slums as something normal and inevitable. This is not to suggest that social change was not a concern of members of the first Dáil; it was, especially in relation to the redistribution of land and the creation of modern industry. The Democratic Programme reflected elements of a Utopian socialism, a product of the influence of the late James Connolly and the teachings of individuals like George Russell. But British sanctions, in the form of the withdrawal of grants during the War of Independence, inhibited financial autonomy. The Minister for Finance, Michael Collins, also found it impossible to introduce a Dáil system of income tax and the Dáil itself never advocated that the Irish should stop paying tax or indeed land annuities to the British.

'cows to milk, hay to save and women to order about'
The Democratic Programme was highly aspirational and contained the resolute intention to abolish 'the present odious, degrading and foreign

poor-law system'; a further promise was to uphold the welfare of children and the elderly. But Brian Farrell suggested that 'The Democratic Programme did not represent the social and economic ideas of the first Dáil. Most of its members had not read the document in advance; the few who had seen it in draft form were reluctant enough to subscribe to it and there was a last minute redrafting of the document only hours before the Dáil met.'[13] Fr Michael O'Kennedy, a prominent Sinn Féin activist, was later to comment that 'it is a pity to mix up Sinn Féin in that land question. Of necessity questions of land, food, industries turn up, but all are of secondary importance and none must obscure our objective.'[14] The practicalities of politics were thus removed from the theory and the kind of propaganda contained in de Blacam's *What Sinn Féin Stands For* when he wrote of 'distributivism' – the system which Catholic social workers proposed in opposition to communism and capitalism. This was, he maintained, distinct from religious dogma so that even 'an atheist can admire it'.[15]

Many of the revolutionaries were low- and middle-ranking government employees whose information was essential for Collins's intelligence network. Tom Garvin suggested that many of the putative revolutionaries had also been profoundly influenced by their primary school teachers:

> The National Teacher's financial and intellectual security and dependence made him a natural source of radicalism that was curiously short of intellectual adventurousness. Teachers were chronically discontented and also thoroughly subordinated. They were spread about the country and had a pervasive effect on the young and in the long run on the general political culture of the entire nation. Intellectually inhibited discontent, economic dependence on both church and state combined with great cultural influence to form a potent mixture. Many IRA veterans ascribed their original indoctrination into extreme nationalism to their local village teachers.[16]

This was one reason why so many ordinary people got involved. It was also the case, as pointed out by David Fitzpatrick, that not all could take to the hills: 'as long as there were cows to milk, hay to save and women to order about, the vast majority of volunteers would have to remain part-timers'.[17] Nonetheless, it is accurate to see the volunteers as mostly representing those with a stake in the country, and it was significant that they defined themselves against a culture of poverty and deprivation and emphasised

their clean living. There was little middle- or upper-middle-class participation in the ranks; the revolutionaries were neither very poor nor very
well off, but in the words of Hart 'the central stratum of "plain people" in
between'.[18] There was an abundance of young, literate, unmarried, practising Catholics. Many of the Cork volunteers were farm workers rather
than casual labourers, or sons of publicans and tradespeople, and few were
unemployed. The same profile of volunteers has emerged in other regional
studies of the revolution, notably at Longford.[19]

'a number of these people imagine that the whole Irish race is pauperised'
The Dáil meetings were rarely disrupted, but it met infrequently: only
21 times between its establishment and the Truce of July 1921, and only
eight times after its legal suppression in September 1919. There was much
success in raising money outside Ireland, a key plank in Sinn Féin's policy
of matching international recognition with external funding. Despite
President Wilson's fobbing off of Sinn Féin in Paris in 1919, de Valera
managed to raise in the region of $6 million in the United States between
January 1920 and October 1921 (which was much more than was raised
in Ireland; perhaps the figure was a reflection of the fact that the United
States' Irish-born population in 1920 was close to one million). Owing
to disputes between different Irish-American factions, much of it never
reached Ireland. It would not be exaggerating to describe Irish nationalism by 1920 as a mass movement in the US; the Friends of Irish Freedom,
established in 1916, claimed nearly 300,000 members by 1919, while the
American Association for the Recognition of the Irish Republic, founded
in 1920, had 700,000 members by 1921. A much smaller group, the
Irish Progressive League, kept the Irish republican cause alive in the face
of increased governmental intolerance and US entry into the First World
War.

Most of the leaders of such groups were wealthy Irish-American professionals, particularly lawyers, though Irish-American labour groups also
played a part, at a time (1916–20) when US trade union membership
more than doubled. The Irish-American Chicago Federation of Labour, for
example, condemned the execution of Irish republican 'prisoners of war'.
Despite a bitter history of racial conflict between Irish and black workers
in the city, there was some support for a boycott campaign of British
goods and black dockers joined in a strike in the wake of the death of
Terence MacSwiney (see below). In 1919, a rally of 8,000 Polish-American

workers in the stockyards of Chicago unanimously called for recognition of the Irish republic, while James Larkin was also active in the States in perpetuating the memory of James Connolly.[20]

The Dáil approached the issue of international recognition with vigour, determination and ambition, though with mixed success. Whatever about the desired recognition not coming from President Wilson, de Valera in private was to find in the autumn of 1921 that the real challenge was to prevent government funds being controlled by strangers. The sheer number of those raising money in the name of Irish independence was a source of worry to the Department of Foreign Affairs. Joseph Connolly, the Irish Consul in New York, articulated his fears about Wall Street exploitation and cynical Irish-American politicians hoping to make connections, pointing out that 'a number of these people imagine that the whole Irish race is pauperised and that we can do nothing for ourselves without Wall Street money'.[21] There was also much uncertainty – Laurence Ginnell, the government's Irish representative in Argentina, was unsure as to the legality of his money-raising exercises. By the summer of 1921 there were Irish envoys in Geneva, Rome, Washington, Madrid and Paris, with trips also undertaken to South Africa, Australia and New Zealand. But Irish representatives of the 'Republic' were often restricted by lack of status and resources. Patrick MacCartan, who was sent to Russia, suggested the *Irish Bulletin* (being published by the government's department of propaganda) was relatively useless there: 'They cannot consistently condemn the shooting of Irishmen by England while they themselves "slice their own bandits". They cannot condemn imprisonment without trial in Ireland while their own jails are full of political prisoners … Russia laughs at the Estonian language as the British are accustomed to laugh at the Irish language.'[22] Nonetheless, propaganda was successful in influencing those who championed self-determination, and the consequences of the War of Independence provided for excellent publicity material. The *Irish Bulletin* enjoyed a healthy circulation in Britain and put pressure on the British government to justify its military policy in Ireland.

It was more mundane matters at home, however, which primarily occupied the new administration. After the laughter that greeted Edward Carson's name in the roll call of the first Dáil in January 1919 came the serious business of wrestling administrative control from the British government, under what were essentially emergency conditions. In March 1921, of the 69 members of the Dáil, 26 were in prison, two had resigned, three had died, two were sick and six were abroad.[23] For those that remained active in directing the clandestine work, preventing any leakage of information was instrumental to successful duplicity. For correspondence outside Dublin, the country was divided into four main districts as served by the Dublin rail termini of Kingsbridge, Amiens Street, Broadstone and Harcourt Street. For transmission, all correspondence had to be bundled together and sent as goods to some ordinary business address. In the summer of 1921 there were complaints that dispatches were becoming too bulky, which prompted Sinn Féin to appoint a director of civil communications. The conditions under which the members of the Dáil were operating undoubtedly posed a considerable strain on their personal lives. De Valera, for example, so often seen as a stern, unemotional political animal, had to endure frequent and prolonged absences from his family, and no doubt often felt the loneliness he had expressed in 1916 in the letter he wrote to his wife from Dartmoor gaol, on hearing of his reprieve from a death sentence. This letter, part of a small series discovered only at the very end of the century, suggested that his only source of anxiety were his wife and children, and read: 'I know the agonies you must have endured during the past few weeks. The suspense at any rate is now over – the sentence of death passed on me has been commuted to penal servitude for life – so you have now only to cope with a certainty.'[24]

'invest him with a dignity'

One of the incidents that ensured international media coverage and indeed outrage was the death of Terence MacSwiney, following an attempt to force-feed him during a hunger strike. One of eight children brought up in poverty, he left school at 15 to become a clerk. MacSwiney was one of the few working-class republicans of the twentieth century who became temporary international icons (a feat also achieved by Bobby Sands in 1981). MacSwiney had articulated his philosophy of self-sacrifice in his 1914 play *The Revolutionist*, ably supported by a rebellious, communist and atheist wife. MacSwiney's evolution as a republican had not been without soul-searching – he had refused to join the Irish Republican Brotherhood because he believed its secrecy was demoralising. But it was the simplicity and courage of MacSwiney's protest – begun in Brixton prison after he had been arrested as Lord Mayor of Cork – which struck a chord around the world: one emaciated individual versus the Empire. The London *Times* had been accurate indeed, at an early stage of the hunger strike (about which, privately, King George V was urging the authorities to compromise), when it suggested that, if he died, his memory would be 'infinitely more eloquent and infinitely more subversive of peace than he himself could ever be. Beyond Ireland his death must sweep aside every petty argument and suspicion and invest him with a dignity from which no subsequent explanations can ever detract.'[25] MacSwiney's funeral in Cork was another significant propaganda coup for Sinn Féin.

On a lighter note, de Valera's standing as an international celebrity seemed to be confirmed in August 1921, when an export cigar manufacturer, Jan Vandereijde, wrote to him requesting permission to manufacture a 'De Valera Series' of first-class cigars, requiring a portrait of de Valera that was duly sent. Sinn Féin's ethical concerns about tobacco smoking were, it seemed, set aside in the national interest.[26]

The heightened profile of the Irish situation was also a reflection of the exhaustive work being done by the department of publicity and propaganda, which had its origins in the aftermath of the 1918 election. At this time, a foreign-relations committee of Sinn Féin had been formed to prepare a series of pamphlets on various aspects of the Irish question. By the summer of 1921 they claimed an *Irish Bulletin* was being sent weekly to 900 newspapers world-wide. In October 1921 Scottish nationalists in a 'Friends of Ireland' group complained bitterly about the paper's generalisations and the liberal use by Irish nationalists of the word 'British' when complaining of imperial oppression.[27]

'so far as this is intended to prevent drunkenness it is an admirable thing'
The courts system established by the first Dáil involved the adoption of a legal system very similar to that operated by the British administration in Ireland. As far back as 1905 Arthur Griffith had put forward the idea of arbitration courts outside the domain of rapacious lawyers. In June 1919, in an attempt to counteract crime, particularly agrarian, the Dáil decreed for the establishment of national arbitration courts in every county. By June 1920 the Dáil had established its own hierarchy of civil and criminal courts: parish courts dealing with summonses of a minor nature; district courts for each of the old parliamentary constituencies; circuit courts, where the judge, a qualified lawyer, was sent periodically to different country parts; and a supreme court in Dublin. The issue of law and order became increasingly difficult, with a preponderance of vigilantism. There was often utter confusion in distinguishing between the authority of the

IRA and the republican police force (IRP) when it came to such issues as the enforcement of the licensing laws. In the summer of 1921 the chief of police warned his officers not to indulge in threatening or intimidating behaviour in the execution of their duties and to have no involvement in boycotts, other than those decreed by the Dáil. The IRA, ever quick in local areas to blur the line between civil and military law (an enduring and pervasive problem of the period), were apt to make their own laws. In October 1921, an angry civil servant wrote to the Minister for Defence concerning the activities of the IRA in certain parts of Mayo imposing a penny tax on the sale of stout:

> The IRA have other means of increasing their income besides this dangerous method … so far as this is intended to prevent drunkenness it is an admirable thing in itself, but the fact that the shopkeepers are being vested with powers to increase already inflated prices and proceed to fleece the public … is nothing short of an incentive to the profiteering evil which has already been carried too far.[28]

'A very fine tenor voice'

The first court under the direct authority of the Dáil sat at Ballinrobe, County Mayo, on 17 May 1920 and was reported with some pride in the national press. Dáil courts were not arenas for weighty trials of political violence (military tribunals and criminal courts constituted under the Defence of the Realm Act and Restoration of Order in Ireland Act 1920 dealt with these) but heard minor civil suits in rundown halls, rooms and outhouses. Banishment was often the preferred punishment, being both severe and inexpensive, though the promptness and efficiency of these courts impressed even some unionists. There were incidents of farce also. The *Limerick Leader*, in 1920, reported on the case of two men who had disobeyed an order of a Sinn Féin court to rebuild a wall they had demolished. 'Banished to an island off the Clare Coast for 3 weeks, a party of the RIC who attempted to rescue them were pelted with stones and abused by the prisoners who declared proudly they were citizens of the Irish republic and that the police had no right to interfere.'[29]

But for all such declarations of faith in native justice, the reality was that the Minister for Defence, Cathal Brugha, had little time for police or courts, seeing them as a deflection from the priority of war. Austin Stack, Minister for Home Affairs, was often bullying and pedantic in his abusive missives to overworked and confused registrars in his attempt to control district courts. Cahir Davitt, son of land reform crusader Michael, and largely responsible for the courts operating in Munster as a circuit judge of the Dáil courts, recalled that after the creation of the hierarchy of courts, most were administering justice as they saw fit, with no prescribed code of law for them to administer and with no rules of court. Overall, it seemed a mixture of efficiency and accessibility but also confusion,[30] mirroring the uncertainty that seemed to exist at the level of government. But with the Truce of July 1921 there was an even more concerted effort to make the Dáil courts work, to illustrate that they were more effective than the imperial legal system. According to David Fitzpatrick: 'however limited their influence, the courts did bring the Republic to some extent into the daily lives of Irishmen, whatever their politics, and it may be that one five shilling decree for trespass in a remote western parish was worth a dozen declarations of independence'.[31]

Conor Maguire, later Chief Justice of the Irish Free State, submitted a statement to the Bureau of Military History concerning his work in connection with the republican courts in 1920–21 in Mayo. Here, land agitation led to the courts considering claims between owners and landless men, these courts thus assuming a jurisdiction for which there was no counterpart in the British system. He suggested that in the initial months of the War of Independence, they were able to operate with relative ease, but had to take certain gambles on arbitration being accepted. He described one incident that:

> took place at the close of one sitting of Kevin O'Shiel's court in an out-of-the-way deserted mansion on the edge of a bog. Michael Maguire, who was chief of the IRA police, presided at a court martial on a prisoner who had been held for some days. He was a young man who looked to be frightened out of his wits. The charge against him was that he had pretended to be an IRA policeman and in that capacity had ordered all the public houses in Multyfarnham to close one evening about 3 hours before closing time. He pleaded guilty and received a sharp lecture from Michael Maguire who fined him £1 and let him go. I well remember the look of relief on the prisoner's face as he left. We then had an unexpected treat in the form of a recital of Gilbert and Sullivan songs by Michael Maguire who had a very fine tenor voice.[32]

The courts cannot be judged to have effectively tackled the social problems of the era but they managed to contain some of them, at least temporarily, in their preoccupation with licensing laws, property and protecting women from abusive language. (In terms of social misbehaviour, temperance continued to be advocated by many religious activists, with a resolution drawn up by the Catholic Total Abstinence Federation in June 1919 expressing the hope that 'the paralysis of British rule in Ireland does not allow Ireland's worst domestic enemy, the liquor traffic, to tighten its stronghold'.[33]) In January 1922, following the signing of the Treaty, it was ordered that the British courts should continue to operate. It was a decision that baffled many district justices, judges and clerks who had put their lives at risk operating the illegal courts. It seemed to render empty much of the rhetoric used in the previous two years concerning the need to protect the public from these enemy courts. It was left to a courts winding-up commission to deal with cases left pending under the old Dáil system.

'taking advantage of the disturbed state of the times'

The local-government brief was enormous, complicated by many vested interests, but with the potential to effect significant change in Irish life. The multitude of problems faced included the attempt to administer the workhouses, recruitment to local government officer posts and enforcing the collection of rates. Disagreements frequently broke out in local-government bodies. In July 1921 William Cosgrave bemoaned the 'deplorable indolence' of members of Meath County Council, with little 'inclination to rise to its responsibilities'. Belmullet in County Mayo was not deemed worthy of serious administrative endeavour because of is geographical remoteness, the poverty of its populace and the contention that its population consumed so much poteen.[34] Members of Cork County Council complained: 'at least 75 per cent of our time is almost invariably taken up with labourers' cottages – rents, arrears of rents, repairs, changing of tenants etc. Some of the tenants are taking advantage of the disturbed state of the times and seem to make no effort to pay the rent or arrears.'[35]

Given the prevailing unemployment, there was also a belief that many local-government officials were corrupt and lining their own pockets. In Limerick in the autumn of 1921 the Irish Transport and General Workers' Union complained of labourers being dismissed, 'many of whom have large families to support and keeping useless officials in luxury, thus creating discontent amongst the workers and furnishing propaganda for reactionaries'.[36] In the first of his two statements to the Bureau of Military History, William Cosgrave stressed the significance of the 'loss of civil control' by the British government in Ireland. As Minister for Local Government, he managed to achieve much with a staff of just 65, one quarter of the number of officials in the British local-government board for Ireland. He recounted how on one occasion 'the chairman of an important County Council walked freely through the city of Dublin with £50,000 on his person'. He also pointed out that many local public representatives paid a heavy price for their activities: 'two lord mayors of Cork were done to death, one outside his own home; one mayor of Limerick, two members of the Limerick Corporation and the chairman of the Limerick County Council'.[37]

Another major source of discontent was the provision of health care, and in particular the hospital amalgamation scheme, which was an attempt to promote home assistance, end dependency on the workhouse and save money by closing some of the more remote and overstaffed hospitals. It was only in County Roscommon that the elimination of the workhouse system and the amalgamation of the hospitals was completed before the Truce.[38] Patients were often forgotten about once they had been admitted and frequently stayed beyond the period of their illness. In Sligo, an irate inspector wrote: 'I found the imbecile and idiot inmates belonging to Tobercurry (about 16 females) huddled together in a small ward, where they have been confined and congested.'[39]

'the dream of all my boyhood pals to join the force'
Whatever about confusion in the ranks of the republican carriers of the torch of justice, these were clearly the most difficult days for the Royal Irish Constabulary, for so long the bulwark of policing in rural Ireland. There were undoubtedly police heroes of the Irish revolution, though until recently history declined to record them. There were 11,000 officers and men in the constabulary, in 1,299 barracks, when war broke out in 1919, but by 1921 the number of barracks had been reduced to 865. Many had come from the poor western seaboard; many others were former farmers or small labourers and their service often became a source of division. During the War of Independence, the force still had 400 who had been members since the era of the land war in the 1870s and 1880s. As early as 1914 a royal commission established to investigate the force had heard of their

fears for the future. It was seen as essential that Sinn Féin undermine them socially, morally and physically after 1919. Until the War of Independence, the RIC was consistently more than 70 per cent Catholic, very close to the recorded population of the period 1861–1911, though 45 per cent of new recruits were Protestant between 1916 and 1920, which had important implications for the likelihood of it being accepted by the public. Between January 1919 and its disbandment in the spring and summer of 1922, 493 were killed, 12 per cent resigned, 12 per cent were dismissed, and 63 per cent of the men who were in the force in January 1919 were still there at the time of its disbandment.[40]

This seemed to account for an unusual degree of loyalty and experience, and indeed maturity, in the midst of duress. However, there was no escaping the fact that this was a civil police force confronted by a guerrilla army. Yet some of the recollections of individual members suggest that even in 1921–2 an RIC sergeant was seen as an important adviser and arbitrator in some rural communities. The reason why it was essential for the IRA to ostracise and demonise them was precisely because of their close ties with the communities they served. A member who joined in 1918 and served in counties Mayo and Sligo recalled:

> I was respected when I joined, but after a while I wasn't. When the trouble started nobody wanted you, but before you were fairly well liked, fairly well. There was always a bit of a slur on them in places, surely, they belonged in the establishment, you know, they called it that, the right word or not. But people were friendly until the troubles … when the troubles got bad you could go out and you wouldn't know when you'd be fired on … In the West of Ireland, you'd meet very little Protestants, but we wouldn't be a bit better in with Protestants than Republicans. We'd be less better in with them. They'd have less to do with us than some of the Republicans, because they were afraid to be accused of giving us news, so they kept away from us all together to keep safe.[41]

The archive of the Bureau of Military History contains much material on the experiences of the RIC during this period. Some of their statements are understandably defensive in tone, given the vilification of the RIC that resulted from the War of Independence. But the assumption that the force was overwhelmingly loyal to the Crown is not supported by those members who contributed to the Bureau. Eugene Bratton, a constable in Meath, maintained that 'in some cases the police actually assisted in the training of the volunteers for a short period, but not for long'.[42] He also contended, and this is repeated elsewhere, that the police resented the conscription threat of 1918. In a scenario that also seems to have been common, he recalled: 'I wanted to resign from the force, but general Boylan of the IRA would not allow me ... I was more useful where I was.' Many RIC members collaborated with the IRA through a mixture of fear and genuine conviction; and to a man, it seems, they strongly resented the coming of the Black and Tans, whom they regarded as morally and professionally reprehensible.

John Duffy, an RIC member who carried out intelligence work for the IRA, advised Michael Collins on how to persuade young men to leave the force. 'Collins sent down a courier by return with instructions in his own handwriting that under no circumstances was I to leave the force and if I did so I would be looked upon as a coward. The word "coward" decided my determination to remain on.'[43] A fascinating but exaggerated and at times self-serving statement by Jeremiah Mee, instigator of a mutiny within the Listowel RIC against the taking over of their barracks by the British military, explains the sentiments behind the mutiny: 'when we joined the police force, we joined with characters second to none and we refused to co-operate or work in any capacity with the British military, men of low moral character who frequented bad houses, kept the company of prostitutes and generally were unsuitable and undesirable characters.' The police also objected strongly to the instruction of Colonel Smyth, in charge of police and military in Munster, to commit open murder of republicans. Mee, who ended up working at republican headquarters in Dublin, also recalled a belief 'that it was the British government's intention to round up the prominent republican leaders, put them on board a ship on the pretence of sending them to a concentration camp and then arrange for an accident at sea'.[44]

Statements from ex-RIC members not only emphasise the moral probity and discipline of the force, but also the men's sense that, by joining, they were attaining a social respectability unachievable in many other jobs. Most insist that the relationship between the population and the police force was relatively good prior to the War of Independence. Understandably, many joined because it provided a secure income and pension, and, as noted previously, even republicans could see the merit in this. Some Irishmen serving with the British army were also angered by events at home – John Flannery, one of the participants in the mutiny of the Connaught Rangers in India in 1920, insisted that the action was prompted by the treatment of their mothers and sisters by the Black and Tans; the mutineers' spokesman:

> put it to the general if it was a fitting reward for the sacrifices that thousands of Irishmen had made on many fronts throughout the Great War and to these men on parade who came through this great ordeal, to return home and learn that our own fellow countrymen and women were being shot down by the orders of the British government.[45]

'They had their loyalties and stuck to them'

The names Dan Breen and Sean Treacy will forever be associated with the beginning of the War of Independence. But it was the true extent of Breen's control over the third Tipperary Brigade of the IRA during their attack on Soloheadbeg which encapsulated the military and civil dilemma of Irish republicans in 1919, given that prior authorisation for the action was neither sought nor received from Dáil Éireann. This was at a time when republicans advocating militarism were dissatisfied that the volunteers were too closely associated with a party which still contained a proportion of Home Rulers and even monarchists. It was significant that it was the two policemen killed, James MacDonnell and Patrick O'Connell, who were well-liked, integrated within their community and in the force primarily for bread-and-butter reasons, whose names history forgot. In transporting gelignite, they were the nearest and most obvious source of ammunition. Whether it was actually necessary to shoot them from the shelter of a ditch when they showed no serious resistance was understandably glossed over in the bluster of post-revolution memoirs. But the attack – no more than the subsequent infamous Kilmichael ambush in November 1920 in which 18 auxiliary policemen were killed – did draw attention to the youth, inexperience and nervousness which sat alongside unbridled idealism and daring.[46]

Seán O'Faoláin, whose father served with the RIC, recalled in his autobiography that 'men like my father were dragged out in those years and shot down as traitors to their country. Shot for cruel necessity – so be it. Shot to inspire terror. So be it. But they were not traitors. They had their loyalties and stuck to them.' Nonetheless, subsequent research by

Peter Hart revealed they were also capable of organising death squads.[47] Richard Abbott points out that after the Kilmichael ambush, a notice appeared in the RIC barracks at Macroom, in County Cork, giving them licence it seemed to kill on sight: 'all male inhabitants of Macroom and all males passing through Macroom shall not appear in public with their hands in their pockets. Any male infringing this order is liable to be shot on sight.'[48]

This period was also notable for the ending of another significant feature of Ireland's military history: the disbandment of the British army's five Southern Irish regiments in 1922. Although generally officered by British and Protestant unionists, the ranks were in the main composed of Irish Catholics. The Royal Munster Fusiliers, originally employed by the East India Company in the eighteenth century, were described by Lord Dunraven in 1918 as a regiment whose bones came from Bengal but whose blood and sinews were Irish. Some were quite content to make the transition from the army of the Empire to the IRA. One of the assassins of loyalist army officer Sir Henry Wilson, in 1922, was Joseph O'Sullivan, who had enlisted in the Munsters in 1915.[49] Nevertheless, between January 1919 and December 1921, 20,000 Irish men enlisted in the British army, over 1,500 coming from Cork, the most violent of the counties during the Troubles, and also the area with the highest incidence of IRA executions of ex-servicemen. Many had returned home as traitors having embarked on their military journeys as heroes, and found little room for manoeuvre in a changed political and social climate. By October 1919, 35,000 ex-servicemen were receiving the out-of-work donation in Ireland, accounting for an unemployment rate of 46 per cent, compared with only 10 per cent in Britain.[50]

'Deadly hunger for land'
As reflected in many of the decrees and resolutions of Dáil Éireann, and indeed the Democratic Programme, land remained a polarising issue in Irish society throughout the period of the Troubles. This was despite the social revolution inspired by successive acts of legislation, and the fact that most agricultural holdings had been purchased by tenants subject to land annuities which were not then a matter of contention. But by the early 1920s up to 3 million acres remained in landlord ownership. The distribution of land was highly uneven, with 32,000 farms of over 100 acres, and a large number of rich farmers in Leinster often at odds with

labourers. Land hunger in the west of Ireland fuelled resentment directed at the ranches. Some landlords retained huge tracts of tenanted land, or took advantage of legislation to mortgage and repurchase untenanted lands from the Land Commission at favourable rates, enabling some to continue to maintain the 'big houses' that dotted the rural landscape. These were obvious emotional and strategic targets for the IRA and between 1919 and 1923 over 300 of them were burnt down (most in fact were burnt during the Civil War, when almost three times as many were destroyed as during the War of Independence). Socio-economic as well as political reasons played a part in their destruction, and it was also the case that the compensation awarded was not enough to support their restoration to their previous splendour.[51]

In the rhetoric employed by the first Dáil, land redistribution was an issue of social justice as well as economic necessity. A decree of the Dáil that every Irish man was entitled to a living on his own land was typical of the era, but the practicalities of effecting such change were complex and emotive. The Dáil decreed that it was more important to channel the national desire for land towards the clearing out of foreign invaders rather than the occupiers 'of this and that piece of land'. This, however, was wishful thinking that overlooked the economic crisis besetting Irish agriculture, a hangover from the boom of the war years, after which there was a sharp fall in prices and a reduced export market because of stiffer competition from countries like Denmark taking advantage of the inferior quality of some Irish produce. In tandem with this there was continued friction between the Irish Farmers Union and the Irish Transport and General Workers' Union over rates of pay for agricultural labourers.

The first Dáil's attempt to deal with claims to land is reflected in the records of the Land Settlement Commission of 1918–22. A Proclamation of the first Dáil in June 1920, relating to claims for land, was rendered necessary by the fact that:

> Such claims are being based on the assertion that the claimants or the ancestors were formerly in occupation of the property so claimed, and whereas these claims are for the most part of old date, and while many of them may be well founded, others seem to be of a frivolous nature and are put forward in the hope of intimidating the present occupiers.[52]

By the summer of 1922 the commission courts had dealt with claims for ownership and transfer of land totalling 13,992 acres. The Land Settlement Commission sought to intervene by arbitrating in contested areas through the operation of district land courts, and was faced with the task of reconciling the central rhetoric of 'land for all' with the reality of local concerns and long-running disputes. Many of the cases dealt with by the commissioners revealed rural areas on the verge of social anarchy. Obduracy could be fuelled by long-term sectarian hatred or in many cases abject poverty, while those seeking land frequently organised themselves into ad-hoc committees to orchestrate agitation, or simply to plead for a fair hearing. Many locals deprived of land took it on themselves to evict Protestant neighbours without recourse to arbitration (cases which were particularly sensitive in the aftermath of the Treaty). Hand-scrawled death threats appeared occasionally when a land dispute ended in deadlock. In May 1922 the *Freeman's Journal* reported on 'Deadly hunger for land', detailing a case in which two men were killed in Loughrea, County Galway, following a land conflict.[53] But what was really striking was the number of Protestant landlords who were prepared to submit to arbitration, whether through fear, pragmatism or sincerity.

Land hunger was also exacerbated by an extraordinary prohibition on emigration, decided by the Dáil on the basis that it was unpatriotic to leave the country in time of war, though it was impossible to enforce this in practice. It was also the case that military engagements by the IRA were convenient screens for manoeuvres that were, in practice, simply land seizures. These not only revealed the relative ineffectiveness of Dublin Headquarters in preventing such moves, but also the determination of many IRA members at grassroots level to implement their own form of vigilantism. With regard to land grabbing, the Bishop of Galway, Thomas O'Dea, remarked that it was greed rather than love of land which prompted the breaking of God's law. Indeed, according to Paul Bew, Connacht's relatively minor contribution to the War of Independence had its roots in a preoccupation with agrarianism and the factionalism such anger inspired. Undoubtedly family tensions also played a part given the number of official 'assisting relatives', who in reality were unpaid labourers waiting for the death of a parent to assume the status of small farmer.[54]

Organised farmers also had an ambiguous attitude to the republican administration (campaigns for non-payment of rates would suit them), but were more assertive in their determination to oppose any redistribution that thwarted their self-interest. Sinn Féin's attempts to prevent the export of food in order to distribute it to the poor were halted when the interests of merchants were at stake.[55]

The violence that the land issue induced could be harrowing. In May 1920, Art O'Connor, the Minister for Agriculture, insisted that the central authority in Dublin was not in favour of land confiscation. This was the same month that Michael O'Toole, a herdsman and father of 13 children, ignored a demand not to work on demesne lands and continued to sow hayseeds. He was attacked by a mob of 20 and beaten with sticks and 'stoned until his skull was opened'. His wife found him at 3 a.m. in the morning, tied to a tree.[56] The IRA leadership may have been distrustful of mixing social agitation with the 'national struggle', but it was significant that districts where the most violent agricultural unrest occurred were not the busiest centres of national struggles. For many, there were other vicious wars to be fought. By 1922 the government was faced with the task of creating a viable agricultural economy, but it could not ignore the underlying class tensions in the rural districts which had prompted many district councils to plead with the central administration not to allow the eviction of cottage labourers (for non-payment of rent) amid fears that the cottages would fall into the hands of the farming classes.

'there were many republics in the world under which the workers were slaves'
Growing social unrest and rebellion against economic deprivation significantly increased in the months after the Truce. Whatever form the constitutional settlement arrived at between the two countries would take, many workers and trade unionists had already turned their heads towards fresh battles. Despite rhetoric from Sinn Féin about the support and sacrifice of workers being intrinsic to the development of the national cause, workers had tired of the postponement of labour issues and growing unrest was evident throughout the country. A series of strikes hit the rail network and other vital industries as workers sought better rates of pay. As well as the more celebrated soviet at the Cleeves factory in Limerick, soviets were established in locations as diverse as Arigna, County Leitrim, where the workers took charge of a mine, and Drogheda, where a foundry was seized. In Cork, 150 workers from the Cork Harbour Board marched through the city, four deep, led by a man carrying a red flag. Though this extreme form of action was celebrated by the Communist Party as an illustration that only through the triumph of the red flag could Irish

workers achieve control, the leader of the Labour Party, Thomas Johnson, was more cautious. He believed such soviets could be only symbolic, and any attempt to expand them was doomed, though the Bishop of Killaloe's belief that communism could be christianised seemed to indicate that even high-ranking members of the Catholic Church were caught up in the general uproar in Munster.[57]

But the 'godless' image of socialism was a further guarantee that Sinn Féin would keep its distance. Aodh de Blacam was insistent that Sinn Féin was in favour of co-operation rather than 'orthodox socialism', because co-operation was based on private ownership. He asserted: 'it is communal but not communistic'.[58] Arthur Griffith also swiped at the British influence of socialism. But the reality was that Johnson and his colleagues were determined there would be no repeat of the 1913 Lockout or any prolonged dispute that would place their organisation at risk. The Labour leadership had to tolerate local outbreaks under the vigorous tutelage of such individuals as Seán Dowling, the ITGWU organiser in Munster, and Peadar O'Donnell, who gave up his teaching job for full-time trade unionism. This weakness of national as opposed to local leadership was another illustration of Labour's seeming inability to place labour issues at the centre of any quest for power, as had happened in 1918.

The agricultural sector was equally shaken by economic disputes. In Kilmallock, County Limerick, in November 1921, the refusal of the Irish Farmers' Union to pay the harvest bonus developed into serious confrontation as labourers and creamery workers marched through the town carrying the red flag. By the following January the IRA had proclaimed martial law in the area after walls around large holdings were knocked down and cattle driven off the land. In County Wexford, a transport union told a group of farm labourers and other workers that:

> some workers were foolish enough to believe that when they got an Irish settlement they would have no more problems to face and automatically they would start driving about in motor cars and living like lords; that an Irish republic would mean peace and plenty for everybody immediately. Let them examine the truth of that ... there were many republics in the world under which the workers were slaves. To the Irish worker, an Irish republic meant a workers' republic – freedom for the working classes – and if they did not obtain that freedom, they would have to fight for it, even after an Irish settlement.[59]

The level of trade union membership rose dramatically during these years, reflecting the economic down-turn, and was seen by many activists as the outstanding achievement of the post-war years because of its key role in establishing a link between mature urban trade unionism and an older tradition of agrarian radicalism. If Labour was to be established as a vital force in Irish life it was essential that it be firmly established in the country's biggest industry, agriculture. The figures seemed to indicate that it was. Previously, precarious employment and impoverishment had militated against any rural labourers joining unions, a situation the war had reversed. The priorities of the ITGWU duly switched from a preoccupation with getting wage levels increased to a determination to maintain wage levels. There were roughly 100,000 Irish trade union members in 1916; this rose to 156,000 in 1919 and 225,000 in 1920, with, in addition, 30,000 union members who were not affiliated to the Irish Trade Union Congress. These figures were to decrease to 196,000 in 1921 and 175,000 in 1924. Emmet O'Connor suggested that:

> The rise of rural trade unionism in Ireland was the outstanding achievement of the post-war years. It constituted a conduit between the agrarian tradition of direct action and advanced trade unionism ... above all, it anchored Labour within the heart of the Irish condition, giving it an interest in the country's biggest industry. In this sense agricultural trade unionism was the measure of Labour's power.[60]

Unfortunately for the labour movement it was never to be quite that simple, nor 'the heart of the Irish condition' that hospitable. The number of days lost through strikes had averaged 200,000 between 1914 and 1916; reached 700,000 in 1917 and 1918; jumped to 1.4 million in 1920; only to fall again to 700,000 in 1921.[61] The tumults of post-war Europe had their echo in the form of a syndicalist movement which was minor though significant, ensuring an uneasy relationship with Sinn Féin. Unlike in France, Germany and Britain where social disturbances often disappeared as a result of economic depression, and divisions between communists and socialists were common, overall militancy was maintained at a high level. But Irish syndicalism also differed from some of its European counterparts in its lack of a theoretical framework of reference, relying solely on direct action and the idea of one big union. Occupational demands for libertarianism were favoured over long-term strategy. Like their counterparts in the Labour Party, there did seem to be a neglect of the concept of state power in the trade union movement. In May 1921, the Labour Party withdrew from the general election, although they had polled one fifth of the votes in the 1920 local elections.

The labour movement also faced the difficulty of class prejudice and integrating their philosophy of class conflict and 'redistributivism' into a Sinn Féin-controlled national movement that placed such a premium on cultural and racial unity and an external rather than internal enemy. Unlike in southern France and central Italy, where socialism was more effectively cultivated among land-owning peasants, this was not a feature in Ireland. Even though Labour could be strongest when it tackled social issues, the development of a broader political hegemony to displace a nationalism which it shared was to prove difficult. Likewise the partition of the country militated against an alliance between industrialised craft workers and semi-skilled and general workers, which was a feature of other parts of Europe in the early decades of the twentieth century. In the context of labour history, the shipyard workers of Belfast represented the greatest concentration of unionised skilled labour in Ireland, numbering about 36,000 in 1919, though unionist leaders had successfully moved in 1918 to establish a unionist labour association in order to stem an independent labour movement challenging its political hegemony. This occurred because it was recognised by unionists that the Northern labour force was a highly complex social group with many divisions and antagonisms.

Whatever about the limitations of the organisational endeavours of the trade union leadership, the extension of syndicalism to the rural world heralded new styles and new forms of struggle. The world war had significantly involved new sections of the salaried classes, including clerks and civil servants, but especially agricultural and general workers, of whom one third were unionised by 1920. The municipal officers of Ireland's trade unions had staged the first-ever clerical workers' strike in Dublin Corporation in June 1920, achieving victory after closing down the city's government for a week. Also active were the Irish Women's Workers' Union, though the decision to establish a separate women's union perhaps owed as much to traditional prejudice against women workers on the part of male trade union membership as to a specific claim for exclusivity on the part of women.

'put machinery out of order and burnt farms'
Dáil Éireann responded with concessions, attempts to outflank labour, or simple repression. This was justified on the same grounds that de Valera had justified the postponement of the implementation of the Democratic Programme and on the same grounds that the Irish Republican Brotherhood had suggested 'internal problems' were only of minor importance; they could be rectified only when British rule was ended. But the 'internal problems' were manifold – paralysed industry, inadequate protection of traders, bank raids, seizure of farms by force and, especially in districts like Clare, cattle driving. Amidst the mayhem, Constance Markievicz, the first woman to be elected to Westminster, and the Dáil Minister of Labour, strove to construct an economic policy.

The Truce it seemed did not hold out hope of alleviation; Markievicz noted after it that:

> In the last few weeks conditions have been growing worse and worse and in many places the workers have taken forcible possession of industries, put machinery out of order and burnt farms and ricks. Each one of these small outbreaks acts as an advertisement and is an encouragement to workers in other places to do similar things. The difficulties of the situation in this country today are intensified by the truce. We do not know whether it is to be war or peace during the next few months that are coming. In the meantime we have an enemy in partial occupation of our country, our government cannot function freely and our supply of money is limited.

Significantly, Markievicz believed that if the war was resumed the blame for unemployment would fall on British occupation; that if there was peace, 'power and money' would enable a native government to alleviate the difficulties. She suggested that if the uncertainty continued, a 'violent and popular' leader could emerge and plunge the country into an industrial relations quagmire,[62] an indication that historians have not given enough attention or credence to the potential for revolutionary working-class unrest in the midst of the revolution. Markievicz had also commented on the problem of infanticide in Ireland in 1919, complaining that 'most were foolish working girls who had got into trouble and had killed their little babies because life with them was impossible, because they had no way of earning a living, nowhere to go and nothing to eat'.[63]

Despite these specific fears, economic policy remained rooted in crude generalisations and vague, if worthy, aspiration. Markievicz was in favour of the organisation of co-operatives to ensure agricultural workers were paid a decent wage, and an increase in roadworks to employ the labourers over the winter. But the government's economic committee continued to draw up general policy statements based on the reclamation and redistribution of land, the encouragement of the fishing industry, and propaganda in favour of a 'national industrial spirit' and the consumption of home-manufactured goods. Some impatient officials were at pains to point out that in the difficult prevailing economic climate, propaganda was an ill substitute for meaningful legislation (in the form of protective tariffs), which would have to include retailers as well as manufacturers to 'ensure that the will of the bulk of the people was not largely nullified by the action of shopkeepers who would kill all Irish industry to earn a fraction more profit'. This was another private admission that for many in revolutionary Ireland the issue of profit was of much more relevance than that of patriotism.[64]

'Her money kept the household going'

As the first woman to be elected to parliament in the UK and the Dáil's only female minister, Markievicz has understandably been given pride of place in the recording of women's contributions during this period. The role played by women in the founding of the state was multi-dimensional; from the elevated position of Markievicz, through the women TDs, Cumann na mBan, women's rights activists, women whose family members were involved, and the great number whose lives were played out in grinding poverty, women were deeply integrated in the move towards independence, though it was often a struggle to be heard. Máire Mhac an tSaoi, the daughter of Seán MacEntee (a leading republican and future Fianna Fáil government minister), suggested the discrimination against women after independence was all the more galling in light of the fact that many of the male revolutionaries frequently had to rely on earning wives to keep the household going. Speaking about her mother, she suggested: 'on women's issues, she had no confidence in male politicians – ever. She had been the main breadwinner. My father had been in and out of jail. *Her* money kept the household going.'[65]

Feminists like Hanna Sheehy Skeffington made much of the fact that the 1916 insurrection was unique in being an occasion where men

fighting for freedom voluntarily included women. In terms of perpetuating a popular culture of quasi-religious martyrdom for the dead 1916
patriots, women had played an instrumental role, not to mention their
orchestration of the powerfully emotive and symbolic receptions that the
internees received on their return to Dublin. However, during April 1917
there was only one woman, Mrs Plunkett, on the council deciding the
strategy of the new Sinn Féin movement, which was seen by many as an
inadequate recognition of the status of women within the new nationalist family. A league of women delegates was promptly formed, proposing
six women to play a part in these negotiations – Kathleen Clarke, Áine
Ceannt, Jenny Wyse-Power, Kathleen Lynn, Helena Molony and Alice
Ginnell – on the grounds that they had taken equal risks in the quest for
a republic; it was necessary to have their organised co-operation in the
continuing struggle; and they could bring greater insight to the social
problems that would arise in the near future (a very early vote of no confidence in the male ability to deal with social problems).

'my weight was reduced to 6 stone'

The women were effectively ignored until the forces of Cumann na mBan,
the Irish Women's Franchise League and the Irish Women Workers' Union
were marshalled together, forcing a concession from Sinn Féin that four
'ladies' would be involved in the new Sinn Féin executive out of 24 (they
had demanded six). This permitted them a vocal presence at the Sinn Féin
convention of 1917, though there were only 12 women among the 1,000
delegates, with only one from outside the capital, Rosamund Jacob from
Waterford.[66] This battle over the convention was only the beginning of
a struggle to be heard – only two women were selected to contest the
1918 general election (where women over the age of 30 with the requisite property qualifications could vote for the first time), though they had
more success in the 1920 local-government elections. There was also an
acknowledgement that the national crisis had left suffrage as a secondary
issue.[67]

The male leaders of Sinn Féin were at best ambiguous, at worst
duplicitous, in their dealings with political women. Michael Collins was
not convinced in June 1921 about the merits of sending Sheehy Skeffington and members of the IWFL to form part of the Women's International League to interview premiers from the British colonies (who were in
London), though de Valera agreed to give them £100.[68] At the level of foot

soldier Cumann na mBan's lines of communication through the provinces were vital to the war effort and their dedication to duty no less passionate. In October 1921 there was great rejoicing in contemporary newspapers when four women political prisoners succeeded in escaping from Mountjoy Prison using a rope ladder. In the aftermath of the escapade a crackdown in the jail brought the five remaining prisoners, three of whom had been sentenced to life, out on hunger strike under the leadership of Commandant Eileen McGrane.

The Bureau of Military History archive contains a total of 149 statements by women. Collectively, they suggest that the involvement of women was comprehensive and wide-ranging, covering the political and military spheres as well as education, promotion of the Irish language, involvement in drama groups and helping to orchestrate the opposition to conscription in 1918. The level of commitment of ordinary volunteers was exceptional and, in some cases, damaging to their health. Brighíd O'Mullane, organising branches of Cumann na mBan, recalled that:

> the life was strenuous, as I generally worked in three meetings a day to cover the various activities of each branch. My meals were, of course, very irregular, and the result of this sort of life, which I led for three years ... was that my weight was reduced to 6 stone. I got many severe wettings and consequent colds, which I was unable to attend to. The reaction to this came during the truce, when I broke down and had to get medical attention.[69]

Cumman na mBan members from branches in Scotland and England also smuggled in arms, often at great personal risk. There was nothing genteel about the revolutionary female's role. In 1921 an IRA division commander wrote that:

> In my area there was no question of girls only helping. In dispatch carrying, scouting and intelligence work, all of which are highly dangerous, they did far more than the soldiers ... were it not for the assistance of the women, organised and unorganised ... at the height of the terror we found that the more dangerous the work, the more willing they were to do it.[70]

'the terrorism of the few self-seeking hot heads'

There were many acts of defiance during the War of Independence which was the most obvious manifestation of a direct change in the tactics of the republican movement. It was of pivotal importance to expand opposition to British rule into an all-out war, both political and military. It was the culmination of a strategy which, directly at odds with the approach of 1916, placed a premium on killing rather than dying for Ireland. In subsequent years an idea of unity, coherence and virtue was often ascribed to the republican fighters of the war, but this rarely existed at the time. As with most wars, the reality was much more a mixture of bravery, contradiction, inconsistency, bluster and brutality, coinciding with clever, imaginative and strategic planning, and perhaps most importantly, the support of much of the general public, though this could also be procured under duress. Flawed military thinking on the part of the British establishment also ensured widespread revulsion at the British presence in Ireland. British ineptitude in this regard was a product of a wholly simplistic interpretation of the Anglo-Irish problem, revealed in the private papers of the viceroy Lord French, who seemed genuinely to believe that the Irish race was 'peculiarly liable to be influenced by their immediate environment', so that Irish people only had to be freed 'from the terrorism of the few self-seeking hot heads'.[71] A similar mentality was also reflected in the papers of Lloyd George and other British ministers of the period; it was based on racial and religious prejudice and an ignorance of the real state of affairs in Ireland that had been much in evidence in the nineteenth century.[72]

The War of Independence led to the death of roughly 1,200 people, though the manner in which it was conducted gave it an impact far beyond what the statistics for fatalities would suggest, and there are no reliable figures for civilian deaths.[73] (Neither are there exact figures for the numbers killed in the Civil War; a figure of 1,100 for military combatants has been suggested.) A significant feature of the war in Cork, for example, was that most of those killed by the IRA did not die in armed combat but as a result of the shooting of unarmed people. Fatality statistics may suggest a military draw but they do not account for the decisive propaganda war which the republicans emphatically won. They not only proved themselves capable of withstanding the British military, but also of developing enough momentum to secure a seat at the negotiating table in Downing Street.

'slay them if necessary to overcome their resistance'

Whatever about the use of words such as murder and massacre – and such semantics in relation to the war have proved emotive and controversial – perhaps the most important point of this era, as enunciated by Michael Laffan, was that at the helm of this war was a political party with a popular mandate. An obsessive preoccupation with the military events of this era can lead to a neglect of the fact that, as Laffan pointed out, Sinn Féin 'was the principal means whereby Ireland's constitutional tradition was transmitted through years of turbulence, and it played an important role in ensuring that governments in independent Ireland would be responsible to the people. Sinn Féin was the democratic face of the Irish revolution.'[74] Of course, there were many other faces too, many of them bloody and contorted. There was overlap too between various groups; the revised Irish Republican Brotherhood Constitution of 1920, for example, had maintained that its Supreme Council was the sole government of the Republic of Ireland, which led to many clashes such as that between Cathal Brugha and Michael Collins. The real fall-out from the War of Independence, and indeed the subsequent Civil War, was the need to contain violence, even if it could not be eliminated completely; ironically, the same challenge was facing Britain during these years.

For many scholars, demystifying the War of Independence was about deconstructing the historical romance of Irish militarism and life in the column on the run, though the reality of course was that most of the young volunteers (and this was overwhelmingly a revolution of the young) remained as part-time players in the drama. Despite confusion about allegiance on the part of the volunteers (it is probably the case that many were confused as to whether their allegiance was to the Dáil, Sinn Féin, the IRA or, for some, the IRB), it had been asserted by *An tÓglách*, the newspaper of the IRA, in the aftermath of the Soloheadbeg episode, that every volunteer was entitled to use 'all legitimate methods of warfare against the soldiers and policemen of the English usurpers and slay them if necessary to overcome their resistance'.[75] Defiant messages to the footsoldiers of the flying columns were, however, only one aspect of this conflict – the use of elements within the establishment, particularly government employees at the lower end of the scale with organisational experience and access to information, was essential, particularly to Collins in his attempt to keep ahead of the Dublin Castle system of intelligence. But for many more, the revolution was to be experienced by those excluded from power who

could focus their political objectives on a romantic and historical continuity of oppression without having to worry about the reality of power
politics for the time being. Meanwhile, propaganda from Britain understandably focused on the idea of murderous thugs intimidating normally
law-abiding people into support for a Dáil which, though proclaiming
democratic legitimacy, was merely a theatre of war.

The British refusal to distinguish between the various arms of the
republican struggle had some legitimacy; well before the Dáil had met,
after all, armed republican forces were in existence. Collins himself
embodied all the ambiguity and the blurring of the lines between civilian
and military, being Finance Minister, President of the IRB and Director
of Intelligence of the Irish Volunteers (now generally being referred to
as the IRA). It was inevitable that tensions would begin to emerge with
individuals like Cathal Brugha, who wanted an army directly controlled
by the Dáil ministry, distrusting the behind-the-scenes influence of the
IRB. On the British side, in any case, it was not until late in 1920 that
police reports began to refer to the IRA, a term covering what was in effect
a hybrid organisation which raised questions as to who was in charge and
whether loyalties were local or national. This was an uncertainty exacerbated by the army's reluctance to accept the autonomy of the Dáil and
indeed the Dáil's reluctance to accept responsibility for their actions. It
was not until March 1921 that de Valera was authorised by the Dáil to
take responsibility for the actions of the IRA, though in time, the limited
extent to which he was in control was to worry both him and others, an
inevitability given his prolonged absence from the country during this
period as he toured the United States.

The extent to which individual volunteers were trained, disciplined
or capable soldiers was another moot point and it was here that, ironically, those who had received training in the allied armies of the First
World War provided invaluable experience to the IRA. Richard Mulcahy,
as Chief of Staff, had noted the need for people to be educated and led
gently into war, but this was perhaps merely camouflaging the fact that
complete centralised control could not compete with the morass of fac-
tional and parochial identities which the struggle inevitably threw up,
particularly with regard to the strong family influences in rural Ireland.
If compromise was achieved, and it was on many levels, this could be
done only with much blurring at the edges, though tensions would have
been eased somewhat by the appointment of a popular and respected

symbol like Michael Collins to both strategic political and military positions.

'We had one old Martini rifle'

Undoubtedly, in some areas officers tended to emerge rather than be elected, but in tandem with a British government crackdown, it was the flying columns, forced on the run and with the time and inclination to develop military ability, who became the essence of the IRA campaign and, in that, the essence of revolutionary youth: sons of labourers, the medium-sized farms and the lower-middle class. Many of the obituaries of the unfortunate would attest to high character, clean living and respectability – not the stuff it seemed of the cabins and the back lanes, despite the emphasis in memoirs on the backing they received from the poorest of the poor, who many of the volunteers saw as ignorant and idle. Volunteers, it seemed, fell distinctly between the middle or upper classes and the unemployed, the classic 'plain people' and not the often reluctant republicans of the farming classes.[76] Many were reared solely by their mothers and in their memoirs saw their volunteering as a natural impulse requiring little elaboration, a collective response to regional identity, though in Dublin it seems the majority came from working-class backgrounds.[77]

How able and numerous were they? The truth was that with a strategic approach of assassination in the city and ambush in rural areas, it was probably not realistic to have more than 1,000 men in flying columns, but it has been argued that modern guerrilla warfare methods first emerged successfully in Ireland, though again, this could be an attempt to suggest an innovativeness that was not in evidence to contemporaries. Regional variation was significant and Dublin, Cork and Clare, for example, tended to be more organised than other parts of the country.

The witness statements in the Bureau of Military History invite reflection on the extent to which the independence struggle was under effective central control. Patrick Cannon, a volunteer in west Mayo, testified that 'we had no information about the enemy and just anticipated that some such would pass that way some time during the day … we had no arms at the time'. In east Mayo, Patrick Cassidy remembered himself and his colleagues as ill-equipped: 'we got no rifles of any sort. We had one old Martini rifle and a large sporting type rifle for which we had no ammunition … we did not appreciate then the importance of intelligence and did not give this subject the value it deserved.'[78] These are among the many statements that, far from being triumphalist or boastful, were frank about the shortcomings of the IRA's campaign. But it is clear other volunteers were relatively well armed and had access to more information; indeed, there is a multitude of statements from those involved in intelligence work of various kinds. The lengthy statement by Ned Broy, Michael Collins's spy in Dublin Castle, is irksome and exaggerated. It recounts long conversations and incidents in great detail with a tone of hero worship of Collins that borders on the homoerotic.[79]

A particularly interesting statement was contributed by James O'Donavan, Director of Chemicals on the IRA's GHQ staff, a university student of chemistry, who detailed the tests and research he carried out in UCD using gelignite, nitro-cresylic acids and poison gas. It comes as a surprise when he mentions the importance of an awareness of 'bacteriological warfare', not a phrase one normally associates with the War of Independence. He suggested that the IRA at one stage considered the possibilities of infecting British military horses with 'glanders or some similar infectious disease' and of spreading botulism. O'Donavan wrote with great passion and pride about his work, relishing the memory of:

> getting a beautiful grenade turned out in a week – a vast improvement on anything that had been done in the way of moulding the wall with its sectional grooves. I always maintained that our final grenade was really superior to the Mills. The whole problem with me, if I was going to produce explosives more or less on an army scale, was that they had to be made so simple that men with practically no knowledge could make them in a farmhouse kitchen and places like that. Yet, they had to be fairly foolproof, because we could not have people all over the country having their heads blown off. We had some accidents, but not many. Training was given and a series of instructions on explosives, incendiaries etc., was gradually given.[80]

'His job was to shoot the drivers of the lorries'

A number of statements describe, sometimes with suspicious exactitude, the details of various ambushes and confrontations, and the carrying out of the sometimes chilling orders volunteers were given. Daniel Cashman, a member of the East Cork Flying Column, recorded that 'In the middle of May 1921, an order was received from Brigade headquarters that all British military personnel in uniform should be shot at sight whether they were

armed or unarmed.' This kind of statement makes one think of the effect
this must have had on young terrified British soldiers who, in going out
on patrol against a guerrilla army who could strike and disappear quickly,
were such vulnerable and in many cases easy targets. Sometimes they were
killed by IRA soldiers who had been trained by their own former British
army colleagues, a theme which crops up in a number of areas. Daniel
Cashman remembered:

> an ex British army man who had been recently demobbed and had
> joined … he was reported to be a crackshot with a rifle and, for that
> reason, he was stationed at a point about 50 yards on the east of the tree
> giving him a clear view of the approaching enemy lorries. His job was
> to shoot the drivers of the lorries.[81]

Statements were also collected from IRA activists who had operated abroad.
James Byrne, a member of the IRB based in Scotland, described how his
colleagues, mostly miners and steel workers, smuggled small numbers of
explosives out of the mines and had them shipped to Dublin via Glasgow,
as well as buying rifles from former British servicemen, and he suggested
the number of automatic rifles passing through his hand was 'about 20 per
week over a period of nine months'.[82] Hugh Early and his colleagues in
the Liverpool Battalion of the IRA, with about 130 active volunteers, also
smuggled arms, set fire to property in Liverpool and attacked the homes
of Black and Tans whose addresses had been secured by raiding the mail
in Ireland.[83]

   The memoirs of Ernie O'Malley, detailing the evident ignorance of
military work at the very end of 1919, were also referred to by Charles
Townshend, one of the historians of the military campaign, who suggested
that 'political dispute, family rivalry, instinctive opposition – in effect
a sort of social banditry – provided the motive force. The means were
dictated by circumstance. Slender resources created the style of warfare
rather than a conviction that it held a real hope of ultimate success.'[84] Such
historical accounts depict separated and irregular units, many of which
were never fully prepared for serious action, an impression endorsed by the
statements given to the Bureau of Military History. But the same statements also highlight the reasons why, in 1921, the IRA could still inflict
damage in the most chilling ways: '5 or 6 of the Westport Volunteers and
an equal number of the Castlebar Volunteers all equipped with small arms

were instructed to go into the respective towns and shoot up any patrols or parties of the enemy they could find.'[85]

Nonetheless, there was a consistency to the military approach; initially raids for arms, attacks on RIC stations and the disruption of transport and essential communications, while Mulcahy attempted to place some order and discipline on the disparate components. In the pages of *An tÓglách*, some semblance of a theory of guerrilla warfare did seem to be emerging, particularly given its references to the IRA developing the practice of guerrilla warfare from a casual thing to 'a science'. Of course, not all got the opportunity to fly in the columns. Seán O'Faoláin observed that:

> the great mass of us rank and filers were given such undemanding if essential jobs as the gathering of more or less useful information, watching over the billets of fighters, scouting, carrying dispatches … helping to trench roads or fell trees … otherwise we hung around, drilled, waited, felt nervy, groused and were supremely proud and happy whenever even the most modest task made us feel we were doing something positive in the struggle for independence.[86]

Townshend dismissed the notion of a degree of professionalism or military expertise, commenting:

> The IRA's campaign was much more casual than scientific … the political position of the IRA within the Republican structure was fraught with the most dangerous possibilities. The failure to subordinate the army to a single legitimate authority and to eliminate the influence of the IRB undermined from an early stage the chance of securing acceptance of the eventual Anglo-Irish settlement and of avoiding civil war. Notwithstanding its faults however, the Republican campaign still demands attention as a remarkable pioneering endeavour. If the reasons for its achievements were not entirely understood, either by the IRA itself or by others, these achievements could be used to establish a new framework for resistance against imperial power. To that extent, at least, *An tÓglách* was right.[87]

The work of Peter Hart also demonstrates the difficulty of categorising acts of violence 'to give them moral and military coherence'. His research makes clear there were many revenge and anonymous shootings, disappearances and nocturnal raids, while by the summer of 1922 the IRA was capable of committing similar abuses to the Black and Tans, British ex-servicemen recruited to augment the troops already in Ireland.[88]

'for many guerrillas, of course, the republic had nothing to do with politics'
One thing which was abundantly clear, however, was that this was a conflict that revealed the extent to which class warfare became an essential feature of the struggle to silence opposition and prevent collusion. Revenge and betrayal were the uncomfortable bedfellows of unity and self-sacrifice during these years; volunteering for many of the working classes or lower-middle classes could become a badge of respectability, but it came at a cost and created confusion about categorising acts of violence morally and militarily. Peter Hart suggested over 700 people died in Cork between 1917 and 1923 as a consequence of the revolution, 400 at the hands of the IRA. The IRA losses amounted to 192 killed, but more than one third of the dead were civilians, which is why the forensic meticulousness of Hart made for such uncomfortable but revealing reading 75 years after the events.[89] His research into County Cork revealed that the IRA deliberately shot over 200 citizens, of whom over 70 were Protestant, one of the reasons for the reduction by 34 per cent of the Protestant population of the south from 1911 to 1926, which Hart suggested was 'the single greatest measurable change of the revolutionary era'.[90]

Hart valiantly documented the forgotten civilian footnotes of the revolution, but also questioned the unchallenged accounts of such events as Tom Barry's Kilmichael ambush in November 1920, in which three IRA members and 17 (or 18 according to some accounts) auxiliary cadets, members of an elite anti-IRA force, were killed. In Hart's view it was a brave ambush that ultimately became a cowardly massacre which involved the deliberate killing of already surrendered soldiers. It was an ambush that became the most venerated IRA victory in the War of Independence, making celebrities of its architects. It led to the imposition of martial law and British recognition that the IRA was capable of defeating its soldiers on the battlefields.

Hart's revision was of course at odds with local myth and triumphalist memoir but served to illustrate the murky reality of such exercises, militarily and morally. If such detailed document hoovering was done for other events it would doubtless rattle the bones of other heroes.

But for all the Tom Barrys, and indeed his namesake Kevin, the Jesuit-educated middle-class martyr, hanged by the British in November 1920, after his part in an ambush, there were many more whose stories remained buried with their spy placards and family shame. Hart suggested that 'Most people were keeping quiet and out of trouble. Uneasy ambivalence seems to have been the feeling of most communities. If support for Volunteers operations was far from universal, fear provided an adequate motive for acquiescence and silence.'[91] Such assertions have to be qualified by an acknowledgement that a guerrilla campaign could not be waged without a significant degree of public support. The role played by women was crucial in this regard, particularly from Cumann na mBan, which evolved into an at times strident rebel organisation, irked occasionally by the criticisms of the likes of Hanna Sheehy Skeffington as to the unequal relationship between CnB and the IRA. Perhaps emboldened by the fact that 43 women had been elected locally in 1920, some women got involved in rifle practice, but for the CnB branches divided into squads of six, one for signalling and the others for first aid and home nursing, it was unlikely they would engage in much shooting.

But the killing of civilians by the IRA does seem unusually high, particularly after the beginning of 1920, when open attacks on crown forces were authorised by IRA Headquarters, leading to many more on the run. Paranoia inevitably increased as information and popular support became more urgent; and those suspected of assisting or indeed tolerating the enemy – whether by accusation, supposition, employment or sentiment – were legitimate targets, often providing a convenient cover for local vendettas. Hart suggested that:

> for many guerrillas, of course, the republic had nothing to do with politics. Having power meant one thing; settling old scores and ridding the country of their enemies. And, in the sudden absence of government or armed opposition, a profusion of grievances and feuds sprang back to life. Once again, anonymous shootings, disappearances and nocturnal raids became commonplace. The dominant theme of the violence ... was revenge.

He also suggested that the war against spies and informers, which tapped a vein of communal prejudice and gossip, was 'a second unacknowledged civil war'.[92]

'a mockery of the Confessional'

Sectarianism too played its part and there was no shortage of abusive political language to identify Protestant enemies ('landgrabber', 'loyalist', 'imperialist', 'Orangeman', 'Freemason') and assert the need for their killing. In the same manner, labelling one an informer could in fact cover a multitude of sins, agrarian and domestic included. Simple non-conformity was also dangerous, as was a refusal to contribute financially to the IRA campaign, or indeed being unfortunate enough to be the victim of local gossip. Although it had been made clear in April 1920 that HQ sanction was needed to execute spies (except when their continued imprisonment endangered the volunteers), lack of evidence and sanction seemed to matter little towards the end of the conflict. Sectarianism remained rampant in certain areas. In early May 1922 there were ten Protestants shot dead in Cork in a single night.[93]

Perhaps inevitably, given the allegiances of the witnesses, there is little information on the IRA's own brutality and crushing of internal dissent in the statements contributed to the Bureau of Military History, though the occasional native dissident appears. A local chemist by the name of Kennedy, in Borris, Co. Carlow, an atheist educated at Trinity College, refused to close his shop in support of an IRA-called strike or for the funeral of Terence MacSwiney. A member of the Carlow IRA claimed he also collaborated with the Black and Tans in firing at the IRA. Kennedy's lack of religious conviction seemed to contemporaries to go hand-in-hand with his pro-British sympathies:

> He was continually passing insulting remarks about the Catholic religion. On one occasion when there was a mission in the parish church in Borris, Kennedy cleared everything out of his shop window and covered it with brown paper. He left two rectangular apertures over one of which he printed the word 'men' and over the other 'women'. This was intended as a mockery of the Confessional. The missionaries were brought to talk to him, but they never made any headway with him. He used to say – 'show me your God, and then I will believe.'[94]

Kennedy's shop was boycotted, and the IRA, the witness maintained, eventually managed to shoot him.

The truth was that the revolution was as much regional as national in nature and much could depend on the traditions of radicalism within particular urban or rural areas, the relative wealth of a particular district or the strength of family connections. Given the relative homogeneity of the population in areas like County Mayo, it is likely a much more symbiotic relationship existed between volunteers and community, a closeness which would have been more difficult in the more diffuse urban areas such as Dublin. In any case, lack of central co-ordination could only breed regional diversity. Joost Augusteijn, who researched the experiences of the ordinary rank and file members, makes the point that 'few of all the columns conformed to the organisational and administrative directions given by GHQ ... a variety of groups emerged ranging in size from about 10 men in less active areas to as many as 100 in Cork'; and furthermore, that 'only a small number of volunteers in a few areas were fully professionalised in their involvement. Activity was continuously limited by a lack of arms, courage and moral and physical willingness.'[95]

'I found my mind preoccupied with the devising of menus'
Rather than reflecting devout ideological commitment, involvement with the IRA could be very much dictated by social context. Reaction to British aggression – such as the hanging of Kevin Barry – was another motivational force, as was the treatment of prisoners on hunger strike. Seán Moylan, a member of an active-service unit of the Cork IRA, described his experiences in prison in a statement to the Bureau of Military History:

> I shall always hate jails and sympathise with prisoners. The food was uneatable; the bullying tones of the warders unbearable; the harsh routine of prison life a constant insult. I went on hunger strike. Then began the struggle for freedom. Day after day I found my mind preoccupied with the devising of menus. Elaborate and often incongruous combinations of food – flesh, fruit, vegetables – passed on the assembly belt of imagination before my eyes, leaving the craving that encompassed me more insistent as the days went by ... wearisome, interminable, the days of the hunger strike dragged out at slow length. Threatened, abused, ridiculed at first, later I was wooed and tempted with specially prepared delicacies. I refused to break.[96]

Frequent raids and searches and the appeal of the history of the Irish resistance to British rule, as had been transmitted to new generations as a result of the commemoration of 1798, and the anti-English sentiment during the Boer War and 1916 Rising, also played their part in sustaining the republican campaign. This was despite the fact that 'very few volunteers actually expressed a clear idea of what Irishness exactly entailed beyond speaking Irish and playing Gaelic games, or what should be done differently once independence was achieved'. But ultimately, the British government's use of force 'only reinforced the idea that complete independence offered the sole solution to Ireland's problems'.[97]

This supports the idea that British government policy in Ireland up to the middle of 1920 was a disaster, with a failure to establish any unity of command, the militarisation of the police and the failure to discourage reprisals.

The increasing severity of the government's approach to republican organisation and defiance was another essential factor in co-ordinating the IRA's strategic plans. But the response of the British government to the Irish crisis was not one-dimensional; peeling back the layers of their various strategies does in fact reveal a multitude of factors at work, and indeed ironies, given Britain's wider concern with preserving its 'liberal' credentials with the world at large. There was much imperial unrest elsewhere in the Empire, particularly in Egypt, India and Mesopotamia, and from 1919 to 1921 all these places, along with Ireland, 'appeared with monotonous regularity on the cabinet agenda'. As Deirdre McMahon has noted: 'the fear of a domino effect in each theatre of Imperial unrest gripped British ministers as they thrashed around for a solution'.[98] It was not until September 1919 that the government declared the first Dáil illegal; but the election which had encouraged Sinn Féin to convene a domestic parliament had also been a moment of domestic triumph for David Lloyd George. The post-1916 British government response to Irish republicanism also has to be seen in the context of the conduct of the First World War. This was an administration presiding over the largest army in British history; a confident, determined government which not only executed the 1916 rebels but also came away from the ill-fated 1917–18 Convention believing that Sinn Féin, who boycotted it, were ultimately misguided, if not unintelligent; a sentiment which was stuck with publicly at least until 1921.

'tinkers and tailors and candle-stick makers'
But it was also the case that the conscription crisis of 1918 and the subsequent 'German plot' arrests not only did much to unite Irish public

opinion, but forced the clever men of Sinn Féin underground and intensified their determination to break the police intelligence system. Their
clandestine activity underlined the simplicity of the attitude evident in
the London *Daily News* in 1919 whose contributor wondered whether a
'respectable' group of idealists at the top would be submerged by grassroots hot heads with little grasp of the reality of power politics.[99] The conscription crisis was an important event in transforming the character of the
Irish attitude from an overt defiance, which often seemed to provocatively
invite arrest, to secret preparation for military conflict by a small group of
committed volunteers who had been tutored in the so-called schools and
universities that their post-1916 prison camps became.

The Viceroy, Lord French, had his own views on the hierarchy of the
volunteers and its relationship with the grassroots, as already seen, and
backed by Walter Long, the cabinet's key man on Irish affairs, initiated
a number of policies, including the recruitment of the Black and Tans.
Patrick Shea, later a successful Catholic civil servant in the North, in his
memoir *Voices and the Sound of Drums*, remembered being in Templemore,
where his father was an RIC officer. He recalled that there was a huge gulf
between the Tans and the RIC men, to the extent that the former frightened even those they had come to help: 'They had all sorts of occupations;
there were lapsed motor mechanics and cooks and retired professional
boxers, overweight jockeys, ex-commercial travellers, unsuccessful university students, unskilled labourers, tinkers and tailors and candle-stick
makers. There were confidence men, petty crooks, congenital loafers, card
sharpers and gun-happy adventurers. There were decent men and scoun-
drels, adventurers and frightened youths, domesticated family men and
fugitives from deserted wives; there were English and Scottish and Welsh,
Jew and gentile.'[100] Walter Long was crucial in convincing the government
in the autumn of 1919 that any offer of dominion status would be transformed by Sinn Féin into complete separation, depicting them as extremists to be crushed rather than a coalition to be persuaded to compromise.
The problem with British policy was that heavy-handed tactics to deal
with the so-called extremists merely brought more so-called 'moderates'
into Sinn Féin's realm, making a mockery in Irish eyes (and ultimately,
beyond Ireland) of the idea that the government was involved in extending
protection to a law-abiding majority against violent corner-boys. In any
case, they were not capable of overcoming the military tactics of their opponents, which eventually led a reluctant Lloyd George to acknowledge in the

summer of 1921 that there was indeed a war (labelled 'small') going on in Ireland; a fact which had not been admitted publicly previously. This was also an acknowledgement that an expanded police force and counter-insurgency methods would not deliver as long as military forces were confined to acting merely as an extension to civil power; hence the decision to bring in the ex-soldiers who constituted the Black and Tans, though it was believed by the Chief Secretary, Hamar Greenwood, that there was still a possibility of pulling the coals of moderate opinion from the fire of the IRA.

'they are savages – they are out for loot'
The Restoration of Order Act of August 1920 was a wholly inadequate response, not rectified until the spring of 1921. The isolation of the Black and Tans and the increasing indiscipline and intensity of the battle led to the Black and Tans' involvement in notorious reprisals – particularly in Balbriggan, Ennistynom and Cork – which, aided by effective Sinn Féin propaganda, blackened Britain's name abroad, but also lowered the threshold of violence. Many Black and Tans and auxiliaries had arrived with predictable anti-Irish stereotypes, which were inflamed by the reaction they were met with on the ground. Harassment by the Black and Tans took a number of forms. John Duffy, a contributor to the Bureau of Military History, explained that:

> it was a common practice for them when they went out the country in their lorries to shoot down fowl and other poultry, the property of poor people, and bring them back to the mess where some of them were cooked for their own use and those that were not required were dispatched to their families in England.

James Collins, a member of the Abbeyfeale IRA and future TD (member of parliament), recalled that one of the Black and Tans' favourite pastimes was 'to shoot sparrows on the wing'. A local priest who condemned the killings of the Black and Tans by the Limerick IRA 'promptly received a despatch from Brigade headquarters, warning him of the consequences of his talk from the altar'.[101] The hatred the Black and Tans engendered was understandable if the account given by Monsignor J. T. McMahon, secretary to Archbishop Clune of Perth, Australia, who mediated between Lloyd George and Collins, is true (and there is no reason to doubt it). McMahon's own experience in Limerick was that:

in one house the Black and Tans found a young family, the wife rocking the cradle. They ordered them out on the street while they sprinkled the house with petrol. The young husband, who was not an active 'Sinn Féiner', muttered something about his house being destroyed. A 'Black and Tan' fired point blank at him and as the young man screamed with the pain of the bullet, they lifted him and threw him into his blazing house.[102]

Lady Gregory's observations of the Black and Tans prompted her to write about their deeds in a series of articles published in the English weekly *The Nation*, though she wrote anonymously in order to ensure the survival of her property. She also recorded details of their house burnings and reprisals in her journals. They emerge from her pages as whiskey-guzzling and blood-thirsty: 'little chaps of 5 foot 6 – and with no character ... are there any gentlemen among them?' In September 1920, a doctor informed her of them dragging men out of their homes, shooting them and setting fire to property. He was moved to remark: 'I used not to believe the stories of English savages whether written or told. I thought they were made up by factions, but now I see that they are true ... they are savages – they are out for loot.'[103]

'Authorised reprisals' or 'official punishments' were in fact gambles that backfired badly for the British government; they were a recognition of the failure of politics in Ireland, which was not lost on substantial sections of the British public. Ironically, they were the long-term effect of a British policy that up to 1919, when Sinn Féin was banned as a seditious organisation, had in fact been moderate. Townshend concluded emphatically that 'between 1916 and 1921 Britain drifted into a piecemeal repressive policy whose illegality – in such sharp contrast to the pious rhetoric of British statesmen – was instrumental not merely in manufacturing Sinn Féiners in Ireland, but also in compromising Britain's liberal credentials in the world at large'.[104] Those who may not have cared less about Ireland could be convinced to care about Britain's standing in an international context, a factor which had not been lost on those in Ireland determined from the beginning to make the Irish crisis an international issue.

'not so near the end that we can afford to start the handshaking'?
The British government also had to balance the sentiments of its own military appointees with the political necessity of damage limitation.

General Macready, the commander of the British forces in Ireland, had been reluctant to take the job, perhaps recognising that the government would be very slow to acknowledge Ireland was a war arena and declare martial law throughout the country, in an attempt to change the guerrilla character of the IRA's campaign. British statesmen, however, were slow to depart from the terminology which depicted the IRA as rebels rather than soldiers. The Black and Tans, later to be referred to by Calwell, the biographer of Sir Henry Wilson, as 'the greatest blot on the record of the coalition and perhaps on Britain's name in the twentieth century',[105] had been reinforced in July 1920 by an auxiliary division composed of ex-officers with more sound military records. But it was events like Bloody Sunday in November 1920 which were an indication of the chilling consequences of the sophistication of Michael Collins's intelligence network. On that day, 14 British officers were assassinated; as Alvin Jackson suggests, it was 'the most sensational counter-intelligence coup of the War, even though only perhaps 11 of those killed were actually agents. One of Collins's victims, a Captain MacCormack of the Veterinary Corps, was a second cousin of Michael Davitt and had been sent to Ireland in order to buy mules for the British Army.'[106] Later that day 12 civilians were killed when British auxiliaries fired into a crowd attending a Gaelic football match at Croke Park, home of the Gaelic Athletic Association. The auxiliaries were, after the earlier assassinations, 'bent on indiscriminate revenge'.[107]

The British determination to be hard-line was complicated by a British Labour Party campaign for peace in Ireland and, in particular, by other organisations campaigning for peace such as the Peace with Ireland Council and the British trade union movement, which had a large Irish component but also represented a considerable cross-section of British public opinion. These groups were able, through focusing on crown atrocities, to hit the coalition and in particular Lloyd George where it hurt – at their claim to be a liberal administration. Sinn Féin activists, notably Art O'Brien, complemented such work with the activities of the Irish Self-Determination League of Great Britain. It was no wonder Lloyd George was to comment acidly on the ability of Irishmen to be natural propagandists for their country. The Sinn Féin propaganda department and the army director of publicity, Piaras Beaslai, continued to circulate their *Irish Bulletin*, not just to the British and Irish press, but also, crucially, to the United States.

With roughly 40,000 troops in Ireland and 10,000 armed police, it seemed the British government was getting little in return. After the sack of Balbriggan in 1920, the *Manchester Guardian* wrote: 'to realise the full horrors of the night one has to think of bands of men inflamed with drink raging about the streets firing rifles wildly, burning houses here and there and loudly threatening to come again tonight and complete their work'.[108] At home, the IRA was not without its own critics. The attitude of the Catholic Church varied, but could be a source of great irritation to republicans. Between January and April 1921, 73 people were found executed accompanied by placards proclaiming their guilt as spies.[109]

Was the British government forced to the negotiating table? The moves in this direction had much to do with the return of de Valera from the United States, as he was anxious to change the character and focus of the war, while conciliatory noises from George V in opening the Northern Irish parliament in June 1921 played a significant, if symbolic, part. The election of May 1921 had seen most Sinn Féin candidates returned unopposed to a second Dáil (six republican women were also elected). Lloyd George's decision to drop his precondition of arms surrender before any possible negotiation gave much room for manoeuvre and a possible rest to a war-weary and stretched IRA, though the extent to which they were on the verge of military bankruptcy has been disputed. The decision by General Smuts, the South African leader, to agree to travel to Dublin in early July was also an indication that public statements of moderation were being matched with a private determination to discover just what de Valera wanted, particularly given that he had maintained in addressing the opening of the second Dáil that 'we are not republican doctrinaires as such'.[110]

Moves towards peace had also much to do with the risks Lloyd George was prepared to take, but in 1921 he could not ignore the advice he was receiving from the Dublin Castle administration and his top military brass in Ireland. At the end of 1920, a tentative peace initiative, involving the use of Archbishop Patrick Clune as an intermediary, had begun at the behest of Lloyd George. A moderate nationalist and native of County Clare, Clune travelled to Dublin and met Sinn Féin representatives to discuss the possibility of a truce. Michael Hopkinson, author of *The Irish War of Independence*, maintains that responsibility for the failure of the mission 'lies squarely with Lloyd George himself', as he backed away from a possible truce in the face of military and Conservative opposition, underlining the difficulties of heading a coalition government with a significant Conservative presence. But retreat from peace moves was not an option by the summer of 1921, and the establishment of the Northern Irish government had made negotiations with the republicans more likely. More importantly, both Macready and John Anderson, Joint Under Secretary, were making it clear that a continued military campaign was not an option. As Hopkinson notes:

> The British Cabinet and its sub-committees weighed up the options during the first half of June, going into some detail about the precise military strategy to be applied if the hawkish option was decided upon. There never seems to have been any possibility that such a course would be followed. It was Macready who made the most effective case against coercion ... he argued that even if military action could succeed, he saw no prospect of a stable government emerging and did not see the necessary support in Britain for an escalation of the conflict. He was also very concerned about the morale and fitness of the troops.[111]

Alfred Cope, the Assistant Under Secretary, who had a type of 'undercover role' during these years, and was regarded in some British quarters as a Sinn Féin sympathiser, had also played an important role in establishing lines of communication with republicans, and was aware of the need for compromise. Unfortunately, he refused to submit a statement to the Bureau of Military History in the early 1950s about his role during this period. His justification for non-cooperation was that he regarded the period as 'the most discreditable in your country's history – it is preferable to forget it – to let sleeping dogs lie'.[112]

The subsequent truce in July, and de Valera's speedy journey to London, was the beginning of the end to the claim for the right to a republic; what was on offer was dominion status; recognition of the right of Northern Ireland to have its own form of Home Rule by consent, and a series of qualifications that allowed a substantial British military presence in Ireland. That such terms were rejected was not perhaps as important as their potential to sow the seeds of division within a movement that had traditionally been a mixture of moderates and hardliners. Another important indication of informal contacts prior to the Truce was de Valera's admission to Collins that 'this particular "peace" move business has been going on for some time. They have tried so many lines of approach that it is obvious they are banking somewhat on it.' Collins's own view was that

'It would be a great pity if well-meaning people queered the position by too much of this peace talk. There are always those who insist on shaking hands before the combat is over and, in my opinion we are not so near the end that we can afford to start the handshaking.'[113]

A tortuous correspondence between Lloyd George and de Valera followed, aided by clever tactics on the British side in publishing the correspondence. Lloyd George referred in a letter to de Valera on 13 August 1921 to:

> The claim that we should acknowledge the right of Ireland to secede from her allegiance to the King. No such right can ever be acknowledged by us. The geographical propinquity of Ireland to the British Isles is a fundamental fact. The history of the two isles for many centuries however it is read, is sufficient proof that their destinies are indissolubly linked. Ireland has sent members to the British parliament for more than a hundred years. Many thousands of her people during all that time have enlisted freely and served gallantly in the forces of the crown. Great numbers in all the Irish provinces are profoundly attached to the throne. These facts permit of one answer and one only to the claim that Britain should negotiate with Ireland as a separate and foreign power.[114]

'you could not raise an army in England to fight for that'

The British government published such correspondence because it was aware it had to recover from some of the bad publicity generated by its military campaign in Ireland, but also to impregnate the public mind with the idea that the issue was now about compromise within the framework of the Empire. The Irish government decided to send delegates to London on 11 October, with not a republic in sight. Michael Laffan points out that 'even the most extreme of all Dáil deputies, Mary MacSwiney, never believed that the negotiations would end in British recognition of an Irish republic'.[115] Surprisingly, the delegation included the notoriously evasive Michael Collins, and was officially sent 'with a view to ascertaining how the association of Ireland with the community of nations known as the British Empire may best be reconciled with Irish national aspirations'. It was a pivotal moment which was to colour the character of Irish politics for the next 40 years and, perhaps unfortunately, the beginning of the process by which two individuals, de Valera and Collins, for many became the prism through which much of the history of this period was assessed.

In the short term, de Valera was to come out the worst, fuelling conspiracy theories as to the reasons for his absence (he knew after all there was not a republic on offer). But it is also simplistic to suggest that in choosing Collins to negotiate he was plucking a 'mere' soldier to negotiate with the heavyweights of Downing Street. Lloyd George maintained Collins was a 'rather stupid man',[116] but Collins's abilities were far more than those of a soldier, despite the focus of the subsequent hagiography of him in Ireland, much of which was based on military iconography.

The instructions to the Irish negotiators (officially termed plenipotentiaries), particularly as to whether they could negotiate and conclude a treaty, or merely negotiate and refer back for approval, were to be a source of controversy. The Irish delegation consisted of Arthur Griffith, Robert Barton, Michael Collins, Eamonn Duggan and Charles Gavan-Duffy, with Erskine Childers as principal secretary. They were facing a formidable team of Lloyd George, Austen Chamberlain, Lord Birkenhead, Hamar Greenwood, Gordon Hewart and Winston Churchill. The Tory element was thus heavily represented as the tense negotiations began. The words 'Collins the murderer' were whitewashed on the footpath outside 22 Hans Place in London where most of the Irish delegates stayed, while Collins himself stayed separately at Cadogan Gardens protected by his own bodyguards.[117]

The next two months were to witness a fair share of tough negotiation, soul-searching, frustration, romance, deception and honest brokering.[118] The four most difficult issues were British insistence on retaining Ireland as a base for military and naval facilities; the exact constitutional status of any putative Irish state; the question of the partition of Ireland; and finally, an oath of allegiance to the British crown. The Irish delegation insisted on the need for compromise on the part of James Craig, Northern Ireland's new prime minister. There was much drafting and redrafting of forms of words, and an eventual agreement to postpone the partition question by incorporating the idea of a Boundary Commission. Amidst all the documentation this entailed, a number of things were clear. The Irish delegation needed to keep the focus on the 'essential unity of Ireland', an issue on which they were sure they could garner the most sympathy, even though, as was often overlooked, the partition of Ireland was already a reality. In contrast, the British need was to keep the focus on Ireland in the Empire, an issue on which they could be assured public support, and over which they could insist they were prepared to resume war. During the negotiations, Chamberlain wrote pointedly to his wife: 'Ulster would be the worst ground to fight on that one can imagine; for the six counties was a compromise, and like all compromises is illogical and indefensible and you could not raise an army in England to fight for that, as we could for crown and empire.'[119]

'The issue was peace or war'

There were also psychological and personal factors that operated on many levels. These were intense, draining negotiations where individual strengths and vulnerabilities were utilised and exploited. The truth from the Irish side was that their range of options was limited. The eventual signing of the Treaty, which involved recognition of the British crown, was partly a generational compromise between what the older Griffith represented and the younger Collins sought; a compromise between dominion status and the elusive republic. The agreement also reflected a desire to avoid a further debilitating military war which perhaps both sides knew they could not win. De Valera undoubtedly knew this too, and seemed deceptive in the reasons he proffered for his refusal to go to London – he later acknowledged it was against the will of the majority of the cabinet – justifying the understandable bitterness of Collins's comment that the compromise was in the acceptance of the invitation to negotiate.

The delegates were also aware that there was a huge welcome for the truce and peace in Ireland. Celebratory bonfires in Dublin after the truce were as much to welcome peace as to celebrate the perceived defeat of the British, as were the emotional crowds who cheered both negotiating teams as they drew up at Downing Street. Celebrations were rife as the curfew was lifted in Dublin; the *Freeman's Journal* reported that 'the jubilation over the abolition of the curfew was continued again last night … bonfires were blazing at street corners, and well into the small hours joyous souls were making echoes with the music of mouth organs and melodeons … social life has once again become possible in Dublin.'[120] Another consideration to be borne in mind was the potential difficulty in reactivating the IRA after a prolonged period of peace.

It was a treaty that was signed reluctantly and with a heavy heart by some; but it was also the case that many of Sinn Féin's English sympathisers believed Sinn Féin should accept dominion status because it conferred on them the substance of freedom. One such sympathiser, C. P. Scott, suggested: 'Sinn Féin has got to travel a good way, I'm afraid, before it realises ... the immense possibilities of the terms offered it.'[121] It may also have been that the difficulties of the Irish delegation were exacerbated by a failure to agree the limits of their concessions prior to travelling.

Many years later, Sinéad McCoole researched the role of such 'society' diplomats as Lady Hazel Lavery, who having been a frequent attender at the trial of Roger Casement in 1916 became passionate about Irish politics, discovering that it was 'positively chic' to be Irish in London during this period. She built up a friendship with Collins – later rumoured to be an affair, of which there is no hard evidence, though she clearly had an influence on him and communicated with British government officials on his behalf.[122]

The starkness of the Irish delegation's position was revealed in the final communication sent by Griffith to de Valera on 6 December 1921, the day on which the Treaty was signed: 'We were on the point four times of breaking on the crown, which I told the cabinet I would not break on. The issue was peace or war. We decided our course and they gave in on fiscal autonomy and other matters.'[123] Griffith's letter was a significant reminder that the Irish were not the only side obsessed with symbols, given that it was Britain who made the oath the sticking point,[124] an oath which eventually read: 'I do solemnly swear true faith and allegiance to the Constitution of the Irish Free State as by law established and that I will be faithful to His Majesty in virtue of the common citizenship of Ireland with Great Britain.' Could the oath of allegiance have been modified to one of fidelity and would this have made any difference to hard-liners at home? Lloyd George played a clever game of bluff on 5 December, as dramatically recorded by Frank Pakenham in his classic account of the negotiations, *Peace by Ordeal*:

> I have to communicate with Sir James Craig tonight. Here are the alternative letters which I have prepared, one enclosing articles of agreement reached by his majesty's government and yourselves and the other saying that Sinn Féin representatives refuse to come into the empire. If I send this letter it is war and war within three days. Which letter am I to send? If the messenger is to reach Craig in time we must know your answer by 10pm tonight. You can have until then, but no longer, to decide whether you will give peace or war to your country.[125]

'*looking for the substance of freedom and independence*'

Erskine Childers, secretary to the Irish delegation, wrote to his wife: 'Everything changed at the last moment. They placed the minority in a frightful position – a cruel position. Nevertheless Barton held out till the last moment. Then he weakened, overcome by MC [Michael Collins] I think.'[126] Pakenham also gave a good indication, having written his book with the benefit of personal contact with many of those involved, of the mentality of Imperial England's negotiators. They were the political titans of their age ('anyone of her leading quartet could have played Prime Minister with distinction') and they, too, were taking political risks. For Chamberlain, for example, an Irish republic 'could scarce do other than contradict a vital principle', while for Birkenhead the concern was with legal exegesis and drafting as a constitutional expert. Churchill, on the other hand, had very much the instincts of the soldier. Lloyd George, ever the pragmatist, had a simple concern: to be able to sell an agreement to Parliament; which made his own ideals irrelevant.

The question of whether or not the Irish delegation could have got better terms will perhaps never be answered, but there seems much truth in Pakenham's observation that 'one can only assume that if the Irish delegates had stuck together and insisted, as they were fully entitled to do, on reference back to Dublin, the negotiations would have dragged on, with the British army still more or less in control in Ireland'.[127] That they did not refer back at the last moment remained a sore point for many years in Irish politics. Collins insisted afterwards that the original credentials given to them empowered them to negotiate and conclude a treaty as representatives of the Irish republic.[128] Griffith, in defending the Treaty to the Dáil on 7 January 1922, cleverly used de Valera's earlier words and maintained: 'we went to London not as republican doctrinaires but looking for the substance of freedom and independence ... to attack us on the grounds that we went there to get a republic is to attack us on false and lying grounds'.[129] He was correct.

Lloyd George had also done his back-bench homework well. On 14 December the size of the majority in the House of Commons in favour of the Treaty was 401 to 58. The view of General Macready was that the only thing which would now solve the Irish question was to let the two sides, pro- and anti-Treaty, fight it out together; an ironic observation given that one of the main weaknesses of the Treaty was that it was designed to suit English rather than Irish requirements. The 'two sides' theory also conveniently shelved the issue of the North. In retrospect, it was easy to criticise the fact that the negotiators on the Irish side did not insist on independent commissioners and a plebiscite as elsewhere in Europe, in relation to deciding the border issue between North and South.[130]

The fall-out from the Treaty involved the return of the delegates to a divided cabinet, emotive Treaty debates and summer elections which resulted in the electorate endorsing the Treaty. Republican defiance of the new Free State government led ultimately to civil war. Confusion abounded in the wake of the signing of the Treaty. Given the exceptional unity that had existed prior to this (at least in theory) within the Sinn Féin movement, any schism that now occurred was going to be raw and highly personal, particularly given the energy which had been poured into the War of Independence at both home and abroad. One thing, however, became clear at quite an early stage: those who signed the Treaty, those who supported it and spoke out in its favour, seemed to conjure up more justifications for it and more arguments in its favour than the two main arguments against it – that it did not deliver a republic and incorporated an oath of allegiance to the crown, however ambiguous the language that oath was couched in.

'any philosophy of nationalism to rely upon'?

The division of the cabinet could not have been closer with four (Griffith, Collins, Barton and Cosgrave) in favour, and three (de Valera, Brugha and Stack) against. Of all the cabinet, it was perhaps Griffith alone who felt honour-bound in signing the Treaty. It was consistent with his original political ideas; this was a factor alluded to by his defenders, especially after his sudden death in August 1922. According to his supporters, there did not exist in the history of Irish journalism a man of more patience and persistence and with a greater talent for propaganda. P. S. O'Hegarty commented, with a degree of truth, in the immediate aftermath of his death, that 'Griffith was the only member of the government who had any philosophy of nationalism to rely upon, who was in touch with the whole stream of Irish nationalist philosophy. In that respect he might well be like to a grown-up amongst children.'[131] But, for the time being, Griffith was a man who had enough of his political sons on board, even if they differed in their estimate of where the benefits of the Treaty lay. While some, like Cosgrave and Barton, emphasised the advantage of tariff autonomy, others urged a view of the Treaty as an interim arrangement.

It was not until 1972 that the private sessions of the Treaty debates, in all their aggression and rawness, were made available to the public. They revealed two divergent arguments within pro-Treaty Sinn Féin: a nationalist/republican strand and a conservative constitutionalist strand, as defined by the historian John Regan.[132] Collins undoubtedly had a personality and a charisma that could inspire different wings of Sinn Féin. He had been forced to use a clever mix of arguments in selling the Treaty, emphasising the stretched resources of the IRA and the futility of all-out war with Britain (particularly if it was not mandated by the people). His most oft-quoted assertion was that it would provide a stepping-stone; not the ultimate freedom that all nations aspire to, but the freedom to achieve that freedom. He was able to convince enough of the merits of his argument but could not prevent civil war.

It became clear relatively quickly that a compromise which would unite the cabinet, never mind a Dáil that had been re-elected in May 1921 on a mandate to conduct a war for a republic, was next to impossible. That Dáil had its fair share of angry young men and women, many of whom had been imbued with a sense of invincibility. This was despite de Valera's repeated acknowledgement that the majority of Irish people were likely to accept the Treaty.[133] De Valera's alternative, his 'Document no. 2', involved the key principle of excluding Britain from the internal affairs of the Irish state, jettisoning dominion status and the oath in favour of a statement that Ireland's association with the Commonwealth would be strictly limited to defence, peace and war and political treaties. In doing so it fell between the two stools of not being republican enough and (from the British perspective) being an unacceptable alteration of the Treaty terms. His alternative to the Treaty was, maintained Joe Lee, an impressive document couched in conciliatory language that carefully avoided the use of the word 'republic'. While it asserted the right of sovereignty, its list of 'purposes of common concern' was lengthy and concentrated on Commonwealth rather than Empire. Lee suggested that it was a recognition that geography demanded some form of special military relationship between Britain and Ireland, particularly its contention that Ireland would have to defend territorial waters if they were being used to invade Britain. This was ironic given that he would not have been able to renegotiate these 'purposes' in the way he renegotiated the military clauses of the Treaty with Chamberlain in 1938 in order to secure Irish neutrality during the Second World

War.[134] Lee maintained Britain should have been more far-sighted in reaction to this document, given that it had the makings of a defence pact, raising the question of what would happen if Ireland's resources failed to permit her to resist invasion by 'a foreign power hostile to Great Britain'.

'hadn't Collins got drunk on English hospitality ...?'

Various levels of secret negotiations to produce an agreed settlement, particularly important for Collins, given his association with the different wings of the republican movement, achieved nothing. While there was worry expressed by Erskine Childers about Britain's retention of Irish port bases for the British navy, on the grounds that it would deny Ireland the right to exercise an independent foreign policy, one of the real surprises of the Treaty debates, as identified by Maureen Wall, was the sheer neglect of the issue of Northern Ireland. She calculated that of the 338 published pages of the Treaty debates printed in the Dáil report, only nine were devoted to the issue, with two thirds contributed by three deputies from County Monaghan. This lack of focus was either because it was assumed that the Boundary Commission would indeed deliver (even though its terms were utterly vague in contrast to the terms of the Versailles Treaty dealing with plebiscites and the demarcation of frontiers), or because the partition issue was seen as a secondary issue to the nature of the state which would emerge in the South.[135]

Along with highly personalised insults (hadn't Collins got drunk on English hospitality and sold the republic down the river? Hadn't de Valera lost control of the Sinn Féin movement in the first place by going to America and opting out of the Treaty negotiations? Wasn't Childers an Englishman and what right had he to comment on Irish affairs?), there were references, too, to the insult the Treaty was to generations of dead patriots. The republican women in the Dáil in particular asserted the right to speak in the name of their dead loved ones. The six women – five of them related to dead patriots – voted against its acceptance. Margaret Pearse insisted her son would not have accepted a treaty that included only part of the country, while Kathleen Clarke saw it as yet another chapter of England's book of divide and conquer.

As the country divided in the aftermath of the Treaty, Cumann na mBan held a special convention on 5 February, which was attended by over 600 delegates. With Mary MacSwiney and Markievicz to the fore, they emphatically rejected the Treaty by 419 to 63 votes. The women were not for turning, although the wider split did not bypass its ranks, and in March a rival, Cumann na Saoirse (freedom group), was established in the Mansion House. The obduracy of the women at this juncture was interesting, in that it was not representative of public or Dáil opinion, where the Treaty was eventually accepted with 57 votes against and 64 in favour, following a Christmas recess which many believed worked to the pro-Treaty side's advantage. The attitude of Church leaders to the Treaty was of paramount importance also. Later, during the Civil War, one of the most ardent of the republicans, Mary MacSwiney, on hunger strike in Mountjoy jail, wrote to the Archbishop of Dublin. She had been refused holy communion for declining to submit to the pastoral of the bishops calling on republicans to desist from armed action:

> I can no more deny the justice of my cause than Joan of Arc could deny hers. Bishops got her burned as a heretic to please England, but the church has now declared her one of God's saints. To God I commend my soul in all humility but in all confidence. You are supporting men who have declared that 'what is wrong with this country is that we are too damned religious – too much spirituality about us and it's a materialism that pays'. These words were actually said by a prominent member of the pro-Treaty party last December … you are supporting perjurists, job-hunters, materialists and driving away those who stand for truth, honour and the sanctity of oaths.

The Archbishop replied: 'With regard to your political beliefs, hopes and aspirations, I have nothing to say … I too have ideals, many of them impossible of realisation.'[136] But there had not necessarily been unanimity in the Church regarding the War of Independence and its consequences.

In spite of the apparent link between Catholic piety and republicanism, the nationalist insurrection had presented the Catholic Church with its own problems, including fears of loss of allegiance and discipline. Bishop Cohalan of Cork, who did not want his statement to the Bureau of Military History to be released for at least 35 years, sought to explain the 'vacillations' in the public statements of his archbishop concerning the IRA. Cohalan spoke out against the IRA even though he was of the same 'blood and stock' as the men who carried out the Kilmichael ambush. His secretary insisted: 'he could have been an IRA man as ardently patriotic as any and more ruthless than most', but the 'theologian in him' could not find a mandate for armed resistance, leading to his famous excommunication order of December 1920.[137]

'in any other country … the clash of episcopal opinion might have meant a schism'

The ageing Bishop Fogarty of Killaloe was also interviewed by the Bureau, and Richard Hayes, chairman of the advisory committee, wrote an account of the interview. Hayes did not want the statement released until the bishop was dead. The impression he got from this interview was that 'the Irish Bishops did not at any time discuss in council the question of the moral justification of the Easter Rising, or the Anglo-Irish conflict that followed'. Generally the attitude of individual bishops was a matter of age, with the older bishops more opposed to republicans. Dr Fogarty:

> gave expression to the view that in any other country except Ireland the clash of episcopal opinion might have meant a schism in the church there. Dr Fogarty maintained that in private conversation with Dr O'Dwyer, Bishop of Limerick, the latter mentioned that the rising in 1916 was morally justifiable … Dr Fogarty declared that in the Anglo-Irish War the national interest would override such unpleasant happenings as the shooting of policemen.[138]

The initial Church reaction to the signing of the Treaty seemed quite neutral and cautious, only suggesting that the Dáil 'will be sure to have before their minds the best interests of the country and the wishes of the people'. But the growing threat of disorder on the part of the anti-Treatyites was to change their stance dramatically, and many of their Christmas sermons in 1921 were, in effect, pro-Treaty speeches.[139]

'The Great Surrender'?

After the Dáil ratified the Treaty, de Valera resigned his presidency of the Republic and was defeated after offering himself for re-election. A new Dáil met on 14 January in accordance with the articles of the Treaty to approve the settlement, meaning there were in effect two parliaments, an anomaly that was to be sorted out with a general election expected within weeks. De Valera, having used emotive language about the danger of people being tempted from the 'straight and honourable path', rejected

Collins's proposal that a Committee of Public Safety be established by both pro- and anti-Treaty sides. A provisional government was duly formed by the pro-Treaty side; it had been agreed with the British government that this (envisaged) temporary arrangement would not be regularised until after the election.

Meanwhile, an Irish Race Congress held in Paris in late January 1922 (it had been planned before the Treaty) proved to be an embarrassing episode in Irish foreign policy. The Minister for Fine Arts (an office soon to be abolished and not revived for 70 years) had hoped it would be an opportunity to celebrate Irish language, literature and music. Despite the enthusiasm of such luminaries as Yeats, who presented a lecture on the plays and lyrics of modern Ireland, the congress was hijacked by anti-Treatyites and became a platform for unadulterated Irish republicanism and a mixture of tragedy and farce.[140] Back home, 200 delegates at an IRA convention in March 1922 articulated utter defiance of the settlement.

The key question, of course, was how the electorate were going to vote (those who during April had to listen to election meetings in the presence of armed soldiers from both sides of the Treaty divide). It was significant that Kevin O'Higgins, a pro-Treaty TD who had worked with Cosgrave in the Department of Local Government, had referred to the fact that welfare had to take precedence over political creed and theories. It was not lost on many of the republicans that much of the farming, business and legal community, not to mention the Church and media, were in favour of the Treaty (some no doubt working on the logic that, if in doubt, think about the economic implications of a return to war). The labour movement too had its divisions. A special congress of the Irish Labour Party and the TUC was held on 21 February to discuss its electoral strategy. Not all were in favour of parliamentary participation and labour leaders resented the fact that they had not been consulted concerning the Treaty. This caused some to assert that they had no responsibility for it, but instead should focus on putting a programme of social and economic reform before the people. The vote in favour of contesting the election was tight, with 115 in favour and 88 against. The National Executive was slow to give direction, leaving it to individual candidates to decide their own position on the Treaty, but an overly republican position would have compromised their electoral participation.[141]

After the ratification of the Treaty, the British army embarked on a process of evacuation that eventually (according to figures cited by the

Freeman's Journal) saw roughly 40,000 soldiers, 7,000 Black and Tans and 6,000 auxiliaries leave the Free State. The transfer of this number of army personnel and their equipment was an enormous logistical exercise that was largely accomplished within six months under the control of a committee chaired by Winston Churchill. Across the country barracks were vacated as the nascent Free State army took control, but no changing of the guard was so significant as the symbolic handing over of Dublin Castle, the centre of British administration in Ireland, to Michael Collins, on 16 January. This was an event which brought the *Freeman's Journal* to comment in an editorial entitled 'The Great Surrender': 'Yesterday, the Castle, with all that it stands for in power and influence, was handed over to the Irish people ... Emmett died in an effort to get hold merely of the material fabric. But the power that it enshrined was surrendered yesterday to Ireland's men.'[142]

'alliances had been formed with the enemy'

Beyond the symbolism of the surrender of the castle stood the reality of the impact the scale and speed of the evacuation had on Irish society. By the end of March there were no British troops left in Connacht, and Cork was the only county in Munster to retain a garrison. By May, it too was evacuated, as was the garrison from the Curragh in County Kildare, leaving only 5,000 troops in the country, all stationed in Dublin. During the evacuation the Royal Irish Constabulary had also been disbanded and the newly formed (and soon to be unarmed) Civic Guard took over policing duties in the country. The sight of British soldiers marching from their barracks was readily seized on as tangible evidence of the extent of independence conferred by the Treaty. Newspapers carried a constant stream of photographs of departing soldiers, but their exit produced a range of conflicting emotions. As well as a sense of triumph with the handing over of the barracks, newspapers carried stories detailing instances where troops commandeered groceries, drink and clothing from shopkeepers and had now left without paying their bills. Collins, ironically but perhaps fittingly, had to deal with a more macabre aspect of the evacuation, having received requests from the relatives of dead soldiers concerning the possibility of disinterring the bodies of British soldiers for proper burial.[143]

Not every section of Irish society greeted the departure of the troops with relish. Garrison towns had grown accustomed to a heavy dependence on the money spent by the British soldiers in their shops and pubs. As well as their personal expenditure, there had been large contracts for townspeople in the provision of a wide range of supplies for the various barracks. Such was the impact of the decline in this commerce in towns such as Fermoy, in County Cork, that a delegation was sent to the provisional government to discuss the matter.[144] The attachment to the departing troops was not merely commercial, but also sexual. The *Freeman's Journal* carried photographs of tearful young Irish women standing on the quayside of the North Wall, waving to a ship carrying soldiers back to England, as during the war, 'it seems alliances had been formed with the enemy'.[145]

But there were more serious challenges facing the new provisional government, aside from the obvious difficult political ones, many being voiced by ordinary people. Land problems remained to the forefront, prompting a series of resolutions to Patrick Hogan, the new Minister for Agriculture, from labour organisations and local authorities, urging compulsory tillage and the acquisition of land for tillage allotments. In comparison to the rousing rhetoric which had appealed for tillage on patriotic grounds, the response of the new minister was muted, reflecting the responsibilities of power, as he insisted it was first necessary to build up government structures, pass necessary legislation and control finances.

'They haven't a perch of land'

Hogan was also receiving queries from farmers' representatives concerning the intention of the new government with regard to the establishment of agricultural colleges and schools. He had no doubt that they were a necessity in a country whose prosperity was so largely based on agriculture, but given the political insecurity, he was loath to make specific predictions regarding the future. In the meantime, he and his civil servants theorised on the need for co-operative endeavours in rural parts and the feasibility of adopting certain foreign co-operative methods for Ireland's rural economy. They recognised, for example, that in Italy government contracts awarded to co-operative movements did much to promote agriculture.

Despite being conversant with international trends, by and large in 1922 a 'wait and see' attitude was adopted regarding both agriculture and methods. Many of the ordinary rural populace did not, understandably, share the belief that such patience was necessary. The Land Settlement Commission files are interspersed with the voices of those beneath the poverty line. Despite the fact that by the summer of 1922 the commission courts had dealt with many claims for ownership and transfer of land, the poor were still the land's most hapless victims. The Ardfert (in County Kerry) Village Tenants' petition to the government was representative of a widespread predicament, particularly after arbitration had been refused:

> Our group comprises tradesmen, small shopkeepers, business hands etc, all married with families. The provision of milk for our children is one of our great difficulties. It is impossible to get grazing for a pony and a pony is a necessity with most of us. We seek only a few acres each, enough to keep a cow and graze a pony, or if it would smooth matters, we would accept less – say, what would keep a cow. Thus among nine of us we would only ask what would scarcely make an economic holding for one person. We live right on the edge of this land and have had to look at the bullocks of the Grazier for years while our children pined for milk. There are among our families 19 children, either babies or little beyond the baby stage. The widow and female orphans of one of our male members who was murdered by the Black and Tans live in a small shop. They haven't a perch of land.[146]

In a society that had become accustomed to the acceptance of a high degree of illegality, the pressures of providing a suitable structural framework for law and order were no less arduous. After the Treaty split, Eamonn Duggan replaced Austin Stack as Minister for Home Affairs. To him fell the task of establishing a viable law and order policy. In January 1922 it was ordered that the British courts continue to operate; the Dáil courts were in turn allowed to absorb criminal and civil jurisdiction, with scant attention devoted to an overall policy. These difficulties were reflected in the records of the Courts (winding-up) Commission, which sought to deal with cases left pending under the old Dáil system. Also evident in these files is a preoccupation with efficiency and consistency rather than clemency, reflecting a desire to establish the provisional government's law and order bona fides. Larceny and shooting were so common that the actions of judges who imposed severe sentences were endorsed. There was concern that, previously, it was too easy to get a reprieve on sentences, undermining the government. This was a reaction to a multitude of petitions on behalf of those imprisoned for petty crime, many ending with the insistence of mothers that their sons' characters were impeccable when they were sober. Once again the issue of poverty was stark – most pleading for leniency or remission because the offender was the family wage earner.[147] Much uneasiness existed over the creation of the new Civic Guard. The officers of the Irish Republican Police believed their contribution to the national struggle was not being recognised and that after the creation of the new force they would be discarded.

It was a sense of lawlessness, coupled with the compromised position of Michael Collins, that allowed the sort of blatant defiance which culminated in the republican occupation of the Four Courts in Dublin city in April 1922. Individuals like Rory O'Connor and Liam Mellows showed none of the at times ambiguous prevarication of de Valera (he was not in a position to take political responsibility for the army leaders whom he did not control and who, in any case, did not look to him for advice) or the caution of Sean Moylan and Liam Lynch, who seemed prepared to postpone conflict to see how the new government fared. Potential exclusion from a new Free State army (many of whose members had not fought in the War of Independence) can only have heightened the bitterness. Collins, preoccupied with the quest to frame a constitution which he still in vain hoped would placate republicans, and also immersed in the logistics of attempting to continue an IRA campaign in the North, not to mention convincing former comrades to come on board, was stretched beyond belief.

Women's suffrage briefly assumed political importance. The June election was to be run under the inherited British franchise, which would allow women over the age of 30 (with the requisite property qualifications) to vote. In an effort to extend the franchise to all women over the age of 21, Kate O'Callaghan introduced a bill in March 1922 for this purpose. It was interpreted as an attempt to further delay the planned election and the bill was defeated, although Arthur Griffith declared that he believed absolutely in full adult suffrage and that it would be introduced as soon as was practicable.[148]

'assert itself or perish'

The election was held on 16 June 1922. In many respects it was a somewhat unreal event, particularly in view of a Collins/de Valera pact that had been agreed four weeks before the election, allowing both pro- and anti-Treaty Sinn Féin to be nominated as national coalition candidates relative to their existing strength in the Dáil. In effect, it was an attempt to avoid putting the Treaty before the electorate, and to avoid electoral contest; the idea was that both supporters and opponents of the Treaty would be 'rubber-stamped' by voters.[149] This was a desperate but flawed attempt to heal the rift that had widened considerably since the Treaty debates. The election was also held in the midst of the occupation of the Four Courts, which began on 14 April. Days previously, Churchill had written to Collins indicating the British government's impatience that the pro-Treaty side was not assertive enough:

> The Cabinet instructed me to send you a formal communication expressing their growing anxiety at the spread of disorder in the 26 counties. Instead of this however, I write to you as man to man. Many residents are writing to this country tales of intimidation, disorder, theft and pillage. There is no doubt that capital is taking flight. Credits are shutting up, railways are slowing down, business and enterprise are baffled. The wealth of Ireland is undergoing a woeful shrinkage ... it is obvious that in the long run the government, however patient, must assert itself or perish and be replaced by some other form of control ... we really have a moral right to ask that the uncertainty as to whether our offer is accepted or rejected should not be indefinitely prolonged ...[150]

This letter raises the question of the extent to which the election about to be held was a truly democratic one, given the threats that then existed. Critics of the republicans at this juncture have made much of the fact that not to accept the result of the Treaty election was profoundly anti-democratic. In 1989 Joe Lee insisted it was a simple issue of democracy versus dictatorship between the Irish pro- and anti-Treaty camps: 'In the event', he wrote, 'the aspiring military dictators were crushed. The mere Irish were not to exchange one jackboot for another. If the civil war illustrated with a vengeance the potential for autocracy lurking in Irish political culture it illustrated even more emphatically the potential for democracy.'

But Lee admitted in 2000 that this was 'too facile a distinction' given that the Treaty had been signed under threat of war and that the fear of violence was what made some people accept it, so in that sense it could not be considered a free vote. He also suggested another anti-democratic aspect of the Treaty: that it made it impossible for Irish people not to be drawn into British wars, whatever their preferred wishes.[151] It is also worth pointing out that the republicans based their opposition to the Free State on the grounds that an all-Ireland republic 'had been lost without a free vote of all the people of Ireland'.[152] This serves to underline that there was much confusion about defining 'democracy' in Ireland in 1922, and some historians of the later twentieth century had a tendency to project a contemporary view of democracy back to 1922.[153]

'a nation and not a rabble'?

Collins produced a constitution that contained no oath of allegiance, a constitution that was keen to preserve the republic 'by a clever process of omission' with no mention of the king and an emphasis on the sovereignty of the Irish people.[154] It was rejected by the British as incompatible with the terms of the Treaty, and amid further threats of war a revised constitution was published on the morning of the election. It conformed to the stipulations of the Treaty and was rejected immediately by its opponents. The results of the election – pro-Treaty Sinn Féin 58 seats, anti-Treaty Sinn Féin 36, Labour 17, Farmers' Party 7 and independents 10 – represented something of a triumph for the Labour Party, but even more significant was the actual breakdown of the votes. Pro-Treaty candidates received 239,195, anti-Treaty 132,161 and others 247,082, suggesting that many voters were tiring of debates about oaths and symbols and were more preoccupied with bread-and-butter issues.[155]

But it was the worsening military situation, particularly the occupation of the Four Courts and the assassination of Sir Henry Wilson, military adviser to the government of Northern Ireland, which allowed Lloyd George to insist on an immediate move against the anti-Treaty IRA. He thundered to Collins:

> The ambiguous position of the IRA can no longer be ignored by the British government. Still less can Mr Rory O'Connor be permitted to remain with his followers and his arsenal in open rebellion in the heart of Dublin in the possession of the Courts of Justice organising and sending out from this centre enterprises of murder not only in the area of your government but also in the six northern counties and Great Britain ... His Majesty's government are prepared to place at your disposal the necessary pieces of artillery which may be required, or otherwise to assist you as may be arranged. Now that you are supported by the declared will of the Irish people in favour of the Treaty they have a right to expect that the necessary action will be taken by your government without delay.[156]

Regarding Ireland's reputation abroad, the Minister for Foreign Affairs, George Gavan Duffy, had been equally stark the previous month, lamenting the fact that no country had ever started its international career with better prospects after the war. He insisted it would now be 'idle to gloss over the fact that we have lost our prestige in recent months … if we are to retrieve the splendid position we held, we must take steps at home without delay to prove that we are a nation and not a rabble'.[157] The steps that were taken marked the beginning of the Civil War.

'You are all abstract fanatics'

George Gavan Duffy's fear of the 'first of the small nations' being viewed as primitive was significant. If the Civil War was to prove anything, it was that the Irish were by no means first in the league of decency, or unique in their capacity for Christian tolerance, unity and indeed spiritualism.[158] Seán O'Casey's controversial play *The Shadow of a Gunman* was first staged just before the ceasefire of May 1923 which ended the Civil War. O'Casey critically challenged the idea of the gunman as hero; in the character of Séumas Shields, according to the words of the stage directions, was manifested: 'the superstition, the fear and the malignity of primitive man'.[159] This, he seemed to be suggesting, was no intellectual battle, and historians have correctly pointed to the sheer dearth of contemporary debate about the ideology of Irish republicanism. Seán O'Faoláin made much of the fact that the revolutionary leaders were not thinkers; they were gallant and idealistic, but very much playing it by ear. His future wife Eileen was more blunt, in maintaining: 'You are all abstract fanatics.'[160]

Those presiding over the new Free State institutions could not of course choose to be abstract. The obvious dilemma for them during the Civil War was to establish and confirm centralised political authority, in the midst of its rejection and of guerrilla warfare, as the means of opposition. Treaty supporters began to make disparaging references to the mystical, hysterical and neurotic worship of the republic exhibited by their Civil War opponents. But excess was also a feature of the pro-Treaty side, ranging from the often conflicting allegiances and actions of Michael Collins, to the sheer violence of both state civil authorities and their soldiers. The events of the Civil War years prompted the subsequent deification and vilification of various individuals, most notably Michael Collins and Eamon de Valera. Superficially, there is much that is attractive in this approach, but it takes little cognisance of the human dilemma these people faced. They were not caricatures; contradictions and inconsistencies abounded, but there was also a fair degree of integrity. Nor was it simply a battle between ministers and gunmen; the events of the previous few years had illustrated how blurred the lines could become between civilian and military life, and this ambiguity lingered. The IRA executive convention of March 1922 seemed like a provocative dismissal of democracy and government, but it was also the case that Richard Mulcahy, chief of staff of the IRA from 1919 to 1921, now Minister for Defence, had given permission in January for the convention to be held.[161]

Of course, the Civil War in one sense was about getting rid of this distinction between military and civil, but it was also going to be the case that the gunmen were to play a pivotal role in the Irish political system in the future. The actions and sentiments expressed during the Civil War would seem to indicate that there was a more even distribution of anti-democrats, beween anti- and pro-Treatyites. It is worth noting, for example, the utter contempt that quickly developed at central-government level for local democracy.[162]

'deserted the people for the fleshpots of Empire'

Contradictions and ironies abounded. In 1922 the holding of a republican prisoner was challenged by way of habeas corpus by a republican judge, who insisted on the appearance of the Minister for Defence and was thrown in jail. Exactly a year before, when Sir Charles O'Connor had issued a similar order in relation to the arrest of Macready, he was acclaimed by the nationalist press and later honoured by a seat on the Supreme Court.[163] The government, in dealing with its first trades dispute, wanted to deny postal workers the right to strike after their 'cost of living' bonus had been cut. The government not only voted against this right to strike, but was determined to use the police and military, who even went as far as shooting a striker in September 1922 while on picket at Merchant Arch (luckily her suspender buckle deflected the bullet). Perhaps the irony of all this was that J. J. Walsh, the postmaster general overseeing such intimidation and bullying, as a trade unionist had previously used Bolshevik rhetoric.[164]

Was this simply a government determined not to be diverted from the main aim – winning the Civil War – or the early signals that this war was also a class war with a government overly hostile to workers? Liam Mellows in September 1922 had sent a letter from Mountjoy (the letter was probably penned by Peadar O'Donnell), weeks before his execution:

'The unemployment is acute. Starvation is facing thousands of people. The official labour movement has deserted the people for the fleshpots of Empire. The Free State government's attitude towards striking postal workers makes clear what its attitude towards workers generally will be.'[165] Mellows's letters to Austin Stack and Ernie O'Malley may have enthused about the idea of communism and seizing the lands of the aristocracy, but the reality was that the Irish Transport and General Workers' Union was in danger of bankrupting itself in 1923 in attempting to support farm strikes, particularly in Kildare and Waterford, and was forced to call them off. That year was also to see the Labour Party's representation in the Dáil decline to 13 seats, while dissent within the trade union movement led to the expulsion of James Larkin from the ITGWU and the formation of the Irish Workers' Union. In many ways, the left in Ireland was weak and internally divided, whatever about any hostility that may have existed on the part of pro-Treaty Sinn Féin, and yet the speed with which Cumann na nGaedheal (the name given to pro-Treaty Sinn Féin when they formed a new party in April 1923) became associated with the 'men of property' was telling.

'The side of his head was torn open'

The Civil War, like the War of Independence, was largely instigated and fought by young men. The conflict, if anything, made young men old, despite the observation by writer Frank O'Connor in *Guests of the Nation* that one was glad to have been young at such a time, giving them much more to brood upon than books or first love.[166] The price that youth had to pay also received much literary airing as a fall-out from the Civil War. The description of the execution of two young republicans in Francis Stuart's *We Have Kept the Faith* (1923) illustrated what it meant for a youth to die at dawn for his country:

> Joe had fallen back against the wall but his feet were still firm on the ground and he was choking with blood and spittle coming out of his mouth and his face turning dark. The other boy fell from his knees and the two boys lay across one another. The sergeant put his gun to the side of Joe's head and fired four or five shots into it. The side of his head was torn open, then he fell sideways with his shoulder slipping down along the wall ...[167]

The figures used by historians in the 1980s concerning the numbers who died in the Civil War are now regarded as greatly exaggerated. There is no formal register and no one knows precisely how many died, but the figure of over 4,000 deaths[168] does not tally with more recent research, which gives the number of national army deaths at about 800 and a republican list of about 400. According to the Registrar General's tabulation, there were about 1,150 homicides, executions and deaths as a result of gunshot in 1922 and 1923.[169] At least as much infrastructural damage was caused as during the War of Independence and the deaths, given that both sides had recently been fighting together, had immense psychological and political implications that made the conflict more vicious.

Historical analysis of the Civil War reveals the difficulties the anti-Treaty IRA members had in supporting each other and that were heightened by the opposition to central control and the distance from Dublin of many of the main republican rural bases. Economic conditions also played a part in deciding whether or not an appetite for war existed in a particular place.[170] This had been a factor throughout this period. In Longford, for example, a dichotomy existed between the north and south of the county, with republicanism proving more congenial to the more impoverished north and less so in the south, where there were better land and larger farms.[171]

The initial fighting was centred in the city of Dublin, leading to the destruction of hotels and claiming one of the first of the high-profile republican victims, Cathal Brugha, though many more, such as de Valera, Austin Stack and Oscar Traynor, escaped with relative ease. Naive ideas about attacking Dublin from Wicklow were abandoned.[172] Resistance in Waterford, Tipperary and Limerick was overcome by more numerous and better-equipped Free State troops, but it was perhaps the use of the sea, allowing heavy armour to be transported to Kerry and Cork, which marked the beginning of the end for the republicans and their withdrawal to the mountains and hills. These landings effectively ended the Civil War as a serious military conflict by taking the so-called 'Munster republic' from the rear; but the month of this manoeuvre, August, also coincided with the shooting of Michael Collins, which altered both the character of the Civil War and in a sense the course of Irish politics.

'what is the position today and tomorrow?'

Collins had walked a tightrope in the aftermath of the Treaty; an inevitability given his multi-faceted role in the conduct of the War of Independence. The reckless decision to travel openly in convoy in Cork resulted in him being shot dead by republicans. In essence, Collins's leadership incorporated all the contradictions within this new regime. The image most used of Collins is of him in full military uniform the week prior to his death, as Commander-in-Chief of the Free State army at the funeral of Arthur Griffith (who Risteárd Mulcahy contended, died from a heart attack[173] – 'no shadow of a doubt' according to Collins – brought on by stress, overwork and mental anguish[174]). This ensured the perpetuation of the popular cult of Collins the gunman at the expense of examining Collins where he was at his strongest, as an administrator. Richard Mulcahy noted: 'he was capable of an intense amount of concentration over what might be called documentary or office work',[175] his life demonstrating that terrorist leaders could also be rational administrators.

Collins's role as a Civil-War commander was but a very short aspect (six weeks) of a career tailor-made for future movies. Collins knew the power of the military image and how to manipulate it. But what he said and wrote in private not only revealed (in correspondence with Kevin O'Higgins) his view that the Civil War was a battle for the foundation of the state and to protect recognition of majority rule; it also made clear that it was a huge personal trauma. It was simply humiliating, as Collins saw it, that the country was in a more lawless state than it had been during the days of the Black and Tans, and he saw this as a serious blow to national hopes, despite Churchill's reassurance to him that following the Four Courts attack, they were now masters of their own house.

He also regretted that long-term national objectives had now to be set aside. He had written some weeks before his death in a memorandum on the contemporary situation: 'What matters is not the past six months but the present position ... the question to be asked is, what is the position today and tomorrow? The rebel leaders have never faced this question. We must face it and keep it before the people.'[176] His sentiments also reflected an irritation at what was seen as much of the 'mystical and neurotic' worship of the republic. Whatever about Collins's ability to balance his contradictions, there was relative unanimity in the press reaction to his death, in both Britain and Ireland. But Collins's death also ensured that his attitude to the Treaty was now open to a multitude of interpretations.

'his blessed heart broke for Ireland'

Perhaps the death of Collins prevented significant reflection on the legacy of Arthur Griffith. For his staunchest supporters, it remained for Ireland to become worthy of Griffith, but he was quickly airbrushed from Irish history. The first signatory of the Treaty, he remained for many an embarrassment because of his attachment to the idea of a dual monarchy, and his ideas of economic self-sufficiency were at odds with the free-trade philosophy of the 1920s. The sneering jibes of republicans were that he had craved a 'King, Lords and commons of Ireland'. His wife Maud was humiliatingly forced to beg the Irish government for assistance in the aftermath of his death, and there were pathetic rows about the size of his burial plot in Glasnevin, with his wife at one stage resorting to threats to disinter his body. After 1923 Griffith was no longer the man they wanted to remember, and suggestions of commemoration came to nothing in the aftermath of Civil War, despite his wife's assertion that 'his blessed heart broke for Ireland'. In 1942 Cosgrave regarded the task of writing his biography as 'an onerous undertaking' and he would want to ensure that 'I'm not mentioned' in any such work.[177] Republicans taunted Cumann na nGaedheal about Griffith's memory and his political arguments, and by the 1960s there was virtually nothing known about him by a younger generation. It was not until 1968 that a simple plaque was placed on his home; Griffith died, in his wife's words, not only 'as poor as the day he entered politics' but also, in the words of Frank O'Connor, 'a peculiarly lonely, unknown man', one who his wife insisted 'had made you all'.[178] But with the death of both Griffith and Collins, the other Treatyite leaders filled the power vacuum decisively and controversially, by insisting that the actions of the republicans represented not ideological but criminal opposition.

For the *Cork Examiner*, news of Collins's death was an 'almost incredible fact':

> Cork was at once plunged into mourning. All the business establish-
> ments ceased work for the day and the trams stopped ... His last words
> when he lay dying on the roadside, when he knew he had only a minute
> or two to live, revealed his greatness as nothing else could have done.
> He said, 'forgive them' and then died.[179]

But it was also the case, as the *Freeman's Journal* pointed out, that 'he had dared death so often in the struggle with England that men felt he could run all risks and emerge unharmed. That he should be killed by an Irish bullet is a tragedy too deep for tears.'[180] It is a measure of the tragedy and the deeply personal divisions of the Civil War that, when arriving in Bandon in Cork, Collins was met by Seán Hales, who commanded national army forces in the area, while a few miles away Hales's brother was waiting to ambush Collins. This was a planned attack that was subsequently called off, but a few had remained to ensure the demise of Collins.

Republican prisoners in Mountjoy were said to have dropped to their knees to pray on hearing the news. Tim Pat Coogan also maintained that Collins was subsequently airbrushed out of Irish history, and that 'from the time of Collins' death there was a constant movement in which historians joined to under-play crucial factors which affected Collins' last days'.[181]

By the end of the century it was recognised that his was a life always waiting to be screened. Michael Collins had truly become an industry, but it was also the case that it was a gross simplification of the era for people to be asked to take sides in terms of de Valera or Collins, or the idea, as one journalist put it in 1999, that both Dev and Collins could be reduced 'to one-dimensional embodiments of the intellectual and emotional discord that precipitated civil war'.[182] Tim Pat Coogan's biography of de Valera was at pains to point out how hostile to the memory of Collins de Valera was.[183] But deifying one to demonise the other took both their lives out of context, lives that for only a short time could be considered parallel, and politically they had ideas for Ireland which were remarkably similar. As pointed out by Joe Lee and John Regan, 'the bulk of Collins's time was not spent in action scenes. It was spent as a manager and an administrator, whether as Minister of Finance or Director of Intelligence.'[184] It was difficult for Collins to wrestle with the demands of diplomacy. But he did it. He was also torn in several directions on the North. He justified his support of the Northern IRA on the grounds that they were entitled to defend themselves from pogroms:

> This is a case which can be settled by Irishmen. By force we could beat them perhaps, but perhaps not. I do not think we could beat them morally. If you kill all of us, every man and every male child, the difficulty will still be there. So in Ulster. That is why we do not want to coerce them. But we cannot allow solid blocks who are against partition in the north of Antrim through a part of Derry and part of

Armagh to Strangford Lough. If we are not going to coerce the North
East corner, the North East corner must not be allowed to coerce.[185]

'the birds were eating the flesh off the trees at Ballyseedy Cross'

The death of Collins also ensured that any attempt by republicans to co-
ordinate a military campaign was weakened. The tendency now was to
break up into smaller groups, as the IRA was forced into more remote
country districts. Erskine Childers, perhaps symbolically, as the republican
director of propaganda, temporarily based himself in a small cottage
in the hills of west Cork. Childers, who some erroneously believed was
the military mastermind of republican opposition, was ultimately to be
a victim of the government's special emergency powers, which allowed
those captured with arms to be tried by court martial. He was executed
while his sentence was still under appeal, and it was suggested, but never
fully substantiated, that the weapon he possessed had been given to him
by Michael Collins. One of the most powerful images of the Civil War was
that of Childers calmly shaking the hands of his firing squad before they
shot him. It was subsequently suggested that Childers's death had been
temporarily delayed as he informed his executioners that there would need
to be a medical officer present, and that after his death, one soldier shot
him in the face in his coffin.[186] Mystery writer, naval hero from the First
World War and a late convert to Sinn Féin in 1919, he came to despise
compromise and denounced the Treaty. His life and death were a further
illustration of the conflicting allegiances of this period in terms of dual
nationality and loyalty. He was to suffer the same fate as the knighted
Roger Casement. Days before his execution, Childers reflected on the
paradox of his situation:

> I have been held up to scorn and hatred as an Englishman who, betray-
> ing his own country, came here to lecture and destroy Ireland. Another
> and viler version is to the effect that so far from betraying England, I
> have been actually acting as the secret instrument of Englishmen for
> ruining Ireland.[187]

Although executions (and it still has not been established how many
were executed during the Civil War, but in the half-year from November
1922, 77 republicans were executed as a result of the government's special
emergency powers[188]) provoked a resurgence of republican violence, it

was limited. The beginning of 1923 saw reduced military activity in the south-west of Ireland, coinciding with the appointment of General Eoin O'Duffy, who had been Assistant Chief of Staff of the Free State army, to the position of Chief Commissioner of the Civic Guard (later renamed An Garda Síochána – Guardians of the Peace). A significant achievement, this body was created in the context of the need to create a new moral force in Irish policing. Its first Commissioner, Michael Staines, saw it as depending for its success on its moral strength as the representative of civil authority, rather than on force of arms or numbers. Approximately 96 per cent of the first 1,500 Civic Guards were ex-IRA members (19 per cent of the guards recruited in the first ten years of independence were RIC men and their experience was valued). A half-hearted mutiny in May and June 1922 involving about 300 guards was a result of many RIC men being quickly promoted to high-ranking positions. An inquiry initiated by Collins resulted in two civil servants recommending that the force should cease to carry arms and that politicians should not be serving members of the force, hence the departure of Staines.[189]

This was a brave move in the midst of civil war, particularly given the propensity to violence within the state. The policy of executions was to leave further deep scars on the infant state, particularly the executions in reprisal for the assassination of Seán Hales TD. Such executions had no legal basis. Not only were 40 republicans executed between the beginning of December 1922 and the end of January 1923, but the IRA also began to attack the homes of many prominent Free State soldiers. A meeting of the association formed by neutral members of the IRA at the La Scala Theatre in Dublin appealing for a truce may not have been a success initially, but that it occurred at all was an indication that this was not a war set to go on indefinitely. Perhaps a measure of the realism entering the equation was Dan Breen's laconic observation that 'in order to win this war you'll need to kill 3 out of every 5 people in the country and it isn't worth it'. Meanwhile, William Cosgrave, who had succeeded Griffith as President of the Dáil government in August 1922, was adamant that 'I am not going to hesitate and if the country is to live and we have to exterminate 10,000 republicans, the 3 millions of our people are bigger than this 10,000'.[190]

De Valera was determined to lead Sinn Féin into the election that Cosgrave was obliged to call when the statutory year of the provisional government's life was up, but he was arrested at Ennis in August 1923 in the aftermath of the Civil War, and the enforced retreat may have been welcome given his increasing impatience with a rejection by hard liners of practical politics in preference to IRA 'democracy'. He too was no doubt tired of being a 'humble soldier' subordinate to the men of faith rather than reason as he claimed to Richard Mulcahy.[191] That the bishops insisted in a joint pastoral in October that, morally, the republican case was 'only a system of murder' was a further blow to republican morale. The increasing barbarity of both sides had been reflected in two particular atrocities: when five Free State soldiers were killed by a mine at Knocknagoshel in County Kerry, in reprisal eight republicans were tied to a mine and blown up at Ballyseedy, Tralee, also in Kerry. According to Dorothy Macardle, for days after 'the birds were eating the flesh off the trees at Ballyseedy Cross'.[192] Richard Mulcahy, who succeeded Collins as Commander-in-Chief of the army, was reluctant to investigate events in Kerry. These were a reminder that no side had a monopoly on virtue during the Civil War. The IRA, as an unpaid army, was perhaps more liable to force its demands on the population in order to survive, but indiscipline and heavy drinking were a feature of the Free State army. A motley crew, many were on short-term contracts, leading to the eventual incorporation of British army veterans in the upper ranks to counteract the IRA veterans. By early 1923, Richard Mulcahy sought to address indiscipline with a measure of the centralisation that had been tried during the War of Independence, but Minister for Defence and Commander-in-Chief was an uneasy mixture. Nonetheless, Kevin O'Higgins, Minister for Home Affairs, had also strongly attacked standards in the army early in 1923 and MacEoin and Lawlor's Western Command were not without their critics. Emmet Dalton also strongly criticised his troops in Cork.[193]

'we must see it through'?

There will always be controversy, given the feebleness of republican military resistance in early 1923, as to whether the intensification of executions was justified or necessary. But whatever about indiscipline and questionable decision making, the stark reality, admitted by de Valera in private, was that this was not a war for which the republicans had a mandate in the aftermath of the vote for peace. But a seemingly delusional de Valera, in the midst of the darkest period of his career, in writing to Joseph McGarrity in Philadelphia, greatly exaggerated the strength of the republicans and the weakness of the Free State, suggesting that:

The Free State are starting the old villainous misrepresentation. I have always tried to think that our opponents are acting from high motives, but there is no doubt that there is a bit of the scoundrel in O'Higgins … already they are divided into a war party and a peace party, almost of equal strength, I am told. We are a far more homogeneous body than they are. If this war were finished Ireland would not have the heart to fight any other war for generations, so we must see it through.[194]

There was little drama to the end of the Civil War and the ceasefire of 25 May 1923 followed a government decision in February to offer amnesty to those prepared to surrender. The government insisted on adherence to majority rule and the dumping (but not publicly and hardly complete) of republican arms, with whatever demands the republicans may have proffered in the negotiations ignored. Neither were the hunger strikes on the part of some of the estimated 13,000 republican prisoners a success. In any case, the anti-Treaty leaders, at an executive meeting in Kilkenny in March, had shown that they could not agree themselves on how best to proceed amid conflicting signals from Liam Lynch, the IRA's Chief-of-Staff.

'a spiritual reality stronger than any material benefits you can offer'

The death of Liam Lynch, who was killed in action in April 1923, undoubtedly intensified demoralisation, while the voices of protest from republican women like Mary MacSwiney only confirmed for those of a sexist hue the unsuitability and inappropriateness of women in politics. MacSwiney insisted, in correspondence with Mulcahy, that 'we hold the republic as a living faith – a spiritual reality stronger than any material benefits you can offer'.[195] Indeed, the historian Margaret O'Callaghan maintained that the male creation of the 'republican virago' was a convenient way of depoliticising women who opposed the Treaty settlement.[196] P. S. Hegarty was later to refer to such women as 'the Furies'.[197] Jenny Wyse Power, who was eventually persuaded to accept the Treaty, was later to reflect on the consequences of so many republican women opposing the new state, and the departure of moderates from Cumann na mBan to form Cumann na Saoirse: 'It is to be regretted that this splendid force of women should have been the first body to repudiate the National Parliament, and thus initiate a policy which has had such disastrous results. The decision had the further effect of limiting Cumann na mBan to purely military work.'[198]

The dying weeks of the war had also raised troubling questions about the relationship between the civilian and military wings of the state, exemplified by tensions between Kevin O'Higgins and Richard Mulcahy, who was reluctant to discuss military matters with the cabinet. O'Higgins was unhappy with the intensity of the army's efforts, an ominous forewarning of the post-war difficulty experienced in trying to demilitarise Irish society.

'Praise God that he did not die in a snuffy bed of a trumpery cough'
The passions of the Civil War ran far and deep and historians have pointed to a number of long- and short-term effects. The war perhaps did not develop a 'revenge dynamic' cycle of killings akin to that of the War of Independence, though in republican areas, according to Peter Hart, 'Free Stater' assumed the same significance as 'informer' in the War of Independence days.[199] Whatever about increased tensions at the level of government, it was also the case that the IRA had not surrendered arms or acknowledged the legitimacy of the new state. Nor was there an abrupt and unequivocal end to IRA violence, which continued at a low but significant level. The fact that in the post Civil War period republican prisoners in Newbridge military camp were being taught courses in constitutional law, local government and Irish history[200] suggested that a mix of constitutionalism and defiance would be the future for some.

The playwright George Bernard Shaw, following the death of Collins, wrote to Collins's sister urging her not to mourn deeply: 'Hang up your brightest colours in his honour and let us all praise God that he did not die in a snuffy bed of a trumpery cough, weakened by age and saddened by disappointment that would have attended his work had he lived.'[201] Shaw's correspondence could be read as highly insensitive, but it was true that Collins was to escape the inevitable post-war tensions in Irish political life and the extent to which many who survived it had virtually no other political reference point, which was good for neither political life nor social maturation. The republican and labour activist Peadar O'Donnell, when asked why he did not bequeath his papers to posterity for historical research, was perhaps only half joking when he replied that he had no desire to start the Civil War again. He subsequently destroyed his personal documentation and correspondence relating to this period.[202] Certain participants of course sought to ensure their version of history won credence and acceptance, but people like O'Donnell saw the war as distracting attention from the social ills affecting Ireland and felt that disagreement over the degree of independence seemed abstract in light of the sheer poverty of Ireland.

'not the harps and martyrs and the freedom to swing a hurley'

Michael Collins had suggested that the essence of the struggle for independence was to secure freedom to control Irish life. But the Civil War ensured very centralised control was the primary political aim. Ivan Reynolds, one of the fictional characters in Roddy Doyle's *A Star Called Henry* (1999), summed up the attitude of certain architects of the state who, in their single-minded pursuit of political self-determination, had precious little to say about social need and want:

> But here's the truth now. All the best soldiers are businessmen. There had to be a reason for the killing and the late nights and it wasn't Ireland. Ireland's an island, Captain, a dollop of muck. It's about control of the island and that's what the soldiering's about, not the harps and martyrs and the freedom to swing a hurley.[203]

This view could be challenged as unduly harsh. The Civil War was fought on both sides by many decent, honest men and women. But it also sank the middle ground. There was no room, it seemed, for waverers. Nor was there room for a socialist utopia, despite the influence of many socialist intellectuals during this period, who were frustrated at best, ignored at worst. Richard English has suggested:

> Not only did their failure reflect the impact of economic background on the political ambitions of people from a variety of classes; but class struggle was seen by most republicans in these years as disruptive of the national harmony they sought to foster between all classes; precisely the kind of approach which O'Donnell and his comrades abhorred. It was also a very Catholic episode as the socialists' provision of an alternative (and their exasperation at its failure) eloquently demonstrated. Socialist intellectuals proclaimed the possibility of class unity overcoming sectarian divisions; the revolutionary years in fact demonstrated the degree to which sectarian self-definitions gave meaning to Irish people's lives.[204]

The tragedy, perhaps, was that what divided Sinn Féin was so little, in practice at least. De Valera, after all, in common with Griffith and Collins, was prepared to accept a connection with Britain with a view to the 26 counties increasing their independence through the evolution of the Constitution. De Valera's contention in the summer of 1921 that 'we are not republican doctrinaires' was perhaps true – if it had not been, it is doubtful he would have stayed in politics. But there was also the question of taking responsibility for assuming a die-hard position. Robert Barton, during the Treaty debates, had insisted: 'For myself, I preferred war. I told my colleagues so, but for the nation, without consultation, I dared not accept that responsibility ... I signed.'[205] De Valera and his followers were to sign too, though belatedly and with fingers crossed.

That they were in time able to gain office and dismantle the Treaty only increased the antipathy felt by those who had supported it. Mulcahy, for example, believed that de Valera 'had a blind pride in seeking power'.[206] This legacy of bitterness was not to be confined to one generation. Richard Mulcahy, could not, despite leading his party in government, assume the office of Taoiseach in 1948 because of his previous military life. He may in any case have been happy to be of service as an unambitious minister, but it is interesting that the career of Mulcahy was overshadowed by others for the simple reason that he was not Michael Collins, or as his son noted, 'he lived to the age of 86 years and was fortunate enough to die in his bed'.[207] And yet, remembering Shaw, he did live to see the disappointments which attended his work – the demobilisation of the army, the tarnishing of his reputation as a result of policy decisions during the Civil War, and the social problems that existed after the foundation of the state. Mulcahy asserted simply that politicians in general did not appreciate or understand the army and the difficulties in establishing a peacetime army after the disaster of the Civil War, but he was frustrated that a country with so many contemporary problems could be so occupied with the past. De Valera became a figure who polarised, inspiring loyalty and hatred in equal measure. He had, at the time, placed the burden of compromise on others, but ultimately, in gaining power in 1932, ensured many of the Treatyites stayed in the political wilderness for over 16 years.

There was a huge financial cost too, which brought the new state perilously close to bankruptcy and imbued its leaders with an eye for financial stringency that made a mockery of the idea that an independent Ireland would flourish economically. There is also much truth in Tom

Garvin's assertion that it imbued the new rulers with a distrust for popular consultation and a penchant for emergency legislation which was to have long-term effects embraced by both the main political parties.[208]

'make all the flags to be carried by the Volunteers'

As revealed in the attitude to Mary MacSwiney, the state's emerging chauvinism may in part have been a reaction to the politics of female republicanism during the Civil War era. Over 400 republican women were taken prisoner during the Civil War. They were held at Mountjoy, Kilmainham and the North Dublin Union. Margaret Buckley, in the *Jangling of the Keys*, indicated they were treated harshly:

> Máire [Comerford] sat on a bench, like a stoic of old with tightly compressed lips, never emitting even a murmur, while a doctor cut away her hair and put three stitches in her head. I had seen [Sheila] Humphreys being dragged out, half conscious from the blow dealt her when she resisted the search.[209]

In July 1923, Polly Cosgrave, a prisoner in the North Dublin Union, wrote to a former prison comrade: 'my jail experience is written in letters of fire across my brain, never to be effaced'.[210] It was a far cry from the domestic chores that many male nationalists had envisaged for Cumann na mBan. An article in the *Irish Volunteer*, written to coincide with the inauguration of Cumman na mBan, had called upon Irish women to 'form ambulance corps, learn first aid, make all the flags to be carried by the Volunteers, do all the embroidery that may be required, such as badges on the uniforms etc. To a patriotic Irish woman could there be any work of more intense delight than that?'[211] In a Dáil debate as late as 1928, de Valera questioned why five republican women prisoners, including Sheila Humphreys, had gone on hunger strike and were being kept in solitary confinement, noting that many of the women were known personally to members of the Dáil:

> I know myself that in the home of Sheila Humphreys the Republican Cabinet met when the Black and Tan regime was in progress. With that home I associate many of the acts of that cabinet, and nothing that this young girl is doing now is different from anything which was

preached in that home by members of the republican cabinet, some of whom are now persecuting her.[212]

After the formation of Fianna Fáil in 1926 Máire Comerford admitted that Cumann na mBan was a 'greatly weakened organisation' and one that 'gathered speed downhill'.[213]

'inconceivable how decent Irish boys could degenerate so tragically'

But the need to reclaim the role of the women during the revolution was only one part of the intellectual legacy of the Civil War. The ceasefire of May 1923, notes Anne Dolan, did not end the revolution: 'It is not a disease cured simply by the cessation of violence, nor a subject grown bland because the guns have been hidden away. After 24 May 1923, revolution is probably at its most revolutionary for it is then that the interpretation, the manipulation begins.'[214] This was something the Catholic Church was acutely conscious of, which was why, during the Civil War, it had moved with great speed to reassert its authority. The bishops' pastoral letter of October 1922 had insisted the Civil War was not a war, but 'morally only a system of murder and assimilation', suggesting it was 'almost inconceivable how decent Irish boys could degenerate so tragically'. More importantly, they asserted that 'disregard for the divine law then laid down by the bishops is the chief cause of all our present sorrows and calamities'.[215] There was a simple subtext to such a statement: obey your prelates and be subject to them. They were relatively mute on the subject of the state execution of republicans during the Civil War.

Many other episcopal pronouncements of the post-Treaty period, as pointed out by Patrick Murray, constituted a powerful affirmation of their own divinely sanctioned authority, and a sense of their relationship with the laity 'as resembling that between master and servant'. The accompanying language was suffused with notions of power, mastery, subjection and obedience, though a considerable number of priests ignored this and continued to support the republicans, being prepared to afford to anti-Treaty republicans 'the moral status of a war of independence'. So the Hierarchy's rhetoric was also directed at rebel priests, who if they supported the republicans in the Civil War would be 'false to their sacred office'. It seemed for the bishops there was now no place for the ambiguity that had surfaced during the War of Independence. An indication of the Hierarchy's mindset at this stage, and a marker for the future, was the contention of Bishop Hallinan of Limerick, in 1923, that bishops and priests had every right to exert their dominance in political affairs given the historical political power and importance of the Irish clergy.[216]

'the long-term character of loyalist government'

In his history of the Irish War of Independence, Michael Hopkinson was critical of the neglect of Northern Ireland in analyses of the conflict and insisted it deserved a more thorough treatment, arguing that:

> The most important consequences of the war of independence related to the six counties of the North-East, despite the fact that little of the fighting occurred in Ulster and that the existence of the Dáil government applied only in theory to the whole island. Ulster unionist resistance, by preventing a settlement along Home Rule lines and by radicalising opinion in the south and west, was the most significant cause of the war. The Truce terminating the conflict followed soon on the establishment of partition: hence the Northern question had been the key factor in dictating the fighting's duration.[217]

Given the existence of a Conservative-dominated coalition, the Government of Ireland Act of 1920, which provided a constitutional framework for the creation of Northern Ireland, was never more than a measure to appease Ulster unionists, though it was easier for them to do this given the blinkered approach to the North by Southern republicans, while any IRA activity in the North, given the isolation of Catholic nationalists, would be primarily defensive.

The sectarian violence that affected the province, partly prompted by fears that migrant Catholic workers had replaced Protestant ex-servicemen in the shipyards, reactivated the Ulster Volunteer Force. The threat posed by the IRA led to repeated calls for more troops in the North, and the British government subsequently went 'virtually the whole way' in satisfying Craig's demand for a new force with the establishment of the A, B and C Special Constabularies, largely recruited from the Orange Lodges and the UVF. This, combined with the failure to act over the shipyard riots, further alienated Ulster's Catholics from the British government. As Hopkinson notes: 'these developments defined the long-term character of loyalist government of the six counties even before the Government of Ireland Bill was passed'.[218]

In the election of May 1921, Unionists won 40 of the 52 seats for the new Northern Ireland parliament, and the new state was marked, during the turmoil in the South, by a digging in of heels. Ernest Blythe, for one, believed a policy of the South boycotting the North, particularly in the area of trade, was a futile exercise. Though some rhetoric emanating from de Valera and others hinted at a federal solution, or a unionist Ulster within the framework of a united Ireland, these ideas blatantly ignored the determination of the Northern state to uphold its new status. It was also ironic that, later, Collins was still ordering IRA activities in the North when the main emphasis elsewhere was on getting people to disarm. The North inevitably had its own share of turmoil, as James Craig and his unionists orchestrated the beginning of the idea of a Protestant state for a Protestant people. Perhaps symbolically, but appropriately, Edward Carson, he who, like the state of Northern Ireland itself for much of its future, exuded 'a manic-depressive mixture of reserve and high spirits',[219] had retired to the Sussex Downs in 1921, though he was to appear spasmodically in the House of Lords to make protests about British treachery.

'What a fool I was! I was only a puppet'

The rise and departure of Edward Carson revealed much about issues of Ulster identity. At the time of their resistance to Home Rule, Ulster unionists may have wanted Empire, but the Empire wanted Home Rule. In this context Carson built a remarkable career by mobilising Ulster Protestants and made a significant impact on British politics, even though it could be argued that his real brilliance was neither as strategic tactician nor ground-breaking lawyer, but as an extraordinary orator who was very aware of the power of symbolism and the need to emphasise the essential 'honesty' of Ulster. This made it easy to depict all that took a different view as essentially dishonest and treacherous. That Carson was also an 'outsider' with a Dublin background was good in terms of leadership credentials (in the sense of an all-Ireland unionism) but the increasing 'Ulsterisation' of the partition issue meant that it would ultimately undermine his authority, particularly when so much of this had been centred around 'speaking of Ulster as if it were Ireland'. Carson could do much, but he could not prevent partition. He acknowledged in private to Bonar Law that 'the duty is to come to terms'.[220] Nor could he fail to acknowledge the raw sectarianism of Northern Ireland; indeed Carson, master of the public performance, no more than many of his Southern counterparts in republicanism, seemed strangely short of ideas on how the future of Northern Ireland would be shaped, and relied instead on emotional sectarian rhetoric and was revered largely for saying 'no'.

But no to what? And had Unionists been used for the purpose of bringing a degree of unity to the Conservative Party? It was striking how quick they came to distrust British governments. In his maiden speech in the House of Lords in December 1921, Carson bellowed: 'What a fool I was! I was only a puppet and so was Ulster and so was Ireland in the political game that was to get the Conservative Party into office.'[221] It was on the idea of unstinting devotion to Empire that much of the political rhetoric of Northern unionism depended. But as Churchill had written to Collins, while he was trying to referee disputes between Collins and Craig, from an imperial point of view there was nothing the British would have liked better than to see North and South joined together. Churchill was naive in insisting 'the bulk of people are slow to take in what is happening and prejudices die hard. Plain folk must have time to take things in and adjust their minds to what happened. Even a month or two may produce enormous changes in public opinion.'[222] This was precisely the opposite to what happened, and also wishful thinking was Collins's vision of the opening up of river traffic across a united Ireland given that Belfast in terms of social organisation and economic development was closer to English cities like Bristol than it was to Dublin.

'imperialism followed the creation of unionism in Ireland'
But it was the attitude to Empire that was perhaps most interesting. Irish attitudes to the Empire were not consistent and at various stages were characterised by affection, indifference and hostility, and there is much truth in the assertion of Alvin Jackson that 'imperialism followed the creation of unionism in Ireland rather than the reverse'. It could also be dictated crudely by economics; before the First World War, Belfast industrialists with an eye on the North Atlantic market were more concerned with free trade than with Empire; but with a trade recession and tariff barriers the Empire seemed to become more important.[223] Economic recession could also expose the class divisions within Ulster unionism. The appearance of the Ulster Unionist Labour Association in June 1918 seemed to be an attempt to move workers away from 'bolshevism', a significant move given that, with 36,000 employees in 1919, the shipyard workers of

Belfast represented the greatest concentration of unionised skilled labour in Ireland. The general strike of that year revealed a complex social group with many antagonisms within it, which was probably the reason why unionist leaders, though conservative, took the step of initiating loyalist groups that could accommodate radical rhetoric.[224] The scale of working-class participation in loyalist politics was confirmed when in the election of 1921 the Ulster Unionist Labour Association provided five of the 40 unionists elected.

'In both cases they have found that they made a mistake'

But nor was there a homogeneous nationalist and Catholic community in Northern Ireland; indeed, it was the continuing divisions within Northern nationalism, along with Sinn Féin's strategy of abstaining from Westminster between 1918 and 1920, which further distanced them from influencing their own fate at a critical juncture. The idea of constructive opposition was a long way off and Joe Devlin in 1921 was to lament the difficulty of contesting the elections given the want of machinery, lack of funds and difficulty of raising enthusiasm, an indication of the effective collapse of the Ancient Order of Hibernians. It was not until the Boundary Commission of 1925 that the uncertainty was dispelled definitively and the need for a unified movement highlighted. Neither could the IRA boast of active resistance – an IRA officer wrote to Moss Twomey (Chief of Staff of the IRA from 1926 to 1936) in 1925, expressing his amazement when he reached Derry city:

> to learn that absolutely no organisation existed in the city or in any part of the county. Such staff as exist was purely nominal and had not even made an effort at organisation for a few months. One of their excuses was that the GHQ officer they met a few months ago laid down an impossible programme, in their opinion, i.e. parading and drilling.[225]

This was also a reminder that certain areas like County Londonderry had never really been hotbeds of republican activity but were more likely to be dominated by nationalists, the Ancient Order of Hibernians being the dominant force in local politics.[226] The papers of Moss Twomey suggest the total strength of the anti-Treaty IRA forces in the Northern Command numbered no more than 1,170 with approximately 400 weapons – one for every three members. As early as 1924 an IRA officer summed up the situation:

> Those of the Catholic population of Ulster who supported the Treaty did so for 2 reasons; firstly, they were strongly influenced by the Boundary Commission clause and secondly, they had an idea there would be a national government in the 26 counties which would safeguard them from political and economical persecution from their own government. In both cases they have found that they made a mistake.[227]

Dublin did not exactly rush to their aid. In the elections of May 1921 for the 52-seat House of Commons, Sinn Féin and the nationalists won 12 between them. It was a disappointing result for the nationalists with, for example, the Catholic 25 per cent of Belfast securing only 6 per cent of its representation. The elections and how Sinn Féin in the South should respond to them, was hotly debated. De Valera believed that, morally, it made more sense to boycott the parliament than the elections, and that by contesting the elections with a view to abstention, the unity of republican Ireland could be preserved:

> Letting the elections go by default would seem to be an abandonment of the North as hopeless for us, and the acceptance in a sense of partition; it would help kill the republican movement in the North by throwing Sinn Féiners practically into the camp of the nationalists – this might produce, later, a dangerous reactionary effect on the south.[228]

'Ulster in the wrong'?

But ultimately propaganda rather than practical politics was to be the hallmark of the approach of the Southern administration to the North during this period. Pamphlets were published by the first Dáil putting 'Ulster in the wrong', a reaction to the expulsion of Catholic employees from Belfast firms in the summer and autumn of 1920. The Dáil maintained that 7,410 Catholic employees had been expelled and decreed a trade boycott of Belfast which did not end formally until 1922. By early 1921 there were 80 local boycott committees under the auspices of local authorities and by October 1921 the government had published a list of over 200 firms in England and Ireland which were distributing from Belfast and thus to be boycotted. Though it achieved some success, it was also true that the Dublin United Tramway Company continually flouted the rules by advertising boycotted firms on its train tickets and refused to pay the fines imposed, to the chagrin of boycott director Joe McDonagh.[229] Hopkinson makes the point that the boycott was 'little more than gesture politics: it was an example of the often counter-productive Sinn Féin policy regarding the North.'[230] The Southern government also circulated weekly Belfast summaries detailing atrocities and pogroms; government figures for November and December 1920 alone recorded 41 deaths. Over 100 people were killed in Belfast during 1921, and in 1922 nearly 300 murders were officially recorded.[231]

For the new prime minister, James Craig, the task of establishing a viable democratic state was complicated by a great amount of political posturing during 1921–2. He welcomed the Treaty negotiations but refused to be bribed by Lloyd George in relation to the supposed economic unviability of Northern Ireland. Secret 'Ulster draft clauses' circulated during the Treaty negotiations, suggesting certain northern constituencies could elect to be directly represented in the southern parliament, also came to nothing. Griffith had written to de Valera detailing meetings between himself, Collins, Lloyd George and Birkenhead: 'the gist of it was that if we would accept the crown they would send for Craig, i.e., force Ulster in as I understand'.[232] The truth, however, was that there had been little coherence on the part of the British government about partition and it was implemented with scant regard for the long-term consequences, though Sinn Féin remained extraordinarily naive in maintaining that a united Ireland would be a prosperous and harmonious entity. That this was a facile contention was recognised by W. B. Yeats, who lost no sleep over partition: 'I have always been of the opinion that if surly disagreeable neighbours shut the door, it is better to turn the key in it before they change their mind.'[233]

Lady Lilian Spender, wife of Wilfred Spender, who had commanded the Ulster Volunteer Force and went on to become the most senior civil servant in Northern Ireland, recorded in her diary her doubts about the Treaty in December 1921:

Up to the last I don't think we ever really believed England would do this thing – would reward murder and treachery and treason and crime of all kinds and penalise loyalty ... [Miss Erskine] an ardent unionist ... [told me] it was the saddest day of her life. 'England doesn't want us', she said, with a depth of bitterness I cannot convey ... And now we know that worse is to come, and further pledges are to be broken, for two of the six counties may be taken from us – Tyrone and Fermanagh.[234]

But in public, particularly after the elections of May 1921, James Craig was more concerned with conveying to Dublin the simple message that it had to come to terms with the reality of a separate Northern state. Craig met de Valera secretly in Dublin in May 1921, Craig amusedly suggesting that the return meeting should take place in an Orange Hall. It seemed to be a futile mutual expression of grievances, though it has been suggested that it was Dublin Castle's way of finding out more about what de Valera wanted. That they met at all in the context of a possible agreement about a truce, fiscal agreements and a prisoner amnesty – anything short of a republic that did not threaten Ulster – 'illustrates how pragmatic de Valera and Craig could be despite their inflexibly dogmatic public stances'.[235]

'huddled together to save ourselves from the stones'

But it was the violence which continued to make the headlines in 1922 despite a series of meetings between Craig and Collins (who was receiving exaggerated reports from London sources that a civil war was being planned in Ulster, enabling more British troops to be stationed in the North, who would later find it necessary to cross the border[236]). Like the imminent civil war in the South, what was striking was the sheer human isolation and personal tragedy which was coming to characterise the North. The Dublin government kept a series of signed statements from victims of loyalist mobs; included was this statement from a Catholic woman in Argyle Street whose house had been looted and set alight:

As we were huddled together to save ourselves from the stones which were coming through the windows, we heard the front door being attacked and then burst open. A leader of the mob who was well dressed compared with the others, came to us and told us to get out, giving us a minute to do so. He called us Sinn Féin bastards and said to do as we were told or we would all be blown up. He then joined the mob outside. This occurred about 5.30am. There was only one other Catholic woman in the street besides ourselves, the rest having been previously cleared.[237]

'unnaturally dependent on the fragments of the internees' lives'

For a settlement or, as Craig put it, a 'supreme sacrifice' which was not requested or wanted, there was certainly no delay in implementing the Government of Ireland Act. By 1922, for example, there were 16,000 'B Specials' in the North and the gerrymandering of local government areas was well under way. As Joe Lee put it: 'the border was chosen explicitly to provide unionists with as much territory as they could safely control. Its objective was not to separate unionists and nationalists in order to enable them to live peaceably apart. It was instead to ensure Protestant supremacy over Catholic even in predominantly Catholic areas.'[238] The priority (similar to the South) given to 'law and order' was reflected in the internments on the prison ship *Argenta*, with 700 incarcerated by May 1922, the first manifestation of the draconian Civil Authorities (Special Powers) Act of March 1922, which gave extensive powers to the executive. The files on the internees released in 1996 allowed the historian Denise Kleinrichert to get an insight into what they endured, the logic of such a penal system and indeed the pride in it; the Unionist minister Dawson Bates later acquired the ship's bell as a souvenir.[239]

Both the internment and the subsequent exclusion orders undoubtedly contributed to the demoralisation and poor organisation of nationalist politics and cultural life. In March 1922 Craig's government had estimated the full strength of the IRA at 112,650 throughout all Ireland, with over 8,000 living in the North. The arrest of those bound for the *Argenta* was the greatest mass arrest in the history of Ireland, and the internees were housed in cages (some containing as many as 56 men) 40 feet long, 20 feet wide and 8 feet high, with rotten food and infectious diseases part of the prisoners' lot. Most of them were nationalist middle-class professionals, and a measure of their resourcefulness and capacity to endure was evidenced by the fact that they managed to produce an *Argenta Bulletin*, hand-written on board and satirising their internment predicament. In October 1923 a hunger strike was begun by 269 of the men, leaving further long-term health legacies. The *Argenta* was not cleared of internees until 1924. Kleinrichert commented that 'the only creatures seemingly aware of and unnaturally dependent on the fragments of the internees' lives were the birds as they hovered above the vessel'.[240]

'not a single penny would they let fall from their tight fists'

But Craig's true priorities revealed much about the peculiar state that

Northern Ireland was to become. The *Freeman's Journal* in February 1922 noted that in the previous three weeks 40 people had been killed and at least 100 wounded; with no arrests and a Catholic population under siege in what the paper called 'a city of death'.[241] At the same time, Craig's longest letters to the Cabinet Secretariat related to the design of concrete fencing posts for the Stormont estate, the home of the parliament buildings, and architecture intended to emphasise Protestant supremacy and the permanence of partition. During 1921 and 1922, Craig was in constant personal touch with the Office of Works, visiting London frequently to discuss progress. It was imperative, he wrote, 'not to go along lines which would appear to the outside world as though we in Ulster itself placed a minor importance on our institution and felt that a small trifling and niggardly treatment of the subject was sufficient for the Ulster people'.[242]

Others were left to countenance, whether Catholic or Protestant, life in the 1920s working-class ghettos of the new Northern Ireland. Robert Harbinson, recalling the plight of his Presbyterian, charwoman mother wrote: 'What depths of shame and pride did she not suffer to borrow a gill of milk, a neighbour's hat to go to church or the skin of an eggshell to put over my blistered heels.' He recalled wanting to grow up to be a binman to discover what 'marvels could be found in the bins of wealthy homes'. Meanwhile, others:

> having made their fortunes from the likes of us and from the mills and factories that scarcely left room for our mean streets to run between, they wanted no other contact with us. It seemed to me that they determined, every fat man jack of them, that not a single penny would they let fall from their tight fists.[243]

- FOUR -

1923-1932

'fanaticism will one day be killed by radicalism'?

In his survey of contemporary Ireland in 1908, the French writer Louis Paul-Dubois suggested that 'fanaticism will one day be killed by radicalism in Ulster, but the struggle is not yet near its end'.[1] Had he been surveying the birth of the Northern state in the early 1920s he may well have written the same thing, or indeed, had he been an observer of the outbreak of the modern troubles in 1969, the same assessment could also have applied. At the birth of their respective states, North and South, despite the obvious different religious complexions, had in fact much in common, particularly in the context of violence, law and order, and class tension, issues that were to dominate the political and social agenda in both parts of the island throughout the 1920s and beyond. In the North, the sectarian issue exacerbated these concerns, with Northern Protestants outnumbering their Catholic counterparts by two to one according to the census of 1926.

A close relationship existed between the Orange Order and the state's new Protestant parliamentarians, though as David Fitzpatrick has pointed out tensions between the two and expulsions from the organisation highlight 'an energetic but far from unchallenged system of management'.[2] This alludes to another theme – the degree to which, having achieved the defeat of an all-Ireland Home Rule settlement, unionists could succeed in ensuring the tensions within unionism, so blatant when Home Rule was not a direct threat, could be kept in check. Another overriding preoccupation was the extent of Britain's financial and political support for the new state and whether or not the Northern state would become an expensive thorn in the side of the British Empire. After all, the (better) Government of Ireland Act, passed in December 1920, had effectively allowed Britain to sidestep the issue of how power in that state would be wielded. The elections of May 1921 followed a year of mass workplace expulsions in Belfast shipyards, mostly directed at Catholics, nationalists and socialists. Unemployment (in June 1921 one quarter of the North's insured workforce was unemployed compared to less than 18 per cent in Britain) and the 'Belfast boycott' in operation in the South, and intense and vicious sectarian riots in Derry, created other tensions.

Increasing levels of violence in the summer of 1921 indicated that this was not going to be a short-term problem, which explains why the law-and-order ticket became so central to the governance of the state, and the effective bypassing of normal judicial process. A sort of permanent state of emergency existed, enforced by a sectarian police regime, particularly the three divisions of special constabulary established in November 1920. By mid-1922, 32,000 had been recruited, and the indisciplined 'B' Specials were intent on targeting Catholics and nationalists in a vicious and premeditated way. That they were allowed to operate in such a manner not only incensed the Southern authorities, but marked, in Fitzpatrick's phrase, 'Britain's belated blessing of bigotry'.[3] This was to remain contentious throughout the century. In May 1922, the regular police force, which had contained many Catholics, was reconstituted as the Royal Ulster Constabulary.

The general election produced for the 52-seat parliament a result which remained relatively consistent for 50 years – 40 unionists, 6 nationalists and 6 Sinn Féin members, the latter 12 abstaining from what became immortalised in the phrase 'A Protestant Parliament for a Protestant People'. This was a description uttered by James Craig, though it was retrospectively asserted that he meant Protestantism in the context of tolerance and freedom of conscience.[4] The transformation of the North was completed in December 1922, when the government invoked the right to opt out of the Treaty clause allowing them to join with the South. The early 1920s were thus important, not only for establishing the character and management of the state, but because the issues centre-stage then were to remain so for the rest of the century. Indeed, the negotiation of the Good Friday Agreement in 1998 was about the extent to which these controversies could be, if not solved, at least diluted in the context of nationalist inclusion in the apparatus of the Northern state.

'innocence was no guarantee for a Catholic then'

The bitter nationalist reaction to the state in the 1920s was inevitable, given the brutality experienced by some of their population, who, like all victims of the corruption of the Northern state (Catholic and Protestant), were mostly working class. Over 100 people died in Belfast alone in 1921, rising to nearly 300 in 1922. It was no wonder that Derry writer Séamus Deane's father 'would not speak of it at all' and that Deane, in his novel *Reading in the Dark*, records the comment of a teacher in the 1950s that 'innocence was no guarantee for a Catholic then. Nor is it now.'[5] David Fitzpatrick estimates that between the summer of 1920 and the summer of 1922 there were in the region of 550 murders, with 80 members of crown forces, 300 Catholic civilians and rebels, and 170 Protestants the victims, the overwhelming majority killed in Belfast.[6] Under the Special Powers Act of April 1922 the Minister for Home Affairs was authorised to delegate his authority to the police forces. The security measures enacted included internment and flogging (which, Cosgrave protested in an angry letter to Churchill, had been legalised by the Firearms Act of 1921) and the use of prison ships to house republican internees.

Thousands were convicted annually in the early 1920s, while the Southern authorities seemed to have little interest in preventing IRA attacks in the North, which raised questions about the extent of their complicity in terrorism in the North. They were more concerned about the treatment of the nationalist population and the attempt to 'reduce the men to the position of common criminals'. A medical doctor in March 1922 insisted that the torture of IRA prisoners, including gas poisoning, needed 'to be made public to the world', to which Craig responded that there was 'no truth in the suggestion that there was anything in the nature of barbarous treatment'.[7]

'an underworld there with deadly feuds of its own'

The Southern government retained files of shocking persecution of Catholics in 1922. It was observed that few of the many Catholics who had established licensed premises in the 'quiet period' up to 1920 had escaped, and that 219 licensed houses had been burnt down. Three publicans and six barmen were murdered, revealing something of what Churchill in a letter to Collins referred to as 'an underworld there with deadly feuds of its own'.[8] Michael Collins was more concerned that, as he put it in a letter to Desmond FitzGerald, 'I feel they are doing better in publicity than we are.' Thus the reports compiled on 'Belfast outrages' began to run to hundreds of pages to describe the murder and mayhem caused by those who believed 'Popish blood is sweet.' An entry for the night of 31 March 1922 read:

> 10.20 pm. Bomb thrown into house of Francis Donnelly, 29, Brown Street, killing his child, Francis, aged 2.5 years and wounding himself and Joseph Donnelly, aged 12. 'Specials fired over heads of Catholic young men playing football in Academy Street. Military arrived on the scene and remonstrated with 'Specials. Both left street together. John Meeney, aged 17, Stanhope Street, shot by sniper last night and died later in Mater Hospital. John Campion, Vintner, 120 Boundary Street, wounded by gunmen on refusing to put up hands. John Sweeney (18) 36 Stanhope Street, wounded previous night, died, this night, in Mater Hospital. Gunner searched Grocery Street 'for arms' and stole money.[9]

When Cosgrave received a deputation of nationalists in October 1922, they complained bitterly of their treatment. Cosgrave suggested Craig himself was anxious to reduce the presence of the B Specials. A priest informed him that three of the B Specials had been removed for cursing the Pope, to which Cosgrave replied: 'that won't do the Pope much good'.[10] While the B Specials may have been bankrolled by the British government, Paul Bew and others have suggested that the degree of support for the unionist security apparatus has been exaggerated, and there was a recognition that many of them were 'the younger and wilder type'. But unionists rowed with Lloyd George over the need for an inquiry into their behaviour. It was suggested in 1922 that 'ministers were too close to their followers', but that there was no need for a judicial inquiry. It clearly annoyed Britain that efforts to encourage more professionalism within the B Specials were constantly blocked, along with the suppression of reports of their atrocities.[11] Interestingly, the delegation to Cosgrave also suggested that their dilemma was not only born of lack of funds and fears about the Boundary Commission, but the absence of cohesion on the part of nationalists, a reminder that not all were automatically actively opposed to the new state. Indeed, Cosgrave had referred to those who 'go out of their way to assist your government' even if they got precious little in return, in a letter to Lord Londonderry (Minister for Education in the North) concerning interned school teachers.[12]

A 'United Catholic Party'?

While the leadership of middle-class nationalism remained the same, a 'United Catholic Party' in 1923 on Belfast City Council represented the interests of businessmen, publicans and clergy. It was largely the Catholic Church that assumed the most obvious leadership position, and in the process became relatively oblivious to Protestant fears regarding its political role. It came to view itself as indispensable in the North, particularly with Sinn Féin so demoralised and nationalism generally weakly organised. In 1921 all but one of the nationalist candidates had been proposed or seconded by Catholic Church personnel.[13] It was no wonder they placed such a premium on exclusively Catholic education, and Londonderry's attempt to prioritise non-denominational schooling in 1923 was scuppered by both churches.

A Catholic boycott involved 700 teachers in over one third of the Northern schools under Catholic management. But it could be legitimately argued that, had there been wide-scale Catholic acceptance of the new state, this would have made little impact on the Protestant view of them. MacRory as Bishop of Down and Connor until 1928, and Archbishop of Armagh from 1928 to 1945, stuck steadfastly to a Belfast ghetto mentality, though from 1924 to 1927 the more instinctively pluralist Patrick O'Donnell led the Hierarchy and managed to break the impasse concerning teacher training. But even had he survived it is doubtful he, or any other bishop, could have pulled the aggrieved flock in a direction it did not want to go, though, as Mary Harris has pointed out, there were those who believed the flock was let down by its leadership.[14]

The reality was that there were divisions among the Catholic Hierarchy, particularly about the extent to which they should be involved in Northern politics. MacRory, for example, accepted an honorary doctorate from Queen's University but would not accept it in person. But ultimately, Mary Harris suggests, 'much of the Church's success in politics depended on accurately assessing public opinion. In cases where there was no lay movement to follow the church's suggestions, nothing happened.'[15] There has also been retrospective questioning of the extent to which, in the light of a new kind of nationalism in the 1960s, the Catholic community during this era were dominated 'by green backwoodsmen obsessed with the partition issue'.[16]

'grimly related to the present tense'

The abolition of proportional representation and the gerrymandering of constituencies created a thoroughly debased and artificial structure for Northern politics, with, for example, 25,000 unionists in County Fermanagh electing 17 representatives on the county council, while 35,000 nationalists could elect only 7.[17] The *Irish Times* noted in 1924 that in the six rural districts of Tyrone, all with a Catholic majority, as a result of gerrymandering, they could not elect a majority in any district. It estimated that in the four areas most largely Catholic, one member was returned by 622 votes, while in the four areas most largely Protestant, 259 votes could return a representative.[18] Local government in the North was complex, and its administration multi-tiered, which contributed to a considerable lack of dynamism. In 1920 there were seven different forms of local government – Boards of Guardians, Borough Councils, Urban District Councils, Rural District Councils, County Councils, Borough Councils and Town Commissions – amounting to 70 separate local-authority bodies. Between 1919 and 1939 a total of only 3,839 houses were erected by local authorities compared to 32,644 by private builders.[19]

Notwithstanding, the *Morning Post*'s representative in Ireland at the end of 1925 met with Joe Devlin, Northern MP for West Belfast, concerning the possibility of him taking his seat in the aftermath of the Boundary Commission, and predicting to Cosgrave 'a happy ending'.[20] Devlin did indeed enter the Northern parliament that year, and by 1927 the other nationalist MPs had followed him. There were 11 nationalists MPs elected in 1929, though this seemed to be the peak of their success, as Devlin's National League went into decline thereafter. The civil service, too, was to be no warm place for Catholics (and the south attempted to frustrate the transfer of civil servants who were prepared to move North by withholding departmental records); the service was dominated by existing Irish officers, imperial servants mostly employed in tax offices, and the new Protestant recruits. War service was the essential criterion for discrimination, along with religion. By 1942 there were 2,000 permanent members and 6,000 temporary officers. But it was not until 1946 that the Whitley system of negotiation was adopted, having been rejected by the Minister for Finance in 1924, the service only having a consultative representative council with no negotiating rights.

The writer Denis Donoghue was brought up in Warrenpoint, County Down, having been born in Carlow, after his father, one of the few Catholics who joined the RUC, became entitled to a transfer there as a member of the disbanded RIC ('He had no choice, no other job was available and the RUC could not reject his application'). In his book *Warrenpoint* Donoghue recalled that religion was practised but never discussed in his house and his father, like many Catholics of that generation in the North, rarely talked about the past: 'he was grimly related to the present tense and determined to gain a better future for his children, so he didn't have much time for nostalgia'. Donoghue also gives a good insight into the intricacies of class differences among the Catholic community: 'By being in uniform he was better dressed than a lower-middle-class Catholic and this made his social image somewhat ambiguous.' But there was nothing ambiguous about relations between Catholics and Protestants. Donoghue's family spoke and shopped only with Catholics, and when growing up: 'I could spot a Protestant at a hundred yards ... In the North a Protestant walks with an air of possession and authority, regardless of his social class. He walks as if he owned the place, which he does. A Catholic walks as if he were there on sufferance.' Distinguishing between Catholic and Protestant, Donoghue maintained, was a social necessity, and, most tellingly: 'I did this upon instinct ... it was not inculcated by my parents, whom I never heard speak a word on the subject.'[21]

'lives seemed to depend on the noises they were able to make'

Northern Protestantism remained morally conservative (and essentially similar to Southern Catholicism, without the obsession with birth control), though Fitzpatrick maintains that 'there was no Protestant consensus concerning the proper bounds of clerical authority'.[22] Concern about violation of the Sabbath led to a licensing act of 1923 prohibiting the opening of pubs on Sundays. A proposal to release women from compulsory jury service was rejected (unlike in the South), and while Parliament did not tend to legislate for discrimination against women in the same manner as in the Free State, 'Orangeism' remained very much a male preserve. The artist John Lavery painted the 12 July parade in Portadown in 1928, and Northern author Susan McKay quotes him as noting the 'austere passion' of the occasion. The drummers' 'lives seemed to depend on the noises they were able to make ... their wrists bleeding and a look in the eye that boded ill for any interference.'[23]

But Protestant and Orange culture was not just about the annual machismo of marching. It was also about media (and often university) backing for an exclusively Protestant ethos which, in the context of the new creation of the Northern state, and to dispel any notion of insecurity, focused instead on their more ancient pedigree. This was in evidence in Ronald Mac Neill's *Ulster's Stand for Union* (1922)[24] while the main unionist papers, the *Belfast Newsletter, Belfast Telegraph* and *Northern Whig*, remained close to the governments, presenting, as Denis Kennedy revealed, almost identical interpretations of events for their readers, coupled with a dismissive and vindictive attitude to the Free State, with a particular focus on the killing of Protestant civilians in the South.[25]

'purify public morals'?

Welfare and labour issues were rarely aired in the new parliament. The extent to which the labour movement was weak in the North was significant in such a class-based, industrialised and, for many, very poor society, as was the extent to which these issues were drowned and dwarfed by unionism. The poet John Hewitt, in a perceptive retrospective essay on his Ulster identity, recalled:

> By the mid-1920s, with the new ministers in gear and the non-entities trooping to the Westminster back benches, it seemed evident that the unionists were a right-wing offshoot of the British Tory party, who at home fought every election on the border, and that the nationalists, the representatives of the Catholic minority, were merely obsolete clansmen with old slogans, moving in an irrelevant dream, utterly without the smallest fig-leaf of a social policy. So my concern went to the Labour Party.[26]

But the labour movement's attitude to partition was divisive. In 1920 the Belfast Labour Party had won ten seats on the Belfast City Council, sidestepping the partition issue. But such avoidance was more difficult in the volatile environment of 1920–22, preventing it from contesting the May 1921 elections, when, instead, four independent candidates were fielded in the labour interest. In December 1923 the Belfast Labour candidate, Harry Midgely, lost only narrowly to a unionist when contesting

the Westminster seat of West Belfast, though the extent to which political expediency was more important than labour principles was revealed in
his electioneering approach, and underlined the difficulties any nascent
labour movement would face in the North. The *Irish News* noted: 'on the
Shankhill Road he stressed his Protestantism and his army service in the
Great War, while in the Falls he hit out against the internment of prisoners and appeared to share the aspirations of his audience to a United
Ireland'.[27]

In March 1924 at a conference in Belfast, the Belfast Labour Party
became the Northern Ireland Labour Party, but once again avoided the
'national' question, and remained Belfast-orientated throughout the 1920s,
winning, for example, 16 seats on the city's corporation in 1926. The fact
that unionist policy was based on duplicating British social legislation also
narrowed the field available to class politics. In 1925 three Labour MPs
were elected, but if there was to be any continuation of the idea of James
Connolly of an Irish workers' republic independent of Britain, the success
of labour nationally would depend on the South ensuring the same kind
of social benefits as existed in the North. Another strand of the North's
labour movement was reflected in William Walker's idea of an Irish labour
movement integrated with Britain in the context of a unionist political
framework, as had been argued as early as 1911.[28] Eventually, the pragmatism of Walker's view, and thus acceptance of the reality of the state,
was chosen by activists like Sam Kyle and Harry Midgely, and generally held sway. This involved a close identification with the British labour
movement, though loyalty to Connolly remained significant, ensuring
there were different strands of the NILP in the 1920s.

Hugh Gemmell, in *Socialism for Ulster* (1927), argued that socialism
would 'purify public morals' and advocated a specific puritanical form of
Ulster socialism with a strong emphasis, as in the British labour movement,
on the need for temperance.[29] Graham Walker suggested the abolition
of proportional representation was a disaster for the labour movement in
the North because it became 'a convenient punch bag both for unionist
and nationalist politicians anxious to preserve the pan class unity of their
respective blocs'.[30] The reality was that it was designed to prevent Protestant splinter groups gaining a political foothold.

Politically, women were marginalised. The first issue of the Ulster
Women's Unionist Council journal, the *Ulsterwomen*, was published in
1919, but publication ceased a year later. There were only two female

Unionist MPs in the 1920s, Dehra Parker and Julia McMordie. (Ten women were elected to the parliament of Northern Ireland between 1921 and 1972, six of them as members of the Ulster Unionist Party.) The opinions they expressed on the role of women in Northern society are thus worthy of scrutiny. As in the South, most expressions of desire to see women involved in public life were qualified by the assertion that it would or should in no sense diminish their contribution to home life. Parker asserted:

> Women's advent into ... branches of public life does not necessarily entail any departures from the confines of home. I am convinced that it is quite possible for her to give the benefits of her advice and help to her county, her district or her town, whilst living at home, looking after that home and in no manner neglecting any of her home duties ... every board would be improved by the presence of one or two sensible women members who in remembering the human and humane side of their duties, would, I am sure, equally remember the financial side and would conserve the interests of the ratepayers whom they represent, and bring their training as housewives to bear upon the running of any institutions under their control.[31]

Another publication of the Ulster Women's Unionist Council appeared in in 1925: *Northern Ireland, Home and Politics: A Journal for Women*. Rather than advocating that women stand for election to parliament, the journal urged them to vote for male Unionists. In 1927 Joe Devlin, the nationalist MP for West Belfast, introduced a bill, extending the franchise to all men and women aged 21 or over. The bill was opposed by the government, which introduced its own bill the following year, granting equality of franchise between men and women, but maintaining a property qualification for local elections. Dehra Parker's initial reaction to Devlin's bill was to announce that 'Personally, I would prefer to have seen universal franchise at the age of 25 ... at the age of 21 years I was far too interested in my home and two children to pay any attention to political matters of any kind.'[32]

'welded together after all in poverty and deprivation'
Regardless of sentiments about humanising and feminising politics, the poor continued to live in squalor, with working-class conditions for many

retaining, in the words of T. W. Moody, 'the suffering character of the industrialised areas of Victorian Britain'.[33] It often seemed elected representatives were determined to deny its severity. In the summer of 1926, Derry city's corporation insisted that 'on the information before us we are not satisfied that the state of distress alleged to exist in the city is such as would justify this Corporation in making application to the Ministry of Home Affairs for an order authorising the Board of Guardians to administer relief out of the workhouse'.[34] It was resentment at a similar attitude in Belfast in the 1930s that caused widespread and violent disturbances.

John Simms, writing about his impoverished boyhood in the unionist Shankhill area of Belfast (the Hammer) in the 1920s, suggested in those years poverty could overcome religious tensions. There was, he maintained, much affection for the Jewish residents because 'we were welded together after all in poverty and deprivation. For a certainty there were no great financiers in the back streets of the Hammer.' Notwithstanding, Jews, 'situated betwixt orange and green ... became more and more the object of mindless bigotry and violence'. The same grinding poverty as existed in the Southern slums afflicted the North also, with 'one-room slums, stricken mothers and meals concocted from pieces of fatty meat scraps. I had an innate sense of being respectful of wealth and authority and of course many kids had little option but to respect rich masters however foul those masters might be. There were times when one just had to grovel.' The Protestant fundamentalism and patriotism of such districts had a similar effect as the at times suffocating Catholic nationalism of the South:

> Sins were constantly brought to our attention at Gospel halls, open air
> meetings, Sunday School, the morning readings at elementary school
> and by the stream of religious tracts that were pushed through our
> doors, a conglomeration of saintly effort that resulted, in my case at
> any rate, not in peace, but in guilt. If sin was one of the certainties of
> our lives, another was our Britishness. We bickered and debated, but
> in general, agreed that Britain had the best government in the world,
> the best soldiers in the world and the best navy and the smartest kings
> and queens.[35]

The Ulster Farmers' Union continually made it clear that their members wanted parity of relief from rates with the farmers in Britain. In

1929 the Antrim branch of the union strongly protested against the extension of medical benefits to labourers. When they sent a delegation to John Andrews, Minister for Labour, he found them implacable, which surprised him, as he saw them as normally 'moderate'.[36] They insisted they had co-operated with the government in livestock, marketing, quality control and land purchase measures, but could not stomach the medical benefits and claimed that agricultural labourers were also opposed to them. The farmers wanted the retention of the dispensary system, rather than a panel system which suffered from lack of public control. They insisted that agricultural labourers would be put at a disadvantage in comparison to directly insured workers, and that agricultural labourers should be segregated from other industrial workers.

Andrews's response was strident, as he explained that Britain could not ratify the 1927 Geneva Convention on sickness insurance owing to the absence of medical benefits in Northern Ireland. He insisted this was an embarrassment to the North's government which it was 'imperative to remove', and said he was looking only for an extra one penny per week from the farmers employing labourers. He pointed out that 'approximately two thirds of the farms in Northern Ireland are of 30 acres or less and on very few farms of that size are any labourers employed'. He further claimed that the de-rating proposals would mean a saving of £500,000 to the farmers, while medical benefit for their workers would cost only £5,000 (the subsequent de-rating of agricultural land in 1929 relieved farmers of most of the rate cost but left local authorities dependent on central funding for over 80 per cent of their expenditure). Andrews criticised them for disingenuously underestimating the ill-health of their employees, arguing that 'the agricultural worker may be healthier in early life, but in later life owing to the incidence of diseases such as bronchitis, catarrh, rheumatism etc., a considerable amount of illness is experienced'. A certain penny-pinching conservatism, it seemed, was not confined to farmers of the South.[37] In urban areas in the early twentieth century, skilled wages may have been above national averages, but unskilled wages were below, which, with attendant low welfare spending, left it up to the new regime to inaugurate populist state spending. But in areas like Belfast, low state spending continued, exacerbating high unemployment and diseases such as TB.

'there will not probably be more than from 20–30 criminal lunatics'
At the beginning of 1922 there was discussion in the Department of Home
Affairs on criminal lunatics ('there will not probably be more than from
20–30 criminal lunatics from Northern Ireland at any one time') and the
question of industrial schools and reformatories. According to files in the
Public Records Office of Northern Ireland, Dawson Bates set up an inquiry
in October 1922, because the managers of such institutions had expressed
concern about the low level of funding and the consequent difficulty of
equipping the children 'physically and mentally for the battle of life'.[38]
Some were in favour of cutbacks in state aid to the schools, arguing that
destitute orphans in England were left to the workhouse or private charity,
but in the North were being sent to industrial schools. It was unfair, the
department maintained, for the state in the North to bear half of the cost
of the 'destitute orphans' in contrast to the situation in England. This was
just one early example of the concern with regional disparities when it
came to welfare. In the years 1903–22, out of a total of 1,085 committals,
142, or 13 per cent were listed as destitute orphans. What was particularly
revealing, as pointed out by D. A. Chart, was that the present institutions were 'on average accommodating not more than two fifths of the
total number for which they were certified' with the overhead charge per
inmate 'inordinately heavy'.[39] But it was clear that the same use of these
institutions was not being made in the North as in the South, and that as
early as 1922 there was a recognition that they were no 'proper substitute
for home', with a consequent need for 'closer supervision'. No such attention was evident in the Free State.

'unemployment insurance would be our greatest problem'
There seemed precious little that Dublin could do to help the Northern
Catholic minority, as the state of Northern Ireland was turned into the
illiberal entity its opponents had warned of. By 1921 Northern nationalists
were locked into a state which had what the satirical magazine *Dublin
Opinion*, in a reference to the abolition of proportional representation in
local elections (extended to general elections in 1929), termed a passion
for 'disproportional representation'.[40] Given the preponderance of the
stereotype of Ulster intransigence, making Dublin readers despise Ulster
was relatively easy, even though this overlooked the political skill which
was involved in managing the divisions within the Unionist Party
between populist and anti-populist factions.[41] But some commentators in

the South, notably in *An Phoblacht*, were also severely critical of Joe Devlin and the Ancient Order of Hibernians, suggesting they were as harmful to national advance as the Orange Order, though it is probably accurate to see the Order as past its sell-by date at this juncture.

While Collins had continued to support IRA activity in Northern Ireland for most of 1922, Eoin MacNeill, the government's representative on the Boundary Commission in February 1923, had mused on the general problem of North–South relations. He suggested there were three options: to regard the Belfast government as subordinate and open discussion through the Belfast government; to have direct relationships with the British government; or 'to drift on doing nothing and this promises no advantage'.[42] Cosgrave expressed a clear preference for 'direct relations with the Belfast government'. Kevin O'Higgins had informed the delegation of Northern nationalists who visited Dublin in 1922 that 'we have no other policy for the North East than we have for any other part of Ireland and that is the Treaty policy'. Significantly, this was asserted in direct response to an appeal from Northern nationalists for funding, but O'Higgins preferred to stress the importance of the need for 'strenuous voluntary work'. Three years later, Cosgrave once again rejected appeals for funds owing to 'heavy calls upon our resources'.[43]

This denial came in the same year the Boundary Commission Report was leaked, an event which was an acute embarrassment to Southern nationalists. It proved the accuracy of the *Morning Post*'s contention in March 1925 that 'it is the coming general election in Northern Ireland, and not the coming report of the Boundary Commission which will settle the frontier line between Northern Ireland and the Free State'.[44] Privately, Irish ministers had been asked to respond as to how the impending report of the commission would affect their departments. The Minister for Finance, Patrick McGilligan, not surprisingly, asserted that 'unemployment insurance would be our greatest problem', an early acknowledgement that in effect the South could not afford to incorporate the Northern state, given its own precarious financial state. The Chief of Staff of the Irish army had written of the need for firm action 'if the government of Northern Ireland decide to adopt an obstructive attitude' with regard to the Boundary Commission Report, though it was subsequently decided to cross this line out.[45]

'Cosgrave burst into tears'

It was the failure of the Boundary Commission to deliver for nationalists which blasted any optimism that may have existed about further 'national advancement'. In November 1925 the *Morning Post* newspaper revealed its recommendations, involving a relatively minuscule transfer of population from Fermanagh and Armagh into the South and just under 3,000 Catholics from the east Donegal region into the North. In other words, a transfer of territory designed merely to copper-fasten the existing border. Cosgrave's subsequent hurried visit to British prime minister Stanley Baldwin was a diplomatic embarrassment, as all Cosgrave could do was complain like a child to Baldwin about what the devious Lloyd George had promised, or given the impression of promising. The most senior Northern civil servant, Wilfred Spender, was later to record that 'Cosgrave burst into tears' at the debacle.[46]

Believing that a large transfer of territory was achievable was tantamount to residence in a fool's paradise as far as both the British and Northern Irish governments were concerned. The issue was ultimately 'solved' in December 1925 by the three governments agreeing to the existing border with the granting to Northern Ireland of jurisdiction over services which under the Treaty had been due to be transferred from Westminster to a Council of Ireland. This damage limitation agreement included some financial concessions concerning Ireland's commitment to the UK public debt, and non-publication of the report. Kevin O'Higgins was subsequently to make the sad admission that the accusation that the Irish government had effectively sold Northern nationalists was 'no more than a half truth'.[47] Cosgrave informed the Dáil that the only security for minorities now lay in the good will of the people amongst whom they lived. Cahir Healy, a Northern nationalist MP, insisted that partition had now been accepted as permanent.[48]

The Boundary Commission episode revealed the practical limits of the Free State's room for manoeuvre, while Craig had ensured through the British-appointed Northern Ireland representative on the Commission, J. R. Fisher, that no serious alteration would take place in the border. Many of the ideas of members of the North-Eastern Boundary Bureau, established by the government in the South to make the Free State case, though showing a familiarity with the idea of plebiscites on Versailles models and the difficulties of minority and majority rights, were rendered useless. Though this was an unwinnable case for the South, they took it seriously, and in the words of Margaret O'Callaghan: 'its outcome to them was not a foregone conclusion'. There were, after all, 56 boxes of files of the North-Eastern Boundary Bureau, revealing that the members weren't, in O'Callaghan's phrase, 'anti-intellectual possessors'.[49]

'you in Ulster are far too sensitive'

In a sense the London Agreement of December 1925, in recognising partition, brought to a formal end the revolutionary struggle, by removing any constitutional framework for Irish unity, despite Eoin MacNeill's statement that 'it was nothing less than an outrage on Ireland, and I may say on civilisation, to be asked to draw a line across this country dividing it on the basis of religious difference'.[50] As the Irish government's representative on the commission, he resigned, though Cosgrave and O'Higgins had been more than willing to do a deal, in order to minimise damage, as was James Craig out of self-interest.

Following this embarrassment, there was to be virtually no contact between Cumman na nGaedheal governments and Northern Ireland, despite an abortive attempt to arrange a personal meeting between Craig and Cosgrave in 1926, Craig being under domestic pressure owing to the release of IRA prisoners. Ronan Fanning makes the point that areas like Derry and Newry, with Catholic majorities, were essential economic urban hinterlands for Northern Ireland, meaning that two of the Boundary Commission's terms of reference had always been mutually contradictory: 'in accordance with the wishes of the inhabitants' and 'in so far as may be compatible with economic and geographic conditions'.[51] The report, not published until 1969, stated clearly that 'The commission is not to reconstitute the two territories but to settle the boundaries between them.' Perhaps this is why, afterwards, Craig was apt to use more promising rhetoric about co-operation for economic prosperity.[52] But sensitivity about the question of the border was never far from the surface. F. E. Smith, Secretary of State for India in 1924, the same individual who had been one of the signatories of the 1921 Treaty and a prominent leader of the resistance to Home Rule in 1912–14, suggested to Lord Londonderry that as Ireland was one island, the two states would be better economically joined, even though this could not happen without the consent of Ulster. He didn't like Londonderry's reply, which he considered pompous and defensive. In a further letter to Londonderry, he wrote: 'The real truth is that you in Ulster are far too sensitive. Even you, who are so largely in touch with Imperial affairs and with English political society, the moment you go back to Belfast become parochialised.'[53]

'neither a wild-eyed revolutionary nor a lank-haired poet'

The growing interest in social history makes it tempting to pounce on a number of quotable utterances by key members of the first Free State government as stark examples of a deliberate and regressive conservatism. Kevin O'Higgins, Free State Minister for Home Affairs (later Justice), famously remarked of himself and his colleagues that 'we were probably the most conservative revolutionaries that ever put across a successful revolution'. The statement was made in the context of justifying heavy-handed tactics in attempting to restore order in Ireland during the Civil War period.[54] But, in a sense, it was a proud boast as well as a plea for understanding.

The shadow of civil war and the poverty of the new state ensured there was little appetite for radical social and cultural change. Politically, a reliance on the structure and indeed the priorities of Westminster government, and a tough approach to law and order, seemed inevitable. Many of the social ideas of the revolutionary period were to become, again in the words of Kevin O'Higgins, 'largely poetry'. But it would be inaccurate to suggest that the republican side in the Civil War, despite the nostalgia of former republicans and their tendency to be more prolific writers, were particularly socially radical. Despite the fact that the new state was one of the few creditor nations in the world in 1923, the Civil War had brought grave warnings of state bankruptcy. This not only led to a preoccupation with the need to balance the books, but also seemed to cement attitudes to the 'undeserving poor'.

While it is true that Cumann na nGaedheal never achieved any degree of populist or emotional appeal (a friend of O'Higgins once remarked that if he woke up one morning and discovered he was popular he would examine his conscience[55]), they were helped in the running of government by the lack of opposition from the defeated and rudderless republican movement. Also helpful was the fact that when it came to the exercise of religion – the high culture of the poor – their credentials and practices were impeccable, to the extent that William Cosgrave, President of the Executive Council (prime minister), had an oratory in his own house and was accorded a number of papal honours. But aside from his religious devotion, his supporters argued that he had a practicality that was needed. The *Irish Times* made this assessment:

> He is neither a wild-eyed revolutionary nor a lank-haired poet. He dresses generally in sombre hues, wears a bowler hat and looks rather like the general manager of a railway company ... unlike so many of the new school of Irish politician he does not believe in talking and has an excellent capacity for work ... he has no violently extremist past to live down and with him the problem of saving face does not arise.[56]

'*felt no urgency about door-to-door canvassing*'

Nearly fifty years after the birth of the new Free State, one of its key ministers, Ernest Blythe, insisted that the government's greatest achievement was 'to bring the country round to the position where the government could be changed without bloodshed'.[57] More than 30 years later, the political descendants of Cumann na nGaedheal, along with sympathetic historians, were asserting the same thing. They claimed the party had used the Treaty to ensure that 'almost nothing' remained of British rule by 1932; that they established an efficient central administration and passed a large body of native legislation, not to mention overseeing the physical reconstruction of the country after the war, having to pay for almost everything out of current revenue. In terms of a return to law and order, success, it was suggested, could be measured by the fact that the army accepted the democratic result of 1932 (when the republicans won the election) to loyally serve 'the new government comprised of people they had defeated in arms a mere nine years earlier'.[58]

The historian Mary Daly has suggested Cumann na nGaedheal was 'atypical' because it was first a government and only subsequently became a party 'in the most difficult circumstances possible'. She maintains that ensuring a functioning democracy in Ireland was all the more remarkable given the fate of the new states after the First World War such as Latvia, Estonia and Czechoslovakia, which failed to survive intact or became dictatorships, while many of the longer-established states came under Fascist control.[59] The degree to which Cumann na nGaedheal was a government first and party second was recognised by a contemporary activist in the 1920s, who suggested that 'government ministers felt no urgency about door-to-door canvassing, or speaking on cold and wet platforms at church gates, or appealing for funds'.[60] Joe Lee reflected on the fact that while the governments of the 1920s were instinctively conservative, and while they could not be classed as failures in comparison with their international contemporaries, they did fail 'in the context of historical expectations'.[61] This was an inevitable failure given the exaggerated rhetoric of expectation and propaganda that all politicians of this era grew up with. Equally understandable was the authoritarian streak that lurked within their political personalities, given that they were entrusted with the task of state building 'before they had a chance to mellow or learn the art of political manoeuvre'.[62]

These assessments are accurate, given the extraordinary circumstances of 1922–3 in which Cumann na nGaedheal took office. Their precarious existence ensured there was a determination during and after the Civil War to assert that there was no distinction between ordinary crime and political crime. In private, in an example of how bizarre some of the circumstances of the government of this time were, in September 1922 the Executive Council agreed that 'the British government would be requested to make the island of St Helena available for the internment of captured republicans'. This would be what an Irish official described as 'an orderly and comparatively contented residence', housed by a British contractor and guarded by British troops.[63] However, the cost of the garrison was prohibitive, ensuring that imprisoned republicans did not become latter-day Napoleons.

'Faces without flesh or colour, only eyes'

There were exceptions to the Free State consensus and the nostalgia or inactivity of the republicans. One example was the social radical, writer and communist activist Peadar O'Donnell, who throughout his varied and full life was to achieve more success in literature than politics as he put pen to paper to depict the struggle for survival in marginal rural constituencies. Perhaps O'Donnell's own personal dilemma – achieving success decrying the harshness of 1920s Ireland, but only in fiction – was a symbol of the degree to which this decade was to prove that the Irish revolution was more political than social. In writing about what was happening around him, O'Donnell was observing the congested districts along the western seaboard that suffered so badly from the bad harvests of the early 1920s, with some of them reaching near-famine conditions by the middle of the decade.

In 1929, O'Donnell published *Adrigoole,* a novel set in Donegal, but based on an actual tragedy in West Cork, in which a mother had starved to death, surrounded by her starving husband and children. It was an event that shocked many, not only being a stark reminder of poverty in isolated communities, but also because of the failure of neighbours to intervene because of a dispute over land boundaries. It seemed to prove that many of the social and class tensions which the land gave rise to were still raw and divisive, despite the fact that the last piece of the land purchase jigsaw had been put in place by the native government in 1923. Enclosed in a mountainous corner of Munster, the family were fictionalised as Hughie Dalach and Brigíd Gallagher, and the overriding theme was one of helplessness and despair. The following passage deals with the eventual gruesome discovery of the family, as powerful a depiction as any of the challenges facing the Free State:

> He pushed the door open softly and entered the kitchen on tiptoe ... he took a cautious step forward and a stream of light attracted his gaze. Where it crossed the hearth a bulk showed black and wan. Against the bulk something white. A face. Brigíd's face ... he jerked the body upright and something banged on the hearth flag and rolled into the starlight. The child ... in the bed something stirred. Nancy was sitting up. They lifted her out. Donal grumbled; Eoin cried weakly. Faces without flesh or colour, only eyes.[64]

Such harrowing accounts were found not only in the realm of fiction. Numerous accounts in state files exist detailing poverty and desperation. Some took the form of pleas from the poor, the forgotten and the marginalised, highlighting the extent to which a central government intent on asserting authority to facilitate survival of the state became more and more removed from the communities it governed. This was particularly true of areas which, ironically, were supposed to contain all that was best about Ireland. This suggests that the assertion of the author Lynn Doyle, in 1935, that 'Ireland was the best place in the world in which to be destitute' was highly fatuous.[65] In March 1922, a deputation from Tory Island, off the coast of County Donegal, informed the government:

> There is a population of 350, of whom two thirds are said to be desti-
> tute. A school roll of 45 of whom 30 attend regularly. Father Carr says
> he has not the heart to force the balance to school knowing that they

would have to go there hungry. At the same time some of the 30 go hungry to school. The deputation ask for help for the 30 families until the herring fishing begins which will be about the middle of May. The Rural District Council of the mainland, under whose sway they are supposed to be, will do nothing for them as they pay no taxes – in which they are no doubt right as they never got any benefits such as police, JPs, poorhouse officials, contracts, etc. ...[66]

'to play football and study Irish behind barbed wire'

There was an inevitability about post-Civil War pessimism, particularly given the number of republicans in prison by the end of the conflict, and that the government's hands were still red with the blood of official executions. It was one thing for George Russell to assert that the republicans had squandered a spirit created by poets, scholars and patriots of a different order, but it was also the case that more Irishmen were executed under Cosgrave's government in 1922 and 1923 than under Asquith's and Lloyd George's governments between 1916 and 1921. Russell remarked that he found 'few people in Ireland deeply concerned about the ethics of civil war or revolution'.[67] By February 1923 there were in the region of 13,000 republican prisoners and internees, reduced to about 9,000 by October 1923. In November, 559 of the remaining prisoners went on hunger strike. By the end of December, only 1,866 remained incarcerated.

The mental distress of de Valera following the Civil War and the death of Collins was but one example of the despondency that can also be gleaned from many of the memoirs of those who fought on the losing side. The continuance of bank robberies, kidnapping and attacks on police barracks gave the government the excuse to keep them imprisoned on national security grounds. In truth, it was a welcome respite for some, a theme common in the writing of authors like Frank O'Connor and C. S. Andrews. Years on the run had taken their toll on what were still very young men; it was almost a relief, in the words of O'Connor, 'to be left to play football and study Irish behind barbed wire'.[68] The failed hunger strikes were also indicative of the disorientation, divisions and confusion in republican thinking, particularly when the government demanded a signed declaration that they would accept the Free State's legitimacy as the price of release. O'Connor's description of the ending of the hunger strikes reveals the sadness and despair of utter defeat:

But the strike dragged on for days before the masterminds of the revolution saw that their own organisation was bleeding to death under their eyes and issued a hasty general dispensation. Immediately the whole camp became hysterical. Even the sentries dropped their rifles and dragged buckets of soup to the barbed wire and the prisoners tore their hands as they thrust mugs through it, pushing and shouldering one another out of the way. Some got sick but came back for more. A tall, spectacled man who had not been invited to join the strike came up to me with an oily smile. 'Well, professor,' he said gleefully, 'the pigs feed', and I turned away in disgust because that was exactly what the scene resembled and I knew it was the end of our magical improvisation. Buckley, Walsh and myself looked on as though it were the funeral of someone we loved.[69]

C. S. Andrews, nearing the end of his own imprisonment, had long since changed his mind on the virtues of a potential republican military dictatorship, ceasing to believe that the IRA leadership would have had the capacity to give the country a stable administration. Seán O'Faoláin, in assessing his options for emigrating or teaching in some remote secondary school, knew 'that I had been given an exceptional vision of the potential wholeness and integrity of human nature in a moment of intense awareness forced on us all; that I had thereby been blinded to the virtues of ordinary, average, common life as it is outside such rare hours'.[70] Some republican women were regarded as the most die-hard; indeed, the virulence of their opposition had led Cosgrave to suggest that it 'was not possible to consider these women as females' as they had caused 'the mainstay of the trouble' and saw all acts of grace as a weakness.[71] Even as late as 1927, the *Irish Statesman* was referring to the 'wild women', their dislike of politics stemming from the fact that they were 'so much more extreme than any of our male intransigents in the preaching of militarism and violence'.[72]

'ever again take their stride from a soldier's boot'

Internally, Cumann na nGaedheal was not without its tensions, and unity of purpose was achieved only after the triumph within the party of a conservative and consolidationist wing, over those who saw themselves as taking a more radical approach to the implementation of the Treaty. Political defeat and the resignation of Richard Mulcahy, Minister for Defence, and Joseph McGrath, Minister for Industry and Commerce, tilted the balance towards O'Higgins and Cosgrave, following the suppression of an army mutiny in 1924. The mutineers were resentful about the lack of government initiative in delivering on Michael Collins's promise that the Treaty would be used to gain further independence, though many of their concerns were more personal and reflected jealousies about promotion prospects. McGrath was their sole ministerial ally. They styled themselves the Irish Republican Army Organisation, and had particular grievances about the promotion of people within the army who had no War of Independence service, as well as the downsizing of the army. At the end of the Civil War there were 50,000 members of the army. Between 1924 and 1927 army strength was reduced from 32,000 to about 12,000 and it was to fall further to about 6,000 by 1932.[73]

The army mutiny, in undermining the stability of the state, also seemed to highlight a naivety on the part of the radical Treatyites. It ensured that the issue of government legitimacy and a loyal army would lie at the core of the government's philosophy at the expense of anything more ambitious. Put another way, the actions of the mutineers meant that the conservatives, still using the rhetoric of Civil War threats, could clear the decks relatively quickly. O'Higgins maintained that it was merely a repetition of the Four Courts episode (in April 1922, republican opponents of the Treaty had occupied the courts). He was determined that 'neither he nor the institutions of the state would ever again take their stride from a soldier's boot'.[74] The mutineers were faced down with relative ease, and the 'republican' sympathisers within the regime were left on the margins.

John Regan makes the important point that, in the context of the mutiny, the radical Treaty supporters confused 'national aspirations with a direct attack on state institutions – still thinking in a mode of revolutionary politics which the Civil War had negated'.[75] The *Irish Times* summed up the reasons why the consolidationists acted the way they did in suppressing the mutineers: 'Thus we are confronted with an undefined amount of political revolt in the army, with some measure of dissension in the government and possibly with a prospect of similar dissension in the ranks of the government's political supporters.'[76]

'to discover a way to the people's confidence and having found it, to keep it'
Cumann na nGaedheal were in an unusual electoral position, not needing and not receiving a majority of the popular vote to govern, because of the refusal of republicans to take their seats in the Dáil. At no election did

CnG secure even two fifths of valid first-preference votes. Even within the Treatyite party there were competing interpretations of the Treaty settlement – one more nationalist, the other more consolidationist – which, particularly after the death of Collins, who could reach out to both sides, were bound to collide. Supporters of the Treaty could justly argue that, unlike republicans, they could not afford to dwell on the past, but had to be preoccupied with contemporary concerns, an urgency that ensured they depicted republican opposition as criminal rather than ideological.

This was the beginning of a very important assertion by CnG which amounted to a declaration of moral monopoly. This became even more pronounced after the departure of McGrath and Mulcahy and the triumph in government of Kevin O'Higgins. Indeed, the phrase 'enemy of the state' was to be applied to simply too much in Ireland during the 1920s. The extent to which the conservative 'strong man' of the government could triumph can be garnered by the fact that by 1927, when O'Higgins was murdered by republicans on his way to mass in a Dublin suburb, he was not only Vice President of the Executive Council and Minister for Justice but also Minister for External Relations. Along with Cosgrave, he had ensured that the motto of CnG going in to every election was 'safety first'. After the assassination of O'Higgins, Cosgrave stated specifically in the Dáil that the prestige and credibility of the country depended more on its administration of justice than on anything else. This was understandable given that the electoral threat from anti-Treaty Sinn Féin was strong; in the aftermath of total military defeat, its performance was quite remarkable, achieving 27.4 per cent of the vote in 1923 as against CnG's 38.9 per cent. Cosgrave remarked:

> If it be true that the prestige and credibility of a country depend more upon its administration of justice than upon any other single test, then what does the country owe to the Minister for Justice, with its courts enjoying the confidence of all its citizens, its unarmed Gardaí respected throughout the land, the whole administration of law functioning without reproach?[77]

But the triumph of the conservative wing also bred an arrogance, and a belief that coalition government was to be avoided at all costs, along with suggestions that the Irish electoral system was ill-served by proportional representation. But there was a positive and honest side also; Cosgrave had an admirable tendency to distinguish between willingness to promise and capacity to deliver. He insisted in the Dáil that he had no intention of being the super policeman of law and order while the country performed disastrously in other areas; but it was precisely because CnG were seen as the party of law and order that made it difficult to connect with voters when a degree of stability had returned. It was highly revealing that by 1932 the private notes for CnG canvassers contained two sections, the first being the record of their administration, and the second, 'points against Fianna Fáil'.[78] The absence of a third section outlining their programme for government seemed to suggest that they wanted to prevent Fianna Fáil from gaining office more than they wanted office themselves, and that a self-preservation mentality was lacking. Years later, after his retirement, Cosgrave was to admit as much when he wrote to a confidante:

> But we must be candid – in the sphere that we considered the least important but which was the most important we failed – viz: to retain popular support. It should not and I believe it is not beyond the capacity of able men to discover a way to the people's confidence and having found it, to keep it.[79]

'silver-buckled shoes, silk stockings, velvet knee breeches'

It also seemed that Cosgrave and his companions enjoyed the trappings of office and prized the new-found friendship with Britain, to the chagrin of many republicans. Austin Clarke, one of Ireland's greatest poets, wrote: 'They are the spit of virtue now/ Prating of law and honour/ But we remember how they shot Rory O'Connor' (one of the Civil War republicans executed by the state).[80] C. S. Andrews wrote satirically about newspaper photographs of the government standing in line dressed in striped trousers, lavender waistcoats and silk hats, indistinguishable from the chorus line of a musical which was showing in London at that time. A feeling that Cumann na nGaedheal were far too quick to ape the manners and indeed fashion of their former conquerors continued to anger republicans. Andrews commented acidly on Cosgrave's trip to Buckingham Palace, and thought that 'his silver-buckled shoes, silk stockings, velvet knee breeches, lace shirt and velvet shirt looked painfully ridiculous'.[81]

But this sartorial manifestation of continuity was also reflected in much else that changed little. Indeed, a favourite sneer of republicans was that nothing had changed in the 1920s except the painting of post-boxes green and evidence of bilingualism in public signs and notices. There was a transfer of 21,000 serving officials to the new state's civil service, and in the sphere of administration the government had no intention of creating novel structures. The chaos of the administration of law, rectified by 1924, was marked in its settling-down phase by barristers who had acted as republican justices during the War of Independence and had been loyal to the Treaty side. The police force, particularly its detective branch, remained, in the words of David Fitzpatrick, 'all too obviously the tools of political parties'.[82] The first recruit to the Gardaí was officially attested in February 1922, and most of the initial recruits came from the ranks of the pro-Treaty IRA, with ex-Royal Irish Constabulary and ex-Irish Republican Police represented as well, causing certain tensions on account of former RIC men being promoted to higher ranks. An initial mutiny on these grounds failed, and a subsequent commission of inquiry 'mapped out a role for the new force which was at variance with that of its predecessor, the RIC. The Civic Guard was to be the servant of the people, not militaristic or coercive. The Commission envisaged a greatly enhanced civilian role for the new police force'; this meant disarming was essential.[83]

This was one of the reasons for the Garda Commissioner Eoin O'Duffy's emphasis on sobriety and clean living (which his own private life was later to make a mockery of); he emphasised that the force was on trial and moral probity essential. As well as bringing a party of 250 guards to visit the Pope in 1928, O'Duffy thundered against alcohol abuse:

> A police officer who has developed a taste for spirituous liquors is always a corrupt official ... the stolen visits to the public houses are noted with an even greater care than the open violation ... the disease is infectious. Evil communications corrupt good manners, and the drunkard, a scourge in every walk of life, is particularly obnoxious in the uniform of a public servant ... no man of any rank who is addicted to drink will be permitted to remain a member of the Civic Guard. This is a penalty which will be rigidly enforced.[84]

In July 1923 the name of the force was changed to An Garda Síochána ('Guardians of the Peace'), and between 1922 and 1952 10,135 men joined, with the sons of farmers strongly favoured over their urban counterparts, and recruits from the western counties preferred to those from the east. It had been important to O'Duffy that 'the son of the peasant is the backbone of the force'. During this era, 50 per cent of the police were former farmers or landworkers, and over 98 per cent Catholic, and while during peaceful times they often had little to do, the shooting dead of a member in January 1924 during a bank raid in Wicklow was a measure of the condition of danger under which they sometimes worked.[85]

'unenthusiastic democrats'?

Cumann na nGaedheal's commitment to strong state centralisation was an inevitable reaction to the Civil War, and presaged an approach to the distribution of power in Ireland which was to become the hallmark of successive administrations. Ernest Blythe, Minister for Local Government, contemptuously dismissed threats from republican local bodies not to function until republican prisoners had been released, suggesting that no important public interests would suffer as a result of their refusal to function. The Civil War undoubtedly contributed to a feeling that strong national leadership was needed at the expense of local autonomy, despite the misty contention of Constance Markievicz that the Irish had a sort of 'feeling for decentralisation'.[86] The consequences of overly centralised government were negative. According to Tom Garvin, 'these unenthusiastic democrats were qualified in their attachment to democratic ideas and were not prepared to trust the people with the powers to run local affairs'.[87]

But there was also a commendable determination to initiate a process of reform in the administration of local government, predicated on the idea of 'cleaning up' a system that was being patently abused. In relation to local government, the 1920s displayed an obsessive concern with administration and personnel rather than with expanding the breadth of services provided. Some notable attempts were made to deal with housing and educational needs, but centralisation took precedence over all other concerns and the move towards management of local government was the most logical step in this direction. Academic support was provided for the government by key scholars, particularly in the pro-government University College Dublin. Political scientists like Michael Cronin (along with James Hogan in University College Cork) criticised from an early stage the fact that local authorities could not be put out of office within an appointed period. Cronin also pointed to extravagance and inefficiency and a huge burden of taxation in the form of rates with very little to show for it: 'The trouble in Ireland', wrote Cronin, 'is that the people are not only apathetic but hardly conscious of anything wrong, otherwise the streets of a city like Cork could not, as at present, be left to a condition of dirt which would disgrace a native village in Central Africa.'[88]

For the more cynical, suspending local councils, including Dublin Corporation, was a way of backing social counter-revolution. But a commitment to introducing fairness into the system of local-government appointments was reflected in the operation of the Local Appointments Commission, while the creation of the Civil Service Commission to preside over the public appointments process demonstrated a determination to ensure ethical standards prevailed. Joe Lee suggested this was 'perhaps the major achievement of the early years and it remains one of the most remarkable achievements in the history of the state'.[89]

'failed lamentably in its duty towards the common people'?

There was little solace for the opponents of such a centralised and essentially conservative state apparatus. A small Irish Communist Party had been formed during the War of Independence by, amongst others, Roddy Connolly, son of James. The Labour Party had demonstrated that it had the capacity to make inroads into the support of Sinn Féin in the aftermath of the Treaty, but it struggled to repeat its success of 1922. George Russell had wondered 'why should not the proletarians in Ireland, suffering from more than middle-class nationalism has ever suffered under British rule, also use physical force to upset a social order which has never brought them physical plenty or intellectual life?'[90] The answer to this was not only weak leadership, but the fact that the state was willing to crush strikes using police and army. That successive governments made so much of opposition to the nascent republican Fianna Fáil movement, established in 1926, was a testament not only to the fear of the republican flair for organisation, but also to the failure of the Labour Party to create a viable and effective left-wing opposition. Progress was also hindered by the open conflict between trade unionists Jim Larkin and William O'Brien over control of the Irish Transport and General Workers' Union.

Labour Party contributions to the Dáil revealed a determination to oppose erosion of individual social, economic and political rights, but the reality was that there was virtually no doctrinaire socialist trend in the party's attitude to legislation, except perhaps on the part of its leader Tom Johnson. If anything, it seemed their time in the Dáil institutionalised their growing conservatism, losing them any potential radical support which could be mopped up by the abstentionist republicans. This was at a time when, as Tom Johnson was to articulate in the Dáil, the government 'has failed lamentably in its duty towards the common people ... and has failed to provide opportunities for willing workers to engage in the creation of wealth by useful, productive labour ... it has denied that it has any responsibility in this regard'.[91]

A more critical analysis would suggest that caution and aspiration to office prevented the Labour Party from effectively championing the poor against cutbacks and political repression. There is much truth in the assertion that in the late 1920s Fianna Fáil was able to mobilise a lower-class electorate which could have been galvanised by a more radical Labour Party (though some political scientists claim that this is a statistical illusion[92]). But severe economic distress, coupled with the deployment of the army and Gardaí, affected the outcome of a wave of strikes against organised wage cuts in 1923, particularly on the part of rural labourers. Trade union membership collapsed dramatically in the 1920s: the ITGWU, which had 100,000 members in 1921, had a membership of 15,453 in 1929. This was not just due to economic depression but also to the split in the ITGWU, a fall-out from the row between Larkin and William O'Brien. This led to the formation of the Workers' Union of Ireland in 1924, when the majority of the Dublin membership (16,000 workers) followed Larkin out of the union he had established.

Larkin led 'Irish Workers' League' candidates against the Labour Party, bringing about the defeat of Tom Johnson in the second general election of 1927. Larkin's most recent biographer, Emmet O'Connor, suggests one of his major weaknesses was 'his inability to distinguish between 1913 and 1923', and that his splitting of the trade union movement was entirely of his own making owing to his 'unbalanced personality'. His 'egomania' meant he could not accept the contemporary trade union/ Labour Party alliance, created when he had left the country, and cemented by Tom Johnson and William O'Brien, 'simply because he could not claim credit for it'.[93] Instead, he maintained that the achievements of the pre-1914 ITGWU had been forgotten, overlooking the fact that he split the unions at the worst time possible, given that employers were demanding wage cuts. In fairness to Larkin, he had correctly identified one of the weaknesses of the contemporary labour movement: 'its stolid refusal to exploit the current political instability to force the government to restrain the employers'.[94]

Historians have expressed little surprise that the Labour Party was utterly devoid of radicalism, as it quickly adapted to the clientelism of Irish politics, with leaders with an Anglocentric bent who could not, or would not, match the nationalistic socio-economic programme of the new Fianna Fáil, who achieved 26 per cent of the first-preference votes in the 1927 election, soon to rise to 35 per cent. On becoming the only communist elected to an Irish parliament in the twentieth century, Larkin concentrated his ire on Labour, in order to discredit the ITGWU, and further his aim of getting the British unions out of Ireland. Larkin remained a quarrelsome, polarising but strangely mesmerising figure, and had agreed in 1924 with British and Soviet communists to undertake the leadership of communism in Ireland, a triangular relationship which failed miserably. His refusal to form a communist party (and his determination to ensure no one else did) meant that British communists would have to work independently of him (indeed the British communists played an important role in Irish communist affairs during the 1920s).[95]

In reality it was an enormous ego that left Larkin averse to accountability, though he was right to be suspicious of a British communist party who were more interested in his value as a figurehead. Communism, which had not yet attracted the depths of opprobrium it was to gain, lacked strong leadership in Ireland in the 1920s. By the time its followers became more organisationally competent, the climate had changed. By 1927, Moscow seemed to place more value on displacing Larkin and courting the IRA and inviting Irish students to study in Russia. Between 1927 and 1935, 20 Irish students enrolled in the Comintern's International Lenin School. Following the collapse of the Soviet Union, the archives dealing with the school were opened, and revealed that the Irish students were a politically self-confident group, having cut their political teeth in the Irish revolution. But they complained of an abundance of theory, finding it difficult to relate to conditions in Ireland. One unfortunate student, Pat Breslin, never returned, dying in a labour camp.[96]

'It is to the wayside crosses that you are loyal'

But it was the formation of Fianna Fáil in the La Scala Theatre in Dublin in 1926 (the same year in which the IRA's membership had declined to only 5,042) that was to transform Irish politics. Led by Eamon de Valera, the party's inauguration followed divisions within anti-Treaty Sinn Féin (of the 1,500 branches of the party before the Treaty, only 16 attended a public meeting to re-establish the party in June 1923) about the future direction of Irish republican politics.[97] The assassination of Kevin O'Higgins the following year prompted the government to introduce legislation stipulating that electoral candidates had to promise to take the oath of allegiance and their seats to be legitimate, leading to a volte-face on the part of Fianna Fáil. They took their seats in the Dáil as the main opposition party in August 1927.

Membership of Fianna Fáil grew from 460 *cumainn* (branches) in November 1926 to over 1,000 by the summer of 1927, paralleling Sinn Féin at its peak a decade previously.[98] De Valera and many others had made a choice between revering a tradition which excluded them from contemporary political participation, and accepting Michael Collins's original argument about the Treaty. That de Valera was prepared to do the latter, but had not been four years earlier, was the source of much personal and political opposition in the coming years. But in completing such soul-searching, republicanism was leaving itself open to the dangers of factionalism. Peadar O'Donnell, for example, fought many battles with other republicans in the 1920s and 1930s. In an argument with Mary MacSwiney in 1927 (the woman who during the hunger strikes Cosgrave had suggested acidly wanted to be 'Queen of Ireland'), he had criticised her version of republicanism as being too idealistic and too spiritual. He also applied these criticisms to both the IRA and Fianna Fáil in the 1930s, particularly to their infatuation with the memory of the dead, and to their vision of the future to the neglect of the social problems of the present. As he put it in the *Bothy Fire and All That*: 'It is to the wayside crosses you are loyal, to the whole tradition of struggle.'[99]

'our real selves; how could we find them?'

Other contemporary republicans were aware of how much myth played a part in the maintenance of the republican culture. Ernie O'Malley, one of the most heroic and driven during the revolution, reflected on how this also posed difficulties in terms of personal identity: 'I could not recognise myself from the legend. That was a difficulty. The confusion between the legendary and the real self. Time jumped a gap with us. People saw us as a myth, which bore little resemblance to ourselves; and our real selves; how could we find them?'[100] For the republican pragmatists, long-term satisfaction could not be derived from hurling abuse at the Free State's supporters on the eve of Poppy Day at College Green in Dublin (in the company of the League against Imperialism), where 5,000 attended in 1930 to hear de Valera speak. It was obvious to pragmatists like de Valera that political careers, particularly given the TDs' inability to represent constituents' concerns practically if they abstained from the Dáil, could not be built on such protest. Or as Seán O' Faoláin put it: 'I used to cackle madly at the role, which Dante assigns to all such prime-souled idealists as myself in the Inferno. He classifies them as the opportunists, racing endlessly through the mists of hell after a wavering flag which they can never overtake.'[101]

'to have a soul and be propagandist'

Addressing themselves to concrete economic grievances was to become a more realistic option than Sinn Féin's insistence that utopia would follow after the establishment of a republic. In the late 1920s, Fianna Fáil carved out an economic philosophy that involved idealising the small property owner and 'national capitalists' alienated from Cumann na nGaedheal by its opposition to economic protectionism.[102] But there was also the question of the new party's connection with the IRA, who were more than a mere collection of gunmen. The pages of *An Phoblacht*, the IRA's newspaper, give much insight into the diversity of thought within the IRA in the 1920s. Though it retained its penchant for seditious language, the Director of Public Prosecutions cautioned against taking legal action against *An Phoblacht* for language that was commonly used in the Dáil.[103] The rhetoric of class warfare was strong in *An Phoblacht* in the 1920s amidst calls for social revolution. It was argued, for example, that the government was driving people out to make way for bullocks, and suggested there was not a thought shown for people crawling in rags through city slums. The paper also took egalitarian stands in relation to women in Irish life, particularly with regard to industrial conditions. It frequently looked at developments in the Middle East, China and India, and gave a fair degree of idealistic coverage to events in Russia. And yet there were limits to its radicalism; the writings of Seán O'Casey and Liam O'Flaherty were strongly criticised, and referred to as 'sewage' in 1928.[104] The paper preferred instead to idealise all aspects of Gaelic Ireland before the conquest and venerated the Gaeltacht.

Some in the republican movement, it seemed, saw themselves as embodying the broad inclusive nationalism of 1798, while others championed a more ethnocentric Catholic outlook. Yet another group adopted a more Marxist anti-imperialist perspective, suggesting a rather uneven interplay of nationalism, Catholicism, socialism and militarism.[105] The success of Fianna Fáil was to lie in dropping the latter two, but gradually, hoping initially to gain support from the IRA. In the context of republican propaganda, the pro-de Valera weekly the *Nation*, which began in 1925 and ran until 1931, was unable to compete effectively with the daily newspapers, most notably the pro-government *Irish Independent*. This led to the foundation of the *Irish Press* in 1931. Heralded by de Valera as 'a people's paper pledged to honesty and truth without bias', it was to become something of an institution and lasted until 1995. Its first edition contained a message to the nation by Douglas Hyde, urging people to speak Irish; an agricultural column entitled 'The Lure of the Grass', emphasising Fianna Fáil's preference for tillage instead of grazing; and an attack on the government over its failure to provide jobs. One letter-writer, wishing the paper well, suggested: 'it was better for a newspaper to have a soul and be propagandist than to have no soul and still be propagandist'.[106]

But some contributors to *An Phoblacht* were anxious to reassure that they were not communists. Fianna Fáil was determined to keep the door open to the IRA in order to maximise electoral support, without giving damaging hostages to fortune. Cumann na nGaedheal's insistence in 1927 that 'Fianna Fáil has got the arms dumps' didn't seem to perturb the Irish electorate unduly, as de Valera and his key colleagues managed to repeat the organisational triumph of pre-Treaty Sinn Féin.

'Is the policy simply to be that this country is to go on as a grass ranch ...?'
Cumann na nGaedheal's relentless insistence on depicting de Valera as being in the shadow of the gunmen, while offering little of their own vision, can, in retrospect, be seen to have been counterproductive. But the sense of fear and resentment, sometimes panic, caused by republicans should not be underestimated. Fianna Fáil, after all, emerged a mere three years after the end of the Civil War. CnG's assertion of the potential for anarchy was the logical culmination of their insistence on a moral monopoly. But after a decade of independence, the 'safety first' slogan was tiresome to some, both within and outside the party. J. J. Walsh, soon to resign as party chairman owing to what he regarded as the pro-imperialist perspective of his colleagues,[107] insisted that people had grown tired of abusive political rhetoric, and that the real problems facing the country were economic decline and emigration. Writing to Cosgrave, he suggested:

another five years of this galloping decline in a country teeming with natural riches must leave us incapable of revival for generations. In my humble opinion, oaths, loans and what Mr so and so said in such a year are merely a cruel kind of joke beside this terrible tragedy, the curing of which in a brief period of time is in the hands of a resolute government.[108]

There was an abundance of economic discontent for Fianna Fáil to exploit in the late 1920s and early 1930s, which was a fact recognised within the ranks of government. The brand of relative economic radicalism proposed by Fianna Fáil promised more welfare measures, which the laissez-faire dogmatism of Cumann na nGaedheal prevented, and offered hope to both industrial employers and workers through protected industrial expansion. Cherishing the smallholder was not only a method of rallying the 'have nots' of Irish society while big business called for the abolition of income tax. It was also useful in creating an emotive, nationalist economic rhetoric which, in continuing the (largely unsophisticated) tradition of believing the British connection was the cause of most of Ireland's economic woes, allowed Fianna Fáil to pillory the free-trade lobby as putting economics above people. Tomás Derrig, a senior Fianna Fáil TD, asked in the Dáil in 1930: 'Is the policy simply to be that this country is to go on as a grass ranch until it ultimately declines to a couple of million people?'[109] William Murphy makes the point that de Valera went as far as to invoke the rhetoric of the eighteenth-century polemicist Jonathan Swift in his *Modest Proposal*, claiming that under a native Fianna Fáil government, no longer would children, like cattle, be brought up for export.[110]

But there had been little scope for economic radicalism in the Free State in 1922, when industry was employing only 100,000 people. In the mid-1920s, 35 per cent of the working population of Northern Ireland were engaged in industry compared to only 14 per cent in the Free State. By December 1923 it was estimated that 80,000 people were unemployed,[111] and new jobs created between 1926 and 1931 totalled no more than 5,000. The idea of promoting industrialisation through a mixture of import substitution and monetary experimentation was rejected, the main focus instead being on the cultivation of a robust agricultural sector (responsible for employing 53 per cent of the workforce), specialising in livestock and dairying. Using the free-market logic, it made sense to import flour and animal food rather than produce it in Ireland, which would have raised costs for the grassland farmer. Industrial bosses did not want tariffs on capital goods. Income tax was reduced from 5 shillings to 3 shillings (25p to 15p) in the pound in 1927–8 in favour of relying on indirect taxes and reduction of old-age pensions (see below).

What tariffs did exist were used to raise revenues rather than promote the idea of protection. Cormac Ó Gráda points out that Ernest Blythe, first Finance Minister of the new state, 'came very close to delivering on his early promise to run the country on £20 million a year'.[112] In this regard, it is important to acknowledge that one of Cumann na nGaedheal's main priorities in the fiscal area was to repair the damage caused by the Civil War, and in particular servicing the large national loan issued in its aftermath. Vast spending on the army amounted to £10.6 million in 1923/4 alone, and compensation payments for property losses were £4.6 million in that year, stark reminders of the economic cost of civil war. But there was also a determination to prove that they could manage the Irish economy. Their policies favoured the well-off and established businesses, and led to a succession of stringent and in retrospect harsh assertions by key government spokesmen. This further underlined the government's distaste for what they seemed to regard as a culture of dependency, which was not only economically but politically at odds with their 'self-help' agenda.

'about one and a half million landless men'

They clung to the belief of Patrick Hogan, the government's high-profile Minister for Agriculture, that national development was synonymous with agricultural development; that the interests of the farmer and the nation were identical. Manufacturing jobs only existed for the few, with brewing accounting for almost 30 per cent of manufacturing output. Neither have comparative assessments been kind to the Free State's performance. In looking at countries like Austria, Hungary and Bulgaria, economic historians, as noted by Ó Gráda, have concluded that economic growth was slower in Ireland than in any of the other newly emerging nations of Europe. Despite the priority given to agricultural exports, the Irish share of the British cattle import market did not experience a sustained rise.[113]

Hogan also gave attention to completing the process of land purchase that predated independence. His success was considerable, given the complicated financial aspects of the Land Act of 1923. Between 1923 and 1933 more than 110,000 holdings were bought under the Land Purchase Acts. It was hoped that increasing land purchase would not only encourage 'independence and thrift' amongst new landowners, but also discourage social unrest in rural areas. Writing to Cosgrave in 1924, Hogan noted: 'there are about 500,000 tenants in Ireland; there are about one and a half million landless men and only about 30,000 holdings for them, and these landless man are at present prepared to exercise their claims with gun and torch'.[114] That Hogan was attempting land reform in this climate was commendable, especially given the constant complaints of the Department of Finance about its cost. But ultimately, it was tenant purchasers rather than those with no land that legislation benefited, with labourers' representatives concentrating instead on wages and conditions rather than the pursuit of the unrealisable goal of land ownership.

The state financing of land division involved the 1923 Act and 13 subsequent Land Acts, involving the appropriation by the Land Commission of large and underdeveloped holdings in the ownership of former landlords and tenants who underutilised their land. The Land Commission in effect became the landlord for untenanted land that it subsequently divided for the benefit of small farmers, ex-republican combatants and others. It was a programme that did not end until the mid-1980s, by which time two and a half million acres had been distributed at a total cost of £287 million. The challenge to civil servants in the 1920s was to begin this process without bankrupting the state, which was why it was financed through borrowing, with those dispossessed compensated in land bonds. In effect, they were forced to lend to the state, meaning the schemes cost little in terms of current expenditure, and the Land Commission became by and large an independent and impartial body, though the dispossessed rarely got market value for their land.[115]

Night Candles are Burnt Out

Not all government members were resolute free traders, and there were disagreements that became apparent after the instigation of a fiscal inquiry committee. But the government was far-sighted regarding state intervention in some areas. They created enduring and valuable legacies by establishing publicly owned corporations such as the Agricultural Credit Corporation and the Electricity Supply Board, but rejected the idea of a national air service. The case of electricity was particularly significant; in the mid-1920s the Free State contained only 36,000 electricity users and only one of its 600 creameries used electrical power.[116] Electricity supply was relatively undeveloped by the standards of other European countries, with roughly 300 producers across the country using a variety of generating systems, both publicly and privately run. The decision to harness the power of the River Shannon for electricity purposes, through the Ardnacrusha (in County Clare) scheme, was not only a far-sighted and innovative move, but also the government's most significant gesture in the direction of industrialisation. It deservedly received huge media coverage, and became an important symbol of the potential for constructive use of Irish natural resources. It was marked symbolically by the government-commissioned paintings of Seán Keating, including *Night Candles are Burnt Out*, which, with its hallmarks of Soviet realism, depicted Ireland's revolutionary gunmen being replaced by bureaucrats intent on modernity. The dangerous, unfortunately sometimes fatal work on the Shannon Scheme was undertaken at camps at Ardnacrusha, Parteen-Weir, O'Briensbridge and Clonlara. It took the huge workforce under the control of Siemens, who won the contract (and placed great store by it as evidenced by over 5,000 photographs of its development at their museum in Germany), four years to complete.[117] The sluice gates were opened in the summer of 1929, and by 1937 the Ardnacrusha power station supplied 87 per cent of system demand in Ireland. It was a notable exception; fiscal inquiries, on the other hand, revealed a cautious government which was loath to tinker with free-trade orthodoxy or scare vested interests, backed by an array of conservative establishment economists who gave academic justification to the government's practice.[118]

'The number of people who lead a parasitic existence'

The tendency of certain government spokesmen to berate any desire or demand for significant welfare measures in the 1920s was partly a reflection of the Victorian climate in which many of them grew to adulthood. The cutting of the old-age pension by a shilling in 1924 reflected the Minister for Finance's determination to balance the budget books, regardless of the social cost. The pension had traditionally been suspect as a result of the notorious number of fraudulent claims which predated independence; indeed, some British military strategists believed that it had allowed young men in the poorer districts, who were freed from contributing to the upkeep of the home as a result of the £1 payment, more time to concentrate on the IRA campaign against the British.[119] The financial cost of the pension to the new government was exceptionally high, but the political cost of reducing the payment was even higher. The language of James A. Burke, Minister for Local Government, was particularly significant in this regard. In suggesting that the day when the pension was fair game because it was not the Irish taxpayer that was exclusively paying for it was over, he asserted: 'One of the most serious defects of the Irish character is this tendency to dependence of one kind or another. The number of people who lead a parasitic existence was increasing relative to the number of people who are striving to make an honest living.'[120] The harsh and judgemental semantics of the 1920s aside, it was incontrovertible that spending on the pension (£3.3 million in 1922/3) towered over spending on areas such as national health insurance (£317,000), unemployment insurance (£284,000) and hospitals (£17,000), and even came close to spending on education (£4.2 million). As Ó Gráda points out: 'the pension was truly in a class of its own; the next radical step in welfare provision, children's allowances, would absorb only 4 per cent of exchequer receipts when introduced in 1944.'[121]

Nonetheless there was opposition even within Cumann na nGaedheal to lowering the pension, some believing that given the prevailing poverty and bad harvests, not to mention the importance of putative by-elections, it would have been wiser to target fraudulent claims before scaling down existing payments. But the hard men of the CnG government, as they did in reacting to most pleas to be sensitive, dismissed such sentiment as part of the 'state of mind which is responsible for a good deal of harm in this country'.[122] This was an indication of the class bias that crept into the political rhetoric in the post-Civil War period, though, as seen during the War of Independence, it was already in circulation privately prior to this. Even though the cut was reversed in 1928, it was of course the initial decision to reduce the payment that was remembered. In 1929 the government was defeated in a vote on a Fianna Fáil bill which aimed to remove a clause in the 1908 Old Age Pension Bill, by which the maintenance of relatives or others was taken into account in calculating the means of a claimant. Inevitably, the claim that the old-age pension was not safe in the hands of CnG was an important part of Fianna Fáil electoral propaganda, and they significantly extended entitlement when in office.

'people may have to die in this country and die of starvation'
And what of the experience of the 'parasites' so denounced by Burke in

the 1920s? The governments of the 1920s clearly could not afford to deliver on the promises of the Democratic Programme of the first Dáil in 1919. One of the most notorious pronouncements in the 1920s was the minister Patrick McGilligan's contention that 'people may have to die in this country and die of starvation'.[123] The real surprise is that more unrest was not shown by those most distressed given that, for example, the number of people affected by overcrowding had increased by 16 per cent between 1911 and 1926. An *Irish Times* campaign over 'Dublin's shame' led to a flood of correspondence in May 1931 after it had been suggested it was 'something of a miracle, for which we must thank the boundless resignation of the Irish poor – that the slums of Dublin have borne no violent revolt against the social order'.[124] The writer suggested that a moral campaign was needed as much as one for material improvement, and called for leadership from, amongst others, the Church. Catholic activists had in fact narrowed the ground available to radicals intent on mobilising the less well-off, through its astute targeting of working-class communities, focusing on spiritual and moral improvement rather than material reform. In the words of Paul Smith, whose novel *The Countrywoman* depicted life in Dublin's slums in the 1920s, what was wrong with priests was 'mostly the way they teach people to accept poverty as a way of life … to accept and endure brutality in the name of God. That's the worst of all … by telling us not to question it at all but to submit, submit like animals.' The mother in the novel believed that 'politics was not the province of the poor'.[125]

In the 11 years from 1922 to 1933 the average output of local-authority dwellings by Dublin Corporation amounted to just 483 a year. The main emphasis in the 1920s was on the supply of good middle-class housing, with government grants, for example, for civil service employees to build large houses. It was not until the early 1930s that there was once again an emphasis on slum clearance. In 1929 the Department of Local Government and Public Health estimated that the total housing need for the country stood at 43,656 units. The Professor of Design at Liverpool University, Patrick Abercrombie, had suggested in 1922 that Dublin was 'a city of magnificent possibilities, containing features of the first order, but loosely co-related and often mirrored by the juxtaposition of incongruities and squalor'. He argued that suburban housing with efficient transit schemes was the solution.[126] But fears about costs were always going to win through in the 1920s, given that the city had only recently been reconstructed following its destruction during the revolutionary years. While town-planning ideas may have been more visible, there was never real unanimity about the merits or drawbacks of suburban or city housing.[127]

'life for the few and death for the many'

The most pressing problem was still poverty; housing was not a problem for people with an adequate income. The rhetoric of land nationalism in the late nineteenth and early twentieth centuries had been avowedly rural and agrarian, overlooking many of the sectional interests in Irish society, and in 1923 the government maintained that it had no intention of framing legislative initiatives to assist town tenants in purchasing their houses, although a Tenants Act of 1931 eventually contributed to an escalation of purchase agreements. Broadly speaking, the Irish government, in the same manner as its British predecessors, accepted the arguments of the landlord class – that granting extensive town tenant rights would undermine urban investment – a smokescreen allowing landlords to continue to neglect their property and its inhabitants.[128] It frustrated social radicals like Constance Markievicz, one of the co-founders of Fianna Fáil, who decried the failure in getting people to understand that politics should be about the organisation of food, clothing and housing, instead of their impulse 'to get behind some idol', the foolish and uneducated falling into 'unthinking battalions'.[129] The organisers of Fianna Fáil in 1926 declared that the resources and wealth of Ireland should be subservient to the needs and welfare of the people, and during the 1927 campaign activists like Markievicz insisted on the need for a pension for mothers and for a focus on child welfare.

It was long overdue. The census of Ireland for 1926 had revealed that there were 800,000 living in overcrowded conditions, while the infant mortality rate in the working-class north of Dublin city was 25.6 per 1,000, compared to 7.7 among the middle classes. Tuberculosis was still causing in the region of 4,500 deaths per year. Outside the cities, where 61 per cent of the population resided, 36,000 farm labourers were still living in their employers' housing.[130] For writers like Seán O'Casey, urban squalor was still stubbornly a fact of Irish life, with Dublin city a little older but as ugly as ever. Independence, he insisted, had made no difference. As he wrote in 1925: 'It isn't a question of English or Irish culture with the inanimate patsies of the tenements but a question of life for the few and death for the many. Irish-speaking or English-speaking, they are all what they are: convalescent homes of plague, pestilence or death.'[131]

Hospital provision during this period came under three separate systems, with the existence of voluntary institutions (many of them in dire financial straits), surviving county infirmaries and fever hospitals, and the former workhouse hospitals (now county hospitals). Mary Daly points out that there was much confusion and disagreement as to the balance that should be struck between public hospitals, voluntary endeavour and state intervention, given the determination of the Church and the medical profession to maintain their autonomy. The position of voluntary hospitals became a matter of increased concern in the 1920s; the national maternity hospital in Holles Street was experiencing grave financial crises, and the ceiling of the gynaecological landing in the hospital was on the verge of collapse.[132] Threatened closure of the hospital was one of the main reasons for the poorly drafted Public Charitable Hospital Act of 1930, which gave certain named hospitals a monopoly on horse-racing sweepstakes, inaugurating one of the most bizarre and corrupt enterprises of twentieth-century Ireland (see Chapter 5). In 1932, the secretary to the Department of Local Government and Public Health insisted it was not desirable for the state 'to assume even remotely any additional liability in connection with hospitals'.[133]

'irredeemable'?

There was little public discussion about the mental hospitals, aside from suggestions that the blame for their financial crisis lay at the feet of the ratepayers for failing to make payments. In 1927, the report of the Commission on the Sick and Destitute Poor made similar recommendations to those made by inquiries twenty years previously, particularly in terms of the need for outpatient services and voluntary admission. It also criticised standards of care in general hospitals, discrimination against the sick poor and general shortcomings in the care of all classes of vulnerable patients.[134] The majority of mentally ill patients were still being labelled incorrectly and archaically as 'dangerous lunatics', when they were no such thing. A very flexible definition of insanity, often without any scientific basis, seemed to exist, becoming a 'catch-all' category that included those suffering from congenital mental deficiency and epilepsy.

There was also a rise in the number of illegitimate births, from 1,520 in 1922 to 1,853 in 1929, though the illegitimacy figures can be seen to be quite low given that 80 per cent of all males between the ages of 25 and 30 were unmarried, as were 62 per cent of all females in the same age group. The Gardaí in Dublin estimated there were about 100 women under the age of 21 engaged in prostitution. In June 1930 a committee, chaired by William Carrigan KC, was established to investigate the problem of juvenile prostitution. Eoin O'Sullivan makes the point that Carrigan had already demonstrated his views on the issue of the age of consent. In a court case in 1927, he commented that the Irish people 'were supposed to be a people of robust virtue; but if this case was heard in England it would not last five minutes, because the jury by direction would find the prisoner guilty … in this country, with all their boasting, they did not protect by law girls over 16'.[135]

There was an excessive focus in the Carrigan report on illegitimacy and prostitution, but little connection made between social conditions and social problems. In private, civil servants were scathing about the simplistic attempt to link immorality with the existence of unlicensed dance halls, at the expense of examining housing, education or unemployment. The obsession with the car as a facilitator of moral decline was another illustration of a misfocused approach.[136]

Kevin O'Higgins was also coming under pressure from social workers to make changes in the law concerning venereal disease. One of the reasons for the pressure was that the Irish Free State lagged behind Britain and Northern Ireland in the field of sex legislation. It is noteworthy that there was debate about sex in religious and government circles, though it was telling that when frank debates on VD in the Irish army took place in the 1920s (including an inter-departmental committee on VD from 1924 to 1925), the cabinet refused to accept it was a public-health issue and it was largely women who were blamed for spreading it. A clear distinction was made between those who were relatively unchaste and those considered 'irredeemable' (meaning professional prostitutes and women born out of wedlock).[137]

'the laying of our hands upon them is contrary to the rules of modesty'
Early in 1925 there was something of a clear-out of the Monto, Dublin's red-light district. The sex problem was very much defined in terms of who could be compelled to restraint – soldiers rather than the general public – while the cabinet approached the Archbishop of Dublin about

whether they could publish the Carrigan report. One interesting aspect of the focus on sex was that there was a whole class of women who were not getting married but who were sexually active – revealing a whole area of Irish sexual activity that had not been explored, similar to the neglect of masculinity and male heterosexual activity. The social historian Susannah Riordan makes the perceptive point that Irish historians have been over-concerned with the denial rather than the experience of sex.[138]

Nor is it the case that there was no knowledge of sexual abuse in Ireland in the 1920s. The Superior General of the Christian Brothers in Ireland informed members of the order in 1920 that 'the fondling of boys, the laying of our hands upon them is contrary to the rules of modesty and is decidedly dangerous'.[139] Six years later a circular issued by the Christian Brother Provincial noted that 'the teacher who allows himself any softness in his intercourse with his pupil, who does not repress the tendency to "pets" and who fondles the young or indulges in other weaknesses is not heeding the danger sign and may easily fall'.[140] In the 1960s, the Department of Education received a letter (which it ignored) from a former inmate of the industrial school at Tralee, County Kerry. He had spent seven years there in the 1920s and 1930s:

> I noticed a great number of atrocities by the so-called Christian Brothers against the boys, i.e. beatings and floggings in the most per-verted way, as if Christ was not present on the altar as a boy as well as a man. I believe such pagan methods are still used against boys who get beatings and run away ... I hope that the truth of what I saw during my time as a boy ... will put an end to this practice of naked beating which is nothing short of homosexuality, and that a Christian method will be used and not degraded pagan methods of keeping order.[141]

The extent of infanticide in early independent Ireland was uncovered in the 1990s by Louise Ryan and Alexis Guilbride. Guilbride suggested that a publication of 1924, *Women of the Gael*, written by a priest, makes it easier to understand why so many single mothers were reduced to prostitution, begging or incarceration in the Magdalen laundries. This publication contended: 'In Ireland, whenever a child is born out of wedlock so shocked is the public sense by the very unusual occurrence that it brands with an irreparable stigma and to a large extent, excommunicates the woman guilty of the crime.'[142] The court files detailed infanticide cases such as the following, in which the new mother was terrified of parental discovery: 'Kate brought the child out of the shed where she attempted, but failed, to strangle her with a sock. She then covered her with wet sacks, on top of which she placed 2 iron window-frames, weighing 40lbs each.'[143] Whatever about the attempts by some to depict women who had killed their children as beyond redemption, there was often a divergence between official and popular attitudes; there was a recognition of the human dilemma and stark loneliness of the single mother, and a frequent refusal by juries to convict women of infanticide or impose the death penalty or unduly harsh sentences.[144]

'avoidance of scandal'

It is also probable that the figures for illegitimacy underestimated the true extent of the incidence of single mothers, as the problem was often exported to England. In the 1920s publications such as the *Irish Ecclesiastical Record* deliberated on the plight of 'fallen women'. The sociologist Eoin O'Sullivan has highlighted one such article from 1922, which recommended 'the continuation of the system of individual treatment provided by a range of Catholic societies, due to its avoidance of scandal'. Nuns opened homes for the 'fallen' in an attempt to lessen the dependence on the County Home, where 70 per cent of unmarried mothers remained in the 1920s.[145] The 1927 report of the Commission on the Sick and Destitute Poor suggested there were 629 unmarried mothers classed as 'first offenders' and 391 mothers 'who had fallen more than once'.[146]

Migration to England was the only option for many, and was a particular concern of the Catholic Rescue and Protection Society that had been established in 1913. This organisation was particularly preoccupied with the threat of proselytism. Not surprisingly, pressure for the repatriation of these women often came from English agencies, no doubt concerned that they were financing an Irish social problem. At home, children born outside of marriage were five times more likely to die prematurely, and in the 1920s one in three registered illegitimate children died in his or her first year.[147] Mothers forced to have their offspring fostered were generally denied all contact with their children, it being a cardinal rule of the Magdalen laundries, for example, that it was 'strictly forbidden for any reference to their past life being made by the penitents in their conversation with the nuns'.[148]

Illegitimacy was also of concern to the Carrigan Committee, which recommended the age for consensual sex be increased from 16 to 18 or 19. According to a contemporary Jesuit campaigner, Richard Devane, this was necessary for the 'simple, innocent girls of an agricultural country like ours'.[149] Many submissions to the Carrigan Committee, whose report was later suppressed, also seemed concerned with a moral laxity they saw as characteristic of the 1920s. The Garda Commissioner Eoin O'Duffy pointed to the incidence of child sexual abuse of girls under the age of 14 and suggested only 25 per cent of cases were being reported, with only a 15 per cent prosecution rate. He maintained that, in any case, 'to impose a sentence of six months on, or to fine, a ruffian who destroys the innocence of a child under 13 is farcical'. There were 31 prosecutions for defilement of girls under the age of 16 in Dublin city between 1924 and 1929. The Carrigan Committee proposals were overshadowed by the need to prevent public discussions of these matters, some believing that commissions were too public and that a small Catholic elite should advise the government 'without public discussion'.[150]

'the character of the national mind'

Such focus on moral panic, which often suited the interests of the Church as well as the conservative middle-class social base of Irish politics, not only inhibited the development of a strong social and labour movement but also facilitated the continued hiding of many of Ireland's social problems. In his memoirs, Noël Browne (Minister for Health from 1948 to 1951) gave one example of the suppression of a discourse based on highlighting social need and want: '"They can come to my back door and ask for it if they need it", said a priest in the course of a sermon denouncing a proposal to provide children with a free school meal as "communism".' [151] Children born into the 'unfortunate' class thus continued to be hidden. A system of legal adoption, introduced in England and Wales in 1926 and Northern Ireland in 1929, was not introduced in Southern Ireland until the 1950s. De Valera, in a contribution to Dáil proceedings in 1928, described as 'savage' a decision to send two 14-year-olds to an industrial school for three years for destroying £2 worth of insulators from the Shannon Electricity Scheme. This was just one footnote in what was subsequently discovered late in the century to be the monstrous history of the Irish industrial-school system.[152]

It was in the 1920s that the crucial decision was made to increase reliance on the system of industrial schools, unlike in Britain, where reform was suggested. By 1924 there were more children in industrial schools in the Irish Free State than there were in all of the industrial schools in England, Scotland, Wales and Northern Ireland combined. Abolished in England in 1933, the system was tenaciously clung to in Ireland. Any chance that the issue of child abuse would be debated in Ireland had been buried with the suppression of the Carrigan Report, which had also pointed to the way the prevailing Irish judicial process operated to the detriment of children. The Minister for Justice, James Geoghean, wanted the report suppressed on the grounds that it exaggerated the extent of declining morality, and also had grave doubts as to the validity of evidence heard from children. The Carrigan Report, in favouring a tightening of the law in relation to the protection of women and children, was also believed not to have struck a balance between considering the culpability of children and women, being too severe on women.[153] The report had referred to the 'objectionable' fact that, in care, unmarried mothers could not be maintained apart from other inmates (the 'decent poor and sick').

The truth was that Ireland was still living under the shadow of the former workhouse system, and the mentality it induced, in its discrimination against the sick poor, those suffering from TB, unmarried mothers, and deserted and orphaned children. It was ironic indeed that, in the introduction to the report of the inquiry into the sick and destitute poor, W. T. Cosgrave had suggested that 'the condition of a nation's poor indicated the character of the national mind'. In truth there was often a tendency to see poverty as representing a flaw in the national character: a lack of thrift, independence or of 'manly desire' to want to earn a living. The government enviously observed the German Elberfield Poor Law system, where the duty of investigation and relief was not the responsibility of central government but voluntary assistants.[154]

'to bounce a boot off her now and then'
Aside from the suffering of many children, the social and political progress of women remained constrained. For many, the gravest danger to their welfare came in the home. This was an issue which the Irish Suffrage Movement's newspaper, the *Irish Citizen*, had drawn attention to before independence (in September 1919), criticising the prevailing ethos, which stipulated that what transpired in the home had to be carefully concealed from the world without. If black eyes had to be kept strictly secret, the American social anthropologists Arensberg and Kimball, who produced

a seminal study of Irish rural life, also recorded that it was acceptable for wives who had 'failed' to get pregnant (this of course being deemed solely their problem) to be beaten or for her husband 'to bounce a foot off her now and again for it'.[155] The countless reports of wife beating in the Irish newspapers were virtually ignored, symptomatic of an attitude that saw domestic violence as petty rather than serious crime. As mentioned earlier, the Civil War and its aftermath had produced a mindset in some that it was women who were more predisposed towards violent hysteria, which prompted a considerable backlash in the 1920s. This was by no means confined to so-called 'conservatives'; one of the most celebrated liberals of the era, Seán O'Faoláin, recalled in his autobiography that during the Civil War 'the women I met were particularly disturbing – driven by that unfeminine animus … they were theatrical, self-dramatising, power-hungry, temperamental but with few warm emotions, ruthless, abstract in discussion and full of terrifying sentimentality'.[156] Neither did P. S. O'Hegarty hold back in his assessment of those women whom he saw during the war as steadily eliminating from themselves every womanly feeling; 'intolerance, swagger, hardness, unwomanliness captured the women and turned them into unlovely destruction-minded arid begetters of violence'.[157] After one of his encounters with Constance Markievicz, Yeats had referred to arguing 'with that steam whistle for an hour'.[158]

It is significant that this sustained vitriolic discourse concerning women has received scant attention from historians. Perhaps it proved that Irish women were politicised at an earlier stage than many of their European counterparts, and their visibility and demands, so obvious during the revolutionary years, were now seen as something of an embarrassment and something to be reined in. In this regard, it is difficult not to be sympathetic with the assertion of the writer Oliver St John Gogarty, when speaking in the Senate on censorship in 1928, that 'it is high time that the people of this country find some other way of loving God than by hating women'.[159]

In the fiction of Peadar O'Donnell, in such novels as *Storm* (1925), *The Knife* (1930) and *Islanders* (1928), the reader is presented with a picture of women continually sidelined, sorrowful and passive, or, if they are seen, as spiritual and their radicalism regarded as something to be curbed. Stereotypical Irish mothers abounded, first to rise and last to go to bed, performing the endless household tasks which is consistent with the picture drawn by Arensberg and Kimball.[160] But O'Donnell also made it clear that many of the women, in carrying out daily chores, were hiding smouldering resentments. This is understandable given that most husbands in Irish fiction regarded their wives as being responsible for whatever difficulties existed in their domestic lives, an idea given a powerful airing in Paul Smith's *The Countrywoman*. Molly Baines, in her desperate bid to keep her children fed, constantly awaits the terrifying return of her abusive and drunken husband, and is observed by her young son 'listening to the sounds his voice made without hearing what he said. She could gauge instantly the extent of his wrath, and, when he was sober, whether or not to expect violence, by the near shading of the rise and fall of a sound that alerted her and put her on her guard.'[161]

It is undoubtedly the case that despite all the outbursts about women and their propensity to violence in the struggle for independence, it was passages such as these that were more representative of Irish women's experience of violence. But the culture of the family, and the strict belief in non-interference, cemented by Catholic social theory and the Catholic sanctity of the marriage vows, ensured that victims of domestic violence had little refuge in Ireland until at least fifty years after independence. Alcohol abuse undoubtedly exacerbated the problem.

Ireland was not unique in developing aspects of a gendered state in the 1920s, but should be seen as reflecting (albeit very stridently) a broader movement within European conservatism, as seen, for example, in the policies of pro-natalism in France, and curtailment of access to contraception across Europe. The government built up an array of legislation discriminating against women, legislation which was to be built on by their Fianna Fáil successors, even though republican women, such as Kathleen Clarke, were instrumental in founding the new Fianna Fáil party. Clarke had stayed quiet about her part in pushing republicans into political as opposed to military opposition. In her memoirs she claimed she did this: 'in a sense to shield de Valera. Some time before, he had been sneered at as being under petticoat government, that Miss [Mary] MacSwiney was running him. I did not want that sneer repeated, with just a change of petticoat.'[162]

In 1925 the right of women to sit for all examinations in the civil service was curtailed. The 1927 Juries Bill was originally designed to prevent women from sitting on juries. Following pressure from women's groups, it included an amendment which allowed women to sit on juries only if they specifically applied. In 1932 compulsory retirement was introduced for married female teachers, and was subsequently extended to the entire civil service. This was perhaps an Irish version of 'republican motherhood', which had also been experienced after the American and French revolutions. In employing much ecclesiastical discourse, it depicted ideal women as self-sacrificing and passive mothers who nurtured a deep patriotism in their children, rather than being active agents of political change.[163] There was female opposition to these legislative initiatives; in 1927 Jenny Wyse Power, former vice-president of Sinn Féin, and now a senator, trenchantly opposed the Juries Bill:

> If this bill becomes law, the civic spirit that is awakening in women will be arrested. In fact, the suggestion that there shall be only male jurors in the future cuts at the very root of this development in the awakening of the civic spirit ... during the last 50 years the men who led political movements and carried them in the main to success, utilised women in order to achieve their object. That utilisation of women helped in a great degree their civic spirit, and some of them encouraged more or less by the way they have been thrust out, as it were, to do work that they never did before, came gradually into public life and have done social work which is generally regarded as successful. It is for that reason I deplore so much the Minister's attitude in this matter, not so much, perhaps, because we want to be on juries, or anything else, but because he is doing such an injustice to what is really a necessary asset to every state, the co-operation of its men and women.[164]

The 'former dignity' of Irish women

The fact that during the 1920s and 1930s there were repeated references to the 'former dignity' of Irish women was more evidence that much of the rhetoric and practice of these years reflected a desire to reimpose acceptable boundaries. Added to this was a form of cultural nationalism which decreed it was a woman's responsibility, given her general management of household incomes, to spend exclusively on Irish products and not, in the words of the *Irish Independent*, on 'such scanty drapery as could only be exceeded in the slave markets of pagan countries'.[165] De Valera suggested, too, on coming to power, that it was the duty of a woman to boast that she was clothed 'from head to foot' in Irish manufacture.[166]

Latter-day liberals and feminists have denounced many of the above sentiments and expressions of a sometimes ribald sexism, but it is worth noting that the excessiveness of the language was not only challenged by contemporary groups such as the Irish Women's Citizens' and Local Government Association and the National Council of Women (established in 1924 to promote welfare issues), but by other disparate groups who worked together on issues which affected the welfare of women and children.[167] The middle-class National University Women's Graduate Association frequently highlighted the imbalance of power between men and women in Irish society. It may also have been that strong discriminatory language was employed by opponents of women's advancement precisely because many women (and not just those who emigrated) were loath to be bound by such restrictions. The research of Caitríona Clear makes clear there was precious little idealisation of the household in popular magazines and literature aimed at women.[168] Interestingly, much the same gender ideology (taking its lead from the papacy) was also in evidence in Fascist Italy, where modern dress, the participation of women in athletic pursuits and attempts to limit women's participation in the workforce were also matters of public and political discourse.[169] A Catholic teacher-training college for women, Mary Immaculate in Limerick, launched the Mary Immaculate Modest Dress and Deportment Crusade in 1927, in response to Catholic bishops' appeals for women to cover up. The rules included a ban on the wearing of dresses 'less than four inches below the knee' or those 'cut in a suggestive style, or so loosely or low about the neck as to allow the collar-bone to appear, or cut equally low at the back'.[170]

Officially, the work of many Irish women remained hidden, a consequence of the pervasiveness of the 'family economy' in the Irish Free State. This was demonstrated by the fact that the 1926 census did not allow more than one woman in a household of less than seven to be recorded as 'engaged in home duties'. According to this census, one third of women were engaged in agriculture, though farmers' wives were not included as members of the agricultural workforce. The difference between the North and the South of Ireland was quite striking regarding female employment. In 1926, only 5.6 per cent of married women in the Free State (8,000 women) had professional occupations, compared with 14.5 per cent in Northern Ireland. Less than 50 per cent of single women aged over 14 were in employment, compared with 87 per cent of men, though the claim that Irish women could achieve independence only by leaving Ireland has remained contested.[171]

'the preserve of their spiritual leaders'?

Combined with low marriage rates and high fertility, emigration ensured that the Irish demographic situation was quite unique. It did not necessarily imply that parents disinherited all but one of their children – perhaps by giving one a solid farm and the others the chance of a life elsewhere, they could provide for both themselves and their children, though undoubtedly many were forced to go. Emigration remained a central feature of the Irish experience in the 1920s and 1930s, making a mockery of much of the rhetoric of the pre-independence era, which had depicted it as solely a consequence of foreign occupation. Between 1926 and 1936, 72,563 males and 94,188 females emigrated.[172]

Though it was an established and accepted stage in the Irish experience of growing to adulthood, the nature of international migration changed in the 1920s. There was a sharp decline in the rate of overseas emigration. As no frontier controls existed between the Irish Free State and Britain, the changing of US immigration policy and declining opportunities there undoubtedly contributed to the sharp increase in 1925 and 1926 in emigration figures from Ireland to Britain, when over 30,000 left the Free State annually. From the mid-1930s Britain was the chief destination for Irish emigrants. This was because it was cheaper to travel to and held out more chance of a return journey, and there was more demand for unskilled labour. The typical migrant was young, rural and unskilled.[173]

Their departure was an inevitable product of the family inheritance system in Ireland and the failure to create a robust economy. Emigration did not become a significant part of political and public discourse in Ireland during these years, which seemed to indicate an acceptance of its inevitability, and this, no doubt, was the sentiment in so many of Ireland's large families. Enda Delaney pointed out that 'Both civil servants and politicians believed that the problems which Irish migrants encountered in Britain were the preserve of their spiritual leaders, not the Irish state.'[174] In the 1920s, the Aliens Board of the House of Commons occasionally turned their attention to the issue of Irish emigrants, particularly where unskilled migrants in urban centres like Glasgow and Liverpool were contributing to class and sectarian tension. Irish emigrants were often depicted as hard workers, but who had a tendency to turn to degeneracy. The Aliens Board made the quite startling assertion in 1928 that the 'elimination' of the Irish from Scotland would reduce the crime statistics by 75–80 per cent. Although this was an exception to what was generally a pragmatic approach to Irish emigration, it did reveal how government thinking could be influenced by public opinion, galvanised by protests in Scotland in the late 1920s, where it was felt the Irish were increasing the level of unemployment.[175]

'half a dozen old parish priests in any diocese can make a bishop pick his words'

If this was an issue for the Catholic Church in Ireland, it was one of a growing list of welfare and spiritual questions that dominated its concerns in the 1920s. Much has been written of the Church's determination to impose its control in the new Free State and to make its authoritative voice heard on a range of social, political and religious topics. Emphatic statements by members of the Hierarchy in support of the Treaty have been accepted generally as indicating a united approach within the Church concerning Civil War and post-Civil War politics. But the most recent research, by Patrick Murray, would suggest that this is an over-simplification; given the complexity and divisiveness of the revolution, it is stretching credulity to believe that the leaders of a religion to which 94 per cent of the population adhered, would not have their own internal divisions. What has been depicted as a monolithic Church was in fact often divided on political issues.[176]

There is room, too, for a comprehensive analysis of both pro-republican clergy and bishops who, significantly, included the rector and the vice-rector of the Irish College in Rome, Monsignor John Hagan and Fr Michael Cronin. They also included in their ranks figures in the Irish diaspora, such as Archbishop Daniel Mannix in Australia and home-based dissidents like Fr Michael O'Flanagan. The local press provides numerous examples of individual members who were prepared to brave the wrath of their superiors in refusing to support the Treaty.[177]

Notwithstanding, the end of the Irish revolution did provide an opportunity for the Church to reassert its moral authority in many areas. The language that had been used by Irish republicans – most emphatically in 1916 – had been the language of Catholic mystics and idealists. They had invoked Christian imagery and concepts of sacrifice to justify a rebellion which in fact contravened Catholic teaching on the subject, which gives some indication of why the Church was in a rather difficult position. Perhaps this is the reason why some of its more high profile members, like Archbishop Walsh of Dublin, seemed to devote little attention to religious issues during the revolution. Significantly, republican hunger strikes were seen by Walsh, it seems, solely in terms of their political impact, rather than the questions they raised about the ethics of hunger striking in relation to the Catholic faith. This was a measure of the sheer pragmatism of Walsh's approach, keeping the Church in tune with popular struggle, and often following the flock when it chose a new path.[178] Towards the end of his life, the increasingly frail Walsh was certainly following rather than leading events. He may not have lived to see the creation of the Free State, but he had played a pivotal role in preparing both Church and society for independence.

Certainly after the signing of the Treaty and the move towards civil war, the language being used by some members of the Hierarchy, determined to be masters in their own backyard, demanded unfailing obedience. When a Vatican representative, Monsignor Salvatore Luzio, came to Ireland during the Civil War period, he was cold-shouldered not only by the government but also by the Church authorities.[179] There was also a determination not to have a repeat of the situation during the War of Independence, when the Catholic Church did not have a clearly defined policy in relation to the Dáil's authority.

Fear of anarchy and social revolution during the Civil War would only add to the Church's belief in itself as the upholder of Catholic Ireland's moral integrity. For Bishop Cohalan of Cork, for example, the concept of obedience was at the core of his teaching on morality, and it could be argued that the Church's attitude during these key years provides a key to understanding its influence in later years. However, many of the Hierarchy's pronouncements were urgent, confused and meandering, not to mention poorly written. Maryann Valiulis has convincingly argued that some of the language they used (sometimes bordering on the hysterical) was not the language of confidence in their authority, but of the panic of those who were unsure about the measure of their power or felt it was slipping.[180]

The existence of republican sympathisers within the Church was crucial in the context of Irish politics because, put simply, it meant that the anti-Treaty republicans, and later Fianna Fáil, were never bereft of some kind of ecclesiastical backing. If such support had been lacking, it may well have led to a more pronounced anti-clericalism among republicans after the Civil War.[181] By 1926 certain key members of the Hierarchy, including Cohalan of Cork and Cardinal O'Donnell, were encouraging the republicans to enter parliamentary politics. Although as Fianna Fáil got closer to power there were some clerical attacks on de Valera, they were relatively few in comparison to the immediate post-Civil War era. One could take this argument further and suggest that the active support of priests was essential to de Valera's political resurrection. In Peadar O'Donnell's novel *The Bothy Fire and All That*, it was noted that priests 'are valuable recruits for de Valera, who is menaced by the Catholic Fascism of the bishops, for half a dozen old parish priests in any diocese can make a bishop pick his words'.[182] De Valera's own tendency to stress spiritual rather than material values obviously helped; indeed, there were those who saw him as 'the new Jesus in a black coat', an individual who assumed for some the style of a lay cardinal, and many of his pronouncements on economic and social issues were seen as indistinguishable from episcopal pastorals.[183]

Many of the older and more established clerics actively supported Cumann na nGaedheal. In the June 1927 general election for example, there were 33 priests involved in the campaign in the Galway constituency, all of whom were government supporters, while the Bishop of Limerick, David Keane, nominated his local CnG candidate.[184] But it is also significant that a new generation of clerics were turning elsewhere, and many of the newly ordained priests coming out of the Irish colleges in Rome, Paris and Salamanca were firm supporters of Fianna Fáil. The truth was that those involved in the Church at all levels reflected the same political and class divisions which affected the rest of society. The inferior status of lay sisters entering convents, for example, who had no dowries and were responsible for more menial duties meant they had no vote in community affairs and were ineligible to stand for election as superior. The manner in which middle-class children were more likely to end up in orphanages than industrial or reformatory schools was also an indication of a Church-endorsed class bias.[185]

'their earnestness is doubtful'

The 'moral panic' created by the Church in the 1920s was also couched, though sometimes privately, in the language of class. Those of a 'weaker moral fibre' were deemed to be in the working- or lower-class categories, particularly those who had, as Cardinal Logue informed a new generation of Catholic priests at Maynooth in 1924, lost their 'reverence' for religion. Rectifying this was one reason for many of the sodalities, Catholic lay and charitable organisations which were such a marked feature of Catholic life after independence. The growth of new devotional cults such as that of Matt Talbot (a reformed alcoholic who turned to God and self-mortification) was also significant. The largest Catholic lay organisation in Ireland remained the Jesuit-run Pioneer Total Abstinence Association, while Frank Duff's' Legion of Mary, originally established in September 1921, had an influence that went far and wide. The Legion had within three decades established itself on all five continents. The Society of Saint Vincent de Paul was also active in charitable work in the major Irish cities. Eamon Dunn suggested their activities 'narrowed the ground' available to left-wing radicals who were keen to politically mobilise impoverished communities.[186]

Missions and retreats were numerous in the Free State, particularly those organised by the Redemptorists, who believed in the value of parish missions as forces for reconciliation. They gave 91 missions in 1922, and 145 in 1924, and for the disillusioned, like the poet Austin Clarke, were a symbol of the repression of the Irish clerical world. One of their earliest targets was excessive and illegal poteen-making in the west of Ireland. There was a sense in which some of these more marginal communities, away from the strict structures and patterns of Catholic life in towns and cities (with their sequence of sodalities, masses and retreats), were utterly pragmatic in their approach to such missions, toeing the line when the preachers appeared, but remaining somewhat anarchic when they had departed. This was something which the Capuchin order had discovered when trying to inculcate sobriety in the opening years of the century. In the 1920s, the Redemptorists in Culnamuck found, as they acknowledged in private, 'a stubborn and ignorant people debauched by poteen. They told barefaced lies and only with great difficulty did they surrender four stills. All but four took the anti-poteen pledge, but their earnestness is doubtful.'[187]

This is a reminder that for all Ireland's legendary institutional adherence to the Catholic faith, there was often an almost underground resentment and resistance to excessive enforced piety. This was despite the wonderfully staged triumphalism of the celebrations marking the centenary of Catholic emancipation in 1929 and the Eucharistic Congress of 1932. For all their indication of mass piety and devotion, with hundreds of thousands thronging the streets of Dublin, they also had elements of the carnival. As Peadar O'Donnell wrote in the *Gates Flew Open*: 'Religion in those days was an atmosphere in which one lived without any parade of piety. We conceal private devotion as much as we conceal our courting. It is, I think, quite common in rural Ireland to distrust people who make a great show of religion.' This is not to belittle or underestimate the success of the Church in inculcating faith and mass attendance, but a reminder once again that behind the monolith there were more varied attitudes to religious expression.[188]

'drunkenness and drunkenness alone'?

In the same way, it would be easy to highlight the various pronouncements of the Catholic Church, or the often-savage fulminations of a publication like the *Catholic Bulletin*, which was published from 1911 to 1939, and conclude that the Church in Ireland in the 1920s was obsessed with issues of sexual morality. There is an element of truth in such an assertion, but it should not be made without taking due cognisance of the intellectual and rhetorical diversity in Irish Catholic life, which a selective reading of contemporary Catholic literature precludes. As Margaret O'Callaghan pointed out, it would be unwise 'to reach conclusions about certain policies by an examination of the worst excesses of their rearguard'.[189]

Certainly, the Church was concerned with what it saw as declining morality. The issue of alcohol abuse and the criticism of licensing laws was one such example, but this was not just a question of the Church imposing its views on the government of the day, but practical action being taken to counteract what was regarded across the religious, political and cultural spectrum as a particularly significant problem. It was a social issue that Kevin O'Higgins seemed determined to confront in order to simplify the complex licensing laws inherited from the eighteenth and nineteenth centuries. They were, as he put it: 'a bewildering maze of statutes and decisions, which, while creating offences also provided ingenious means of escape for unscrupulous people, and for people otherwise honest but who were driven to lie and worse in the struggle for existence'.[190]

There was nonetheless a drop in the convictions for drunkenness: down from 15,339 in 1914 to 6,862 in 1925. The 1924 Licensing Act had prohibited the sale of drink after 10.30 p.m., and sought to tighten the procedures in relation to the compulsory endorsement of licences after conviction of an offence and the leniency of district justices in their application of the law. The legislation reflected O'Higgins's determination that the judiciary should be aware of its subservience to the state. Given the power of the licensed vintners as a lobby group determined to protect their interests, there were inevitably concessions to the trade, but the government did succeed in ensuring a cut in the number of trading hours. But O'Higgins was loath to state explicitly that Ireland was a nation of drunks. He insisted he was not hostile to the licensed trade, or indulging prohibitionists. Instead he seemed to occupy that vague middle ground, so beloved of Irish public representatives when speaking about the role of alcohol in Irish society:

> What is excessive drinking? I do not take it that excessive drinking means that you fall over a man every five yards on your way home. If we are drinking beyond our resources there is excessive drinking. £17.5 million was spent across the counter on drink in the financial year 1925–6. Is that excessive drinking? Some would say no. Some people would say very differently. At any rate I object to the criterion that drunkenness and drunkenness alone is to be the test of whether or not there is excessive drinking.[191]

'setting his snares for unwary feet'

It was also the case that the quest for moral rectitude was being processed in a country that had become accustomed to violence and lack of discipline. The programme for Seán O'Casey's *The Shadow of a Gunman* included a note advising the audience that any gunshots heard during the performance were part of the play, and requested the audience to remain seated.[192] The Catholic Church, which for so long had been accustomed to crusading in the context of identifying an external enemy, now needed to police a newly identified target. In the same way that republicans had traditionally insisted that moral corruption was a result of English influences, the Church had also decided that this was the case, but the focus was now on attacking, in particular, the social life of their flock. As enunciated in the Hierarchy's pastoral of 1927, following a national council at Maynooth: 'the evil one is ever setting his snares for unwary feet. At the moment his traps for the innocent are chiefly the dance hall, the bad book, the motion picture, the indecent fashion in female dress – all of which tend to destroy the virtues characteristic of our race.'[193]

One could quote a succession of such declarations in isolation; what is less easy to establish is the extent to which they succeeded in transforming the lives of people. It is surely ironic, given the constant references to 'alien influences', that the Irish population became one of the heaviest cinema-going populations in the world, and were keen to drink as much as possible and dance from one end of the country to the other. The middle classes were delighted to hear jazz music and imitate the social forms of London, leading to utterly exaggerated comments from excitable Irish priests that activities which in other countries were confined to brothels were being seen without hindrance on Irish roadsides. Many contemporaries refused to take such assertions seriously. It should also be noted that large numbers attended novenas and sodalities because they were an important social outlet, or in the words of George Russell 'the high culture of the average man and especially the poor'.[194] One suspects that with the passing of time the activities of the Church may have been exaggerated in the interests of literary flourish, though this may simply be smug scepticism on the part of a younger generation who were reared in the midst of the decline of the Church's influence. Writing in the 1950s, the Kerry writer Bryan MacMahon suggested, in relation to the clergy's obsession with dance, that in the 1920s 'wooden road-side platforms were set on fire by curates, surer still, the priests drove their cars backwards and forwards over the timber platforms; concertinas were sent flying into hill streams and those who played music at dances were branded as outcasts'.[195]

'Well Done Mayo!'

There was also a proliferation of vigilance groups such as the Catholic Truth Society, mocked in future literary memoirs, and ridiculed by future liberals, though it could be argued that the members of such groups were more representative of Irish people than those who wrote books. The pressure groups had a key part to play in providing the impetus for censorship legislation. But the idea that this was a simple case of Church controlling state overlooks the popular culture of Catholicism and the fact that legislators and civil servants did not make much of a distinction between Church and state. In other words they did not separate the job of governing from their own Catholic consciences. Governments of the 1920s did not need to aggressively secure Church support through such legislation; it was already a part of their identity. If they had needed to secure it, why, for example, in a notorious case in 1930, did they suspend Mayo County Council against the grain of popular opinion because the council had refused to stand over the appointment of a Protestant librarian? Although the librarian was eventually removed, it was only when the government had withstood much pressure, including belief in party circles that if the government defied Catholic opinion, there was a danger of a 'Catholic Centre Party emerging', while the *Catholic Bulletin* had screamed in a headline: 'Well Done Mayo![196]

In other words, they had refused to take the easy option, which would support the contention that the government were 'moderate, educated and unself-conscious Catholics'.[197] Nonetheless, the sustained onslaught from Catholic opponents of a Protestant librarian, dressed up in the rhetoric of continuing Catholic sacrifices, illustrated the pressure that could be brought to bear. The parish priest who proposed the rejection of the librarian commented: 'If the people of Mayo cannot have a Carnegie library without a Protestant librarian being made director of the literature distributed to their children, they will do without a Carnegie library. They have made bigger sacrifices in the past.'[198] But Hubert Butler, an insightful (Protestant) commentator on both Irish and European affairs, identified in relation to the Mayo library case a Protestant weakness also. He argued that 'it was usually through their own inertia that Irish Protestants lost cultural influence in the provinces'; that they rarely attended the meetings of the Carnegie library committees and thus lost places reserved for them. When the library controversy erupted in 1931, he maintained: 'the government supported the Protestant candidate, but they received only lukewarm support from the Protestant community and ultimately the government capitulated'.[199]

In the same vein, while elements of Catholic triumphalism, anti-Protestantism and anti-Semitism could be whipped up by the bishops and Catholic press, this did not mean that the political culture of the time was dominated by these sentiments. Despite the cynical remark of Mr Deasy in James Joyce's *Ulysses* that 'Ireland ... has the honour of being the only country which never persecuted the Jews ... because she never let them in', by 1926 there were 3,686 Jews in the Free State, and some politicians were close to the Jewish community. Indeed, during the War of Independence, Dermot Keogh suggested, Jews opted for the cause of radical Irish nationalism 'to a greater extent than is recognised'. In *Ulysses*, Joyce mischievously has Bloom come up with the idea of Sinn Féin, subsequently giving the idea to Arthur Griffith.[200] The truth was that, rather than slavishly following a Catholic triumphalist approach, behind the scenes there was more of an attempt to juggle obligation to minorities with the demands of some of the more extremist Catholic voices. The row, for example, over divorce in the Free State in 1923 was not a simple matter of the government removing the existing right of divorce. The transfer of powers from Westminster had included the possibility of petitioning for divorce through a private bill in the Dáil, and it became necessary to provide standing orders to deal with this, as with every other private bill. It was thus for the government more of a legal issue, but they were conscious that its abolition would be regarded as a poor indication of its determination to protect the rights of Protestants (who were not demanding extension of the facility). Cosgrave was accurate in suggesting that the confusion was about legal procedure rather than a debate about divorce on sectarian grounds, but when the Bishop of Cork got wind of it, it was he who claimed that Protestants were clamouring for divorce procedures.[201]

It was this that forced Cosgrave to receive advice from Archbishop Byrne of Dublin, who predictably informed him that it was not an option. The chairman of the Senate, Lord Glenavy, an ex-unionist landowner, who moved the motion against removing the standing order, was subsequently vilified in the Catholic press. This was a reminder that the Senate had been intended as a safeguard for minority interests, though some of the minority of Catholic extremists would have preferred to see it replaced by a House of Bishops. The same extremist contributors to publications turned what was a confusion about legal procedure into a sectarian bear pit by insisting disingenuously that there was a vast gulf between Catholics and Protestants on issues of personal morality. The political upshot was anything but an example of Catholic triumphalism; the government withdrew the proposed standing order and divorce by private bill remained technically possible, though the attempt was not taken up.[202]

How accurate was the prediction of W. B. Yeats that the responsibilities of self-government and the growth of political freedom would dissolve what he termed the 'iceberg' mentality of the Catholic majority towards minorities? Approximately 7 per cent of the population were registered as Protestants in the census of 1926, which represented a decline of about one third since 1911; most were found in the border counties and professional Dublin. There is little evidence of a mass emigration by Irish Protestants as a result of religious discrimination in the Irish Free State, though the rate of migration for Irish Protestants in the 1920s and 1930s was higher than that for Catholics. Most, it seemed, had adjusted to the new state and its governing party though without much enthusiasm. The *Church of Ireland Gazette* remained loyal but relatively mute. Protestants tended to enjoy separate social lives, while the *Irish Times* kept them abreast of imperial and royal affairs. Rather than focusing on reluctant acceptance, however, some historians, like F. S. L. Lyons, suggested there was a battle of two civilisations, Gaelic Ireland versus Anglo-Ireland, pointing to divergent publications such as the *Catholic Bulletin* and George Russell's *Irish Statesman*.[203]

Certainly, the idea that a single Gaelic culture existed was promoted by the *Catholic Bulletin*, which consistently attacked the government for not making the state more 'Catholic'. But the idea of a single Catholic and Gaelic culture overlooks the class divisions permeating Irish life between such groups as large and small farmers, and professions and trades, and within the middle classes. In essence, it overlooks the fact that Gaelic culture meant different things to different people. Devoted language revivalists, for example, were not necessarily representative of any sustainable 'mass' movement, given the continuous demand for English publications and English modes of entertainment. Russell's *Statesman* bemoaned the lack of cultural diversity and innovation in the new Free State and expressed a wish for a nationality that would incorporate a diversity of cultures. This was not a neat sectarian issue, however, being instead a common reaction of writers and artists to conservatism, as was the case in every other European country.

'indecent or obscene'?

It is also worth noting that certain legislation identified as being promoted exclusively by the Catholic Church against the interests or 'spirit' of Anglo-Ireland was in fact broadly supported by all churches. Representatives from the Protestant Church were included in consultations before the framing of such legislation. Censorship was one such example. The introduction of film censorship was passed quietly and without fuss in 1923, establishing the office of official censor of films and the censorship of films appeal board. Contemporary government memoranda, compiled after hearing deputations, tended to refer to an 'ever increasing body of public opinion', but the popularity of the cinema belied any so-called 'public revulsion'. Department of Justice files suggest that deputations to wholesalers to prevent the sale of English newspapers were unsuccessful, as was their 'enrolment' crusade.[204] More contentious, however, was the Censorship of Publications Act of 1929.

Lists of respected writers whose books were banned in this period may illustrate the dourness of Irish cultural life, but it should be acknowledged that much similar legislation existed elsewhere, supposedly as a 'purging antidote to the perceived permissiveness of the 1920s'.[205] But at the time it represented for many Irish writers a kind of betrayal, and biographers have recorded the personal frustration and humiliation that resulted, Maurice Harmon noting that Seán O'Faoláin 'felt infuriated and humiliated and regretted his mother's distress'.[206] The idea of two warring factions in relation to censorship – Catholic organisations such as the Catholic Truth Society and the Knights of Columbanus, versus liberal intellectuals such as Yeats, Shaw, O'Faoláin and Frank O'Connor – is superficially appealing. But it is highly unlikely that either elite represented the concerns of the general population, or was intimately connected to the reality of Irish readership habits and interests. Indeed, it is difficult to sustain the contention that it was censorship which primarily retarded the nation's intellectual development given that the country was served by an education system that excluded many. In the 1924/5 school year, there were 493,382 pupils on primary-school rolls and only 22,897 in secondary schools,[207] and there was no sustained demand for intellectual literature.

The 1929 Act came about as a result of an inquiry by the Committee on Evil Literature, established by Kevin O'Higgins in 1926, which included representatives from both the Catholic and Church of Ireland churches as well as three laymen. An indication of the evidence it heard was that over one quarter of its report was concerned with birth control and the circulation of information advocating the prevention of conception. The other main concern was to widen the definitions of 'indecent' and 'obscene', with a proposal for a board of from nine to twelve people, eventually in legislation reduced to five, to advise the Minister for Justice on books that were unsuitable for public consumption. Part two of the Act stated it was unlawful to print 'any indecent matter, the publication of which would be calculated to injure public morals', and material that advocated 'or might reasonably be supposed to advocate the unnatural prevention of conception or miscarriage, or any method, treatment or appliance to be used for such prevention or procurement'.[208]

This legislation was also influenced by the obsession of individuals like the Jesuit Richard Devane, who sought for legal standards of morality to be brought into greater harmony with the Ten Commandments. He energetically hunted out groups who would be interested in making submissions to the Committee. Whether or not such associations were representative of public opinion, they certainly had an influence on the government. A measure of their determination was that even after the legislation was introduced they were insisting that 'evil' literature was managing to evade the censors, though it should be noted that this extremism often irritated civil servants and government ministers, particularly the threatening and hectoring tone of some of the correspondence. In October 1929, the Department of Justice informed the Secretary of the Catholic Truth Society he could not undertake to refer to the Censorship of Publications Board a book 'merely because on one page out of four hundred there are a certain number of rhetorical questions recording doubts on the question of contraception running through the mind of the hero. The book, whilst it perhaps treads on delicate ground, could scarcely be called indecent or obscene.'[209]

That such impatience existed was important in the context of the eventual 1941 amendment to the Act, where it was laid down that when examining texts the Board had to take into consideration 'the literary, artistic, scientific or historic merit or importance and the general tenor' of the book. Even at the end of the 1920s cognisance was being taken of what was the main complaint against the Board – that it failed to take into account the overall book but could, and often did, ban it on the basis of an isolated paragraph, sentence or even word. While the pressure groups were successful in persuading governments in the late 1920s, future governments were to be found less susceptible to pressure.

Among those who opposed censorship were some of the most creative writers to emerge in Ireland in the twentieth century, who by their very nature were not going to be representative of the general public. The initial intellectual reaction centred on individuals such as Yeats, Russell, Oliver St John Gogarty and Bernard Shaw. Yeats, Ireland's greatest living poet, who may have entertained hopes of becoming Minister for Fine Arts, instead had to satisfy himself with an appointment to the Senate in December 1922. He had returned to live in Ireland in April 1922, encouraged by Lady Gregory, who felt the government could do with his support. Kevin O'Higgins had even envisioned a place for Yeats as a member of the Censorship of Films Board, though this never materialised.[210]

In a letter to William Cosgrave, in June 1923, Yeats expressed a concern that:

some of the recent art work which has received the official sanction of the Free State has not, we have reason to think, done justice to the real intellect and force of the Irish government. I would be greatly obliged if you would grant me an interview that I may lay before you a suggestion that might I think remedy this in future. I want to suggest to you the formation of an unpaid committee which could advise the government. Sir John Lavery [the artist] is prepared to act upon this committee, crossing to Ireland for the purpose whenever necessary, and both he and I are certain other artists of eminence would be ready to act.[211]

Yeats served as a senator until July 1928 and then left politics, disillusioned at the manner in which a prohibition ethos was developing, and formed the anti-censorship Irish Academy of Letters in 1932.

'made for the hillsides and the fields and the sea'

In any case, it cannot be said that Irish authors agreed on what was best for Ireland. The writer Liam O'Flaherty had criticised Russell's *Irish Statesman* in 1925 as being 'not national' or representative of the 'the cultural forces that are trying to find room for birth in this country at present'.[212] O'Flaherty, it seemed, wanted a symbolic art which would arouse patriotic sentiment; he informed foreign tourists in 1929 that the Irish peasant was the only honourable and natural type of human being in the country.[213] O'Flaherty's characters in such works as *The Informer* (1925) were corrupted by the city, which was inevitable because those coming to the city from rural areas 'were made for the hillsides and the fields and the sea. That's our life.' For O'Flaherty this was about the past, his interpretation of land very much bound up with the Aran Islands experience of the nineteenth century. And yet O'Flaherty was perhaps confused in his own approach to the theme of the Irish peasant and the issue of country versus city – he was angry at the American director Robert Flaherty's film *Man of Aran* because, in its presentation of idealised primitivism and individualism, it avoided dealing with the deep social divisions of the island.[214]

It was understandable that there was much confusion among writers in the 1920s given that independence had yet to be solidified and no one was sure how decolonisation would progress. But those who revered country above city life were well aware of the negative aspects of country life, despite what may have been written for the American tourist market. O'Flaherty's 1932 novel *Skerret* was the beginning of an engagement with not only the relationship between humanity and the soil, but also hunger and insubordination, obvious themes from his childhood. What he discovered, and what he articulated, was not the cosy rural consensus of Arensberg and Kimball, but, as with Peadar O'Donnell, a rural Ireland that had exchanged external masters for a native set. What was characteristic of the rural environment was, it seemed, conflicts over money, land hunger and sexual repression, rather than the peasants being, in Daniel Corkery's words, 'the descendants of greatness, and of a cultivated greatness', who were linked intrinsically with the noble Gaelic society of the past, and whose job it was to maintain the primacy of the countryside over the city.[215]

'passages of that brutal frankness'

Frank O'Connor too, retrospectively commenting on the Civil War period, disputed such idealisation: 'what neither group saw was that ... what we were bringing about was a new establishment of Church and state in which imagination would play no part and young men and women would emigrate to the ends of the earth, not because the country was poor but because it was mediocre'.[216] Such mediocrity was born of materialism and greed, seen by many writers as being the hallmark of the new state. Ironically, at the heart of it all stood Corkery's treasured Gael, no longer fuelling a pure nationalist ideology but representing meanness of spirit, controlled by, in Seán O'Faoláin's phrase, the 'hateful rigour' of Maynooth, training ground for Ireland's future priests. In O'Connor's *Guests of the Nation*, set during the War of Independence, the narrator finds that in the midst of patriotic deeds 'I was somehow very small and very lonely.'[217]

Seán O'Faoláin's *Midsummer Night Madness* was introduced controversially by Edward Garnett, who castigated the censorship, clerical domination and backwardness of Ireland. He praised the story, not just for its sensitiveness to place and emotional mood but because it was 'punctuated by passages of that brutal frankness which is the conscience of the new generation'. That 'conscience' created a tale which included the seduction of a young rebel by an Anglo-Irish lady, and an unsympathetic depiction of the IRA during the revolutionary era, a volunteer being challenged by one of their enemies who criticised their lack of success: 'Look at them today. As dirty as ever, as poor as ever, as backward as ever ... where are our crafts? What can we show? What have we ever done? Except dig ditches and plough fields?'[218] Nonetheless, there were those prepared to develop Corkery's thesis – the poet F. R. Higgins in his collection *The Dark Breed* argued strongly that 'the racial strength of a Gaelic aristocratic mind' with its 'vigorous colouring and hard emotion' was easily recognisable in Irish poetry, reflecting the richness of life and the 'intensity of a dark people still part of our landscape'; in other words, those of the Gaelic-speaking west of Ireland.[219]

Maintaining a false opposition of the country against the city was important in the maintenance of a conservative political culture. Although writers like Lady Gregory recognised the reality, they were reluctant to dismiss hope of a revival of a golden era. Synge had admitted:

> there are sides to all that Western life, the groggy patriot publican general shop man who is married to the priest's half sister and is second cousin once removed of the dispensary doctor that are horrible and awful ... all that side of the matter of course I left untouched in my stuff ... I sometimes wish I hadn't a soul and then I could give myself up to putting these lads on the stage ... in one place the people are starving, but wonderfully attractive and charming and in another place, when things are going well, one has a rampant double chinned vulgarity I haven't seen the like of.[220]

It was this vulgarity that Synge's literary successors seemed to be faced with, perhaps one of the reasons why, particularly in the case of O'Flaherty, O'Faoláin and O'Connor, they sought refuge in the short story. These generally dealt with childhood and showed reverence for a past rustic simplicity (though with attacks on the revolution recently fought), a more palatable creative exercise than dealing with what O'Faoláin saw as the moral decay of the present, a native, acquisitive middle class (though ironically he later became a writer of the Catholic upper-middle class). Fintan O'Toole pointed out that even city writing, especially in the tenements, particularly in the work of Seán O'Casey and George Fitzmaurice, was essentially 'urban drama in rural form in its presentation of self-contained communities'.[221]

'knitted with common life'?

The disillusionment of such writers was perhaps an inevitable part of post-revolution adjustment, which also seemed to involve the polarisation of intellectual pursuit into the political journal on the one hand, and literary endeavour on the other. It was one thing for George Russell to insist that he did not want cultural uniformity, but it was the very uniformity of purpose in a political sense that had galvanised such writers as active participants in the Irish revolution, and who were now living in a time of transition, relatively authoritarian government and economic insecurity. The revolutionary legacy was underpinned for some by the belief that the revolution was by no means complete.

Any ambitions writers had must be seen in the context of the insecurity of those who had, in a sense, arrived too late for the original literary revival. They respected it but were unsure of the value of its legacy. Terence Brown points out that in distinguishing his own generation of writers from those of the Yeats's era, Seán O'Faoláin wrote that his peers 'were faced with problems far more insistent: social, political and even religious; they 'had grown up in a period of revolution, were knitted with common life and could not evade its appeal. As time went on these problems became strangely acute.'[222]

Thus the accusation that the country had become sectarian, utilitarian and provincial. Much of it repulsed this generation and they came to realise relatively quickly that many of these aspects would not be rendered redundant under native rule. Another writer dealing with the harsh reality of rural existence was the poet Patrick Kavanagh, whose first poem to reach a wide audience appeared in the *Irish Statesman* in 1929, though it was not until the 1940s that the full extent of his realism would become apparent. In Austin Clarke's *Pilgrimage and Other Poems* (1929), anger at a suffocating societal approach to sexuality and religion were apparent. But artists were also, in looking to the past to depict a historical balance between Christianity and paganism, reflecting disappointed republican idealism mixed with a certain conservatism in wanting to be an essential part of the new state. Overall though, there was much resentment about the new middle class, whose version of nationalism was narrowly defined for the purposes of self-aggrandisement.[223]

Notwithstanding, *Dublin Opinion*, launched by two middle-class civil servants in 1922, achieved a circulation of 40,000 per month by 1926. The fact that the editors were permitted to lampoon the government with impunity pointed not only to a middle-class desire for satire but also to the political maturity of the state. It managed to ridicule both sides of the political divide, not only Ulster and Britain, but also the 'four horsemen of the Irish Apocalypse' – civil war, profiteering, taxation and unemployment. In sending up both rich and poor, it was ideal middle-class entertainment. It also savagely satirised the glorification of the Irish past with its series of 'peeps into Irish history'. Anne Dolan has suggested that this was the staple diet of a self-confident bourgeoisie – which the cultural historian Terence Brown denied existed – representing an Ireland that had been hidden by the revolution: Catholic and nationalist, but also smug and conceited.[224]

Some nationalist- and Catholic-sponsored publications also sought to profile the importance of Irish culture – the *Capuchin Annual,* launched in 1930, had an obvious nationalist allegiance, but relatively little religious content, and it prized high culture. Brian Kennedy observed that 'to be the subject of a series of tributes in the *Capuchin Annual* was to enter the pantheon of acclaimed Irish artists'.[225] Ireland's greatest writer, however, James Joyce, chose to live outside Ireland, and a misunderstanding of his genius was by no means confined to Ireland. The British Foreign Office had opened a secret file on Joyce in 1918, one so hostile to the writer that London considered revoking his British passport (which, had it happened, would have confined him to Ireland). In 1922 the English Director of Prosecutions, Archibald Bodkin, banned *Ulysses* after reading just 42 of its 732 pages and admitted he could not make 'head nor tail of it … I can discover no story'. The ban remained in force until 1936.[226] The book was also banned in the United States, and Virginia Woolf, it seemed, had judged it according to the social class of the author, thinking it was 'underbred' and 'reeling with indecency'.[227]

'never talking politics with a woman'

State-sponsored art was not a significant feature of the 1920s, with the exception of the Abbey Theatre, which in 1925 had accepted an annual grant of £850 from the government. The directors of the theatre had offered the theatre as a gift to the Irish government the previous year, as it was on the verge of bankruptcy. Partly because of its association with Yeats, it was also a republican target during the Civil War, when it was necessary for soldiers to be present to ensure the theatre stayed open. The government, particularly Ernest Blythe, decided to subsidise rather than take over the theatre, and the first director appointed was George O'Brien, Professor of National Economics at University College Dublin, which seemed to indicate that there was more of an interest in ensuring the financial rather than the artistic survival of the theatre.[228] Nonetheless, there were a series of successful plays in the 1920s, but the death of Lady Gregory, probably the most able Abbey director, and the success of the new Gate Theatre, as well as a change to a less sympathetic government, put the theatre under considerable strain. So did pressure from Irish-American lobbyists, who claimed that *The Playboy of the Western World* and *Juno and the Paycock*, by Synge and O'Casey respectively, did nothing to elevate the Irish character, holding up drunken and foul-mouthed murderous Irish characters to be scoffed at by foreign audiences. The truth was that the Abbey had a tendency to reject what was new and different in Irish theatre, not through government pressure, but because of its dependency on populist taste and its association with conservative management and sometimes players. Seán O'Casey's *The Shadow of a Gunman*, presented in 1923 at the height of the Civil War, was a huge success, as was his *Juno and the Paycock* the following year, and the Abbey seemed to be reaching working-class audiences for the first time.

But it was O'Casey's third full-length play, *The Plough and the Stars,* which opened in 1926, that saw a return to riots at the Abbey. It would be too simplistic to see it as a spontaneous protest against the appearance of a prostitute and the tricolour (the national flag) in a pub, and individual 'offensive' lines, despite Yeats's appearance on stage to tell the audience they had disgraced themselves again. The producer and many of the cast had objected to the language, and criticism was not directed from anti-intellectual quarters, being led by feminist and pacifist Hanna Sheehy Skeffington. It was a play that dealt with the 1916 Rising in the context of the underbelly of Dublin tenement life, and most importantly: 'it did not glorify those who fought for Irish freedom at a time when many of them were hungry for glory'. The government's representative on the Abbey board, George O'Brien, attempted to censor the play, but Gregory made it clear that she placed more value on artistic freedom than government subsidy. It was a battle Gregory and Yeats won: the play continued to be staged, the theatre remained full for subsequent performances, and the government subsidy was not lost. Significantly, in contrast to the aftermath of the *Playboy* riots, there was no public debate at the theatre, perhaps because, as was noted by Colm Tóibín, most of the rioters were women and Gregory had a rule of 'never talking politics with a woman'.[229]

Writers including O'Flaherty, F. R. Higgins and Austin Clarke complained to the newspapers about O'Casey's exploitation of the working class in the tradition of an outdated Anglo-Irish literature.

Perhaps the Abbey shared in the cultural confusion, being accused of staging anti-national plays and yet defending artistic freedom, but this overlooks the fact that Yeats's speech was well planned in advance. He thrived on shocking Dublin, and in any case he was not committed to the work of O'Casey, his snobbery leading him to ignore and patronise the playwright. He was in general dictatorial about which plays should and should not be staged; perhaps he was confirming Seán O'Faoláin's observation on the generational gap, wanting poetic visions rather than the realism that marked young Irish writing. The Abbey rejected O'Casey's *The Silver Tassie* in 1928 (which he believed was his best work). O'Casey was understandably furious at Yeats's insistence that the playwright knew nothing of the Great War because 'you never stood on its battlefields', and after O'Casey published the correspondence between the two in the *Observer*, the controversy extended to Britain and America.[230] O'Casey was subsequently to suggest that government censorship of literature could not be much worse than the effective censorship of Yeats, and kitchen comedies were to remain the staple Abbey diet.

There was considerable pressure on the state's new radio service, 2RN, and its 18 employees to do their bit in the quest for national revival. Maurice Gorham, an early employee, recalled that the station was:

> expected to do a great many things that were not demanded of other national radio services, most of them far better equipped. It was expected not merely to reflect every aspect of national activity but to create activities that did not yet exist. It was expected to revive the speaking of Irish; to foster a taste for classical music; to revive traditional music; to keep people on the farms; to sell goods and services of all kinds from sausages to sweep tickets; to provide a living and a career for writers and musicians; to reunite the Irish people at home and those overseas; to end partition. All this in addition to broadcasting's normal duty to inform, educate and entertain. And all in a programme amounting (if advertising time was excluded) to some five and a half hours a day.[231]

'not of any spontaneous force emanating from the Irish-speaking districts'

The most notable government-sponsored initiative in the field of culture was the attempt to revitalise the use of the Irish language. The Constitution of 1922 had recognised Irish as the national language but gave equal recognition to the English language. Irish-language proficiency was compulsory for entrance to the civil service from 1925 onwards. Prior to independence, it was the Irish National Teachers' Organisation, encouraged by Timothy Corcoran, the anglophobic Professor of Education at University College Dublin, who sought to take responsibility for raising the status of Irish, and suggested that in infant classes all work should be done through Irish. A conference in 1925 classified schools according to the degree to which Irish was used as a medium of instruction, with salary increments for teachers more competent in Irish, leading to teachers flocking to government-funded summer schools. By 1926 approximately 50 per cent of primary-school teachers had achieved a standard of Irish that was regarded as satisfactory. Of the 2,000 members of the Association of Secondary Teachers in Ireland in 1922, one third had no Irish.[232] In the 1920s the Gaeltacht (now defined by the state as electoral divisions where more than 80 per cent of the people were able to speak Irish) had a population of only 165,000 while the population of the partly Irish-speaking areas was estimated at 295,000 (it was not until 1956 that the government drew a line on the map to define the Gaeltacht geographically).[233]

Eoin MacNeill, Minister for Education in 1925, drafted an essay on the 'Vicissitudes of the Irish Language' and set the historical context for the problem: 'under a political ban for three centuries, the use of Irish became restricted to expressing the needs of religion, of rural life. Excluded from the great world of modern politics and science and industrial development, it did not keep pace with these in vocabulary and terminology.'[234] There were thus the problems of the absence of a standardised language in spelling, grammar and terminology, many of which were not solved until the 1950s. The Irish-language crusade failed to regenerate economically the Gaeltacht or to ensure Gaeltacht children would enjoy equality of opportunity, or that the state apparatus in the Gaeltacht would be marked by competent Irish-speakers. The failure to involve native Irish-speakers in the formulation of a solution was also notable. The *Leader* concluded in 1928 that 'the modern Irish language revival was the result of an Anglo-Irish conviction and not of any spontaneous force emanating from the Irish-speaking districts'.[235]

'the evicted tenants of the race'?
Initially, there had been even more of an urgency about the issue because of the acceptance of partition, the attempt at revival being Cumann na

nGaedheal's attempt to demonstrate their commitment to a distinctive nationalist ideal. Though it was a genuine conviction rather than an opportunistic appeal to national sentiment, it is necessary to distinguish between those who were committed to the language itself and those who saw it as more important for political reasons. The most notable activities of the Gaelic League were campaigns against the appointment of non-Irish-speakers to educational or cultural posts, as they aligned themselves with the zealots of the *Catholic Bulletin*. The fact that the key figure behind the revival was Ernest Blythe was significant, as he was also Minister for Finance; a man committed to an Irish culture based on high aesthetic principles rather than the mucky localism of the dwindling Gaelic League brigade; a man who preferred experimentation to propaganda. His statement to the Bureau of Military History, which ran to over 200 pages, significantly began with the sentence: 'I had always wanted to learn the Irish language', and as an Ulster Protestant he immersed himself in the activities of the language revival, seeing it as an essential part of the Irish revolution.[236]

The real obstacle to the Irish-language policy was the failure of adults to make the language a part of their daily lives, which had much to do with the grim and stern manner in which the issue was presented. The determination to impose compulsion in the schools did little to whet the appetite. Rather than presenting it as an enjoyable part of native culture, a hectoring approach was adopted by governments. Their rhetoric was contradictory, implying that Gaeltacht inhabitants held the nation's reserves of piety, heroism and the ancient characteristics of the race, but also that the same people were standing in the way of the ideal nation, a favourite phrase being the 'slave mentality'. Ernest Blythe was eventually to blame parents for continually complaining about the teachers of the language in the presence of their children. It was to children, too young to object and too young to have absorbed Anglocentric culture, that the government looked. But it was this focus, and the association of education policy almost solely with the Irish language, that created resentment and deprived children of a broader education.

It was also an economic issue. A correspondent of MacNeill informed him in 1933 that 'unless the government can keep them in a state of comparative comfort in their own homes they will leave those homes and lose the language'.[237] The government gave this issue considerable attention. In 1925 a Gaeltacht Commission, under the chairmanship of Richard Mulcahy, discovered a low standard of national schools and lack of secondary schools, with no children proceeding to university from the Gaeltacht areas. For all the recommendations that were made regarding improved access, and the appointment of Irish-speakers to the civil service and army, the economic reality was that children had to be taken out of the education system after primary level to work. This was the real problem and not, as the commission seemed to believe, that priests and teachers were using English, leading to a belief that inhabitants of the Gaeltacht were not valued highly enough. The commission seemed more interested in the language than the speakers; despite detailed economic statistics, one fisherman was the only local recorded as having given evidence. Instead, the commission reverted to the well-worn tradition of praising a destitute but heroic people: 'These people are not only uneconomic holders, but they are the evicted tenants of the race. Through all their particular vicissitudes they have, in preserving the national language as their traditional speech, carried with them an undeniable title and claim to a footing in the soil of their country.'

To the government's credit, following the publication of the Gaeltacht Commission report in 1926, considerable progress was made in the area of agriculture through the work of the Land Commission, and assistance was given to the fishing and textile industries. Some industrial centres were established in the Gaeltacht areas, a far-sighted initiative ahead of its time, though most of the projects were small-scale. But the overall failure to distinguish between social and economic problems and language revival issues rankled with certain members of the Gaeltacht community. This resentment was later articulated in An t-Éireannach, the first Irish-language weekly newspaper published in the Gaeltacht. It had a circulation of only 500 and was shunned by the 'official' Irish-language movement because it highlighted the realities of poverty for the ordinary people of the Gaeltacht, which stood in marked contrast to the romanticism of the Dublin-centric Gaelic League. In highlighting the speakers rather than the language itself, it reaffirmed that language revival was a social and economic issue rather than a cultural and educational one. It was no coincidence that the paper also condemned the excessive centralisation of European administrators and governments and the resultant lack of empathy with the majority of citizens.[238]

The government wished to convert the western grasslands into economic holdings, to have a band of Irish-speaking families from east to west, and to settle English-speaking families with claims to land outside the Gaeltacht. But the Land Commission recognised this was not feasible, and that it was inequitable to distinguish between Irish- and English-speaking families in this matter. Whatever about a commitment to Gaelicisation, being sponsors of eviction in rural Ireland could not be countenanced by any native government.

By 1931, 38 per cent of teachers still had no formal qualification in Irish, while only 30 per cent were qualified to use Irish as a medium of instruction. Blythe concluded: 'we have to do the best that we can with them, but a great many of them are hardly competent even to teach Irish satisfactorily'.[239] The percentage of national schools that used Irish as a medium of instruction rose from 4 per cent in 1930 to 12 per cent in 1940 and fell to 11 per cent in 1950, while the voluntary use of Irish in the civil service remained small-scale. A 1935–6 inter-departmental commission into the matter concluded that 'with the exception of offices who are employed in Irish-using sections, which have been set up by certain departments, the majority of civil servants find little occasion to use Irish in their official duties'.[240] The focus remained on compulsion in the national schools and a reduction of time allotted to other subjects in order to make time for Irish, a language few of these children (so many of whom would emigrate) would find little practical use for. A cynical contributor to the *Bell* magazine in 1942, under the title 'Twenty years a-withering', suggested: 'Publishing a Gaelic newspaper with horse-racing news, making Gaelic compulsory in all official functions, publishing in Gaelic all books banned by the censor, and finally, if all measures failed, making it a crime to speak Gaelic. Overnight, the Irish people's militancy would be brought back to life.'[241]

'grows green beneath thy sparkling dew'

Governments of the 1920s also had a concern with how Ireland's nationality was presented abroad, though little progress was made with the vexed question of a new national anthem. In June 1924, the *Dublin Evening Mail* suggested Ireland needed a new anthem, but the standard of entries to their competition was so abysmal that the judges, including Yeats and James Stephens, decided none of the entries was worthy. Following a further competition in 1925, the winning song was utterly clichéd, the chorus running: 'God of our Ireland by whose hand her glory and her beauty grew, just as the Shamrock o'er the land, grows green beneath thy sparkling dew.'[242] Given such a standard it was understandable that it was decided to stick with 'The Soldier's Song', which was played at the close of transmission of Radio Éireann, the state's new broadcasting service from 1926. It seemed to be too difficult to find a 'safe' anthem which wouldn't ignite political agitation.

There was controversy in 1929 when Trinity College invited the Governor General (the Crown's representative in Ireland), James McNeill, to their college sports. The college suggested that a rendition of 'God Save the King' rather than 'The Soldier's Song' was appropriate for the occasion. McNeill maintained that as the monarch's Irish representative, he should be greeted with 'The Soldier's Song'. Although Trinity conceded the option of playing neither anthem, McNeill instead declined the invitation, on the advice of the Irish government.[243]

Despite such controversy, the previous year Ireland's gold medallist in the hammer event at the Olympic Games expressed joy at his win, not for the victory itself, but because the world had been shown that 'Ireland has a flag, that Ireland has a national anthem, in fact, that we have a nationality'.[244]

While the Gaelic Athletic Association continued to be a dynamic force in Irish sporting endeavour, and was important in healing Civil War divisions, it had ceded its role in athletics to the National Athletic and Cycling Association of Ireland, which was amalgamated into the Irish Amateur Athletic Association. This meant that for the first time there was a single governing authority for Irish athletics, North and South (an Irish Olympic Council was established at the same time), though a subsequent rift with Ulster members led them to establish a Northern Ireland AAA. Much to the chagrin of the Free State, this was formally recognised by the English AAA. The refusal of the Free State to recognise it, and its insistence on a 32-county organisation, led to the Free State's dismissal from the International Amateur Athletics Federation, which meant there was no Irish team at Hitler's Olympic Games in Berlin in 1936. It was not in fact until 1952 that the International Olympic Committee conceded the right of Irish citizens born in Northern Ireland to compete for Ireland, just one example of the 'cold war' that existed between North and South during these years.

The political turmoil of these years inevitably had an impact on Irish sport, though the Gaelic Athletic Association recovered relatively quickly, despite its failure to relax the ban and failed attempts to bring the two sides of the Civil War together. While in 1922 the playing fields of the GAA were practically deserted, they had made a significant recovery by the summer of 1923, though many of the Ulster clubs remained in a disorganised state until well into the 1920s. Catholic priests seem to have become more and more involved in the national organisation. Croke Park in Dublin was developed into a formidable stadium after 1924, while the decision to inaugurate national league games in hurling and football in 1925 ensured a level of interest in the games from the end of one championship season to the start of another. In August 1926, with the arrival of Irish radio, an all-Ireland hurling semi-final became the 'first radio commentary outside America on a field game'.[245]

There was much pageant and sentimentality associated with the organisation of the Tailteann Games in August 1924, the revival of an idea first raised in the 1880s of showcasing Irish sports and pastimes such as hurling, football, handball, athletics and shinty. Although the Games were not controlled by the GAA, it played a major part in organising the 16–day festival, and it brought the Association closer to the government, some of whose members enthusiastically endorsed the Games. There was trouble, however, when it came to organised soccer, with a split in the Football Association of Ireland. Free State newspapers continued to carry advertisements for matches in Dublin as being under the auspices of the Football League of Ireland, while games in Belfast were referred to as 'Belfast and district'. The FAI was determined to remain the governing body for the whole country, but noted in its 1926–7 report: 'It is regretted no improvement in the relations of the two associations can be recorded. The stupid policy of labelling the small northern province as "Ireland" continues to be favoured by England, Scotland and Wales so that the Northern Association has no incentive to come to an agreement.'[246]

'a lot of cloudy waffle about indivisible crowns'

The Free State achieved more success at international level. Anglo-Irish and Commonwealth concerns were one preoccupation, but membership of the League of Nations and Ireland's bilateral European contacts were also important. Nonetheless, within the League, many Irish actions and decisions sought to clearly demonstrate the Free State's independence of other dominions, but especially of Britain. The Irish campaign of 1923–4 to register the Anglo-Irish Treaty with the League was an example of this strategy. Beyond this, however, the early years of membership were undistinguished; a fact admitted by Ernest Blythe, a delegate to the

1926 Assembly, who conceded frankly: 'during the last two years Ireland has been absolutely negligible at the Assembly neither saying or doing anything whatsoever'.[247] The Irish representatives sought to rectify this in the next few years, by increasing preparation and staff numbers, with Irish delegates soon active in League committees on internal League reform, codification of international law and League economic policy. They were also successful in 1930 in getting elected as a non-permanent member of the League Council. The permanent Irish representative at Geneva, Seán Lester, was subsequently appointed League Commissioner at Danzig, a significant tribute to the standing of Ireland abroad.

It was also the case that in such a small diplomatic service resourcefulness was required at all times. At one international gathering a Free State minister, Patrick McGilligan, a poor speaker of French, having checked his place at the formal dinner in advance, discovered he was seated between two fluent French-speakers who knew no English. He promptly swapped his place-setting with one from another table to ensure that he sat between two English-speaking delegates.[248] While Cumann na nGaedheal ministers undoubtedly attempted to extend the parameters of the Treaty to increase their independence in international affairs, Joe Lee makes the point that the dismantling of the Treaty had more to do with 'the attitude of Australia and South Africa in demanding greater autonomy for dominions achieved through the Statute of Westminster (which prevented Britain from legislating for the dominions), than with any direct development in Anglo-Irish relations'.[249] This has been disputed by Deirdre McMahon, who maintains that the Canadians, Irish and South Africans were much more active in demanding autonomy than the Australians. The representatives of the Irish Free State were active in the Imperial conferences of 1926, 1929 and 1930. McMahon argued that what successive Irish governments wanted was precision regarding the constitutional independence of the Commonwealth, but what they got (until they left the Commonwealth in 1948) was 'a lot of cloudy waffle about indivisible crowns and indissoluble unity'.[250]

The Free State also had much work to do if it was to market Ireland abroad as a desirable holiday location. Tourism was regarded by some in the 1920s as the greatest of Ireland's undeveloped resources, waiting to be exploited. The London Midland and Scottish Railway Company had made one of Paul Henry's paintings (which depicted a frugal though it seemed satisfying landscape) into a poster promoting tourism, helping to create what became a typical view of the Irish landscape: idyllic rustic scenes unsullied by technological modernisation.[251] An Irish Tourist Association was established in January 1925 (which Craig told the Northern Irish Tourist Board they were to remain aloof from[252]), at a time when the tourist trade was worth only three quarters of a million pounds to the Irish exchequer. There were nearly 600 hotels in Ireland, but standards of hygiene, comfort and irregular classification and charges were a problem. So was the fact that, although Ireland was one of the culturally richest countries in western Europe in terms of the remains of antiquity, art and architecture, and a capital city situated so close to the sea, many of these assets were not being protected or preserved properly, perhaps unsurprising given the material poverty of the state. And then there was the food. A contemporary observer noted: 'our food is simple without being good, never ingenious and not always agreeable. Hotels and restaurants but reflect this general or national defect.'[253] The new tourist board had much work to do.

FIVE

1932-1945

'an almost Stalinist antagonism to modernism'?
Social historians should be sceptical of the phrase 'de Valera's Ireland', often used to describe the 1930s and 1940s. The research of a new generation has undermined the validity of simplistically labelling Irish society in terms of the political personalities of the era. While the political context changed considerably with the electoral triumph of Fianna Fáil in 1932, there was also much continuity, and many of the issues associated with maximising cultural and political sovereignty were in practice merely an extension of the solid, if sometimes flawed, state-building of the 1920s.

Contradictions abounded during these years, particularly the gulf between the vision and the actual limitations of the new political party, Fianna Fáil, which presented itself as the champion of the dispossessed, or the 'men of no property'. Despite Ireland's supposed glorious isolation, it was often external events – political and economic but also cultural – which decided the parameters of the Irish social experience, culminating in the Emergency (1939–45), a word used to describe the period of the Second World War, when Ireland remained neutral. Despite neutrality, the years of the war have rightly been recognised as something of a watershed in Irish life. It highlighted many of the contradictions of the era: a period when, in theory, Ireland went its own way, but also an era that shattered the illusion that Ireland could continue to plan for the future on the basis of unfettered independence from the rest of the world.

Vitriol pervaded the politics of these years, as those who had taken the losing side in the Treaty debates and subsequent Civil War returned to dominate parliamentary politics for 16 years. Fianna Fáil convincingly sold the electorate a simple message, but the party was a complex coalition of traditionalists, modernisers, visionaries, conservatives, radicals, cranks and optimists; a party which denied it was a sectional grouping, asserting to the contrary that it was a national movement. While increased cultural sovereignty and a heightened sense of Irish identity may have gathered new momentum when the party gained power, the issues which dominated the politics of the 1920s – most notably stability and security – continued to be equally relevant. When deemed necessary, threats to the stability of the state were responded to with ruthless force, and the Department of Justice files of the era reveal an exceptionally high level of low-intensity violence. There certainly were new ideas on economics, the role of the state and the relationship with Great Britain, but Ronan Fanning was also accurate in asserting that the 1937 Constitution was a validation of values established over 15 years of Irish independence, and not just the priorities of Fianna Fáil after taking office in 1932.[1]

Those who considered themselves the real political radicals found little solace in Ireland of the 1930s, and a literary minority were prone to asserting that, whatever about the extent of political sovereignty, there remained a paucity of indigenous intellectual creativity. In the phrase of Thomas MacGreevy, delivering a lecture to the Irish Society in London in 1934, there was 'no Irish cultural republic; no republic of the Irish mind'. A more stark rendition of this complaint was offered by Terence Brown in the late 1970s when he referred to Ireland in the 1930s as experiencing 'an almost Stalinist antagonism to modernism ... combined with prudery and a deep reverence for the Irish past'.[2] Such emotive rhetoric does little justice to the complex layers of Irish society during this era. Equally unsatisfactory is Tom Garvin's assertion that while, figuratively speaking, a Catholic elite was replaced with people from humbler backgrounds, the stagnation of Ireland in this period was the result of the dreams of de Valera of 'a moral community which was authentic, egalitarian, pious, static and intellectually homogeneous'.[3] In fact there was a robust, if ultimately ineffective, opposition to what was becoming a crusade for complete state centralisation on the part of Irish governments. This opposition was often expressed by Catholic social theorists or proponents of vocational organisation (or devolution), and though it was not developed to a sophisticated or indeed practical degree, it is quite legitimate to see it as a Catholic intellectualism which was sometimes loud and self-conscious.

Such debates, however, were inevitably conducted at an elite level. Survival and subsistence remained the goal for the majority of what Seán O'Faoláin was to refer to as the 'plain people of Ireland'.[4] Their idealisation exposed further contradictions, particularly given that the rhetoric extolling them – de Valera was apt to stress that the Irish genius had always stressed spiritual and intellectual rather than material values – was not always matched by a practical commitment to their welfare. The Economic War of the 1930s over a refusal to pay land annuities to the British government may have exacerbated class tensions in rural Ireland, but in the cities (particularly in Dublin) the middle class remained comfortable.

And yet, there were socially progressive aspects to the policies of Fianna Fáil. These were evident in its commitment to use land legislation to empower the Land Commission to expropriate land deemed suitable for redistribution among small farmers. They also introduced measures to improve housing, increase unemployment assistance, and provide for the aged, blind and widowed. These initiatives coincided with a continuance of censorship and laws governing sexual morality, and an overt discrimination against women in the workforce. From the perspective of cynics writing in the 1980s, it was 1930s oppression, and a failure to modernise, which meant that Ireland was simply not an interesting place to live during this era. This, as Brian Fallon has recognised, ignores the degree of cultural vitality that continued to exist in Ireland; and just because much of this culture was imported does not mean it should be ignored. Popular tastes were in fact dominated by Anglo-American culture, undermining the contention that Ireland was 'a chauvinistic statelet shutting its doors and windows on international currents'.[5]

'he hasn't been seen lately in the lanes of Limerick'

Despite nationalist rhetoric, most remained utterly pragmatic about their priorities. Things that were regularly denounced by the Church – cinema and imported tabloid newspapers, for example – were loudly criticised precisely because they were so popular. People continued to be quite capable of distinguishing between their theoretical devotion to faith and patriotism, and their practice. For all those who bowed to intimidation there were those like the mother of novelist John Banville who was, he recalled, 'one of the last breed of Irish Catholics who were more pagan than Christian. She treated priests with a mixture of deference and cloaked distaste; they were fine in their place, she said, but you wouldn't want to have them in the house.'[6] Likewise, for all those who endured the poverty of the era and silently acquiesced in the Church-sponsored sanctification of poverty (sometimes it seemed to be presented as a national asset), there were those, like Frank McCourt, who later got a sort of revenge by exposing the cruelty of class bias in Irish life. His 1996 memoir, *Angela's Ashes*, was blunt about the chasm between theory and practice: 'Mam says she's sure God is good for someone, somewhere, but he hasn't been seen lately in the lanes of Limerick,' or 'If you tell her the child is dying in your arms she'll say the doctor is in the country riding his horse.'[7]

Perhaps it was only towards the end of the century that some of McCourt's generation could begin to deal with the difficult and cruel aspects of society's failure during this era to place a premium on equality. There was no shortage of detractors lining up to criticise McCourt's book in the 1990s. Roy Foster suggested that McCourt, 'apparently trading on misery, actually sells on synthetic moral uplift, contributing to the genre of idealised Irish personal history ... if any message is to be read out of the book, it is that you have to get out early as you can and head west.'[8] The weakness of this criticism is that it fails to acknowledge that for many this was a necessity rather than a choice.

Of course it was not all despair. Despite legislative discrimination and the confinement of women to a limited sphere, the successful attempts to organise women collectively to further their comfort and status have been overlooked. There was diversity as well as commonality in the Ireland of this era, behind the labels and artificially defined monoliths. There were rabidly nationalist and Catholic editorials as well as brave publications which sought a return to George Russell's idea of recognising the hybridity of Irish society. There were assertions of the necessity of matching revolutionary spirit with the intellectual and moral qualities to ensure its success; attempts to look abroad for social, cultural and economic ideas. Elite debates about censorship or contraception were of little relevance to the majority, who carried on reading the westerns and romances they desired and having the children they felt duty-bound to. It was also the case that those with impeccable Catholic and nationalist credentials were just as likely to be censored if they exposed filth, poverty and discrimination.

'the only hope of securing political peace and social progress'?

What Fianna Fáil preached and practised remained central to some of the ambiguities and contradictions outlined above. The kind of sentiments expressed by de Valera on self-sufficient frugal living were not necessarily backward when one considers some of the more extreme ideas being propagated in parts of Europe in the 1930s. Perhaps it was an image which gained a broad acceptance precisely because it masked the diversity in the ranks of de Valera's team. Within Fianna Fáil, one could find de Valera celebrating a chance to implement the teaching of James Connolly and using the airwaves (in a very modern way) to articulate elements of his pastoral image; while his Minister for Education, Tomás Derrig, insisted that the idiom of Irish music could give expression to sentiment not experienced by Bach or Beethoven. His Minister for Industry and Commerce, Seán Lemass, aggressively sought to fill the green hamlets with factories, while the long-winded Minister for Finance, Seán MacEntee, sat in the Shelbourne Hotel bar sipping dry sherry, looking like a Tory straight out of the House of Commons.

The truth was that Irish ministers in the 1930s were quite capable of taking action with little reference to ideology, despite the claim of de Valera at the hustings that no man was worth more than £1,000 a year. If private capital would work better in some areas and state intervention in others, then both would be used; if women were useful in employment in some spheres but curtailing the employment of men in others, then they would be both encouraged and prevented. Civil protest would be encouraged when seeking office but civil rights sometimes ignored when in office. It is therefore no surprise that pragmatism has been one of the words continually associated with the essence of Fianna Fáil, a party that within a year of its foundation in 1926 had established 1,307 branches nationwide. It has also eluded an agreed classification by political scientists; but the essence of its success in the 1930s and beyond involved building support across class boundaries which enabled it to manage class conflict more effectively. It took advantage of the weakness of class politics in Ireland by developing a language which seemed occasionally socialist, but practices which were comfortably capitalist, undermining a Labour Party which adopted the rhetoric of welfarism but seemed devoid of plans for economic growth.[9]

In presenting themselves as saviours of the working classes, Fianna Fáil also managed to portray those who advocated class politics as champions of an exploitation that would hinder the development of a strong and autonomous trade union movement. Fianna Fáil, having broken the connection with the old Sinn Féin, also learned from the mistakes of that movement, particularly regarding Sinn Féin's lack of attention to social policy and the failure to think in terms of a long-term strategy. Two other essential ingredients in their success were discipline within the ranks and skilful leadership, which is why so much attention has justifiably been given to the career and methods of de Valera, who from the mid-1920s became the greatest political tactician of twentieth-century Ireland.

Fianna Fáil also benefited from the integrative effects of Catholicism in a state that was so religiously homogeneous. Before the 1932 general election, the Cork academic Alfred O'Rahilly, in a stinging rebuke of Cumann na nGaedheal, insisted:

> Everyone who has the temerity to disagree with the present ministers is declared to be an indifferent Catholic, a dishonest lawyer, an indiscriminate economist ... even at the risk of excommunication, I declare publicly that unless President Cosgrave and the fellow members of his new-fangled synod give up their attempt to intimidate us by issuing impertinent Lenten pastorals, unless they proceed to argue fairly and squarely against the perfectly legitimate alternative policy put forward by their opponents, I for one am going, for the first time, to vote for Fianna Fáil as the only hope of securing political peace and social progress in this country.[10]

Given the victory of Fianna Fáil in 1932, his sentiments were likely to have been shared by a significant proportion of the Irish electorate, who in giving Fianna Fáil 44 per cent of first-preference votes were rejecting the idea that Cumann na nGaedheal knew what was good for the people better than the people themselves. But the fear (and loathing) of de Valera was understandable in the context of the previous decade. The IRA, whilst maintaining its insistence on a 32-county republic, suggested with satisfaction that 'the terrorist rule of traitors is being superseded by the peaceful rule of honest men',[11] a verdict they would soon drop.

In the run-up to the 1932 election, individual Fianna Fáil members had been apt to sing from different hymn sheets depending on the audience. In different weeks in February 1932, for example, de Valera promised social radicalism but pledged that private property would be safeguarded as well as by a Fianna Fáil government as by a Cumann na nGaedheal government. But he also claimed that the state had a right to interfere when private property was being worked against the interests of the community.[12] Meanwhile Seán Lemass, architect of the famous phrase that Fianna Fáil was 'a slightly constitutional party', had suggested, according to the *Irish Times*, that Fianna Fáil policy was 'a constructive alternative to communism'. Cumann na nGaedheal, of course, was quick to pounce on associations with anything unorthodox, claiming on a front-page advertisement on election day in 1932 that 'the gunmen and the communists are voting for Fianna Fáil today'.[13] (In fact, those who voted for communists made little impact in 1932, and the three general election candidates for the party were defeated.)

'democracy is not just a technique to be improved by technicians'
In February 1932 the *New York Times* suggested that the secret of de Valera was that he was 'anything but a firebrand, this mild, academic, lean and tight-lipped man who lectures his audience and leaves it to his lieuten-ants to revive emotions of more troubled times'.[14] Whatever about the degree to which the past was invoked during this period, de Valera was intent on articulating a commitment to social and economic change while maintaining the apparatus of the state that had been inherited by Fianna Fáil. They not only won the general election of 1932, but a further 'snap' general election of 1933 which increased their vote. De Valera also retained a penchant for phrases such as 'as far as is practicable', and a nationalism which seemed to have a basis in nineteenth-century philosophies, particu-larly with regard to the importance of a distinctive national language and a reversal of the extent to which English culture had permeated Ireland. He invoked the Christian and Catholic theme of Irish identity to empha-sise Ireland's moral superiority in this sphere. In reality this was a defen-sive reaction to the fact that the two countries had much in common, or what Freud called the 'narcissism of trivial differences': exaggerating the relatively minor differences in order to mask obvious similarities.[15]

De Valera seemed to work on two levels. He maintained his distance from notions of devolved government or decentralisation, because they would challenge the type of strong centralised and bureaucratic state that Fianna Fáil was comfortable with. But he was also careful not to disassociate himself publicly from the concept of local autonomy because its proponents shared much of the language he used about the need to regenerate rural life and revitalise demoralised communities. In tandem with this, he was practical enough to recognise that economic leadership and institutional continuity in areas such as banking practice were desirable. The report of the Banking Commission, published in August 1938, pleased him because it endorsed the status quo, despite his criticisms of Cumann na nGaedheal in the 1920s for following a system they had inherited from Britain. The reality was that de Valera believed in state control of all areas of Irish life. This continuity had also been seen in the civil service, when the Brennan Commission of 1936 blandly reinforced the status quo.

There was a striking change in the language used after the consolidation of power, with the desire to work the existing machinery of government rather than restructure it. In 1940 (albeit during the Emergency), in a radio broadcast, de Valera asserted that 'the very notion of the state is futile if it not be conceded that there exists within the state one single and sovereign power having the supreme right effectively to co-ordinate all wills in the pursuit of the common end'.[16] Despite the attention historians have given to de Valera's reflections on the rural idyll, it is this sort of sentiment that is much more relevant to an analysis of state power in Ireland in the 1930s and 1940s. These centralising tendencies were not just picked up by eminent Catholic intellectuals (see below) and politicians like James Dillon, who criticised the increased tendency to rule by ministerial order, but also academics like the Cork historian James Hogan, who centred his intellectual endeavour on the relationship between ethics and the coercive power of government.

This was an understandable preoccupation with those who had experienced such a blurring of the lines between civilian and military power during the revolution. Hogan was one of the few commentators in the 1930s who advocated an alliance between Fianna Fáil and Fine Gael (as Cumann na nGaedheal became after 1934) in order to re-create the revolutionary period opposition to British influence; and by the 1940s he had become an admirer of strong authoritarian governments.[17] In any case, Fianna Fáil shared the distaste that Cumann na nGaedheal had shown for decentralisation and popular representation, summed up in Seán Lemass's memorable contention that the Irish people needed a strong central government owing to their 'fissiparous tendencies',[18] one of a number of profoundly anti-democratic sentiments expressed during this era. They had little time for the view of Seán O'Faoláin that 'this combination of the influence of fear and the desire for power is a typically bourgeois synthesis ... democracy is not just a technique to be improved by technicians. It is a state of mind or it is nothing.'[19]

'poor by reason of the fact that they served the state'

Despite the Fianna Fáil party building up a formidable organisational network that was very much based on localism, some in the party effectively wanted to abolish local government. A government memorandum from 1933 suggested not only that local government was an unfortunate relic of British rule, but that 'governmental intervention and supervision is now feasible in respect of all national activities. The retention of local government bodies is, therefore, gradually becoming an expensive anachronism.' Administration of taxation and social services, it suggested, should be completely reviewed, and any such review 'would logically point to the complete abolition of local governing bodies and the merger of their functions with those of the central government'.[20]

The significance of such sentiments transcended their obvious illustration of a government fed up with what it viewed as irksome and expensive local councils. At their core was a belief in the necessity of a powerful central state. It was equally significant that frank views on centralism were being expressed in the 1930s, the decade in which totalitarianism flourished. Many contemporary Catholic intellectuals were gravely worried about the implications of such views, but were faced with the dilemma of pitching Catholic social theory, which looked for as much decentralisation as possible, against the actual practice of government in an infant state. The interaction between the Catholic Church, local activists and central government can thus be seen as a struggle between different facets of middle-class Ireland. Each sought to establish its authority in the shaping and consolidating of the new state's administrative framework, and indeed, social outlook. If there was confrontation, it was a fight which central government won decisively. Whatever about diversity within the ranks of Fianna Fáil, they seemed to share the scepticism of the community's capacity for voluntary self-reliance.[21] But it was also the case that the disunity and incompetence of various political groupings (most notably the ideological confusion of Fine Gael in the 1930s) allowed Fianna Fáil to develop such a mentality.

Neither, however, can the Fianna Fáil politicians of this era be accused of hiding their views. The memoirs of Senator Joseph Connolly, who became Controller of Censorship during the Emergency, reveal a man who was typical of the era. He held the traditional nationalist belief in a nation of smallholders and decentralised industries, and feared emigration and depopulation. He was also typical of a generation who were undoubtedly capable administrators with perhaps unrealistic political beliefs; urban-centred, but idealising the rural way of life; distrustful of debate and 'weak' government (any government that was not Fianna Fáil or composed of more than one party). They were also puritanical to a certain extent (de Valera discouraged socialising with the opposition and did not approve of the Dáil bar), and yet it was a puritanism that produced a social conscience unimaginable in those who came to dominate the party in the late twentieth century.[22] This is not to suggest that unmitigated altruism dominated their approach to politics, but like their Cumann na nGaedheal counterparts in the 1920s, whatever about ego, and it was in abundance, there was a devotion to an honest politics which had little to do with personal material aggrandisement. In 1937, William Norton, the leader of the Labour Party, in making the case for retirement allowances for ministers, said: 'I do not think I am breaking any confidence when I say that many of these people are poor by reason of the fact that they served the state …'[23]

'a gradualist approach to the Republic'?

Perhaps the chief difference between the two larger parties was that Cumann na nGaedheal had been shaped by external factors whereas Fianna Fáil was driven by a more domestic ideological agenda. Fianna Fáil was determined to change the shape and manner of Anglo-Irish relations, and in doing so de Valera proved, to the understandable anger of his political opponents, the truth in Collins's assertion that the Treaty could be a basis for further independence. The acceptance of this realisation was in fact the reason why the handover of power in 1932 had been relatively smooth, despite the exaggerated claim of James Dillon that Fianna Fáil were 'swaggering around the place with revolvers bulging out of their pockets'.[24] While there were highly amusing and somewhat farcical incidents in the quest to undermine the status of the Governor General, the British Crown's representative in Ireland (Fianna Fáil ministers and their wives fled from a function at the French Legation as soon as the presence of James McNeill was known), the serious side of the reshaping of Anglo-Irish relations was expressed in a number of initiatives. The External

Relations Act of 1936 abolished the post of Governor General; the oath of allegiance was also dropped and the government decided to refuse to pay land annuities (the annual repayment of loans made by the British government to Irish tenants under pre-independence Land Acts). The British government responded by placing a 20 per cent duty on most Irish exports to Britain, with Ireland responding in kind, leading to the Economic War of 1934–8 (see below).

The resolution of this crisis involved a one-off payment by Ireland of £10 million to Britain, but also, more importantly, the return to Ireland of the ports maintained by Britain under the Treaty, which were essential to Ireland exercising an independent foreign policy in the event of European conflict. In Anglo-Irish relations, de Valera was thus able to match his rhetoric with negotiating skill. In 1984 Deirdre McMahon's classic work on Anglo-Irish relations in the 1930s, *Republicans and Imperialists*, revealed the extent to which myopic British politicians failed to appreciate that it was not only the Civil War that poisoned Irish political life, but also Anglo-Irish relations. Partition remained pivotal in de Valera's preoccupations, but there was a failure to understand that he was not a republican die-hard, but a cautious diplomat who responded stage by stage 'to the failures of his approaches to the British government' in seeking an independent united Ireland in association with the Commonwealth. Refusing to learn the lessons of history, it seemed, the British government made 'little conscious effort to understand the new Irish government'.

De Valera assumed complete control of Anglo-Irish affairs, in contrast to the disunity prevailing on the British side.[25] John Bowman's seminal *De Valera and the Ulster Question 1917–73* confirmed that de Valera appreciated the intractability of the partition problem and explicitly stated that unity was not available in the short term. He placed little emphasis on it in the 1932 election campaign: 'In conflict with the British government within weeks of his election victory and in talks with them by July, de Valera was anxious to debate "fundamentals" including partition. But if the latter proved, at least for the moment, non-negotiable, he was content to pursue a gradualist approach to the Republic.'[26] That British ministers continued to describe him as 'a complete dreamer' and an 'impractical eccentric' revealed more about their own preconceived notions and historical prejudices than any supposed obsessions on de Valera's part. By the end of the Second World War, the gradualist approach ensured 'the Irish relationship with the Commonwealth was almost invisible'. But significantly, de

Valera did not want to leave the Commonwealth as long as it was accepted no allegiance to the Crown was involved. This was a stance encouraged by the fact that the partition issue remained in Southern eyes unresolved, but it also revealed that he was in no sense a republican die-hard; perhaps he wanted to prove that his idea of 'external association', proposed as an alternative to the Treaty, was workable.

'a virtual volkisch sense of community'

Successful Anglo-Irish diplomacy towards the end of the 1930s was made possible not only by a change of attitude on the part of Britain in view of the exacerbated tensions in its dealings with the rest of Europe, but also because de Valera had managed to complete another section of his independence jigsaw the previous year: the Irish Constitution of 1937. This was an expression of the sovereignty he desired, but also a means by which to resolve the Economic War without the loss of Irish constitutional rights (though as Irish neutrality was to prove (see below), arrangements between Britain and Ireland could be suitably ambiguous to the satisfaction of both sides). When asked after the Ports Agreement if neutrality would be compatible with continuing the supply of food to Britain, de Valera replied that 'the truth is that in modern War there is not any neutrality'.[27]

The Constitution, about which de Valera consulted widely, contained a preamble which sought to depict a liberal state on the one hand with, in the words of Joe Lee, 'a virtual volkisch sense of community on the other'.[28] Lee also makes the point that its moderation demonstrated political maturity on the part of de Valera, given the international climate of the 1930s and the scope in the original 1922 Constitution for the imposition of autocracy, but that the Constitution was ultimately despised because of the oath of fidelity to the Crown 'in virtue of the common citizenship of Ireland with Great Britain'. The preamble of the 1937 document stated that it was needed 'so that the dignity and freedom of the individual may be assured; true social order attained and the unity of our country restored and concord established with other nations'. The Irish electorate voted for the Constitution by a margin of 685,000 to 527,000, a reminder that endorsements of de Valera's initiatives were by no means foregone conclusions.

While de Valera had consulted John Charles McQuaid, the future Archbishop of Dublin, when drafting it, the Constitution did not declare Catholicism the state religion, to the disappointment of many zealous

Catholic activists. It included a provision ensuring the Constitution could be amended only by referendum and created a new senate, symbolically but superficially based on vocational representation, but ultimately chosen by a restricted political electorate. It also created the office of President, with few real powers, while giving to the prime minister (Taoiseach) a powerful constitutional position, alongside firm commitments to human rights. More controversial in the eyes of unionists were articles 2 and 3, insisting that the state was defined as a 32-county one, de Valera presumably attempting to ensure he would not be accused of betraying the ideal of a United Ireland. It also incorporated the assertion in article 44 that by her life in the home a woman made a contribution to the state without which it could not prosper. Kate O'Brien's autobiographical novel *Pray for the Wanderer* (1938) attacked this idea and questioned the idealisation of marriage that it implied ('life might fruitfully be a lonely track or a jealously personal adventure'). The male protagonist in the novel was scathing about de Valera and his Constitution: 'a dictator's country too ... subtle but dictatorial and obstinate ... Ireland, newly patrolled by the Church would be unlikely to vote against the Holy Trinity' (which was invoked in the Constitution's preamble).[29]

Nonetheless it was a document which was to survive, perhaps because of the degree to which it contained scope for renewal and change.[30] While it did not declare a republic, leaving open the nature of Ireland's future association with the British Crown, it was significant that there was repeated use of the word 'sovereignty', which during the course of the next sixty years would be a matter of significant debate.

Abroad, de Valera was a respected speaker at the League of Nations in Geneva, where Ireland had been elected to the Council in 1930, though ultimately Irish neutrality during the Second World War would unravel much of the goodwill garnered during the preceding years. In a case like the question of sanctions against Italy over the invasion of Abyssinia, there were few financial or security implications for Ireland – Ireland's undoubtedly sincere and committed participation did not have a high price, unlike the situation pertaining in other European countries such as France and England. Irish diplomats continued to labour under the somewhat misguided assumption (particularly on the part of those like Seán Lester) that Ireland was much more independent than other dominions; a view of an acquiescent Empire certainly not shared in London.[31] With regard to its own defence, it was a measure of the triumph of rhetoric over reality that a state which had achieved independence through armed struggle and claimed territorial rights over the North, and whose defence policy was based on the principle of neutrality, had 'such a miserably equipped defence establishment'.[32]

'a disorganised and howling wilderness in three months'?

There was, of course, precious little scope for extravagant spending on defence in the depressed years of the 1930s, but there was an attempt to reshape the economics of the state as Fianna Fáil sought to make a radical departure from the policies of their predecessors. The economic historian Brian Girvin suggested: 'it is very questionable if Fianna Fáil could have achieved significant political success between 1926 and 1932 if it had not adopted an active socio-economic policy'.[33] Much of this was bound up with the quest for political independence, and the two frequently dove-tailed in the 1930s, ensuring the wrath of economists such as Trinity's Professor George Duncan and University College Dublin's George O'Brien. The opposition to economic nationalism was also expressed by another Trinity academic, Joseph Johnston, in his *Nemesis of Economic Nationalism* (1934), where he equated the new economic philosophy as presaging a regimentation of Ireland's economic life along Bolshevik lines. But it was also the case that it was civil servants rather than professional economists who effectively controlled the economic and financial machinery of the state, making use of their training in the British administrative system. Committees of inquiry and financial commissions seemed intent on endorsing existing government policy, despite the criticism of the Swede Per Jacobsen that there was no effective co-ordination of Irish economic policy.[34]

The conservative conclusions of the Banking Commission (which recommended the creation of a Central Bank, eventually set up in 1943 but with limited powers) pleased those who sought to belittle the claims of contemporary critics that the Irish monetary system was excessively concerned with money profit to the exclusion of issues of social justice. Although the twin pillars of Irish economic policy in the 1930s and 1940s – agricultural and industrial self-sufficiency – failed to transform the economy, the international crisis of the 1930s was perhaps felt less in Ireland than in other European countries. It was undoubtedly the case that it hit large farmers the most and there was a whole litany of sorrows to befall them in the 1930s. They were affected not just by worldwide economic depression but the shift towards agricultural protectionism in the UK, Fianna Fáil's emphasis on tillage at the expense of dairy farming, the Economic War and the Emergency, which pushed them off the pedestal of comparative advantage.

Although by the 1940s agriculture still directly employed almost half of the active work population, unemployment stood at 120,000 in 1936, and by the late 1930s it seemed clear that Fianna Fáil's economic policies had reached the end of their shelf life. While there was success in creating industrial employment, with up to 7,000 jobs a year being created in the 1930s (figures equalled not even in the 1960s), this was a short-term adjustment rather than an industrial revolution, as local industries emerged to plug the holes left by the increased cost of imports and the Control of Manufacturing Acts (which restricted foreign ownership of domestic firms, though the legislation was not rigidly enforced). Such firms were almost totally geared towards a home market with little potential for growth. Most ironically, these firms did not represent the essence of self-sufficiency because the expansion of domestic industry actually raised the reliance on imported raw materials – other than in the food sector, the value of imports actually rose during the 1930s.[35] While the trade unions supported protectionism, the attempts to be self-sufficient in flour resulted in the British company Rank buying control of flour-milling in Ireland, following the collapse of talks between the Department of Industry and Commerce over government intervention and credit. Rank then divided the Irish market between British and Irish millers, giving Irish millers a higher quota than they had in the 1920s but 'much of the quota was controlled by Ranks'.[36]

Theory and practice differed sharply. Despite nationalist rhetoric, governments allowed considerable monopoly powers to foreign companies, and, as Mary Daly pointed out, while the policies resulted in a new economic elite, the existing elite did not suffer.[37] A white paper on national income and expenditure for the years 1938–44 revealed that roughly the top 3,000 took 5 per cent of all income in 1943, suggesting that not enough was being done to decrease the gap between rich and poor. Labour's share of domestically generated national income fell from 51 per cent in 1938 to 44.3 per cent in 1944. The one elite to suffer badly were the cattle farmers during the Economic War. The quotas introduced by the British government in January 1934 meant that there were no Irish exports of beef to Britain, so the government introduced a free-beef scheme for the poor and encouraged farmers to slaughter calves. The settlement of this dispute in 1938 included an agreement to swap British coal for Irish cattle. Essentially, this was a return to the status quo, in the sense of 'concentrating resources once again on the export of cattle to the British market, a minimalist state and close control over expenditure'.[38] A measure of the bleakness facing the Irish economy in the 1930s was recorded by David Gray, the US envoy in Dublin (there were no ambassadors until 1949), who suggested that 'If Britain completely cuts off coal and gasoline, this place would be a disorganised and howling wilderness in three months ... it probably would be a wise thing to do to explode this nationalistic dream of self-sufficiency.'[39]

This bleak scenario overlooked the fact that almost complete import substitution was achieved in some sectors – only 200,000 pairs of shoes were imported in 1938/9 compared to 4 million pairs in 1929/30, for example – but such sectors were unimportant in overall economic terms. In terms of self-sufficient vehicle assembly, for instance, it was hardly significant, given there were only 7,480 private cars licensed in Ireland in 1939, falling to a mere 240 in 1941 as a result of the Emergency.[40] As well as trade union weakness and infighting, the poor performance of the economy also explained the large rise in the gap between British and Irish wages in the late 1930s and early 1940s. Wage freezes were introduced in 1941 and 1942 and strikes outlawed. Despite a strike in the building industry in 1937 (the biggest in the history of the state) it was not until the late 1940s that labour militancy emerged (see below). Seán Lemass as Minister for Industry and Commerce did achieve some success in reorganising the economy, helped by the market forces encouraging protection (the establishment of the Industrial Credit Corporation was a notable achievement), but he was somewhat isolated. Brian Girvin suggested he remained 'the only major dynamic force attempting to promote change in the economy',[41] but he was hampered by a resurgent conservatism in the Department of Finance. While Fianna Fáil was pragmatic in its approach to semi-state bodies, whose numbers increased dramatically during this period, the Control of Manufacturing Acts (1932–4) also led British firms to bypass tariffs by setting up subsidiaries in Ireland to serve the domestic market, with the Guinness brewery safeguarding its market in Britain by building a brewery in London's Park Royal. Although Ireland's national debt may not have been large by contemporary European standards, control of credit was curtailed by the link with sterling, and despite the establishment of a Central Bank in 1943, Irish bank lending was still heavily concentrated in the City of London.[42]

If any more proof was needed that economic self-sufficiency was an irrational and unachievable quest, it was provided with the Emergency, though the war also focused Irish economic planners on change and adaptation. Industrial output fell by one fifth during the Emergency, rationing was introduced (in 1943 Ireland had only 28 per cent of its normal requirements for its beloved tea) and a wide-scale turf development plan was implemented. But it is fair to assert that stagnation, inflation and a fall in living standards were not the only developments which contained lessons for Irish economic planners. The concept of long-term planning was also given a boost by a recognition that the economy could be directed and guided, particularly in the context of general European post-war reconstruction and recovery plans. The increased power of bureaucracy – exemplified in the exceptional powers given to the Minister for Supplies, Seán Lemass (who could now control exports, imports, transport, prices and wages, and with other cabinet members was already by 1942 discussing post-war economic planning[43]) – initiated the rise of economic planning and state capitalism and the collection of crucial data to allow such planning to be informed. The Social and Statistical Inquiry Society of Ireland also helped to facilitate discussion of Keynesian economics in an Irish context.[44]

'a peculiar people in their own land'

Pastoral imagery remained important in the 1930s, and the 'rural ideal', if it can be termed such, was still common to all shades of opinion, but became even more pronounced owing to Fianna Fáil's courting of the small-farm electorate and their goal of self-sufficiency. It was also a continuation of what Michael Collins and others had spoken of in terms of getting a glimpse of what Ireland could become again, though those who idealised the rural landscape continued to be conveniently selective in their imagery. There was a gulf, too, between what was said about the rural populace in public and in private. De Valera may have spoken of them on occasion as 'rightful princes', but Seán MacEntee, as Minister for Local Government and Public Health, in his frustration at failed attempts to get rural communities to embrace the idea of social insurance, preferred to see a very substantial part of them as still taking 'a ... fatalistic attitude in regard to their personal hygiene and in regard to the conditions under which they live'.[45]

Gearóid Ó Crualaoich argued that the perpetuation of a folk image in the 1930s was a continuation of the romanticism of previous centuries, perhaps reinforcing Irish cultural sovereignty while leaving that actual society relatively unaltered.[46] Article 45.2 of the 1937 Constitution aspired towards establishing on the land in economic security 'as many families as in the circumstances shall be practicable'. In 1933 land legislation had empowered the Land Commission to redistribute land to landless labourers, though a drift to the right caused members of the government to question the economic value of this practice. In the same year as the new Constitution was approved, the small farmers of Bantry, County Cork, informed the Minister for Agriculture of the pitiful quality of their land, the disastrous condition of their roads, poor reclamation and the fact that only 12 marriages had taken place in the previous year.[47]

And yet, even in literary journals which were aiming to challenge an outdated and narrow national identity, such as *Ireland Today*, it was still maintained: 'If there is one country in the world where one man symbolises nearly all national life and nearly the whole content of the national struggle, that country is Ireland and that man is the Irish peasant.'[48] Cynicism about such assertions does not have to extend to the contention that rural Ireland was a community on the verge of death. The American sociologists Arensberg and Kimball, who wrote about rural life in Clare in the 1930s, found themselves in a small-farm economy in which co-operative effort was controlled by the social forces operating within the family with links based on family, age, sex, labour and economic exchange. They concluded it was a self-contained society capable of continued and viable existence.[49] De Valera, however, was often naive about this issue; during the Emergency he examined the idea of grants for building a second house (or 'dower house') – essentially a house for parents so that generations could live side by side – and was puzzled that farmers seemed to care for it so little. This was a significant reminder that certain attempts at the 'modernisation' of rural Ireland could in fact be frustrated by rural communities who retained a suspicion and often hostility towards attempts to improve their material comfort, a factor the Department of Local Government and Public Health sometimes commented acidly on.[50]

There were many exceptions. The founding of Muintir na Tíre in 1937 was an attempt to revitalise rural life through community action, self-help schemes and, later, the encouraging of farmers to embrace modern farming methods. This organisation was a grassroots manifestation of the intellectual Catholic social theory debates of the 1930s which pitched visions of 'organic', 'functional' and 'communal' societies against the corollaries of 'individualism', 'statism' and even 'totalitarianism'. Certain members of the Catholic Hierarchy, such as Cornelius Lucey, the future Bishop of Cork, extolled the virtues of organising rural workers in corporations to achieve autonomy in controlling their interests. For Fr John Hayes, founder of Muintir na Tíre, it was an advantage to treat rural areas as virgin soil through which to plough new 'anti-centrist' structures.[51] For the more cynical this was merely a nostalgic medievalism that conveniently ignored economic depression; satirist Flann O'Brien saw this quest for a rural utopia as amounting to 'an ignorance of the impulses that condition human behaviour'.[52]

Many in government and the Land Commission agreed, as reflected in the reaction to the Report on Vocational Organisation (see below) with its proposals to restructure rural life. This report was a profession of faith in a pyramidal construction of parish agricultural organisations, parish guilds, county guilds and national agricultural councils. These could do little, the report's detractors believed, to rectify the ingrained habits of scattered farmers who were stubbornly individualistic in mentality.[53] Perhaps the same traits were what led Ernest Blythe in 1931 to be somewhat unsure of how rural communities would react to the building of parish halls for communal purposes, as if they were some kind of museums for the living Irish peasant. Blythe warned that they would 'not consent to be made a sort of "peculiar people in their own land"', though Muintir na Tíre leaders sought to dispute this by continually insisting that the Catholic parish was the natural territorial unit in which to organise Irish rural life.[54]

'Rural Ireland is real Ireland'?

Such concerns emerged in the 1930s because land and rural life were so central to contemporary debate. Land redistribution was still contentious, the technicalities of farm ownership were of paramount concern, and rural inhabitants were finding that there was an increasingly complex range of functions which the unevenly divided land had to satisfy. This was all the more so as a result of Fianna Fáil's promotion of a tillage policy and discouragement of grazing. But for John Hayes, it was a simple and spiritual Christian equation; according to him: 'Rural Ireland is real Ireland and rural Ireland is Ireland true to Christ.' In fostering what became something of a parish council movement, Hayes enlisted the support of Catholic intellectuals, who were conversant with what was going on in similar parish movements on the continent, such as the *mairies* in France, *sindicos* in Italy and the *Bürgermeisters* in Germany. Underpinning their more ambitious aims was a barely concealed distrust of and hostility towards centralisation, the influence of Dublin and the ranks of civil servants seen as championing a bureaucracy devoid of empathy with the culture and conditions of rural life.[55]

The report of the Civil Service Commission in 1935, which contained a strong attack on the merits of regional planning under the direction of independent bodies, had previously rubbed salt into rural reformers' wounds. Likewise, in debates about the degree of autonomy associated with local government, it suited the central government to insist, in the words of MacEntee, that 'the true spirit of local government cannot be created by an act of the Oireachtas. It must spring from the people themselves.'[56]

But it was also ironic that many of the proponents of rural reform were urban-based academics, and many had specialised ideas of rural life based on their own memories rather than the contemporary conditions prevailing. Roy Foster pointed to the significance of the Irish Folklore Commission, which in 1935 was founded at a time when the society it celebrated was entering its final stages. De Valera, too, in the 1940s was anxious to have a state-commissioned history of the Famine which reflected the ordinary victims he had recalled his grandmother mentioning. The academics were unable or unwilling to produce such a volume and instead produced what was in effect a history of the administrative response to the Famine.[57]

But it was poverty that was inimical to the development of thriving parish movements or councils. Of 380,147 holdings in the 26 counties of the Free State only 80,000 were over 50 acres or more in the 1930s. There were also issues of more pressing concern to those with a vested or aspirational interest in the land than cleaning up the local cemeteries or sharing recipes for jam-making, despite the fact that 1.25 million acres of land were redistributed by the Irish Land Commission between 1923 and 1953. Commissioner's conferences were frequently convened to deal with contentious and difficult cases, and the land bond scheme was often severely criticised. Politicians may have pretended that they had the ear of the commission when deciding on applications, but attempts to breach confidentiality and compromise the independence of the Commission rarely succeeded. In 1957 Fianna Fáil's Erskine Childers was dismissive of the 'fiction' that TDs could influence its operations:

> Suggestions have been made from time to time that deputies have very considerable power in securing land for people. This is not so and I should like to deny the suggestion … that up to 1948, it was possible for a member of an FF club, who had paid a shilling, to get land from the Land Commission. Such a suggestion is a gross insult not only to the Minister of the day but also to the Land Commission itself and the fine body of 138 Land Commission Inspectors against whom not a single sustainable damage of serious corruption has been made as long as I can remember.[58]

Studies of agricultural labourers have shown that rises in the standard of living lagged behind aspirations in these decades, and yet Muintir na Tíre berated the 'indecency' of agricultural 'civil war' waged by striking labourers in Kildare in the 1940s.[59]

The brief of an organisation like Muintir na Tíre was in fact far too wide. Their prose was at its most purple in times of national crises such as the economically depressed years of the 1930s or the Emergency. But undermining this, and in contrast to their more pragmatic political representatives, the language used and the ideas offered left precious little space for compromise, which was why the commissions and reports they endorsed were received coldly. In any case, Catholic social theory was not seen as capable of doing much to alleviate the vulnerability of those who farmed the poorest soil in Ireland, and there is much validity in the argument that the 'parish council movement', with its emphasis on selfless solidarity, was too contrived by European standards and at odds with the more practical Irish co-operative philosophy set down by a more secular-minded Protestant Ascendancy in the closing years of the nineteenth century.[60]

Nonetheless a belief in the moral and social superiority of the rural way of life persisted, and it was one which Fianna Fáil was not satisfying. This was evidenced by the emergence in 1937 of the Irish Farmers' Federation, who built support on the back of a no-rates campaign. They became involved in a commodity strike in 1939 and were harshly treated by a government quick to use emergency powers legislation to suppress protest. But the movement also exposed class tensions within the farming community. Given the view in the west of Ireland that large farmers in more prosperous areas should not be relieved of all their rates obligations, there was not going to be unanimity on the issue of derating agricultural land. Clann na Talmhan ('party of the land') did emerge as a dynamic grass-roots organisation in the 1930s and used strong language in condemning politicians, financiers and produce processors, but also suggested that politics was of no use to them. But the state's refusal to consult with farm organisations during the war pushed them into the arena of party politics (it became a political party in 1938), and in demanding minimal prices for agricultural produce, tillage subsidies and a reduction of higher public-sector salaries, they won ten seats in the general election of 1943. Notwithstanding, they still could not agree on the balance to be struck between the demands of eastern and western agriculture within Ireland, which was one of the main reasons why they could not build on their initial success. This highlighted class tension and Fianna Fáil's ability to place itself above this; the inequities in Irish farming in terms of size, region and specialism were seemingly inimical to sustaining a farmers' party that could command a wide and permanent appeal.[61]

'no shortage of answers for you'

Whatever about the rural mainland, members of the island communities emerged into the national and sometimes international spotlight in the 1930s and 1940s. This was largely as a result of the remarkable literary endeavours of some members of the Blasket island community off the coast of the Kerry Gaeltacht, the most westerly point in Europe. It was ironic that this emergence coincided with the beginnings of the exodus from the same islands; indeed, the twentieth century witnessed their almost complete demise. In 1911 there were 124 inhabited islands off the Irish coast, with a population of 24,000; by 1961 the figure had dropped to 92 islands with a population of 14,262 and by 1991 there were only 21 inhabited with a population of just 3,055.[62] Between 1930 and 1960, the populations of five of the islands were moved to the mainland with government assistance, because despite the strong market orientation of their fishing, it was a market in decline. Ironically, in view of the praise heaped on rural living, successive governments had no definable 'island policy'; frequent petitions from islanders were passed around various government departments, all of whom absolved themselves from responsibility.[63]

Similarly, despite fishing disasters in the 1920s in which over 50 men were drowned off the west coast, recommendations from the Gaeltacht

Commission designed to help such communities were ignored. Although the migration of island inhabitants to Gaeltacht communities in Meath was regarded by the Land Commission as a success, it was still the case that no department wanted responsibility for the islands (indeed it was not until 1992 that the islands were assigned a particular department), and ultimately it was the islanders themselves who would often request the evacuation of their homes. In one sense they were strangers in their own land; many of the Blasket islanders, for example, felt closer to the United States, where the majority of their families went, than they did to Dublin. Thus it was highly ironic that the state came to institutionalise the Blasket literature within the schooling system as a representation of national identity.

The islands had long attracted visitors from abroad. E. M. Forster and George Thompson introduced Maurice O'Sullivan's *Twenty Years a-Growing* (1933), which followed Tomás O'Crohan's *Islandman* (1929), as dealing with 'a Neolithic civilisation', a hyperbolic description to say the least. And yet for such small, marginalised and relatively primitive societies to produce such a volume of literature did represent something exceptional. Because they represented the antithesis of institutionalisation and urbanisation, their environment gave them great physical and mental freedom. And yet as seen clearly in *Peig* (1936), a book dictated by the Blasket storyteller Peig Sayers, the literature also drew attention to the realities behind living so dangerously and so exposed, particularly in the absence of medical care and the danger of being cut off from essential foodstuffs.[64] It was also biography that lacked self-consciousness, containing little, if any, interior dialogue. The language and conversation electrified visitors like Thomson who were keen to imbibe its resonances before its imminent demise. Literary critics have made bold (some would argue extravagant) claims for this literature; Declan Kiberd wrote that each text demonstrated an energising homage to past culture, accompanied with an invincible pride: 'the islanders are scarcely part of the literate world yet they speak a kind of elegant poetry. They live in a sort of socialist commune, where all share a common danger and poverty. Yet they bred themselves with the beautiful reserve and considered manners of rural aristocrats. They are the ultimate in radical traditionalism.'[65]

But it should be acknowledged that many of the islanders were aware of the irony of their endeavours being lauded by the establishment, or becoming living museum pieces as the Gaeltacht region crumbled around them. The demise of the Blaskets was finally brought to a conclusion by the death of a young islander following his failure to get medical treatment in 1953, and was beautifully chronicled by an English journalist, Cole Morton, in *Hungry for Home*. Morton noted de Valera's decision to travel to the Blaskets personally in 1947. But little good came of it. So disgusted with government hypocrisy was Maurice O'Sullivan that he refused to meet de Valera, even as the latter waited outside the house of the celebrated author when O'Sullivan had moved to the mainland in Galway.[66] Seán O'Crohan, another of the Blasket authors, in *A Day in Our Life* also commented acerbically on the new-found interest in the Blaskets which coincided with their demise (by 1945 they had a mere 45 inhabitants, down from 160 in 1911). Writing of the visitors, he commented:

> Another thing I let fly at them was that the high up learned professors and people with a sound knowledge of Irish were well paid to tease out the knotty problems for them; it was all a cod to be coming to myself looking for answers, while others were paid to give them. 'But', says I, 'when I am paid in the same way as the professors are paid on your behalf there will be no shortage of answers for you.'[67]

'possible to limp and hobble along'

More than anything else, however, it was emigration that made a mockery of any idealisation of rural life, providing successive governments in the 1930s and 1940s with evidence of the failure of policies designed to keep people on the land. A moderation in the departure rates in the 1930s was a result of international depression, but its resurgence during the Emergency posed new challenges, as did the large number of women emigrating. From the mid-1930s onwards Britain was the chief destination, and despite certain controversies over Irish migration to areas like Liverpool, which dissipated, the British government declined to take action to restrict emigration. It is tempting to view the lack of honest appraisal of the problem by clergy and politicians as a blatant hypocrisy, given the simultaneous demand that Ireland cherish its rural population. In truth, argued Gearóid Ó Crualaoich, emigration was a safety valve which enabled Ireland to successfully navigate the transition from a traditional rural society to a modern rural one.[68]

However, such explanations imply a certainty or definitive endorsement in relation to the culture of emigration from Ireland which was not in existence in the first few decades of independence. Patrick McGilligan conceded in 1937 that it was only because so many were emigrating to England that 'we still found it possible to limp and hobble along', though McGilligan also revealed his class bias, worrying that the 'taxation of the meagre comforts of the middle class' would tempt them into emigrating too, along with those with no obvious financial stake in the country.[69] Fianna Fáil seemed to believe that advising emigrants on how to cope was more important than the hopes they left behind, while the Church chose to focus on the 'moral welfare' of Irish female emigrants in particular, with a Catholic Emigrant Welfare Bureau eventually established under the auspices of John Charles McQuaid. Following the deaths of ten Irish emigrants from Achill in a bothy fire in Kirkintilloch, Scotland, in September 1937, an inter-departmental committee on seasonal migration to Britain made the dubious assertion that evidence from emigrants or organisations was not necessary. Not for the last time, the views of emigrants were deemed largely irrelevant, the report concluding abruptly that it was up to the labourers themselves to prevent exploitation. An official inquest found that their deaths were accidental, though because of the anti-Irish Catholic racism of the period some continued to maintain it was arson.[70]

Such lack of sympathy for the plight of emigrants was also reflected in the views of some rural activists; a contributor to the report of the Vocational Commission suggested that emigrants should have to pay 'at least five hundred pounds' before they would be allowed to emigrate. A Muintir na Tíre activist could only write laconically that 'a good working definition of a patriotic Irishman is a man who never lets himself grow resigned to fewness of people',[71] hardly a ringing endorsement of the need for action. In the 1930s there was virtually no support for the view that a restriction on emigration would lead to increased indigenous economic growth.

With the outbreak of war in 1939 there was a much sharper focus on the issue, with interesting implications for Anglo-Irish relations, given that, unlike the situation pertaining during the First World War, Irish workers in Britain were now citizens of a neutral state. The most significant feature of the period was the involvement of the state in the regulation of cross-channel migration. The Irish government at certain periods during the war imposed restrictions: on those under the age of 33, those from an area with a population of fewer than 5,000, those already in employment and those with more than three months' experience of agricultural work. It was interesting that Irish civil servants, aware that the cost of living was increasing dramatically in Ireland (it rose by 70 per cent in the period 1942–6), saw migration as an important means of relieving potential social unrest, while British officials at the ports of application noted the degree to which potential emigrants were aware of the multitude of regulations and the ways around them. The truth was that both countries had much to gain: emigration provided a convenient pool of labour for the British war effort, and contributed to alleviating unemployment in Ireland, whilst the governments maintained control over the numbers leaving and the categories of workers permitted to travel. By July 1944 nearly 100,000 Irish people were working in Britain, and over two thirds of the males who were granted permits were under 30 years of age.[72]

More worrying for the Irish Department of External Affairs was that more women emigrating were under 22 years of age than over it, partly reflecting a shortage of trainee nurses in England. While most women were working for the Ministry of Supplies, building contractors employed most men, and finding suitable accommodation could be troublesome in areas like Birmingham and Coventry. In 1943, 48,324 travel permits were issued for workers, and many more may have taken advantage of a loophole allowing intending emigrants to indicate holidays or visiting a relative as reasons for travelling. An estimated £21 million was remitted from emigrants in Britain to Ireland during the war. Dublin County Borough had the second-highest rate of emigration (72 per 1,000) in the years 1940–43, surpassed only by County Mayo.[73]

... men 'who will no doubt have imbibed a good deal of leftism in England'

One of the most unpleasant aspects of the emigration experience was the delousing procedures performed in Dublin, introduced because of unease in Britain about the spread of infectious diseases. They had unfortunate resonances of the nineteenth-century Great Famine, and Ireland's chief medical officer recorded that 'the atmosphere of shame and fear and outrage was easy to feel'.[74] Between 1943 and 1947, 55,000 people were processed by the health embarkation centres in Dublin. It is perhaps more difficult to assess how emigrants fared, partly owing to the rigorous censorship in Ireland of reaction to emigration, but one significant development was that the patterns of settlement during the war had changed, with more now travelling to the north, Midlands and east as well as the large cities of lowland Scotland, Lancashire and London. Such new settlements by the Irish were important in determining the direction of the much more extensive emigration of the 1950s. Equally significant, the demand for Irish labour in Britain for post-war reconstruction meant that Irish officials did not have to countenance the mass return of displaced workers. The Department of Industry and Commerce during the war had worried about the 'dumping' home of 100,000 men 'who will no doubt have imbibed a good deal of leftism in Britain'.[75]

Despite complaints that Irish migration to Britain was 'conscription in disguise', the Irish government had received assurances in the summer of 1941 that Irish migrants would not be subjected to conscription, and was more concerned with losing potential workers on the land who could help maximise the production of fuel and food. The Department of External Affairs, having witnessed the granting of 15,000 travel permits in August 1941, exclaimed dramatically: 'we won't have anyone left to work the land',[76] though such alarmist sentiments were tempered by those reminding government departments that the worker had a right to dispose of his or her labour in whatever market would bring the best advantage. It was also pointed out that it was anachronistic and iniquitous to prevent workers from certain 'scheduled areas' (rural areas with a population of under 5,000) emigrating, given that it could lead to different policies being applied to adjacent areas with higher populations in which the material circumstances were exactly the same, perhaps one of the reasons why there was a certain ambiguity when it came to enforcing such regulations.[77] At the end of the war the Irish Times, although insisting that the Irish were 'not emigrants by nature', did not feel that it was a subject on which the government should be criticised. Early the following year, the former Cumann na nGaedheal minister Richard Mulcahy was branded an 'emigration agent' because he chose to describe some of England's attractions, one of the relatively few occasions when the subject of migration publicly entered Irish political discourse.[78]

The participation of Irish emigrants in the British war effort, directly or indirectly, highlights the difficulties in assessing the true extent of Ireland's neutrality. It is perhaps unfair, given that so many were travelling to find work they could not find in Ireland, to suggest that they were making any emphatic judgement on Ireland's status as a non-belligerent. A. V. Judge, an economic historian at the London School of Economics, completed an account of Irish labour in Britain in 1948. As pointed out by Enda Delaney, he encountered resistance to suggestions that the Irish authorities had co-operated with the British government during the war, later acknowledging that reference to the Irish government would have to be handled with great diplomatic sensitivity.[79] This was just one of a host of ambiguities associated with Ireland's neutrality. Irish history chose largely to forget the Irish volunteers in the war effort, even though a British liaison office was established in Dublin to operate the arrangements agreed between the two countries. Many of the volunteers also believed that their war-time endeavours were not incompatible with an Irish national identity, or a demonstration of hostility to neutrality – there was, after all, a long tradition of Irish service in the British armed forces. Others joined for their anti-fascist beliefs or simply in search of military excitement.

In any case, they were largely assisted by an Irish government whose main concern was 'to allow Irish workers to go to Britain without being implicated in the process'.[80] The Irish government must also have been aware it was likely to benefit diplomatically from the efforts of Irish volunteers. According to British figures, in December 1944, 37,440 men and 4,510 women born in the then 26 counties of the Free State were with the British armed forces, while during 1945 the number increased to 50,000. The true number is likely to have been much higher because these figures did not include volunteers from the South recruited in Northern Ireland. The correct figure may have been closer to 70,000, with up to 10,000 fatalities (Southerners won a total of 780 decorations, including seven Victoria Crosses). In the aftermath of the conflict the Irish government seemed determined to prevent any expression of commemoration of Irish involvement in the Allied war effort, and banned a remembrance march in November 1945. It was not until 1995 that an Irish government formally sponsored a memorial to those who had participated.[81]

'calling the world to witness that this is no affair of ours'

The government's post-war suppression of Allied remembrance was but a further extension of the ruthless censorship that operated in Ireland during the Emergency, helped by a political consensus that Ireland's neutrality was the only viable policy. The reports of the speeches of the single Dáil deputy to oppose neutrality – James Dillon – were censored, and he

was forced to resign from his party. Dillon, ever the individualist, castigated neutrality, which he said involved 'washing our hands and calling
the world to witness that this is no affair of ours'. The novelist Elizabeth
Bowen, who supplied some intelligence to the British authorities during
the war, concluded in relation to Dillon that 'the country is frightened
of him'.[82] This was only one aspect of a censorship that knew no bounds.
Arland Ussher, in *The Face and Mind of Ireland* (1947), found Irish apathy
perplexing and exasperating to one who felt himself to be not only an
Irishman, but also a European. He noted that Frank Aiken, the minister
with responsibility for co-ordination of defence measures, would not allow
Irish parents who had lost a son in the conflict to add the Latin phrase
'*Dulce et decorum est*' to death notices in the national press.[83] Ruthless censorship also made the subsequent details of Nazi atrocities all the more
incredible to Irish ears.

Aiken saw his mission as 'keeping the temperature down', both within
the state and between Ireland and the combatants, and censorship covered
both press and publications of all kinds, as well as film, radio and theatre,
and postal, telegraphic and telephonic communications. In neutralising
war news, Ireland went further than anything done in Switzerland and
Sweden; or in the words of Donal O'Drisceóil: 'the Irish authorities refused
to allow the war to be placed in a moral framework'.[84] The religious publication the *Irish Messenger of the Sacred Heart* managed to slip through some
information from London about the armed forces and the experiences of
Catholic combatants, on the grounds that faith had to take precedence
over government priorities, though in 1945 reports of the mistreatment
of Irish religious missionaries by the Japanese were also censored. In April
1943 references to concentration camps in a play called *The Refugee* in
Dublin's Peacock Theatre, featuring a Jewish refugee attempting to escape
from German persecution, were omitted, with Special Branch detectives
attending the opening night to ensure there was no breach of the censor's
order.[85]

Censorship also helped to perpetuate the belief that Irish suffering
was somehow unique, and encouraged belief after the war that reports of
Nazi atrocities were merely British propaganda. There was still a tendency
in Ireland at the end of the war to believe that Irish suffering was more
marked than that experienced anywhere else in Europe, a narrow mindset
which government policies facilitated. Germany managed to broadcast to
Ireland between two and four times a day, often recalling British atrocities

in Ireland; the voices of Francis Stuart and William Joyce (Lord Haw Haw) were a regular feature of the airwaves. The broadcasts did not unduly hinder military intelligence, being mostly in favour of Irish neutrality, and simplistically ignored Anglo-Irish and Irish-American links; only one official complaint was made to the Germans when Francis Stuart attempted to comment on the Irish general election of 1943.[86]

Ireland had little of a track record in relation to receiving immigrants, who under the Aliens Order of 1935 could not land without the permission of an immigration officer. According to official figures there were only 2,354 aliens in Ireland in 1939, including 1,143 Americans, 194 Germans and only one each of Japanese and Chinese.[87] Some of the more distinguished guests during the war included the poet John Betjeman and the nuclear physicist Erwin Schrödinger. Despite telegrams from Isaac Herzog, former Rabbi of the Jews in Dublin, and friend of de Valera, outlining the plight of persecuted Jews, de Valera's desired liberalism in relation to the taking in of Jewish refugees was overshadowed by the inflexibility of the Department of Justice. The department frequently reiterated its views that Jews were not wanted as permanent residents owing to the difficulty of assimilation and the danger of exacerbating existing anti-Semitism. Though small organised anti-Semitic groups were active in Dublin during this period, they were robustly challenged by eminent Catholic lay activists, who sought to establish counter-societies to foster dialogue between Christians and Jews. As with dominions such as Canada, Australia and New Zealand, Ireland failed the Jews during the war, Dermot Keogh suggesting the number of persecuted Jews accepted as refugees may have been as low as 60.[88]

The bombing of Dublin's North Strand, in which 43 were killed, was as close as Ireland got to the Blitz (aside from Blitz washing powder produced to fill a gap created by the cessation of British imports). The North Strand episode seemed trifling compared to the Belfast Blitz of April and May 1941, a mere 103 miles away from Dublin. De Valera's decision to send Irish fire brigades was a noble humanitarian gesture, though doubtless many of a unionist persuasion were irritated by his assertion that the South assisted because 'we are one and the same people'. With 100,000 made homeless and 53 per cent of the houses in Belfast damaged, it can be seen how relatively tranquil the South was during the war. In comparison to the North the Free State's priorities seemed almost embarrassingly trivial, but were not necessarily so. The production of turf was essential to keep Ireland self-sufficient in fuel. Prior to 1939 the country's annual fuel consumption amounted to 2.5 million tons of imported coal and 3.5 million tons of turf. Given the loss of coal (down to 735,000 tons by 1941), and the general fuel crisis, 5 million tons of turf in excess of normal requirements were needed for industrial and domestic use. Averting a fuel famine was a success; between 1941 and 1944 output of turf hovered between 4.6 and 4.5 million tons, overseen by the publicity-shy but highly effective and austere Hugo Flinn, who marshalled the turf forces like an army general. By 1942 there were 26,441 people employed on 803 bogs, many of them having been diverted from local-authority road and construction employment. These endeavours also laid the foundations for a modern turf industry in the post-war period. If this was as close as most Irish people got to digging in the trenches it is also the case that, like soldiering, it invoked a sense of camaraderie and a spirit of co-operation; a severe test had been successfully met. The same spirit saw the country grind to a standstill as de Valera made a dignified but firm response to Winston Churchill's infamous attack on Irish neutrality over the airwaves after the war – de Valera's response, in the words of Joe Lee, was 'a magisterial performance, exquisitely tuned to the emotional needs of his flock'.[89]

'who are we neutral against?'

There is a consensus that de Valera successfully met the political test of neutrality in overseeing the ultimate expression of Irish independence, and concluded it by asserting the rights of small nations to be masters of their own political and military destinies. It is also the case, however, that this could not have been achieved without a huge degree of moral and political ambiguity, not to mention utter pragmatism. Whatever about the achievement in maintaining control of the Treaty ports, given Northern Ireland's involvement in the war, the ports were not strategically vital to the Allies, whose forces could operate from Northern bases, without which, as Eisenhower noted, it was difficult to see how they could have countenanced the invasion and defence of Europe. The successful maintenance of neutrality needed the assistance of British and American restraint, which de Valera was well aware of. Public perception and actual practice were poles apart during the war. The British cabinet in 1945 admitted they had not been denied by 'neutral' Ireland the co-operation they needed, and listed 14 areas in which this was the case. (The Irish government had even agreed to the establishment of a British 'radar' station on Irish soil for use against German armed forces.)

Fury was expressed at de Valera's decision to visit the German embassy in Dublin on 2 May 1945 to express his condolences on the death of Hitler. This was very much a lone decision by de Valera, and against the advice and wishes of his officials at the Department of External Affairs. De Valera, in his own words, scorned the idea of excusing himself on the grounds of 'diplomatic illness'. Writing of Dr Hempel's (the German representative in Ireland) 'irreproachable' conduct during the war, 'in marked contrast' to the American Minister in Dublin, David Gray, he insisted he 'certainly was not going to add to his humiliation in the hour of defeat'.[90] He added, quite legitimately, that there had been little publicity given to the fact that the Dáil had been adjourned on the death of President Roosevelt. The American media understandably excoriated de Valera's visit to the embassy; indeed it won him few friends anywhere and placed him in the company of dictators Salazar of Portugal and Franco of Spain. History was to find it difficult to place the visit outside the context of details of the atrocities of German concentration camps, and recorded it as a massive blunder (Switzerland and Sweden did not offer such condolences). In truth it was a further indication of the dangers and diplomatic tightrope that came with an ambivalent neutrality. J. P. Duggan noted at the very end of the century that the question still was: 'who are we neutral against?', and went on to suggest: 'De Valera never really understood the primal reality, in the final analysis, of wicked war. He got away with it and he knew it. He could not foresee a repetition of such a fall-out from future wars. Endemic anomalies in evolving defence doctrine are still with us in the ongoing neutrality dilemma.'[91] Neutrality was to remain for some a sacrosanct tenet of Irish independence; for others a duplicitous and sometimes shameful abrogation of Ireland's moral and security responsibilities.

But what choice did de Valera have in relation to a declaration of neutrality? He contended in 1941 that 'for a divided nation to fling itself into this war would be to commit suicide', which was why the previous year the Irish cabinet rejected the offer by Britain of a declaration in favour of Irish unity in return for the ending of Ireland's neutrality. How such a commitment could have endured the opposition of 'loyal' Ulster was the obvious question, and it demonstrated a certain disingenuity on Britain's part, but was also understandable given Ireland's geographical position 'as the backdoor of Britain's defences, a springboard for the final blow against Germany's only surviving European enemy'. Robert Fisk pointed out that Germany had indeed photographed the Irish coastline and possible invasion beaches and that German intelligence work in Ireland was 'detailed, thorough and only occasionally careless', but that 'no attempt was made to conduct any serious analysis into the politics of the partitioned island'. Britain certainly had no excuse for overlooking those politics, which was why, in the event of an invasion, there was huge sensitivity about 'secret plans that would have enabled British and Irish soldiers to fight shoulder to shoulder against the Nazis in defence of Ireland'. But in terms of unity, it was, according to Frank Aiken, 'a sheer waste of time' to discuss proposals that were not practical.[92] Ulster unionists thoroughly agreed, as was evidenced by Craig's 'proud, impertinent and explosive' telegram to Chamberlain when he got wind of the proposal of a British declaration in favour of Irish unity. In retrospect, neutrality was depicted unduly smugly; in 1942 newsreel in Ireland informed cinema audiences: 'yes, its been a hard war ... but no sacrifice, no hardship can ever be too great when the reward is our own homeland', while in 1945 the first prize at a fancy-dress ball went to 'the Beast of Belsen' at a time when the first newsreels of the Nazi camps were being shown.[93]

Neutrality also coincided with significant discussion about the manner in which Ireland would plan for the future in a whole host of areas, despite the fact that during the war the Irish were perhaps less informed than any other people in Western Europe. They had, however, comforts that others did not enjoy – plentiful supplies of meat, for example – while drinking and sport continued to thrive as national pastimes: in 1944, 79,245 people attended the All-Ireland Gaelic football final. Many writers and artists of various hues found in Ireland a peace unavailable elsewhere, and were undoubtedly mildly surprised at the availability of steak and alcohol and bright lights. De Valera used the presence of Erwin Schrödinger to promote his pet project, the Dublin Institute for Advanced Studies, leading to some suggestions that he was trying to satisfy his vanity with a pretence of scholarship while war threatened.[94] That Ireland could become a world centre for the elucidation of theoretical physics at the time of its most obvious isolation does seem ironic, but is evidence of a certain cultural vitality that existed during the Emergency. Schrödinger found in the Irish a refreshing determination to continue living as they saw fit, in contrast to the culture of obedience and prohibition that then existed in Germany.[95]

But to suggest that the Free State conspired in creating the fiction that Europe and the wider world did not exist is to oversimplify; whatever about protecting Ireland's evolving independence to date, Joe Lee suggested that it was not neutrality 'but the manner in which the Irish chose to misinterpret the nature of the experience that deprived it of much of its value for the education of a people in genuine self-reliance'.[96] This, however, underestimates the extent to which policies being pursued in Ireland were placed under a new scrutiny. In a contribution to a debate in the Senate in May 1945 on the impact of the war, Professor William Fearon suggested that the lesson of the war was that Ireland could no longer hide behind its own independence because it was in fact utterly dependent: 'I think we have learned our history lesson. I respectfully suggest that we should learn that we are not an island outpost on the Atlantic, but part of the great family of nations. Justice, our geographical position and commerce should make us appreciate that our partnership is linked up with other nations; that we are linked up with their welfare.'[97]

'that's why children die. People don't know'

In relation to domestic welfare, it is unsurprising that by the end of the Emergency criticisms of social conditions were mounting, despite the genuine attempts by Fianna Fáil during this period to instigate measures conducive to greater social justice. Memoirs of those growing up in Ireland at this time contain a mixture of the cynical and the belief that a kind of 'dignity of aspiration' compensated for material deprivation. Respect for tradition, love of family and place, are evident in spite of the poverty of the era, but also given prominence is the humiliation of the poor, which was a product of the dispensary medical system, the indignity of queuing for handouts and a basic ignorance of healthcare. When one of his brothers died, Frank McCourt remembered that 'Dad said he didn't know and Mam said she didn't know and Dr Troy said that's why children die. People don't know.'[98]

Reports from the National Society for the Prevention of Cruelty to Children from the mid-1940s did not point to numerous deliberate instances of cruelty to children, but rather to the generally appalling physical environment in which the vulnerable lived. In a typical case, recorded by the Dublin District branch in 1944–5, it was observed that:

a man, his wife and three children, from 14 months to 8 years lived in a room 14 feet by 8 feet; there is just room for a bed and a cot, a stove and a minute table. The moral and physical effects of such squalor are deplorable. And the only remedy very often is to break up the family for the sake of the children and have the children committed to approved schools.[99]

For those experiencing life in the slums, poverty was always relative; self-made entrepreneur Bill Cullen, who hailed from such a background in Dublin, noted in another best-selling memoir:

> It was okay to be living in an 'uninhabitable dwelling' but you had to be in a 'dangerous building' to be moved. Number 28 wasn't too bad, as it officially housed only 49 residents. There were 128 people living in number 24. So, as Mary said, we should always count our blessings – things could be a lot worse.[100]

It was ironic that a society which placed such a premium on the family and the home environment was still prepared to incarcerate children in institutions where childhood was all but non-existent, while legal adoption continued to be resisted on the grounds that it would threaten the religious welfare of children. The notion that the state should not intervene in the affairs of the family was not adhered to in relation to incarceration in institutions run by Irish religious orders, which were funded directly by the state. There was, however, a divergence between the views of the Department of Health, which encouraged keeping children in their families of origin or fostering, and the Department of Education, which officially continued to believe in the benefits of institutional care, even going so far as to prevent children being boarded out of them in the 1940s. Local authorities concurred; they were primarily concerned with minimising costs; and it was cheaper to maintain the culture of institutionalisation.

'I had no idea what intact meant'

The report of a Commission of Inquiry into industrial schools in 1936 (the Cussen Report) revealed much poverty and neglect and a lack of contact with the outside world. A fire in an industrial school in Cavan town in 1943, in which 36 children died, raised further questions about the manner in which juveniles were being cared for. Until the 1950s there were still roughly 6,000 children in such schools at any one time. Mary

Norris, who experienced such committal in the mid-1940s, recalled that 'we were like sheep going to a fair, to a slaughter. We all stood there in front of this judge and he put us away.'[101] Norris and her seven siblings were taken from their widowed mother and sent to institutions because her mother had formed a new relationship after her husband died. Mary ended up in an industrial school in Killarney, County Kerry, run by the Sisters of Mercy. When she reached the age of 16 the nuns got her a job working for a family in Tralee. She was allowed out one night a week, but one week went out twice, to the cinema, and was hauled back to the nuns in Killarney, and locked in a room:

> The next day, I was taken down to a doctor, and he examined me, gave me an internal examination. And I remember him saying to the Matron who had brought me down, 'What in the name of God is wrong with them up there, this girl is intact.' But I had no idea what intact meant. The next day I was sent to the Good Shepherd Convent. I wasn't even allowed to say goodbye to my sisters, to anybody. The Good Shepherds was what they used to threaten us with if we were bold. It was a Magdalen laundry in Cork. I was sent there to work, to slave in that laundry. The nuns in Killarney had no right to do this – I had turned sixteen and was out from their power. But I didn't know that at the time. I thought I had to do what I was told, as always. The way I see it now is that it was one load of nuns giving servants, skivvies, to another lot of nuns to run their laundry, their workroom.[102]

The industrial-school system was abolished in Britain in 1933 but remained in place in Ireland, even though the Cussen Report acknowledged that Ireland was behind the rest of Europe in dealing with this social issue. A medical inspector appointed in 1939 began to compile reports which, at their worst, gave glimpses of starvation, neglect and abuse. Despite an increase in funding following a Children Act of 1941, the Department of Education in the mid-1940s was well aware of the grave situation in respect of feeding and clothing such children. Anna McCabe concluded in one of her many reports that 'semi-starvation seems to be a tradition' and that there was 'no human interest whatsoever in the children'.[103] In the 1990s, it was discovered that the most glaring omissions from the archive files of the industrial-school system related to information concerning the deaths of children – it is highly unlikely that those missing or unaccounted for wandered innocently outside the gates of industrial schools and became lost and untraceable.[104] It is more probable, though difficult to prove conclusively, that a small number of Irish children were beaten to death in state-financed, religious-run institutions.

What is most striking about the testimony of inmates who were asked to tell their stories is the level of abuse and humiliation directed at the very young. An inmate at an orphanage in County Dublin in the 1940s, John, talked about the practice of demeaning bed-wetters, and his account is representative of many such memories. The orphanage was run by the nuns of the Daughters of Charity (how ironic the names of many of these orders of priests and nuns seemed by the end of the century):

> They had a special punishment for children who wet the bed. I think they really believed we did it on purpose just to defy them. They would hold you up by your hands and feet, naked, and duck you into an ice-cold bath of water four or five times. You'd be blue in the face and gasping for air. It was lay staff who used to do these drownings to us. The nuns never beat me. We'd be forced out of bed in the middle of the night and made to sit on rows of potties for up to an hour. I used to try and stay awake so I wouldn't wet the bed. There'd be children crying in their beds, knowing they were going to get a drowning in the morning in the freezing water. And remember that in this dormitory, we were all under five years old ... in bed you had to display the sign of the cross – all night you had to lie on your back in that position. If you moved, you'd be woken up with a beating, often with one of the staff hitting us with her big pair of siscors [sic].[105]

'crying for simple shelter'

Although during the 1930s all the major notifiable diseases were declining in incidence, infant mortality remained a concern in Dublin, partly because legislation to provide maternity and child welfare services was not mandatory, and government policy was to look to voluntary organisations to provide services of this nature. An indication of their success was that infant mortality showed a continuous decline in urban areas from the mid-1920s to the mid-1930s. But in Dublin in 1932, Kerry Reddin, in charge of the child and maternity welfare services for Dublin Corporation, noted that large numbers of babies were still dying unnecessarily in the first month of life, which was attributed to ignorance on the part of mothers concerning baby care, inadequate diet and the conditions in which expectant mothers were living. A Department of Local Government and Public Health survey of 1941 suggested 60 per cent of Dublin mothers were unable to breastfeed on account of their own malnourishment.[106]

The overall infant mortality rate in Ireland in the 1930s was almost 7 per cent of births, which was high by European standards; while the Free State during this decade was also unique in Western Europe in that the male survival rates exceeded the female at any age. The outbreak of war and shortage of funds not only curtailed slum clearance but also overburdened the public-health infrastructure, which encouraged innovative thinking on the part of Ireland's health administrators. It was badly needed. Inflation and unemployment tended to erode the living standards of the working classes in the city over and above the erosion suffered elsewhere (not having the means to purchase or store large amounts of coal they were often exploited by street hucksters), to the extent that the government had to introduce supplemental food allowances in September 1941. This was frowned upon by some Catholic activists, who resented this 'interference' with the family, a foretaste of some of the rancorous debates which were to follow.[107]

Likewise the concern of the government following the publication of the report of inquiry into working-class housing heralded new approaches to the problem. Lack of amenities for children, poor living conditions and general nutritional problems meant that they were hit badly by TB and rickets (in 1943 an estimated 173 per 1,000 children were suffering from some form of rickets). In 1938, 111,950 people were living in 6,307 tenement houses, half of which were reckoned incurably unfit for habitation. Successive governments had shirked the challenge of buying out professional slum landlords, which could have been done to benefit both state and tenant. The *Irish Press*, which had done much to expose their conditions, had called on the government (which the paper supported) to recognise their plight: 'if this is the second century of slumdom; it is also the 14th year of a self-governed state, when the babies of 1916 are still, as men and women, crying for a happier life for their babies, crying for simple shelter'.[108]

Although some progress had been made on the housing front in Dublin in the 1930s (7,637 dwellings were provided between 1933 and 1939), the problem was that the most impoverished families could not afford to rent them. In 1939 the overall infant and child mortality rates per 1,000 of the population of the Irish Free State was 66; for the Dublin County Borough it was 90. Death rates from TB per 1,000 of the population in the same year were 1.13 nationally, but 1.48 in Dublin.[109] Statistics were one thing, but the emotive memoirs which recall the sheer suffering that TB inflicted give some sense of the unfolding human tragedy. Noël Browne, future Minister for Health, and crusader against TB, recalled that his brother was 'unwanted, crippled and unable to fend for himself or communicate his simplest needs, except to the family; he was unable to mix with his peers. It is impossible to imagine the awesome humiliation and desperation of his life. I have never understood its purpose.'[110] As late as 1945 a report of the TB committee established by the government noted that practical problems such as unpasteurised milk had still not been tackled, and claimed that Dublin slums were littered with crippled children because they were drinking contaminated milk and enduring overcrowding while living at or below the poverty limit. Dr Robert Collis, paediatrician in the National Children's Hospital, maintained in 1941 that approximately 40,000 people in Dublin were trying to feed themselves on sixpence a day and he grew weary of giving medicine to poor children who really needed food.[111] The Catholic Social Services Conference, established by Archbishop McQuaid, ran 27 food centres in Dublin, supplying 250,000 meals per month.

Such problems provided the impetus for post-war attempts to ameliorate the situation, though it was largely through the efforts of women like Dr Dorothy Price, the author of *TB in Childhood* (1942) and a physician in the Royal City of Dublin Hospital, that the BCG vaccination began to be used in Ireland in the 1930s, predating its introduction in the UK. This was indicative of a determination to pioneer a scientific approach to medicine despite resistance (by 1955 a nationwide BCG vaccination programme ensured the administration of 100,000 vaccinations).[112]

'a level below that which is compatible with decency'

Juvenile unemployment was also recognised as socially corrosive; unemployment among adolescent males was much higher than in England and Northern Ireland. In the early 1940s, 30 per cent of boys between 16 and 17 were unemployed, compared with 11.3 per cent in England and Wales and 17.2 per cent in Northern Ireland. Dublin city's unemployment figure at the beginning of the war, 23,250, more than quadrupled to 96,000 at the height of the Emergency.[113] It was often left to voluntary activists, particularly through the Catholic Church, to instigate charity schemes, and in some ways the 1940s witnessed the beginning of a more realistic approach to the problem of poverty, unlike in the 1930s, when distinctions were still being made between the 'deserving' and 'undeserving' poor, with the personal morality of the individual often being blamed for the existence of poverty. But it was still the case that Catholic charities like the Society of Saint Vincent de Paul, Dublin's most active charity group, did not see its duty or function to suggest solutions, given that its aim remained that of self-sanctification in the relief of distress: a middle class urged to elevate itself spiritually by assisting the poor. Their decision not to get involved in campaigns for better housing illustrated the limitations of these charitable organisations in the actual relief of poverty, though individual members worked hard and heroically. According to the *Irish Catholic Directory* of 1945, the Legion of Mary was concerned with the 'careful selection of men whose inadequate moral and material equipment causes them to live on a level below that which is compatible with decency and who are accordingly undergoing a process of degradation'.[114] But it was also the case that a growing demand for professional training in the area of social services was one of the effects of evolving public-health awareness.

Bewilderment was also expressed about a lack of will or initiative on the part of those experiencing social degradation to demonstrate a commitment to improvement or progress. Charity activists in Dublin during the Emergency expressed frustration at the apathy and unwillingness in the ranks of the working classes when it came to helping themselves. In rural areas, many schemes aimed at providing water and sewerage schemes were stymied because some communities showed little interest in connecting themselves to new supplies. The truth was that there was a broad acceptance of substandard accommodation in many districts of Ireland, with some regarding the ownership of property, however dilapidated and under-serviced, as an end in itself. This was something Seán MacEntee, Minister for Local Government and Public Health, had frequently drawn attention to in private, noting that residents were slow to embrace schemes designed to improve their welfare and lamenting what he termed the 'conservative outlook' of the Irish farmer.[115] It was often left to the women of rural Ireland, chiefly the Irish Countrywomen's Association (see below), to challenge this inertia and provide the impetus for rural communities to embrace modernisation, particularly with regard to initiatives which would lighten labour-intensive domestic work through the provision of electricity and running water. It was still the norm in rural Ireland in the 1930s and 1940s for house-dwellers (nearly always the women) to travel significant distances to water pumps and wells.

Those who were not in a position to help themselves owing to mental illness were afforded little succour in the 1930s and 1940s. The experience of victims seemed to provide further proof that the family unit could mask the harshest attitudes of all, as the problem of mental health was swept under the carpet. The removal of those suffering from mental illness from the fabric of the family perpetuated the stigma and ignorance associated with the condition. A psychiatrist writing in the *Bell* in 1944 believed that medical experts working in the field in the year 2000 would write of 'the crude, unscientific treatment of mental disease' in early independent Ireland.[116] Ireland was certainly not at the forefront of innovative research in the field of psychiatry, though by 1945 methods of modern treatment were being used in most mental hospitals. The 1945 Mental Health Act was by no means radical, but rather a belated amendment of Georgian and Victorian lunacy laws that dated back to 1821, and which had been amended in Britain in 1930. It marked an attempt to prevent mental homes remaining dumping grounds for the unwanted, replacing the description 'lunatic' with 'person of unsound mind', and reforming the system of admission. Official figures for those receiving treatment for mental illness in 1945 stood at 19,358.[117] While at least they were now officially being depicted as patients rather than prisoners, with new categories of temporary and voluntary patients, the institutions in which they were cared for remained decidedly Victorian.

'the greatest bleeding heart racket in the world'

Fianna Fáil made a firm commitment to increased spending on social services on coming to office in 1932, and the figures illustrate that social spending rose from £8 million in 1929, 36 per cent of the government's budget, to £12.6 million or 40 per cent of the budget by 1939. Within their first year of office the greatest advances were made in the areas of housing, pensions and unemployment relief. Cottages for the agricultural labourers had become something of a catch-cry on the hustings in 1932. Successful schemes from earlier decades resulted in over 40,000 labourers' cottages being built by 1932, meaning that in some districts labourers were actually living in better conditions than the small farmers. Fianna

Fáil wanted to develop these schemes, partly to prevent rural class agitation from dominating the political arena, but also because it followed logically from their ideas on rural self-sufficiency and their commitment to the prosperity of the countryside. In 1932 they increased the government subsidy for cottage building from 36 to 60 per cent of the local authorities loan repayments, with the 1936 Labourers Act allowing many cottage tenants the opportunity to buy their cottages.[118]

Aimed at married labourers and rural workers in permanent employment, Fianna Fáil's cottage scheme occasionally caused contention when it came to compulsory acquisition of sites, inquiries into which exposed many of the iniquities associated with land distribution in Ireland. Between 1932 and 1940, 16,526 cottages were built. Although sanitary conditions remained poor, overall housing conditions in rural areas were improving, to the extent that the average number of persons per room in rural areas declined from 1.9 in 1926 to 1.08 in 1936, to one person per room in 1940. There was also significant disparity between local demand and the numbers of cottages built (it was ironic that more were built in Wicklow, where the number of labourers declined, than in Clare, where the number of labourers increased). Although wider economic influences and emigration meant that there was little chance of rooting enough labourers to the land, the building of cottages may have slowed the decline and made a significant contribution to relatively peaceful class relations in certain parts of rural Ireland.[119]

Fianna Fáil also managed to make the old-age pension, so contentious an issue in the 1920s, less so. Expenditure on it rose significantly in the early 1930s and more appeals relating to means were decided in favour of the claimants. As well as the introduction of populist measures such as free-milk schemes, income generated by the hospitals sweepstakes meant considerable money could be spent on improving the hospital services in most counties (the Public Hospitals Bill of 1933 shifted responsibility for overseeing the sweepstakes from the Minister for Justice to the Minister for Local Government and Public Health, and established a Hospitals Commission, to which all hospitals could apply for funding). Given the increased number of working- and middle-class people seeking hospital treatment, the needs of the community rather than the needs of individual hospitals were deemed more important, with some concern at the number of patients capable of paying being catered for in voluntary hospitals at the expense of the poor.

With National Health Insurance Acts in 1933 and 1941, initiatives were also undertaken to providing protection for the working class against the cost of hospital treatment, with a corresponding effort to increase control of local-government activities in health care.[120] There was an improvement in health care in the 1930s, partly because the county and district hospitals that had replaced the workhouses were offering free medical treatment to the poor. The government was also able to employ the funds rolling into the hospitals sweepstakes, operating as a sort of national lottery, to embark on an ambitious programme of hospital building, and the funding from the sweepstakes undoubtedly contributed to an improvement in standards, with hospital care of a high quality by international standards. By the summer of 1931 the sweepstakes had raised about £1 million for the participating hospitals, an enormous sum given that in 1933 the 52 voluntary hospitals had a combined annual income of less than £400,000.[121] The government insisted that voluntary hospitals remain charitable institutions (and thus more egalitarian) in order to be eligible for public funds. But by 1935, only 40 per cent of patients in the voluntary hospitals were treated for free, and 'the hospitals were perceived to favour paying patients'.[122]

Cumann na nGaedheal's decision to legalise the sweepstakes had not only been a response to the financial difficulties of the voluntary hospitals, but also a pragmatic admission that many sweepstakes and lotteries were already operating, and were hugely popular, even though they were illegal under Lottery Acts of the nineteenth century. In the early 1920s, Thomas Johnson, the Labour Party leader, had spoken out against any moves to legalise them for fundraising purposes, on the grounds that they would 'exhibit the sores of Ireland and the poverty of Ireland to the world'. But by the late 1920s and early 1930s, the need to counteract the hospital crisis took precedence. The legislation governing them and the public limited company established to administer them was sufficiently loose to make huge fortunes for their promoters, including Richard Duggan, a mastermind of sweepstakes in the 1920s, and Joe McGrath, a War of Independence veteran. What constituted legitimate promoters' expenses was not established, and audited accounts did not account for all the money that was spent. As one former employee of the sweepstakes put it: 'you couldn't print in the audit accounts an amount allocated to smuggling and bribing'.

Between 1930 and 1987, it is estimated that £247 million was paid out in prize money, with £133 million raised for Irish hospitals. The sweepstakes caused tremendous excitement (and employed over 3,000 women in Dublin by the mid-1940s); the prizes were astronomical (for the 1932 Grand National the prize fund was £2.3 million), and international media attention accompanied the glamorous parades in Dublin where the tickets were brought to their mixing destination, with further elaborate ceremonies for the carrying of tickets out of mixing machines. The sweepstakes process inaugurated smuggling rackets on a grand scale, as tickets were sold illegally outside Ireland in 150 countries worldwide, with the counterfoils and money sent back to false addresses in Ireland. There were frequent complaints from Britain and America about the circulation of tickets, as lotteries were illegal in these countries. A network of republican veterans oversaw their distribution in America, and the profits may have helped to finance endeavours that could not have been further removed from medical care, such as the purchase of the IRA's tools of war. Successive governments turned a blind eye to the blatant illegalities and personal riches the sweepstakes conferred on its promoters and on those behind the smuggling rackets and 'kickback' payments (in this regard it's worth noting that the directors of the sweepstakes company were substantial political donors). The latitude the promoters had was extraordinary; even the tame *Reader's Digest* described the sweepstakes as 'the greatest bleeding heart racket in the world'. It was not until the 1970s that journalists could reveal that only a small fraction of the money raised actually went to the hospitals.[123]

In terms of staffing, those in the medical profession experienced many fears and frustrations during the 1930s and 1940s. The doctors in the service of local authorities had to rely in the main on private patients for most of their income; while Irish doctors were much in demand in Britain. The position of nurses was much worse, with poor pay (a dispensary midwife could earn as little as £25 per annum in the early 1940s), long hours and little provision for old age. One of the difficulties was the lack of a unified organisation that could speak for all nurses. At a symposium in 1942 dealing with the nursing profession and its needs, a prominent Dublin Jesuit, P. J. Gannon, referred to Irish nurses as the 'ill-used stepdaughter of the community'.[124]

To cure and to care?
There was also debate during the war about the introduction of children's

allowances, widows' and orphans' pensions having been introduced in
1935. Here, the debate was starting later than it had done in Britain,
though ultimately in Ireland children's allowances were to be introduced before they were in Britain; a development undoubtedly influenced
by concerns about population decline. But the Department of Finance
baulked at the idea of taxing higher incomes to finance them, arguing:
'the principle has not been generally accepted that the state has responsibility for the relief of poverty in all its degrees'.[125] A decision was made
to introduce an allowance scheme by compulsory contributory insurance, payable through the employer, some members of the government
being worried that a non-contributory scheme would provoke the ire of
Catholic sociologists by being seen as undue state interference in family
life. Although allowances had originally been envisaged to relieve large
families, it was a payment which was to apply to all families. Unlike in
England, a proposal that the payment should be made to the mother was
defeated in the Dáil, Seán Lemass referring to the view that it could begin
the process of increasing the economic independence of married women as
'rather revolutionary'.[126]

Population decline was always a concern, but what carried the measure
within government circles was an increasing awareness that the state had a
more active role to play in relieving poverty. Ideologically, it also seemed a
more appropriate way to combat family poverty, as opposed to increasing
the employment of wives, which was at odds with Fianna Fáil's position
on the merits of females in the labour force. The accompanying debates
were also an indication that the Free State, in combining aspects of British
social thinking on the welfare state with its own Catholic social thought,
was by no means immune from the influence of European developments
during and immediately after the war. In a sense Fianna Fáil was entering
the second period of expansion in social-welfare legislation from the early
1940s on; and developments in Britain obviously precipitated new ideas,
though both contemporaries and historians questioned the wisdom of
an agricultural country using an industrial nation as an appropriate role
model.

But if there was a certain Christian pragmatism in the welcome
accorded the Beveridge plan in 1942, a more dogmatic conservatism was
also to emerge in Ireland in relation to the role of the state in providing for welfare. Through membership of such groups as the International
Social Security Association, Irish officials were up to date on social policy

across Europe. As far back as 1934 the management committee of the National Health Insurance Society had travelled to Yugoslavia to examine the workings of an equivalent insurance society. Indeed, the repeated reference to the experiences of other countries by senior Irish civil servants would suggest that Ireland's intellectual insularity during this period has been exaggerated. The government had also shown itself impatient with proposals from Catholic social thinkers in the area of social welfare that did not seriously address cost, or the problem of amending and altering existing structures of power.

In October 1944 the Bishop of Clonfert, Dr John Dignan, proposed a national insurance scheme, suggesting Irish social services should be unified and transferred to an insurance basis to be administered by an enlarged version of the National Health Insurance Society, of which he was chairman. There were many shortcomings to his proposal; not least the paradox of believing the bureaucracy of the Irish social services could be overcome by creating an enlarged system of centralisation which would not be answerable to parliament. The Minister for Local Government and Public Health, Seán MacEntee, reacted angrily (no plan, after all, had been submitted to the government). Significantly, he was hostile to the Beveridge Plan also because of its emphasis on dependence on the state for benefits and his opposition to compulsory insurance benefits. He also disliked its emphasis on the regimentation of labour and the placing of economic policy above and beyond changes of government.[127] MacEntee asserted his ministerial authority by dismissing Dignan from his chairmanship of the NHIS and introduced a bill to give him 'clear and unequivocal power' to keep the NHIS out of political debate. Susannah Riordan points out that this was not an anti-Church crusade – MacEntee was in fact very sympathetic to Catholic social thought – but rather an assertion of power and the primacy of existing parliamentary forms which Dignan had misused his position to challenge, thereby shooting himself in the foot by undermining the very type of vocational body he sought to champion.[128]

There were inconsistencies, too, in relation to MacEntee's position, given his opposition to the Beveridge report and his support for centralising and interventionist measures such as the Public Health Bill of 1945. The war years were in fact a time of vigorous activity in the areas of health and welfare administration, helped by the appointment of James Deeny, an expert on the links between nutrition and poverty, as Chief Medical Officer in 1943. He later penned a robust, informative but rather self-serving account of his time in the position, *To Cure and to Care* (1989). A separate Department of Health was established in 1947 and there was a gradual re-evaluation of the role of the state and, by extension, the role of local authorities in relation to public health, and the need to be more interventionist about such matters as the isolation of those with infectious diseases. New proposals were not just centred on the move towards preventive rather than curative medicine and the availability of specialists and services to a wider range of the population than previously, but also on the desire to integrate general practice, maternity care, child services and public health, and to provide these services in so far as possible free of cost to break the link between health services and public assistance. They were thus radical proposals, but as Ruth Barrington pointed out, unlike the author of the Beveridge report in England, those who reported and proposed reform in the Irish health services 'were not independent of the system and free to toss ideas into the political and administrative court' without serious consequences.[129]

Although the instigators of new departures did not see themselves as proposing socialised medicine, there were already rumblings from the medical profession and the Catholic Church, which so venerated the medics. Catholic commentators in such journals as *Studies* were quibbling about the implications for Ireland of the inexorable rise of what some saw as a 'planning fever', spreading after a long incubation in Moscow. The explicit warning was that while all wanted improved public health, limitations of possibility in the Irish context needed to be recognised and human liberty preserved.[130]

'getting rid of the Bishop of Galway on the grounds of War Economy'
It was understandable that most of these unsettling noises were being made by the vocationalist lobby within the Catholic Church, which had first made its presence felt in the 1930s and commanded enough attention by 1939 to instigate the Commission on Vocational Organisation, which sat until 1943. The chief problem, as identified by Eamonn McKee, was that 'as a philosophy of government vocationalism was ill-conceived, in that it did not address itself to the problem of amending or supplanting the existing derivation of power'.[131] Those who championed vocationalism included prominent Dublin-based Jesuits like Fr Edmund Coyne and Fr Edward Cahill, author of *Framework of a Christian State*, and influential Catholic lay academics such as Alfred O'Rahilly and Michael Tierney,

future presidents of University College Cork and University College Dublin respectively. It has already been seen how these ideas were thought suitable for the regeneration of rural Ireland; but their proposals irked the defenders of strong central government who were loath to share or decentralise the structures they commanded.

Given the climate of fascism in Europe it was also perhaps inevitable that the lines of distinction between 'vocationalism', 'corporatism', 'the corporate state' and indeed 'dictatorship' would be somewhat blurred. Vocationalists continually attacked excessive bureaucracy, and the simple idea, as noted by an anonymous contributor to *Studies* in 1933, that 'half a dozen cabinet ministers, the "strong" personalities of a given cabinet and a dozen or so civil servants, heads of departments or experts, literally dominate all the social and a great deal of the economic activity of the citizens of a country. Citizens, deprived of any scope for the social side of their nature, become virtually individualists, each intent on his own affairs.'[132] The truth, however, was that Catholic 'experts' could not agree on an exact definition of vocationalism, and it tended to simmer uncomfortably under the surface rather than erupting into a concrete political framework. Joe Lee suggested it revealed certain intellectual shortcomings on the part of the Church in attempting to counteract centralisation,[133] but the reality was that they more than met their match in governments determined not to allow challenges to their authority, as Bishop Dignan was to find in relation to his plans for social insurance.

Many activists wrote of the potential power of vocational structures to redefine democracy for the new state, by organising the various professions and interest groups in the country into councils which could regulate sectional interests and be answerable to an overall national vocational assembly. These ideas were fleshed out in the report of the Vocational Commission, which, chaired by the redoubtable Bishop Browne of Galway, had 25 members, and met 312 times before producing its substantial report in 1943. Its publications provoked both indifference and hostility. Mussolini and Salazar had no shortage of admirers in Ireland, but some vocationalists saw the danger in taking corporate ideas too far. One academic sympathiser from Cork, J. A. Busteed, writing to the editor of *Studies*, in a letter preserved in the Jesuit Archives in Dublin, had written the word 'corporate' but crossed it out in favour of 'organic'; yet he said he was still not clear 'as to the distinction between the desirable corporate scheme of affairs and the undesirable state absolutism of Mussolini'.[134]

Catholic intellectuals may have felt that they were in a strong position in the 1930s to launch a campaign for reform, given there was now a conservative land-owning rural class to dominate, the backing of the papal encyclical *Quadragesimo Anno* on the reconstruction of the social order, and seemingly pious politicians who were still basking in the glory of having hosted the Catholic Eucharistic Congress of 1932. But they also recognised that their knowledge was largely theoretical. De Valera tended to be more sympathetic to English rather than continental ideas. He viewed favourably the Whitley system of administration in the UK, where district councils operated in conjunction with national councils in the arbitration of industrial disputes. In any case, it was more politically convenient to defer action by accepting the proposal of Michael Tierney to form a commission which would considerably delay having to take any concrete action, and would also provide a convenient talking shop for like-minded Catholic intellectuals (who heard evidence from over 200 organisations). The war was also to militate against the Commission's effectiveness, and indeed its *raison d'être*, de Valera reminding the Commission at the outset that the post-war world would be very different from the one they were to prescribe cures for.

The Commission's report offered a Catholic social interpretation of Ireland; one which few of its inhabitants could relate to, one which irritated serving government ministers (owing to criticism about the way their departments were run), and one which, in the long term, left the Church looking stubbornly, and impractically, idealistic. In taking evidence and compiling its report, the Commission sometimes seemed more interested in judging than inquiring. From the outset, it annoyed the administrators of government, an official in the Department of Finance suggesting: 'there would be a certain grim satisfaction in getting rid of the Bishop of Galway on the grounds of War Economy'.[135] Browne admitted in private that it was difficult to convince all the members of the Commission to be as devoted to its labours and ideas as were himself and the Jesuit Edmund Coyne. When the report appeared Flann O'Brien dismissed it as an impractical 'monument of verbosity', deriding its recommendation of layers of new structures based on parish and county units. He suggested the proposed institutes, conferences and boards were unnecessary given that nearly every profession had some class of organisation to represent and defend it.[136]

The insistence that the alternative to vocational organisation was 'competitive anarchy' or 'state regimentation' seemed far-fetched to most. The fact that it was, however, being debated both publicly and privately, and in a wider European context, was one illustration that vocational-ism represented in Ireland a developed Catholic intellectualism. This was reflected in the pages of *Studies*, *Irish Monthly* and *Irish Ecclesiastical Record*, and it is fallacious to see the report as merely a repository of Catholic extremism.

In any case, Fianna Fáil ministers hardly saw themselves as being out of touch with Rome, and it was common in the early 1930s for them to suggest that their policies were in line with Catholic social teaching as endorsed by the Vatican. De Valera visited the Pope in 1933, part of an attempt by him and his officials to remove any doubt that may have existed about their commitment to the Church given the events of the Civil War period, when some republicans had been excommunicated. Con-sidering Ireland's contribution to international Catholicism, the Vatican had reason to foster good relations with the Irish Church regardless of which party was in power. Joseph Walsh, future Irish ambassador to the Holy See, made plenty of explicit statements about Ireland's commitment to Rome, and as Dermot Keogh notes was at pains to point out in 1933 that 'more members of the Irish Free State government have gone to Rome for the Holy Year than of any other government in the world'.[137] The Irish constitution, too, did much to remove any residual suspicion which may have lingered. Notwithstanding their commitment to Catholicism, Irish representatives in Rome still had to negotiate the parameters of Vatican politics and were not always afforded a position of prestige.

De Valera was clever in how he framed the parameters of his relation-ship with the Church and Catholic social teaching, skilfully keeping at arm's length from vocationalism but not explicitly dissociating himself from the concept; indeed, the same approach coloured much of his attitude to Church–state relations. He did not share the belief that there was a need for vigorous Catholic 'reconstruction' as championed by newspapers like the relaunched *Standard* in 1938,[138] and the more firmly entrenched his power became, the less anxiety there was to establish his Catholic cre-dentials. By the time the Vocational Commission reported he had been in office for 11 years and was to win another general election in the same year.

'nobody was self-conscious about sweat'

There are thus many levels at which the influence of the Catholic Church in the 1930s and 1940s can be assessed. The percentage of the Catholic population in the Free State increased throughout this period, accounting for 92.6 per cent in 1926, 93.4 per cent in 1936 and 94.3 per cent in 1946. The Eucharistic Congress, held in Dublin in 1932, involved the close collaboration of Church, state and citizens. The centenary celebrations of Catholic emancipation in 1929 had already set a precedent for large-scale, often dramatic expressions of the Free State's religious identity for both domestic and foreign audiences, with a heavy emphasis on the idea of survival amidst centuries of oppression before ultimate triumph. Such commemorations were also used to draw attention to the plight of Catholics in Northern Ireland. There was a tendency, too, to emphasise that Irish Catholicism knew or recognised no class boundaries; the *Catholic Emancipation Centenary Record* had been at pains to point out that 'profuse and brilliant as the display in the centres of fashion, that made by the poor in the back streets was of surpassing excellence'.[139] The display in 1932 was on an even grander scale, as a National Congress League collected funds and launched a crusade of prayer, encouraging the city's poor to give their tenements a face lift, seeing no irony in the vulgarity of spending £2,000 to provide a cavalry escort in special dress uniform for the Papal Legate.[140]

Nonetheless, for such a homogeneously Catholic state, the Eucharistic Congress was as least divisive an event as could be found, and the national press commented on it as an occasion that demonstrated the union of Christian ideals and 'national endeavour' that had been manifest in all important Irish historical events. In Dublin it was estimated there was 12 miles of bunting, and one million people participated in the ceremonies,[141] making it difficult to avoid the conclusion that this was indeed a Catholic state for a Catholic people. It was this demonstration of the democracy of the Irish faith which so impressed English Catholics like G. K. Chesterton, as seen in his book *Christendom in Dublin* (1932).

But such images of unity, and often triumphalism, should not be the only yardstick with which to measure the impact of religion in Ireland at this time, given the whole host of mediating structures through which Catholicism operated in Irish life. Debates continued to rage about the morality of dance halls and jazz music, and the amount some of the bishops had to say about these issues seemed to indicate not only how seriously the Church took them, but also the degree to which their directives were being ignored. The complaints eventually resulted in the Dance Halls Act of 1935, which vested power in district justices to grant licences. The truth was that this legislation had little long-term impact on Irish social life. There was a lack of uniformity among the district justices as to what constituted a threat. Writing sardonically in *The Bell* in 1941, Flann O'Brien estimated there were 1,200 licensed dance halls in the 26 counties, accounting for perhaps 5,000 dances annually, but he suggested there were another 5,000 unlicensed. Such entertainment was, it seemed, strictly class-based; O'Brien distinguished between dances for the wealthy (which even some of the district justices attended) and the cheap dances, held in school prefabs with poor ventilation, 'where nobody was self-conscious about sweat'.[142]

In January 1934, in Mohill, a small village in County Leitrim, a campaign against jazz music was launched following Church condemnation of this form of entertainment. But any chance that there would be legislation against such a foreign imposition was diminished by the secretary of the Gaelic League's denunciation of the Minister for Finance for selling 'the musical soul of the nation for the dividends of sponsored jazz music' on Irish radio.[143] Such groups as the secretive Knights of Columbanus were also active in supporting campaigns like these. Although the Knights received recognition from the Irish Hierarchy in 1934, it was very much up to individual bishops whether or not to support it. It is significant that de Valera was hostile to the idea of members of Fianna Fáil joining the group, maintaining that it was absurd, in a country where 93 per cent of the population was Catholic, to have an organisation for the protection of Catholic interests.[144]

Although de Valera took advice from senior Church figures in drafting the Constitution (and accepted much of their advice on social matters), he resisted the demand that Catholicism should be recognised as the state religion. Instead, de Valera recognised its 'special position' in the Irish Free State, while safeguarding the rights of minority churches, whose leaders he also widely consulted, being particularly friendly with the Chief Rabbi of Ireland's Jewish community, Dr Isaac Herzog. De Valera, too, was capable of withstanding the complaints of bishops who criticised the Economic War and his refusal to support the Franco regime in Spain (see below). This did not mean there were question marks over his religious devotion, but rather reveal a politician who did not want Ireland to become a theocracy or clerical state. Throughout his career he proved adept at handling Church–state relations, and was one of the few politicians able to face down the Church when he thought necessary, in contrast to the more subservient, at times sycophantic, attitude of leaders of the other political parties.

While the 1937 Constitution was endorsed by the Church, which was particularly happy with the clauses venerating the family unit, there was nothing uniquely Irish about this; the Church was an important ideological pillar in the Vichy regime in France from 1940 to 1944, for example. Seán MacEntee shared some of the sentiments of Vichy familiasts concerning the wisdom of adult suffrage, suggesting voting in the senate and local elections should be confined just to married men and women with family responsibilities.[145] Although this was a complaint about universal suffrage rather than a legislative initiative, it was an extreme view shared by thinkers such as Edward Cahill, and demonstrates that such moralising about 'traditional' gender roles was by no means the preserve of the leaders of the Irish Catholic Church in the 1930s and 1940s; as in France, it was a case of Catholic vision and national needs coinciding.[146]

Charges of insularity and narrow-mindedness cannot be levelled at all aspects of Catholic activism. Not only did they make an enormous contribution to education, but apart from the Irish labour movement, the leaders of the Catholic social movement seemed to be the only group making a noise about social problems. McQuaid, following his appointment as Archbishop of Dublin in 1940, demonstrated a concern about poverty and ill health, albeit as long as it was tackled or highlighted on his terms, and he did not want to challenge the basis of the Irish health system. Missionary work was also an important part of Irish clerical endeavour, particularly in Africa, Asia and South and Central America. This was not only an expression of zeal for the faith but was also presented in the 1930s as a re-enactment of Ireland's glorious past. Whatever about stressing the need for catechism and conversion, these were also modern missions in terms of the emphasis on scientific, technical, welfare and educational issues.[147] Irish priests and nuns abroad, it seemed, could often be more liberated and radical than they could be at home, as exemplified by the pioneering Dubliner Marie Martin, who in 1936 founded the Medical Missionaries of Mary.

'immediate and admirable docility'

Those who grew to adulthood in the 1930s and 1940s found both solace and discomfort in their experience of Irish Catholicism. The novelist John McGahern, who was born in 1935, lost his faith in later life, but as an adult expressed great gratitude for the spiritual remnants of his upbringing. He had positive experiences of the sense of equality, mystery and wonderment that religion created, but also of the sense of security it gave many young Irish Catholics, centred around their identification with home, school and church. He also saw many of the preaching Redemptorists as performers, appreciated like horror novels. But interestingly, he drew attention to the issue of class and Irish religion, and recalled that:

> In those days it took considerable wealth to put a boy through Maynooth and they looked and acted as if they came from a line of swaggering, confident men who dominated field and market and whose only culture was cunning, money and brute force. Though they could be violently generous and sentimental at times, in their hearts they despised their own people.[148]

McGahern had his own reasons to be bitter about the Catholic Church (see chapter 7), but his reflections are important in the context of the mixture of appreciation and alienation which many people took to adulthood.

Others, like the poet Patrick Kavanagh, in his poems *Lough Derg* and *The Great Hunger*, depicted a Church repressing instinct, pleasure and creativity, but still felt they could not be apart from it or escape it, attempting instead to marry modern Catholicism with the freedom of an older, pagan church. Nonetheless, institutional adherence to the Catholic Church in Ireland remained exceptionally high. McGahern's description of such priests could also be applied by critics to John Charles McQuaid (referred to by his most recent biographer as 'ruler of Catholic Ireland'), who was Archbishop of Dublin from 1940 to 1972 and a man of exceptional talent, cunning, faith and ruthlessness. He was for many the ultimate symbol of clerical domination of Irish life throughout these decades. There was no acre of the Catholic field in Dublin during these decades that was not observed and maintained by McQuaid, who believed the diocese of Dublin had lacked leadership under his predecessor, Archbishop Byrne. In princely and dogmatic style, he also kept an extensive archive with exceptional diligence. The collection reveals his superb talent for administration, but also his obsession, first as headmaster of Blackrock College and later as Archbishop of Dublin, with control. His advice was given whether sought or not, and he had a direct line to government which was unsurprising given that his appointment had been championed by both the Taoiseach and Papal Nuncio, although as seen in relation to the Constitution his 'suggestions' were not always taken on board.

McQuaid was also an effective fundraiser and champion of pet projects such as the Catholic Social Services Conference and the Emigrant Welfare Bureau, and in the words of John Cooney 'was particularly adept at persuading the state authorities to finance church involvement in the voluntary sector, while retaining ecclesiastical control of projects'.[149] But McQuaid was also critical of many of the Catholic lay organisations such as the Society of Saint Vincent de Paul, the Legion of Mary and Muintir na Tíre, partly because he did not feel their devotion was sustained by sufficient ecclesiastical knowledge. He was also excessively hostile to any outside criticism of conditions prevailing in his diocese, and did his utmost to curtail the influence of Protestants in Dublin, while dismissing their theological competence, suppressing, for example, the Mercier Society, which had been established to promote inter-Church dialogue. When it was wound up he thanked the members for the 'immediate and admirable docility' shown towards his command.[150]

'well-intentioned young men occupied learning to form fours'

Whatever breaches may have occasionally taken place in the relative consensus between Church and state, hard-liners of both the left and right retained a presence in Ireland of the 1930s and 1940s. The mainstream Labour Party failed to develop into a political force capable of challenging the two larger parties, partly because Fianna Fáil had stolen many of their ideological clothes in the early 1930s. Indeed, many Fianna Fáil members were to maintain throughout the century that they were in effect the real Labour Party of Ireland. In 1933 the Labour Party had only 8 TDs, despite the separation of the Irish Trades Union Congress and the political party. In 1939 one sixth of the Irish workforce was in industry, and 150,000 workers unionised, and at the outset of the war trade unions were politically confused and organisationally fragmented, while the Labour Party, in the words of one trade union historian, continued to laud James Connolly as a prophet 'while his teachings were gingerly put aside'.[151] There were continuing divisions between indigenous trade unions and those that were

British-based. The presence of British trade unions at the 1939 reform congress incensed the more nationalist unions, and much of the future faction sniping can be traced back to the divisions of these years, given the ongoing conflict between William O'Brien and James Larkin. What exacerbated tension even more was a divisive process of voluntary and government-sponsored trade union reform. The 1941 Trade Union Act, which sought to recognise the trade union movement and rationalise bargaining structures, had the tacit support of the Irish Transport and General Workers' Union, whereas it was opposed by Larkin's Workers' Union of Ireland and a large number of British-based unions. The Act was controversial on account of the inclusion of the power to restrict wages, but the ITGWU leadership eschewed the syndicalist rhetoric of the founding fathers and the militant campaigning of the grassroots, and sought refuge and excuses in the political consensus which surrounded neutrality.[152]

The Labour Party recovered to capture 17 seats at the general election of 1943, after the number of Labour Party branches grew from 174 in 1941 to 750 in 1943, demonstrating a frustration with Fianna Fáil's unbroken electoral dominance. But the party then split in 1944, as five of the eight TDs who were ITGWU members formed the National Labour Party, rejecting the Larkinite wing of the party, who were deemed too close to communism in political outlook. They quickly lost the seats they had gained, and it was unfortunate and unwise for the Labour Party to have allowed the personalities of both O'Brien and Larkin to have overshadowed so much. The divisions in the labour movement in the early 1940s were paradoxically caused by greater unionisation and mobilisation of labour militancy, reflected in the pages of the *Torch*. If O'Brien had been instrumental in bringing Labour into the established political fold, by the early 1940s new ideas and indeed loyalties had gained currency, and found O'Brien's leadership selfish (it was said he talked of principle while he thought of power[153]). A measure of the conservativeness of the party was that it expelled Owen Sheehy Skeffington in 1943 for publicly engaging in controversy with a priest over the nature of socialism. Sheehy Skeffington hosted meetings of the Secular Society in Dublin, where those of various affiliations, but united in the belief of free expression, would gather.[154] Meanwhile, critics of Fianna Fáil saw it as a party that during the Emergency was able both to launch attacks on workers and still come to an understanding with sections of the trade union hierarchy.

Accusations that communists were an intrinsic part of the Fianna Fáil party were flung during the general election of 1932, reflecting the fears of Church and state about an upsurge in left-wing activity in the early 1930s. The Department of Justice was keeping detailed notes on groups such as the IRA, Cumann na mBan, Irish Friends of Soviet Russia, the Workers' Revolutionary Party of Ireland and the Irish National Unemployed Movement. The appearance of Saor Éire in 1931 provided evidence for many of a conspiracy between the IRA and communists to undermine the Irish Free State, partly prompting the coercive Public Safety Act, which appeared in the same year. Red scares were effective in undermining any support which the extreme left in Ireland hoped to gain, and in the long term would contribute to the IRA's return to a narrow guerrilla war philosophy as well as heralding the departure of talented social activists such as Peadar O'Donnell. The truth was that most of these subversive groups had tiny memberships. Although there may have been an IRA hardcore of up to 5,000 in 1931, it was clear relatively soon after Fianna Fáil came to power that there would be no fruitful collaboration between them and the IRA, the organisation being declared illegal in 1936, with de Valera's speeches beginning to place a premium on the idea of the 'rule of order'. Having increased in the early 1930s, IRA membership plummeted from 7,358 in 1935 to 3,844 in 1936.[155]

In forming Saor Éire as a political party, an attempt had been made to link the IRA with the prevalent social upheaval and was an important historical revision for the IRA, an organisation that prided itself on tradition and continuity. Peadar O'Donnell recognised that the absence of a commitment to real political campaigns would render it relatively worthless, and that it could be easily used by the IRA leadership as merely a political alibi. The creation of Saor Éire was an attempt by some in the IRA to apply the principles of 'class against class' in Ireland; or to create a new political forum for disgruntled radicals within republicanism.[156] It was in effect a recognition of the limitations and narrowness of the IRA's Civil War strategy, as had been noted by individuals such as Liam Mellows.

Similar aims were attributed to the Republican Congress of March 1934, but the desire to engage in 'mass struggles' was being attempted by a movement that did not have an overall radical ethos; quite simply, there were more non-socialist republicans than there were socialist republicans, and their proposed alternative to the widely acknowledged injustices in Ireland of the 1930s was unconvincing. In many ways, what the IRA experienced at this juncture was an unfocused radicalism which came to be complemented by an explicit anti-communism.[157] The withdrawal of leading members of the IRA from the Republican Congress facilitated this and exposed the ideological incoherence and contradictions within republicanism; those on the left wanted to target industrial workers, small farmers and traders as well as the Northern working class. It was the first organised attempt to mobilise such forces as a group distinct from the conservative middle-class leadership, working on the basis that there were precedents for working-class confrontational politics in Irish history, particularly during the First World War. In the words of George Gilmore, one of the IRA leaders in the 1930s, if the IRA did not go down this path it would simply keep 'well-intentioned young men occupied learning to form fours, instead of working for national and social progress'.[158] Peadar O'Donnell and his ilk were perhaps justified in believing that in the early 1930s the political space existed for a radical movement, but it seemed his progressive instincts were directed into communism and the IRA, where they were subsumed by the elitist assumptions of both movements. O'Donnell's contention that he 'knew the insides of the minds of the mass of folk in rural Ireland' was somewhat delusional, this assessment coming from a revolutionary socialist who cultivated links with the rich and powerful, collected fine art and speculated on the Stock Exchange.[159] The most recent history of the IRA in the 1930s, by Brian Hanley, reveals a movement plagued by contradictions; but the belief that social and political campaigns would 'divert our minds and divide our energies', and undermine armed struggle, ensured the maintenance of a militarist ethos amongst those who felt that the revolution of 1918–23 was by no means over.

'Come on lads and we'll kick the fu---rs out of town!'
The Communist Party, formed in June 1933, was reported to have had a maximum of 300 members with perhaps only 50–60 of them active, which may make James Hogan's *Could Ireland Become Communist?* (1935) seem highly alarmist; it was a party that was to become increasingly moderate by the time of the Emergency, abandoning its attachment to anti-capitalist policies, with the Dublin branch dissolving itself into the Labour Party by 1941. Hogan's chief concern had been to depict those sympathetic to communism in the IRA as a threat to democracy and religion, believing there could be no 'Christian communists' in Ireland, to which Peadar O'Donnell replied by accusing him of being

the theoretician of fascism in Ireland.[160] In any case, the enormous popularity enjoyed by the Blueshirts ensured anti-communist hysteria became populist and afforded Eoin O'Duffy a political platform he embraced with gusto.

It is important to locate Hogan's intellectual outpourings in the almost frenzied and paranoid atmosphere of the early 1930s, which facilitated the emergence of the Blueshirts, a group which by 1934 had between thirty and forty thousand members and undoubtedly possessed certain fascist traits, though not in the sense of German or Italian fascism. An appreciation of fascism was remote from the concerns of the rank-and-file members, who were more preoccupied with the hardships that the Economic War foisted on the farming community. Members enjoyed the sense of belonging at recreational level, whether through dances, picnics, Gaelic football, cycling or boxing matches.[161] The emergence of the Army Comrades' Association, a forerunner of the Blueshirt movement, was very much a product of the Economic War and a movement designed, in theory, to protect freedom of speech and assembly and oppose the policies of Fianna Fáil. In February 1933, having been dismissed as Commissioner of the Gardaí, O'Duffy was invited to lead the Army Comrades' Association, which subsequently became the National Guard. Banned in 1933, it subsequently amalgamated with the Centre Party and Cumann na nGaedheal to become Fine Gael. O'Duffy, not an elected politician, became its president, with Cosgrave leading the political party in the Dáil. O'Duffy was quickly ousted in 1934, a wise decision, given that, according to a Garda report, he was boasting that 'we have as much guns as the IRA'.[162]

The secret Garda reports of the early 1930s give a good overview of the menace, vitriol, violence and fun that were a part of the Blueshirt era. The campaign of lawlessness to prevent the collection of land annuities (de Valera's retention of them being a part of the Economic War that so damaged farming interests) marred the countryside; in Cork alone between July 1934 and January 1935 there were 197 violent attacks. The Blueshirt meetings, frequently with a strong recreational element, were often attacked by republicans, with the Gardaí becoming uncomfortable buffers. At a Fine Gael meeting at Kilrush, County Clare, in June 1934, republican opponents rounded on the speakers:

The shouting consisted of expressions such as 'to hell with O'Duffy', 'To hell with f---ing Blueshirts' 'Come on lads and we'll kick the fu---rs out of town!', 'Up Dev' and 'up the IRA' ... the baton charge dispersed the crowd and afterwards everything was comparatively peaceable until the Blueshirts were leaving town. Further disorderly conduct again occurred at this stage and the same party were again prominent.[163]

The same year, in County Monaghan, a Garda report gave an indication of the sense of self-importance of O'Duffy and his followers:

about 1,400 persons attired in Blueshirts, including about 100 girls, formed up in Main Street in processional order and marched to Classford Cross where they met General O'Duffy and other speakers who arrived by motor car from Dublin. This procession was headed by 15 horsemen and accompanied by four bands ... at about 6pm, 20 young men, 4 or 5 of whom were intoxicated, assembled in Main Street and marched towards the meeting shouting 'up de Valera' and 'Up the IRA'. The Gardaí at the rear of the meeting immediately formed a cordon across the street to prevent a clash between the parties.[164]

If these were seen as relatively tame confrontations, it is also the case that the Gardaí were aware of the constant potential for serious violence, a report from County Waterford in the same year noting: 'Blueshirts were armed with offensive weapons and would have charged into the unarmed crowds.'[165]

The Blueshirt movement was something of an aberration in Irish political and social life, an economically disgruntled group, organised along parish and county lines with separate women's and children's divisions, utilising trappings of fascism. It was divided and confused as a result of the gulf between the overtly political ambitions of its leaders and the more mundane, but immediate, concerns of its grassroots membership who were reacting to the perceived threat of an autocratic de Valera/ IRA partnership. Mike Cronin pointed out that 'the gap between the populist rhetoric of Fianna Fáil and the reality of the experience of the Blueshirt members who suffered at the hands of Fianna Fáil policies is very real and did most to motivate those wearing the shirt'.[166] At leadership level, the Blueshirts were not monolithic, with the bombastic O'Duffy following a different agenda from the likes of Richard Mulcahy, whose primary allegiance was to party politics. Catholic academics such as Alfred O'Rahilly,

Michael Tierney and James Hogan did much to justify the movement, by linking it to developments on the continent and the teachings of papal encyclicals that criticised state centralisation. But keeping this curious coalition united, particularly given O'Duffy's refusal to accept the political advice of his peers, proved impossible, and facing them down, as the government did, was an important turning point in the consolidation of Irish democracy.

'the remarkable military feat of returning home with more men than they went out with'

Some Irish left-wing activists found an outlet to fight for their beliefs during the Spanish Civil War, which gave them an opportunity to engage in conflict on a scale unavailable in Ireland. Of the approximately 900 Irishmen who fought in Spain, three quarters fought on the nationalist side in support of Franco. For many republicans, too, it was a defining era in their lives, though they were largely vilified and isolated in their own land. Thomas O'Brien, a political activist, dramatist and publisher, suggested in a letter to his sister from Spain in July 1938, where he was a Republican volunteer, that 'Spain and its war are not realities to people in Ireland'. He was referring to the fact that the issue of democracy was ignored by most, who could not distinguish Spanish republicanism from anti-Catholic and thus anti-Irish communist ideology.[167]

A measure of the impact of the reports of the anti-clerical atrocities during the Civil War was the attendance of over 40,000 people at a pro-Franco meeting in Dublin's College Green, organised by the Irish Christian Front, through which the Catholic Church urged Irish Catholics to raise funds. These developments, along with Eoin O'Duffy's commitment to international fascism, and the decline of his political influence in Ireland, saw him, too, travelling to Spain with a pro-Franco Irish brigade. It was a brigade that was under-strength and disorganised, and tended to contain more of the rural Blueshirt members, in contrast to the mostly urban origins of the Republican International Brigade members, of which Frank Ryan was a notable leader.[168] O'Duffy's men were showered with miraculous medals and sacred hearts as they left Dublin with robust renditions of *Faith of Our Fathers* ringing in their ears. In Spain, as revealed by Fearghal McGarry, hostility between O'Duffy and his officers was not helped by his excessive drinking and ostentatious lifestyle in the Gran Hotel in Salamanca. They had a low casualty rate compared to the Irish on the Republican side, prompting the playwright Brendan Behan's remark that they had achieved 'the remarkable military feat of returning home with more men than they went out with'.[169] But as the twentieth century progressed, posterity was kinder to the men of the International Brigade and their anti-fascism; in 1991 an Irish memorial to Irishmen who fought in Spain at Liberty Hall in Dublin commemorated only the Republicans, even though three times as many Irishmen fought for Nationalist Spain. Duffy's brigade, no more than the Blueshirts, was too embarrassing to be afforded memorials by the establishment, and Mike Cronin likened Fine Gael's attitude to the O'Duffy era as akin to the embarrassment felt at the antics of a drunken uncle at a sedate wedding.

Domestically, if any further evidence was needed that de Valera was washing his hands thoroughly of the IRA, it was provided during the Emergency. Refusing to give in to republican hunger strikes in which three died was not only an assertion by the Justice Minister, Gerald Boland, of the determination to rout the IRA, but also a response to the decision of Sean Russell, chief of staff, to launch an IRA bombing campaign in Britain which killed seven people and injured 200. The explosion of a bomb in Dublin Castle and the shooting of two Gardaí exacerbated the situation, leading to the execution of six IRA members. Nearly 1,000 were interned during this period and hunger strikes were resorted to. The lesser evil, reasoned de Valera, was to see IRA men die rather than endanger the safety of the whole community. His hard-line approach (representing the poacher turned gamekeeper to his critics) coincided with the zenith of coercive legislation in Ireland (the Offences against the State Act became law in 1939). Joe Lee suggested that the 26 IRA men who died during the Emergency 'were the logical products of the official political culture that now sought to suppress them'.[170]

'modern girls'

Some of the recent research on women of this era has focused on groups that were more interested in improving the lot of women in the home and were active in voluntary work, rather than on issues that came to dominate the women's movement from the 1970s such as political representation, access to paid employment, equal pay, divorce and contraception, subjects that did not regularly feature as part of the political and societal discourse of the 1930s and 1940s. Influential and vocal groups included the National Council of Women, the Joint Committee of Women's Societies and Social Workers, the Catholic Federation of Women's Secondary School Teachers, the Irish Countrywomen's Association and the Irish Housewives Association. Various terms have been used to describe their work, such as 'maternalist' 'recreational welfare' or 'social feminism',[171] and they were at various stages called on to give evidence to government commissions. Female journalists such as the *Irish Independent*'s Gertrude Gaffney were also apt to defend the much derided 'modern girls' and their rights as workers and citizens.[172]

Irish women were faced with restrictive legislation regarding employment and contraception, which was the lot of women in Europe and the United States also, and the Catholic social theory that depicted women primarily as wives and homemakers, though sometimes more explicit in Ireland, was not unique. In Ireland such a view was reflected in article 41.2 of the Constitution, which affirmed that the most important and valuable contribution a woman could make to Irish society was by her life in the home; that she should not be forced to work through economic necessity. Caitríona Clear has suggested that de Valera was influenced by the accounts of the ill-health of women and children as a result of industrialisation, as elucidated in Ivy Pinchbeck's *Women Workers and the Industrial Revolution*,[173] though this may have been only one of several influences.

Few of the main political parties seemed to offer women a chance for involvement in politics, and with notable exceptions, there was also very little scope for trade union involvement, given the sometimes misogynist outlook of the labour movement in Ireland. Hanna Sheehy Skeffington's attempt in 1943 to get elected to the Dáil as a member of the Women's Social and Progressive League witnessed her losing her deposit, which seemed indicative of a marginalisation of radical female political activism. Her electoral address was based on the idea that women 'are responsible for the feeding, the clothing, and the nursing of the sick, the tending of the aged, the running of the home. They will play an immense part in the rebuilding of the world in the present chaotic condition.'[174] It was an appeal that fell on deaf ears, but a telling statistic was that 2.2 per cent of TDs in 1942 were female, compared to 1.5 per cent of MPs elected to Westminster in the same era.[175]

In any case, Catholic periodicals such as the *Irish Messenger*, *Irish Monthly* and later *Christus Rex* promoted the idea of women in public life (and occasionally, politics). The *Irish Monthly* in 1924 had encouraged women to form their own Catholic societies, and to get involved in publishing, the writing of history and the promotion of public libraries.[176] But industrial policy undoubtedly reflected a preference for creating jobs for men, with unemployment benefit designed to supplement the income of small farmers and casual labourers who were mostly male, and many women left their jobs during the Emergency because of a shortage in raw materials for factories. Women were receiving equal pay in 9 out of 33 categories of government work, but were excluded from many civil service positions. An examination into the operation of the civil service revealed that there was only one woman in receipt of a salary above £500 a year.[177]

The most prominent female trade unionist of the era, Louie Bennett, general secretary of the Irish Women's Workers' Union, in her capacity as Irish Trades Union Congress president in 1932, had occasionally questioned the usefulness of women working at all, arguing it had not raised standards of living, was a menace to family life and blocked the employment of men, and she believed there were certain jobs women were not suited to.[178] The marriage ban imposed on female primary teachers from 1934 to 1958 seemed to attract little public comment, despite the fact that many untrained single teachers were replacing trained married female teachers. The Irish National Teachers' Organisation was not vocal in objecting on the basis of gender equality, and whatever opposition existed in the union was overshadowed by its campaigns on wage levels.

A minority of vocal activists made known their opposition to the clauses of the Constitution concerning women. A letter of protest was sent to the government from the Joint Committee of Women's Societies and Social Workers, formed in 1935 from nine societies concerned with the welfare of women and children. The purpose of this group was to make recommendations regarding legislation affecting women, and at their first meeting they had recommended the establishment of a female police force, and the restoration of the right of jury service to women. The letter was primarily concerned with the clauses in the Constitution which they believed would interfere with women's economic rights. They posed the question: 'who would decide whether the economic necessity in a household was such as to oblige the mother to do outside work or not. Would there be an inquiry into the needs and finances of the household, and if so, would such an enquiry not be resented?' They also objected to the use of the phrase 'the inadequate strength of women', on the grounds that 'the question of the adequacy or inadequacy of strength for any particular work is one which arises in the case of men, as much as in the case of women

... much of the heaviest work done by women is in the home, or on the farm.'[179]

There were few corresponding campaigns directed towards improving the health of women. Ironically, given the obsession in some circles with unwarranted state interference, it was often the Catholic Church representatives who were most active in this regard. The Catholic Social Services Conference, for example, orchestrated the campaign for a children's hospital, obviously a matter of concern for women, as were the pre-natal centres run by the CSSC, while the Church also sought to champion the role of religious sisters in hospital management at the expense of lay nurses. Maternal mortality declined in Ireland from the first half of the 1940s, which may suggest that economic factors such as children's allowances played a part in improving the health of mothers.

But birth was still a traumatic experience. In her memoirs, Mary Healy from Kilkenny reminisced about giving birth to six children in the space of seven years in the 1940s, a time when 'nobody went into hospitals to have their babies'. She concluded: 'I never considered the rearing of my children a burden, even though I had no running water for several years and had only an outside dry lavatory. The only thing I dreaded was the labour involved in bringing children into the world, and with each child, this was long and difficult.'[180] Ireland's marital fertility rates remained exceptionally high, aided by the ban on contraception introduced in 1929 and extended in 1935, although some urban middle-class couples may have engaged in forms of birth control. It does seem that most Irish women did not have the means to engage in social and political activities outside the home, which would explain why organisations emerged with a concern for women based in the home, particularly rural women. There was not yet in Ireland a large concentrated mass of suburban housewives.

'she stuffed grass into its mouth to silence it'

The Criminal Law Amendment Act of 1935, which banned the sale and importation of contraceptives, was the culmination of four years of debate following the Carrigan Report on sexual offences, which was never made public on the grounds that its sweeping statements relating to immorality in Irish life were too embarrassing, if not exaggerated. Statutes passed for England and Scotland in 1922 and 1928 and for Northern Ireland in 1923 meant the law concerning sexual offences against minors was more lenient in the 26 counties than the United Kingdom.[181] The 1935 Act raised the age of consent from 16 to 17 years and raised from 13 to 15 the age at which carnal knowledge would be classed as a felony, which resulted in more prosecutions of those who defiled underage girls; between 1936 and 1940 one hundred such offenders were imprisoned. This would suggest that there was 'a range of discourse' about the sexual abuse of children in Ireland at this time.[182] The 1935 Act, in allowing for a complete ban on the import and sale of contraceptives, was preceded by debates that revealed differences of opinion, and the demand for a ban was not confined to Catholics. There were disagreements from an all-party committee as to how severe the prohibition should be and whether or not doctors should be allowed to prescribe small amounts for 'legitimate purposes'. One TD questioned whether it was legitimate 'to enforce moral principle by statute', but the view from the Department of Justice that 'no exceptions whatsoever are to be made' prevailed, despite the fear that it would lead to an increase in abortion and infanticide.[183]

Undoubtedly, some women did travel to England to procure abortions, and it was telling that during the Emergency, when restrictions were imposed on women leaving the country, both illegitimacy and infanticide rates increased. Between 1940 and 1946, when travel bans were lifted, at least 46 cases of infanticide came before the courts, but fewer than 20 such cases were tried from 1925 to 1940. Many cases were dealt with by the district courts, with the women charged with 'concealment of the birth of an infant', rather than in the central criminal courts as capital offences. One case from the 1940s concerned Mary, a woman whose parents were dead, and who lived with her two brothers in a farmhouse in County Kilkenny. It is unclear how she became pregnant, but in 1948 she gave birth on her own in an outhouse, at the age of 23:

> She was terrified that her older brother would hear the child cry and be angry with her for bringing shame on the family, so she carried the baby out to a field where she stuffed grass into its mouth to silence it. She covered the body with large stones and rocks and left it there, where it was later found and reported to the Gardaí. Mary was sentenced to 12 months in the Magdalen laundry in Gloucester Street, Dublin.[184]

'all the little matters that come under my notice'
But sex and contraception were, it seemed, of little interest to female

public representatives. During a war-time debate on the shortages and rationing experienced by rural women, Fianna Fáil's Senator Helena Concannon stated: 'as a woman I am never interested in great ideas but all the little matters that come under my notice'.[185] Indeed, it was women who were being asked to notice such things: the Department of Finance had issued circulars in the 1930s on the management of household income and distinguished between the 'housewife' and the 'careless housewife' when it came to buying Irish products, suggesting that those buying foreign instead of Irish goods were losing Irish manufacturers £38 million a year.[186] But whatever about the political construction of Irish motherhood, this did not mean there was a complete 'idealisation' of women's experience of the home. Contemporary publications aimed at women were well aware that Irish women desired modernity in a new consumer era, not just in obvious areas like electricity and running water, but in respect of recreation, appearance and relationships. The best-selling *Woman's Life* magazine in the 1930s and 1940s offered as role models not only independent unmarried working women, but women in arts, culture and sport,[187] though those in urban centres who were deemed too modern for the era received short shrift from the Church, particularly if they moved into what were traditional male bastions, including public houses.

Many rural women found an outlet in the Irish Countrywomen's Association, originally founded in 1910 as the United Irishwomen, under the auspices of the co-operative movement backed by the remnants of the Protestant Ascendancy. As it was taken over by the Catholic middle class in the 1930s, it prioritised the domestic economy, health care, handicrafts and education, markets for farm produce and improved cooking methods. Many who joined what became the largest women's organisation in Ireland were those with a degree of leisure time unavailable in poorer parts of the country.[188] Nevertheless, the ICA was skilful in carving out its own niche, as it sought to prioritise practice over theory. Its leaders became effective lobbyists on the basis that government assistance could be procured only when the women of rural Ireland knew exactly what they needed, and articulated their demands to what were initially unsupportive governments. It was pointed out in 1937 that of 80 similar organisations affiliated to the Associated Country Women of the World, New Zealand and Ireland alone received no grant, a statistic the Department of Agriculture chose to ignore.

Their role was also of paramount importance in providing a social outlet in an attempt to move women beyond the confined sphere which the social anthropologists Arensberg and Kimball had identified as deciding the parameters of a rural woman's life. The ICA were also apt to dismiss the romantic idealisation of life on the farm. Alice Curtayne, a prominent member, insisted in 1940 that 'the romantic and sentimental lovers of the land are beyond classification. They have one thing positively in common. Few of them derive their income from the land. Even fewer of them live on it.'[189] But they also attempted to avoid excessive negativity, deciding in 1943 against a proposal to ask the novelist Elizabeth Bowen to speak to their members on 'the sad plight of the Irish countrywomen'. Certain ICA activists demanded membership of parish councils on the grounds that their experience as practical economists justified a public role, a reminder that many women controlled the purse strings in rural homes. It was also significant that by the end of the war they realised they would have to work with (and if possible manipulate) the machinery of national, county and local authority administration to achieve some of their aims, an important recognition that foreshadowed many of their successes of the 1950s. It was comparative statistics that often prompted such action; the ICA commissioned a comparative analysis with other European countries, which revealed that in Ireland in 1945 only 2 per cent of rural homes had electricity; for rural Denmark and Holland the figures were 85 and 98 per cent respectively.[190]

Hilda Tweedy, founder of the Irish Housewives' Association in 1942, explained that the term 'housewife' was used in the name of the association to defy critics who jeered at the label. It was in fact quite a feminist organisation during this period, demanding women's rights as consumers. The association originated out of women who signed petitions sent to every TD before budget day, demanding action on the distribution of food, free milk for expectant mothers and children, and protection of the poor and unemployed. In essence it was a women's organisation that wanted a say in all spheres of community planning, and at various stages looked for legalised contraception, equal pay and consumer rights, as well as supporting female candidates for the Dáil, and thereby gave women the confidence to claim their rights and the capacity to lobby publicly.[191] In 1948, Hilda Tweedy explained the purpose of the association in its annual journal, the *Irish Housewife*:

women are all feeling the pinch, they are all trying alike to adapt their means to meet the ever-increasing cost of living ... let us listen to what these women are saying: 'Eggs at 4/ – a dozen in July! And the price of cheese gone up! What are we going to eat? ... I can't manage at all on the butter ration, I hope it won't be reduced in the winter.' These are the problems women are discussing every day, these are the problems which the Irish Housewives' Association is trying to solve.[192]

'a young man from Cobh named Jack Doyle'

The idea that the 1930s and 1940s were an era of cultural poverty has been refuted in recent years, most notably by Brian Fallon, who has asserted that Ireland, given its appetite for Anglo-American popular culture, its links with the London literary establishment, its commitment to modern art (with its artists looking to Spain and France), its challenging critical intellectual journals and active theatre scene, should not be characterised as excessively inward-looking.[193] Granted, between 1930 and 1939, 1,200 books and 140 periodicals were censored with little attention given to artistic merit. But it was also the case that behind the scenes governments were often hostile to the hysterical tone of some of the more extreme correspondence received from Catholic vigilance groups, having, for example, little time for the strict censorship of theatrical productions.[194] Likewise the fulminations of the small group of literary intellectuals who opposed censorship were not representative or indeed close to the concerns of the average Irish reader, who had little appetite for the books about which both 'Catholic right' and 'literary left' were campaigning. As Seán O'Casey was to point out, most of those who read serious literature had read the banned books, and advocates of censorship seemed wonderfully informed on the content of foreign filth. Much of the censorship mentality was seen as representing an unhealthy interest in sex, or a sexual prudery. As a contributor to the *Bell* put it in 1941, the Irish mind 'either runs away from sex or it runs after it; it never seems able to stand and look at it objectively'.[195]

There was truth in Arland Ussher's contention that censorship existed primarily for the purposes of 'baiting the intellectual', and those who cast doubt on religion, language and sexual purity were pilloried and excited great anger. This was much in evidence during a farcical four-day debate in the Senate in 1942, concerning the banning of Eric Cross's *Tailor and Ansty*, while much of the rest of Europe was at war. But what many historians have ignored is popular reading habits – the cheap novels, newspapers and periodicals; happy-ever-after tales with, when Irish, a smattering of nationalism and Catholicism. Popular magazines such as *Ireland's Own* and the *Catholic Fireside*, and books such as the romances of Charlotte Brame and the westerns of Zane Grey, as well as the *Irish Rosary*, and collections of the lives of saints and Catholic icons, were devoured. The Irish also remained fascinated with the British royal family: in 1937, 750,000 orders were placed for the programme of the King's coronation, while domestically produced titles like *Our Boys* (with cowboys called Seán) also proved highly popular.[196]

In 1933 customs duties were extended to imported daily newspapers, which meant that by 1939 the circulation of the *Irish Independent* reached 110,000 and that of the *Irish Press* 140,000. In extending its readership base to academics and civil servants, the *Irish Times* under the editorship of the difficult and eccentric Robert Smyllie ensured its survival in Catholic Ireland, and became required reading for those in government as well as an outlet for original talent and serious reporting of foreign affairs.[197] Although the *Irish Press* was established as a Fianna Fáil organ, it could also produce balanced and thought-provoking reporting, particularly on social issues. It also pioneered the reporting of Gaelic games, which was a further illustration of the need to feed the interest in popular culture.

If it is true the Irish could not be objective about sex, it is also true they were not objective in their passion for their hurling and football club and county teams. The Gaelic Athletic Association remained popular as a mass movement, though its enforcement of the ban on foreign games continued to be ignored and resented by many. The Irish president, Douglas Hyde, ignored it in 1938 to attend a soccer international. The devotion of GAA fans was evident not just in their passionate commitment to parish identity (the GAA's greatest success) but also in the willingness of nearly 80,000 people, in the midst of the Emergency and travel difficulties, to descend on Croke Park for an All-Ireland final. The GAA experience involved collective expression, triumphalism and heartache, and was continually linked in the press to the past; not just to Ireland's past, but even to the athleticism of the ancient Greeks, and given the speed, skill and athleticism involved in hurling this was not necessarily far-fetched.[198] Less high-profile and illegal entertainments such as cock-fighting were followed no less passionately in some quarters, and raising a cock was an illicit experience crossing class boundaries, though the details of training methods, of necessity, remained highly secret. In 1946, a contributor to the *Bell* reported that:

> Somewhere in Munster during the past few days has been the scene
> of an international cock-fight ... Birds smuggled from England and
> Northern Ireland gave a striking display with silver spurs in one of
> the biggest arranged during the past 20 years. Bookmakers took front
> seats perched on tree-tops, while members of the exclusive club passed
> wads of currency in the moonlight. Before the company dispersed at
> dawn all evidence of the conflict was collected feather by feather.[199]

Ireland produced boxers of note during this era, none more so than
Jack Doyle, and his rise and fall captivated sports fans. As Con Houlihan
reminisced, during an era of economic depression:

> people hungered for heroes, for a sign that there were some on whom
> the gods had not turned their backs. Never were sporting heroes more
> revered and the demand seemed to create a supply ... in this country
> we had our own heroes on the playing fields but we needed an icon of
> international status. The gods delivered him in the person of a young
> man from Cobh [County Cork] named Jack Doyle.

Initially a labourer, he enlisted in the British army, only to be coaxed
out by a promoter who launched him on a career as a heavyweight boxer.
Within months he had become a national hero and was embraced by
Britain also ('he was their Irishman from folklore'), and between April
1932 and July 1933 he beat a string of heavyweights. He earned a quarter
of a million pounds in 1933, squandered it, and was disqualified for a low
punch when fighting Jack Petersen for the heavyweight championship of
Britain. There was a (completely unjustified) outcry in Ireland led by the
morning papers, maintaining he had been hard done by. His subsequent
quest to dazzle the boxing world in the USA failed, and he launched a
singing career with his actress wife, but on his return to Dublin his last
fight during the war (witnessed by 23,000 spectators in Dublin) was a
pathetic affair, which Doyle prepared for by getting drunk on brandy. The
contest ended after round one, and Doyle's last recorded fight, Houlihan
sadly recorded, 'was in a pub', earning him two weeks in Mountjoy jail in
Dublin: 'Thenceforth he went down as a person as rapidly as he had risen
as a pugilist.'[200] A move back to London eventually resulted in destitution
and acute alcoholism, though he lived until 1978 and remained a hero for
many of his generation.

'night-club queens covered by a few spangles'

Fianna Fáil in the 1930s occasionally attempted to create the impression that traditional Irish music was second only to the Irish language in distinguishing Gaelic from Anglo-Saxon culture, though the standard of music on the Irish radio was rarely uplifting. Those with a concern for the future of Irish music decried the paucity of native Irish composers and the fact that a country with a great tradition in folk music was not developing an art music of its own, and lamented an education system that music gave a very low priority. While there was widespread participation in native pastimes, Irish audiences also yearned for the faraway hills, and remained avid cinema-goers. In 1943, 22 million cinema tickets were purchased. Predictably, those on the Catholic right lambasted this failure to resist the invasion of what they characterised as cheap foreign filth. That their primary purpose was entertainment and escapism was lost on B. G. McCarthy, a lecturer in education from University College Cork:

> It is interesting to consider the average farm labourer walking five or six miles into Bruff [County Limerick], let us say, to go to the pictures and then that long walk home again in our Irish rain. What has he seen that has the slightest relation to life as he knows it? He has seen night-club queens covered by a few spangles, Chicago gangsters talking a peculiar argot, society playboys babbling aridly of Reno divorce. He has seen crooning cowboys, coal-black mammies, typists clad in Schiaparelli, models living in luxurious flats and millionaires living in Babylonian palaces. He is going home to fall into his bed in the loft, to rise next morning and feed the pigs. What does he make of it all?[201]

'Tá an iomad muiníne ag ár múinteoirí as leabhair'

For all the focus on the Irish language in education and administration (competence in Irish became compulsory in 1937 for entry to the civil service and the Gardaí), by 1931, 38 per cent of teachers had no formal qualifications in Irish, while only 30 per cent were qualified to use Irish as a medium of instruction. By 1934 only 19 per cent of the 314 secondary schools used Irish as the sole medium of instruction.[202] The emphasis on written rather than spoken Irish continued to frustrate the quest for revival. Teachers were often blamed, a report of the Department of Education noting that 'Tá an iomad muiníne ag ár múinteoirí as leabhair' ('Our teachers have too much trust in books'), an ironic assertion given that the same department continued to allow the education system to be subjugated to the language revival. James Dillon suggested in the Dáil in 1936 that it was necessary to teach Irish and provide education at the same time.[203] The linking of salary increments to knowledge of Irish was found unlawful by the Supreme Court in 1940, but the fact that there were so few opportunities to use Irish outside of the schools continued to be ignored, as was the folly of the belief that schools alone could solve the issue.

The conditions of many of the schools themselves was appalling, frustrated by the Church's stubbornness in refusing to accept reforms in the management system of primary schools. In relation to the teaching of history, the Department of Education's notes for teachers (in use until the early 1960s) suggested history was about articulating and illustrating 'sublime examples of patriotism in order to refute the calumnies of Ireland's enemies'.[204] But at third level a new departure resulted from the labours of T. W. Moody and Robin Dudley Edwards, who inaugurated the Irish Historical Society in 1936 to facilitate a scientific, 'value free' approach to the subject, and studiously avoided modern history. The popular appetite for bombastic accounts of much more recent events was demonstrated by the huge success of Dan Breen's *My Fight for Irish Freedom* (1931), an account of the War of Independence. But whatever about reading, in the sometimes poisoned political atmosphere of the 1930s, when political opponents were despised rather than just resented, many studiously avoided discussing their revolutionary days amongst themselves or in front of a new generation. At the end of Fianna Fáil's second year in office in 1933, the Minister for Education, Tomás Derrig, suggested in a letter to the Department of Defence that it would be desirable to take steps to collect and preserve the political records of the War of Independence period for historical posterity. He mentioned that the issue had come up 'on more than one occasion' in cabinet discussions, and suggested Fianna Fáil *cumainn* around the country would be ideal as potential collectors of this material. Derrig professed concern at the ignorance of students of this period, in particular 'lack of knowledge of the 1916 leaders and of the events subsequent to 1916 displayed by boys with the leaving certificate'. What was needed, he surmised, was 'a record of facts' from 'the Irish point of view' to match the prevailing British view of the period.[205]

University representation in the Dáil continued until 1934 and many individual academics served in the 1930s and 1940s, including Michael

Tierney (who admitted that the history of University College Dublin was not a particularly exciting chapter in the public life of Ireland), and Eoin MacNeill. Some of the more zealous Fianna Fáil members berated UCD for debasing 'national feeling' in its failure to promote the Irish language. University College, though secular by statute, maintained a Catholic ethos, and an attempt to stage Wilde's *The Importance of being Earnest* in the early 1930s was prevented by the president. Trinity College was still viewed by many Catholics as a citadel of unionism. Although by the 1940s toasts to the British royal family were less common, the college witnessed a riot and siege in 1945 when, after the surrender of Germany, Trinity students displayed the flags of the Allies, to which nationalist students, including future Taoiseach Charles Haughey, responded by burning the Union Jack. The Catholicisation of both UCD and University College Cork is rightly regarded by historians as having been smug and self-congratulatory; the UCD handbook boasted in 1932 of 'there being rarely more than a dozen non-Catholic students'.[206] But by the mid-1940s, the 1930s optimism was replaced by more debate in UCD about professional and liberal education rather than Catholicism and nationalism, and writers like Anthony Cronin fulminated against the lack of intellectual excitement and the desertion of Newman principles, originality and idealism.[207]

'the enemy is no longer external'

These were also difficult decades in which to be a dissenting writer, or in Seán O'Faoláin's case one who wished to be characterised as much European as Irish. In his book *The Irish* he decried the fact that histories of Ireland were nationalist, patriotic, political and sentimental; championed by the new middle class or native bourgeoisie, whose approach to their ancestry, to rural life and to their own revolution was emotional rather than intellectual and frequently dishonest. For writers, as he saw it, 'the enemy is no longer external'.[208] Unlike Joyce and Beckett, O'Faoláin remained at home; Benedict Kiely was later to comment on the importance of this – that because of his presence, visibility and audibility, O'Faoláin was a huge influence on those who came after him. Flann O'Brien, though almost obsessive about James Joyce, did not follow in his footsteps, but stayed at home and seemed to show little interest in foreign affairs, but his work was of such a quality that literary critics wondered whether he was a pioneering post-modernist or a disciple of Russian formalism.[209] Disillusionment was a preponderant sentiment of the era – or as a War of

Independence veteran was to remark in John McGahern's *Amongst Women*: 'look at where it brought us. Look at the country now. Run by a crowd of small-minded gangsters out for their own good. It was better if it never happened.'[210]

The response of O'Faoláin and others was to argue that the only cultural sanity was to be found in the novels of the realists, whose authors were uncompromised moral authorities. Samuel Beckett, too, swiped at a land where 'history's ancient faeces were sniffed up by patriots on all fours; faces a-glow': the company of such 'Gaels' in *Murphy* is described as 'irksome beyond endurance',[211] which explained his preference for France in war to Ireland at peace. O'Faoláin, in launching the *Bell* magazine in 1940, no longer wanted 'to sniff at Brian Boru, Cathleen Ní Houlihán and Roisín Dubh'; or as shown in his *King of the Beggars* (a biography of Daniel O'Connell), there was little point in attempting to bring to life the corpse of eighteenth-century Ireland.

Patrick Kavanagh believed he was connected to common life in a way the early twentieth-century writers were not; but it was the sheer inadequacy of Irish life (which in his words 'froze for want of Europe') that comes through in his early poetry, where a stultifying Catholicism wins out over pagan naturalism. Indeed, the tone of resignation in Kavanagh's and O'Faoláin's earlier work is what is most striking, and may have prevented them being more ambitious in their writings. Joyce, writing in the pre-independence era, did not have to worry so much about writing about the ordinary because the generation he used for his raw material were not burdened with the same sense of social and political responsibility and consequently feelings of failure and disappointment.[212]

In other ways Irish literary disillusionment in the 1930s was just a version of a wider international despair at the shortcomings of the political order. But the 1930s and 1940s were also a great era for the Irish short story, exemplified in the work not just of Sean O'Faoláin but also Frank O'Connor, Liam O'Flaherty and Mary Lavin, where the few pleasures of provincial life 'almost have to be stolen'. This gave their work an emotionalism where, in the words of Terence Brown 'passion and encounter are matters of fleeting privacies, where disillusionment dogs individual hope and disappointment enforces bitter submission'.[213] Mary Lavin's female characters nonetheless sought to move in their own direction, outside the context of a strict religious and moral code. Her superb short stories offered a view of Ireland in which women ran farms, made decisions, chased men, and fought with each other and with authority. Sexual morality is by no means the only yardstick by which the women judge each other in small Catholic rural communities. 'In this alone', as recognised by Sarah Briggs, she explores 'a subject which is largely unresearched in terms of Irish writing.' Briggs points to the opening paragraph of the short story *Sarah* (1942) as an example of this debunking of stereotype: 'Sarah had a bit of a bad name. This was the worst her neighbours would say of her, although there was a certain fortuity about her choice of fathers for the three strapping sons she'd borne – all three out of wedlock.'[214]

Ireland, Brian Fallon insisted, also had 'a thoroughly secure, liberal upper-middle class', and there were intellectuals like George Russell (who died in 1935) who sought to bring a continental dimension to Dublin literary gatherings in preference to rejecting the country.[215]

'laugh boisterously, make love and eat oranges'

There was vitality, too, in Dublin theatre life, propelled by the genius of the utterly cosmopolitan Micheál Mac Liammoir at the Gate Theatre, the success of which revealed an appetite for serious, challenging drama. The Abbey, on the other hand, because of its financially precarious position, was not, in O'Faoláin's view, searching the nation's consciousness, but merely going for 'the insincere laughter of the crowd'. The theatre continued to reject plays in the 1930s that dealt with issues of religion and sexual morality in a controversial way. The appointment of Ernest Blythe in 1940 as director raised new questions as to what constituted suitable material, and in keeping with his own obsessions, Irish-language plays became a central feature of the theatre's repertory. In the 1930s, 104 new plays were produced, but in the 1940s only 62, though there was still much pride in what was, after all, 'a national institution'.

The audiences, according to Mervyn Wall, had 'shrunk to those who laugh boisterously, make love and eat oranges'.[216] The theatre was also accused of treating young writers discourteously. The Gate, on the other hand, was being adventurously modernist, further illustrating that whatever stagnation may have existed culturally in these decades was being balanced by creativity and innovation. This was also demonstrated by the courage of Mainie Jellet and Evie Hone in introducing modernism to Irish art in the early 1940s; the work of these women suggested the powerful pastorals of Seán Keating would not be representative of post-war Ireland.[217]

'barefoot children, the means test and increasing malnutrition'

A survey of a Belfast working-class area in 1938–9 revealed that 36 per cent of the people assessed were living in absolute poverty. This is a reminder, according to the labour historian John Boyle, that 'the thirties were the years of barefoot children, the means test and increasing malnutrition'.[218] The extent of this suffering, if it was known, was rarely alluded to at government level, or was occasionally rejected as greatly exaggerated. The prime minister, James Craig, had visited Australia and New Zealand, and told his cabinet on his return he was 'quite satisfied with the social position as it existed in Northern Ireland compared with the dominions', but that he was particularly interested in the education system of New Zealand ('which was free, compulsory and non-religious').[219] The cabinet decided to defer action on the issue of child and maternity welfare, but a telling indication of the attitude of some was the contention of the Minister for Finance, Hugh Pollock, that, given the sums being distributed by the government on social services, he found it hard to believe 'that there can be marked abnormal distress'.

On humanitarian grounds, Pollock accepted the need for an extended maternity and child welfare scheme in Belfast, but rejected Belfast Corporation's demand that the government should contribute 50 per cent of the cost of the scheme. The Corporation, he suggested, had 'endeavoured to throw on the government the whole moral responsibility for its adoption or rejection'. In tandem with this, there was the oft-repeated warning that the same grants that were available to British towns could not be paid in Northern Ireland as there were no comparable liabilities. It was pointed out, for example, that the cost of elementary education totalled approximately £530,000, with the Corporation paying only £12,000 of this and the state the rest, whereas the local authority of a British city would be paying in the region of £265,000. Significantly, he felt that the attitude of Belfast Corporation disclosed 'complete ignorance of the present advantages which they enjoy', noting that the conclusions he reached were applicable to local authorities as a whole.[220]

Dissatisfaction with local government was common, and the local authorities were not exempt from the sort of maladministration and at times corruption existing in the South. In 1927, the Lord Mayor of Belfast had written to Lord Londonderry, indicating his determination to put local government on a clean, sound and efficient basis, recognising the 'element of intrigue and patronage which has to be combated'.[221] As in the

South, the distribution of power in Northern Ireland was very centralised, perhaps inevitably given the widespread distrust and difficulty associated with devolution, particularly in the context of security, education and finance, not to mention gerrymandering. Ninety per cent of county and rural councillors' seats were not contested between 1924 and 1939, and in urban areas less than one fifth obtained a mandate in 1932.[222]

'the public conscience has been aroused'

Whatever about these difficulties, it was financial dependence on Britain that made meaningful autonomy almost impossible. David Fitzpatrick points out that the Northern parliament was responsible for spending over four fifths of the province's revenue in the early 1930s, but only one fifth of that revenue was raised under its auspices. So Pollock's righteousness was not only somewhat hollow, but a defensive reaction to the government's dependence on the Imperial exchequer; a British official quoted by Fitzpatrick noted the 'series of dodges and devices' necessary to give Northern Ireland subventions within the terms of the Government of Ireland Act 'to save Northern Ireland from coming openly on the dole'.[223]

This had serious implications for the North's ability to provide for the welfare of its citizens, and those most in need of assistance often had to rely on the charity of volunteers, who were continually short of resources. City-based charities in particular felt the pressure of having to cater for the rural poor who migrated to the city. The minute book of the Belfast Midnight Mission for Unmarried Mothers, for example, reveals that their maternity home contained far too many girls from country districts, with an average of 32 births per month. Not only was there a high level of infant mortality, but there was also a preponderance of married women with nowhere else to go.[224] These women, judging from the tone of the minutes, were treated more compassionately than their Southern counterparts, and generally there seems to have been more debate about these issues at an earlier stage of the state's development than in the Free State.

Of the 32 rural districts in Northern Ireland, only 11 had child and maternity welfare schemes in operation. In 1930 the rate of childbirth mortality was 4.8 per 1,000, compared to 4.1 in England and Wales. The Home Affairs Minister, Dawson Bates, wanted to take action to reduce the rate of infant mortality as had happened in England (where the rate had been reduced from 96 per 1,000 in 1917 to 73 per 1,000 in 1927), but the Minister for Finance would not sanction spending. Bates concluded that because 'the public conscience has been aroused ... the government is open to attack on this matter and has little ground of defence',[225] a view that seems more realistic and frank than in the South.

Cultural and religious differences inevitably affected the Protestant attitude to large Catholic families and their associated health problems. Moya Woodside, a surgeon's wife living in South Belfast, recorded in her war-time diary her impressions of a typical Catholic working-class mother:

> She said she was 28 but looked to be 40 – toothless, haggard, under-nourished, thin lank hair ... the mother of 8 living children, 3 of them tubercular, was suspected of TB, and her husband of course long-term unemployed Catholic ... I try not to be intolerant, but a religion which turns women into reproductive machines, regardless of the effect on health and happiness is brutal and inhumane ... there are thousands and thousands like her in this city alone.[226]

Sexually transmitted diseases, as in the South, were also of concern; in 1929 Derry Corporation had appointed a committee to examine the issue and insisted a local centre for treatment needed to be established 'without delay'.[227] The other welfare and sanitary issues that dominated the proceedings of Southern local authorities – housing, sewerage, water, TB, public entertainment – also preoccupied Northern authorities, rather than issues of sectarianism or party politics. Attitudes to the treatment of children were also discussed; in the late 1930s there was much attention given to the alleged maltreatment of children in the Shamrock Lodge and Victoria homes, with a concern that Shamrock Lodge, originally opened in Belfast in 1881 by the Belfast Women's Temperance Association, was 'accepting mentally defective children without a murmur', with many eventually ending up in the workhouse.[228]

'I would recommend that all flock pillows be replaced by feather ones'
In May 1938 a civil servant who visited Shamrock Lodge had no unfavourable comments to make, but noted shrewdly that, as the committee of the institution was there at the time of his arrival, 'I may just possibly have seen conditions at their best.' The Belfast Council of Social Welfare wanted the institutions to be more accountable in view of the public donations

which helped keep them afloat. Their chief fears about the 98 children in the two homes was that the institutions were badly managed and there was a tendency not to segregate criminal and non-criminal. Crucially, they wanted 'to be allowed to inspect the school at any time without warning', but the Home Affairs Ministry criticised their 'whispering campaign' and the idea that they were 'blackmailing the homes that if their requirements are not met public support will be withdrawn from the voluntary side of the school'.[229]

As there was no reformatory for females, Shamrock Lodge was the only place to which Protestant girls in the North could be sent. The BCSW was successful in bringing pressure to bear on the authorities, and raising these issues publicly. In December 1938 the assistant inspector of reformatories and industrial schools in Northern Ireland felt conditions in Shamrock Lodge were generally good and added: 'I would recommend that all flock pillows be replaced by feather ones'.[230] In 1939 the Home Affairs Ministry intervened in the case of two other voluntary homes in Belfast, where there were allegations of maltreatment of children, and misuse of funds collected from the public but not spent on the children. Although only a warning was given, 'the managers deemed it wiser to bring their activities to a sudden stop and in both cases promptly closed down their premises voluntarily'. It was also agreed, at the insistence of the BCSW, that a woman be appointed as assistant inspector.[231] While the number of children involved was much smaller in the North than the South, these issues were being dealt with frankly, and pressure was successfully brought to bear on the authorities, in marked contrast to the Free State, where Catholic institutions remained unaccountable and impervious to political and moral pressure. This is not to suggest that children were not subjected to cruelty in Northern institutions, but it does suggest that a greater care, on the reading of the documented evidence, was being shown for their welfare, in the absence of sufficient local-authority attention.

What was similar to the South was the high levels of poverty, unemployment and the failure of an effective socialist movement to challenge the establishment, along with the determination of the main churches to contain social agitation in areas like Belfast, where roughly 50 per cent of the Catholic male workers were semi-skilled or unskilled. From the late nineteenth and early twentieth centuries there was much focus on Catholic social organisation, with such groups in existence as the Society of Saint Vincent de Paul, the Catholic Truth Society and the Knights of

Saint Columbanus. Mary Harris points out that in the year ending 1933 the Society of Saint Vincent de Paul distributed £14,000 among the poor, assisting 5,840 individuals, and by 1938 had established a secretariat to help the poor secure benefits in Belfast, while the Ladies of Charity were also active, as was the Catholic Young Men's Society.[232]

'no poverty beneath the blankets'?

While all such groups were concerned with education, poor housing and loan sharks, the ethos remained one of the sanctification of volunteers, as in the South. But their compassion was far ahead of that being displayed by those administering the Poor Law, who added the further humiliation of the names of successful applicants being posted on gable walls. It was in the interests of the Catholic Church to be active in welfare issues, owing not only to their distrust of state intervention, but also to the hostility of officialdom to the Catholic religion. This was memorably summed up by one Board of Guardians official's acid comment, in relation to large Catholic families seeking assistance, that 'there was no poverty beneath the blankets'.[233] Catholic social activism was dominated by the middle classes, and in their attitude to poverty they often shared a view with the more Calvinistic of the Protestants that the unemployed and poor had themselves to blame through laziness or sin, or that many of them, as one priest put it, would not 'get up off your backsides and go out and do something yourselves'.[234]

The harshness of the Belfast Board of Guardians did affect Catholics disproportionately, in that Protestant workers were less likely to suffer uninterrupted long-term unemployment, fall out of benefit and thus be forced to turn to the Guardians for relief. But poverty crossed sectarian boundaries, and tensions exploded in 1932 with the refusal by the Board of Guardians to grant outdoor relief, leading to notorious riots that eventually forced the state to take responsibility for the able-bodied poor. In September 1932 there were 72,000 registered unemployed in Northern Ireland, with an estimated 30,000 unregistered, with unemployment benefit limited to a maximum of 156 days a year. If transitional benefit could not be obtained from the Guardians it was necessary to seek outdoor relief, and the rates for a family of three were only 12 shillings a week. The riots and marches in 1932 (with an estimated 60,000 marching in October looking for reform) were matched by police brutality, more pronounced in nationalist areas, and led to the imposition of the first curfew since

1922.[235] The extent to which it was a pre-revolutionary anti-imperialist struggle has been doubted by many who partook, and the 'unity' of the strike was short-lived, partly also due to the 'red scare' that all religious leaders encouraged. The strike lasted about two weeks, with some reforms, though not all demanded, being introduced. Unemployment insurance schemes were widened in 1936 to include agricultural workers, and in 1937 extended local-authority powers to distribute outdoor relief were granted.

'8 butchers unemployed who have full knowledge of this work'

The reality was that, as with the building of houses (only 50,000 built between 1919 and 1939[236]), neither Catholic nor Protestant requirements were being met, a reminder that 'sectarianism is not the totality of the Belfast experience'.[237] Belfast witnessed the kind of unemployment riots also in evidence in cities like London and Liverpool. Those intent on building a socialist movement on the momentum created by the unemployment protests had a mountain to climb; even fascists in Northern Ireland assisted the election of unionists, given that the overriding priority was to help in the work of fighting communism.[238]

Likewise, in nationalist areas those who wished to repel the threat of labour played the sectarian card, as did many in opposition to the Socialist Party of Northern Ireland formed in 1932. According to Joe Devlin, the Church was 'the greatest obstacle facing the Labour movement if it hoped to appeal to the Catholic working-class'.[239] While the communists had influenced the events of 1932 there seemed little chance they would make a breakthrough in the North, since the more moderate Labour Party was experiencing difficulties also. The minutes of the Labour Party branch of which Patrick Agnew was a member, housed in the Public Records Office of Northern Ireland, reveal a concern not only with unionist jobbery ('a sub sanitary officer is being sent to Newry for a course of training as meat inspector at ratepayers' expense, which qualification he should have held on his appointment whilst there are at least 8 butchers unemployed who have full knowledge of this work'), but also with low unemployment benefits, the administration of child welfare, housing and public health, and 'seizure of branch literature by police'.[240]

'five shillings to keep a dog in a dogs' home'

The main concerns of most of the impoverished population were food and rent, with many experiencing the queues for stale bread and the prevalence of TB, rickets and pneumonia. One contributor to an oral history of Belfast in the 1930s recalled her mother reading that 'It costs five shillings to keep a dog in a dogs' home and they gave us two shillings to keep a child.'[241] During the 1920s and 1930s 'the number of children under one year who died per 1,000 live births never fell below 70'.[242] The pawnshop was the last resort for many, but those who suffered also recall a strong sense of self-sufficiency and community spirit.

Poverty was not of course confined to city areas; Patrick Shea, then a young Catholic civil servant, was struck in the 1930s by the number of old men in tumbledown cottages living on very little in rural Fermanagh, while he, in contrast, 'found myself in parties going on long journeys to hunt balls'.[243] It was Shea's job at that stage to make people aware of their social-welfare entitlements. John Mogey, in his seminal *Rural Life in Northern Ireland*, estimated that in 1944 there were 91,699 holdings of one acre or more and almost one third of these remained in the class of ten acres or under, while only 13,000 farms out of 92,000 regularly employed wage labourers. In Fermanagh, it was found that 58 per cent of the houses were either totally unfit for habitation or were overcrowded and 'not a single labourer's cottage has been erected by any rural district council in the county between the wars'.[244] For many, it seems the state was quite distant, with a general impression before the war that 'the state was the rate collector, the policeman on punitive raids against after hour drinkers … the customs man on the border and not much else'.[245] The viciousness of the sectarian riots of 1935, however, ensured that many came face to face with the security apparatus of the state, with conditions once again close to civil war and the widespread expulsion and victimisation of Belfast Catholics. A typical slogan brandished at the Harland and Wolff shipyard was 'Catholics who cannot swim, learn to before Monday'. It was estimated that 2,241 Catholics were intimidated out of Protestant areas and mob rule reigned for some time, underlining the strength of populist deep-rooted sectarianism. The Communist Party was active to a certain extent, without seeming to have a permanent presence. Passions had been stirred at the same time as the silver jubilee of King George V in May 1935, when Protestant bands encroached on Catholic territory, and subsequent Orange parades were fired on near Belfast city centre. An original ban on the parade, imposed by Dawson Bates, had been lifted, following pressure from the Orange Order. Thomas Hennessey quotes a contemporary letter from a prominent Northern nationalist, Cahir Healy, to Sir Thomas Inskip, the British Solicitor General, concerning the riots: 'the identification of certain Northern Ministers with the Ulster Protestant League, whose watchword is "Protestants employ Protestants", indicates that they have been ... the moving spirits in a most intolerant and reactionary effort to stir up old animosities amongst the most ignorant and excitable classes in the community'.[246]

'Our ideas? We didn't stop to think an awful lot about that'

The railway strikes of 1933 had been another outlet for the Communist Party's radical militancy but they received precious little support as political candidates. Socialists did not fare much better; in 1927 only 28 per cent of workers were in trade unions, compared to 41 per cent for the UK as a whole, and organisational efforts were hampered by the preponderance of casual labour. It was estimated that there were only 150 members in the Socialist Party in the 1930s, with one activist suggesting that they were always 'walking a tightrope on the national question'.[247] The IRA also emerged as players in the 1933 strikes, though it was significant that an interviewee in the oral history of Belfast, when asked about the IRA's ideas responded: 'Our ideas? We didn't stop to think an awful lot about that.'[248] Activists like Peadar O'Donnell believed that the IRA in the North was relatively useless without Protestant participation. Brian Hanley's study of the IRA in the 1930s reveals they made more of an effort to achieve cross-community support than previously thought. He quotes Peadar O'Donnell's 'address to the men and women of the Orange Order', to which the response was pathetic. Surprisingly, there was some co-operation between the B Specials and the IRA during the railway strikes, but the suggestion of the Chief of Staff of the IRA, Moss Twomey, that there had been 'a realignment within the ranks of the Orange population upon a class basis' was highly delusional. The IRA was not speaking with one voice in the North in the 1930s because of regional and personnel differences, and sectarianism tended to make them revert to their traditional role. But to see them solely as a Catholic militia force would be too narrow an interpretation, given their radical rhetoric, which continually called for cross-community action and criticised the bigotry of their own supporters. Nonetheless, the fundamental point remained that they did not have a sufficient understanding of unionist hostility to republicanism and retained a certain suspicion of the Dublin leadership.[249]

Left-wing activists in the North were involved in debating the international issues of the rise of fascism and the threat to democracy in the 1930s. John Hewitt reminisced that he and others were active in the Left Book Club and the Belfast-based Peace League. But with regard to the latter, he recalled 'being wedged in a cruel paradox, working for international peace, for international sanctions against Italy because of her aggression against Abyssinia. At the same time, in my native city, Catholics were burnt out of the York Street area and fled to the new houses of the Glenard Estate.'[250]

'unpardonable ignorance of Irish matters'

It suited the unionist establishment that the 1938 Northern election was once again fought on the issue of partition, the same year de Valera had suggested a united Ireland and a devolved parliament for the North, with its powers based in Dublin. For unionists this served to underline the fact that the South was still a threat, which also fed their need to reinforce support within their own ranks and to show a united front to the outside world. As Londonderry put it in a letter to his godson in the same year:

> There is a strange and unpardonable ignorance of Irish matters in the minds of the great majority of English people. They fail to understand the differences in outlook between the population of the six counties in the North and the population in the South and they have a sort of idea that if only the North would be more amenable, Ireland would be a happy, prosperous and contented country.[251]

Perhaps this was one of the reasons why unionists had to ensure loyalty in their own ranks and constantly reiterated the need for unionists never to forget their political heroes. This led to the orchestration of a number of elaborate ceremonies and celebrations, such as the unveiling of the Carson statue outside the Stormont Parliament in 1933, the Silver Jubilee celebrations of George V in Belfast in 1935, the funeral of Carson and the Royal Coronation visit in the same year. All provided an opportunity to emphasise the North as a homogeneous community with an emphasis on shared heroes and class unity, or as Gillian McIntosh put it: 'in death Carson became even more of an embodiment of ideal unionism and the ideal unionist'.[252] Mirroring the experiences of the South in the 1932 Eucharistic Congress, there was much theatre and spectacle, as soil from each of the six counties was taken from a silver bowl and placed on Carson's coffin. A flattering biography of Carson by Edward Majoribanks and Ian Colvin stressed the honesty and fearlessness of the Northerners in contrast to the whimsical and mercurial Southerners, while royal visits were an opportunity to restate loyalty to crown and Empire.

At the heart of unbridled declarations of devotion was insecurity. In 1938 Craig was quoted as saying in an interview: 'I firmly believe that public opinion in the UK would rise in indignation if any British government showed the slightest signs of its intention to betray the loyalists of the North of Ireland', a sentiment that was wishful thinking. A determination that cracks would never appear in the unionist edifice, as well as genuine sectarianism, was also the reason why the 1930s was the decade of the anti-Catholic sound bite, including the most quoted about 'a Protestant Parliament for a Protestant People' and Craig's assertion that 'I am an Orangeman first and a politician afterwards'.[253] Along with the idea that Protestants should not employ Catholics, there was the unionist insistence that 'any inequities resulted not from Protestant discrimination, but from Catholic alienation and voluntary abstention'.[254] Middle-class Catholics with a vested interest in the establishment, like Patrick Shea, refused to protest against the anti-Catholicism of their employers because they 'would give support to those bigots who saw us as agents of a foreign church seeking always to undermine democratic government'.[255]

The truth, as elucidated by Paul Bew and others, was that there was often disagreement within unionist government between the populists who succumbed easily to local pressure and those who were more interested in strict financial control; a form of 'little Ulsterism' best represented by Craig, in contrast to the more imperial-minded like Sir Wilfred Spender, head of the civil service, who thought of unionist supremacy in the context of imperial security, and, in the words of Thomas Hennessey, 'strove to keep policy in line with pre-Keynesian financial policies in Britain'.[256] Those differences were central to tension within government and between government and the Dominion Office, with Britain happy not to intervene to impose 'normal government' if it felt 'strategic figures' in the Northern Irish administration were 'attempting to implement British methods'.[257]

There remained precious little contact between North and South. A ban on Free State medics working as dispensary doctors in the North unless they were of British parentage, and had at least five years' residential qualification in the UK or Northern Ireland, was upheld by the Northern High Court in 1937.[258] Cattle smuggling became an important part of cross-border traffic in the 1930s, following the reintroduction of tariff barriers. The irregular 240 mile path that was the border was ideal territory for smuggling: 'no less than 180 roads crossed the border and in some 35 to 40 instances they defined it, with the frontier lying in the middle of a crossing point every mile'. This meant in theory that a farmer could be prosecuted for bringing turnips (a dutiable commodity in the 1930s) from one of his fields to another across the border. The judiciary often remarked on the prevalence and indeed acceptance of smuggling across the border, with perhaps up to 100,000 cattle smuggled in 1934 alone.[259] Other cross-border traffic did not go unnoticed. In July 1938 de Valera and Frank Aiken attended the consecration ceremony for St Patrick's Cathedral in Armagh. It was remarked in the Belfast column of the *Irish Times* that 'possibly nowhere else in the world would the prime minister of one state motor into the territory of another for an official engagement without, even as a matter of courtesy, informing his opposite number'.[260]

'possible to "do it" in quite a number of surprising positions'

In many respects, Belfast was the city most unprepared for the devastation wreaked by German air raids in 1941, and it paid a massive price. Perhaps many had shared the hope of Patrick Shea that 'our patch on the outer edge of Europe would have a pretty low rating in the Germans' plans'.[261] That it was bombed, however, retrospectively became an ideological gain as well as a material loss. John Blake's government-sponsored *Northern Ireland in the Second World War*, eventually published in 1956, but commenced in 1941, was once again an opportunity to stress the determination and doggedness of the Ulster character, also serving as a narrative that could emphasise the Ulster unionist continuity between opposition to Home Rule and their support for the war effort, in direct contrast to the Free State. Yet underlying it all, according to Gillian McIntosh, was the age-old fear of British abandonment.[262]

Elizabeth McCullough, born into the middle-class outskirts of Belfast in 1928, wrote about how the importance of the year one was born in dawned on her as an adult, in terms of how the war impacted on any given life and the guilt of those who were young enough to pass the war years in a relatively frivolous manner. With the arrival of American troops in Ulster, she recalled that 'Mrs Toner formed a vigilante group that patrolled the grounds of Belfast City Hall at night, torchlight in hand, spotlighting some of the intimate acts performed by the soldiers and their local pickups on the benches or the grass. I gathered it was possible to "do it" in quite a number of surprising positions.'[263]

The conflict had huge political and social implications, including a much closer relationship between Stormont and Westminster. Contemporary Ulster was subjected to much censorship, particularly with regard to information about labour unrest at home and suffering abroad. The arrival of 300,000 troops in the province altered the complexion of many communities, particularly County Londonderry. The intensity of the war was not felt in Ulster in the initial stages. Brian Barton quotes one observer in March 1940 as noting: 'we are umbombed and we have no conscription, there is still plenty to eat and life is reasonably normal'.[264] De Valera had not only resisted British invitations to join the war effort, but nationalists generally were vocal in their opposition to conscription, which was not imposed in Northern Ireland. The message from the Northern bishops was that it would be 'a further outrage on rights already invaded' and folly to make the same mistake as was made in 1918. In May 1939 the *Irish Press* reported: '2,000 republicans with hurley sticks and blackthorns headed by a party of men carrying a banner bearing the inscription "down with conscription" carried out a surprise parade in the Falls Road district of Belfast tonight'.[265] The parliament of Northern Ireland did not have the power to impose conscription. Craig agitated for conscription to be extended to the North, a pressure that increased at Westminster following the 1941 bombings, his logic being that 'the principle of equality of sacrifice underlying conscription is essential to promote the degree of corporate discipline which a united population must have' to defeat the enemy. But as Blake pointed out, the arguments against it 'were not less impressive', given the experience of 1918 and the opposition of the labour movement and nationalists. To impose it against the will of many, believed the US ambassador in London, would 'absorb as many men as conscription in Ireland would have added to the armed forces'. Churchill wisely decided it was not worth pursuing.[266]

'so many broken bodies in one place'
When monthly recruitment levels in the North were low early in the war Winston Churchill complained to Roosevelt that 'young fellows of the locality … loaf about with their hands in their pockets', and in the early

days munitions factories' output was low, and a certain apathy prevailed regarding civil defence, though there was an impressive increase in tillage output by the North's farmers. The government was presided over by the increasingly incapacitated James Craig, who died in 1940, and the Belfast mortuary services had emergency plans to deal with only 200 bodies. The bombings of April and May 1941, which left 1,100 dead, 56,000 houses in the city damaged and 100,000 temporarily homeless, changed much. A Belfast air-raid warden recalled in his memoirs the horror of the makeshift morgue at the Falls Road Baths:

> How could anyone have visualised seeing so many broken bodies in one place? No text books, no training pamphlets could have prepared us for the grim task we were about to undertake. Some were whole and others hardly resembled human beings. The scene could only be compared in a small way to the pictures released some years later of the mass graves at Belsen and other German death camps.[267]

A contemporary nurse described corpses 'with tangled hair, staring eyes, clutching hands, contorted limbs, their grey-green faces covered with dust'.

The writer Brian Moore, whose father was a Catholic surgeon in Belfast city, also witnessed the air raids and worked in the morgue. His biographer suggested the war was the most crucial event of his early life, and his own novel *The Emperor of Ice-cream* would suggest it was also somewhat empowering. Given the 'liberating orgy of destructiveness being enacted all around him', the days of the ARP (Air Raid Protection volunteers) being depicted as boozing unemployed misfits was over. As he described it: 'The world and the war had come to him at last ... tonight, history had conferred the drama of war on this dull, dead town in which he had been born.' As the bombs began to fall he roared: 'Blow up a few capitalists ... and the Bishop of Down and Connor ... and Stormont and Lord Carson's statue ... and the House of Bloody Parliament.' But the reality of the human cost quickly dawned as he began to place the dead in coffins.[268] Meanwhile, politically, Spender believed John Andrews (who replaced Craig) and his government had fostered complacency by failing to offer 'leadership and sacrifice'.[269]

'familiar with the position on paper'

Andrews did not last long (he was replaced by Sir Basil Brooke in 1943), which said much about the way the Northern unionist establishment was affected by the war. There was a realisation there would have to be much closer co-operation between business and politics, a grasping of the idea of a managed economy, and a need to respond to the political pressures of the working class. Many of these themes dominated cabinet discussions and committees of the war years. Andrews was worried enough in 1942 to note that 'the minds of our people have been directed more than ever before towards what is called "a new order" or a "fair deal", "the scandal that poverty should exist" and "the horrors associated with the slums"'.[270] In losing by-elections to labour candidates, the danger to unionism was all too apparent, as was the need to reconcile middle- and working-class Protestant interests. It was divisions over how best to achieve this that ensured Andrews's demise, as he began to make what were regarded as incautious promises of social expenditure.[271]

In October 1941 the government's Town Planning Committee was quick to place on record that this 'was a UK problem', and had to be factored as such into an overall plan. Months later more caution was the order of the day, as the secretary to the Minister for Home Affairs pointed out that until they knew what London had planned: 'a city or an area could be in an unfavourable position to press its claims if it has its reconstruction proposals all planned and complete'.[272] Belfast faced acute problems. Infant mortality, it was noted at government level, was 'appallingly high', with a figure of 66 per 1,000 births for London in 1936 compared to 101 for Belfast, which had actually risen to 122 in 1940. Another worry was the high density of population in Belfast, with 18.3 people per square mile compared to 11.84 for the Greater London area, with no satisfactory distribution of water supplies and sewerage systems.

Clearly, it had taken the devastating German assault to bring home the seriousness of the problems, a government official admitting: 'I must confess that while I was familiar with the position on paper, its practical disadvantages were really only brought home to me when we found that it was a practical impossibility to establish satisfactory hutment camps except in one or two restricted areas.' There was a danger, he concluded, that the province would 'stagnate in matters of public health and development generally'.[273] It was also noted that only 10,422 labourers' cottages were built between 1921 and 1941. The cabinet was divided on whether to define policy first and then establish the relevant machinery or vice versa, while a meeting of November 1943 concluded it was desirable 'to avoid the rubber stamp policy of doing something merely because it is being done in Great Britain'.[274]

'lavatories are either the field or a hut with a bucket'

The bombings had clearly done much to expose the poor state of housing in the city of Belfast and beyond. The interim report of the Planning Advisory Board on Housing in Northern Ireland revealed that of 323,052 houses in Northern Ireland, only 51,127 did not require repairs, while over 42,000 were totally unfit for habitation or required repairs of more than £200. Betty Sinclair, a member of the Communist Party, and a trade union activist, campaigned for more money to be spent on slum clearing in the cities, but she also recognised the dilemmas facing rural women as a result of squalor:

> In 85 out of every 100 [rural] homes, every drop of water has to be carried from outside, candles and lights must take the place of up-to-date methods of lighting, there is no other method of cooking ... lavatories are either the field or a hut with a bucket, termed a dry lavatory. The burden for women is intolerable. The difficulties of keeping everything, including the occupants of the house, clean is something which we can now begin to understand. Is it any wonder that great numbers of evacuees decided to face the bombs rather than stay in the 'safe' areas?[275]

But at government level there was recognition that Britain would determine the financing of reconstruction and the measure of parity between Britain and Northern Ireland. While unemployment in Northern Ireland was virtually nil by 1944, and the ratio of Northern Ireland to UK incomes grew from 55 per cent in 1938 to 67 per cent in 1945, there was consternation about how to employ 'some 50,000 men and women' who would be released from the forces at the end of the war, and the need for 'the provision of a colony for mental defectives', as well as concern about 'too rigid' an approach to parity in the area of public health. Much attention was also given to the radical Housing Trust that would centralise responsibility for housing.[276]

While such discussions were taking place at cabinet level, the grassroots contribution to the war effort increased, as did the province's strategic geographical significance. Real effort and sacrifice were involved, not just in military terms but also in doubling the acreage under the plough, providing Britain with vital foodstuffs. Between 1940 and 1944, 140 warships were built, as well as 1,200 Sterling bombers, 30 million shirts were produced, and 38,000 men and women from the North enlisted in the armed forces. There was also 'a strikingly high number of Irishmen in senior British military positions' and four wartime field marshalls had an Ulster background, including John Dill and Alan Brooke.[277]

In the absence of the Treaty ports, it was essential to keep sea lanes open during the Battle of the Atlantic, by diverting convoys around the north coast of Ireland, resulting in warm tributes from British statesmen and from General Eisenhower, future American president, who in August 1945 said: 'without Northern Ireland, I do not see how the American forces could have been concentrated to begin the invasion of Europe'.[278] While the prosperity that transpired with the business of war may have reduced intercommunal tension, some of the nationalists of Derry were not always happy about the vital role their city played in the war effort, reflected in the assertion of the writer Brian Moore's father that 'when it comes to grinding down minorities, the German jackboot isn't half as bad as John Bull'.[279]

- SIX -

1945-1960

'It's your money Éire is after'

It was revealing that by the early post-war period, the Free State government was keeping detailed files of comparisons 'between South and
North' in the social and economic but not the political sphere. Much of
this was undoubtedly prompted by the extension to Northern Ireland
of the British welfare state. Between 1945 and 1947 Northern Ireland
received the benefits of the Family Allowances Act of 1945, the Northern
Ireland Insurance Act of 1946, the Industrial Injuries Act of 1946 and
the National Health Services Act of 1946. Also in 1946, services and
taxation parity between Northern Ireland and the rest of the UK was
formally agreed. A comparison of economic and social trends North and
South, written by Labhrás Ó Nualláin for the Social and Statistical Inquiry
Society of Ireland in December 1945, observed that the North had colder
winters and summers, more rainfall, less sunshine, a younger population
than the South with higher and earlier marriage rates, but lower fertility.
It suggested 98 per cent of the total land area in the North was used productively in agriculture, compared with 68 per cent in the South. It also
detailed the extent to which industry was more significant in the North
but stressed that greater progress had been made in house building in the
South.[1]

Within two years, however, Northern Ireland's Minister for Home
Affairs wrote in the *Sunday Times* that 'the standards of living in the two

parts of Ireland are so dissimilar as to be scarcely comparable'.[2] This was particularly true, he asserted, in respect of social services, giving the example of children's allowances, where a woman with three children received 2s 6d per week in the South, compared with 10s in the North. He also maintained that the annual revenue per head in Northern Ireland was just over £41 compared to just under £23 in the South. De Valera responded by insisting that the North had almost double the taxation, and that 'if the people here are prepared to bear the burden of double taxation then we will provide them with higher social services'.

Thus the arrival of the welfare state in Northern Ireland prompted a battle of statistics, the South responding with the rather weak argument that in the North there were four towns with a population of over 1,000 that had no piped water whereas there were only two such towns in the South. While it was noted, on the basis of a 1943 survey, that there were similar housing deficiencies in both parts, Southern civil servants conveniently ignored the bombing of Belfast in the Blitz. They also maintained that with regard to education in the South, the Protestant minority were treated 'as generously as the majority if not more generously', given that denominational boards were asked for only a very small contribution with the state paying the lion's share.[3] De Valera also maintained in the Dáil that the standard of living in Dublin and Cork was higher than that of Belfast, and essential foodstuffs were not rationed in the South, while the *Belfast Telegraph* argued that not only were social services neglected in the South, but 'the government of Éire is more kind to the rich and more harsh to the poor'.[4]

In developing the propaganda war about the 'prosperous North and the poverty-stricken South', the prime minister, Basil Brooke, continued to maintain that the Northern government was a champion of working-class welfare. An Ulster Unionist Council leaflet was issued entitled 'It's your money Éire is after'.[5] An economist, Kieran Kennedy, estimated that living standards in Northern Ireland were better than in the South on the basis of a 20 per cent higher per capita disposable income.[6] Whatever about the reservations some unionists may have had about the adoption of the welfare state, it was certainly useful in terms of the North–South propaganda battle, though they neglected to point out that some unionists objected to the cost of family allowances owing to the size of Catholic families.[7] Despite the welfare state, which led to the winding up of the Poor Law, with new health and welfare committees at local and central level, poverty continued to be the experience of many in the North, but not to the extent of the pre-war era. The young Bernadette Devlin, a future nationalist MP, maintained that many Catholics felt that the welfare being paid to them was paid by a state that 'made us feel they were paying out money to the unworthy poor … our poverty wasn't extreme, but it was a kind of bottom-level poverty, the minimum necessary to support life in decency'.[8] Séamus Deane's novel *Reading in the Dark* describes women and girls streaming home from the shirt factories in Derry in the early 1950s, being watched by many unemployed men, 'most of whom stood at the street corners'.[9]

The welfare state did contribute to a change in some of the unionist political rhetoric, and influenced some women to appeal to the electorate on the basis of their concern for quality of life. Patricia Ford, elected as a unionist MP for the North Down constituency in 1953, urged voters to support her precisely because she was a woman:

> I feel perhaps that there may be a prejudice amongst some of you at the thought of a woman being able to tackle the problems which lie ahead, but I do feel, as a mother and a housewife myself, that on certain questions – such as children, food, housing, family allowances and health, a woman's angle is the more practical and realistic.[10]

'baths were luxuries for working-class homes'

Some unionists condemned the reported remarks of a Northern Ireland senator that 'baths were luxuries for working-class homes', the Derry Labour Party maintaining that housing conditions were 'utterly barbaric', while the Ulster Unionist Council condemned landlords for taking advantage of the housing shortage to increase rents.[11] Derry Corporation was very preoccupied with temporary housing in the post-war era, particularly the overcrowding and insanitary conditions of the Springtown camp, and maintained they would manage huts and temporary accommodation 'provided we are not required to give any priority in regard to permanent housing'.[12]

The post-war period also witnessed the publication of John Mogey's *Rural Life in Northern Ireland* (1947) in response to the 1938 claim of the Chairman of the Northern Ireland Council of Social Services that 'there had been no serious investigation of rural problems for over a century'. Mogey's findings revealed that 56 per cent of farms were less than 30 acres and that 93 per cent of houses lacked piped water and a lavatory. But it acknowledged that the wartime boom had changed the fortunes of rural Ireland and that Northern farmers were easily out-performing their Southern counterparts.

Agriculture still employed one worker in six in Northern Ireland in 1950, but there was huge variation in farming conditions between, for example, depressed areas of south Armagh and prosperous parts of Antrim.[13] Education, of course, was another pillar of the welfare state; secondary intermediate schools were a new departure of the post-war era, and the 1944 Education Act provided new opportunities for Catholics. In 1947, the Ministry of Education upheld and raised the grants for voluntary schools (which were mostly Catholic) despite objections, and the Education Act of that year instigated a new structure for primary, secondary and further education, and single, reconstituted education committees for each county and city. It also 'laid obligations on education authorities to provide extensive free services to all schools, relating to medical treatment, transport, school meals and milk, books and stationery'.[14]

In the midst of discussion on education reform in the North, the *Irish Times* suggested it was an embarrassment to the South, where so many children of the poor were leaving school at 14.[15] But many of the traditional barriers in relation to employment were still in stark evidence. In 1943, Wilfred Spender, the head of the civil service, had admitted to John Andrews that in relation to the employment of Catholics in the civil service 'he would find it a source of embarrassment if he produced any statistics or defended himself in this matter'.[16]

Given that a Labour government in Britain was responsible for many of the post-war changes, it is interesting to observe how labour parties in Northern Ireland fared and the extent to which unionism stole its political clothes. In 1944, a 44–hour working week was introduced, closing the gap between skilled and general workers. New arbitration procedures for industrial disputes were introduced, though Northern Ireland retained measures on strikes that had been repealed in Britain. The 1945 Northern Ireland election was certainly dramatic for labour, where non-nationalist labour parties, including the Northern Ireland Labour Party, the Independent Labour Party of Northern Ireland and the Commonwealth Labour Party, received 70 per cent of the vote in Belfast, 'with only the electoral system and a divided opposition limiting unionist losses to three seats'. In the Westminster election that followed, the unionists could hold on to barely 50 per cent of the vote in Belfast, something of a humiliation; but once again, anti-partition rows split the Northern Ireland Labour Party, as did pressure resulting from the declaration of the Irish Republic.[17]

The minutes of one branch of the Northern Ireland Labour Party's post-war meetings, in the papers of Patrick Agnew, reveal rancorous disputes, it being claimed in November 1946 that the party 'was being run by a couple of dictators', with internal critics warning that they wanted 'some definite arrangements whereby all decisions made at meetings would be adhered to'.[18] Jack Macgougan, chairman of the NILP, made the astonishing admission in 1947 that 'I have never found out the exact extent to which the Northern standard of life and social services are subsidised by Britain'. By the time of the Stormont general election of October 1953 there were four labour–nationalist groups contesting Belfast seats – the Irish Labour Party, Independent Labour, Republican Labour and Independent Irish Labour. Macgougan was to refer bitterly to the 'myopia induced by the pursuit of unity'.[19]

'permanently in the job'?

There were battles in the unionist family also, and there were many Brookes, depending on one's standpoint – antagonist, sectarian loyalist, tame squire – but ultimately it was his tactical and executive skills that kept him in power until 1963. He had more of an imperial outlook than the parochial Craig, and he came to power to head an aged and incompetent government, being perhaps the only minister of that era who had not been subjected to criticism. It was significant, in view of some of the discontent within the younger ranks of the party, that his chosen public image was that of a restless reformer who warned his cabinet that they should not consider themselves 'permanently in the job',[20] even though he remained there for 20 years and was occasionally utterly nonchalant about his job, preferring, it seemed, trout fishing. This casualness was a common attitude. Sir Roland Nugent, Minister for Commerce, admitted in the Northern Ireland Senate: 'sometimes when I meet strangers I do not tell them I am a minister. I say I am a farmer or a retired businessman, because I know that in this country it is a shameful thing to be a minister.' He was speaking in a Senate that, in the view of G. Duggan, the former Comptroller and Auditor-General for Northern Ireland, remained utterly ineffective: 'too much of a home for discards or the aged'.[21]

Unionists were heartened by the Northern Ireland Act of 1949 (in response to the Declaration of the Irish Republic), which confirmed that in no circumstances would 'Northern Ireland or any part thereof cease to be part of His Majesty's dominions without the consent of the parliament of Northern Ireland'. In introducing this legislation, Clement Attlee touched a raw nerve in Irish nationalism by announcing that he had to 'conclude that the government of Éire considered the cutting of the last tie which united Éire to the British Commonwealth was a more important objective of policy than ending partition'.[22] But fears remained concerning the extent to which Northern Ireland could embrace the welfare state whilst 'resisting the erosion of its autonomy by other aspects of Westminster legislation'.[23]

Divisions of this kind did not prevent Brooke from posing as a champion of popular working-class interests, and he maintained in 1947 that 'the backbone of unionism is the unionist Labour party', adding that the welfare state posed no threat to the middle classes, who were supported by industrial policy. For good measure there was a share of anti-Catholic rhetoric thrown in, stigmatising Catholics who claimed welfare benefit but rejected the state. His stance was aided by the anti-partition campaign of some Southern politicians. After the 1949 election, Brooke was able to reflect on the effective merging of these arguments, by recording in his diary 'a magnificent victory ... all socialists knocked out'.[24] The truth, as recounted by the poet Michael Longley, was that prosperous Belfast citizens were always anxious 'to separate themselves safely from the ghettoes of the bellicose working-classes'.[25] Meanwhile, the Festival of Britain in 1951 and the Coronation of Queen Elizabeth in 1953 were further opportunities to present the government-approved image of loyal Ulster as essentially British but with its distinct and unique state and people.[26]

'we want the Ulster accent'

It would be misleading, however, to assume there were no differences of opinion as to what the unionist identity encapsulated. Some observers like Duggan believed representation at Westminster was unnecessary, with some Northern MPs making a 'show of business' and others indistinguishable from British Conservatives. He also maintained that 'outside the marshalled ranks of voters', Ulster provincialism was very strong; he mentioned not only the emphasis put on the differences between Ulster and the rest of Ireland, but also the pride of the Ulsterman in his province and ultimately his Irish heritage; indeed, too often 'have members brought the provincialism of the local councillor into the seats of government'.[27] Maurice Hayes recalled that, in the 1950s, 'you could tell the location of county councillors houses, if not by the better state of the roads leading to them, by the string of cars driving round at weekends and on the clear evenings when teaching appointments were being made'.[28]

Unionists often complained of the 'Englishness' of the BBC in Ulster but, as Gillian McIntosh has pointed out, rejected local cultural programmes because of the danger of acknowledging cultural differences in the state. She argues that the war forced Ulster to rely more on its own resources, with a consequent focus on the meaning of its own identity, and a new emphasis on regionalism at the radio station.[29] The cabinet in the summer of 1952 was very sensitive about the BBC programme *Opinion* creating an unfavourable view of the North, the Minister for Home Affairs suggesting that 'perhaps the BBC in selecting Imperial MPs as the unionist representatives were under the impression that they spoke for the Northern Ireland government'. Likewise during the war, it had been felt that data for the Ulster news should be prepared by someone independent of the BBC – they did not, it seemed, 'want the Oxford accent; we want the Ulster accent'.[30]

'offended both camps beautifully'

There was also critical questioning of the quality of Northern Irish culture and literature in the post-war period, and complaints that the state had not produced writers, playwrights or poets of sufficient excellence. The emergence of individuals like Sam Hanna Bell, John Hewitt, W. R. Rodgers and Louis MacNeice was significant in this regard. They did not beat the established unionist drum, but were more inclined to examine the disharmony and diversity of Ulster life, which was at odds with the official presentation of cultural unity. John Hewitt was delighted, for example, that W. R. Rodgers 'offended both camps beautifully'. The adoption of a regionalist perspective was one of the consequences of the war, with Ulster depicted as an entity emerging out of colonisation, but not yet a nation, with many finding a forum in the BBC for the articulation of their ideas.[31] Hewitt, although critical of sectarian nationalists, was deprived of the directorship of the Belfast Museum for being too provocative, while the novels of Hugh Sherman, who in his history-writing was essentially an apologist for the Northern Irish government, displayed a certain hostility to England and the religious and class diversity within the Northern State. Sam Hanna Bell's novel *December Bride*, in focusing on themes similar to those of the rural South – craving for land, familial tension and prevailing morality – 'actively sabotages the notion of a homogenous Protestant enclave'.[32] But even by the mid-1950s Hewitt was sceptical in his correspondence with Rodgers about the extent to which Ulster had a distinct literary voice. In the summer of 1955 he wrote: 'actually there is nothing like a movement. We have writers who migrate to London, to Dublin, to the rest of the world – a very few who stay at home ... the best we can say is that for the novelists, most draw their material from Ireland ... a new novel which has received good notices – I haven't seen it yet – is a case in point. The scene is laid in Belfast ... but the author [Brian Moore] is now a Canadian citizen and the dialogue is peppered with transatlanticisms. Here, as a Belfast man, he apparently showed no signs of literary interest. Can we call him an Ulster author?'[33]

Edna Longley examined the work and careers of individuals like the playwright Sam Thompson to make the point that 'Left-wing Ulster Protestants have a distinctive tale to tell.' She suggested that Thompson's exposure of sectarianism in the shipyards in his play *Over the Bridge*, written in 1957 and performed in 1960, revived the dissenting spirit of the 1930s. The play was originally supposed to be performed at the Belfast Group Theatre in 1957 but was dropped when the head of programmes at BBC Northern Ireland, a member of the theatre's board of management, 'set alarm bells ringing at Stormont'. A successful three-year battle to get the play staged commenced, with controversy raging in the press and at Stormont. The support of people like Louis MacNeice for Thompson was particularly significant; it was, MacNeice insisted, 'a play about something ... social consciousness seems to have become, among the younger generation, a dirty phrase [so] it is very refreshing to encounter a work such as this which reaffirms the eternal commonplaces of the misery – and the dignity – of man'.[34]

The censorship that affected the South was also in evidence in the North. Derry city councillors, for example, made regular trips to screenings to decide what films could and could not be viewed. In 1949 they permitted the *Snake Pit* but in April 1952 they were divided on *A Streetcar Named Desire*, the chairman's vote saving the day.[35] Towards the end of the war concern was also expressed that Northern Ireland should not fall behind Great Britain in the area of library development; as in the South, there was some puzzlement as to why libraries came under the auspices of the Department of Health and Local Government rather than the Ministry of Education. The problem, as in the South, was lack of uniformity in the provision of facilities, and in many areas neither a school service nor a public library was available.

The assistant secretary to the Minister for Education had noted in 1938 that 'in only a few areas does it appear that the facilities can be regarded as reasonably satisfactory'.[36] In 1944 the Minister for Local Government and Public Health suggested that the civil service input to the library service amounted to 'the time of one man, for one week per annum'. There were far too many urban and rural districts working as independent units, and by 1949 there was a call for an advisory Northern Ireland Library Council, a year in which it was revealed there were just 17 libraries in Northern Ireland, established and maintained by local authorities under the Public Libraries Act. But having removed the limits of expenditure of rates on libraries in 1946, the Ministry believed 'there was nothing much else' they could do to accelerate development. In 1958 Harry Diamond suggested the library facilities in Northern Ireland 'were the worst in the British Isles' as Stormont said 'No' to grants for libraries.[37]

'Didn't the nuns kidnap little girls'?

To what extent was there pressure on unionists in the North to develop closer ties with Ulster nationalists? Henry Patterson suggests the career of Brian Maginess, a historically neglected figure who attempted to broaden the mind of unionism, revealed the limits of liberal unionism. Appointed Minister for Labour in 1945, and later Minister for Finance, he believed the welfare state could create a nationalist constituency conscious of the benefits of the Union who needed to be embraced by Northern society rather than the continuance of what he referred to in 1959 as 'a policy of apartheid'.[38] He earned further wrath by his banning of certain Orange parades. But for the existence of the border, he suggested to Brooke: 'our own people would have begun to clamour for a government which had more real powers than we possess'. Although in favour of a locally controlled economy, Patterson argues that Maginess was in effect patronising Catholics and ignored the huge unemployment problem they faced.

In any case, in many respects a new generation of Protestants was being taught to ape the ignorance and condescension of their parents. In the 1950s, Michael Longley, later a renowned poet, craved the bond of shared fears and superstitions which a Protestant education fostered. The Orange Order and the B Specials dominated Protestant schoolchildren's conversations, and there was little on the curriculum to suggest they were living in Ireland, as schoolboys were taught to despise Dublin and be suspicious of Catholics. 'Didn't the nuns kidnap little girls and imprison them behind the suspiciously high walls of the big convent at the top of the Ormeau Road?'[39]

He also noted how class-ridden Belfast was, but the same class divisions and use of religion operated on the nationalist side also. The idea that an educated Catholic middle class emerging from the welfare state would liberate the Catholic working class was something of a myth. There was little change in either the education or the social background of nationalist leaders, and they still, it seemed, received little support from the South. The nationalist MP Eddie McAteer, a leading light in the Anti-Partition League, complained bitterly in Galway in 1948 that Southerners were 'more interested in the price of beef and eggs while Northern Catholics were being driven from their homes'.[40] Bernadette Devlin's *The Price of My Soul* also gives an insight into the class snobbery operating within Northern Catholicism, her family shunned because her mother had married a lower-class Catholic and did not 'observe the rituals of Cookstown's bourgeoisie', and was thrown out of her house as a result. The only reason her family subsequently obtained a house from the Housing Trust was because local Presbyterians were prepared to give them a reference.[41]

'such a happily disenfranchised part'?

The two aunts in Séamus Deane's novel *Reading in the Dark* are 'treated like skivvies and boarded in a henhouse', his father's aunt informing his father when his father's family were scattered to various relatives: 'you eat margarine ... butter's for the children of this house only'. The religion teacher in the novel summed up the attitude (in 1954) of a middle-class Catholicism which stressed conservatism and resentment simultaneously:

> there is no need to exhort you people to be simple. You achieve that condition effortlessly. But I shall, in this and in succeeding years, exhort you to believe that education can be conducted in such a manner as to confirm that simplicity rather than disturb it. It is of course a gratuitous exercise, but one demanded by the society of which you form such a happily disenfranchised part.[42]

Bernadette Devlin's fanatical republican teacher, a nun, also suggested, even though she was the most political teacher in the school, that 'politics is a waste of time'. Of course, for those who refused to be quiet there were other prejudices to be faced that sparked defiance; the mother in Deane's novel questioned why they should 'go back to being unemployed, gerrymandered, beaten up by every policeman who took the notion, gaoled by magistrates and judges'. The IRA cast a shadow over the early life of Deane and his family as a result of activities in the 1920s and they were 'a marked family' after being interrogated about weapons, ensuring 'the police smell took the oxygen out of the air'.[43]

But the IRA border campaign of the late 1950s (see below) made no sense to many. What struck Ben Caraher, a veteran Belfast lawyer in the 1990s, who had grown up in Crossmaglen in the 1950s, was: 'the absolute irrelevance of it ... what on earth was it all about?' In 1959 Sinn Féin polled only 74,000 votes in the North, down from 152,000 in 1955, despite what they maintained was the 'pathetic ineffectuality cum petty corruption' of nationalist leaders, and they were to complain of the lack of support from Northern nationalists for their military strategy at this stage. The nationalist MP Anthony Mulvey, who represented Fermanagh–Tyrone from 1945 to 1947, had received some harsh correspondence from a parish priest in County Down, which revealed a naive belief that de Valera could still deliver on the partition issue ('we should not doubt his real earnestness and attention to the border issue'). The priest saw a need to arouse the 'drooping spirits' of Northern nationalists and lambasted their lack of attention to partition, urging Mulvey 'to shake the dust off your boots' and fight hard at Westminster. He complained that to sit down and accept as slaves every 'slap in the lug' should not be the Irish approach to any British government: 'This sort of thing gives me a very painful political headache.' This priest was highly delusional in believing nationalists who wished to be 'a persistent international nuisance'[44] would be guaranteed a sympathetic audience. Of course, nationalists were also frustrated by the inbuilt majority against them; in 1958 Eddie McAteer was reduced to token protest resolutions that had no chance of being carried on the gerrymandered Derry Corporation, proposing for example that the words 'with great regret' be deleted from the finance report that deplored the closure of the Royal Naval Air station in Eglinton.[45]

'mutually hostile and irreconcilable?'

But the 1950s did produce a certain amount of co-operation between North and South relating to the drainage of the River Erne, the Foyle Fisheries Commission, foot and mouth disease, electricity and the Great Northern Railway Board, and customs authorities. By 1957 the Department of External Affairs in the South was looking at the idea of a formal commission to encourage co-operation between North and South, to destroy the 'prevalent idea that the northern Irish and the southern Irish are mutually hostile and irreconcilable' and strengthen 'the hands of moderate elements at present in the unionist camp'.[46] Dismissed by Brooke, it was a suggestion Seán Lemass, who succeeded de Valera as Taoiseach in 1959, was keen to pursue. There was no agreement, however, on extradition, with accusations that the Southern government was morally responsible for raids on the RUC.

Whatever about 'moderate' elements within unionism, it was the critical voice that continued to dominate the headlines. In 1958 a unionist MP suggested that the version of Irish history taught in schools in the South glorified assassination, blaming contemporary IRA outrages on such propaganda. An official in the Commonwealth Relations Office disagreed and suggested that most teaching was in fact 'quite objective' and that the real reason for IRA activism was unemployment and boredom. He suggested 'the real niggers in the woodpile over this stoking of ancient hates' were teachers from the religious orders.[47] There was an irony of course in such unionist concern, given the accurate assessment of Northern journalist Martin Wallace in 1956 that unionists were 'forever attempting to justify themselves' and unduly sensitive to outside opinion. It was unfortunate, suggested David Harkness, that it was in the 1950s 'that opportunity to adapt was overlooked'.[48] The poet John Hewitt, who had spent many years attempting to define his Protestant Ulster identity, hinted that the need to adapt was more pressing than ever in his poem 'The Colony' (1953), which used the phrase 'the curfewed ghetto' in relation to the Catholic minority. He had already, in the poem 'Conacre' (1943), established that 'this is my home', being forced to focus on regional identity owing to the isolation caused by the war, but had not yet found that 'this nation is my own'. Another poem, 'Once Alien Here' (1948), established the claim that he was an Ulsterman, through his lineage and physical identity with the province. But in 'The Colony' the narrator turns his attention to the future and concludes his plea to Protestant Ulster to:

admit our load of guilt

and would make amends by fraternising

by small friendly gestures

hoping by patient words I may convince my people and this people

I may convince my people and this people we are changed from the raw
    levies which usurped the land

and each gain something from proximity.

It was telling that when the poem first appeared few paid much heed, but by the time violence broke out, nearly twenty years later, it was being quoted liberally.[49]

'Here, if ever was, is a climate for the death wish'

Historians have invariably used words such as 'doom', 'drift', 'stagnation', 'crisis' and 'malaise' to describe Ireland south of the border in the 1950s. It has not only been those with the benefit of hindsight who have employed the semantics of despair. In July 1954, in the last issue of the *Bell* magazine, the writer Anthony Cronin described what he saw as an illness, affecting not only Irish writers, but also Irish society at large:

> One looks out of the window at the wet Sunday morning, ineffable grey
> above melancholy deep green and dull red bricks; at the girls hurrying
> to mass in their glowing mackintoshes, at the man with the six soaked
> Sunday newspapers under his arm and a face as grey and expressionless
> as the sky. Here, if ever was, is a climate for the death wish.[50]

It would be difficult to find a gloomier account of Irish culture and society, as the country, it seemed, was left in the economic and cultural doldrums while much of the rest of Europe was benefiting from a sustained post-war boom.

Writing some 20 years later, Cronin suggested Ireland's neutrality during the war had left a wound, 'set up complexes in many, including myself, which the post-war period did little to cure'.[51] Those of a creative bent who left Ireland seemed to have fared better: the playwright Denis Johnston, who spent his childhood in Dublin, had joined BBC Northern Ireland in 1936 and went on to become a producer with the BBC television service. He recalled in his autobiography the success of the Irish in British television and the 'luxury' of debating television issues, 'the exciting things that we all used to argue about in working out the techniques of an entirely new medium'.[52]

'the stupid propaganda of the calamity mongers'

But at home economic malaise was eating away at Irish confidence like a cancer, and while the census of 1951 recorded a population increase of 5,000 over that of 1946 – the first recorded increase in population since 1841 – this slight rise was confined almost entirely to Dublin and five other counties, and was quickly consumed by emigration on a scale startling by international standards. In 1958 alone nearly 60,000 people left Ireland, at the end of a decade that saw some rural areas lose exceptionally large chunks of their population, both male and female. Unemployment continued to rise and it was estimated that from 1949 to 1956 real national income rose by only 8 per cent, at a time when the average increase in Europe was about 40 per cent. There were many who, out of frustration, conviction, impatience or sheer boredom, sought to counteract such malaise, but they were up against significant barriers, and a stubborn, defensive refusal to face reality. An article in *Studies* in 1951, for example, acknowledged that capital and labour still regarded each other with suspicion but insisted that:

> poverty fifty years ago was real, now it is comparative ... the poor are still with us, but actual destitution if it is still to be found in Ireland is rare and avoidable ... unless we are deliberately determined to drift into communist slavery let us stop repeating the stupid propaganda of the calamity mongers who, day in day out, declare that we were never so badly off as we are now, when, in actual fact, we are more fortunate than most nations and have the power to continue advancing if we have the will.[53]

These observations were highly deceptive, and indicate that many of those attempting a constructive critique of the Irish state's failures (such as those, for example, involved in unemployment protest movements) were conveniently, unfairly and often lazily branded communist. Particularly in the context of the international Cold War, such accusations became a potent weapon in the hands of the Catholic Church, which continued to command an exceptional degree of obedience, but which in doing so also began, particularly in its high profile opposition to a welfare state, to sow seeds of dissent. This was a factor commented on, though rather exaggeratedly, by Tom Garvin, when he wrote that 'rather like the Communist regimes of Eastern Europe, the Catholic Church in 1950s Ireland had begun to educate itself out of power; her own secondary schools were hatcheries of sceptics and anti-clericals. An undercurrent of anti-clericalism ran through the steadily growing educated stratum of a relatively under-educated nation.'[54]

While Archbishop McQuaid seemed to reign supreme, many were also finding the constant expressions of outrage from the Catholic right irksome, and this is seen in a growing liberalism in relation to, amongst other things, censorship. It is important in this context to acknowledge that, culturally, in many ways the 1950s was the decade in which an ethos which tolerated, if not encouraged, the sanctification of deprivation was to be challenged, not just by those emigrating but also by the growing resentment of those left at home. In some ways, the logic which economist Liam Kennedy applied in looking at the modern industrialisation of Ireland, applied to other areas also:

> The 1950s are etched in the popular imagination as the decade of crisis and stagnation in the Republic. Yet ... it was during the 1950s that the foundations for a decisive break with a mediocre past were laid. Investment in infrastructure and, even more importantly, a variety of institutional innovations, helped lay the basis for future development.[55]

Politically, the 1950s were also important in establishing that the Fianna Fáil monopoly on power could be broken and that, though sometimes difficult to manage, coalition governments could work effectively in Ireland. Not only was there the arrival of new and younger politicians, exemplified by the dramatic rise and decline of Clann na Poblachta, but also, by the end of the IRA border campaign (1957–62), a growing recognition of the immaturity of the 'official' Irish attitude to partition, while Ireland's involvement with the United Nations indicated a willingness to expand foreign-affairs horizons.

Women in rural areas, particularly through groups like the Irish Countrywomen's Association, became more effective lobbyists, and expanded the spheres in which Irish women could operate. The trade unionist Louie Bennett publicly derided an education policy which decreed that domestic science was the be all and end all for Irish female education, and women were instrumental in bringing long-needed change and innovation to Ireland, particularly in the context of running water and electricity. But it was not until the 1990s that there was any willingness to face up to the sad continuity in both Church, state and societal attitudes towards the vulnerable and poor in Irish society; notably children in religious-run institutions such as the industrial schools, but also unmarried mothers, who were left in many cases in appalling physical and psychological circumstances, making a mockery of the assertion, above, that 'actual destitution' in Ireland was rare. Whatever about physical destitution, emotional destitution and humiliation were rife in post-war Ireland, alongside a near obsession with public devotion to Marianism within the ranks of the Catholic Church, making the lack of charity all the more ironic.

In cultural terms, revision was a notable feature of the historiography of the period, helping to balance the view of Ireland as utterly introverted. Brian Fallon suggested there was a battle between conservatism and renewal being fought virtually everywhere: in the United States, an unrest among the young about the stifling mores of their parents; an angry young man generation in England; in France a new critical generation which responded to the authoritarianism of de Gaulle. These movements were in turn attacked by a rear-guard action, exemplified by Poujadisme in France and McCarthyism in America: 'so Ireland, though more often than not without knowing it, was mostly in step with the times, in her own odd way and at her own peculiar gait'.[56] Fallon offers an impressive list of cultural innovations and liberating events, episodes, institutions and individuals of the 1950s in the areas of literature, art, theatre, historical research and writing, with the gauntlet thrown down to the Catholic right by a new commitment to public criticism.

'Ireland is building'?

There is much merit in Fallon's thesis, but what many of the other countries had that Ireland lacked were healthy, if not booming, economies in the post-war period. In contrast, in the late 1940s less than 1 per cent of Irish exports were going to the United States, highlighting the huge dollar deficit, and the sterling crisis of 1947, when London limited the convertibility of its currency, took Ireland by surprise and exposed another weakness in her economic dependency. Between 1951 and 1961, 412,000 people emigrated from Ireland, and in 1956 and 1957 Ireland was alone in Europe in being a country where the total volume of goods and services consumed fell. Employment in industry fell by 38,000, or 14 per cent of the industrial labour force, between 1951 and 1959, while between 1941 and 1961 the agricultural workforce was depleted by 200,000.

Economic prospects had not seemed that bleak in the immediate post-war period, helped by the fact that during the war national income had not declined, unlike in many other European countries. While unemployment stood at 14 per cent in 1945, from 1945 to 1950 personal expenditure rose by 25 per cent, industrial output rose by one third, investment was recovering, and the Irish economist James Meenan noted a new form of earning through tourism that was unknown before the war.[57]

The coalition government that came to power in 1948 had promised, in a brochure designed to lure home Irish emigrants, that *Ireland is Building*, announcing a ten-year plan for the building of 110,000 houses, while in the 1948/9 local-government financial estimates 88 per cent of expenditure was allocated for housing. The years 1947–52 duly witnessed something of a boom in house-building, with the total number of houses built with state aid growing from 1,600 in 1947 to 14,000 in 1953. Cutbacks and an emphasis on conserving existing house stock quickly followed, but during the 1950s housing continued to absorb a huge percentage of the public capital programme.[58]

These positive developments, however, were soon to be subsumed by the economic failings that became the hallmark of the 1950s, a time when 35 per cent of Ireland's top 115 companies were externally controlled. These included balance of payment crises, increases in income and direct taxes, and, often most damaging in the eyes of the public, the removal of food subsidies on basic foodstuffs. The budget of 1952, with Fianna Fáil back in power, was regarded as something of a bleak turning point since it was a departure from the Keynesian-inspired policy of the first coalition government of 1948–51. (Gross National Product had been rising owing to the European Recovery Programme, but the Korean War and balance of payments problems were added economic pressures.) The 1952 budget inaugurated several years of stagnant national income, with, as Ó Gráda noted, Irish economic growth slower than anywhere else in Western Europe.[59]

The introduction of married women to the workforce, as was being experienced in the United States in the 1950s, was not considered in Ireland; according to the 1946 census, out of a total of over 450,000 married women, only 11,000, or 2.5 per cent, were classified as employees. In Britain the figure was 25 per cent. Irish conservatism in this regard was reflected in concerns about fertility and threats to 'home life', though there was an increased demand for the lifting of marriage bars in certain professions. The social-welfare system in Ireland was centred around the idea of the dependent wife and children and breadwinner husband, while there was no support whatsoever in financial terms for unmarried mothers. It is also significant that even in the late 1950s there was a suspicion about the word 'planning', given its association in the mind of Catholic social theorists with the ever-encroaching paternal state.[60]

But despite this hostility, Ireland had been forced to begin to see itself in the context of its relationship with its European neighbours, particularly regarding Marshall Aid funding from the United States and the beginnings of European post-war reconstruction. The debate as to whether Ireland should be a recipient of Marshall Aid funds suggested it was in the interests of the US to have Ireland involved to provide more food for export. Even though there were those in the US who wished to isolate Ireland as a result of neutrality, there was a perceived security need to tie Ireland into the American-sponsored reconstruction, while, interestingly, there was also a perception that excluding Ireland would intensify anti-partitionism. It was also significant that the US ambassador in Dublin from 1948 to 1950, George Garrett, erroneously believed that Ireland was as vulnerable as any other country to communist infiltration owing to its economic depression, despite Ireland's seemingly impeccable anti-communist credentials. Over four years, despite the government's arrogant insistence that they should get grants rather than loans (and the US was by no means disposed towards being overly generous), a token grant of only $18 million was given, with the bulk of $149 million coming in loans.

'the quality of the thought that informs public policy'

The Marshall Aid period was significant in that it focused much attention on the difficulties of directing the economy away from protection towards more openness. Alongside this, there was much diplomacy involved between Britain, the US and Ireland, which was to dominate Irish foreign policy until the late 1950s. It also forced much debate in the civil service, particularly in the context of the overwhelmingly negative attitude of the Department of Finance and the protective mindset of the Department of Industry and Commerce (elements of the Department of Agriculture were much more optimistic, according to Bernadette Whelan).[61] But because of the huge demand for immediate employment, loans were not always spent productively or with a long-term perspective; indeed, there was much comment on Ireland's low rate of productive investment in the 1950s, and internal government squabbling did not help. Money was spent on afforestation, land reclamation, the Electricity Supply Board, bog land development and construction. Arguments were not resolved, but as Bernadette Whelan has powerfully argued, the accompanying debates were important in terms of modernising the context in which economic policy-making debate took place, while the statistical reviews and planning exercises which were a compulsory part of the process of the European Recovery Programme and the Organisation for European Economic Co-operation exposed the fundamental weaknesses of the economy and forced economists into making comparative analyses with other countries that were way out-performing Ireland.

It was no coincidence that in 1953 Patrick Lynch, a lecturer in economics in University College Dublin, directed attention to the quality of official advice and exhorted civil servants to 'recognise the necessity for revealing the quality of the thought that informs public policy'.[62] A new interest in economics (it was significant that governments would begin to fall on the issue of managing the economy) was signalled by a series of articles in 1954 by a rising economist, Garret FitzGerald (a Taoiseach in the 1980s). The views he expressed were closely akin to those of T. K. Whitaker, a senior civil servant and architect of the economic-recovery programmes of the late 1950s. But it was also significant and an indication of the old-school mentality that George O'Brien, Professor of Political Economy in UCD, when appointing FitzGerald as a lecturer in economics, 'dismissed as irrelevant my lack of qualifications in the subject, pointing out that he himself had no degree in economics'. The innocence of it all is striking.

'clear all the rocks out of Connemara'

There had also been comment in the early 1950s on the government's conservative attitude towards the Central Bank of Ireland, a cautious institution at all times. Writing in the *Irish Times* in January 1951, during a strike by bank officials, Flann O'Brien suggested an Irish bank, in the sense of a banking concern dedicated to furthering the interest of Ireland, did not exist. He wrote:

It is almost a cliché that this country is chronically undercapitalised, that money for productive capital works cannot be got. The administration recently started formidable capital works concerned with land reclamation and drainage and is about to clear all the rocks out of Connemara. With money borrowed from the banks deposited by thrifty farmers? Not on your life. With borrowed American dollars which are roughly twice as costly as pounds.[63]

He was suggesting a reconsideration of the link with sterling. The truth, however, was that Irish politicians did not seem to want to interfere with the banking system. The Central Bank was cautious about public spending, and in the late 1950s reiterated the view that prosperity could not be attained by financial devices, and irritated the government by lamenting inflation, wage demands, and rises in expenditure and taxation. In any case Ireland's attempt at an independent monetary policy in the mid-1950s, by not following an increase in the British bank rate, was not a success.[64]

The Irish agricultural sector continued to disappoint and pro-tillage policies failed. An Anglo-Irish trade agreement which removed quotas imposed on Irish livestock did not herald the boom anticipated, owing to the British deficiency payments system. There was progress in the meat-processing industry, with the export of frozen meat to the US beginning in 1950 (Aer Lingus inaugurated a transatlantic route in 1958). The tragic depletion of what had been a marvellous railroad network continued in the 1950s. There were, however, new industrial incentives and subsidies created during the decade, though they did not have an immediate effect on the tariff-based outlook. Córas Tráchtála, a state export promotion agency, was created in 1952, export tax reliefs were introduced in 1956, and the Industrial Development Authority, established in 1948, was given an industrial promotions role in 1952, while An Fóras Tionscáil (the Irish Management Institute) and Bord Fáilte (the Irish Tourist Board) were also established. Perhaps the earlier publications of the Irish Tourist Board were indicative of some of the paradoxes holding back the Irish economy generally. While they sought to depict Ireland as modern in terms of its 'convenience' and 'luxury', there was also a heavy emphasis on 'primitive' Ireland and indeed 'life at Europe's edge'.[65]

'the impression of being an economic slum'
Such ambiguities were understandable, but perhaps militated against a
more effective development of tourism. They certainly did not impress a
Bank of England official who holidayed in Ireland in 1957. His impressions
of the visit were unearthed by Cormac Ó Gráda in the Bank of England
archives, and serve as a useful summary of the dilemmas facing the Irish
economy, though even this observer would have been unlikely to predict
the speed with which things were to improve dramatically:

> The fundamental weaknesses remain, namely that too much has been
> spent on unproductive capital schemes, particularly building, too little
> devoted to increasing the productivity of agriculture and there is too
> much nationalism as regards the introduction of industry from abroad
> … Foreign industries are welcomed in theory, but are hampered by
> the Control of Manufactures Act which prescribes that the majority
> interest should be in Irish hands and tends to locate business in out-
> landish parts of the country to reduce unemployment. It is impos-
> sible to maintain lower wage rates than the UK owing to the demand
> for labour in Great Britain; good skilled labour tends to emigrate at
> once. The result is that the country gives the impression of being an
> economic slum from which there is a constant outflow of emigrants
> who have any initiative and any desire to better themselves.[66]

The following year, James Dillon of Fine Gael spoke for many, in informing Fianna Fáil that they had two choices: 'I often grow weary of the
codology that goes on in this house [the Dáil]. Either Fianna Fáil wants
foreign capital or it does not want foreign capital. If it wants it, it should
open its doors to it.'[67]

'our second national debt'
It was easier for external observers to be more frank about Irish emigration than Irish officials and commentators, who often seemed at a loss to
explain, or to be honest about, what became known as the 'decade of the
vanishing Irish'. As the figures suggest, it was an extraordinary outflow,
and attempting to put a human face on it is important. Perhaps one of the
sadder aspects was that so many intended, or at least pretended, that their
emigration would be short-term. And yet fifty years later, at performances
of a play centred on Irish emigrant life in London, *The Kings of the Kilburn*

High Road by Jimmy Murphy, Irish audiences were informed of a 'safe home' programme for the repatriation of Irish emigrants who wished but could not afford to return. The focus in particular was on two forgotten groups of older Irish people, 'the first being the sad silent migration of ... people to far away institutions when they were most vulnerable and alone and the second the group of our older Irish emigrants who had done so much for this country and many of whom need our help now'. An insert in the play's programme pointed out that many of the latter were living in dreadful conditions in the bigger urban centres of England. But there was a strong political point to be made also:

> the emigrants' remittances are testimony to the sacrifices made so self-lessly by our emigrants to sustain our Irish economy over the years. These unique people rebuilt Britain after the Second World War, and were our original 'Celtic Tiger', helping us pay off our own national debt. Now the Irish economy is booming, it is time that we pay off our second national debt, which is due to our emigrants, not in charity, but in justice.[68]

This was a long overdue recognition of something which many in Ireland had refused to accept in the post-war period, including those who had gone so far as to accuse those who did not stay at home of being unpatriotic, even though so much emigration in the 1950s was born of necessity. There had been no real sustained examination of the emigration issue until well into the 1940s, particularly in the context of the outflow that had been witnessed during the war and the fact that in the post-war period, between 1946 and 1951, for every 1,000 males emigrating, there were 1,365 females. There was much double-speak associated with attitudes to emigration; even in the 1950s it was common for the champions of rural development to lament that providence had provided sufficient room for the youth of Ireland to stay at home, with an attendant emphasis on the supposed evils awaiting them abroad. In 1950, one such crusader, the Irish journalist and novelist Aodh de Blacam, who was a member of the government-appointed Commission on Emigration (1948–54), stated that:

> No normal man or woman, able to make a living at home, prefers a living abroad for the sake of an increase in salary. What is a hundred pounds'

increment when balanced against separation from one's kindred, one's own class fellows, one's home town and nation, the rearing of one's children in the right spiritual environment? The flight from Ireland, now that we have control of its resources and our personal future, is abnormal, morbid and one might add absurd.[69]

In 1989, Joe Lee seemed to suggest that spiritual considerations were utterly irrelevant, arguing that 'few people anywhere have been so prepared to scatter their children around the world in order to preserve their own living standards',[70] a judgement which may appear unduly harsh, but at least recognised the extent to which emigration was an economic safety valve. This was a factor in other European migration; the Irish case had parallels with what was going on in southern Europe, especially Italy, Spain, Portugal and Greece, in terms of movements from underdeveloped agricultural economies to advanced capitalist ones, and in the region of 10 million migrant workers moved to Western Europe (particularly France, West Germany and the Netherlands) from more impoverished Mediterranean regions between the end of the Second World War and the mid-1970s.[71]

'an old and evil tradition'?

But for Irish emigrants it was a case of crossing national boundaries at an unprecedented rate, and clearly the period of the Second World War was a watershed in terms of Irish presence in Britain in both the armed forces and industry, presaging the massive labour emigration of the 1950s. But even by the late 1940s, the best an internal memorandum compiled by various Irish government ministers could do was to conclude that it was 'simply an old and evil tradition in this country with its roots deep in our national history'. There was little indication in this document of a desire to curtail emigration, but rather a fear that it would be Britain that would impose restrictions, as historically the Irish had unrestricted access to Britain.[72]

After December 1947 there were no restrictions imposed on the employments that migrants could take up in Britain, allowing males and females who received travel permits to migrate without official assistance from the British Ministry of Labour. There was, however, continued concern about the young age of Irish emigrants; Enda Delaney points out that over 70 per cent of applicants for travel documents between 1947 and 1951 were under the age of 30, while 72 per cent of female applicants were under the age of 24.[73] Even after the declaration of the Irish Republic, Irish citizens in Britain had a special 'non-foreign' status, enabling them to take up employment without restrictions. Despite the presence of anti-Irish racial prejudice, they were white, which meant that there was little desire to bring them under immigration control, and the 1951 British census recorded a total number of 537,709 persons who were born in the Irish Republic.[74]

The election of the new coalition government in 1948 seemed to herald a new questioning of emigration, partly because it had featured prominently in the election, partly as a result of a public statement from the Catholic Hierarchy in 1947 decrying the number of women emigrating. Such concerns gave rise to the Commission on Emigration and other Population Problems, which sat between 1948 and 1954, a motley group of 16 that included civil servants, workers' and women's organisations, clerics, rural activists and economists. Under the chairmanship of P. J. Beddy of the Industrial Development Authority, the Commission held 115 meetings. While it represented a fair cross-section of Irish society, and while contemporary newspapers heralded it as a long overdue attempt to confront the problem, its deliberations took so long that some began to wonder cynically whether the Commission itself had emigrated.[75] The fact that only two women sat on the Commission was criticised by women's organisations, given the preponderance of female emigration at this time. Others saw it as relatively useless exercise given the prevailing economic climate; cynics could snigger at a *Dublin Opinion* cartoon in December 1949 which depicted the 'Dublin Opinion Commission on Emigration': 'The Commission furnishes its report after having sat for five seconds. The people emigrate because they think they will do better elsewhere. They will return when they think they will do better here.'[76]

'her natural vocation'?

While the Commission sat, there was much attention focused on the situation of Irish emigrants in Britain and the high number of women emigrating. It was no surprise so many women were leaving; according to the 1946 census one third of all 'occupied girls' under the age of 20 and one quarter of all occupied women were employed as domestic servants, indicating a severe lack of career options. This was reinforced by the report of a Commission on Youth Unemployment of 1951, which suggested that 'domestic service helps to train a girl for her natural vocation – the care and management of home and children'. More interesting was the widespread contention that young women leaving was humiliating for the country. This was a suggestion that deeply angered the Irish Country Women's Association, who exposed the double standards in relation to this subject in their evidence to the Commission on Emigration, writing that 'our members are emphatic that loss of social standing is involved in entering domestic service in Ireland, but menial work may be undertaken in England without such loss'.[77]

This was a point further reinforced by the Irish Housewives' Association, which suggested: 'the domestic worker in Great Britain gets recognition as a human being while she does not get it here'.[78] The Irish Country Women's Association argued that rather than focusing on national humiliation, the government needed to ameliorate the drudgery of Irish rural life through piped water, light and sanitation schemes, and improved housing. It was significant in this context that surveys conducted by the Commission revealed a unanimity on the unattractiveness of life in rural Ireland compared with the experience in urban areas.

Some critics of emigration wanted to ban women under the age of 22 from emigrating, seeing their departure as a threat to the population's proportion of women of marriageable and child-bearing age; but both Church and state recognised this would represent an unacceptable invasion of civil rights and be repugnant to moral law. There were many Irish men who despaired at Irish women's new-found liberation in this regard. Seán O'Faoláin suggested that what Irish men wanted from their women was 'not love, not romance, not passion, not companionship, not charm, not wit, not intelligence, but simply the plain homespun qualities of housekeeper and mother ... they are extremely sceptical about the capacity of the modern young Irishwoman to fill these very simple requirements'.[79] This was the kind of view excoriated by trade unionist Louie Bennett, who lambasted the establishment's refusal to see female ambition beyond the home as desirable. Instead, it was decided to target English employment and recruitment agencies, which even in the late 1950s were still regarded in some quarters as culpable for much female emigration.

There was also a frequent denial that the state had any responsibility for the economic, spiritual or social welfare of Irish citizens abroad, with the burden of responsibility often left to both Irish and English ecclesiastical authorities, who oversaw the opening of Catholic hostels and mission schemes to ensure emigrants fulfilled their religious obligations. Particularly active in this regard was Cardinal Griffin, Archbishop of Westminster. The Catholic Church in England certainly had sizeable Irish flocks to deal with; by 1961 there were 780,000 people of Irish birth living in Britain, the Irish being the largest immigrant racial group in the greater London area, with other significant Irish populations in Coventry and Birmingham. Catherine Dunne's *An Unconsidered People: The Irish in London*, draws on the personal testimony of emigrants to highlight the extent to which the emigration experience was diverse, and the difficulties created by conflicting loyalties. Neither nostalgic nor self-pitying, her interviewees provide evidence not only of discrimination by the host country, but internal exploitation by the Irish themselves (such as the activities of unscrupulous Irish landlords) and the degree to which London was a refuge for those unwelcome at home, such as Irish women who had mixed-race children.[80] Ultan Cowley, who traced the experiences of the Irish navvy (building labourers) in Britain, entitled his book *The Men Who Built Britain*, a reference to the fact that the Irish were critical to the completion of many of the post-war British civil engineering projects in the building boom; they were the heavy diggers who dominated the groundworks aspects of British construction. Although they could undoubtedly earn more than at home, better wages came at a price, which included a sometimes lonely, nomadic lifestyle, with workers frequently accommodated in poorly equipped lodging houses. The labourers tended to refer to their work as a preliminary to repatriation to Ireland, a common attitude which was a manifestation of a collective and defensive response to enforced dislocation. This affected not just the emigrants, but those they left behind, as Cowley has illustrated:

> A few emigrants expressed guilt because they'd 'run out' on those at home, but countered it with the assertion that 'Everyone was going at that time, you'd feel strange staying behind' meaning that anyone with any 'go' in him would have done the same. Most offer the explanation that the family holding could not sustain the numbers of children reared on them and off-farm employment in Ireland was unavailable. Many who remained, and prospered, have repressed guilty feelings around the plight of emigrants by describing them as 'shiftless', 'unreliable', 'lacking staying-power', or 'unable to settle down for the long haul'. We are only now finding out the true extent of this deep-seated tension and its ultimate consequences for Irish society.[81]

'anything is good enough for the Irish'

Some found the secular British cities liberating, while others had crises of faith or felt abandoned by the local clergy, though the Church was to the forefront in promoting and protecting their spiritual and material welfare. The Church was sufficiently concerned about the religious welfare of Irish emigrants in Birmingham to authorise a clandestine mission by the Young Christian Workers' Association to compile a report on the Irish in that city in 1951, causing much controversy and embarrassment in both countries. The report suggested a certain moral degeneration and the undermining of Catholic values, including the formation by Irish women of relationships with 'black men'.[82] Though alarmist, the report was relatively innocuous and thoroughly predictable given the organisation under whose auspices it was compiled. That the author spent more time talking to representatives of the Catholic associations in England than the emigrants themselves was indicative of its bias. Nonetheless, there was much truth in its assertions about overcrowding and deplorable housing conditions for the Irish labourers.

But it was the manner in which the report was exploited by de Valera at a Fianna Fáil function which caused controversy, with his reference to the harshness of life in Birmingham, and particularly his comment during his plea for them to return home that 'the prestige of our people generally suffers by the suggestion that anything is good enough for the Irish'. Peadar O'Donnell noted caustically that 'it has become fashionable to look on emigration as an expression of some sort of mental weakness in our people'. De Valera received many telegrams critical of his handling of the affair and the Irish media printed letters from emigrants in Birmingham asking the government either to provide jobs at home or else to 'leave us alone and not make it difficult and embarrassing for us over here'.[83] De Valera, it should be stressed, had no monopoly on such delusion, if not hypocrisy; but, as Delaney notes, it was British embassy officials who were articulating what Irish civil servants and politicians would not admit publicly; that if Ireland could not export surplus Irish labour to the UK 'an impossible unemployment situation would result in the Republic'.[84] The Irish government also rejected an appeal for state funds on behalf of a group promoting the Irish Community Trust Fund. In dismissing their request, the Department of External Affairs drafted a letter to the effect that 'the Irish government would be only too happy to look after them if they came home', but the sentence was deleted by the Taoiseach's Office.[85] It was also being pointed out by Roy Geary of the Central Statistics Office that there was no reason for the Irish population to have a kind of guilt complex about emigration – according to him, the contemporary attitude was an inheritance from the period of the independence struggle, when it was politically convenient to blame England, a position no longer tenable.[86]

'come on out of here to Hell'

Emigration had thrown up many complexes, including guilt. The searing realism of the Irish playwright Tom Murphy's examination of the emigration issue is noteworthy in this regard, in plays that were deemed unfit for Irish audiences, but which critics were later to see as depicting Irish society at a particular time of crisis and demoralisation. This was particularly true in the context of the impossibility of escape from certain dilemmas, including forced departure and all the identity issues that arose as a result. It was difficult for young people, who in the words of Fintan O'Toole were 'pursued by the past, a past that is both the flesh of his own family and the sour spirit of a haunted, marginalised people'.[87] Overtly male, menacing and filled with violent language, plays that were once castigated as a racial slur on the Irish were in fact depicting the hurt and confusion associated with attempts to escape a society that could not provide for them as families, but which still idealised the family unit, sometimes through sheer brute force.

There is no doubt that violence and alcoholism were a part of life for some Irish emigrants. What Murphy in *A Whistle in the Dark* (1961) seemed to be suggesting was that it was a violence born of enforced dislocation. The closing line of his 1959 play *On the Outside* suggests emigration is the only option as one character invites the other to 'come on out of here to Hell'.[88] But it was not all bleak; Dónal Mac Amhlaigh, who wrote an account of his years as an Irish emigrant labourer in England in the 1950s, had a routine of which much was pleasant: observing mass, drinking in Irish pubs, trips to the cinemas and experiencing the freedom of regular mobility. He found that class did not seem to matter as much as it did at home, because unlike at home there was only one kind of Irish man: the worker.

And yet, insights into humiliation, class discrimination and confusion, as well as sheer loneliness and lack of education, permeate the plays and written accounts of Irish migrants in Britain. Mac Amhlaigh was saddened by:

seeing the little groups of Irish walking aimlessly around town every Sunday evening with no interest in anything at all – only waiting for the pubs to open – it's hard enough on young Irish men who were reared out in the country to have nowhere to go on their day off except the pubs. It's small wonder we are getting a bad reputation over here.[89]

Mac Amhlaigh was embarrassed by fellow emigrants who were frank enough to speak of Ireland's poverty and unemployment in front of the English, even though he knew they were speaking the truth.

But he also recognised, and this was the crucial point also recognised by many women, that Britain's welfare state highlighted the class inequality and degradation that existed in parts of Ireland. Noting the lack of external devotion to religion in England, he suggested, notwithstanding, that:

> it has many qualities that are closer to Christian values than much at home in Ireland … at home, such as I saw of it, if you can get a ticket to go to the doctor, you have to wait in an old ruin of a house. Look around you and all you see is poverty, despair and dirt, both on people themselves and on their clothes. The people go in to the doctor as they used to go into the aristocrats or the landlords long ago – shaking with humility. In England he'll give you to understand that you are a person and not a beggar.[90]

In this regard it is worth noting that the most violent language used in Murphy's A Whistle in the Dark is not in relation to gang warfare or racial strife, but the humiliation of an Irish boy in school as his teacher searches for headlice: 'lifting your hair like that. Holding his breath in your ear. Them 'munchen them nuts, moving on to the next place in your head and slobbery bits of white nuts slobbering outside his lips.'[91]

When the Report of the Commission on Emigration was finally published in 1954 it did not reveal any insight into such prejudices, but the appearance of The Vanishing Irish by John O'Brien in the same year caused something of a stir, its provocative title alone giving cause for consternation. It was a collection of essays that went some way towards attacking the lazy intellectual, economic and social assumptions of Irish ecclesiastical and political leaders. But the book was overly facile and sentimental, particularly in its use of the words 'extinction' and 'dying', its reiteration of Ireland's Catholic credentials, its denial that there was any class strife in Ireland and its contention that the drinking Irish bachelor was 'the enigma of the modern world' and certainly not the desired object of young Irish women. There was scant mention of what women did or did not want, aside from a so-called 'craze for pleasure', and the Irish mother was regarded as 'the most jealous and unreasoning female on the face of the earth'. Nonetheless, it was trying to make a serious point – alongside emigration: 'in short, 64% of Ireland's population is single, 6% widowed and only 30% married – the lowest in the civilised world'.[92]

'idle to pursue'?

The report of the Commission did much to present the emigration statistics in context, provided interested parties with a useful source for the social and economic history of modern Ireland, and facilitated the presentation of a cross-section of cultural attitudes. The report sought to reject the supposedly alarmist belief that the exodus constituted a nation in decline, contending that emigration rates would not be dramatically whittled away through a transformation in the Irish economic and social structure. Though it did suggest not all emigration was bad for the country, there was an acknowledgement that some of it was involuntary and unnecessary. But there were still many hints of a dated attitude to rural Ireland and its populace: the belief, for example, that women really went abroad in search of marriage, perpetuating an approach which viewed male emigration as economic but female emigration as sociological. In the same vein, the religious journal *Christus Rex* had suggested 'romantic paranoia has done much to render Irish women intolerant of reality',[93] which was a refusal to acknowledge the higher status afforded to women in Britain.

The report also suggested that there was an insufficiently developed sense of responsibility towards the family, with a new generation more concerned with individualistic material interests than national well-being, and that as there were 'relatively few' large families in Ireland, it was unreasonable to assume that Ireland's family pattern imposed an 'undue strain' on mothers in general. Whether or not emigration amounted to loss or gain for the country, the Commission decided it was 'idle to pursue'.

But there were practical proposals also: the need to improve diet, clothing and housing, the necessity for a land utilisation body and the need to attract industry to rural areas, though the report was ambivalent as to how some of those plans could be financed. The authors rejected the idea of a government prohibition on emigration, cash grants on marriage and, most hilariously, a tax on bachelors. It exonerated governments from blame but did suggest that continuing emigration was producing an environment unfavourable to the 'latent potentialities' of the Irish population, and admonished educators to avoid fostering an 'urban mentality'. A mute conclusion was that, while the role of government was instrumental in preventing excess emigration, the decision to leave was very much 'a personal matter'.

'those whose forefathers were driven to the mountains and bogs by Cromwell'
It also acknowledged that higher wages for unskilled labourers in England were an obvious incentive to emigration. More pointedly, an obvious, though rarely discussed, fact was highlighted:

> the ready outlet of emigration has provided the remaining population with a reasonably satisfying standard of living and this has been responsible for an acquiescence in conditions of underdevelopment which are capable of considerable improvement. The absence, over the country as a whole, of severe pressure on resources has failed to establish the need for drastic action and has made the need for full development of our economic resources less compelling.[94]

This was to have a continued relevance into the 1960s; Catherine Dunne's survey suggested that in 1961 alone emigrants sent £13.5 million home in remittances to relatives, almost equalling the £14 million spent on primary and secondary education in Ireland. In certain respects the report cast aspersions on the morality of Irish emigrants. Peadar O'Donnell, in his qualification to the main report, took umbrage at sullying references to the behaviour of Irish emigrants abroad, which for him exposed an utter hypocrisy: 'there is no more justification for a paragraph on moral delinquency among exiles than in relation to life in Ireland itself'.[95]

Changes of government and general indifference ensured that the recommendations of the Commission were largely ignored, and advising emigrants how to cope abroad, in the absence of domestic economic regeneration, seemed to be the best state and Church could offer. A particular interest in the spiritual welfare of emigrants remained, leading to the inauguration of the Irish emigrant chaplaincy service in 1957. The previous summer, the Bishop of Kerry, Dr Moynihan, had travelled to England to meet emigrants, and estimated that 95 per cent of them were 'doing well', suggesting reports of widespread loss of religious faith were greatly exaggerated. However, there was a marked reluctance by the supposed pillars of Irish society to face the reality of the multitude of factors compelling young Irish people to leave the country. In a remarkably narrow-minded letter to the Taoiseach in 1956, the Garda Commissioner concluded: 'there are only two categories of emigrants: those who did not accept Irish institutions and laws and preferred to live elsewhere, and finally, those whose forefathers were driven to the mountains and bogs by Cromwell and who have been living on uneconomic holdings'.[96]

'the arresting of the Führer mentality'

Nonetheless, the decision by the new coalition government of 1948 to investigate emigration had signalled a growing concern with the failure of the Irish economy to meet the needs of the domestic labour market, an issue on which Fianna Fáil was being increasingly criticised after the war. It was significant that when Clann na Poblachta ('party of the republic') emerged as a new political party in 1946, much of its rhetoric concerning the need for radical social and economic change tended to echo that used by Fianna Fáil in 1932, only now it was being used against them. Clann na Poblachta was also clever in using the first modern 'spin doctors' for political purposes and made effective use of the media, particularly in their efforts to show the victims of poverty in a pre-election film that shed light on Ireland's darker corners. It was of course important to illustrate that there was a possible alternative government to Fianna Fáil, but the first coalition government, which lasted until 1951, was also significant in terms of salvaging the electoral future of Fine Gael and healing divisions in the Labour Party.

John A. Costello, who became Taoiseach because the leader of the Fine Gael party, Richard Mulcahy, was unacceptable (an indication of unhealed Civil War wounds), presided over an administration of five political parties and independents, an unusually large cabinet and a wide range of cabinet committees (16 in 1950). He also had to contend with brazen and regular breaches of collective responsibility, and the extent to which decisions were agreed and properly recorded lay at the heart of the row over the declaration of a republic in 1949.[97] The decision to exclude Maurice Moynihan, secretary to the previous government, and one of twentieth-century Ireland's most able civil servants, added to this government's administrative tawdriness.

As has been seen, although the coalition was deeply divided on economic issues, its introduction of capital budgets was a turning point in Irish economic planning, though in the long run it was Fianna Fáil who ultimately benefited from the new departures in economic thinking by taking subsequent advantage of what were, by the early 1950s, acceptable new economic discourses and philosophies. The coalition government thus deserves recognition as a reforming administration and not just one that presided over the declaration of the Republic, the Mother and Child controversy (see below) and the internal squabbling of Clann na Poblachta.[98] This new party was an acute disappointment, promising so much in terms of new policies and younger politicians, but sinking quickly under the weight of individual members' arrogance; a party which was searching for a 'populist' issue of social concern, to emphasise ideological purity in a hybrid government, but lacked the skill to handle government or inter-party relations effectively.

Despite its self-proclaimed radicalism it was led by a sometimes petty-minded Seán MacBride. As John Bowman discovered, his obsequiousness to the Church was even more pronounced than that of most of his pious contemporaries.[99] Whatever about the difficulties of Clann na Poblachta they could at least take credit for introducing to Irish politics younger radicals, who, though often impatient and egotistical, were nonetheless essentially noble and independent-minded, such as Noël Browne (who was appointed Minister for Health on his first day in the Dáil and admitted in his memoirs he was not quite sure what the party stood for[100]), Noel Hartnett and Jack McQuillan. In June 1946 it was suggested there were five tendencies within Clann na Poblachta: extra-parliamentary, Catholic intellectual, parliamentary, social reform and Fenian, though, as Jack McQuillan noted, the overriding imperative was unswerving loyalty to the leadership.[101]

Fianna Fáil, on the other hand, in its cabinet composition of the 1950s, continued to rely on its Civil War era and 1930s stalwarts when it got back into power. Seven out of the 12 members of the 1951–4 cabinet had been members of the 1932 government. Many members of Fine Gael seemed intent on occasional appearances in the Dáil while they concentrated on more lucrative and seemingly more satisfying professional careers; the lethargy and frustration prompted by 16 years out of office were matched in their opponents' view by an arrogance which rendered them ineffectual constituency politicians. But by the end of the 1950s new, younger members contributed a new intellectual vitality to the party by establishing a research and information council.

It had been important for de Valera's opponents to prove that he could be at least temporarily deposed through the formation of coalition government, or in the words of Liam O'Bríain, writing to Michael Hayes in 1950, to ensure 'the arresting of the Führer mentality which had and has reached such dangerous heights in that section of the Irish people – the infallibility and superhuman quality of Dev'.[102]

'what ideological differences, if words retain their meaning'?

The Labour Party remained on the margins, outside and inside government, as witnessed by the difficulties the party experienced in government when attempting to push through their desired welfare reforms. Terence De Vere White had noted sardonically in 1949: 'the issues that divided the people of Southern Ireland are dead; the Labour Party alone can boast a right to exist on the grounds of recognisable identity; unfortunately that is its only cause for boasting'.[103] The party leader, William Norton, chose to depict the new government as the logical culmination of the effective use of proportional representation, and a pooling of the nation's resources for the task of reconstruction, something which was commonplace at that time in continental Europe. Pretending there were distinct ideological furrows for Irish politicians to plough was dismissed in the summer of 1951 by Fine Gael's James Dillon when he reasonably asked: 'what ideological differences, if words retain their meaning, divide any two deputies on any side of this house?'[104] Three years later the *Irish Times* urged the formation of a Fianna Fáil–Labour government.

Nonetheless, the Dáil in the 1950s was a cantankerous and bad-tempered place, where occasional fisticuffs were witnessed. Whatever about hysterical incidents in the national parliament, the excessive preoccupation of politicians with matters local was still in evidence. In 1952 a British journalist, Lawrence Earl, found material for a full book in the 'Battle of Baltinglass'. This occurred in 1950, when the residents of this small County Wicklow town refused to accept the appointment by the Labour Party minister James Everett of a Labour Party political activist to the post of sub-postmaster, because it involved displacing the serving postmistress, Helen Cooke, whose family had run the post office for 80 years. The residents finally got the appointment rescinded after threatening to wage pitched battle against the minister, who was accused of blatant corruption.[105]

The 1940s had been characterised by unease amongst councillors, many regarding themselves as mere puppets, with others slavishly following the party line, though successive governments showed no intention of lessening their control or centralising tendencies. In 1945 a critic writing in the *Bell* magazine had suggested that the introduction of the county management scheme implied 'a rather awesome admission of failure, an admission that we were not, in some respects, fit for self-government'.[106] In February 1946, the *Irish Independent*, reflecting the views of many local authorities, attacked the minister Seán MacEntee under the heading 'Dictators at the Custom House', as a bill was going through the Dáil which would enable the government, through a ministerial inquiry, to order a local authority to strike a higher rate, under threat of dissolution if they refused to co-operate.[107] But whatever about the diminution in powers, given Ireland's size, it seemed the parish pump remained crucial in securing a lengthy political career, and section four of the City and County Management Act of 1955, which should have been used to uphold the public interest against damaging or indifferent administration by giving councillors power to override certain management decisions, became instead an essential ingredient in the clientelist system of politics.

'determined to do nothing about it except blather every now and then'
In terms of political and national identity, the declaration of the Irish Republic in 1949 had raised interesting questions about the constitutional status of Southern Ireland and its external relations. The decision to declare a republic and leave the Commonwealth was controversial, not least because critics claimed the Taoiseach, John A. Costello, announced the decision without cabinet approval, on a visit to Canada. 'In fact he did nothing of the sort', was the verdict of David McCullagh, historian of this coalition government. The decision to repeal the External Relations Act (which authorised the British king to sign letters of credence for Irish diplomats) had been taken by the cabinet, but it was not properly recorded or communicated to Britain.[108] The technicalities of the External Relations Act were largely academic, given that Ireland was a republic in all but name, but there had been some questioning of the exact constitutional status of the state by Clann na Poblachta, and both Costello and MacBride

found the Act irritating. The British representative in Dublin suggested the declaration was an attempt by Fine Gael to steal the 'Long man's clothes' (de Valera's). Costello's decision may have been impulsive, but he perhaps believed he was merely enunciating government policy. There was no question of Fianna Fáil making an issue out of it; indeed, why they hadn't done it themselves was puzzling. Deirdre McMahon argued that de Valera had held back to see what happened in India. In any case, Costello did not appear to consider the option of repealing the Act but remaining in the Commonwealth. This was ironic, given that British officials 'were actually suggesting to the Indians that they use the External Relations Act as a basis for staying in the Commonwealth'.[109]

In 1948, Britain's Nationality Act recognised Ireland's separate nationality, the securing of which had seemed more important to successive governments than the question of Irish unity. Reciprocal trading and citizenship rights were regarded as the most practical solution for the new Irish position. The 1956 Irish Nationality and Citizenship Act made Irish citizenship more accessible to the descendants of Irish emigrants and those born outside of the state (who no longer needed to register for citizenship, and a grandchild of any person born in Ireland could claim citizenship irrespective of age), as well as those born in Northern Ireland. According to Mary Daly, this wish to extend Irish citizenship as widely as possible reflected a desire to encourage emigrants to visit Ireland in response to the huge exodus of the 1950s, but also coincided with a renewed anti-partition campaign.[110] The future Northern Ireland prime minister, Terence O'Neill, was distinctly unimpressed, suggesting it was 'an attempt by a small pastoral republic to create a vast empire of citizens, many of whom, scattered all over the world, will be quite unaware of the honour which has been conferred upon them'.[111]

Anti-partitionism still seemed to unite all shades of political opinion in the South in the post-war period, though an indication of the extent to which practical political considerations would take precedence over the issue was that the same Southern politicians were not impressed when the Northern-based Irish Anti-Partition League, created in 1945, intruded in Southern elections. In 1949, the response in the South to an election campaign fundraising collection for Northern nationalists was abysmal, which questioned the representativeness of the posters that appeared in Dublin streets asserting it was timely to 'arm now to take the North'.[112] It also seemed myopic for an Irish delegation at the Council of Europe in 1949 to use this forum to raise the question of partition, while de Valera took time in opposition to visit Australia, the US, Britain and New Zealand to champion Irish unity. Opposition to partition was also the reason given for Ireland's refusal to join NATO.

The reality was that Ireland's breakaway from the Commonwealth while Northern Ireland remained seemed only to reinforce partition, and Fianna Fáil were conveniently more vocal on the issue when in opposition than when in government. The truth was that there was no consensus among nationalists as to how to end partition, the same reason why the Anti-Partition League of Britain was unsuccessful. In 1949, Ernest Blythe, in *Towards a Six County Dominion*, suggested 'a gentle policy of persuasion'. There was certainly more realism by the end of the 1950s, perhaps a recognition of the observation of John Bowman that 'such is the nature of partition that frontal pressure tended only to reinforce it'.[113] By 1956 Seán Lemass was attempting to develop economic links between North and South, though he still needed to wait for the departure of de Valera, who rejected the idea of a commission to support social, cultural and economic co-operation between the two jurisdictions.

It was thus not until 1959 that Lemass could publicly speak of 'practical co-operation even in advance of any political arrangement' in his Oxford Union address, and he raised the possibility of exploring useful co-operation without any prior conditions.[114] It was also being suggested that Ireland's attitude to the outside world and its isolationism were based on emotion rather than reason. This was a result, the argument went, of hiding behind the excuse of partition, with not enough debate on foreign affairs but instead attacks on personal character, such as the attack experienced by Frank Aiken when he voted in favour of a discussion on China's entry to the United Nations. Liam O'Bríain, mentioned earlier, believed that:

> what you should do and every southern member of the Dáil and senate should do is visit Belfast and Derry twice a year and talk to the people there. The long and short of it is that we have partition and are determined to do nothing about it except blather every now and then – and by we I mean all of us without exception since 1925.[115]

'middle-aged men who make the same martial music today'

This was perhaps an illustration of an honesty that was more likely to be relayed in private, but a more serious issue was the extent to which such 'blather' contributed to the IRA border campaign of 1956–62. Some suggested it assisted the re-emergence of the IRA, given the emotion of the language frequently used, seen in phrases such as 'occupied Ireland' and references to the 26 counties as 'free Ireland'. These implied, according to Donal Barrington in 1957, that the North was in need of an idealistic and just liberation struggle.[116] As early as 1949 Terence De Vere White had warned Irish anti-partitionist propagandists that as they were so 'touchy' about their own symbols and loyalties (indeed they had been thought worthy of a civil war), they should recognise unionist loyalties, and that with the propagation of the idea of recruiting to 'force' Ulster, 'we have in our midst middle-aged men who make the same martial music today'.[117]

The border campaign that began eight years later came after a period of exceptional quiet for the IRA. There had been few signs of life in the organisation by the end of the Second World War, consisting as it did largely of isolated units, though constitutional republicanism was still a force, given that at least 22 of the 27 members of Clann na Poblachta's provisional executive had been active in the post-Treaty IRA at one time or another.[118] Many Clann members had been appalled by the death of the IRA prisoner Seán McCaughey on hunger strike, following four and a half years naked in solitary confinement, after which Seán MacBride, in representing the prisoner at the inquest, got the prison doctor to admit he would not keep a dog in such circumstances. Nonetheless, Clann na Poblachta was never accepted by the remnants of the IRA, because they took their seats in a 'partition parliament', or as they put it in a statement in January 1948, entitled *Ireland's Call to Arms*: 'for all those who would wish to make any claims to sincere republicanism there can be no connection or tinkering with pseudo-Republican political parties, old or new'.[119] It was significant that as early as 1949 Tony Mangan, Chief of Staff of the IRA, was indicating that, in a determination not to repeat the mistakes of the Second World War, he would restrict IRA activity to the North, as well as inculcate a new puritanism in members concerning their social behaviour.

That many of the raids were daring, in the sense of volunteers being prepared to engage in open battle with the British army, may explain many of the sympathetic resolutions carried by various local authorities in the South. The campaign itself began on 12 December 1956, the logic being that guerrilla campaigns and methods were the most effective way for the

IRA to proceed. That the Gardaí were caught off guard is understandable, given that their official report on crime in 1956 listed only 12 organised crimes of violence, eight of an agrarian and four of a political nature.[120] A disastrous attack on Brookeborough Barracks in Fermanagh in 1957 created two martyrs, Seán South from Limerick and Fergal O'Hanlon from Monaghan, the funerals of whom became a public-relations coup for the IRA. The burial of two young Irish 'soldiers' with full military honours from the IRA in front of thousands of mourners was not only a powerful image, but also indicative of the high degree of emotional support for the IRA, and resentment at the border, though subsequently the border campaign lost momentum and public support. Sinn Féin was able to get 65,640 first-preference votes in the March 1957 general election, winning four seats in the Dáil, from which they abstained, though it would be inaccurate to view the IRA as having anything like the full support of the Republic's population.

At the end of the campaign, the IRA seemed in almost exactly the same position as at the end of the Second World War; leaders in jail, weapons seized or dumped and low morale; though perhaps, as with other disastrous campaigns, they learned exactly what not to do the next time. It was also significant that in responding to the security threat the Taoiseach, John A. Costello, had been under political pressure not to deploy army troops and Gardaí towards the border. But in deciding in January 1957 that republicans were to be rounded up under the Offences against the State Act, Costello addressed the nation in very trenchant terms in a radio broadcast supported by de Valera and the British government:

> It is the deep and earnest conviction of my colleagues and myself that partition cannot, and never will, be ended by force. We believe that, even if it were practicable to subdue by arms – and hold in subjection – those Irishmen who now wish to remain apart from us, the resentment which they feel would thereafter divide us more deeply and more lastingly than ever before.[121]

By the end of January the IRA leadership was in jail, a fact even more difficult for them to swallow given that the IRA's plans had been based on an expectation of tolerance from Dublin. 'The theory', wrote John Bowyer Bell, 'was that the IRA's policy of quietism in the 26 counties would induce Dublin to tolerate the campaign.'[122] Seán MacBride duly pulled the plug on the government for its hostility to the IRA, later claiming his opposition was based on economic reasons, though it was notable that the subsequent election decimated Clann na Poblachta and MacBride lost his own seat, with the republicans' enemy, de Valera, returned to power. Joe Lee suggested: 'it would have been instructive to have watched de Valera's reaction in a situation where Sinn Féin TDs, with the wit to take their seats, held the balance of power'.[123]

The extent to which the border question could still muddy the wider republican waters and embarrass former gunmen was reflected in Jack McQuillan's contribution to a debate about the border campaign in the Dáil. He pointed out that these men were nurtured on heroic tales of 1916, and that:

> the type of history lesson that all these young men were taught was that it was necessary to fight Britain with her own weapons, that blood must be spilled if anything was ever to be taken from Britain. Their belief, and that is where their teaching and where the example of the past came to life, is the very same belief as was held by members of the front bench of Fianna Fáil and Fine Gael 30 or 40 years ago.[124]

Perhaps it was a tacit acknowledgement of the truth of this that led to a new stress on the primacy of constitutional action and cross-border initiatives.

'Cork 1920 – Budapest 1956'

Other political dissidents and left-wing activists remained more concerned with poverty than the border, but enjoyed little support and faced stern state reaction in the 1950s. A measure of the degree to which a certain paranoia lurked in the establishment about communism is revealed in the autobiography of Garret FitzGerald. He recalled: 'In 1949 I wrote an article for a British news magazine, *Cavalcade*, in which I imported Communist leanings to several quite innocent organisations such as the Irish Housewives' Association and the Irish Association of Civil Liberty.'[125] Much attention had been given to the communist 'purge' of the Labour Party in 1944, and in 1948 Dublin communists regrouped as the Irish Workers' League, despite the fact that Irish communists seemed incapable of sustaining a consistent analysis of Irish class forces owing to the Russian ideological stranglehold. It was also the case that politicians like

Seán MacEntee and newspapers like the *Standard* went out of their way to encourage witchhunts in order to uncover any who might be remotely tainted with communist associations, Jim Larkin being the most obvious victim in 1943.

The sheer virulence (and sometimes violence) of attitudes towards communists was striking; a year after Archbishop McQuaid had raised £40,000 in a matter of days to fight communism in Italy, up to 150,000 are estimated to have joined an anti-communist march in Dublin, led by the city's Lord Mayor, with a platform dominated by trade unionists. The Irish Workers' League could not publish their paper, *Irish Workers' Voice*, in Ireland because of the fears of printers, and members were also physically beaten, as happened in the early 1950s when they were campaigning for peace and the banning of atomic weapons. Mike Milotte points out that 'the Communist-inspired peace movement failed to attract any section of the labour movement in the 26 counties and in the end, only 3,000 signatures were collected'.[126]

Meanwhile the *Standard* newspaper was able to boast that communism had been purged in Dublin (the leader of the party, Michael O'Riordan, managed to poll only 295 votes as a general election candidate). The Hungarian uprising and subsequent invasion in 1956 also had a huge impact on Irish public opinion, and between July and December 1956 the anti-communist pro-Catholic rhetoric of the Irish media, in particular the *Irish Independent* (the largest selling daily at this time), managed not only somehow to link the uprising with Ireland in 1916 and during the War of Independence – in Cork 200 students marched behind a banner which read 'Cork 1920 – Budapest 1956' – but also to create something of a personality cult centred on the imprisoned Cardinal Mindszenty.[127]

'tough realism and resilient idealism'

The issue of communism and Catholicism in Eastern Europe had also caused controversy in 1952, when at a meeting in Dublin the Irish essayist Hubert Butler highlighted the forced conversion of orthodox Serbs by Croatian collaborators. This was at a time when Archbishop Septinac was being depicted by sympathetic Catholics as a martyr of anti-communist persecution. The Papal Nuncio walked out of the meeting and the resultant publicity forced Butler to resign from the Kilkenny Archaeological Society he had helped to establish. The reviews editor of the *Bell*, and a Protestant nationalist with a vision of a cosmopolitan Irish identity that encompassed European as well as local loyalties, Butler had travelled extensively in Eastern Europe and played a part in helping Jews to relocate in the 1930s and 1940s. He had reflected widely on the fate of Protestants in Ireland, proud of their free thinking and ability to 'put their Bishops in their place' and yet shared George Bernard Shaw's view that the true nature of Irish Protestantism was 'distorted into conservatism and conformity by its association with an Ascendancy class'. He was thus proud of his heritage, aware of its shortcomings and committed to both Ireland and Europe, and sad that many writers felt it necessary to leave Ireland. Butler was, in the words of Roy Foster, one who looked 'forward as well as back with that blend of tough realism and resilient idealism'. But in the paranoid atmosphere of 1952 his attempt to bring home the reality of Eastern Europe was responded to crudely in Ireland with the simple accusation that he was a crypto-communist and anti-Catholic.[128]

'communism to protest for three meals a day'?

Those agitating against unemployment in the main urban centres also had to run the gauntlet of anti-communist hysteria, despite peak unemployment figures of 100,000 in the 1950s. Unemployment benefit in the mid-1950s for a family was 50 shillings (even for a family of up to ten), which obliged those on welfare to live on a diet of bread and margarine, milk and tea, with many pensioners unable to afford fuel, while Erskine Childers of Fianna Fáil suggested that unemployment could be solved only under a dictatorship.[129] In 1953, a year when unemployment reached 86,604, a Dublin Unemployed Association emerged but quickly collapsed a year later to be followed by the Unemployed Protest Committee in early 1957. The demands such groups were making were basic, in terms of payment of benefit for each child and the reintroduction of food subsidies, but it was the street marches and sit-ins that seemed to worry those whose anti-communist radars were on full alert.

Whilst there was undoubtedly communist involvement, it was also pointed out in the summer of 1953 by one of the leaders of the Dublin Unemployed Association, Tom Pearle, that 'this is not communism or any other ism – if it is communism to protest for three meals a day, then all of you are reds'. Evanne Kilmurray has pointed to the harshness shown towards those who were unemployed, to the extent that a mother of three children whose unemployed husband was dying in a Dublin hospital had her home assistance cut from 37 to 35 shillings as, according to the relief officer, 'she had one less mouth to feed'.[130] This was some years after a Department of Health survey of nutrition in the late 1940s had shown serious malnutrition among the unemployed. Police intimidation, however, including the prevention of basic street protest, ensured the collapse of the DUA.

The diet of bread and tea was to continue well into the 1950s. There was a particular crisis in the building trade (the level of employment in building and construction fell from 74,000 in 1955 to 56,000 in 1958), and, as members of the Unemployed Protest Committee pointed out, building workers were lying idle while 6,000 people lived in Dublin slums. The Unemployed Protest Committee managed to get one of their members, Jack Murphy, a republican (it was decided not to let a communist stand), elected to the Dáil for Dublin South Central, home of the city's largest labour exchange, in 1957, making him the first 'unemployment candidate' to be elected to the Irish parliament. But his subsequent hunger strike in opposition to the removal of food subsidies in the May 1957 budget lasted only four days, and also saw the beginning of internal dissension in the group between communist and non-communist members. Murphy resigned in March 1958, ostensibly on account of his powerlessness in the Dáil, the split in the UPC and the indifference of the main political parties, but in reality because of the intervention of Archbishop McQuaid. Though he insisted in public he could not interfere in political affairs, McQuaid was active behind the scenes in persuading Murphy to exit the Dáil stage, warning him of the dangers of communism. Murphy subsequently emigrated to Canada, and Fianna Fáil won back the seat.[131]

'so much Christianity was taught but so little practised'

Murphy was a sad and lonely symbol not only of a depressed economy, but also of the fate of organised left-wing activism (and a still partially prevalent belief that it was not the duty of the government to provide employment) and the Church's refusal to devote the same energy and rhetoric to physical as to spiritual well-being. During the UPC era, while protestors marched with empty coffins, John Conroy, president of the Irish Transport and General Workers' Union, had lamented that 'nowhere in the world was there a country where so much Christianity was taught but so little practised'.[132] But it was also the case that during the 1953 protests the Congress of Irish Unions had refused to support the DUA. The Industrial Relations Act of 1946 had dissipated much of the militancy of the Irish labour movement by establishing the Labour Court, which brought trade unions much closer to the establishment, and by providing for wages orders made licensed trade unions the logical choice for low-paid employees in pursuit of pay claims. Between 1945 and 1950 trade union membership in Ireland rose from 172,000 to 285,000. The Catholic Church ensured a role for itself by providing lectures in Catholic social teaching to trade unionists, enabling Catholic social theorists to assert that the Irishman's propensity towards strikes was an indication that he would not easily submit to the 'octopus embrace' of the paternal state,[133] but also allowing the Church to influence the pace and militancy of industrial disputes. The departure of both James Larkin and William O'Brien, whose personality clashes had exemplified many of the tensions between the Irish Trade Union Congress and the Congress of Irish Unions, was marked by a dramatic plea from Larkin's son for them to reunify, which did not happen until the very end of the 1950s.

Strikes by farm labourers were common after the war and the newly emergent Federation of Rural Workers also had to endure red-scare tactics by Fianna Fáil and the *Standard* newspaper. After initial strike action in Kildare, by the summer of 1947 the Federation had a membership of about 17,000 in 21 counties, and they managed to get four of their members elected to the Dáil in 1948. By 1951 they had secured a weekly half-day with pay for rural labourers (although they were not given parity with industrial workers where public holidays were concerned until 1969).[134] But for most of the 1950s, with the trade union movement divided into two congresses, it was difficult to establish a united front in dealing with governments, and union influence on the inter-party governments seemed to be quite negligible. The healing of the split in 1959 was important and well timed given that Seán Lemass seemed closer to union thinking on economic matters than de Valera. This decade also represented the end of the road for William Norton, a pale shadow of the energetic Labour Party leader of the 1930s, who in his constituency focus seemed to symbolise the conservative and clientelist focus of Labour Party deputies. In 1956 James Larkin's son, also James, and a TD, emphasised that government policy from the point of view of the left was dominated by cuts and economies; but the subsequent collapse of that coalition government (in power from 1954 to 1957) seemed to induce a reticence in the Labour Party towards coalition, which they were pointedly to avoid for most of the next two decades.[135]

Ireland's most high-profile female trade unionist, Louie Bennett, general secretary of the Irish Women's Workers' Union until 1955 and president of the Irish Trades Union Congress in 1932 and again in 1947–8, seemed to personify the dilemma of the left in Ireland. She was seen as too conservative in her views on equality between the sexes and too middle class to be an effective or genuine spokeswoman for working women. Throughout the 1950s the IWWU seemed unsure about whether to endorse equal pay for all women, which was damaging to women in the long term, though Bennett had been successful in directing a 14-week strike of women laundry workers in 1945, achieving two weeks' paid holiday. She admonished her trade union colleagues for not uniting in the late 1940s to challenge more effectively what she believed were totalitarian methods of state control. Seán O'Casey noted after her death in 1958: 'she was a trades unionist and contented to go no further, which in its way was good, but left a lot undone.'[136] This was a comment which did not do justice to her lengthy career, and she was by no means the only woman with conflicting feelings about women in the workforce; James Larkin could also point out that his motion to Dáil Éireann promoting equal pay did not receive the vote of any female TD, even though they received equal pay with their male colleagues. In 1951, Helen Chenevix was elected president of the Irish Trades Union Congress, one of only three women ever to hold that position. In her presidential address to congress in the same year she raised the issue of equal pay ('whatever should be the basis of wage standards, it should not be the sex of the worker'), but gave even more attention to educational inequality, as this was where 'the inequality between higher and lower income groups is most glaringly obvious'.[137]

'Although her father still called her a girl, Bridie was thirty-six'
The sheer loneliness affecting women left on the land through no choice of their own in the 1950s and 1960s, as many others emigrated or left to work in urban areas, was poignantly captured by William Trevor in his short story 'The Ballroom of Romance'. The women danced with bachelors wedded only to whiskey and stout or old mothers in the hills:

> settling for second, even third best. Just settling. 'It's a terrible thing for you girl,' her father used to say, genuinely troubled, 'tied up to a one-legged man.' He would sigh heavily, hobbling back from the fields, where he managed as best he could. 'If your mother hadn't died,' he'd say, not finishing the sentence. 'Amn't I as happy here as

anywhere?' she'd say herself, but her father knew she was pretending and was saddened because the weight of circumstances had so harshly interfered with her life. Although her father still called her a girl, Bridie was thirty-six.[138]

There was certainly an abnormal reluctance to marry in Ireland at this time, or what Malthus had labelled 'a decay of the passion between the sexes', coinciding with a period when marriage was proving more popular in the rest of Europe. In 1948 almost half of all grooms were at least five years older than their wives, though the 1951 census figures recorded a rise in the proportion married in the young adult age groups. In the 1960s, Edna O'Brien, in such books as *Girls in Their Married Bliss*, managed to depict a private world of unmarried Irish women in the 1950s that had not previously found any literary expression.[139]

'home managers and agricultural producers'

The largest women's group in Ireland remained the Irish Countrywomen's Association, which in the post-war years not only provided an essential social outlet for many rural women but also managed to become much more vocal in decrying the lack of progress in rural living conditions for women. The mechanics of post-war planning presented them with an opportunity to stake their claim to participation in the evolution and improvement of post-war rural life, while Catholic social theorists urged them to provide certainty in the home and the backbone to rural life when so much outside was uncertain. Public debate about women was still often focused on defining women's relationship to the domestic world, and much weight was still placed on the maintenance of tradition, with the inculcation of 'proper' housewifery skills seen as a way in which to manage the women's social environment. The literature aimed at women often tended to be frivolous, ignoring not only the reality of women's daily existence, but also the fact that the aspirations of young rural and urban women were moving a lot closer than those of the previous generations.[140] Despite, for example, regular reports from medical officers and the ICA's determination to draw attention to the back-breaking consequences of carrying water long distances, at an inquiry in Limerick into a compulsory purchase order for the purposes of building houses, the county medical officer, Dr McPolin, 'admitted that neither he nor his medical officers investigated the water supply to the proposed cottages and stated that he did not consider distances of over half a mile from cottages to water supply as unreasonable'.[141]

Perhaps what was important about the ICA was that they began to see that their role was to articulate not just the transformations they wished to see in rural Ireland, but the means by which these changes could occur, including access to their own money. In encouraging debate about the differences between the urban and the rural experiences of Irish women, they sought to challenge the notion that changeless and archaic practices in rural Ireland were inherently positive and enhanced the fabric of Irish society. The ICA sought to use its estimated 350 guilds to pressure the government for grants, which they began to receive in 1951, while they increased their involvement with state and local services, including participation on housing, agricultural, library and vocational committees, and wanted to be consulted as professionals, insisting government departments send official plans to their organisation for detailed comment. It was no coincidence that it was also during the 1950s that some ICA executive members began to refer to countrywomen 'in their double capacity of home managers and agricultural producers', such descriptions indicating a departure from the semantics of the 1930s.

There were changes too in women's participation in the labour force, with a move into large-labour industry, and to a limited degree the professions, though even in the early 1950s it was considered by the Department of Education undesirable, because of pregnancy, to employ married women in mixed schools. This was an argument put forward in favour of retaining the marriage ban on primary teachers, which was eventually repealed in 1958.[142] There was still an ethos predicated on the idea that a woman working was acceptable in terms of economic necessity, but intolerable in the context of them having independent career ambitions. Women were nonetheless making small inroads into the professions; the number of female doctors, which accounted for 10 per cent of the total number in 1926, had risen to 17 per cent by 1951, while female solicitors and barristers increased their representation from 1 per cent in 1926 to 4 per cent in 1951.[143] The secondary-school system seemed to secure the place of women teachers; in 1949 they accounted for 53.5 per cent of secondary teachers, making them somewhat privileged among professional women, though a campaign by the Association of Secondary Teachers of Ireland for a special wage rate for married men was conducted at the expense of agitating for equal pay. Officially, the marriage bar did not affect secondary teachers because they were employed by the private sector, but a Department of Education memorandum from 1953 stated that 'in most cases secondary schools dispense with the services of women teachers when they marry'.[144]

'dreamy and unpractical people remote from the realities of the present day'?
Superficially at least, Irish social conditions were improving somewhat in the post-war period, but full-scale modernisation was a long way off. In 1949 Ireland still had the highest rates of infant and maternal mortality in Europe. Poverty was still endemic; during the great freeze of 1946–7 the Archbishop of Dublin granted a dispensation from Lenten fasting to his diocese owing to its under-nourishment. While Dublin Corporation made efforts to begin housing programmes on the outskirts of the city in places like Rialto, Ballyfermot and Cabra, in 1948, 80,000 people in Ireland still lived in one-roomed dwellings, with 23,000 in Dublin alone. According to the census of 1946 there were 310,265 houses in the country without any sanitary facilities, and while the size of families had fallen from an average of eight children in 1911 to five in 1946, these figures were still double those of Britain. In October 1949 the Censorship of Publications Board banned the Report of the British Royal Commission on Population, on the grounds that it advocated contraception, the first time an official report had been banned.[145]

The fears expressed about rural depopulation and migration to towns were not unique to Ireland, and the scale of the changes coupled with emigration forced Irish sociologists to match their European counterparts in examining the changes in traditional Irish society and suggest remedies beyond the age-old appeal to appreciate the green hamlets and bemoan the morally corrosive cities. In 1958, Jeremiah Newman suggested the need for 'rurbanisation', after examining the county of Limerick where, of 51 town and villages, only four had a population of over 1,000, while 19 had a population of between 500 and 1,000 and 19 of less than 200, some even less than 100. He urged the development of six or eight larger towns in each county to ensure the survival of the smaller villages.[146] In 1958 the Bishop of Clonfert, William Philbin, suggested that Ireland was largely responsible for its classification as an underdeveloped nation and for the loss of many of its more adventurous citizens, who would look for the rewards that more advanced economies could offer:

our own writers have gained currency for the notion that we live in a Celtic twilight, that we are dreamy and unpractical people remote from the realities of the present day. It was important to consider where we stood in this connection. Even though we believed that there were higher and better things in life than the material and the mechanical, it did not follow that these might be neglected. We live in a mechanical and scientific age and the community that failed to come to terms with the age in which it lived would shortly be subsisting in a primitive economy.[147]

Such observations were an indication that clerical sociologists of the 1950s saw as their duty to point out the failures of rural self-sufficiency, which 40 years previously had been a key feature of Irish revolutionary rhetoric. They were no doubt emboldened by the irony that it was now England that was providing many with the option of achieving material self-sufficiency. While Irish farmers were managing to become more effective organisationally and there were positive developments in terms of Muintir na Tíre's parish activism and championing of farm modernisation, such initiatives were still hampered by the insistence that they disturbed vested interests. Opposition members in the Dáil did not seem to see the irony, for example, in decrying the appointment of agricultural advisers in rural Ireland to advise on modernisation as blows to local government and further steps in the cementing of the 'highly centralised state', a card that was used when it suited them for narrow political purposes.[148] Understandably, by the 1950s, many small farmers were prepared to leave their land to take up unskilled off-farm work, partly because there was no effective 'farming ladder' in rural communities; the average age of succession to farms in the country was between 38 and 40, while of all the male farmers and relatives assisting, 57.6 per cent were unmarried.[149]

But it was also important to recognise that many farmers were apathetic or accepting of a subservient standard of living. It was pointed out, for example, that the 1946 census recorded a very low standard of social amenities even amongst larger farmers who could have afforded much better. The experience of local government also indicated that some local politicians were reluctant to embrace local-authority schemes for improved sanitation, water supply, electrification and the acquisition of land for social housing. Many of the schemes for social housing, including in some cases compulsory acquisition orders, led to heated protests, with the territorial mindset of landowners and seekers coming to the fore. Given its pervasiveness in the Irish social and cultural psyche, it was unsurprising that the issue of land gave rise to such passion, captured memorably in John B. Keane's *The Field* in 1965.

Roads also remained chronically underdeveloped. By 1945, as a result of wartime lack of petrol, there were only 7,845 licensed private cars on Irish roads. During the 1950s, the absence of a national road policy meant that roads could not cope with the increased volume of traffic. In the six years after the end of the war, the number of cars had increased to 156,000, but minor rather than major routes were given priority. Mary Daly suggested that:

> nothing which could be remotely identified as a national roads policy existed by 1956. The far-sighted plans of the war-time years had been eroded by a combination of lack of funds, government pandering to local political interests and the pressure of unemployment statistics. The road fund, originally established to provide finance for main roads, was being used for a variety of quasi-social purposes.[150]

After its inception in 1945, Córas Iompair Éireann (responsible for road and rail transport) was expected to provide a quasi-social service based on commercial criteria, and this ambiguity in purpose left them unable to plan for the future, while the demise of the rail network seemed to indicate a triumph of the accountant over the social planner, which was to return to haunt Ireland at the end of the century.[151]

'It is not perhaps a matter for wonder if farmers today take short views'

The electrification of rural Ireland began in 1946 and over the following 30 years meant drastic improvements for most, with the erection of 75,000 miles of new line, as against the total of about 2,000 miles that then existed, while the recruitment and training of young engineers was another of the plan's attractions. Electricity was initially viewed by many as too expensive an alternative to the oil lamp or candle there were many conservative attitudes towards it to be overcome. In writing his minority report for the Commission on Emigration in 1954, the economist James Meenan sought to explain the reactive mindset of many Irish farmers:

> The average age of male farmers was 55 years in 1946. The average

farmer would thus have been 23 years old when the First World War broke out in 1914. Since then, he has lived through two world wars, the Anglo-Irish war and a civil war; two collapses in prices including a major depression; four devaluations of currency, the 'economic war' and all the business of reconstruction after 1918, 1922, 1938 and 1945. It is not perhaps a matter for wonder if farmers today take short views and are reluctant to embark on improvements that, however excellent they may be in theory, are only hostages to the fortunes of prices and the political and economic events that control prices.[152]

Nonetheless, electrification and ultimately running water were to be successfully introduced. By 1962, 96 per cent of the 800 areas designated for modernisation had an electricity supply. The remark of a War of Independence veteran, that 'it wasn't for street lamps we fought', rang hollow indeed.[153] The Irish Countrywomen's Association made much of the fact that, according to the census of 1956, the environment the 1.4 million Irish rural inhabitants were living in corresponded with the communities the World Health Organisation defined as having 'a lack of diversity of skill and of organised community services'. At a conference in 1960 on rural water supply, the Minister for Local Government, Neil Blaney, laid the blame for inadequate provision of basic rural amenities squarely at the foot of the Irish male, and suggested it was up to the women to break down their conservativeness in the matter of rural improvements.

The substantial immigration of the rural population to urban areas, most notably Dublin, was also a pronounced feature of the post-war era, and involved the kind of families interviewed by the sociologist Alexander Humphreys in his seminal *New Dubliners*, published in 1966, but based on field work completed in 1948–9. Ultimately he was to find that there was a greater intimacy and more maturity in relations between parents and children and more frankness in discussing sex (it suggested some birth control practices among the manager class) than there had been among the previous generation. But while suggesting that 'the new Dubliners still frequently take as models of class behaviour, the norms of the old Anglo-Norman Ascendancy', Humphreys chose to emphasise instead the similarities that existed in the family lives of the new Dubliners regardless of wealth, though he acknowledged they had an acute sense of class, trying to outstrip each other in all things, typified by the tendency to criticise the higher classes, but 'striving to emulate the people criticised'.[154] For all the changes that the new urbanisation brought, there were remarkable consistencies concerning not just class, but the role of women and religious observance, three themes that were to be particularly pertinent when it came to the issue of health and welfare reform in post-war Ireland.

'the doctors who want to remain gentlemen and not let officials near them or their tax returns'

During this period there was a general re-evaluation of the role of the state and, by extension, local authorities in relation to public health. As a result, the need to be more interventionist, with a concentration on the principles of preventative rather than curative medicine, was recognised. This new recognition had important implications for the welfare of mothers and children and was championed by Dr James Deeny, chief medical adviser to the government. In 1946 he initiated a national nutritional survey and secured the co-operation of the maternity hospitals in a campaign to eradicate gastro-enteritis, and further developments in this regard led logically to what became controversial Mother and Child schemes. Although schemes of immunisation against child-killing diseases were prevalent by the 1940s, Catholic social theory influenced some members of the medical profession, who argued that it was unacceptable for the state, through the local authorities, to interfere with the private welfare of families and their children. The identification of the national maternity hospital at Holles Street with Catholic moral doctrine also led to the practice of symphysiotomy: the widening of a woman's pelvis during difficult labours. Dr Arthur Barry, Master of Holles Street, boasted that between 1949 and 1954 he had performed over 100 symphysiotomy operations. He insisted it was a better procedure than a caesarean operation, and that 'all the bogies and pitfalls' mentioned in books critical of the procedure were 'sheer flights of the imagination on the part of inexperienced writers'. It was, in fact, a harmful procedure that was abandoned in the 1960s. Many Irish women suffered permanent pain as a result of it.[155]

Initiatives taken with regard to the prevention of TB have been well documented, as has the career of their greatest champion, Noël Browne, who was appointed Minister for Health in 1948. By 1947, before his appointment, streptomycin was generally available and deaths were declining sharply, but much shame was still attached to the condition, with friends of victims often not writing to the sanatorium, but to nearby addresses instead.[156] As a result of a mixture of wartime awareness and Browne's subsequent initiatives, in conjunction with more efficient administration, the death rate from TB fell from 1.25 per 1,000 in 1945 to 0.54 in 1952 and there were no new cases of the disease recorded in 1958.

But obstacles to a comprehensive reform of the health services, beyond the issue of TB, were many, coinciding with winds blowing in the direction of change, including influences from abroad, the arrival of radical young politicians and young doctors, evolution in medical knowledge and a commitment to put resources into a more controversial health service that was still too dependent on the dispensary system. The Health Services Act of 1947, introduced by Fianna Fáil, sought to provide for the expansion of the health services by taking the financial burden away from local authorities and passing it instead on to a central fund, and, crucially, by employing more dispensary doctors. The Act was the culmination of a 1945 bill that included the idea of free medical services for mothers and children, which was followed in 1946 by separate departments for health and social welfare. The Irish Medical Association, however, saw these plans as a threat to private medicine.

Seán MacEntee, as Minister for Local Government and Public Health, had recognised after the war that 'it may be taken as absolute fact that the threat of insecurity is no longer accepted by the modern world in a fatalistic spirit and no government can afford to ignore this trend of opinion'.[157] But whatever about the sentiments within Fianna Fáil, it was left to Noël Browne to implement the changes, and the proposals of a child health council he established to advise him, and who reported in 1950, were for free mother and child health services to be administered without a means test. Browne's failure to get this through on account of opposition from the medical profession and the Church, and the refusal of his government to support him, as well as the machinations of his own party, became one of the most celebrated and vitriolic controversies of twentieth-century Ireland. Often referred to as a Church–state clash, it was in reality far too multi-layered for such a label to do justice to it. While the Church may have featured prominently in the latter stages, a contemporary, Liam O'Bríain, was perhaps closer to the truth when he wrote to Michael Hayes of Fine Gael that:

> When Browne talked of pre-natal education, it was clear he meant
> to have nothing whatever morally objectionable but merely ordinary
> advice such as doctors are giving and have been giving everyday. The

only point of the bishops was that an anti-religious government, if elected, could use these regulations in a very different way! A queer point. Such a government would only be elected if the Irish people had profoundly changed and would quickly make up its own regulations. No, I and many can't resist the feeling that the bishops were pulled by the doctors who want to remain gentlemen and not let officials near them or their tax returns.[158]

Browne was in many ways admirable but difficult, and there were many inaccuracies and deliberate omissions in his autobiography, *Against the Tide*, a phenomenal success following its publication in 1986 (it quickly became the largest-selling biography in Irish publishing history). Vituperative, angry and intent on settling old scores, its early chapters also gave an indication of the sense of injustice in Irish society that propelled him. But Browne was determined to be evasive towards the last stages of a remarkable life, personally and politically, during which he always polarised opinion, frequently enraged, but often enthralled. He was also – and this was crucial with regard to the Mother and Child Scheme – relatively innocent of the reality of power politics, and the Mother and Child Scheme controversy ensured that other aspects of his career have been overlooked, particularly the creation of the National Blood Transfusion Service and BCG tests for children.

As his biographer, John Horgan, points out, Browne was also disingenuous in being unwilling to admit subsequently that his proposals were not as egalitarian as he pretended. But the saga was also about a complicated power play within Clann na Poblachta itself.[159] The voluminous archives of Archbishop McQuaid, opened to researchers in the late 1990s, illustrate not only the role the bishop played in blocking legislation, but also that Browne gave undertakings to McQuaid which question the credibility of the reasons he gave for his own resignation. Such documents reveal the contradictions that often surrounded Browne, 'dismissive and supine by turns', in his dealings with the Hierarchy. Horgan concluded that Browne's appeal lay in his ability 'to project undeniable human needs as a basis for legitimate positive and creative public emotion'.[160] It was also an ability which highlighted the injustices that surrounded him, and the refusal of the Catholic Church to place health and welfare on a par with the so-called 'spiritual welfare' of Irish mothers and children because of its fear of 'state paternalism'. The Church's ability to project that fear was in large part due to the determination of the Irish Medical Association to bring them on board. The famous assertion by the *Irish Times*, to whom Browne gave some of his correspondence with John Charles McQuaid, which they subsequently published (unprecedented for an Irish newspaper), that the Catholic Church seemed to be 'the effective government of Ireland',[161] was in this sense a one-dimensional interpretation of what had been not just a religious and medical issue but also one of entrenched class interests.

'fed, housed, herded and driven as cattle are'

The Department of Health was, of course, acutely conscious of the development of the welfare state in Britain, but seems to have concluded that it was not as relevant to Ireland, where it was felt necessary merely to unify the fragmented public-health system as it already existed. The proposals of the Irish Medical Association – for a voluntary state-subsidised insurance scheme for financing the health services – were not compatible with the administrative structures existing in Ireland, and the government maintained that such a scheme would cover only a small section of the population.[162] The IMA reduced debate about health reform into a simplistic argument between vocationalism and bureaucracy. Those sympathetic to the doctors' case – with the Church to the forefront in venerating the medical profession – maintained that:

> the state cannot give without first taking away. What is called free must somehow and by somebody be paid for. When it provides everything, as some would have the state do, men and women will be fed, housed, herded and driven as cattle are, but freedom will have disappeared. It is happening, even here, yet the danger is being ignored by those who ought to guard against it.[163]

Such assessments invariably went on to insist harmony could be created only by the spirit of the people themselves and that there were things of value which the state could not supply. But this created the false impression that those in power, who, as Eamon McKee has suggested, represented a tradition of restraint in government in these matters, were obsessed with bureaucratic control.

Whatever about the opposition of the Church with regard to parental rights, gynaecological care, confidentiality and class, it was the doctors who mobilised the Catholic Hierarchy and Catholic social activists, and in mobilising them they created an impression which tempted historians to see the saga as a clash between Noël Browne and McQuaid. The truth actually lay in the observation of J. J. Mc Elligott, Secretary to the Department of Finance, which could just have easily been articulated by the Irish Medical Association:

> There was at one time in the country the belief – perhaps it still persists – that to take 'a red ticket' involved a certain loss of caste, and that the doctor should be paid if the money could be found at all. That very proper pride will surely be strictly diminished if the farmers' sons and daughters can get this medical benefit without any transfer of cash. That spirit of independence was very valuable and I am not actuated by financial considerations when I say it is a pity that it should be helped to disappear.[164]

Rather than solely being concerned with financial considerations, he was also, it is tempting to conclude, motivated by class considerations, just as the doctors were.

'sick and tired of being asked where I came from'

Nearly all the memoirs of Irish childhood during this period are mindful of these class distinctions. They underline the huge gulf between the rhetoric of aspiration that coloured so many of the expressions of the supposed advantages of Ireland as an unsullied classless rural idyll, and the reality of a society that failed hopelessly to live up to such rhetoric. One such author, Bernadette Fahey, in *Freedom of Angels*, noted the irony of the fact that soon after she and her siblings were placed in an orphanage in the 1950s, ostensibly because of their mother's inability to look after them, her mother was offered and took a job rearing the children of a wealthy business family in Dublin.[165] Fahey eventually moved to England, and her comfort there led her to trenchantly denounce the class snobbery that had forced her out of Ireland:

> I left Ireland for several reasons, chief amongst which was the feeling that I didn't belong to anyone, anything or anywhere. I was also sick and tired of being asked where I came from and who I was. In common with hundreds of others who were raised in orphanages, I was ashamed of my past and did all in my power to hide it. England was a useful

place to evade these issues. It was less parochial. People were happy enough to know which country you came from and leave it at that. For that reason alone it became the safe haven of thousands of orphans who couldn't bear the daily pressures that Irish society put on them. We were constantly confronted with our lack of roots and identity. This was extremely painful in a society that laid so much emphasis on one's family pedigree, place of birth and religious persuasion. These were the barometers by which individuals, families and groups were acceptable or not.[166]

George O'Brien, who went on to pursue an academic career in the United States, was vividly struck by the differences in the status of the poor in 1950s Waterford, between those in the Main Street and those in the Church Lane Cabins: 'it was', he wrote, 'impossible not to be struck by the unbridgeable, inscrutable gulf which the mere turn of a corner could evidently create'.[167] Many of those educated in Ireland were to experience class divisions also, with those of the middle classes educated by the Jesuits less likely to experience violence in the classroom than those educated by the Christian Brothers.

Gene Kerrigan, a pioneering journalist of the 1980s, who was reared in 1950s working-class Dublin, recalled that despite the absence of public discussion about class, children were under no illusions that 'there was a right way to be born and a wrong way' and that mothers who gave birth outside of marriage were risking 'stone-faced rejection and years of misery'.[168] Many such single mothers were hidden either domestically in institutions, or sent away to Britain, which raised serious questions about Irish society's view of its own responsibilities in this regard. Halliday Sutherland, in his journey through Ireland in the mid-1950s, pointed out to Bishop Browne of Galway the contention of English priests that most of the Irish lost their faith within six months of coming to England, to which the bishop responded: 'then why don't your English priests look after the Irish instead of throwing bastards in our face?' Sutherland suggested that the crusade of rescue in the Diocese of Westminster between 1950 and 1953 had dealt with applications from 1,693 pregnant Irish women, of which 485, or 28 per cent, had become pregnant in Ireland; girls who resisted the idea they should return to Ireland for their confinement because they would be placed in Catholic institutions for up to two years, though it was pointed out that the illegitimate birth rate in Ireland was lower than that in England; in 1949 there were 31 illegitimate births per 1,000 compared to 50 in England and Wales.[169]

There is little doubt that abortions were being performed in Ireland, despite the legal prohibition. In 1956 a nurse stood trial for performing abortions at a private house in Merrion Square, an opulent part of the city, after one of her operations went horribly wrong. The trial was reported in only one newspaper, as if this was a subject too reprehensible to merit coverage. Hubert Butler questioned whether this supposedly vehement opposition to abortion was in fact genuine. Why, he wondered, had nobody stepped in earlier, given that there was knowledge of what went on behind the doorway in Merrion Square? 'For years we have passed it by, laymen and professionals, with at most a disapproving shrug, a cynical observation. True feeling expresses itself otherwise.'[170]

'drinking to ward off the thirst that may come at ten, at eleven, or even not at all'

Though life expectancy figures were rising in the post-war period, they were still surprisingly low. Visitors to Ireland noted the chronic tobacco addiction that was prevalent in all parts of the country; indeed, Heinrich Böll in his *Irish Journal* insisted there would be a rebellion if smoking in cinemas was prohibited. Members of all classes smoked voraciously. Pauline Bracken, who grew up in an affluent suburb of south County Dublin, wrote that:

> smoking was part of living. It was expected that adults would smoke and every provision made that they did so in comfort ... the trip on the morning bus was a cacophony of throat clearing and the church was not much better ... even for women, diamond rings and nicotine stains were not mutually exclusive.

While, as elsewhere, advertisements idealised smoking for the well-adjusted person.[171]

In the 1950s Ireland also continued to be a nation of extremes when it came to drinking, with both excessive drinking and a robust temperance movement in the form of the Pioneer Association. Heinrich Böll ridiculed the Irish licensing laws that allowed pubs on Sunday to open only from 12 to 2pm and from 6 to 8pm, which seemed to make people even more determined to obtain drink by cycling or travelling to take advantage of bona-fide laws, or made people drink too much too quickly: 'at five minutes to eight the crush at the bar is tremendous; everyone is drinking to ward off the thirst that may come at ten, at eleven, or even not at all'.[172] But the Pioneer Association was claiming in 1952 that 100 new members were joining every week. There was also an increased recognition and understanding of the concept of alcoholism and new associations such as Alcoholics Anonymous (which perhaps appropriately opened its first European branch in Dublin in 1946) sought to deal with drink abuse in an increasingly practical, scientific and medical manner, as opposed to the strictly spiritual approach of the Catholic temperance groups.

'it is not a problem in this country'

Pioneer Association propaganda was still often gendered, particularly the idea that the home with a drinking wife was 'rudderless, miserable, reckless', though some contemporary writers and future sociologists were apt to point out that it did the Irish male no favours in terms of their social development, with the pub becoming, according to Tom Inglis, 'a type of perpetual secondary school for males'.[173] The Association continued to organise mass public rallies that were tremendous spectacles, and illustrative of a high degree of demonstrative faith, but the extent to which they could significantly dilute the Irish drink culture was doubtful.

By the latter half of the 1950s there were calls for the licensing laws to be modified and liberalised, with the powerful Licensed Vintners' Association demanding extended Sunday opening. The report of the Intoxicating Liquor Commission in 1957 did recommend extended Sunday opening, and while it admitted that the 11,953 licensed premises in the country were in excess of reasonable requirements, it did not recommend corrective action. What was more surprising was the fallacious contention that 'drunkenness has ceased to be a problem in the state. In 1955 prosecutions for drunkenness totalled 3,782 as compared with 7,165 in 1925 and 45,670 in 1912.' This supposed increase in sobriety was attributed to education, standards of living, alternative recreation and temperance groups.[174] But it was also the case that figures revealed in 1958 suggested that, while tobacco consumption had declined by 21 per cent in the 1950s because of high prices and an awareness of cancer (receiving publicity in England), the breakdown of the average household expenditure indicated that 34.1 per cent of income was spent on food, 8.1 per cent on alcohol and 7.9 per cent on tobacco; in other words, nearly half of what was spent on food was spent on stimulants.[175]

The government stood firm in the face of Church opposition to the liberalisation of opening hours in legislative proposals introduced in 1959. Séan Lemass squared the circle of episcopal disapproval by suggesting that 'drunkenness is a sin for which men are responsible to a higher court than ours'. But John Charles McQuaid was also correct in suggesting that, given the increase in the consumption of drink, aligned with a falling population and a high percentage of abstainers, it was surely obvious that there was heavier drinking by fewer people. As a result of his comments the Department of Justice asked the Department of Health about the scale of the problem of alcoholism in Ireland, and the reply was an indictment of the ignorance that existed concerning drink abuse, and again characterised the ambivalent attitudes to the Irish drinking culture that existed, despite the efforts of the Pioneers: 'off hand the Department of Health have said that it is not a problem in this country; that fewer than 400 persons are received into institutions (public or private) for treatment in any year'.[176]

'formerly white but is now a blackish green colour'

Drink was also undoubtedly a contributory factor to the suicides and mental illness that continued to plague Ireland. In his autobiography, *Downstart*, Brian Inglis noted that there was a tendency at the coroner's court to rule that suicides were 'accidents'; an indication, according to the coroner, that it was guided not only by the laws of evidence, but also by the laws of charity, which seemed to confirm the impossibility of getting reliable statistics for Irish suicide.[177] But despite the Mental Health Treatment Act of 1945 requiring the Inspector of Mental Hospitals to inspect every mental hospital in the country once a year, and present a report to both houses of the Oireachtas, this was a promise continually reneged on (the last report of any detail was written in 1956), and overcrowding of mental hospitals became a serious problem during the 1950s. By 1959 the number of patients aged over 65 who were admitted to mental hospitals was 1,666.[178]

Dr Dolphin, who was appointed Inspector of Mental Hospitals in 1953, had pointed to the dangers of using the mental hospital as a solution to purely social problems, and 'he clearly thought that too many elderly people were in mental hospitals because of their home conditions rather than an illness'. The conditions of the institutions were appalling; an unpublished account of conditions in Clonmel District Mental Hospital in 1958 referred to 58 female patients using one bath, which was 'formerly white but is now a blackish green colour' and three or four patients were bathed in one lot of water. There were 17 square feet for each of the patients, some of whom slept on floors; cabbage was chopped up with a 'garden edging tool' and cooking utensils were kept in the lavatory. The civil servant who was principal officer for medical services wrote: 'we are keeping patients at a low level of animal existence and actively destroying any little bit of individuality, confidence or self-respect they may have left'.[179] Despite, or perhaps because of, this recognition, the report was not circulated, even to members of the mental hospital boards, while proposals for specific legislation with regard to mental handicap were also abandoned in the 1950s. It seemed cruelly ironic that in 1959 all the mental hospitals were renamed with saints' names, and while the state in the 1950s invested in general hospitals and the grant-aided voluntary system, long-stay patients in mental hospitals were ignored, even though it was recognised that such hospitals were unsuitable places for unmarried mothers and children.

'cannot conceive any sadism emanating from men ... trained to have devotion'

The extent of the harsh treatment of many of the unmarried mothers and their children was not publicly debated until the 1990s. There is no doubt there was knowledge of what was going on, despite the contention in 2000 of the Catholic Church's communications officer that 'we did indeed have the "stuff" of scandals in the Ireland of the 1940s, 1950s and 1960s ... but nobody knew'.[180] Gene Kerrigan suggested that for the majority experiencing a happy childhood, what was going on behind closed doors was not known:

> the other stuff – the kids being pawed and raped by their biological fathers and by fathers of the cloth, the secret sicknesses that wouldn't be talked about for decades, the abuse of orphans, the secret arrangements to export bastard kids – all that was as alien to us as the dark side of the moon, we who were living through the best years of our lives.[181]

But it stretches credulity that there was no adult knowledge of what was

occurring. One girl who was sent to an industrial school in County Roscommon because her mother was unmarried was referred to as 'red boy …
as in the devil'. She recounted:

> one time when I was quite small I knocked against a door and it pushed
> against a nun. She grabbed me and belted me across the head and then
> she threw me down the stairs. They were hard stone steps. When I fell,
> I couldn't get up, so I was dragged by the hair down into the bucket
> cupboard, where they kept all the cleaning stuff. And I was locked in
> there. I was afraid they'd forget about me in there, and it used to be full
> of rats. So what I did was sing at the top of my voice – all I knew were
> hymns, so I sang them all. After a long time, I heard the nun outside
> the door saying 'Get that red boy out of there'. But I couldn't walk,
> my leg just gave out from under me. They brought me to hospital, and
> it turned out my leg was broken in five places. I told the doctor and
> the nurses about the nuns throwing me down the stairs. I always felt
> they kind of believed me, but that they weren't going to say anything
> to the nuns.[182]

The industrial-school system remained important in the abrogation
of the state's responsibility towards 'problem' children, and any of those
who queried the merits of placing healthy children in institutions were
always quick to qualify their comments by insisting that there was no
question of criticising the management of those institutions. At the end
of 1954 there were 5,513 children in industrial schools and the lie that
they were all 'well fed and exceptionally cared for' was still being pro-
pounded.[183] As Paddy Doyle, in his harrowing account of 1950s institutional abuse in *The God Squad*, saw it: 'I used to hear people refer to me
as "one of the children from the orphanage" which was the phrase locals
used to soften the brutal reality of the industrial school in their midst.'[184]
Given what is now known, it is ironic that the Irish Society for the Prevention of Cruelty to Children in the early 1950s was pointing out that most
people's impression was that the committal of children to such schools was
a remedy for unhappiness or unsuitable conditions in the home, despite
the fact that the Society in 1948–9 had argued that it would be better if
they could avoid such institutions.[185]

How these children were viewed, both during and after their incarceration was revealed in a Dáil debate in 1947. The subject of the discussion

was a 19-year-old boy who had been boarded out of an industrial school
and was forced by a County Leitrim farmer to sleep in a manure cart, as a
result of which he developed TB and had to spend three years in hospital.
The Minister for Justice claimed that trying to supervise such cases would
be too large a task for the Gardaí to undertake.[186] Stories of abuse in industrial schools, though known to certain politicians, civil servants and religious orders, rarely leaked into the public domain. One of the few lengthy
references came in the Dáil in 1954, when a TD raised the concerns of
a constituent whose son, an inmate of Artane Industrial School, was in
hospital after a vicious beating by a Christian Brother. The response of the
minister revealed much about the contemporary view of such institutions
and those who managed them:

> I cannot conceive any deliberate ill treatment of boys by a community
> motivated by the ideals of its founder. I cannot conceive any sadism
> emanating from men who were trained to have devotion to a very
> high purpose. The point is that accidents happen in the best-regulated
> families and in this family there are about 800 boys. These boys are
> difficult to control. At times maybe it is essential that children should
> be punished. This is an isolated incident; it can only happen again as
> an accident ... I would point out to parents that any guarantee I give
> them of full protection of their children is no licence to any of the
> children to do what they like.[187]

When, in 1956, John Charles McQuaid assumed control of the ISPCC,
the challenging and graphic case studies of neglect, squalor and parental
irresponsibility were no longer a feature of the annual reports. The awkward
questions posed about adoption and industrial schools were jettisoned, to
be replaced with superficial feel-good stories with happy endings because
fathers had come to their senses and stopped drinking. The exposure, it
seemed, of the underbelly had ground to a halt. (McQuaid had targeted
organisations like the ISPCC that traditionally had a strong Protestant
membership and effectively swamped them with Catholic recruits, who
manoeuvred themselves into a position of control.) Likewise, politicians
were not prepared to admit that the whole system of detention in industrial schools was outdated. It is noteworthy that there were still over 800
children in county homes (the old workhouses) in 1950, and in the workhouse in Cork children, segregated by sex, wore numbers on their backs.[188]

In 1951 religious orders running industrial schools refused to provide financial accounts for government scrutiny, in a bid, it seems, to avoid state interference, even though in 1945 the secretary of the Department of Education had acknowledged the 'grave situation which has arisen regarding feeding and clothing of children detained in industrial schools'. But when Fr Edward Flanagan, of the famed and lauded 'Boys Town' at Omaha in the United States, travelled to Dublin in 1946 and branded the Irish industrial schools and prison system 'a disgrace to the nation' (and insisted the true facts were being covered up), he was ridiculed by both press and politicians.[189] His death in 1948 deprived inmates of one of their few friends. Department of Education correspondence made it clear it had suspicions that state funds were not always spent on the children; but it abandoned attempts to make the institutions more accountable, after the religious orders refused to co-operate, and the neglect continued. In 1955 a report on St Conleth's Industrial School in Daingean, County Offaly, suggested cows were being cared for better than children.

'He didn't even have the goodness to bugger you in private'

Tom Sheehan, who spent ten years in industrial schools, from the mid-1940s to the mid-1950s, did not feel his experiences did him lasting damage, but he was blunt about the acceptance of routine assault:

> We always knew that the Brothers could do what they liked. There was no one to stop them. They could kill you, and no one would know. I remember one Brother punched a boy in the refectory, in front of everyone, and knocked him out cold … I got a kicking one night, I was about ten. This brother pulled me out of my bed and punched and kicked me all over the place. The only explanation was that he thought I was playing with myself. But he never really said why. We never saw any sexual abuse. But there was definitely sadism there. Maybe they got pleasure from that.[190]

But others bore their physical and mental scars for the rest of their lives. An inmate at Artane Industrial School, Barney, recounted horrendous experiences of abuse in the 1950s. He remembered not only vicious beatings ('some of the boys were so badly beaten they used to suffer from what they call head staggers, like when boxers get punch drunk'), but also rape and sexual abuse, perpetrated by a well-known figure in Ireland, Brother Joseph O'Connor, who worked with the Artane Boys Band at the school:

> I was in his class once – he taught school as well as the band – and I had said or done something, and he put me out on the line at the edge of the classroom. Then he told me to take off my clothes. And right there in front of the whole class he sat down on his desk with his foot on the bench where the boys would sit and write, and his other foot on the ground. He opened his cassock and put me across it and put his left hand under my private parts. He was squeezing me and beating the living hell out of my bare backside. He was foaming at the mouth, jumping and bopping. He was having a sexual orgasm in front of the whole class of boys. And I wasn't the only boy he done. It just hurts you to be degraded in such a manner. He didn't even have the goodness to bugger you in private. He was a bastard. And yet he would march around there on parade with the band like he was King Tut. He was evil. He did things to me that I couldn't even tell my wife about, they were so shameful. One of the things he'd do when he'd be sexually molesting you was that he'd be trying to choke you as well. He'd be foaming at the mouth during it. Some of the things he did I can't even talk about now. It's too painful. And yet many others suffered the same fate as me, or even worse. Especially the young boys from the convents in the country who had absolutely nobody. If something happened to them, even if they had disappeared, nobody would have missed them.[191]

When Halliday Sutherland interviewed the Mother Superior of a convent in County Galway which was home to one of the Magdalen laundries, she was evasive about the degree to which the girls were happy, insisting that the highest form of punishment was to 'stop their food, only one meal'. Her comment that 'last week one girl made such a row that we let her go. That night she was ringing the bell and begging to be readmitted' was hardly proof of the girl's happiness, given that there was nowhere else for her to go. Neither was the comment: 'on Sundays they're allowed to use cosmetics'.[192] Many of the women sent here were unmarried mothers forcefully removed from their children, and Sutherland was also struck, in the children's home he visited, by the 'pathetic' scene of children clamouring to get the attention of visitors who could be potential adoptive parents.

'A. Concealment of fall. B. Prevent local scandal'

Another side to the experience of some unmarried mothers that did not receive much publicity until the very end of the century was the 'adoption' of babies who were sent abroad, often without the knowledge or genuine permission of their mothers. It was a system in which the state occasionally colluded with Church agencies to facilitate the export of children born to single mothers, mostly to the United States, regulated by McQuaid and helped by the Department of External Affairs, who issued passports so the children could be taken out of the country. According to Mike Milotte, in his book *Banished Babies*, 2,100 children were sent to America under this scheme between 1949 and the end of 1973.[193] This was done at a time when the number of births outside marriage was increasing, and there was no restriction on their entry to the US, but the 'consent' of young and vulnerable women was in many cases no such thing, leading to heartache and guilt. While it is true many of the children were afforded a quality of life in America that would never have been available at home, the fact that so many grew to adulthood under assumed names created serious issues of confused identity when the truth was revealed or found out, as did the fact that the real mother's name was in some cases deleted from the record.

It was not an issue of child abuse (in the sense that the Catholic charities by and large did a good job and children were well matched with families), as experienced by many in institutions, but rather the exploitation of mothers. And it exposed the fact that some Americans rejected as adoptive parents in their own country were in effect permitted to buy Irish babies ('contributions' were made to the institutions that housed the mothers), who were white, which was important for many in race-conscious America in the 1950s. Potential adopters were invariably informed the mothers of the children were unmarried 'but respectable and well-educated'. To the relief of the religious orders, they were being taken from orphanages and institutions that were overcrowded. Moreover, the process began before legal adoption was available in Ireland.

The Church and state's primary concern in this regard remained the religious welfare of these children, and to ensure that stories such as appeared in the German newspaper *Uhr Blatt* in December 1951 were avoided: 'Ireland has become a sort of hunting ground today for foreign millionaires who believe they can acquire children to suit their whims'; or in the *British Empire News* in June 1956: 'Babies sold to US in secret.'[194] When it became clear by the mid-1950s that there was a question over the safeguards the Irish and American churches had put in place, the Church grew worried, while Tom O'Higgins, Minister for Health, reacted furiously to local authorities becoming involved. His concerns were in turn rebuffed by the Department of External Affairs. But those who wanted the details kept secret even went as far as to suggest in the Dáil that questions on the issue were 'anti-national', while the memoranda of civil servants who wrote frankly of their worries about the practice were sanitised or spiked.

By the end of the 1950s the schemes were standardised and the Adoption Act of 1952, while allowing for a very limited legal adoption in Ireland, did outlaw the exchange of money. It was not until 1996 that the vulnerable mothers, many of whom, unbeknownst to them, had relinquished the child 'for ever', were acknowledged by the Irish government, whose Tánaiste (deputy prime minister), Dick Spring of the Labour Party, spoke of the children as having been 'removed from their young and frightened mothers at the most vulnerable possible time in the lives of those mothers'. The sting in the tail was that owing to the constitutional right to privacy and archives legislation, the mothers could not get access to the files of such adoptions.[195]

The pressures on single mothers in mid-century Ireland, as well as the attitudes of those in authority, were revealed in notes compiled by a senior Fine Gael politician, Seán MacEoin, when he reflected on the need for legal adoption: 'Reasons for adoption: A. Concealment of fall. B. Prevent local scandal. C. Revulsion to child because of inconvenience to mother, employment, maintenance etc. D. Mental stress before and during.' When it was eventually introduced, adoption legislation was based primarily on maintaining the Catholic faith of the child. C. F. Casey, Ireland's Attorney General, in an address to a college society, insisted that Ireland was unique in its concern for spiritual welfare, and wondered: 'how can a Catholic logically demand or permit any legislation which would endanger the soul of a single child?'[196] The mental well-being of thousands of Irish mothers was always a secondary consideration, if it was considered at all, the same attitude that characterised the approach to abortion throughout the century. The post-war reports of the English Catholic 'rescue' workers, who were apt to complain about the number of Irish women travelling to

England, revealed that many young Irish pregnant women refused to go home because of the threat of a prolonged stay, perhaps up to two years, in a 'Mother and Baby' home in Ireland. In many ways the children of those who stayed in England formed part of a 'hidden diaspora'.[197]

Though it was not fashionable to admit it towards the end of the century, many of the members of religious orders had worked hard under difficult conditions to educate and provide for vulnerable children. The fact that they displayed such arrogance when it came to acknowledging hurt, admitting wrong and simply being accountable reflected the sheer confessionalism of the Irish state, and the status afforded to the Church by the 1950s, accompanied by a deliberate discouragement of ecumenism. Nonetheless, one can have some sympathy with the contention of Patrick Touher, an inmate of Artane Industrial School, that 'on the whole the [Christian] Brothers were doing their best, within limited circumstances in hard times and with frightening numbers. They too shared in the hard rigid life. They had no luxuries, nothing to look forward to, except more of the same.'[198]

'the first experience I had of completeness'
What struck critics of Irish Catholicism as scandals unfolded in the 1990s was the sheer gulf that existed between external piety and devotion, and a meaningful emphasis on internal spirituality and codes of behaviour. Franz Werfel's reverential novel *The Song of Bernadette* was a bestseller in Ireland in the 1940s, and the 1950s witnessed the cult of Marianism and all its attendant sodalities, shrines and worship, as well as a fascination with Lourdes and Fatima, religious devotion that extended well beyond the traditional parochial structures.[199] Devotion to the rosary became the cornerstone of many Catholic families' daily prayer, while according to the *Irish Catholic* the formula for peace in time of Cold War and communism was a pair of rosary beads lying on the table of every house in Ireland. There was a concomitant exaggerated rhetoric around the threat of communism gaining a foothold in Ireland. A book published in 1948, *Communism and Ireland*, by Seán MacEoin, depicted the country as flooded with communists, and 150,000 Catholics protested in Dublin against the imprisonment of Cardinal Mindszenty and Archbishop Stepinac, while communist endeavour in China and Korea further fuelled the articulation of pious outrage.

Historians have placed much emphasis on the Church's obsession with sexual morality, and this was undoubtedly strong, but there was also an emphasis on stoicism and honesty and an absence of serious and regular crime. Mary Kenny points out that in 1950, there were only 469 men and 68 women in Irish prisons.[200] It is also the case that many children continued to find comfort, security and warmth in religion as well as inclusiveness, the same sense of belonging felt by John McGahern mentioned in the previous chapter. George O'Brien, in *The Village of Longing*, an account of his boyhood in Waterford in the 1950s, presided over by a grandmother devoted to her Catholic faith, remembers how he too came to cherish the unity that religion brought: 'being an altar boy was the first experience I had of completeness ... the notion that the show couldn't go on without me gave rise to a feeling of integration'. Meanwhile, temporarily thinking that he had a religious vocation left him feeling thankful and strangely cleansed.[201]

'a personal investment in the cycle of failure'?

Others writing memoirs, however, still had to try and make sense of the logic of, for example, groups of contemplative nuns, their lives shut off from the world, their love confined to God, being allowed to have complete charge of children deprived of normal family life. Bernadette Fahey recounted how the nuns in Goldenbridge Orphanage in Dublin predicted the children would turn out just like their 'fallen' mothers: 'It was as if they had a personal investment in the cycle of failure.'[202] But there is evidence, too, that for those who loyally stuck to religious routine, it did not have to crush them or smother them with guilt. Rules, after all, were made to be broken, and if forgiveness could be sought and procured, why not break the rules again? Dermot Healy, in his novel *The Bend for Home*, having received absolution in confession, skipped out of the church and 'then with a giddy heart I stood on the steps of the Cathedral ready to start all over from scratch again'.[203] These observations do not serve to negate the intense Catholic faith of Ireland in the 1950s, but reveal how an institution, usually interpreted as monolithic and unyielding with a vice-like grip on all, did not in reality invoke a common reaction, or indeed faith, on the part of its audience. Acknowledging the diversity of the private experience of Irish Catholicism is important given the emphasis on public show, procession, spectacle and conformity, which also underlined the considerable distance between shepherd and flock. It is tempting to believe Halliday Sutherland's observation in his *Irish Journey* that 'a priest told me that the greatest example of purity he had ever met was a middle-aged Irish woman who had left the Catholic Church for two years when she discovered that priests and nuns used the lavatory'.[204]

'how many children of Mary from Eire are now prostitutes in Piccadilly'?
But Sutherland, as an English Catholic author whose book *Laws of Life* had been banned in Ireland because it mentioned the rhythm method of contraception, also noted that its censoring was a result of an account of the function of sex, and that in Ireland many people, including clerics, 'regard ignorance as synonymous with innocence', adding: 'those persons should enquire how many children of Mary from Eire are now prostitutes in Piccadilly'.[205] It was an important point, given that most young Irish people in the post-war era still grew up with a surprising degree of ignorance in this regard, and the fact that sex was rarely, if ever, discussed. Ironically, when talking to the priest sociologist Alexander Humphreys, interviewees exhibited a surprising frankness about the subject, which he suggested was because he was a priest, underlining the fact that they still felt they were discussing something sinful, but believed because the interviewer was a man of the cloth, there would be no moral price to play in terms of guilty conscience. It was quite clear that they did not talk to each other about sex, and that many women never enjoyed guilt-free sex.

Humphreys noted that the attitude that sex was somehow evil was widely prevalent and was expressed quite explicitly. Lack of sexual awareness was reflected in the belief that before marriage the union was deemed to be a matter of companionship, and children 'just came somehow'. One woman suggested that 'there is something repulsive about it and nothing will get that out of my system'. It was men rather than women, it seemed, who got enjoyment out of the marriage when it came to sex.[206]

And yet, in other areas, Irish Catholics were capable of pragmatically compartmentalising their religion. The 'sin' of drunkenness, as temperance reformers were to discover, was one in which many indulged frequently, while in October 1955 over 21,000 soccer supporters defied John Charles McQuaid's instruction not to attend a soccer match between Yugoslavia and Ireland. Many were incensed at McQuaid's perceived bullying of the Football Association of Ireland and there was a feeling that he was overstepping a line. But every important junction in the lives of young Catholics remained church-centred. Out of a total of 17,525 marriages in

Ireland in 1946, only 31 were celebrated by civil contract in the registrar's office, the rest being religious ceremonies.[207]

'a slight move on my part could have precipitated a crisis'
The words and actions of John Charles McQuaid reflected many concerns (if not obsessions), and though it is tempting from a latter-twentieth-century perspective to see him as unduly preoccupied with sex and the control of his diocese, who along with sanctimonious priests and politicians retarded any development towards 'modernisation' in Irish Catholic life, this does scant justice to the multitude of tasks he performed. He was an educationalist, a church administrator and reformer, pioneer of social services and theologian, and facilitated the construction of schools and hospitals. To make him (along with de Valera) a scapegoat for an authoritarian, repressed and censorious society ignores both the scale of the social change that was occurring during his tenure as archbishop (1940–72) and the views and activities of other members of the Irish Hierarchy, about which very little has been written.

Yet there is merit in Noël Browne's scathing attacks, as when he depicted the Church of this era seeing its duty as keeping the flock in perpetual ignorance about matters of the 'flesh' and instinctively opposed to any measures that sought to improve their 'bodily welfare'. But McQuaid, unlike many other members of the Hierarchy, who because of their farmer class background were relatively removed from and unsympathetic to issues of urban life and poverty, could not be classed in this category, given his action with regard to TB, VD, the sick, and the physically and mentally handicapped. Nonetheless, McQuaid had his own class bias, and wondered: 'why it was necessary to go to so much trouble and expense simply to provide a free health service for the 10 per cent necessitous poor'.[208] In his denunciation of the encroachment of state power he was reacting to the state's assumption of a more interventionist role in social and economic life, and his was by no means the sole voice in the Hierarchy in this opposition.

But when bishops were deemed to have gone too far, the government was becoming more apt, as the 1950s progressed, to call a halt to their gallop. Dermot Keogh, for example, revealed how the Irish Minister to the Holy See was active in ensuring McQuaid did not become a cardinal owing to resentment at his tendency to interfere.[209] It is also important to note the sheer sycophancy of certain politicians who, as soon as they assumed political power, insisted they would 'always welcome any advice' from McQuaid, a very direct invitation to him to become involved in the legislative process in the 1940s and 1950s. Civil servants requested permission from McQuaid to read Marxist literature when their duties as diplomats required it.[210] The archives of McQuaid reveal the extent to which even perceived radicals like Noël Browne could be submissive, McQuaid writing a note to the effect that Browne 'apologised for all in which he had been faulty'.[211]

Of course, as with anyone with too much power, there was also a nasty, uncharitable side to McQuaid, as when he backed the attempted takeover of the Meath Hospital management, which saw leading non-Catholic physicians discharged or resign. He also used 'moles' in the Department of Health during the Mother and Child episode to arm himself with inside information. This easy access led to an extraordinary arrogance in McQuaid, as when in 1951 he wrote to Bishop of Staunton of Ferns: 'a slight move on my part could have precipitated a crisis within the cabinet and caused a general election at any moment since January.'[212] He took pride in being depicted as a noble enemy of socialism in the London-based Catholic journal the *Tablet*. McQuaid's utter certainty about what was right and wrong led to a preoccupation with the 'evils' of sex, reflecting in many ways his own personal repression. He was aware, for example, that 'the drawings of women modelling underwear used in *Irish Press* advertisements actually revealed a *mons veneris* if one employed a magnifying glass' (which was true; the boy in John McGahern's *The Dark* used such ads for masturbation). He regarded the threat of liberalism as coming especially from a small group of Protestants in Trinity College (again reflecting an inferiority complex about the former colonisers), and he sought to control academic life in University College Dublin in relation to the chairs of ethics, logic, psychology, education and sociology.[213]

'frustrated, provincial and profoundly uncultured'?
But McQuaid's proud boasts that Ireland had more successfully resisted 'modern aberrations' than any other country also reflected a deep insecurity, as did his insistence that a belief in Catholic social theory would uphold the traditional view of the Catholic Church and the role of the state, even though it was becoming clear that this was growing more and more difficult. The fact that McQuaid had sour relations with so many of the groups who claimed their Catholic social credentials were impeccable

was an indication not only of an obsession with control born of insecurity, but also of the extent to which McQuaid could cause great irritation, as revealed in his thorny relations with groups such as the Legion of Mary. Its founder, Frank Duff, was later to lament that 'anyone who wants to work in Ireland will be cribbed, cabined and confined ... even when the world has more or less taken up the Legion, Ireland looks on it suspiciously.'[214]

Such divisions within the Catholic social movement encouraged some to take a more extremist approach and support groups like Maria Duce, described by the anti-Catholic polemicist Paul Blanshard in 1954 as proto-fascist, 'frustrated, provincial and profoundly uncultured, resembling the least literate, super-fundamentalist leaders in the Southern states of the US'.[215] Its supporters were people who were often resentful and bewildered precisely because in many respects Ireland was showing signs of increasing secularisation. This group was viewed within mainstream Catholicism as being alarmist, often misfocused and sometimes anti-Semitic. They were avowedly anti-communist and initiated a campaign to prevent the actor Gregory Peck appearing in Dublin in 1949, because of his alleged communist sympathies, which Peck denied. They were also central to a campaign to amend article 44 of the 1937 Constitution in order to seek recognition of the 'one true church', which isolated them among other Catholic activists. They were treated dismissively by politicians, and by McQuaid, who disliked their exhibitionism and doubted their theological competence.[216]

'A lieutenant may think his Captain's orders stupid'

Tom Garvin suggested that in some ways the Mother and Child controversy led to a resentment in middle- and working-class circles and that 'a common remark of the period was "this time the bishops have gone too far".'[217] The extent of this sentiment is difficult to gauge, but what was clear by the end of the 1950s was the degree to which politicians were prepared to give the go-ahead to civil servants to write: 'The Bishop's letter does not merit a response.' Liam O'Bríain, a War of Independence veteran and language professor at University College Galway, had wondered in 1951 in the aftermath of the Mother and Child episode: 'how far is one entitled to say publicly, "I disagree with the Bishops?" Apparently there is a question of discipline and scandal in it. A lieutenant may think his Captain's orders stupid but he is to remain silent out of respect and carry them out.'[218] This was a view being increasingly challenged as the 1950s progressed. The Fianna Fáil government, which returned to power in 1951, was felt by McQuaid, for example, to be pursuing 'a policy of distance' from the Church. De Valera was in fact being politically astute, but McQuaid realised that precedents of this kind threatened his domination.

When a coalition government was returned to power in 1954, the Minister for Agriculture, James Dillon, was determined to pursue his plans for an Agricultural Institute, despite the Church's fear that this would represent an attack on the Church's control of higher education, and the danger of 'Protestant' input from Trinity College. Dillon suggested in private that the intervention of individual bishops in public controversy was becoming tiresome and destructive, but when asked why he did not take them on in public, he summed up the dilemma of his generation of politicians by suggesting that engaging in public debate with them 'carried with it the possibility of consequences in a wider field, out of all proportion to the advantage which is served by their public correction'.[219] But increasingly, the urgent letters from the Hierarchy about state 'encroachment' were not responded to, which was something of a new departure. That same sense of irritation was also apparent when it came to the implementation of the Intoxicating Liquor Report at the end of the 1950s. McQuaid's anger that his directives were not being accepted led to some heated correspondence and tetchy meetings between himself and the secretary of the Department of Justice, but once again the government stood firm, indicating that by the end of the decade a much clearer line was being drawn between Church and state when it came to the framing of legislation: 'His Grace's letter does not call for a reply' was Lemass's instruction to a civil servant wondering how to respond to a letter from McQuaid that criticised the government's refusal to consider the opposition of the Hierarchy.[220]

'Let the round tower stand aloof'?

Some literary critics contend that the introversion which accompanied Irish neutrality extended well into the 1950s. In support of this Declan Kiberd quotes the poet Louis MacNeice: 'let the schoolchildren fumble their sums in a half-dead language ... Ourselves alone! Let the round tower stand aloof in a world of bursting mortar.'[221] The long-time social activist Peadar O'Donnell, having taken over the editorship of the *Bell* from Seán O'Faoláin, saw a need to give more attention in the journal

to young writers in order to challenge the inertia created by his generation, and there was concern expressed at the London-centred focus of Irish
writers. John D. Sheridan bemoaned the death of the fiery idealism that
had marked the national revival of the early twentieth century, suggesting most good Irish writers were abroad, seeing London as their literary
capital. He maintained there were only two types of Irish writer, those
who wrote about pagan morality and sex and those who avoided these
things altogether, and he pleaded for a literature 'Catholic in tone and
written, published and read in Ireland'.[222]

His protestations seem quite naive and almost quaint when one
thinks of the sheer anger and frustration, but also subtlety and boldness,
of some of the contemporary Irish writers who were continually subvert-
ing the stereotype of their often rural and republican backgrounds. Patrick
Kavanagh and Flann O'Brien had already done this in the early 1940s,
but it was significant that by the late 1940s it was even being done in the
Irish language by Martin Ó Cadhain, whose *Cré na Cille* (1949) centred on
a dead woman's monologue about class status in a western peasant community. Later, the plays of John B. Keane, Tom Murphy and Brian Friel
sought to give voices to Ireland's peripheral communities in their con-
tinual obsession with ownership of land, ancient feuds, avarice and drink.

There was perhaps something ironic in the fact that many of the
Dublin-based writers of the 1950s also indulged in their share of the vices
they sometimes savagely satirised and never realised their full potential.
Brendan Behan, an original, funny and 'Rabelaisian talent', continued
the tradition of offering a critique of Irish republicanism begun by Liam
O'Flaherty. Both Brian Inglis and Anthony Cronin movingly described
how his alcoholism was exacerbated as his later plays attracted huge
London audiences, but in the words of Inglis such commercial plays were
'Behan at one remove, filtered through the needs of a script for the actors
to learn'.[223] Even Kavanagh, who had written so savagely of rural Ireland
and who remained obsessed, in the words of Kiberd, with 'expressive
underdevelopment', suggested in the *Bell* in 1954 that Irish authors had
manufactured a 'lower order' to allow a new middle class to feel smug and
superior: 'great liberality is permitted towards these mythical characters
in the case of murder, infanticide, drunkenness and outrageous brawling.
The new middle class audience of theatre and books is falling backwards
in an effort to prove itself broad-minded.'[224]

'He doesn't know what he wants'

Kavanagh, though never doubting his own greatness, was a restless soul, who like Flann O'Brien had been trapped by the war. He moved between Dublin, London and Monaghan, frequently penniless, and in the words of a contemporary: 'like the wandering Jew… up and down, in and out. God help him. He doesn't know what he wants.'[225] His unsuccessful libel trial against the *Leader*, following an unflattering portrait of him, revealed the true bitchiness of Dublin literary life in the 1950s, and made him one of the most famous characters in the country. In the witness box for a total of 13 hours, he maintained that literature, far from being the activity of 'wild bohemians', was in fact a religion: 'a wild life is total anathema to me'. Unfortunately for him, cross-examination also revealed 'the far more vicious and personal streak in the poet's own criticism'.[226] Simultaneously, in some fabulous poems written in the 1950s he sought to transfer the rural idyll to an urban setting.

Mary Lavin, on the other hand, chose to focus on human emotions in her masterful portraits of small-town life, by dramatising the small, seemingly irrelevant details, or in the words of Colm Tóibín: 'the moments of pure truth'.[227] Such work, formally conservative, was also being produced by the short-story writers Bryan MacMahon and Frank O'Connor. Meanwhile, Samuel Beckett (who had been transformed by the war and was honoured for his work with the French Resistance), in *Waiting for Godot* (1957), subverted any sense of ordered life the observer or reader had and continued to make himself unavailable personally, while the rancour of Seán O'Casey was still prevalent, even though he was absent from Ireland. He withdrew his play *The Drums of Father Ned* from the Dublin Theatre Festival, citing clerical interference. The wider world of Irish poetry witnessed distinctive new voices with the work of Anthony Cronin, John Montague and Thomas Kinsella, while the brilliance of Austin Clarke was sustained and publications such as *Poetry Ireland* and *Envoy* inaugurated. It seems a certain freedom of spirit was enduring. Terence Brown suggested:

> Austin Clarke's satire of the 1950s was vigorously sane, the persona adopted that of a man who has transcended parochial absurdities in a broad, humanistic vision of Irish identity and who finds aberration from this tiresome and infuriating. In the 1950s too, Patrick Kavanagh abandoned the crude, boisterous satire, bred of anger and frustration,

that he had produced in the late 1940s and early 1950s for a lyrical celebration of everyday Irish experience.[228]

Brian Fallon points out that the 1950s also saw the inauguration of many enduring festivals, including the Wexford Opera, Cork Film and Dublin Theatre, while Radio Éireann was going through something of a golden era, and was beginning to engage in a more frank and open discussion of issues which in the pre-war era were taboo.[229] The emergence of the intellectual group Tuairim ('Opinion') in 1954 was also indicative of a restlessness about the lack of debate about existing social and economic policies, and was later described by Garret FitzGerald as 'a combined think tank and debating club, which from the late 1950s sought to stimulate the discussion of political, economic and social issues' with a role in the modernisation of Ireland that was subsequently largely ignored.[230] Independent of party politics, the group produced pamphlets that challenged outmoded practices in arts, education, the law and the treatment of children, as well as critically questioning the culture of Irish politics and the merits of economic nationalism.

'in the remotest hamlet and up in the hills'
Attempts were also made in the post-war era to encourage more widespread reading among the public, and a Public Libraries Bill introduced in 1947, creating the Irish Library Council, was an attempt to instigate improvements at local level and take over some of the previous duties of the United Kingdom Carnegie Trust. They were reforms badly needed, given that attitudes to reading and public library facilities were still often rooted in the Victorian era. It was difficult to refute the claim of the Limerick TD, Donnchadh Ó Bríain, in a Dáil debate, that it was 'one of the most starved of all the services we have'. The government had refused the request of the Library Association of Ireland for a commission of inquiry into the library services in 1937. In 1943, at a meeting in Dublin City Hall, members of the association expressed their frustration and dissatisfaction with the existing public library service and they submitted a statement to this effect to the Minister for Local Government and Public Health, Seán MacEntee. They not only drew attention to the effect of general wartime scarcity on an already suffering service; they also wanted the abolition of the limitation set on the public library rate and a central advisory body to be established by the government to assist the improvement of the library service. Given

these demands, it was unsurprising that they broadly welcomed the 1947 Public Libraries Act.[231]

In presenting the proposed legislation to the Dáil, Erskine Childers of Fianna Fáil highlighted the deficiencies of the public library service and with the new Act seemed to be promising dramatic improvements. The rhetoric he employed was ambitious; there was no reason, he suggested, why the library service could not become what he called the 'new nucleus' of an adult education movement. It was important, he said, not only for children to read during the long winter nights, but also that people knew about their own history and indeed the complexity of the wider world: 'In many cases,' he said, 'they only begin to do that when they reach the age of 25 or 30.' He went on to say:

> we can no longer be isolationists, since what goes on in China is indirectly of importance to this country, so that the more one learns about foreign countries and their customs and ways the better ... an immense amount of good can be done everywhere – in the remotest hamlet and up in the hills – by improvement of the services.[232]

Childers's promised crusade seemed redolent of the insistence many years earlier of George Russell that a nation can become cultivated only insofar as the average man, not the exceptional person, is cultivated and has knowledge of the thought, imagination and intellectual history of his nation. Childers's fears about the lack of suitable reading material were underlined by disappointing figures in relation to library funding and borrowing in Ireland. Prior to the passing of the bill, in a typical county where the library service was relatively well organised, 75,000 books were issued in a year, of which 20 per cent were non-fiction, two thirds of that 20 per cent relating to travel, biography, history and social science. But the number of active borrowers in a county area varied from between 7 and 15 per cent of the population. In the years before the bill, total expenditure on the library service was a miserly £90,000, of which about half was devoted to salaries and one third to books. In the Dáil, a Labour Party TD, Brendan Corish, bemoaned the lack of books in the Irish language which could be substituted for 'some of the tripe we are used to'. When it was pointed out that there was tripe in every language, he replied: 'I agree, but there is tripe and tripe and we get the tripe.'

In the context of the demand for popular fiction, Dermot Foley, former librarian for County Clare, and later first chairman of the Library Council, recalled that in Clare his library was 'whipped into serving up an Irish stew of imported westerns and sloppy romances'. The real problem, as he saw it, was the operation of censorship, which made a mockery of plans to bring books to the people; a cultivated taste for civilised reading was, he wrote, for an entire generation rejected by a conspiracy of closed minds: 'It became', he elaborated, 'a statutory, inexhaustible bean feast for the bigots and obscurantists and in due time made a dog's dinner of defenceless people, who above all things badly needed a bit of leadership to lift them out of the morass of ignorance they had for so long endured.' One rural TD, in his contribution to the Dáil debate, was less sanguine:

> anybody who comes across the beautiful pieces of crochet that used to be made in the rural areas 30 or 40 years ago must admit that the girl who devoted her time to the making of these things was as usefully employed – I would say more usefully employed – than if she were to spend her spare time in reading books ... I feel there is a danger that in extending library services we might be overdoing it ... I have seen mothers, a few, who got so keen on the reading that they kept their children away from school while they themselves read.[233]

There was thus no wholesale embracing of 'quality literature'. Nonetheless, there was much reading of newspapers – Dublin alone had three evening newspapers in the 1950s – and it was clear that the attempts made in earlier decades to discourage the reading of 'foreign' (meaning British) Sunday newspapers, which by the end of the 1940s were arriving by air early on Sunday mornings, had not succeeded. The *Furrow* periodical recorded the details of a survey of March 1950, carried out 'in a department of a factory with 28 girls' in which '8 get and read *The News of the World*. This paper is officially banned'.[234] At the other end of the scale, in middle-class Dublin, Pauline Bracken recalled the periodicals coming into her home as including *Irish Tatler and Sketch* (to keep abreast of fashionable upper-class weddings), *Life* magazine from America and the *National Geographic Magazine*.[235]

In the early 1950s, the circulation of the high-brow *Irish Times* was a modest 35,421, and while it introduced innovative and irreverent political journalism, it did not remotely approach the circulation of the other nationals, the *Irish Independent* (203,206) and the *Irish Press* (198,784), while the *Sunday Press*, established in September 1949 (another Fianna Fáil-supporting paper), came to dominate the Sunday domestic market (selling 378,454 weekly in March 1953), along with the *Sunday Independent* (selling 395,507 in the same period).[236] Controversy erupted over the ownership and control of the *Irish Press* in 1958, Noël Browne later justifying his attempts to get to the bottom of the shareholding issue on the grounds that 'The *Irish Press* was funded by one pound notes collected from rank and file republican supporters of the party. It was the intention that it should become a national newspaper and certainly not the political play thing and enormous financial asset of the de Valera family which it later became.'[237] Browne claimed that de Valera had systematically over a number of years become a majority shareholder, paying only a nominal price to ordinary shareholders, and maintained de Valera's continuing role as Controlling Director was incompatible with his role as Taoiseach, particularly given that as far back as 1932 he had announced that no members of his cabinet could continue to hold directorships in any commercial concerns. It was an embarrassing charge that was not answered adequately by the soon to retire de Valera, who insisted his position did not bring significant personal financial reward.

A 'paper wall'?

Many established journalists had first worked for provincial newspapers, many of which survived on account of the fierce loyalty of readers and the belief it was necessary to have a representative voice outside of Dublin promoting the interests of a particular region. The playwright Lennox Robinson regarded the *Kilkenny People* and the *Kerryman* 'as the two classic weeklies in Ireland',[238] though Michael O'Toole, a future *Irish Press* journalist working on the *Limerick Weekly Echo* (Limerick had three local newspapers), remembered that 'the bohemians and the eccentrics were still thick on the ground'. There were often excellent editors, according to O'Toole, with no formal training, who were devoid of cant: 'the chief – and only – reporter had been a barber and he had drifted into journalism through bringing in snippets of news that he had picked up in his shop.'[239] In 1994 the journalist Hugh Lambert recalled that during the 1950s, when he began his career, it was not particularly important for a paper to develop a particular personality or view of the country and its problems: 'News and sport were what we were about. Features were little added extras not

essential to the paper. It was vital to have a good selling story on page one
... papers need much stronger personalities now.'[240]

There was still the occasional warning about the dangers of the
'foreign press', but the attempt by the coalition government of 1948–51
to create an Irish News Agency did not succeed because it was too closely
associated with the state and it neglected the domestic press. It was seen
as a way of challenging the 'paper wall', a phrase originally used by Sinn
Féin early in the century to suggest that most of the news about Ireland
reaching foreign audiences was filtered through British vested interests.
The new body was championed by Seán MacBride, who lamented the
'gross distortions' being perpetuated about Ireland.[241] Up until then, Irish
papers received most of their foreign stories from British and other foreign
agencies.

It was also envisaged that the INA would have a significant anti-
partitionist function; but the truth was that the idea of a 'paper wall' was
given little credence by journalists or politicians. The INA had to rely on
a state subsidy and the decision to operate commercially meant that to be
taken seriously it could operate only without government interference.
Irish papers largely refused to co-operate with it and were quite prepared
to be incorporated into the British news system, given the well-established
integrity of the Press Agency/Reuters relationship, and indeed, in line
with so many other aspects of Irish culture and media, those managing the
Irish media were happy to accept British codes of practice. The primary
weakness of the INA, according to its critics, was that it did not develop
as a response to the needs of the Irish newspaper sector, but was imposed
by the government as a diplomatic and propaganda tool.

Progress was, however, being made in other areas of the media, notably
the quadrupling of the broadcasting estimate for radio and the expansion
of its news staff in the late 1940s, while innovative Catholic periodicals
like *Furrow* sought to give a forum to fresh voices regarding religion in
Ireland. Although the radio may have been more closely controlled than
the BBC, there were innovative attempts to create new sports, children's
and music programmes, along with encouragement of original artistic
talent. Radio in some ways became more interactive and controversial in
the 1950s, and did contribute to a liberalisation of public discourse.[242] A
close eye was also being kept on the beginnings of television in England,
with suggestions that Ireland was not ready for it until governments could
be sure it would preserve national culture, though individuals like Leon

Ó Broín, secretary to the Department of Posts and Telegraphs, tried to get politicians to be more realistic about the inevitability of demand for a domestic television service, which materialised in 1961.[243]

The Thomas Davis Lectures, inaugurated on radio in 1953, succeeded in making the work of academic historians more accessible. In the context of honest accounts of Ireland's past, it was also significant that the first report from Michael McDunphy, Director of the Bureau of Military History, referred to the importance when taking evidence from the period 1913–21 to steer interviewees 'carefully in the realm of remembered fact, free as far as possible from hearsay, speculation, romance or prejudice'.[244] This coincided with the insistence of a generation of historians such as Robert Dudley Edwards, Desmond Williams and Conor Cruise O'Brien (who in 1957 published his seminal *Parnell and His Party*) that 'careful research' must be prioritised rather than using history as propaganda, with a key emphasis on sources. There was also an interest in hitherto taboo areas such as the Civil War, though the 50-year rule then in operation concerning the release of state papers meant that *Irish Historical Studies* did not publish studies of history after 1900. But there was great encouragement given to those willing to challenge the established historiography of events prior to that period. Initially, however, there was little direct criticism of the philosophy of history teaching in the schools, and significant reform was not instigated at this level until the 1970s.

'No communal excitement about ideas and their application to life, art and politics'
There was a certain pessimism in the post-war period in relation to lack of progress in education, the Irish language and the universities. In 1944, in the *Irish School Weekly*, it was noted: 'the pity is that the tradition of bad school buildings, underpaid teachers and rigid bureaucratic control is as strong as it ever was.'[245] Such sentiments presaged the kind of discontent evident in the protracted national teachers' strike of 1946 by the Irish National Teachers' Organisation, in pursuit of higher salaries, following a salary offer in 1945 that did not remotely placate discontent. Another indication of troubled waters for the government on this issue was that the Archbishop of Dublin was the first to be informed of the result of the strike ballot. The length of this strike also allowed a trenchant long-term resistance to government to evolve, while, in October 1946, 70 teachers in black coats invaded the pitch at Croke Park during an All-Ireland final

(without the approval of their union). Ultimately, the strike was defeated and the teachers, with the prompting of McQuaid, returned to work, though there was much anger created by the fact that a special payment was to be made to teachers who made their services available during the strike. The education minister, Tomás Derrig, seemed to reflect the arrogance of 15 years of uninterrupted power in rejecting calls for Ireland to follow the educational reforms being put in place in post-war Europe. He argued that during the war: 'Bhíomar saor ó aon ní do chuirfheadh bac ar ár scéimeanna oideachais' ('we were free from any hindrance to our educational schemes').[246]

As the first full-blown use of the strike weapon by a professional group in Ireland, impinging on almost every home in the country, it was a significant episode. Despite the collapse of the strike it laid much of the groundwork for the INTO's emergence as an increasingly powerful force in the educational sphere in the 1950s, as well as improving the morale and solidarity of the teachers. In 1957, a year in which only 10,000 students sat the leaving certificate, it was suggested in *Studies* that secondary teachers were being undermined by a system in which the security of their positions depended on examination results. Teacher unrest also reflected a certain degree of frustration over the failure of the Irish language revival. In 1956 the government finally decided to establish a ministry for the Gaeltacht, and money began to be spent on promoting native handcrafts and other ways of promoting the distinctiveness of this region, but the prognosis for sustained social and economic regeneration seemed bleak.

Third-level education remained for the elite, though not immune to criticism. The numbers attending the National University of Ireland colleges grew to 4,560 in 1948–9; but the proportion of national-school students who went on to university remained tiny. The university experience was still limited to under 2 per cent of students. By the end of the 1950s there were only 8,653 students at all third-level institutions. The Catholic educational gurus of the period, such as Michael Tierney and Alfred O'Rahilly in University College Dublin and University College Cork respectively, duly attended their boards, meetings and commissions, saturated Catholic periodicals, and sought to preserve the Catholic ethos of their colleges as presidents. They often sparked controversies well beyond their areas of expertise, though some students of a more artistic bent were utterly pessimistic about the university experience. Writing in UCD's *National Student* in 1946, the young poet Anthony Cronin suggested:

> There is in fact no intellectual life worth mentioning in this college at this time. No communal excitement about ideas and their application to life, art and politics; neither a hard won originality of outlook nor a susceptibility to the ideas that are warming the youth of the world to fervour. And there is no idealism.[247]

But there was occasional audacity, as when two Irish students travelled to London in April 1956, and in broad daylight stole a Hugh Lane painting from the Tate Gallery. The painting was safely returned, but the theft succeeded in renewing debate about the codicil to Lane's will that had directed his paintings be left to Ireland. As the codicil was not witnessed, the pictures had controversially remained in London, and the *Irish Times* pointed out, the day after the theft, that 'almost every year since 1915 claims have been put forward for the return of the pictures from London'.[248] The student stunt played a part in ensuring that, eventually, the collection would be shared between the two countries.

'Bastards, bastards'

There was a growing liberalism with regard to censorship (an appeals board had been established in 1946), though even by the mid-1950s the list of books illegal for sale in Ireland included the Church of England's *Threshold of Marriage*, and works by Graham Greene, George Orwell, Kate O'Brien, Simone de Beauvoir, Seán O'Casey and Ernest Hemingway. In May 1962, Dermot O'Flynn of the Knights of Columbanus, writing to McQuaid, noted that 'ever since the liberals scored a victory in the court over the *Rose Tattoo* the authorities are slow and hesitant in taking any action'.[249] This was a reference to the arrest, though he was subsequently vindicated, of Alan Simpson, owner of the tiny and radical Pike Theatre in Dublin city, after the staging of a performance of the Tennessee Williams play, said to be indecent and obscene. It was one of the uglier episodes of Irish cultural history in the 1950s, which once again featured the clandestine spying of Archbishop McQuaid. The theatre, despite the fact that a court decided there was no basis for a prosecution, never recovered.[250]

This theatre, run by Simpson and his wife Carolyn Swift, had staged the debut of Brendan Behan's *The Quare Fellow* and one of the first English-language productions of Beckett's *Waiting for Godot*, which became the longest continuous run in Irish theatre history up to that point; clearly there was a strong appetite in Dublin for Beckett's European avant-garde.[251] Only much later were the devastating human consequences of the abuse of power that shut the theatre recognised, including social ostracism, bankruptcy and the breakdown of Simpson and Swift's marriage. A book published in 2002, *Spiked*, argued (using evidence that was 'compelling, though circumstantial') they became the victims of an attempt by de Valera to outflank McQuaid on a separate issue: the Censorship of Publications Board.[252] It seemed the action was deemed necessary to forestall a demand by the bishops for a more stringent approach to censorship, with the Department of Justice anticipating a row with the Catholic right over control of the Censorship Board. The government did not want to afford their critics an opportunity to depict them as 'unsound' on the censorship question. In August 1957 Samuel Beckett wrote a note of condolence to Simpson: 'Sorry about all your trouble over the Rose Tattoo. Bastards, bastards.'[253]

'very exaggerated notions of what is indecent'

In this sense, the contention of the Irish Association for Civil Liberties that censorship propagated intellectual malaise in the 1950s may have been justified, but the existence of the Pike Theatre illustrates how literary and theatre-conscious Ireland remained throughout the 1950s. While the correspondence of the IACL may have been treated with indifference by the government, they were increasingly dismissive of the Catholic far right also, and it was significant that the government was seeking to absolve itself from tedious responsibility on this issue. The Minister for Justice, Gerald Boland, suggested in 1953 that 'the problem was one jointly for the home, school and Church and he felt if they could not solve it, the state could not'. He also criticised the hysteria of neurotic parents, a recognition that concepts of morality were changing; or as he wrote in September 1957, responding to the righteous thunder of the League of Decency: 'It is apparent from communications received from their secretary over a number of years that the league have very exaggerated notions of what is indecent and any discussions with them could not fail to be embarrassing.'[254] The government was now apt to point out that official statistics did not provide any evidence of a decline in sexual morality, despite McQuaid's role in the late 1950s in orchestrating a campaign against 'foul books' and his rallying of other Catholic organisations to the cause. It was also suggested privately within the Department of Justice that these Catholic organisations attempted to force on the Irish population 'a standard of propriety that exists nowhere else in the world'.[255]

Far removed from such debates and concerns, most Irish people continued to entertain themselves in the manner they saw fit. The Gaelic Athletic Association 'ban' remained counterproductive and unnecessary, and though in the 1950s emigration could kill off a GAA parish team, as recognised in the 1952 report to its congress, the association, on a diet of loyalty, passion, tribalism, fitness and parish consciousness, remained exceptionally robust. Irish radio audiences were also enthralled when Ronnie Delaney won the gold medal for the 1,500 metre race at the Melbourne Olympics in 1956, reviving interest in athletics.

While those involved in professional music despaired at the dearth of national composers, and the idea that male students seemed to see music as a frivolous occupation fit only for girls, there were signs of a change of outlook in relation to this in the teacher-training colleges in the early 1950s.[256] The work of Frederick May, perhaps the most important Irish composer before Seán Ó Ríada in the 1960s, and director of the Abbey Theatre Orchestra for 15 years, was largely forgotten. May was frustrated and artistically imprisoned within the narrow confines of the Abbey Theatre, being bullied by Ernest Blythe, the theatre manager, whose grave May was later reputed to have danced upon. Having studied in Vienna in the 1930s, he produced a marvellous string quartet, which he finished in Dublin in 1936, but which only got due public attention over a decade later. Because it was his early work, according to the writer of the notes for the CD produced in 1995, its only recording, it was therefore 'untainted by the increasing embitterment he felt on his later return to Ireland'.[257]

SEVEN

1960–1970

'The best of decades'?

One of the most outstanding journalists of his generation, Michael Viney charted new ground in investigative social affairs reporting in the *Irish Times* in the 1960s. Becoming almost a one-man department of sociology, he uncovered a whole series of 'hidden Irelands' in his examination of poverty, alcoholism, marriage breakdown, mental illness and old age. His findings were often harrowing, but also encouraging, in that the balanced and meticulous approach to his research was coupled with a certain degree of optimism that, given the increased wealth of Ireland, and a growing awareness of social problems, there was a hope that they could be not only recognised and discussed but more effectively tackled and ultimately alleviated.

Viney's work in many ways highlighted what was good and bad about the 1960s in Ireland: squalor and neglect in the midst of a new-found opulence; the degree to which promises of a more egalitarian Ireland had been continually reneged on over 40 years of Irish independence; but also a public discourse, aided by an expanding media, that, at the very least, was shedding light on dark, often shameful, corners. Although there may be a tendency to exaggerate the economic success of Ireland in the 1960s (it was not very high by European standards), it was certainly the case that national poverty no longer sufficed as an excuse for social neglect. There was also a new generation coming to the fore – in politics, the media, health services, sport, musical, cultural and legal life, and religion – who seemed to have little patience with or tolerance of conditions their elders had endured, and they refused to indulge in the sanctification of deprivation which had persisted in some quarters of Irish nationalist thinking. Young entrepreneurs Michael Smurfit and Tony O'Reilly emerged during this decade, starting relatively modest businesses in cardboard packaging and processed foods respectively, only to expand through trading partnerships, foreign acquisitions and takeovers. They went on to become the two richest men in the country.

It is that sense of optimism which has coloured the view of Ireland in the 1960s as confidently swinging, a perspective summed up in the title of one of the few established reference works for the period, *The Best of Decades* by Fergal Tobin, published in 1984. No doubt the reappearance of economic depression and emigration in the 1980s heightened this perception of the 1960s as a golden era, given the virtual absence of the emigration that had become a standard feature of Irish life since independence. But as a label it does not do justice to the complexities and subtleties of the decade. For all the steps taken forward, there was still much stagnation and class snobbery. For all the reforms in education, for example, an area utterly neglected until the 1960s, access to third-level education for the majority of the working class remained elusive. Joe Lee has rightly made much of the intellectual capacity to respond to new economic thinking and planning in the minds of politicians and public servants, but in a small open economy much of the wealth generated served to widen the gulf between rich and poor.

Outside of the inevitable embracing of the free-trade philosophy, the political imagination was not particularly adventurous. Fine Gael had made significant gains in the general election of 1954 and had formed another coalition government, this time with the Labour Party and Clann na Talmhan, but struggled to counteract economic stagnation. Fianna Fáil returned to power in 1957 with 77 seats in a Dáil of 147 members, but according to Lee: 'it was more of a vote of no confidence in the other parties than of confidence in Fianna Fáil, whose popular vote rose only marginally.'[1] Fianna Fáil remained in power throughout the 1960s, their dominance sustained after the departure of de Valera in 1959, partly because the party was managed very effectively by Seán Lemass, who was not only astute but broadminded enough to introduce new and younger blood, but also owing to the increasing inefficiencies of the opposition. The Irish

Labour Party enticed newer recruits also, but even when it became brave enough to use the word 'socialism', it still had problems in establishing a national 'socialist' identity, while Fine Gael's attempt to move to the left always seemed at best half-hearted.

There was little prolonged or meaningful debate on European integration. Urban–rural divides also seemed to be exacerbated during this period and farmers became militant and impatient with their perceived marginalisation, as Lemass opened new industrial outlets at a quickening pace. There were worthy attempts to improve the structure and administration of the health services, but still a tendency to settle for less than ambitious targets. The same was true regarding housing, with action often forced only when decaying buildings were collapsing around the heads of the poorer tenants.

Care for welfare of the underprivileged was another area in which progress was made, but there was a continued refusal to abolish the 'shame and hide' approach. Young pregnant women were still being committed to Magdalen laundries run by Irish Catholic nuns for their 'crimes'. A culture of shame and fear was matched by the sometimes violent enforcement of a regime of heavy physical labour, ironing 100 shirts a day at the age of 15, with no access to the outside world, and, most cruelly of all, their babies snatched away from them when they were barely out of the womb, so they could contribute almost immediately to sustaining the material profits of these institutions.[2] Up to 30,000 young women and girls are estimated to have been sent to such laundries (the last one in Drumcondra, Dublin, did not close until 1996), many for the 'crime' of being unmarried mothers, simple-minded, assertive, pretty or even having suffered rape and talked about it. While they raised serious questions about the Church's approach to vulnerable women, they could not have been operated without co-operation from society at large, particularly the many parents who consented to their daughters being sent there, and co-operated with the Church to force them to give up their babies.

Their sentence to these institutions was sometimes indefinite and their existence was a measure of the social values of the era; many had nowhere else to go owing to abandonment and some stayed their entire lives, being buried in unmarked graves. A play by Patricia Burke Brogan, *Eclipsed*, first performed in 1992, was set in a Magdalen laundry in 1963. It is illustrative not only of physical suffering and institutionalisation, but of the extent to which the women were blamed for their own situation:

'they have not only been "contaminated" by sexual sin, but are also seen as possible contaminators of society.'[3] But many of the nuns who ran them also lived and worked in unnatural conditions, and were regarded highly by the many thousands of girls whom they educated and sometimes clothed in a multitude of schools and institutions.[4] Professional and educated women fared better, and the decade ended with a commitment to establishing the Commission on the Status of Women, following pressure from various women's groups who demanded equality, respect and the redress of historic wrongs.

The Vatican II reforms in the Catholic Church were also significant in democratising the practice and scope of Irish Catholicism, to the extent that arch-conservatives could not effectively resist or turn back the tide. Here, generation change was also important, as enlightened clergy sought to move the Church into areas that previously had not been debated or questioned. John Charles McQuaid was quick to recognise that the Church needed to become media literate and in 1961 sent the young Fr Joe Dunn to a television course in Manchester and subsequently a three-month course in the Academy of Broadcasting Arts in New York. Dunn went on to establish the religious programme *Radharc*, travelling the world making often hard-hitting and high-quality documentaries about oppression and difficulties in the development of the Third World. He recalled that McQuaid 'told us to go ahead, not to worry about failure'.[5]

'drinka pinta milka day'

The state-controlled RTÉ, which launched its television service in 1961, often had a difficult time in trying to establish and measure the extent of its true independence, given the ease with which political and social pressure could be brought to bear when it was deemed to have strayed beyond its brief. But independence was also undermined by its reliance on imported cultures and programmes. These concerns are a reminder of the extent of cultural failure, which was also a hallmark of debates about the Irish language, amongst other things, where, by the 1960s, both the pro- and anti-compulsion lobbies were literally taking swipes at one another. In 1965, the civil servant and Irish-language activist Seán de Fréine published a book called *The Great Silence*, a scholarly, provocative and perceptive attempt to explain the decline of an indigenous Irish culture. He perhaps exaggerated the degree of social progress in Ireland – lauding Irish diet, housing, health and transport services – but it was difficult to refute his assertion that English culture was more pervasive in Ireland than the native one:

> English cultural influence is reflected in the interest aroused in Ireland in any matter which is topical in England. Practically all the issues of post-war life in Britain, such as the welfare state, the death penalty, the ombudsman, have become subjects for the Irish debating societies. England's domestic affairs – the big law cases and murder trials, her political doings, financial affairs and sports events – are extensively reported in Ireland; far more so than similar events on the continent … English influence is reflected in many ways, from the introduction of prize bonds, PAYE, zebra crossings and 'honest face loans', to football pools, bingo and the adaptation of the slogan 'drinka pinta milka day'.[6]

Later, the poet John Montague was also to castigate the discarding of native culture in the poem 'Farewell to the English', taking a swipe at the new embrace of materialism:

> Gaelic is the conscience of our leaders? the memory of the mother-rape
> they will not face
> the heap of bloody rags they see and scream at in their boardrooms of
> mock oak
> they push us towards the world of total work
> over politicians with their seedy minds and dubious labels, communist
> or capitalist
> none wanting freedom – only power. All that reminds us we are not
> human
> and therefore not a herd
> must be concealed or killed or slowly left to die
> or microfilmed to waste in space
> For Gaelic is our final sign that we are human
> therefore, not a herd.[7]

Nonetheless, it would be trite and misleading to subvert Tobin's title to the 'worst of decades'. Ireland matured greatly in the 1960s and showed itself as a society well capable of necessary adaptation in many areas. Many young people embraced secularisation and liberalisation with gusto. But the process of maturation and adaptation was often derivative and exclusive. The public service ethos was still strong and served by often exceptional people, but there was no way all ghosts could be laid to rest as a result of a few years of unprecedented economic confidence. There was still much of what Seán O'Faoláin referred to as the 'traditional Irish-life concept', which was, he wrote: 'too slack, too cosy, too evasive, too untense'.[8]

'the interests of the individual rather than the state'

This was a description that could not be applied to some members of the legal profession, and a number of supreme court judgements in the 1960s dramatically expanded the notion of individual constitutional rights, as Irish judges looked to 'American precedent' for inspiration. In the 1950s there had been a reluctance to use the Constitution in this manner because most inhabitants of the Irish law library had been educated in a British tradition that emphasised the primacy of parliament over the law. But two Supreme Court judges in the 1960s, Cearbháll Ó Dálaigh and Brian Walsh, were responsible for a 'revolution' in the interpretation of the Irish legal system. As Colm Tóibín pointed out, in 1961 they 'set out in a coherent and premeditated fashion to establish a set of legal principles and precedents which would change the face of Irish law and make significant differences to Irish society'.[9] They sought to curb the tendency of governments to give themselves arbitrary powers; to protect citizens' rights in the area of criminal law; and to expand the rights of individuals under the Constitution. A judgement delivered in 1965 concerning the legality of the fluoridation of Irish water (the woman who took the case, Gladys Ryan, insisted that fluoride was dangerous and an infringement of her constitutional 'right to bodily integrity'), while dismissing the idea of fluoride as harmful, resulted in the Supreme Court asserting its right to define the unidentified 'rights' mentioned in the Constitution, and that 'the court's point of departure in defining these rights would be the interests of the individual rather than the state'. More generally, the judges' willingness to hear the grievances of prisoners caused consternation in the Department of Justice, but most significant in the long term was the general 'de-Anglicisation' of the courts, with the sovereignty of the people taking precedence over parliament.

'a pace of reorganisation and development'

The success of the initial Programme for Economic Expansion, as enunciated by the Secretary to the Department of Finance, T. K. Whitaker, in 1958, must have taken even its instigators by surprise, given that the report's tone still revealed a certain caution about free trade. There was a rise in the value of the country's exports of 35 per cent from mid-1959 to mid-1960 alone, while the worries of foreign debt and inflation seemed to be a thing of the past. Unilateral tariff reductions in the years 1963 and 1964 set the tone for the Anglo-Irish Free Trade Agreement of 1965, which Lemass had initiated in a letter to the British prime minister Harold Macmillan, by suggesting it would be useful in maintaining 'a pace of reorganisation and development which will bring us, as soon as possible, to a sufficiently high degree of economic strength and competitiveness to keep our place in a world of freer trade and to assume, when the time comes, the obligations of membership of the [European] community'.[10] The agreement was that all tariffs between the two countries would be phased out by 1970.

Whatever about the technicalities of Anglo-Irish trade, it was the slowing down of human traffic that seemed to highlight the success and potential of a more open economy. The average annual emigration rate (per 1,000 of the population), which had been about 14 between 1951 and 1961, dropped to less than 5 between 1961 and 1971. While 44,427 emigrated in 1961, only 12,226 did so in 1963. By 1966 the population had risen by 66,000 above the 1961 level of 2.8 million, and by the early 1970s 'the numbers immigrating remained over a sustained period higher than the numbers leaving', as some of those who had emigrated in the 1950s returned with their families. Those in the 1960s who still chose or were forced to leave had new income and career goals, fuelled by education, and unlike in previous decades there was an importance attached 'to the active vision of being able to return home if circumstances so dictated'.[11]

Another new departure involved making Ireland attractive to foreign investors by offering the same incentives that applied to Irish firms, and it was to this that hundreds responded. Cormac Ó Gráda points out that, by 1973, overseas firms accounted for almost one third of manufacturing employees.[12] Another important developing sector was tourism, income from which doubled in Ireland in the 1960s. Continental and American visitors increased fourfold to 1.2 million in 1964 (despite the rain 'which falls steadily through most post-war Irish travel accounts and veils the promised beauty of hill and lake'), a healthy return on overseas promotional work. The rising standard of living at home witnessed for the first time an expansion in internal tourism, with working-class families appearing in holiday resorts that had previously been confined to the middle classes. The democratisation of travel was a mixed blessing for certain tourist resorts such as the seaside towns of Kilkee in County Clare and Bray in County Dublin. Single people were now much more likely to take inexpensive package holidays abroad, while the wealthier sought more exclusive resorts at home. Continental package holidays to beach resorts were introduced to the Irish market in 1960 and by the early 1970s 'over 110,000 Irish people a year were taking holidays abroad'.[13]

There were also developments in the banking sector and the emergence of the larger Allied Irish Bank and Bank of Ireland groups which modernised and expanded in conjunction with the increase in free trade. The importance of the analysis of younger economists was also significant, particularly those who saw Ireland's economic future as resting in a well-planned free-trade economy in Europe. Garret FitzGerald, a University College Dublin economics lecturer and future Taoiseach, was described memorably by Tobin as arriving on the Irish political and economic scene 'in a cloud of statistics and high-velocity opinions'.[14]

'to cater on their own terms for all the people born in Ireland'

Whatever about the pragmatism of individuals like Lemass when it came to economics – Fintan O'Toole described his approach as one of 'ad hoc socialism, state planning and a policy of dividing the economy into public and private sectors'[15] – younger economists like FitzGerald were responding to the challenges raised in the late 1950s by the economist Patrick Lynch, who, as part of the Tuairim study group, insisted it was time to shatter the contradictory 'Sinn Féin' myth in Irish economic thinking. Lynch had written truthfully about Irish emigration: 'it is because so many emigrate that those who remain at home are able to afford a standard of living that could not be maintained if Irish political independence implied the obligation to cater on their own terms for all the people born in Ireland since the state was established.'[16] The myth that the ending of partition would lead to a robust economy, by giving the South access to resources it lacked, was also dismissed, it being realised that the interdependence of the Irish and British economies had to be consciously recognised, and that there was a need to be unapologetic in attitudes to public enterprise and systematically plan for it.

Many such views influenced economic planning, but for some

sectors there was a price to pay. There may have been a less restrictive fiscal stance and a readiness to be adventurous, but this also meant in practice the erosion of the predominance of the agricultural sector, despite the suggestion in the first programme for economic expansion that agriculture had to be the main focus for growth. The targets set in the second programme (an annual average growth rate of 4 per cent) were not met; it was abandoned by its due completion date, and there was some doubt about the success of economic planning in conjunction with competitiveness and incomes policy. Important new bodies such as the Committee on Industrial Organisation and the National Economic and Social Council presaged the approach to centralised pay bargaining, leading to national wage agreements from 1964 to 1966, though they were controversial, and industrial unrest in Ireland was rife by the end of the decade as a system of decentralised bargaining returned.

The more research that has been done on the economic management of the 1960s, the more critical economic historians have become, perhaps confirming the accuracy of a contemporary American industrialist and head of the Shannon Steel Company, when he insisted Ireland 'has to develop something unique besides tax forgiveness and low labour rates to sustain industrialisation in the long-run'.[17] The reforms of the 1960s were in fact a culmination of innovations that had begun in the 1950s, including the introduction of export profits tax relief in 1956, which had the support of most of the political and business establishment. Whitaker's programme was also drawn up in the context of unofficial discussions with the World Bank, and, as Kieran Allen points out, in the mid-1950s the way had been cleared for the US multinationals, when the Irish government guaranteed there would be no expropriation of the investments of US citizens and no ban on the reconversion of their earnings into dollars. 'In general,' concludes Allen, 'the welcome for the multi-nationals was overwhelming and any action against them was viewed as akin to national sabotage.' This, he argued, was a shared perspective between Fianna Fáil and trade union leaders, because the newly created Irish Congress of Trade Unions refused to affiliate to the Labour Party. It was thus not something 'imposed on a reluctant bourgeoisie', as has been argued in earlier studies of Lemass.[18]

It is also too simplistic to see Whitaker's and Lemass's contribution as 'the bridge between the insularity and despondency that characterised the Irish inter-war scene' and an 'era of buoyant growth and confident expectations in a free trade environment'.[19] As the most recent biographer of Lemass, John Horgan, points out: 'It would be plainly ahistorical to put it all down to a grand design.' While there was abandonment of the idea of a high degree of state economic control (a core value of de Valera), and while this involved bravery and considerable risk, it is also the case that the accompanying rhetoric of self-esteem and public confidence 'also acted to generate unreal expectations and economic conflict, whose full dimensions were only becoming apparent as Lemass retired' (in 1966).[20]

One thing perhaps was certain: with the republic's integration into the international economy, it was more vulnerable to outside economic fluctuations. Brian Girvin suggested that the state in turn failed to produce a positive socio-economic programme or make the right developmental choices, ultimately abdicating responsibility to sectional interests within Ireland (such as the farmers), and outside interests, in the form of foreign capital. Domestic agencies such as the Industrial Development Authority and specialist accountants were also pushing a sectional agenda, with political parties differing very little in maintaining the myth of a class consensus in Ireland through a corporatist approach that did little to identify the winners and losers of their policies.[21]

'top convent wife with Ulysses in her handbag'

And who exactly were the winners and losers? To what extent was the promise, in 1966, of Kevin Boland, one of the younger ministers appointed by Lemass, kept, that economic expansion was not designed to assist individuals to amass large fortunes, but to improve the lot of all, so that 'hardship would be reduced and eventually eliminated'?[22] Retrospectively, there seemed great irony in the fact that when he spoke such words some of his political contemporaries were amassing large fortunes through property speculation (which may have been why he said what he did). But what of the rest? Alan Bestic, author of *The Importance of being Irish*, returned to the country in the late 1960s having been away for 15 years, and noted with surprise that there were 3,728 people assessed for surtax who had incomes of over £3,000. He went on to record his observations of the gulf between those who benefited from economic development and those still deprived:

> The scampi-belt, the Bacardi brigade. They own a house in Foxrock
> and have a Mercedes on the firm. The wife has a Mini for shopping

and a swimming pool for the garden is on order. There is a cottage in Connemara – 'I can really think down there' … wine namedroppers, BA (pass), top convent wife with *Ulysses* in her handbag. Oyster festival but not Galway races. Hard tennis court, yacht in the front garden during winter … unhappy people with easy laughs and eyes that are always moving, looking for Murphy, wondering whether he is watching and whether he has a mohair suit too … blurred carbons of English suburbans from the mock stockbroker belt … there are street cleaners who went on strike this summer because they earned no more than £12 a week. How do they live? I simply do not know.[23]

'no room in this country for Nazis'

One of the notable failures to make good use of the economic improvement was in the area of planning. There had been little interest shown in the Town Planning Act of 1934 by local authorities, and during the Second World War, the Irish president did not attend a national planning exhibition in Dublin because it was felt planning was not sufficiently developed in Ireland and attendance 'might eventually bring the president into ridicule'.[24] Change seemed to be imminent with the Planning Act of 1963, framed after consultation with the United Nations. This allowed for the creation of 87 planning authorities, required to deliver plans concerning land re-zoning, provision of services and removal of obsolete areas, and dictated that anyone wishing to undertake development would have to obtain planning permission from their local authority in advance. It was difficult to administer (in the case of Dublin Corporation the first review of development was not completed until 1980); regional planning was still neglected and approaches to planning were criticised because of what were considered negative regulatory controls being implemented by the planning and legal professions.

While there was a new recognition given to the relationship between economic and physical planning, it was economic planning that took precedence rather than a national developmental strategy. The Irish Georgian Society, for example, looked on with horror as a succession of Georgian buildings were demolished to make way for buildings for the Electricity Supply Board on Fitzwilliam Street. Lack of continuous monitoring meant that the five-year plans adopted owed more to a pre-war British planning philosophy. As the historian of Irish planning points out:

the absence of a statutory role for regional planning was to leave Ireland almost alone in Europe in not having legal provision for regional planning – such an omission was particularly serious since only through a strong tier of regional plans could the government achieve its objective of linking local planning to national, social and economic policies.[25]

At local level, it was also in the 1960s that the benefits to the individual of land speculation came to be recognised, with the use of provisions from the City and County Management (Amendment) Act of 1955. These were used to override management decisions by councillors pushing through 'section 4' motions in relation to local land re-zoning, and were abused by a minority for clientelist purposes or to create personal wealth at the expense of co-ordinated planning. The acquisition of property by non-nationals also became controversial in the 1960s, and by 1965 legislation had been passed that prohibited their purchase of land without the prior sanction of the Land Commission (though land under five acres that might be used for residential purposes was not included). The logic of such regulation was that land purchase should be regarded as part of the pool of resources required for small-farm enlargement policies. A curious feature of the hostility shown towards foreigners buying land was the reappearance of an organisation bearing the subtitle 'land league', insisting the government should buy back land owned by foreigners to raise uneconomic holdings to a more profitable level. Gradually, such sentiments took on a more racist tone, with county committees of agriculture demanding that the government 'preclude aliens from acquiring land in Ireland'.[26] There was also resentment at the level of tourism, which prompted the establishment of non-Irish companies for the purposes of acquiring development land and other property.

By the end of the decade, such opposition had gathered momentum, and was being abused by various elements to suit their own sectional agendas, to the extent that questions in the German Bundestag were being asked by the opposition FDP Party about what measures were being taken to protect German farmers who were being dispossessed in Ireland. The National Land League exploited fears by asserting that 'the land of Ireland for the people of Ireland has as much meaning today as it had in Lalor's day [James Fintan Lalor, a nineteenth-century advocate of land nationalisation], and no other solution will be tolerated by this or any future generation of Irishmen or women'.[27] The IRA duly stepped into the breach, affirming its opposition to 'this new cheque book attack' on the property rights of the Irish people, and began to raid a number of properties owned by non-nationals, with the burning of German-owned farms in counties Louth and Meath. While it is true that rising prices were making it difficult for smaller farmers to enlarge their holdings, it was foreigners, in particular Germans, who were being wrongly blamed for inflating prices. Condemning such extremism, the *Irish Times* pointed out in August 1969: 'In this year, when man has left his footprints on the moon and has sent cameras to Mars, we have suddenly seen the range of vision of some Irishmen shrinking to a condition of myopia.'[28]

This was also a reaction to the shameless attempt of one of Ireland's most conservative politicians, Oliver J. Flanagan, who in the 1930s had shown no qualms about using anti-Semitic rhetoric in his pursuit of local political dominance, to heap opprobrium on German property-owners. In a style Enoch Powell would have been proud of, he asserted at a meeting of the General Council of Committees of Agriculture that 'there is no room in this country for Nazis ... I am not at all as opposed to an Englishman having a holding here as a German, and the sooner we take steps the better'; a curious repositioning of traditional Irish republican allegiances.[29] The poet Thomas Kinsella, who worked in the Department of Finance, also dealt with the German investors issue in his poem 'Nightwalker', satirising the department officials who boasted about:

> our labour pool
> the tax concessions to foreign capital
> how to get a nice estate through German.

But in a violent shift in the tone of the poem he revealed his indignation at having to deal with the heirs of Nazi Germany:

> I cannot take my eyes from their pallor
> A red glare plays on their faces
> livid with little splashes of blazing fat. The oven door closes.[30]

The Department of Lands identified a more subtle approach, suggesting any idea circulating abroad that there was land to spare in Ireland should be effectively discouraged. There was something ironic, too, in the failure to recognise that it was Irish nationals who were in fact often leading the way in land speculation and acquisition through new prosperity and political contacts.

'popular esteem as the upholder of a traditional way of life'?

But the fears expressed concerning land were part of a wider concern about the status of rural Ireland, agriculture as a way of life and the standing of the farming community. All those orchestrating the economic expansion of Ireland from the late 1950s on had been at pains to emphasise the continued importance of agriculture to the Irish economic, social and cultural condition. Patrick Lynch had suggested in 1959 that the agricultural sector needed to be developed with the same emphasis on efficiency, education and technical knowledge as was evidenced in relation to manufacturing. He suggested the practice of allowing the less intellectually endowed sons of rural Ireland to inherit the land was retarding development and undermining progress. But, interestingly, Lynch also foreshadowed the increased protests that were to become a part of the rural sector, with his assertion that 'popular esteem as the upholder of a traditional way of life is poor compensation for the farmers whose economic status marks him as a second class citizen'. This was a recognition that a cultural clash between the farming community and the champions of industrial expansion was inevitable, particularly when some small farmers in Ireland were earning as little as £14 per year.[31] This seemed a poor return, given that even in the second Programme for Expansion, 'primary attention' was focused on agriculture, while acknowledging that most extra employment would come from industry. Cormac Ó Gráda points out that by the time of the third Programme (1969–72), it was estimated agriculture would contribute only 8 per cent of the projected economic output, justifying the pessimism of the classic post-war work on Irish agriculture by Raymond Crotty, *Irish Agricultural Production*.[32]

These fears threw down the gauntlet to the National Farmers' Association. This body had been established in 1955 and in its early years had been dominated by the upper classes of the farming community, who seemed strangely unrepresentative of most Irish farmers. They now had, with the emergence of the Irish Creamery Milk Suppliers' Association, serious rivals, but both groups came to share a resentment at the advances in pay made by public sector workers through centralised pay bargaining. Such tension was to reach crisis and confrontation point in the late 1960s, though some hoped to benefit from common European agricultural policies.

Many of the difficulties of the farmers stemmed from the gross inequality in size and distribution of holdings and the earnings of the 10 per cent of farmers with holdings of one hundred acres or more. Was rural Ireland inevitably to wither during an era in which primacy was given to the industrial entrepreneur? Farm organisations that emerged in the 1950s were faced with a stark decline in the number of small farms and the size of the rural population, where the total labour force fell by 17.5 per cent, while in the latter part of the 1950s, the number of 5–15 acre farms fell by 20 per cent, and those of 15–30 acres by 12 per cent. From 1953 to 1959 the output of the industry as a whole increased by less than 2.5 per cent.[33] That 'modernisation' was such an important concept in the 1960s served only to underline the educational, research and mechanical deficiencies of Irish agriculture, which lacked the essential foundations to build an effective system. An (often petty) sniping fuelled much of the relationship between farmers and bureaucracy, to the detriment of the smooth workings of the Agricultural Institute. Rows about a rural home economics advisory service were endemic between agricultural and education departments. Paul Rouse points out that the poverty of agricultural education was revealed by the fact that, in 1964, only 449 sat the subject for the Higher Certificate, while 'an *Irish Farmers' Journal* columnist wrote in 1962 that every year 7,000 farmers' sons left school to go into farming, but probably not more than 200 receive training in an agricultural college'.[34] Farm apprenticeship schemes were hampered by a lack of adequate funding, and while an interdepartmental committee on the problems of small western farmers criticised the poverty of agricultural instruction, it was also the case that even when schemes were in place the farming community was not enthusiastic about embracing them, a point that had been made by senior Church figures in the 1950s.

Trying to impose uniform agricultural advisory services also proved difficult, which meant that progress was a matter left to individual county authorities, with widely different results, mostly indifferent. Under-investment also impeded the whole process of mechanisation, which assumed a particular importance given the mechanisation of Ireland's agricultural competitors. There were 43,697 tractors in Ireland in 1960, and 84,349 in 1970, but over half of all Irish holdings were still relying on horses. There were rows also over the value of income supplements and pilot area programmes, which tended to cover only minute areas of the country. But the insecurity of rural Ireland also meant that many farmers feared over-investment as well as under-investment, in the sense of worrying about where increased production would find remunerative markets. In any case, 'the inability of agricultural communities to innovate or expand at as precipitate a rate as industry was not peculiarly Irish but represented an enduring world-wide phenomenon'.[35] Between 1964 and 1966 growth in the agricultural sector was estimated by the Department of Agriculture to have been only 1.5 per cent, only marginally above the average growth over the previous 20 years of 1.25 per cent.

'class distinction was almost entirely absent in this country'

For some, the relative decline in the fortunes of rural Ireland was even more difficult to accept given the traditional reverence for the rural way of life in Irish cultural and economic thinking. The traditional idea that material progress was not in itself enough seemed even more pronounced when officialdom was referring to the farming community. Well into the 1960s they were still spoken of as a people apart to which different standards should apply. Writing in his capacity as Minister for Agriculture in 1966, Charles Haughey suggested precisely this:

> we must always think of farmers as people. We must not listen only to
> the economist and the bureaucratic planner who think of agriculture as
> simply another sector of the economy and who are concerned only with
> output, return or investment and so on. Agricultural policy cannot be
> measured by the norms that are applied to policies for other sectors.[36]

There was something rather hollow about such rhetoric in the 1960s, and the sentiments expressed were also ironic given that the farmers' main complaint in confrontation with individuals like Haughey was precisely that they were not being dealt with in the same way as other sectors. Four years previously, the *Irish Times* had criticised the government's policies towards the small farmers and Gaeltacht areas and highlighted the gap between policy and promise and the resultant abuse, as they saw it, of the public's confidence.[37] It was not only politicians who perpetuated the myth about the rural populace being somehow above materialism and indeed class antagonism. A judge in the Limerick circuit court in 1963, Barra O'Bríain, asserted, in rejecting the evidence by counsel for the accused that there was a social cleavage between farmers and labourers, that 'while we may not have a classless society, in his experience, class distinction was almost entirely absent in this country'.[38] The truth was that rural Ireland remained as class conscious as it always had been, if not more so, as a result of the increased prosperity of other sections of the community.

'the unequal struggle with stubborn rock and creeping water'

The development of social sciences and sociological surveys of rural Ireland, in particular the *Limerick Rural Survey*, published in 1964, raised serious questions about perceptions of rural society and the fears farmers had about their own status and standing, even within their own families. The survey drew attention to the opposition that existed among an older generation to the theoretical study of farming by their sons:

> It is important to understand that the farmer's attitude is not just one of indifference. He is positively opposed to agricultural education. What is involved is not education as such, but the farmer's own status. He is the teacher and transmitter of a craft – by virtue of his under-standing of that craft he is head of the family as an economic unit. To admit new methods which he does not understand and which are introduced by his son is to resign his position of authority.[39]

In this sense the rural community was not a victim just of administrative inertia, or state under-funding, but of the prejudices within its own community.

There were those who attempted to respond constructively. The activities of Fr James McDyer in West Donegal in the 1960s generated much interest and hope as he sought to revitalise the fortunes of that area through galvanising the local populace to help themselves. It was the beginning of a 'Save the West' campaign, a slogan that was to be used by champions of the rural community for the rest of the twentieth century, as they placed a premium on increased levels of co-operative endeavour and discouraging emigration. But the attention devoted to them often had as much to do with the passion, erudition or energy of particular high-profile individuals, and their concrete achievements were in fact few. Emigration from these areas remained common and bishops of the west continued to lament the closing of smaller rural schools. The western areas were also crippled with high rates, which were rigorously protested against, to the extent that in 1965 a Connacht newspaper called for the abolition of taxes and duties in the region, while some motorists refusing to pay tax went to jail protesting against conditions on their roads, 'and in the villages more homes were shuttered up by small farmers who gave up the unequal struggle with stubborn rock and creeping water'.[40] The dilapidated state of fishing harbours was also a measure of the decline in the fortunes of that particular way of life. At the beginning of the 1960s there were fewer than 800 full-time fishermen in the west of Ireland. Also symptomatic of this rural decay was the further depopulation of the island communities. A sociological survey of Gola island, off the remote west coast, revealed there were only ten inhabitants (down from 200 in 1930); the closure of the school meant all families with children had no option but to leave, and it seemed the only thing that could adapt such communities to modernity was emigration, mass communications and tourism, all of which involved an assimilation into urban attitudes and standards. Between 1961 and 1966 the population of Ireland's inhabited islands (92 listed in the official census and 90 per cent of them off the west coast) decreased by 10 per cent, compared to a 3.1 per cent decrease for the population of the republic as a whole, and 6.1 per cent for the rural areas of Connacht. The islands of County Donegal lost 16.5 per cent of their population. One person in three in the west of Ireland was described as 'chronically isolated'.[41]

'Let them run a campaign on the theme – "farming is a wonderful way of life"'

In this sense it is unsurprising that representatives of rural communities, such as the farmers' organisations, became more vocal and militant, with a whole succession of protests, blockades and strikes. Unlike the urban protest movements of the 1950s, they were not tainted with the charge of communism, given their traditional allegiances and identification with the national rural ideal of economic and cultural self-sufficiency. Their growing dissatisfaction was a recognition that what was happening was irreversible. In 1966 the Irish Creamery Milk Suppliers' Association picketed the Dáil demanding higher milk prices, and that summer over 450 members were arrested, tactics that the National Farmers' Association saw fit to follow. These waves of unrest were also indicative of the failure of farmers to be adequately represented by political parties. As far as the new generation of farmer activists were concerned, the experience of a party like Clann na Talmhan (see Chapter 5) was proof of the inadequacy of direct involvement in party politics as a strategy for Irish farmers. But the government's view, as enunciated by Minister Neil Blaney in 1968, was that the government's function was to aid farmers 'rather than enter into negotiations with them on an employer–employee basis'.[42]

The NFA responded by asserting that the British government did not employ British farmers, yet they negotiated farm prices and agricultural policy as part of an annual review. Irish farm leaders saw the creation of a National Agricultural Council as denying their right to negotiate directly with the government. The government privately acknowledged that arresting farmers for picketing (rather than for road blockades) presented them with a particular problem because it was a form of protest 'in which there is no interference with other people's rights: it is "pure protest"'.[43] But it was differences within the two main farmers' groups, the ICMSA and the NFA, over who was the legitimate voice of dairy farmers, that created the real difficulties. Their failure to solve internal tensions militated against a unified front, which allowed the government, by the end of the 1960s, to sit back and insist they could not make progress until farmers put their own house in order, particularly regarding who had the right to represent dairy farmers on the milk issue, while the NFA's resentment against senior figures in the Department of Agriculture put the government on the defensive.

It was also the case that the negative tactics of the farmers, though born of genuine grievance, gave rise to complaints which were to persist (particularly as the economic boom had peaked) that farmers were setting unrealistic demands and presenting themselves as deprived out of all proportion. An *Irish Times* editorial noted in November 1968:

> We have had a record summer; the farmers have done well, yet they have been so busy telling politicians and the rest of us their difficulties that they never seem to let us know of their advantages. Let them run a campaign on the theme – farming is a wonderful way of life. After all, industry is not afraid to blazen its attractions.[44]

'sons of their dead das, publicans and the rest'

Some of the younger generation of politicians and public servants cut their political teeth in getting to grips with the dissatisfied elements of Irish society in the 1960s. This gave them much negotiating and tactical experience, and opened their eyes to a growing level of protest and intolerance with what their parents' generation had created. Lemass's leadership of Fianna Fáil began in 1959 and ended in 1966; long enough for a relatively old man of the revolutionary generation. Yet Lemass's place in history was secured precisely because he is regarded as having led like a politician at the beginning rather than at the end of his career. In the words of John Horgan, he was 'forever prodding and chivvying his own followers rather than following meekly in their wake'.[45] Significantly, this also meant taking crucial decisions about those of his contemporaries who he felt were ready for retirement, allowing for a rejuvenation of Fianna Fáil that helped to keep them in power until 1973.

There were many reasons for such electoral dominance. The cynical insistence of a voter, in conversation with the writer Christabel Bielenberg, that Irish politicians were 'sons of their dead das, publicans and the rest – nothing but holy chancers' belies their passionate commitment to politics, though some of them may have shared her view that de Valera's reign had been over long and 'thus successfully retarded not only Ireland's ultimate unity, but also her advance into the twentieth century'.[46] This was an overly simplistic assertion given the sophistication of de Valera's legacy and his astute management of politics, but in terms of the prevailing increased yearning for material advancement, it was the common judgement of a new generation. Lemass's eagerness to drop the holy grail of self-sufficiency was undoubtedly helped by the departure of de Valera, particularly after Lemass won his first general election in 1961.

Critics delighted in contrasting the sexy, youthful and smiling John F. Kennedy on his visit to Ireland in 1963 with the ageing and blind President de Valera as symbols of Ireland past and future. The flying visit of Dean Rusk, American Secretary of State, and the arrival of his public relations team ahead of Kennedy were a measure of the stage management involved, though the Irish authorities decided against laying out a red carpet in case it might rain and ruin the carpet 'at a total cost of £250'.[47]

The visit was important in bringing Ireland back into the American-led Western fold, despite its military neutrality and reluctance to embrace NATO, and there was praise for Irish inspections of Eastern-bloc aircraft at Shannon airport en route to Cuba during the Missile Crisis and of Ireland's UN resolutions concerning Kashmir and India and Pakistan. During the Kennedy visit, Lemass also gave an indication of a more realistic approach to the issue of partition, insisting: 'this is a question which must be settled in Ireland and that any form of international pressure would not alter the basic situation'. Equally significantly, he suggested: 'we had seen in membership of the EEC the solution of certain problems, including our commercial relations with Britain, our participation in European political integration including defence, and the economic consequences of partition' – admissions that would scarcely have been uttered five years previously. Such diplomatic manoeuvring and honest assertions were, however, overshadowed by the media circus that followed Kennedy and the decision of upper-class Ireland to throw dignity to the wind by mobbing Kennedy at a garden party in what was nothing short of a dangerous stampede. Retrospectively, however, people preferred to remember the rhetoric Kennedy employed in comparing suffering communist Eastern-bloc regimes with Ireland, with the reminder that countries struggling for independence should remember 'the constancy, faith, endurance and final success of the Irish'.[48]

'Let Lemass lead on'

But it was important, too, that while accepting the '800 years of oppression' version of Irish history he also acknowledged that the violent stage of Irish history was now finished and lauded Ireland's 'principled' foreign policy and UN peace-keeping efforts (and why wouldn't he, given Lemass's assertion in 1962 that the US was 'the guardian of the free world'). Of course, there was much that was sentimental and superficial about Kennedy's visit (it was also a perfect domestic US media story; the return of a great-grandson of an Irish emigrant). But superficiality and sentimentality were, at the same time, being quickly discarded by Fianna Fáil under the leadership of Lemass, who in his call for an upsurge in patriotism in his first speech as leader had meant a very different kind of patriotism from that of the revolutionary years, one which involved a serious co-ordination, elaboration and enlightenment in policy outlook and economic performance.

Lemass was also a positive election campaigner and sought to encourage new thinking about the Constitution and the organisation of the public services, although he failed to reduce the degree of interchangeability of civil servants in government departments and state boards.[49] Their detractors may have decried Fianna Fáil as conservative materialists and traditional nationalists, but it was precisely this pragmatism which meant they appealed to the electorate more than the other parties, who often failed collectively to expose Lemass's tendency to downplay the loss of sovereignty which would be involved in membership of the EEC. In any case, as pointed out by Stephen Collins, a measure of Lemass's command of the leadership of Fianna Fáil was that their slogan during the 1965 election was 'Let Lemass lead on', stressing the personality of the leader, while the other parties had no such leaders to whom this kind of obedience and loyalty could be secured.[50] By 1969, under the leadership of Jack Lynch, the election slogan was 'Let's back Jack.'

The same sort of slogans, of course, had been used about de Valera, who was now president, though his grip on this office was shown to be less than watertight in 1966, when he barely scraped back into office after a strong challenge from Tom O'Higgins of Fine Gael. The election of de Valera indicated to some that Fianna Fáil 'looked upon the presidency as a kind of honorary doctorate',[51] and an inevitable arrogance was a part of continued electoral success. In 1963 the same arrogance had been displayed in a pamphlet, *Some Facts about Ireland*, prepared in a very hurried fashion by the Department of External Affairs.[52] The decision, in compiling the section dealing with the evolution of Irish politics, to omit all reference to the governments of Cumann na nGaedheal from 1922 to 1932 was shameless in the extreme. The offending piece read that following the approval of the Treaty:

> a civil war broke out which ended in May 1923 in the defeat of those who wished to maintain the Republic and were opposed to the Treaty. In 1926 Mr Eamon de Valera, who as president of the Republic had opposed the Treaty, founded the Fianna Fáil party. Following the 1932 election the Fianna Fáil party came to power.

Seemingly, some 'facts about Ireland' were interchangeable with some facts about Fianna Fáil.

'I admit that this is rather an alarming prospect'

In any case there seemed to be few threats coming from the opposition benches as Fine Gael, which at times seemed like a part-time political party, continued to drift. Their front bench in the early 1960s functioned spasmodically at best, with a neglect of organisation and structure and a preference among TDs to concentrate on their farming, business and legal affairs. A significant turning point seemed to arrive with the departure of Costello, who did not believe in the concept of full-time leadership ('wrong in principle in a small democracy, where average incomes are low'), and the election to leadership of the most outstanding parliamentary orator of his day, James Dillon, formerly a lone voice against neutrality and Minister for Agriculture in the inter-party governments. Dillon, as his biographer Maurice Manning recognised, was cast in an Edwardian mode with little empathy for the concept of modernisation, and looked with unease on younger members who desired a new infusion of ideology into the party and who were unsympathetic to his obsession with matters agricultural.[53]

The real difficulty for Fine Gael in the 1960s was to prove the extent to which it had an ideology distinct from Fianna Fáil; and Dillon, it seemed, had little more to offer than what Lemass was already delivering. Clever and insightful, Dillon was tailor-made for the cut and thrust of robust parliamentary exchange. But he seemed incapable or unwilling to attempt to match Fianna Fáil's organisational strength on the ground, to the extent that he made an extraordinary admission to his predecessor in 1961, predicting that, following the election: 'Fine Gael will be the largest party in Dáil Éireann. I admit that this is rather an alarming prospect but it is one that I do not suppose we can avoid facing, if it arises.'[54] It was little wonder that younger party members like Declan Costello were frustrated at the naivety and laziness (not to mention deluded sense of their own appeal) of the Fine Gael hierarchy, which was why they sought to shift the party to the left. Costello pointed out that not even party members could elaborate on how they differed from their opponents. Their decision in 1961 to advocate the abolition of compulsory Irish in the schools was the most notable difference, which gave their opponents an opportunity to label them anti-national. But, in any case, Dillon did not believe there was a need for serious ideological differences in Irish politics, a position which spoke volumes about political complacency. Garret FitzGerald was much more blunt, a year before he was elected a senator for the party, asserting that 'Fine Gael does not understand what is meant by the formation of economic, social and cultural policies under modern conditions'.[55]

Dillon was patronising to the younger element in Fine Gael eager for change (in marked contrast to Lemass). He eventually accepted Costello's eight-point *Just Society* document in 1965, which had an emphasis on economic planning in both the public and private sector, greater control over commercial banks, more investment in social capital, and the abolition of the dispensary doctor services, amongst other things. But the reality of parliamentary arithmetic was that they could not be implemented without the Labour Party, which ruled out coalition prior to the election. After the election, in which he managed to increase the Fine Gael vote and temper talk of the party's demise, Dillon quit, admitting to his nephew that he had even begun to bore himself.[56]

'Christian socialists, not rip-roaring Marxists'

The Labour Party had little to cheer about either. William Norton had resigned in 1960 to be replaced by Brendan Corish, at a time when the party was utterly disorganised, with few staff or resources. Despite their structural weakness, they had the power to dictate the course of Irish politics through Corish's pledge not to participate in a coalition, a position they maintained until 1973. Their progress in the 1960s, with the benefit of hindsight, seemed to be about becoming a more recognisably social-democratic party. 'Socialist' was a word rarely uttered by the party in the 1950s, though this changed somewhat with the launch of the '1913 Club' in 1958, composed of younger radicals. That they believed 1913 had been the most recent year 'in which the two ideals of national independence and social justice had been in harmony' spoke volumes about the weakness of the left in Ireland.[57]

In the whole of Dublin in 1961 Labour had only a single Dáil seat, the same year in which Corish was keen to quote papal encyclicals and assert that the party was composed of 'Christian socialists, not rip-roaring Marxists'. Lemass continued to deride the conservative positions of the Labour Party, consistent with his contention that Fianna Fáil was in effect the real Irish Labour Party. But by the time of the 1965 election, the future looked brighter for the party; they not only doubled their vote in Dublin city (and won 22 seats nationally), but also began to use the word socialist, and in 1968 reaffiliated with the Irish Transport and General Workers' Union. But the expulsion of the author and Irish language campaigner Proinsias Mac Áonghusa in 1967, for criticising union dominance and the 'do nothing backwoodsmen', was an indication of differences of emphasis within the party, and, for some, evidence of an anti-intellectualism.

The optimistic insistence that 'the seventies will be socialist' was misplaced, as evidenced by the continuing discomfort of many party members with the concept of socialism and the inability to bridge the gap between the sentiments expressed at annual conferences and the caution of the parliamentary party. Michael Gallagher quoted David Thornley, a talented academic Marxist, as describing Labour as a right-wing 'band of hard working parliamentarians' and 'a firebreathing party congress, whose ideological purity is in inverse ratio to its political realism'.[58] This was underlined by the tendency of rural Labour Party TDs to distinguish between socialism in theory (in favour) and socialism in practice (against). Although more intellectual credibility was on offer with the arrival of Conor Cruise O'Brien in the late 1960s (by the end of the decade eight Labour TDs had university degrees compared with two in 1965), any talk of a workers' democracy still sent shivers down many a Labour spine and led to the use of the red smear by political opponents. Labour faced electoral disappointment in 1969 (having nominated 99 candidates), and it suffered accusations of being an advocate of Cuban socialism with 'a Dublin TD claiming it would confiscate the Guinness Brewery'.[59] Although it increased its vote, it lost seats (nationally, down to 18), while making significant gains in Dublin. It had neither the ideological uniformity nor the personnel (and too many running mates) to deliver on the promise that the seventies would be socialist. Kieran Allen suggested the labour and trade union movement in the 1960s was being pushed in two contradictory directions, wanting higher wages and improved working conditions but also, like Fianna Fáil, embracing development and the battle for exports: 'They often swung between the demands made on them as social partners of the government and a desire to stay in touch with their members. As the 1960s progressed, these conflicting pressures were stretched to breaking point.' In response, the Labour Party reacted to growing militancy with an increasingly shrill plea for 'normalisation', and 'as always, the Labour Party proved that its own conservatism was the best ally Fianna Fáil had'.[60]

'the first big money subscription'
Whatever about the more widespread use of the term 'socialist', the 1960s was also notable for the emergence in political circles of unabashed capitalists, who were prone to use their political affiliations and connections to become richer, in marked contrast to the previous generation of political leaders like Lemass, who acquired little significant wealth during his political career. Fianna Fáil attempted to institutionalise the connection between rich business and politics with the formation of Taca (an Irish word meaning support), in which businessmen were given access to ministers in return for contributions to party (and personal) coffers, a prac-

tice partially halted after rumours about an unhealthy alliance between Fianna Fáil and the building industry, and after this the courting of the business community was done more subtly. But the precedent had been established. Kevin Boland later recorded that his father, a life-long party activist, 'always ascribed the beginning of the degeneration of Fianna Fáil to the receipt and acceptance of the first big money subscription'.[61] His father's generation had thought it essential 'to keep aloof from the financial and commercial establishment'.

Towards the end of the 1960s some of the younger Fianna Fáil members were critical about the practice of property speculation, their resentment fuelled by the wealth being amassed by Charles Haughey, Minister for Finance and son-in-law of the Taoiseach, Lemass, and himself a future Taoiseach. Undoubtedly an exceptional minister in various portfolios, he was also to become the most polarising, controversial and corrupt politician of his generation. Intriguing, sharp-witted and often enlightened, he was described memorably by Conor Cruise O'Brien in 1969:

> He was an aristocrat in the proper sense of the word; not a nobleman or even a gentleman, but one who believed in the right of the best people to rule and that he himself was the best of the best people. He was at any rate better, or at least more intelligent and interesting than most of his colleagues. He was considered a competent minister and spoke in parliament with bored but conclusive authority. There were enough rumours about him to form a legend of sorts.[62]

'I could never do that, it's Christmas morning!'

But for all the intense interest in the likes of Haughey, there was little sustained investigation of Dáil deputies and the practice of politics and political institutions in Ireland, though certain criticisms did begin to emerge. The work of Irish TDs was still dominated by the concerns (chiefly welfare) of individual constituents, exacerbated by the fact that of the 144 TDs elected in 1965, 58 per cent were serving on local authorities also. The preponderance of multi-member constituencies ensured this would continue, as Irish voters prized (and sometimes abused) their level of access to their TDs. Barry Desmond, a Labour Party minister in the 1980s, recalled in his memoirs a story told by another minister, of a local supporter calling to his house on Christmas morning:

'I thought I would get you in! Will you ever fill in the form for me?'
The minister duly signed the form and pointed out that it needed to
be certified by a doctor and suggested the constituent should go to the
GP's residence to finalise the form. 'Ah Minister, I could never do that,
it's Christmas morning!'[63]

TDs had plenty of criticism to make of this system, but the Irish electorate
were not for turning on the issue of proportional representation, which
Fianna Fáil, having failed in 1959, again attempted to abolish in 1968,
through a constitutional referendum. Vigorous opposition by the main
opposition parties (indeed they briefly discussed the possibility of merger
in the event of PR's abolition), coupled with a prediction unveiled by
political scientists on RTÉ that Fianna Fáil could secure 100 of the 144
seats with just 40 per cent of the vote, ensured its rejection by a margin
of 60/40.

In the event there was little change in either political parties or the
political system in the 1960s. There still seemed to be no fundamental
ideological gulfs between the different parties, such as those around which
other western European party systems had developed, with the three main
parties receiving in the region of 95 per cent of first preference votes. The
idea that increased societal change would alter the voting habits of the
electorate could not be applied to Ireland in the 1960s, given that, in the
1965 election, minor parties and independents won only 2.9 per cent of
the vote. A significant change was that Labour's strength in Dublin rose
greatly, from 8.4 per cent in 1961 to 28.3 per cent in 1969; but overall
the picture was not altered dramatically, particularly with regard to the
education of TDs. Whatever about the stirrings within the Labour Party,
the largest party, Fianna Fáil, saw little reason to be worried, given their
direct relationship with their party membership through local *cummainn*.
What did reveal much about the TDs' self-perception was that they all
tended to portray themselves as being to the left of the other parties.

'deep below the surface of politics'
In 1964, David Thornley raised the question of who was making the really
important decisions in Ireland:

few would deny that the publication of the first and second economic
programmes were the most important political events of the last

decade. Where were these policies hammered out? On the hustings? At the Árd Fhéiseanna [annual conferences] of the political parties? In the columns of the press? In the cabinet room? Or deep below the surface of politics, in a creative dialogue between a group of first-class non-partisan administrators and a handful of politicians who had enough courage and common sense to recognise stark necessity when they saw it?[64]

He added that, in the analysis of power in Ireland, not enough was known of the social breakdown of the country, of class structure, and the decision-making bodies and pressure groups and community elites.

Thornley saw in such neglect the danger of politics becoming a side-show to the business of government and there was a growing body of criticism which maintained that there was little dynamism from below in Irish political culture, with authority still seen in terms of being conferred from above, which further accentuated the urban–rural divide through the maintenance of a city-centre focus. Others saw the conception of the state's function in the 1960s reduced to it being merely a facilitator and dispenser of material interests and nothing else. According to Tom Garvin, policy was still an issue to be decided by cabinets, civil servants, interest groups and clergy, and he suggested the average Irish parliamentary representative 'is deferential to tribal symbols such as the language, 1916, the tricolour and anti-partitionism, but his deference is essentially verbal and is denied by his utterly pragmatic everyday behaviour'.[65] Notwithstanding, the *Irish Times* annual review of 1965 suggested that 'partition, the republic, the language, and all the old constitutional questions were completely replaced by the social and economic questions of the new era',[66] as well as a new generation of leaders. Perhaps the most effective way of managing such change was to continue a reverence for certain aspects of the past whilst getting on with the pragmatic business of charting the future.

'disturbed by the fierce and vengeful tone of the poem'

The year 1916 remained important in this context, particularly the fiftieth anniversary of the rebellion in 1966. In appointing a commemoration committee to plan the celebrations, the government was able to include those still alive who had been associated with the Rising. The main emphasis seemed to be on pride in the past and confidence in the future, but the repetition of such sentiment was always in danger of becoming increasingly hollow, given how little progress had been made in delivering on the idealism and equality promised in the Proclamation of 1916. It was significant that individuals like Lemass had different conceptions of how the commemoration should be used from the traditionalists like de Valera and Frank Aiken. Lemass tended to focus on the idea of providing another opportunity to emphasise a new era of national development, rather than simply the traditional reiteration of Pearse's rhetoric.

While de Valera gave much rhetorical attention to the language revival theme as part of the commemoration, Conor Cruise O'Brien suggested in the *Irish Times* that the nation had 'no cause in this anniversary year for self-congratulation'.[67] The Minister for Local Government, Neil Blaney, oversaw the creation of a supposedly innovative and far-sighted legacy of 1916: the building in Dublin of the Ballymun block of modern high-rise flats, with the blocks named after the 1916 signatories. No more than the 1916 Proclamation, the hopes of the Ballymun project remained unfulfilled. Failure to back up the project with adequate facilities and services meant they became a symbol of acute social and economic depression and enduring controversy. Meanwhile the cabinet, against the advice of the Secretary of the Department of the Taoiseach, failed to ensure an ecumenical tone to the service accompanying the opening of the Garden of Remembrance in Dublin city, having caved in to McQuaid's opposition to sharing a blessing with non-Catholic clergymen.[68] A dramatic, wholly romanticised reconstruction of the events of 1916, *Insurrection* by Hugh Leonard, was screened by RTÉ, and in subsequent years (in tandem with the outbreak of the Northern troubles) was criticised as an inappropriate glorification of violence and was never rebroadcast. A perceptive Lemass, when pondering the suitability of Pearse's poem 'Invocation' as an inscription on the memorial wall in the Garden of Remembrance, 'was disturbed by the fierce and vengeful tone of the poem, which was entirely appropriate to the circumstances of 1916, but will be less so to those years after 1966'.[69]

The British government returned the flag that had been hoisted over the General Post Office when the Republic was proclaimed in 1916; a year previously they had also agreed to allow the Irish government to lay another ghost of 1916, Roger Casement, to rest at home, his body having been buried in Pentonville Prison after his execution. Casement had remained a source of endless fascination, not only because of his political career as knighted humanitarian turned Irish republican, but also because of the endless rumours and conspiracy theories about his 'black diaries' revealing rampant homosexual encounters while on his humanitarian missions. The return of Casement's body was an issue de Valera had pushed strongly with Churchill since the 1930s. Churchill resisted on the grounds of not wanting to change legal precedent or revive old controversies. But, as pointed out by Deirdre McMahon, de Valera (and other administrators who probably suspected the diaries were genuine) were determined to separate the issue of the diaries and the question of his remains.[70]

A succession of books and articles in the 1950s dealing with the life of Casement kept the issue alive, as did the question of who had access to the diaries. There was increased pressure in the 1960s about the issue of where Casement's body should finally rest, because of the impending centenary of his birth in 1964. Paul Keating, an official at the Irish embassy in London, explained the Irish case:

> As far as the Irish people were concerned, the Casement diaries were completely irrelevant to the question of the return of the remains or of the respect in which Casement himself was held … in the event the diaries, if genuine, showed a strange aberration which had little to do with the character of the man as he was known by his friends. Our main concern was the return of Casement himself.

In the end Harold Wilson agreed to the return, on condition of it being done secretly. The exhumation was carried out in darkness in Pentonville Prison, supervised by Irish and British officials; later the prison officers involved in the digging were presented with a Waterford crystal glass, having been praised by Irish officials for 'the humanity and even reverence' shown during the task. The British home secretary paid for the coffin of Roger Casement.[71]

In the event, the Irish government was determined to steer clear of the disputed diaries and happy to see them placed in the Public Record Office in London. In 2002, following an investigation paid for by the companies that made documentaries about Casement for the BBC and RTÉ, they were deemed to be genuine, an assertion generally, though not unanimously, accepted.

'not exactly the way we had planned'

The following year, there was less political controversy about the blowing up of Nelson's Pillar by Irish Republicans in March 1966. It had been a landmark in the centre of Dublin's O'Connell Street since 1808. All that was now left was the stump, destroyed shortly afterwards by the Irish army, though, in the words of an Irish army official, 'not exactly the way we had planned', a reference to the shattering of the windows of business premises on O'Connell Street. There were few tears shed over the destruction of Nelson, even though Dublin Corporation was worried about malicious injury claims anticipated from the trustees of what had been a significant tourist attraction. In the autumn, mischievous Irish students were said to have stolen the surviving head of Nelson from a Corporation yard and it was to turn up on stage at the Gate Theatre in the same year, to the delight of a crowd gathered to hear popular Irish folk band the Dubliners. (There were actually several heads in circulation, with each claiming to be the genuine article.[72]) The nationalist view of the destruction of the pillar, for which no one was to be convicted, was summed up in a letter sent to the Taoiseach by an Irish-American attorney:

> The English have every right to have monuments to their heroes in their own country, but they never had any right to jam their heroes down the throat of Ireland ... every leniency should be shown towards the boys who blew up Lord Nelson and if they have to be punished at all for the look of things, it shouldn't be more than 'a slap on the wrist.'[73]

'the political ammunition of the people before firing the gun'

In any case, the Irish republican movement, having gone quiet in the aftermath of the abandonment of their border campaign, changed their focus in the 1960s to the extent that Tim Pat Coogan, when compiling his history of the IRA, felt it necessary to give only 10 out of 480 pages to the IRA from 1962 to 1970.[74] It was not that the IRA had any intention of disappearing, but rather it went underground and reorganised, while Southern republicans seemed to find a new socialist direction through groups such as the Dublin Wolfe Tone Society (1963 was the bicentenary of the birth of Wolfe Tone). A handbook for members of the IRA in 1967 made it clear that the leadership wanted members and republicans generally to become more socially active, through infiltrating civil-rights organisations, trade unions and farmers groups, so that the radicals of the movement could be accepted 'in leading positions in the mass organisations of the people'.

Such a belief led to them identifying with the rights of small farmers and championing the housing issue in Dublin, the Dublin leadership almost ignoring the issue of partition in their political programme. As Cathal Goulding was to comment: 'if political power comes out of the barrel of a gun it is necessary to gather the political ammunition of the people before firing the gun.'[75] In the aftermath of the ending of the border campaign in 1962, there was a succession of resolutions from Irish local authorities calling for the release of republican prisoners in Britain and by 1963 there was only a single IRA prisoner in jail in Britain, Joseph Doyle, sentenced for his part in an attack on the Aborfield Barracks. There were 29 IRA prisoners in the North, one third of whom were from the South. The government felt that public agitation demanding Doyle's release or the 'direct approach' would be counterproductive, even though by 1963 civil liberties groups and the National Union of Journalists were also calling for his release. In March 1963 the *Evening Herald* quoted a resolution from Waterford Corporation, suggesting that 'never during the past 700 years had the relations between Britain and Ireland been on a more friendly basis, whether taken on a governmental or individual level'.[76]

'a gross abuse of that term'

Trade unions in Ireland had much re-evaluating to do in the 1960s, particularly in the context of the quest for consensus on issues such as income policy and economic planning. The government was careful to incorporate them through various government-sponsored bodies in the realignment of economic policy. At the beginning of the decade there were 123 trade unions, and though 84 of them had a membership of fewer than 1,000, Ireland remained a heavily unionised country. In 1959 the Irish Congress of Trade Unions had been inaugurated, marking a healing of the split in the trade union movement and the dissolution of the Irish Trade Union Congress and the Congress of Irish Unions. The ICTU now represented a membership of well over half a million workers, three fifths of them in the republic.[77] Most of their demands and strike action in the 1960s stemmed from a preoccupation with relativities in pay, though tensions were often compounded by the degree of fragmentation within the unions, as they sought to strike a balance between commitment to long-term planning and the short-term threat of loss of relativities. This was why the government sought to give them more input into formulation of policy, through the National Industrial Economic Council and the National Economic and Social Council. But this in itself raised questions about the viability and effectiveness of existing trade union structures.

There were different views within the unions on the partnership approach, which resulted in the collapse of the 1964 wage agreement after 18 months. This led to the resignation of the Minister for Agriculture, Patrick Smith, owing to what he called the disregard by the unions and their leadership of the wage agreement, 'the complete indiscipline of their union members and their own utter lack of leadership'.[78] A contentious dispute commenced between the EI Company, a subsidiary of General Electric, at Shannon and the ITGWU, over recognition of the union, a time when 'bus-burning allied with the nineteenth-century tradition of collective bargaining by riot made a fleeting reappearance'.[79] Highly destructive strikes by craftsmen were a feature of industrial discontent towards the end of the 1960s, with sectionalised pay bargaining increasing the risk of conflict and the emergence of an unprecedented white-collar militancy. There were strikes in construction, the National Busmen's Union, the Electricity Supply Board (in 1966 the government rushed through legislation to make it illegal for ESB personnel to strike in some circumstances) and, most bitterly, among maintenance craftsmen in 1969. Tobin suggested the latter was 'prosecuted with single-minded and inflexible purpose', which ended with the capitulation of the employers and a 20 per cent pay rise for the strikers. But it also 'humiliated the official trade union movement' through selective picketing, a departure from the spirit of union solidarity, lack of discipline and authority; it seemed difficult to establish who exactly was speaking for whom.[80]

Greater security in employment had made for increased membership of unions and greater independence, but this was not matched by the assertion of strong authority at congress level, since a number of unions remained outside. A member of the executive council of the ICTU admitted in 1964 that 'a reduction in the number of unions and a more rational form of organisation is essential'. In the same year, John Conroy, general president of ICTU, said that 'others have so small a membership that the description "trade union" is a gross abuse of that term'. One journalist commented on the degree of directness and practicality that Northern Irish delegates brought to congress discussions, and on a uniting of Northern and Southern delegates on issues of health, housing and education.[81]

Many employers chose to conduct their own pay bargaining with skilled employees, though there was a new centralised pay agreement in 1970.

The appeal of the far left, through the Communist Irish Workers' Group, remained insignificant (in 1965, their general secretary, Michael O'Riordan, polled only 180 first preferences despite the group's seeming acceptance of incomes policy and less denunciation of the Church), though the Irish Socialist Group, founded in 1961, and the Connolly Youth Movement, begun in 1965, were somewhat more successful. Sinn Féin also proved more attractive to radicals in the 18–25 age bracket, who prided themselves on the use of force 'as an instrument for obtaining social justice', though they continued the policy of abstention from the Dáil. On the far left, the tiny Trinity College Dublin Maoist Group, established in 1965, was importing books directly from the Peking People's Press, but an *Irish Times* journalist noted wryly that, in order for their book shop to become commercially viable, 'recently the writings of Patrick Pearse have made a rather incongruous appearance alongside the "Thoughts of Mao"'.[82]

'It was female anger, subtle, veiled but there'

One notable feature of trade union activity was the increased female membership, pointing to the growing visibility of women in industrial employment and other areas of Irish life. Crucially, their involvement in the employment sector gave them some access to an independent income for the first time. The appointment of a women's advisory committee by the ICTU in 1959, though hardly making huge waves, did provide a platform for the discussion of women's issues. There was still only a tiny fraction of married women working: 5.2 per cent, compared to 20.6 per cent in England and Wales and 20 per cent in Finland. Overall, in 1961, women accounted for 29 per cent of the workforce and sex segregation continued to the extent that, in 1962, 77 per cent of women were in occupations where women accounted for 90 per cent of the workforce.[83] Politics remained largely a male preserve; in the 1967 local authority elections, women won only 20 seats nationally, only seven more than in 1934, and it was not until 1969 that Ireland's first elected feminist since Constance Markievicz, Mary Robinson, arrived in the Senate.

The Income Tax Act of 1967 regarded a married woman's income as her husband's income for income tax purposes, with married women paying higher tax than married men or single people, and this was not challenged constitutionally until 1980. Law and legislation became powerful weapons in the emergence of a women's liberation movement and demands for equality. June Levine, one rising feminist and later author of the acclaimed *Sisters*, summed up the growing frustration with inequality in Irish society when it came to gender:

> the sixties were a good time for the boys. Lemass's Ireland was flour-ishing, business booming, high hopes. There was money around, and employment and optimism. And if one had been a mite more sensitive, it would have been possible to recognise the anger that was mounting under the surface as the decade went on. It was female anger, subtle, veiled but there. It was an anger the cause of which was only partly recognised or understood. It was a hangover, an almighty international hangover. It was an anger which clearly said: 'ok the awful fifties are gone, things were going right for a change. Going right for the boys. But what about us?'[84]

A committee on equal pay in the ICTU in 1965 reflected a growing anger at the failure to include women workers as equals in the 1964 wage agreements. In 1960, female workers received 53 per cent of the male rate, which was to rise to only 54 per cent in 1969 and 59 per cent in 1971. Child benefit was not paid directly to mothers until 1974, while until 1968 there was no provision for the widows of civil servants who died in service. Charles Haughey, as Minister for Finance, devoted particular attention to widows through the Succession Act of 1965, and in budgets in the late 1960s that prioritised public service pensions for widows and orphans. The Succession Act was introduced at a time when there was a 50 per cent intestacy rate, and sought to deal with the fact that, particularly in the farming community, there was often a failure to provide for widows. Now the surviving spouse was entitled to a share of the estate whether or not a will existed. How the lack of a succession act affected women and their perception as the lesser sex was revealed in an observation articulated by John A. Costello, and quoted by Finola Kennedy:

> There was a man who had seven daughters and finally a son was born and the son was the apple of his eye. He explained as the boy grew up what he was going to do for him; he would send him to the best school and then to university and his attitude was summed up when he said

'you would like to do the best you can for the one child you have'. The
seven daughters were in the halfpenny place.[85]

Women were eligible but not obliged (unlike males) to serve on
juries. Only nine women between 1963 and 1973 applied to have their
name inserted in the jury list, of which only three served on a jury, making
assessment of criminality an entirely male preserve. It was not until 1976,
when judgement was delivered in the Attorney General versus De Búrca
case, that this was deemed to be unconstitutional, after Mairín De Búrca
and others challenged the 1927 Juries Act as being discriminatory on
grounds of sex and property. One of the judges asserted that all male juries
'fall short of minimum constitutional standards'. In 1969, it was also left
to a woman, Josie Airey, to challenge her prevention from seeking a judicial separation from her husband because she had no right to legal aid.
Such aid was essential, given the only option of separation proceedings
was through proceedings in the High Court. She appealed to the European
Court of Human Rights, who found the Irish government in breach of its
obligations, and forced them to change their position on legal aid.[86]

'sacrificial tolerance of the unhappy marriage'
This came at the end of a decade in which marriage was at least being
discussed more; an institution recognised by outsiders as being idealised
in Ireland was finally coming under close scrutiny. The journalist Dorine
Rohan, in *Marriage: Irish Style*, found women eager to speak about their
problems in this regard, and she suggested the high Irish birth rate prevented women from striking out on their own, despite the fact that so
many were deprived of respect, financial independence, and a loving and
fulfilling sex life. But she concluded that, on the whole, their fears of marriage break-up were economic rather than moral or emotional (an argument effectively used by anti-divorce campaigners in the 1980s). Rohan
also encountered a good deal of revulsion and ignorance about sex, no
doubt fuelled by a belief, articulated by novelist Edna O'Brien, that 'the
men's way of testing their heroism and bravery and overdrinking seems to
be a compensation for their fears of themselves as lovers'.[87]

Notwithstanding, there seemed to be a consensus that a bad marriage
was better than a divorce or separation, and there certainly was no public
support for divorce. The Minister for Justice, Brian Lenihan, was told by
an administrator of the Dublin Catholic Diocese in 1966 that there would

be 'violent opposition' from the Hierarchy to any proposal to allow divorce in the state.[88] But at the end of the 1960s Michael Viney identified an increasing impatience with a 'sacrificial tolerance of the unhappy marriage', more frequent use of the Guardianship of Infants Act of 1966 as a comparatively cheap way of securing a judicial separation (lack of access to expensive legal help meant there were only five judicial separations in 1967), along with the growing loss of the priest's credibility as an effective marriage counsellor.[89] The government had at least introduced a deserted wives allowance, an acknowledgement of the difficulty of enforcing court maintenance orders. This development was also an implicit recognition of the reality of a peculiar 'Irish' form of divorce: Irish husbands 'getting lost' overseas, because Irish court maintenance orders were unenforceable in Britain. Six hundred husbands were estimated to have deserted in the year 1969–70. Some were eventually traced by the persistence and perseverance of the Irish Society for the Prevention of Cruelty to Children.[90]

This is not to suggest that all married Irish emigrants were on the run; but as long as legal separation remained the preserve of the rich, there was little chance of a realistic approach to Irish marriage breakdown, or of challenging the blind eye being turned to domestic violence. In any case Justice John Kenny, a judge of the High Court, informed Viney that there was no discussion about divorce in the Irish legal world; instead many Irish dioceses witnessed the emergence of Catholic marriage advisory centres. The number of children born outside of marriage was still relatively small: 1,638 in 1969. Finola Kennedy has suggested the introduction of legal abortion in Britain in 1967 led to a reduction in Church condemnation of extra-marital births, for fear that it could encourage women to abort in England. Although it is impossible to put a figure on it, June Levine also made it clear that some wealthy Irish women availed themselves of the service in Britain; a young upwardly mobile woman 'took leave of her husband for a shopping spree in London and returned "honeymoon fresh". That was the phrase. Suddenly, in my predicament, everyone seemed to know about abortion.'[91] What may have begun as a trickle inevitably became a flood, and remained a problem Irish society exported for the rest of the century.

Given the traditional religious observance of Irish Catholics, the widespread anger at the reaffirmation of the Catholic Church's ban on artificial contraception with the papal encyclical *Humanae Vitae* in 1968 was noteworthy. The encyclical was unveiled with glee by the Archbishop of Dublin. Many Irish women had already decided to confine this issue to the realm of their own conscience, using the pill but maintaining their religious observance, but such a public assertion of 'wrongdoing' jarred. Dermot Keogh suggested that 12,000 women were taking the contraceptive pill in the Republic at this time, while an opinion poll taken for the *Irish Medical Times* suggested 65 per cent of doctors were opposed to *Humanae Vitae*.[92]

Nonetheless, the first family planning clinic in Ireland, offering the pill from 1967 in Dublin's Holles Street, was closed as a result of pressure exerted after *Humanae Vitae*. In 1969 the Irish Fertility Guidance Company (later renamed the Irish Family Planning Association) got around the 1935 Criminal Law Amendment Act prohibiting the sale of contraceptives by offering the pill free of charge but charging a fee for medical advice. Although in 1965 there were 9,000 families in Ireland with eight or more children in receipt of children's allowances, and while there was an upsurge in the number of Irish marriages in the 1960s, women were having fewer children. The number of births for married women between the ages of 15 and 44 had dropped significantly by 1961.[93] The idea of distinguishing between commercial importation of the pill and importation solely for personal use was recognised as a potential problem by Peter Berry, Secretary of the Department of Justice. He wrote that 'If importation otherwise than for sale is allowed, the practical result may not be very much different than allowing them to be sold here.' Privately, the government acknowledged the widespread prescription of the pill by GPs for 'medical reasons' and preferred to make references to 'a matter for one's conscience', while by the end of the decade the *Irish Medical Times* was demanding that 'reasonable quantities' be allowed for personal use.[94]

'women can emerge from the Celtic twilight'

Irish women's groups had remained active throughout the period after independence. Rather than dwell on issues of sexual morality or reproduction, the Irish Countrywomen's Association concentrated on the need for essential services for rural women and was particularly active in the early 1960s in a less than fully successful campaign, in conjunction with local authorities, to bring running water to all rural areas. According to the 1971 census over 42 per cent of rural homes still lacked running water. Lemass heralded water schemes as a revolutionary step in improving rural conditions, as well as an important way of bridging the gulf between urban and rural areas. He was assisted by modernisers such as Neil Blaney, Minister for Local Government, despite discontent in certain quarters of the National Farmers' Association who blamed rising local-authority rates on the provision of water. According to Mary Daly, that they were able to partially frustrate the government's campaign revealed much about the status of women in rural Ireland.[95] For many women the burden of house-work was alleviated by the arrival of modern electrical appliances and the disposable income to purchase them. Peter Sheridan, in his memoir *44: A Dublin Childhood*, remembered the excitement generated in a working-class house when the first washing machine was purchased: 'Mrs Sheridan, it's only beautiful. It's a dream machine. You won't know yourself. Look at the shine off it … the white enamel box with the blue top and the blue hose. A twin tub … the housewives' friend and more reliable than a husband.'[96]

But the ICA had also begun to stress the importance of women having access to their own incomes, which became a crucial objective of women's groups. This was also an indication that certain organisations, often depicted as conservative, had maintained a discourse (albeit low key) about the need to recognise the separate concerns of women, as was the case with the ICA and Irish Housewives' Association. These groups joined other long-standing professional and businesswomen's organisations (such as the Association of Business and Professional Women) in forming an ad hoc committee on women's rights, perhaps emboldened by the fact that the number of married women at work rose by almost 60 per cent between 1966 and 1971. Their extensive lobbying and research led to the establishment of the First Commission on the Status of Women in 1970.

Declarations on the political rights of women and elimination of dis-crimination against women from the United Nations were also putting the Irish government under pressure, as they sought qualifications to be made concerning the employment of married women in the public sector before these resolutions could be implemented in Ireland. Debate on these issues led to more frequent parliamentary questions about the issue of equal pay. In July 1967, the Minister for Labour, Patrick Hillery, suggested in the Dáil that the practical implementation of the equal-pay principle would not arise until Ireland joined the EEC, while the Taoiseach, Jack Lynch, at the same time lauded the higher value placed on home life by Irish women compared to other countries. He commented: 'I don't regard Irish women as being in a Celtic twilight that was imposed on them, but I think that women can emerge from the Celtic twilight by their own actions rather than by anybody else facilitating the women in doing this.'[97]

'frustrated lesbians sublimating everything nice … into a grotesque campaign'?

Women's organisations seized on remarks made by government ministers regarding the desirability of women taking a greater role in public life by pushing the equal-pay demand. Paddy Hillery admitted in private to Lemass that the situation on unequal pay in the civil service was becoming indefensible, and that 'I believe that we will be increasingly embarrassed by publicity and pressure for the adoption of international standards in relation to women's rights.' They were also under pressure from the International Labour Organisation and the Council of Europe. The government finally adopted the 1952 UN convention on the political rights of women in 1968, with a reservation on the employment of married women, Hillery believing 'public opinion in this country would not at present favour a general removal of barriers on employment of married women in public employment, particularly in view of the substantial extent of male unemployment'.[98] This was also an issue on which the Department of Finance urged caution. In 1969, when Charles Haughey decided to establish the Commission on the Status of Women, he asserted that Ireland had no reason to be ashamed of its record on the legal status of women; citing the Widows and Pensions Act, the Succession Act and the Guardianship of Infants Act, he conveniently avoided the issue of equal pay. The reason for his muteness on the issue of equal pay was revealed in his private thoughts on the value of a commission on the status of women: 'this would provide the government, if required, with an answer to groups seeking to force them to move too precipitately towards equal pay.' The ad hoc women's committee reacted angrily to the idea that the question of equal pay in the public service would be referred to the Commission, arguing it should not be used to delay action.[99]

The *Irish Times* journalist, and later Ireland's best-selling novelist, Maeve Binchy, wrote an open letter to the Commission at the end of 1969, reflecting on the challenges facing it, her advice falling far short of advocating a storming of the barricades: 'Women demanding better conditions for women are too often and too widely dismissed as frustrated lesbians sublimating everything nice and normal into a grotesque campaign … you will have to make it "respectable" to seek a new and improved status for the women of Ireland.'[100] Certain male preserves did open their doors to women during this decade, including the Garda Síochána. Women were first admitted in 1959 (200 women were interviewed for 18 vacancies), their role initially perceived as 'dealing with children and young girls who got into trouble with the law'. By 1969, out of a total force of 6,500 there were five women sergeants and only 23 of ordinary Garda rank.[101]

'dreams of moral leadership may, for the moment at any rate, be put aside'
There was a recognition that future membership of the EEC would force the government to adopt legislation they were slow to initiate domestically, and it was interesting that ministers wrote about membership as a certainty if not an inevitability. Despite the government's just boast that Ireland was the first country to recognise the compulsory jurisdiction of the European Court of Human Rights, there was little sustained debate on membership of the Community, although there was a view in some quarters that it would force Fianna Fáil and Fine Gael closer together, given the political groupings on the Christian Democrat benches at European level. Considering Ireland's status within the Community, David Thornley, writing for the Tuairim group, suggested that 'dreams of moral leadership may, for the moment at any rate, be put aside', suggesting Ireland should adopt a common policy with the Benelux countries.[102]

The feeling that if Britain was accepted for membership Ireland would automatically follow was widespread, which some contemporary commentators claimed was making the government stand watching on the sidelines rather than initiate developments. The same point was being made by the Irish Council of the European Movement. It asserted in 1966 that Ireland needed to make a much greater effort to make its presence felt diplomatically, given that in Europe it was the country the least known politically, had one of the smallest populations, was the furthest from the mainland, and had the least developed economy, which, in any case, was regarded as a subsidiary of Britain.[103] Ireland's diplomatic presence in Europe, it was believed, was not strong enough, given Ireland's tiny embassy in Brussels (with a staff of only three), and the fact that the Irish ambassador to the Common Market, Frank Biggar, was also ambassador to Belgium and non-resident ambassador to Luxembourg. Irish delegates to the Council of Europe were regarded as being party political rather than Europhile, although some were concerned about defence issues.[104] The first visit by an Irish parliamentary group to European institutions took place in October 1965, and Denis Corboy of the ICEM strenuously objected to a sneering report that appeared in the *Business and Finance* magazine in June 1966, which suggested:

> Our TDs are better acquainted with local parish happenings than with national and international developments. When we send them abroad on the odd trip designed to broaden their understanding of world affairs they are more likely to be found in the bars than in the conference rooms. You lose no first preferences through getting drunk in Brussels.[105]

'like a dental operation performed by an apprentice blacksmith'

Despite such cynicism, the truth was that, with an expanded media and diplomatic corps and a growing awareness in Irish society of outside developments, there was much more of an interest in foreign policy as well as more vigorous debate at home about world affairs. Frank Aiken, from the old guard of Fianna Fáil, remained at the helm as Minister for External Affairs, and while his standing may not have been particularly high within the cabinet, he was justly praised for his enormous contribution to the 1961 UN resolution on nuclear non-proliferation, and when the treaty was eventually ratified in 1968 he was invited to be its first signatory. The Irish army's participation in the UN's peace-keeping mission in the Congo from 1960 to 1964 also played a part in revitalising Irish foreign policy, during an era in which the Irish diplomat F. H. Boland was elected president of the General Assembly of the UN, and Ireland took its turn as a member of the Security Council in 1962.

While the Irish army had previously sent soldiers on peace-keeping missions to the Middle East in 1958, and as observers of the UN operational group in the Lebanon, the Congo mission was a much more significant departure for the armed forces, particularly given the small size of the Irish army at this period (it had only 8,400 soldiers, though its approved strength was 12,500), and its insular and administrative character. As Aiken pointed out, in terms of peace-keeping duties, there were few European nations that were acceptable politically to a newly independent African nation.[106] The inexperience of Irish troops and the UN's own lack of expertise in deploying large peace-keeping missions made conditions difficult for the 600 Irish soldiers, the first of whom departed in July 1960. That the British War Office was asked to supply health manuals for the Irish troops also pointed to a lack of resources, but a measure of their success was that an Irish soldier, Seán McKeown, was chosen as commander of the military forces in the Congo in 1961. This appointment came after the gravity of the mission had been brought home to the Irish soldiers, and the Irish public, following the ambush and killing of nine soldiers at Niemba. The weakness of the UN mission was specifically a UN weakness; for the Irish army the mission was certainly a positive development in terms of the modernisation of equipment it led to, of how the Irish army compared with other armies and improvement in the army's public image.

A close eye was kept on other military conflicts in which Ireland had no direct involvement, but was morally bound by the culture of the 1960s to engage with, as the country experienced the protest and anti-violence marches that were a feature of many other parts of the Western world. Though only a tiny crowd protested in Dublin against the invasion of Czechoslovakia in 1968, the government advised the Cork International Film Festival organisers to be wary about banning entries from Eastern European countries in protest, on the grounds that the Department of Justice 'has doubts whether policies of economic sanctions and ostracism towards the USSR etc would do much good'. In the event, the organisers decided to withdraw the entries from the Soviet Union.[107]

Opposition to the Vietnam War was much more evident on the streets of Dublin towards the end of 1967, with an Irish protest movement calling for an unconditional cessation of the bombing, backing the similar call by the Secretary General of the UN, U Thant. The official view of the Department of External Affairs was that the only hope of halting the violence was for the nations of south-east Asia, including Vietnam, to organise themselves into a neutral area of law and limited armaments.[108] There were criticisms of such a policy; particularly, as Ireland was a member of the UN, for its failure to back U Thant's initiative and support the Pope's call for such an initiative in solving the conflict (in which 21 Irish soldiers were killed). More controversially, the Taoiseach, Jack Lynch, in office since 1966, angered many by appearing to say that he was inclined to back the American approach, while the Department of External Affairs was making vague assertions that it was up to Ireland to do all it could as a small power (in public and private) to help bring conflicts to an end, and that a temporary cessation would not bring warring parties to the table. It was even suggested in 1968 that the government could be potential hosts for peace talks.[109] In February 1968 an *Irish Times* editorial lambasted the perceived timidity of the government:

> Such sentiments would be admirable if they were not impossibly vague. It would be reassuring to be able to believe that the government is doing all it can in private, for there is no evidence that it is doing anything at all in public. This country showed a sense of identity and the courage of independence in the early years of its UN membership, for example in its position vis-à-vis China's claim to be seated. In recent years the impetus and sense of pride have gone by the board and the impression has grown that we must say nothing to offend the American establishment – which, particularly at this moment in time, is not the same as the American people. The tone of the few official pronouncements on Vietnam which have been extracted with considerable difficulty – like a dental operation performed by an apprentice blacksmith – suggests pusillanimity at the least and the illusion, that somehow or other, integrity can be preserved by silence and expressions of ambitious high-mindedness.[110]

'a mistake to give publicity to the facts'

During the same period much Irish attention was focused on the Nigerian Civil War, after the declaration of the Republic of Biafra, an interest heightened by the fact that up to 500 of the country's 800 priests were Irish. There were many Irish citizens in the eastern region of Nigeria, practically all missionaries who the Irish Catholic bishops were reluctant to withdraw, feeling it would be seen as an abandonment of their flocks. The Irish missionaries were held in high regard in Nigeria, and the Irish ambassador, Kevin Rush (Ireland's only African embassy was in Lagos), had regular access to General Gowan and also compiled detailed reports of atrocities against the Ibos committed by troops of the federal government and their supporters. But the Department of External Affairs decided 'it would be a mistake to give publicity to the facts in this matter', on the grounds that embarrassing the federal government could do damage to the status and future of Irish missionaries in the region.

This was a convenient way for Frank Aiken to try and discourage debate on the issue in Ireland, particularly following the calls of people like Conor Cruise O'Brien for Ireland to intervene. Missionaries, and indeed the Irish public, were overwhelmingly sympathetic to the Ibos, but the government argued that it had good standing with both sides and could not recognise the secession of Biafra, while some missionaries also felt the government was wary of antagonising Britain, which was providing arms for use against the Biafrans. Aiken was disingenuous about the extent of his knowledge of the African massacres, and remained mute about the vivid and detailed reports he was receiving from Kevin Rush.[111]

More controversy was generated by the RTÉ programme *Seven Days*, which highlighted divisions between the missionaries and their superiors. These were understandable given that Irish missionaries ran nearly 2,500 schools catering for over half a million pupils as well as 47 religious-run hospitals. It was also unsurprising that press coverage was pro-Biafran, or that there was tension between the African-aid agency Concern and the government. The new medium of television also made this conflict more accessible for the Irish public; huge sums of money were raised by the *Independent* newspaper group and the Catholic Church, while the government donated money to the Irish Red Cross. There was further controversy in October 1968 when the Nigerian commissioner for home affairs suggested some Irish Holy Ghost fathers were involved in gun-running. It was clear the Civil War presented the Church with a particular dilemma given its delicate presence in what was overwhelmingly a non-Christian country.[112]

The Civil War also brought about the creation of the Africa Concern and Górta organisations, marking something of a turning point in the nature of Irish overseas aid. A *Radharc* documentary on the issue was censored, resulting in the cutting of remarks by the Biafran leader, Ojukwu, to the effect that the Irish people's attitude to the conflict was different from that of their government. Enda Staunton pointed out that 'privately, the Irish authorities were under no illusion about their countrymen's involvement' in arms purchasing, but that foreign policy in relation to Nigeria, as generally, remained neutral with an emphasis on the peaceful resolution of the dispute. They had, maintained Staunton, little choice: 'For an Irish government almost pathological in its attitude to subversion within its own boundaries, to have supported Biafra and in the process undermined Ireland's image and position on a continent in which it enjoyed close ties would have been political suicide.'[113]

South Africa's oldest newspaper, the *National Witness*, attacked and lampooned Ireland's refusal to host an official reception for the South African rugby team in November 1969, suggesting that given the state's export of products to Ireland and the degree of sectarian tension in Ireland, it was an utterly hypocritical decision. The government was not prepared, however, to accede to the demand of the Irish anti-Apartheid movement that the match be prevented, not believing it 'should go so far as to interfere with sporting or similar competitions on political grounds'.[114]

'it was far more problematic being a poof'

While it was undoubtedly the case that events in Africa were of acute concern to many in the Irish Church, and politicised missionaries and domestic priests, there were plenty of stirrings at home during the 1960s which highlighted for critics the narrowness of traditional Catholic aims and teaching. The Archbishop of Dublin, McQuaid, who remained in his position until 1972, sought to resist the winds of modernisation and ecumenism blowing with some gusto after the Vatican II reforms. He continued to object to growing secularising trends in education, and remained preoccupied with the need to counteract the influence of Trinity College Dublin, though he eventually gave in to the inevitability of the removal of the ban on Catholic students attending the college unless they had a special dispensation from the Archbishop. Meanwhile, in University College Dublin, John Whyte, author of the seminal *Church and State in Modern Ireland*, was instructed not to write his book on the grounds that it would be interference in the affairs of the Dublin diocese. He subsequently went to Queens University Belfast, something of an irony, as pointed out by Tom Garvin, given Whyte's own pious Catholicism; furthest from his mind was a hatchet job on the Catholic Church.

This episode was an indication that bullying and denial of academic freedom were an integral part of clerical politics at Ireland's largest university while McQuaid was still Archbishop.[115] But many who were studying at and graduating from UCD were becoming less patient. In June 1960, the religious periodical the *Furrow* reported on a gathering of 200 priests in Donegal who had convened to smugly discuss the shortcomings of modern youth but were 'quickly chastised when, in the first lecture, Peter Dunn, a young UCD graduate, turned the tables by voicing the criticisms of university youth of the clergy, their sermons and parish organisation'.[116] This was one small indication of a trend that was to gather momentum. In the same periodical, much attention was now being given to the role of ecumenism in the modern Church, and a practical interest in the spiritual welfare of Irish Protestants, though there was much embarrassment in 1966 when, at an unprecedented ecumenical meeting at the Mansion House in Dublin, the Church of Ireland Archbishop, George Simms, was left seated in the audience rather than on the platform beside the Catholic bishops.

From 1946 to 1961 the Protestant population fell almost five times faster than the overall population, and by the end of the 1960s the entire Protestant population stood at only 130,000. The Church of Ireland's Sparsely Populated Areas Commission had to oversee the closure of many churches and schools. The community as a whole, however, suffered little poverty, and their religious affiliation was not a significant factor in employment discrimination. More pain was caused by the *Ne Temere* decree and the unpredictability and inconsistency of Church rulings in this regard, but it was also the case that Protestant social events deliberately did little to encourage younger Protestants to mix with their Catholic counterparts. A prominent Southern Protestant recalled at the end of the century:

> At that time the Catholic Church insisted on people in mixed religion marriages getting married not only in a Catholic Church, but at a side altar therein, preferably early in the morning when no one was around to witness the ceremony. Prods, after all, could not get into heaven. I had to take the *Ne Temere* decree. The kindly Dublin priest told me it was a 'gentleman's agreement' and I replied that it was one to which my wife and I would not be paying too much attention. He did not seem to care as long as I signed the document ...[117]

Notwithstanding such pragmatism, much pain had been caused by the boycotting of Protestant businesses in the small Wexford town of Fethard-on-Sea in 1957, when the Protestant wife of a Catholic man defied the local priest who insisted their children had to be educated at the local Catholic school. The silence of Irish bishops about this shameful episode of open sectarianism spoke volumes, and no formal apology was made until the end of the 1990s. Although the wife was absent for some time with the children, her brave husband did not give in to intimidation, and, when she returned, the children were eventually educated at home. In this sense, it is understandable that a Protestant bishop referred to 'denominational apartheid' when reflecting on his experiences of growing up in Dublin, but he pointed out that 'in North Dublin it was Apartheid by mutual consent. Roman Catholics and members of the Church of Ireland would have treated each other with genuine courtesy, would have been good neighbours to one another, but the overwhelming sense was one of difference. We were different'. Thus it can be seen as a partly self-imposed separateness, but there was hurt caused by a prevalent view that they were 'not really Irish'. But despite the stereotype and the myth of a privileged, aloof class, most were fiercely proud of their Irish heritage. David Norris, later to be a senator and Ireland's leading gay-rights campaigner, recalled: 'Growing up, I was never greatly troubled by being a Protestant; it was far more problematic being a poof ...'[118]

'incapable of transcending the theological approach'
Certain opulent areas such as Malahide, Greystones and West Cork, were, in the words of Michael Viney: 'genteel ghettos for the disengaged West Briton ... in [Harold] Wilson's Britain he would be an anachronism, in Lemass's Ireland he is an irrelevance'.[119] But McQuaid, in contrast to others, continued to lay stress on the doctrinal divisions separating the two religions, though his reluctance to engage with Vatican II reforms was shared by other conservative bishops, who looked askance at the more questioning theological journalism appearing in England. But in the 1960s McQuaid's self-righteousness was much more likely to be criticised, and despite the willingness of younger politicians like Haughey and Hillery to consult him concerning legislation, the blanket uncritical media coverage he had been accustomed to was coming to an end. Although McQuaid recognised the value and power of television and encouraged priests to train in television techniques, it was becoming clear that he would not be in a position to exert the same control over this powerful medium as he had over radio.[120]

Other criticisms began to be made of the extent to which the lay potential in the Church was not being adequately recognised. The research of the American Jesuit Bruce Francis Biever, for example, may have confirmed the degree of outward manifestations of loyalty, but particularly among higher-educated Catholics this was masking an impatience and resentment at traditional Church controls. Biever found that nearly 90 per cent believed the Church was the greatest force for good in contemporary Ireland, much more so than the state, but four fifths of those educated to third level believed Church dominance was too strong. The decision of the provincial of the Jesuit community in Ireland to withstand pressure from McQuaid and allow the publication of an article critical of Church control in education by Seán O'Connor (see below) was a measure not only of McQuaid's loosening grip, but of a belief in freedom of expression and tolerance of criticism, even if the Catholic Church was the target.

McQuaid's nasty authoritarian streak nonetheless remained, as evidenced by the transfer to the West Indies of the editor of the Redemptorist magazine *Reality* and the tendency to move other questioning priests to fringe parishes. It is easy to go overboard in criticising McQuaid; personally still capable of great generosity and charity, he found it difficult to adapt to the culture of the 1960s, all the more so because he had exercised power at a time when criticism of Church control was non-existent and his moral vigilantes roamed freely. He was in a sense a prisoner of his rigorous training. John Cooney points out that:

> It is clear from private conversations which McQuaid had with Mrs Simms [wife of the Church of Ireland Archbishop of Dublin] that he had made an attempt to understand the changing attitudes of a younger generation towards organised religion, but that he was incapable of transcending the theological approach which he had been taught as a student at Kimmage.[121]

Deirdre McMahon, in a perceptive analysis of McQuaid's career, points out that by the mid-1960s, when a contemporary cleric, Roland Burke-Savage, refuted charges of excessive interference by McQuaid in a special edition of *Studies*, 'there was a defensive and occasionally obscure quality about his comments that failed to convince critics'. Although a man of great integrity and pastoral concern, McQuaid was neither socially minded nor an effective communicator, and his pastorals in the 1960s became 'increasingly formulaic and abstract'. As McMahon concludes, while for clerics a careless move during McQuaid's tenure could cause great hardship for the transgressor, by the mid-1960s 'assertive lay voices could not be silenced so easily'.[122]

'class distinction was wounding Christ'
In any case, McQuaid was not representative of the totality of the Catholic Church in 1960s Ireland, and there has been too much attention focused on his personal rigidity at the expense of an analysis of those who strove to make the Church more adaptable, relevant and accessible. Alan Bestic,

for example, was to find that 'some of the most energetic agents of change were the priests themselves', as they voiced their concerns on issues such as housing, poverty, the travelling community and third-world development. Mary Kenny points out that in place of tirades against the evils of communism, a 'new theme generally in sermons was that class distinction was wounding Christ'; and priests sought to give serious attention to film and literature rather than instinctively favouring censorship as always the lesser evil. In doing so, they helped prepare for an acceptance of the need for legislative reform.[123]

In modernising, the Church was capable of both leading and following. Irish Catholics in the main were wholly welcoming of ecumenism as they finally got a peep inside Protestant churches they had long been curious about, and indeed on gaining entry wondered what all the fuss was about. Bishop Lucey of Cork was vocal, not only on the marginalisation of Irish rural communities, but also issues of public health, and the connection between business and politics. He was a consistent and stern critic of successive governments' lack of social and economic innovation. Lucey disliked pretentiousness and those who embraced the trappings of office, disputing the idea that culture 'is a matter of exotic learning and polish. It is no such thing. The cultured or cultivated person is the person who is making the best use of all the powers God has given him. True culture then, is the growth of your own mind and your own personality.'[124] Lucey admonished politicians for allowing the small farm communities to decline, and his criticisms irritated the government. Fellow Cork man Jack Lynch, when Minister for Industry and Commerce, was moved to suggest that the pronouncements of bishops should extend only to matters of faith and morals, and he went on to insist pointedly: 'lest silence on my part be construed as acquiescence, I as a member of the government who is also a member of his Lordship's flock, regretfully feel constrained to refer to the criticism which, I feel, does not instil in the public respect for civil authority.'[125]

Meanwhile, Bishop Peter Birch of Ossory pioneered a new approach to the administration of social services in Kilkenny, challenging his diocese to develop a vision of charity equal in size to the vision of modern industrialism and science. He was praised for advances made in the creation of support systems for the disadvantaged and mentally handicapped.[126] Also active at home and abroad was the Irish Red Cross Society, which had greatly expanded its humanitarian work following its foundation in

1939, and to which the government gave £23,600 in 1964/5. The IRC were active in launching monetary appeals for refugees, to which the Irish responded with exceptional generosity.

'we have not paid sufficient attention to the weaker sections of the community'

In this context it was important for the Church to try and highlight the need for a social conscience, and indeed a social vision, in a society that was creating more wealth but had much progress to make in the areas of welfare, health, social provision and care, even though McQuaid insisted on defending criticisms of the Catholic Social Services Centre by asserting that 'no measures of social security can eliminate human poverty'.[127] In many ways Irish people had a standard of life which was comfortable; according to UN figures they enjoyed a high consumption of calories per head and were thus well nourished. Dubliners spent less (10 per cent) on their houses than they did on drink and tobacco (15 per cent); crime rates were low (885 crimes reported against people in 1962 of which 830 were detected); while life expectancy stood, more disappointingly, at 62 for males and 67 for females.[128] There was a high rate of hospital beds per head of the population and relatively low levels of illiteracy; while the establishment of the Economic and Social Research Institute in 1960 meant there was a new level of awareness of the importance of sociological and economic information.

But there was a growing recognition by the mid-1960s that the provision of social services was not keeping pace with economic expansion. Many working-class estates were filled with early school leavers who married young and were surviving on diets of bread and tea, who were soft targets for money lenders, with people still often being treated cruelly by officials for their 'social failings'. Pride in children's appearances seemed to be confined to attendance at religious functions, and lack of privacy and excessive drinking were features of areas that were the supposed solution to city slums, but were now becoming problem estates in the suburbs of the larger cities. They demonstrated the futility of the idea that 'urban populations need only roads and houses'.[129]

Class snobbery was still rampant in most parts of the country, evidenced by the continuing practice of reading from the altar parishioners' contributions to church funds, beginning with the highest and ending with the lowest. Some younger Fianna Fáil ministers felt there was an onus on the party to put its money where its mouth was. Kevin Boland informed the Minister for Finance that there was 'a general feeling that we have not paid sufficient attention to the weaker sections of the community and that there has not been an equitable distribution of the increased prosperity to which we point as an achievement'. The minister responded by suggesting Boland was attempting to wreck the Second Programme for Economic Expansion by calling for increases in social welfare, an important indication of the priorities of a government that did not equate economic expansion with increased redistribution.[130]

The care of deprived children continued to reveal archaic practices and values. The advocates of reform in the Tuairim group suggested it would come as a surprise to many that the legislation used in Ireland to care for deprived children in the mid-1960s was 60 years old, and long since discarded in England, the country of its origin. In England, institutions (particularly after the 1948 Children Act) were a last-resort alternative to the family, unlike in Ireland, where they still seemed to be first port of call. Although in Ireland fosterage had been regularised under the 1957 Children Act, adoption was still confined to children of 'good class' parentage; in 1965, while 1,782 children were in some form of foster care, there were 3,419 children in industrial and reformatory schools, institutions which received no information on the child's medical, social or educational history.[131] The probationary service in Ireland was woefully underdeveloped, with few welfare officers or child care workers to do preventive or after-care work outside schools. Lack of sex education and the practice of sex segregation meant the issue of physical and sexual abuse was only occasionally alluded to. The London branch of the Tuairim study group concluded of the Irish child that 'provided he is physically healthy, well clothed, obedient and can speak Irish, officialdom is satisfied'. It urged the establishment of a subsidiary children's department at government level, arguing the government should give the same attention to these issues as it was now giving to the mentally handicapped, where it had been forced to act as a consequence of a waiting list of 24,000 for institutional care.[132]

Tuairim's publications also criticised what was in effect the export of deprived youth once they left institutions, with many emigrating to England. By 1961 there were 130,000 Irish-born in London. Many unmarried labourers in particular still had a reputation for excessive drinking and were living in poor accommodation. Of the 41,746 males committed into prisons and borstals in England and Wales in 1961, 3,267 or 8 per cent stated their place of birth as the Irish Republic. Women formed 230 of the 2,561 committed, also 8 per cent. Given that they formed only 2 per cent of the population, these figures were strikingly high.[133] The Catholic Church in Ireland was particularly concerned about those emigrating under the age of 18, and admitted to the government that the task of supervising them, particularly young prostitutes, 'was getting beyond' their chaplains. The Irish government rejected the idea of placing restrictions on travel between the two countries given the potential for court or constitutional challenges, and was loath to fund Irish Church charities in England because it would be 'incapable of being kept within fixed limits'.[134] This was a euphemistic way of asserting that this was not so much a civil issue as a spiritual welfare issue for the Irish Church. The Church operated Irish 'centres' for the rank and file of manual labourers, and Irish 'societies' for the well-to-do, ensuring Irish class divisions were a reality for emigrants also. At home, by 1966, the Irish Society for the Prevention of Cruelty to Children was dealing with 2,086 cases, involving 7,516 children, and noted a rise in what they termed 'immoral offences'; their priority remained the reuniting of families torn apart by drink, neglect and violence, though it was not until 1968 that they employed social science graduates.

'get me out of this fucking place'

Corporal punishment was being used widely, often viciously, in Irish schools. Although legal, it was not supposed to go beyond light caning or be inflicted for failure at lessons, but the official journal of the Irish National Teachers' Organisation admitted in January 1964 that this was being widely ignored.[135] A journalist from the London *Daily Telegraph Magazine* in April 1969 expressed astonishment at the toleration of public beatings in schools, asserting that in Irish church schools in particular, 'every day many endure thrashings which, in England, would be enough to close the school and start an inquiry'. It was going on in England, the journalist suggested, but not to the same extent. The truth was that it was not taken seriously, despite the efforts of Reform, a small group of parents who campaigned on the issue. The *Daily Telegraph* reported how this group backed the first ever successful legal action taken against a teacher of a religious order for excessive punishment, after a nine-year-old child, partially blind and deaf in one ear, was savagely beaten by a Christian Brother at a Dublin school. As was reported, the family 'were awarded one shilling in damages and punished with £400 costs. The Brother is still teaching in Dublin, but the [family] have emigrated to Canada.'

The Minister for Education, Brian Lenihan, believed that there were difficulties in either abolishing or retaining corporal punishment, and decided to retain the status quo. This was the same minister who in 1968 visited Artane Industrial School and was informed of weekly beatings. His response was: 'Get me out of this fucking place.'[136] But soon the inmates were to get out, too, as a result of the establishment of the Kennedy Committee in 1967, at a time when religious orders were beginning to close some of the schools and operate more child-centred units, and the Department of Education was recognising the need for more psychiatric care. The damning report of the Kennedy Committee, which criticised not only the industrial schools, but also inadequate state supervision, recommended the abolition of the system. The full extent of abuse was by no means uncovered, partly because the Department of Education did not co-operate fully with the committee by refusing to give it a list of all the complaints received.

The report came after a period when there had been widespread embarrassment at press coverage in England following the case of eight girls whose heads were shaved after they escaped from an industrial school in Donegal. There were repeated accounts of maltreatment and hunger, criticisms were made of a small number of professional groups and politicians, and a senior Department of Justice official witnessed naked beatings.[137]

'the workhouse mode of thought'

At the other end of the scale, Ireland's ageing population was also becoming a matter of concern during the 1960s, with an increase of over 10 per cent in the volume of the dependent age groups since the 1930s. By 1966, 11.2 per cent of the population was over the age of 65 (while 31.2 per cent were aged 14 or under). In Dublin alone, in 1961, the population over the age of 65 was 59,000 and had increased at a rate of 1,000 per year since 1940. There was an attendant interest in low-quality institutional care in county homes and mental hospitals, and a consequent failure to develop home-care services. By the end of the 1960s, life expectancy had increased to 68 for males and 72 for women.

In the west of Ireland, where there was traditionally a higher rate of emigration, the proportion of elderly people was higher again; it was small wonder that a consequent depression afflicted many of these areas, as revealed by Hugh Brody in *Inishkillane*, published in 1973. While there were improvements made in geriatric care, there were too few doctors who had experience of working with the elderly. The system of institutionalising them in the 34 remaining county homes meant scant recognition of them as a separate medical class, which was why a suggested solution was voluntary home assistance, though as in other cases of welfare local authorities were slow to respond. This was why the initiative of Bishop Birch in Kilkenny was so important. He stressed the necessity of working with the elderly rather than merely providing money, and he contended that Irish society was becoming more selfish, in the sense that neighbours had a tendency to shun those in need of care as if there was a social or moral stigma attached to them; another reason why they ended up in the county homes.

Michael Viney wondered why 'the county homes have to be so utterly shut off from the communities around them … the truth is that many county homes have still not shaken off the workhouse mode of thought; and many communities still regard the resident of the county home as a social pariah. This is just what the authorities meant to happen when they built these stark barracks a century ago.'[138] Ambitious schemes and housing complexes for the elderly were in place in Dublin, and housing authorities had the power to provide reserved housing for the aged, but rural areas were making little use of these powers. It was hoped the establishment of a national council for the elderly would effect a more constructive alliance of official and voluntary activity.

'tower block mania'

Housing was particularly crucial in view of the crisis which began to affect Dublin in the early 1960s, particularly after a tenement housing collapse in Dublin in which a number of people were killed. It was estimated that nearly 13,000 new houses were required annually, double the number being built in the early 1960s.[139] This era also saw the emergence of a militant Dublin Housing Action Committee in 1968, in which many republican activists became involved. The government defended the record of Dublin Corporation, pointing out that in the Dublin area alone the number of new houses built had risen from 2,631 in 1963–4 to 5,502 in

1967–8 and that 'few other local authorities in Europe, if any, have done as much to house their people as Dublin Corporation'.[140] According to housing activists, there was a need not just to build new houses but also to improve the substandard condition of existing housing, and they claimed there were 10,000 living in intolerable conditions in Dublin alone, while suitable premises were either being turned into offices or decaying. Their protests were loud and confrontational, and they made frequent accusations of Garda brutality. A local authority survey of 1963 suggested that, nationwide, there were 60,000 occupied houses that were unfit for human habitation, with 32,000 of them incapable of repair (27,000 of them in rural areas), while trade union leaders deplored the cessation of direct labour in the building of new houses.[141]

The building of offices caused much anger, particularly when habitable dwellings were being demolished to make way for office blocks, with few restrictions imposed by the Fianna Fáil governments or planning authorities. These new developments also prompted the formation of the Georgian Society to lobby for the retention of the magnificent buildings and edifices of eighteenth-century Dublin. In a powerful polemic, *The Destruction of Dublin*, published in 1985, Frank McDonald argued that before the economic boom the city at least had some coherence, and quoted a wry observation from the 1960s to the effect that 'the only reason why Dublin remained for so long the beautiful eighteenth-century city the English built is that the Irish were too poor to pull it down. This, unfortunately, is no longer the case.'[142] In 1960 there were no supermarkets in the city, and the only large modern office block was Busáras, designed by Sam Stephenson, a pioneering construction highly regarded by European architects. But as McDonald pointed out, unlike cities like Edinburgh, there were few professionals living in Dublin city who had 'enough political clout to secure its preservation' as the decade progressed.

The speculators moved to buy vacant properties for new office developments, and planners and city councillors largely ignored the Royal Institute of Architects' recommendations concerning the preservation of the Georgian city, relenting in relation to only small pockets of the city. Instead, developments like Liberty Hall in 1965 were a product of the 'tower block mania of the early 1960s', as were the ugly O'Connell Bridge House and Apollo House in Hawkins Street. There were impressive buildings too, such as the Irish Life development at Mespil Road and the award-winning new RTÉ buildings in Donnybrook, a southside suburb. Indeed, one of the most significant architectural developments was the tendency to concentrate much of the new building in the southside suburbs, such as the new University College Dublin campus at Belfield, and new super-markets in Dundrum and Stillorgan, and there was an increase in church building also. But the city centre itself became one of 'anonymous office blocks', making it unattractive as a place of residence.[143]

'Duine le Dia'

Mental illness also received new attention during the 1960s, including a Commission of Inquiry in 1961. It reported in 1966, and called for the development of community services, psychiatric units and a national advisory council, arguing the need for a commitment to psychiatric ser-vices to bring the mental-health services out of the dark ages. In 1963 seven out of every 1,000 Irish people were in mental hospitals (19,656 people); in certain counties like Roscommon and Leitrim it was over 11 in 1,000, making the severity of Ireland's mental health problem unique. Many should not have been in institutions, or were detained far too long. The 19 district mental hospitals had almost all been built between the 1820s and the 1860s, and most, but not all, were beginning to throw off their workhouse atmosphere.[144]

Some patients were being committed on the basis that they were 'persons of unsound mind' when they were no such thing, and there was a low percentage of voluntary admissions. In Michael Viney's view, 'the stigma historically attached to mental illness has taken longer to fade in Ireland than in most European countries', and he pointed out that the World Health Organisation in 1963 had drawn international attention to Ireland's extraordinary mental health statistics. Improvements were made in outpatient clinics for those suffering psychosis – the Irish language euphemised these individuals to 'Duine le Dia' ('one especially belonging to God') – but Viney also suggested that many rural GPs were still hostile to psychiatry, in comparison to the progressive attitudes of St Patrick's Institution in Dublin (which was private). While Britain had 82 psychiatric units in general hospitals, Ireland had none. The 2,000 mentally handicapped adults and children in the district mental hospitals were still being referred to as 'mental defectives', and there was still much to be done to challenge specifically Irish attitudes. Viney perceptively observed:

Indeed the preoccupation of other countries with matters of psychology and psychiatry is here often found rather comic or incomprehen-
sible, or regarded as symptoms of social failure in materialistic, pagan
or 'overcivilised' nations. Part of this attitude is a concealment of the
fear and suspicion which still surrounds in Ireland the topic of mental
illness. Part of it too, may result from a popular confusion of the roles
of priest and psychiatrist, in which the functions of one are held to be
a substitute for those of the other.[145]

In the same context, an unprecedented study published in 1961, *The Priest
and Mental Health*, suggested that seeing mental illness as a spiritual malaise was a 'facile aim to cross fertilise the priest and the psychiatrist.[146]

'moving around in clouds of alcoholic vapour'

There was also increased recognition given to the problem of alcoholism,
with the opening in 1961 of a special alcoholic unit at St John of God's
hospital in Dublin, and particular concern expressed about the growing
number of female alcoholics. While statistically Ireland's per capita alcohol consumption did not seem to indicate a heavy drinking nation, these
figures did not take into account the substantial membership of the Pioneer Association, which may suggest that those who drank were more
inclined to drink excessively. Figures supplied by the Central Statistics
Office to Seán Lemass in 1960 showed that in 1958 Ireland consumed per
head of population 64.3 litres of beer and 1.2 of spirits; figures for Britain
were 79.1 and 1.1 respectively.[147]

There was little official interest shown in attempting to estimate the
number of Irish alcoholics, the government preferring to focus its attention on drunken Irish stereotypes in the British media. Lemass noted that
'even the BBC rarely, if ever, presents a play about Ireland without the
characters moving around in clouds of alcoholic vapour'.[148] The assistant
medical director of St John of God's believed 70,000 alcoholics nationwide was a conservative estimate, and that the 785 alcoholic admissions
to hospitals in 1962 were but a tiny fraction of the real problem, and he
noted there were more women opting for voluntary admittance.[149] Alcoholic admissions formed about 5 per cent of all admissions to mental hospitals in 1962. The 1960s were a painful and challenging time for the
Pioneer Association, particularly as a result of the battle between those
who felt that the Pioneer method and message (life-long abstention in

devotion to the Sacred Heart) was overly simplistic and harsh in its depiction of the Irish drink problem and its solution. There was an acknowledgement that traditional propaganda was no longer appropriate given its tendency to depict drinker and abstainer as representing two extremes. Drinking continued unabated; between 1948 and 1970 consumption of alcohol rose by 60 per cent, with consumption increasing by a full litre per person in the years 1965–70.[150] The American journalist Donal Conery admitted the problem of alcoholism, but contended that 'the pub is a booby-trap for anyone trying to take a true measure of Irish life ... there are far more homes than pubs in Ireland and it is in the homes that one must look for the Irish man as he is most of the time.'[151] Nonetheless, recognition of excessive drinking as a health issue was finally hitting home, and in November 1966 the Minister for Health announced the establishment of an Irish National Council on Alcoholism, headed, notably, by a reformed alcoholic. From 1960 to 1967 admissions to psychiatric hospitals for drink-related illnesses rose from 404 to 2,015, and by the end of the decade, despite the existence of nearly 2,700 Pioneer centres, there were about 800,000 drinkers in the Republic, who spent £80 million a year on alcohol.

'the typical vices of the underprivileged'

The sheer range of inquiries and commissions into areas of Irish life that had been neglected, or individuals who had been traditionally ignored, was a crucial feature of Irish social discourse and activism in the 1960s. Ireland's travelling community was one such group, about which strong prejudice and hostility had existed. The deliberations of the government-appointed Commission on Itinerancy began in 1960 and they reported in 1963 at a time when there were about 1,100 travelling families. Attempts to settle them were often thwarted by the protests of local residents and the adoption by local councillors of popular racist rhetoric. The Commission had made much of their visit to the Netherlands, where the traveller population was 20,000 and was provided with accommodation facilities and education.

The report suggested the real solution lay in coaxing the travellers into becoming settled; one of the more worrying findings was that more than 1,600 itinerant children between the ages of six and 14 received no education. The report provided little insight into the plight of the female travellers, partly because only one woman was appointed to the

Commission, and travellers themselves did not give any evidence. Travellers were also subjected to police harassment; in 1965 two farmer's sons were sentenced to two years in prison after being convicted of the manslaughter of a traveller, while in the same year a traveller was sentenced to seven years for assaulting someone in a street brawl.[152] In 1961 the *Irish Times* had summed up the beliefs and prejudices of most, and in refusing to acknowledge the legitimacy of the travelling lifestyle suggested:

> Nobody will claim that tinkers as a class are more sinned against than sinning, but their vices are the typical vices of the underprivileged – petty thieving, trespassing, begging, brawling, committing nuisance of various kinds. There is no reason to doubt that, given a better life, these would not largely disappear.[153]

Health reform was not as politically contentious as it had been in the 1940s and 1950s, although younger social activists were becoming impatient with what they saw as an over-emphasis on conservatism and means testing, and the tendency to identify the concept of the welfare state with socialism rather than welfare capitalism. In 1964, 110,000 people received the means-tested non-contributory old age pension of £1 17s 6d a week, regarded by the social-policy academic Anthony Coughlan as 'ludicrously low', given the fact that the UK national assistance rate was over double that rate and included a rent allowance. Irish governments were still spending a lower proportion of money on social-security payments than other countries in Western Europe, while the health services remained tiered according to class and income.

Significantly, Coughlan also suggested that the local authority means test determining entitlement to hospital care was not uniform throughout the country, and questioned whether local authority areas were the best administrative units in which to organise a hospital service.[154] In terms of community welfare, it was also surprising that so many social science graduates of University College Dublin and Trinity College Dublin were going to work in Britain; of the 17 who qualified in UCD in 1962 only four were employed in Dublin.[155] The 1960s did not herald a brand new liberal dawn when it came to health services; a 1966 white paper on the health services, as Ruth Barrington pointed out, reaffirmed the government's opposition to the idea of the state providing medical services free of cost to all sections of the community. What was proposed was a choice of doctor in the general medical service and a commitment to further centralise the health services through the creation of regional health boards, effectively answering Coughlan's criticisms of the local authority units as inappropriate for the administration of the health services. From 1960 to 1966 the costs of health administration had doubled from £16.6 million to over £30 million, rising to £47 million for the year 1968/9.[156] Local rates were not sufficient to meet these expenses, and the cost of health services was not equally distributed between the different health authorities.

The replacement of the dispensary system with a choice of doctor was important, the *Irish Press* asserted, in helping to counteract the 'hangover of nineteenth-century Poor Law attitudes'. The imposition of the new changes was free from the kind of political and ideological conflict of former years, which had much to do with the fact that the bishops and medical profession (crucially, the doctors were now involved in administration) were largely singing from the same hymn sheet. Health authorities were being offered relief in the rates in order to surrender their authority, though this was temporary, and there was controversy towards the end of the 1960s about striking a rate for health charges, which led to the dismissal of Dublin city council in 1969.[157]

'a dark stain on the national conscience'
There was also a much more realistic investigation into the failures of the Irish education system and an acknowledgement of the sheer volume of progress that was required, which was revealed by the OECD-sponsored *Investment in Education* report in 1966. This came after certain improvements had been made in terms of access. In 1961 the scholarship system was extended, and in 1964 state capital grants for secondary schools were introduced, as were state-funded comprehensive schools, along with special schools for the blind and those suffering from mental handicap. A common intermediate course was introduced in 1966. State subsidies for the upkeep of national schools were also introduced, as were posts of responsibility for national teachers and a reduction in the number of very large classes. As a result, thousands of Irish children were receiving a high standard of education, and the innovations revealed Patrick Hillery as a reforming and effective Minister for Education between 1959 and 1965, one who 'brought co-ordination of provision and extension of educational opportunity'. He also initiated a modified scholarship scheme for third-level education, appointed the Commission on Higher Education and

initiated the *Investment in Education* study in 1962.[158] In 1964 only 36 per cent of 16-year-olds and 14 per cent of 18-year-olds were in full-time education. The report revealed as well the extent to which class determined access to education: 46.5 per cent of children of professional people aged 15–19 were in full-time education in 1961 but less than 10 per cent of the children of semi-skilled and unskilled workers. A new emphasis on educational inequality was backed up by increased research in psychology and sociology. *Investment in Education* also revealed that of those who did honours leaving certificates in 1963, 43 per cent of boys but only 19 per cent of girls went on to university.

The new young minister for education, Donogh O'Malley, caused a huge stir (not least among the ministers in his own cabinet, who had seen no costings) by announcing the introduction of free secondary education in 1966. He was also in a hurry to steal a march on Fine Gael, who were working on their own plans for education.[159] The Department of Finance was astonished that such a major change in education policy was announced at a weekend seminar of the National Union of Journalists. Lemass rather mildly rebuked O'Malley (and repeated the Department of Finance's warning that there was no guarantee of extra money), but was indulgent of him, perhaps impressed by his fresh idealism. Relatively unrepentant, O'Malley wrote to him: 'I believe that it is essential for a government from time to time to propound bold new policies which both catch the imagination of the people and respond to some widespread, if not clearly formulated, demand on their part.'[160]

O'Malley had also been prompted to act by UNESCO figures which revealed that in the Republic 36 per cent of children aged 14–19 were at secondary and technical schools, half the rate of some other European countries and, indeed, well behind that of Northern Ireland. As he put it:

> Every year, some 17,000 of our children finishing their primary schools course do not receive any further education. This means that almost one in three of our future citizens are cut off at this stage from the opportunities of learning a skill and denied the benefits of cultural development that go with further education. This is a dark stain on the national conscience, for it means that some one third of our people have been condemned – the great majority through no fault of their own – to be part educated unskilled labour, always the weaker who go to the wall of unemployment or emigration.[161]

What would remain contentious in this context, however, was whether or not the changes introduced actually facilitated social mobility in practice, or just consolidated the advantages of the middle classes.

Debates about education also drew attention to the sorry state of many national schools; the number over 50 years old in 1968 stood at 1,913,[162] and 45 per cent of the school buildings dated from the nineteenth century. There was a very high teacher–pupil ratio; by 1971, 35 per cent of pupils were still in classes of more than 40, two thirds being one- or two-teacher schools, over 200 of which did not have basic sanitary facilities.[163] A concentrated push was made to decrease the number of one- and two-teacher schools, and a beginning was made to upgrade the school curriculum. This was needed to provide children with outlets for their creativity and counteract the idea prevalent in the 1954 Council of Education report on primary education that a child was born in a state of sin.[164] While certain elements of the attitude that the school was subsidiary to the family and the Church survived, Vatican II reforms and a questioning of traditional Church control also impinged on the education debate. In 1968 an article in *Studies* by Seán O'Connor suggested the Church should be partners rather than masters, and stressed the need for decentralisation and shared decision-making. This confirmed the Church's fear that growing secularisation was leading to a sinister denigrating of the role played by the clergy in education.[165]

'Spur him on with that report'

There were 12,132 full-time students in Irish universities in 1964, four years after a commission on higher education had been established, although its bulky report did not appear until 1967. The waiting became something of a joke in university circles, prompting O'Malley to write to Lemass in 1966 concerning Chief Justice Cearbháll Ó Dálaigh, who chaired the commission: 'Spur him on with that report. The Australian university commission were given three months to report and did so in that time. Granted they had not our problems – but still ...'[166] The problems he alluded to included overcrowding, lack of resources (George Colley in 1966 had predicted a 'financial crisis within a year or two in the universities') and a staff appointments procedure that was inhibiting applications. There was also a growing demand for regional universities and a preoccupation with the intricacies of university politics, which, according to Joe Lee, 'were more eagerly addressed than the national condition'.[167] There was an almost complete absence of working-class students in universities. Also controversial, but ultimately unsuccessful, was the suggested merger of Trinity College Dublin and University College Dublin. The logic of this, as enunciated by the Minister for Education in April 1967, was that in the capital city there were two separate and differently constituted university institutions, both ploughing separate furrows with no formal or informal co-ordination of their efforts or sharing of resources: 'Why, for instance, should the state have to pay University College Dublin £160,000 annually and Trinity College £86,000 annually towards the support of 2 distinct veterinary faculties, when these 2 faculties annually produce about 45 and 10 veterinary graduates respectively?'[168] The proposal came to nothing, winning little support in the university sector, and O'Malley's premature death in 1968 also impeded any chance of change.

Students, too, made their dissatisfaction with the administration of universities known, though not with the same passion or militancy as some of their European counterparts. What became known as the 'Gentle Revolution' in UCD in the late 1960s was nothing of the sort, or in the words of one of the participants, the journalist Kevin Myers, 'gentle it was, revolution it was not'. Any radicalism was drowned out by moderates and by the ideological failure to link the discontent to a wider class critique of Irish society. Students for Democratic Action represented only a small minority of the students, and there was little intellectual lead given from the staff. Myers concluded that 'the majority of the teaching staff in UCD are as unaware of ideology as are the majority of the students'.[169] But the introduction of third-level student grants by the end of the 1960s, 'grudging and ungenerous though they might be', altered somewhat the social composition of colleges like University College Cork, with a shift within the 'middle-class' student body, from the offspring of propertied and professional families 'to those of a new urban middle-class'.[170] Because of the relatively small student grants, most Irish students lived modestly, in comparison to some of their European counterparts. A student at UCD in the 1960s remembered 'how much we envied English students who were here on grants and lived like Pashas in splendid flats with their own bathrooms. Irish students for the most part when they had to rent rooms lived in bedsits and queued for the one bathroom on draughty landings.'[171]

'Is fearr leathbhairín ná bheith gan arán'
The Irish language once again came under the microscope, examined both

by those with an interest in trying to revitalise its use and those tired of
the insistence on compulsion, or what they felt was a tiresome effort to
flog a dead horse. The problems of the Gaeltacht were given an airing by
the government white paper on the restoration of the Irish language in
1965, which for some was the beginning of a new crusade to 'save' the language. For writers like David Thornley, the idea that Ireland faced national
extinction through neglect of the language was a gross exaggeration; and
he suggested it was better to leave well enough alone on the basis that 'Is
fearr leathbhairín ná bheith gan arán' ('Half a loaf is better than no bread').
Gay Byrne, presenter of *The Late Late Show*, who chaired debates on virtually all the contentious topics in Irish society in the 1960s, found Irish
language activists among the most fanatical of any group in the country.[172]
Their frustration was a reaction to a public opinion that was in the main
indifferent, and unconcerned with the claims of activists about 'an imita-
tive insecurity and mediocrity in the face of British and North American
culture that is the direct result of language loss'.[173] The casual acceptance
of linguistic decline infuriated revivalists, who castigated the view that 'a
distinctive language has no real significance, other than aesthetic, in the
life of the community whose form of speech it is and that such a language
can be abandoned with impunity'.

By the mid-1960s Fianna Fáil's approach to the language was to
encourage people to use it freely, even if ungrammatically, but the failure to revive the language through the education system was patently
clear by the 1960s, as was the failure to encourage the use of spoken
Irish outside of the schools. There was criticism too of it being a compulsory part of civil service entry requirements. The 1969 Devlin report
on the civil service suggested it was leading to recruitment difficulties,
and a reason why private industry was attracting more highly qualified
personnel. In 1959 it had been estimated that only 14 per cent of all
public-service employees were fluent in Irish, and the idea that more
weight was being attached to linguistic rather than other qualifications
seemed ludicrous in some areas of public service. Meanwhile, the Irish
National Teachers' Organisation was calling for a reduction of the time
spent on teaching the language. But the 1960s also witnessed advances
in debates on the methods of teaching Irish, with an effort being
made to develop scientific teaching methods. The issue also permeated
party politics, with the Labour Party in 1963 criticising the approach
that made learning Irish a form of 'grammatical drudgery'. Fine Gael, in

making it clear they would abolish compulsory Irish in schools, called for a recognition that previous policies had been inimical to the educational development of the child. A commission to enquire into the use of Irish in schools suggested those 'who condition the mind of a child by constantly associating the adjective "compulsory" with Irish' were doing a disservice. In 1967, the government publications office produced Buntús Cainte ('rudiments of speech'), the first multi-media graded course in Irish for beginners, based on books, audio tapes, and radio and television series.[174] Although it was undoubtedly the case that some Irish students became bilingual, and many had a reasonable command of Irish, Adrian Kelly suggested the *Investment in Education* report 'showed what limited use was being made of Irish as a teaching medium'; of the 4,550 schools outside of the Gaeltacht areas, only 135 used Irish as the medium of instruction.[175]

Critics of the neglect of the economically depressed Gaeltacht regions occasionally wondered aloud why there seemed to be more interest in preserving the language than in the social and economic well-being of the people. Perhaps one of the reasons why the language groups became so quarrelsome was because opposition to the methods of the revival was simplistically presented as opposition to the concept of revival or indeed the language itself. In 1966 some Irish authors and other activists went on a seven-day hunger strike to focus attention on the issue. There was no such silent dignity attached to a meeting of the Language Freedom Movement, a group advocating greater choice and less emphasis on compulsion, when they met in the Mansion House in the same year. They were attacked by militant revivalists. The following day, the *Irish Times* reported the scenes:

> As John B. Keane rose to speak, a man in the front of the audience jumped on the stage and seized the tricolour, shouting that it should not be displayed at a meeting of this kind … a struggle ensued … jeers from hecklers, bursts of applause and derisive shouts continued to interrupt the speakers … small Union Jacks were waved in confusing profusion, and at one point as if at a given signal, a large Union Jack surrounded by smaller duplicates was raised, with derisive shouts of 'Judas! Speak Irish!'[176]

'take the whine out of their voice'

There was much cultural upheaval in other areas also, particularly after the arrival of television in Ireland in 1961. It was estimated that by the late

1950s British television broadcasts were available to 40 per cent of the population in the Republic, which was reason enough for an Irish version as far as cultural nationalists were concerned. There were warnings about the potential for decadence and moral corruption in television content, though politicians became more concerned with the idea that they could be called to account by truculent interviewers. Lemass suggested broadcasters should 'take the whine out of their voice' and avoid the 'God help us' approach to social issues. This was indicative of the government's view, later articulated by Lemass in 1966, that the state broadcaster should not be, 'either generally or in regards to its current affairs and news programmes, completely independent of government supervision'.[177]

The result was that the broadcasting authority was not allowed the autonomy it hoped for. Conflict with the government in this regard was inevitable, as witnessed by rows over how politicians and interest groups were presented, and RTÉ television crews were also prevented from travelling to political hotspots such as Vietnam and Africa. Given this interference, and a sometimes censorious approach to current affairs, or, as the *Irish Times* put it, 'the sheer craven fear that the speaker of home truths in public will suffer for it privately', it was perhaps unsurprising that there was an undue emphasis on less serious television.[178] In this context it was significant that what began as a light talk show, *The Late Late Show*, became the surprise facilitator of questioning of accepted political and social orthodoxies, its live format adding to its uniqueness (it went on to become the longest-running chat show in the world). The novelist Colm Tóibín suggested that, without it, it would have been possible for people to have lived and died in twentieth-century Ireland without ever having heard any discussion of sex.[179]

'they get into bed, they embrace, and you cut'

But it is important to recognise that it was not foisting these subjects on the Irish people. As its host, Gay Byrne, honestly admitted, the producers could not impose discussion on a society that was not ready for it.[180] Irish society, it seemed, was ready to talk about what Christabel Bielenberg referred to as 'tragedies lurking beneath the surface of such a rigid regime', and when they surfaced they were manifold, intriguing, sometimes tragic and often funny, but ultimately issues that all had an interest in, and thus both presenters and guests were emboldened. The fact that so many priests became telegenic was significant too.

Other programmes, particularly urban and rural dramas, were also exploring the family unit and the position of women as well as pioneering an approach to outdoor location work. They avoided romanticism and sentimentality, and once again exposed myths by shedding light on aspects of the Irish psyche, or, in the words of Luke Gibbons, 'by disengaging the family from the cycle of inhibition, authority and conservatism in which it had been traditionally enclosed'.[181] But the overall reliance on imported programmes was not only a commercial inevitability for a small state broadcaster; it was also the case that, as John Horgan pointed out, the appetite for Anglo-American culture remained undiminished: 'the Irish mass audience for television has never found it difficult to combine a deeply rooted and at times even visceral republicanism with a deep fascination with the activities of the House of Windsor'.[182] Irish filmmakers also tackled the legacy of independence, the Church's attitude to contraception and sexual promiscuity, as seen in *Paddy* (1969), adapted by the Irish writer Lee Dunne from his novel *Goodbye to the Hill* (1965). The film was banned in Ireland. Dunne recalled:

> There was a scene of Maureen Toal getting into bed with Des Cave, an Irish actress and an Irish guy. They're going to make love; they get into bed, they embrace, and you cut. The film was banned. There was nothing else … this was just a picture about a kid who was scared and hungry and frightened and promiscuous and just looking for someone to be warm and this woman who had a need.[183]

'My mother hates skirts, but doesn't everybody's mother?'

An embracing of foreign culture was reflected in the showband craze that reached Ireland in the 1960s. Touring was essential for these bands, and new audiences were guaranteed owing to increased social mobility. The home parish was no longer regarded as the only unit in which entertainment could be sought or procured. The first of the big Irish showbands, the Clipper Carlton, were playing an average of 240 nights a year by 1963; soon there were over 450 ballrooms nationwide and they became an industry employing 10,000 people, including 4,000 singers and musicians. They also created huge opportunities for a new generation of businessmen and impresarios such as Albert Reynolds (a future Taoiseach), Jim Aiken, Oliver Barry and Noel Pearson, who became 'architects of a minor social revolution' according to the historian of the showbands, though certain signs of decline were evident by the mid-1960s, with discos with alcohol licences proving more appealing. The broadcaster Gay Byrne was frank about the reasons for the decline:

> In fact, people were going to grotty, dirty, filthy ballrooms around the country with no amenities at all and, by and large, listening to fairly indifferent musicians banging out their few chords. But we were all young, vigorous, in love or on the hunt, or whatever, and all this has an effect when you look back. The ballroom people were so short-sighted they didn't realise they would have to improve their surroundings ... people got a bit more sophisticated and time caught up with the ballroom owners.[184]

Women in particular became disenchanted with the 'cattle market environment' of the dances. A female student at University College Dublin remembered her contemporaries' preoccupation with not just cinema and politics, but also with fashion, which 'changed enormously as we started out dressed like young ladies in tweed and sensible shoes but ended up in boots and mini skirts hoping we would look like Julie Christie'.[185] The feminist June Levine, in her acclaimed *Sisters*, recalled the obsession with new hair styles and skirts; her contemporary, the journalist Mary Kenny, remarked: 'My mother hates skirts, but doesn't everybody's mother? ... It's worse for her when I come home with a ladder in my stocking and she knows I've been seen like that, maybe in Grafton Street, for heaven's sake.'[186]

'Puritan Ireland's dead and gone'

Songwriting and originality had not been necessary for the ballroom industry to thrive, as the showbands were not performing Irish music. Indeed, the lack of attention to a creative Irish music sector was frustrating many in the 1960s. Until the 1950s the Royal Irish Academy of Music was receiving only a miserly £350 a year in grants from the government, with composers frustrated by the assumption that the works of an Irish composer would always be the arrangement of an Irish air. Trying to wed the European and Irish musical traditions was difficult. Seán Ó Ríada, influenced initially by European modernism, developed a heightened awareness of Irish music and its potential, and he became the best-known composer of his generation, by using traditional instrumentalists with novel arrangements of the native repertory. His music for film was also hugely popular and he gave a start to traditional Irish musicians whose arrangements became popular all over the world for the rest of the century.

In 1967 the Dubliners folk band delighted British audiences with their rendition of 'Seven Drunken Nights', and the Clancy Brothers became worldwide bestsellers, though the purists warned of the danger of failing to distinguish between what was popular and what was traditional. A number of European singers got their first international opportunities in Wexford at the annual opera festival, while the RTÉ orchestra was of a high standard. Dublin in the 1960s had a varied range and high standard of public music performance; the folk singing of Luke Kelly, a member of the Dubliners, was unparalleled in its intensity and beauty.

Summer musical festivals, in the form of the Fleadh Cheoil ('festivals of music'), were hugely popular and liberating for the hordes of youngsters who revelled in their version of Woodstock. The poet John Montague, in 'The Siege of Mullingar', captured the sense of rebelliousness and excitement:

At the Fleadh Cheoil in Mullingar there were two sounds
the breaking of glass and the background pulse of music
Young girls roamed the streets with eager faces shoving for men
Bottles in hand, they rowed out a song
Puritan Ireland's dead and gone, a myth of O'Connor and
O'Faoláin.[187]

The screams of teenagers, and occasionally adults, deafened Dublin with the arrival of the Beatles for a concert in 1963, followed two years later by the Rolling Stones. Regarding the latter, the *Irish Times* reported on its front page: 'The Rolling Stones, travelling much the same ground as the Beatles nearly two years ago, last night gyrated through two shows in the Adelphi Cinema, Dublin and left thousands of youngsters hoarse, exhausted and very bruised ... just like the Beatles' "concerts" it was impossible to hear their songs.'[188] But by the end of the decade every note of the Beatles was being savoured. Peter Sheridan, in his book *44: A Dublin Memoir*, memorably described the arrival of the album *Sergeant Pepper*:

The needle hit the groove and made its way towards track one, side one. It was straight into an urgent guitar solo and vocals that felt like they'd always existed. Had we heard these words in another existence before we were born? ... This wasn't a record, it was an experience from another world. The second track followed without a break, just like a symphony. A continuous stream of music with everything related to what went before and what came after. This was better than a symphony. Better than Mozart, Beethoven and Brahms. Better than Handel and his *Messiah*.[189]

'the rule is a mockery'

The Gaelic Athletic Association continued to thrive, retaining its status as Ireland's most successful sporting organisation. The prediction of the *Limerick Rural Survey*, published in 1964, that the passionate attachment to hurling would die out because an individualistic urban approach to leisure would pervade rural areas was proved spectacularly wrong, as it simplified and sanitised the tribalism, loyalty and commitment to parish and county sport, which the survey clinically analysed as an insecure and immature psychological need. But the 1960s did see the emergence of controversy surrounding the GAA ban on foreign sports, as a campaign by the persistent and courageous Tom Woulfe of the Civil Service Football Club led to an intense debate in the media and the GAA. In 1962, J. D. Hickey, the leading sportswriter of his day, was adamant that 'in many places – and they are not all in Dublin – the rule is more honoured in the breach than in the observance – as matters stand, the rule is a mockery rather than a cornerstone of the association. All over the country the rules are openly flouted.'[190]

The activities of vigilance committees, particularly now that television meant 'foreign games' were being widely watched, but could not be attended, also ensured, in Woulfe's words, that the ban was 'a dead letter'. RTÉ coverage of the 1966 World Cup guaranteed further interest in soccer. There was strong opposition from traditional GAA supporters to the dropping of the ban, but its eventual removal in 1971 perhaps meant, in the words of Paul Rouse, that most now saw the GAA 'not in terms of an Irish-Ireland body, but rather as a purely sporting organisation'.[191] Donogh O'Malley, who did not live to see the ban rescinded, was defiant in opening a rugby pavilion in January 1968 and expressed the view of many of his generation when he contended that 'rugby and soccer people were sick and tired of having the finger pointed at them as if they were any worse Irishmen for playing these games. When Ireland was asked for sons to call to the colours we were there and were not asked what shape of a ball we used.'[192]

'nothing here soon but Scobers, tinkers and tourists'

Embarking on a career in public life in the mid-1960s, Garret FitzGerald was perplexed by what he saw as 'the strong anti-cultural bias of a large part of the community'.[193] This was shortly after the Professor of Psychology in University College Dublin, E. F. O'Doherty, suggested that Ireland was going through 'a deep and far-reaching cultural revolution', with a consequent need to examine 'the social institutions, beliefs, practices and taboos in our midst', in order to establish which could be preserved and which altered. Such an assertion may be deemed too sweeping, but it is fair to suggest that Irish writers were playing their role in a new critical evaluation, even if it was not quite revolutionary. Perhaps the more mundane truth was that it was a growing awareness and acceptance of materialism that was outweighing attachment to tradition. In this sense, many of the changes reflected in government policy, institutional entities and indeed creative writing were reflecting the choices which ordinary Irish people were making.[194]

Certain writers in the early 1960s, encouraged by a huge increase in paperback publishing, were upbeat. John Montague and the poet Thomas Kinsella, for example, in a book published by Liam Miller's Dolmen Press which did much to promote new poetry, suggested emerging Irish writers were the most interesting since the realists of the 1930s. This reflected a change of sensibility and a more experimental form of writing, with authors like Brian Moore, John McGahern and James Plunkett avoiding a particular form of Irishism, 'whether leprechaun or garrulous rebel'.[195] In 1962, Seán O'Faoláin touched on the same theme by suggesting Irish writers could no longer continue to write about Ireland 'within the narrow confines of the traditional Irish-life concept', urging them not to perish as regionalists, but to take the local and universalise it.[196] This was done by the playwright Tom Murphy in his depiction of the tensions of small-town life and its personalities; an angry confrontation between a young man and a society he found full of inertia, but also, crucially, the theatrical tradition he found equally disappointing.

Eugene McCabe's first play, *King of the Castle*, which won the Irish Life award at the Dublin Theatre Festival in 1964, broke new ground by containing an on-stage rape scene. But the play was also about the greedy machinations of the sexually impotent character Scober, the native who acquires a mansion. The play reflected 'a countryside embittered by change' and anger at the failure to redistribute possessions: 'Combines, groups and the co-ops ... all for Scober and the go-go men and we're the corn they'll fatten on, we're the chaff they'll blow to Birmingham, for good if they get their way. There'll be nothing here soon but Scobers, tinkers and tourists.'[197] Although the Dublin Theatre Festival held out some hope and amateur drama was thriving, Irish theatre as a whole was not in a healthy state, because of its attachment to outmoded traditions and the dramatists and plays of a different era. The question remained, according to the critic T. P. O'Mahony, why the conditions of modern Ireland were not being explored theatrically: 'Where are the writers? And where are the plays relevant to contemporary Ireland?'[198]

'both halves of the book should be sent in separate brown envelopes'

Brian Friel's *Philadelphia Here I Come* had caused something of a stir in 1964, displaying a distinct ambivalence towards tradition; seemingly adapting the norms of the Abbey kitchen comedy of the 1950s, it in fact subjected the form to a modern interrogation, and examined tensions between different generations and other aspects of social, political and cultural change. Friel was also to satirise the idea that tourism was the only salvation of rural Ireland in the *Mundy Scheme*, presenting Ireland as a retirement commune for European industrialists. Edna O'Brien not only portrayed traditional male pillars of Irish society with a new subtlety and bite, but also, according to Declan Kiberd: 'the unerring accuracy of her eye and the deft rightness of her phrase convinced many that there were believable, fallible, flesh and blood women; neither paragons nor caricatures.'[199] John McGahern, too, wrote powerfully of the generation that had grown up in an oppressed rural Ireland.

Both O'Brien and McGahern were duly banned, reaffirming that those intent on making the writer a social pariah had at least a few gasps left. A bookseller from Galway wrote to McGahern's publishers with an order for *The Dark*, insisting that 'the dust jacket be torn off and discarded; that the book then be torn in half and that both halves of the book should be sent in separate brown envelopes'.[200] McGahern was to retain his interest in the family unit and the notion that nothing could be changed within it; while for others, like William Trevor, exile, and writing books that had nothing to do with Ireland, remained the more attractive option. In 1962, Frank O'Connor, at a debate in Trinity College Dublin, opposed Justice Kevin Haugh, then chairman of the Censorship Appeals Board, on a motion that 'Irish censorship is insulting to Irish intelligence'. O'Connor's winning contribution was anecdotal and devoid of the bitterness that had characterised the censorship debate 20 years previously, but he asserted that it was still a significant threat to artistic and personal liberty, particularly the invidious manner in which it was imposed: 'I don't want to depend for protection on any individual, whatever his taste and judgement. As a citizen of this country I want to depend for protection on the Constitution and the courts.'[201] There was still a personal price to pay for the censored writer. Edna O'Brien protested strongly against censorship, speaking at public meetings, bringing her books into the South across the border from Northern Ireland, and she encountered such hostility from her own community that some of her books were 'burned in the chapel grounds'. She was in no doubt such books as *Girls in Their Married Bliss* (1964) were banned because people were disturbed by her treatment of women and because she refused to yield, in her own words, to 'codology ... that sort of colleen image, being very pretty and unblemished, sitting at the hearth ... I admitted their sexuality and unhappy married life – a young girl yearning and, indeed, eventually having sex with a much older married man.'[202]

In 1967, however, greater liberalisation prevailed regarding censorship, when Brian Lenihan introduced a bill limiting the period for which a book could be banned as indecent or obscene to 12 years, with the consequent automatic unbanning of several thousand titles. Charles Haughey also introduced tax exemption for artists, a unique measure in state financial policy, while the Irish Arts Council strove to develop an effective appreciation of art, including sponsoring a Picasso exhibition at Trinity College Dublin, about which the lack of controversy reflected a new maturity. The opening of a new wing in the National Gallery in 1968 suggested there was much to nourish the visual imagination. In the eyes of its critics, the Arts Council remained a small and exclusive body that did not do enough to support small independent projects. According to its director, Donal O'Sullivan, in 1969, internationally Ireland was still in an artistic backwater.[203]

Newspapers responded more quickly to societal change. Douglas Gageby, appointed editor of the *Irish Times* in 1963, realised that the paper could become more 'than the voice of an embattled minority', and attempted to expand the paper's remit, recognising the importance of women, the younger generation and 'a more independent-minded Catholicism'. It also facilitated a more irreverent coverage of politics and became the first Dublin paper to have a full-time office in Belfast and employed a number of talented female journalists.[204] The *Irish Press* also employed many able young journalists such as Tim Pat Coogan and Brian Inglis, and enjoyed huge success with the *Sunday Press*, which by the early 1960s had a circulation of over 400,000.[205]

'15 *in House. 6 years on list*'

Poverty was the reason for much of the social and political upheaval in Northern Ireland in the 1960s. When the prominent Derry journalist Nell McCafferty published a collection of her writings in 1985, she dedicated her work to Bridget Bond from Derry city, 'who started the fight for civil rights, when it was neither fashionable nor popular'.[206] It was appropriate that McCafferty, a pioneer in the art of eyewitness-style journalism who looked closely at the vulnerable and poor in Irish society, North and South, recognised that this was precisely what Bond had been doing in the late 1960s.

It was also appropriate because it was often left to women to initiate demands for social change, and it was women who were to the forefront in organising the community networks that became so important in the 1960s and 1970s. A group of women activists published *Picking Up the Pieces* in 1983, and recalled the growing suburbanisation of Belfast; the plans to 'put cars before people' by placing link roads through inner city areas, destroying supportive social networks. The solution was deemed to lie in building flats; an expensive and destructive mistake, which carved up local communities. It was primarily the women who fought back. The authors of *Picking Up the Pieces* posed the question:

> Why did women take on this role, particularly in a society where men had always been traditionally associated with action? Logically it was the women who had to deal with the realities of disintegrating communities. In the 1970s women formed the backbone of most community action right across Northern Ireland, because problems in local areas were clearly affecting these women's lives and those of their children. Women had been brought up to see the home and the family as their

primary responsibility, and the survival of these was being threatened increasingly by the state. It is paradoxical really, that our society should seek to keep women passive, yet by threatening the basis of that passivity, the society provokes action from the same women.[207]

Women were also prominent in campaigning against religious discrimination in the allocation of public-sector housing, in the early 1960s, their protests being central to the establishment of the Northern Ireland Civil Rights Association. The historian Catherine Shannon pointed out that 'a glaring example of Northern women being written out of the history of the Northern Irish Troubles is the failure of most historical accounts to mention that the very first protests against discriminatory housing policies by Unionist dominated local government councils were initiated by women'.[208]

As evidenced by her archival collection in the Guildhall in Derry, Bridget Bond chronicled the poverty of Derry city, and the housing dilemmas of its Catholic population. Her case notebook on housing contains entries for the year 1967, the same year in which the Northern Ireland Civil Rights Association was born: '1967: 1 small room. 1 bed. 1 kitchen. 1 handicapped. Children always suffering from bad colds owing to dampness. Wife expecting fifth child and suffering with nerves and depression and husband afraid of something happening.' Another entry read: '15 in house. 6 years on list. 4 children living with Mother-in-law. 7 children. Eldest five years, youngest five weeks. 3 bedrooms. Boys 14 years sleeping in same room as girl of 19 years. Twins, boy and girl 8 years and boy, 12, sleeping with mother.'[209]

This was in the same county where in 1951 Catholics accounted for 43 per cent of the population, but fewer than 8 per cent of the non-manual government employees of Derry Corporation.[210] Nationalist councillors elected to the Corporation found themselves continually frustrated in their efforts to highlight the housing problem. They pointed to a total of only 302 houses built from 1959 to 1968, a number not even enough to house the number of new applicants for local-authority housing in a single year. There were 1,650 families homeless, with a marriage rate for Derry city of 400 per year, of whom 360 applied for houses each year. The council had been continually told of the housing crisis and the amount of homes unfit for human habitation, but appeals for special meetings to discuss the situation were refused throughout

1966, as were attempts to get more detailed progress reports. Perhaps it was symbolic that in 1961 the Corporation had refused permission to screen the film *Too Hot to Handle*.[211]

'emigration might prove the least expensive and least painful solution'

The concern with housing and unemployment was not exclusively Catholic; indeed, one of the main aims of the NICRA was to unite Catholic and Protestant, who shared many working-class grievances. But the pattern of investment in Northern Ireland had disproportionately adversely affected Catholic areas, and revealed institutional bias. Between 1963 and 1969 Brian Faulkner, as Minister for Commerce, persuaded 104 companies to invest in the province, but Catholic unemployment remained much higher west of the River Bann, and the retention of infrastructure in already prosperous unionist areas ensured any new industry was inevitably propelled in that direction. The result was that 70 per cent of Faulkner's new factories were located east of the Bann.[212] The traditional large employers were in decline: 8,000 shipyard workers were let go in 1961, while the linen industry, which employed 58,300 in 1949, was employing only 25,300 by 1968. This was a decade after Sir Roland Nugent had suggested: 'emigration might prove the least expensive and least painful solution to Ulster's economic difficulties'.[213]

'vastly different from that in Great Britain where there was a loyal opposition'

Labour in Northern Ireland did seem to be making serious headway in the early 1960s. The Northern Ireland Labour Party received 26 per cent of the vote and won 4 seats in the election of 1962. To a certain extent there was more awareness of the levels of inequity in Northern society. Maurice Hayes went as far as to suggest that:

> It was the very adoption of economic and social planning by [Terence] O'Neill and the use of the planner's tools of quantification, estimation, demographic forecasting and outcome measurement that exposed the conflicts latent in the society and began to impose strains which its members could not bear. Inequality could be fudged or ignored (as can poverty or social disadvantage or poor housing) so long as it was not quantified.[214]

But there was a much more pragmatic political reason for the emergence of 'O'Neillism' in the 1960s, after Captain Terence O'Neill had succeeded Lord Brookeborough as prime minister. It was an attempt to continue the same process of previous decades of keeping the diverse Protestant family united, in order to prevent the Labour Party from eating into the unionist votes, as it had done in the 1958 and 1962 Stormont elections. There was uncertainty over how far these efforts at unity could proceed. Partition was no longer a live political issue, but O'Neill knew, according to Patterson, 'that assimilatory policies that went beyond economic and social improvement were incompatible with the populist dynamics of the Unionist Party's electoral hegemony'.[215] In other words, there were many in the middle-class professional community who, while they may have accepted the need for a modicum of reform, rejected a fundamental reorganisation of the power bases of Northern Irish society. Thus the main worry of O'Neill's Unionist Party was losing the power to control events, hence, in Feargal Cochrane's words: 'a dominant dynamic of retrenchment, of getting back something that has been lost, or which soon will be'.[216] Eventually, O'Neill's resignation was forced by his inability to keep enough of his MPs on board.

A similar attitude had been displayed in May 1963, revealing the unionist preoccupation with controlling both media and political opposition. As with the system prevailing at Westminster, the *Belfast Telegraph* wanted access to parliamentary papers on a confidential basis, up to 48 hours in advance of official release. The Minister for Education opposed this on the basis that:

> the position in Northern Ireland was vastly different from that in Great Britain where there was a loyal opposition. It was certain that nationalist members received assistance in the preparation of their speeches from members of the press gallery and if the latter were to be briefed on the lines suggested the results would probably soon be reflected in speeches from the nationalist benches.[217]

This was a classic example of the articulation of a one-party state mentality. But it was also the case, as pointed out by Paul Bew, that a large segment of the Protestant working class did not necessarily examine local economic decline through an orange haze. Bew saw the opposition to O'Neillism as 'a backlash against a shift in the state machine towards more power for bureaucracy' and a 'presidential style of politics' along with an awareness that the acceptance of the shelving of regional problems could no longer be continued.[218]

'not an unmitigated pleasure to occupy the chair at the head of the cabinet table'

Academic studies had highlighted the lack of resilience in the economy and the archaic structure and narrow vision of local businesses, to the extent that questions were being raised as to their loyalty to the working classes. The new shift towards a focus on economic growth was partly in order to steal Labour's clothes. But once again, despite symbolic gestures suggesting a new direction, the real issue was to try and solve conflicts within the unionist 'bloc'. In November 1966, O'Neill wrote privately to Jack Lynch: 'no doubt you are already finding it is not an unmitigated pleasure to occupy the chair at the head of the cabinet table'. He was resentful at those who 'expose us to misunderstandings by the extravagance of their remarks'. But the truth was that there was virtually no strategy for reform in relation to civil rights and discrimination.[219] O'Neill specifically denied that when he spoke of a 'new Ulster' this meant the Ulster of Carson and Craig was dead, and his primary loyalty was to Britain and the British state.[220]

'the power which they were beginning to feel was real'

Nationalist politics in areas like Belfast employed occasional leftist rhetoric, but was factionalised and depended on personal following and brokerage. Nationalists did not necessarily have coherent opposition plans and were, according to Michael Farrell in *The Orange State*, overly grateful for O'Neill's gestures, and the increasing activity in 1968–9 did not by any means ensure unity. According to Bew, the ability to get the working classes protesting on the street had much to do with the traditional non-secular and territorial nature of demonstrations in Ulster.[221] This, however, may underestimate the sense of grievance outside the conservative leadership of nationalism, and the injection of youth into nationalist opposition campaigns, due to the fact that, according to Eamonn McCann, 'we came very early to our politics'.[222] McCann and others resented the traditional idea that nationalist candidates were anointed rather than selected, with a very real fear that it was somehow sinful not to vote for them in a city like Derry, where 80 per cent of the births were Catholic and 'children skipped to songs of cheerful hatred' and worshipped abstract heroes like de Valera with 'uncensorious fervour'. One of the reasons for the launch of the tiny Campaign for Social Justice in 1964 was a belief that the nationalist representatives were ineffectual in putting the minority's case. Thomas Hennessey points out that it differed from previous minority groups 'in that it focused its efforts on British public opinion' in relation to housing discrimination, local-authority corruption and prejudice in public employment.[223] While NICRA, launched in April 1967, had a constitution which set out its objectives – to defend the rights of the individual and freedom of speech, highlight abuses of power and inform the public of their lawful rights – it was composed of those who were looking both for revolutionary change and for gradual reform. They organised public protests in the summer of 1968, including a march in Dungannon opposing sectarian discrimination in the allocation of housing, which were well controlled and relatively peaceful. But on 5 October 1968 a civil rights march in Derry, which had been banned, went ahead, leading to large-scale rioting and confrontation with the RUC, with television coverage maximising the impact.

But while many nationalists may have feared the young activists' 'communist ideas', there were none who could defend Derry Corporation, the mayor of which was granting houses secretly to Protestants while the Catholic enclave was 'a teeming, crumbling area of ugly, tiny terrace houses'. The strategy, according to McCann, a native of Derry city and a senior member of People's Democracy, a radical students' group formed in 1968, was to provoke over-reaction and then channel the reaction to that, which of course scared the Nationalist Party. But they did not expect, he wrote, 'the animal brutality' of the RUC. The middle-class Derry Citizens' Action Group sought to take control, with John Hume at their head, but the emergence of the more radical Derry Citizens' Defence Association in 1969 reflected the different layers of nationalist opposition. O'Neill's promises of change – including reformed local government (in 1967 there were 909,842 voters on the parliamentary franchise, but only 694,483 voters on the local-government franchise[224]), a points system for the allocation of housing, the appointment of an ombudsman and a review of special powers legislation – rather than inviting closure, confirmed to the Catholic masses 'that the power which they were beginning to feel was real'.[225]

That was the crucial point about a community that for so long felt disenfranchised; people were applauding, not the leftist rhetoric, but the manner in which it was expressed; the feeling of liberation and the fact that the young unemployed had something to do. When the riots were temporarily stalled in 1969 they found they did not want a return to 'the anonymous depression which had hitherto been their constant condition'.[226]

'My God, we might be socialists'

It was significant of course that the civil-rights movement was not about a united Ireland, but about, as nationalist MP Gerry Fitt saw it, making the British government face up to the facts of discrimination and honour the rights of nationalists as citizens of the UK. Fitt had been a merchant navy seaman, as he often reminded the House of Commons. He recalled a party of nationalist Stormont MPs received by Roy Jenkins, Chancellor of the Exchequer in 1967. When an aide suggested to Jenkins something needed to be done, he reportedly replied that nothing would be done 'because any Englishman who set foot in Northern Ireland affairs would be setting a foot in his political grave', a comment heard, according to Fitt, by the *Observer* journalist Mary Holland, who chose to break the silence that pervaded the British media in relation to Northern Ireland at that time.

Fitt brought her to Derry to a civil-rights march, and what she saw filled her with outrage, anger and pity, as she phoned her story from a fish and chip shop in Duke Street, Derry, amidst water cannons and blood.[227] She went on to become one of the most perceptive commentators on the North, having been outraged at the sight of police batoning a Westminster MP, though Fitt was subsequently admonished for abusing his position as MP to bring attention to, if not invite, the violence in Derry.

An emphasis on British citizenship was essential. Bernadette Devlin, one of the leaders of People's Democracy, who helped to organise a controversial march in January 1969, maintained that the march, denounced by the mainstream leadership of the civil-rights movement who wanted O'Neill's reforms tested, was designed to relaunch the civil-rights movement as a mass movement, and to expose O'Neill, so as to 'pull the carpet off the floor and show the dirt that was under it'.[228] She maintained: 'If they're going to make us British by law, we must be British by standard of living as well', goading the police for 'disgracing Northern Ireland' though 'we still had the attitude "My God we might be socialists"'.[229] The sense of excitement, camaraderie and optimism is palpable from Devlin's account of the initial civil-rights marches (she who had found more politics in the folk music society at Queen's than in the political parties). Also striking is the speed with which violence and defiance took over ('Policemen always call me a stupid bitch and I deny that I'm stupid'). One Unionist MP described her memorably as 'Fidel Castro in a mini skirt', and neither Dublin nor London regarded her as an ideal role model.[230] In parallel with the turmoil in Derry, violence in Belfast worsened, and in the summer of 1969 some 1,820 families fled their homes, 1,505 of them Catholic, and it is estimated that 30 per cent of the city's Catholic population was displaced.[231]

'the same equality of treatment and freedom from discrimination'?

Tensions inevitably increased between socialists and more cautious nationalists over tactics. Devlin pointed to the degree to which leadership of the Civil Rights Association wanted 'majority rule in Catholic areas where they could be rulers' and the irony of 'Catholic slum landlords marching virtuously beside the tenants they exploited'. Her election to parliament caused a sensation in 1969, as she was the youngest female MP ever elected, but tensions abounded because in the peculiar circumstances of the election, she estimated that only one quarter of the voters believed in her policies, the others wishing her to be a model of Catholic respectability.[232] Many campaigners in the summer of 1969, the time the British army came on the streets, claimed that working-class interests were not represented by nationalist politicians, but all agreed on the importance of the media in bringing the civil-rights issue to a worldwide audience. There was also a belief that great opportunities were squandered in the late 1960s to make progress. Many rioters had, in the words of Gerry Adams, 'visions of boy martyrs uppermost' in their juvenile minds when experiencing their first riots in the mid-1960s, but also believed 'a few changes here and there and we'd all be happy'.[233]

That optimism was perhaps understandable, given Harold Wilson's Downing Street declaration of 1969 that 'every citizen of Northern Ireland is entitled to the same equality of treatment and freedom from discrimination as obtains in the rest of the UK, irrespective of political views or religion'. He went on to make it clear that the problems of Northern Ireland were an internal matter for the UK alone.

But such pious rhetoric did not reflect what civil-rights activists began to witness, and it was all the more jarring given that the unemployed action groups continually emphasised in Derry that 'no retaliation' should be offered in the face of persecution and that 'anyone joining our march with the express intention of using it to foment religious or sectarian strife is not welcome'.[234] Almost all their demands were strictly economic, including equal pay for women, a state-sponsored industry and a motorway linking Derry and Belfast, and as the Derry Housing Action Committee anniversary publication of 1968–9 put it, the need for 'equal earnings with British workers' and an end to 'local government puppets in John Bull's political slum'. But it was difficult to move away from a sectarian framework. One community activist recalled a nationalist councillor saying at council: 'For God's sake will somebody speak because I have been here for 11 years and I don't know the sound of a man's voice, I only know the colour of his hand when he raises it against me.'[235] A determination developed not to fulfil the unionist desire that the activists should accept O'Neill's proposed reforms and 'crawl back into their rat-infested Rachmanist flats'. In the same way they had demonstrated, with the success of the Derry Credit Union, that they could achieve control over their own financial affairs, they now wanted control over their political futures. In short, they did not want community associations to be taken over by politicians.

'It's the old handshake yet again'

Much of the attention focused on Dublin's attitude towards the outbreak of the Troubles has centred on the extent to which strong and decisive leadership was lacking. The evidence available does little to support the idea that Jack Lynch was in control of the situation, being caught between the opposing poles of the Fianna Fáil party: hard-line and emotional or cautious and realistic.[236] There had been positive developments in terms of North–South co-operation, including the freeing up of trade and cross-border tourism, Brian Faulkner suggesting in January 1966: 'I am not going down to Dublin on any begging mission, but I am very ready and anxious to talk to Dublin ... to accelerate the lowering of tariffs.'[237] The celebrated meeting of Lemass and O'Neill in the spring of 1965 was repeated in January 1968, when O'Neill travelled to Dublin; 'It's the old handshake yet again', was his rather weary comment.[238] But there was no wholehearted consensus between the Dublin government and the Northern Nationalist Party led by Eddie McAteer, who had adopted a policy of non-violent civil disobedience, and little attempt to understand the civil-rights issue; calling for 'wholesome community relations' was the rather meek response.

There was a low-key response also to loyalist attacks on the People's Democracy marches. When Lynch had met O'Neill in January 1968, for a lobster lunch at the Russell Hotel, McAteer pleaded for a meeting with Lynch in March 1968 'for public appearances sake', demanding the same reception as O'Neill and to be 'lunched' accordingly. He had to be satisfied with lunch in Leinster House and the humble main course of lamb.[239] Notes circulated by Frank Aiken in August 1969 suggested nationalist politics in the North had been 'weak, contradictory and unrealistic' and tellingly: 'the use of the term "our people" in the North can only be used in times of crisis, if at all'.[240] He commented on the need to tap into the desire of the 'several hundred thousand people' who would support moderate reform, in order to avoid the revival of the IRA and a 'rethinking of our unity policy'.

Neil Blaney, another cabinet minister, was already insisting that partition, having been imposed by Britain, could only be undone by Britain, to which a note attached to a file on North–South policy for the Taoiseach responded: 'It is much too naive to believe that Britain simply imposed it on Ireland.'[241] A certain hardening of stance was in evidence from the beginning of 1969, with O'Neill insisting he had met Lemass in 1965 to expose 'the grandiose and empty claims of Éire's constitution'. In December 1968 the British ambassador in Dublin had expressed concern that certain comments in the South could serve as a justification 'for the already-alleged intervention of extreme nationalist groups in the affairs of the North'.[242] Within nine months the *Sunday Independent* was suggesting that unity 'would cost us £100 million', which was one third of all tax revenue in the Republic. O'Neill was under increasing pressure from unionists, who believed that issues such as local-government reform were merely a cover 'for destabilising the state', and that support for civil-rights associations was not based on civil-rights grievances, but was a way to discredit unionists to the outside world. Such a view led to the resignation of Brian Faulkner from the cabinet. He wanted O'Neill to demonstrate explicitly that he would either resist reform or admit there were reforms which were necessary, instead of dithering and undermining confidence in the government. Eight days later, 12 Unionist MPs demanded O'Neill's removal in order to keep the party united.

The subsequent general election called by O'Neill split his party and was exploited by Ian Paisley's evangelical Protestant unionism. Thirty-nine Unionists were elected, 27 supporting O'Neill, 10 opposed and two undecided.[243] Two months later, an announcement that the Northern Ireland government would accept adult male suffrage in local elections prompted the resignation of James Chichester-Clark, Minister for Agriculture, and it was clear O'Neill's premiership was drawing to a close. He resigned on 28 April 1968, suggesting that the election had demonstrated that old prejudices were too strong for people 'to break out of the mould of sectarian politics once and for all'. He was succeeded by Chichester-Clark.

'unruly natives in a far-flung colony'

The IRA was hardly robust in the South in the 1960s, and the Chief of Staff of the organisation, Cathal Goulding, was arrested for possession of a pistol. The Gardaí had estimated IRA membership at 923 in 1965, up from 657 in 1962, with 3,339 Sinn Féin members. Internal security papers suggested 'occasions such as (a) the 1966 commemoration ceremonies, or (b) the Paisley sectarian riots, might serve as an excuse for the recommencement of a campaign of violence if the organisation were otherwise ready', with evidence they were inculcating 'a strong sense of military discipline' among their members. In the same year the Stormont Minister for Home Affairs said IRA activities were 'no longer a matter of concern'.[244]

In 1969, the Irish government was slow to monitor events in the North and to assess their significance, and though Aiken as Tánaiste stressed that caution and internal reform were the way forward, Lynch seemed to be temporarily siding with the hawks, in view of the Southern elections in June of that year. But the reality was that he was caught in the middle, not even being sure whether officially to 'regret' the resignation of O'Neill, that word being struck out in a draft statement, and he admitted to the British ambassador that he was 'subject to certain pressures' concerning his Northern policy. Aiken had rowed with the leader of the Conservative Party, Edward Heath, over Dublin intervention in the North, but the fact that Aiken retired at the 1969 election was a blow for moderation in the Dublin cabinet. Both Dublin and London remained reactive and hoped for too much, with the British Foreign Secretary using language in private that seemed to indicate, according to Michael Kennedy, that those at loggerheads in Derry 'were merely unruly natives in a far-flung colony'.[245] Meanwhile, the Irish government discussed options which included military involvement and the use of UN observers, and, more critically, the idea of Irish defence forces sending field hospitals to the border. Lynch asserted in his address to the nation that 'the Irish government can no longer stand by and see innocent people injured and perhaps worse', which was greeted with acclaim by Derry nationalists. But it was a speech that had been rewritten by the hardliners in the cabinet and it was that small group – Haughey, Boland and Blaney – who were, it seems, to the fore, defining policy while Lynch dithered. He sent Patrick Hillery, who replaced Aiken as Minister for Foreign Affairs, to London to seek agreement on the use of Irish and British armies as a joint force. Hillery was informed that John Hume had insisted, when in contact with the Foreign Office, that 'we must have British troops on the streets of Northern Ireland'.[246]

More controversial was the decision of the cabinet on 16 August to provide a sum of money, 'the amount and the channel of distribution of which would be determined by the Minister for Finance ... to provide aid for the victims of the current unrest'. The Minister for Finance, Charles Haughey, thus had sole control of the money. This came three days after a group of Northern republicans, including Paddy O'Hanlon and Patrick Kennedy, came to Dublin looking for arms. They had said: 'as regards guns, nothing need be done openly or politically – a few hundred rifles could easily be lost and would not be missed'.[247] Subsequently, the Public Accounts Committee investigating the 'Arms Crisis' could not trace this money. As the hawks seemed to dominate Lynch, Harold Wilson and the new Northern prime minister, Chichester-Clark, were in talks that would lead to the Downing Street Declaration and Lynch seemed more concerned with securing the 26 counties against violence, and being seen to encourage the involvement of the United States. In tandem with this, the Government Information Bureau worked as much as 'eighteen hours a day' to present its case on Northern Ireland to the world's press, with the secondment of about 20 senior public-relations executives from state bodies. It was a short-lived exercise, ending in November, and according to the *Irish Times* 'produced little'.[248]

A memorandum from the Department of the Taoiseach on 25 November 1969 suggested there was a danger of sinking back to the level of uninterest which had resulted in caustic remarks that 'our mass media and general public opinion here only "discovered" the six counties on the 5 October 1968'.[249] The desire to involve the UN was in a sense a distraction, since the Irish government knew that the UN approach would be to seek an Anglo-Irish solution. By September, Lynch was thus moving in a new direction, with peaceful reform, unity by consent and condemnation of force now the official line from the government. The problem for Lynch was that there were rumours circulating in the South that some government ministers were sending arms across the border, while in December Blaney was insisting the use of force in relation to Northern Ireland could not be ruled out. Whatever about London and Dublin pulling back from the brink through diplomatic channels, what was going on in Dublin behind the scenes was far from clear (see Chapter 8). But, in the words of Michael Kennedy, Dublin had finally, for the first time since 1925, been forced to take a real look over the border.[250]

EIGHT

1970–2000

I

'*By the beginning of* 1971 *they were being told by* 15-*year-olds to fuck off*'
The degree to which the British army was welcomed on to the streets of
Northern Ireland in the summer of 1969 has been contested, an indication that nationalists were unsure how the military presence would affect
the rising tensions in areas like Derry and Belfast. This was particularly
significant given the growing number of youths for whom, in the words of
Eamonn McCann: 'the Saturday riot became a regular thing. It was known
as the "Matinee". People did their shopping in the morning so as to get
home before the riot.' Tensions were exacerbated by the 1970 Criminal
Justice Act, allowing mandatory sentences of six months for disorderly
behaviour, and by the sneering attitude of the judiciary and counsel
towards the working classes, a recurrent theme over the next thirty years.
As regards the moderates, the young Trotskyist McCann noted that 'by
the beginning of 1971 they were being told by 15-year-olds to fuck off'.
But the radicals had little success in attempting to unite the left, and the
civil rights and protest groups were riven with divisions from the beginning.[1]

The Minute Book of the Derry Civil Rights Association reveals many
of the tensions between the disparate civil rights agitators. In February

1970 the CRA condemned 'the *Derry Journal* on its vicious editorial attacking the civil-rights movement and asked the meeting if a paid advertisement should be put in the papers explaining the role of the so-called left-wing in the CRA'. Reference was also made 'to the activities of Mr Eamonn McCann in tearing up his membership card on leaving St Mary's Hall, Belfast', and worry expressed about conflict between themselves and the Derry Unemployed Action Committee. By the end of the year it was determined to 'Challenge Hume and the Social and Democratic Labour Party [formed at the end of August; in 1969, John Hume had replaced Eddie McAteer, leader of the nationalists since 1964, as MP for Foyle] on why there were no fireworks in Stormont as promised by him and his party in their statement on non-support of march'. It admitted its own need for better public relations: 'so that we can let the people know there is a CRA committee at work in Derry'. The following month the committee threatened 'to resign en bloc if John Hume speaks from a civil rights platform'. Later that year it also admonished the legal profession, who, with few exceptions, had been 'absent from our struggle so far'. This was an indication that many comfortable middle-class professionals saw no reason to get involved.[2]

The acrimonious split in the IRA ranks, between 'Provisionals' and 'Officials' at their army convention of 1969, complicated the situation. The division was a product of the debate in the 1960s about the merits of political involvement, the Provisionals opting for a purely military strategy, while the Officials eventually 'suspended' operations in May 1972, though they had been responsible for much violence in the interim. There was also a growing recognition that the British army had the potential to be part of the problem, rather than part of the solution. From an early stage both wings of the IRA were offering advice on business normally the preserve of local authorities, a telling signal of the power vacuum that existed and republicans' determination to fill it. The Catholic Church was quick to move to ensure the republican left did not control community associations in Belfast.

But ultimately there was no general agreement and no single representative body. In 1979, McCann argued that the IRA was entitled to see itself as the legitimate inheritor of the civil-rights movement, because the late-1970s members of the IRA 'were the rioting children of a decade ago', and it had dawned on Catholics that talk of reform and new structures really meant 'that a few Englishmen would be given supervisory positions at the top of the old structures'. If the machinery of government was not democratic, the logic went, the fight for democracy had to be a fight against the state itself. McCann also contended that in this context 'partition was irrelevant'.[3] In this sense, perhaps the 1973 plea of the Derry Civil Rights Association to people 'to sign a pledge rededicating themselves to the struggle to win democracy' was a desperate admission that they could no longer shape the parameters of the conflict, though it is debatable if they ever had.[4]

The NICRA submission to a committee examining the operation of the 1973 Emergency Provisions Act disputed the belief that the nature of the conflict had been transformed to one involving 'relatively small numbers of ruthless and vicious killers'. They insisted this was a dishonest and convenient British assessment, which ignored the fact that there was precious little difference in the conditions of suffering nationalists. If the British assessment was true, they argued, people would have rallied around the idea of a power-sharing executive.[5]

'Potentially, though, it had ten times that number the day after'

In the meantime, other developments exposed the belief of the British government that they were dealing with just small numbers of ruthless murderers as wishful thinking. Internment was one. On 9 August 1971 about 340 men were seized by British soldiers and RUC men, who smashed their way into Catholic homes in the middle of the night. Eamonn McCann pointed out that 'in fact, the IRA had nowhere near 340 members that day. Potentially, though, it had ten times that number the day after', and internment put paid to the idea that civil disturbance held out any hope of change.[6] The failure of the trade union movement to explicitly denounce internment strengthened the image of the Provisionals as sole defenders of the Catholic working classes, the unions deciding they were going to play the 'non-sectarian' card rather than take a stand. While this was understandable given the particular religious sensitivities of Northern society, the labour historian Andrew Boyd pointed to the irony of the fact that the Northern Committee of the Irish Congress of Trade Unions 'was the only representative body in all of Europe, east or west, which failed to condemn internment'.[7]

That this was indeed a labour issue was reflected in a NICRA survey of internees' families in February 1972, which identified 'a positive correlation between unemployment and internment', and crucially, in terms of support for the IRA, that it was children who suffered most, the majority of them in the 7–13 age range. Such was the effect of a policy which one community activist described as 'an issue politically explosive, emotionally charged, immorally based and crassly used', which raised serious questions about the concept of the rights of individuals, and where collective responsibility began and ended.[8] As the young journalist Rosita Sweetman argued in 1972, internment was also something which particularly burdened women; the 'wire widows' of Northern Ireland whose husbands, brothers and fathers were being interned without trial: 'they have lived the last year without any heroism attached to their names, bruised victims of a brutal system, watching their children grow up warped by a violence that's loose in their streets, watching their menfolk used as political hostages in a massive political game.'[9]

Displacement was another factor which would ensure the longevity of the bitterness, as did the belief that there was a constant one-sided presentation of violence in the media. In 1974, a community relations report suggested that 8,180 families were forced to evacuate their houses in the Greater Belfast area between August 1969 and February 1973, 80 per cent estimated to be Catholic, and by 1973, 23 out of the 30 Catholic-owned bars in North Belfast had been bombed by loyalists.[10] The shooting and bombing of the Provisional IRA became more intense, backed, as Ed Moloney noted, by 'traditional conservative, republican values'. Like their predecessors in the 1930s and 1940s, the Provisionals were obsessively anti-communist and devoutly Catholic, insisted on military status in prison, and were often fearless and vicious: 'they were quite happy sitting in their cells reading the *Sun* or the *Mirror* boasting about operations. They were purely militarists – hit, hit, keep on hitting.'[11]

'it was murder, gentlemen. Sheer unadulterated murder'

On 30 January 1972, Bloody Sunday was another lifeline to the IRA, as was the British government's response, which obliged the families of those involved to embark on a 30-year crusade to prove the truth of the Derry coroner's contention that 'it was murder, gentlemen. Sheer unadulterated murder.'[12] The quest for answers about Bloody Sunday centred around questions of political motivation and responsibility for the killing of 13 unarmed civilians on a civil-rights march, a march that had been prompted by anger at internment affecting the working-class, 30,000 strong Bogside–Creggan district of Derry. It was suggested that a subsequent cover-up spanned the highest levels of the political and legal establishment, with the likelihood that it was planned in advance and that the Lord Chief Justice's report concealed the truth, though it was not until the early 1990s that it became a significant feature on the Anglo-Irish agenda.

Two days after the event a meeting between the British prime minister, Edward Heath, Lord Chief Justice Widgery and the Lord Chancellor, Lord Hailsham, took place, at which Widgery, appointed to chair a tribunal of inquiry into the event to commence the following day, was told that 'it had to be remembered that we were in Northern Ireland, fighting not just a military war, but a propaganda war'.[13] He duly ignored the 700 eye-witness statements from Derry people, particularly the repeated insistence that shots had been fired over the city walls, and medical evidence which suggested that people had been shot from above. The scandalous and ultimately discredited Widgery report (39 pages long and published 71 days after the event on the basis of the evidence of 114 witnesses) maintained that shots had been fired only at ground level, and asserted as well that 'there was no reason why they should have ... begun to shoot unless they had come under fire themselves'. Nail bombs had also been planted in one victim's pockets, the only 'evidence' that aggression from the protestors was planned.

Given the political pressure Brian Faulkner was under (he was the last prime minister of Northern Ireland), the paratroopers' attempt to entice the IRA into battle backfired disastrously, the ultimate political question being whether or not it was approved in advance by the Northern Irish Committee of the British government. There is no doubt that the event encouraged IRA recruitment. By the summer of 1972 the Derry CRA was opposed 'to specific marches against the Provisionals at this time' but they decided against a commemorative march the following year because 'certain groups were planning to use it for their own ends'.[14]

Bloody Sunday was also a milestone because of the reaction in the South, which was highly vocal, emotional and occasionally violent (the British embassy was burnt down in Dublin city). Like never before, in the words of McCann, there was 'a sense of oneness in shared, raging sorrow with nationalists corralled in the north', and thus in its way it represented 'the highpoint of 32 county nationalism in the history of the southern state'.[15]

'this was a provocative march today'

Irish government files, released in 2003, reflect the tension that existed between the British and Irish governments following the killings, as the Taoiseach, Jack Lynch, phoned the prime minister, Ted Heath, on the night of Bloody Sunday. Trying to restrain his emotions, Lynch raised the question of Britain's control of the army in Northern Ireland. Heath's tone was a mixture of disdain and business-like terseness: 'Well then, this was a provocative march today … I cannot therefore take this as a criticism of Stormont.'[16] It is no exaggeration to assert that relations between Dublin and London were close to breaking point in 1972, and Heath was critical of Dublin's failure to stamp out IRA active service units operating across the border, even going so far as to try and enlist the support of Pope Paul VI. In July, in the aftermath of Bloody Friday, when the IRA detonated 26 bombs in Belfast, killing 11 and injuring 130, the British government even devised a plan for the forcible re-partition of Ireland, by moving thousands of Catholics and Protestants into 'safe enclaves', which, it was admitted, would require 'ruthless force'. Earlier in the year, when the government was preparing to suspend the Stormont government of Northern Ireland, Heath ordered a list of sanctions against the Republic in the event of the Irish government refusing to co-operate, including identity cards and work permits for Irish immigrants in London, and the freezing of Ireland's sterling balances.[17]

But the evolving priority of Irish governments was to contain and control republican sentiment, and ensure it did not unsettle politics in the South, or put more crudely, to maintain a partitionist mindset. In this they were quite successful, particularly after loyalist bombs killed 34 people in Dublin and Monaghan in 1974. By 1977 a poll conducted for the current affairs magazine *Magill* revealed that, in theory, 63 per cent of those polled in the South were in favour of a united Ireland, but only 35 per cent suggested aiming for unity 'whatever the problems'. The high level of theoretical attachment to the idea of a united Ireland was also evidenced by the fact that 64 per cent were opposed to the dropping of articles 2 and 3 of the Irish constitution (over 95 per cent were happy to see them go in the context of an overall settlement by 1998).[18] With the abolition of the Stormont parliament in March 1972, however, it was the British government that was now responsible for direct rule, and the response of the IRA was to claim it as a victory and step up its campaign, hoping it would bomb the British to negotiations. Moloney has suggested the fall of Stormont 'opened up a fault line within nationalism that would never really close. Moderate nationalist opinion now sought a political deal and reform, while the IRA fought on for revolution and the elusive republic.'[19] The growing complexity of the relationship between Heath and Lynch (John Bowman suggests Heath was a 'slow learner' when it came to Anglo-Irish affairs) encouraged Lynch to emphasise the need for power-sharing, and Heath eventually became more open to this idea.[20]

'an attempt to con'?

The doomed Sunningdale agreement of 1973, the first attempt to initiate a political settlement based on a power-sharing executive, with militant republicans and unionists excluded from discussions, was followed by the Loyalist Workers' Strike of 1974 (a period of 'raw Nazism' according to Patrick Shea[21]). Both experiences suggested the political outlook was bleak, after workers were beaten out of factories, while the RUC consorted openly with masked Ulster Defence Association men and the British army expressed outrage at the release of internees. According to McCann, the proposed executive failed because it was an attempt 'to devise a square circle'. The functions of the proposed 78-member assembly and the Council of Ireland designed to encourage cross-border security and economic co-operation were, in the opinion of Bernadette McAliskey (formerly Devlin), 'an attempt to con nationalists into thinking they have gained a great victory, and loyalists into believing they have lost nothing'.[22] The assembly elections resulted in seats being won by 22 power-sharing Unionists, 28 anti-power-sharing Unionists, 19 SDLP, eight Alliance (the Alliance party had been formed in April 1970, representing centrist interests demanding the abolition of sectarian strife) and one Labour. Lack of unanimity in the unionist family and the 'threat from within' was thus as important in unionist thinking as anything else. The variety of 'unionisms' included Ian Paisley's Democratic Unionist Party, Craig's Vanguard Unionists, the Official Unionists of Harry West and Brian Faulkner's Unionist Party of Northern Ireland. At the end of 1978, the UDA talked of its plans for independence for Ulster, rejecting the close alliance with the UK urged by Unionist politicians, and suggested a bill of human rights, a parliamentary democracy for an independent Northern Ireland which could join the EEC. This, they argued, would create normal class politics in the North. Seamus Mallon recalled that when, in 1978, the SDLP resolved that the North should be the focus of a joint effort by the British and Irish governments to break the deadlock, they were 'laughed at'.[23]

'areas of dereliction and rat-infested bricked-up houses'

The conditions of the republican and loyalist ghettos became bleaker as the conflict intensified. These were the areas where most of the 2,100 people in jails at the end of 1977 came from, and where most of the one quarter of a million house searches between 1973 and 1977 were carried out.[24] The Derry CRA publicised the fact that in 1975 Derry was the worst black spot in the region as regards children in low-income, large families, single-parent families and overcrowded housing. Many of these features were also a fact of life in Belfast for Catholics and Protestants, one of the reasons why between 1969 and 1977 over 50 community organisations came into existence in both Catholic and Protestant areas. The Roden Street area of West Belfast was an example of a district that prior to 1969 had been a well-integrated working-class community, but was reduced to a derelict wasteland, as a buffer zone between the lower Falls and the Protestant Sandy Row. It was a victim not only of the conflict, but of bad planning, with a Belfast urban motorway breaking through it. By the end of 1973 fewer than 100 of the original 995 householders in the Roden Street area remained, with families segregated into enclaves divided by the army 'peaceline'.[25] In November 1977 Kevin Myers wrote powerfully in *Magill* magazine about the Short Strand area, one of the poorest and most violent ghettos in Belfast. This was a republican hinterland where the population had dropped from 8,000 to 2,500 in just six years, with 54 in jail on internment charges. Myers reminded readers that 'one person's terrorist is another person's child', something Nell McCafferty was to reiterate in writing about the lives young IRA men had led. Myers also pointed out that the high arrest rate was an indication that confidential calls were being made to police, perhaps demonstrating a resentment of the IRA's exceptional arrogance in their own areas, an arrogance that was often barbaric. Unemployment stood at over 30 per cent in the Short Strand, with squalid housing amidst prospering drinking clubs that fed alcoholism. But the hospitality and strong family ties were also exceptional, even though 'community leaders' often meant 'men with guns', which Myers saw as a consequence but not a cause of the war. In 1976, only four out of 28 final-year pupils in the area qualified for grammar school. Myers continued:

1970–2000 631

In that quarter square mile of 27 streets are 2 bookies, 7 drinking
clubs, one pub, 2 churches (one of them Protestant), two schools, one
police station, one army base, 2 playgrounds (both closed because of
vandalism), 3 paramilitary organisations, lots of committees, areas
of dereliction and rat-infested bricked-up houses and about two and
a half thousand people, including a sprinkling of Protestants, with
about 300 pensioners, living in some 800 households.[26]

In Derry's Creggan estate, women were criticised by a tenants' association
for spending too much time with their mothers outside Creggan, travelling back and forth four or five times a week, leading to a feeling of being
'exiled in Creggan'.[27]

'The idea that a republican woman would have an orgasm was blasphemy'
But throughout the 1970s women continued to be involved in community
action; and not just on the issues prioritised by the Northern Ireland Civil
Rights Association. In 1971, a number of mothers in the Ormeau Road
area of Belfast mounted a campaign in opposition to Margaret Thatcher's
decision (as Minister for Education) to stop the supply of school milk for
children over the age of seven. The sectarianism of Belfast ensured allegations surfaced that the milk campaign was a Catholic conspiracy. As Lynda
Edgerton, a founder member of the Northern Ireland Women's Rights
Movement, remembered: 'even this apparently straightforward issue of
social concern was to be damned by the age-old tensions of Orange and
Green politics'.[28]

The Troubles ensured many women became politically active in order
to protect the well-being of their families, or because they 'could sympa-
thise and feel solidarity with other women when they were under attack'.
The focal point for working-class families, particularly with the policy of
internment, as recognised by Margaret Ward, was 'the release of prisoners, an end to debt legislation and better housing'.[29] As a result of male
imprisonment, many women had to shoulder full responsibility for the
households; rent and rate strikes in response to internment, supported by
over 25,000 people, resulted in the Payment by Debt Act, which allowed
rent arrears to be deducted at source from wages or social security. For
many, feminism was a luxury they could not afford, given the daily battle
for subsistence. But collectively women ensured their voices were heard,
and some sought to challenge the masculine political traditions their male

family members embraced; and they did gain recognition (though not without opposition) as 'political actors within the community'.

Not surprisingly, women also became involved with paramilitary organisations. Many teenage girls joined the IRA in the 1970s, and were particularly active in carrying weapons and intelligence gathering. The journalist Catherine Cleary noted that some were also given the role of the 'honey-pot' – to meet up with British soldiers at dances or pubs and entice them back to an IRA hit squad. But the paramilitaries remained sexist in their attitude to these women; indeed, the papacy and the army council of the IRA had a lot in common, according to one woman imprisoned as a result of her membership of the IRA: 'As a republican woman, if you died you were supposed to be a virgin on your death bed, with a rifle in one hand and rosary beads in the other. The idea that a republican woman would have an orgasm was blasphemy'. It was also the case, according to this activist, that the authorities were more vindictive towards female terrorists; women engaged in killing were deemed to be in a 'sub-human' category of their own.[30]

'a tube of toothpaste'
The increasing intensity of military conflict in the 1970s ensured that the attitude of police and judiciary became an even more overtly political issue. In 1979, Mary Holland wrote extensively about police brutality directed against republicans and of the fact that the complaints of police doctors (who had little sympathy for the IRA) were being ignored. This was due to the obsession of Roy Mason, the British Labour government's Northern Ireland Secretary from 1976, with the conviction rate, and his keenness to announce how many people he had put in jail. He had promised to roll up the IRA 'like a tube of toothpaste'.[31] Such determination meant much hardship for the young men of the British army, many being housed in primitive conditions in a war far removed from their personal interests. It seemed that after 1976 the British had effectively abandoned hope of a political solution, preferring to seek military victory or containment. The Secret Intelligence Service was also involved in deliberately leaking sensitive intelligence reports to encourage political promises of tougher action and more personnel, while in the South, in 1976, the Gardaí deliberately suppressed vital evidence, in co-operation with the RUC, in order to protect an agent for British military intelligence. Throughout the 1970s, allegations of Gardaí and British security force collusion were

rife. Special category status for paramilitary prisoners came to an end on
31 March 1976.

Initial success in extracting confessions from IRA members in new
police interrogation centres emboldened Mason's rhetoric, though eventually Gerry Adams and others ensured the IRA developed anti-interroga-
tion training, based on avoiding any relationship with their interrogators.
They learnt many other things also, Moloney pointing out that 'IRA men
have always used their time in prison well', one of the reasons why they
evolved into such a sophisticated military and then political force. Some of
those involved in compiling British intelligence, such as Brigadier James
Glover, who became the British army's commander of land forces in the
North, pointed out how few people the IRA needed to continue their
war. This was due to discipline and long-term strategy; far from being
mindless thugs and unsophisticated murderers, the IRA was training and
using members 'with some care', enabling them to 'retain popular support
sufficient to maintain secure bases in the traditional republican areas'.[32]
That was all they needed to maintain a long war.

But being able to depict Britain as sponsors of human-rights abuses
was important also. Amnesty International expressed concern about the
lack of guidelines from judges on the behaviour of interrogators, and the
fact that between 75 and 80 per cent of the convictions in the Diplock
Courts (non-jury courts established in 1973) were on the basis of confessions alone.[33] Between 1972 and 1978 there were 1,612 allegations of
ill treatment, and not a single prosecution as a result, though in 1978
the European Court of Human Rights acknowledged the 'inhuman and
degrading treatment' of prisoners. This was in the midst of one of the
darkest periods of the Troubles, with indiscriminate sectarian killing 'in
which the loyalists and the IRA vied with each other ... the latter refusing
to admit its attacks or seeking refuge behind fictitious cover names, the
former glorying openly and proudly in the carnage'.[34] The period witnessed the rise of the Shankhill Butchers, Ulster Volunteer Force killers
who hacked victims to death with knives and axes, while the IRA targeted
Protestant pubs, killing many innocent civilians.

'can only operate in a community which supports him'?
A long war had not been the aim of the IRA movement at the beginning
of the Troubles, and it made many mistakes along the way. But whatever
about the revulsion the IRA's acts of destruction caused, it was unlikely

that working-class Catholics would back the British against them. McCann maintained that individual killings by the SAS 'drove hundreds of Derry people back to the Provos'. After a spate of bombings late in 1978, including the notorious La Mon House hotel bomb, in which 12 Protestants were incinerated because of the failure of the IRA to give adequate warning, the IRA first declared its commitment to 'a long war'. It was a strategy around which there was no unanimity within the movement, given that the nature of the war they could wage was limited. An added threat was the viciousness of the splinter groups, as revealed by the feud between the Irish Republican Socialist Party and the Officials in 1975. In December 1979, Mary Holland concluded that the IRA had laid to rest the classic theory of guerrilla warfare, 'that the guerrilla fighter ... can only operate in a community which supports him'. Holland further suggested that apathy concerning the protests of republican prisoners in the H-Blocks prison at Long Kesh (400 'on the blanket' by the end of 1978, many being treated brutally) was an indication of a low level of support for the IRA. (Prisoners who refused to wear prison clothes in pursuit of the restoration of political status were confined to their cells for breaching prison discipline, with just blankets to cover them.) What the IRA had was the 'quiescent ambivalence' in Catholic areas of Belfast and Derry: 'which may fall short of active support but still ensures that almost nobody is prepared to go out on a limb to co-operate with either the army or the RUC'.[35]

'modern media techniques and the liberation of women'?

But, significantly, by 1979 Gerry Adams admitted that 'our most glaring weakness to date lies in our failure to develop revolutionary politics'.[36] This was an indication that change was on the way in terms of linking provisional republicanism to anti-imperialist and socialist rhetoric. Meanwhile, the Irish-Americans of the National Association for Irish Freedom and the Irish Republican Clubs were squabbling about violence and whether to share platforms with civil-rights groups.[37]

A much-heralded peace movement had emerged in 1976, which allowed both sides of the community to question the ethics of violence in a unique cross-sectarian display of unity. It was the expression of a particular mood of frustration rather than a coherent political entity, and was marred by disputes over the three separate financial structures within the movement and the decision of Mairéad Corrigan and Betty Williams, awarded the Nobel Peace Prize, to keep the prize money. In one sense it was a very genuine coalition of emotion in response to the killing of children, but it ignored fundamental political and sectarian issues in the noble but naive belief that mere goodwill could solve the problem. It lost independence by inevitability aligning itself with the forces of law and order and thus the contested state. It also lost autonomy on account of the extent to which external organisations that funded it could dictate its agenda. The international media craze that followed the 'peace women' (understandable given that at last there was good news coming out of Belfast) also created pressures. According to Nell McCafferty, reviewing the rise and fall of the movement in 1980, despite its failure it was significant because 'it resulted from the convergence of two historical phenomena – modern media techniques and the liberation of women – was fuelled by the worldwide threat to parliamentarians of armed guerrilla movements and was sustained locally by a genuine sense of war weariness'.[38]

'segregated, suspicious, surreptitious, sneaking about'

While there was a huge volume of literature on the political and military aspects of the Northern Troubles as the conflict lengthened, there was relatively little exploration of how ordinary people lived and reacted on both sides of the divide. Two notable exceptions were Fionnuala O'Connor's *In Search of a State*, an examination of Catholic feelings about the Northern state, and Susan McKay's *Northern Protestants*, an extensive survey of a range of Protestant viewpoints. Alongside these the journalism of Eamonn McCann, Nell McCafferty and Mary Holland analysed the ordinary (mostly working-class) communities who bore the brunt of a long and vicious conflict. After 30 years, the parameters of the conflict had shifted considerably, and it was as if an opportunity now existed to peek behind the headlines and the armies to shine a light at those on whose behalf the war was supposedly being fought.

There was undoubtedly a political context to this also; looking at internal rather than external forces seemed timely in light of the 1998 Good Friday Agreement, particularly given the belief, articulated by the historian Tom Bartlett in the same year, that 'it is now self-evident that if Britain has no selfish, strategic or economic aim in holding on to Northern Ireland, then Dublin has likewise no selfish, strategic or economic ambition to take it over'. He concluded that the solution to the problem lay in a separate Northern Ireland within a European federal structure.[39] This realisation, though of course not accepted by all, meant very different things according to which side of the political divide one was from. It was written at a time when the conflict had, since 1968, caused 3,330 killings, with the IRA and other republicans responsible for 1,959 (59 per cent), Loyalists 920 (28 per cent) and the security forces 355 (11 per cent). Such statistics, of course, will never explain the depth of feeling which gave rise to such violence and the scale of the pain, disruption and loss of youth experienced. As one interviewee put it to Susan McKay, in certain parts of the North the violence meant that 'my growing up was segregated, suspicious, surreptitious, sneaking about, knowing where you could go and where you couldn't. One wee piece of violence a day, a bomb, a murder. It absolutely paralysed a psyche.'[40] For those in the South, its impact was more abstract, if not relentlessly monotonous. In the mid-1980s, Colm Tóibín suggested that for many people 'the North became a dizzying spiral of abstractions and statistics, statements of aspirations and numbers of dead, wounded, convicted and imprisoned'.[41]

A number of things were clear by the end of the century, aside from the intentions of Dublin and London. Protestants generally were feeling more vulnerable and politically fragile than at any other time since the first threat of Home Rule, with, for example, in the Shankhill district, quarrels among gangsters rooted in rivalries over drugs and territories promising only more dysfunctional generations, making 'a once proud district leaderless and demoralised'. A gable wall mural depicted warrior ghouls and skeletal characters with gun in one hand and Ulster flag in the other.[42] In contrast, the Catholic community seemed more politically in the ascendant, their numbers increasing, and their murals more confident and demanding. Many in both communities, however, continued to experience political and material poverty, and their political representatives, preoccupied with a solution to the war, were rarely heard discussing the bread-and-butter issues of socio-economic development, being instead obsessed with religious and party political allegiance.

Eamonn McCann critically questioned the value of a solution based on the hemming in and bedding down of sectarianism, rather than focusing on the desperation of poverty, which was a lifeline to extremism. What was needed, he contended, was 'a vision which might bring us together rather than police us apart'.[43] McKay's survey of Northern Protestants also recorded the grievances many Protestants had about poverty, but they had traditionally been told 'not to shout about it'.[44] It was also the working class that did most of the killing, who died in greatest numbers and spent longest in jail.

'how to formally identify the nature of the enemy'

Having settled down for a 'long war' in the late 1970s the republican paramilitaries and their opponents ensured that the 1980s and 1990s produced countless atrocities, sadness and tragedy, though for much of the period channels remained open between the warring sides, whatever about what was acknowledged in public. For all the skilful management of republicanism, there were mistakes, and one of the most striking features of the Troubles was the extent to which paramilitaries on both sides did such damage to their own communities, the ones they were supposedly protecting. In 2000, in the midst of a debate about the need for IRA decommissioning of arms, Fintan O'Toole pointed out that:

> the largest number of republican paramilitaries killed in the conflict were murdered, not by the RUC or the British Army, or the loyalist terror gangs, but by their own comrades. The INLA and the IRA have been responsible for the deaths of 164 of their own members. The British Army, RUC, UDR and loyalist paramilitaries killed 161.[45]

By the 1990s, senior republicans often traced the beginnings of the Peace Process back to key developments in the 1980s, even though, according to Henry Patterson, they often seemed to be unaware of these milestones at the time.[46] This is a view that has been somewhat revised. Ed Moloney's authoritative and absorbing history of the modern IRA argues that an indirect channel was opened up between Gerry Adams and the Northern Ireland Secretary Tom King as early as 1986. Although this will be disputed by some, it was noticeable that the explicit demands for a united Ireland became less frequent, with the more ambiguous (and elastic) phrase 'national self-determination' being employed instead. It was also the case that Britain, as identified by Peter Taylor, ensured that language became a victim of this process, with the emphasis on their side also on prevarication and ambiguity. As was pointed out by Taylor:

> neither could the British decide how to formally identify the nature of the enemy: was it political, terrorist or criminal? Should it be negotiated with or squashed? This confusion led to off-the-record political

talks taking place at the same time as interrogation techniques were being used that were later condemned by the [European] court of human rights.[47]

By the 1990s, constitutional nationalists in search of a solution were effectively looking for a new power-sharing agreement which was likely to divide unionism, creating difficulties in their relationship with Britain, but which they could sell to republicans as a transitional settlement preceding Irish unity. The difficulty would lie in how much Britain could give against the wishes of Ulster unionists, but also, as Bernadette Sands, sister of the martyred republican hunger striker Bobby, who died in 1981, pointed out, how republicans would manage those who regarded it as a sell-out: 'my brother didn't die for cross-border bodies'.[48] The response of Adams was to ruthlessly but skilfully sideline potential internal opponents.

The evidence, absorbed by Moloney over many years of reporting on the conflict, was that some time in 1986, courtesy of Fr Alec Reid, a Redemptorist priest in Belfast, a secret line of communication was opened between the Northern Ireland Secretary, Tom King, and the Sinn Féin leader, and later between 1988 and 1992, with his successor, Peter Brooke. The Peace Process was thus, in the words of Moloney, 'not a spontaneous phenomenon, tossed around by forces outside its control, nor was it forced upon its architects by the fortunes of war', but rather 'an exercise in management toward an already decided outcome'. That was why all sides had to be so careful, and why senior republicans became not only longsighted, politically dedicated and strategically sophisticated, but also 'pragmatic, cunning and all too often duplicitous. They were also utterly ruthless.' Moloney maintained that in the process Adams became 'one of the largest figures in Ireland's long and sad history, a revolutionary leader who deservedly ranks alongside those competing founders of Irish independence, Michael Collins and Eamon de Valera, a man whose qualities, both negative and positive, are fit to be measured alongside theirs'. When the Nobel Peace Prize in December 1998 went to John Hume and David Trimble, Adams was 'forced to stay silent, biting his lip lest by accepting the praise of the establishment he undermine the Peace Process in the eyes of supporters'.[49]

This in turn infuriated his opponents, but it also frustrates the historian, who in Adams's bestselling autobiography *Before the Dawn* (1996),

gets precious little information on the most important periods of his political and military life. Roy Foster pointed out that because he was on his
way 'to constructing a new establishment of the kind he made his career
fighting against ... a decisive amount of retrospective remodelling is necessary'. Foster noted:

> Adams was born in 1948, but his book takes 263 pages to reach the
> year 1978; while events since then are compressed into sixty-two,
> many of them dealing with the hunger strikes by republican prisoners
> demanding 'political status' in 1981. The book effectively ends there
> ... there is a deliberate structure of evasion and conflation ... breath-
> takingly, there is absolutely no discussion of the evolving attitude of
> British governments from the mid 1960s up to the dramatic Hillsbor-
> ough Accord of 1985 and the subsequent Downing Street Declaration
> of 1993.[50]

'strategically, physically and morally opposed to a hunger strike'

By the 1980s there was a recognition, identified by John Whyte in 1990,
that many Northern Catholics would settle for a solution falling far short
of a united Ireland and that, in any case, the Republic would not be able
to cope economically with a united Ireland.[51] In the late 1970s a younger,
more radical IRA that had little experience of life other than violence was
not focusing on such realities. But the move away from a purely military
strategy was not far off. As early as 1980, Gerry Adams was boasting that
the move to the left in the republican movement was 'the most successful
radicalisation of the republican movement since the republican congress
[of 1934], and it didn't cause a split'.[52]

The republican hunger strikes the following year, in pursuit of political status for prisoners, and the resultant political upheaval, did much
to convince military purists of the potential value of a political strategy.
That a significant level of support and sympathy was evident in the South
broadened the impact of the hunger strikes. But initially there was much
opposition from the IRA, who feared they would not be able to control
the hunger strikers, and they often clashed with the relatives' action committees. The issue at stake was not only the personal will of the hunger
strikers, but the forces that their deaths could set in motion, and how they
would be directed. Particularly notable was the degree to which young
working-class people, North and South, became involved in politics as

a result. For some, the H-Block hunger strikes raised questions about republicans and their place in Northern society, but it was significant that initially they had got little support. Gerry Adams had informed Bobby Sands in the early stages of his hunger strike that 'we are tactically, strategically, physically and morally opposed to a hunger strike', believing it to be a diversion from the war.[53] Indeed, one of the reasons for the adoption of the ultimate protest was the degree to which the prisoners felt their plight was not getting enough attention outside. However, when the republican leadership came on board, their military and authoritarian mindset ensured they took control. They attempted to sideline those, like Bernadette McAliskey, who were not under their discipline, as well as preventing the families of the strikers doing solo runs.

Successive meetings between Church, republican and government representatives went on behind the scenes, muddied by the fact that so many different people were looking for different things from the strikers. A suspicious Dublin government looked for active intervention, and believed the IRA was sabotaging a settlement, while a duplicitous British government put its own spin on the situation, in an attempt to discourage US involvement. According to Joe Lee, the British government's handling of the crisis, during which ten hunger-strikers died, was 'inept to the point of criminality'.[54] The deaths and election victories by hunger strike candidates, with the first, Bobby Sands, elected as MP for Fermanagh–Tyrone in 1981, can be said to have altered the political environment in which the IRA operated. It was notable that funeral attendees applauded when the IRA firing parties appeared, and talk of class, social inequality and sister liberation movements soon followed. One of the ironies of the career of Gerry Adams was that his political support base was significantly broadened by the actions of those he had initially opposed. But now, 'the politicisation of the masses' was a phrase that began to emanate regularly from Sinn Féin leaders.

By 1983 they could confidently proclaim that they were out to replace the SDLP as the voice of the nationalist people of the North, and this had strong elements of a class crusade, frowned upon by the Catholic Church. Michael Farrell summed up the situation in Belfast in 1983, prior to Adams winning a Westminster seat in the general election, when Sinn Féin won 13.4 per cent of the vote compared to 17.9 per cent for the SDLP:

the offices illustrate the contrast. The Sinn Féin supporters are young, unemployed ex-prisoners. So are most of their candidates. They live in the working-class ghettos; they speak the people's language, they experience their problems. The SDLP candidates are all middle class. Three of the four candidates in Belfast are doctors. Most of their workers are middle class too. On election day they have to pay people to staff their polling booths. Sinn Féin have no trouble getting volunteers ... In West Belfast Sinn Féin have set up specialised housing and welfare departments with full-time staff, to get to know the regulations inside out.[55]

'fighting for their streets'?

But there was a belief in some quarters that the electoral ceiling had been reached in 1983, with little possibility of Sinn Féin receiving more than 100,000 votes in the North, and no question at this stage of politics taking precedence over a military campaign. Adams, as he was to do for the next twenty years, insisted that the republican movement should not make grandiose predictions about short-term sweeping electoral successes, but adopt a carefully orchestrated long-term policy of targeting specific local constituencies. Though Sinn Féin political representatives were shunned by many, in 1984 an Irish government embargo on dealings with Sinn Féin's 28 local-authority representatives in the South was conveniently ignored when council, senate or mayoralty votes were needed.[56]

Nonetheless, Adams's victory in West Belfast in 1983 was a significant electoral inroad, given that during the Stormont years the only seats won by Sinn Féin had been in the rural areas of Mid-Ulster and Fermanagh–South Tyrone. But the extent to which the 1983 campaign was a victory for republicanism, or a reflection of communal anger, is debatable, raising the question of the extent to which success in elections could be seen as ideological victory. At this stage, Adams tended to use the words 'nationalism' and 'republicanism' interchangeably. The books by ex-IRA members that had appeared by the end of the century, including those by Seán O'Callaghan, Raymond Gilmore and Eamonn Collins, as McCann pointed out, rarely mentioned political discussions or Irish unity, but rather suggested that these people were in effect 'fighting for their streets'. Support for the IRA was often given 'through gritted teeth', but was there nevertheless because of the daily humiliation 'of being seen as second-class in your own home place'.[57]

It remained difficult to get the better of an articulate republican debater. One interviewee in Fionnuala O'Connor's book observed:

> You're sitting there talking to republicans for hours, arguing. You just have a feeling there are no goalposts here, there's no framework you'd agree on. A smile comes over their faces at the end of the night; because you have a threshold, they don't ... but there's so many like me. I'm a classic example, that can't 100 per cent come out and just say in black and white – they're wrong, they have no justification.[58]

The tyranny and knee-capping of their own communities at local level was justified by fostering the idea that they were moral as well as political guardians. When the issue of child abuse arose, for example, since there was in effect no support for the RUC in areas the IRA controlled, 'even SDLP supporters tend to look to the IRA when they want direct action against local criminality'.[59] The IRA developed an extraordinary capacity to ignore violence that did not fit their own concepts of legitimacy, and the RUC bore the brunt of much of it, being particularly vulnerable because of their place at the coal-face, and the hatred that existed in oppressed working-class republican areas.

'as busy politically as the Provisionals are militarily'

The largely middle-class SDLP operated from a completely different conception of what the Northern state was about, as was revealed in their manoeuvres in the New Ireland Forum and the background to the Anglo-Irish Agreement of 1985. Much of this went hand-in-hand with John Hume's endorsement by the Southern establishment, cemented by his opposition to violence of any kind and the use of utterly non-contentious rhetoric (some considerable achievement in the North of Ireland). But, according to his critics, he was not in reality saying anything. He was tailor-made for the 'statesman of the Troubles' role, particularly given his determination and persistence in influencing external opinion, the European and US channels in particular. His skill as a lobbyist and political broker and advocate of non-violence were extraordinarily stretched, and often very effectively employed, but what ultimately secured Hume's place in history was taking the risk to engage with the IRA. This was a significant move from the leader of a party that had been caught between the two stools of wanting to be more critical of the Northern state and its institutions, but not wanting to strengthen the hand of the IRA by employing overly critical language. Thus, as Olivia O'Leary wrote in 1984, Hume was 'desperate to be seen to be as busy politically as the Provisionals are militarily', a business that often heightened tensions within his own frequently divided party.[60] In the eyes of many, John Hume was the party. He was certainly accurate in his contention that while the British political establishment could give much time to the symptoms of Northern Ireland's condition, it did not seem interested in addressing the causes of that condition.

'conciliatory language which masks traditional demands'?

The New Ireland Forum was a group established by constitutional nationalists in the North and South to discuss ways of solving the Northern crisis. They were worried about the threat of Sinn Féin, but also, according to Garret FitzGerald, welcomed the Forum as 'an opportunity for the Unionist viewpoint to be presented to the public in our state'. There was no mention of Irish unity in the terms of reference, but it was also notable that FitzGerald, as Taoiseach, got 'an almost uniformly negative reaction' from his colleagues when he introduced the idea, as they thought it would divert him from pressing domestic issues.[61]

The difficulty with ideas like the Forum was the extent to which they were open to abuse by those in the South who, because of factions within their own party, wished to play the green card and reiterate their desire to see unity. This was the case with Charles Haughey, leader of Fianna Fáil. Critics of the Forum came to see it as deceptive; its apparent openness belied, insisted Mary Robinson, 'the skilful manipulation of public opinion by the use of a conciliatory language which masks traditional demands'.[62] But it was reassuring for those who felt the North's problems were at least a factor in Southern rhetoric, and who sought a joint moderate nationalist approach as desired by Hume and FitzGerald. Ultimately, it was Margaret Thatcher's rhetoric of 'Out, out, out' which lingered, this being her response to the three options proffered by the Forum: joint authority in Northern Ireland by British and Irish governments, confederation of the two states or a unified Ireland.

The reality by the mid-1980s was that there were few nationalists who trusted Dublin to protect their best interests, despite the Anglo-Irish Agreement, which gave a formal advisory role in the affairs of the North to the Irish government. A common argument of staunch unionists was that the agreement involved an assault on the civil rights of unionists, which was far greater than that ever suffered by nationalists during the Stormont years. In many respects the agreement vindicated the view in the SDLP in the late 1970s that the North should be the focus of a joint effort by both the British and the Irish governments. The issues it was concerned with included reform of the Diplock courts, an international fund, RUC practices, flags, emblems, funerals and the use of Irish street names. Sinn Féin hoped to demonstrate that the agreement by-passed most of the nationalist community, conscious that politically it was designed to take the ground from under them.

But one of the main problems was the lack of co-ordination of British policy towards Ireland, while opposition politicians in the South in 1988 accused Haughey of not using the machinery of the agreement to bring about change. In his autobiography, FitzGerald insisted that the extent of change brought about by the agreement was significant, and that the Irish government made a mistake in largely going along with the British government's downplaying of the worth of the agreement for fear of provoking unionists further. The result of this mistake, he insisted, was that when:

> this euphoria in the nationalist community wore off, as it inevitably did, the minority were left with no clear sense of the remarkable number of changes effected through its mechanisms, and as a result the longer-run impact of the agreement among nationalists was much less than we intended, although it was clearly sufficient to consolidate the drop in IRA support that had begun while it was under negotiation.[63]

A later judgement, that of Ed Moloney, supports this, contending that Dublin diplomats skilfully used the agreement 'to smooth the rough edges of Britain's security policy thereby reducing the grievances that nourished Catholic support for the IRA'.[64]

But the fact that the Anglo-Irish Agreement was signed illustrated that British policy had aspects of both continuity and the capacity for tactical adjustment, though ultimately a lack of co-ordination. This was partly because the Northern Ireland issue remained marginal in British politics, even if it was true there was still strong integrationist feeling within the Conservative party.[65] But there was little prospect of Britain being allowed to forget the North, politically or economically. By 1986 the IRA had killed 80 people in Britain; by 1994 one third of the North's GDP came from Westminster's financial subvention, and four out of every ten workers were employed directly by the British state. There had been a significant fall in manufacturing employment, from 183,600 in 1960 to 101,300 in 1985. By 1996 only 2,000 were employed in the ship-yards and the Troubles undoubtedly affected investment; the De Lorean car plant fiasco in 1982 cost the British taxpayers £85 million. By 1990, foreign-owned plants employed more than twice as many people in the South than in the North. This was not all a result of the Troubles, since Northern economic performance more or less paralleled that of Britain. Nonetheless, Cormac Ó Gráda has noted that an estimate of the annual cost of the Troubles to Northern Ireland of £339 million is too low because it 'does not take account of industrial jobs diverted elsewhere because of the Troubles'.[66]

Policing also remained a hugely significant issue for Britain and Northern society, financially and politically. It has been estimated that an analysis of statistics for arrests would suggest one in four Catholic men between the ages of 16 and 44 were arrested during the conflict.[67] Between 1971 and 1989, Fr Denis Faul, a Catholic priest vocal about nationalist suffering and a critic of the IRA, submitted 2,000 complaints against the British army and Ulster Defence Regiment, with no success.[68] A sense of injustice on the Catholic side was often compounded by the operation of a blatant judicial double standard. At the time of the hunger strikes, a young loyalist received a suspended sentence, having been found guilty of gun possession; the same charge for which Bobby Sands had been sentenced to 14 years in prison. In November 1986, an Old Bailey jury jailed for life Irish men found guilty of conspiring to cause explosions. Two days later in the Old Bailey a self-confessed fascist was jailed for three years for making and possessing explosives.[69] In the early 1980s the lack of thorough inves-tigation of shoot-to-kill policies in the RUC was also decried.

The supergrass system also became widely discredited. Twenty-six men, for example, were jailed in 1986 on the word of Harry Fitzpatrick. Between 1982 and 1986 almost 400 men and women had been arrested, charged and remanded in custody on the word of informers, being held for an aggregate of 1,000 years before coming to trial, while it could take up to two years to have an appeal heard. There were distressing court scenes in 1983 when the informant Ray Gilmore was due to give evidence against republicans. The IRA had threatened to kill his father, who they were holding captive, if he did not withdraw his evidence. As Gilmore 'turned to face the people he had grown up with' there was mayhem, and his three sisters were beaten from the court.[70] In the South, the Irish Supreme Court gave contradictory judgements on articles 2 and 3 of the Irish Constitution concerning the territorial claim over the North. In 1976 it was stated that they professed merely a political claim, not a legal one, a decision reversed by the court in 1990, where it was deemed to be 'a declaration of the extent of the national territory as a claim of legal right'.[71]

'many ... do not actually believe in the same God'

Intense political debate from the 1970s onwards posed new challenges for a unionism that had been artificially shielded by the Stormont regime, a transition made more difficult by the fact that, as Alvin Jackson pointed out in 1989, 'unionism does not demand a complex vision of its own past' and 'as the demands of Anglo-Irish politics have become more intricate, so the political and historical perceptions of unionism have become simplified'. This often involved sacrificing the past 'to a caricature of the present' to serve current political ends, particularly in order to ignore the historic divisions within unionism. The result was more attention being devoted to extremists like Paisley (three biographies by the late 1980s, but none of Molyneaux, the leader of the Ulster Unionist Party from 1979 to 1995), and much focus on loyalism and paramilitaries instead of official unionism and the distinctions within unionism. Historians faced the added burden of being 'informally bound to an agenda devised by government', given the partisan nature of the state. This is common to all historians of official archives, but it is even more pronounced in Northern Ireland.[72]

Academic work challenging the nationalist case became more visible in the late 1980s;[73] it particularly focused on the disastrous economy in the South to rubbish the idea that the South could ever afford unity. Opinion polls which demonstrated a lack of appetite in the South for unity were highlighted, and the need to accept the will of the majority was emphasised, a necessity some felt was being ignored, given the attention devoted to the misgovernment of the Stormont era. But it was still the case that the emphasis on 'not a united Ireland' from the unionist perspective was not accompanied by a positive cultural identity. The comments about lack of interest in the South in unity were nonetheless accurate; documents in the British Public Records Office released in 2003 reveal that, as early as 1972, the Taoiseach Jack Lynch had told the British ambassador that voters in the South 'could not care less' about reunification.[74]

But the unionist siege mentality revealed a quite desperate lack of confidence. The failure of the loyalist strike of 1977, reflecting amongst other things the demand for greater autonomy in the North, was in stark contrast to the strike of 1974, and a tactical disaster for Ian Paisley, who prematurely backed those who would quickly retreat. It was also the case in the 1980s and 1990s that while there was a diversity and sincerity about unionist beliefs in Northern Ireland, the diversity of unionism's social composition was both a strength and a weakness. Cohesion was evident when opposing undesirable developments, but there was a tendency towards disintegration when solutions or ways forward needed to be formulated. As Feargal Cochrane put it, social and cultural diversity within unionism ensured that 'far from singing from the same hymn sheet many [unionists] do not actually believe in the same God'.[75]

The need for unity, for example, in opposition to the Anglo-Irish Agreement, seemed to ensure that potentially divisive decisions concerning strategy were avoided, with the result that unionist opposition lost a sense of direction. Susan McKay observed: 'the unionist cliché that the other side is far better at propaganda than us all too readily became a form of denial'.[76] Alvin Jackson pointed out that for the Ulster Unionist Party the 'memories of the party's travails in the early 1970s remained all too alive and resonant in the late 1990s', which suggests a serious failure of adaptation, even though there was no shortage of intellect and vibrant personality within the unionist ranks. The legacy of the failed United Loyal Campaign of Opposition to the Anglo-Irish Agreement compounded the malaise, and it became a legacy of 'broken unionist confidence and internal recrimination'.[77] The party was frequently caught napping by the evolution of British policy, David Trimble later acknowledging that it failed to keep its finger on the pulse of British government thinking.

'You destroy the talent. Dishearten the community'

As the IRA's campaign raged, the activities of loyalists also became a recurring theme of Anglo-Irish conference meetings. The 6,400-strong Ulster Defence Regiment (many former members of the B Specials) was the focus of much discussion in the 1980s. By 1989, 16 UDR members were serving life sentences for murder, while from 1969 to 1989 more than 100 were jailed for serious offences, including passing information to loyalist paramilitaries, and there was overlap in membership of the Ulster Volunteer Force and Ulster Freedom Fighters. The Unionist MP John Taylor asserted that 'the loyalist paramilitaries achieved something which perhaps the security forces would never have achieved, and that was, they were a significant contribution to the IRA finally accepting that they couldn't win'.[78] Like the IRA, the loyalist paramilitaries could be unpredictable, with a propensity to savagery as revealed in the actions of the Shankhill Butchers, and their murder tally was high; they killed far more, for example, in 1975 than republicans, following the previous year's bloodiest day of the Troubles when the UVF killed 33 people and injured over 100 in a single day, detonating bombs in Monaghan and Dublin. The extent of secret British involvement remained highly controversial. It was certainly clear by the end of the century that many questions needed to be answered about the activities of British military intelligence (MI5) in Ireland, the failure of the Gardaí to investigate them adequately, and indeed the extent to which, in the mid-1970s, MI5 were influencing the activities of C3, the security branch of the Gardaí, as well as the RUC Special Branch, who, it was alleged, were running loyalist gangs on behalf of British intelligence.

The degree of expertise involved in the 1974 Dublin and Monaghan bombs was well beyond that demonstrated by loyalists previously, which would suggest collusion with others, and crucial evidence in the aftermath of the bombs was deliberately sent outside the state. But what was often as surprising as the paramilitary death tallies was what McCann referred to as the 'astonishing quiet decency' of victims' families in the aftermath of bereavement. Another Unionist MP, Ken Maginnis, pointed out to Susan McKay that the republican paramilitaries chose their targets well, in terms of inflicting maximum damage on small unionist communities in Fermanagh: 'the people who were targeted were carefully selected. You destroy the talent. Dishearten the community. It is a take-over.'[79]

'not even a dialogue of the deaf can occur'

In terms of religious identity, the local parish dynamic was often more significant than central Church structure and leadership. While Ulster Protestantism was diverse in terms of denominational divisions and conservative/liberal splits, most were united in their fear of the Catholic Church and what role they would play in a united Ireland. They were genuine fears, a point made by Cahal Daly, Archbishop of Armagh, in the *Price of Peace* (1991), in which he demonstrated an understanding of Protestant Ulster and emphasised that there was a strong religious dimension to the conflict, which some Catholics minimised or denied. In 1991, the census showed that the Catholic population was 41.4 per cent and rising and the Protestant share 54.1 per cent and falling (in 1971 the Catholic share had stood at 34.7 per cent, an indication of the speed of the rise). As was indicated in the *Opsahl Report* (1993), the result of an independent commission of inquiry into the possibility of political progress in the North: 'demography is all; uncertainty breeds insecurity; insecurity breeds violence'.[80]

In 1993, it was estimated that about one half of the province's 1.5 million people lived in areas more than 90 per cent Protestant or 95 per cent Catholic, with fewer than 110,000 people living in areas with roughly equal numbers of Catholics and Protestants.[81] In South Armagh, the Protestant population near the border dropped from 19 per cent to 1 per cent between 1971 and 1991, while the Catholic population rose from 67 per cent to 91 per cent in the same period. There was much of what a 1990 report referred to as 'cultural blindness', this report examining the tendency of people from both communities to say that they enjoyed good community relations, when in reality there was minimal contact between the two religions.[82] Reflecting on the *Opsahl Report*, Tom Garvin noted that people tended to talk past each other: 'an eerie symbol of this is provided by the fact that Catholic and Protestant deaf children are actually taught different sign languages. In Ireland, not even a dialogue of the deaf can occur.'[83]

Clearly, any progress would require the discarding of so many certainties. In the late 1980s the 50 or so Hare Krishna followers in Belfast were a strange and unique presence, but one devotee suggested: 'it transcends everything here. It gets me out of the mess and rot of being a Catholic or a Protestant.'[84] Many young people who emigrated from the North to England enjoyed the fact that people there did not care about their religion, a welcome liberation from the suffocating reality of sectarianism at home.[85] It permeated all aspects of society: Cliftonville, the main Catholic-supported soccer team in the North, made headlines for non-sporting reasons, not even being able to play their home matches against Linfield on their own ground. But there was a tendency for people to deny the existence of sectarianism in their own bailiwicks; McKay made the point in relation to the killing of the Quinn children, three Catholic brothers who burned to death after their house was petrol bombed in July 1998, that theirs was an experience which cautioned against expecting too much from integration: 'they were boys who were well integrated. They went to school with Protestant children, ran about with them and used the same community centre. They spent the evening of 11 July 1998 at the Loyalist bonfire they'd help to build. Hours later, their house was ablaze and they were dead.'[86]

'a major mystification to Protestant onlookers'

The Gaelic Athletic Association, which had remained a 32-county organi-sation, managed to survive the Northern conflict, but not without paying a significant price. Its members and property frequently came under attack. Desmond Fahey's book, *How the GAA Survived the Troubles*, demonstrates the degree of self-reliance required in order for the GAA to continue oper-ating, given that it appealed only to nationalists. It was 'like a lifebuoy and we clung on doggedly ... anything the GAA got, it got for itself'. It could not avoid politics; in 1981, during the hunger strikes, the organisation was involved in a delicate balancing act, and found it could not remain aloof from the demands of individual clubs to demonstrate against government policy. The fact that they spent the 1990s defending the retention of the rule prohibiting membership of the security forces also 'yoked the GAA to the most contentious issue of the Peace Process – policing'.[87]

But the 1990s proved to be a golden age for the GAA in Northern Ireland, despite murderous attacks. Protestants found its appeal difficult to fathom, and Fionnuala O'Connor pointed out that, when it came to the GAA, 'one lot genuinely does not know what makes the other tick'. The increase in nationalists' devotion to the GAA in the 1990s was a measure of confidence rather than triumphalism. O'Connor noted perceptively: 'a sport that crosses all classes, drawn on local talent with the strongest local support, is enviable in Protestant eyes. Theirs is a thinner sense of com-munity, the Orange hall a local hub for only one section ... the fierce alle-giance of GAA fans is a major mystification to Protestant onlookers.'[88]

Despite vast improvements, religion still affected employment chances. In 1998 in Portadown, the stage for an annual stand-off between Orange Order Drumcree marchers and the Catholic Garavaghy Road residents, 25 per cent of the residents of the Garavaghy Road had been unemployed for five years or more and 50 per cent for over one year, whereas unemploy-ment for the whole Portadown area (6,000 nationalists, 24,000 unionists) was only 9–10 per cent.[89] But Protestant identity was also affected by class; McKay found that among the wealthy middle class 'the least vehement in their loyalism were the most obvious in their Britishness'.[90] The virulently anti-Catholic rhetoric of the leader of the Democratic Unionist Party, Ian Paisley, appealed to a working-class constituency but also to propertied unionism. As he had said, as early as 1969, it was the Catholic system not the Catholic people he despised. This was typical of Northern society; those who espoused hatred of a religion in one breath expressed pity for its adherents in the next: 'I hate the system of Roman Catholicism, but, God being my judge, I love the poor dupes who are ground down under that system. Particularly I feel for their Catholic mothers who have to go and prostitute themselves before old bachelor priests.'[91]

Its critics maintained there was an arrogance about Ulster Catholicism, witnessed in its dismissal of its Protestant counterpart. Edna Longley pointed out: 'the conviction of a superior culture, a coherent identity in some, also relies on adherence to a religion that has always proclaimed itself the one true church from which all Protestants are Schismatics'.[92] But the rise of a Catholic middle class also created tensions within Catholicism, with a belief that many who benefited from the civil-rights movements of the 1960s were putting little back into the working-class communities that still, according to a leaked 1992 civil service memo called *Targeting Social Need*, were more likely to be unemployed, uneducated and sick and to experience poor housing than Protestants.[93] Dissent within Northern Catholicism was treated in much the same harsh and arrogant way as in the South. Cahal Daly allegedly told the rebel priest Pat Buckley: 'when I look out in the ocean of priests I don't want to see your head above the water'. Buckley found the Catholic Church too timid, but also contended that Daly did not match his action to his rhetoric: 'always calling for reconciliation, but he won't budge an inch on integrated education.' Buckley, who was fired by Daly, discovered he had a strange kind of freedom as he began to operate independently: 'I find up here that the Catholic Church doesn't have the absolute power to hammer someone like me into the ground. I know several priests in the South in my position who were annihilated.'[94]

At various stages the Catholic Hierarchy in the North was criticised for being either too vocal or too quiet or, indeed, too selective in what it chose to address or ignore. Gerry Adams easily side-stepped the issue of the irreconcilability of republican violence and Church law by

insisting: 'it's my church as well as Cardinal Daly's'. Others believed it
was up to Church leaders to protect working-class Catholics from the
IRA. The same snobbery and preoccupation with respectability as in the
South was apparent in the North, as was a reactionary attitude to education which saw the Church, even in 1993, warning teachers to stay away
from the new inter-church syllabus. Critics of the Catholic Church could
also legitimately argue that it was somewhat hollow to be talking about
a united Ireland when there was obviously little willingness to make the
changes necessary in Southern society to accommodate unionism. But by
the 1980s and 1990s there was a decided shift away from the rhetoric of
the 'fourth green field', and more of a tendency to criticise nationalists for
their lack of understanding of unionist fears, North and South. In 1995,
Garret FitzGerald pointed out that during the revolutionary period of the
early twentieth century many of the Protestant minority had experienced
what they felt were successive betrayals of their British/Irish identity. He
continued:

> It is important to remember that this disillusioning Southern Protes-
> tant experience remains valid today in the memory of many Northern
> Protestants. For this fact may explain more than we would like to
> believe of Northern Unionists' reluctance to trust to our oft-preferred
> but never defined 'generosity' in reaching a possible settlement of the
> Northern Ireland problem.[95]

'native, traditional Irish nationalism'

The attitude of Irish-Americans and United States governments became
more important as the Troubles endured. In the 1980s, NORAID (the
American-Irish Northern Aid Committee) unsuccessfully attempted to
resist pressure to disclose all the sources and uses of its funds, and in
1984 was forced by the courts to register as an agent of the IRA. Its
returns to the Department of Justice were a good indication of Irish-
American reaction to British policy and tactics. It collected vast sums
during internment and the aftermath of Bloody Sunday, but money was
less forthcoming when the IRA's campaign involved civilian deaths.
NORAID established roots in places as diverse as Montana and Ohio,
but pressure from the American and British governments led to an FBI
crackdown in the 1980s, the same FBI which in 1971 had described the
old IRA American leadership as 'conservative and respectable'. NORAID

was capable of attracting support from conservative quarters who saw the war simply as a British–Irish struggle; social and economic analysis did not seem to figure much in its thinking. The selection taken from the IRA's newspaper *An Phoblacht*, to be published by NORAID's paper, *Irish People*, conveniently left out references to socialism, the Middle East, Thatcher and American foreign policy in places like Chile and Cuba.[96] NORAID supporters were assured that 'the main impulse of the Irish republican movement is native, traditional Irish nationalism and is avowedly anti-Communist', though there were elements who supported the leftward shift in Irish republicanism. There is no doubt that events like the hunger strikes swelled the coffers of NORAID, and presumably the money collected not only went to dependants of prisoners but was also spent on arms. But as Brian Hanley was to point out, NORAID's politics did not remain static over the course of the Troubles, and 'while NORAID would not have existed without the Northern Ireland conflict, it was also rooted in a section of Irish America and profoundly influenced by American ethnic politics'.

Its emergence had coincided with an increased awareness of ethnicity across America and it sought to represent an ethnic identity under attack, it believed, not just from Britain, but also from 'what it saw as an Anglophile American establishment'. It encouraged Irish-Americans to emulate other ethnic groups, and resist negative portrayals of the Irish. It was never a mass movement; in 1983 the *Irish People* had a print run of just 12,500, which by 1989 had fallen to only 6,000.[97] No senior republicans were allowed to visit the US from 1972 until 1994, the year of the IRA cease-fire. With a supportive president, Bill Clinton, now in power, Sinn Féin had an exceptional level of access to the White House, supported by Congressional and corporate allies. Clinton was keen to get involved, not just because of the size of the Irish-American vote and the need for foreign policy success, but because the American government had the same interest in stability as did the British and Irish governments. American involvement had precious little to do with ideology; Clinton's National Security Advisor informed the *Irish Times* journalist Conor O'Clery that 'I don't really care whether there is a united Ireland or not'.[98]

For those in the media, reporting on the North was often difficult and dangerous, but broadcasting bans North and South frustrated many journalists and at times operated farcically, as when RTÉ was unwilling to interview a teacher dismissed because of pregnancy, due to the fact that she was living with a member of Sinn Féin, despite the subject of the interview being her dismissal.[99] There was always a danger of propaganda masquerading as news, which often led to the conflict being depicted as completely irrational. David Miller suggested that this propaganda machine was funded by the British government to the tune of £20 million sterling,[100] though perhaps it was a measure of the success of the republican movement's own propaganda skills that both Irish and British governments felt the need for such extreme measures. The extent to which senior republicans had a 'hotline' to RTÉ has been exaggerated, particularly in relation to the news division. The nature of the broadcasting ban was accepted by many, McCann has suggested, 'with a shrug of indifference', probably through a mixture of boredom and resentment at intimidation. In contrast to republicans who worked hard at media presentation, unionism, Enda Longley maintained, suffered from 'an extraordinary lack of public relations skills'.[101]

Neither was there academic consensus on whether the conflict was primarily political or religious (or whether, indeed, these could be seen as separate categories in the North), or on the reasons why substantial reform did not result in a diminution of violence. Some historians sought to empathise with all sides and blame the conflict on the backwardness of Northern Ireland's two cultures and economy,[102] and attempted to write histories acceptable to the middle ground of Northern society, even though the middle-class Alliance party had little success in trying to do this politically. The biggest weakness of the historiography of Northern Ireland remained the failure to examine history through non-sectarian concepts – power, class and gender – which was why McKay's and McCann's work, amongst others, was so valuable. They often analysed working-class communities and their attitudes, rather than the traditional 'pillars' of Northern society. But because of the violence of the North and the acrimonious political rhetoric it was difficult for historians to be frank and break new ground; Alvin Jackson pointed out that 'even the most disinterested historian is [as] bound to the sectarian arena as the most vitriolic polemicist'.[103] One of the most influential academic works, John Whyte's *Interpreting Northern Ireland*, referred to over 500 studies. He accepted the conflict as essentially religious and estimated that at the time of writing two thirds of the published analyses of the North adopted what he called the 'internal conflict' interpretation, looking at internal community divisions. Whyte also debunked the myth that Britain was the only stumbling block to a solution, suggesting the Northern Ireland problem would continue to exist regardless of Britain.

But what was missing in many analyses was an assessment of the role class and poverty played in prolonging the Troubles. A common Protestant complaint heard by McKay was that both Protestants and Catholics had experienced great poverty, but Protestants were discouraged from being vocal about it: 'that the Protestants lost out twice – they didn't recognise how badly off they were back then and now they feel that Catholics have overtaken them'. McCann was accurate, too, in asserting that 'people who claim that class has no relevance are wrong'; the IRA emerged from a community under pressure and was sustained by community networks, which was why, in the words of McCann, 'even people sickened by IRA violence can nonetheless feel an association with the IRA's presence'.[104]

'god-mothers of hatred'

But for the first 20 years of the conflict, the obsession was with security and constitutional concerns, instead of looking at structural inequality, education and community relations. There was much more focus on the latter during the 1990s, along with an examination of regional variations within Northern Ireland. In this context, women became more visible, though the extent to which they were more respected is debatable; only 11 per cent of members of local authority councils in 1989 were women, while in 1992 there were no women among the 17 MPs and three MEPs. By 1985 the four published works on women and the Troubles were exclusively republican. In 1992, Catherine Shannon criticised the tendency 'of the British tabloid press to portray Northern women as passive victims of paramilitary mobsters or bomb-throwing viragos and god-mothers of hatred'.[105] It was difficult for women to get their grievances taken seriously, but the middle-class feminist consciousness was given a certain outlet through the Equal Opportunities Commission and the Women's Law and Research group, while working-class women were to the fore in compiling data on the impact of poverty and poor social conditions. Shannon noted the pragmatic and non-hierarchical methods employed in women's collaborative work, though many felt that lack of social contact in the 1980s and 1990s (in contrast to that of the 1940s and 1950s) was contributing to considerable psychological ill-health among women.[106]

'There is menstrual blood on the walls of Armagh Prison'

By 1999 there were up to a thousand local women's groups, some of which became adept at networking and getting EC grants, though Susan McKay discovered a lot of young loyalist men who had difficulty taking women seriously. Gary Mitchell, a Protestant playwright, suggested that Protestant men's attitude was 'to silence them, keep them at home, protect them – don't allow them to do anything'.[107] Enda Longley was scathing about the identification of feminism with nationalism; she argued that nationalists had hijacked Irish feminism: 'at least Unionism [despite its 'cult of male chieftains'] does not appropriate the image of women, or hide its aggressions behind our skirts.'[108] But in the 1980s women from different religious and political backgrounds began to meet to discuss issues of common concern, as seen with the emergence of the Women's Information Group. They succeeded in 'asserting our own interpretation of what we are doing and our own definition of what we are'.[109]

Monica McWilliams of the Women's Coalition, which was represented in the Good Friday Agreement Northern Assembly, observed in the midst of discussion about paramilitary decommissioning in the 1990s that there was no reference to the use of military weapons in relation to domestic violence, and that 'the militaristic nature of the state means that weapons have been more available than in other states and that these weapons have been used against women'.[110]

There was no more telling indication of the immaturity of unionist political culture than the contempt with which it treated the Women's Coalition in the 1990s, in particular the ribald sexism of the Democratic Unionist Party. Negotiations between the Ulster Unionist Party leadership and Tony Blair also resulted in the removal of Mo Mowlam as the Secretary of State for Northern Ireland in 1999. She was the first woman to hold the office, and the unionist campaign against her included disparaging her mental abilities while she was still convalescing from a brain tumour operation.[111] The Women's Coalition was attacked precisely because it was offering something new, though the journalist Suzanne Breen criticised the lack of rigorous journalistic probing of what exactly this was. One of its leaders, Bronagh Hinds, emphasised that 'it credited the experience and skills that women brought and targeted those in community action. It gave women the belief that they had the ability to stand for election.'[112]

The difficulty Southern feminists had in deciding their attitude to Northern republican female prisoners had been revealed in 1980. Nell

McCafferty, in perhaps the most powerful opening line of her journalistic career, wrote about the women in Armagh Prison on 'dirty protest' and the brutality they were subjected to, facing sterility and death: 'There is menstrual blood on the walls of Armagh Prison in Northern Ireland.'[113] Whether or not this was a feminist issue was not something that McCafferty's feminist contemporaries could agree on. Women's community groups were given a heightened profile by President Mary Robinson in the 1990s, a reminder that it was often poverty rather than violence or sectarianism which made change in Northern Ireland difficult, though the trade unions often avoided key issues, fearing accusations of political partisanship. But by 1997 all of the political parties in the North had formulated policies on women's issues, and both the SDLP and Sinn Féin had introduced positive discrimination to ensure more women served on the executives of their parties. Women also remained prominent within dissident republican groups.[114] Bríd Rogers, a member of the SDLP talks team during the Good Friday negotiations, praised the aspiration in the agreement to advance the role of women in public life. But she acknowledged in the same year that 'the struggle for women's rights is in many ways comparable to the struggle for equality of rights between nationalist and unionist in Northern Ireland. The essential and often the most difficult first step is to get society to recognise that there is a problem.'[115]

'History creaks on its bloody hinge'

In some respects the 'Peace Process' was about institutionalising difference rather than its eradication, with the advantage for the Southern establishment of getting Sinn Féin to move away from one of the key tenets of republican orthodoxy by accepting the authority of the Dublin government. One of the ironies of the process was the very different things it meant to different sides; talk of prospects of peace was almost always accompanied by assertions that civil war was imminent. This was perhaps inevitable given the divisions of the society, and the schism the process engendered in the unionist family. It also demonstrated a lack of trust, which is perhaps why, according to McCann, the Good Friday Agreement provided for structures 'designed to contain sectarian rivalries, not get rid of them', and accept them as natural parts of Northern life.[116] But it was continually asserted that the alternative was bleaker, and the process had the added attraction of the backing of corporate Irish-America. This was one of the reasons why the arguments of the likes of McCann swayed few, and instead there was much delusional if genuinely idealistic rhetoric employed about making 'people rather than territory the touchstone of political identity'.[117] The Good Friday Agreement provided for power-sharing within Northern Ireland, North–South bodies with executive power, and new institutional links with both parts of Ireland and the devolved parliaments of Scotland and Wales.

The idea that the war could be over was what propelled 94.5 per cent of the Southern electorate and 71.2 per cent of the Northern electorate to back the Agreement in 1998, while the Omagh bomb, in some respects, cruelly sealed it. Detonated by dissident republicans styling themselves the 'Real IRA', it killed 29 people in August 1998, and the poet John Montague despaired that 'History creaks on its bloody hinge and the unspeakable is done again.' There were scenes, a witness to the bomb recalled, 'like an abattoir after someone has gone crazy; blood and burning flesh ... I saw my son walking with a woman and she had a young boy's foot in her hand. The lid of a manhole had been blown off and when I went to lift it I found there was an amputated leg under it.' The reaction was significant in that it was one of the few occasions, if not the only one, where the bulk of a divided population seemed to share grief equally.[118]

What had gone on behind the peace talks revealed the different tight-ropes republicans and unionists were walking, and the different degrees to which they could find a balance. Republicans performed infinitely better; David Trimble as leader of the Ulster Unionist Party after 1995 found it more difficult, under pressure from three governments, IRA ceasefires (the first, in 1994, was broken in 1996 and restored the following year), and a belief that unionists could face a worse future if no one negotiated for them. But as one journalist put it, he was 'an undecided man leading unenthusiastic followers'.[119] Republicans, on the other hand, had a care-fully planned and long-term strategy, demoting, dismissing and sidelin-ing hard-liners to ensure they could sustain the inevitable threat posed by dissidents. But in any case, as Fionnuala O'Connor had noticed, dissidence was traditionally less tolerated and pronounced in republican culture than within unionism: 'the major difficulty the rebel in northern Catholic society has always found, is the impossibility of being taken at his or her word as an independent agent; stepping outside the tribe equated with going to the enemy'. This was Sinn Féin's real trump card.

'I won't bend on the simple principle'

The discipline of the republican movement guaranteed exceptional faith in the leadership at least publicly, bolstered by a war-weariness and a recognition that, while negotiations would not produce a unified Ireland, neither would another 30-year conflict. While there was fragmentation, intimidation and tyranny, mastered over many years, republican leaders ensured there would never be a haemorrhage of support, and skilful media performances and public relations served them well. It also helped that from 1997 the Irish Taoiseach, Bertie Ahern, was regarded as an affable, pragmatic and ideologically indifferent negotiator. Stephen Collins has suggested that 'none of his colleagues is really sure whether he is possessed of all the deviousness and cunning attributed to him by [Charles] Haughey or whether he simply suffers from chronic indecision disguised as political shrewdness'. But what was more important in the context of the Peace Process, was that he was conciliatory and patient, and these traits 'were vital to the negotiation of the three national agreements with the social partners which delivered industrial peace for almost a decade'.[120]

In any case, this was a process that Ahern had inherited: it was largely through the efforts of Charles Haughey that contact had been kept open with republican intermediaries, and his 1991 suggestion of a joint declaration with John Major's government establishing the principle of a possible settlement would eventually bring the republicans into mainstream politics. Especially important after Haughey's resignation in 1992 was the no-nonsense businesslike approach of the deal-maker Albert Reynolds, and it was this that made the first ceasefire possible. Through the idea of a pan-nationalist consensus, Reynolds as Taoiseach began, in the words of his press secretary, Seán Duignan, 'carefully reeling the IRA in'. His insistence that 'I'm not going to pull back' was politically brave, as he was increasingly being accused of using pro-Sinn Féin language, and of using his influence and connections with the US Clinton administration to assist Sinn Féin, despite British opposition. But his response to these accusations was revealing, in that he made it clear Sinn Féin would also have to make sacrifices for the process: 'I asked Reynolds if he worried about being regarded as being too "green"', Seán Duignan recalled in his memoir of his time in government. He replied:

> It just has to be done, despite what your politically correct pals in the media are saying. What they don't notice, which may be just as well,

is that I'm also telling Sinn Féin that I won't bend on the simple principle that self-determination by the people of Ireland as a whole cannot be exercised without the agreement and consent of the majority of the people of Northern Ireland. They don't like hearing that there are no buts or maybes, no short cuts, and no way around that.[121]

Reynolds was a formidable deal-broker despite the sneers of his detractors and his short-lived premiership (see below).

'Sunningdale for slow learners'?

In many respects, Trimble agreed a package he could not sell, while ironically the DUP, who rejected the agreement, enjoyed working the resultant assembly, and the trappings of office. Trimble may have reckoned that their hypocrisy – wanting to be in government and opposition at the same time – would eventually sicken unionists. He became an unusual mixture: formed by traditional passions and fears, but also courageously bringing unionists into uncharted waters and happy to take the praise of academia in the process.[122] Republicans cleverly shifted the debate on a united Ireland to talk of unity in the context of a federal state. It was, as Séamus Mallon quite rightly pointed out in the most brilliant line of the Peace Process, 'Sunningdale for slow learners'.[123] This did not upset the tempo of the republicans as they drowned the media. In March 1999, the journalist John Waters described the interviewers' frustration: 'all Sinn Féin leaders have a series of mantras and mini-speeches which they seek to get into every interview regardless of the questions. The task of the journalist is to avoid setting off these reflex responses.'[124] Their disarming (some unionists would add chilling and sinister) politeness made this a difficult task. IRA dissidents and the Loyalist Volunteer Force, with fewer than 400 members between them, waited in the wings; unpredictable and often indisciplined and brutal.

John Hume could end his career in satisfaction, and there was truth in the Nobel Prize citation (the Prize awarded to him and Trimble in 1998) that 'his has been the clearest and most consistent advocacy of the principles reflected in the Good Friday Agreement'. More controversial was the contention of Ed Moloney that Gerry Adams too would have been a worthy recipient given his role in bringing the IRA military campaign to an end. The irony for Hume and the SDLP was that by succeeding they were endangering the *raison d'être* of their party and allowing Sinn Féin to expand, Trimble being in the same position vis-à-vis the DUP. It was telling that Trimble allegedly told Adams that he saw himself not as a leader but as a chairman; the problem was that because the unionists were so divided, they could not 'tell the people and keep on telling them what republicans have given up'.[125]

For republican grassroots, the line preferred was that the IRA 'haven't gone away you know', for which they offered the occasional chilling reminder. The journalist Suzanne Breen pointed out in 2003 that:

> since the cease-fire the IRA has dealt harshly with many in its own community. Former IRA prisoner Paddy Fox was abducted and beaten in 1999 for criticising Sinn Féin ... in 1998, former Derry internee Mickey Donnelly suffered a broken leg when he was beaten with iron bars for criticising Sinn Féin. That year, Andy Kearney bled to death in a 'punishment attack' after he had clashed with a Belfast IRA commander.[126]

It was difficult to trust republicans given that the leadership was inclined to tell their grassroots not to listen to 'what's being said publicly', and some unionists' dignity on the subject of their own suffering at the IRA's hands was outstanding. But perhaps the most significant truth, and what ensured the conflict was coming to an end, was that there was no obvious support for a return to violence. In a sense, that was the deal by the close of the century: contained violence and agonised progress and setbacks, with large dollops of dissidence, sectarian outbursts and traditional paranoia, along with a significant media and propaganda battle. But more importantly, institutions finally seemed preferable to guns.

Whether a culture of integration, the end of an often understandable obsession with security and politics, and a concentration on social issues could be achieved, however, was another matter. It could be argued that the new language of respect for 'two traditions' and 'tolerance of diversity' reinforced some of the cultural isolationism it aimed to rectify. There were still, it seemed, only two labels and two colours to be tolerated. 'Both sides want to be left alone' was the enduring impression that Fionnuala O'Connor was left with. On their joint post-Good Friday travels, unionists and republicans stayed resolutely apart. David Ervine, a leader of one of the fringe unionist parties that supported the agreement, noted that on a visit to South Africa republicans and unionists travelled on separate planes, drank in separate bars and ate in separate dining rooms: 'we went to South Africa and reintroduced Apartheid'.[127]

II

'the most expensive type, the £1.2 million type, is called after Beckett, poor bastard'
Writing at the end of the 1960s, Seán O'Faoláin, who had written prolifically throughout the Irish experience of independence, reflected on his fellow natives:

> time was when common words on every lip in every Irish pub were partition, the civil war, the republic, the gun. The vocab of the mid fifties and sixties was very different – the common market, planning, growth, rates, strikes, jobs, education opportunities or why this factory failed and that one flourished.[128]

Thirty years later these latter subjects were still of immediate relevance to most Irish people, many of whom had experienced huge change, cycles of boom and bust economically, and a politics that was at times exciting and productive but sometimes corrupt, bland and indifferent as the century drew to a close. Other issues too could now be added to O'Faoláin's list: the troubled health system, serious traffic problems, the high cost of living, the Euro, child abuse, the environment, racism, drink-induced violence, the fortunes of the Irish football team in world cups, military neutrality, and the belief that high taxation was a persecution which, through their suffering in the 1980s, the middle classes had earned the right to be absolved from. Ireland finished the twentieth century richer than could have been imagined, even during the relative affluence of the 1960s. A new middle-class generation, on the cusp of adulthood in the late 1990s, had never known anything but economic prosperity.

It is still jolting to read the opening line of one of the books that sought to explain what became known as the 'Celtic Tiger': 'Ireland has had the fastest growing economy in the world in the last years of the twentieth century.'[129] After decades of under-development and stagnation, 'Ireland' had become rich. But what was done (and not done) with that wealth would remain a source of fierce debate. Critical observers depicted a society that had become vulgar in its opulence, and indifferent to redistribution. The journalist Anne Marie Hourihane, in her book *She Moves through the Boom*, cast a cynical eye on the palatial mansions appearing in south County Dublin, as the new residents outdid their 1960s counterparts, and adorned their neighbourhoods with the ghosts of Irish literary and cultural icons:

> Out of eight houses that are occupied on the left-hand side of the cul-de-sac we count four jeeps, one Jaguar and a Porsche ... As you look around the development from the Japanese-style pond, at the yellow apartments with palms, at the top balconies, you wonder where you are. It could be a holiday village in Southern Spain or perhaps Florida, rather than a housing estate in South Dublin ... there are seven different types of houses in Carrickmines Wood and the most expensive type, the £1.2 million type, is called after Beckett, poor bastard.[130]

Many Irish left-wing activists, and social justice and religious groups, criticised the fact that the misdirected wealth increased the gap between rich and poor, failing to create a fairer society. External observers were capable of marvelling at and praising the wealth creation, but were also stinging in their end-of-century rebuke of misplaced priorities. A human-development report of the United Nations Development Programme, based on data collected in 1997, and published in 2002, observed that Ireland had the highest level of poverty in the Western world outside the United States and was one of the most unequal among Western countries, with the richest 10 per cent of the population 11 times wealthier than the poorest 10 per cent. This was despite the fact that Ireland was ranked as the fourth richest country in the world, with a per capita GNP exceeded only by Luxembourg, the United States and Norway. It was estimated that 15.3 per cent of Irish people were living in poverty, largely caused by the fact that 23 per cent of the population was functionally illiterate.[131] In 1987, the top 10 per cent of full-time employees earned 3.6 times more in gross weekly pay than the bottom 10 per cent, but by 2000, the figure had dropped to 3.3 times. Given the tax cuts favouring the rich, the degree to which this was a serious attempt at redistribution was questionable. But significantly, one study claimed that the percentage in persistent poverty fell from 11 per cent of the population in 1997 to 6 per cent in 2000.[132]

Ireland was becoming a more intolerant society also. The writer John

Ardagh, who compiled his book *Ireland and the Irish* in the early 1990s, remarked: 'if Asiatics or Africans were ever to arrive in some numbers, would the Irish remain so tolerant?'[133] Judging by the racism evident in Ireland by the end of the 1990s, the answer was a resounding no. Refugees and asylum seekers were often subjected to much the same prejudice that had been shown towards native marginalised groups in Ireland. Aside from such uglier aspects, there was a great deal of discussion about the new-found confidence of the Irish, the 'feel-good' factor and the sense of pride emanating from an economic performance which surpassed that of the traditionally dominant European economies.

But it is indisputable that many of the problems in evidence at the time of Irish independence remained unsolved, and there was still very little ideological soul-searching among those in a position to mould a new society or politics. Despite a few false dawns, virtually every political party (with the exception of the Greens, Sinn Féin and the tiny Socialist Party), old and new, was in power at some stage from the 1970s to the 1990s, as the electorate, after 1977, rejected single-party government for the rest of the century. The fact that they were so quick to rotate spoke volumes about the triumph of the middle ground in Irish politics. This may have been convenient when economic success was evident; but in many ways it was postponing the inevitable question that economic cycles of boom and recession would leave: how would public services be paid for when it was politically unacceptable to advocate tax increases? It was in this context that the general failure in the post-war period to consolidate and rebuild infrastructure and health and education systems, financed by consensual tax rises, became most problematic. It seemed to be the case that the concept of wealth was private rather than public, with a lack of debate about the merit of low taxes or high social provision and public investment. By the end of the twentieth century some Irish schoolchildren were still being taught in dilapidated rat-infested Victorian primary school buildings, despite living through a sustained economic boom.

'a parallel stream of information'

There was a growing awareness of the many failures of independent Ireland, particularly with regard to its treatment of vulnerable children, and the appalling treatment many of them endured. Giving a voice to victims became a major cultural concern in the 1990s, aided by a vastly expanded media. Irish people were listening to and seeing things that would have found no outlet in the 1970s. Their tales revealed a sorrowful bounty for the social historian; indeed, they depicted a hidden Ireland which had to be aired, as if to prove the salience of the point made by Eavan Boland, one of Ireland's best-known poets, when she cautioned that 'one of the things that acquisition and the pursuit of wealth induces is amnesia ... and those who seek them will not only forget, but want to forget, the levels of strength and survival and near-to-the-edge dispossession that we once had as a people'.[134]

The recounting of miserable Irish childhoods became something of an international phenomenon in the 1990s, underscored by Frank McCourt's *Angela's Ashes* in 1996. This success led in turn to the accusation that such childhoods were fictitious and imagined for commercial gain, or traded cynically on the nostalgia industry, though the evidence presented in earlier chapters would suggest that this was patently not the case. The books also served as a reminder that other accounts of difficult pasts, published before the boom but neglected because they were not believed, or were unfashionable in the sense that society was not ready for them, needed to be re-examined. In June 2000, the archivist and literary critic Catriona Crowe suggested:

> the whole business of untold stories is at the heart of our fascination with these revelations. The private domain of personal experience has always been at odds with the official stories which were sanctioned, permitted and encouraged by the state and the Catholic Church ... these memoirs run like a parallel stream of information alongside the official documentary record and complement it with their personal immediacy and vibrancy. The official record can tell us what happened, but rarely what it felt like.[135]

Greater openness about physical abuse, sexuality and public and political morality also facilitated discussion of dark pasts, as did widespread reportage of contemporary events such as concealed pregnancies, rape, corporal punishment and sex abuse. But by the end of the century it could be argued that the media occasionally went overboard, to the extent that one newspaper in reviewing the year 1997 referred to it as 'the year of the paedophile priest', narrowing the scope of a discussion and reflection that needed to go much further than that. Nevertheless, it was understandable that newspapers sought to make amends for their lack of pursuit of such issues in the past, though they could hardly be blamed given the environment in which they existed. The criticisms levelled at the Church were at times ferocious and the power of the Church in Ireland was shattered in many ways, though to suggest that the end of its dominance can be dated to the 1990s is misguided; it was in fact well under way by the 1970s.

'Aphrodite rising from the waves'

Another dominant theme of these years was the huge change in attitudes to the family, and birth control. Ireland finally began to reflect European demographic norms, revealing a society utterly transformed. This was the case in terms not only of the availability of contraception and the legalisation of divorce, but also the relative youth of the population. According to the 1991 census, 44 per cent of the population was under the age of 25, by far the highest proportion in the European Union, and a huge gulf existed between their outlook and that of the preceding generation. The divide between rural and urban widened as well, to the extent that the viability of some farming communities was seriously in doubt by the 1990s. The status of women also drew much comment and analysis, though the women's movement in the 1970s was to have a chequered history. Forty per cent of married women were in the workforce by the end of the century, compared to only 5 per cent in 1966. Between 1975 and 1995 the probability of marriage for women declined by one third, from 90 to 60 per cent.[136]

It was not until 1973 that an unmarried mother's allowance was introduced, which Finola Kennedy suggested, in ideological terms, 'was like stepping on to a new planet'. The Family Planning Act of 1979 (as a result of a 1973 Supreme Court decision that marital privacy was protected under the Constitution) allowed only married couples access to contraception through prescription, and was indicative of the timidity of politicians in the face of pressure from the Catholic right. But, as Kennedy noted, throughout the century, governments were happy to avoid taking responsibility for the welfare of families 'until stimulated to do so by some element of public demand, or left with no option due to a decision of the courts'.[137]

Linda Connolly, the first author to chart the history of the different Irish women's movements of the twentieth century, considers that an undue concentration on women and nationalism has distorted a recognition of the hybridity of the history of the Irish women's movement, as has the lack of attention given to numerous Protestant middle-class female reformers. She also challenges the simplistic assumption that a backward Irish women's movement suddenly modernised in the 1960s and 1970s; or as Hilda Tweedy of the Irish Housewives' Association put it, 'so many people believe that the women's movement was born on some mystical date in 1970, like Aphrodite rising from the waves'.[138] The network of women's organisations of the mid twentieth century was in fact 'the direct catalyst' for the establishment of the ad hoc committee on women's rights in 1968, which resulted in the establishment of the First Commission on the Status of Women in 1970 and the formation of the Council of the Status of Women in 1972. This was a particularly significant development given that 'in no other European country today is there an organisation like the CSW, a co-ordinated organisation directed by paid, professional staff and funded by the state'.[139] However, the emergence of ideological debates and tensions within Irishwomen United was a reminder of the numerous divisions within Irish feminism during the 1970s.

Nonetheless, the extent to which these women succeeded in bringing to the fore issues that had been considered private and taboo, such as domestic violence, rape and discussion of parenthood, was striking. The backlash of the 1980s, including the abortion and divorce referenda, was an indication of the ability of small groups of Catholic activists to divide women, leading to what Connolly called 'a highly unsuccessful and deferential campaign' to oppose the pro-life amendment campaign in 1983, which in the short and long term was a disaster. The degree to which there was a convergence in the direction of the mainstream, with the increasing professionalisation of the women's movement, and a certain dichotomy between grassroots community and professional activism in the 1990s, raised the question of how far the women's movement could remain radical.[140]

'only a few hundred ever marched to protest against unemployment'
Revelations of political corruption may have been shocking in terms of the extent to which individual politicians and state-sponsored institutions lined their own pockets, but the traditional larger parties continued to dominate policy and government, and outrage seldom translated into civic protest if the middle-class individual was not affected. In 1987, the historian and journalist Tim Pat Coogan made the important observation that

three quarters of a million people marched against income tax in the great marches of the 1970s, 'but only a few hundred ever marched to protest against unemployment'.[141] It would perhaps be inaccurate to see Irish politics as being particularly corrupt, as those on the take were matched by those championing ethics, and in 1997 Ireland had far-reaching and progressive freedom of information legislation, in advance of most developed countries. The political establishment was not the only one to come under negative scrutiny; so did the legal profession and the Gardaí, who, before the 1970s and 1980s, had virtually never been called to account.

If it is true that Irish identity was thrown into the melting pot, it is also the case that with regard to certain issues the Irish experience remained constant. Alcohol abuse continued to leave deep scars. John Ardagh, writing about pre-boom Ireland in the early 1990s, suggested that 'one old image that certainly needs to be revised, if indeed it was ever valid, is that of the Irish as violent drunkards. They are now drinking less and many pubs are doing quite badly; alcohol has risen sharply in price, the Irish are now better educated and they have other things to do.'[142] This trend was not to continue. Between 1989 and 1999 there was a 41 per cent increase in alcohol consumption in Ireland, whereas in ten other European countries it dropped. In the remaining four EU states, the increase was much less over the same period. There was now one pub for every 290 people in the state, and public order offences increased by 97 per cent between 1996 and 2000, most of them alcohol-related.[143]

A 1999 survey on drinking habits revealed that over half of men and nearly two thirds of women in the 18–24 age group engaged in high-risk drinking, and male deaths from homicide seemed to be closely related to changes in the consumption of alcohol. By the beginning of the twenty-first century, alcohol was an industry worth £5 billion annually, and alcohol accounted for 13 per cent of the average household expenditure, with alcoholism now as likely to affect women as men. There was a four-fold increase in the number of teens intoxicated in public places; alcohol abuse was responsible for 7 per cent of all health costs and 80 per cent of public-order offences. One expert in the field contended that alcoholism was being treated 'as something suffered by individuals rather than a reflection of an entire societal approach to drink'.[144] It also seemed ironic that what was blamed on poverty at the end of the nineteenth century was blamed on affluence by the end of the twentieth century.

'our politicians have propelled us towards economic and social calamity'

The performance of the Irish economy was affected by a number of external as well as internal factors, including entry into the European Economic Community in 1972 and the oil crisis of 1973. But irresponsible internal management of the economy from the 1970s ensured that by the 1980s politicians were making grave declarations that the country was spending way beyond its means. Basic lack of information about the economy was a hindrance to effective management and planning. As far back as 1969, the Third Programme for Economic Development specifically referred to the need for more information regarding the distribution of incomes. The lack of statistical data was also singled out by the National Economic and Social Council in the 1970s, highlighting the immature state of economic forecasting.

The distribution of the payment of tax was something which came sharply into focus, with PAYE contributions to the overall total increasing dramatically, from 71.4 per cent in 1975 to 86.5 per cent in 1978. There was much resentment that, for example, in the period 1974–8 PAYE workers paid £1,800 million in income tax, self-employed people £320 million and farmers just £20 million. A substantial number of farmers paid no tax at all, a factor which no doubt contributed to the anger of those white-collar workers who took to the streets in protest. Over time, there was also resentment that EEC grants were providing some small farmers with middle-class incomes; in 1973, 80 per cent of farmers in the Republic had been classed as transitional and, consequently, were heavily subsidised.[145]

But economists in the 1970s and 1980s were also alarmed at the extent to which governments would not place the economic well-being of the country above party politics. Put more crudely, they were accused of being prepared to risk national bankruptcy in order to buy votes, as happened when Fianna Fáil won the last overall majority of the twentieth century in 1977, promising a massive give-away which would have been deemed totally imprudent and unpatriotic by a previous generation. In 1982, Vincent Browne, the most dynamic investigative journalist of his generation, and editor of the innovative current-affairs magazine *Magill*, sought to raise the concept of accountability in many areas, including economic management. He editorialised: 'our politicians have propelled us towards economic and social calamity in the last decade. Wild, irresponsible election promises and commitments, reckless public expenditure schemes, uncontrolled deficit budgeting and an unprecedented falsification of budget figures have coalesced to create the most serious economic crisis the state has ever known.'[146] The figure owed in foreign debt was equivalent to £6,000 for every income tax payer in the country, and at one point virtually all the money collected in income tax was only serving the interest owed on the debt.

Ireland's renowned economic planner T. K. Whitaker pointed to two policy errors in the 1970s that began the process of decline: the decision in 1972 to resort to borrowing for current budgetary purposes, and the misplaced (and irrational) optimism which underlay the resumption of economic planning in 1977.[147] The huge rise in public spending did not generate the productive capital hoped for, nor did the desired private-sector investment materialise.

There was much decrying too of what was regarded as an overstaffed and inefficient public service – in 1971 there were 38,200 civil servants, which had risen by 58 per cent to 60,500 in 1981 – and a failure to index taxation bands. This meant that many of the lower paid were being propelled into the higher income tax bands as their wages rose in line with inflation, while tax allowances and exemptions were aimed largely at the middle class. A 1974 wealth tax was abandoned in 1977, while the middle class rebelled against a residential property tax in 1994. By 1984, nearly 30 per cent of the adult population was receiving some form of social welfare, with roughly one sixth of all households being fully reliant on social welfare payments as their only source of income.

While the economy and employment had continued to grow in the 1970s, tax reductions and increases in public spending as a result of the 1977 promises simply did not provide the growth to sustain them, and interest rate increases risked crippling the economy entirely. Though Ireland's reaction to the oil crisis in this regard was not unique in Europe, according to Cormac Ó Gráda, the managers of the Irish economy seemed much slower to learn the lesson of its mistakes.[148] In 1973, employment stood at 1.05 million, as it had been in 1961, but between 1979 and 1985 unemployment rose from 7.8 per cent to 18.2 per cent. In the middle of that period, a serious debate began about the extent of poverty in Ireland, with the Combat Poverty Agency estimating one third of the population, or one million people, were living in poverty, and this poverty rate was exceeded only by Spain, Greece and Portugal. By 1985, 26 per cent were living below a poverty threshold set at 40 per cent of average income in the EU, while the average EU rate had fallen to 16 per cent.

Farmers on marginal holdings, and labourers without skills, were perhaps the most stranded and least socially mobile, as was the case in Greece, Portugal and Spain. EU subsidies did help to close some of the gaps between rural and urban Ireland. Critics argued that preoccupation with this sort of redistribution and with winning elections by subsidising key groups of voters dominated Irish politics and undermined business confidence. Multinationals had been a feature of the economy since the 1970s and tended to perform better than the native Irish companies (by 1983 the multinationals employed 87,600). Criticism was made of an industrial policy that paid too much attention to promoting foreign companies and capital, to the neglect of infrastructural investment in communications and the environment. But such concerns evaporated with the success of multinational investors in the mid-1990s, and by late 1996 about 300 computer and electronic firms employed over 10,000 people in Ireland.[149] Many of the US pharmaceutical giants also located in Ireland, while much use was made of the Irish Financial Services Centre which was established in 1987, to meet the the huge growth in financial services. Seemingly, Ireland had recovered from a culture which, according to some management strategists in the mid-1980s, had constrained entrepreneurial action, Irish men and women having traditionally found it easier to make money abroad.

Progress was also helped by the fact that the attitude of the trade unions changed. The Irish Congress of Trade Unions took a hard-line stance in the midst of much industrial unrest in the 1970s and 1980s. They rejected the idea that pay increases in the public sector should be based on the government's capacity to pay, and flexed their muscles in the industrial and public sector spheres. Their actions were defensive, in order to maintain wages and employment, particularly after the collapse of pay bargaining. But there was a successful attempt to bring to Irish industrial relations more harmony than existed in Britain towards the end of the 1980s, leading to programmes for National Recovery (1987), Economic and Social Progress (1991), Competitiveness and Work (1994) and Prosperity and Fairness (2000). Trade union leaders, in stark contrast to their militant founding fathers, became champions of social stability and consensus.

'Things Irish are truly swinging in London right now'

But before such consensus was established, it was emigration which once again became the only option for thousands of unemployed workers and graduates. In the years 1985–6, over 30,000 emigrated, and between 1983 and 1988 there was a net outflow of 130,000. Many of them naturally went to England, which was understandable given that by 1970 it was claimed there were almost one million Irish-born people living in Britain. This was the same year in which a weekly newspaper, the *Irish Post*, was launched to serve the emigrant community. By 1986 it had a circulation of 78,000. During St Patrick's Week (not just day!) in 1986, it proclaimed: 'Things Irish are truly swinging in London right now. 3 month long festivals of Irish culture – 3 seasons of Irish film – and ever so much more. Dublin offers nothing to compare to it. The young London Irish who have come on stream have spiritedly claimed their heritage.'[150]

But this optimism and confidence belied the complexity and difficulty of that heritage, the consequences for those that left and those left behind. In 1970, a survey undertaken by the residents of Achill Island in County Mayo, for example, showed that 75 per cent of the fathers or heads of households on the island were working outside the country. By 2000 it was estimated there were 850,000 Irish-born people living in Britain, 600,000 of whom were from the Republic; and the 1950s exiles were more poorly educated than the 1980s NIPPLES (New Irish Professional People Living in England). Of those who earned primary university degrees in Ireland in 1988, 36 per cent went on to emigrate. A 1997 report for the British Commission for Racial Equality, *Discrimination and the Irish in Britain*, pointed out that while 11.5 per cent of black African women in Britain were in the lowest social class, 14 per cent of Irish women were, and that poor housing, health problems and high mortality rates were striking features of the lives of the older Irish in Britain. These were facts that the economic boom at home tended to completely overshadow, raising the question of whether there was an onus on Ireland as it became rich to do more for their welfare, if not bring them home.[151] Irish men in Britain were the only migrant group whose mortality rate was higher in Britain than it was in their country of origin.

'sneaking into hostels after hours, with illegally-held keys'

Though the 'New Irish' were much better educated than their 1950s counterparts, their task could still be daunting. Tim Pat Coogan recalled meeting a group of young civil engineers, who had a photograph of their graduation class:

> Of the 47 beaming young faces in the photograph only one had a permanent job in Ireland, two had temporary work and the other 44 were emigrants ... they had been doubling up in friends' bedsitters, sneaking into hostels after hours with illegally-held keys and generally subsisting in a variety of ways never envisaged by themselves or their parents as they worked their way through 16 difficult, costly years of education.[152]

But there were compelling reasons to stay abroad. Five years later John Ardagh met a 23-year-old Irish man in London who told him: 'I'm now earning £20,000 a year here in London as a civil engineer. In Ireland, I would find it hard to get any such job and if I did, it would pay only half that and be far more highly taxed. That's why I'm still here. But I miss the warmth of Ireland.'[153]

America, too, provided a new outlet for the wandering Irish, where earlier in the century they had established themselves at the centre of the labour movement, the politics of the cities, the Church and even literature. Their legal status was one of the foremost concerns in the 1980s. Although 9,900 emigrated legally in 1989, many more went illegally to cities like New York, Boston and Chicago, and became active in the Irish Immigration Reform Movement. A notable success of their campaign was the Immigration Reform and Control Act. Of the 40,000 green cards available under this scheme, 16,329 went to Irish applicants, a measure of the social and political influence they could generate in America, though many Irish women ended up once again in private homes looking after children and the elderly.[154] As with Britain, it was the fact that the emigrants were better educated which facilitated their more innovative pursuits, with many finding their way into journalism, publishing and television, making an impact beyond their numbers. Perhaps they were attempting to discard the psychological baggage that had marked a previous generation of Irish emigrants. In October 1996 the *New York Times* declared: 'The Irish are ascendant again'; some even managed to sell a message about triumph over misery which had an enormous appeal to the Americans, as Frank McCourt was to discover. The writer Pete Hamill suggested: 'many members of this new generation are not living a postponement or a sacrifice, they are having their American lives now'.[155] The influential *Irish Voice* newspaper commenced publication in 1987 in response to increased Irish-American activity, and its first headline sold a message of defiance: 'We'll never return – Young Illegals'. But ten years later, the *New York Times* told a different story: 'Irish eyes turning homeward as a country's moment comes'. The unprecedented economic boom in Ireland was making even confirmed expatriates reconsider where their futures lay.[156]

'consistently outperforms its partners in the EU'

The roots of this boom lay in a communal political appetite for change (Alan Dukes as leader of Fine Gael after 1987 promised not to obstruct Fianna Fáil's plans for economic revival), along with the granting of increased EU aid, and the growing participation in the workforce, including a huge increase in the number of women working. In 1987 the rate of labour force participation for women was 40 per cent, which increased to 48 per cent by 1997 (but was still well below the UK rate of 67 per cent). There was an effort to rationalise parts of the public sector, and the decision of numerous multinationals to locate and invest in Ireland was facilitated by exceptionally favourable tax breaks, very low corporation tax and a healthy external economic environment.

The creation of new jobs averaged more than 1,000 a week between 1994 and 2000. Between 1986 and 2000, 513,000 new jobs were created, an increase of 47 per cent, hence the 'Celtic Tiger' label, as Ireland's economy grew at a pace akin to the 'tiger' economies of south-east Asia. There were 1.71 million employed by 2000, up from 1.08 million in 1986. Paul Sweeney pointed out that in the 16 years to 1996, Irish non-agricultural growth, at 26 per cent, exceeded that of the 12 European Union countries (only 7 per cent growth) and the US (with 15 per cent growth), and while the problem of long-term unemployment was not eradicated, unemployment fell to 6.4 per cent. Sweeney quotes the *Financial Times* assessment of 1995: 'Ireland has been one of the unsung success stories of the past few years. With a productivity record which would be the envy of the Germans and a balance of payments surplus in line with Switzerland or Japan, Ireland consistently outperforms its partners in the EU.'[157]

With a population of 3.72 million in 1999, and a very low population density, only 8 per cent of the workforce were now involved in agriculture (compared to 37 per cent in 1960), another indication of the transformation of the economy. The overwhelmingly positive media reporting of the economy, both at home and abroad, however, encouraged a lack of critical thought as to how the money should be spent, or what constituted sustainable or holistic development. While unemployment assistance and pension payments rose, some economists estimated that, particularly from 1994 – using a poverty line of 60 per cent of average income in 1987 – the proportion of the population in poverty in 1987 was 16 per cent, falling to 15 per cent by 1994 and 10 per cent by 1997.[158] Though these figures were disputed, the increase in inequality in Ireland could not be denied. In the late 1980s, the top 10 per cent of households held one half of the total wealth of the country, and the top 5 per cent about 20–25 per cent.[159] There was also a failure to tackle Ireland's appalling transport, infrastructure and housing problems. A critic noted in 1998 that 'if the recession of the 1980s brought too little criticism of Ireland's dependent industrialisation strategy, the economic expansion of the 1990s brought even less critical thought'.[160] External factors and the vulnerability of a small open economy also meant that predicting continuing spectacular growth rates was a risky business. Neither was there any attempt to tackle the monopoly privileges enjoyed by the elite in the legal and medical professions.

'the atmosphere of a noisy real estate agency or pork belly futures market'
With regard to housing, it was ironic that a hundred years after the end of the Irish Land War, a native class of landowners and speculators aped many of the traits of the worst landlords of the nineteenth century. Many of those who profited from the Celtic Tiger spent fortunes on property speculation that by the end of the 1990s had contributed to hugely inflated house prices. This was the culmination of a building boom, which began after EEC entry, leading to so-called 'Bungalow Blight'. By 1976, 5,500 new private bungalows were being built every year in rural Ireland. By the early 1980s that figure had doubled to 11,517.[161] In urban areas, vulnerable people in rented accommodation had to endure the vagaries and whims of landlords who took advantage of a lack of legislation protecting tenants, and the fact that no government was prepared to tackle the building industry. In November 1989 it was estimated that 70 per cent of people in private rented accommodation were on week-to-week tenancies, the same year in which the Gardaí investigating planning corruption referred to a 'nest of vipers'.[162]

In the late 1970s, the price of land for residential development rose steeply and sparked a series of what were to become controversial land rezoning resolutions by local authorities. This procedure was abused by certain county councillors to secure benefits for individual business people and political supporters, particularly in Dublin, by granting permission for rezoning and developments that would more than likely have been refused by officials. The environmental journalist and author Frank McDonald described how:

> meetings of Dublin County Council to deal with successive county development plans ... took on the atmosphere of a noisy real estate agency or pork belly futures market. You could almost smell corruption in the air. The tiny public gallery was often packed beyond capacity by landowners, speculators, developers and their agents waiting for favourable rezoning decisions often involving hundreds of acres of land ... according to reliable sources, almost every major rezoning adopted by the [Dublin County] Council during the early 1990s was contaminated by corruption.[163]

The truth was that from the 1960s very little progress was made in terms of regional and physical planning. Commissioned reports recommending planning in an integrated way were ignored; rather than plan along existing railway lines, planners favoured motorised city-led developments in which public transport would play a very small role (the decision to close so many railway lines in the 1950s was to prove costly indeed). What was regarded as the expanding 'Dublin Region', or commuter belt, resulted in the 1990s in the growth of towns like Mullingar, where, observed Ann Marie Hourihane, the streets were 'festooned with the signs of Dublin estate agents'.[164] A price was being paid for ignoring a 1974 report that recommended development land be compulsorily acquired by the local authorities at a small margin above its existing use value (an effective solution to housing landless labourers in the early years of independence). The arrest of George Redmond, the former Assistant Dublin City and County Manager, at Dublin Airport in February 1999, on suspicion of taking bribes, was a fitting if sad way for a century of local government in Ireland to end, in tandem with the establishment of a number of tribunals of inquiry to investigate corruption. By 1996 the value of the construction industry's output was £6.1 billion, a 48 per cent increase on the 1994 level. Everything, it seemed, was for sale, one journalist acerbically remarking that 'indeed, if this government got a decent offer for the Rock of Cashel tomorrow morning, they would probably take it'.[165]

'tribunals are about as useful as tits on a bull'

Money, and the abuse of power in its pursuit, came to dominate the headlines in the second half of the 1990s, the outrage deepened by the fact that much of the revelations concerned the 1980s, when the economy was in recession. But the outrage was rarely translated into a wider debate about fairness. Dick Walsh, political correspondent of the *Irish Times*, noted that the 1997 general election campaign, 'which really was about fairness, public service and the nature of society, ended with a lopsided populist appeal which reduced all issues to one: tax reductions at any cost'.[166] Perhaps if the revelations had come to the surface in the 1980s, the Dáil could have become Ireland's Bastille, though it should be noted that there were politicians who spurned advances and bribes and fought hard for ethics, standards and the minute raking of the past in order to serve accountability, even if one tribunal witness, a developer, was to rage that 'tribunals are about as useful as tits on a bull'.[167]

Not only corruption by politicians and businessmen was being investigated; many victims of unaccountable institutions were also to see their tormentors exposed. By the end of 2000 there were six tribunals: the Moriarty Tribunal investigating payments to Charles Haughey and Michael Lowry, a former Fine Gael minister; the Flood Tribunal on allegations of planning corruption; the Laffoy Commission in the abuse of children in institutions; the Lindsay Tribunal on the infection of haemophiliacs by contaminated blood products; the Barron inquiry on the Dublin, Monagahan and Dundalk bombings of 1974; and a non-statutory Dunne inquiry into organ retention by hospitals. The fees paid to lawyers were astronomical, and the work of the tribunals grindingly slow, not helped by the stalling mechanisms and legal challenges of various parties, some of whom had used offshore bank accounts to avoid the paying of tax. The early 1990s had also witnessed an investigation into the collusion of government and business in the beef trade.

'I've taken this shit long enough. I'm not taking another minute of it'

The details of the tribunals were often complicated, made barristers into millionaires, and rarely looked like they would end in prosecutions for the wrongdoers, who could take some comfort in the fact that the tribunals were not courts of law. Tribunals were also an indictment of the lack of investigation at home into these issues. It often took outsiders to unfold the truth, as with the exposure by Susan O'Keefe of the BBC of the beef industry in the 1991 documentary *Where's the Beef?* She concluded in 1993 that there was far too much indulgence in Irish society of unethical behaviour and malpractice and that a culture of silence prevailed. The tribunal of inquiry into the beef industry gave a good insight into how power operated in Ireland. Private beef processors were given huge amounts of government export credit in order to trade with Iraq, and in the summer of 1990 the Dáil reconvened for an emergency session during its holidays, in order to pass emergency legislation allowing the courts to appoint an examiner rather than a liquidator for the Goodman beef companies. In the words of Fintan O'Toole, the 'possible collapse of a private beef company was treated as a national emergency'.[168] The onset of the Gulf War left the Goodman group with uncollectable credits of £180 million. Failure by governments to carefully control and regulate the beef industry had allowed individuals like Larry Goodman, who owned 74 companies in 1986, to amass fortunes, particularly after the EU began to buy beef into intervention. This was the system whereby the EC had guaranteed to keep the price of beef from falling by setting a basic price above the general world price of beef, and then buying large quantities of beef if market prices within the EC fell below the set price. Beef companies were paid to debone and store the meat before it would eventually be sold. This had been designed as an emergency measure, but because of the over-supply of beef was a huge business in itself. The Beef Tribunal heard evidence of an enterprise plagued by the forgery of documents and stamps, the alteration of declared weights, tax dodging and forays into the politics of the Middle East. Also noteworthy was the absence of investigations into the source of the beef. Eighty-four per cent of beef exported to Iraq by Goodman was intervention beef, and non-Irish beef was being used for the Iraq contracts. Even when two of his plants were under criminal investigation, this did not alter state support for the company. He thus 'not only had the state subventing his purchase of the beef for Iraq, he also had it guaranteeing payment for it'.[169] The judge who presided over the tribunal suggested that 'if the questions that were asked in the Dáil were answered in the way they are answered here, an awful lot of time and money could have been saved'.[170]

Ultimately, however, the full truth could not emerge because a

Supreme Court ruling on cabinet confidentiality decided the interest of government confidentiality took precedence over the public interest. (Maurice Moynihan, secretary to governments in the early decades of independence, dismissed this judgement as 'all nonsense'.[171]) Rather than greater public awareness resulting from the inquiry, the issues most salient were lost in the mire of legal wrangling and squabbling politicians battling over any sentence they claimed would vindicate their reputation. Seán Duignan, press secretary to the government, recalled the night a copy of the tribunal report was procured, and the Taoiseach Albert Reynolds's determination that the Labour Party's hope that it would lead to his downfall would be foiled. (Reynolds had been Minister for Finance when many of the decisions concerning the Goodman Group were made and he was now uncomfortably in coalition with the Labour Party.) 'I was summoned to the Taoiseach's office where members of his beef tribunal legal team were examining a copy of the tribunal report which had been obtained through the Department of Agriculture.' They:

> had divided the report into a number of sections which were being simultaneously scrutinised between them while the Taoiseach sat awaiting their verdict. After about a half hour, a quick check around the table produced a consensus that the findings, apart from criticising certain of the Taoiseach's decisions, did not question his motives or impugn his integrity. Someone said, 'You're in the clear.' 'Are you sure?' asked Reynolds. 'Yes,' came the reply. 'OK,' said Reynolds. 'I've taken this shit long enough. I'm not taking another minute of it. Tell the pol corrs I'm vindicated, Diggy.'[172]

'The demons summoned by the cocaine he had snorted'

The payments to politicians scandals emerged by accident, when a member of Ireland's best-known supermarket dynasty, Ben Dunne (who had previously survived a kidnapping by the IRA in 1981), was arrested snorting cocaine with a prostitute in Florida. Journalist Sam Smyth described a scene in a Florida hotel that nobody could have predicted would have serious consequences for Irish politics:

> The demons summoned up by the cocaine he had snorted on the seventeenth floor were still torturing Ben Dunne as police officers tried to get him through the hotel to the ambulance at the front door. He was

hog-tied, cuffed at the wrists and ankles, with policemen supporting each end of a pole, carrying him trussed up like a beast prepared for a barbeque. He continued to struggle and bellow.[173]

When his fellow heirs sought to dethrone him, they discovered Dunne had given huge sums to certain politicians, which led to the McCracken enquiry of 1997, the findings of which led to a wider Tribunal into payments to politicians. The extent to which Charles Haughey, dragged out of peaceful and opulent retirement, had been dependent on huge handouts from businessmen, and had his debts written off by banks, confirmed what many suspected but was still shocking in its scale. Another investigation was initiated in 1999 to reveal the truth about the Ansbacher operation, used by 120 of Ireland's wealthiest business people, and handled by Haughey's accountant, involving the placement of money offshore to avoid the paying of tax. The monies were routed through London, the Cayman Islands and back to Dublin.

Another fact revealed by such investigations was the extent to which bankers, accountants and benefactors colluded and were untouched for so long. By reducing capital gains tax from 40 to 20 per cent, governments encouraged the idea that heavily taxing the rich was completely off the political agenda. Perhaps most scandalous, given that it got the endorsement of the Labour Party while in coalition with Fianna Fáil in 1993, was the tax amnesty, when tax defaulters were given a total amnesty on payment of just 15 per cent of the tax they owed to the state, and a guarantee of absolute confidentiality (which undoubtedly benefited many who had contributed generously to the funds of political parties). Another revelation was that Irish Life Insurance had taken £4.5 million out of customers' accounts, and placed the money in sales schemes designed to earn commission for staff, but against the interests of policy-holders. One could be forgiven for wondering whether the Irish Revenue Commissioners actually existed. Between 1989 and 1993, the Allied Irish Bank operated over 50,000 bogus overseas accounts in order to avoid paying DIRT (Deposit Interest Retention) tax, and in a secret deal with the Revenue Commissioners it was agreed to keep the issue secret and to impose no penalties. More and more often the phrase 'banana republic' was to be heard, and there was justifiable worry that corruption was often uncovered only by accident.

In 1999, the Taoiseach, Bertie Ahern, suggested that there was a 'culture' of tax evasion in Ireland, and perhaps this was a culture that operated not only among the wealthy, which may explain why there was relatively little political fallout or criminal prosecution as a result of the revelations. In the 1980s, after all, many farmers had conspired to defraud the taxpayers through using loopholes in the TB eradication scheme, whereby farmers nominated their own vets, a connivance which could not have succeeded without the co-operation of the veterinary profession and members of the civil service. Irish farmers had strongly resisted paying any tax.

The Irish section of a European Values System study found that while the Irish were less tolerant than other Europeans when it came to sexual morality or orientation, they were much less likely to disapprove of issues such as social welfare fraud or tax evasion: 'on a range of one to ten, where one meant that a certain kind of behaviour was never justified and ten meant that it was always justified, cheating on your taxes scored 2.64 in Europe as a whole. In Ireland the score was 3.35.' Materialism, it seemed, even overrode marital fidelity: 'people in the Republic disapproved more strongly of stealing your neighbour's car than of stealing his or her spouse'. In 1998, the EU anti-fraud unit announced that in 1997 there were 149 known acts of fraud against EU funds in Ireland, to the value of £7 million.[174]

'bought off the conservative heartlands of rural Ireland'?

Perhaps the above observations lend credence to the idea that for Ireland membership of the European Economic Community was primarily about financial considerations. Certainly, these were to play a huge part in strategic thinking concerning membership. Ireland signed the Accession Treaty in 1972, and given its military neutrality (though this was not expressed constitutionally) the idea of an EEC to promote peace in Europe was not a major factor in Ireland's 'ideological commitment' to Europe. A euro barometer taken in autumn 1974 found that 82 per cent of Irish people polled considered that the most important aspect of the community was economic rather than political. While both the Labour Party and Sinn Féin campaigned against joining, the issue of sovereignty did not form a significant part of the referendum campaign, in contrast to the importance of this issue in countries such as Britain, Denmark and Norway. In rural regions, the prospect of higher prices for agricultural produce and subsidies for farmers ensured support for membership was strong and contributed to the 83 per cent vote in favour (70 per cent of the electorate voted). The Irish electorate stayed broadly in favour; according to a euro barometer in June 1994, 79 per cent polled believed 'membership a good thing' compared to 58 per cent in the European Community as a whole.[175]

The decision to join was one that ended Ireland's pretence to isolation and self-sufficiency, or, put more cynically, 'bought off the conservative heartlands of rural Ireland'.[176] Garret FitzGerald, one of the leading advocates of European co-operation, suggested that the argument in the referendum was narrowly focused on the farm issue, to the detriment of the gains Ireland was likely to secure through foreign investment. Opponents had argued that economic activity would draw away from the peripheral countries in favour of a 'golden triangle' at the heart of Europe and affect Irish neutrality. In the event, it was in the realm of internal market policy, along with agricultural, monetary, and regional policy, that the effects of EEC membership were most clearly seen. The Common Agricultural Policy ensured an increase in the output and incomes of one third of Irish farmers, or, as a more cynical assessment would have it: 'the Irish farmers did not get into the EEC agricultural market – they got into intervention'.[177] Garret FitzGerald admitted to John Ardagh that 'yes for most people the EU is a matter of economic self-interest, not of idealism or emotion'. This belief was enhanced by the £7.2 billion received in structural funds between 1994 to 1999, while there was always deep consternation about reform of the CAP, which initially encouraged over-production and guaranteed price regardless of output.[178]

'Paddy the amiable pick-pocket'?

At the time of membership, the government had estimated that one third of Irish farms were not economically viable, so there was much that was attractive in an EEC that would rid Ireland of its dependence on the British market, and hold European prices above world prices through import levies, intervention buying and export subsidies, with the use of a social fund for underdeveloped regions. Irish negotiators succeeded in having a protocol added to the Irish Treaty of Accession, which committed the Community to 'making adequate use of the Community's resources to aid Ireland's development effort'. Price increases, coupled with the devaluation of the punt (Irish pound), did bring higher prices for Irish farmers. By 1970, the direct gain from the CAP was 5 per cent of GNP, and by 1978 per capita incomes for farmers were more than double their

1970 level. Membership also brought the farmers' organisations closer to governments, after the difficulties of the 1960s. There were no sectional disputes about competition for EU funds; only the desire to get as much as possible.

Ireland was also quick to press for the establishment of the regional fund, though it could be argued that this encouraged a tendency to see disadvantaged areas as purely monetary rather than social problems, with a lack of serious debate on the nature of spending. What was categorised as 'training' was often in effect a replacement for unemployment assistance. Between its initial payout from the regional fund in 1975 and 1981, Ireland received £159.38 million. There is thus much truth that there was an essentially pragmatic approach to EEC membership in terms of how much could be got out of it: the idea of Ireland with the begging bowl, or, as Joe Lee put it, 'Paddy the amiable pickpocket', rather than membership encouraging expression of a European identity. During the first direct elections to the European Parliament in 1979, the focus was on domestic rather than European issues, though it is interesting that the Green Party had more success in European elections towards the end of the century than in domestic politics, as if the environment was perceived to be a 'European' rather than an 'Irish' issue.

In his 1984 paper *Reflections on Ireland in the EEC* Joe Lee suggested the 'begging bowl' approach merely continued the tradition of Irish 'under-performance', a tendency to look externally rather than at domestic issues, and the absence of an intellectual approach to policy. He identified a lack of long-term perspective, concluding the national interest might be better served if the time devoted to politics were devoted to the marketing of milk (though ironically Lee's paper, as he acknowledged, could not have been written without the financial support of the European Commission).[179] When Ireland held the European presidency, it was politically adroit, emphasising the need for respect for majority voting in Council and strengthening the European Commission.

Irish representatives were also forced to develop policies on international issues not dealt with before, which sometimes resulted in wider debates at home on these issues. Garret FitzGerald maintained, in his *Reflections on the Irish State*, that the prosperity and success of Ireland in the 1990s was based not only on political and economic independence from Britain, but also on Ireland's place in Europe. He argued that, 'far from there being any contradiction between our demand for independence from Britain and our later accession to the EC, Irish membership of the EC ultimately justified that independence', given that participation in the EC without independence would not have been on the terms accorded to a sovereign state, but as a region of the UK.[180]

'all gains and no losses in an Irish context'

Brigid Laffan suggested that 'in the area of equal rights there are all gains and no losses in an Irish context' (of EEC membership), particularly regarding social policy and the status and rights of women. The women's movement that predated membership had ensured that there was a wider concern with equality in any case, as witnessed by the non-EU-imposed end to the marriage bar in public service employment and the introduction of maternity leave. But pressure from the EEC further advanced entitlements. The Social Welfare Act of 1973 reduced the qualifying age for old-age pensions from 70 to 69 years and increased payment by £1 a week. Equality directives were also important, an equal-pay directive coming into effect in 1976, though the government announced it would be unable to apply it to the public sector. As a result of lobbying of the European Commission by women, the Commission refused to consider deferral. Two acts in 1977 were also significant, the Employment Equality Act of 1977 and the Unfair Dismissals Act, though the 1978 directive on equal treatment for men and women in social welfare caused difficulties, owing to the assumption in Ireland that married women were dependants and unavailable for work, and did not become law until 1986, after married women were forced to take a case to the European Court to have the provisions of the directive deemed directly applicable.

In the mid-1970s, pilot schemes to combat poverty, influenced by the EEC's social action programme, eventually led to the establishment of the Irish Combat Poverty Agency in 1986, though the degree to which the EEC promoted changes in Irish attitudes to poverty is debatable. Rhetoric was one thing; in the mid-1970s the Minister for Social Welfare, Frank Cluskey, suggested one definition of poverty which had arisen out of EEC discussions was that a person was in poverty 'if his command over his resources, including money, social services and community services, is so far below the normal standards of the community that he is in effect excluded from normal integration in that community'. But translating this into direct action was different (and difficult). However, membership of the EEC enabled Irish pressure groups with a concern for social welfare, or the lack of it, to compare standards in Europe when looking for direct action, rather than merely using Britain and Northern Ireland as the standard comparisons.

One of the more surprising aspects of involvement in the EEC was the exceptional ignorance that existed about the way it operated, even more surprising given that, constitutionally, major decisions had to be put to referendum. A 1995 report showed that 50 per cent of people in Ireland were unaware that the European parliament was directly elected, with 65 per cent feeling they were not well informed enough about the EU. 'Yes' votes in referenda decreased, from 83 per cent in 1972 to 69.1 per cent in 1992, as did turnouts, from 70.9 per cent in 1972 to 57.3 per cent in 1992. The majority of the electorate thus voted in favour of the EU project on only one occasion: 1972.[181]

'something to which our people are so firmly attached'
In the conduct of foreign policy, the occasional desire to act differently from Britain may suggest that enthusiasm for Europe was partly bound up with the self-conscious need to be different from the former coloniser. But it could be argued that, given Ireland's independent stance at the UN prior to EEC membership, an independent foreign policy was compromised by joining. Like Denmark, Ireland tended to abstain rather than vote against EEC resolutions dealing with international disputes. An exception, souring Anglo-Irish relations, was the Falklands War, where Ireland broke ranks with the EEC, reversed its original stance and opposed imposing sanctions on Argentina. Ireland was also the first EEC country to accord recognition to the Palestine Liberation Organisation and proclaim the Palestinians' right to statehood, but tended to be muted with regard to US alarmism over countries like Iran and Afghanistan, and did not want to boycott the 1980 Moscow Olympics. In the 1980s, while Ireland adopted a high moral tone at the UN regarding South African apartheid, it did not support the idea of a total trade embargo because of substantial South African investment at Shannon. It was, in fact, strikers at Dunne's Stores, Ireland's leading indigenous supermarket chain, dismissed for refusing to handle South African produce, who selflessly forced the 1982–7 Fine Gael/Labour coalition to take unilateral action as a result of support for the workers and intense public pressure.[182]

The growing debate about the intensification of European defence eventually made life difficult for Irish governments, particularly with regard to military neutrality, and the merits of a common European defence policy. Historically, the reality was that statements made by Lemass and Patrick Hillery in the late 1960s suggested that neutrality was not a matter of principle, and there would be little difficulty in abandoning it. Instead, it was contended that, for the present, membership would not require Ireland to enter into any military agreements. In a Dáil debate in February 1969, when extolling the virtues of EEC membership, Jack Lynch observed that Ireland 'had never been ideologically neutral'. Liam Cosgrave, Taoiseach from 1973 to 1977, asserted that 'those participating in the new Europe must be prepared to assist, if necessary, in its defence'.[183] By the 1990s, some of the smaller parties, like Sinn Féin and the Greens and other Eurosceptics, managed to revert to traditional arguments about small nations upholding their sovereignty in the midst of a European superstate, and Irish people tended to rediscover their nationalistic impulses when it suited them, or when EU funds were drying up.

Sceptics could easily pounce on the disingenuous and ambiguous fudging that even individuals of the intellectual calibre of Garret Fitz-Gerald could articulate, as quoted in the *Irish Times* of February 1983:

> I think that the Irish people have a very strong attachment to the situation in which we are not a member of a military alliance. The word neutrality is used by different people in different ways and gives rise to a great deal of confusion. But something to which our people are so firmly attached is inevitably firmly embedded in our foreign policy.[184]

Neutrality, it seemed, was so ingrained in the national psyche that it did not need to be defined. It was no wonder, out of office and retired from politics, FitzGerald referred to the 'aberrant eccentricity' of Irish attitudes to common European defence.[185]

There was often concern expressed about the possibility of NATO membership, and nuclear proliferation, but Eunan O'Halpin noted that Irish politicians 'generally prefer to avert their eyes from questions of European security and defence'. While there was a political consensus that Ireland would not join NATO, it was also the case that Ireland had endorsed the growing foreign policy co-ordination of European partners, while allowing for the 'semantic caveats to avoid the charge that Ireland has sacrificed neutrality'.[186] This was an ambiguity that was by no means solved by the end of the twentieth century, and no political party was prepared explicitly to advocate the abandonment of 'neutrality', whatever it in fact meant.

It was not until 1996 that the first ever government white paper on foreign policy was published. Anglo-Irish and Northern Irish affairs were omitted from this paper because of political sensitivities, a measure of the caution that governed political articulation of foreign-policy issues. But from the 1980s there was an attempt to reappraise the role and structure of the Irish defence forces, prompted by a desire to save money by closing outdated barracks. While there was an expansion of the number of permanent defence force members, one of the more interesting developments was the emergence of a representative body for army officers, which meant there was a voice given to serving soldiers on issues of defence policy and practice, which, as O'Halpin points out, could not have been aired previously. These were positive developments in light of criticisms of a report of 1990 which depicted 'an army militarily ineffective in proportion to its size, strangled by red tape, mainly engaged in essential non-military duties, and with remarkably elderly soldiers who had come to see the army as a job for life'.[187] In the 1980s public perception of the army was also influenced by an 'army wives' campaign to achieve better pay for their spouses, and in the 1990s by numerous claims taken against the government for hearing damage caused during training. But towards the end of the century improvements were made in pay and promotion procedures which for too long had been based on politics, not merit, though to some it still seemed 'ludicrous' that they possessed just two modern armoured personnel carriers. There was continued involvement with UN forces in Cyprus until 1974 and from 1978 in southern Lebanon, and a gradual move towards involvement with UN peace enforcement.

Following Fianna Fáil's victory in the 1969 general election there were nine governments over the course of the next 30 years. Politically, the 1980s were a period of great instability, marked by factionalism within parties, divisions over leadership and the demise of single-party government. This was combined with the emergence of smaller parties, notably the Progressive Democrats in 1985, formed mostly by Fianna Fáil dissidents, who placed themselves on the right of the political spectrum regarding economic policies. Opinion polls became the essential tool of every party in deciding political strategy, particularly after the Fine Gael/Labour coalition went into the 1977 general election without commissioning one, believing they were going to win, and lost heavily. With the election of

Garret FitzGerald as leader of Fine Gael in 1977, the party was injected with great enthusiasm and vigour, while the Labour Party, with 19 TDs in 1978, flirted with socialism but effectively abandoned it for moderate social democracy. The Fianna Fáil party, after the departure of the populist Jack Lynch in 1979, was led until 1992 by Charles Haughey. During his tenure, the party (and often the country) was preoccupied with his ego-driven crusade in pursuit of an overall majority. FitzGerald was disarmingly honest about the state of his party, asserting in 1978 that 'Fine Gael is not a political party. It will be, but it isn't yet.'[188] He stressed that the challenge was to both attract the young and capture the middle ground, and, crucially, to be more than just anti-Fianna Fáil; in effect to create a new Fine Gael as much as to reform it, which he succeeded in doing, coming within a few seats of matching Fianna Fáil's Dáil representation.

'failure of the cabinet to discuss openly policy in relation to Northern Ireland'

Fianna Fáil had been thrown into chaos by the Arms Crisis of 1970, after the Fine Gael leader, Liam Cosgrave, informed Jack Lynch he was aware of a plot by senior members of the government to assist the importation of arms into the state to be used by Northern republicans. By the end of 1970, two ministers, Neil Blaney and Charles Haughey, were sacked and a third, Kevin Boland, resigned in solidarity. Blaney, Haughey, an army captain, James Kelly (who had kept Col. Michael Hefferon, Director of Army Intelligence, fully informed of his activities), and a Belgian businessman, Albert Luykx (who had little reason to believe he was not acting on behalf of the Irish state given the approach to him came from cabinet ministers[189]), were subsequently tried and acquitted. James Kelly insisted he was acting under the instruction of the Minister for Defence, James Gibbons, who vehemently denied this, though Kelly's acquittal clearly meant that the jury believed the Minister for Defence was lying. The judge presiding over the case stated that one of the two ministers on trial had clearly perjured himself.

Controversy raged for the next 30 years about what precisely went on, the consensus being that Jack Lynch had prevented civil war with his belated and decisive action to counteract the threat of collusion between an army intelligence officer and cabinet ministers to arm nationalists in the North. The reality, however, as seen in the previous chapter, was that Lynch did not have control over his cabinet and it was the contradictions of policy on Northern Ireland which led directly to the crisis, with a cabinet of hawks and doves battling to control policy. It was only after Lynch flushed the hawks out that he achieved control, but it has been argued that Haughey's decision, as Minister for Finance in 1969, to permit funds voted for the relief of distress in the North to be used to purchase guns for the defence of nationalists there was not at the time at variance with government policy.

There were clearly ideological and generational differences within the IRA about how to approach the Dublin government. There was also a tendency for Southern armchair-republicans to behave like excitable boys, getting ready to travel to the Continent to purchase guns with cash stuffed in a brown paper bag. There is little doubt that Haughey lied about his knowledge of the affair, but according to Vincent Browne in 1980:

> there Charlie Haughey's culpability ends and it is not terribly serious … suggestions that he was involved in an attempt to overthrow the state or was guilty of treason are simply outrageous … the real genesis of the Arms Crisis was in the failure of the cabinet to discuss openly policy in relation to Northern Ireland generally.[190]

It was a pity that what was regarded as Ireland's most sensational trial was shrouded in such ambiguity. Further allegations emerged with the release of state papers in 2001. These centred around the alleged doctoring of an army statement in relation to the case, and changes to statements in the book of evidence for the trial, deleting reference to the knowledge of the Minister for Defence and whether or not such changes had been made in the Department of Justice. This prompted a 6,000-word statement from the minister who replaced Charles Haughey, Des O'Malley, in his (O'Malley's) defence. The papers also made it clear that James Kelly should never have been brought to trial and had no case to answer, as he had merely been carrying out the instructions of his seniors.[191]

'The Republican card was now operating at a discount'

There was no evidence to suggest O'Malley played any part in altering statements, and new documentation did not prompt a completely new perspective on the trial or prove to be a political time-bomb. It is likely the definitive story of the arms trial will never be told satisfactorily, at least not until all the documentation is released, despite the contemporary view of the *Cork Examiner* that 'the country has been in the throes of a crisis of a magnitude greater than anything experienced since those stormy far-off days of the Treaty debates'.[192] Captain James Kelly, forced to resign from the army, felt particularly aggrieved despite his acquittal, believing his political masters had betrayed him. It was not until his death in 2003 that the state acknowledged that he had always acted honourably and 'on what he believed were the proper orders of his superiors'.[193] Col. Hefferon, an honest and honourable man, was adamant James Gibbons had perjured himself by denying that Hefferon had been keeping him informed of developments, and that Gibbons had contacted him by phone before the trial to ensure 'our memories are the same'. Despite the pressure and intimidation, Hefferon refused to commit perjury and was ostracised by his colleagues; both his health and his family suffered as a result. Unlike Kelly, he never received an apology from the state, though he clearly merited one.[194]

Justin O'Brien maintained that the crisis represented 'the greatest threat to the stability of the state in a generation and arguably since its foundation' and that:

> the way in which Dublin responded to the crisis provides a compelling insight into the working of nationalist politics during times of upheaval. The actions taken by a deeply divided administration in the pivotal years 1969–70, operating to a myriad of competing agendas, hastened the split in the militant republican movement and set the scene for the emergence and eventual dominance of the provisional IRA ... the fact that the conclusion of this power struggle took place in the aftermath of the Ballymurphy riots in Belfast in April 1970 is a crucial fact often overlooked. The riots marked the first overt confrontation between the provisional IRA and the security forces. Dublin was in effect making it clear that it was one thing to be the moral guardians of the nation's ideology, quite another to take on the British Army. The Republican card was now operating at a discount, and the ministers most publicly associated with a hawkish line were fundamentally exposed.[195]

'rejected voices from the past counselling extremism'
The crisis not only forced Haughey into the political wilderness until the end of the 1970s; it also ensured, along with the evolving Northern crisis,

that the Fine Gael/Labour coalition of 1973–7 was dominated by security concerns, owing to the extent of republican and loyalist violence. In 1974, loyalist bombs caused carnage in Dublin and Monaghan and killed 34 people, the *Irish Times* commenting:

> we do not always recognise the implications of the phrases which are so often bandied about – phrases about the inalienable rights of this or that section of people, phrases about the freedom to do this or that. When any man fails to reckon his neighbours' freedom as important as his own, the result can be released in explosions like those in Dublin yesterday.[196]

The mayhem prompted new security legislation, and increased powers were given to the Gardaí, which would, in time, cause much trouble. A measure of the contemporary climate was that when the president, Cearbhall Ó Dálaigh, referred the Emergency Powers Bill (allowing terrorist suspects to be detained for up to seven days) to the Supreme Court to test its constitutionality, an allegedly tired and emotional Minister for Defence, Patrick Donegan, referred to him as 'a thundering bollocks' (some maintained he said 'thundering fucker') and it was the president rather than the minister who resigned. In refusing to demand the resignation of Donegan, the Taoiseach, Liam Cosgrave, had, suggested Garret FitzGerald, been 'fatally betrayed by his own excessive loyalty to one of his ministers'.[197]

The coalition of 1973 had been formed after the leader of the Labour Party, Brendan Corish, had suggested it would be 'an act of irresponsibility' not to give the electorate the opportunity to elect an alternative government to Fianna Fáil. But given the divisions in Fine Gael, it was in fact the impact on the South of the crisis in the North that was a political salvation for Liam Cosgrave, leader of the party, and son of William. Stephen Collins wrote that:

> virtually all his TDs and senators were in the process of walking out of the Fine Gael party room in disgust at their leader's determination to vote with Fianna Fáil in support of emergency security legislation. Suddenly a loud thud was heard and the windows of Leinster House vibrated. The first Loyalist bombs had gone off in Dublin. They killed two people and saved Cosgrave's political life.[198]

But it was economics that had dominated the election campaign of 1973, and Fianna Fáil's attempt to shift the debate to the Northern issue failed through lack of public interest, and the subsequent transfers between Fine Gael and Labour ensured the ousting of Fianna Fáil. Cosgrave dismissed the republican rhetoric, suggesting the electorate 'rejected voices from the past counselling extremism, doctrinaire solutions and violent ways as a method of solving the problems of the present or the future'.[199] Quiet, gentle, but stern and extremely private, Cosgrave presided over a talented government that attempted to protect the social-welfare constituency, and succeeded in building more houses despite the oil crisis. The introduction of a wealth tax in 1974, amidst much internal and external opposition, back-fired badly on the government. In his memoirs, Garret FitzGerald, the architect of the plan, gives a good insight into the attitudes to redistribution of wealth, and in this instance the extent to which civil servants played a key part in undermining the tax, which Fianna Fáil abolished in 1977. Referring to 'a most unscrupulous campaign by some among the wealthy people affected by it' for its abolition, he recalled:

> This campaign had been designed to arouse irrational fears amongst people of quite modest means who were in no danger of even being found liable to pay wealth tax. The deeply ironic result was that the net effect of all my efforts over a decade to substitute a more effective method of limiting the accumulation of wealth in too few hands, which would at the same time bear more equitably on those paying it, achieved the exact opposite result: a much lighter burden of capital tax than hitherto. When we returned to government in 1981 in a new coalition with the Labour Party, the weight of 'popular' opinion amongst the middle classes against the reintroduction of wealth tax prohibited my party from responding from continuous pressure from Labour to restore the system that we had succeeded in introducing in 1974 against so many obstacles.

Regarding the resistance of civil servants, he suggested it demonstrated 'the distance civil servants can go in challenging government policy rather than the distance they normally do go in warning governments of the consequences of their actions'.[200]

Cosgrave also demonstrated his independence and stubbornness, as well as a conservative Catholic faith, by voting against his government's own contraceptive legislation in 1974 (permitting contraceptives to be imported and sold to married people only). But, as Stephen Collins points out: 'Northern Ireland was the first major issue confronted by Cosgrave's government and it was to dominate his term of office.' This was all the more significant given that the attitude of both Fine Gael and Labour to Northern Ireland had been transformed after the outbreak of the Troubles. Conor Cruise O'Brien, in particular, made the intellectual arguments within the Labour Party regarding a recognition of the consent principle, and 'Cosgrave accepted without a quibble O'Brien's involvement in everything to do with Northern policy'.[201] This was an important factor in forwarding the power-sharing Sunningdale proposal. But there was inevitably controversy about the toughening of security legislation and allowing terrorist suspects to be detained for up to seven days.

'diffidence and an absence of fanaticism'
Jack Lynch, a former hurling star with the Cork GAA team, revered in his native county and generally regarded as an affable and decent man, performed wonders with Fianna Fáil in terms of attracting the popular vote on a scale his successors could not match. But, internally, the fact that Lynch had succeeded Lemass, who had encouraged ministers to act independently, made it difficult for Lynch subsequently to put his stamp of authority on his cabinet. The party, after his prevarication during the arms trial, had to deal with its legacy and was divided on the merits of seeking a more co-operative approach with Britain. This was despite the fact that Lynch convinced the British prime minister, Edward Heath, that the Republic had a legitimate interest in the affairs of Northern Ireland. Because Lynch also stressed non-intervention in the North, many have contended he has to be assessed historically in terms of what he might have prevented, something his followers would see as one of his major achievements. It was interesting that, after he died in 1999, one journalist noted that 'diffidence and an absence of fanaticism – suspect qualities in the party – proved a powerful attraction outside', which proved to be 'the paradox of one of the most highly successful – and consequently vulnerable – careers in modern Irish politics'.[202] But the decision to go along with the give-away manifesto that secured an overall majority in 1977 was ill-judged, as was his decision to make Haughey's comeback possible (he brought him back into the cabinet). But he was also brave in deciding to transfer the fixing of constituency boundaries from local government

to a non-party commission, making it much more difficult for his own party to achieve an overall majority, and he insisted on putting a motion to the Fianna Fáil party, reaffirming the right of the Taoiseach to hire and fire ministers. As the first Taoiseach with no Civil War baggage, Lynch's political rise had represented a discernible break with the past, and:

> Lynch was fond of pointing out in later years that the War of Independence hero, Tom Barry, who ran in the 1946 by-election, polled fewer votes than Communist Party candidate Michael O'Riordan. It was Lynch's oblique reply to critics of his in Fianna Fáil who decried the fact that that his family did not have an IRA record in the War of Independence.[203]

'would the alternative be worse still?'

Haughey's comeback was executed brilliantly and uniquely, to the extent that by 1979 he was elected leader of the party in succession to Lynch without the active support of a single cabinet minister. He relied instead on the sometimes fanatical loyalty of backbenchers, a measure of his charisma and careful networking. But it was also one of the more unusual and democratic leadership contests in modern Irish politics, the backbenchers, as one journalist put it, not 'providing mere lobby fodder for a party oligarchy'.[204]

The politics of the 1980s, however, were to be dominated by the economy and the tendency of politics to be debased by budgets based on political expediency. A measure of the despair was reflected in the view of Vincent Browne in June 1981 that 'the present government under Charles Haughey is certainly the worst government the country has ever endured. The question is: would the alternative be worse still?'[205] This period was also the first time that the question of the funding of political parties was raised, an issue shrouded in mystery, particularly with regard to the source, size and uses of campaign funds. This was all the more pertinent given there were three general elections between 1981 and 1982. In particular, Fianna Fáil's fund-raising activities seemed to be organised in such a way as to encourage the belief that business contributors could buy favours, with their requests channelled to the highest levels, not to mention the fact that builders and planners were benefiting from lax planning and tax controls.

While Fianna Fáil was not the only party to pursue funds in this

manner, it was telling that while Fine Gael and Labour had no hesita-
tion in advocating the state funding of political parties, there was no such
enthusiasm in Fianna Fáil. The journalist Brian Trench claimed in 1981
that 'the party has shaped its organisation and its politics on the least
accountable party political system in Europe. And it has done well by
it.'[206] There was no obligation to disclose public companies' political contributions, as recognised under British laws since 1948 for contributions
over £200.

In June 1981, the general election resulted in a hung Dáil, making
possible a brief coalition between Fine Gael, Labour and independents.
Their budget in January 1982 was defeated, resulting in another general
election in February, which Fianna Fáil narrowly won. In November 1982,
yet another general election confirmed a country in crisis. Both Fianna
Fáil and Fine Gael had much to consider concerning the preferences of
the Irish electorate. Haughey managed to retain 45 per cent of the vote,
while Fine Gael made a breakthrough under Garret FitzGerald, achieving 36.5 per cent of the vote and its highest number of seats ever. The
Labour Party, partly because of equivocation regarding their identity and
weak leadership, did not make significant electoral gains. While Haughey
could not achieve an overall majority, FitzGerald's open style of leadership
and national touring campaign to raise the profile of the party drew many
young people into the party.

Aside from the crisis of public finance (indeed there was even a suggestion that a constitutional amendment should be passed prohibiting
politicians borrowing more than a certain proportion of GNP for current
or capital purposes), there were also questions raised about Dáil reform.
These were to re-emerge spasmodically over the next 30 years, partly owing
to the fact that, on average, the Irish Dáil was meeting half the number of
days the British House of Commons met, and for at least one hour less per
day. In 1971 the Dáil had been increased in size from 148 to 166 seats. Up
to 40 per cent of the senate was filled with defeated Dáil candidates, and
there was a lack of political will to allow decentralisation. Proposals in the
1970s for local-government reform were halted by political and bureaucratic inertia and a growing school of thought in the 1970s and 1980s
began to reflect angrily on the implications of relentless centralisation. Joe
Lee developed many of the arguments of Tom Barrington of the Institute
of Public Administration, noting the gap between the myth of the self-
reliant community, so intrinsic in terms of historical propaganda about the

ability of the Irish to run their own social, economic and political affairs, and the 'stern realities' of the centralising state. European regional local authorities accounted for a much higher proportion of public expenditure than in Ireland, and Lee argued that intellectually and emotionally the Irish had conditioned themselves to think English rather than borrowing from European models of decentralisation.[207]

Charles Haughey's career provided journalists with much fodder. Despite his acknowledged talent as a minister in the 1960s, he was a poor and indecisive party leader, with question marks over his credibility because of his relentless ambition and the amassing of a huge fortune while holding public office. Fine Gael was home to both radicals and conservatives, but FitzGerald sought to move the party to the left, by claiming that future redistribution of wealth could not await future economic growth. His commitment to constitutional and legislative change (dubbed a 'crusade') was far-sighted if difficult to deliver on. But for the time being, the media still failed to elicit honest answers to pivotal questions about the state of the nation's finances. Another notable development, given the Dáil's increasingly tight arithmetic and the absence of single-party government, was the exaggerated significance of independents and smaller parties holding the balance of power. Even though this rarely reflected the wishes of the electorate, it was to become a consistent feature of the political landscape; dividing the spoils between the two large parties had come to an end, particularly with the Labour Party in the middle, the Workers' Party on the left and, later, the Progressive Democrats on the right.

'backbenchers who always threatened revolt'
The November 1982 election seemed to confirm resolutely the maxim that a week is a long time in politics, resulting in a coalition between Fine Gael and Labour (now led by the young Dick Spring) that survived until 1987. It was a government that faced enormous challenges, particularly with regard to halting the open-ended increases in expenditure in such areas as the public service, the health services and the self-perpetuating large institutions. Much time was also spent on what Tom Garvin called the 'politics of denial and cultural defence' – abortion and divorce – to the detriment of developing democratic institutions and addressing the abuse of their power. Such abuses were common because the Irish Constitution did not provide for the rights and duties of the major organs of state. There was little progress made in developing the welfare state and

implementing reform of the public sector (the Devlin Report into the public service, published in 1969, had recommended sweeping changes in the decision-making structures, a challenge successive governments avoided).

Despite his ability to revitalise his own party, it was beyond the capabilities of even Garret FitzGerald to ensure effective financial management whilst also liberalising Irish society. There was significant success in reducing the ratio of debt to GNP, but economic policies inevitably caused tensions. Being in government with FitzGerald at the helm involved excruciatingly long cabinet meetings. The Minister for Education, Gemma Hussey, who published her 1982–7 cabinet diaries, lamented that:

> during the four years in government I spent what must amount to several months shut up in the cabinet room ... we knew that Fianna Fáil, nationally and locally, would oppose any expenditure cut ... they were, therefore, a constant and predictably destructive force – but it was their effect on the constantly wavering Labour backbenchers which was the real worry.. All the time we were in government I was conscious of two things: the affection and respect in which the Taoiseach and Tánaiste held each other, the almost fatherly concern of Garret for Dick [Spring] and the terrific burden Dick carried of acute worry about the malcontents on his backbenches who always threatened revolt when the heat of public hostility rose.[208]

'in the national interest'?

For all the acres of newsprint Charles Haughey generated up to his retirement in 1992, what was most significant was his insistence that he had no ideology, from which one of his protégés, Bertie Ahern, Taoiseach from 1997, was later to reap much political benefit. Both presented themselves as equally concerned with wealth creation and social justice, with little mention of class or inequality, while socialism, according to Haughey, was 'an alien gospel of class warfare, envy and strife, is also inherently unIrish and therefore unworthy of a serious place in the language of Irish political debate'.[209] Haughey was back in charge of a minority administration after the 1987 general election, but there continued to be a huge gap between the images politicians portrayed in campaigns, and the reality of the politics they practised once in power. Fianna Fáil, for example, came to power in 1987 condemning health cuts and within days adopted and intensified these policies as their own. Haughey, it seemed, had been converted to fiscal rectitude, and was listening to economists with greater care. Public-sector borrowing had to be reduced, in the words of Bruce Arnold, to 'honour the new, reborn monetarist leader'.[210]

Fine Gael's Michael Noonan correctly asserted when the budget was introduced in 1987 that 'this is grand larceny of our policy as put before the electorate'.[211] But Fine Gael, it seemed, had little option but to support government economic policy, which in turn created an identity crisis for post-FitzGerald Fine Gael under the leadership of Alan Dukes. Nonetheless, his decision to endorse government economic policy was historic and politically courageous. The leader of the Labour Party, Dick Spring, one of the most shrewd and respected politicians of his generation, came to be associated with the provision of effective political opposition, as he moved to silence the left of his own party and safeguard a middle-class political base. Haughey only occasionally realised his potential, a contradictory mixture of restlessness and conservatism ensuring his career ended in relative failure, all the more disappointing because his talents were manifold. Going into coalition in 1989, having come out so strongly against it, was just another illustration of how debased the phrase 'in the national interest' was becoming.

The Progressive Democrats party that emerged in 1985 claimed it had more policy than any other party. Its core group of strategists worked in senior management positions and championed private enterprise, the ethical high ground regarding standards in public life, and the 'liberal agenda' on sexual morality. They were led by one of the more enlightened, if prickly, politicians of the 1980s, Des O'Malley. But by the end of the century the party, which started promisingly, winning 15 seats in 1987, was reduced to a rump, ironically, given that most other parties began to adopt its policies. It happily coalesced with Fianna Fáil in 1989–92 and 1997–2002, and its claim to be ethical watchdogs had little credibility the longer they were in power. It was, however, a powerful presence in terms of championing competition, low taxation (which had obvious consequences in relation to public spending, which was low by international standards), and the break-up of monopolies, especially under the leadership of Mary Harney, who succeeded Des O'Malley to become the first female leader of an Irish political party. The Labour Party often decried such policies, but was utterly ambiguous about committing itself to a return to higher taxation.

'a golf handicap of 7'

In the midst of all this political upheaval, it was one of the ironies of modern Irish politics that the political institution most transformed was the one with little real power, the Irish presidency. The election of Mary Robinson in 1990 was dramatic, and many on the left felt they were on the verge on a historic breakthrough having thrown Fianna Fáil into disarray. Their presidential candidate, Brian Lenihan, became embroiled in controversy over whether or not he had made phone calls in 1982 to the outgoing president, Patrick Hillery, encouraging him not to dissolve the Dáil. Hillery had served two terms (14 years), the maximum permitted, in what until then had been a ceremonial office, with little publicity attached. Writing tongue-in-cheek (and unfairly) about Hillery in 1983, the journalist Gene Kerrigan noted: 'with a golf handicap of 7 the president of Ireland has the lowest handicap of any European head of state. So the past six years haven't been entirely wasted'.[212]

The Labour Party's decision to choose as its candidate Mary Robinson, a liberal academic lawyer from Trinity College, with a strong commitment to human rights, was inspired. It made for a fascinating election, though critics suggested quite legitimately that in talking of 'opening up' the office of presidency she was exaggerating the potential of what was largely a ceremonial office. Her message was based on inviting people to be courageous enough to step out 'from the faded flags of the Civil War' (the presidency usually seen as a retirement bonus for senior Fianna Fáil politicians), to vote for a woman to advance the quest for equality in Ireland, and to reach out to emigrants abroad and acknowledge exiles at home.[213]

She was successful, in spite of the fact that both Fianna Fáil and Fine Gael had introduced the 'red scare' into the campaign, Fianna Fáil patronising voters on the morning of the election by taking out advertisements wondering: 'is the left right for the park?' (The Phoenix Park in Dublin is where the president resides.) Pollsters were divided on whether or not she would have been elected if scandal had not engulfed the Fianna Fáil candidate. Robinson became extraordinarily popular and visible, and stretched the Irish presidency as far as it could go. She had a deliberate agenda, and inspired an almost religious loyalty in some, using an intense moral rhetoric about exclusion and social justice, her favourite phrase being: 'we must also find the ability to listen to the narrative of each other's diversities'. She annoyed some Catholics for talking of social democracy without alluding to religion. The editor of the *Irish Catholic*, David Quinn, maintained: 'she does not realise that without religion there is no moral basis for freedom or justice'.[214] But Robinson was clever enough, as John Waters noted, to emphasise that in moving to a new Ireland not all of the 'old Ireland' had to be left behind.[215] The fact that her campaign centred on visiting neglected but traditional Ireland was important in this regard, as was her focus on the Third World, and traditional ideas of the nation.

Another woman with an academic and legal background, Mary McAleese, succeeded her in 1997, in a campaign that caused some controversy as she was a Northern Catholic ('a tribal timebomb' according to one of her most vociferous critics). Another candidate of serious intellect, with a warm manner and outstanding communication skills, she too sought to build on the idea of a caring presidency, without the pointed political agenda of Robinson, whose ambition and concern for international social justice propelled her to the position of UN High Commissioner for Human Rights. A journalist in 1999 described McAleese, unkindly, but not wholly inaccurately, as 'a nice woman with pronounced social-worker tendencies and a grab bag of beliefs that satisfy most of the people most of the time'.[216]

Nonetheless, Robinson and McAleese at least created a situation where presidents could make important and powerful gestures about the need for a more mature and inclusive concept of Irish identity, as was seen with the new embrace of Remembrance Day, signifying a growing maturity within Irish nationalism, and the enthusiasm for ecumenism. That voters in 1990 were prepared to move away from traditional party loyalty was also an indication that the two largest parties between them could secure the allegiance of only a little over half of the voters. By the end of the century, this was further in evidence, with left-wing voters opting not only for the Labour Party, but also the Greens, Sinn Féin and a variety of independents, though there was still little prospect of these forming a coalition government.

'the realisation that it was time for change'?

Notwithstanding the 'Robinson effect', the Labour Party by the end of the century did not make the huge breakthrough it desired and sometimes predicted. Dick Spring, a skilful and icy orator, backed by skilled tacticians and advisers, routed the hard left of the party in a manner not achieved in Britain until much later. He led the Labour Party to 33 seats in 1992, only to subsequently pay the price for entering a coalition with Fianna Fáil, the Labour Party losing half those seats in 1997. Spring's main adviser, Fergus Finlay, maintained that the period 1993–7 'was one of the most productive periods of government that Ireland has ever seen … the glue that bound us together was Dick Spring … he has one major fault and I suppose I share it. He's always been unwilling to articulate the sense of vision and commitment that's in his gut.' But, he maintained, 'he is simply the outstanding leader of his generation. And nothing became him more than the realisation that it was time for change.'[217] However, for many who voted for Labour in 1992, 'time for change' was about putting Fianna Fáil out of office rather than keeping them in.

To the left of the Labour Party, the Workers' Party was riven with internal debate about where to situate themselves on the political map after the collapse of communism in Eastern Europe. Originally Official Sinn Féin, and regarded by some as having undue influence in RTÉ and in the trade union movement, some of its strategists had suggested it opt instead for social democracy, or socialist values within a market economy. The party's historical links with republican violence were an embarrassment in the Ireland of the 1990s, despite their now vociferous opposition to the IRA. Most of them subsequently regrouped as Democratic Left, home to some of the most able left-wing TDs in the Dáil, and their party had merged with the Labour Party by the end of the 1990s. Democratic Left had served in a coalition government with Fine Gael and Labour, under the leadership of the Fine Gael leader, John Bruton (one of the party's dominant intellects), after the break-up of the Fianna Fáil/ Labour coalition of 1992–5. Fine Gael also found itself drowned by the shift to the centre, and was rarely able to respond coherently when being questioned as to what it stood for beyond opposition to Fianna Fáil. Labour still found it difficult to make significant gains, partly because they were being outflanked on the left by the smaller groupings, and partly because Fianna Fáil, as they had since the 1930s, stole so many of their clothes. Though their performance in government was certainly competent, it by no means marked them out as champions of the underdogs in Irish society.

'so securely entrenched as to hearken back to its nineteenth-century predecessors'

And how were the underdogs faring, those who became subjects for discussion during this period in stark contrast to earlier decades? Public discourse about injustice was facilitated by the growth of talk radio, investigative reporting and a more liberal climate in relation to gender, sexuality and repression. But it is too simplistic to portray Ireland in the 1980s and 1990s as a simple battleground with, as one observer put it, 'shining progressive crusaders everywhere doing battle with the dark forces of reaction'.[218] John Waters also noticed that 'to listen to the radio one would think the entire country was tearing itself apart. Although I approved of most of what the voices on the radio wanted to achieve, I did not like their tone, which was hectoring and dismissive.'[219]

In a sense, poverty had been 'discovered' only in the 1970s, influenced by the activities of many prominent Church people. A figure of one million people living in poverty was suggested by one campaigner for the homeless, Sr Stanislaus Kennedy, in the early 1980s. The extent of social inequality was revealed by the proportion of income which went to the poorest: 30 per cent smaller than anywhere else in the EEC.[220] Almost 800,000 people, of whom over one third were children, were exclusively or largely dependent on weekly social-welfare or health board payments, while in the late 1970s spending on social welfare was a declining proportion of overall government spending, falling from 16 per cent in 1975 to 13 per cent in 1979.

Another problem was that housing expenses were not recognised in the means test for assistance payments, the original means test mentality assuming people owned the house they lived in. But many welfare recipients were now in private rented accommodation. The Society of Saint Vincent de Paul (raising up to £8 million yearly and with 10,000 members, indicating a high degree of personal charity) conducted a survey among old people living alone in 1978 and uncovered appalling depths of poverty, while the Combat Poverty Agency engendered an awareness of inequality, as did the Conference of Religious Orders in Ireland. The latter consistently criticised budgets for favouring the rich, and clashed with economists who insisted that the need to create employment should take precedence over raising the level of welfare payments. Despite impressive building programmes – in 1975 local authorities built 9,000 new dwellings, and the National Building Agency was put at the disposal of local government – social housing went somewhat 'downmarket' in the 1970s and the 1980s.[221] In 1981 there were 35,000 on the housing waiting lists, which had risen to 100,000 by 2000, with an estimated 8,000 homeless adults. A measure of the crisis was that between 1997 and 2000 homelessness doubled. In 1994 the average house price was 4.3 times the average industrial wage; by 2000 it stood at 8.2 in Dublin and 6.4 in the rest of the country, and there was strong opposition from the building trade to a proposal which would see 20 per cent of all houses built reserved for social housing.[222]

All this was at a time when, in the midst of the Celtic Tiger, there were more people with an income level below the poverty line than there had been in the late 1980s, a time of recession. Of the EU countries, only Portugal was spending less on social welfare than Ireland, and while the depth of some people's poverty was certainly reduced by increased social mobility, this was done at the expense of the less poor rather than the well off. Seemingly in late twentieth-century Ireland there was still a 'deserving' and an 'undeserving poor'.[223] In 1982, an Economic and Social Research Institute paper recorded how deeply implanted class differences were, and predicted: 'Ireland may enter the twenty-first century with an upper-middle class so securely entrenched as to hearken back to its nineteenth-century predecessors.'[224]

'as much character as a second rate knacker's yard'

Combat Poverty schemes that emerged in the 1970s set themselves modest aims. An EEC study of 1977 revealed that there was a low awareness in Ireland regarding the structural causes of poverty. Fifty-five per cent of Irish people believed poverty was caused by personal misfortune (25 per cent) and laziness (30 per cent), other Europeans tending to show a greater awareness of social structures as a cause of poverty. Surprisingly, 56 per cent of those surveyed stated they did not think there were any poor people.[225] Lack of social mobility and residential segregation spawned many more problems; urban decline was one of them, particularly significant in view of the fact that from 1971, for the first time, the majority of the Irish population (52 per cent) was living in urban areas. The once classical thoroughfare of O'Connell Street in Dublin became home to filth, fast-food outlets and slot machines, one lord mayor of Dublin, Jim Mitchell, describing the city as having 'about as much character as a second rate knacker's yard'.[226]

In October 1978, 20,000 marchers protested about the fate of the Wood Quay site, in a spontaneous challenge to Dublin Corporation's decision to build new offices on this important archaeological site, associated with the Viking foundation of Dublin from the ninth and tenth centuries. Although the National Museum was prepared to give the go-ahead to developers after limited salvation work was done, Wood Quay was in effect seized by protestors, preventing the bulldozers entering for almost a month. Although the site was eventually built on, many artefacts were recovered and maps of a large part of the site were completed. The historian of this episode, Thomas Heffernan, wondered whether the debt owed to the lawyers, historians and literary figures who spearheaded the opposition was 'more a cultural one for saving the archaeological treasures or a political one for demonstrating that the country's citizens are in control of their own political destiny. Or at least can be if they want to.' That last sentence was particularly relevant, given the contention of Douglas Gaegby, editor of the *Irish Times*, that 'all of this talk about heritage – it's so selective' (being noticeably Dublin-centric).[227] Michael Lucey, the property investment manager of Irish Life, the state-owned insurance company, shocked conservationists by calling for the abolition of planning controls so the development of the city could be left to 'free market forces', which was precisely what dictated the shape of late twentieth-century Dublin. Out of the total of 300 office blocks built in the 25-year period after 1960, only 33 were located north of the river Liffey, the area most in need of urban renewal.[228]

'worse than comparable figures for the New York ghettos'
In 1977, looking at the deprived areas of Dublin's inner city, Gene Kerrigan observed that once the trouble spilled on to O'Connell Street, 'the obsession of the press and the establishment with the behaviour of Dublin's wilder kids is not matched by any official willingness to analyse the problem', by breaking down police, corporation, educational and medical statistics to give a true picture of the conditions in any single area.[229] Community activists emerged to battle gallantly, and in 1980 Dublin Corporation was forced to declare a housing emergency, as activists marched through the streets of Dublin from the affected areas, demanding action. In 1981 the Rent Restrictions Act was deemed unconstitutional with as many as 40,000 tenants losing legal protection as a result. Dublin's notorious Dunne family (not the supermarket chain owners) were

estimated to control more than 40 per cent of the heroin market in Dublin in the early 1980s, and a Concerned Parents against Drugs group was established in north Dublin city in 1987. They instigated a controversial policy of house evictions, and battled allegations that they were a front for IRA supporters.

This was a few years after a Health Board-commissioned report showed that in the Dublin North Central area, 10 per cent of those aged 15–24 were on heroin, while in the 15–19 age group the figure was 12 per cent and among girls aged 15–19 it was 13 per cent: 'the statistics for female users were worse than comparable figures for the New York ghettos.' In combating this problem it was often women who took the initiative on the ground, but the policy of not co-operating with the Gardaí and a resort to vigilantism (which was initially successful in clearing out pushers) led to much political infighting and resentment. No one agreed on how many were addicted; the Gardaí estimated a figure of 2–3,000, while Concerned Parents against Drugs suggested a much higher figure of 8–10,000, with up to half believed to have AIDS anti-bodies.[230] In 1997, the Garda Research Unit estimated there were 4,105 hard-drug users in the Dublin area, 91 per cent of whom had left school by the age of 16 and 87 per cent of whom were unemployed.[231] The economic boom also allowed many of the middle classes to indulge in cocaine habits.

Dublin also became a much more congested city. In 1991, there were 248 cars per 1,000 people in the greater Dublin area, which had risen to 344 by 1996.[232] This should not have created traffic chaos, given that Ireland was far from the saturation level of 500 per 1000 in other European cities. But Ireland simply did not have a matching public-transport system. One of the country's historical treasures – its nineteenth-century extensive rail network – was long gone; in 1920 there had been 3,442 miles of railway (including Northern Ireland); in 1957, 2,557, and in 2003 only 1,250.[233] What constituted the Dublin region changed dramatically, with a new world of housing estates springing up within a 60-mile radius of the city: 'a North American style "edge city" sprawled far out into Leinster' owing to cheaper house prices outside the city, with a prediction that car-orientated sprawl would damage the social fabric of the country as a consequence of time spent travelling. Unfortunately, planning for these new communities took second place to land rezoning.

Bishops in the west of Ireland deemed the problems of their communities serious enough to launch a 'Save the West' campaign in the early

1990s. But in 1985 an article in *Studies* argued that social anthropologists had placed undue emphasis on the west, that social damage was less complex and less destructive of community values than the literature would suggest, and that there was a need for more representative areas to be examined. This was an implicit criticism of Nancy Scheper-Hughes's argument in her book *Saints, Scholars and Schizophrenics* that 'rural Ireland is dying and its people are consequently infused with a spirit of anomie and despair'.[234]

'no doctor would dream of putting alcoholism on a patient's certificate'

Alcohol abuse, however, continued to affect all parts of the country. In 1968, 58 per cent of the population drank alcohol; a decade later nearly 70 per cent drank. While Ireland featured low in the European drinking table in terms of litres of 100 per cent alcohol (8.7 in Ireland compared with 16.5 in France and 12.7 in Italy), due to high duties and low income per capita, Ireland spent more of its consumed expenditure on alcohol than any other EEC country. The Pioneer Association began to fade in importance and visibility, finding it more difficult to appeal to young people. There was no government that was prepared to seriously challenge the licensed vintners. Charles Haughey, as Minister for Health in 1978, insisted: 'there is no question of condemning young people. My generation has not by its own performance earned the right to do that.'[235]

Under-age drinkers received much attention in the 1970s and 1980s, but perhaps Haughey was correct in implying that they would get little by way of a good example from an older generation: certainly the younger generation had inherited a very ambivalent attitude to alcohol, growing up in an environment in which some totally abstained and some drank heavily. In 1971, it was estimated that there were 66,000 alcoholics in the country, but alcohol problems among those under the age of 25 increased by 360 per cent between 1970s and 1985. It is likely this was only the tip of the iceberg; 'no doctor would dream of putting alcoholism on a patient's certificate', Tim Pat Coogan noted in 1975. More than 20 years later, the Department of Health's *National Alcohol Policy* publication seemed delusional, claiming: 'There is evidence that the description of the Irish as a particularly alcohol-prone race is a myth. Indeed it is doubtful whether Ireland ever occupied a prominent role with regard to alcohol use or misuse.'[236]

Alcohol abuse undoubtedly contributed to many other social

problems, including ill-health and domestic violence, which began to receive more attention in the 1970s and 1980s, as the traditional sanctuary of the home was questioned. Mental health also worsened; between 1945 and 1995 the rate of suicide in Ireland rose from 2.38 per 100,000 of the population to 10.69 per 100,000. For young males (aged 15–24) the level of suicide was equal to a rate of 19.5 per 100,000 of population, and was particularly a rural problem. This was at a time when expenditure on mental health was actually falling. In 1994, 9.4 per cent of non-capital health expenditure was spent on this area, but by 2001 the figure was 7.2 per cent, with the emphasis on courses of drugs to stabilise patients, rather than intensive therapy.[237] From the 1970s, the suicide rate among elderly Irish men doubled, and it was a social problem that received little attention. Neither did the still sorry state of Ireland's psychiatric hospitals, where there were 14,000 patients in 1980, many living in conditions of squalor and indifference to their particular requirements as psychiatric patients.

'virulently hostile reaction from entrenched vested interests'

Endless debates and controversies about the Irish health system raged in the 1980s and 1990s, and the health portfolio was a poisoned chalice for an ambitious minister. Barry Desmond of the Labour Party resolutely defended his tenure as Minister for Health in the 1982–7 coalition government, and, political partisanship aside, gave some indication in his memoirs of the challenges:

> I was under enormous political pressure after three years plus of grinding endeavours to control health and social welfare expenditures and to initiate long-overdue reforms. I had faced down the cynical Fianna Fáil dominated health boards whose accounts were often submitted to the department years out of date. I had challenged the proliferation of private beds in publicly funded hospitals which were a licence to print money for some very well paid consultants under the extremely generous common contract given to them by Charles Haughey when he was Minister for Health. And I had attempted to turn around the conservative ethos of psychiatric hospitals, some of which fully merited closure. Others were in dire need of fully integrated nursing care. On the public health policy side, my legislative reforms in relation to the nursing profession, contraception, clinical trials, childcare and tobacco

advertising had met virulently hostile reaction from entrenched vested interests.[238]

The two-tier aspect to hospital care was never seriously challenged by any political party. A cycle of investment and cutbacks developed; the investments of the 1970s were quite dramatically cut back in the 1980s only to rise sharply again in the 1990s. One of the many problems, it seemed, was the denial of GP care to poorer families unable to afford doctor's fees. Also problematic was private patients' preferential access to public hospitals; salaried public-hospital consultants earning private fees in public hospitals and also working in private hospitals; too much pressure and responsibility on junior doctors; too many small sub-standard hospitals; and inefficient health boards. Cutbacks in the late 1980s had reduced spending to 57 per cent of the EU per capita average by 1989, and spending was not to exceed the EU average until 2001. But given the decades it had taken France and Germany to build their health care system, Ireland was, it seemed, in for a long wait, particularly when the number of hospital beds was remaining static despite the fact that the population grew by 8 per cent between 1996 and 2002.

'until such time as they decided'

The insistence of hospital consultants on their right to practise privately remained a constant obstacle to reform, and, more than anything else, exposed the class bias of Irish vested interests. In 1974, they threatened strike action and defeated the attempt of the Labour Party leader and Minister for Health, Brendan Corish, to extend free hospital care to the entire population, seeing in the proposals a future as salaried state employees. It was an important turning-point, and a battle the medical establishment won decisively, and they won it without the support of the Catholic Hierarchy, unlike previously. Addressing the Dáil, Corish decried the undermining of the democratic will of parliament and government:

> To my intense regret I have received neither the understanding nor the co-operation which I could have expected as Minister for Health charged with the responsibility of implementing a policy decided upon by the government elected by this Parliament. Instead, repre-sentatives of the medical consultants opposed the introduction of my scheme until such time as they decided the population should have free

hospital and medical services.[239]

In 1981, the consultants were offered a contract of employment that gave them public-service pensionable employment and a right to unlimited private practice. In 1991, health care was made free to all income groups, but a bed designation system was also introduced which guaranteed patients who opted to pay private fees a number of specified beds (typically 20 per cent of the total), ensuring consultants would retain the benefit of a continued source of private income. The Minister for Health at that time, Fianna Fáil's Rory O'Hanlon, believed such a two-tier system 'served the nation well'. In this way, according to Maev-Ann Wren, government 'conspired to retain a system in which those with money can buy faster access and better care than those without', an unusual situation internationally.[240] The insistence on the right to private practice had echoes of the disputes in the early 1950s, and it seemed the medical profession still emphatically owned the Irish public health care system.

For decades, public-health spending had remained below the European average, reaching its nadir in 1989. Despite a massive shift in spending in the 1990s, the two-tier system ensured that poor people queued, while, as Wren put it, those who could pay were able to 'jump the queue'. This two-tier system, according to Tom Garvin, was 'the child of history and the survival of the interest group veto, as are so many other irrationalities and anomalies in Irish public service systems, ranging from transportation to town planning'.[241]

Another difficulty was the degree of decentralisation and fragmentation of the health services, closely linked to local politics. In 1975 there were 54 general hospitals in the Republic, despite the fact that the 1968 Fitzgerald Report had recommended four regional and 12 general hospitals for the entire country. But the electorate played its part in prioritising local and short-term interests, often themselves strangling opportunities for reform by keeping the debate local. Although local health boards were being harshly criticised in the 1990s, one historian of public health in Ireland, Ruth Barrington, argued that they did not get enough credit for the contribution they had made. Barrington noted that when health boards were established in 1970 they took over the health functions of local authorities, which at the time were funding half the cost of health services through local taxation. This was a major reason why elected local-authority representatives constituted the majority of members on a health board. In 1994, when the government decided to replace local-authority funding with central taxation, the job of local politicians changed to one of securing as much central funding for the development of health services in their region as they possibly could. Barrington lamented the fact that all the criticism of health boards and their political nature had included no analysis of the financial incentives 'that give rise to the behaviour that is seen as hostile to the implementation of national strategies'.[242]

'the solution does not lie ... primarily in the system of funding'

It was clear vast amounts of money were being spent on a system (often benefiting consultants, pharmacists and drugs companies) that was not sufficiently rationalised, while the health of the community marginally worsened. In the late 1980s, cuts in community care services affected public-health nursing, social work and child psychiatry, and there were hospital and ward closures, while the home and child care crisis deepened. Overall, in the 1980s there was a reduction of 16 per cent in the proportion of GNP allocated to health expenditure. But it was not just an issue of finance. The most quoted sentence from the Report of the Commission on Health Funding in 1989 stated that 'the solution to the problem facing the Irish health services does not lie primarily in the system of funding but rather in the way that services are planned, organised and delivered.' Forty per cent of the population were enrolled in the two voluntary health insurance schemes, though deaths from cancer and heart disease remained high, with Irish life expectancy still below the European average.[243] By 1998, 25 per cent of public expenditure went on the health services (a massive increase on past figures), and overspending health boards were made more accountable. Waiting lists remained chronic, but management and patients' views rather than just the medical profession were receiving more attention. More doctors and nurses and administrative staff were employed (by 2001 the public health service workforce was 93,000), but public patients were still waiting nearly twice as long for access to a bed in public hospitals as private patients. There was a strong belief in some quarters that health boards needed to be abolished, and replaced by a national health service executive and more centralisation, a recommendation that had also been forcefully made in 1989 by the Commission on Health Funding. There was a need, it seemed, not only to concentrate services in centres of excellence, but also to employ more consultants on lower salaries (similar to the UK), and phase out subsidies to private care and ensure public-salaried doctors worked solely for the public system.

The Blood Transfusion Board was engulfed in scandal in the 1990s when 1,500 people, mostly women, were infected with the hepatitis C virus when this virus contaminated the anti-D virus. The lack of accountability and compassion shown to victims was quite staggering, and the decision of the Minister for Health, Fine Gael's Michael Noonan, to defend a court case taken by one of the victims caused uproar. She died just days before her case was due to be heard in the High Court. The scandal dated back to 1976, when plasma was taken from a pregnant woman, without her knowledge, for the manufacture of anti-D, which was given to women to prevent illness in babies who had a different rhesus blood type. The anti-D became contaminated because the women became jaundiced during treatment, and despite being aware of this the Blood Transfusion Board continued to use her plasma, and some women began to show symptoms of hepatitis C. More than a decade later, plasma donations were taken from a patient with hepatitis, apparently without proper testing. This plasma was also used to make anti-D, and more women were infected. A tribunal into the affair in 1997 found that the Board had clearly breached its own standards, had failed to recall contaminated batches, and had acted unethically in the first place in using a patient's plasma without her permission.

Many individual tragedies resulted from the mistakes made by the health system. When it came to light that unnecessary caesarean hysterectomies had been systematically carried out – one doctor was alleged to have performed more than sixty – many women's claims were not believed. The fact that maternity hospitals were not obliged to publish annual statistics made it more unlikely that this problem would be highlighted. One woman, who later took successful court action over the issue, was told in 1992 simply 'to go home and get on with my life'.[244]

The economic boom witnessed more money being invested in the health system, but in the short term, there was not enough progress made to take health out of the headlines, or to make it a remotely desirable ministerial job. Brian Cowen, minister from 1997, memorably referred to the Department of Health as 'Angola' because of the endless political landmines, and the failure to agree on health service investment and reform. Given the degree to which health spending was rising from such a low base it was, according to Wren, 'the Boston [low taxes, low public spending] versus Berlin [higher taxes, higher public spending] debate reduced to its essentials. Which matters more – low taxes or public services?' It was interesting to see Fianna Fáil, which from the 1930s to the 1960s had been regarded as a party of health care reform, and delivered free hospital care for most of the population, grapple with the fear of taxing higher earners in order to make the system more equitable.[245] As Wren pointed out, this was in a country where by the beginning of the twenty-first century public spending had been reduced to 42 per cent of national income compared with 54 per cent in France.[246]

Nor was there enough action being taken regarding lifestyle. Reform of the health structures was one thing, but if the Irish continued to smoke (just under 30 per cent of the population smoked at the end of the century), drink and eat to excess, any putative structural reforms would be offset. As in the rest of the western world, along with cancer and alcoholism, obesity was becoming a matter of concern. In 2000, one of Ireland's leading food critics, Helen Lucy Burke, pointed out that while some countries were dancing towards the millennium, 23 per cent of all food shopping in Ireland was for convenience food, slightly lower than the UK at 30 per cent:

> Healthy eaters the Irish? Judging by clinical obesity levels we are no such thing ... the UK advances at a heavy trot, having Europe's [highest] obesity levels at 37 per cent of the adult population. Figures for Ireland are not available – but we eat the same TV dinners on a tray, many from England, and our trot may be even heavier and slower.[247]

'is it correct to rake up the past now?'

In 1997, the Department of Health became the Department of Health and Children, indicating the extent to which the welfare of minors had assumed more political and social significance. In the 1970s and 1980s there was little political will to update child abuse laws and reform the 1908 Children Act. By 1980 the official 90 confirmed and 271 suspected cases of child abuse by no means represented the totality of what was happening, and the community care service was understaffed. At that stage, legislation did not go far enough, in that it applied only to cases of criminal physical assault on children, and there was little consistency in judgements on child abuse and neglect cases.[248] Abuse and its cover-up still often involved collaboration between Church, state and society. A

Department of Education file, opened on a paedophile teacher in 1982, was typical, illustrating how civil servants could ignore allegations and allow abusing teachers to remain in the system. Referring to a teacher who began abusing boys in 1940, it read: 'If Mr Dunne had served as a secondary teacher – in girls' schools – for the last 13 years without coming under any notice, is it correct to rake up the past now?'[249]

In 1979, the journalist Rosita Sweetman, in a survey of changing attitudes to sexuality, referred to 'a hidden aspect of Ireland ... which is officially denied'. Interviewing young girls in Dublin's inner city, she found that:

> everything to do with sexuality in their experience seemed linked with violence, ignorance, and fear. There was the fear of pregnancy, the fear of intercourse, the fear of giving birth, the fear of men. Yet all women said they wanted to get married. Why? To get out of home, which was overcrowded, and get a place of their own; and to get out of work which was unskilled and underpaid. Their information came from rumour, half-heard stories of terrible happenings (usually to do with pregnancies) and their experience of men: their fathers and the young lads of the area.

Sweetman also bravely wrote about child abuse within the family, writing of a girl who 'transferred to a professional psychiatrist and under hypnosis walked straight back to her bedroom where, as a child aged four, her father had repeatedly molested her and finally raped her aged eight'.[250]

Perhaps such issues had been hidden for so long because of the reluctance to confront the questions of sexuality, marriage as an institution, pregnancy and sex education, all of which came under the spotlight in the 1980s and 1990s. As early as 1978, *Magill* magazine reported evidence of a sex explosion in Ireland, on the basis of the available figures on marital infidelity and births outside marriage, VD and abortions. It was suggested that 20,000 marriages had broken down, 60,000 unmarried people were cohabiting as partners, and that there were over 27,000 cases of VD diagnosed in 1977. Over 2,000 women travelled to Britain for abortions in the same year, up from 1,400 in 1974, while 60,000 women were believed to be on the pill. All these figures were highly contentious and probably conservative.[251] By 1979, the family planning clinics were estimated to have

100,000 clients, the same year in which new contraceptive legislation was proposed, five years after the Supreme Court upheld the constitutional right to privacy, including the rights of married couples to use contraceptives.

'the abominable crime of buggery'

By the end of the 1970s, 350,000 condoms were imported into Ireland each month and distributed through the non-profit family planning clinic network. (By 1985 it was legal for over-18s to purchase condoms and in 1992 the age of restriction was lowered. Condom-vending machines appeared the following year.) Eileen Desmond, a Labour Party TD, articulated the frustration of those who found it socially outdated to be debating the rhythm method, and ridiculous that married people had to get prescriptions for contraceptives: 'our Irish conscience has been conditioned to agonise most about sex and sex-related matters. Would that we felt so strongly about other issues such as drink abuse, hunger, the elderly and violence.'[252]

But, in any case, fertility statistics revealed Irish couples and their doctors were making their own choices, as did the extraordinary number of Irish women taking the pill, supposedly on account of their irregular periods. By the end of the century births to unmarried mothers stood at 30 per cent of the total, rising from 1,600 in 1921 to over 15,000 in 1998.[253] By the early 1980s only 20 per cent of chemists stocked condoms, but by 1987 this had risen to 70 per cent.[254] The world of prostitution also came under the spotlight, when in 1983 *Magill* won a Supreme Court victory enabling them to publish a story about the prostitution underworld, after a pimp burned to death a former prostitute and her mother in revenge for her leaving him.[255]

In 1989, the same publication published the diary of a young gay man dying of AIDS, which gave a graphic insight into gay life in Ireland in the 1970s and 1980s. But it would take a Supreme Court challenge by Ireland's most high-profile openly gay man, David Norris, a Trinity academic and future senator, and a further case to the European Court, for Irish homophobia to be sufficiently challenged to force a change in the law. For Norris, the early days with the Gay Rights Movement established in 1974 and the Irish Homosexual Law Reform Campaign begun in 1977 were also the days 'when vituperous letters arrived through the mail box, one enclosing a dog turd'. But he recalled that 'it was important to move it out of Trinity, which most Irish people regard with suspicion anyway, and go publicly gay'.[256]

The laws relating to homosexuality were draconian, and dated from 1861, when section 61 of the Offences against the State Act stipulated: 'whosoever shall be convicted of the abominable crime of buggery, committed either with mankind or with any animal, shall be liable ... to be kept in penal servitude for life.' Norris began his proceedings in 1977, seeking a declaration that the law transgressed the constitutional right to privacy. As Norris recalled, the difficulty was not just a legal one, but also 'a barrier in terms of popular and political prejudice'. When his High Court case was dismissed in 1980, he appealed to the Supreme Court, which also rejected his case, the Chief Justice, Tom O'Higgins, asserting that 'the deliberate practice of homosexuality is morally wrong, that it is damaging both to the health of individuals and the public and finally, that it is potentially harmful to the institution of marriage. I can find no inconsistency with the Constitution in the laws which make such conduct criminal.' Norris duly initiated a case under the European Convention on Human Rights. There was no political will in favour of changing the law, and Barry Desmond recalled that 'the advice available to the government from counsel was that the AIDS argument should be used if it was a factor in the government's thinking on the desirability of retaining present laws'. Norris won his case in 1988 at the European Court of Human Rights. The Church remained opposed. The law was not changed until 1993, when homosexual relations between adults were decriminalised.[257]

'What was the quality of the pain?'

The reality of child pregnancies and infanticide also came into the public domain in the 1980s. In February 1984, a 15-year-old died in childbirth under a grotto in Granard, County Longford. Her parents were, the subsequent inquest was told, unaware of the pregnancy. There was an extraordinary response to the deaths in the form of letters read by the broadcaster Gay Byrne on RTÉ radio, as people revealed intimate accounts of their own experiences. Fintan O'Toole argued: 'a sort of secret history of modern Ireland emerged that day with stories from every decade since the 1940s, stories that had been told to no one, stories that had been bottled up and swallowed down'.[258] The events also began a process whereby there was virtually nothing that could not be discussed in an intimate way on Irish radio, facilitating the exposure of further 'hidden Irelands'.

The Kerry babies case of 1985 was similarly dramatic: another concealed pregnancy, and the finding of two dead babies, with conflicting stories as to what had occurred. There were allegations of ill-treatment by the Gardaí, and another ordinary Irish family was in the spotlight over the unwritten code of silence that prevailed about pregnancy outside of marriage, this one the result of an extra-marital affair. A 77-day tribunal into the handling of the case was marred by confusion, innuendo and crude rhetoric. The central question was whether the Gardaí had concocted confessions and intimidated the family into signing them; but the adversarial approach created the impression of a criminal trial of a vulnerable woman who, with her family, had confessed to crimes which forensic evidence suggested they could not have committed. The discrediting of the family's story took much of the spotlight off the Garda handling of the case. As she was taken through a detailed description of giving birth in a field, the woman was asked: 'What was the quality of the pain?' It was a mystery that remained unsolved.[259]

'The introduction of internment in Ireland: for 14–year-old girls'

More women continued to travel to England for abortions, and marriages continued to break down, with no legal provision for divorce. There were referenda on both subjects; on abortion in 1983 and 1992, and on divorce in 1986 and 1995, with the words 'bitter' and 'divisive' the most oft quoted in relation to them. Although there was no widespread demand for a change in the abortion laws, a tiny group managed to put pressure on the government in the early 1980s to insert a pro-life amendment in the Constitution. The debate that followed was one of the most poisonous witnessed in twentieth-century Ireland. Groups whose titles had echoes of 1920s zeal, such as the League of Decency and the Irish Family League, were still operating on a small scale. They had emerged to attack Fiona Poole, a known supporter of family planning when she ran (successfully) for the post of President of the Irish National Teachers' Organisation in 1978. Poole was also targeted because she was separated from her husband, and a significant factor in her election was the support she received from INTO members from the North of Ireland. Usually, the Northerners were not active in such elections, but they may have been prompted to have their say given the attempt of the Catholic right (and indeed conservative elements within the INTO) to undermine Poole.[260]

Weak political leadership was the foremost factor in allowing a small anti-abortion lobby to advance the idea that a constitutional amendment asserting the right to life was necessary, which it patently was not, given that abortion was already illegal in Ireland under the Offences against the Person Act of 1861. Once passed (66.45 per cent of the voters agreed to its adoption), the amendment was to cause countless problems, not just for its opponents, but also for the numerous pro-life groups who differed when it came to tactics and militancy, the largest of which, the Society for the Protection of the Unborn Child, emerged in 1980. A measure of the intensity, extremism and gratuitousness that existed was the posters in 1982 announcing: 'the abortion mills of England grind Irish babies into blood that cries out to heaven for vengeance'.[261] While all organisations had passionate and articulate front men and women, much of the campaigning (and often intimidation) was of a backroom, discrete, some would say sinister kind. The intellectuals on the Catholic right claimed that those looking to liberalise the laws were attempting to turn the Republic back into a mere province of the UK.[262] The Women's Right to Choose group also split internally, and by 1990 one of its former leaders, Ruth Riddick, lamented that not only was a fundamentally feminist demand overwhelmingly rejected at the polls, but that 'the focus of subsequent debate became the *practical* right of access to information about (lawful) abortion services abroad ... a consideration of women's *moral* right to choose has been virtually abandoned'.[263]

The campaigns of the 1980s graphically highlighted the tendency in Ireland towards denial, and a hypocrisy that saw Ireland's abortion issue dealt with in England. In 1992, the country was again engulfed in debate about abortion, after a 14–year-old girl, pregnant as a result of rape, was prevented from leaving the country to have an abortion. Following a legal appeal on behalf of the girl (referred to as 'X'), the Supreme Court decided the pro-life amendment of 1983 protected the life of the mother also, and that in cases like this the mother's life had to take precedence if there was a threat of suicide. In the same year, following a further referendum, the pro-life amendment was amended to include the right to travel and information for the purposes of abortion. But a proposed third amendment, legalising abortion if there was a risk to the life of the mother was rejected as being too liberal by those who opposed abortion on all grounds, and too restrictive by those advocating the general legalisation of abortion. During the X case, the *Irish Times* cartoonist Martyn Turner sketched one of the most powerful images of the twentieth century, which depicted a young girl clutching a teddy bear in the middle of a map of Ireland surrounded by barbed wire. The caption read: 'The introduction of internment in Ireland: for 14–year-old girls.'[264]

The issue had still not been resolved by the close of the century, some wanting to legislate for the 1992 Supreme Court decision, others wanting to overturn it; but there was no significant political support for an abortion law similar to England's in either the North or South. The legal position remained that abortion was legal under the terms of the Supreme Court judgement in the X case. According to a 1998 survey, social and economic pressures were considerable factors influencing the decision to have an abortion. In 1999 over 6,000 women giving addresses in the Irish Republic had abortions in England and Wales.[265]

'You can't have a civil right to break a contract'

In 1980, supporters of divorce legislation inaugurated a campaign at Liberty Hall in Dublin, the organisers believing it could take 20 years to achieve their goal. In the first referendum to legalise divorce the proposal was rejected by nearly a two to one majority, while in the 1995 referendum it was accepted by the slimmest majority (50.5 to 49.5 per cent). Economic issues were to the fore on both occasions. The importance attached to the family in the Irish Constitution was not matched with sufficient state support in the area of welfare and family allowances. But, ironically, the same professional and well-connected anti-abortion lobby was determined in 1986 to present divorce as involving huge financial sacrifice, and it managed to elbow out the extreme groups like the League of Decency. This was a clever campaign which sought to instil fear, not about the idea of family break-up, but the idea of being poor. Indeed, it was central to Finola Kennedy's thesis in her seminal book *Cottage to Crèche: Family Change in Ireland* that economic influences have been more important in the long term than the social and moral teaching of the Catholic Church in shaping the family.

Emily O'Reilly, in her book *Masterminds of the Right*, described the Divorce Action Group's campaign in 1986 as 'shambolic'. One of the leading DAG campaigners, Mags O'Brien, acknowledged the validity of this assessment, but pointed out that the majority of them were separated people looking for a second chance, and lacked the political skills that the Anti-Divorce Campaign had learned through the 1983 abortion referendum campaign. More importantly, the DAG:

lacked the massive funds that their opposition used so effectively for advertising. ADC posters appeared targeting different socio-economic areas stating: We Want Jobs, Not Divorce; Divorce Kills Love; God Says No ... a leaflet from the Irish Family League read: 'Taxpayer pays all – Divorce will cost IR£200 million p. a., IR£17 per week extra out of each taxpayer's pocket.'[266]

Garret FitzGerald, Taoiseach at the time of the 1986 campaign, noted that the debate was between two sets of people whose views he did not accept. With regard to religious opposition, he insisted 'marriage was being destabilised through the absence of divorce' in the sense that marriage was being undermined through the frequency of second unions not recognised by either Church or state. But he also maintained that the idea of divorce as a civil right was 'a nonsense. You can't have a civil right to break a contract that was indissoluble.' This would suggest it is too simplistic to treat FitzGerald's initiatives in the 1980s as a liberalising constitutional crusade to wrestle Ireland from the dark ages. Attitudes were a lot more complicated. He was certain, however, that in 1986 'property was the fact that defeated the divorce referendum. No doubt about that.'[267] The property argument held great sway in a country where, by 1991, 80 per cent of homes were owner-occupied compared with 53 per cent in 1946. FitzGerald later contended that one of the paradoxes in relation to marriage breakdown was that 'the delay in the introduction of civil divorce may have contributed to the undermining of marriage'.[268]

But by 1995 the ideal notion of the family could not be sustained in light of the social reality of changed perceptions of marriage (which included the fact that, in the absence of divorce, the courts liberalised their attitude on nullity). Pro-divorce campaigners were helped by the fact that many of those seeking divorce were materially better off than in the 1980s. Notwithstanding the improved economic environment, moving the debate towards the idea of compassion and pluralism was also important, and managed with considerable aplomb by John Bruton, leader of Fine Gael and Taoiseach of the coalition government from 1995 to 1997. Initially, there was no great rush to the divorce courts, but, in any case, what constituted the traditional Irish family unit had been transformed by the end of the century with so many more women working outside the home and the increase in single-parent families. Lack of adequate state support in offsetting childcare costs put more pressure on parents, and contributed to smaller family size, while some parents had to resort to the courts to force the state to provide for the educational rights of the disabled.

Young Irish people were certainly having more unsafe sex in the 1980s and 1990s: 32 per cent of those attending clinics for sexually transmitted diseases at the end of the century were teenagers. But there were positive developments also. In 1921, the rate of maternal mortality had been 4.8 per 1,000, but by 1994 Ireland had the lowest rate of maternal mortality in the world. The infant mortality rate fell from 99 to 6 per 1,000 live births between 1900 and 1995. Although some of these improvements were a product of government intervention, successive governments often sought to avoid taking responsibility for the welfare of families (and the same applied to homosexuals) until they were forced to as a result of legal action.[269]

'a special language designed to confuse and terrorise the defendants'

But taking legal action could be an intimidating process. Experience of the courts by the Irish working class was chronicled with great humanity, anger and often incredulity by Nell McCafferty. She had noted in 1974:

> the total irrelevance of the defendant to the legal machinations of the court. The game is one between solicitors, justice and policemen. Between them they decide on a man's innocence or guilt and liberty or deprivation of it ... the Guards and the legal eagles address the Justice as 'your worship' or 'Lordship' and make their cases with respect ... the defendant who ignores these procedures incurs the displeasure of the Almighty, and prejudices his case from the outset. He can, of course, be told to shut up, or be threatened with seven days in the clink for contempt. Or the Justice can restrain himself and take it out later and increase the sentence ... the Justices, Guards and members of the legal profession use a special language designed to confuse and terrorise the defendants.

This affected women in particular, McCafferty observing: 'There's no place like a courtroom to dismiss the nonsensical notion entertained by housewives that they are in any degree independent of their husbands.' She detailed the case of a woman who appeared, offering herself as bonds-woman for her friend who had been convicted of shoplifting:

'Do you do any work other than housework?' she was asked. No, she did not. 'Are you dependent upon your husband for money?' 'Yes,' she said. 'I cannot accept you then,' said the justice. It was as short, simple and brutal as that. In the world where money matters, women matter not.[270]

Nearly 30 years later, incredulity was still expressed at the obsequiousness of barristers and their archaic gestures. One caustic observer remembered: 'various barristers frequently addressed the judge as "Milord" adding a hint of a curtsy. Momentarily, I was transported to the Old Bailey. I was sure that I could not be hearing a form of address so inimical to the Irish republic, so opposed to the equality of the citizenry unburdened by a monarchy.'[271]

III

'free sedatives for neurotic elephants'
Women's rights were being debated in a more forthright manner from the 1970s onwards. In *Chains and Change*, the 1971 publication of the Irish Women's Liberation Movement, it was stated dramatically that 'upon marriage a woman in Ireland enters a state of civil death'. In the same year, a Women's Political Association was established to support women seeking public office (women were not normally involved in the professions that gave a prominent constituency profile). The collective organisation of women was enhanced by the inauguration of the First Commission on the Status of Women in the early 1970s, but the women's movement had its fair share of divisions and conflict. This was partly because the more radical elements insisted on a confrontational approach, which was perhaps understandable, given that, as pointed out by feminist June Levine, 'no government of the seventies spontaneously passed a law which improved women's lives'.[272]

Some of the tensions within the broad feminist family were revealed in Nuala Fennell's letter of resignation from the Irish Women's Liberation Movement in 1971. Her and other resignations illustrated, she wrote, that:

Irishwomen, for all the discrimination and deprivations they suffer, are not the nation of blinkered female donkeys that the small policy making central group of Women Liberationalists thought them to be … I can no longer work for these changes with the elitist and intolerant group who are using Women's Liberation as a pseudo-respectable front for their own various political ends, ranging from opposition to the Forcible Entry Bill [which allowed the Gardaí to evict squatters, who were supported by the socialists in the IWLM], to free sedatives for neurotic elephants.[273]

The historian of the women's movement in Ireland, Linda Connolly, was later to contend that tensions were evident because Irish women 'are now considered to have suddenly changed from being late developers to rapid developers. Irish women internationally today have an image of prosperity, mobility and modernity', but this at a time when women remained under-represented in many areas.[274] In the late 1970s women held only 7 per cent of senior positions in the civil service and local authorities, where there was a high concentration of female workers; there were only five women out of 148 TDs, and no women in the High Court or Supreme Court, with only a handful of women on the boards of the 100 top public companies in Ireland. There were still a handful of pubs in Dublin that would not serve women in the bar.

In 1973, the ban on married women working in the public service was removed. This was the same decade in which women were organising marches against rape and other violent crimes against women. But after its foundation in 1975, an 'Irish Women United' group began to tear itself apart, when socialist women argued that working-class men were more oppressed than middle-class women.[275] In 1981 an attempt was made to launch a sister publication to *Magill* for female readers, and it lasted for only ten editions. According to its editor, Pat Brennan, 'the antipathy towards the magazine was stunning'. Ironically, the last edition documented the absence of women from positions of power.[276] Many of the demands of the Council for the Status of Women – equal pay and education, equality before the law, justice for deserted wives, widows and unmarried mothers – had been at least partly met by the end of the 1990s. Priorities had changed over time; adequate child care so women could work outside the home, a demand reflected in the report of the Second Commission on the Status of Women published in 1993, had been viewed as 'a decidedly second-best option' by the First Commission on the Status of Women.[277]

'only one sin in Ireland and only women can commit it'

The Employment Equality Agency was set up in 1979, and equality for men and women in social security was eventually established. While it is true there was a continuity to Irish feminist activism throughout the century, perhaps what the women's liberation movement achieved was to make private life public life, and to focus attention on the social, economic and political structures that defined that life. Increasing professionalisation and paid leadership also advanced the causes of women, as mainstream and marginal groups coalesced, and they became active agents of change themselves. According to Nuala Fennell, such organisations helped to expose 'the Pandora's box of the Irish family'. Fennell, one of the founders of Women's Aid in 1974, noted that at that time the deserted wife had to wait six months before qualifying for an allowance, and had to prove that she had attempted to trace her husband.[278] Whatever about evolving legislation, enhanced by equality directives from the EEC, societal discrimination was deep rooted. As one female journalist put it in 1985, 'the unmarried mother is still a pariah and her child is still a bastard, because there is only one sin in Ireland and only women can commit it'.[279] (In 1987 the concept of 'illegitimacy' was effectively abolished when an Act gave children of unmarried parents the same rights as children of married parents.) Such attitudes contributed to a determination to establish services for women, run by women, to deal with issues such as rape, single parents and domestic violence.

Though the 1980s exposed the extent of conservative reaction to women's advancement, this decade also revealed the variety of feminisms that existed, and eventually a belief by some that masculinity was being neglected, or sometimes demonised. It was suggested that 'the difficulty with family laws in those strange years was not that they were designed to oppress women but to burden men'. This was particularly true in relation to the family law courts, with the failure to alter the in-camera rules for family law cases, and the degree to which the rights of unmarried fathers, and the estranged father in cases of marital breakdown, were not being adequately recognised in the courts. Privacy – as facilitated by the in-camera rule – in reality meant secrecy, which led to much ignorance about the workings and judgements, and an inbuilt anti-male prejudice in the family law courts. There was also a lack of consistency in judgements. In 1998, the future Chief Justice, Ronan Keane, stated in a judgement on in-camera hearings that 'the most benign climate for the growth of corruption and abuse of powers, whether by the judiciary or members of the legal profession, is one of secrecy'. But the reality was that it was up to the legislature to change the rules, which it chose not to do.[280]

By 1994, there were 19,000 women in management positions, as against 58,000 men, though a 1995 survey of the top 15 publicly quoted Irish companies showed that just 3.5 per cent of directors were women.[281] A record number of women were elected to the Dáil in 1992, and the following year a ministry for equality and law reform was given full cabinet status. Most Fianna Fáil female politicians did not enter politics through the women's movement. In 1993, one such TD, Mary Coughlan, defended this, on the grounds that her constituents did not want her to specialise in feminist issues. She insisted she was 'probably happier talking about the state of farming or the level of headage payments or the conditions of the roads, than about gender balance'.[282]

In 1998, the National Women's Council of Ireland had 124 women's organisations with a membership of 300,000, the same year the European Court of Justice ruled against the government in relation to indirect discrimination against female clerical officers. By the end of the century there was increased poverty in female-headed single-parent households, and women were more concentrated in part-time insecure employment. These women did not feature in debates about financial compensation for women in the home, or those needing child-care, the focus instead being on professional women.

'condemned to spend her life as a mother and a homemaker'
Some feminists in the 1990s got thoroughly fed up with the selective coverage of women's lives by the media. Mary Cummins in the *Irish Times* was scathing about the belief of some foreign journalists that 'Irish women equal the X case, condoms, abortions, the Kerry babies, Granard and Mary Robinson. Not all Irish women spend their weekends having abortions or burying their babies.'[283] In contrast, she celebrated unsung women doing ordinary but desperately necessary work, and the manner in which women and men related to each other. Perhaps one of the reasons why the Irish journalist Nuala O'Faoláin's memoir, *Are You Somebody?*, struck such a chord with the Irish public on its publication in 1996 was her depiction of her relationship with her mother, and her generation's determination to try and avoid being cast in a role they did not want, or were not suited to. Her mother, she remembered, who gave birth 13 times, did not want anything

to do with child-rearing or housework: 'But she had to do it. Because she fell in love with my father and they married, she was condemned to spend her life as a mother and a homemaker. She was in the wrong job.' But this process of demoralisation of Irish women began at a much earlier stage, O'Faoláin defiantly reminding the reader that 'the emotions we felt as schoolgirls were volatile and exaggerated, and they have always been despised by the world. But they were not trivial.'[284] What made her book so appealing was that it was a powerful testament to the fact that neither were the emotions of middle-aged women trivial, particularly those who had chosen unconventional, sometimes lonely paths.

By the end of the century there was resentment in certain quarters of a prevailing belief that the task of liberating Irish women had been completed. Pat O'Connor, writing in 1998 in *Emerging Voices: Women in Contemporary Irish Society*, maintained:

> The reality of Irish society in the past twenty-five years has been trans-
> formed by individual incremental change, as reflected in family size,
> women's education, women's participation in paid employment etc.
> Of course these things have been facilitated by technology, and by a
> post-modern deconstruction of taken-for-granted ideologies. Ironically
> perhaps, the ability of women to change the parameters of their own
> private lives has generated in some an optimism which fails to recog-
> nise the implicit male bias in these systems ... this optimism is legiti-
> mated by ideas about meritocracy and equality ... the implication is
> that there is no need for women to face the gendered reality of power;
> that their differences are no different to anyone else's (i.e. men's) and
> that their attempts to suggest this are divisive and unhelpful.[285]

'under-serviced and distinctly unfriendly'

More generally, discrimination continued to exist in Ireland, as witnessed in attitudes towards marginalised communities. By 1976, many members of the travelling community had been settled in houses or on serviced sites, though there were about 862 families still on the roads, and many of the young travellers in Dublin fell victim to habits such as glue sniffing. Treated very harshly in suburban Dublin, where, in the early 1980s they were sometimes burnt out, the travellers came in for scathing criticism because of their lack of family planning and strict divisions between poor and poorer, accompanied sometimes by violence and filth. The reality was that relocating to the cities, as many had done in the 1960s, presented them with as many problems as possibilities, as did the manner in which they were settled in already deprived areas, often on under-serviced sites. Gradually, the ethos of equality emanating from the left of the political spectrum, and sometimes Europe, ensured that their plight became a political issue and they gave themselves political leadership. While legislation sought to prevent the settled community discriminating against them, the racism against them was both personal and institutionalised, seen for example in the obstructionist behaviour of local councillors.[286]

Conor Cruise O'Brien's contention in 1971 that the 'Irish character was peculiarly resistant to racism' rang hollow over time. A seminal study, *Prejudice and Tolerance in Ireland*, published in 1977 by the campaigning Jesuit Mícheál Mac Gréil, revealed a 'high and severe degree' of racial prejudice, and this stood out as one of the survey's most significant findings. A lingering anti-Semitism was also uncovered. While there was a higher degree of tolerance towards unmarried mothers and deserted wives than previously, the same charity was not extended towards travellers, socialists, alcoholics, criminals and atheists, but most especially people of different races. By 2000, a leading Irish MEP suggested racism was 'endemic' in Dublin, with a clear lack of political leadership on the issue; particularly ironic for a country that prided itself on its empathy with the Third World and had such a long history of emigration.[287]

Between 1995 and 2000, about 10,000 people sought asylum in Ireland, a development unprecedented in the twentieth century. They received disproportionate media attention precisely because most were not white. While some electioneering politicians were quick to cash in on the potential vote-getting value of racist soundbites, both the courts and the health boards battled valiantly to uphold human rights in the absence of an effectively run refugee appeals board.[288] Many foreigners seeking pleasure in Ireland on holidays were also in for something of a rude shock by the 1990s, to the extent that in the legendary 'land of the thousand welcomes' it was necessary to inaugurate a tourist victim support service in 1994. An extraordinarily cavalier attitude to public filth remained, to the extent that one survey of tourists found that 'although one in six innocent souls expected the Republic to be cleaner than their own countries, one in four concluded afterwards that it was dirtier'. Despite tourism being a £2 billion industry by 1999, the 'new' Ireland was 'overpriced, under-serviced and distinctly unfriendly'. David Rose, an English journalist, suggested that Ireland had become 'not quite rude, but almost brusque; businesslike, pressed for time and keen to get on to the next customer'. Also described was 'a two hour wait just to get into the city on a Saturday night. Getting out again is something else. Three English guests who joined a taxi queue in the city centre at 3am finally made it to Dún Laoghaire at 6.30am.'[289]

'the courts system is log-jammed and it's my people who are putting them there'

Law and order also became a more frequent topic of debate, and by the 1990s the Gardaí were coming under a scrutiny the force had avoided for most of its existence. In 1977, serious questions were raised about the Garda fingerprint section following the investigation into the July 1976 assassination of the British ambassador by the IRA. Garda officers reportedly attempted to frame a suspect by falsifying fingerprint evidence, and successive justice ministers were reported to have covered up the scandal.[290] Other questions raised included the issue of secret Garda surveillance on the Director of Public Prosecutions, Eamon Barnes (the office had been created in 1974). The first reports on suspected brutality by the Gardaí appeared early in 1977 and were condemned by Amnesty International. Their main concern was with C3, the section that co-ordinated anti-subversive activities.

The previous year, the Garda Commissioner, Edmund Garvey, had fallen out with the Garda representative bodies, after they criticised him in their monthly publication. He attempted to sue them for sedition, a notion derided and dismissed by the DPP. Stories of harsh discipline, and irregular transfers and promotions, abounded, as did the idea that the Gardaí were being forced to prosecute a specific number of summonses. Collectively, these events saw an unusual degree of attention focused on the internal activities of the Gardaí. Amnesty International also criticised the non-jury Special Criminal Court, for failing to scrutinise allegations of maltreatment with regard to admissibility of statements. Illegal phone tapping became part of the culture of policing and government in the early 1980s, with prominent journalists surveyed, clearly a hangover from the early 1970s (the coalition government of 1973–7 was strongly anti-media, and newspapers and the current-affairs magazine *Hibernia* were taken to court charged with printing material that cast doubt on the behaviour of the Gardaí and Special Criminal Court). It worried many that by the late 1970s up to 80 per cent of convictions for serious crimes were being secured by confessions, with the inevitable likelihood of miscarriages of justice.[291]

Every few months someone was dying in a Garda station, the deaths often violent and rarely satisfactorily explained. From 1980 to 1983, 15 people died in Garda stations and prisons. Many allegations of Garda brutality came from members of subversive groups, which meant little attention was paid, given the ferocity of much of the paramilitary crime of the period. Promised inquiries never materialised, which not only meant allegations were not substantiated, but also that Gardaí against whom allegations were being made did not have an opportunity to clear their names. But the level of retracted confessions after suspects got out of custody or gained access to the law was too high to be coincidental, though the courts nearly always accepted that statements were made voluntarily.

In the mid-to-late 1980s arrests under section 30 of the Offences against the State Act (originally introduced in 1939 and allowing the Gardaí to arrest and incarcerate for up to 48 hours) had reached an all-time high. Between 1981 and 1986, 382 such arrests were made, the law often being employed as a method of harassment and intimidation. There were 11,000 Gardaí in the state at the end of the century, and while they deservedly did not suffer the crisis of public confidence experienced by the police in some countries, owing to the empathy that existed between the force and society, police accountability remained poor. By the end of the 1990s internal investigations of Garda corruption were ongoing, as indeed were complaints about the force investigating themselves, which suggested a lack of external accountability. In August 1998, the Garda commissioner, Pat Byrne, remained defiant, boasting: 'people have criticised this force, but the prisons are full, the courts system is log-jammed and it's my people who are putting them there'.[292]

Some miscarriages of justice perpetuated by corrupt Garda practices took years to unravel, particularly notable being the case of Nicky Kelly. A member of the Irish Republican Socialist Party, he was wrongfully imprisoned for a train robbery near Celbridge in 1976, and not released until 1984 on humanitarian grounds, but without a pardon. In their book on the case, the journalists Derek Dunne and Gene Kerrigan reproduced extracts from statements in the book of evidence, revealing almost identical statements from Gardaí who were:

supposedly recalling separately and individually the facts of one incident in the case … There is a substantial body of evidence that a number of Gardaí committed crimes of assault during the investigation of the train robbery and that a number of Gardaí perjured themselves during the subsequent trial. It is prima facie evidence, consisting of allegations, inconsistencies in explanations which are themselves contradicted by the facts, medical evidence and statements by Gardaí which appear to have been made in collusion. This body of evidence has been ignored by the authorities and the Gardaí over whom this shadow hangs have been promoted. Whether or not that evidence would stand up in an independent inquiry is not the point – the point is the fact that the authorities by not initiating an inquiry wilfully covered up substantial evidence of a possible crime.[293]

This was a situation that could not be divorced from the political context of the time. The degree of paranoia in the South about republican activities came at the expense of civil liberties; but it was also the case that Gardaí had been killed in the line of duty by paramilitaries.

'governance of the country is now performed by lawyers'
Increased legal activity and the proliferation of tribunals contributed to the wealth of many lawyers, who themselves were an exceptionally unaccountable group, particularly in terms of the vast amounts they earned and the fact that their methods of training remained archaic and elitist. Piecemeal reform was introduced in Irish prisons in the 1970s, but there was little in the way of training and rehabilitation of prisoners, and conditions remained poor, as frequently noted by independent visiting committees and European human rights groups. Prisons remained overwhelmingly the preserve of the working class, despite, as Paul O'Mahony put it, 'the occasional imprisonment of an embezzling solicitor or an angel-dusting farmer and the significant increase in sex offenders from all occupations'.[294] Reports of child sexual abuse rose from 37 in 1983 to 2,441 in 1995, and by 1997 there were 250 convicted sex offenders in Irish prisons, one in eight of the sentenced male prison population. In Mountjoy, there were only 10 places for roughly 500 drug addicts on the detoxification programme.[295]

The media afforded crime much more attention in these years, partly because in such a small country, single violent incidents were inevitably given extensive coverage. But Ireland was by no means a crime-ridden country. The year 1947 had been the first when the number of indict-able crimes was recorded, and by 1981 there was a six-fold increase, but crime figures were still relatively low. The late 1970s and early 1980s witnessed an escalation; from 1973 to 1991, the figure for annual indict-able crimes increased from 38,000 to 94,000, and by 1995 the 100,000 mark was breached, only for the figure to fall again, partly attributable to the strong performance of the economy. But the Irish ratio of police to members of the public was one of the most favourable in the world in the early 1990s.[296] The reality (rarely reflected in the media) was that with the exception of the Dublin area, which did have high levels of theft, Ireland was less crime-ridden than most developed nations. The most worrying trend towards the end of the 1990s was the significant rise in the number of murders, which increased from 46 in 1996 to 53 in 1997 to 72 in 2000, from an average of about 30 in the previous 20 years.[297]

There were criticisms about lack of coherent sentencing policy, with an overuse of short sentences for minor offences; and the inability of the health boards to provide facilities for troubled children came in for sustained crit-icism, as most ended up in remand centres. A prominent and vocal judge, Peter Kelly, took the drastic step in 1998 of issuing an injunction against the Minister for Justice that required him to do something about provid-ing secure accommodation, following a landmark 1995 decision that the state had an obligation to do precisely that. Kelly said the treatment of troubled children was 'a bureaucratic and administrative quagmire … [It is] no exaggeration to characterise it as a scandal.'[298] (Kelly's decision to injunct the minister was later overturned by the Supreme Court.) Journal-ists, too, felt let down by a legal situation (including the law of contempt) that led to a sustained onslaught on them in the libel courts. This tended to inhibit comment on public matters, contributing to a tradition in which judges did not feel they had to explain themselves to the public.

The High Court expanded rapidly in the 1970s, in response to an explosion of litigation. In 1957 it had only six judges, but had 14 by 1982. There was a growth in the use of specialised tribunals outside the regular courts system, in the areas of employment appeals and criminal injuries, while in 1975 the Law Reform Commission was established. In February 1985, as *Magill* editor, Colm Tóibín was the first journalist to investigate the workings of the Supreme Court. He noted that it was the single institution that had the most profound effect on Irish society in the previous twenty years, and was 'praised by some, damned by others, ignored by most'.[299] John Kelly's 1980 edition of the *Irish Constitution* cited only 480 cases for constitutional and public law matters in the history of the state. By 1984, when he published an updated version, there were 650 cases to cite. In the preface to this edition, he wrote: 'If the judgement of the average liberal observer were asked for, he would probably say the overall impact of the courts on modern Irish life, in their handling of constitutional issues, has been beneficial, rational, progressive and fair.'[300] Those concerned with property rights, homosexuality and abortion may have dissented from such a view.

By the end of the 1990s, there was concern about the reliance of the political establishment on legal advice and lawyers, a preoccupation exacerbated by the tribunals. It was legitimate to argue that, in this context, parliament was becoming less relevant. The journalist Kevin Myers went so far as to argue that the ambition to have open and accountable government had been abandoned, in the sense that lawyers were advising the government on whether or not to change the law and setting their own exorbitant fees: 'governance of the country is now performed by lawyers and by professional officials advised by lawyers. Elected representatives are reduced to being clientelist technicians.'[301] Although the Supreme Court was generally regarded as being independent of politics in its judgements, senior judicial appointments (to the High Court, Supreme Court and Circuit courts) were decided by the government, who frequently sought to appoint or promote those close to the political parties in power. In November 1994, Albert Reynolds resigned as Taoiseach, after uproar concerning the appointment of Harry Whelehan as President of the High Court: Whelehan had been Attorney General at a time when the Attorney General's office was embroiled in controversy over the extradition of a paedophile priest from the North.

The enforcement of the law in relation to the environment remained another thorny issue, with the management of both planning and environment systems depending heavily on the threat of legal sanctions. In the early 1980s, Frank Convery insisted: 'this is the Achilles' heel of the Irish environmental management system. Our post-colonial cultural and social traditions and attitudes mean that the enforcement process is not seen to have the legitimacy and popular social sanctions which such a system enjoys in most other Northern European countries', thus diminishing the degree of social opprobrium associated with breaking the law. At that time, it was still not a mainstream concern. A series of pollution scandals, particularly in rural areas, slowly changed attitudes. The pollution caused by pig slurry and agricultural waste and illegal dumping was endemic. As the waste management crisis gathered momentum, the Irish attitude seemed to be selective, and the idea of having to pay for it was baulked at. Pollution caused by local authorities reached scandalous proportions; the agencies charged with the task of enforcing the Waste Pollution Act were themselves often in breach of legislation. This was at a time when loud noises were being made about the Sellafield nuclear reprocessing plant pumping radioactive waste into the Irish Sea, accompanied by much popular protest and outrage. Ireland was slow to implement EURATOM directives, and while its stand on nuclear waste issues in the international field was toughened, the record on such waste at home was poor, and was itself internationally criticised.[302] At a time when import of radioactive substances was increasing in the late 1980s, Ireland, unlike Britain, had no collection service for its radioactive wastes.

'no effort to apply their theology to Irish life'
The Catholic Church was another institution that came under the microscope as never before. Undoubtedly, the birth control issue made many young people more hostile to the Church, and priests were ill-equipped, as male celibates, to give advice to Catholics struggling with their conscience over matters of family planning. In the 1970s and 1980s this did not seem to affect mass attendance figures significantly. Nearly two million Irish people welcomed Pope John Paul II in 1979. The visit was an exceptional organisational endeavour, and perhaps it was appropriate that 'the 1,400 lavatories assembled in Knock for the Pope's visit were assembled by a London firm called Archangel interiors'.[303] Seen as an intense, communal experience, paralleled to that of the Eucharistic Congress of 1932, in retrospect it seems to have been one last blast, given that some of the indicators of a demise in the power of the Church were already in place.

Between 1967 and 2000, the number of priests, brothers and nuns declined from 34,000 to fewer than 20,000, or a 41 per cent reduction. Ordinations to the priesthood fell from a peak of 412 in 1965 to only 44 in 1998. The historian James Donnelly pointed out that in 1998 'deaths and departures from the religious life among Irish priests, diocesan and regular, outnumbered ordinations by a factor of almost five to one'. In 2000, there were 10,987 Irish nuns at home and abroad, down from 14,130 in 1990, 16,361 in 1980 and 18,662 in 1970. There were just 21 admissions to nuns' orders in 1999, compared to 227 in 1970, and at the end of the century 70 per cent of Irish nuns were aged over 60.[304]

The liturgical, theological and Church governance changes inaugurated as a result of the Second Vatican Council (1962–5) were a challenge to an Irish Catholic Church that was, in the words of James Donnelly, 'authoritarian in its governance, Manichaean in its general approach to the modern world ... devoid of a scriptural tradition in either scholarship or popular piety and strongly inclined to privilege "externalism" in religious practice over interior spirituality'.[305] Vatican II reforms stood in marked contrast to all the above, and the Church adapted well to many of them, but found itself embarrassingly bare in other respects. Liturgical renewal was a success, and mass attendance remained above 80 per cent, with much greater lay involvement in the mass, but not in the governance of the Church, and ecumenical activity remained minimal.

Rosary devotion declined, and the demise of Marian devotion was reflected in figures for membership of the Legion of Mary; by 1995 there were fewer than 8,000 members, down from over 25,000 in the 1950s. Decline in mass attendance became more noticeable in the 1990s. While an Irish marketing survey in 1997 suggested most people's religious beliefs had been unaffected by Church scandals, more than half believed the Church had been permanently damaged, and that mass attendance figures had substantially dropped. Attendance had remained exceptionally high by international standards in the 1970s and 1980s, but a national survey revealed attendance had fallen to 78 per cent in 1992, with a figure as low as 65 per cent recorded for 1997; the decline was most pronounced among urban youth.

Significantly, while the Pope in 1979 had spoken repeatedly about the need for an end to IRA violence, he had also chastised Irish bishops for failing to identify with the poor in Ireland. In January 1980, Latin America's leading Catholic theologian suggested Irish theologians were competent 'but seem to make no effort to apply their theology to Irish life'[306] (though it was also the case that many Irish missionaries in South America did apply theology in criticising US foreign policy). Whatever about the sense of optimism pervading the Church during the Pope's visit, the promise of a new golden age for Irish Catholicism, punctuated by relevance, modernity and compassion, was not to materialise. There was still an arrogance and impatience displayed by senior Church figures, who decried the general discussion of issues they felt should have remained the preserve of theologians and Church-office holders. Similarly, some of their views on the unchanging nature of Catholic dogma held out little hope for ecumenism or compromise, though traditionalists admired them precisely because of this.

'should not feel it necessary to apologise'?

Notwithstanding, many priests, nuns and bishops continued to inspire and lead at home and abroad, continuing, for example, their tradition of helping oppressed minorities and Irish emigrants. But what Garret Fitz-Gerald was to refer to as the 'irrationality' of their position on many issues was to be their undoing, and their wealth and astute financial management (controlling over £100 million in assets in the Dublin region alone in the early 1980s) attracted critical attention unthinkable in previous years. So was their seeming hypocrisy when it came to rhetoric and reality. In 1983, for example, the Archbishop of Armagh, Cahal Daly, promised young pregnant women they would be treated with Christian kindness and compassion, but then supported a parish priest in his diocese who refused to allow a 16-year-old mother back to school.[307] Senior Church figures gave an uncompromising presentation to the New Ireland Forum; they could see no reason why the state should dilute its Catholic ethos in the interests of Christian unity 'and should not feel it necessary to apologise'.[308]

There was a continuing concentration on bureaucracy and maintaining Church control in health and education. This was particularly true of successive archbishops of Dublin, still representative of the old-style academic tradition, who inspired fear or obedience rather than affection, and were at odds with the concerns of those administering on the ground (particularly regarding the idea that the clergy should no longer live as a group apart). This was revealed in 1985, when the Archbishop of Dublin, Kevin MacNamara, insisted that 'religious teachers should not be afraid to ask children to memorise what they do not yet fully understand'.[309] These children were being taught in the same schools in which the electorate voted, in classrooms littered with Catholic artefacts. But bishops were divided, for example, in the 1983 abortion referendum on whether to include in their statements advocating a 'yes' vote the sentence 'We recognise the right of each person to vote according to conscience', some clearly not approving, while some of the more liberal bishops did.

In the *Furrow*, one the most influential voices of Irish Catholicism, celibacy was a recurrent theme, and there were frequent demands for the Church to tolerate sexual diversity, again an indication that there was a significant range of opinion in Irish Catholicism on these issues. Perhaps this was inevitable given that the Church became so closely involved in issues of public morality and social criticism. This had an added significance, given what Joe Lee called 'the very shallowness of "traditional" civic culture' in Ireland.[310] Nonetheless, only half of those surveyed for the European Values Study in the early 1980s felt that the Church provided adequate answers on individual moral problems and needs, particularly in relation to family life. Less than 40 per cent of those under the age of 45 considered it important to teach children religious faith. But in comparison to the rest of Europe, Irish church attendance remained high, and in 1985 thousands flocked to a grotto in Cork where 'moving statues' were reported. It was, of course, in the interests of the chip van and pub owners to insist on the 'miracles',[311] but cynicism aside they vividly demonstrated the need of many for public devotion and certainty of faith during a time of great change. A few years earlier, Bishop Peter Birch admitted: 'we have failed to provide a richly Christian body of thought on any social topic'. This was essentially the crux of the issue; despite the bravery and activism of many individual clerics and nuns, the Church was not prepared or able to deal with the revelations of the 1990s.[312]

'the morals characteristic of Imperial Rome in its declining years'

It was a ferocious onslaught of tragedy and occasional farce which led one priest in the west of Ireland to complain that the media had declared open season on priests, presenting them as 'closet sexual deviants'.[313] It was unfortunate that the issue of child sexual abuse was lumped together with that of clerics involved in consensual adult relationships, as if they formed a seamless robe that symbolised the difficulties of the Church in the 1990s. Eamon Casey, the Bishop of Galway and in 1992 revealed to be the father of a teenage boy, was a popular left-wing bishop with a strong interest in human rights. Representing the first high-profile exposure of Church scandal, he was retrospectively and inaccurately regarded as having opened the floodgates, though he chose to pay the price by removing himself from Ireland to the poverty of Ecuador after his fraudulent use of diocesan funds to finance his family commitments was revealed (the money was subsequently repaid).

In November 1994, a Dublin priest died in a gay sauna, while two other priests gave him the last rites. In the same year, Fr Brendan Smyth's catalogue of paedophilia came to public light, north and south of the border. A request that he be extradited by the RUC remained for seven months in the office of Harry Whelehan, the Attorney General, and some Irish ministers were alleged to have had knowledge of the case. The Taoiseach Albert Reynolds's determination to still appoint Whelehan as President of the High Court brought down the government. Although Reynolds insisted: 'Harry did not know about the priest', perhaps through simple personal stubbornness, he refused to relent, and was, in his own words, 'led to my execution', as accusations flew that he and his ministers had misled the Dáil about their knowledge of cases in the Attorney General's office.[314] Whelehan was also forced to resign as President of the High Court. Mary Kenny noted the evolving impression that the Irish priesthood was:

> steeped in the morals characteristic of Imperial Rome in its declining years ... On one Monday in November 1994 the three leading stories on RTÉ were the political repercussions following the Brendan Smyth case; the collapse and death of the Dublin priest in a Gay sauna club and the conviction of a Galway priest for a sexual assault on a young man.[315]

In 1995, the hypocrisy of the country's best-known priest, Fr Michael Cleary, was exposed after his death. He had used his own radio show and newspaper column to espouse his extreme conservatism in relation to celibacy and matters of sexual morality, and was now revealed to have had a child with his live-in house-keeper.

Emboldened by the new climate of revelation, documentary makers and victims of abuse in various orphanages, industrial schools and reformatories run by religious orders unravelled a series of brutal 'hidden Irelands', stretching back many decades. So many had endured a painful silence that was now shattered, and the media response was ferocious. There was anger, too, at the leniency of some of the sentencing in relation to sex abuse. After the Sligo incest case, which revealed the story of Sophia McColgan and the years of rape and torture she endured at the hands of her father, the seven-year sentence he received, the maximum sentence for incest with a 15-year-old, was considered too lenient, leading to an Act of 1995 which increased the maximum sentence to life in prison.[316] In June 2000, there were 354 sex offenders, all males and 30 per cent over the age of 50, in custody, compared with 98 in 1990.[317]

Many new guidelines for both Church and state institutions were drawn up in relation to how to deal with child abuse. In May 1999, the government apologised to the victims, and a commission was established to investigate abuse in industrial and reformatory schools following the broadcast of the *States of Fear* series on RTÉ. The testimony in the programmes was harrowing and relentless, and revealed that abuse had been commonplace right up to the 1970s. Mary Raftery, producer of the documentary, suggested that up to 40,000 people were still alive in 1999 who had been inmates of the industrial school system at one time or another. She declared that 'virtually no industrial-school where there were boys over ten has not had or is not having a Garda investigation into sexual abuse, and this includes the schools for the deaf [and] the mildly handicapped'.[318] As the financial sponsor of such institutions, the state was directly implicated, and Department of Education files revealed the extent to which they had ignored complaints about the institutions.

Much of the abuse, of course, was not unique to Ireland, and it is important to point out that 31 Catholic clerics (priests and brothers) were convicted in Ireland of child sexual abuse between 1991 and 1998, out of a total of about 9,013 Irish Catholic priests (2,000 of them overseas). The media construct of the 'paedophile priest' was criticised by the sociologist Harry Ferguson as being too selective in confronting the issues abuse raised about men, masculinity, the family and sexuality in general, given that males from all social backgrounds had committed such crimes. Awareness was not solely a development of the 1990s. A number of social workers in 1983 had hosted a workshop on child sexual abuse and the Rape Crisis Centre had identified survivors of child abuse in the mid-1980s as a major client group.[319]

Some became angry that when Harry Whelehan was questioned and denied the existence of a Catholic conspiracy within the Attorney General's office, he felt the need to defend his right to be a practising Catholic. Others maintained that not only was it important for the victims' anger to be visible, but that it should be recognised that many of those who joined clerical life were often ill-suited to the priesthood, some of them victims of abuse themselves who lacked the freedom to make a proper decision about their vocation. While there had been severity and abuse, the Church had also offered genuine care to many people. Undoubtedly though, the revelations contributed to a hardening of attitudes against celibacy; an RTÉ poll in 1995 suggested 71 per cent wanted an end to the rule on clerical celibacy.[320]

'a catch-all commission'?

In any case, the problem was much greater than the Catholic Church, though the Church leadership did not exactly do themselves any favours by remaining so distant and less than honest in some of their responses. The 'we feel your pain' message was often simply not credible. There were some exceptions, such as Bishop William Walsh of Killaloe, who urged the Church to be contrite and avoid the appearance of trying to defend the indefensible. There was also an opportunity for closure on past mistakes. In 1998 Bishop Brendan Comiskey of Ferns apologised for the events at Fethard-on-Sea in the late 1950s (but later came in for criticism over his failure to respond adequately to allegations of sex abuse in his own diocese). A measure of the changing times was that the following year, in a film of the events at Fethard-on-Sea, *A Love Divided*, the hero was the local publican, the only atheist in town. Mary Kenny also cautioned against writing off the Church, given that a eurobarometer of 1999 revealed young Irish people as the most spiritual in Europe, with 48 per cent of 15–24-year-olds believing in God and practising their faith, compared to 8 per cent in France.[321]

The extent to which the state was culpable too, not to mention society at large, given that parents, the Gardaí, judges and the Department of Education had played a central part in incarcerating children in institutions, was not adequately addressed or debated. The demonisation of individual clerics and nuns at the expense of posing these wider questions was convenient, and often understandable, but inadequate and selective. The commission established by the government to seek redress quickly proved to be contentious, as 1,700 victims wanted to have their claims heard independently, and sought answers as to why the abuse had continued unchecked. The legislation for the inquiry was put in place in April 2000, but there was immediately confrontation. The government could not agree legal fees for the lawyers of victims' groups, who wanted legal representation for complainants appearing before the commission, given that religious orders would have their own legal representation.

Another controversial issue was compensation, with victims seeking a compensation tribunal, instead of recourse to the High Court. This was a proposal greeted with scepticism by the government, who felt it would lead to the state rather than the religious orders bearing the brunt of the cost. The journalist Liam Reid maintained that 'in its attempt to create a catch-all commission that would be all things to all people, the government created a vehicle with the potential to become the longest-running and most expensive inquiry in the Republic's history'.[322] In autumn 2000, the chairperson of the commission, Justice Mary Laffoy, publicly criticised the government for not showing 'a more obvious willingness to speedily address' these issues.[323] In November 2000, the government finally announced a compensation tribunal, in the form of a Residential Institutions Redress Board, and that religious orders had agreed to make a 'meaningful contribution' to its costs. What precisely was meant by a 'meaningful' contribution, and how much the state would have to contribute, were questions for the twenty-first century. So was the issue of the vacuum that had been left by the widespread loss of faith and respect for the Church. Even radical journalists like Vincent Browne 'almost wished to be back in those days of rosaries and the valley of tears'. The sense of camaraderie and solace that had been experienced in communal religious devotion had been replaced, he mused, by the individual subscribing 'to the anonymous society, acquisitive, rootless, unbonded'.[324]

The Protestant churches in Southern Ireland ended the century more confidently, even though their population was only 3.4 per cent of the recorded total in 1981 (down from 10 per cent in 1911). Ten years later, there were only 90,000 Church of Ireland members in the Republic. From the early 1970s, 30 per cent of Church of Ireland members' marriages were to Catholics and special commissions were needed to help dispose of idle churches. They had other important decisions to make: permitting the ordination of women priests in 1990, and in 1995 allowing divorcees to remarry in the church. It was significant, not only that 'Change' was the theme selected by the primate of the Church of Ireland, Robin Eames, during the 1996 General Synod, but also that Protestants had an increasing confidence in their place in Irish society on the basis that they were quite well equipped to make a contribution to what was becoming, in many ways, a more pluralist society.

'from driving Volkswagen cars to flying Concorde'

There were many manifestations of cultural upheaval after 1970, with the growth in the Irish media particularly notable. The country's state broadcaster, RTÉ, was often under political pressure, particularly in the context of Section 31 of the Broadcasting Act that banned the airing of interviews with paramilitaries. In 1972, the entire RTÉ Authority was fired. The investigative aggression of current-affairs programming, which the government seemed to think was too intrusive and troublesome, was replaced with much softer political programmes. Fianna Fáil was seemingly resentful at a small group of what they regarded as hostile intellectuals in RTÉ, and challenging producers were shifted out of the current-affairs domain while others resigned. Many were frustrated that they were obliged by law to give coverage to the Northern conflict as the criminal doings of small and unrepresentative groups of republicans and loyalists, and were unable to depict its scale and complexity or report on it impartially. In 1976 Gene Kerrigan noted that a *Here and Now* interview with an expert from the London Institute of Strategic Studies had the line 'after all, guerrilla movements always win in the end' cut out, even though the reference was to Zimbabwe.[325]

RTÉ radio not only faced the challenge of domestic private stations, but competition from the BBC and ITV. RTÉ Radio One, strong in the news and current-affairs areas, performed well in this context, and Gay Byrne continued to show the intuition and awareness that made him a unique broadcaster. The continued success of *The Late Late Show* was a further testament to his media skills. But by 1999, RTÉ's share of the total radio audience fell below 50 per cent (dropping to 49 per cent) for the first time. The opening of the airwaves to commercial competition, subsequently shrouded in controversy over alleged bribing in relation to the award of contracts, put RTÉ under further pressure, as did criticisms of poor financial management and lack of quality and volume in home-produced programming. Nonetheless, John Horgan noted that RTÉ managed to retain, by the early 1990s, 'more than 50 per cent of the audience in the 70 per cent of homes which had access to multi-channel viewing'.[326] RTÉ was further tested by the launch of TV3 in 1998, as a national commercial TV competitor. As a station, it depended on imported light television, though there were limits on the advertising revenue it could raise. It consequently claimed RTÉ's dual system of licence fee funding and advertising was unfair. An Irish-language station, TG4, heavily subsidised by the state, began broadcasting in 1996, and after a shaky start commanded a small loyal audience.

The influence of the UK media was also debated, and ownership and management of Irish newspapers underwent dramatic shake-ups, particularly with the arrival of business tycoons like Tony O'Reilly into the media domain. The appearance of the *Sunday World* in 1973 tested the large public appetite for a home-based tabloid, though broadly speaking, unlike in the UK, the private lives of politicians remained out of bounds.[327] Many external entrepreneurs tapped into the large demand for newspapers in Ireland, and blurred the lines between native and non-native media, the Independent Group's share of the indigenous Irish Sunday market eventually reaching 71.2 per cent. The *Irish Press* titles finally collapsed in 1995, amidst much recrimination. Tim Pat Coogan, who left the paper in 1987, suggested it fell victim to 'ego and incompetence' and the 'contempt' shown to its flagship publication was heightened by management's treatment of workers:

> Labour relations were worsening all the time. Alone of all the major Irish newspaper groups, the Press papers managed to create a strike over the introduction of computerised typesetting. To the people who had to operate the visual display units as opposed to the old hot metal typesetting, the new technology was the equivalent of going from driving Volkswagen cars to flying Concorde. Yet a derisory couple of weeks was all that was allowed for training.[328]

In the last years of the 1990s, advertising revenue for newspapers almost doubled and the best quality Irish newspaper, the *Irish Times*, managed a circulation of over 100,000 for the first time. It continued to increase coverage of science, the law, and environmental, social and health issues, along with setting up more overseas offices, eventually making the mistake of spending too lavishly during the boom. The provincial-newspaper sector remained robust, and the introduction of the Freedom of Information Act was seen as an opportunity to make politicians more accountable. Politicians were not the only targets; there was a significant rise in the industriousness of crime journalists and a national outcry when the *Sunday Independent* crime journalist, Veronica Guerin, was shot dead in 1996 by a criminal gang member as a result of her investigations. Later, questions were raised as to the manner in which she operated and the risks the newspaper was prepared to expose her to.[329]

The government subsequently introduced tougher legislation for dealing with organised crime, and to allow seizure of criminal assets, with mixed success. Broadly speaking, however, there was a decline by the 1990s in critical and investigative journalism, particularly in the Sunday newspaper sector, and unlike in the 1980s an emphasis instead on lifestyle, celebrity and the journalist as personality. Brian Trench, a former editor of *Magill,* pointed out that, despite the fact that science and technology had been dramatically altering the nature of Irish society, 'an outmoded Irish media has dramatically failed to keep us adequately informed ... science is reported largely in its own specialist context and technology is covered mainly in a business context'.[330]

'rock and roll is finally part of their culture'

The youth of the Irish population, and the ability of its musicians to absorb historical musical influences while creating something new, ensured that the Irish music scene was vibrant and noisy from the 1970s. Van Morrison became one of the world's leading rock stars, while the 'Irish renaissance' also spawned the Boomtown Rats. Most influential and successful were U2, the greatest rock band in the world in the 1980s and 1990s, making it to the cover of *Time* magazine in 1987, but with a strong commitment to maintaining their home base in Ireland. One of Ireland's greatest folk singers, Christy Moore, suggested that the key to his success lay in the fact that in the 1970s and 1980s he was more excited by Irish music than he had been previously by American and British rock and roll. The 1970s were an innovative decade for Irish traditional and folk music, with a creative interaction of folk, blues, country and rock with groups like Planxty, Dé Dannan and the Chieftains bringing traditional Irish music to a very wide audience with rock interpretations of Irish instrumental music.[331]

Christy Moore, who was to make over 30 albums, including those with Planxty in the 1970s and Moving Hearts in the 1980s, was a phenomenal collector of music as well as an unrivalled solo performer. He absorbed many influences and was highly political when it came to social justice and his republican sympathies. Writing his autobiography through explanations for his songs, he noted: 'There are songs that need to be set up and benefit from a great intro. There are songs that I cannot perform without setting a landscape in which they can live. But there are others that are best left completely alone, songs that can touch the hearts and minds without any embellishment.'[332] In 1977, one broadcaster suggested: 'our traditional music has never been so popular in Ireland and outside Ireland amongst young and old, and this must go down as one of the major developments in the Irish social history of the last twenty-five years'.[333] The phenomenal success of *Riverdance* in the 1990s modernised traditional Irish dancing, but its high energy may have left some of the traditional dance masters reeling in their graves. A historian of Irish dance had noted in 1971 that restraint was the ideal of the old school of dancers:

> who discouraged flinging the hand about or flourishing them at the level of the head. As well as being cutting of such acrobatic steps as Léim an bhradáin (the salmon leap). The good dancer, it was said, could dance on eggs without breaking them and hold a pan of water on his head without spilling a drop.[334]

Lovers of European kitsch celebrated Ireland becoming the most successful country in the history of the Eurovision Song Contest, winning the competition a record seven times, bringing much headache to RTÉ who had to host the show each year after victory. In the early 1990s, Paul McGuiness, the manager of U2, suggested: 'The Irish now feel that rock and roll is finally part of their culture. I doubt that in many countries would the manager of a rock band be appointed to the Arts Council, as I have been.'[335] Much of this was part of a conspicuous youth culture, but by the end of the century, serious criticisms were being made of decline in the quality of pop music. The 1990s were marked (and marred) by the rise of the manufactured boy bands, dependent not on musical talent, but skilful marketing, and in this league the Irish enjoyed phenomenal success. In 2000, the journalist Liam Fay pointed out that when musicians like Bob Geldof and the Boomtown Rats appeared on *The Late Late Show* in the 1970s, while half the nation were 'balling their fists in fury' the younger half were delighted, because they represented for them an alternative culture and a new generation who had angry things to say, but that 'during the past decade or so mainstream Irish popular music has become slurry-soft, all the easier to channel into the ongoing campaign to sell Ireland abroad and to ourselves as a bucolic idyll peopled with happy-clappy bodhrán rapping riverdancing rustics'.[336]

'there to administer to our shared passion'
In the 1970s, state support for sport remained minimal, depending on

massive armies of volunteers, but interest in Irish sporting endeavour entered a new phase when the Irish soccer team qualified for its first European championships in 1988, and its first World Cup in 1990, where it reached the quarter finals under the management of Jack Charlton. Charlton, a member of the 1966 World Cup-winning English team, became a national hero, despite purists' disgust that his management tactics were based on preventing other teams from playing the way they wanted to, leading to banal, defensive and negative football. Ireland's best-known football writer, Eamon Dunphy, became a pariah figure for criticising this approach, and what he perceived as Charlton's bullying manner. English journalists were surprised at the lack of criticism and the degree of self-censorship of Irish journalists at the 1990 World Cup, and indeed Dunphy's treatment after he criticised the team's style.[337]

But a country that had little to celebrate in the 1980s revelled in watching the team on a world stage, and understandably most were oblivious to the concept of 'pure' play. Abroad, the fans who travelled were regarded as exceptionally good-natured, and the streets of Dublin came close to the atmosphere of Rio in carnival time in the summer of 1990. That some of the soccer team were English (and could play because they had Irish grandparents or parents) was of little concern, though Dunphy's criticisms proved to be salient and accurate, and after the departure of Charlton in 1996 there was a noticeable move towards a more open and attacking style.

There was criticism too of the 'insular autocracy' that controlled the Gaelic Athletic Association, but the organisation remained successful, and developed Croke Park in Dublin into a world-class sports stadium, and continued to work hard at local level, nurturing talent, for example, in the Dublin suburbs. Hurling underwent something of a renaissance in the 1990s, with traditional 'non-hurling counties' coming to the fore. When it is played at its best, there is no sport to rival it in the world; the fact that the teams remained amateur when so many of their colleagues in other sports were earning vast sums made the success of the GAA all the more remarkable. Broadly speaking, the voluntary unpaid ethos was cherished and the creation of a Gaelic Players' Association witnessed players demanding respect and better treatment by management rather than elaborate salaries. The GAA at times revealed itself to be exceptionally narrow-minded and insensitive, as when in 1984 during its centenary year it would not allow members of the British army to participate in games, or exempt English teams from the archaic rule that required all team lists to be submitted in the Irish language. They continued to forbid soccer to be played in Croke Park. Notwithstanding, little compared to an all-Ireland hurling or football final day, when, in the words of Nuala O'Faoláin, there was a marvellous 'feeling of the nation as an entity'.[338]

Breandán Ó hEithir's book *Over the Bar* (1983) remained the best book on the GAA, as it set life against the sporting backdrop. It was a book of added significance because the GAA, for all its influence on Irish culture and society and the huge level of participation it engendered at local and county level, did not inspire an equally significant literature that contextualised the association and placed it at the heart of the community.[339] With a membership of three quarters of a million country-wide, the GAA managed, partly owing to the success of a Dublin 'glamour' Gaelic football team in the 1970s, to keep the games alive in the city, and yet continued its identification with rural homeplace, tradition, history and the passing of bloodlines. Tom Humphries, one of the greatest of the twentieth-century chroniclers of the game, suggested in 1996: 'its impact is emotional, visceral ... the GAA is more than a sports organisation, it is a national trust, an entity which we feel we hold in common ownership. It is there to administer to our shared passion.'[340]

'*a wild feral thing, and it's beautiful to watch*'

Many Irish footballers, like Liam Brady and later Roy Keane, thrived in the professional English leagues and the athletic achievements of Eamon Coughlan, John Treacy and Sonia O'Sullivan ensured continued attention was devoted to Irish track performances, particularly after John Treacy won an Olympic silver medal for the marathon at the Los Angeles Olympics in 1984. Sonia O'Sullivan's achievements surpassed those of any Irish athlete. A world and European gold-medal championship winner, she also had an appealing vulnerability, partly as a result of over-training and disappointing performances in the big Olympic races; partly because of the huge pressure on her from a small country, or, as she put it: 'so many athletes aren't the focus of attention in their country'. She finally became the first Irish female athlete to win an Olympic track medal in the 2000 Games, winning a silver medal in the 5,000–metre race. Tom Humphries, who followed O'Sullivan in the year leading up to the Olympics, memorably described the pressure and eventual elation that allowed O'Sullivan to finally 'stand still for a while':

If you've ever watched Sonia O'Sullivan, watched her race on a good day, you've seen some of the love. Of running and of racing. It's written on her face and in her flashing eyes and fluid stride. When she goes, when she kicks, it's a wild feral thing and it's beautiful to watch. People lean forward in their seats and clench their fists. There are few greater sights in sport than watching Sonia do what she loves to do ... It was one of those occasions. Nation as village. Children were herded into assembly halls to watch. Office workers gathered around small televisions. College students gathered on concourses. Traffic stopped. The woman in whom Ireland had invested so much emotion and hope was on the track again. People roared and people cried. Adults watched from behind the cracks in their own fingers. People turned away from the screen. Too raw. Go on girl! Silver. 'So close,' said Sonia, and then broke into a smile that spread across the face of the country that loves her. Silver. Bronze. Didn't matter. She'd just run faster than we thought possible. She'd just laid herself bare again. She was back. Ireland's greatest ever athlete restored.[341]

In contrast, the unbelievable achievement of Michelle Smith, in winning three gold medals in the Atlanta Olympics in 1996, remained precisely that, following interference with a urine sample during a drug test, and her banning from competition.

The cyclists Seán Kelly and Stephen Roche put their stamp on world cycling in the 1980s, Stephen Roche winning the Tour de France in 1987, and Irish boxers continued to perform strongly at the Olympics. The Irish rugby team of the 1980s was one of the strongest of the century, winning Triple Crowns in 1982 (for the first time since 1949) and 1985. They were managed by Mick Doyle, and it was noted in 1985 that the performances of the Irish team were significant not just in domestic terms, but because 'it was essential for the wellbeing of the game in Europe that someone other than France should reject the awful game of kick and chase'. The pursuit of an expansive type of play was not always successful, and the physical size of the Irish players was sometimes an obstacle to delivering on the vision of the team's managers. But the results of the 1980s revealed the potential for success with 'a fighting Irish pack that can either control or spoil'.[342]

'*deliberate, collective amnesia*'?

A revisionism in academic writing was evident from the 1970s, as some historians attempted to downplay the significance of violence in Irish history, particularly in view of the ongoing crisis in the North. It was notable that in 1991, the seventy-fifth anniversary of the 1916 Rising was greeted with almost silence, a fact that angered some who deplored what was called a 'deliberate, collective amnesia'.[343] But by the end of the 1990s the 'revisionist debate' was jaded, and historical writing had moved on to a post-revisionist stage. Historians demonstrated themselves more than capable of depicting both the noble and uglier sides of the course of twentieth-century Irish history and saw little need to disown the young republicans of the War of Independence era on the basis that their actions were foolish and unnecessary, or that to remember them with pride was to glorify murder. But neither did younger historians shirk the task of exposing the murkier and bloody aspects of the War of Independence and Civil War.

A new generation with the benefit of distance and modernised curricula generally chose to remember what actually happened as opposed to what revisionists thought could have happened, or believed should have happened. The 'official' state attitude had in any case matured, as seen for example in the commemoration of the forgotten Irish soldiers who fought in the world wars. Looking for ideological consistency in the years 1916–23 with the benefit of hindsight seemed a futile exercise, and it sometimes seemed that an arrogant academic, political and journalistic establishment believed the Irish history-loving public could not distinguish between past or present, or fail to recognise the changing context of Irish republicanism. The reality was more complex. In 1991, 65 per cent of those surveyed by the *Irish Independent* felt pride in 1916; but this did not mean they supported the modern IRA campaign.

Nonetheless, it is understandable that many of the generation born after independence had mixed feelings about 1916–23, feeling shame at the manner in which the IRA abused and falsified the passion and mandate of the 1916–23 generation, in order to wage terror in the North. The debates from the 1970s to the 1990s in this regard were thus significant, not perhaps in relation to the quality or range of historical writing they prompted, but for what they revealed about a society's relationship with its past, the attitude of the Republic to the Northern crisis, and the intellectual inheritances of a particular generation of (often English-trained) historians. At times, the debates seemed like a tiresome re-run of the Treaty debates in 1922.

In a seminal article, written in 1966 but not published until 1972, Francis Shaw insisted it was necessary to reject the myth of 1916 which depicted the Rising as 'the beginning and the end of Ireland's struggle for freedom'. He suggested the veneration of violent resistance had done much to ensure the permanence of partition, and though he had little to say on the unionist perspective, the timing of the publication of his thesis was significant given the Troubles in Northern Ireland.[344] That the challenge to reinterpret Irish history was also coming from such a ubiquitous intellect as Conor Cruise O'Brien was also notable given his media appearances, essays, journalism and academic work such as *States of Ireland* (1972). He roundly criticised the ambivalence to partition that existed in the South, and the lazy resource to history to justify threatening the contemporary peace of Ireland.

O'Brien remained 'fascinated and puzzled' all his long life by nationalism and religion, 'the interaction of the two, sometimes in unison sometimes antagonistic; and by the manifold ambiguities in all of this'. He castigated in particular what he saw as the mystical messianic Catholic nationalism of Patrick Pearse. In 1979, on the occasion of the centenary of his birth, he suggested Pearse 'was a maniac, mystic nationalist with a cult of blood sacrifice and a strong personal motivation towards death. A nation which takes a personality of that type as its mentor is headed towards disaster.'[345] O'Brien's criticisms were not just about targeting republican purists, but attempting to create greater awareness about the depth and nature of Ulster unionism and the continuity of Irish nationalist history.

In this sense, according to Terence Brown, he was repeating (or updating) the criticisms of Seán O'Faoláin and George Russell, in the sense that they too had challenged nationalist complacency. Brown suggested that because of his profile and public office (a serving minister in the 1973–7 coalition), Cruise O'Brien 'was better placed to argue his case than his predecessors, and was rewarded with better success'; and there were vocal unionist politicians being seen on screens in the South, providing 'compelling evidence of the substance of O'Brien's thesis'.[346] Indeed, Séamus Heaney credited Cruise O'Brien with creating 'some kind of clarity' in Southern thinking about the Protestant community in the North. But there was truth too in Brown's contention that a weakness of

Cruise O'Brien's revisionism was its 'unhistorical quality', because implicit in his writings in the 1970s was the suggestion that:

> Ireland would have achieved as much as it did had the Easter Rising of 1916 not taken place ... the reasons why in the colonial circumstances of maladministered nineteenth-century Ireland a myth of the inde-structibility of the Irish nation, of the seamless garment of Irish his-torical continuity had developed, why indeed Irish historiography had become dominated by a sense of the repetitive successes and failures of the national struggle, were almost entirely ignored.

These developments, noted Brown, 'could not simply be talked or legislated away'.[347] Cruise O'Brien may have criticised the 'unhealthy intersection' between literature and politics, but by the end of the 1990s he felt it necessary to oppose the Good Friday Agreement in the North by standing as an anti-agreement unionist politician in Northern elections.

Younger historians were nonetheless absorbing the new perspective. There was much truth in Roy Foster's contention in 1976 that the 'myths' of Irish history were not used in a creative way, and that 'their function is rather as a refuge in which to evade analysis', his concern being with the failure to acknowledge those who had never embraced extreme nationalism. Ten years later, in 1986, Foster suggested there should be enough cultural self-confidence in the South to critically question the national consensus and that to say 'revisionist' should be just another way of saying 'historian'.[348] Critics questioned his own work, for failing to appreciate the legitimacy or complexity of the republican inheritance, and not acknowledging the refusal of Britain to recognise the democratic wishes of the Irish people (for example after the 1918 general election). His call for more mature reflection also seemed politically convenient, given the new emphasis on Anglo-Irish relations in the search for an inclusive settlement of the Northern problem. But the unfortunate reality was that the focus of historians remained narrow – republicanism, violence and the continuing fixation with intransigence in the North – whereas revisionism also needed to look at so many other neglected areas of Irish history that had little to do with that triangle. Thirty years later, it was at least being recognised that social history had been neglected by researchers, while others continued the line of inquiry of F. S. L. Lyons, who had done much to stress division, in terms not just of political differences, but also separate cultures.

Foster's work was also criticised for being heavily influenced by five decades of revisionist history, the charge being that in claiming to be getting away from an approach marked by an obsession with the relationship with England, he and his ilk in fact remained obsessed with it – that Irish history was still being written in the context of the British Isles, or a 'two nation theory' of Irish identity that made partition the most sensible solution. This was influenced by seminal work such as Lyons's *Culture and Anarchy* and his contention that 'the coexistence of several cultures, related but distinct, has made it difficult, if not impossible, for Irishmen to have a coherent view of themselves in relation to each other and to the outside world'.[349]

But Foster's contention in 1986 that history is a constant process of revision – 'that we are all revisionists now' – could scarcely be denied (indeed the history of Ireland North and South in the following decade was to prove him correct). Events in the North ensured that the preoccupation with the Anglo-Irish axis was to remain until well into the 1990s, meaning that a true estimation of what native rulers had succeeded or not succeeded in doing after 1922 was delayed. Notwithstanding, individual historians were clearly becoming more interested in native failings, rather than externally created problems. The 'revisionist' debate grew wearisome and it is no surprise younger scholars sought refuge or escape in social, cultural and economic history, using literary and oral as well as documentary sources. They built on the lead given by such publications as *Irish Economic and Social History* and *Soathar* (the journal of Irish labour history), which commenced in the 1970s. This strand of research was initiated by a generation who had received higher education in the 1960s, had a greater interest in economic than political matters and were writing prior to the outbreak of the Northern troubles. In any case, the revisionist debate was conducted by a small group of scholars and it remained a parochial debate, at a time when international historiography was developing the concept of comparative studies and encouraging the writing of women's history.

As noted earlier, in 1978, Margaret MacCurtain, a University College Dublin historian and the pioneer of women's history in Ireland, pointed out that many Irish women had been deprived of information about their historical role and the resources to explore it. Her quest for historical material about Irish women was groundbreaking, in terms of changing women's relationship with history and their own status in the historical narrative. As she wrote in the book *Women in Irish Society: The Historical*

Dimension, the first collection by historians on women's role in Irish history, 'many Irish women find it difficult to learn about their historical identity, or their role in the life of the country because they have neither the information readily available, nor the skills of evaluation at their disposal'. She was later to see this book as 'an expression of the vitality of the intellectual and creative energy of the 1970s'.[350] She had provided the spade for women to dig themselves out of obscurity, and ten years later followed this up with Mary Cullen by establishing the Irish Association for Research in Women's History.

It was both a political gesture and a call for women 'to search their houses, open the tea chests, scour the attic to find the letters, diaries, and committee books of their grandmothers and mothers'. In 1997 Mary O'Dowd maintained that, having been trained in the methodology of *Irish Historical Studies*, 'the approach of the women graduates is now virtually indistinguishable from that of their male peers'. But there was still a sting in the tail: 'Less dramatic has been the growth in the numbers of full-time [female] academic staff and consequently, women historians still form a tiny minority of staff employed in history departments in Irish universities, and for most, promotion within their profession has remained elusive.'[351]

Historical writing was only one discipline undergoing change. Economics and sociology became equally important in the 1980s and 1990s, as did what was loosely termed 'cultural studies'.

'A post-Catholic pluralist republic'?

This new vogue of cultural studies in the 1980s and 1990s emphasised 'diversity', 'variety of cultures' and 'modernity versus tradition' in attempting to contextualise Irish identity as something complex, but ultimately pluralist. In 1996, the Minister for Finance, Ruairi Quinn of the Labour Party, described Ireland as a 'post-Catholic pluralist republic'. This was somewhat premature, because whatever about the new rhetoric of equality and inclusiveness, promoters of cultural studies often left the analysis of class and economic issues to others. One observer, Jim Smyth, in a contribution to *History Ireland*, was more accurate in maintaining that:

> cultural studies in Ireland and elsewhere may well be a redemptive
> substitute for the failure to engage with the material reality of Irish

life: a class-ridden corrupt society with levels of inequality and deprivation unrivalled in Europe. If Irish historians have sanitised history, the
denizens of cultural studies have evaded it by ignoring that, cultural
crisis or otherwise, Ireland possesses a class and power struggle apparently immune to change.[352]

Richard Pine, a contributor to the *Irish University Review*, argued there
was an unhealthy obsession with establishing and defining Irish identity
– an exceptional effort expended on self-definition – at the expense of
concentrating on the more prosaic but relevant challenges of eliminating
injustice, resisting the devaluation of the concept of community, and
addressing the failure to develop a decentralised state and society.[353]

John Waters argued that public discourse was dominated by the
single generation that benefited from the Lemass era. As he put it: 'all
our political classes, economists, sociologists, media managers and
leading commentators emerged from the big lie of the 1960s. This lie
was that the past was over and the future had begun and the rising tide
was lifting all boats.'[354] Was this the same lie of the Celtic Tiger of the
1990s, given that there was still such a neglect of the prevalence of
social inequality? Interestingly, in the 1980s, there was a more sustained
criticism of indigenous government and society in relation to issues that
had traditionally been attributed to British misrule in Ireland. Joe Lee
lambasted the failure to develop a system of 'native thought' and the
tendency to cling to authoritarianism and centralisation, suggesting
a degree of post-colonial attitudinal schizophrenia along with a lack of
public morality.[355] Notwithstanding, sympathetic commentators pointed
to a high degree of social progress in Ireland since the 1920s and accused
critics of imbuing their comments with an exaggerated moralism. But
there seemed much truth in John Ardagh's suggestion in 1994 that 'as
the church enjoyed a moral monopoly, Ireland has never really developed
the alternative found in many other countries of a liberal, humanist or
socialist ethic of civic-cum-personal responsibility'.[356]

Attitudes to the Irish language continued to reveal a gulf between
theory and practice, even 50 or 60 years after independence. Declan Kiberd
pointed out that a 1975 government report showed that three quarters of
the people still believed it essential to Irish identity, but less than one
quarter believed it would still be thriving in the twenty-first century.
There was a new trend favouring Irish-language schools in the cities and an

Irish-language TV station, but Irish speakers were now ironically, if with a degree of success, making their case on the basis of minority rights.[357] In relation to the rural–urban divide, a common belief persisted, articulated by John Waters, that the so-called 'Dublin 4 state of mind' meant one part of the country had no interest in understanding the rest.[358]

The education system did little to develop a culture of equality or tolerance, but it did increase social mobility by the 1990s. From the 1970s to the end of the century, there was a sixfold increase in the scale of the higher-education system.

In 1977, Ireland's first multi-denominational primary school was opened; ten years later there were still only six, with just 1,200 pupils.[359] Educational subsidies for the training of graduates were funded largely through the taxes of those who had little access to the third-level system, a system that remained obsessed with its territorial sphere, with over-duplication of faculties and courses. Joe Lee was scathing in the 1980s of the under-performance of Irish universities, and suggested they had made a negligible contribution to the social development of the state. 'Ireland desperately needed thinkers capable of synthesising varieties of experience', he wrote; 'unfortunately, her institutional structures forced most of her best minds to think sectorally.'[360] This was not as true in the 1990s, as critical attention was devoted to rectifying the absence of cross-disciplinary activity and research.

While a new educational curriculum for the primary sector had been introduced in 1971, it was not updated for 30 years, and by the very end of the century one in ten Irish children had difficulties with reading and writing, a statistic that had not changed in almost 20 years.[361] But many Irish schools were producing highly educated students, and Irish teachers were paid better than many of their European counterparts. The numbers attending second and third level increased dramatically during this period. One half of all 17-year-olds remained in full-time education in 1979, while between 1964 and 1979 there was a two-thirds growth in participation at third level. But the children of unskilled workers remained vastly under-represented. In 1979, while 21 per cent of the population of County Dublin consisted of higher socioeconomic groups, their children constituted 72 per cent of the entrants to higher education.[362] In 1993, the Dé Butléir report on third-level student support made it clear that declared incomes were being rigged by those outside of the PAYE sector in order to qualify for grants, and that the means test 'ignores the accumulated wealth of individuals'.[363] But census data revealed the positive role the Irish education system played in rapid social change. As highlighted by Garret FitzGerald, throughout the 1990s, the level of education of the workforce rose rapidly, and did much to contribute to a booming economy:

> Between 1991 and 2002, the number of workers who in their youth received only primary education was reduced by nearly 200,000, or almost 30 per cent, while the number with third-level education more than doubled, from 300,000 to 650,000. Economic studies suggest that this upskilling of the labour force accounts for almost 1 per cent extra national output each year.[364]

'cultural democratic ideas'?

The extent to which the education system could contribute to the development of the arts was also debated during these years. The Irish Arts Council was slow to acknowledge the place of Irish traditional music in what constituted the arts. Music was given a lowly status in the area of education, and much of the success of Irish artists seems to have been achieved in spite, rather than because, of it. But there were positive developments also, with the opening of a national concert hall, and many Irish cities played host to high-quality performance arts, with open-air concerts and free cultural events being staged regularly and with great expertise and professionalism. After restructuring in 1973, the Arts Council in the 1980s focused on community and regional arts, only to take a more businesslike approach in the 1990s. In the early 1990s, Ciarán Benson, Professor of Psychology at University College Dublin, suggested: 'a comprehensive arts policy in which cultural democratic ideas are reconciled with contemporary artistic and aesthetic ones is still an aspiration'.[365] But Brian Kennedy, Assistant Director of the National Gallery of Ireland, maintained that from the 1950s to the early 1980s, the Arts Council went from being artistically elitist and politically inoffensive to being a 'challenging and independent institution', though he highlighted a lack of recognition of any value in the non-heritage arts.[366]

'an excavation of unactualised spaces'?

In the realm of literature and theatre, Irish writers continued to excel and command international attention. In the late 1970s, new publications such as *The Crane Bag* excited the new artists by posing key questions about what exactly Irish identity meant, and the need to examine 'the plural of the consciousness' and the 'deeply rooted schizophrenia in the Irish psyche'.[367] The poet Séamus Heaney remembered:

> the editorial in the first number is full of sentences which thrill because they tempt us towards the idea of renewed possibility. In the zestless mood of Ireland in the late 1970s the merriment of its way of thinking and challenging stirred us with its boast that it would promote an excavation of unactualised spaces within the reader, which is the work of constituting the fifth province.

In philosophy, history and discussion of contemporary literature, tradition was reinterpreted, and an attempt made to articulate this 'fifth province' of the imagination innovatively.

Heaney ensured that poetry was a part of this also, and it was fitting that he was so keen, given his own artistic journey that saw him awarded the Nobel Prize in 1995. According to Séamus Deane, Heaney had to reinvent his heritage and change the conception of what writing can be, by considering his literary heritage more carefully and attempting to 'interrogate it in relation to his Northern and violent experience; to elicit from it a style of survival as poet'. Thomas Kinsella too had to subsume his eclectic knowledge of so many areas, working on a large canvass 'but with a concentrated, even finicky precision'.[368] It was telling that another innovative new publication, the *Irish Review*, which began publication in 1986, was opened with an article by Roy Foster in which he stated baldly that 'the last generation to learn Irish history only from the old nationalist textbooks will soon be middle-aged men and women ... in a country that has come of age, history need no longer be a matter of guarding sacred mysteries'.[369]

'refused to place these writers in any tradition of Irish writing'

In 1978, Christopher Murray identified four new areas in which Irish playwrights were being innovative: frankness about sexual themes, religion being treated as a metaphysical rather than a socially conservative question, an embryonic working-class theatre, and aspects of the Northern conflict.[370] Twenty years later, the playwright Sebastian Barry wrote about the dozens of new companies of actors and directors that exulted in presenting new work. This was at a time when in the region of half of all theatrical productions in Ireland were premieres, drawing on some of the oldest elements of Irish culture, but confronting contemporary problems:

> It's sometimes said that there is a new theatrical resurgence going on comparable to the national theatre movement, as orchestrated by Lady Gregory in the 1900s, but this time there is no controlling mind along the lines of the Yeatsian model, as one might say, and really, the new playwrights are quite separate entities and do not strictly speaking form a group. This accidental fact has unexpectedly given it a unique strength and independence. The new Irish theatre is a moveable feast, that moves quite naturally and lightly between Dublin, Belfast, London and New York.[371]

Séamus Heaney, Brian Friel and Tom Murphy flourished in the 1980s, and the period also witnessed the emergence of a vibrant film industry. Film- and documentary makers re-examined Irish culture, and questioned the traditional narrative of Irish history, though the more commercially successful films tended to marry history with nostalgia, notably in the 1990 film *The Field*. Other films of the 1990s tended to eschew modernity and focus on the small rural community, and depict traditional gender roles and resourceful children. As one of those involved suggested, it was 'a case of trying to capture the state of the community they have here and that I think a lot of the world yearns to regain'.[372] But filmmakers also confronted contemporary Ireland in productions such as *The Snapper* (1993) and *Guiltrip* (1995).

Given economic recession and emigration, it was understandable that there was a bleakness to the tone of many Irish plays and novels of the 1980s, and there was still an unhealthy concentration on priests and politicians. In *The Journey Home*:

> Dermot Bolger took the name of a 1916 patriot, Plunkett, for a corrupt gombeen-politician, and filled the narrative with anger against the Christian Brothers, nuns (who beat girls for possessing such pagan names as Sarah) and rural immigrants in Dublin suburbs, who after three decades in the city, persisted in calling Kerry or Cork home.[373]

In the early 1990s, in his *Picador Book of Contemporary Irish Fiction*, Bolger celebrated a confident yet challenging and dissenting young literature, and deliberately 'refused to place these writers in any tradition of Irish writing'. Roddy Doyle, in humorous and satirical takes on traditional Irish pieties, was not only artistically powerful, but also a powerful social analyst. According to Kiberd, 'this new generation effortlessly assured the attention of the world as a natural right' and were novelists on their own terms, after absorbing the experiments of the 1970s.

'They want to be the same as everyone else'

In *Birchwood* (1973), John Banville had bravely satirised an Irish history of rebellion, land war and famine, and dismissed the idea of belonging to any literary movement or tradition. The narrator in *Birchwood* tellingly insists: 'we imagine that we remember things as they were, while in fact all we carry into the future are fragments which reconstruct a wholly illusory past'. He continued to revise traditional narrative and specific texts for parodic ends.[374] In the following decade, writers focused on themes of exile, violence, conservatism and post-nationalism. William Trevor continued the tradition of Irish melancholy, but also could write 'with equal conviction whether he is dealing with an Irish spinster or an English general', his writing full of black comedy but also compassion. Jennifer Johnson wrote about the failure of integration and reconciliation among Ireland's two 'nations', which she believed stemmed from the First World War. This was due to the fact that a generation of young men was massacred and to the embittering of a large number of people who remained. She contended: 'In Ireland it was the beginning of the Troubles we are now in.'[375]

In 1999, it was pointed out by Colm Tóibín that:

In Ireland now, for the first time, the exiles tell their own story to the whole country. Writers like Edna O'Brien, Julia O'Faoláin, Desmond Hogan, Patrick McCabe, Joseph O'Connor, Frank Ronan, Colum McCann and Emma O'Donoghue can explore Irish identity in England or the United States or Europe. In the nineteenth century and for much of the twentieth, the emigrants were too busy finding work to write stories.[376]

Tóibín and others were keen to:

banish the concept of an historical identity, any special theory of the nation or Ireland … and because the state is not partisan, because it has no rational purpose other than to exist … it sponsors this range of 'private fictional universes', and the writing of simple, forensic prose that is 'non-judgmental and non-evaluative'.[377]

They thus carved out their own niche, without a shared context or memories for writers and individuals to share. The detachment and liberalism of such prose seemed central to Denis Donoghue's contention in 1998 that:

many Irish people have grown tired of being told that they are interesting beyond their numbers or that the trajectory from race through nation to state has made them distinguished among their European associates. They want to be the same as everyone else, the same as England to begin with and as the United States later on. It is their right.[378]

In 1999, however, Ray Ryan maintained that this was an attempt to withdraw, and represented a failure to evaluate liberalism; their task should be to 'offer some substantive and coherent conception of what is good, not to withdraw to hermetic and private universes in defence of the right not to be assaulted by tradition and history'.[379] But there was nothing hermetic and private about most of this fiction: the grief and madness that were a part of the fabric of small-town rural Ireland in Patrick McCabe's *Butcher Boy* (1992), for example; the political and sexual turmoil of contemporary Argentina in Colm Tóibín's *Story of the Night* (1996); or the humour-filled mayhem of Dublin working-class life in Roddy Doyle's *The Snapper* (1990).

'What was it all for?'

John McGahern remained prince of the Irish novelists, producing the most impressive body of work in the latter part of the century, charting the fortunes of family and rural life, and the timeless themes of land, family and human dilemma. These were all powerfully enunciated in *Amongst Women* in 1990. The central character, Michael Moran, a War of Independence veteran, felt he and his comrades had fought for independence at the best time of their lives, only for native misrule to render it somewhat meaningless: 'some of our own Johnnies in the top jobs instead of a few Englishmen. More than half of my own family work in England. What was it all for? The whole thing was a cod.'[380] When Moran died, it was perhaps appropriate that the tricolour flag of the Irish Republic that draped his coffin was so faded. For Moran, so alienated from public life, the republican dream had long since vanished, though his involvement in the local themes of family, survival, money and the repression of women was always apparent, making him an appropriate symbol of twentieth-century Ireland. But apart from his insight about character and what propels people, McGahern was also able to write beautifully about nature and rural Ireland, gentle, small and independent communities and local concerns, employing rich dialogue and an acute sense of place. These positive aspects of Irish identity were, if not dying by the close of the twentieth century, at least being left further behind by a pragmatic, dismissive and ideologically indifferent Ireland. McGahern's work remains both an indictment of the failures of Irish independence and a celebration of Ireland's distinctiveness. It is difficult for the historian to disagree with his assessment.

NOTES

Introduction

1. See F. S. L. Lyons, *Ireland since the Famine* (London, 1971); John A. O'Brien (ed.), *The Vanishing Irish* (New York, 1954); and Fergal Tobin, *The Best of Decades: Ireland in the 1960s* (Dublin, 1984).

2. Interview with A. T. Q. Stewart, *History Ireland*, vol. 1, no. 2, Summer 1993, pp. 55–9.

3. *Magill*, August 2000.

4. Fintan O'Toole, *The Irish Times Book of the Century* (Dublin, 2000), p. 313.

5. J. J. Lee, *Ireland 1912–85: Politics and Society* (Cambridge, 1989).

6. Quoted in Liam O'Dowd, 'Neglecting the material dimension: Irish intellectuals and the problem of identity', *Irish Review*, no. 3, 1988, pp. 8–18.

7. R. F. Foster, *Modern Ireland 1600–1972* (London, 1988), and *Irish Historical Studies*, vol. xxiv, May 1989, p. 304.

8. Interview with Seán Ó Mordha, *Irish Times*, 19 February 2000.

9. *Seven Ages: The Story of the Irish State*, produced by Seán Ó Mordha. Shown on Radio Telefís Éireann, February and March 2000.

10. J. J. Lee, 'A sense of place in the Celtic tiger', in Harry Bohan and Gerard Kennedy (eds.), *Are We Forgetting Something? Our Society in the New Millennium* (Dublin, 1999), pp. 71–94.

11. Finola Kennedy, *Cottage to Crèche: Family Change in Ireland* (Dublin, 2000), p. 140.

12. Interview with John McGahern, *Irish Times*, 13 October 1990.

13. Fintan O'Toole, editorial, *Magill*, May 1986.

14. Michael Viney, *Growing Old in Ireland* (Dublin, 1967), p. 14.

15. Mary Raftery and Eoin O'Sullivan, *Suffer the Little Children: The Inside Story of Ireland's Industrial Schools* (Dublin, 1999), p. 380.

16. Quoted in Tony Canavan, 'The profession of history: The public and the past', in Ray Ryan (ed.), *Writing in the Irish Republic: Literature, Culture, Politics, 1949–1999* (London, 2000), pp. 226–41.

17. See Diarmaid Ferriter, 'Suffer little children? The historical validity of memoirs of Irish childhood', in Joseph Dunne and James Kelly (eds.), *Childhood and Its Discontents* (Dublin, 2002), pp. 69–107.

18. David Thornley, 'Ireland: The end of an era?', *Studies*, vol. LIII, no. 209, Spring 1964, pp. 1–18.

19. Tony Farmar, *Ordinary Lives: Three Generations of Irish Middle-class Experience* (Dublin, 1991), p. 168.

20. Colm Tóibín, 'Thomas Murphy's volcanic Ireland', in Christopher Murray (ed.), *Irish University Review, Thomas Murphy Issue*, vol. 17, no. 1, Spring 1987, pp. 24–31.

21. Farmar, *Ordinary Lives*, p. 169.

22. Liam Ryan, *Social Dynamite: A Study of Early School Leavers* (Dublin, 1967), p. 32.

23. Eamonn McKee, 'Church–state relationships and the development of Irish health policy: The Mother and Child Scheme 1944–53', *Irish Historical Studies*, vol. XXV, no. 98 (1989), pp. 159–94.

24. Fintan O'Toole, *A Mass for Jesse James: A Journey through 1980s Ireland* (Dublin, 1990), pp. 174–5.

25. Gay Byrne with Deirdre Purcell, *The Time of My Life: The Autobiography of Gay Byrne* (Dublin, 1989), p. 155.

26. Tom Garvin, 'The politics of denial and cultural defence: The referenda of 1983 and 1986 in context', *Irish Review*, no. 3, 1988, pp. 1–8.

27. *Irish Times*, 2 March 1929.

28. Susan McKay, *Sophia's Story* (Dublin, 1998).

29. Mark Patrick Hederman, 'Climbing into our proper dark – Ireland's place in Europe', in Bohan and Kennedy (eds.), *Are We Forgetting Something?*, pp. 34–52.

30. Elizabeth Russell, '"Holy crosses, guns and roses": Themes in popular reading material', in Joost Augusteijn (ed.), *Ireland in the 1930s: New Perspectives* (Dublin, 1999), pp. 11–29.

31. Published Debates of *Dáil Éireann* (hereafter *Dáil Debates*), 31 March 1937.

32. Donál Mac Amhlaigh, *An Irish Navvy: The Diary of an Irish Exile* (London, 1964), p. 123.

33. John Horgan, *Irish Media: A Critical History since 1922* (London and New York, 2001), p. 80.

34. John Whyte, *Church and State in Modern Ireland, 1923–70* (Dublin, 1971); Tom Inglis, *Moral Monopoly: The Catholic Church in Modern Irish Society* (Dublin, 1987); Patrick Murray, *Oracles of God: The Roman Catholic Church and Irish Politics, 1922–37* (Dublin, 2000); and Mary Kenny, *Goodbye to Catholic Ireland* (Dublin, 2000).

35. John Cooney, *John Charles McQuaid: Ruler of Catholic Ireland* (Dublin, 1999).

36. Patrick Touher, *Fear of the Collar* (Dublin, 1991), p. 173.

37. Cooney, *John Charles McQuaid*, p. 390.

38. James Donnelly, 'A church in crisis: The Irish Catholic Church today', *History Ireland*, vol. 8, no. 3, Autumn 2000, pp. 12–27.

39. A. M. Mac Sweeney, 'A study of poverty in Cork city', *Studies*, vol. 4, no. 13, March 1915, pp. 93–104.

40. J. A. Nolan, *Ourselves Alone: Emigration from Ireland, 1885–1920* (Lexington, 1989), p. 91.

41. J. Anthony Gaughan (ed.), *Memoirs of Senator Joseph Connolly (1885–1961): A Founder of Modern Ireland* (Dublin, 1996), pp. 127–8.

42. University College Dublin Archives Department (UCDAD), Papers of Michael Hayes, P53, 263, 18 June 1951.

43. Seán de Fréine, *The Great Silence* (Dublin, 1965), p. 207.

44. Eunan O'Halpin, *The Decline of the Union: British Government in Ireland, 1892–1920* (Dublin, 1987), p. 98.

45. Sari Oikarieu, *A Dream of Liberty: Constance Markievicz's Vision of Ireland, 1908–1927* (Helsinki, 1998), p. 196.

46. Charles McCarthy, *The Distasteful Challenge* (Dublin, 1969), p. 42.

47. John Coakley, 'Society and political culture', in John Coakley and Michael Gallagher (eds.), *Politics in the Republic of Ireland* (Galway 1992), pp. 23–40.

48. National Archives of Ireland (NAI), Department of the Taoiseach S Files (DT S), 1636B, Report on Vocational Organisation, 'Departmental views: Industry and commerce', November 1944.

49. Susannah Riordan, '"A political blackthorn": Seán MacEntee, the Dignan Plan and the principle of ministerial responsibility', *Irish Economic and Social History*, vol. XXVII, 2000, pp. 44–63.

50. Stephen A. Royle, 'Leaving the "dreadful rocks": Irish island emigration and its legacy', *History Ireland*, no. 4, Spring 1998, pp. 34–8.

51. *Irish Times*, 22 August 1931. See also Jude McCarthy, 'State-aided island migration, 1930–60', unpublished MA thesis, University College Dublin, 1997.

52. *Irish Times*, 23 May 2002.

53. *Dáil Debates*, 13 June 1951.

54. Michael Marsh and Michael Gallagher, *Days of Blue Loyalty: The Politics of Membership of the Fine Gael Party* (Dublin, 2002).

55. Garret FitzGerald, *All in a Life: An Autobiography* (Dublin, 1991), pp. 78–9.

56. *Irish Times*, series of articles February and March 1963.

57. *Irish Independent*, 27 August 1923.

58. William Cosgrave to Michael Hayes, 3 July 1944, UCDAD, Papers of Michael Hayes, P53 (258).

59. *Irish Independent*, 6 and 12 February 1932.

60. Diarmaid Ferriter, *Lovers of Liberty? Local Government in Twentieth-Century Ireland* (Dublin, 2001), p. 25.

61. Dermot Bolger (ed.), *Letters from the New Island* (Dublin, 1991), pp. 19–21.

62. John Banville, 'The Ireland of de Valera and O'Faoláin', *Irish Review*, nos. 17–18, Winter 1995, pp. 142–53.

63. Ronan Fanning, *The Irish Department of Finance, 1922–58* (Dublin, 1978); Mary E. Daly, *The Buffer State: The Historical Roots of the Department of the Environment* (Dublin, 1997); and Mary E. Daly, *The First Department: A History of the Department of Agriculture* (Dublin, 2002).

64. Garret FitzGerald, *Reflections on the Irish State* (Dublin 2002), foreword.

65. See for example Peter Hart, *The IRA and Its Enemies: Violence and Community in Cork, 1916–23* (Oxford, 1998); Michael Farry, *Sligo 1914–1921: A Chronicle of Conflict* (Trim, 1992); and Marie Coleman, *County Longford and the Irish Revolution, 1910–1923* (Dublin, 2003).

66. Interview with A. T. Q. Stewart, *History Ireland*.

67. Hart, *IRA and Its Enemies*, introduction.

68. Diarmaid Ferriter, 'On the State Funerals', *Dublin Review*, no 5, Winter 2001–2, pp. 5–15.

69. David Fitzpatrick, *The Two Irelands: 1912–1939* (Oxford, 1998), p. 124.

70. Seán O'Faoláin, *Vive Moi! An Autobiography* (London, 1965), p. 165.

71. Ernie O'Malley, *The Singing Flame* (Dublin, 1978).

72. Richard English, *Ernie O'Malley: IRA Intellectual* (Oxford, 1998), and Tom Garvin, 'Many young men of twenty said goodbye in 1920, many young men of 20 said hello in 1970', *Irish Review*, vol. 23, Winter 1998, pp. 176–8.

73. Deirdre McMahon, 'Ireland, the Empire and the Commonwealth, 1886–1972', in Kevin Kenny (ed.), *Ireland and the British Empire* (Oxford, 2004), pp. 182–219.

74. Senia Paseta, *Before the Revolution: Nationalism, Social Change, and Ireland's Catholic Elite, 1879–1922* (Cork, 1999), pp. 4 and 148–9.

75. Patrick Maume, *The Long Gestation: Irish Nationalist Life 1891–1918* (Dublin, 1999).

76. Colm Tóibín (ed.), *The Penguin Book of Irish Fiction* (London, 1999), p. ix.

77. W. F. Mandle, *The GAA and Irish Nationalist Politics 1884–1924* (London, 1987). See also John A. Murphy's review, 'Academe and playing fields', *Irish Review*, no. 4, Spring 1988, pp. 139–42.

78. Eamon Phoenix, *Northern Nationalism: Nationalist Politics, Partition and the Catholic Minority in Northern Ireland, 1890–1940* (Belfast, 1994).

79. T. W. Moody, 'Irish history and Irish mythology', *Hermathena*, nos. CXXIV-CXXVII, 1978–9, pp. 7–25.

80. Desmond Fennell, 'Against revisionism', in Ciaran Brady (ed.), *Interpreting Irish History: The Debate on Historical Revisionism* (Dublin, 1994), pp. 184–5.

81. Ronan Fanning, '"The Great Enchantment": Uses and abuses of modern Irish history', in Brady (ed.), *Interpreting Irish History*, pp. 138–56, and R. F. Foster, 'We are all revisionists now', *Irish Review*, no. 1, 1986.

82. Séamus Deane, *Reading in the Dark* (London, 1996), pp. 20–22.

83. Brian Fallon, *An Age of Innocence: Irish Culture 1930–1960* (Dublin, 1998), p. 11.

84. Cecil. J. Barrett, 'The dependent child', *Studies*, vol. XLIV, Winter 1955, pp. 419–28.

85. Declan Kiberd, *Irish Classics* (London, 2000), p. 592.

86. Tobin, *Best of Decades*, passim.

87. NAI, DT 96/6/707, 'Corporal punishment', July 1967–April 1969.

88. *Some of Our Children: A Report on the Residential Care of Deprived Children in Ireland* (Tuairim, London, 1966), p. 10.

89. NAI, DT 97/6/85, 'Social Services', 15 January 1965.

90. *Irish Press*, 12 June 1969.

91. NAI, Department of Justice (hereafter DJ), 12 January 1924, Kevin O'Higgins view re: Town Tenant Branches.

92. Lee, *Ireland 1912–85*.

93. Interview with J. J. Lee, *History Ireland*, vol. 3, no. 2, Summer 1995, pp. 44–8.

94. Catriona Crowe, 'Testimony to a flowering', *The Dublin Review*, no. 10, Spring 2003, pp. 42–69.

95. Martin Mansergh, review of Patrick O'Mahony and Gerald Delanty, *Rethinking Irish History: Nationalism, Identity and Ideology* (Basingstoke, 1998), *History Ireland*, vol. 7, no. 1, Spring 1999, p. 53.

96. *Irish Times*, 26 January 1999.

I: 1900–1912

1. Paseta, *Before the Revolution*, passim.

2. Maume, *Long Gestation*, passim.

3. T. J. Clancy, *Ireland in the Twentieth Century* (Dublin, 1892), pp. 8ff.

4. *The Leader*, 1 September 1900.

5. Fintan O'Toole, *Irish Times Book of the Century*, p. 22.

6. Lyons, *Ireland since the Famine* (London, 1971).

7. Maume, *Long Gestation*, pp. 85–6.

8. F. S. L. Lyons, *Culture and Anarchy in Ireland, 1890–1939* (Oxford, 1982), p. 27.

9. Colm Tóibín, *Lady Gregory's Toothbrush* (Dublin, 2002), p. 44.

10. Frank Callanan, *T. M. Healy* (Cork, 1996), pp. 268–9.

11. Seán O'Casey, *Mirror in My House: The Autobiographies of Seán O'Casey*, vol. 1 (New York, 1956), pp. 74–5.

12. NAI, Bureau of Military History (hereafter BMH), Witness Statement (hereafter WS) 205, Maud Griffith.

13. Maume, *Long Gestation*, pp. 85ff.
14. NAI, BMH, WS 1316, John Flanagan.
15. NAI, BMH, WS 839, Patrick Sarsfield.
16. NAI, BMH, WS 25, Patrick Higgins.
17. Maume, *Long Gestation*, pp. 48–59.
18. Eunan O'Halpin, *The Decline of the Union*, passim.
19. D. G. Boyce, *Nineteenth-Century Ireland: The Search for Stability* (Dublin, 1990), p. 229.
20. Donal Murphy, *Blazing Tar Barrels and Standing Orders: Tipperary North's First County and District Councils, 1899–1902* (Tipperary, 1999), p. 18.
21. See O'Halpin, *Decline of the Union*, pp. 44–50.
22. Alan O'Day, 'Irish Home Rule and Liberalism', in Alan O'Day (ed.), *The Edwardian Age: Conflict and Stability 1900–1914* (London, 1979), pp. 113–33.
23. ibid., p. 120.
24. ibid., pp. 2–3.
25. Deirdre McMahon (ed.), *Their New Ireland: Moynihan Family Correspondence in Peace and War, 1908–1918* (Dublin, 2004), pp. 53–4.
26. Ferriter, *Lovers of Liberty?*, p. 36.
27. Sally Warwick-Haller, *William O'Brien and the Irish Land War* (Dublin, 1990).
28. Daniel Mulhall, *A New Day Dawning: A Portrait of Ireland in 1900* (Cork, 1999), p. 143.
29. *Report of the Commission on Emigration and Other Population Problems* (Dublin, 1956), p. 115.
30. Robert Lynd, *Home Life in Ireland* (London, 1909), p. 13.
31. '1902 resolution of the Standing Committee of Irish Archbishops', *Irish Ecclesiastical Record*, vol. 11, 1902.
32. *Catholic Times*, 11 November 1889.
33. Joseph Robins, *Fools and Mad: A History of the Insane in Ireland* (Dublin, 1986), pp. 175–83.
34. *Irish Peasant*, 19 May 1906.
35. David Fitzpatrick, *Irish Emigration 1801–1921* (Dundalk, 1984), pp. 29 and 41.
36. Louis F. Paul-Dubois, *Contemporary Ireland* (Dublin, 1908), p. 305.
37. Jeremiah Murphy, *When Youth was Mine: A Memoir of Kerry* (Dublin, 1998), p. 20.
38. Nolan, *Ourselves Alone*, p. 92.
39. Patrick MacGill, *Children of the Dead End: The Autobiography of an Irish Navvy* (London, 1914), pp. 36–7.
40. Declan Kiberd, *Inventing Ireland: The Literature of the Modern Nation* (London, 1995), p. 311.
41. See Eimear Burke, '"Our boasted civilisation": Dublin Society and the work of the DSPCC, 1889–1922', *UCD History Review*, 1991, pp. 1–6, and Ferriter, 'Suffer little children?', pp. 69–107.
42. Frances Finnegan, *Do Penance or Perish: A Study of Magdalen Asylums in Ireland* (Kilkenny, 2001), p. 197.
43. Ferriter, 'Suffer little children?'
44. Jacinta Prunty, *Dublin Slums 1800–1925: A Study in Urban Geography* (Dublin, 1999), p. 153.
45. Raftery and O'Sullivan, *Suffer the Little Children*, p. 69.
46. Elizabeth Malcolm, 'The house of strident shadows: The asylum, the family and emigration in post-Famine rural Ireland', in Greta Jones and Elizabeth Malcolm (eds.), *Medicine, Disease and the State in Ireland, 1650–1940* (Cork, 1999), pp. 177–95.
47. Jeremiah Murphy, *When Youth was Mine*, p. 31.

48. Cormac Ó Gráda, '"The greatest blessing of them all": The old age pension in Ireland', *Past and Present*, no. 175, May 2002, pp. 124–61.
49. ibid.
50. Mulhall, *New Day Dawning*, p. 53.
51. Murray Fraser, *John Bull's Other Homes: State Housing and British Policy in Ireland* (Liverpool, 1996), p. 36.
52. ibid., pp. 66–114.
53. Fintan O'Toole, *Irish Times Book of the Century*, p. 47.
54. Colm Tóibín and Diarmaid Ferriter, *The Irish Famine: A Documentary* (London, 2001), p. 109.
55. Paul-Dubois, *Contemporary Ireland*, p. 144.
56. Fintan O'Toole, *Irish Times Book of the Century*, p. 6.
57. Ruth McManus, *Dublin, 1910–1940: Shaping the City and Suburbs* (Dublin, 2001), p. 32.
58. ibid., p. 41.
59. Prunty, *Dublin Slums*, p. 331.
60. Fraser, *John Bull's Other Homes*, pp. 17–26.
61. ibid.
62. ibid.
63. Kevin Kearns, *Dublin Tenement Life: An Oral History* (Dublin, 1994), p. 184.
64. See Eimear Burke, 'The treatment of working class children in Dublin by statutory and voluntary organisations 1889–1922', unpublished MA thesis, University College Dublin, 1990.
65. Greta Jones, 'The campaign against TB in Ireland, 1899–1914', in Jones and Malcolm (eds.), *Medicine, Disease and the State*, pp. 158–77, p. 167.
66. Fintan O'Toole, *Irish Times Book of the Century*, p. 48.
67. Ruth Barrington, *Health, Medicine and Politics in Ireland, 1900–1970* (Dublin, 1987), p. 49.
68. Diarmaid Ferriter, *A Nation of Extremes: The Pioneers in Twentieth-Century Ireland* (Dublin, 1999), p. 65.
69. ibid.
70. Peter Beresford-Ellis, *A History of the Irish Working Class* (London, 1985), and E. T. McDonnell, 'The Dublin labour movement 1894–1967', unpublished MA thesis, University College Dublin, 1977, pp. 6off.
71. ibid.
72. ibid.
73. Andy Bielenberg and David Johnson, 'The production and consumption of tobacco in Ireland, 1840–1921', *Journal of Irish Economic and Social History*, vol. 25, 1998, pp. 1–22.
74. Tom Inglis, *Moral Monopoly*, p. 222.
75. Maurice Harmon, 'Cobwebs before the wind: Aspects of the peasantry in Irish literature from 1800 to 1916', in Daniel J. Casey and Robert E. Rhodes (eds.), *Views of the Irish Peasantry, 1800–1916* (Hamden, Connecticut, 1977), pp. 129–60.
76. Finola Kennedy, *Cottage to Crèche*, p. 208.
77. Harmon, 'Cobwebs before the wind'.
78. Lynd, *Home Life in Ireland*, p. 12.
79. Tóibín and Ferriter, *Irish Famine*, p. 6.
80. Mulhall, *New Day Dawning*, p. 30.
81. Stephen Ball, *A Policeman's Ireland: Recollections of Samuel Waters, RIC* (Cork, 1999), and W. J. Lowe and E. L. Malcolm, 'The domestication of the RIC, 1836–1922', *Irish Economic and Social History*, vol. 19, 1992, pp. 27–49.

82. ibid.

83. Seán O'Faoláin, *Vive Moi!*, p. 86.

84. NAI, BMH, WS 509, J. J. McConnell.

85. David Fitzpatrick, 'Militarism in Ireland, 1900–1922', in Tom Bartlett and Keith Jeffery (eds.), *A Military History of Ireland* (Cambridge, 1996), p. 382.

86. Donal P. McCracken, *The Irish Pro-Boers 1877–1902* (South Africa, 1989).

87. Quoted in Jonathan Bell, 'The improvement of Irish farm techniques since 1750: Theory and practice', in P. Flanagan (ed.), *Rural Ireland 1600–1900: Modernisation and Change* (Cork, 1987), pp. 22–44.

88. Arthur Smith, 'Agricultural education in Ireland', *New Ireland Review*, vol. 23, 1905.

89. Monsignor O'Riordan, *Catholicity and Progress* (Dublin, 1906), p. 60, and Horace Plunkett, *Ireland in the New Century* (Dublin 1905), p. 45.

90. ibid.

91. Patrick Bolger, *The Irish Co-operative Movement: Its History and Development* (Dublin 1977), and Liam Kennedy, 'The early response of the Irish Catholic clergy to the Co-operative movement', *Irish Historical Studies*, vol. XXI, 1977–8, pp. 55–75.

92. ibid., and Cyril Ehrlich, 'Sir Horace Plunkett and agricultural reform', in J. M. Goldstrom and L. A. Clarkson (eds.), *Irish Population, Economy and Society* (Oxford, 1981), pp. 271–85.

93. Fergus Campbell, 'Rewriting the ranch war: Agrarian conflict in Ireland, 1903–14', paper delivered at conference, *Land, Politics and the State*, National University of Ireland, Maynooth, 10 May 2003.

94. Brian Inglis, 'Moran of the *Leader* and Ryan of the *Irish Peasant*', in Conor Cruise O'Brien (ed.), *The Shaping of Modern Ireland* (London, 1960), pp. 108–23.

95. Paul-Dubois, *Contemporary Ireland*, p. 444.

96. Liam Kennedy, *Colonialism, Religion and Nationalism in Ireland* (Belfast, 1996), p. 136.

97. Tom Garvin, *Irish Nationalist Revolutionaries, 1858–1928* (Oxford, 1987), pp. 90–93.

98. Bolger, *The Irish Co-operative Movement*, pp.158–60 and 240–81.

99. ibid.

100. Quoted in Kennedy, *Colonialism, Religion and Nationalism*, p. 160.

101. Filson Young, *Ireland at the Crossroads: An Essay in Explanation* (London, 1903), p. ix.

102. *Irish Homestead*, 9 April 1904.

103. Diarmaid Ferriter, *Mothers, Maidens and Myths: A History of the Irish Countrywomen's Association* (Dublin, 1995), pp. 3–10.

104. Susan Parkes, 'Education in twentieth-century Ireland', in Angela Bourke, Siobhán Kilfeather, Maria Luddy, Margaret MacCurtain, Gerardine Meaney, Máirín Ní Dhonnchadha, Mary O'Dowd and Clair Wills (eds.), *The Field Day Anthology of Irish Writing: Volume V, Irish Women's Writing and Traditions* (Cork, 2002), p. 667 (hereafter *Field Day Anthology V*).

105. Joanna Bourke, *Husbandry to Housewifery: Women, Economic Change and Housework in Ireland, 1890–1914* (Oxford, 1993).

106. Paseta, *Before the Revolution*, pp. 90–93.

107. Lambert McKenna, *The Church and Working Women* (Dublin, 1913).

108. Paseta, *Before the Revolution*, pp. 90–93.

109. Maria Luddy, 'Women and politics in Ireland, 1860–1918', in *Field Day Anthology V*, p. 83.

110. Sinéad McCoole, *No Ordinary Women: Irish Female Activists in the Revolutionary Years* (Dublin, 2003), p. 21.

111. ibid., p. 23.

112. Luddy, 'Women and politics', p. 85.

113. Maria Luddy, 'The labour movement in Ireland, 1800–2000', in *Field Day Anthology V*, p. 550.
114. Tom Garvin, 'The anatomy of a nationalist revolution: Ireland 1858–1928', *Comparative Studies in Society and History*, vol. 28, 1986, pp. 468–501.
115. C. S. Andrews, *Men of No Property* (Dublin and Cork, 1982), pp. 10ff.
116. P. S. O'Hegarty, *The Victory of Sinn Féin* (Dublin, 1924, new edition with introduction by Tom Garvin, Dublin, 1998), p. x.
117. Andrews, *Men of No Property*.
118. Conor Cruise O'Brien, *States of Ireland* (London, 1972), p. 53.
119. John A. Murphy, *The College: A History of Queen's/University College Cork* (Cork, 1995), p. 185.
120. Paseta, *Before the Revolution*, p. 84.
121. David Dickson (ed.), *The Gorgeous Mask: Dublin 1700–1850* (Dublin, 1987).
122. P. J. Corish, *Maynooth College 1795–1995* (Dublin, 1994), pp. 283–96.
123. Patrick Maume, *'Life that is exile': Daniel Corkery and the Search for Irish Ireland* (Belfast, 1993).
124. ibid., p. 59.
125. ibid., p. 62.
126. Michael Laffan, *The Resurrection of Ireland: The Sinn Féin Party 1916–1923* (Cambridge, 1999), pp. 16–18.
127. ibid., p. 21.
128. Caitríona Clear, *Nuns in Nineteenth-Century Ireland* (Dublin, 1987).
129. Harry Levin (ed.), *James Joyce: The Essential James Joyce* (London, 1990), pp. 138–75.
130. Tom Garvin, 'Priests and patriots: Irish separatism and the fear of the modern, 1890–1914', *Irish Historical Studies*, vol. xxv, no. 97, May 1986, pp. 67–81.
131. McMahon, *Their New Ireland*, p. 22.
132. Paseta, *Before the Revolution*, pp. 103ff.
133. Thomas J. Morrissey, *William J. Walsh: Archbishop of Dublin, 1841–1921* (Dublin, 2000), p. vi.
134. ibid., pp. 350–55.
135. Alec R. Vidler, *The Modernist Movement in the Roman Church* (Cambridge, 1934), p. 217.
136. *Irish Ecclesiastical Record*, vol. xxii, July–December 1907, p. 561.
137. W. P. Ryan, *The Pope's Green Isle* (Dublin, 1912), p. 12.
138. Joseph Flood, 'The priest and social action', *Irish Monthly*, vol. 43, 1915.
139. Seán O'Faoláin, *Vive Moi!*, p. 21.
140. Austin Clarke, *Twice around the Black Church* (Dublin, 1962), p. 21.
141. Fintan O'Toole, *Irish Times Book of the Century*, p. 49.
142. Séamus Ó Buachalla, *Education Policy in Twentieth-Century Ireland* (Dublin, 1988), pp. 115–21.
143. Derry City Council Archives (hereafter DCCA), Harbour Museum, Derry, Corporation Minute Book, 23 January 1907.
144. See John Logan, *Teachers Union: The TUI and Its Forerunners in Irish Education, 1899–1994* (Dublin, 1999).
145. John Coolahan, *Irish Education: Its History and Structure* (Dublin, 1981), p. 70.
146. Ó Buachalla, *Education Policy*, pp. 115–21.
147. *Irish Times*, 16 March 2002.
148. Catherine Candy, *Priestly Fiction: Popular Irish Novelists of the Early Twentieth Century* (Dublin, 1995), pp. 12–26.
149. Nolan, *Ourselves Alone*, p. 91.
150. Dermot Keogh, *Jews in Twentieth-Century Ireland: Refugees, Anti-Semitism and the Holocaust* (Cork, 1998), p. 14.

151. ibid., pp. 56–7.

152. Kiberd, *Inventing Ireland*, pp. 115–16.

153. Maume, *Long Gestation*, pp. 9–10.

154. Maume, *'Life that is exile'*, p. viii.

155. ibid., p. 92.

156. Quoted in G. J. Watson, *Irish Identity and the Literary Revival; Synge, Yeats and O'Casey* (London and New York, 1979).

157. Tóibín, *Lady Gregory's Toothbrush*, p. 71.

158. Liam O'Dowd, 'Intellectuals in twentieth-century Ireland: The case of George Russell', *Crane Bag*, vol. 9, 1985, pp. 6–26, and Nicholas Allen, *George Russell and the New Ireland, 1905–1930* (Dublin, 2003).

159. Patrick O'Farrell, *Ireland's English Question* (New York, 1971), pp. 1–15, and Declan Kiberd, 'Inventing Irelands', *Crane Bag*, vol. 8, 1984, pp. 11–26.

160. Tóibín, *Penguin Book of Irish Fiction*, pp. xiii–xv.

161. Watson, *Irish Identity*, pp. 23ff.

162. R. F. Foster, *W. B. Yeats, A Life: Volume 1: The Apprentice Mage 1865–1914*, (Oxford, 1997), pp. 258–62.

163. ibid., pp. 305–29.

164. Kiberd, *Inventing Ireland*, pp. 166ff.

165. ibid., pp. 163–91.

166. ibid.

167. P. J. Hannon, 'Peasant thinkers and students', *New Ireland Review*, August 1901, p. 364.

168. Watson, *Irish Identity*.

169. R. F. Foster, 'Writing a life of W. B. Yeats', *Irish Review*, no. 21, Autumn/Winter 1997, pp. 92–103.

170. Ann Saddlemyer (ed.), *J. M. Synge: Collected Works, Volume IV: Plays Book II* (London, 1968), pp. 51–179.

171. R. F. Foster, 'Writing a life'.

172. Tóibín, *Lady Gregory's Toothbrush*, pp. 43–65.

173. Fintan O'Toole, *Irish Times Book of Century*, pp. 39ff.

174. Tóibín, *Lady Gregory's Toothbrush*, pp. 43–65.

175. R. F. Foster, 'Writing a life'.

176. R. F. Foster, *W. B Yeats: A Life: Volume I*, p. 494, and Robert O'Byrne, *Hugh Lane, 1875–1915* (Dublin, 2000).

177. *Sunday Tribune*, 20 November 2000.

178. Denis Carroll, *They Have Fooled You Again: Michael O'Flannagan* (Dublin, 1993).

179. Thomas J. Morrissey, *Towards a National University: William Delaney (1835–1924)* (Dublin 1983), pp. 321–45.

180. Tóibín, *Lady Gregory's Toothbrush*, p. 40.

181. Morrissey, *Towards a National University*.

182. Adrian Kelly, *Compulsory Irish: Language and Education in Ireland 1890s-1980s* (Dublin, 2002), p. 125; Seán O'Tuama (ed.), *The Gaelic League Idea* (Dublin, 1983); and Corish, *Maynooth College*, p. 289.

183. W. P. Ryan, *Pope's Green Isle*, pp. 52–63.

184. Helen Brennan, *The Story of Irish Dance* (Dingle, 1999), pp. 31–3.

185. Paul Rouse, 'Sport and the politics of culture: A history of the GAA ban on foreign games, 1884–1971', *The International Journal of the History of Sport*, vol. 10, no. 3, December 1993, pp. 333–60.

186. ibid.

187. Breandán Ó hEithir, *Over the Bar* (Dublin, 1991).

188. Padraig Purséil, *The GAA in Its Time* (Dublin, 1982).

189. Edmund Van Esbeck, *One Hundred Years of Rugby in Ireland* (Dublin, 1974), p. 73.

190. Jeremiah Murphy, *When Youth was Mine*, p. 57.

191. *Irish Times*, 20 January 2003.

192. Patrick O'Sullivan, 'Ireland and the Olympic Games', *History Ireland*, vol. 6, no. 1, Spring 1998, pp. 40–46.

193. Kevin Rockett, Luke Gibbons and John Hill, *Cinema and Ireland* (New York, 1988), p. 10.

194. Brendan Grimes, 'Carnegie libraries in Ireland', and Diarmaid Ferriter, 'The post-war public library service: Bringing books "to the remotest hamlets and the hills"', in Norma McDermott (ed.), *The University of the People: Celebrating Ireland's Public Libraries* (Dublin, 2003), pp. 31–43 and pp. 67–79.

195. Tomás Ó Canainn, *Traditional Music in Ireland* (London, 1978).

196. William Henry Grattan-Flood, *A History of Irish Music* (Dublin, 1905), p. ix.

197. Richard Pine (ed.), *Music in Ireland 1848–1998* (Cork, 1998), pp. 22–33.

198. Flann Campbell, *The Dissenting Voice: Protestant Democracy in Ulster from Plantation to Partition* (Belfast, 1991), p. 351.

199. NAI, BMH, WS 632, Elizabeth Bloxham.

200. J. C. Beckett, *Belfast: The Origin and Growth of an Industrial City* (London, 1967), J. C. Beckett, *Belfast: The Making of the City: 1800–1914* (Belfast, 1983); and Sybil Gribbon, *Edwardian Belfast: A Social Profile* (Belfast, 1982), Jonathan Bardon and Stephen Conlin, *Belfast: 1000 Years* (Belfast, 1985).

201. Gerry Adams, *Falls Memories* (Dingle, 1983), p. 49.

202. Margaret Neill, 'Homeworkers in Ulster, 1850–1911', in Janice Holmes and Diane Urquhart (eds.), *Coming into the Light: The Work, Politics and Religion of Women in Ulster, 1840–1940* (Belfast, 1994), pp. 2–23, p. 22ff.

203. Public Records Office of Northern Ireland (hereafter PRONI), BG/7/A/67, Belfast Board of Guardians Minute Book, 8 January 1901 and 2 April 1901.

204. John W. Boyle, 'Industrial conditions in the twentieth century', in T. W. Moody and J. C. Beckett (eds.), *Ulster since 1800: A Social Survey* (London, 1957), pp. 128–38.

205. Greta Jones, 'Eugenics in Ireland; The Belfast Eugenics Society, 1911–1915', *Irish Historical Studies*, vol. XXVIII, no. 109, May 1992, pp. 81–113.

206. Austen Morgan, *Labour and Partition: The Belfast Working Class, 1905–1923* (London, 1991).

207. ibid.

208. Mats Greigg, '"Marching through the streets and singing and shouting": Industrial struggle and trade unions among female linen workers in Belfast and Lurgan, 1872–1910', *Soathar*, vol. 22, 1997, pp. 29–47.

209. Ruth Taillon and Diane Urquhart, 'Women, politics and the state in Northern Ireland, 1918–66', in *Field Day Anthology V*, p. 353.

210. Luddy, 'Women and politics', p. 87.

211. Ruth Dudley Edwards, *The Faithful Tribe: An Intimate Portrait of the Loyal Institution* (London, 1999), pp. 181–207.

212. Flann Campbell, *The Dissenting Voice*, p. 351.

213. F. S. L. Lyons, 'The twentieth century', in Moody and Beckett (eds.), *Ulster since 1800*, p. 55.

214. DCCA, Rural District Council Minute Book, 6 May 1911.

215. Flann Campbell, *The Dissenting Voice*, p. 381.

216. ibid., p. 369.

217. ibid., p. 395.

2: 1912–1918

1. Luddy, 'Women and politics', p. 69.
2. Stephen Gwynn, *Irish Books and Irish People* (Dublin, 1919), foreword.
3. Stephen Gwynn, *Ireland* (Dublin, 1924), pp. 73–7.
4. ibid., p. 119.
5. Michael Laffan, *Resurrection of Ireland*, p. 15.
6. NAI, BMH, WS 279, Liam Brady.
7. James Connolly, *Labour in Irish History* (Dublin, 1917), p. 2.
8. Leonard Piper, *Dangerous Waters: The Life and Death of Erskine Childers* (London, 2003), p. 116.
9. P. J. Matthews, *Revival: The Abbey Theatre, Sinn Féin, the Gaelic League and the Co-operative Movement* (Cork, 2003).
10. J. M. Synge, 'Le mouvement intellectuel irlandais', translated by M. Egan, quoted in Matthews, *Revival*.
11. Conor Cruise O'Brien, *States of Ireland*, p. 70.
12. James Connolly, *Labour in Ireland* (Dublin 1917, with an introduction by Robert Lynd), p. xiv.
13. Martin Mansergh, 'A rising curve from subversion to statecraft', *Fortnight*, February 1991, pp. 28–31.
14. Martin Mansergh, review of Margaret O'Callaghan, *British High Politics and Nationalist Ireland* (Cork, 1994), *History Ireland*, vol. 3, no. 1, Spring 1995, pp. 56–7.
15. A. T. Q. Stewart, *The Ulster Crisis* (London, 1967).
16. Jonathan Bardon, 'Belfast at its zenith', *History Ireland*, vol. 1, no. 4, Winter 1993, pp. 46–52.
17. *Cork Examiner*, 12 April 1912.
18. Sophia Hillan King and Seán McMahon (eds.), *Hope and History: Eye Witness Accounts of Life in Twentieth-Century Ulster* (Belfast, 1996), p. 7.
19. John Wilson Foster, *Recoveries: Neglected Episodes in Irish Cultural History, 1860–1912* (Dublin, 2002), pp. 66–8.
20. Alvin Jackson, 'Unionist history', *Irish Review*, no. 7, Autumn 1989, pp. 58–67.
21. Alvin Jackson, *Colonel Edward Saunderson: Land and Loyalty in Victorian Ireland* (Oxford, 1995).
22. Jackson, 'Unionist history'; Alvin Jackson, *Sir Edward Carson* (Dublin, 1993); and Alvin Jackson, 'Unionist myths, 1912–85', *Past and Present*, no. 136, 1992, p. 164.
23. Lynd, *Home Life in Ireland*, p. 65.
24. Diane Urquhart, '"The female of the species is more deadlier than the male": The Ulster Women's Unionist Council, 1911–40', in Holmes and Urquhart (eds.), *Coming into the Light*, pp. 93–126.
25. Taillon and Urquhart, 'Women, politics and the state', p. 355.
26. Alvin Jackson, 'The Larne gun running, 1914', *History Ireland*, vol. 1, no. 1, Spring 1993, pp. 35–9.
27. Charles Townshend, *Political Violence in Ireland: Government and Resistance since 1848* (Oxford, 1983), pp. 250–54.
28. See Martin Mansergh, review of Paul Bew, *Ideology and the Irish Question: Ulster Unionism and Irish Nationalism, 1912–1916* (Oxford, 1994), *History Ireland*, vol. 3, no. 1, Spring 1995, pp. 56–7.
29. Paul Bew, *Ideology and the Irish Question*.
30. Gillian McIntosh, *The Force of Culture: Unionist Identities in Contemporary Ireland* (Cork, 1999), p. 20.

31.   Michael Foy, 'Ulster unionist propaganda against Home Rule', *History Ireland*, vol. 4, no. 1, Spring 1996, pp. 49–54.
32.   Patrick Maume, 'The political thought of Arthur Clery', *Irish Historical Studies*, vol. XXXI, no. 122, November 1998, pp. 222–40.
33.   Michael Laffan, *Resurrection of Ireland*, pp. 13–14.
34.   McIntosh, *Force of Culture*, pp. 11ff.
35.   F. X. Martin and F. J. Byrne (eds.), *The Scholar Revolutionary: Eoin MacNeill, 1867–1945* (Shannon, 1973), pp. 84–94.
36.   Michael Laffan, *Resurrection of Ireland*, pp. 10–13.
37.   *Irish Volunteer*, 22 May 1915.
38.   Thomas Kettle, *The Open Secret of Ireland* (Dublin, 1912).
39.   Stephen Brown, 'What is a nation?', *Studies*, vol. 1, September 1912.
40.   O'Casey, *Mirror in My House*, pp. 145ff.
41.   Arthur Clery, 'Thomas Kettle', *Studies*, vol. 5, no. 2, December 1916, pp. 503–16.
42.   ibid.
43.   Paul Bew, *Conflict and Conciliation in Ireland, 1890–1910: Parnellites and Radical Agrarians* (Oxford, 1987).
44.   Paul Bew, 'The Easter Rising: Lost leaders and lost opportunities', *Irish Review*, 1991–2, pp. 9–13.
45.   Phoenix, *Northern Nationalism*, p. 33.
46.   *Freeman's Journal*, 21 September 1914.
47.   Ruth Sherry, 'The story of the National Anthem', *History Ireland*, vol. 4, no. 1, Spring 1996, pp. 39–43.
48.   Alvin Jackson, *Ireland 1798–1998: Politics and War* (Oxford, 1999), p. 198.
49.   ibid., pp. 238–9.
50.   Bulmer Hobson, *A Short History of the Irish Volunteers* (Dublin, 1918), p. 9.
51.   Lennox Robinson (ed.), *Lady Gregory's Journals, 1916–1930* (London, 1946), p. 130.
52.   Hobson, *A Short History of the Irish Volunteers*, p. 156.
53.   Michael Laffan, *Resurrection of Ireland*, p. 13.
54.   NAI, BMH, WS 279, Séamus Dobbyn.
55.   NAI, BMH, WS 939, Ernest Blythe.
56.   Maume, *Long Gestation*, pp. 101–30 and 118–19.
57.   Tom Garvin, 'The Rising and Irish democracy', in Máirín Ní Dhonnchadha and Theo Dorgan (eds.), *Revising the Rising* (Derry, 1991), pp. 21–9.
58.   Nicholas Mansergh, 'John Redmond', in Conor Cruise O'Brien (ed.), *The Shaping of Modern Ireland* (London, 1960), pp. 38–50.
59.   Paul Bew, *John Redmond*, (Dundalk, 1996), pp. 43–5, and 23–6.
60.   Maume, *Long Gestation*, pp. 118–19.
61.   Bew, *John Redmond*, and Stephen Gwynn, *John Redmond's Last Years* (London, 1919), pp. 259ff.
62.   *Sunday Tribune*, 20 August 2000.
63.   *Freeman's Journal*, 17 September 1914.
64.   Keith Jeffery, *Ireland and the Great War* (Cambridge, 2000).
65.   Kevin Myers, *From the Irish Times Column, An Irishman's Diary* (Dublin, 2000), pp. 263–5.
66.   Fitzpatrick, 'Militarism in Ireland'.
67.   F. X. Martin, '1916: Interpreting the Rising', in D. G. Boyce (ed.), *The Making of Modern Irish History: Revisionism and the Revisionist Controversy* (London, 1996), pp. 163–88.
68.   Thomas Dooley, 'Politics, bands and marketing: Army recruitment in Waterford city,

1914–15', *Irish Sword*, vol. 18, no. 72, 1991, and Dooley, *Irish men or English soldiers* (Liverpool, 1995).

69. Jeffery, *Ireland and the Great War*, pp. 19ff.

70. McIntosh, *Force of Culture*, p. 11.

71. Deirdre MacMahon, 'Ireland, the Empire, and the Commonwealth'.

72. Elizabeth Bowen, *The Last September* (London, 1948).

73. R. F. Foster, *W. B. Yeats, A Life, Volume II: The Arch Poet: 1915–1939* (Oxford, 2003), pp. 123–7.

74. Jeffery, *Ireland and the Great War*.

75. Mary Kenny, *Goodbye to Catholic Ireland*, p. 54.

76. McMahon, *Their New Ireland*, pp. xii–xl.

77. ibid.

78. NAI, BMH, WS 1766, William O'Brien; WS 1316, John Flanagan; and WS 939, Ernest Blythe.

79. Ben Novick, *Conceiving Revolution: Irish Nationalist Propaganda during the First World War* (Dublin, 2001), p. 150.

80. ibid., p. 182.

81. *Irish Times*, 30 December 1999.

82. Garvin, 'The Rising and Irish democracy'.

83. FitzGerald, *Reflections on the Irish State*, p. 3.

84. Jackson, *Ireland 1798–1998*, p. 201.

85. O'Faoláin, *Vive Moi!*, pp. 100–103.

86. Michael Laffan, *Resurrection of Ireland*, p. 34.

87. ibid., p. 39.

88. Maume, *Long Gestation*, pp. 173–81.

89. Ruth Taillon, *The Women of 1916* (Belfast, 1996), pp. 37–8.

90. Margaret Ward, 'Gender: gendering the Irish revolution', in Joost Augusteijn (ed.), *The Irish Revolution 1913–23* (London, 2002), pp. 168–86.

91. Taillon, *Women of 1916*, p. xviii.

92. NAI, BMH, WS 31, Bulmer Hobson and WS 1754, Mrs Tom Barry.

93. Jackson, *Ireland 1798–1998*, p. 202.

94. Michael Laffan, *Resurrection of Ireland*, p. 37.

95. James Connolly, *Labour in Ireland*, p. xiii.

96. ibid., pp. xxiff.

97. NAI, BMH, WS 1343, James Cullen.

98. NAI, BMH, WS 346, Captain E. Gerard.

99. NAI, BMH, WS 705, Christopher Brady.

100. NAI, BMH, WS 1766, William O'Brien.

101. Dhonnchadha and Dorgan (eds.), *Revising the Rising*, pp. ix–x.

102. *Irish Times*, 30 December 1999. See also Ruth Dudley Edwards, *Patrick Pearse: The Triumph of Failure* (London, 1977).

103. ibid.

104. *True Lives*, documentary on Patrick Pearse, shown on Radio Telifís Éireann, 9 April 2001.

105. ibid.

106. J. J. Lee, 'In search of Patrick Pearse', in Dhonnchadha and Dorgan (eds.), *Revising the Rising*, pp. 122–39.

107. O'Casey, *Mirror in My House, Vol. 1* (New York, 1956), p. 351.

108. Séamus Ó Buachalla (ed.), *A Significant Irish Educationalist: The Educational Writings of P. H. Pearse* (Dublin, 1980), p. 373.

109. Lee, 'In search of Patrick Pearse'.

110. Declan Kiberd, 'The elephant of revolutionary forgetfulness', in Dhonnchadha and Dorgan (eds.), *Revising the Rising*, pp. 1–21.
111. Ernie O'Malley, *On Another Man's Wound* (London, 1936), pp. 32ff.; C. S. Andrews, *Dublin Made Me*, p. 90 and Frank O'Connor, *An Only Child* (London, 1958), pp. 170–83.
112. O'Malley, *On Another Man's Wound*.
113. Brian Barton and Michael Foy, *The Easter Rising* (Gloucestershire, 1999), pp. 124–60.
114. W. K. Anderson, *James Connolly and the Irish Left* (Dublin, 1994), p. 8.
115. Morrissey, *William J. Walsh*, p. 290.
116. NAI, BMH, WS 1754, Mrs Tom Barry.
117. NAI, BMH, WS 550, Thomas Duggan.
118. Gwynn, *Ireland*, p. 98.
119. O'Brien, *States of Ireland*, pp. 70ff.
120. Leah Levenson, *With Wooden Sword: A Portrait of Francis Sheehy Skeffington: Militant Pacifist* (Boston and Dublin, 1983), p. 217.
121. Charles Townshend, 'The suppression of the Easter Rising', *Bullán*, vol. 1, no. 1, 1994, pp. 27–40.
122. Jackson, *Ireland 1798–1998*, p. 206.
123. Townshend, 'The suppression of the Easter Rising', p. 44.
124. *Sunday Tribune*, 20 August 2000.
125. Michael Laffan, *Resurrection of Ireland*, pp. 50–51.
126. Townshend, 'The suppression of the Easter Rising'.
127. NAI, BMH, WS 357, Kathleen Lynn.
128. NAI, BMH, WS 939, Ernest Blythe.
129. Keith Jeffery and Hamilton Norway (eds.), *The Sinn Féin Rebellion As They Saw It* (Dublin, 1999), p. 42.
130. *Irish Times*, 4 August 1916.
131. NAI, BMH, WS 588 and WS 253, A. M. Sullivan.
132. *Irish Times*, 30 December 1999.
133. Michael Smith, *An Unsung Hero: Tom Crean, Antarctic Survivor* (Cork, 2000).
134. *Irish Times*, 30 December 1999.
135. O'Casey, *Mirror in My House*, p. 74.
136. Tim Corcoran, 'Social work and the Irish universities', *Studies*, vol. 1, no. 3 September 1912, pp. 534–49.
137. Enda McKay, 'The housing of the rural labourer, 1883–1916', *Saothar*, vol. 17, 1992, pp. 27–40.
138. Ruth McManus, *Dublin, 1910–1940*, pp. 17–26 and 147–62.
139. Fraser, *John Bull's Other Homes*, p. 8.
140. William Crofton, 'The TB problem', *Studies*, vol. 6, no. 23, September 1917, pp. 443–55.
141. Frank O'Connor, *An Only Child*, pp. 32–3.
142. Padraig Yeates, *Lockout: Dublin 1913* (Dublin, 2001), p. xviii.
143. Prunty, *Dublin Slums*, introduction.
144. Robins, *Fools and Mad*, p. 174.
145. Mac Sweeney, 'A study of poverty', pp. 93–104.
146. S. Shannon-Mullen, 'Child life as a national asset', *Journal of the Social and Statistical Inquiry Society of Ireland*, December 1915, p. 301.
147. Janet Dunwoody, 'Child welfare', in David Fitzpatrick (ed.), *Ireland and the First World War* (Dublin, 1988), pp. 69–75.
148. Lambert McKenna, 'School attendance in Dublin', *Studies*, vol. 17, no. 3, March 1916, pp. 109–18.

149. ibid.
150. Alfred O'Rahilly, 'The social problem in Cork', *Studies*, vol. 6, no. 22, June 1917, pp. 177–89.
151. *Freeman's Journal*, 7 May 1917.
152. Ferriter, *Nation of Extremes*, p. 71.
153. ibid., p. 51.
154. PRONI, D1812, Minute Book of the Women's Working Association, Fisherwick Presbyterian Church, Belfast, 21 February 1916.
155. O'Casey, *Mirror in My House*, pp. 27–8.
156. Yeates, *Lockout*, p. 564.
157. Peter Murray, 'Electoral politics and the Dublin working class before the First World War', *Saothar*, vol. 6, 1980.
158. Emmet O'Connor, 'Jim Larkin and the Communist Internationals, 1923–9', *Irish Historical Studies*, vol. 31, 1998–9, pp. 357–73.
159. Yeates, *Lockout*, p. 564.
160. Austen Morgan, *James Connolly: A Political Biography* (Manchester, 1988), and Richard English, 'Unities contradicted', *Irish Review*, no. 5, Autumn 1988, pp. 109–11.
161. Maurice Goldring, *Pleasant the Scholar's Life: Irish Intellectuals and the Construction of the Nation State* (London, 1993), pp. 95–112.
162. Eric Talpin, 'James Larkin, Liverpool and the National Union of Dock Labourers', *Saothar*, vol. 4, 1978, pp. 1–7. See also Emmet O'Connor, *James Larkin* (Cork, 2002), and Emmet Larkin, *James Larkin: Irish Labour Leader 1876–1947* (London, 1977).
163. Henry Patterson, 'James Larkin and the Belfast dockers and carters strike of 1907', *Saothar*, vol. 4, 1978, pp. 8–14.
164. Andy Bielenberg, 'Entrepreneurship, power and public opinion in Ireland: The career of William Martin Murphy', *Irish Economic and Social History* vol. 27, 2000, pp. 25–44, and Dermot Keogh, 'William Martin Murphy and the origins of the 1913 Lockout', *Saothar*, vol. 4, 1978, pp. 15–35.
165. *Irish Homestead*, 13 September 1913.
166. *Irish Times*, 7 October 1914.
167. Morrissey, *William J. Walsh*, p. 249.
168. E. M., 'The Church and Labour', *Irish Monthly*, vol. 42, 1914, pp. 25–30, and Lambert McKenna, *The Church and Labour* (Dublin, 1914).
169. Yeates, *Lockout*, p. xi and p. 75.
170. Interview with James Plunkett, shown on Radio Telifís Éireann, 12 June 2003.
171. David Fitzpatrick, 'Strikes in Ireland, 1914–21', *Soathar*, vol. 6, 1980, pp. 26–40.
172. ibid.
173. Thomas Crean, 'Labour and politics in Kerry during the First World War', *Saothar*, vol. 19, 1994, pp. 27–41.
174. Dan Bradley, *Farm Labourers: Irish Struggle: 1900–1976* (Belfast, 1988), p. 31.
175. John W. O'Hagan (ed.), *The Economy of Ireland: Policy and Performance* (Dublin, 1987), p. 21; Kieran Kennedy, *The Economic Development of Ireland in the Twentieth Century* (London, 1988); Maume, *Long Gestation*, p. 151; and Mary E. Daly, *A Social and Economic History of Ireland since 1800* (Dublin, 1981), p. 138.
176. See R. M. Fox, *Louie Bennett: Her Life and Times* (Dublin, 1958), and Rosemary Cullen Owens, *Louie Bennett* (Cork, 2001).
177. Margaret MacCurtain and Donncha Ó Corráin (eds.), *Women in Irish Society: The Historical Dimension* (Dublin, 1978).
178. Margaret Ward, *The Missing Sex: Putting Women into Irish History* (Dublin, 1991).
179. Fitzpatrick, *Irish Emigration*, p. 7.
180. Nolan, *Ourselves Alone*, p. 49, and Yeates, *Lockout*, p. 54.

181. Margaret Ward, *Hanna Sheehy Skeffington: A Life* (Cork, 1987).

182. Hanna Sheehy Skeffington, *Reminiscences of an Irish Suffragette* (Dublin, 1975), and Luddy, 'Women and politics', pp. 91–9.

183. Luddy, 'The labour movement', pp. 550–51.

184. Mary Jones, *These Obstreperous Lassies: A History of the IWWU* (Dublin, 1988), pp. 12–14.

185. Maria Luddy, *Hanna Sheehy Skeffington* (Dundalk, 1995), p. 16.

186. Luddy, 'Women and politics', pp. 91ff.

187. *Irish Citizen*, 23 May 1914.

188. Ferriter, *Mothers, Maidens and Myths*, pp. 1–9.

189. ibid., p. 10.

190. *An Claidheamh Soluis*, November 1913.

191. McCoole, *No Ordinary Women*, pp. 60–63.

192. Michael Laffan, *Resurrection of Ireland*, pp. 81–6.

193. ibid., p. 94.

194. Hart, *IRA and Its Enemies*, p. 50.

195. Marie Coleman, 'Mobilisation: The South Longford by-election and its impact on political mobilisation', in Augusteijn (ed.), *Irish Revolution*, pp. 53–70.

196. Michael Laffan, *Resurrection of Ireland*, p. 110.

197. Joost Augusteijn, *From Public Defiance to Guerrilla Warfare: The Experience of Ordinary Volunteers in the Irish War of Independence, 1916–1921* (Dublin, 1996), p. 85.

198. Fitzpatrick, *Two Irelands*, pp. 34–5, and G. K. Chesterton, *Irish Impressions* (London, 1919), pp. 121–2.

199. Pauric Travers, 'The priest in politics: The case of conscription', in Oliver MacDonagh, W. F. Mandle and Pauric Travers (eds.), *Irish Culture and Nationalism, 1750–1950* (Dublin, 1983), pp. 161–82.

200. NAI, BMH, WS 467, Eugene Bratton.

201. R. F. Foster, *W. B. Yeats: A Life: Vol. 2: The Arch Poet,* pp. 131–2.

202. Michael Laffan, *Resurrection of Ireland*, p. 146.

203. Joost Augusteijn, 'Motivation: Why did they fight for Ireland?: The motivation of volunteers in the revolution', in Augusteijn (ed.), *Irish Revolution*, pp. 103–21.

204. Michael Laffan, *Resurrection of Ireland*, p. 151.

205. *Sunday Tribune*, 17 September 2000.

206. Michael Laffan, *Resurrection of Ireland*, pp. 201–4.

207. ibid., pp. 156–7.

208. James Murray, *Galway: A Medico-social History* (Galway, 1996), p. 139.

209. David Mitchell, *A Peculiar Place: The Adelaide Hospital, Dublin* (Dublin, 1991), pp. 154–5.

3: 1918–1923

1. NAI, Dáil Éireann files (hereafter DE) 2/84, 3 May 1921.

2. David Fitzpatrick (ed.), *Revolution? Ireland 1917–23* (Dublin, 1990), p. 8, and Charles Townshend, 'Historiography: Telling the Irish revolution', in Augusteijn (ed.), *Irish Revolution*, pp. 1–17.

3. Quoted in Peter Hart, 'Definition: Defining the Irish Revolution' in Augusteijn (ed.), *Irish Revolution,* pp. 17–34.

4. ibid., pp. 78 and 84.

5. Michael Hopkinson, *The Irish War of Independence* (Dublin, 2002), p. 126.

6. UCDAD, Papers of Robert Dudley Edwards, LA 22, 335 (183), 31 March 1952.

7. ibid., 333 (149), 22 February 1958.

8.   NAI, BMH, WS 632, Elizabeth Bloxham.
9.   Canon Sheehan, *The Graves at Kilmorna: A Story of '67* (London, 1915),
     pp. 74–5.
10. Aodh de Blacam, *What Sinn Féin Stands For* (London, 1921), pp. 125ff.
11. Conor Kostick, *Revolution in Ireland: Popular Militancy 1917 to 1923* (London, 1996),
     p. 11.
12. P. Lynch, 'The social revolution that never was', in T. D. Williams (ed.), *The Irish
     Struggle 1916–26,* (London, 1966), p. 98.
13. Brian Farrell, 'The first Dáil and its constitutional documents', in Brian Farrell (ed.),
     The Creation of the Dáil (Dublin, 1994), pp. 61–75.
14. Kostick, *Revolution in Ireland*, p. 31.
15. De Blacam, *What Sinn Féin Stands For*, pp. 231–2.
16. Garvin, *Irish Nationalist Revolutionaries*, pp. 24–7.
17. David Fitzpatrick, *Politics and Irish Life, 1913–21: Provincial Experience of War and
     Revolution* (Dublin, 1977), pp. 178–92.
18. Hart, *IRA and Its Enemies*, p. 213.
19. ibid., p. 157, and Coleman, *County Longford*, p. 148.
20. David Brundage, 'American labour and the Irish question', *Saothar*, vol. 24, 1999,
     pp. 59–67.
21. NAI, DE 2/450, December 1921.
22. Keiko Inoue, 'Propaganda II: Propaganda of Dáil Éireann', in Augusteijn (ed.), *Irish
     Revolution*, pp. 87–103.
23. NAI, DE 2/14, March 1921.
24. *Irish Times*, 25 November 2000.
25. Francis J. Costello: *Enduring the Most: The Life and Death of Terence MacSwiney* (Dingle,
     1996), and *Times*, 2 September 1920.
26. NAI, DE 2/526, July 1921.
27. NAI, Department of Foreign Affairs, Provisional Government (hereafter DFA) 34/35,
     October 1921.
28. NAI, DE 14/72, October 1921.
29. Mary Kotsonouris, *Retreat from Revolution: The Dáil Courts, 1920–24* (Dublin, 1994),
     p. 24.
30. ibid.
31. Fitzpatrick, *Politics and Irish Life*, pp. 174–84.
32. NAI, BMH, WS 708, Conor Maguire.
33. Ferriter, *Nation of Extremes*, p. 82.
34. ibid.
35. NAI, Dáil Éireann, Local Government files (hereafter DELG), 6/9, July 1921.
36. NAI, DELG, 17/4, September 1921.
37. NAI, BMH, WS 449, William Cosgrave.
38. Tom Garvin, *1922: The Birth of Irish Democracy* (Dublin, 1996), pp. 72–81.
39. NAI, DELG 26/9, October 1921.
40. Richard Abbott, *Police Casualties in Ireland, 1919–22* (Cork, 2000), pp. 7 and 298–325.
41. John D. Brewer, *The RIC: An Oral History* (Belfast, 1990), pp. 81–2.
42. NAI, BMH,WS 467, Eugene Bratton.
43. NAI, BMH, WS 467, John Duffy.
44. NAI, BMH, WS 379, Jeremiah Mee.
45. NAI, BMH, WS 287, John Flannery.
46. Kevin Haddock Flynn, 'Soloheadbeg: What really happened?', *History Ireland*, vol. 5,
     no. 1, Spring 1997, pp. 43–7.
47. Seán O'Faoláin, *Vive Moi!*, pp. 135–8, and Hart, *IRA and Its Enemies*, pp. 10–11.

48. Abbott, *Police Casualties*, pp. 156ff.

49. Tom Dooley, 'The Royal Munster Fusiliers', *History Ireland*, vol. 6, no. 1, Spring 1998, pp. 33–40.

50. Fitzpatrick, 'Militarism in Ireland', p. 399.

51. Terry Dooley, *The Decline of the Big House in Ireland: A Study of Irish Landed Families* (Dublin, 2001), p. 189.

52. NAI, Land Settlement Commission files (hereafter LSC), Miscellaneous, October 1920.

53. *Freeman's Journal*, 6 May 1922.

54. Paul Bew, 'Sinn Féin, agrarian radicalism and the War of Independence', in D. G. Boyce (ed.), *The Revolution in Ireland, 1879–1923* (London, 1988), pp. 217–36.

55. Augusteijn, *From Public Defiance to Guerrilla Warfare*, p. 258.

56. Bew, 'Sinn Féin, agrarian radicalism and the War of Independence'.

57. Emmet O'Connor; *Syndicalism in Ireland, 1917–1923* (Cork, 1988), pp. 87–8, and Emmet O'Connor, *A Labour History of Waterford* (Waterford, 1989).

58. De Blacam, *What Sinn Féin Stands For*, pp. 149–214.

59. NAI, DE 2/483, October 1921.

60. Emmet O'Connor, *Syndicalism in Ireland*, p. 125.

61. David Fitzpatrick, 'Strikes in Ireland'.

62. NAI, DE 2/483, October 1921.

63. Finola Kennedy, *Cottage to Crèche*, p. 38.

64. NAI, DE 2/483, October 1921.

65. Finola Kennedy, *Cottage to Crèche*, p. 85.

66. Margaret Ward, 'The League of Women delegates and Sinn Féin', *History Ireland*, vol. 4, no. 3, Winter 1996, pp. 37–42.

67. Fitzpatrick, *Two Irelands*, p. 38.

68. NAI, DE 2/486, June 1921.

69. NAI, BMH, WS 450, Brighíd O'Mullane.

70. McCoole, *No Ordinary Women*, p. 73.

71. Fitzpatrick, *Two Irelands*, p. 74.

72. McMahon, 'Ireland, the Empire and the Commonwealth'.

73. Fitzpatrick, *Two Irelands*, p. 85.

74. Michael Laffan, *Resurrection of Ireland*, p. 465.

75. *An tÓglách*, 31 March 1919.

76. Hart, *IRA and Its Enemies*, pp. 138ff.

77. Augusteijn, *From Public Defiance to Guerrilla Warfare*.

78. NAI, BMH, WS 830, Patrick Cannon and Patrick Cassidy.

79. NAI, BMH, WS 1280, Ned Broy.

80. NAI, BMH, WS 1713, James O'Donavan.

81. NAI, BMH, WS 1523, Daniel Cashman.

82. NAI, BMH, WS 828, James Byrne.

83. NAI, BMH, WS 1535, Hugh Early.

84. Charles Townshend, 'The Irish Republican Army and the development of guerrilla warfare, 1916–1921', *English Historical Review*, vol. 94, no. 371, 1979.

85. NAI, BMH, WS 830, Patrick Cannon.

86. Seán O'Faoláin, *Vive Moi!*, pp. 135–8.

87. Townshend, 'The Irish Republican Army'.

88. Hart, *IRA and Its Enemies*, p. 118.

89. ibid.

90. Peter Hart, 'The Protestant experience of revolution in Southern Ireland', in Richard English and Graham Walker (eds.), *Unionism in Modern Ireland: New Perspectives on Politics and Culture* (London, 1996), pp. 81–9.

91. Hart, *IRA and Its Enemies*, chapter 4.
92. ibid., pp. 114 and 314–15.
93. ibid., pp. 273–7.
94. NAI, BMH, WS 1496, Kennedy.
95. Augusteijn, *From Public Defiance to Guerrilla Warfare*, pp. 181 and 132.
96. NAI, BMH, WS 505 and WS 838, Seán Moylan.
97. Augusteijn, 'Motivation', p. 117.
98. McMahon, 'Ireland, the Empire and the Commonwealth'.
99. Augusteijn, 'Motivation', p. 117.
100. Patrick Shea, *Voices and the Sound of Drums: An Irish Autobiography* (Belfast, 1981), pp. 44–5.
101. NAI, BMH, WS 1272, James Collins.
102. NAI, BMH, WS 362, Mgr McMahon.
103. Lennox Robinson, *Lady Gregory's Journals*, pp. 135–45.
104. Charles Townshend, 'British policy in Ireland, 1906–1921', in Boyce (ed.), *The Revolution in Ireland*, pp. 173–93.
105. D. G Boyce, *Englishmen and Irish Troubles: British Public Opinion and the Making of Irish Policy, 1918–22* (London, 1972), pp. 56–9.
106. Jackson, *Ireland 1798–1998*, p. 248.
107. ibid., p. 255.
108. Boyce, *Englishmen and Irish Troubles*, pp. 51–2.
109. John Bowyer Bell, *The Secret Army: The IRA* (New Jersey, 1996), p. 25.
110. *Freeman's Journal*, 17 August 1921.
111. Hopkinson, *Irish War of Independence*, pp. 194 and 185.
112. NAI, BMH, WS 469, Alfred Cope.
113. NAI, DE 2/247, October 1921.
114. NAI, DE 2/302, 13 August 1921.
115. Michael Laffan, *Resurrection of Ireland*, p. 347.
116. ibid., p. 347.
117. Sineád McCoole, *Hazel: A Life of Lady Lavery, 1880–1935* (Dublin, 1996), p. 73.
118. Frank Pakenham, *Peace by Ordeal* (London, 1935).
119. Boyce, *Englishmen and Irish Troubles*, p. 163.
120. *Freeman's Journal*, 18 July 1921.
121. Boyce, *Englishmen and Irish Troubles*, p. 147.
122. McCoole, *Hazel*, pp. 63–77.
123. NAI, DE 304/1, December 1921.
124. *Sunday Tribune*, 24 September 2000.
125. Pakenham, *Peace by Ordeal*, pp. 239–40.
126. McCoole, *Hazel*, p. 81.
127. Pakenham, *Peace by Ordeal*, pp. xiv, 104–7, 111.
128. *Freeman's Journal*, 15 December 1921.
129. Alan O'Day and John Steven (eds.), *Irish Historical Documents since 1800* (Dublin, 1992), p. 329.
130. *Irish Times*, 25 May 1998.
131. P. S. O'Hegarty, Alice Stopford Green, James Stephens and Robert Mitchell Henry, 'Arthur Griffith', *Studies*, vol. 11, September 1922, pp. 337–55.
132. John M. Regan, *The Irish Counter-Revolution, 1921–1936* (Dublin, 1999), pp. xii–xvi.
133. *Freeman's Journal*, 15 December 1921 and 21 December 1921.
134. *Sunday Tribune*, 12 November 2000.
135. Quoted in F. S. L. Lyons, 'The Great Debate', in Brian Farrell (ed.), *The Irish Parliamentary Tradition* (Dublin, 1973), pp. 246–57.

136. NAI, DT S 1369/9, November 1922.
137. NAI, BMH, WS 550, Thomas Duggan.
138. NAI, BMH, WS 271, Bishop Fogarty of Killaloe.
139. Patrick Murray, *Oracles of God*, p. 35.
140. NAI, DFA, Irish Race Congress, 11 November 1921.
141. Charles McCarthy, *Trade Unions in Ireland, 1894–1960* (Dublin, 1977).
142. *Freeman's Journal*, 17 January 1922.
143. NAI, DT S 3827, February 1922.
144. NAI, DE, Finance, 35/9, June 1922.
145. *Freeman's Journal*, 18 January 1922.
146. NAI, LSC, Kerry 150, March 1922.
147. NAI, DE 14/71, May 1922.
148. NAI, DE 2/521, March 1922.
149. Jackson, *Ireland 1798–1998*, p. 264, and Michael Gallagher, 'The Pact general election of 1922', *Irish Historical Studies*, vol. 21, no. 84, 1979, p. 413.
150. NAI, DT S 1283, June 1922, and Benjamin Kline, 'Churchill and Collins 1919–22: Admirers or adversaries?', *History Ireland*, vol. 1, no. 3, Autumn 1993, pp. 38–44.
151. Lee, *Ireland 1912–85*, pp. 62–9, and *Sunday Tribune*, 17 September 2000.
152. Brian P. Murphy, 'Nationalism: The framing of the Constitution of the Irish Free State, 1922 – the defining battle for the Irish Republic', in Augusteijn (ed.), *Irish Revolution*, pp. 135–51.
153. See Michael Hopkinson's review of Garvin, *1922, Irish Historical Studies*, vol. 30, 1996–7, pp. 628–9.
154. Garvin, *1922*, p. 137.
155. Michael Gallagher, 'The Pact general election'.
156. NAI, DT S 1283, June 1922.
157. NAI, DFA 37/1–2, April 1922.
158. Garvin, *1922*, p. 150.
159. Ronald Ayling (ed.), *Seven Plays by Seán O'Casey* (London, 1985), pp. 1–45.
160. Seán O'Faoláin, *Vive Moi!*, p. 165.
161. Risteárd Mulcahy, *Richard Mulcahy (1886–1971): A Family Memoir* (Dublin, 1999), pp. 167–84.
162. Ferriter, *Lovers of Liberty?*, pp. 13–14.
163. Kotsonouris, *Retreat from Revolution*, pp. 28–30.
164. Alexis Guilbride, 'A scrapping of every principle of individual liberty: The postal strike of 1922', *History Ireland*, vol. 8, no. 4, Winter 2000, pp. 35–40.
165. ibid.
166. Frank O'Connor, *Guests of the Nation* (London, 1931), p. 215.
167. Francis Stuart, *We Have Kept the Faith* (Dublin, 1923), p. 9.
168. Ronan Fanning, *Independent Ireland* (Dublin, 1983), p. 39.
169. Fitzpatrick, *Two Irelands*, pp. 133–4.
170. Michael Hopkinson, *Green against Green: The Irish Civil War* (Dublin, 1988), pp. 158–61 and 173–202.
171. Coleman, *County Longford*.
172. Hopkinson, *Green against Green*, pp. 123–42.
173. Mulcahy, *Richard Mulcahy*, p. 130.
174. *Irish Times*, 14 August 1922.
175. Mulcahy, *Richard Mulcahy*, p. 2.
176. John Regan, 'The politics of reaction: The dynamics of Treatyite government and policy 1922–33', *Irish Historical Studies*, vol. 30, no. 20, November 1997; and John

Regan, 'Demilitarising Michael Collins', *History Ireland*, vol. 3, no. 3, Autumn 1995, pp. 17–23.

177. Anne Dolan, 'Arthur Griffith', paper delivered to St Patrick's College History Society, Dublin City University, 9 December 2002; and Anne Dolan 'Commemoration: "Shows and stunts are all that is the thing now" – the revolution remembered, 1923–52', in Augusteijn (ed.), *Irish Revolution*, pp. 186–219.

178. ibid.

179. *Cork Examiner*, 23 August 1922.

180. *Freeman's Journal*, 23 August 1922.

181. *Cork Examiner*, 6 February 1997, 'Big Fella' supplement.

182. *Irish Times*, 5 August 1999.

183. Tim Pat Coogan, *De Valera: Long Fellow, Long Shadow* (London, 1993).

184. *Cork Examiner*, 26 February 1997.

185. ibid.

186. *Sunday Tribune*, 26 November 2002.

187. Piper, *Dangerous Waters*.

188. Colm Campbell, *Emergency Law in Ireland, 1918–1925* (Oxford, 1994).

189. Liam McNiffe, *A History of the Gárda Síochána* (Dublin, 1997), p. 23.

190. Garvin, *1922*, p. 163.

191. Mulcahy, *Richard Mulcahy*, pp. 131–53.

192. Dorothy Macardle, *Tragedies of Kerry, 1922–1923* (Dublin, 1924), pp. 14–17.

193. Eoin Neeson, *The Civil War 1922–23* (Dublin, 1966).

194. NAI, DFA 47, February 1923.

195. Garvin, *1922*, p. 151.

196. Margaret O'Callaghan, 'Women and politics in independent Ireland, 1921–68', in *Field Day Anthology V*, pp. 120–35.

197. ibid., p. 123.

198. McCoole, *No Ordinary Women*, p. 87.

199. Hart, *IRA and Its Enemies*, pp. 142–54.

200. Garvin, *1922*, p. 136.

201. Quoted in James McKay, *Michael Collins: A Life* (Edinburgh, 1996), pp. 296–7.

202. Peter Hegarty, *Peadar O'Donnell* (Cork, 1999), p. 301.

203. Roddy Doyle, *A Star Called Henry* (London, 1999), p. 313.

204. Richard English, 'Socialist intellectuals and the Irish Revolution' in Augusteijn (ed.), *Irish Revolution* p. 217.

205. Treaty Debates, 19 December 1921. See *Private Sessions of the Second Dáil* (Dublin, 1972), p. 27.

206. Mulcahy, *Richard Mulcahy*, p. 138.

207. ibid., p. 3.

208. Garvin, *1922*, pp. 156–79.

209. Margaret Buckley, *The Jangling of the Keys* (Dublin, 1938), p. 50.

210. McCoole, *No Ordinary Women*, p. 137.

211. Margaret Ward, 'Gender', in Augusteijn (ed.), *Irish Revolution*, p. 172.

212. *Dáil Debates*, 7 June 1928.

213. Uinseann MacEoin, *Survivors* (Dublin, 1987), p. 52.

214. Anne Dolan, 'Commemoration', in Augusteijn (ed.), *Irish Revolution*, p. 186.

215. Patrick Murray, *Oracles of God*, chapter 3.

216. ibid., p. 23.

217. Hopkinson, *Irish War of Independence*, p. 153.

218. ibid., pp. 158–60.

219. A. T. Q. Stewart, *Edward Carson* (Dublin, 1981), p. 4.

220. Andrew Gailey, 'King Carson: An essay on the invention of leadership', *Irish Historical Studies*, vol. XXX, no. 117, May 1996, pp. 66–87.

221. ibid.

222. Quoted in Kline, 'Churchill and Collins', p. 38.

223. Alvin Jackson, 'Irish unionists and the Empire, 1880–1920: Classes and masses', in Keith Jeffery (ed.), *An Irish Empire? Aspects of Ireland and the British Empire* (Manchester, 1996), pp. 123–49.

224. John Lynch, 'Harland and Wolff: Its labour force and industrial relations, Autumn 1919', *Saothar*, vol. 22, 1997, pp. 47–63.

225. Ronan Gallagher, *Violence and Nationalist Politics in Derry City, 1920–1923* (Dublin, 2003), pp. 54–65.

226. Phoenix, *Northern Nationalism*, pp. 50ff.

227. Ronan Gallagher, *Violence and Nationalist Politics*.

228. NAI, DE 2/266, January 1921.

229. NAI, DE 2/110, January 1921.

230. Hopkinson, *Irish War of Independence*, p. 161.

231. Fitzpatrick, *Two Irelands*, pp. 118–19.

232. NAI, DE 2/304 (1–8), October 1921.

233. R. F. Foster, *W. B Yeats: A Life, Vol. 2*, p. 213.

234. Taillon and Urquhart, 'Women, politics and the state', pp. 358–9.

235. Hopkinson, *Irish War of Independence*, p. 163.

236. NAI, DE 2/338, February 1922.

237. NAI, DE 2/353, July 1921.

238. Lee, *Ireland 1912–85*, p. 45.

239. Denise Kleinrichert, *Republican Internment and the Prison Ship Argenta, 1922* (Dublin, 2001), p. xvi.

240. ibid., pp. 5, 157 and 199.

241. *Freeman's Journal*, 28 February 1922.

242. Alan Greer, 'Sir James Craig and the construction of Parliament buildings at Stormont', *Irish Historical Studies*, vol. XXXI, no. 123, May 1999, pp. 373–88.

243. Robert Harbinson, *No Surrender: An Ulster Childhood* (Belfast, 1960), pp. 42–72.

4: 1923–1932

1. Paul-Dubois, *Contemporary Ireland*, p. 109.

2. Fitzpatrick, *Two Irelands*, p. 10.

3. ibid., p. 98.

4. Patrick Buckland, *The Factory of Grievances: Devolved Government in Northern Ireland, 1921–1939* (Dublin, 1979), p. 72.

5. Deane, *Reading in the Dark*, p. 23.

6. Fitzpatrick, *Two Irelands*, p. 118.

7. NAI, DT S 5750/1, 3 March 1922.

8. NAI, DT S 5462, 'Northern Ireland: Outrages 1922', 14 March 1922.

9. ibid., 20 March 1922 and 31 March 1922.

10. NAI, DT S 11209, 11 October 1922.

11. Paul Bew, Peter Gibbon and Henry Patterson, *Northern Ireland, 1921–1994: Political Forces and Social Classes* (London, 1995), p. 35.

12. NAI, DT S 5750/2, 16 April 1923.

13. Enda Staunton, *The Nationalists of Northern Ireland, 1918–1973* (Dublin, 2001), p. 41.

14. Mary Harris, *The Catholic Church and the Foundation of the Northern Irish State, 1912–30* (Cork, 1993), p. 258.
15. ibid., p. 260.
16. Staunton, *The Nationalists of Northern Ireland*, p. 259.
17. Bew, Gibbon and Patterson, *Northern Ireland*, p. 15.
18. *Irish Times*, 4 April 1924.
19. Alvin Jackson, 'Local government in Northern Ireland, 1920–1973', in Mary Daly (ed.), *County and Town: One Hundred Years of Local Government in Ireland* (Dublin, 2001), pp. 56–61.
20. NAI, DT S 4782, 20 December 1925.
21. Denis Donoghue, *Warrenpoint* (London, 1991), pp. 46–7.
22. Fitzpatrick, *Two Irelands*, p. 236.
23. Susan McKay, *Northern Protestants: An Unsettled People* (Belfast, 2000), p. 136.
24. Jackson, 'Unionist history', p. 61.
25. Denis Kennedy, *The Widening Gulf: Northern Attitudes to the Independent Irish State, 1919–1949* (Belfast, 1988).
26. Tom Clyde (ed.), *Ancestral Voices: The Selected Prose of John Hewitt* (Belfast, 1987), p. 146.
27. Graham Walker, 'The Northern Ireland Labour Party in the 1920s', *Saothar*, vol. 10, 1984, pp. 19–29.
28. ibid.
29. ibid.
30. ibid.
31. Taillon and Urquhart, 'Women, politics and the state', p. 361.
32. ibid., pp. 364–5.
33. T. W. Moody, 'The social history of modern Ulster', in Beckett and Moody (eds.), *Ulster since 1800*, pp. 224–35.
34. DCCA, Corporation Minutes, 7 June 1926.
35. John Simms, *Farewell to the Hammer: A Shankhill Boyhood* (Belfast, 1992), pp. 42–9.
36. PRONI, D/1050/13/a/a 1–53, Minutes of the Executive of the Ulster Farmers' Union, 26 January 1928.
37. ibid.
38. PRONI, Home Affairs (hereafter HA), 10/9, 12 October 1922.
39. ibid., 10/10, Report of Departmental Committee.
40. *Dublin Opinion*, vol. 1, 8 October 1922.
41. Bew, Gibbon and Patterson, *Northern Ireland*, pp. 10–11.
42. NAI, DT S 1730, 27 February 1923.
43. NAI, DT S 10948, 3 April 1925.
44. *Morning Post*, 11 March 1925.
45. NAI, DT S 4563A, 22 July 1925.
46. Bew, Gibbon and Patterson, *Northern Ireland*, p. 10.
47. Enda Staunton, 'The Boundary Commission debacle 1925: Aftermath and implications', *History Ireland*, vol. 4, no. 2, Summer 1996, pp. 42–6.
48. ibid.
49. Margaret O'Callaghan, 'Old parchment and water: The Boundary Commission of 1925 and the copper-fastening of the Irish border', *Bullán*, vol. 4, no. 2, pp. 27–55 and 38.
50. Michael Kennedy, *Division and Consensus: The Politics of Cross-border Relations in Ireland 1925–69* (Dublin, 2000), p. 9.
51. Fanning, *Independent Ireland*, pp. 86–92.
52. Bew, Patterson and Gibbons, *Northern Ireland*, p. 10.
53. PRONI, Papers of Lord Londonderry, D/3099/2/7/117–36, 26 April 1927.
54. *Dáil Debates*, 1 March 1923.

55. Paul A. Carthy, 'Kevin O'Higgins in Government, 1922–7', unpublished MA thesis, University College Dublin, 1980.

56. Stephen Collins, *The Cosgrave Legacy* (Dublin, 1996), p. 35.

57. *Irish Times*, 6 February 1970.

58. ibid.

59. *Irish Times*, 7 April 2003.

60. Thomas J. Morrissey, *A Man Called Hughes: The Life and Times of Séamus Hughes, 1881–1943* (Dublin, 1991), p. 69.

61. Lee, *Ireland 1912–85*, p. 173.

62. ibid.

63. Paul Murray, 'On Saint Helena's bleak shore', *History Ireland*, vol. 11, no. 1, Spring 2003, pp. 10–11.

64. Peadar O'Donnell, *Adrigoole* (london, 1929), p. 314.

65. Lynn Doyle, *The Spirit of Ireland* (London, 1935), p. 5.

66. NAI, DE 2/413, March 1922.

67. George Russell, 'Lessons of revolution', *Studies*, vol. 12, no. 4, March 1923, pp. 345–6.

68. Frank O'Connor, *An Only Child*, p. 263.

69. ibid., p. 270.

70. Seán O'Faoláin, *Vive Moi!*, p. 177.

71. Charlotte Fallon, 'Republican hunger strikes during the Irish Civil War and its immediate aftermath', unpublished MA thesis, University College Dublin, 1980.

72. *Irish Statesman*, 29 January 1927.

73. Eunan O'Halpin, 'The army in independent Ireland', in Bartlett and Jeffery (eds.), *Military History of Ireland*, pp. 407–31.

74. John Regan, *The Irish Counter-Revolution*, p. 197.

75. Regan, 'The politics of reaction', pp. 542–64.

76. *Irish Times*, 12 March 1924.

77. *Dáil Debates*, 12 July 1927.

78. Paul A. Kelly, 'The electoral appeal of Cumann na nGaedheal, 1923–32', unpublished MA thesis, University College Dublin, 1981.

79. UCDAD, Papers of Michael Hayes, P53, 258, 3 July 1944.

80. Liam Miller (ed.), *Austin Clarke, Collected Poems* (Dublin, 1974), p. 178.

81. Andrews, *Dublin Made Me*, pp. 306–7.

82. Fitzpatrick, *Two Irelands*, p. 170.

83. McNiffe, *A History of the Garda Síochána*, p. 23.

84. Ferriter, *Nation of Extremes*, pp. 106–7.

85. McNiffe, *A History of the Garda Síochána*, pp. 39–56.

86. Ferriter, *Lovers of Liberty?*, p. 146.

87. Garvin, *1922*, p. 95.

88. Michael Cronin, 'City administration in Ireland', with 'Comment' by James Hogan, *Studies*, vol. 21, no. 47, September 1923, p. 359.

89. Lee, *Ireland 1912–85*, p. 107.

90. George Russell, 'Lessons of revolution'.

91. *Labour Advocate*, November 1926.

92. Kieran Allen, *Fianna Fáil and Irish Labour: 1926 to the Present* (London, 1997), and Richard Dunphy, *The Making of Fianna Fáil Power in Ireland, 1923–48* (Oxford, 1995), pp. 120–21.

93. Emmet O'Connor, *James Larkin*, p. 70.

94. ibid., p. 79.

95. Emmet O'Connor, 'Jim Larkin and the Communist Internationals', pp. 357–73.

96. Barry McLoughlin, 'Delegated to the "New World": Irish communists at Moscow's

International Lenin School, 1927–37', *History Ireland*, vol. 7, no. 4, Winter 1999, pp. 37–40.

97. Michael Laffan, *Resurrection of Ireland*, pp. 435–7.

98. Fitzpatrick, *Two Irelands*, p. 288.

99. Peadar O'Donnell, *The Bothy Fire and All That* (Dublin, 1937).

100. O'Malley, *The Singing Flame*, p. 275.

101. Seán O'Faoláin, *Vive Moi!*, p. 169.

102. William Murphy, 'Prophets or patsies: The influence of Swift and Berkeley on nationalist rhetoric', *UCD History Review*, vol. 10, 1996, pp. 15–23.

103. NAI, DT S 1899, c. 1930.

104. *An Phoblacht,* 8 December 1928.

105. Brian Hanley, *The IRA, 1926–1936* (Dublin, 2002), pp. 175–90.

106. Mark O'Brien, *De Valera, Fianna Fáil and the Irish Press* (Dublin, 2001), pp. 36–7.

107. Regan, *Counter-Revolution*, p. 275.

108. NAI, DT S 5470, 'Third Executive Council Appointement, including details of J. J. Walsh's rift with Cumann na nGaedheal', June–September 1927.

109. *Dáil Debates*, 4 June 1930.

110. William Murphy, 'Prophets or patsies'.

111. Fitzpatrick, *Two Irelands*, p. 212.

112. Cormac Ó Gráda, *A Rocky Road: The Irish Economy since the 1920s* (Manchester, 1997), p. 67.

113. ibid.

114. NAI, DT S 3192, 7 April 1924.

115. David Seth Jones, 'Land reform, legislation and security of tenure in Ireland after independence', *Éire-Ireland*, vol. 32, 1997–8, pp. 116–43, and David Seth Jones, 'State financing of land division in the Irish Republic', paper delivered to *Land, Politics and the State*, NUI Maynooth Conference, 10 May 2003.

116. Andy Bielenberg, 'Keating, Siemens and the Shannon Scheme', *History Ireland*, vol. 5, no. 3, Autumn 1997, pp. 43–9.

117. ibid.

118. Ronan Fanning, 'Economists and governments: Ireland 1922–52', in Antoin E. Murphy (ed.), *Economists and the Irish Economy from the Eighteenth Century to the Present Day* (Dublin, 1983), pp. 138–57.

119. Ó Gráda, '"The greatest blessing of them all"'.

120. Ó Gráda, *Rocky Road*, p. 91.

121. Ó Gráda, '"The greatest blessing of them all"'.

122. ibid.

123. Ó Gráda, *Rocky Road*, p. 91.

124. *Irish Times*, 15 May 1931.

125. Paul Smith, *The Countrywoman* (London, 1962), p. 138.

126. McManus, *Dublin 1910–1940*, p. 56.

127. ibid., p. 91.

128. R. J. Graham and Susan Hood, 'Town tenant protest in late nineteenth- and early twentieth-century Ireland', *Irish Economic and Social History*, vol. 21, 1994, pp. 39–58.

129. Oikarieu, *Dream of Liberty*, p. 126.

130. *Census of the Population of Ireland* (Dublin, 1926).

131. David Krause (ed.), *The Letters of Seán O'Casey* (London, 1975), p. 131.

132. Marie Coleman, 'The origins of the Irish hospitals sweepstake', *Irish Economic and Social History*, vol. XXIX, 2002, pp. 40–56.

133. Mary E. Daly, '"An atmosphere of sturdy independence": The state and the Dublin

hospitals in the 1930s', in Jones and Malcolm (eds.), *Medicine, Disease and the State*, pp. 253–67.

134. Robins, *Fools and Mad*, p. 189.

135. Eoin O'Sullivan, "'This otherwise delicate subject'": Child sexual abuse in early twentieth-century Ireland', in Paul O'Mahony (ed.), *Criminal Justice in Ireland* (Dublin, 2002), pp. 176–201.

136. Finola Kennedy, 'The suppression of the Carrigan Report: A historical perspective on child abuse', *Studies*, vol. 89, no. 356, Winter 2000, pp. 354–63, and Mark Finnane, 'The Carrigan Committee of 1930–31 and the moral condition of the Saorstát', *Irish Historical Studies*, vol. 32, 2000–2001, pp. 519–36.

137. Susannah Riordan, 'VD in the army: Moral panic in the Irish Free State in the 1920s', paper delivered to the St Patrick's College History Society, November 2001.

138. ibid.

139. *Irish Times*, 5 October 1996.

140. Eoin O'Sullivan, "'This otherwise delicate subject'".

141. Raftery and O'Sullivan, *Suffer the Little Children*, pp. 224–5.

142. *Irish Times*, 30 October 1995, and Louise Ryan, 'Infanticide in the Irish Free State', *Irish Studies Review*, no. 14, Spring 1996.

143. ibid.

144. ibid.

145. Eoin O'Sullivan, "'This otherwise delicate subject'".

146. P. M. Garrett, 'The abnormal flight: The migration and repatriation of Irish unmarried mothers', *Social History*, vol. 25, no. 3, 2000, pp. 330–43.

147. Sandra L. MacAvoy, 'The regulation of sexuality in the Irish Free State, 1929–1935', in Jones and Malcolm (eds.), *Medicine, Disease and the State*, pp. 253–67.

148. Finnegan, *Do Penance or Perish*, p. 30.

149. Eoin O'Sullivan, "'This otherwise delicate subject'".

150. ibid.

151. Noël Browne, *Against the Tide* (Dublin, 1986), p. 26.

152. *Dáil Debates*, 2 March 1928.

153. Finola Kennedy, 'The suppression of the Carrigan Report'.

154. Joseph E. Canavan, 'The Poor Law Report', *Studies*, vol. 16, no. 4, 1927, pp. 631–44.

155. Elizabeth Steiner-Scott, "'To bounce a boot off her now and then'": Domestic violence in post-Famine Ireland', in Maryann Gialanella Valiulis and Mary O'Dowd (eds.), *Women and Irish History* (Dublin, 1997), pp. 125–44.

156. Seán O'Faoláin, *Vive Moi!*, p. 169.

157. F. X. Martin (ed.), *Leaders and Men of the Easter Rising*, p. 227.

158. R. F. Foster, *W. B. Yeats: A Life, Vol. 1*, p. 384.

159. Quoted in the *Irish Times*, 30 October 1995.

160. C. Arensberg, *The Irish Countryman* (New York, 1937), and C. Arensberg and S. Kimball, *Family and Community in Ireland* (Harvard, 1940).

161. Paul Smith, *The Countrywoman*, p. 115.

162. Kathleen Clarke, *Revolutionary Woman: An Autobiography* (Dublin,1991).

163. Mary Daly, "'Oh, Kathleen Ní Houlihán, Your way's a thorny way!'": The condition of women in twentieth-century Ireland', in Anthony Bradley and Maryann Gialanella Valiulis (eds.), *Gender and Sexuality in Modern Ireland* (Amherst, Ma, 1998), pp. 102–26.

164. *Seanad Éireann Debates*, 30 March 1927.

165. *Irish Independent*, 17 October 1926.

166. Maurice Moynihan, *Statements and Speeches of Eamon de Valera 1917–1973* (Dublin and New York, 1980), p. 252.

167. Caitriona Beaumont, 'Women and the politics of equality: The Irish women's movement, 1930–1943', in Valiulis and O'Dowd (eds.), *Women and Irish History*, pp. 159–73.

168. Caitríona Clear, *Women of the House: Women's Household Work in Ireland, 1926–1961* (Dublin, 2000).

169. Maryann Gialanella Valiulis, 'Neither feminist nor flapper: The ecclesiastical construction of the ideal Irish woman', in Mary O'Dowd and Sabine Wichert (eds.), *Chattel, Servant or Citizen: Women's Status in Church, State and Society, Historical Studies 19* (Belfast, 1995), pp. 168–79.

170. Margaret O'Callaghan, 'Women and politics in Independent Ireland', in *Field Day Anthology V*, pp. 155–6.

171. Rita Rhodes, *Women and the Family in Post-Famine Ireland: Status and Opportunities* (New York, 1992).

172. *Commission on Emigration and Other Population Problems* (Dublin, 1954), p. 115.

173. Enda Delaney, *Demography, State and Society: Irish Migration to Britain, 1921–1971* (Liverpool, 2000), p. 68.

174. ibid.

175. ibid., p. 86.

176. Patrick Murray, *Oracles of God*, pp. 19–23.

177. ibid., pp. 117–22.

178. Morrissey, *William J. Walsh*, pp. 350–55.

179. Dermot Keogh, *Ireland and the Vatican: The Diplomacy of Church–State Relations, 1922–60* (Cork, 1995), pp. 12–27.

180. Valiulis, 'Neither feminist nor flapper', pp. 168–79.

181. Patrick Murray, *Oracles of God*, pp. 266–73 and 283–4.

182. Peadar O'Donnell, *The Bothy Fire and All That*, p. 8.

183. John A. Murphy, 'The achievement of Eamon de Valera', in John A. Murphy and John P. O'Carroll (eds.), *De Valera and His Times* (Cork, 1986), pp. 1–17.

184. Patrick Murray, *Oracles of God*, pp. 298–9.

185. Margaret MacCurtain, 'Fullness of life: Defining female spirituality in twentieth-century Ireland', in Maria Luddy and Cliona Murphy (eds.), *Women Surviving* (Dublin, 1990), pp. 233–64, and Raftery and O'Sullivan, *Suffer the Little Children*, pp. 53–89.

186. Eamon Dunn, 'Action and reaction: Catholic lay organisations in Dublin in the 1920s and 1930s', *Archivium Hibernicum*, vol. XLVIII, 1994, pp. 107–18.

187. Brendan McConvery, 'Hell, fire and poitín: Redemptorist missions in the Irish Free State', *History Ireland*, vol. 8, no. 3, Autumn 2000, pp. 18–22.

188. Peadar O'Donnell, *Gates Flew Open* (Dublin, 1932), p. 157.

189. Margaret O'Callaghan, 'Language, nationality and cultural identity in the Irish Free State, 1922–7', *Irish Historical Studies*, vol. 24, no. 94, November 1984, pp. 226–45.

190. Ferriter, *Nation of Extremes*, p. 93.

191. *Dáil Debates*, 16 February 1927.

192. Ayling (ed.), *Seven Plays by Seán O'Casey*, pp. 1–45.

193. Evelyn Bolster, *The Knights of Saint Columbanus* (Dublin, 1979), p. 50.

194. Liam O'Dowd, 'Intellectuals in twentieth-century Ireland'.

195. Brennan, *The Story of Irish Dance*, p. 123.

196. *Catholic Bulletin*, vol. XXI, no. 2, February 1931, and NAI, DT S 2547, December 1930.

197. O'Callaghan, 'Language, nationality and identity', pp. 226–45.

198. *The Standard*, 13 December 1930.

199. Hubert Butler, *In The Land of Nod* (Dublin, 1996), pp. 22–6.

200. Keogh, *Jews in Twentieth-Century Ireland*, p. 40.

201. See *Catholic Bulletin*, March 1925, NAI, DT S 4127, Archbishop Byrne to Cosgrave, 4 March 1924, and David Fitzpatrick, 'Divorce and separation in modern Irish history', *Past and Present*, no. 114, 1987, pp. 172–96.
202. ibid.
203. Lyons, *Culture and Anarchy in Ireland*, pp. 1–17.
204. NAI, DJ 7/1/1–3, February–December 1926.
205. Gavin Ahern, 'Censorship in Independent Ireland: Catholic morality versus intellectualism', unpublished MA thesis, St Patrick's College, Dublin City University, 2001.
206. Maurice Harmon, *Seán O'Faoláin* (Dublin, 1984), p. 98.
207. Coolahan, *Irish Education*, p. 56.
208. Michael Adams, *Censorship: The Irish Experience* (Dublin, 1968), pp. 35ff.
209. NAI, DT S 2325, 19 October 1929.
210. NAI, DT S 3026, 'Censorship of Films Act, 1923', May–June, 1923.
211. NAI, DFA, Pres. off, 98/1, June 1923.
212. *Irish Statesman*, 20 January 1925.
213. Liam O'Flaherty, *A Tourist's Guide to Ireland* (London, 1929), p. 15.
214. Peter Costello, 'Land and Liam O'Flaherty', in Carla King (ed.), *Famine, Land and Culture in Ireland* (Dublin, 2000), pp. 169–80.
215. Daniel Corkery, *The Hidden Ireland: A Study of Catholic Munster in the Eighteenth Century* (Dublin, 1925), and Maume, *'Life that is exile'*, p. 60.
216. Frank O'Connor, *An Only Child*, p. 210.
217. Frank O'Connor, *Guests of the Nation*, p. 19.
218. Seán O'Faoláin, *Midsummer Night Madness and Other Stories* (London, 1932), p. 42.
219. Richard Loftus, *Nationalism in Modern Anglo-Irish Poetry* (Wisconsin, 1964), p. 264.
220. Fintan O'Toole, 'Going west: The country versus the city in Irish writing', *Crane Bag*, 1985, pp. 111–16.
221. ibid., p. 112.
222. Terence Brown, *Ireland's Literature: Selected Essays* (Dublin, 1988), p. 94.
223. W. J. McCormack (ed.), *Austin Clarke: Selected Poems* (London, 1992).
224. Anne Dolan, '"Fumbling in the greasy till": Dublin opinion and the Irish bourgeoisie 1922–32', unpublished MA thesis, University College Dublin, 1996.
225. *Irish Times*, 26 June 1999.
226. *Irish Times*, 16 November 2000.
227. Richard Ellmann, *James Joyce* (New York and London, 1959), p. 457.
228. Susannah Riordan, '"The unpopular front": Catholic revival and Irish cultural identity', in Mike Cronin and John M. Regan (eds.), *Ireland: The Politics of Independence, 1922–49* (Basingstoke, 2000).
229. Tóibín, *Lady Gregory's Toothbrush*, p. 113.
230. R. F. Foster, *W. B. Yeats, A Life, Vol. 2*, pp. 365–76.
231. Maurice Gorham, *Forty Years of Irish Broadcasting* (Dublin, 1967), pp. 17–54.
232. Adrian Kelly, *Compulsory Irish*, pp. 14–40, and Coolahan, *Irish Education*, pp. 223–7.
233. Desmond Fennell, 'The last years of the Gaeltacht', *Crane Bag*, 1981, pp. 8–12.
234. UCDAD, Papers of Eoin MacNeill, LAI/J/49, c. January 1925.
235. *The Leader*, 12 May 1928.
236. NAI, BMH, WS 939, Ernest Blythe.
237. UCDAD, Papers of Eoin MacNeill, LAI 53/3, 3 December 1933.
238. Eamon Ó Ciosáin, *An t-Éireannach 1934–37: Nuachtan Soisíalach Gaeltachta* (Dublin, 1993).
239. *Dáil Debates*, 21 May 1931.
240. NAI, DT S 6777, January 1936.

241. Naosc A'Ghleanna, 'Twenty years a-withering', *The Bell*, vol. 3, no. 5, February 1942, pp. 379–86.
242. Ewan Morris, '"God Save the King" versus "The Soldier's song": The 1929 Trinity College National Anthem dispute and the politics of the Irish Free State', *Irish Historical Studies*, vol. 31, 1998–9, pp. 72–91.
243. ibid.
244. Patrick O'Sullivan, 'Ireland and the Olympic Games', pp. 40–46.
245. Marcus de Burca, *The GAA: A History* (Dublin, 1980), p. 162, and Purséil, *The GAA in Its Time*, p. 194.
246. Malcolm Brodie, *100 Years of Irish Football* (Belfast, 1980), p. 19.
247. Michael Kennedy, *Ireland and the League of Nations* (Dublin, 1995), pp. 168ff.
248. Michael Kennedy, '"In spite of all impediments": The early years of the Irish Diplomatic Service', *History Ireland*, vol. 7, no. 1, Spring 1999, pp. 18–22.
249. *Sunday Tribune*, 12 November 2000.
250. McMahon, 'Ireland, the Empire and the Commonwealth'.
251. Marie Bourke, 'Yeats, Henry and the western idyll', *History Ireland*, vol. 11, no. 2, Summer 2003, pp. 28–34, and Catherine Nash, 'Embodying the nation: The west of Ireland landscape and national identity', in Barbara O'Connor and Michael Cronin (eds.), *Tourism in Ireland: A Critical Analysis* (Cork, 1993), pp. 86–115.
252. Fitzpatrick, *Two Irelands*, pp. 140–41.
253. Constantine P. Curran, 'Tourist development at home and abroad', *Studies*, vol. 15, no. 58, June 1926, pp. 299–308.

5: 1932–1945
1.   Fanning, *Independent Ireland*, pp. 116–18.
2.   Terence Brown, *Ireland: A Social and Cultural History 1922–79* (London, 1981), p. 147, and Brian P. Kennedy, 'The failure of the cultural republic: Ireland 1922–39', *Studies*, vol. 81, no. 321, Spring 1992.
3.   Tom Garvin, 'Political power and economic development in Ireland: A comparative perspective', in Maurice O'Connell (ed.), *People Power: Proceedings of the Third Annual Daniel O'Connell Workshop* (Dublin, 1993), pp. 32–7.
4.   Seán O'Faoláin, 'The plain people of Ireland', *The Bell*, vol. 7, no. 1, October 1943, pp. 1–8.
5.   Brian Fallon, *Age of Innocence*, p. 11.
6.   John Banville, 'The Ireland of de Valera and O'Faoláin', *Irish Review*, nos. 17–18, Winter 1995, pp. 142–53.
7.   Frank McCourt, *Angela's Ashes: Memoir of a Childhood* (London, 1996), p. 102 and p. 145.
8.   R. F. Foster, *The Irish Story: Telling Tales and Making It Up in Ireland* (London, 2001), pp. 164–87.
9.   Richard Dunphy, *The Making of Fianna Fáil Power*, pp. 118–22.
10. *Irish Press*, 1 February 1932.
11. *An Phoblacht*, 4 February 1933.
12. *Irish Independent*, 6 and 12 February 1932.
13. *Irish Times*, 16 February 1932.
14. Maurice Manning, *James Dillon: A Biography* (Dublin, 1999), p. 51.
15. Michelle Dowling, '"The Ireland that I would have": de Valera and the creation of an Irish national image', *History Ireland*, vol. 5, no. 2, Summer 1997, pp. 37–42.
16. Moynihan, *Statements and Speeches of Eamon de Valera*, p. 423.

17. Tom Garvin, 'Hogan as political scientist', in Donncha Ó Corráin (ed.), *James Hogan; Revolutionary, Historian and Political Scientist* (Dublin, 2001), pp. 177ff.

18. NAI, DT S 13552, 'Report of the Commission on Vocational Organisation', November 1944.

19. Seán O'Faoláin, 'All things considered', *The Bell*, vol. xi, no. 4, January 1946, pp. 877–87.

20. NAI, DT S 4964, April 1933.

21. Ferriter, *Lovers of Liberty?*, pp. 19–21.

22. Gaughan (ed.), *Memoirs of Senator Joseph Connolly*, pp. 388–433.

23. *Dáil Debates*, 25 February 1937.

24. Manning, *James Dillon*, p. 53.

25. Deirdre McMahon, *Republicans and Imperialists: Anglo-Irish Relations in the 1930s* (London, 1984), pp. 287–8.

26. John Bowman, *De Valera and the Ulster Question 1917–73* (Oxford, 1982), p. 109.

27. *Dáil Debates*, 27 April 1938.

28. J. J. Lee, 'The Irish Constitution of 1937', in Seán Hutton and Paul Stewart (eds.), *Ireland's Histories: Aspects of State, Society and Ideology* (London and New York, 1991), pp. 80–94.

29. Eibhear Walshe, 'Lock up your daughters: From ante-room to interior castle', in Eibhear Walshe (ed.), *Ordinary People Dancing: Essays on Kate O'Brien* (Cork, 1993), p. 55.

30. ibid.

31. Douglas Gageby, *The Last Secretary General: Seán Lester and the League of Nations* (Dublin, 1999), p. 220–21.

32. Eunan O'Halpin, *Defending the State: Ireland and Its Enemies since 1922* (Oxford, 2000), p. 133.

33. Brian Girvin, *Between Two Worlds: Politics and Economy in Independent Ireland* (Dublin, 1989), p. 59.

34. Fanning, 'Economists and governments', p. 149.

35. Ó Gráda, *Rocky Road*, pp. 108–13.

36. Mary E. Daly, *Industrial Development and Irish National Identity, 1922–39* (Dublin, 1992), p. 50.

37. ibid., pp. 171ff.

38. Girvin, *Between Two Worlds*, p. 114.

39. Ó Gráda, *Rocky Road*, p. 4.

40. Daly, *Buffer State*, p. 393.

41. Girvin, *Between Two Worlds*, p. 95.

42. Ó Gráda, *Rocky Road*, p. 114.

43. Brian Farrell, 'The unlikely marriage: De Valera, Lemass and the shaping of modern Ireland', *Etudes Irlandaises*, vol. 10, December 1985, pp. 215–22. See also Bernadette Whelan, *Ireland and the Marshall Plan, 1947–57* (Dublin, 2000).

44. Mary E. Daly, *The Spirit of Earnest Inquiry: The Statistical and Social Inquiry Society of Ireland* (Dublin, 1997), p. 127.

45. UCDAD, Papers of Seán MacEntee, P67 (261), c. June 1935.

46. Gearóid Ó Crualaoich, 'The primacy of form: A "folk ideology" in de Valera's politics', in J. P. O'Carroll and John A. Murphy (ed.), *De Valera and His Times*, pp. 47–62.

47. NAI, DT S 9636, 'Small farmers in West Cork', 1937.

48. Quoted in Brian P. Kennedy, 'The traditional Irish thatched house: Image and reality, 1793–1993', in Adele M. Dalsimer (ed.), *Visualising Ireland: National Identity and the Pictorial Tradition* (London, 1993), pp. 165–81.

49. Arensberg and Kimball, *Family and Community in Ireland*.

50. Ferriter, *Lovers of Liberty?*, pp. 108–24.
51. Stephen Rynne, *Fr John Hayes: Founder of Muintir na Tíre* (Dublin, 1960), and see Hayes's introduction to *Muintir na Tíre: Official Handbook* (Dublin, 1943), and Jesuit Archives, Dublin (hereafter JA), Papers of Edmund Coyne, 'Notes on Muintir na Tíre'.
52. *Irish Times*, 19 September 1944.
53. NAI, DT S 13552, 'Commission on Vocational Organisation: Departmental views on Report', 1945.
54. UCDAD, Papers of Ernest Blythe, P24 (304), July 1931.
55. Ferriter, *Lovers of Liberty?*, p. 17, and NAI, DT S 13552, 'Departmental views: Industry and commerce', 30 November 1944.
56. UCDAD, Papers of Seán MacEntee, P67, (571), June 1941, and NAI, DT S 10509 'Parish councils: General file'.
57. Tóibín and Ferriter, *Irish Famine*, pp. 19–20.
58. Patrick Sammon, *In the Land Commission: A Memoir, 1933–1978* (Dublin, 1997), p. 229.
59. Bradley, *Farm Labourers,* pp. 74–93.
60. James Horgan, 'The preconditions of a rural revival', *Irish Monthly*, vol. 67, 1939, pp. 457–75; Patrick Bolger, *The Irish Co-operative Movement*; and Stephen Rynne, 'A decade of terrible peace', in *Rural Ireland*, 1955.
61. Tony Varley and Peter Moser, 'Clann na Tamhlan: Ireland's last Farmers' Party', *History Ireland*, vol. 3, no. 2, Summer 1995, pp. 39–44.
62. Royle, 'Leaving the "dreadful rocks"'.
63. Jude McCarthy, 'State-aided island migration'.
64. Margaret MacCurtain, 'Fullness of life'.
65. Kiberd, *Irish Classics*, chapter 29.
66. Cole Morton, *Hungry for Home: Leaving the Blaskets: A Journey from the Edge of Ireland* (Harmondsworth, 2000), pp. 56–61.
67. Seán O'Crohan, *A Day in Our Life* (Dublin 1969; new edn, Oxford, 2000),
68. Ó Crualaoich, 'Primacy of form', p. 53.
69. UCDAD, Papers of Patrick McGilligan, P35, 259 (3), c. 1937.
70. *Report of the Inter-Departmental Committee on Seasonal Migration to Great Britain* (Dublin, 1938).
71. *Report of the Commission on Vocational Organisation* (Dublin, 1944), Addendum no. 2, and *Muintir na Tíre: Official Handbook* (Dublin, 1945), p. 25.
72. Delaney, *Demography, State and Society*, pp. 116–60.
73. Gerard Fee, 'The effects of World War II on Dublin's low income families', unpublished PhD thesis, University College Dublin, 1996.
74. James Deeney, *To Cure and to Care: Memoirs of a Chief Medical Officer* (Dublin, 1989), p. 78.
75. NAI, DT S 11582, 'Irish Labour emigration', August 1941.
76. ibid.
77. Delaney, *Demography, State and Society*, p. 138.
78. *Irish Times*, 14 July 1945 and 22 February 1946.
79. Delaney, *Demography, State and Society*, pp. 144ff.
80. Brian Girvin and Geoffrey Roberts, 'The forgotten volunteers of World War II', *History Ireland,* vol. 6, no. 1, Spring 1998, pp. 46–52. See also Brian Girvin, *Ireland and the Second World War: Politics, Society and Remembrance* (Dublin, 2000).
81. ibid.
82. Manning, *James Dillon*, p. 160.
83. Mary Kenny, *Goodbye to Catholic Ireland*, p. 153.
84. Donal O'Drisceóil, '"Moral neutrality": Censorship in Emergency Ireland', *History*

Ireland, vol. 4, no. 2, Summer 1996, pp. 46–51, and Donal O' Drisceóil, *Censorship in Ireland, 1939–45: Neutrality, Politics and Society* (Cork, 1996).

85. ibid.
86. Brendan Barrington (ed.), *The Wartime Broadcasts of Francis Stuart, 1942–1944* (Dublin, 2000), and J. A. Cole, *Lord Haw Haw – and William Joyce: The Full Story* (London, 1944).
87. Keogh, *Jews in Twentieth-Century Ireland*, p. 192.
88. ibid.
89. Mary M. Field, 'The politics of turf, 1939–45', unpublished MA thesis, University College Dublin, 1990, and Lee, *Ireland 1912–85*, p. 264.
90. Dermot Keogh, 'De Valera, Hitler and the visit of condolence, May 1945', *History Ireland*, vol. 5, no. 3, Autumn 1997, pp. 58–61.
91. J. P. Duggan, review of Brian Barton, *Northern Ireland in the Second World War*, *History Ireland*, vol. 4, no. 1, Spring 1996, p. 61.
92. Robert Fisk, *In Time of War: Ireland, Ulster and the Price of Neutrality, 1939–45* (London, 1943), pp. 172–220.
93. *Irish Times*, 19 October 1999.
94. J. Walter Moore, *A Life of Erwin Schrödinger* (Cambridge, 1994).
95. ibid.
96. Lee, *Ireland 1912–85*, pp. 258–71.
97. *Séanad Debates*, 9 May 1945.
98. McCourt, *Angela's Ashes*, p. 82.
99. *National Society for the Prevention of Cruelty to Children: Annual Report 1944–5* (Dublin, 1945), National Library of Ireland.
100. Bill Cullen, *It's a Long Way from Penny Apples* (Dublin, 2001), p. 39.
101. Raftery and O'Sullivan, *Suffer the Little Children*, p. 30.
102. ibid., pp. 37–8.
103. ibid., p. 127.
104. ibid., pp. 233–4 and 271–4.
105. ibid., p. 137.
106. Lindsey Earner-Byrne, 'In respect of motherhood: An Irish Catholic social service, 1930–60', paper delivered to Irish Historical Society, Dublin, November 1999.
107. Fee, 'The effects of World War II on Dublin's low income families'.
108. *Irish Press*, 3 November 1936.
109. Fee, 'The effects of World War II on Dublin's low income families', and T. W. Dillon, 'Slum clearance: Past and future', *Studies*, vol. 34, March 1945, pp. 13–20.
110. Browne, *Against the Tide*, p. 124.
111. Margaret Ó hÓgartaigh, 'Dr Dorothy Price and the elimination of childhood TB', in Augusteijn (ed.), *Ireland in the 1930s*, pp. 67–83.
112. ibid.
113. Fee, 'The effects of World War II on Dublin's low income families'.
114. Eamon Dunn, 'Action and reaction'.
115. UCDAD, Papers of Seán MacEntee, P67 (261), October 1945.
116. A Psychiatrist, 'Insanity in Ireland', *The Bell*, vol. 7, no. 4, January 1944, pp. 303–11.
117. Paul Hamilton, 'The reformation of mental health legislation in Ireland, 1945–61', unpublished MA thesis, University College Dublin, 1997.
118. Ferriter, *Lovers of Liberty?*, pp. 76–94, and Adrian Kelly, 'Social security in Ireland, 1922–52' *Irish Economic and Social History*, vol. XXIV, 1997, pp. 113–15.
119. Ann-Marie Walsh, '"Root them in the land"; Cottage schemes for agricultural labourers', in Augusteijn (ed.), *Ireland in the 1930s*, pp. 47–67.

120. Ruth Barrington, *Health, Medicine and Politics*, pp. 113ff.
121. Daly, '"An atmosphere of sturdy independence"', p. 238.
122. Maev-Ann Wren, *Unhealthy State: Anatomy of a Sick Society* (Dublin, 2003), p. 30.
123. Coleman, 'The origins of the Irish hospitals sweepstakes'; *Hidden History*, a documentary on the Irish hospitals sweepstakes, shown on RTÉ, 2 December 2003; Daly, '"An atmosphere of sturdy independence"'; and *Irish Times*, 6 December 2003.
124. Henry Moore, 'The nursing profession and its needs', *Studies*, vol. 31, September 1942, pp. 273–95.
125. Mel Cousins, 'The introduction of children's allowances in Ireland, 1939–44', *Irish Economic and Social History*, vol. XXVI, 1999, pp. 273–95, and Susannah Riordan '"A political blackthorn": Seán MacEntee, the Dignan Plan and the principle of ministerial responsibility', *Irish Economic and Social History*, vol. XXVII, 2000, pp. 44–63.
126. *Dáil Debates*, 2 December 1943.
127. Riordan, '"A political blackthorn"'.
128. ibid.
129. Ruth Barrington, *Health, Medicine and Politics*, p. 154.
130. George O'Brien, 'A challenge to the planners', *Studies*, vol. 33, June 1944, pp. 210–18.
131. Riordan, '"A political blackthorn"', p. 43.
132. John J. Horgan, 'The problem of government', *Studies*, vol. 22, December 1933, pp. 538–60.
133. J. J. Lee, 'Aspects of corporatist thought in Ireland: The Commission on Vocational Organisation, 1939–43', in Art Cosgrove and Donal McCartney (eds.), *Studies in Irish History: Presented to R. Dudley Edwards* (Dublin, 1979), pp. 324–47. See also John Swift, 'Report of the Commission on Vocational Organisation and its times', *Saothar*, vol. 6, 1975, pp. 54–63.
134. JA, Papers of Patrick Connolly, Busteed to Connolly, 3 November 1933.
135. NAI, DT S 10677, 7 June 1940.
136. JA, Papers of Edmund Coyne, 'Notes on Vocational Organisation'; *Irish Times*, 12 September 1944; and Edmund Coyne, 'Vocation structures of Ireland', *Irish Monthly*, vol. 66, 1938, pp. 386–94
137. Keogh, *Ireland and the Vatican*, p. 107.
138. John A. Murphy, 'The achievement of Eamon de Valera'.
139. *Catholic Emancipation Centenary Record* (Dublin, 1929), p. 43.
140. Maurice Hartigan, 'The Eucharistic Congress, Dublin, 1932', unpublished MA thesis, University College Dublin, 1979, and Maurice Hartigan, 'The religious life of the Catholic Laity of Dublin, 1920–1940', in James Kelly and Dáire Keogh (eds.), *A History of the Catholic Diocese of Dublin* (Dublin, 2000), pp. 331–44.
141. ibid.
142. Flann O'Brien, 'The Dance Halls', *The Bell*, vol. 1, no. 5, February 1941, pp. 44–53.
143. *Irish Press*, 2 January 1934, and Rex Cathcart, 'Broadcasting – the early decades', in Brian Farrell (ed.), *Communications and Community in Ireland* (Dublin, 1984), pp. 39–51.
144. Bolster, *Knights of Saint Columbanus*, p. 72.
145. NAI, DT S 1217A, 19 September 1940.
146. Patricia Harkin, 'Family policy in Ireland and Vichy France', unpublished MA thesis, University College Dublin, 1992.
147. Edmund M. Hogan, *The Irish Missionary Movement: A Historical Survey, 1830–1980* (Dublin, 1990), p. 129.
148. John McGahern, 'The church and its spire', in Colm Tóibín (ed.), *Soho Square 6* (London, 1993).
149. Cooney, *John Charles McQuaid*, p. 141.
150. ibid.

151. Charles McCarthy, *Trade Unions in Ireland, 1894–1960*, p. 7.

152. ibid., pp. 178–229.

153. Michael McLoughlin, 'One step forward, two steps back: A labour history of the Emergency', unpublished MA thesis, University College Dublin, 1993.

154. Andrée Sheehy Skeffington, *Skeff: The Life of Owen Sheehy Skeffington, 1909–70* (Dublin, 1991), p. 168.

155. S. Cronin, *The McGarrity Papers: Revelations of the Irish Revolutionary Movement in Ireland and America, 1900–1940* (Tralee, 1972), p. 166.

156. Brian Hanley, *The IRA, 1926–36* (Dublin, 2002), pp. 95 and 200, and Brian Hanley, 'Moss Twomey, radicalism and the IRA: A reassessment', *Saothar*, vol. 26, 2001, pp. 53–61.

157. ibid.

158. Michael McInerney, *Peadar O'Donnell: Irish Social Rebel* (Dublin, 1974), p. 144.

159. Donal O'Drisceóil, *Peadar O'Donnell* (Cork, 2001).

160. *Irish Press*, 4 June 1936.

161. Mike Cronin, *The Blueshirts and Irish Politics* (Dublin, 1997), pp. 5–22.

162. NAI, DJ 8 D 32/36, 17 March 1935.

163. NAI, DJ 8/8, 17 June 1934.

164. NAI, DJ 8/137, 22 April 1934.

165. ibid., 1 June 1934.

166. Mike Cronin, *Blueshirts and Irish Politics*, pp. 11–17.

167. Gustav Klaus (ed.), *Strong Words, Brave Deeds: The Poetry, Life and Times of Thomas O'Brien* (Dublin, 1994).

168. Fearghal McGarry, *Irish Politics and the Spanish Civil War* (Cork, 1999), and Fearghal McGarry, *Frank Ryan* (Cork, 2002).

169. McGarry, *Irish Politics and the Spanish Civil War*.

170. Lee, *Ireland 1912–85*, p. 224.

171. Daly, '"Oh, Kathleen Ní Houlihán"'.

172. Louise Ryan, *Gender Identity and the Irish Press, 1922–37: Embodying the Nation* (New York, 2002), pp. 92 and 119–35.

173. Caitríona Clear, '"The women cannot be blamed": The Commission on Vocational Organisation, Feminism and Home Makers in independent Ireland in the 1930s and 1940s', in O'Dowd and Wichert (eds.), *Chattel, Servant or Citizen*.

174. Margaret O'Callaghan, 'Women and politics', in *Field Day Anthology V*, p. 168.

175. Daly, '"Oh, Kathleen Ní Houlihán"'.

176. M. H. McInerney, 'Constructive work for Catholic Irish women', *Irish Monthly*, vol. LII, no. 610, April 1924, pp. 188–94.

177. Mary E. Daly, *Women and Work in Ireland* (Dublin, 1997), p. 50.

178. Cullen Owens, *Louie Bennett*, p. 73.

179. NAI, DT S 9880, 24 May 1937.

180. Caitríona Clear, 'Women of the house in Ireland, 1800–1950', in *Field Day Anthology V*, p. 607.

181. Finola Kennedy, *Cottage to Crèche*, pp. 158–60.

182. Eoin O'Sullivan, '"This otherwise delicate subject"'.

183. Finola Kennedy, *Cottage to Crèche*, pp. 158–60, and NAI, DJ 8/20, 19 February 1934.

184. *Irish Times*, 30 October 1995.

185. *Seánad Debates*, 8 August 1940.

186. UCDAD, Papers of Patrick McGilligan, P35 (258), 1937.

187. Caitríona Clear, 'No feminine mystique: Popular advice to women of the house in Ireland 1922–54', in Valiulis and O'Dowd (eds.), *Women and Irish History*, pp. 189–206.

188. Ferriter, *Mothers, Maidens and Myths*, pp. 10–18.
189. ibid., pp. 19–20.
190. ibid., pp. 43ff.
191. Hilda Tweedy, *A Link in the Chain: The Story of the Irish Housewives' Association* (Dublin, 1992).
192. O'Callaghan, 'Women and politics', in *Field Day Anthology V*, pp. 168–9.
193. Brian Fallon, *Age of Innocence*, p. 11.
194. NAI, DT 97/9/433, c. 1943.
195. C. B. Murphy, 'Sex, censorship and the Church', *The Bell*, vol. 2, no. 6, September 1941, pp. 65–76.
196. Elizabeth Russell, '"Holy crosses, guns and roses"'.
197. John Horgan, *Irish Media*, pp. 37–48, and Tony Gray, *Mr Smyllie, Sir* (Dublin, 1991).
198. De Burca, *The GAA*.
199. P. O'Crannlaighe, 'Cock fighting', *The Bell*, no. 6, March 1946, pp. 510–13.
200. *Magill*, September 2003, pp. 46–7.
201. Aloys Fleischmann, 'The outlook of music in Ireland', *Studies*, vol. 24, no. 93, March 1935, pp. 121–31, and B. G. McCarthy, 'The cinema as a social factor', *Studies*, vol. 33, March 1944.
202. Adrian Kelly, 'Cultural imperatives: The Irish language revival and the education system', in Augusteijn (ed.), *Ireland in the 1930s*, pp. 29–47.
203. Manning, *James Dillon*, pp. 58–9.
204. Pauric Travers, 'History in primary school: A future for our past?', *History Ireland*, vol. 4, no. 3, Autumn 1996, pp. 13–16.
205. NAI, DT S 13081 A, 7 December 1933.
206. *National University of Ireland Handbook* (Dublin 1932), p. 106.
207. See chapter 6. See also *National Student*, no. 99, December 1946.
208. Seán O'Faoláin, *The Irish* (London, 1947), p. 128.
209. Keith Hopper, *Flann O'Brien: A Portrait of the Artist As a Young Post-Modernist* (Cork, 1995).
210. John McGahern, *Amongst Women* (London, 1991).
211. Quoted in David Cairns and Shaun Richards, *Writing Ireland: Colonialism, Nationalism and Culture* (Manchester, 1988), p. 136.
212. Terence Brown, *Ireland's Literature*, pp. 103–15.
213. Terence Brown, *Ireland: A Social and Cultural History*, pp. 147ff.
214. Sarah Briggs, 'Mary Lavin, questions of identity', *Irish Studies Review*, no. 15, Summer 1996.
215. Brian Fallon, *Age of Innocence*, pp. 80–90.
216. *Ireland Today*, vol. 1, no. 4, September 1936, p. 59.
217. Bruce Arnold, *Mainie Jellet and the Modern Movement in Ireland* (London and New York, 1991).
218. Boyle, 'Industrial conditions in the twentieth century'.
219. PRONI, CAB/4/252, 'Child and maternity welfare', March 1930.
220. ibid.
221. PRONI, Papers of Lord Londonderry, D/3099/2/7/1/1–136, 5 November 1927.
222. Fitzpatrick, *Two Irelands*, p. 179.
223. ibid., p. 145.
224. PRONI, D2072, Minute Book of the Belfast Midnight Mission, 12 December 1934.
225. PRONI, CAB/4/252, 11 March 1930.
226. Brian Barton, *Northern Ireland in the Second World War* (Belfast, 1995), p. 126.
227. DCCA, Corporation Minutes, 22 October 1929.
228. PRONI, HA/10/25, 24 May 1938.

229. ibid., 20 October 1938.

230. ibid., 21 December 1938.

231. ibid., 27 January 1939.

232. Mary Harris, 'Catholicism, nationalism and the labour question in Belfast, 1925–1938', *Bullán*, no. 1, 1997, pp. 15–32.

233. Paddy Devlin, *Yes We Have No Bananas: Outdoor Relief in Belfast, 1920–39* (Belfast, 1981).

234. Ronnie Munck and Bill Rolston, *Belfast in the 1930s: An Oral History* (Belfast, 1997), p. 83.

235. ibid., p. 32.

236. Fitzpatrick, *Two Irelands*, p. 210.

237. Munck and Rolston, *Belfast in the 1930s*, p. 5.

238. James McLoughlin, 'Northern Ireland and British fascism in the inter-war years', *Irish Historical Studies*, vol. XXI, no. 116, November 1995, pp. 537–52.

239. Mary Harris, 'Catholicism, nationalism and the labour question'.

240. PRONI, Papers of Patrick Agnew, D1676/1/1, 15 November 1933 and 24 September 1933.

241. Munck and Rolston, *Belfast in the 1930s*, p. 68.

242. ibid., p. 74.

243. Shea, *Voices and the Sound of Drums*, pp. 121–2.

244. John M. Mogey, *Rural Life in Northern Ireland: Five Regional Studies* (London, New York and Oxford, 1947), pp. 21–33.

245. Maurice Hayes, *Minority Verdict: Experiences of a Catholic Public Servant* (Belfast, 1995), pp. 4–5.

246. Thomas Hennessey, *A History of Northern Ireland, 1920–1996* (Dublin, 1997), p. 68.

247. ibid., p. 149.

248. ibid., p. 169.

249. Hanley, *The IRA, 1926–1936*, p. 59.

250. Hewitt, *Ancestral Voices*, pp. 146ff.

251. PRONI, Papers of Lord Londonderry, D/3099/2/7/117–36, 1 March 1938.

252. McIntosh, *Force of Culture*, p. 50.

253. Jonathan Bardon, *A History of Ulster* (Belfast, 1992), p. 539.

254. Fitzpatrick, *Two Irelands*, p. 236.

255. Shea, *Voices and the Sound of Drums*, p. 172.

256. Hennessey, *A History of Northern Ireland*, p. 58.

257. Bew, Gibbon and Patterson, *Northern Ireland*, p. 60.

258. NAI, DT S 9616, 1937.

259. D. S. Johnson, 'Cattle smuggling on the Irish border, 1932–8', *Journal of Irish Economic and Social History*, vol. 6, 1979, pp. 41–64.

260. *Irish Times*, 29 July 1938.

261. Shea, *Voices and the Sound of Drums*, p. 147.

262. McIntosh, *Force of Culture*, p. 159.

263. Elizabeth McCullough, *A Square Peg: An Ulster Childhood* (Dublin, 1997), pp. 114–15.

264. Brian Barton, *Northern Ireland in the Second World War*, p. 16.

265. *Irish Press*, 1 May 1939, and NAI, DT S 12432, 'NI: Conscription', 1940.

266. John William Blake, *Northern Ireland in the Second World War* (Belfast, 1956), p. 195.

267. James Doherty, *Post 381: The Memoirs of a Belfast Air Raid Warden* (Belfast, 1989), p. 52.

268. Patricia Craig, *Brian Moore: A Biography* (London, 2002), pp. 74ff.

269. ibid., p. 57.

270. Bew, Gibbon and Patterson, *Northern Ireland*, p. 82.

271. ibid., p. 17.
272. PRONI, CAB 4a/20/1/1, 7 October 1941.
273. PRONI, CAB 4a/20/1/2, 3 December 1941.
274. PRONI, CAB 4a/27/1/1, 4 November 1941.
275. Taillon and Urquhart, 'Women, politics and the state', p. 368.
276. ibid.
277. Girvin and Roberts, 'The forgotten volunteers'.
278. Brian Barton, *Northern Ireland in the Second World War*, pp. 81–108.
279. ibid., p. 122.

6: 1945–1960
1. Labhrás Ó Nualláin, 'A comparison of the economic position and trend in Éire and Northern Ireland', *Journal of the Social and Statistical Inquiry Society of Ireland*, ninety-ninth session, 1945–6, pp. 504–41.
2. *Sunday Times*, 6 November 1947.
3. NAI, DT S 14186, 'Twenty-six counties versus Northern Ireland: Contrast of conditions, 1947'.
4. *Belfast Telegraph*, 8 December 1947.
5. *Irish Independent*, 13 August 1949.
6. Kieran A. Kennedy, Thomas Giblin and Deirdre McHugh, *The Economic Development of Ireland in the Twentieth Century* (London and New York, 1988), p. 129.
7. Ó Gráda, *Rocky Road*, p. 92.
8. Bernadette Devlin, *The Price of My Soul* (London, 1969), p. 49.
9. Deane, *Reading in the Dark*, p. 59.
10. Taillon and Urquhart, 'Women, politics and the state', p. 370.
11. PRONI, HLG 1/2/7, 1945.
12. DCCA, Corporation Minutes, 20 December 1945.
13. Ó Gráda, *Rocky Road*, p. 95.
14. Hennessey, *A History of Northern Ireland*, p. 96.
15. *Irish Times*, 12 December 1944.
16. Bew, Gibbon and Patterson, *Northern Ireland*, p. 17.
17. Terry Cradden, *Trade Unionism, Socialism and Partition: The Labour Movement in Northern Ireland 1939–53* (Belfast, 1993).
18. PRONI, Papers of Patrick Agnew, D1676/1/2, 20 November 1946.
19. Christopher Norton, 'The Irish Labour Party in Northern Ireland, 1949–1958', *Saothar*, vol. 21, 1996, pp. 42–54.
20. Brian Barton, *Brookeborough: The Making of a Prime Minister* (Belfast, 1988), pp. 216–18.
21. *Irish Times*, 1 May 1950.
22. David Harkness, *Northern Ireland since 1920* (Dublin, 1983), p. 82.
23. Bew, Gibbon and Patterson, *Northern Ireland*, p. 93.
24. ibid., p. 101.
25. Michael Longley, *Tuppeny Stung: Autobiographical Chapters* (Belfast, 1994), p. 25.
26. McIntosh, *Force of Culture*, p. 105.
27. *Irish Times*, 26 April 1950.
28. Hayes, *Minority Verdict*, p. 20.
29. McIntosh, *Force of Culture*, p. 81.
30. PRONI, CAB 4A/26. 53 and CAB 4A/26, 'Publicity committees', 29 July 1953 and 16 December 1943, and McIntosh, *Force of Culture*, p. 73.
31. McIntosh, *Force of Culture*, p. 181.

32. ibid., p. 196.
33. PRONI, Papers of John Hewitt, D/2833/c/1/8/1, 9 July 1955.
34. Enda Longley, *The Living Stream: Literature and Revisionism in Ireland* (Newcastle-upon-Tyne, 1994), p. 128.
35. DCCA, Corporation Minutes, 14 October 1949 and 25 April 1952.
36. PRONI, HLG, 'Libraries Act 1924', 18 July 1938.
37. ibid., 16 November 1949, and *Irish News*, 9 July 1958.
38. Henry Patterson, 'Brian Maginess and the limits of Liberal Unionism', *Irish Review*, vol. 25, 1999/2000, pp. 95ff.
39. Michael Longley, *Tuppeny Stung*, p. 25.
40. Staunton, *The Nationalists of Northern Ireland*, pp. 163 and 259.
41. Bernadette Devlin, *Price of My Soul*, pp. 15–26.
42. Deane, *Reading in the Dark*, pp. 43 and 181.
43. ibid., p. 203.
44. PRONI, Papers of Anthony Mulvey, D/1862/f/7, 17 June 1948.
45. DCCA, Corporation Minutes, 22 May 1958.
46. NAI, DT S 16272 A, 'Social, economic and cultural co-operation between 26 and 6 counties', and Michael Kennedy, 'Towards co-operation: Seán Lemass and North–South economic relations, 1956–65', *Irish Economic and Social History*, vol. XXIV, 1997.
47. PRONI, HO/5/4/7, April 1958.
48. McIntosh, *Force of Culture*, p. 221, and Harkness, *Northern Ireland since 1920*, p. 84.
49. Clyde (ed.), *Ancestral Voices*, p. 146.
50. Anthony Cronin, 'This time, this place', *The Bell*, vol. XIX, no. 8, July 1954, pp. 5–7.
51. Anthony Cronin, *Dead As Doornails: Bohemian Dublin in the Fifties and Sixties* (Oxford, 1976), p. 2.
52. Denis Johnston, *Orders and Desecrations: The Life of the Playwright Denis Johnston* (Dublin, 1992), p. 106.
53. Séamus O'Farrell, 'The changing pattern of Irish life', *Studies*, vol. 40, December 1951, pp. 428–36.
54. Tom Garvin, 'A Quiet Revolution: The remaking of Irish political culture', in Ray Ryan (ed.), *Writing in the Irish Republic*, pp. 187–204.
55. Liam Kennedy, *The Modern Industrialisation of Ireland, 1940–1988* (Dublin, 1989), p. 13.
56. Brian Fallon, *Age of Innocence*, p. 271.
57. James Meenan, 'National income and expenditure', *Studies*, vol. 40, June 1951, pp. 177–85, and James Meenan, *The Irish Economy since 1922* (Liverpool, 1970).
58. Daly, *Buffer State*, pp. 321–80.
59. Ó Gráda, *Rocky Road*, p. 27, and Michael J. McCormac, 'Crisis in Ireland's balance of trade', *Studies*, vol. 40, September 1951, pp. 257–69.
60. Finola Kennedy, *Family, Economy and Government in Ireland* (Dublin, 1989), p. 15.
61. Whelan, *Ireland and the Marshall Plan*, pp. 109–10 and 249–50.
62. Patrick Lynch, 'The economist and public policy', *Studies*, vol. 42, Autumn 1953, pp. 241–60.
63. *Irish Times*, 10 January 1951.
64. Ó Gráda, *Rocky Road*, p. 49.
65. Michael Cronin and Barbara O'Connor, 'From gombeen to gubeen: Tourism, identity and class in Ireland, 1949–99', in Ray Ryan (ed.), *Writing in the Irish Republic*, pp. 165–87.
66. Ó Gráda, *Rocky Road*, p. 73.
67. *Dáil Debates*, 19 March 1958.
68. *Safe Home Programme* (Dublin, 2001).

69. Aodh de Blacam, 'Emigration: The witness of geography', *Studies*, vol. 39, September 1950, pp. 279–88.
70. Lee, *Ireland 1912–85*, pp. 374–84.
71. Delaney, *Demography, State and Society*, pp. 7–36.
72. NAI, DT S 11582, 30 December 1947.
73. Delaney, *Demography, State and Society*, p. 164.
74. ibid., p. 213.
75. NAI, DT S 14294 A2.
76. Ó Gráda, *Rocky Road*, p. 213.
77. Ferriter, *Mothers, Maidens and Myths*, pp. 34–40.
78. Delaney, *Demography, State and Society*, p. 185.
79. John A. O'Brien (ed.), *Vanishing Irish*, p. 108.
80. Catherine Dunne, *Unconsidered People: The Irish in London* (Dublin, 2003).
81. Ultan Cowley, *The Men Who Built Britain : A History of the Irish Navvy* (Dublin, 2001), pp. 136–7.
82. NAI, DT S 11582 C, 'Irish labour emigration', 23 July 1951.
83. *Irish Press*, 31 August 1951, and *Irish Independent*, 11 September 1951.
84. Delaney, *Demography, State and Society*, p. 194.
85. NAI, DT S 11582, 30 January 1954.
86. *Irish Independent*, 10 May 1954.
87. Fintan O'Toole, *The Politics of Magic: The Work and Times of Tom Murphy* (Dublin, 1987), p. vi.
88. ibid.
89. Mac Amhlaigh, *Irish Navvy*, p. 44.
90. ibid., pp. 64–5.
91. O'Toole, *Politics of Magic*, p. 53.
92. John A. O'Brien, *Vanishing Irish*, p. 33.
93. G. J. Shannon, 'Woman: Wife and mother', *Christus Rex*, vol. 5, 1951, pp. 155–74.
94. *Report of the Commission on Emigration and Other Population Problems* (Dublin, 1954), par. 139.
95. ibid., Reservations, nos. 1–9.
96. NAI, DT S 11582G, 'Irish labour emigration', 23 October 1956.
97. David McCullagh, *A Makeshift Majority: The First Inter-Party Government, 1948–51* (Dublin, 1998), pp. 73–87.
98. ibid.
99. *Irish Times*, 13 November 1999.
100. Browne, *Against the Tide*, and John Horgan, *Noël Browne: Passionate Outsider* (Dublin, 2000).
101. Browne, *Against the Tide*, pp. 22–3 and 198–201.
102. UCDAD, Papers of Michael Hayes, P53, 260 (7), 11 December 1950.
103. Terence De Vere White, 'An aspect of nationalism', *Studies*, vol. 38, March 1949, pp. 8–14.
104. *Dáil Debates*, 13 June 1951.
105. Lawrence Earle, *The Battle of Baltinglass* (London, 1952).
106. Mark Osborne, 'Those county managers', *The Bell*, vol. 9, no. 4, January 1945, pp. 304–14.
107. Ferriter, *Lovers of Liberty?*, pp. 65–7.
108. McCullagh, *Makeshift Majority*, p. 73.
109. McMahon, 'Ireland, the Empire and the Commonwealth'.
110. Mary Daly, 'Irish nationality and citizenship since 1922', *Irish Historical Studies*, vol. XXXII, no. 127, May 2001, pp. 377–408.

111. ibid.
112. *Irish Times*, 18 May 1949.
113. Bowman, *De Valera and the Ulster Question*, p. 276.
114. *Irish Press*, 13 August 1959, and Michael Kennedy, 'Towards co-operation'.
115. UCDAD, Papers of Michael Hayes, P53, 260(7), 29 January 1951.
116. Donal Barrington, 'Uniting Ireland', *Studies*, vol. 46, Winter 1957, pp. 379–402.
117. De Vere White, 'An aspect of nationalism', p. 8.
118. Kevin Rafter, *The Clann: The Story of Clann na Poblachta* (Dublin, 1996), p. 23.
119. UCDAD, Papers of Seán MacEntee, P67, 1542, January 1948.
120. *Garda Report* (Dublin, Stationery Office, 1957).
121. NAI, DT S 11564, 4 January 1957.
122. Bowyer Bell, *The IRA*, p. 205.
123. Lee, *Ireland 1912–85*, p. 329.
124. Quoted in NAI, DT S 15078A.
125. FitzGerald, *All in a Life*, p. 48.
126. Mike Milotte, *Communism in Modern Ireland: The Pursuit of the Worker's Republic* (Dublin, 1984), p. 219.
127. *Irish Independent*, 29 October 1956.
128. R. F. Foster, *Irish Story*, pp. 190ff.
129. *Irish Times*, 14 December 1956.
130. Evanne Kilmurray, *Fight, Starve or Emigrate: A History of the Unemployed Associations in the 1950s* (Dublin, 1988), p. 19.
131. ibid., p. 35.
132. ibid., p. 38.
133. Michael Tierney, 'Strikes and the Labour court: A comment', *Studies*, vol. 36, December 1947, pp. 394–6.
134. Bradley, *Farm Labourers*, pp. 76–92.
135. Michael Gallagher, *The Irish Labour Party in Transition* (Manchester, 1982), pp. 2–29.
136. Cullen Owens, *Louie Bennett*, p. 131.
137. Luddy, 'The labour movement', pp. 561–2.
138. William Trevor, *The Ballroom of Romance and Other Stories* (London, 1972), p. 51.
139. O'Callaghan, 'Women and politics', in *Field Day Anthology V*, p. 171.
140. Clear, *Women of the House*, pp. 25–6.
141. NAI, DENV Reg, box 415, Limerick, 1952.
142. NAI, DT S 6231, Department of Education Memo, 1953.
143. Belinda Farrington, 'The democratisation of higher education and the participation of University women in the labour force, 1920–1950', unpublished MA thesis, University College Dublin, 1985.
144. NAI, DT S 6231, 14 February 1953.
145. Brendan Walsh, 'Marriage in Ireland in the twentieth century', in Art Cosgrove (ed.), *Marriage in Ireland* (Dublin, 1985), pp. 132–51.
146. Jeremiah Newman, 'The future of rural Ireland', *Studies*, vol. XLVII, 1958, pp. 388–409.
147. *Irish Times*, 4 February 1958.
148. Manning, *James Dillon*, p. 300.
149. Rouse, *Ireland's Own Soil*.
150. Daly, *Buffer State*, pp. 400ff.
151. Micheál O'Riain, *On the Move: Corás Iompair Éireann, 1945–95* (Dublin, 1995).
152. Michael J. Sheil, *The Quiet Revolution: The Electrification of Rural Ireland, 1946–1976* (Dublin, 1984), p. 114.
153. ibid., p. 131.

154. Alexander J. Humphreys, *New Dubliners: Urbanisation and the Irish Family* (London, 1966), p. 196.
155. *Irish Times*, 19 September 2003.
156. Gene Kerrigan, *Another Country: Growing Up in '50s Ireland* (Dublin, 1998), p. 84.
157. UCDAD, Papers of Seán MacEntee, P67, 261, 68, 'The problem of extending social insurance', October 1945.
158. UCDAD, Papers of Michael Hayes, P53, 263, 18 June 1951.
159. John Horgan, *Noël Browne*, pp. 292–4.
160. ibid.
161. Whyte, *Church and State*, pp. 239–45.
162. Ruth Barrington, *Health, Medicine and Politics*, pp. 224–5.
163. Séamus O'Farrell, 'The changing pattern of Irish life', p. 430.
164. McKee, 'Church–state relationships', p. 171.
165. Bernadette Fahey, *Freedom of Angels: Surviving Goldenbridge Orphanage* (Dublin, 1999), p. 146.
166. ibid., p. 194.
167. George O'Brien, *The Village of Longing* (Mullingar, 1987), p. 42.
168. Kerrigan, *Another Country*, p. 205.
169. Halliday Sutherland, *Irish Journey* (London, 1956), p. 82.
170. Hubert Butler, *Grandmother and Wolfe Tone* (Dublin, 1996), p. 76.
171. Pauline Bracken, *Light of Other Days: A Dublin Childhood* (Dublin, 1992), p. 104.
172. Heinrich Böll, *Irish Journal* (Cologne, 1961; London, 1967), p. 88.
173. Ferriter, *Nation of Extremes*, p. 181.
174. ibid., p. 188.
175. *Evening Herald*, 22 December 1958.
176. NAI, DT S 15990, 5 June 1959, and *Dáil Debates*, 25 November 1959.
177. Brian Inglis, *Downstart: The Autobiography of Brian Inglis* (London, 1990), p. 90.
178. Annie Ryan, *Walls of Silence: Ireland's Policy towards People with a Disability* (Kilkenny, 1999), p. 22.
179. ibid., pp. 23ff.
180. John Dardis, 'Speaking of scandal', *Studies*, vol. 89, no. 356, Winter 2000, pp. 309–24.
181. Kerrigan, *Another Country*, p. 52.
182. Raftery and O'Sullivan, *Suffer the Little Children*, p. 320.
183. Cecil J. Barrett, 'The dependent child'.
184. Paddy Doyle, *The God Squad* (Dublin, 1988), p. 38.
185. *Irish Society for the Prevention of Cruelty to Children, Annual Reports 1948–9 and 1953–4*, National Library of Ireland.
186. *Dáil Debates*, 28 January 1947.
187. *Dáil Debates*, 23 April 1954.
188. Peter Somerville Large, *Irish Voices: 50 Years of Irish Life, 1916–1966* (London, 1999), p. 258.
189. Raftery and O'Sullivan, *Suffer the Little Children*, p. 90.
190. ibid., pp. 146–8.
191. ibid., pp. 272–3.
192. Sutherland, *Irish Journey*, pp. 77–85.
193. Mike Milotte, *Banished Babies* (Dublin, 1997), p. 16.
194. ibid., p. 54.
195. ibid., pp. 188ff.
196. UCDAD, Papers of Seán MacEoin, P151 (481), and C. F. Casey, 'Adoption in Ireland'.
197. Garrett, 'Abnormal flight'.
198. Touher, *Fear of the Collar*, p. 173.

199. James Donnelly, 'The peak of Marianism in Ireland, 1930–60', in Stewart J. Brown and David W. Miller (eds.), *Piety and Power in Ireland 1760–1960* (Belfast, 2000), pp. 252–84.
200. Mary Kenny, *Goodbye to Catholic Ireland*, pp. 183–96.
201. George O'Brien, *Village of Longing*, pp. 94–116.
202. Bernadette Fahey, *Freedom of Angels*, p. 146.
203. Dermot Healy, *The Bend for Home* (London, 1996), p. 103.
204. Sutherland, *Irish Journey*, pp. 174.
205. ibid.
206. Humphreys, *New Dubliners*, pp. 138–9.
207. Mary Kenny, *Goodbye to Catholic Ireland*, pp. 183–96.
208. Cooney, *John Charles McQuaid*, p. 253.
209. Keogh, *Ireland and the Vatican*, pp. 202–3.
210. Cooney, *John Charles McQuaid*, p. 229.
211. *Irish Times*, 6 November 1999 and 13 November 1999.
212. Cooney, *John Charles McQuaid*, p. 267.
213. ibid., p. 282.
214. Somerville Large, *Irish Voices*, p. 259.
215. Paul Blanshard, *The Irish and Catholic Power: An American Interpretation* (London, 1954), p. 198.
216. Enda Delaney, 'Fr Denis Fahey and Maria Duce 1945–54', unpublished MA thesis, National University of Ireland, Maynooth, 1993.
217. Garvin, 'A Quiet Revolution', p. 192.
218. UCDAD, Papers of Michael Hayes, P53, 262, 18 June 1951.
219. Manning, *James Dillon*, p. 300.
220. NAI, DT S 165243, Lemass to Coyne, 3 November 1959.
221. Kiberd, *Inventing Ireland*, p. 473.
222. John D. Sheridan, 'Irish writing today', *Studies*, vol. 44, Spring 1955, pp. 81–5.
223. Brian Inglis, *Downstart*, p. 195.
224. Kiberd, *Irish Classics*, p. 592.
225. Antoinette Quinn, *Patrick Kavanagh: A Biography* (Dublin, 2001), p. 419.
226. ibid., p. 327.
227. Tóibín, *Penguin Book of Irish Fiction*, p. xxvi.
228. Terence Brown, *Ireland: A Social and Cultural History*, p. 228.
229. Eileen Morgan, 'Question time: Radio and the liberalisation of Irish public discourse after World War II', *History Ireland*, vol. 9, no. 4, Winter 2001, pp. 38–422.
230. FitzGerald, *Reflections*, p. 177.
231. Ferriter, 'The post-war public library service'.
232. ibid.
233. ibid.
234. Christopher Walsh, 'What do we read?', *Furrow*, vol. 1, no. 2, March 1950.
235. Bracken, *Light of Other Days*, p. 73.
236. John Horgan, *Irish Media*, pp. 56ff.
237. Mark O'Brien, *De Valera, Fianna Fáil and the Irish Press*, p. 85.
238. Hugh Oram, *The Newspaper Book: A History of Newspapers in Ireland, 1649–1983* (Dublin, 1983), p. 284.
239. Michael O'Toole, *More Kicks Than Pence: A Life in Irish Journalism* (Dublin, 1992), p. 22.
240. Ivor Kenny, *Talking to Ourselves: Conversations with Editors of the Irish News Media* (Galway, 1994), pp. 150–56.

241. Michael Lawlor, 'The Irish News Agency, 1949–57', unpublished MA thesis, University College Dublin, 1989.

242. Eileen Morgan, 'Question time'.

243. John Horgan, *Irish Media*, p. 68.

244. Diarmaid Ferriter, '"In such deadly earnest": The Bureau of Military History', *Dublin Review*, no. 12, Autumn 2003, pp. 36–65.

245. *Irish School Weekly*, 6 May 1944.

246. *Irish Times*, 20 March 1947.

247. Anthony Cronin, 'The time and the place', *National Student*, no. 99, December 1946, pp. 3–6.

248. *Irish Times*, 14 April 1956.

249. Gavin Ahern, 'Censorship in independent Ireland'.

250. Gerard Whelan and Carolyn Swift, *Spiked: Church–State Intrigue and the "Rose Tatoo"* (Dublin, 2002).

251. *Irish Times*, 19 November 2002.

252. Whelan and Swift, *Spiked*, pp. 21 and 301–3.

253. ibid.

254. NAI, DT S 2321A and B, 27 September 1957.

255. ibid.

256. Denis Donoghue, 'The future of Irish music', *Studies*, vol. 44, Spring 1955, pp. 109–14.

257. *Frederick May String Quartet*, Marco Polo, DDD 8223888, 1996. Sleeve notes by Joseph J. Ryan.

7: 1960–1970

1. Lee, *Ireland 1912–85*, p. 327.

2. *Sunday Tribune*, 24 March 2002.

3. Maria Luddy, 'Magdalen asylums, 1765–1992', in *Field Day Anthology V*, p. 747.

4. *Irish Times*, 1 November 2002.

5. Joe Dunn, *No Tigers in Africa* (Dublin, 1986), p. 31.

6. De Fréine, *The Great Silence*, pp. 230ff.

7. John Montague, *Collected Poems Vol. 1* (Dublin, 1984), p. 162.

8. Seán O'Faoláin, 'Fifty years of Irish writing', *Studies*, vol. LI, 1962, pp. 93–105.

9. Colm Tóibín, 'Inside the Supreme Court', *Magill*, February 1985.

10. Paul Rouse, *Ireland's Own Soil: Government and Agriculture in Ireland, 1945–1965* (Dublin, 2000), p. 239.

11. Enda Delaney, *Irish Emigration since 1921* (Dublin, 2002), p. 26.

12. Ó Gráda, *Rocky Road*, p. 144.

13. O'Connor and Cronin, *Tourism in Ireland*, pp. 25–55.

14. Tobin, *Best of Decades*, p. 137.

15. Fintan O'Toole, *Irish Times Book of the Century*, p. 180.

16. Patrick Lynch, *The Economics of Independence* (Dublin, 1959), p. 2.

17. Tobin, *Best of Decades*, p. 107.

18. Kieran Allen, *Fianna Fáil and Irish Labour: 1926 to the Present* (London, 1997), p. 109, and Paul Bew and Henry Patterson, *Seán Lemass and the Making of Modern Ireland* (Dublin, 1982).

19. Fíonán Ó Muircheartaigh (ed.), *Ireland in the Coming Times* (Dublin, 1997), p. 5.

20. John Horgan, *Seán Lemass: The Enigmatic Patriot* (Dublin, 1999), p. 351.

21. Girvin, *Between Two Worlds*, pp. 169–201.

22. *Irish Press*, 14 January 1966.

23. Alan Bestic, *The Importance of being Irish* (London, 1969), pp. 35–9.
24. NAI, DT S 13469, 26 August 1942.
25. Michael Bannon (ed.), *Planning: The Irish Experience, 1920–1988* (Dublin, 1989), pp. 128ff.
26. NAI, DT 96/6/49, 1 July 1968.
27. *Irish Press*, 23 and 25 September 1969.
28. *Irish Times*, 7 August 1969.
29. NAI, DT 96/6/49, 'Property in Ireland: Acquisition by non-nationals', February–October 1965.
30. Thomas Kinsella, *Collected Poems 1956–94* (Oxford, 1996), p. 76.
31. Patrick Lynch, *Economics of Independence*, p. 13.
32. Raymond Crotty, *Irish Agricultural Production: Its Volume and Structure* (Dublin, 1966), and Ó Gráda, *Rocky Road*, pp. 146–7.
33. Rouse, *Ireland's Own Soil*, p. 139.
34. ibid., p. 156.
35. ibid., pp. 180–207.
36. ibid., p. 209.
37. *Irish Times*, 25 April 1962.
38. *Irish Times*, 1 February 1963.
39. Jeremiah Newman (ed.), *The Limerick Rural Survey, 1958–64* (Tipperary, 1964), p. 214.
40. *Irish Times Annual Review*, 3 January 1966.
41. F. H. A. Aalen, *Gola: The Life and Last Days of an Island Community* (Dublin, 1969), pp. xvi and 84–114.
42. *Irish Times*, 8 February 1968, and NAI, DT 99/1/407, 'National Farmers' Association', February–November 1968.
43. ibid.
44. *Irish Times*, 22 November 1968.
45. John Horgan, *Seán Lemass*, p. xvi.
46. Christabel Bielenberg, *The Road Ahead* (Bantam, 1992), p. 174.
47. Ian McCabe, 'John F. Kennedy in Ireland', *History Ireland*, vol. 1, no. 2, Winter 1993, pp. 38–43.
48. ibid.
49. John Horgan, *Seán Lemass*, pp. 213–52.
50. Stephen Collins, *The Power Game: Ireland under Fianna Fáil* (Dublin, 2000), pp. 21ff.
51. Tobin, *Best of Decades*, p. 143.
52. NAI, DT S 5932 c/2/63, 'Some facts about Ireland', 17 October 1963.
53. Manning, *James Dillon*, pp. 324–9.
54. ibid., pp. 329ff.
55. ibid., pp. 345–63.
56. ibid., p. 375.
57. Michael Gallagher, *The Irish Labour Party*, p. 34.
58. ibid., p. 76.
59. ibid., p. 100.
60. Allen, *Fianna Fáil and Irish Labour*, pp. 148 and 121.
61. Kevin Boland, *The Rise and Fall of Fianna Fáil* (Dublin, 1982), p. 66.
62. Owen Dudley Edwards (ed.), *Conor Cruise O'Brien Introduces Ireland* (London, 1969).
63. Barry Desmond, *Finally and in Conclusion: A Political Memoir* (Dublin, 2000), p. 171.
64. Thornley, 'Ireland: The end of an era?', p. 2.
65. Tom Garvin, 'Change and the political system', in Litton (ed.), *Unequal Achievement: The Irish Experience 1957–82* (Dublin, 1982), pp. 21–43.
66. *Irish Times Annual Review* (Dublin, 1965), p. 5.

67. *Irish Times*, 7 April 1966.
68. NAI, DT S 96/6/193, February 1966.
69. ibid., DT S 8114 C/61, February 1968.
70. Deirdre McMahon, 'Sir Roger Casement: An account from the archives of his reinterment in Ireland', *Irish Archives*, vol. 3, no. 1, Spring 1996, pp. 3–13.
71. ibid.
72. *Irish Press*, 6 September 1966.
73. NAI, DT 97/6/18, 8 March 1966.
74. Tim Pat Coogan, *The IRA* (London, 1980).
75. Rosita Sweetman, *On Our Knees: Ireland 1972* (London, 1972), p. 138.
76. NAI, DT S 11575 B/94, 'IRA activities in Great Britain', February and March 1963.
77. Donal Nevin (ed.), *Trade Union Century* (Dublin, 1994), p. 96.
78. *Irish Independent*, 9 September 1966.
79. Nevin, *Trade Union Century*, p. 151.
80. Tobin, *Best of Decades*, p. 207.
81. *Irish Press*, 13 April 1964, and *Irish Times*, 5 September 1964.
82. *Irish Times*, 4 December 1968.
83. Daly, *Women and Work*, pp. 45–6.
84. June Levine, *Sisters: The Personal Story of an Irish Feminist* (Dublin, 1982), pp. 92–3.
85. Finola Kennedy, *Cottage to Crèche*, p. 130.
86. Mary T. W. Robinson, 'Women and the new Irish State', in MacCurtain and Ó Corráin (eds.), *Women in Irish Society: The Historical Dimension* (Dublin, 1978), pp. 58–71.
87. Dorine Rohan, *Marriage: Irish Style* (London, 1969), p. 29.
88. NAI, DT 96/6/364, 'Status of women', 17 February 1966.
89. Michael Viney, *Marriage Breakdown*, p. 16.
90. ibid.
91. Levine, *Sisters*, pp. 98–9.
92. Cooney, *John Charles McQuaid*, p. 394.
93. David Rottman and Philip O'Connell, 'The changing social structures of Ireland', in Litton (ed.), *Unequal Achievement*, pp. 63–89.
94. NAI, DT 2000/6/67, 9 February 1969, and *Irish Press*, 22 February 1969.
95. Mary E. Daly, '"Turn on the tap": The State, Irish women and running water', in Valiulis and O'Dowd (eds.), *Women and Irish History*, pp. 206–20.
96. Peter Sheridan, *44: A Dublin Childhood* (Dublin, 1999), p. 71.
97. NAI, DT 96/6/184, 20 July 1967, and *Irish Times*, 29 August 1967.
98. *Irish Times*, 24 October 1968.
99. ibid., 12 October 1969.
100. ibid., 13 November 1969.
101. McNiffe, *A History of the Garda Síochána*, p. 161.
102. David Thornley, *The European Challenge* (Dublin, 1963), pp. 34–5.
103. NAI, DT 96/6/679, 'The European Movement: Ireland and the Common Market', 14 June 1966.
104. *Irish Times*, 24 June 1966.
105. NAI, DT 96/6/679, 'The European Movement', July 1966.
106. NAI, DFA 305/384/2 (2), 22 November 1960.
107. NAI, DT 96/6/648, 'Czech crisis', 27 August 1968.
108. NAI, DT 99/1/443, 'Republic of Vietnam War', February 1968.
109. *Irish Press*, 20 April 1968.
110. *Irish Times*, 26 February 1968.
111. NAI, DT 97/6/227, 'Nigeria', October 1967–April 1968.

112. William L. Smith, 'The forgotten war: The Catholic Church and Biafra, 1967–70', *History Ireland*, vol. 8, no. 3, Autumn 2000, pp. 44–9.
113. Enda Staunton, 'The case of Biafra: Ireland and the Nigerian civil war', *Irish Historical Studies*, vol. XXXI, 1998–9, pp. 513–35.
114. NAI, DT 96/6/292, 'Religious, racial and political persecution', October and November 1969.
115. Tom Garvin, 'The strange death of clerical politics in UCD', *Irish University Review*, vol. 2, Winter 1998, pp. 308–15.
116. Desmond Mullin, 'Christus Rex Congress, 1960', *The Furrow*, vol. 11, no. 6, June 1960, pp. 305–15.
117. Colin Murphy and Lynne Adair (eds.), *Untold Stories: Protestants in the Republic of Ireland, 1922–2002* (Dublin, 2002), pp. 38–43.
118. ibid., pp. 158–62.
119. Michael Viney, *The Five Per Cent: A Survey of Protestants in the Republic* (Dublin, 1965).
120. Cooney, *John Charles McQuaid*, p. 347.
121. ibid., p. 390.
122. Deirdre McMahon, 'John Charles McQuaid: Archbishop of Dublin, 1940–1972', in Kelly and Keogh (eds.), *History of the Catholic Diocese of Dublin*, pp. 340–81.
123. Mary Kenny, *Goodbye to Catholic Ireland*, pp. 197–221.
124. *Cork Examiner*, 18 January 1952.
125. *Dáil Debates*, 17 May 1962.
126. Bernard J. Canning, *Bishops of Ireland 1870–1987* (Donegal, 1987), p. 223.
127. Cooney, *John Charles McQuaid*, p. 400.
128. Farmar, *Ordinary Lives*, p. 190.
129. Liam Ryan, *Social Dynamite*, p. 32.
130. NAI, DT 97/6/85, 15 January 1965.
131. Tuairim, *Some of our Children: A Report on the Residential Care of the Deprived Child in Ireland* (London, 1966), p. 10.
132. ibid., p. 15, and *Irish Society for the Prevention of Cruelty to Children, Annual Report 1964* (Dublin, 1964).
133. Matthew Russell, 'The Irish delinquent in England', *Studies*, vol. 53, Summer 1964, pp. 136–48.
134. NAI, DT 96/6/702, 6 February 1965.
135. NAI, DT 96/6/707, 'National Schools; corporal punishment', February–April 1969.
136. Raftery and O'Sullivan, *Suffer the Little Children*, p. 380.
137. ibid., pp. 232–380.
138. Viney, *Growing Old* p. 16.
139. Tobin, *Best of Decades*, p. 83.
140. NAI, DT 2000/6/423, 'Dublin Housing Action Committee', January–March, 1969.
141. Ferriter, *Lovers of Liberty?*, pp. 76–94.
142. Frank McDonald, *The Destruction of Dublin* (Dublin, 1985), p. 6.
143. ibid., pp. 8–37.
144. *Irish Times*, 23 October 1963.
145. *Irish Times*, 30 October 1963.
146. F. O'Doherty and D. McGrath, *The Priest and Mental Health* (Dublin, 1963), p. 16 and p. 53.
147. NAI, DT S 16920A, 8 July 1960.
148. ibid.
149. *Irish Times*, 6 and 9 April 1964.
150. Ferriter, *Nation of Extremes*, p. 203.
151. Donal Conery, *The Irish* (London, 1969), pp. 97–100.

152. Grattan Puxon, *The Victims: Itinerants in Ireland* (Dublin, 1967), p. 13.
153. *Irish Times*, 25 July 1961.
154. Anthony Coughlan, *Aims of Social Policy: Reform in Ireland's Social Security and Health Services* (Dublin, 1966), p. 4.
155. ibid.
156. NAI, DT 97/6/612, 'Health Services, White Paper, 1966', January 1966.
157. Ruth Barrington, *Health, Medicine and Politics*, p. 265.
158. Ó Búachalla, *Irish Education*, p. 281.
159. NAI, DT 96/6/356, 'Education; Developments, 1966–67', September 1966.
160. ibid., 14/9/66.
161. *Irish Times*, 14 September 1966.
162. *Dáil Debates*, 7 November 1968.
163. D. G. Mulcahy and Denis O'Sullivan (eds.), *Irish Education Policy, Process and Substance* (Dublin, 1989), p. 34.
164. Seán Farren, *The Politics of Irish Education, 1920–1965* (Belfast, 1995), pp. 222–9.
165. Seán O Connor, 'Post-primary education: Now and in the future', *Studies*, vol. LVII, no. 227, Autumn 1968, pp. 233–50.
166. NAI, DT 97/6/272, 19 July 1966.
167. Lee, *Ireland 1912–85*, p. 562.
168. 'University Education in Dublin: Statement of Minister for Education, 18 April 1967', *Studies*, vol. 56, Summer 1967, pp. 113–21.
169. Philip Pettit (ed.), *The Gentle Revolution: Crisis in the Universities* (Dublin, 1969), p. 65.
170. John A. Murphy, *The College*, pp. 311–40.
171. Anne McDonagh (ed.), *From Newman to New Woman: UCD Women Remember* (Dublin, 2001), p. 148.
172. Byrne and Purcell, *Time of My Life*, p. 155.
173. De Fréine, *Great Silence*, pp. 226–8.
174. Adrian Kelly, *Compulsory Irish*, pp. 33 and 58.
175. ibid., p. 58.
176. Tobin, *Best of Decades*, pp. 152–4.
177. John Horgan, *Irish Media*, p. 84, and Luke Gibbons, *Transformations in Irish Culture* (Cork, 1996), p. 79.
178. Fintan O'Toole, *Irish Times Book of the Century*, p. 57.
179. Colm Tóibín, 'Gay Byrne: Irish life as cabaret', *Cranebag*, vol. 8, no. 2, 1984.
180. Byrne and Purcell, *Time of My Life*, p. 155.
181. Gibbons, *Transformations*, p. 65.
182. John Horgan, *Irish Media*, p. 80.
183. Julia Carlson, *Banned in Ireland: Censorship and the Irish Writer* (London, 1990), p. 84.
184. Vincent Power, *Send 'Em Home Sweatin': The Showbands' Story* (Dublin, 1990), pp. 397–8.
185. McDonagh (ed.), *Newman to New Woman*, p. 135.
186. Levine, *Sisters*, p. 112.
187. John Montague, *Collected Poems* (Oxford, 1982), p. 62.
188. *Irish Times*, 8 January 1965.
189. Peter Sheridan, *44*, pp. 243–4.
190. *Irish Times*, 19 April 1962.
191. Rouse, 'Sport and the politics of culture', p. 75.
192. *Gaelic Weekly*, 6 January 1968.
193. FitzGerald, *All in a Life*, p. 65.
194. Finola Kennedy, *Cottage to Crèche*, p. 40.
195. John Montague and Thomas Kinsella, *Dolmen Miscellany* (Dublin, 1962), foreword

196. Seán O'Faoláin, 'Fifty years of Irish writing'.

197. D. E. S. Maxwell, *A Critical History of Modern Irish Drama, 1890–1980* (Cambridge, 1984), p. 170.

198. T. P. O'Mahony, 'Theatre in Ireland', *Éire–Ireland*, vol. iv, no. 2, 1969, pp. 93–100.

199. Kiberd, *Inventing Ireland*, p. 566.

200. *Irish Times*, 13 October 1990.

201. Carlson, *Banned in Ireland*, pp. 15–16.

202. ibid., pp. 71–3.

203. Anthony Butler, 'The Irish art scene', *Éire-Ireland*, vol. iv, no. 1, 1969, pp. 114–17.

204. Fintan O'Toole, *Irish Times Book of the Century*, p. 245.

205. Oram, *The Newspaper Book*, chapter 7.

206. Nell McCafferty, *The Best of Nell* (Dublin, 1985).

207. Monica McWilliams, 'Women and political activism in Northern Ireland, 1960–1993', in *Field Day Anthology V*, pp. 378–9.

208. ibid., p. 379.

209. DCCA, Bridget Bond Collection (hereafter BB), 52, 'Case notebook: Housing'.

210. Susan McKay, *Northern Protestants*, p. 331.

211. DCCA, BB (40–49), 'Council's record' and Council Minutes, 31 May 1961, 29 December 1966 and 22 February 1961.

212. *Magill*, November 1978, p. 57.

213. NAI, DT S 14814, 11 January 1956.

214. Maurice Hayes, *Minority Verdict*, p. 5.

215. Marc Mullholland, *Northern Ireland at the Crossroads: Ulster Unionism in the O'Neill Years, 1960–69* (London, 1999).

216. Feargal Cochrane, '"Meddling at the crossroads": The decline and fall of Terence O'Neill', in English and Walker (eds.), *Unionism in Modern Ireland*, pp. 148–69.

217. PRONI, CAB 4/A 26/113, 9 May 1963.

218. Bew, Gibbon and Patterson, *Northern Ireland*, p. 113.

219. NAI, DT 97/6/59, 'Social, cultural and economic co-operation between 26 and 6 counties', 15 November 1966; *Irish Press*, 14 December 1966; and Bew, Gibbon and Patterson, *Northern Ireland*, p. 174.

220. Hennessey, *Northern Ireland*, pp. 131–6.

221. Bew, Gibbon and Patterson, *Northern Ireland*, p. 149, and Michael Farrell, *The Orange State* (London, 1980).

222. Eamonn McCann, *War in an Irish Town* (London, 1980), p. 9.

223. Hennessey, *Northern Ireland*, pp. 134–8.

224. Jackson, 'Local government in Northern Ireland', p. 61.

225. McCann, *War in an Irish Town*, p. 43.

226. ibid., pp. 73–4.

227. *Magill*, July 1983, p. 43.

228. Hennessey, *Northern Ireland*, p. 145.

229. Bernadette Devlin, *Price of My Soul*, p. 119.

230. Michael Kennedy, *Division and Consensus: The Politics of Cross Border Relations in Ireland 1925–1969* (Dublin, 2000), pp. 327–8.

231. Susan McKay, *Northern Protestants*, p. 82.

232. Bernadette Devlin, *Price of My Soul*, p. 155.

233. Gerry Adams, *Falls Memories*, p. 135.

234. DCCA, BB, 43/3, Unemployed Action Committee.

235. DCCA, BB 24 (1), Paddy Doherty – 'Community action, local authorities and government'.

236. Michael Kennedy, *Division and Consensus*, pp. 332–68.

237. *Irish Press*, 11 January 1966.
238. NAI, DT 99/1/281, 25 March 1968.
239. ibid.
240. ibid., 2000/6/659, August 1969.
241. ibid., 99/1/283, 1 November 1968.
242. ibid., 2000/6/657, 'Partition: Government policy', 6 December 1968.
243. Hennessey, *Northern Ireland*, p. 157.
244. NAI, DT 98/6/495, 25 April 1966.
245. Michael Kennedy, *Division and Consensus*, pp. 301–17.
246. ibid.
247. NAI, DT 2000/6/658, 13 August 1969, notes of Secretary of Department of External Affairs.
248. ibid., 2000/1/497, 1 September 1969.
249. Michael Kennedy, *Division and Consensus*, pp. 332–68.
250. ibid.

8: 1970–2000
1. McCann, *War in an Irish Town*, pp. 78–9.
2. DCCA, BB, 50–59, Minute Book of Derry Civil Rights Association, 18 February 1970, 1 December 1970, 5 January 1971 and 21 August 1971.
3. McCann, *War in an Irish Town*, p. 129.
4. DCCA, BB, 50–59, CRA Minute Book, 3 November 1973.
5. DCCA, BB, 40–49, 'Submission on 1973 Emergency Act'.
6. Eamonn McCann, *War and Peace in Northern Ireland* (Dublin, 1998), p. 64.
7. ibid., pp. 14–15.
8. DCCA, BB, 75, NICRA, and BB, Community Development Folder, Joe Mulvenna, 'A road: 1969–77'.
9. Rosita Sweetman, *On Our Knees*, p. 257.
10. Fionnuala O'Connor, *In Search of a State: Catholics in Northern Ireland* (Belfast, 1993), pp. 64 and 161.
11. Ed Moloney, *A Secret History of the IRA* (London, 2002), p. 80.
12. *Magill*, October 1978, p. 7.
13. ibid., February 1998, p. 16.
14. DCCA, BB, 52, DCRA Minute Book, 28 June 1972 and 19 November 1972.
15. McCann, *War and Peace*, p. 206.
16. *Irish Times*, 1 and 2 January 2003, and NAI, DFA/2003/13.
17. ibid.
18. *Magill*, October 1977, p. 3.
19. Moloney, *A Secret History*, p. 112.
20. *Irish Times*, 2 January 2003, and NAI, DFA/2003/13.
21. Shea, *Voices and the Sound of Drums*.
22. McCann, *War in an Irish Town*, p. 140.
23. *Magill*, June and December 1978.
24. *Magill*, January 1978, p. 21.
25. DCCA, BB, 45, 'The Roden Street Report'.
26. *Magill*, November 1977, p. 30.
27. DCCA, BB, 50–59, 'Creggan Estate Tenants' Association', April 1970.
28. McWilliams, 'Women and political activism', p. 382.
29. ibid., p. 383.

30. ibid., pp. 399–400.
31. *Magill*, April 1979, p. 17.
32. Moloney, *A Secret History*, p. 174.
33. *Magill*, April 1979, p. 17.
34. ibid.
35. ibid., December 1979, p. 35.
36. McCann, *War in an Irish Town*, p. 175.
37. DCCA, BB, 73, Letter from National Association for Irish Freedom to the NICRA Executive Committee, 25 January 1979.
38. *Magill*, August 1980, p. 21
39. Tom Bartlett, 'Ulster 1600–2000: Posing the question', *Bullán*, vol. 4, no. 1, Autumn 1998, pp. 5–19.
40. Susan McKay, *Northern Protestants*, p. 336.
41. *Magill*, January 1985, p. 22.
42. *Irish Times*, 21 February 2003.
43. McCann, *War and Peace*, p. 133.
44. Susan McKay, *Northern Protestants*, p. 109.
45. *Irish Times*, 5 February 2000.
46. Henry Patterson, *The Politics of Illusion: Republicanism and Socialism in Modern Ireland* (London, 1989).
47. Peter Taylor, *Loyalists* (London, 1999); Peter Taylor, *Provos: The IRA and Sinn Féin* (London, 1997); and *Guardian*, 7 July 2001.
48. McCann, *War and Peace*, p. 237.
49. Moloney, *A Secret History*, p. xvi.
50. R. F. Foster, *Telling Tales*, p. 179.
51. John Whyte, *Interpreting Northern Ireland* (Oxford, 1990).
52. *Magill*, September 1980, p. 22.
53. *Magill*, August 1981, p. 9.
54. Lee, *Ireland 1912–85*, p. 454.
55. *Magill*, June 1983, p. 3.
56. ibid., September 1984, p. 61.
57. McCann, *War and Peace*, p. 264.
58. Fionnuala O'Connor, *In Search of a State*, p. 98.
59. McCann, *War and Peace*, p. 102.
60. *Magill*, March 1984.
61. FitzGerald, *All in a Life*, p. 464.
62. Mary Robinson, 'Rhetoric and reality' (a review of Clare O'Halloran, *Partition and the Limits of Irish Nationalism* (Dublin, 1987)), *Irish Review*, vol. 3, no. 1, pp. 127–9.
63. FitzGerald, *All in a Life*, p. 575.
64. Moloney, *A Secret History*, p. 241.
65. Whyte, *Interpreting Northern Ireland*, and Cunningham, *British Government Policy*.
66. Susan McKay, *Northern Protestants*, p. 94, and Ó Gráda, *Rocky Road*, p. 131.
67. Anthony Jennings (ed.), *Justice under Fire: The Abuse of Civil Liberties in Northern Ireland* (London, 1988).
68. *Magill*, October 1989, p. 8.
69. *Magill*, September 1982, p. 87, and February 1989, p. 42.
70. McCafferty, *Best of Nell*, pp. 102–115.
71. *Magill*, April 1998.
72. Jackson, 'Unionist history', p. 68.
73. Arthur Aughey, *Under Siege: Ulster Unionism and the Anglo-Irish Agreement* (Belfast, 1989); Paul Teague (ed.), *Beyond the Rhetoric: Politics, the Economy and Social Policy in*

Northern Ireland (London,1987); and Tom Wilson, *Ulster: Conflict and Consent* (Oxford, 1989).

74. *Sunday Tribune*, 25 May 2003.

75. Cochrane, *Unionist Politics*, p. viii.

76. Susan McKay, *Northern Protestants*, p. 290.

77. Jackson, *Ireland 1798–1998*, p. 412.

78. Taylor, *Loyalists*, p. 284.

79. Susan McKay, *Northern Protestants*, p. 213.

80. Quoted in Patrick Roche and Brian Barton (eds.), *The Northern Ireland Question: Myth and Reality* (Aldershot, 1991).

81. Enda Longley, 'A Northern turn', *Irish Review*, no. 15, Spring 1994, pp. 1–14.

82. Susan McKay, *Northern Protestants*, pp. 198–9.

83. Tom Garvin, 'Dialogue for the deaf' (review of Andy Pollak (ed.), *The Opsahl Report on Northern Ireland* (Dublin, 1993)), *Irish Review*, no. 15, Spring 1994, pp. 123–5.

84. *Magill*, April 1990, p. 4.

85. Susan McKay, *Northern Protestants*, p. 78.

86. ibid., p. 276.

87. Desmond Fahey, *How the GAA Survived the Troubles* (Dublin, 2001), pp. 13–16.

88. *Irish Times*, 3 October 2003.

89. *Magill*, June 1998, p. 38.

90. Susan McKay, *Northern Protestants*, p. 36.

91. Jackson, *Ireland 1798–1998*, pp. 408–9, and Marrian, *Man of Wrath*, p. 184.

92. Enda Longley, 'A Northern turn', p. 2.

93. Fionnuala O'Connor, *In Search of a State*, p. 175.

94. *Magill*, November 1989.

95. *Irish Times*, 16 December 1995.

96. *Magill,* April 1987.

97. Brian Hanley, 'The politics of NORAID', lecture delivered to Trinity College Dublin seminars in Contemporary Irish History, May 2003.

98. Conor O'Clery, *The Greening of the White House* (Dublin, 1996), p. 138.

99. Bill Rolston (ed.), *The Media and Northern Ireland* (Belfast, 1991), p. 91.

100. David Miller, *Don't Mention the War: Northern Ireland Propaganda and the Media* (London, 1994).

101. *40 Years of Irish News*, documentary broadcast on RTÉ, 19 December 2002; McCann, *War and Peace*, p. 99; and Susan McKay, *Northern Protestants*, p. 209.

102. Sabine Wichert, *Northern Ireland since 1945* (Harlow, 1991), p. 4.

103. Jackson, 'Unionist history'.

104. Susan McKay, *Northern Protestants*, p. 110, and McCann, *War and Peace*, p. 114.

105. Catherine B. Shannon, 'Recovering the voices of the women of the North', *Irish Review*, no. 12, Spring/Summer 1992, pp. 27–34.

106. Mary Ferris and Anna McGonagle (ed.), *Women's Voices: An Oral History of Women's Health in Northern Ireland* (Dublin, 1992).

107. Susan McKay, *Northern Protestants*, p. 118.

108. Mary O'Dowd, 'Women and politics in Northern Ireland, 1993–2000', in *Field Day Anthology V*, p. 404.

109. ibid., p. 410.

110. Megan Sullivan, *Women in Northern Ireland: Cultural Studies and Material Conditions* (Florida, 1999), p. 4.

111. Mary O'Dowd, 'Women and politics', p. 443.

112. ibid., p. 426.

113. McCafferty, *Best of Nell*, p. 130.

114. Mary O'Dowd, 'Women and politics', p. 414.
115. ibid., p. 452.
116. McCann, *War and Peace*, p. 241.
117. *Irish Times*, 25 May 1998.
118. *Magill*, September 1998, pp. 3–4.
119. Fionnuala O'Connor, *In Search of a State*, pp. 44–97.
120. Collins, *The Power Game*, p. 298.
121. Seán Duignan, *One Spin on the Merry Go-Round* (Dublin, 1996), p. 138.
122. *Magill*, November 1999, p. 14.
123. *Magill*, January 1999.
124. *Magill*, March 1999, p. 9.
125. *Magill*, August 1999, p. 28.
126. *Irish Times*, 24 May 2003.
127. *A House Divided*, documentary shown on RTÉ, 24 May 2003.
128. Seán O'Faoláin, *The Irish* (new edition, London, 1969).
129. Paul Sweeney, *The Celtic Tiger: Ireland's Economic Miracle Explained* (Dublin, 1998), p. 1.
130. Ann Marie Hourihane, *She Moves through the Boom* (Dublin, 2000), p. 148.
131. *Irish Times*, 24 July 2002.
132. *Irish Times*, 16 November 2002, and *Irish Times*, 17 June 2003.
133. John Ardagh, *Ireland and the Irish: Portrait of a Changing Society* (London, 1994), pp. 305–40.
134. Frank McDonald, *The Construction of Dublin* (Dublin, 2000), p. 25.
135. *Sunday Tribune*, 18 June 2000.
136. Finola Kennedy, *Cottage to Crèche*, pp. 22–7.
137. ibid., p. 239.
138. Linda Connolly, *The Irish Women's Movement: From Revolution to Devolution* (Basingstoke, 2002), pp. 71–2.
139. ibid., p. 105.
140. ibid., p. 166.
141. Tim Pat Coogan, *Disillusioned Decades, Ireland 1966–1987* (Dublin, 1987), p. 116.
142. Ardagh, *Ireland and the Irish*, p. 3.
143. *Irish Times*, 29 May 2002.
144. *Irish Times*, 21 September 2002.
145. *Magill*, April 1979, p. 71.
146. *Magill*, January 1982, p. 32.
147. *Magill*, October 1982, p. 7.
148. Ó Gráda, *Rocky Road*, p. 30.
149. ibid., p. 120.
150. *Magill*, August 1986, p. 46.
151. *Irish Times*, 19 September 2000.
152. Coogan, *Disillusioned Decades*, p. 150.
153. Ardagh, *Ireland and the Irish*, p. 315.
154. Kevin Kenny, *The American Irish: A History* (Harlow, 2000), p. 223.
155. ibid., foreword.
156. Ray O'Hanlon, *The New Irish Americans* (Dublin, 1998), p. 157.
157. Sweeney, *Celtic Tiger*, p. 5.
158. O'Hagan (ed.), *The Economy of Ireland*, pp. 40–41.
159. Ó Gráda, *Rocky Road*, p. 90.
160. Denis O'Hearn, *Inside the Celtic Tiger: The Irish Economy and the Asian Model* (London, 1998), p. x.
161. Fintan O'Toole, *Mass for Jesse James*, p. 108.

162. ibid.
163. McDonald, *Construction of Dublin*, pp. 202ff.
164. Hourihane, *She Moves through the Boom*, pp. 48–9.
165. Ferriter, *Lovers of Liberty?*, pp. 26–8, and *Magill*, December 1997, p. 37.
166. *Irish Times*, 27 April 2002.
167. ibid., and Paul Cullen, *With a Little Help from My Friends: Planning Corruption in Ireland* (Dublin, 2002).
168. Fintan O'Toole, *Meanwhile Back at the Ranch: The Politics of Irish Beef* (London, 1995).
169. ibid., p. 241.
170. ibid.
171. Deirdre McMahon, 'Maurice Moynihan (1902–1999), Irish civil servant: An appreciation', *Studies*, vol. 89, no. 353, Spring 2000, pp. 71–7.
172. Duignan, *One Spin*, p. 113.
173. Sam Smyth, *Thanks a Million Big Fella* (Dublin, 1997), p. 98.
174. *Irish Times*, 19 March 2002, and Paul O'Mahony, 'Modern criminality: A response', *Studies*, vol. 88, no. 350, Summer 1999, pp. 120–25.
175. *Irish Times*, 19 March 2002.
176. Fintan O'Toole, *Irish Times Book of the Century*, p. 289.
177. Patrick Keatinge (ed.), *Ireland and EC Membership Evaluated* (London, 1991), p. 279, and Coogan, *Disillusioned Decades*, p. 147.
178. Ardagh, *Ireland and the Irish*, pp. 328–9.
179. J. J. Lee, *Reflections on Ireland in the EEC* (Dublin, 1984).
180. FitzGerald, *Reflections*, p. 102.
181. Richard Sinnott, *Knowledge of the European Union: Irish Public Opinion* (Dublin, 1995), p. 95.
182. Brigid Laffan, *Ireland and South Africa: Irish Government Policy in the 1980s* (Dublin, 1988).
183. *Magill*, January 1998, p. 29.
184. *Irish Times*, 5 February 1983, and Coogan, *Disillusioned Decades*, p. 152.
185. *Magill*, January 1998, p. 31.
186. O'Halpin, *Defending the State*, p. 346.
187. ibid., p. 341.
188. *Magill*, April 1978, p. 21.
189. *Sunday Business Post*, 20 July 2003.
190. *Magill*, May 1980, p. 33.
191. See article on the arms trial controversy by Ronan Fanning, *Sunday Independent*, 13 May 2001.
192. *Cork Examiner*, 30 August 2001, special 160th anniversary edition.
193. *Irish Times*, 19 July 2003.
194. Author's discussion with Colm, Tom and Martin Hefferon, sons of Michael Hefferon.
195. Justin O'Brien, *The Arms Trial* (Dublin, 2000), p. xii.
196. Fintan O'Toole, *Irish Times Book of the Century*, pp. 283–4.
197. Collins, *Cosgrave Legacy*, pp. 187–94.
198. ibid., p. 115.
199. ibid., p. 144.
200. FitzGerald, *All in a Life*, pp. 300–301.
201. Collins, *Cosgrave Legacy*, p. 174.
202. *Irish Times*, 23 October 1999.
203. *Sunday Tribune*, 24 October 1999. See also, Bruce Arnold, *Jack Lynch: Hero in Crisis* (Dublin, 2001), and T. P. O'Mahony, *Jack Lynch: A Biography* (Dublin, 1991).
204. *Magill*, January 1980, p. 22.

205. ibid., June 1981, p. 7.

206. ibid., p. 35.

207. Tom Barrington, *From Big Government to Local Government: The Road to Decentralisation* (Dublin, 1975), and J. J. Lee, 'Centralisation and community', in J. J. Lee (ed.), *Ireland: Towards a Sense of Place* (Cork, 1985), p. 84.

208. Gemma Hussey, *At the Cutting Edge: Cabinet Diaries 1982–1987* (Dublin, 1990), p. 7.

209. *Magill*, February 1987, p. 19.

210. Bruce Arnold, *Haughey: His Life and Unlucky Deeds* (London, 1993), p. 236.

211. ibid., p. 240.

212. *Magill*, June 1983, p. 54.

213. Fergus Finlay, *Mary Robinson: A President with a Purpose* (Dublin, 1990), p. 8.

214. David Quinn, 'An icon for the new Ireland: An assessment of President Robinson', *Studies*, vol. 86, no. 43, Autumn 1997, pp. 207–15.

215. John Waters, *Jiving at the Crossroads* (Belfast, 1991), p. 3.

216. *Magill*, August 1999, p. 17.

217. Fergus Finlay, *Snakes and Ladders* (Dublin, 1998), p. 328.

218. See Peter Donnelly's review of Ardagh, *Ireland and the Irish*, *Studies*, vol. 84, no. 336, Winter 1995, pp. 396–8.

219. Waters, *Jiving at the Crossroads*, p. 57.

220. *Magill*, April 1980, p. 14.

221. Tony Fahey, 'Housing and local government', in Daly (ed.), *County and Town*, pp. 120–30.

222. *Sunday Tribune*, 9 April 2000.

223. *Magill*, November 1997, p. 21.

224. John Sweeney, 'Upstairs, downstairs – the challenge of social inequality', *Studies*, vol. 72, Spring 1983, pp. 6–19.

225. Frank Sammon, 'The problem of poverty in Ireland: Lessons from the Combat Poverty Agency Programme', *Studies*, vol. 71, Spring 1982, pp. 1–13.

226. Quoted in Ferriter, *Lovers of Liberty?*, p. 191.

227. Thomas Farel Heffernan, *Wood Quay: The Clash over Dublin's Viking Past* (Texas, 1988), pp. 132–40.

228. McDonald, *Destruction of Dublin*, pp. 6ff.

229. *Magill*, October 1977, p. 17.

230. *Magill*, August 1988, p. 23.

231. *Magill*, April 1998, p. 7.

232. McDonald, *Construction of Dublin*.

233. *Irish Times*, 13 March 2003.

234. Harry Bohan, Liam Kennedy, Patrick Cummins, and Thomas Nevin, 'Rural Ireland', *Studies*, vol. 74, no. 295, Autumn 1985, pp. 239–386, and Nancy Scheper-Hughes, *Saints, Scholars and Schizophrenics: Mental Illness in Rural Ireland* (California, 1979), p. 4.

235. Ferriter, *Nation of Extremes*, p. 239.

236. Diarmaid Ferriter, 'Sobriety and temperance', in Shane Kilcommins and Ian O'Donnell (eds.), *Alcohol, Society and the Law* (Chichester, 2003), pp. 1–33.

237. *Magill*, November 2001, and June 2003, p. 8.

238. Desmond, *Finally and in Conclusion*, p. 312.

239. Wren, *Unhealthy State*, pp. 50–52.

240. ibid., and *Irish Times*, 2 June 2003.

241. *Irish Times*, 14 June 2003.

242. *Irish Times*, 18 June 2003.

243. Austin L. Leahy and Miriam Wiley (eds.), *The Irish Health System in the Twenty First Century* (Dublin, 1998), p. 3.

244. *Irish Times*, 16 January 2002.
245. *Irish Times*, 31 May 2003.
246. Wren, *Unhealthy State*, pp. 341–5.
247. *Magill Special*, 2000, p. 74.
248. *Magill*, January 1982, p. 32.
249. *Magill*, April 1999, p. 27.
250. Rosita Sweetman, *On Our Backs: Sexual Attitudes in a Changing Ireland* (London, 1979), p. 127.
251. *Magill*, April 1978, p. 14.
252. *Magill*, May 1979, p. 12.
253. Finola Kennedy, *Cottage to Crèche*, pp. 241–2.
254. *Magill*, November 1988, p. 28.
255. *Magill*, December 1983.
256. Sweetman, *On Our Backs*, p. 142.
257. Desmond, *Finally and in Conclusion*, p. 295.
258. Fintan O'Toole, *A Mass for Jesse James*, pp. 174–5.
259. Nell McCafferty, *A Woman to Blame: The Kerry Babies Case* (Dublin, 1985).
260. *Irish Times*, 24 and 25 March 1978.
261. *Magill*, July 1982, p. 23.
262. Desmond Fennell, *Nice People and Rednecks: Ireland in the 1980s* (Dublin, 1986).
263. Frances Gardiner and Mary O'Dowd, 'The women's movement and women politicians in the Republic of Ireland', in *Field Day Anthology V*, pp. 268–9.
264. *Irish Times*, 18 February 1992.
265. Finola Kennedy, *Cottage to Crèche*, pp. 39–42.
266. Gardiner and O'Dowd, 'The women's movement', p. 272, and Emily O'Reilly, *Masterminds of the Right* (Dublin, 1992).
267. Finola Kennedy, *Cottage to Crèche*, p. 236.
268. FitzGerald, *Reflections*, p. xxvi.
269. Finola Kennedy, *Cottage to Crèche*, p. 239.
270. McCafferty, *Best of Nell*, p. 93.
271. *Irish Times*, 17 June 2003.
272. June Levine, 'The women's movement in the Republic of Ireland, 1968–80', in *Field Day Anthology V*, p. 177.
273. ibid., p. 201.
274. Linda Connolly, *The Irish Women's Movement*, p. 220.
275. *Magill*, April 1979, p. 46.
276. *Magill Special*, 2000, p. 34.
277. Finola Kennedy, *Cottage to Crèche*, p. 112.
278. *Irish Times*, 23 May 2000.
279. *Magill*, January 1985, p. 60.
280. *Irish Times*, 2 November 1999, and *Sunday Tribune*, 15 June 2003.
281. *Magill*, November 1997, p. 7.
282. Gardiner and O'Dowd, 'The women's movement', p. 247.
283. Mary Cummins, *The Best of About Women* (Dublin, 1996), p. 32.
284. Nuala O'Faoláin, *Are You Somebody?* (Dublin, 1996), p. 40.
285. Pat Ó Connor, *Emerging Voices: Women in Contemporary Irish Society* (Dublin, 1998), p. 250.
286. Jim Mac Loughlin, *Travellers and Ireland: Whose Country, Whose History?* (Cork, 1995), p. 81.
287. Mícheál Mac Gréil, *Prejudice and Tolerance in Ireland* (Dublin, 1977), and *Irish Times*, 26 February 2000.

288. Paul Cullen, *Asylum Seekers in Ireland* (Cork, 2000).

289. *Irish Times*, 23 January 1999.

290. *Magill*, November 1978, p. 34.

291. ibid., February 1984, p. 31.

292. *Sunday Tribune*, 10 June 2001.

293. Derek Dunne and Gene Kerrigan, *Round Up the Usual Suspects* (Dublin, 1984), pp. 13 and 206–7.

294. Paul O'Mahony, 'Modern criminality', pp. 120–26.

295. ibid., and Eoin O'Sullivan, '"This otherwise delicate subject"'.

296. Paul O'Mahony, *Crime and Punishment in Ireland* (Dublin, 1993), p. 72.

297. *Irish Times*, 30 July 2002.

298. *Magill*, March 1999, p. 37.

299. *Magill*, February 1985.

300. John M. Kelly, *The Irish Constitution* (2nd edn, Dublin, 1984), p. xxix.

301. *Irish Times*, 6 October 2002.

302. *Magill*, June 1987, p. 30.

303. *Magill*, October 1979, p. 94.

304. James Donnelly, 'A church in crisis', and *Irish Times*, 1 November 2002.

305. ibid., p. 12.

306. *Magill*, January 1980, p. 6.

307. ibid., October 1983, p. 39.

308. ibid., January 1984, p. 13.

309. ibid., April 1985, p. 18.

310. J. J. Lee, 'Society and culture', in Litton (ed.), *Unequal Achievement*, pp. 1–18.

311. *Irish Times*, 14 August 1985.

312. Harry Ferguson, 'The paedophile priest: A deconstruction', *Studies*, vol. 84, no. 335, Autumn, 1995, pp. 247–57.

313. Marcus Turner, *Ireland's Holy Wars: The Struggle for a Nation's Soul, 1500–2000* (London, 2001), pp. 387–8.

314. Duignan, *One Spin*, p. 155.

315. Mary Kenny, *Goodbye to Catholic Ireland*, p. 219.

316. Susan McKay, *Sophia's Story*.

317. Eoin O'Sullivan, '"This otherwise delicate subject"', p. 176.

318. Raftery and O'Sullivan, *Suffer the Little Children*, p. 9, and James Donnelly, 'A church in crisis', p. 16.

319. Eoin O'Sullivan, '"This otherwise delicate subject"', p. 179, and Ferguson, 'The paedophile priest', p. 250.

320. *Irish Times*, 1 March 1995.

321. Mary Knny, *Goodbye to Catholic Ireland*, p. 320.

322. *Irish Times*, 6 September 2003.

323. ibid.

324. *Irish Times*, 24 September 2003.

325. *Magill*, September 1985, p. 26.

326. John Horgan, *Irish Media*, p. 154.

327. ibid., p. 112.

328. Mark O'Brien, *De Valera, Fianna Fáil and the Irish Press*, p. xviii.

329. Emily O'Reilly, *Veronica Guerin: The Life and Death of a Crime Reporter* (London, 1998).

330. *Magill Special*, 2000, p. 23.

331. Nuala O'Connor, *Bringing It All Back Home: The Influence of Irish Music* (London, 1991), p. 133.

332. Christy Moore, *One Voice – My Life in Song* (London, 2000), p. 39.

333. Terence Brown, *Ireland: A Social and Cultural History*, p. 276.

334. Breandán Breatnach, *Folk Music and Dances of Ireland* (Cork, 1996), p. 53.

335. Ardagh, *Ireland and the Irish*, p. 98.

336. *Magill Special*, 2000, p. 23.

337. *Magill*, July 1990, p. 13.

338. *Irish Times*, 13 October 2001.

339. *Magill*, December 2000, p. 67.

340. Tom Humphries, *Green Fields: Gaelic Sport in Ireland* (London, 1996), p. 3.

341. Tom Humphries and Patrick Bolger, *Sonia O'Sullivan: Running to Stand Still* (Dublin, 2001), pp. 4 and 85.

342. *Magill*, April 1985, p. 53.

343. Dhonnchadha and Dorgan (eds.), *Revising the Rising*, p. ix.

344. Francis Shaw, 'The canon of Irish history: A challenge', *Studies*, vol. 61, Summer 1972, pp. 117–51.

345. *Irish Times*, 15 November 1979.

346. Terence Brown, *Ireland: A Social and Cultural History*, p. 285.

347. ibid., p. 290.

348. R. F. Foster, 'We are all revisionists now', p. 5, and Lee, *Ireland 1912–85*, p. 652.

349. Lyons, *Culture and Anarchy*.

350. MacCurtain and Ó Corráin (ed.), *Women in Irish Society*, and Mary O'Dowd, 'From Morgan to MacCurtain: Women historians in Ireland from the 1790s to the 1990s', in Valiulis and O'Dowd (ed.), *Women and Irish History*.

351. ibid., p. 56.

352. Jim Smyth, review of Conor McCarthy, *Crisis and Culture in Ireland, 1969–1992* (Dublin, 2001), *History Ireland*, vol. 10, no. 2, Summer 2002.

353. Richard Pine, 'The suburban Shamrock: the embourgeoisement of Irish culture', *Irish Review*, no. 2, 1987, pp. 49–58.

354. John Waters, *An Intelligent Person's Guide to Modern Ireland* (London, 1997), pp. 131–47.

355. Lee, 'Centralisation and community', and Mac Gréil, *Prejudice and Tolerance*, p. 544.

356. Ardagh, *Ireland and the Irish*, p. 13.

357. Kiberd, *Inventing Ireland*, p. 652.

358. Waters, *Jiving at the Crossroads*, p. 3.

359. *Magill*, September 1987, p. 4.

360. Lee, *Ireland 1912–85*, p. 634.

361. *Sunday Tribune*, 9 April 2000.

362. Litton (ed.), *Unequal Achievement*, p. 72, and Ó Buachalla, *Education Policy*, p. 76.

363. *Irish Times*, 27 May 2003.

364. *Irish Times*, 25 October 2003.

365. Ciarán Benson, 'Towards a cultural democracy', *Studies*, vol. 81, no. 321, Spring 1992, pp. 23–34.

366. Brian P. Kennedy, *Dreams and Responsibilities: The State and Arts in Independent Ireland* (Dublin, 1991), p. 2.

367. Séamus Heaney, preface to Mark Patrick Hederman and Richard Kearney (eds.), *Crane Bag Book of Irish Studies, 1977–81* (Dublin, 1982).

368. Séamus Deane, *Celtic Revivals: Essays in Modern Irish Literature* (Winston-Salem, NC, 1987), p. 186.

369. R. F. Foster, 'We are all revisionists now'.

370. Terence Brown, *Ireland: A Social and Cultural History*, p. 320.

371. John Farleigh (ed.), *Far from the Land : New Irish Plays* (London, 1998), foreword.

372. Ruth Barton, 'From history to heritage: Some recent developments in Irish cinema', *Irish Review*, no. 21, Autumn/Winter 1997, pp. 41–57.

373. Kiberd, *Inventing Ireland*, p. 609.

374. Rudiger Imhof (ed.), *Contemporary Irish Novelists* (London, 1990), p. 221.

375. ibid., pp. 113–27, and Rudiger Imhof, *The Modern Irish Novel: Irish Novelists after 1945* (Dublin, 2002).

376. Tóibín, *Penguin Book of Irish Fiction*, p. xxxii.

377. Ray Ryan, 'The Republic and Ireland: Pluralism, politics and narrative form', in Ray Ryan (ed.), *Writing in the Irish Republic*, pp. 82–105.

378. ibid.

379. ibid.

380. McGahern, *Amongst Women*, p. 5.

BIBLIOGRAPHY

Primary sources

National Archives of Ireland, Bishop Street, Dublin
Bureau of Military History (BMH)
Dáil Éireann, including the Land Settlement Commission and the Dáil Éireann
   Courts (Winding-Up) Commission (DE)
Department of the Environment (DENV)
Department of Foreign Affairs (DFA)
Department of Justice (DJ)
Department of Local Government (DELG)
Department of the Taoiseach (DT)

Public Records Office of Northern Ireland, Belfast
Belfast Board of Guardians Minute Books (BG)
Cabinet Secretariat (CAB)
Department of Home Affairs (HA)
Department of Housing, Local Government and Planning (HLGP)
Home Office (HO)
Ministry of Health and Local Government (HLG)
Minute Book of the Belfast Midnight Mission for Unmarried Mothers
Minute Book of the Women's Working Association, Belfast
Minutes of the Executive of the Ulster Farmers' Union
Papers of Anthony Mulvey
Papers of John Hewitt
Papers of Lord Londonderry
Papers of Patrick Agnew
Papers of W. R. Rodgers

Derry City Council Archives, Harbour Museum, Derry City
Bridget Bond Civil Rights Collection
Corporation Minute Books, 1900–1969
Minute Book of the Council of the County Borough of Londonderry, 1906–1913
Minute Book of the Rural District Council, 1908–1949

University College Dublin, Archives Department, Belfield, Dublin
Papers of Desmond FitzGerald
Papers of Donnachadh O'Briain
Papers of Eoin MacNeill
Papers of Ernest Blythe
Papers of Michael Hayes
Papers of Michael Tierney
Papers of Patrick McGilligan
Papers of Richard Mulcahy
Papers of Seán MacEntee
Papers of Seán MacEoin
Papers of Robert Dudley Edwards

Jesuit Archives, Leeson Street, Dublin
Papers of Edmund Coyne
Papers of Edward Cahill
Papers of Patrick Connolly

National Library of Ireland, Kildare Street, Dublin
Vocational Organisation Commission: Minutes of Evidence

Official publications
Report of the Commission on Agriculture (1924)
Report of the Fiscal Inquiry Committee (1924)
Report of the Commission of Inquiry into Intoxicating Liquor (1925)
Report of the Commission on the Gaeltacht (1926)
Report of the Commission of Inquiry on the Relief of the Sick and Destitute Poor (1927)
Report of the Committee on Evil Literature (1927)
Report of the Committee of Inquiry on Widows and Orphans Pensions (1933)
Report of the Commission of Inquiry into Banking, Currency and Credit (1938)
Report of the Inter-Departmental Committee on Seasonal Migration to Great Britain (1938)
Report of the Dublin Housing Inquiry (1943)
Report of the Tribunal of Inquiry on the Fire at St Joseph's Orphanage, Main Street, Cavan (1943)
Report of the Commission on Vocational Organisation (1944)
Report of the Committee on Youth Unemployment (1952)
Report of the Commission on Emigration and Other Population Problems (1956)

Report of the Commission of Inquiry into the Operation of the Laws Relating to the Sale and
   Supply of Intoxicating Liquor (1957)
Programme for Economic Expansion (1958)
Report of the Commission on Itinerancy (1963)
Report on Progress and Prospects by the Minister for Local Government (1964)
Health Services and Their Further Development (1966)
Investment in Education (1967)
Report of the Committee of Inquiry on Mental Illness (1967)
Report of Public Services Organisation Review Group (Devlin Report) (1969)
Membership of the European Communities: Implications for Ireland (1970)
Reformatory Schools: Report of the Committee (1970)

Newspapers and periodicals
An Claidheamh Soluis
An Phoblacht
An tÓglách
Belfast Newsletter
Belfast Telegraph
Catholic Bulletin
Christus Rex
Cork Examiner
Crane Bag
Daily Telegraph
Dublin Opinion
Dublin Review
Economist
Evening Herald
Financial Times
Freeman's Journal
Guardian
Ireland's Own
Irish Catholic
Irish Ecclesiastical Record
Irish Examiner
Irish Farmers' Journal
Irish Homestead
Irish Independent
Irish Monthly
Irish News
Irish Peasant
Irish Times
Irish Worker
Journal of the Social and Statistical Inquiry Society of Ireland
Labour Advocate
Limerick Leader

Times (London)
Magill
Morning Post
National Student
New Ireland Review
Observer
Phoenix
Standard
Studies
Sunday Business Post
Sunday Independent
Sunday Press
Sunday Tribune
The Bell
Torch

Academic journals
Éire–Ireland
Hermathena
History Ireland
Irish Archives
Irish Economic and Social History
Irish Historical Studies
Irish Review
Irish Studies Review
Irish Sword
Past and Present
Rural Ireland
Saothar

Books, articles, theses and other

Aalen, F. H. A., *Gola: The Life and Last Days of an Island Community* (Dublin, 1969)
Abbott, Richard, *Police Casualties in Ireland, 1919–22* (Cork, 2000)
Adams, Gerry, *Falls Memories* (Dingle, 1983)
Adams, Michael, *Censorship: The Irish Experience* (Dublin, 1968)
Allen, Kieran, *Fianna Fáil and Irish Labour: 1926 to the Present* (London, 1997)
Allen, Nicholas, *George Russell and the New Ireland, 1905–1930* (Dublin, 2003)
Anderson, W. K., *James Connolly and the Irish Left* (Dublin, 1994)
Andrews, C. S., *Dublin Made Me* (Bristol, 2002)
Andrews, C. S., *Men of No Property* (Dublin and Cork, 1982)
Ardagh, John, *Ireland and the Irish: Portrait of a Changing Society* (London, 1994)
Arensberg, C., *The Irish Countryman* (New York, 1937)
Arensberg, C. and S. Kimball, *Family and Community in Ireland* (Harvard, 1940)
Arnold, Bruce, *Haughey: His Life and Unlucky Deeds* (London, 1993)
——*Jack Lynch: Hero in Crisis* (Dublin, 2001)

———*Mainie Jellet and the Modern Movement in Ireland* (London and New York, 1991)

Aughey, Arthur, *Under Siege: Ulster Unionism and the Anglo-Irish Agreement* (Belfast, 1989)

Augusteijn, Joost, *From Public Defiance to Guerrilla Warfare: The Experience of Ordinary Volunteers in the Irish War of Independence, 1916–1921* (Dublin, 1996)

———'Motivation: Why did they fight for Ireland? The motivation of volunteers in the revolution', in Augusteijn (ed.), *Irish Revolution*, pp. 103–21

——— (ed.), *Ireland in the 1930s: New Perspectives* (Dublin, 1999)

———*The Irish Revolution 1913–23* (London, 2002)

Ayling, Ronald (ed.), *Seven Plays by Seán O'Casey* (London, 1985)

Ball, Stephen, *A Policeman's Ireland: Recollections of Samuel Waters, RIC* (Cork, 1999)

Bannon, Michael (ed.), *Planning: The Irish Experience, 1920–1988* (Dublin, 1989)

Banville, John, 'The Ireland of de Valera and O'Faoláin', *Irish Review*, nos. 17–18, Winter 1995, pp. 142–53

Bardon, Jonathan, *A History of Ulster* (Belfast, 1992)

———'Belfast at its zenith', *History Ireland*, vol. 1, no. 4, Winter 1993, pp. 46–52

Bardon, Jonathan and Stephen Conlin, *Belfast: 1000 Years* (Belfast, 1985)

Barrett, Cecil J., 'The dependent child', *Studies*, vol. XLIV, Winter 1955, pp. 419–28

Barrington, Brendan (ed.), *The Wartime Broadcasts of Francis Stuart, 1942–1944* (Dublin, 2000)

Barrington, Donal, 'Uniting Ireland', *Studies*, vol. 46, Winter 1957, pp. 379–402

Barrington, Ruth, *Health, Medicine and Politics in Ireland, 1900–1970* (Dublin, 1987)

Barrington, Tom, *From Big Government to Local Government: The Road to Decentralisation* (Dublin, 1975)

Bartlett, Tom, 'Ulster 1600–2000: Posing the question', *Bullán*, vol. 4, no. 1, Autumn 1998, pp. 5–19

Bartlett, Tom and Keith Jeffery (eds.), *A Military History of Ireland* (Cambridge, 1996)

Barton, Brian, *Brookeborough: The Making of a Prime Minister* (Belfast, 1988)

———*Northern Ireland in the Second World War* (Belfast, 1995)

Barton, Brian and Michael Foy, *The Easter Rising* (Gloucestershire, 1999)

Barton, Ruth, 'From history to heritage: Some recent developments in Irish cinema', *Irish Review*, no. 21, Autumn/Winter, 1997, pp. 41–57

Beaumont, Caitriona, 'Women and the politics of equality: The Irish women's movement, 1930–1943', in Valiulis and O'Dowd (eds.), *Women and Irish History*, pp. 159–73

Beckett, J. C., *Belfast: The Making of the City: 1800–1914* (Belfast, 1983)

———*Belfast: The Origin and Growth of an Industrial City* (London, 1967)

Bell, Jonathan, 'The improvement of Irish farm techniques since 1750: Theory and practice', in Flanagan (ed.), *Rural Ireland 1600–1900: Modernisation and Change*, pp. 22–44

Bell, Jonathan Bowyer, *The Secret Army: The IRA* (New Jersey, 1996)

Benson, Ciarán, 'Towards a cultural democracy', *Studies*, vol. 81, no. 321, Spring 1992, pp. 23–34

Beresford-Ellis, Peter, *A History of the Irish Working Class* (London, 1985)

Bestic, Alan, *The Importance of being Irish* (London, 1969)

Bew, Paul, *Conflict and Conciliation in Ireland, 1890–1910: Parnellites and Radical Agrarians* (Oxford, 1987)

——*Ideology and the Irish Question: Ulster Unionism and Irish Nationalism, 1912–1916* (Oxford, 1994)

——*John Redmond* (Dundalk, 1996)

——'The Easter Rising: Lost leaders and lost opportunities', *Irish Review*, 1991–2

——'Sinn Féin, agrarian radicalism and the War of Independence', in Boyce (ed.), *The Revolution in Ireland, 1879–1923*, pp. 217–36

Bew, Paul and Henry Patterson, *Seán Lemass and the Making of Modern Ireland* (Dublin, 1982)

Bew, Paul, Peter Gibbon and Henry Patterson, *Northern Ireland, 1921–1994: Political Forces and Social Classes* (London, 1995)

Bielenberg, Andy, 'Entrepreneurship, power and public opinion in Ireland: The career of William Martin Murphy', *Irish Economic and Social History*, vol. 27, 2000, pp. 25–44

——'Keating, Siemens and the Shannon Scheme', *History Ireland*, vol. 5, no. 3, Autumn 1997, pp. 43–9

Bielenberg, Andy and David Johnson, 'The production and consumption of tobacco in Ireland, 1840–1921', *Irish Economic and Social History*, vol. 25, 1998, pp. 1–22

Bielenberg, Christabel, *The Road Ahead* (Bantam, 1992)

Blake, John William, *Northern Ireland in the Second World War* (Belfast, 1956)

Blanshard, Paul, *The Irish and Catholic Power: An American Interpretation* (London, 1954)

Bohan, Harry, Liam Kennedy, Patrick Cummins and Thomas Nevin, 'Rural Ireland', *Studies*, vol. 74, no. 295, Autumn 1985, pp. 239–386

Bohan, Harry and Gerard Kennedy (eds.), *Are We Forgetting Something? Our Society in the New Millennium* (Dublin, 1999)

Boland, Kevin, *The Rise and Fall of Fianna Fáil* (Dublin, 1982)

Bolger, Dermot (ed.), *Letters from the New Island* (Dublin, 1991)

Bolger, Patrick, *The Irish Co-operative Movement: Its History and Development* (Dublin, 1977)

Böll, Heinrich, *Irish Journal* (Cologne, 1961; London, 1967)

Bolster, Evelyn, *The Knights of Saint Columbanus* (Dublin, 1979)

Bourke, Joanna, *Husbandry to Housewifery: Women, Economic Change and Housework in Ireland, 1890–1914* (Oxford, 1993)

Bourke, Marie, 'Yeats, Henry and the western idyll', *History Ireland*, vol. 11, no. 2, Summer 2003, pp. 28–34

Bourke, Angela, Siobhán Kilfeather, Maria Luddy, Margaret MacCurtain, Gerardine Meaney, Máirín Ní Dhonnchadha, Mary O'Dowd and Clair Wills (eds.), *The Field Day Anthology of Irish Writing: Volume V, Irish Women's Writing and Traditions* (Cork, 2002)

Bowen, Elizabeth, *The Last September* (London, 1948)

Bowman, John, *De Valera and the Ulster Question 1917–73* (Oxford, 1982)

Boyce, D. G., *Englishmen and Irish Troubles: British Public Opinion and the Making of Irish Policy, 1918–22* (London, 1972)

——*Nineteenth-Century Ireland: The Search for Stability* (Dublin, 1990)

Boyce, D. G. (ed.), *The Making of Modern Irish History: Revisionism and the Revisionist Controversy* (London, 1996)

——*The Revolution in Ireland, 1879–1923* (London, 1988)

Boyle, John W., 'Industrial conditions in the twentieth century', in Moody and Beckett (eds.), *Ulster since 1800*, pp. 128–38

Bracken, Pauline, *Light of Other Days: A Dublin Childhood* (Dublin, 1992)

Bradley, Anthony and Maryann Gialanella Valiulis (eds.), *Gender and Sexuality in Modern Ireland* (Amherst, MA, 1998)

Bradley, Dan, *Farm Labourers: Irish Struggle: 1900–1976* (Belfast, 1988)

Brady, Ciaran (ed.), *Interpreting Irish History: The Debate on Historical Revisionism* (Dublin, 1994)

Breatnach, Breandán, *Folk Music and Dances of Ireland* (Cork, 1996)

Brennan, Helen, *The Story of Irish Dance* (Dingle, 1999)

Brewer, John D., *The RIC: An Oral History* (Belfast, 1990)

Briggs, Sarah, 'Mary Lavin, questions of identity', *Irish Studies Review*, no. 15, Summer 1996

Brodie, Malcolm, *100 Years of Irish Football* (Belfast, 1980)

Brown, Stephen, 'What is a nation?', *Studies*, vol. 1, September 1912

Brown, Stewart J. and David W. Miller (eds.), *Piety and Power in Ireland 1760–1960* (Belfast, 2000)

Brown, Terence, *Ireland: A Social and Cultural History 1922–79* (London, 1981)

——*Ireland's Literature: Selected Essays* (Dublin, 1988)

Browne, Noël, *Against the Tide* (Dublin, 1986)

Brundage, David, 'American labour and the Irish question', *Saothar*, vol. 24, 1999, pp. 59–67

Buckland, Patrick, *The Factory of Grievances: Devolved Government in Northern Ireland, 1921–1939* (Dublin, 1979)

Buckley, Margaret, *The Jangling of the Keys* (Dublin, 1938)

Burke, Eimear, '"Our boasted civilisation": Dublin Society and the work of the DSPCC, 1889–1922', *UCD History Review*, 1991, pp. 1–6

——'The treatment of working class children in Dublin by statutory and voluntary organisations 1889–1922', unpublished MA thesis, University College Dublin, 1990

Butler, Anthony, 'The Irish art scene', *Éire–Ireland*, vol. IV, no. 1, 1969, pp. 114–17

Butler, Hubert, *Grandmother and Wolfe Tone* (Dublin, 1996)

——*In the Land of Nod* (Dublin, 1996)

Byrne, Gay with Deirdre Purcell, *The Time of My Life: The Autobiography of Gay Byrne* (Dublin, 1989)

Cairns, David and Shaun Richards, *Writing Ireland: Colonialism, Nationalism and Culture* (Manchester, 1988)

Callanan, Frank, *T. M. Healy* (Cork, 1996)

Campbell Colm, *Emergency Law in Ireland, 1918–1925* (Oxford, 1994)

Campbell, Fergus, 'Rewriting the ranch war: Agrarian conflict in Ireland, 1903–14', paper delivered at conference, Land, Politics and the State, National University of Ireland, Maynooth, 10 May 2003

Campbell, Flann, *The Dissenting Voice: Protestant Democracy in Ulster from Plantation to Partition* (Belfast, 1991)

Canavan, Joseph E., 'The Poor Law Report', *Studies*, vol. 16, no. 4, 1927, pp. 631–44

Canavan, Tony, 'The profession of history: The public and the past', in Ryan (ed.), *Writing in the Irish Republic*

Candy, Catherine, *Priestly Fiction: Popular Irish Novelists of the Early Twentieth Century* (Dublin, 1995)

Canning, Bernard J., *Bishops of Ireland 1870–1987* (Donegal, 1987)

Carlson, Julia, *Banned in Ireland: Censorship and the Irish Writer* (London, 1990)

Carroll, Denis, *They Have Fooled You Again: Michael O'Flannagan* (Dublin, 1993)

Carthy, Paul A., 'Kevin O'Higgins in Government, 1922–7', unpublished MA thesis, University College Dublin, 1980

Casey, Daniel J. and Robert E. Rhodes (eds.), *Views of the Irish Peasantry, 1800–1916* (Hamden, Conn., 1977)

Cathcart, Rex, 'Broadcasting – the early decades', in Farrell (ed.), *Communications and Community in Ireland*

Chesterton, G. K., *Irish Impressions* (London, 1919)

Chubb, Basil, '"Going around prosecuting civil servants": The role of the Irish parliamentary representative', *Political Studies*, vol. XI, no. 3, 1963

Clancy, T. J., *Ireland in the Twentieth Century* (Dublin, 1892)

Clarke, Austin, *Twice around the Black Church* (Dublin, 1962)

Clarke, Kathleen, *Revolutionary Woman: An Autobiography* (Dublin, 1991)

Clear, Caitríona, *Nuns in Nineteenth-Century Ireland* (Dublin, 1987)

—— *Women of the House: Women's Household Work in Ireland, 1926–1961* (Dublin, 2000)

—— 'No feminine mystique: Popular advice to women of the house in Ireland 1922–54', in Valiulis and O'Dowd (eds.), *Women and Irish History*, pp. 189–206.

—— '"The women cannot be blamed": The Commission on Vocational Organisation, Feminism and Home Makers in Independent Ireland in the 1930s and 1940s', in O'Dowd and Wichert (eds.), *Chattel, Servant or Citizen*

—— 'Women of the house in Ireland, 1800–1950', in Bourke et al. (eds.), *Field Day Anthology V*, p. 607

Clery, Arthur, 'Thomas Kettle', *Studies*, vol. 5, no. 2, December 1916, pp. 503–16

Clyde, Tom (ed.), *Ancestral Voices: The Selected Prose of John Hewitt* (Belfast, 1987)

Coakley, John, 'Society and political culture', in Coakley and Gallagher (eds.), *Politics in the Republic of Ireland*, pp. 23–40

Coakley, John and Michael Gallagher (eds.), *Politics in the Republic of Ireland* (Galway, 1992)

Cochrane, Feargal, '"Meddling at the crossroads": The decline and fall of Terence O'Neill', in English and Walker (eds.), *Unionism in Modern Ireland*

Cole, J. A., *Lord Haw Haw – and William Joyce: The Full Story* (London, 1944)

Coleman, Marie, *County Longford and the Irish Revolution, 1910–1923* (Dublin, 2003)

—— 'Mobilisation: the South Longford by-election and its impact on political mobilisation', in Augusteijn (ed.), *Irish Revolution*, pp. 53–70

—— 'The origins of the Irish hospitals sweepstake', *Irish Economic and Social History*, vol. XXIX, 2002, pp. 40–56

Collins, Stephen, *The Cosgrave Legacy* (Dublin, 1996)

—— *The Power Game: Ireland under Fianna Fáil* (Dublin, 2000)

Conery, Donal, *The Irish* (London, 1969)

Connolly, James, *Labour in Ireland* (Dublin 1917, with an introduction by Robert Lynd)

—— *Labour in Irish History* (Dublin, 1917)

Connolly, Linda, *The Irish Women's Movement: From Revolution to Devolution* (Basingstoke, 2002)

Coogan, Tim Pat, *De Valera: Long Fellow, Long Shadow* (London, 1993)

—— *Disillusioned Decades, Ireland 1966–1987* (Dublin, 1987)

Coolahan, John, *Irish Education: Its History and Structure* (Dublin, 1981)

Cooney, John, *John Charles McQuaid: Ruler of Catholic Ireland* (Dublin, 1999)

Corcoran, Tim, 'Social work and the Irish universities', *Studies*, vol. 1, no. 3, September 1912, pp. 534–49

Corish, P. J., *Maynooth College 1795–1995* (Dublin, 1994)

Corkery, Daniel, *The Hidden Ireland: A Study of Catholic Munster in the Eighteenth Century* (Dublin, 1925)

Cosgrove, Art (ed.), *Marriage in Ireland* (Dublin, 1985)

Cosgrove, Art and Donal McCartney (eds.), *Studies in Irish History: Presented to R. Dudley Edwards* (Dublin, 1979)

Costello, Francis J., *Enduring the Most: The Life and Death of Terence MacSwiney* (Dingle, 1996)

Costello, Peter, 'Land and Liam O'Flaherty', in King (ed.), *Famine, Land and Culture in Ireland*

Coughlan, Anthony, *Aims of Social Policy: Reform in Ireland's Social Security and Health Services* (Dublin, 1966)

Cousins, Mel, 'The introduction of children's allowances in Ireland, 1939–44', *Irish Economic and Social History*, vol. XXVI, 1999, pp. 273–95

Cowley, Ultan, *The Men Who Built Britain : A History of the Irish Navvy* (Dublin, 2001)

Cradden, Terry, *Trade Unionism, Socialism and Partition: The Labour Movement in Northern Ireland 1939–53* (Belfast, 1993)

Craig, Patricia, *Brian Moore: A Biography* (London, 2002)

Crean, Thomas, 'Labour and politics in Kerry during the First World War', *Saothar*, vol. 19, 1994, pp. 27–41

Crofton, William, 'The TB problem', *Studies*, vol. 6, no. 23, September 1917, pp. 443–55

Cronin, Anthony, *Dead As Doornails: Bohemian Dublin in the Fifties and Sixties* (Oxford, 1976)

—— 'The time and the place', *The National Student*, no. 99, December 1946, pp. 3–6

—— 'This time, this place', *The Bell*, vol. xix, no. 8, July 1954, pp. 5–7

Cronin, Michael, 'City administration in Ireland', with 'Comment' by James Hogan, *Studies*, vol. 21, no. 47, September 1923, p. 359

Cronin, Michael and Barbara O'Connor, 'From gombeen to gubeen: Tourism, identity and class in Ireland, 1949–99', in Ryan (ed.), *Writing in the Irish Republic*, pp. 165–87

Cronin, Mike, *The Blueshirts and Irish Politics* (Dublin, 1997)

Cronin, Mike and John M. Regan (eds.), *Ireland: The Politics of Independence, 1922–49* (Basingstoke, 2000)

Cronin, S., *The McGarrity Papers: Revelations of the Irish Revolutionary Movement in Ireland and America, 1900–1940* (Tralee, 1972)

Crotty, Raymond, *Irish Agricultural Production: Its Volume and Structure* (Dublin, 1966)

Crowe, Catriona, 'Testimony to a flowering', *Dublin Review*, no. 10, Spring 2003, pp. 42–69

Cullen, Bill, *It's a Long Way from Penny Apples* (Dublin, 2001)

Cullen, Paul, *Asylum Seekers in Ireland* (Cork, 2000)

Cullen Owens, Rosemary, *Louie Bennett* (Cork, 2001)

Cummins, Mary, *The Best of About Women* (Dublin, 1996)

Cunningham, Michael J., *British Government Policy in Northern Ireland, 1969–1989: Its Nature and Execution* (London, 1991)

Curran, Constantine P., 'Tourist development at home and abroad', *Studies*, vol. 15, no. 58, June 1926, pp. 299–308

Dalsimer, Adele M. (ed.), *Visualising Ireland: National Identity and the Pictorial Tradition* (London, 1993)

Daly, Mary E., *The Buffer State: The Historical Roots of the Department of the Environment* (Dublin, 1997)

——*The First Department: A History of the Department of Agriculture* (Dublin, 2002)

——*Industrial Development and Irish National Identity, 1922–39* (Dublin, 1992)

——*A Social and Economic History of Ireland since 1800* (Dublin, 1981)

——*The Spirit of Earnest Inquiry: The Statistical and Social Inquiry Society of Ireland* (Dublin, 1997)

——*Women and Work in Ireland* (Dublin, 1997)

——'"An atmosphere of sturdy independence": The state and the Dublin hospitals in the 1930s', in Jones and Malcolm (eds.), *Medicine, Disease and the State*

——'Irish nationality and citizenship since 1922', *Irish Historical Studies*, vol. XXXII, no. 127, May 2001, pp. 377–408

——'"Oh, Kathleen Ní Houlihán, Your way's a thorny way!": The condition of women in twentieth-century Ireland', in Bradley and Valiulis (eds.), *Gender and Sexuality in Modern Ireland*

——'"Turn on the tap": The State, Irish women and running water', in Valiulis and O'Dowd (eds.), *Women and Irish History*

—— (ed.), *County and Town: One Hundred Years of Local Government in Ireland* (Dublin, 2001)

Dardis, John, 'Speaking of scandal', *Studies*, vol. 89, no. 356, Winter 2000, pp. 309–24

de Blacam, Aodh, *What Sinn Féin Stands For* (London, 1921)

——'Emigration: The witness of geography', *Studies*, vol. 39, September 1950, pp. 279–88

de Burca, Marcus, *The GAA: A History* (Dublin, 1980)

de Fréine, Seán, *The Great Silence* (Dublin, 1965)

De Vere White, Terence, 'An aspect of nationalism', *Studies*, vol. 38, March 1949, pp. 8–14

Deane, Séamus, *Celtic Revivals: Essays in Modern Irish Literature* (Winston-Salem, NC, 1987)

——*Reading in the Dark* (London, 1996)

Deeney, James, *To Cure and to Care: Memoirs of a Chief Medical Officer* (Dublin, 1989)

Delaney, Enda, *Demography, State and Society: Irish Migration to Britain, 1921–1971* (Liverpool, 2000)

——*Irish Emigration since 1921* (Dublin, 2002)

——'Fr Denis Fahey and Maria Duce 1945–54', unpublished MA thesis, National University of Ireland, Maynooth, 1993

Desmond, Barry, *Finally and in Conclusion: A Political Memoir* (Dublin, 2000)

Devlin, Bernadette, *The Price of My Soul* (London, 1969)

Devlin, Paddy, *Yes We Have No Bananas: Outdoor Relief in Belfast, 1920–39* (Belfast, 1981)

Dhonnchadha, Máirín and Theo Dorgan (eds.), *Revising the Rising* (Derry, 1991)

Dickson, David (ed.), *The Gorgeous Mask: Dublin 1700–1850* (Dublin, 1987)

Dillon, T. W., 'Slum clearance: Past and future', *Studies*, vol. 34, March 1945, pp. 13–20

Doherty, James, *Post 381: The Memoirs of a Belfast Air Raid Warden* (Belfast, 1989)

Dolan, Anne, 'Arthur Griffith', paper delivered to St Patrick's College History Society, Dublin City University, 9 December 2002

——'Commemoration: "Shows and stunts are all that is the thing now" – the revolution remembered, 1923–52', in Augusteijn (ed.), *Irish Revolution*, pp. 186–219

——'"Fumbling in the greasy till": Dublin opinion and the Irish bourgeoisie 1922–32', unpublished MA thesis, University College Dublin, 1996

Donnelly, James, 'A church in crisis: The Irish catholic Church today', *History Ireland*, vol. 8, no. 3, Autumn 2000, pp. 12–27

——'The peak of Marianism in Ireland, 1930–60', in Brown and Miller (eds.), *Piety and Power in Ireland*, pp. 252–84

Donoghue, Denis (1), 'The future of Irish music', *Studies*, vol. 44, Spring 1955, pp. 109–14

Donoghue, Denis (2), *Warrenpoint* (London, 1991)

Dooley, Terry, *The Decline of the Big House in Ireland: A Study of Irish Landed Families* (Dublin, 2001)

Dooley, Thomas, *Irish Men or English Soldiers* (Liverpool, 1995)

——'Politics, bands and marketing: Army recruitment in Waterford city, 1914–15', *Irish Sword*, vol. 18, no. 72, 1991

——'The Royal Munster Fusiliers', *History Ireland*, vol. 6, no. 1, Spring 1998, pp. 33–40

Dowling, Michelle, '"The Ireland that I would have": De Valera and the creation of an Irish national image', *History Ireland*, vol. 5, no. 2, Summer 1997, pp. 37–42

Doyle, Lynn, *The Spirit of Ireland* (London, 1935)

Doyle, Paddy, *The God Squad* (Dublin, 1988)

Doyle, Roddy, *A Star Called Henry* (London, 1999)

Dudley Edwards, Owen (ed.), *Conor Cruise O'Brien Introduces Ireland* (London, 1969)

Dudley Edwards, Ruth, *The Faithful Tribe: An Intimate Portrait of the Loyal Institution* (London, 1999)

——*Patrick Pearse: The Triumph of Failure* (London, 1977)

Duggan, J. P., review of Brian Barton, *Northern Ireland in the Second World War*, *History Ireland*, vol. 4, no. 1, Spring 1996, p. 61

Duignan, Seán, *One Spin on the Merry Go-Round* (Dublin, 1996)

Dunn, Eamon, 'Action and reaction: Catholic lay organisations in Dublin in the 1920s and 1930s', *Archivium Hibernicum*, vol. XLVIII, 1994, pp. 107–18

Dunn, Joe, *No Tigers in Africa* (Dublin, 1986)

Dunne, Catherine, *Unconsidered People: The Irish in London* (Dublin, 2003)

Dunne, Derek and Gene Kerrigan, *Round Up the Usual Suspects* (Dublin, 1984)

Dunne, Joseph and James Kelly (eds.), *Childhood and Its Discontents* (Dublin, 2002)

Dunphy, Richard, *The Making of Fianna Fáil Power in Ireland, 1923–48* (Oxford, 1995)

Dunwoody, Janet, 'Child welfare', in Fitzpatrick (ed.), *Ireland and the First World War*

E. M., 'The Church and Labour', *Irish Monthly*, vol. 42, 1914, pp. 25–30

Earle, Lawrence, *The Battle of Baltinglass* (London, 1952)

Earner-Byrne, Lindsey, 'In respect of motherhood: An Irish Catholic social service, 1930–60', paper delivered to Irish Historical Society, Dublin, November 1999

Ehrlich, Cyril, 'Sir Horace Plunkett and agricultrural reform', in Goldstrom and Clarkson (eds.), *Irish Population, Economy and Society*, pp. 271–85

Ellmann, Richard, *James Joyce* (New York and London, 1959)

English, Richard, *Ernie O'Malley: IRA Intellectual* (Oxford, 1998)

——'Unities contradicted', *Irish Review*, no. 5, Autumn 1988, pp. 109–11

English, Richard and Graham Walker (eds.), *Unionism in Modern Ireland: New Perspectives on Politics and Culture* (London, 1996)

Fahey, Bernadette, *Freedom of Angels: Surviving Goldenbridge Orphanage* (Dublin, 1999)

Fahey, Desmond, *How the GAA Survived the Troubles* (Dublin, 2001)

Fahey, Tony, 'Housing and local government', in Daly (ed.), *County and Town*

Fallon, Brian, *An Age of Innocence: Irish Culture 1930–1960* (Dublin, 1998)

Fallon, Charlotte, 'Republican hungerstrikes during the Irish Civil War and its immediate aftermath', unpublished MA thesis, University College Dublin, 1980

Fanning, Ronan, *Independent Ireland* (Dublin, 1983)

——*The Irish Department of Finance, 1922–58* (Dublin, 1978)

——'Economists and governments: Ireland 1922–52', in Murphy (ed.), *Economists and the Irish Economy from the Eighteenth Century to the Present Day*

——'"The Great Enchantment": Uses and abuses of modern Irish history', in Brady (ed.), *Interpreting Irish History*, pp. 138–56

Farleigh, John (ed.), *Far from the Land: New Irish Plays* (London, 1998)

Farmar, Tony, *Ordinary Lives: Three Generations of Irish Middle-class Experience* (Dublin, 1991)

Farrell, Brian, 'The first Dáil and its constitutional documents', in Farrell (ed.),
    Creation of the Dáil
—— 'The unlikely marriage: de Valera, Lemass and the shaping of modern Ireland',
    Etudes Irlandaises, vol. 10, December 1985, pp. 215–22
Farrell, Brian (ed.), *Communications and Community in Ireland* (Dublin, 1984)
—— *The Creation of the Dáil* (Dublin, 1994)
—— *The Irish Parliamentary Tradition* (Dublin, 1973)
Farrell, Michael, *The Orange State* (London, 1980)
Farren, Seán, *The Politics of Irish Education, 1920–1965* (Belfast, 1995)
Farrington, Belinda, 'The democratisation of higher education and the participation
    of University women in the labour force, 1920–1950', unpublished MA
    thesis, University College Dublin, 1985
Farry, Michael, *Sligo 1914–1921: A Chronicle of Conflict* (Trim, 1992)
Fee, Gerard, 'The effects of World War II on Dublin's low income families',
    unpublished Ph.D. thesis, University College Dublin, 1996
Fennell, Desmond, *Nice People and Rednecks: Ireland in the 1980s* (Dublin, 1986)
—— 'Against revisionism', in Brady (ed.): *Interpreting Irish History*, pp. 184–5
—— 'The last years of the Gaeltacht', *The Crane Bag*, 1981
Ferguson, Harry, 'The paedophile priest: A deconstruction', *Studies*, vol. 84, no. 335,
    Autumn, 1995, pp. 247–57
Ferris, Mary and Anna McGonagle (eds.), *Women's Voices: An Oral History of Women's
    Health in Northern Ireland* (Dublin, 1992)
Ferriter, Diarmaid, *Lovers of Liberty? Local Government in Twentieth-Century Ireland*
    (Dublin, 2001)
—— *Mothers, Maidens and Myths: A History of the Irish Countrywomen's Association*
    (Dublin, 1995)
—— *A Nation of Extremes: The Pioneers in Twentieth-Century Ireland* (Dublin, 1999)
—— '"In such deadly earnest": The Bureau of Military History', *Dublin Review*, no.
    12, Autumn 2003, pp. 36–65
—— 'On the State Funerals', *Dublin Review*, no 5, Winter 2001–2, pp. 5–15
—— 'The post-war public library service: Bringing books "to the remotest hamlets
    and the hills"', in McDermott (ed.), *The University of the People: Celebrating
    Ireland's Public Libraries*
—— 'Sobriety and temperance', in Kilcommins and O'Donnell (eds.), *Alcohol,
    Society and the Law*
—— 'Suffer little children? The historical validity of memoirs of Irish childhood',
    in Dunne and Kelly (eds.), *Childhood and Its Discontents*, pp. 69–107
Field, Mary M., 'The politics of turf, 1939–45', unpublished MA thesis, University
    College Dublin, 1990
Finlay, Fergus, *Mary Robinson: A President with a Purpose* (Dublin, 1990)
—— *Snakes and Ladders* (Dublin, 1998)
Finnane, Mark, 'The Carrigan Committee of 1930–31 and the moral condition of
    the Saorstát', *Irish Historical Studies*, vol. 32, 2000–2001, pp. 519–36
Finnegan, Frances, *Do Penance or Perish: A Study of Magdalen Asylums in Ireland*
    (Kilkenny, 2001)

Fisk, Robert, *In Time of War: Ireland, Ulster and the Price of Neutrality, 1939–45* (London, 1943)

FitzGerald, Garret, *All in a Life: An Autobiography* (Dublin, 1991)

——*Reflections on the Irish State* (Dublin 2002)

Fitzpatrick, David, *Irish Emigration 1801–1921* (Dundalk, 1984)

——*Politics and Irish Life, 1913–21: Provincial Experience of War and Revolution* (Dublin, 1977)

——*The Two Irelands: 1912–1939* (Oxford, 1998)

——'Divorce and separation in modern Irish history', *Past and Present*, no.114, 1987, pp. 172–96

——'Militarism in Ireland, 1900–1922', in Bartlett and Jeffery (eds.), *Military History of Ireland*

——'Strikes in Ireland, 1914–21', *Soathar*, vol. 6, 1980, pp. 26–40

Fitzpatrick, David (ed.), *Ireland and the First World War* (Dublin 1988)

——*Revolution? Ireland 1917–23* (Dublin, 1990)

Flanagan, P. (ed.), *Rural Ireland 1600–1900: Modernisation and Change* (Cork, 1987)

Fleischmann, Aloys, 'The outlook of music in Ireland', *Studies*, vol. 24, no. 93, March 1935, pp. 121–31

Flood, Joseph, 'The priest and social action', *Irish Monthly*, vol. 43, 1915

Flynn, Kevin Haddock, 'Soloheadbeg: What really happened?', *History Ireland*, vol. 5, no. 1, Spring 1997, pp. 43–7

Foster, John Wilson, *Recoveries: Neglected Episodes in Irish Cultural History, 1860–1912* (Dublin, 2002)

Foster, R. F., *The Irish Story: Telling Tales and Making It Up in Ireland* (London, 2001)

——*Modern Ireland 1600–1972* (London, 1988)

——*W. B. Yeats, A Life: Volume I: The Apprentice Mage 1865–1914* (Oxford, 1997)

——*W. B. Yeats, A Life, Volume II: The Arch Poet: 1915–1939* (Oxford, 2003)

——'We are all revisionists now', *Irish Review*, no. 1, 1986

——'Writing a life of W. B. Yeats', *Irish Review*, no. 21, Autumn/Winter 1997, pp. 92–103

Fox, R. M., *Louie Bennett: Her Life and Times* (Dublin, 1958)

Foy, Michael, 'Ulster unionist propaganda against Home Rule', *History Ireland*, vol. 4 no. 1, Spring 1996, pp. 49–54

Fraser, Murray, *John Bull's Other Homes: State Housing and British Policy in Ireland* (Liverpool, 1996)

Gageby, Douglas, *The Last Secretary General: Seán Lester and the League of Nations* (Dublin, 1999)

Gailey, Andrew, 'King Carson: An essay on the invention of leadership', *Irish Historical Studies*, vol. XXX, no. 117, May 1996, pp. 66–87

Gallagher, Michael, *The Irish Labour Party in Transition*, (Manchester, 1982)

——'The Pact general election of 1922', *Irish Historical Studies*, vol. 21, no. 84, 1979, p. 413

Gallagher, Ronan, *Violence and Nationalist Politics in Derry City, 1920–1923* (Dublin, 2003)

Gardiner, Frances and Mary O'Dowd, 'The women's movement and women politicians in the Republic of Ireland', in Bourke et al. (eds.), *Field Day Anthology V*

Garrett, P. M., 'The abnormal flight: The migration and repatriation of Irish unmarried mothers', *Social History*, vol. 25, no. 3, 2000, pp. 330–43

Garvin, Tom, *1922: The Birth of Irish Democracy* (Dublin, 1996)

—— *Irish Nationalist Revolutionaries, 1858–1928* (Oxford, 1987)

—— 'The anatomy of a nationalist revolution: Ireland 1858–1928', *Comparative Studies in Society and History*, vol. 28, 1986, pp. 468–501

—— 'Change and the political system', in Litton (ed.), *Unequal Achievement*

—— 'Dialogue for the deaf' (review of Andy Pollak (ed.): *The Opsahl Report on Northern Ireland* (Dublin, 1993)), *Irish Review*, no. 15, Spring 1994, pp. 123–5

—— 'Hogan as political scientist', in Ó Corráin (ed.), *James Hogan*, pp. 177ff.

—— 'Many young men of twenty said goodbye in 1920, many young men of 20 said hello in 1970', *Irish Review*, vol. 23, Winter 1998, pp. 176–8

—— 'Political power and economic development in Ireland: A comparative perspective', in Maurice O'Connell (ed.), *People Power: Proceedings of the Third Annual Daniel O'Connell Workshop*, pp. 32–7

—— 'The politics of denial and cultural defence: The referenda of 1983 and 1986 in context', *Irish Review*, no. 3, 1988, pp. 1–8

—— 'Priests and patriots: Irish separatism and the fear of the modern, 1890–1914', *Irish Historical Studies*, vol. xxv, no. 97, May 1986, pp. 67–81.

—— 'A Quiet Revolution: The remaking of Irish political culture', in Ryan (ed.), *Writing in the Irish Republic*, pp. 187–204

—— 'The Rising and Irish democracy', in Dhonnchadha and Dorgan (eds.), *Revising the Rising*, pp. 21–9

—— 'The strange death of clerical politics in UCD', *Irish University Review*, vol. 2, Winter 1998, pp. 308–15

Gaughan, J. Anthony (ed.), *Memoirs of Senator Joseph Connolly (1885–1961): A Founder of Modern Ireland* (Dublin, 1996)

Ghleanna, Naosc A', 'Twenty years a-withering', *The Bell*, vol. 3, no. 5, February 1942, pp. 379–86

Gibbons, Luke, *Transformations in Irish Culture* (Cork, 1996)

Girvin, Brian, *Between Two Worlds: Politics and Economy in Independent Ireland* (Dublin, 1989)

—— *Ireland and the Second World War: Politics, Society and Remembrance* (Dublin, 2000)

Girvin, Brian and Geoffrey Roberts, 'The forgotten volunteers of World War II', *History Ireland*, vol. 6, no. 1, Spring 1998, pp. 46–2

Goldring, Maurice, *Pleasant the Scholar's Life: Irish Intellectuals and the Construction of the Nation State* (London, 1993)

Goldstrom, J. M. and L. A. Clarkson (eds.), *Irish Population, Economy and Society* (Oxford, 1981)

Gorham, Maurice, *Forty Years of Irish Broadcasting* (Dublin, 1967)

Graham, R. J. and Susan Hood, 'Town tenant protest in late nineteenth- and early twentieth-century Ireland', *Irish Economic and Social History*, vol. 21, 1994, pp. 39–58

Grattan-Flood, William Henry, *A History of Irish Music* (Dublin, 1905)

Gray, Tony, *Mr Smyllie, Sir* (Dublin, 1991)

Greer, Alan, 'Sir James Craig and the construction of Parliament buildings at Stormont', *Irish Historical Studies*, vol. XXXI, no. 123, May 1999, pp. 373–88

Greigg, Mats, '"Marching through the streets and singing and shouting": Industrial struggle and trade unions among female linen workers in Belfast and Lurgan, 1872–1910', *Saothar*, vol. 22, 1997, pp. 29–47

Gribbon, Sybil, *Edwardian Belfast: A Social Profile* (Belfast, 1982)

Grimes, Brendan, 'Carnegie libraries in Ireland' in McDermott (ed.), *University of the People*, pp. 31–43

Guilbride, Alexis, 'A scrapping of every principle of individual liberty: The postal strike of 1922', *History Ireland*, vol. 8, no. 4, Winter 2000, pp. 35–40

Gwynn, Stephen, *Ireland* (Dublin, 1924)

——*Irish Books and Irish People* (Dublin, 1919)

——*John Redmond's Last Years* (London, 1919)

Hamilton, Paul, 'The reformation of mental health legislation in Ireland, 1945–61', unpublished MA thesis, University College Dublin, 1997

Hanley, Brian, *The IRA, 1926–1936* (Dublin, 2002)

——'Moss Twomey, radicalism and the IRA: A reassessment', *Saothar*, vol. 26, 2001, pp. 53–61

——'The politics of NORAID', lecture delivered to Trinity College Dublin seminars in Contemporary Irish History, May 2003

Hannon, P. J., 'Peasant thinkers and students', *New Ireland Review*, August 1901

Harbinson, Robert, *No Surrender: An Ulster Childhood* (Belfast, 1960)

Harkin, Patricia, 'Family policy in Ireland and Vichy France', unpublished MA thesis, University College Dublin, 1992

Harkness, David, *Northern Ireland since 1920* (Dublin, 1983)

Harmon, Maurice, *Seán O'Faoláin* (Dublin, 1984)

——'Cobwebs before the wind: Aspects of the peasantry in Irish literature from 1800 to 1916', in Casey and Rhodes (eds.), *Views of the Irish Peasantry*

Harris, Mary, *The Catholic Church and the Foundation of the Northern Irish State, 1912–30* (Cork, 1993)

——'Catholicism, nationalism and the labour question in Belfast, 1925–1938', *Bullán*, no. 1, 1997, pp. 15–32

Hart, Peter, *The IRA and Its Enemies: Violence and Community in Cork, 1916–23* (Oxford, 1998)

——'The Protestant experience of revolution in Southern Ireland', in English and Walker (eds.), *Unionism in Modern Ireland*

Hartigan, Maurice, 'The Eucharistic Congress, Dublin, 1932', unpublished MA thesis, University College Dublin, 1979

——'The religious life of the Catholic Laity of Dublin, 1920–1940', in Kelly and Keogh (eds.), *A History of the Catholic Diocese of Dublin*

Hayes, Maurice, *Minority Verdict: Experiences of a Catholic Public Servant* (Belfast, 1995)

Healy, Dermot, *The Bend for Home* (London, 1996)

Heaney, Séamus, preface to Hederman and Kearney (eds.), *The Crane Bag Book of Irish Studies, 1977–81*

Hederman, Mark Patrick and Richard Kearney (eds.), *The Crane Bag Book of Irish Studies, 1977–81* (Dublin, 1982)

Hederman, Mark Patrick, 'Climbing into our proper dark – Ireland's place in Europe', in Bohan and Kennedy (eds.), *Are We Forgetting Something?*, pp. 34–52

Heffernan, Thomas Farel, *Wood Quay: The Clash over Dublin's Viking Past* (Texas, 1988)

Hegarty, Peter, *Peadar O'Donnell* (Cork, 1999)

Hennessey, Thomas, *A History of Northern Ireland, 1920–1996* (Dublin, 1997)

Hillan King, Sophia and Seán McMahon (eds.), *Hope and History: Eye Witness Accounts of Life in Twentieth-Century Ulster* (Belfast, 1996)

Hobson, Bulmer, *A Short History of the Irish Volunteers* (Dublin, 1918)

Hogan, Edmund M., *The Irish Missionary Movement: A Historical Survey, 1830–1980* (Dublin, 1990)

Holmes, Janice and Diane Urquhart (eds.), *Coming into the Light: The Work, Politics and Religion of Women in Ulster, 1840–1940* (Belfast, 1994)

Hopkinson, Michael, *Green against Green: The Irish Civil War* (Dublin, 1988)

——*The Irish War of Independence* (Dublin, 2002)

——review of Garvin, *1922*, *Irish Historical Studies*, vol. 30, 1996–7, pp. 628–9

Hopper, Keith, *Flann O'Brien: A Portrait of the Artist As a Young Post-Modernist* (Cork, 1995)

Horgan, James, 'The preconditions of a rural revival' *Irish Monthly*, vol. 67, 1939, pp. 457–75

Horgan, John, *Irish Media: A Critical History since 1922* (London and New York, 2001)

——*Noël Browne: Passionate Outsider* (Dublin, 2000)

——*Seán Lemass: The Enigmatic Patriot* (Dublin, 1999)

Horgan, John J., 'The problem of government', *Studies*, vol. 22, December 1933, pp. 538–60

Hourihane, Ann Marie, *She Moves through the Boom* (Dublin, 2000)

Humphreys, Alexander J., *New Dubliners: Urbanisation and the Irish Family* (London, 1966)

Humphries, Tom, *Green Fields: Gaelic Sport in Ireland* (London, 1996)

Humphries, Tom and Patrick Bolger, *Sonia O'Sullivan: Running to Stand Still* (Dublin, 2001)

Hussey, Gemma, *At the Cutting Edge: Cabinet Diaries 1982–1987* (Dublin, 1990)

Hutton, Seán and Paul Stewart (eds.), *Ireland's Histories: Aspects of State, Society and Ideology* (London and New York, 1991)

Imhof, Rudiger, *The Modern Irish Novel: Irish Novelists after 1945* (Dublin, 2002)

Imhof, Rudiger (ed.), *Contemporary Irish Novelists* (London, 1990)

Inglis, Brian, *Downstart: The Autobiography of Brian Inglis* (London, 1990)

——'Moran of the *Leader* and Ryan of the *Irish Peasant*', in O'Brien (ed.), *The Shaping of Modern Ireland*, pp. 108–23

Inglis, Tom, *Moral Monopoly: The Catholic Church in Modern Irish Society* (Dublin, 1987)

Inoue, Keiko, 'Propaganda II: Propaganda of Dáil Éireann', in Augusteijn (ed.), *Irish Revolution*, pp. 87–103

Jackson, Alvin, *Colonel Edward Saunderson: Land and Loyalty in Victorian Ireland* (Oxford, 1995)

——*Ireland 1798–1998: Politics and War* (Oxford, 1999)

——*Sir Edward Carson* (Dublin, 1993)

——'Irish unionists and the Empire, 1880–1920: Classes and masses', in Jeffery (ed.), *Irish Empire?*

——'The Larne gun running, 1914', *History Ireland*, vol. 1, no. 1, Spring 1993, pp. 35–9

——'Local government in Northern Ireland, 1920–1973', in Daly (ed.), *County and Town*

——'Unionist history', *Irish Review*, no. 7, Autumn 1989, pp. 58–67

——'Unionist myths, 1912–85', *Past and Present*, no. 136, 1992

Jeffery, Keith, *Ireland and the Great War* (Cambridge, 2000)

—— (ed.), *An Irish Empire? Aspects of Ireland and the British Empire* (Manchester 1996)

Jeffery, Keith and Hamilton Norway (eds.), *The Sinn Féin Rebellion As They Saw It* (Dublin, 1999)

Jennings, Anthony (ed.), *Justice under Fire: The Abuse of Civil Liberties in Northern Ireland* (London, 1988)

Johnson, D. S., 'Cattle smuggling on the Irish border, 1932–8', *Journal of Irish Economic and Social History*, vol. 6, 1979, pp. 41–64

Johnston, Denis, *Orders and Desecrations: The Life of the Playwright Denis Johnston* (Dublin, 1992)

Jones, David Seth, 'Land reform, legislation and security of tenure in Ireland after independence', *Éire–Ireland*, vol. 32, 1997–8, pp. 116–43

——'State financing of land division in the Irish Republic', paper delivered to Land, Politics and the State, NUI Maynooth Conference, 10 May 2003

Jones, Greta, 'The campaign against TB in Ireland, 1899–1914', in Jones and Malcolm (eds.), *Medicine, Disease and the State*

——'Eugenics in Ireland; The Belfast Eugenics Society, 1911–1915', *Irish Historical Studies*, vol. XXVIII, no. 109, May 1992, pp. 81–113

Jones, Greta and Elizabeth Malcolm (eds.), *Medicine, Disease and the State in Ireland, 1650–1940* (Cork, 1999)

Jones, Mary, *These Obstreperous Lassies: A History of the IWWU* (Dublin, 1988)

Kearns, Kevin, *Dublin Tenement Life: An Oral History* (Dublin, 1994)

Keatinge, Patrick (ed.), *Ireland and EC Membership Evaluated* (London, 1991)

Kelly, Adrian, *Compulsory Irish: Language and Education in Ireland 1890s–1980s* (Dublin, 2002)

——'Cultural imperatives: The Irish language revival and the education system', in Augusteijn (ed.), *Ireland in the 1930s*, pp. 29–47

——'Social security in Ireland, 1922–52' *Irish Economic and Social History*, vol. XXIV, 1997, pp. 113–15

Kelly, James and Dáire Keogh (eds.), *A History of the Catholic Diocese of Dublin* (Dublin, 2000)

Kelly, John M., *The Irish Constitution* (2nd edn, Dublin, 1984)

Kelly, Paul A., 'The electoral appeal of Cumann na nGaedheal, 1923–32', unpublished MA thesis, University College Dublin, 1981

Kennedy, Brian P., *Dreams and Responsibilities: The State and Arts in Independent Ireland* (Dublin, 1991)

—— 'The failure of the cultural republic: Ireland 1922–39', *Studies*, vol. 81, no. 321, Spring 1992

—— 'The traditional Irish thatched house: Image and reality, 1793–1993', in Dalsimer (ed.), *Visualising Ireland*, pp. 165–80

Kennedy, Denis, *The Widening Gulf: Northern Attitudes to the Independent Irish State, 1919–1949* (Belfast, 1988)

Kennedy, Finola, *Cottage to Crèche: Family Change in Ireland* (Dublin, 2000)

—— *Family, Economy and Government in Ireland* (Dublin, 1989)

—— 'The suppression of the Carrigan Report: A historical perspective on child abuse', *Studies*, vol. 89, no. 356, Winter 2000, pp. 354–63

Kennedy, Kieran A., Thomas Giblin and Deirdre McHugh, *The Economic Development of Ireland in the Twentieth Century* (London and New York, 1988)

Kennedy, Liam, *Colonialism, Religion and Nationalism in Ireland* (Belfast, 1996)

—— *The Modern Industrialisation of Ireland, 1940–1988* (Dublin, 1989)

—— 'The early response of the Irish Catholic clergy to the Co-operative movement', *Irish Historical Studies*, vol. xxi, 1977–8, pp. 55–75

Kennedy, Michael, *Division and Consensus: The Politics of Cross Border Relations in Ireland 1925–1969* (Dublin, 2000)

—— *Ireland and the League of Nations* (Dublin, 1995)

—— '"In spite of all impediments": The early years of the Irish Diplomatic Service', *History Ireland*, vol. 7, no. 1, Spring 1999, pp. 18–22

—— 'Towards Co-operation: Seán Lemass and North–South economic relations, 1956–65', *Irish Economic and Social History*, vol. XXIV, 1997

Kenny, Ivor, *Talking to Ourselves: Conversations with Editors of the Irish News Media* (Galway, 1994)

Kenny, Kevin, *The American Irish: A History* (Harlow, Longman, 2000)

—— (ed.), *Ireland and the British Empire* (Oxford, 2004)

Kenny, Mary, *Goodbye to Catholic Ireland* (Dublin, 2000)

Keogh, Dermot, *Ireland and the Vatican: The Diplomacy of Church–State Relations, 1922–60* (Cork, 1995)

—— *Jews in Twentieth-Century Ireland: Refugees, Anti-Semitism and the Holocaust* (Cork, 1998)

—— 'De Valera, Hitler and the visit of condolence, May 1945', *History Ireland*, vol. 5, no. 3, Autumn 1997, pp. 58–61

—— *Twentieth-Century Ireland: Nation and State* (Dublin, 1994)

—— 'William Martin Murphy and the origins of the 1913 Lockout', *Saothar*, vol. 4, 1978, pp. 15–35

Kerrigan, Gene, *Another Country: Growing Up in '50s Ireland* (Dublin, 1998)

Kettle, Thomas, *The Open Secret of Ireland* (Dublin, 1912)

Kiberd, Declan, *Inventing Ireland: The Literature of the Modern Nation* (London, 1995)

—— *Irish Classics* (London, 2000)

—— 'The elephant of revolutionary forgetfulness', in Dhonnchadha and Dorgan (eds.), *Revising the Rising*

—— 'Inventing Irelands', *The Crane Bag*, vol. 8, 1984, pp. 11–26

Kilcommins, Shane and Ian O'Donnell (eds.), *Alcohol, Society and the Law* (Chichester, 2003)

Kilmurray, Evanne, *Fight, Starve or Emigrate: A History of the Unemployed Associations in the 1950s* (Dublin, 1988)

King, Carla (ed.), *Famine, Land and Culture in Ireland* (Dublin, 2000)

Kinsella, Thomas, *Collected Poems 1956–94* (Oxford, 1996)

Klaus, Gustav (ed.), *Strong Words, Brave Deeds: The Poetry, Life and Times of Thomas O'Brien* (Dublin, 1994)

Kleinrichert, Denise, *Republican Internment and the Prison Ship Argenta, 1922* (Dublin, 2001)

Kline, Benjamin, 'Churchill and Collins 1919–22: Admirers or adversaries?', *History Ireland*, vol. 1, no. 3, Autumn 1993, pp. 38–44

Kostick, Conor, *Revolution in Ireland: Popular Militancy 1917 to 1923* (London, 1996)

Kotsonouris, Mary, *Retreat from Revolution: The Dáil Courts, 1920–24* (Dublin, 1994)

Krause, David (ed.), *The Letters of Seán O'Casey* (London, 1975)

Laffan, Brigid, *Ireland and South Africa: Irish Government Policy in the 1980s* (Dublin, 1988)

Laffan, Michael, *The Resurrection of Ireland: The Sinn Féin Party 1916–1923* (Cambridge, 1999)

Larkin, Emmet, *James Larkin: Irish Labour Leader 1876–1947* (London, 1977)

Lawlor, Michael, 'The Irish News Agency, 1949–57', unpublished MA thesis, University College Dublin, 1989

Leahy, Austin L. and Miriam Wiley (eds.), *The Irish Health System in the Twenty First Century* (Dublin, 1998)

Lee, J. J., *Ireland 1912–85: Politics and Society* (Cambridge, 1989)

—— *Reflections on Ireland in the EEC* (Dublin, 1984)

—— 'Aspects of corporatist thought in Ireland: The Commission on Vocational Organisation, 1939–43', in Cosgrove and McCartney (eds.), *Studies in Irish History*, pp. 324–47

—— 'Centralisation and community', in Lee (ed.), *Ireland: Towards a Sense of Place*

—— 'In search of Patrick Pearse', in Dhonnchadha and Dorgan (eds.), *Revising the Rising*

—— 'The Irish Constitution of 1937', in Hutton and Stewart (eds.), *Ireland's Histories*

—— 'A sense of place in the Celtic tiger', in Bohan and Kennedy (eds.), *Are We Forgetting Something?*

—— 'Society and culture', in Litton (ed.), *Unequal Achievement*

—— interview in *History Ireland*, vol. 3, no. 2, Summer 1995, pp. 44–8

Lee, J. J. (ed.), *Ireland: Towards a Sense of Place* (Cork, 1985)

Levenson, Leah, *With Wooden Sword: A Portrait of Francis Sheehy Skeffington: Militant Pacifist* (Boston and Dublin, 1983)

Levin, Harry (ed.), *James Joyce: The Essential James Joyce* (London, 1990)

Levine, June, *Sisters: The Personal Story of an Irish Feminist* (Dublin, 1982)

—— 'The women's movement in the Republic of Ireland, 1968–80', in Bourke et al. (eds.), *Field Day Anthology V*

Litton, Frank (ed.), *Unequal Achievement: The Irish Experience 1957–82* (Dublin, 1982)

Loftus, Richard, *Nationalism in Modern Anglo-Irish Poetry* (Wisconsin, 1964)

Logan, John, *Teachers Union: The TUI and Its Forerunners in Irish Education, 1899–1994* (Dublin, 1999)

Longley, Enda, *The Living Stream: Literature and Revisionism in Ireland* (Newcastle upon Tyne, 1994)

———'A Northern turn', *Irish Review*, no. 15, Spring 1994, pp. 1–14

Longley, Michael, *Tuppeny Stung: Autobiographical Chapters* (Belfast, 1994)

Lowe, W. J. and E. L. Malcolm, 'The domestication of the RIC, 1836–1922', *Irish Economic and Social History*, vol. 19, 1992, pp. 27–49

Luddy, Maria, *Hanna Sheehy Skeffington* (Dundalk, 1995)

———'The labour movement in Ireland, 1800–2000', in Bourke et al. (eds.), *Field Day Anthology V*, p. 550

———'Magdalen asylums, 1765–1992', in Bourke et al. (eds.), *Field Day Anthology V*

———'Women and politics in Ireland, 1860–1918', in Bourke et al. (eds.), *Field Day Anthology V*, p. 83

Luddy, Maria and Cliona Murphy (eds.), *Women Surviving* (Dublin, 1990)

Lynch, John, 'Harland and Wolff: Its labour force and industrial relations, Autumn 1919', *Saothar*, vol. 22, 1997, pp. 47–63

Lynch, P., 'The social revolution that never was', in Williams (ed.), *The Irish Struggle 1916–26*

Lynch, Patrick, *The Economics of Independence* (Dublin, 1959)

———'The economist and public policy', *Studies*, vol. 42, Autumn 1953, pp. 241–60

Lynd, Robert, *Home Life in Ireland* (London, 1909)

Lyons, F. S. L., *Culture and Anarchy in Ireland, 1890–1939* (Oxford, 1982)

———*Ireland since the Famine* (London, 1971)

———'The Great Debate', in Farrell (ed.), *The Irish Parliamentary Tradition*

———'The twentieth century', in Moody and Beckett (eds.), *Ulster since 1800*

Mac Amhlaigh, Dónál, *An Irish Navvy: The Diary of an Irish Exile* (London, 1964)

Mac Gréil, Micheál, *Prejudice and Tolerance in Ireland* (Dublin, 1977)

Mac Lochlainn, Alf, 'Gael and Peasant, a case of mistaken identity', in Casey and Rhodes, *Views of the Irish Peasant, 1800–1916* (Hamden, Connecticut, 1977)

Mac Loughlin, Jim, *Travellers and Ireland: Whose Country, Whose History?* (Cork, 1995)

Mac Sweeney, A. M., 'A study of poverty in Cork city', *Studies*, vol. 4, no. 13, March 1915, pp. 93–104

Macardle, Dorothy, *Tragedies of Kerry, 1922–1923* (Dublin, 1924)

MacAvoy, Sandra L., 'The regulation of sexuality in the Irish Free State, 1929–1935', in Jones and Malcolm (eds.), *Medicine, Disease and the State*

MacCurtain, Margaret, 'Fullness of life: Defining female spirituality in twentieth-century Ireland', in Luddy and Murphy (eds.), *Women Surviving*

MacCurtain, Margaret and Dhonnacha Ó Corráin (eds.), *Women in Irish Society: The Historical Dimension* (Dublin, 1978)

MacDonagh, Oliver, W. F. Mandle and Pauric Travers (eds.), *Irish Culture and Nationalism, 1750–1950* (Dublin, 1983)

MacEoin, Uinseann, *Survivors* (Dublin, 1987)

MacGill, Patrick, *Children of the Dead End: The Autobiography of an Irish Navvy* (London, 1914)

Malcolm, Elizabeth, 'The house of strident shadows: The asylum, the family and emigration in post-Famine rural Ireland', in Jones and Malcolm (eds.), *Medicine, Disease and the State*, pp. 177–95

Mandle, W. F., *The GAA and Irish Nationalist Politics 1884–1924* (London, 1987)

Manning, Maurice, *James Dillon: A Biography* (Dublin, 1999)

Mansergh, Martin, 'A rising curve from subversion to statecraft', *Fortnight*, February 1991, pp. 28–31

—— review of Bew, *Ideology and the Irish Question*, *History Ireland*, vol. 3, no. 1, Spring 1995, pp. 56–7

—— review of O'Callaghan, *British High Politics and Nationalist Ireland*, *History Ireland*, vol. 3, no. 1, Spring 1995, pp. 56–7

—— review of O'Mahony and Delanty, *Rethinking Irish History*, *History Ireland*, vol. 7, no. 1, Spring 1999, p. 53

Mansergh, Nicholas, 'John Redmond', in O'Brien (ed.), *Shaping of Modern Ireland*, pp. 38–50

Marsh, Michael and Michael Gallagher, *Days of Blue Loyalty: The Politics of Membership of the Fine Gael Party* (Dublin, 2002)

Martin, F. X., '1916: Interpreting the Rising', in Boyce (ed.), *Making of Modern Irish History*, pp. 163–88

—— (ed.), *Leaders and Men of the Easter Rising* (London, 1967)

Martin, F. X. and F. J. Byrne (eds.), *The Scholar Revolutionary: Eoin MacNeill, 1867–1945* (Shannon, 1973)

Matthews, P. J., *Revival: The Abbey Theatre, Sinn Féin, the Gaelic League and the Co-operative Movement* (Cork, 2003)

Maume, Patrick, *'Life that is exile': Daniel Corkery and the Search for Irish Ireland* (Belfast, 1993)

—— *The Long Gestation: Irish Nationalist Life 1891–1918* (Dublin, 1999)

—— 'The political thought of Arthur Clery', *Irish Historical Studies*, vol. XXXI, no. 122, November 1998, pp. 222–40

Maxwell, D. E. S., *A Critical History of Modern Irish Drama, 1890–1980* (Cambridge, 1984)

McCabe, Ian, 'John F. Kennedy in Ireland', *History Ireland*, vol. 1, no. 2, Winter 1993, pp. 38–43

McCafferty, Nell, *The Best of Nell* (Dublin, 1985)

—— *A Woman to Blame: The Kerry Babies Case* (Dublin, 1985)

McCann, Eamonn, *War and Peace in Northern Ireland* (Dublin, 1998)

—— *War in an Irish Town* (London, 1980)

McCarthy, B. G., 'The cinema as a social factor', *Studies*, vol. 33, March 1944

McCarthy, Charles, *The Distasteful Challenge* (Dublin, 1969)

—— *Trade Unions in Ireland, 1894–1960* (Dublin, 1977)

McCarthy, Conor, *Crisis and Culture in Ireland, 1969–1992* (Dublin, 2001)

McCarthy, Jude, 'State-aided island migration, 1930–60', unpublished MA thesis, University College Dublin, 1997

McConvery, Brendan, 'Hell, fire and poitín: Redemptorist missions in the Irish Free State', *History Ireland*, vol. 8, no. 3, Autumn 2000, pp. 18–22

McCoole, Sinéad, *Hazel: A Life of Lady Lavery, 1880–1935* (Dublin, 1996)

——*No Ordinary Women: Irish Female Activists in the Revolutionary Years* (Dublin, 2003)

McCormac, Michael J., 'Crisis in Ireland's balance of trade', *Studies*, vol. 40, September 1951, pp. 257–69

McCormack, W. J. (ed.), *Austin Clarke: Selected Poems* (London, 1992)

McCourt, Frank, *Angela's Ashes: Memoir of a Childhood* (London, 1996)

McCracken, Donal P., *The Irish Pro-Boers 1877–1902* (South Africa, 1989)

McCullagh, David, *A Makeshift Majority: The First Inter-Party Government, 1948–51* (Dublin, 1998)

McCullough, Elizabeth, *A Square Peg: An Ulster Childhood* (Dublin, 1997)

McDermott, Norma (ed.), *The University of the People: Celebrating Ireland's Public Libraries* (Dublin, 2003)

McDonagh, Anne (ed.), *From Newman to New Woman: UCD Women Remember* (Dublin, 2001)

McDonald, Frank, *The Construction of Dublin* (Dublin, 2000)

——*The Destruction of Dublin* (Dublin, 1985)

McDonnell, E. T., 'The Dublin labour movement 1894–1967', unpublished MA thesis, University College Dublin

McGahern, John, *Amongst Women* (London, 1991)

——'The church and its spire', in Tóibín (ed.), *Soho Square 6*

McGarry, Fearghal, *Frank Ryan* (Cork, 2002)

——*Irish Politics and the Spanish Civil War* (Cork, 1999)

McInerney, M. H., 'Constructive work for Catholic Irish women', *Irish Monthly*, vol. LII, no. 610, April 1924, pp. 188–94

McInerney, Michael, *Peadar O'Donnell: Irish Social Rebel* (Dublin, 1974)

McIntosh, Gillian, *The Force of Culture: Unionist Identities in Contemporary Ireland* (Cork, 1999)

McKay, Enda, 'The housing of the rural labourer, 1883–1916', *Saothar*, vol. 17, 1992, pp. 27–40

McKay, James, *Michael Collins: A Life* (Edinburgh, 1996)

McKay, Susan, *Northern Protestants: An Unsettled People* (Belfast, 2000)

——*Sophia's Story* (Dublin, 1998)

McKee, Eamonn, 'Church–state relationships and the development of Irish health policy: The Mother and Child Scheme 1944–53', *Irish Historical Studies*. vol. XXV, no. 98 (1989), pp. 159–94

McKenna, Lambert, *The Church and Labour* (Dublin, 1914)

——*The Church and Working Women* (Dublin, 1913)

——'School attendance in Dublin', *Studies*, vol. 17, no. 3, March 1916, pp. 109–18

McLoughlin, Barry, 'Delegated to the "New World": Irish communists at Moscow's International Lenin School, 1927–37', *History Ireland*, vol. 7, no. 4, Winter 1999, pp. 37–40

McLoughlin, James, 'Northern Ireland and British fascism in the inter-war years', *Irish Historical Studies*, vol. XXI, no. 116, November 1995, pp. 537–52

McLoughlin, Michael, 'One step forward, two steps back: A labour history of the Emergency', unpublished MA thesis, University College Dublin, 1993

McMahon, Deirdre, *Republicans and Imperialists: Anglo-Irish Relations in the 1930s* (London, 1984)

———'Ireland, the Empire and the Commonwealth, 1886–1972', in Kenny (ed.), *Ireland and the British Empire*

———'John Charles McQuaid: Archbishop of Dublin, 1940–1972', in Kelly and Keogh (eds.), *History of the Catholic Diocese of Dublin*, pp. 331–44

———'Maurice Moynihan (1902–1999), Irish civil servant: An appreciation', *Studies*, vol. 89, no. 353, Spring 2000, pp. 71–7

———'Sir Roger Casement: An account from the archives of his reinterment in Ireland', *Irish Archives*, vol. 3, no. 1, Spring 1996, pp. 3–13

McMahon, Deirdre (ed.), *Their New Ireland: Moynihan Family Correspondence in Peace and War, 1908–1918* (Dublin, 2004)

McManus, Ruth, *Dublin, 1910–1940: Shaping the City and Suburbs* (Dublin, 2001)

McNiffe, Liam, *A History of the Garda Síochána* (Dublin, 1997)

McWilliams, Monica, 'Women and political activism in Northern Ireland, 1960–1993', in Bourke et al. (eds.), *Field Day Anthology V*

Meenan, James, *The Irish Economy since 1922* (Liverpool, 1970)

———'National income and expenditure', *Studies*, vol. 40, June 1951, pp. 177–85

Miller, David, *Don't Mention the War: Northern Ireland Propaganda and the Media* (London, 1994)

Miller, Liam (ed.), *Austin Clarke, Collected Poems* (Dublin, 1974)

Milotte, Mike, *Banished Babies* (Dublin, 1997)

———*Communism in Modern Ireland: The Pursuit of the Worker's Republic* (Dublin, 1984)

Mitchell, Arthur, 'Alternative government: Exit Britannia – the formation of the Irish national state 1918–21', in Augusteijn (ed.), *Irish Revolution*

Mitchell, David, *A Peculiar Place: The Adelaide Hospital, Dublin* (Dublin, 1991)

Mogey, John M., *Rural Life in Northern Ireland: Five Regional Studies* (London, New York and Oxford, 1947)

Moloney, Ed, *A Secret History of the IRA* (London, 2002)

Montague, John, *Collected Poems* (Oxford, 1982)

———*Collected Poems Vol. 1* (Dublin, 1984)

Montague, John and Thomas Kinsella, *Dolmen Miscellany* (Dublin, 1962)

Moody, T. W., 'Irish history and Irish mythology', *Hermathena*, nos. CXXIV–CXXVII, 1978–9, pp. 7–25

———'The social history of modern Ulster', in Moody and Beckett (eds.), *Ulster since 1800*

Moody, T. W. and J. C. Beckett (eds.), *Ulster since 1800: A Social Survey* (London, 1957)

Moore, Christy, *One Voice – My Life in Song* (London, 2000)

Moore, Henry, 'The nursing profession and its needs', *Studies*, vol. 31, September 1942, pp. 273–95

Moore, J. Walter, *A Life of Erwin Schrödinger* (Cambridge, 1994)

Morgan, Austen, *James Connolly: A Political Biography* (Manchester, 1988)

———*Labour and Partition: The Belfast Working Class, 1905–1923* (London, 1991)

Morgan, Eileen, 'Question time: Radio and the liberalisation of Irish public discourse after World War II', *History Ireland*, vol. 9, no. 4, Winter 2001, pp. 38–422

Morris, Ewan, '"God Save the King" versus "The Soldier's song": The 1929 Trinity College National Anthem dispute and the politics of the Irish Free State', *Irish Historical Studies*, vol. 31, 1998–9, pp. 72–91

Morrissey, Thomas J., *A Man Called Hughes: The Life and Times of Séamus Hughes, 1881–1943* (Dublin, 1991)

——*Towards a National University: William Delaney (1835–1924)*, (Dublin 1983)

——*William J. Walsh: Archbishop of Dublin, 1841–1921* (Dublin 2000)

Morton, Cole, *Hungry for Home: Leaving the Blaskets: A Journey from the Edge of Ireland* (Harmondsworth, 2000)

Moynihan, Maurice, *Statements and Speeches of Eamon de Valera 1917–1973* (Dublin and New York, 1980)

Mulcahy, D. G. and Denis O'Sullivan (eds.), *Irish Education Policy, Process and Substance* (Dublin, 1989)

Mulcahy, Risteárd, *Richard Mulcahy (1886–1971): A Family Memoir* (Dublin, 1999)

Mulhall, Daniel, *A New Day Dawning: A Portrait of Ireland in 1900* (Cork, 1999)

Mullholland, Marc, *Northern Ireland at the Crossroads: Ulster Unionism in the O'Neill Years, 1960–69* (London, 1999)

Mullin, Desmond, 'Christus Rex Congress, 1960', *The Furrow*, vol. 11, no. 6, June 1960, pp. 305–15

Munck, Ronnie and Bill Rolston, *Belfast in the 1930s: An Oral History* (Belfast, 1997)

Murphy, Antoin E. (ed.), *Economists and the Irish Economy from the Eighteenth Century to the Present Day* (Dublin, 1983)

Murphy, Brian P., 'Nationalism: The framing of the Constitution of the Irish Free State, 1922 – the defining battle for the Irish Republic', in Augusteijn (ed.), *Irish Revolution*, pp. 135–51

Murphy, C. B., 'Sex, censorship and the Church', *The Bell*, vol. 2, no. 6, September 1941, pp. 65–76

Murphy, Colin and Lynne Adair (eds.), *Untold Stories: Protestants in the Republic of Ireland, 1922–2002* (Dublin, 2002)

Murphy, Donal, *Blazing Tar Barrels and Standing Orders: Tipperary North's First County and District Councils, 1899–1902* (Tipperary, 1999)

Murphy, Jeremiah, *When Youth was Mine: A Memoir of Kerry* (Dublin, 1998)

Murphy, John A., 'Academe and playing fields', review of W. F. Mandle, *The GAA and Irish Nationalist Politics 1884–1924*, *Irish Review*, no. 4, Spring 1988, pp. 139–42

——'The achievement of Eamon de Valera', in Murphy and O'Carroll (eds.), *De Valera and His Times*

——*The College: A History of Queen's/University College Cork* (Cork, 1995)

Murphy, John A. and John P. O'Carroll (eds.), *De Valera and His Times* (Cork, 1986)

Murphy, William, 'Prophets or patsies: The influence of Swift and Berkeley on nationalist rhetoric', *UCD History Review*, vol. 10, 1996, pp. 15–23

Murray, Christopher (ed.), *Irish University Review, Thomas Murphy Issue*, vol. 17, no. 1, Spring 1987, pp. 24–31

Murray, James, *Galway: A Medico-Social History* (Galway, 1996)

Murray, Patrick, *Oracles of God: The Roman Catholic Church and Irish Politics, 1922–37* (Dublin, 2000)

Murray, Paul, 'On Saint Helena's bleak shore', *History Ireland*, vol. 11, no. 1, Spring 2003, pp. 10–11

Murray, Peter, 'Electoral politics and the Dublin working class before the First World War', *Saothar*, vol. 6, 1980

Myers, Kevin, *From the Irish Times Column, An Irishman's Diary* (Dublin, 2000)

Nash, Catherine, 'Embodying the nation: The west of Ireland landscape and national identity', in O'Connor and Cronin (eds.), *Tourism in Ireland*

Neeson, Eoin, *The Civil War 1922–23* (Dublin, 1966)

Neill, Margaret, 'Homeworkers in Ulster, 1850–1911', in Holmes and Urquhart (eds.), *Coming into the Light*

Nevin, Donal (ed.), *Trade Union Century* (Dublin, 1994)

Newman, Jeremiah, 'The future of rural Ireland', *Studies*, vol. XLVII, 1958, pp. 388–409

Newman, Jeremiah (ed.), *The Limerick Rural Survey, 1958–64* (Tipperary, 1964)

Noland, J. A., *Ourselves Alone: Emigration from Ireland, 1885–1920* (Lexington, 1989)

Norton, Christopher, 'The Irish Labour Party in Northern Ireland, 1949–1958', *Saothar*, vol. 21, 1996, pp. 42–54

Norway, Hamilton, *The Sinn Féin Rebellion As They Saw It* (Dublin, 1999)

Novick, Ben, *Conceiving Revolution: Irish Nationalist Propaganda during the First World War* (Dublin, 2001)

Ó Buachalla, Séamus, *Education Policy in Twentieth-Century Ireland* (Dublin, 1988)

Ó Buachalla, Séamus (ed.), *A Significant Irish Educationalist: The Educational Writings of P. H. Pearse* (Dublin, 1980)

Ó Canainn, Tomás, *Traditional Music in Ireland* (London, 1978)

Ó Ciosáin, Eamon, *An t-Éireannach 1934–37: Nuachtan Soisíalach Gaeltachta* (Dublin, 1993)

Ó Connor, Pat, *Emerging Voices: Women in Contemporary Irish Society* (Dublin, 1998)

Ó Connor, Seán, 'Post-primary education: Now and in the future', *Studies*, vol. LVII, no. 227, Autumn 1968, pp. 233–50

Ó Corráin, Donnchadh (ed.), *James Hogan; Revolutionary, Historian and Political Scientist* (Dublin, 2001)

Ó Crualaoich, Gearóid, 'The primacy of form: A "folk ideology" in de Valera's politics', in O'Carroll and Murphy (ed.), *De Valera and His Times*

Ó Gráda, Cormac, *A Rocky Road: The Irish Economy since the 1920s* (Manchester, 1997)

——'"The greatest blessing of them all": The old age pension in Ireland', *Past and Present*, no. 175, May 2002, pp. 124–61.

Ó hEithir, Breandán, *Over the Bar* (Dublin, 1991)

Ó hÓgartaigh, Margaret, 'Dr Dorothy Price and the elimination of childhood TB', in Augusteijn (ed.), *Ireland in the 1930s*, pp. 67–83

Ó Muircheartaigh, Fíonán (ed.), *Ireland in the Coming Times* (Dublin, 1997)

Ó Nualláin, Labhrás, 'A comparison of the economic position and trend in Éire and Northern Ireland', *Journal of the Social and Statistical Inquiry Society of Ireland*, ninety-ninth session, 1945–6

O'Brien, Conor Cruise, *States of Ireland* (London, 1972)
—— (ed.), *The Shaping of Modern Ireland* (London, 1960)
O'Brien, Flann, 'The Dance Halls', *The Bell*, vol. 1, no. 5, February 1941, pp. 44–53
O'Brien, George, *The Village of Longing* (Mullingar, 1987)
—— 'A challenge to the planners', *Studies*, vol. 33, June 1944, pp. 210–18
O'Brien, John A. (ed.), *The Vanishing Irish* (New York, 1954)
O'Brien, Justin, *The Arms Trial* (Dublin, 2000)
O'Brien, Mark, *De Valera, Fianna Fáil and the Irish Press* (Dublin, 2001)
O'Byrne, Robert, *Hugh Lane, 1875–1915* (Dublin, 2000)
O'Callaghan, Margaret, *British High Politics and Nationalist Ireland* (Cork, 1994)
—— 'Language, nationality and cultural identity in the Irish Free State, 1922–7', *Irish Historical Studies*, vol. 24, no. 94, November 1984, pp. 226–45
—— 'Old parchment and water: The Boundary Commission of 1925 and the copper-fastening of the Irish border', *Bullán*, vol. 4, no. 2, pp. 27–55
—— 'Women and politics in independent Ireland, 1921–68', in Bourke et al. (eds.), *Field Day Anthology V*
O'Carroll, J. P. and John A. Murphy (eds.), *De Valera and His Times* (Cork, 1996)
O'Casey, Seán, *Mirror in My House: The Autobiographies of Seán O'Casey, vol. 1* (New York, 1956)
O'Clery, Conor, *The Greening of the White House* (Dublin, 1996)
O'Connell, Maurice (ed.), *People Power: Proceedings of the Third Annual Daniel O'Connell Workshop* (Dublin, 1993)
O'Connor, Barbara and Michael Cronin (eds.), *Tourism in Ireland: A Critical Analysis* (Cork, 1993)
O'Connor, Emmet, *James Larkin* (Cork, 2002)
—— *A Labour History of Waterford* (Waterford, 1989)
—— *Syndicalism in Ireland, 1917–1923* (Cork, 1988)
—— 'Jim Larkin and the Communist Internationals, 1923–9', *Irish Historical Studies*, vol. 31, 1998–9, pp. 357–73
O'Connor, Fionnuala, *In Search of a State: Catholics in Northern Ireland* (Belfast, 1993)
O'Connor, Frank, *Guests of the Nation* (London, 1931)
—— *An Only Child* (London, 1958)
O'Connor, Nuala, *Bringing It All Back Home: The Influence of Irish Music* (London, 1991)
O'Crannlaighe, P., 'Cock fighting', *The Bell*, no. 6, March 1946, pp. 510–13
O'Crohan, Seán, *A Day in Our Life* (Dublin 1969; new edn, Oxford, 2000)
O'Day, Alan, 'Irish Home Rule and Liberalism', in O'Day (ed.), *The Edwardian Age*
O'Day, Alan (ed.), *The Edwardian Age: Conflict and Stability 1900–1914* (London, 1979)
O'Day, Alan and John Stevenson (eds.), *Irish Historical Documents since 1800* (Dublin, 1992)
O'Doherty, F. and D. McGrath, *The Priest and Mental Health* (Dublin, 1963)
O'Donnell, Peadar, *Adrigoole* (London, 1929)
—— *The Bothy Fire and All That* (Dublin, 1937)
—— *Gates Flew Open* (Dublin, 1932)

O'Dowd, Liam, 'Intellectuals in twentieth-century Ireland: The case of George Russell', *The Crane Bag*, vol. 9, 1985, pp. 6–26

—— 'Neglecting the material dimension: Irish intellectuals and the problem of Identity', *Irish Review*, no. 3, 1988, pp. 8–18

O'Dowd, Mary, 'From Morgan to MacCurtain: Women historians in Ireland from the 1790s to the 1990s', in Valiulis and O'Dowd (eds.), *Women and Irish History*

—— 'Women and politics in Northern Ireland, 1993–2000', in Bourke et al. (eds.), *Field Day Anthology V*

O'Dowd, Mary and Sabine Wichert (eds.), *Chattel, Servant or Citizen: Women's Status in Church, State and Society, Historical Studies 19* (Belfast, 1995)

O'Drisceóil, Donal, *Censorship in Ireland, 1939–45: Neutrality, Politics and Society* (Cork, 1996)

—— *Peadar O'Donnell* (Cork, 2001)

—— '"Moral neutrality": Censorship in Emergency Ireland', *History Ireland*, vol. 4, no. 2, Summer 1996, pp. 46–51

O'Faoláin, Nuala, *Are You Somebody?* (Dublin, 1996)

O'Faolain, Seán, *The Irish* (London, 1947; new edn London, 1969)

—— *Midsummer Night Madness and Other Stories* (London, 1932)

—— *Vive Moi! An Autobiography* (London, 1965)

—— 'All things considered', *The Bell*, vol. XI, no. 4, January 1946, pp. 877–87

—— 'Fifty years of Irish writing', *Studies*, vol. LI, 1962, pp. 93–105

—— 'The plain people of Ireland', *The Bell*, vol. VII, no. 1, October 1943, pp. 1–8

O'Farrell, Patrick, *Ireland's English Question* (New York, 1971)

O'Farrell, Séamus, 'The changing pattern of Irish life', *Studies*, vol. 40, December 1951, pp. 428–36

O'Flaherty, Liam, *A Tourist's Guide to Ireland* (London, 1929)

O'Hagan, John W. (ed.), *The Economy of Ireland: Policy and Performance* (Dublin, 1987)

O'Halloran, Clare, *Partition and the Limits of Irish Nationalism* (Dublin, 1987)

O'Halpin, Eunan, *The Decline of the Union: British Government in Ireland, 1892–1920* (Dublin, 1987)

—— *Defending the State: Ireland and Its Enemies since 1922* (Oxford, 2000)

—— 'The army in independent Ireland', in Bartlett and Jeffery (eds.), *Military History of Ireland*

O'Hanlon, Ray, *The New Irish Americans* (Dublin, 1998)

O'Hearn, Denis, *Inside the Celtic Tiger: The Irish Economy and the Asian Model* (London, 1998)

O'Hegarty, P. S., *The Victory of Sinn Féin* (Dublin, 1924; new edn, with introduction by Tom Garvin, Dublin, 1998)

O'Hegarty, P. S., Alice Stopford Green, James Stephens and Robert Mitchell Henry, 'Arthur Griffith', *Studies*, vol. 11, September 1922, pp. 337–55

O'Mahony, Patrick and Gerald Delanty, *Rethinking Irish History: Nationalism, Identity and Ideology* (Basingstoke, 1998)

O'Mahony, Paul, *Crime and Punishment in Ireland* (Dublin, 1993)

—— 'Modern criminality: a response', *Studies*, vol. 88, no. 350, Summer 1999, pp. 120–25

O'Mahony, Paul (ed.), *Criminal Justice in Ireland* (Dublin, 2002)

O'Mahony, T. P., *Jack Lynch: A Biography* (Dublin, 1991)

—— 'Theatre in Ireland', *Éire–Ireland*, vol. IV, no. 2, 1969, pp. 93–100

O'Malley, Ernie, *On Another Man's Wound* (London, 1936)

—— *The Singing Flame* (Dublin, 1978)

O'Rahilly, Alfred, 'The social problem in Cork', *Studies*, vol. 6, no. 22, June 1917, pp. 177–89

O'Reilly, Emily, *Masterminds of the Right* (Dublin, 1992)

—— *Veronica Guerin: The Life and Death of a Crime Reporter* (London, 1998)

O'Riain, Micheál, *On the Move: Corás Iompair Éireann, 1945–95* (Dublin, 1995)

O'Riordan, Monsignor, *Catholicity and Progress* (Dublin, 1906)

O'Sullivan, Eoin, '"This otherwise delicate subject": Child sexual abuse in early twentieth-century Ireland', in O'Mahony (ed.), *Criminal Justice in Ireland*

O'Sullivan, Patrick, 'Ireland and the Olympic Games', *History Ireland*, vol. 6, no. 1, Spring 1998, pp. 40–46

O'Toole, Fintan, *The Irish Times Book of the Century* (Dublin, 2000)

—— *A Mass for Jesse James: A Journey through 1980s Ireland* (Dublin, 1990)

—— *Meanwhile Back at the Ranch: The Politics of Irish Beef* (London, 1995)

—— *The Politics of Magic: The Work and Times of Tom Murphy* (Dublin, 1987)

—— 'Going west: The country versus the city in Irish writing' *The Crane Bag*, 1985

O'Toole, Michael, *More Kicks Than Pence: A Life in Irish Journalism* (Dublin, 1992)

O'Tuama, Seán (ed.), *The Gaelic League Idea* (Dublin, 1983)

Oikarieu, Sari, *A Dream of Liberty: Constance Markievicz's Vision of Ireland, 1908–1927* (Helsinki, 1998)

Oram, Hugh, *The Newspaper Book: A History of Newspapers in Ireland, 1649–1983* (Dublin, 1983)

Osborne, Mark, 'Those county managers', *The Bell*, vol. 9, no. 4, January 1945, pp. 304–14

Pakenham, Frank, *Peace by Ordeal* (London, 1935)

Parkes, Susan, 'Education in twentieth-century Ireland', in Bourke et al. (eds.), *Field Day Anthology V*

Paseta, Senia, *Before the Revolution: Nationalism, Social Change, and Ireland's Catholic Elite, 1879–1922* (Cork, 1999)

Patterson, Henry, *The Politics of Illusion: Republicanism and Socialism in Modern Ireland* (London, 1989)

—— 'Brian Maginess and the limits of Liberal Unionism', *Irish Review*, vol. 25, 1999/2000, pp. 95ff

—— 'James Larkin and the Belfast dockers and carters strike of 1907', *Saothar*, vol. 4, 1978, pp. 8–14

Paul-Dubois, Louis F., *Contemporary Ireland* (Dublin, 1908)

Pettit, Philip (ed.), *The Gentle Revolution: Crisis in the Universities* (Dublin, 1969)

Phoenix, Eamon, *Northern Nationalism: Nationalist Politics, Partition and the Catholic Minority in Northern Ireland, 1890–1940* (Belfast, 1994)

Pine, Richard, 'The suburban Shamrock: the embourgeoisement of Irish culture', *Irish Review*, no. 2, 1987, pp. 49–58

Pine, Richard (ed.), *Music in Ireland 1848–1998* (Cork, 1998)

Piper, Leonard, *Dangerous Waters: The Life and Death of Erskine Childers* (London, 2003)

Plunkett, Horace, *Ireland in the New Century* (Dublin, 1905)

Pollak, Andy (ed.), *The Opsahl Report on Northern Ireland* (Dublin, 1993)

Power, Vincent, *Send 'Em Home Sweatin': The Showbands' Story* (Dublin, 1990)

Prunty, Jacinta, *Dublin Slums 1800–1925: A Study in Urban Geography* (Dublin, 1999)

Psychiatrist, A, 'Insanity in Ireland', *The Bell*, vol. 7, no. 4, January 1944

Purséil, Padraig, *The GAA in Its Time* (Dublin, 1982)

Puxon, Grattan, *The Victims: Itinerants in Ireland* (Dublin, 1967)

Quinn, Antoinette, *Patrick Kavanagh: A Biography* (Dublin, 2001)

Quinn, David, 'An icon for the new Ireland: An assessment of President Robinson', *Studies*, vol. 86, no. 43, Autumn 1997, pp. 207–15

Rafter, Kevin, *The Clann: The Story of Clann Na Poblachta* (Dublin, 1996)

Raftery, Mary and Eoin O'Sullivan, *Suffer the Little Children: The Inside Story of Ireland's Industrial Schools* (Dublin, 1999)

Regan, John, 'The politics of reaction: The dynamics of Treatyite government and policy 1922–33', *Irish Historical Studies*, vol. 30, no. 20, November 1997

——'Demilitarising Michael Collins', *History Ireland*, vol. 3, no. 3, Autumn 1995, pp. 17–23

——*The Irish Counter-Revolution, 1921–1936* (Dublin, 1999)

Rhodes, Rita, *Women and the Family in Post-Famine Ireland: Status and Opportunities* (New York, 1992)

Riordan, Susannah, '"A political blackthorn": Seán MacEntee, the Dignan Plan and the principle of ministerial responsibility', *Journal of Irish Economic and Social History*, vol. XXVII, 2000, pp. 44–63

——'"The unpopular front": Catholic revival and Irish cultural identity', in Cronin and Regan (eds.), *Ireland: The Politics of Independence*, pp. 63–89

Robins, Joseph, *Fools and Mad: A History of the Insane in Ireland* (Dublin, 1986)

Robinson, Lennox (ed.), *Lady Gregory's Journals, 1916–1930* (London, 1946)

Robinson, Mary, 'Rhetoric and reality', review of O'Halloran, *Partition and the Limits of Irish Nationalism*, *Irish Review*, vol. 3, no. 1, pp. 127–9

Robinson, Mary T. W., 'Women and the new Irish State', in MacCurtain and Ó Corráin (eds.), *Women in Irish Society*

Roche, Patrick and Brian Barton (eds.), *The Northern Ireland Question: Myth and Reality* (Aldershot, 1991)

Rockett, Kevin, Luke Gibbons and John Hill, *Cinema and Ireland* (New York, 1988)

Rohan, Dorine, *Marriage: Irish Style* (London, 1969)

Rolston, Bill (ed.), *The Media and Northern Ireland* (Belfast, 1991)

Rottman, David and Philip O'Connell, 'The changing social structures of Ireland', in Litton (ed.), *Unequal Achievement*

Rouse, Paul, *Ireland's Own Soil: Government and Agriculture in Ireland, 1945–1965* (Dublin, 2000)

——'Sport and the politics of culture: A history of the GAA ban on foreign games, 1884–1971', *The International Journal of the History of Sport*, vol. 10, no. 3, December 1993, pp. 333–60

Royle, Stephen, A., 'Leaving the "dreadful rocks": Irish island emigration and its legacy', *History Ireland*, no. 4, Spring 1998, pp. 34–8.

Russell, Elizabeth, '"Holy crosses, guns and roses": Themes in popular reading material', in Augusteijn (ed.), *Ireland in the 1930s*, pp. 11–29

Russell, George, 'Lessons of revolution', *Studies*, vol. 12, no. 4, March 1923, pp. 345–6

Russell, Matthew, 'The Irish delinquent in England', *Studies*, vol. 53, Summer 1964, pp. 136–48

Ryan, Annie, *Walls of Silence: Ireland's Policy towards People with a Disability* (Kilkenny, 1999)

Ryan, Liam, *Social Dynamite: A Study of Early School Leavers* (Dublin, 1967)

Ryan, Louise, *Gender Identity and the Irish Press, 1922–37: Embodying the Nation* (New York, 2002)

——'Infanticide in the Irish Free State', *Irish Studies Review*, no. 14, Spring 1996

Ryan, Ray, 'The Republic and Ireland: Pluralism, politics and narrative form', in Ryan (ed.), *Writing in the Irish Republic*, pp. 82–105

Ryan, Ray (ed.), *Writing in the Irish Republic: Literature, Culture, Politics, 1949–1999* (London, 2000)

Ryan, W. P., *The Pope's Green Isle* (Dublin, 1912)

Rynne, Stephen, *Fr John Hayes: Founder of Muintir na Tíre* (Dublin, 1960)

——'A decade of terrible peace', *Rural Ireland*, 1955

Saddlemyer, Ann (ed.), *J. M. Synge: Collected Works, Volume IV: Plays Book II* (London, 1968)

Sammon, Frank, 'The problem of poverty in Ireland: Lessons from the Combat Poverty Agency Programme', *Studies*, vol. 71, Spring 1982, pp. 1–13

Sammon, Patrick, *In the Land Commission: A Memoir, 1933–1978* (Dublin, 1997)

Scheper-Hughes, Nancy, *Saints, Scholars and Schizophrenics: Mental Illness in Rural Ireland* (California, 1979)

Shannon, Catherine B., 'Recovering the voices of the women of the North', *Irish Review*, no. 12, Spring/Summer, 1992, pp. 27–34

Shannon, G. J., 'Woman: Wife and mother', *Christus Rex*, vol. 5, 1951, pp. 155–74

Shannon-Mullen, S., 'Child life as a national asset', *Journal of the Social and Statistical Inquiry Society of Ireland*, December 1915

Shaw, Francis, 'The canon of Irish history: A challenge', *Studies*, vol. 61, Summer 1972, pp. 117–51

Shea, Patrick, *Voices and the Sound of Drums: An Irish Autobiography* (Belfast, 1981)

Sheehan, Canon, *The Graves at Kilmorna: A Story of '67* (London, 1915)

Sheehy Skeffington, Andrée, *Skeff: The Life of Owen Sheehy Skeffington, 1909–70* (Dublin, 1991)

Sheehy Skeffington, Hanna, *Reminiscences of an Irish Suffragette* (Dublin, 1975)

Sheil, Michael J., *The Quiet Revolution: The Electrification of Rural Ireland, 1946–1976* (Dublin, 1984)

Sheridan, John D., 'Irish writing today', *Studies*, vol. 44, Spring 1955, pp. 81–5

Sheridan, Peter, *44: A Dublin Memoir* (Dublin, 1999)

Sherry, Ruth, 'The story of the National Anthem', *History Ireland*, vol. 4, no. 1, Spring 1996, pp. 39–43

Simms, John, *Farewell to the Hammer: A Shankhill Boyhood* (Belfast, 1992)

Sinnott, Richard, *Knowledge of the European Union: Irish Public Opinion* (Dublin, 1995)

Smith, Arthur, 'Agricultural education in Ireland', *New Ireland Review*, vol. 23, 1905

Smith, Michael, *An Unsung Hero: Tom Crean, Antarctic Survivor* (Cork, 2000)

Smith, Paul, *The Countrywoman* (London, 1962)

Smith, William, L., 'The forgotten war: The Catholic Church and Biafra, 1967–70', *History Ireland*, vol. 8, no. 3, Autumn 2000, pp. 44–9

Smyth, Jim, review of Conor McCarthy, *Crisis and Culture in Ireland, 1969–1992* (Dublin, 2001), *History Ireland*, vol. 10, no. 2, Summer 2002

Smyth, Sam, *Thanks a Million Big Fella* (Dublin, 1997)

Somerville Large, Peter, *Irish Voices: 50 Years of Irish Life, 1916–1966* (London, 1999)

Staunton, Enda, *The Nationalists of Northern Ireland, 1918–1973* (Dublin, 2001)

—— 'The Boundary Commission debacle 1925: Aftermath and implications', *History Ireland*, vol. 4, no. 2, Summer 1996, pp. 42–6

—— 'The case of Biafra: Ireland and the Nigerian civil war', *Irish Historical Studies*, vol. XXXI, 1998–9, pp. 513–35

Steiner-Scott, Elizabeth, '"To bounce a boot off her now and then": Domestic violence in post-Famine Ireland', in Valiulis and O'Dowd (eds.), *Women and Irish History*, pp. 125–44

Stewart, A. T. Q., *Edward Carson* (Dublin, 1981)

—— *The Ulster Crisis* (London, 1967)

—— interview in *History Ireland*, vol. 1, no. 2, Summer 1993, pp. 55–9

Stuart, Francis, *We Have Kept the Faith* (Dublin, 1923)

Sullivan, Megan, *Women in Northern Ireland: Cultural Studies and Material Conditions* (Florida, 1999)

Sutherland, Halliday, *Irish Journey* (London, 1956)

Sweeney, John, 'Upstairs, downstairs – the challenge of social inequality', *Studies*, vol. 72, Spring 1983, pp. 6–19

Sweeney, Paul, *The Celtic Tiger: Ireland's Economic Miracle Explained* (Dublin, 1998)

Sweetman, Rosita, *On Our Backs: Sexual Attitudes in a Changing Ireland* (London, 1979)

—— *On Our Knees: Ireland 1972* (London, 1972)

Swift, John, 'Report of the Commission on Vocational Organisation and its times', *Saothar*, vol. 6, 1975, pp. 54–63

Taillon, Ruth, *The Women of 1916* (Belfast, 1996)

Taillon, Ruth and Diane Urquhart, 'Women, politics and the state in Northern Ireland, 1918–66', in Bourke et al. (eds.), *Field Day Anthology V*

Talpin, Eric, 'James Larkin, Liverpool and the National Union of Dock Labourers', *Saothar*, vol. 4, 1978, pp. 1–7

Taylor, Peter, *Loyalists* (London, 1999)

—— *Provos: The IRA and Sinn Féin* (London, 1997)

Teague, Paul (ed.), *Beyond the Rhetoric: Politics, the Economy and Social Policy in Northern Ireland* (London, 1987)

Thornley, David, *The European Challenge* (Dublin, 1963)

—— 'Ireland: The end of an era?', *Studies*, vol. LIII, no. 209, Spring 1964, pp. 24–31

Tierney, Michael, 'Strikes and the Labour court: A comment', *Studies*, vol. 36, December 1947, pp. 394–6

Tobin, Fergal, *The Best of Decades: Ireland in the 1960s* (Dublin, 1984)

Tóibín, Colm, *Lady Gregory's Toothbrush* (Dublin, 2002)

—— *Soho Square 6* (London, 1993)

—— 'Gay Byrne: Irish life as cabaret', *The Crane Bag*, vol. 8, no. 2, 1984

—— 'Inside the Supreme Court', *Magill*, February 1985

—— 'Thomas Murphy's volcanic Ireland', in Murray (ed.), *Irish University Review, Thomas Murphy Issue*

Tóibín, Colm, (ed.), *The Penguin Book of Irish Fiction* (London, 1999)

Tóibín, Colm and Diarmaid Ferriter, *The Irish Famine: A Documentary* (London, 2001)

Touher, Patrick, *Fear of the Collar* (Dublin, 1991)

Townshend, Charles, *Political Violence in Ireland: Government and Resistance since 1848* (Oxford, 1983)

—— 'British policy in Ireland, 1906–1921', in Boyce (ed.), *The Revolution in Ireland*, pp. 173–93

—— 'Historiography: Telling the Irish revolution', in Augusteijn (ed.), *Irish Revolution*, pp. 1–17

—— 'The Irish Republican Army and the development of guerrilla warfare, 1916–1921', *English Historical Review*, vol. 94, no. 371, 1979

—— 'The suppression of the Easter Rising', *Bullán*, vol. 1, no. 1, 1994, pp. 27–40

Travers, Pauric, 'History in primary School: A future for our past?', *History Ireland*, vol. 4, no. 3, Autumn 1996, pp. 13–16

—— 'The priest in politics: the case of conscription', in MacDonagh, Mandle and Travers (eds.), *Irish Culture and Nationalism*, pp. 161–82

Trevor, William, *The Ballroom of Romance and Other Stories* (London, 1972)

Tuairim, *Some of our Children: A Report on the Residential Care of the Deprived Child in Ireland* (London, 1966)

Turner, Marcus, *Ireland's Holy Wars: The Struggle for a Nation's Soul, 1500–2000* (London, 2001)

Tweedy, Hilda, *A Link in the Chain: The Story of the Irish Housewives' Association* (Dublin, 1992)

Urquhart, Diane, '"The female of the species is more deadlier than the male": The Ulster Women's Unionist Council, 1911–40', in Holmes and Urquhart (eds.), *Coming into the Light*, pp. 93–126

Valiulis, Maryann Gialanella, 'Neither feminist nor flapper: The ecclesiastical construction of the ideal Irish woman', in O'Dowd and Wichert (eds.), *Chattel, Servant or Citizen*, pp. 168–79

Valiulis, Maryann Gialanella and Mary O'Dowd (eds.), *Women and Irish History* (Dublin, 1997)

Van Esbeck, Edmund, *One Hundred Years of Rugby in Ireland* (Dublin, 1974)

Varley, Tony and Peter Moser, 'Clann na Tamhlan: Ireland's last Farmers' Party', *History Ireland*, vol. 3, no. 2, Summer 1995, pp. 39–44

Vidler, Alec R., *The Modernist Movement in the Roman Church* (Cambridge, 1934)

Viney, Michael, *The Five Per Cent: A Survey of Protestants in the Republic* (Dublin, 1965)

——*Growing Old in Ireland* (Dublin, 1967)

Walker, Graham, 'The Northern Ireland Labour Party in the 1920s', *Saothar*, vol. 10, 1984, pp. 19–29

Walsh, Ann-Marie, '"Root them in the land"; Cottage schemes for agricultural labourers', in Augusteijn (ed.), *Ireland in the 1930s*, pp. 47–67

Walsh, Brendan, 'Marriage in Ireland in the twentieth century', in Cosgrove (ed.), *Marriage in Ireland*, pp. 132–51

Walsh, Christopher, 'What do we read?', *Furrow*, vol. 1, no. 2, March 1950

Walshe, Eibhear, 'Lock up your daughters: From ante-room to interior castle', in Walshe (ed.), *Ordinary People Dancing*

Walshe, Eibhear (ed.), *Ordinary People Dancing: Essays on Kate O'Brien* (Cork, 1993)

Ward, Margaret, *Hanna Sheehy Skeffington: A Life* (Cork, 1987)

——*The Missing Sex: Putting Women into Irish History* (Dublin, 1991)

——'Gender: gendering the Irish revolution', in Augusteijn (ed.), *Irish Revolution*, pp. 168–86

——'The League of Women delegates and Sinn Féin', *History Ireland*, vol. 4, no. 3, Winter 1996, pp. 37–42

Warwick-Haller, Sally, *William O'Brien and the Irish Land War* (Dublin, 1990)

Waters, John, *An Intelligent Person's Guide to Modern Ireland* (London, 1997)

——*Jiving at the Crossroads* (Belfast, 1991)

Watson, G. J., *Irish Identity and the Literary Revival; Synge, Yeats and O'Casey* (London and New York, 1979)

Whelan, Bernadette, *Ireland and the Marshall Plan, 1947–57* (Dublin, 2000)

Whelan, Gerard and Carolyn Swift, *Spiked: Church–State Intrigue and the "Rose Tattoo"* (Dublin, 2002)

Whyte, John, *Church and State in Modern Ireland, 1923–70* (Dublin, 1971)

——*Interpreting Northern Ireland* (Oxford, 1990)

Wichert, Sabine, *Northern Ireland since 1945* (Harlow, 1991)

Williams, T. D. (ed.), *The Irish Struggle 1916–26* (London, 1966)

Wilson, Tom, *Ulster: Conflict and Consent* (Oxford, 1989)

Wren, Maev-Ann, *Unhealthy State: Anatomy of a Sick Society* (Dublin, 2003)

Yeates, Padraig, *Lockout: Dublin 1913* (Dublin, 2001)

Young, Filson, *Ireland at the Crossroads: An Essay in Explanation* (London, 1903)

INDEX